World Civilizations

The Global Experience

Volume 1: Beginnings to 1750

Seventh Edition

Peter N. Stearns
George Mason University

Michael Adas
Rutgers University

Stuart B. Schwartz
Yale University

Marc Jason Gilbert
Hawaii Pacific University

D1296807

PEARSON

Boston Columbus Indianapolis New York San Francisco Upper Saddle River
Amsterdam Cape Town Dubai London Madrid Milan Munich Paris Montreal Toronto
Delhi Mexico City Sao Paulo Sydney Hong Kong Seoul Singapore Taipei Tokyo

Editor-in-Chief: Dickson Musslewhite
Executive Editor: William Grieco
Project Manager: Rob DeGeorge
Program Manager: Emily Tamburri
Director of Marketing: Brandy Dawson
Executive Marketing Manager: Wendy Albert
Marketing Assistant: Rebecca Schoenfeld
Senior Operations Supervisor: Mary Ann Gloriande
Senior Art Director: Maria Lange
Interior Design: Red Kite Consulting

Manager, Visual Research & Permissions: Beth Brenzel
Cover Design: Depinho Design
Cover Photo: © Danita Delimont/Alamy—Painting of Chinese women in traditional dress, Tang Dynasty.
Media Director: Brian Hyland
Media Editor: Elizabeth Roden Hall
Composition/Full-Service
   Project Management: SPi Global/Bruce Hobart
Printer/Binder: Courier/Kendallville
Cover Printer: Lehigh-Phoenix Color/Hagerstown

This book was set in 10/12 Minion Pro

Credits and acknowledgments borrowed from other sources and reproduced, with permission, in this textbook appear on page C-1.

Library of Congress Cataloging-in-Publication Data
Stearns, Peter N.
  World civilizations : the global experience / Peter N. Stearns, George Mason University, Michael Adas, Rutgers University, Stuart B. Schwartz, Yale University, Marc Jason Gilbert, Hawaii Pacific University. — Seventh edition.
      pages cm
  Earlier edition entered under title.
  Includes bibliographical references and index.
  ISBN 978-0-205-98630-9 (combined) — ISBN 978-0-205-98629-3 (vol. 1) — ISBN 978-0-205-98628-6 (vol. 2)
  1. Civilization—History. 2. Civilization—History—Sources. I. Title.
  CB69.W666 2015
  909—dc23
                                                                                            2013040835

10 9 8 7 6 5 4 3 2 1

Combined Volume	ISBN 10: 0-205-98630-7
	ISBN 13: 978-0-205-98630-9
Instructor's Review Copy	ISBN 10: 0-205-98631-5
	ISBN 13: 978-0-205-98631-6
Volume 1	ISBN 10: 0-205-98629-3
	ISBN 13: 978-0-205-98629-3
Volume 1 A La Carte	ISBN 10: 0-205-98859-8
	ISBN 13: 978-0-205-98859-4
Volume 2	ISBN 10: 0-205-98628-5
	ISBN 13: 978-0-205-98628-6
Volume 2 A La Carte	ISBN 10: 0-205-98851-2
	ISBN 13: 978-0-205-98851-8

PEARSON

Brief Contents

Contents

PART III

THE POSTCLASSICAL PERIOD, 600–1450: NEW
FAITH AND NEW COMMERCE   235

Special Features

MAPS

Preface

World history explores the human past, around the globe, to help us understand the world we live in today. It seeks to identify how major forces have developed over time, like patterns of migration or world trade. It explores the cultures and political institutions of different regions, to help explain commonalities and differences. World history builds on a growing amount of historical scholarship, some of which has truly altered the picture of the past. It involves a rich array of stories and examples of human variety, intriguing in themselves. It helps develop skills that are vital not just to the history classroom, but to effective operation in a global society—skills like comparing different societies, appreciating various viewpoints, identifying big changes and continuities in the human experience. Always, however, it uses the past as a prologue to the present. World historians argue that no one society, past or present, can be understood without reference to other societies and to larger global forces. They argue, even more vigorously, that the present—which clearly involves relationships that embrace the whole world—cannot be grasped without a sense of the global historical record.

From its first edition, *World Civilizations: The Global Experience* has aimed at capturing a truly global approach by discussing and comparing major societies and focusing on their interactions. The goal is to present a clear factual framework while stimulating analysis about global contacts, regional patterns, and the whole process of change and continuity on a world stage. This kind of world history, focused on the development over time of the forces that shape the world today, helps students make sense of the present and prepare to meet the challenges of the future. It is hard to imagine a more important topic.

Embracing the whole world's history obviously requires selectivity and explicit points of emphasis. This text gains coherence through decisions about time, about place, and about topic. In all three cases, the book encourages analysis, relating facts to vital issues of interpretation. Through analysis and interpretation students become active, engaged learners, rather than serving as passive vessels for torrents of historical facts. Underpinning analysis, the issues of time, place, and topic are the three keys to an intelligible global past.

DECISIONS ABOUT TIME: PERIODIZATION

This text pays a great deal of attention to periodization, or the identification of major points of change in the global experience. This is an essential requirement for coherent presentation—going well beyond the one-thing-after-another type of chronology—and ultimately a precondition of relating the past to the present.

World Civilizations: The Global Experience identifies six periods in world history. Each period is determined by three basic criteria: a geographical rebalancing among major civilizational areas, an increase in the intensity and extent of contact across civilizations (or, in the case of the earliest period, cross-regional contact), and the emergence of new and roughly parallel developments in many major civilizations. The book is divided into six parts corresponding to these six major periods of world history. In each part, basic characteristics of each period are referred to in chapters that discuss the major societies in the Middle East, Africa, Asia, Europe, and the Americas, and in several cross-cutting chapters that address larger world trends. Each period offers a distinctive set of themes, or Big Concepts, that are defined in general terms and then explored in terms of particular regions. Part introductions identify the fundamental new characteristics and new levels of interaction that define each period.

Part I, *Early Human Societies, 2.5 Million–600 B.C.E.: Origins and Development*, sketches the hunting-and-gathering phase of human existence, then focuses on the rise of agriculture and the emergence of civilization in parts of Asia, Africa, Central America, and southeastern Europe—the sequence of developments that set world history in motion from the origin of the human species until about 3000 years ago.

Part II, *The Classical Period, 600 B.C.E.–600 C.E.: Uniting Large Regions*, deals with the growing complexity of major civilizations in several areas of the world. During the classical period, civilizations developed a new capacity to integrate large regions and diverse groups of people through overarching cultural and political systems. Yet many regions and societies remained unconnected to the increasingly complex centers of civilization. Coverage of the classical period of world history, then, must consider both types of societies.

The period covered in Part III, *The Postclassical Period, 600–1450: New Faith and New Commerce*, saw the emergence of new commercial and cultural linkages that brought most civilizations into contact with one another and with nomadic groups. The decline of the great classical empires, the rise of new civilizational centers, and the emergence of a network of world contacts, including the spread of major religions, are characteristics of the postclassical era.

Developments in world history over the three centuries from 1450 to 1750 mark a fourth period in world history, which is covered in Part IV, *The Early Modern Period, 1450–1750: The World Shrinks*. The rise of the West, the intensification of global contacts, the growth of trade, and the formation of new empires define this period and separate it from the preceding postclassical period.

Part V, *The Dawn of the Industrial Age, 1750–1900*, covers the period of world history dominated by the advent of industrialization in western Europe and growing European imperialism. The increase and intensification of commercial interchange, technological innovations, and cultural contacts all reflected the growth of Western power and the spread of Western influence.

The Newest Stage of World History: 1900–Present, the focus of Part VI, defines the characteristics of this period as the retreat of Western imperialism, the rise of new political systems such as communism, the surge of the United States and the Soviet Union, and a variety of economic innovations, including the achievements of Japan, China, Korea, and the Pacific Rim. Part VI deals with this most recent period of world history and some of its portents for the future.

UNDERLYING ISSUES

Two related themes and one standard historical complexity rise above the six-stage world history periodization. The first involves the interaction between tradition and change—and in recent periods, modern change. Many societies established key ideas and institutions early on, at least by the classical period. These traditions would then condition responses to change and modernity. Elements of this interplay become visible from the post-classical period onward; the tradition-change encounter remains vivid in the 21st century, though in forms very different from a thousand years ago. Each world history period involves important shifts in the interaction between change and tradition.

Theme two involves divergence and convergence. Societies emerged separately in many parts of the world, though the process was almost always affected by some wider contacts. This is part of the first phase of the human experience. Separation, or divergence, did not always mean difference, for many societies solved key problems in similar ways; but it did tend to produce separate identities. With growing contacts over time, opportunities and pressures produced various forms of imitation and convergence. The interplay between divergence and convergence is lively in the 21st century, but its shape has changed greatly over time. Here, too, each period involves a different statement of the balance between divergence and convergence.

Periodization emphasizes change, including changes in the basic frameworks in which traditions interacted with new forces and in which separate identities confronted new levels of convergence. Always, however, change must be complicated by recognition of key continuities from the past. At various points in human history, including recently, huge new forces prompt some people to claim that "everything has changed." In fact, strong traces of the past always linger. The challenge is to figure out how the balance works.

PLACE: REGIONS AND CIVILIZATIONS

Usable world history requires decisions about coherence in place as well as time. Even in the present day, and certainly in the past, key developments did not occur evenly across the whole globe: regional conditions always come into play. At the same time, not every definable society can be encompassed—early hunting-and-gathering bands of humans, after all, could number no more than sixty people. No world history survey can even approach that level of detail. World history seeks legitimate ways to define larger regions and societies that serve as the basis for meaningful contacts and reactions to global forces.

Major regions of the world depend on a combination of geography and historical developments in the form of shared institutions and beliefs. This book uses several regions as frameworks for discussing patterns of activity and larger interactions: east Asia; south and southeast Asia; the Middle East, ultimately with the addition of north Africa; sub-Saharan Africa; Europe, often with some division between eastern and western; and the Americas. Australia and key island groups, and also patterns in central Asia, must be added in as well.

In several regions, beginning in key cases several thousand years ago, major civilizations helped organize and define regional characteristics. East Asia, to take one example, would be profoundly shaped by emerging features of Chinese civilization. Civilizations used economic surpluses, beyond basic survival needs, to generate relatively elaborate political institutions, cities, and trading networks. They also emphasized particular kinds of institutional arrangements and value systems that would provide a recognizable identity, differentiating their civilization from other societies. Using, but also debating, the concept of civilization helps organize the geographical foundation of world history by introducing not only key regions but regional characteristics and identities. Civilizations provide the basis for key comparisons, with each other and in terms of regional reactions to larger forces for change. The internal developments in major civilizations, along with mutual interaction and responses to broader factors like migration or missionary religions, form much of the stuff of world history for the past 5000 years. At the same time, other types of societies, including nomadic groups, played a vital role throughout world history, particularly as they long dominated strategically vital regions like central Asia. Most of these other societies were smaller than civilizations, in terms of population, but they played crucial functions in world history and developed successful cultural and institutional forms.

Attention to the major regions of the world does more than set the stage for comparative analysis in each of the chronological periods in world history. It also promotes a sense of geographic balance that is vital to the field. Many earlier historical efforts understandably focused on developments in one's own society, assuming that the rest of the world was unimportant or somehow revolved around what was happening nearer home. Until recently, many Americans were urged to pay primary attention to the history of western Europe and the expansion of Western civilization across the Atlantic. These remain valid themes, but in the world history context they become only a part of a larger and more complicated civilizational pattern. The transition from Western to world history is still under discussion, but the global context gains ground steadily because it more accurately mirrors the world around us today. This book, paying attention to Western developments as part of the larger world story, and showing their interaction with other societies and other influences, strives to distribute appropriate attention to all the major regions and to their changing roles in the larger global story.

TOPICS AND THEMES

A final way to focus world history, intersecting with decisions about time and place, involves the kinds of human and social activities that are highlighted. The first theme follows obviously from the uses of periodization and the need to deal coherently with world history over time: *World Civilizations: The Global Experience* deals consistently with change and continuity and with the causes of basic changes in global dynamics from one period to the next.

Interactions among the major regions and societies, the second theme, focus attention on the ways individual regions and civilizations were shaped by contacts with other areas. Contacts include trade, of course, but also war, diplomacy, and international organizations from religious entities to the multinational companies and global agencies of more modern times.

A cluster of factors deal with economic activities and population patterns as they affect people, societies, and the environment. Technology has a key role here, but also population structures and disease, labor systems, migrations, plus manufacturing and agriculture. Each civilization must be discussed with these patterns in mind, as well as the broader diffusion of trade, technologies, and population exchange as they formed core parts of the larger patterns of interaction.

Each society featured characteristic social and gender structures that organized and tried to justify various systems of inequality. Dealing with how social systems changed over time and comparing them from one region to the next are core features of world history; social systems could also be affected by changing patterns of contact.

The fifth thematic area clusters around culture—belief systems, values, and artistic styles—as these emerged in religions, intellectual systems, and science. Here too, change over time and the results of interactions among societies form key elements in the cultural dynamics of world history.

Finally, politics demands emphasis: the functions and structures of states, as they formed and changed, along with ideas about politics and political identity (political culture). In modern centuries, this topic embraces the emergence of nation states and also their limitations in global context.

The topical themes of this book help organize discussions of change over time but also the possibility of developing comparisons from one society to the next. Interactions among the themes—how new trading patterns affected, and were affected by, cultural systems, for example—help structure more challenging analytical efforts.

What Is New to This Edition?

The seventh edition of *World Civilizations: The Global Experience* has been revised to reflect the latest developments in historical research and benefits from the addition of a host of new features to assist student learning. The most significant pedagogical innovation has been the seamless integration of documents, maps, videos, illustrations, and other resources from MyHistoryLab into the textbook. A new pedagogically driven design highlights a clear learning path through the material and offers a visually stunning learning experience in print or on a screen. With the Pearson eText, featuring a new streamlined design for tablet devices, students can transition directly to MyHistoryLab resources such as primary source documents, videos, and maps.

Learning Objective questions have been added to each chapter to highlight central themes and ideas. Each question is linked to one of the chapter's main sections. Critical Thinking Questions were added at the end of each chapter to reinforce important concepts covered in the chapter and to serve as possible essay or class discussion topics. Further Readings were updated in most chapters, bringing the scholarship for the new edition up-to-date. In many chapters, the authors reference cultural regions that were underrepresented in earlier editions of the book—particularly the Middle East and Oceania.

Specific changes in the content of this edition are as follows:

- In Chapter 1, there are new sections on animism and pastoralism and the section on first cities has been expanded.
- In Chapter 3, there is an increased focus on environmental factors.
- Chapter 4 features an increased emphasis on the impact of political and technical change on the environment. Also, there are extensive changes in the Further Readings.
- Chapter 5 includes expanded treatment of Persia.
- In Chapter 7, there is now a comparison of Roman and Chinese empires. Coverage of Rome's development has been expanded and there is new coverage of Rome's environmental impact. Finally, there is a new section called Cities of the World: Rome
- Chapter 8 now includes an explanation of the Mayan system of assigning dates to events and features expanded coverage of Chavín culture.
- In the Chapter 9 Further Readings, scholarship on New Zealand has been added or updated.
- In Chapter 10, the section on the Spread of World Religions has been expanded.
- Chapter 12, the discussion of Sufis and their roles in science and philosophy has been expanded.
- Chapter 14 includes increased coverage of the Byzantine Empire. Also, there are new sections titled Cities in World History: Kiev and Global Connections and Critical Themes: Eastern Europe and the World.
- Chapter 16 features a stronger, more effective comparison of Aztecs and Incas.
- Chapter 18 includes new coverage of the importance of women in Vietnamese resistance movements and in society in general.
- In Chapter 19, the Further Readings have been expanded.
- Chapter 20 includes expanded coverage of the fifteenth century as a transition. There is a new section called The Structure of Transregional Trade. Coverage of critical themes of the Italian Renaissance has been revised. And there is new coverage of the impact of the Mongol era.
- In Chapter 22, there is expanded coverage of changes during the early modern period and an explanation of cultural changes during the 18th century.

FEATURES

The features in *World Civilizations: The Global Experience* have been carefully constructed and honed over the course of seven editions. Our aim has been to provide students with tools to help them learn how to analyze change and continuity.

Part Introductions

Part introductions, reviewed for this edition, discuss the conditions that set the stage for the developments that define each new period in world history. They identify the characteristics of the period of world history covered in the part, and recap the continuities that exist from one period to the next. Two world maps at the beginning of each part introduction provide a graphic reference for the major changes of the period. Part timelines list the major events of the chronological period covered.

End-of-Part Analysis

Following the final chapter in each part is an essay that revisits the dominant cross-civilizational (or cross-regional) contacts and divisions that occurred during the era under examination. These sections encourage analysis of the dominant contact patterns in the period as well as the relationship to them of major individual societies.

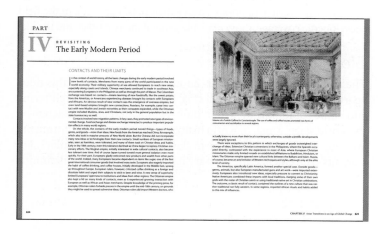

Chapter Introductions

Each chapter introduction tells a compelling story about a particular pattern, individual, or incident to spark students' interest and introduce chapter material in an engaging and dramatic way. The opening story concludes with an explanation of how the story relates to the chapter content and the key themes and analytical issues that will be examined in the chapter.

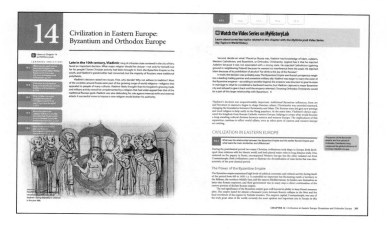

Timelines

In addition to the timeline in each part introduction, each chapter includes a timeline that orients the student to the period, countries, and key events of the chapter.

Learning Objectives

Each of the main chapter headings is followed by a Learning Objective for the section that follows. These Learning Objectives also appear on the first page of the chapter, giving students an idea of important concepts they will encounter when reading the chapter.

Section-Opening Focal Points

Focal points listed next to each of the main chapter headings identify for the student the principal points to be explored in the section.

Visualizing the Past

The Visualizing the Past feature of each chapter supports visual literacy by showing students how to read and analyze visual material such as maps, charts, graphs, tables, or photos to interpret historical patterns. Text accompanying the illustrations provides a level of analysis, and a series of questions draws the students into providing their own analyses.

Documents

Substantial excerpts from selected original documents put students in contact with diverse voices of the past, and many have been revised for this edition. We share a firm commitment to include social history involving women, the non-elite, and experiences and events outside the spheres of politics and high culture. Each document is preceded by a brief scene-setting narration and followed by probing questions to guide the reader through an understanding of the document and to encourage interpretive reflections and analysis.

Thinking Historically

Each chapter contains an analytical essay on a topic of broad application related to the chapter's focus but extending across chronological and geographical boundaries. Critical thinking questions at the end of each essay prompt the reader to think beyond the "who, what, where, and when" of historical events and consider instead the far-reaching implications of historical developments.

Global Connections

Each chapter ends with a Global Connections section that reinforces the key themes and issues raised in the chapter and makes clear their importance not only to the areas of civilization discussed in the chapter but also to the world as a whole.

Critical Thinking Questions

Critical Thinking Questions can be found at the end of each chapter as well as at the end of each part. These questions reinforce important topics and themes explored in the text and also serve as possible essay or class discussion topics.

Further Readings

Each chapter includes several annotated paragraphs of suggested readings, substantially updated for this edition. Students receive reliable guidance on a variety of books: source materials, standards in the field, encyclopedia coverage, more readable general interest titles, and the like.

Glossary

The comprehensive glossary is another feature that sets this book apart. It includes conceptual terms, frequently used foreign terms, and names of important geographic regions, and key characters on the world stage. Much of world history will be new to most students, and this glossary will help them develop a global vocabulary. For students' convenience, the glossary terms, along with their definition and, in many cases, pronunciation, can also be found in the margins of each chapter where the term is first used in the narrative.

MyHistoryLab Icons

Throughout each chapter are MyHistoryLab icons paired with images, maps, and portions of the narrative that lead students to additional resources—documents, images, maps, videos, and more—found on MyHistoryLab, giving students a deeper understanding of the topics covered in the text and leading to a more thorough integration between the book and online resources.

ACKNOWLEDGMENTS

Grateful acknowledgment is made to the following colleagues and reviewers, who made many useful suggestions during the development of the text: Melanie Bailey, Piedmont Valley Community College; Stefan Bosworth, Hostos Community College; Andria Crosson, University of Texas at San Antonio; Robert Crout, College of Charleston; Frank Gregory, Wesley College; Michael Noble, Eastfield College; Patricia O'Neill, Central Oregon Community College; and Tao Peng, Minnesota State University, Mankato.

Peter N. Stearns
Michael Adas
Stuart B. Schwartz
Marc Jason Gilbert

Supplementary Instructional Materials

FOR INSTRUCTORS	FOR STUDENTS
Break Through to Improving Results with MyHistoryLab (www.myhistorylab.com) MyHistoryLab helps students better prepare for class, quizzes, and exams—resulting in more dynamic experiences in the classroom and improved performance in the course. And, the immersive Pearson eText—with videos and interactive activities just a click away—truly engages students in their study of history, and fosters learning within and beyond the classroom.	
Instructor's Resource Center www.pearsonhighered.com/irc This website provides instructors with additional text-specific resources that can be downloaded for classroom use. Resources include the Instructor's Resource Manual, PowerPoint presentations, and the Test Item File. Register online for access to the resources for *World Civilizations*, Seventh Edition.	**CourseSmart** www.coursemart.com CourseSmart eTextbooks offer the same content as the printed text in a convenient online format—with highlighting, online search, and printing capabilities. For more information, or to purchase access to the CourseSmart eTextbook, visit **www.coursesmart.com**
Instructor's Resource Manual Available at the Instructor's Resource Center, at **www.pearsonhighered.com/irc**, the Instructor's Resource Manual contains learning objectives from the text, chapter outlines, chapter summaries that cover each section in the text, key terms from the text, lecture suggestions, and class discussion questions. It also contains a MyHistoryLab syllabus and suggestions for integrating MyHistoryLab into your course.	**Books à la Carte** These editions feature the exact same content as the traditional printed text in a convenient, three-hole-punched, loose-leaf version at a discounted price—allowing students to take only what they need to class. Please contact your Pearson sales representative for details.
The Test Item File Available at the Instructor's Resource Center, at **www.pearsonhighered.com/irc**, the Test Item File contains a diverse set of over 2,200 multiple choice and essay questions, supporting a variety of assessment strategies. The large pool of multiple-choice questions for each chapter includes factual, conceptual, and analytical questions, so that instructors may assess students on basic information as well as critical thinking.	**Documents in World History** Volume I, Sixth Edition (The Great Traditions: From Ancient Times to 1500) and Volume II (The Modern Centuries: From 1500 to the Present), both edited by Peter N. Stearns, Stephen S. Gosch, Erwin P. Grieshaber, and Allison Scardino Belzer, is a collection of primary source documents that illustrate the human characteristics of key civilizations during major stages of world history. (Vol.1: ISBN 0-205-05023-9; Vol. 2: ISBN 0-205-05024-7)
MyTest Available at **www.pearsonmytest.com**, MyTest is a powerful assessment generation program that helps instructors easily create and print quizzes and exams. Questions and tests can be authored online, allowing instructors ultimate flexibility to access existing questions and edit, create, and store using simple drag-and-drop and Word-like controls.	Titles from the renowned **Penguin Classics** series can be bundled with *World Civilizations*, Seventh Edition, at discounted prices. Please contact your Pearson sales representative for details.
PowerPoint Presentations Available at the Instructor's Resource Center, at **www.pearsonhighered.com/irc** and correlated to the chapters of the book, each presentation includes a lecture outline and a wealth of images and maps from the textbook.	*Library of World Biography Series* www.pearsonhighered.com/educator/series/Library-of-World-Biography/10492.page Each interpretive biography in the Library of World Biography Series focuses on a person whose actions and ideas either significantly influenced world events or whose life reflects important themes and developments in global history. Titles from the series can be bundled with *World Civilizations*, Seventh Edition, for a nominal charge. Please contact your Pearson sales representative for details.

FOR INSTRUCTORS	FOR STUDENTS
	The Prentice Hall Atlas of World History, Second Edition Produced in collaboration with Dorling Kindersley, the leader in cartographic publishing, the updated second edition of *The Prentice Hall Atlas of World History* applies the most innovative cartographic techniques to present world history in all of its complexity and diversity. Copies of the atlas can be bundled with *World Civilizations*, Seventh Edition, for a nominal charge. Contact your Pearson sales representative for details. (ISBN 0-13-604247-3)
	A Guide to Your History Course: What Every Student Needs to Know Written by Vincent A. Clark, this concise, spiral-bound guidebook orients students to the issues and problems they will face in the history classroom. Available at a discount when bundled with *World Civilizations*, Seventh Edition. (ISBN 0-13-185087-3)
	A Short Guide to Writing about History, Seventh Edition Written by Richard Marius, late of Harvard University, and Melvin E. Page, Eastern Tennessee State University, this engaging and practical text helps students get beyond merely compiling dates and facts. Covering both brief essays and the documented resource paper, the text explores the writing and researching processes, identifies different modes of historical writing, including argument, and concludes with guidelines for improving style. (ISBN 0-13-205-67370-8)

BREAK THROUGH TO IMPROVING RESULTS WITH MYHISTORYLAB

A fully integrated learning program, MyHistoryLab for *World Civilizations: The Global Experience*, Seventh Edition helps students better prepare for class, quizzes, and exams—resulting in more dynamic experiences in the classroom and improved performance in the course. And, the immersive Pearson eText—with videos and interactive activities just a click away—truly engages students in their study of history, and fosters learning within and beyond the classroom.

PEARSON ETEXT WITH AUDIO

Contained within MyHistoryLab, the Pearson eText enables students to access their textbook online—through laptops, iPads, and tablets. Download the free Pearson eText app to use on tablets. Students may also listen to their text with the Audio eText.

NEW MYHISTORYLIBRARY

A new release of Pearson's MyHistoryLibrary contains some of the most commonly assigned primary source documents, delivered through Pearson's powerful eText platform. Each reading may also be listened to in the Audio eText companion.

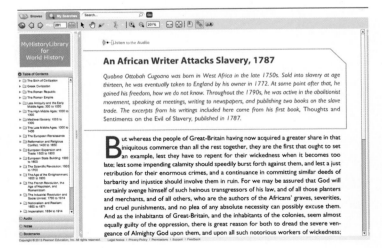

MYHISTORYLAB VIDEO SERIES: KEY TOPICS IN WORLD HISTORY

This comprehensive video series helps students get up-to-speed on key topics. Correlated to the chapters of *World Civilizations*, each video focuses on a key topic discussed in each chapter, readying students to get the most from the text narrative. The videos feature seasoned historians reviewing the pivotal stories of our past, in a lively format designed to engage and inform.

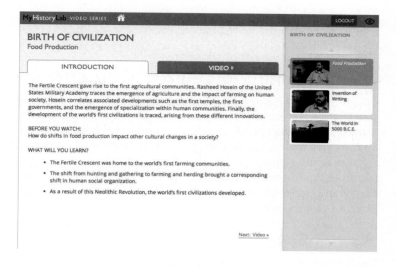

WRITING SPACE

Better writers make great learners—who perform better in their courses. To help you develop and assess concept mastery and critical thinking through writing, we created the Writing Space in MyHistoryLab. It's a single place to create, track, and grade writing assignments, provide writing resources, and exchange meaningful, personalized feedback with students, quickly and easily. Plus, Writing Space includes integrated access to Turnitin, the global leader in plagiarism prevention.

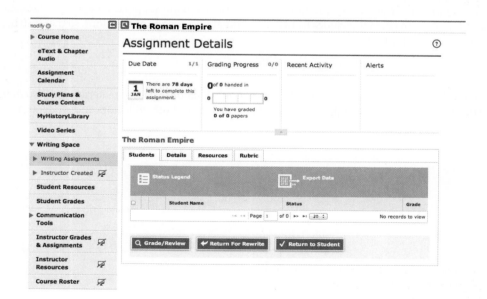

KEY SUPPLEMENTS & CUSTOMER SUPPORT

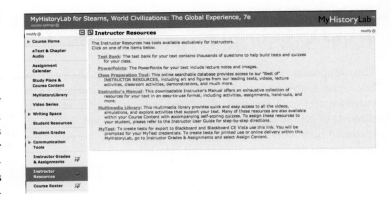

Annotated Instructor's eText

Contained within MyHistoryLab, the *Annotated Instructor's eText* for your Pearson textbook leverages the powerful Pearson eText platform to make it easier than ever for you to access subject-specific resources for class preparation. The *AI eText* serves as the hub for all instructor resources, with chapter-by-chapter links to PowerPoint slides, content from the Instructor's Resource Manual, and to MyHistoryLab's ClassPrep engine, which contains a wealth of history content organized for classroom use.

Instructor's Resource Manual

The Instructor's Resource Manual for *World Civilizations*, Seventh Edition, contains learning objectives from the text, chapter outlines, chapter summaries that cover each section in the text, key terms from the text, lecture suggestions, and class discussion questions. It also contains a MyHistoryLab syllabus and suggestions for integrating MyHistoryLab into your course.

PowerPoint Presentations

Strong PowerPoint presentations make lectures more engaging for students. Correlated to the chapters of your Pearson textbook, each presentation includes a lecture outline and a wealth of images and maps from the textbook.

MyTest Test Bank

Containing a diverse set of multiple choice and essay questions, the MyTest Test Bank supports a variety of assessment strategies. The large pool of multiple choice questions for each chapter includes factual, conceptual, and analytical questions, so that instructors may assess students on basic information as well as critical thinking.

Customer Support

Pearson's dedicated team of local representatives will work with you not only to choose course materials but also to integrate them into your class and assess their effectiveness. Moreover, live support for MyHistoryLab users, both educators and students, is available 24/7.

About the Authors

PETER N. STEARNS

Peter N. Stearns is provost, executive vice president, and university professor of history at George Mason University. He received his Ph.D. from Harvard University. He has taught at Rutgers University, the University of Chicago, and Carnegie Mellon, where he won the Robert Doherty Educational Leadership Award and the Elliott Dunlap Smith Teaching Award. He has taught world history for more than 25 years. He also founded and is the editor of the *Journal of Social History*. In addition to textbooks and readers, he has written studies of gender and consumerism in a world history context. Other books address modern social and cultural history and include studies on gender, old age, work, dieting, and emotion. His most recent book in this area is *Satisfaction Not Guaranteed: Dilemmas of Progress in Modern Society*.

MICHAEL ADAS

Michael Adas is the Abraham Voorhees Professor of History and a Board of Governor's chair at Rutgers University, New Brunswick. Over the past couple of decades his teaching has focused on courses dealing with European and American colonial expansion and African and Asian responses as well as global history in the 20th century. In addition to texts on world history, Adas has written numerous books and articles on the impact of and resistance to Western colonialism and the importance of technology in those processes. His books include *Machines as the Measure of Men: Science, Technology, and Ideologies of Western Dominance*, which won the Dexter Prize in 1992, and more recently *Dominance by Design: Technological Imperatives and America's Civilizing Mission*. In 2012, he was awarded the Toynbee Prize for his lifetime contributions to global history and cross-cultural understanding. He is currently working on a comparative study of the ways in which British and American soldiers' responses to the wars of attrition in the trenches of World War I and in Vietnam contributed to the decline of each of these global powers.

STUART B. SCHWARTZ

Stuart B. Schwartz was born and educated in Springfield, Massachusetts, and then attended Middlebury College and the Universidad Autonoma de Mexico. He has an M.A. and Ph.D. from Columbia University in Latin American history. He taught for many years at the University of Minnesota and joined the faculty at Yale University in 1996. He has also taught in Brazil, Puerto Rico, Spain, France, and Portugal. He is a specialist on the history of colonial Latin America, especially Brazil, and is the author of numerous books, notably *Sugar Plantations in the Formation of Brazilian Society* (1985), which won the Bolton Prize for the best book in Latin American History. He is also the author of *Slaves, Peasants, and Rebels* (1992), *Early Latin America* (1983), and *Victors and Vanquished* (1999). He has held fellowships from the Guggenheim Foundation and the Institute for Advanced Study (Princeton). For his work on Brazil he was decorated by the Brazilian government. His book *All Can Be Saved* (2008) won the Bolton Prize as well as three awards from the American Historical Association.

MARC JASON GILBERT

Marc Jason Gilbert is the holder of the National Endowment for the Humanities Endowed Chair in World History at Hawai'i Pacific University in Honolulu, Hawaii. After receiving his Ph.D from UCLA, he was for many years co-Director of Programs in South and Southeast Asia for the University System of Georgia and was recognized by that System as a Board of Regent's Distinguished Professor of Teaching and Learning. He has benefited from various fellowships which have enabled him to study in Afghanistan, Burma, Cameroon, India, Tanzania, and Yemen. He has directed world history academic conferences and workshops for teachers in Cambodia and Vietnam. He is also a past President of the World History Association and the current editor of a WHA affiliated journal, *World History Connected*. His publications explore the histories of India, Vietnam, and global cultural exchange. His most recent work is *Cross-Cultural Encounters in Modern World History* (2012), with Jon Thares Davidann.

Prologue

The study of history is the study of the past. Knowledge of the past gives us perspective on our societies today. It shows different ways in which people have identified problems and tried to resolve them, as well as important common impulses in the human experience. History can inform through its variety, remind us of some human constants, and provide a common vocabulary and examples that aid in mutual communication.

The study of history is also the study of change. Historians analyze major changes in the human experience over time and examine the ways in which those changes connect the past to the present. They try to distinguish between superficial and fundamental change, as well as between sudden and gradual change. They explain why change occurs and what impact it has. Finally, they pinpoint continuities from the past along with innovations. History, in other words, is a study of human society in motion.

World history has become a subject in its own right. It involves the study of historical events in a global context. It does not attempt to sum up everything that has happened in the past. World history focuses on two principal subjects: the evolution of leading societies and the interaction among different peoples around the globe.

THE EMERGENCE OF WORLD HISTORY

Serious attempts to deal with world history are relatively recent. Many historians have attempted to locate the evolution of their own societies in the context of developments in a larger "known world": Herodotus, though particularly interested in the origins of Greek culture, wrote also of developments around the Mediterranean; Ibn Khaldun wrote of what he knew about developments in Africa and Europe as well as in the Muslim world. But not until the 20th century, with an increase in international contacts and a vastly expanded knowledge of the historical patterns of major societies, did a full world history become possible. In the West, world history depended on a growing realization that the world could not be understood simply as a mirror reflecting the West's greater glory or as a stage for Western-dominated power politics. This hard-won realization continues to meet some resistance. Nevertheless, historians in several societies have attempted to develop an international approach to the subject that includes, but goes beyond, merely establishing a context for the emergence of their own civilizations.

Our understanding of world history has been increasingly shaped by two processes that define historical inquiry: detective work and debate. Historians are steadily uncovering new data not just about particular societies but about lesser-known contacts. Looking at a variety of records and artifacts, for example, they learn how an 8th-century battle between Arab and Chinese forces in central Asia brought Chinese prisoners who knew how to make paper to the Middle East, where their talents were quickly put to work. And they argue about world history frameworks: how central European actions should be in the world history of the past 500 years, and whether a standard process of modernization is useful or distorting in measuring developments in modern Turkey or China. Through debate come advances in how world history is understood and conceptualized, just as the detective work advances the factual base.

WHAT CIVILIZATION MEANS

Humans have always shown a tendency to operate in groups that provide a framework for economic activities, governance, and cultural forms such as beliefs and artistic styles. These groups, or societies, may be quite small; hunting-and-gathering bands often numbered no more than 60 people. World history usually focuses on somewhat larger societies, with more extensive economic relationships (at least for trade) and cultures.

One vital kind of grouping is called civilization. The idea of civilization as a type of human society is central to most world history, though it also generates debate and though historians are now agreed that it is not the only kind of grouping that warrants attention. Civilizations, unlike some other societies, generate surpluses beyond basic survival needs. This in turn promotes a variety of specialized occupations and heightened social differentiation, as well as regional and long-distance trading networks. Surplus production also spurs the growth of cities and the development of formal states, with some bureaucracy, in contrast to more informal methods of governing. Most civilizations have also developed systems of writing.

Civilizations are not necessarily better than other kinds of societies. Nomadic groups have often demonstrated great creativity in technology and social relationships, and some were more vigorous than settled civilizations in promoting global contacts. Moreover, there is disagreement about exactly what defines a civilization—for example, what about cases like the Incas where there was no writing?

Used carefully, however, the idea of civilization as a form of human social organization, and an unusually extensive one, has merit. Along with agriculture (which developed earlier), civilizations have given human groups the capacity to fundamentally reshape their environments and to dominate most other living creatures. The history of civilizations embraces most of the people who have ever lived; their literature, formal scientific discoveries, art, music, architecture, and inventions; their most elaborate social, political, and economic systems; their brutality and destruction caused by conflicts; their exploitation of other species; and their degradation of the environment—a result of changes in technology and the organization of work.

The study of civilizations always involves more, however, than case-by-case detail. World history makes sense only if civilizations are compared, rather than treated separately. Equally important, civilizations (and other societies) developed important mutual contacts, which could have wide impact in reshaping several societies at the same time. And civilizations responded to still wider forces, like migration, disease, or missionary activity, that could reshape the frameworks within which they operated. Civilizations in these wider contexts—as they changed through internal dynamics, mutual interactions, and responses to broader forces—form the basic patterns of world history for the past 5000 years.

Early Human Societies, 2.5 million–600 B.C.E.: Origins and Development

These prehistoric paintings of animals, on the wall of a cave in Lascaux, France, date from 15,000 to 10,000 B.C.E. They show the centrality of meat, hides, and bones taken from wild animals in the economy and symbolism of hunting and gathering peoples.

PART OUTLINE

THE OVERVIEW: MIGRATIONS AND REVOLUTIONARY CHANGES IN HUMAN ECONOMY AND ORGANIZATION

The earliest known, fully human species lived in east Africa about 2.5 million years ago. Gradually, humans developed a more erect stance and greater brain capacity. Early humans lived by hunting and gathering. Because hunting-and-gathering economies require a great deal of space—on average about 2.5 square miles per person—populations remained small, and people lived in small groups. Even a modest population increase in a hunting-and-gathering group required part of the group to migrate in search of new game. Tens of thousands of years ago, the most advanced of the human species, *Homo sapiens sapiens*, migrated from Africa into the Middle East, then into Europe and Asia, and later into Australia and the Americas. Early humans developed tools, first using stones, sticks, and other natural objects. Gradually, people learned to fashion tools and weapons from stone, bone, and wood.

Domestication of animals and techniques of crop growing ultimately created alternatives to the hunting-and-gathering economy. Herding activities constituted one option, but agriculture was the more important innovation. Agriculture began at different times in different places, from about 10,000 years ago onward. It developed independently in at least three regions and perhaps more. The top map on the next page shows the early centers of food production. Gradually, agriculture spread widely, although not universally, from these initial centers.

The development of agriculture was a radical change in humans' way of life. By providing a dependable source of food, it allowed people to live in larger groups. Later on, toolmaking technology advanced with the discovery of metalworking, which in turn further increased agricultural production. Increased production freed some members of the society to perform other kinds of work. This in turn encouraged a further series of organizational changes we call civilization.

Early civilizations arose in several different sites, four of them along the fertile shores of great rivers. Most of these early civilizations arose independently of each other. The map of early civilizations on the bottom of the next page makes another point clear: large parts of the world were not involved in these developments. Early world history focuses on agricultural civilizations, but it must also pay attention to regions that developed different kinds of economies and different organizational structures.

Big Concepts

Each of the key phases of the long period of early human history (2.5 million B.C.E.–1000 B.C.E.) can be characterized by a central topic or Big Concept. The first of these is the development of human hunting skills, the adaptation of those skills to the shifting geography and climate of the ice age, and above all the patterns of human migration that brought humans to so many different areas. The second Big Concept is the rise of agriculture and the changes in technology associated with the Neolithic revolution (9000 and 4000 B.C.E.). These changes set in motion the agricultural phase of the human experience that lasted until just a few centuries ago. The final Big Concept is the appearance of increasingly distinctive human societies through agriculture or nomadic pastoralism, and the earliest contacts among these first societies, particularly after 3500 B.C.E. when larger and more formally organized societies,

Bone tools show the increasing intentionality of tool use among hunting and gathering peoples, as implements were shaped for various purposes.

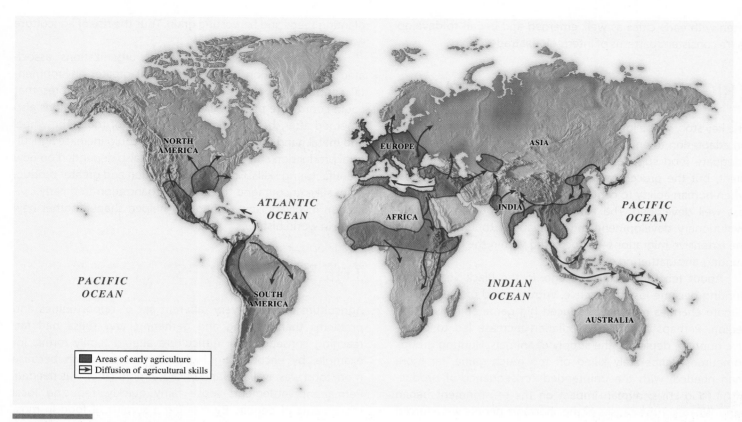

Initial Centers and Spread of Agriculture

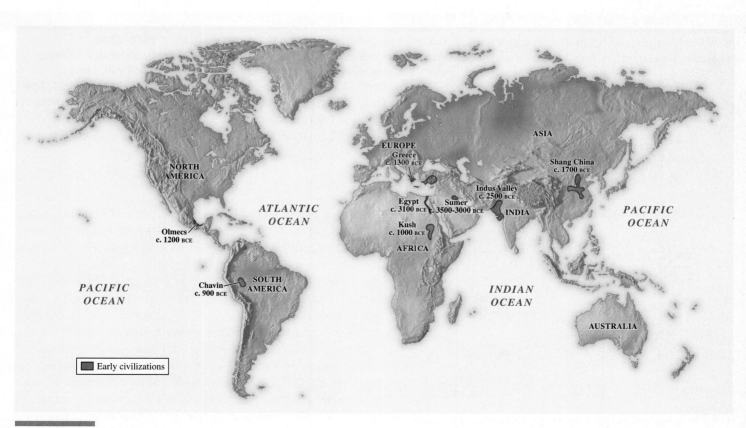

Early Centers of Civilization

often with early cities as well, emerged and began to develop more consistent patterns of interregional trade.

TRIGGERS FOR CHANGE

The key story in the long early phases of human history focuses on adaptation to environments, and particularly the search for adequate food supplies. Humans still react to their environment, but the process was more apparent in earlier periods, when human ability to control aspects of the environment was less well developed. The early changes in human history—evolutionary development, more advanced tool-making, and the extensive migrations—all occurred within the context of a hunting-and-gathering economy.

About ten thousand years ago, in the Black Sea region, hunting became less productive. With the end of the ice age, climate changes may have reduced big game animals in the region. Perhaps a human population increase led to excessive hunting, depleting the supply of animals. Hunting groups sometimes deliberately killed off too much game, far more than needed, with the unintended consequence of producing a food crisis; human impact on the environment began early. Whatever the causes of the shortage, people were forced to look for new sources of food. Women, as gatherers, had undoubtedly become aware of the possibility of deliberately planting seeds and harvesting grain. Thus the rise of agriculture was under way.

Even the advent of new social organizations associated with civilization involved efforts at greater environmental control. Early civilizations provided social structures that could coordinate projects like irrigation. Early civilizations also emerged after the invention of new kinds of tools. The wheel and metal hand tools, initially of bronze, could increase agricultural production and transport. But they also depended on new manufacturing skills. Greater specialization and greater productivity alike encouraged the kind of organization that early civilization involved. New technology helped shape another new stage in world history.

THE BIG CHANGES

Agriculture offered a very different set of opportunities and problems than hunting and gathering, and these had far-reaching consequences. Agriculture altered family forms, for example, by encouraging higher birth rates, both because more food was available and because more labor was needed. Permanent settlements arose fairly quickly, reducing local movements of people. By creating a surplus of food in most years, agriculture permitted a portion of the population to engage in occupations other than food production. This led to

2.5 million B.C.E.	1.25 million B.C.E.	150,000 B.C.E.	30,000 B.C.E.	10,000 B.C.E.
2.5 million Emergence of *Homo sapiens* in eastern Africa	**1 million** Emergence of *Homo erectus*, an upright, tool-using human **600,000** Wide spread of human species across Asia, Europe, Africa; control of fire	**120,000** Emergence of *Homo sapiens sapiens*, which displaces other human species	**30,000–25,000** Passage of first people to Americas **15,000–12,000** Domestication of dogs	**8500–6500** Domestication of sheep, pigs, goats, cattle **8500–3500** Neolithic Age; development of farming in Middle East

the development of unprecedented levels of social inequality, including heightened inequality between men and women. Agriculture altered the environment, sometimes resulting in overcultivation that depleted the soil. It encouraged humans to live in larger groups, and by doing so it created new vulnerability to communicable diseases. While agriculture clearly generated a mixture of advantages and disadvantages, its greater food production allowed more population growth. This in turn helps explain why agriculture tended to spread and why many people were willing to change basic aspects of their lives to accommodate to this new economy.

In the most fertile areas, agricultural centers ultimately developed the organizational forms associated with civilization, most notably formal political structures and cities. Not all did so: Stateless, loosely organized agricultural societies persisted in quite a few places until relatively modern times. But more formal political structures—states—plus larger urban centers—cities—as places to exchange goods and ideas could further the direction of agricultural economies. It was no accident that the first four centers of civilization developed along river valleys, with their opportunities for irrigation: Civilization resulted from the prosperity of this kind of agriculture but also responded to its organizational needs, for it took coordination to run irrigation systems. Civilizations also helped direct many of the surpluses of agricultural economies to upper-class groups—rulers, landlords, and sometimes priests. As with agriculture,

although to a lesser extent, the arrival of civilizations had wider consequences. Most early civilizations, for example, developed monumental buildings often associated with religion and more formal art and culture were standard features of this final great innovation in early human history.

CONTINUITY

While the development of agriculture brought enormous changes, it is important to remember that major continuities persisted as well. Changes took place very slowly. It took thousands of years for humans to develop New Stone Age technologies such as fashioning tools rather than simply picking up suitably shaped objects, such as rocks.

The slow pace of change had two causes. First, inventing fundamentally new devices took time. In some cases, it never occurred at all: Impressive agricultural societies flourished without ever developing the wheel or metal tools. In addition, many people remained attached to old ways. Because the food supply was so precarious, the risk of innovation probably seemed dangerous. This was one reason why agriculture, although it did fan out from its initial centers, took so long to spread widely. People cherished the habits long associated with local migrations. Many men valued the challenge of hunting. Many groups held out against agriculture, even when they knew of it.

8000 B.C.E.	6000 B.C.E.	5000 B.C.E.	4000 B.C.E.	2000 B.C.E.
7000 First town at Jericho	**5600** Beans domesticated in Western Hemisphere	**5000** Domestication of maize (corn) **5000–2000** Yangshao culture in north China	**4000–3000** Development of writing, bronze metalworking, wheel, plow in Middle East **3500–1800** Sumerian civilization **3100–1087** Founding and flowering of Egyptian civilization **25600–1300** Indus civilization in south Asia **1500** Beginning of Polynesian migrations in Pacific	**1850** Origins of Shang kingdom in China **1800** Formation of Babylonian Empire in Middle East **1700–1300** Rise of village culture in Mesoamerica **1600** Beginning of Indo-European invasions of India and parts of the Mediterranean and Middle East **1600** Spread of civilization to Crete (Minoan) **1500–800** Olmec Civilizations in Central America **1250** Moses and Jewish exodus from Egypt (according to Jewish belief) **1200–700** Vedas composed (India) **1122–770** Zhou Kingdom in China **900** Beginning of Maya (Central America) **850** Beginnings of Chavin culture (Andes) **800** Beginnings of Bantu migration in Africa **800** Initial Greek city states **760–600** Meroe (Kush) rules Egypt

Even as change occurred, it could produce efforts to preserve older values in new ways. In hunting-and-gathering societies, men and women both had key productive roles; the roles were very different, but they generated some mutual respect. With agriculture, men took on functions that probably seemed rather feminine, because they were linked to food gathering, which had been women's responsibility before. Men had far less time to hunt or to enjoy the masculine rituals associated with hunting. So men looked for ways within agriculture to emphasize manhood. One common response was to claim new levels of superiority over women. This was a key change in gender relations, but it can also be seen as a kind of compensation. To this extent, men could feel that not all traditions were being lost. Polytheistic religions in many agricultural societies also preserved older emphases, with gods and goddesses dedicated to the hunt, even as they added rituals linked to planting and harvesting.

Once established, agriculture generated its own impulses toward continuity. Many peasant farmers clung fervently to traditional techniques and village structures, regarding further change with great suspicion. Thus, a tension between change and continuity was built into early human experience.

IMPACT ON DAILY LIFE: CHILDREN

Children are an important part of any human society. Some aspects of children's lives are doubtless natural, part of human experience at any time, in any place. But the arrival of agriculture had huge implications for children. Hunting-and-gathering societies depended on a relatively low birth rate, with few children per family. Too many children would overwhelm resources; and no family could easily transport more than one young child during migrations. So hunters and gatherers limited births, mainly by breast-feeding each child for up to four or five years, which created chemical changes in women's bodies that reduced the chances of new conception.

With agriculture, however, more children could be supported, and indeed children became a vital part of the family labor force. Infants began to be weaned at about 18 months on average, a huge change from earlier human patterns. Birth rates shot up—agricultural families usually averaged five to seven children, although some would die because infant mortality rates were high. Childhood began to be defined in terms of work. Even young children had obligations. And by the time they were teenagers, their families depended on their labor.

This was a dramatic redefinition of childhood, even as children became more numerous in the population at large.

Civilization, as an organizational form, had less impact on children, but it added its own changes. Most civilizations developed written language, although only a minority could afford the time to learn to write. As a result, the vast majority of children worked, but an elite minority were sent to school. Also, civilizations used codes of law and other prescriptions to emphasize the duties of children to their families. All agricultural civilizations emphasized the authority of parents over children and children's obligation to obey their parents. In this way, civilizations tried to instill in children a willingness to work for the benefit of their families. An early Chinese saying stated simply: "No parent is ever wrong." Children could be loved and could flourish, but there was a distinctive tone of strict discipline and obedience in agricultural civilizations that bolstered the necessity of children's labor.

Small wonder that some hunting-and-gathering or herding groups, when they encountered civilizations, were shocked at how rigorously children were handled. Many American Indians were appalled by the harsh physical discipline European immigrants dealt out to their children. Here was an example of agriculture's profound impact on daily life.

SOCIETIES AND TRENDS

Chapter 1 focuses on the development of agriculture and the ways in which it changed the lives of early humans. It then describes how farming led, in fertile river valleys, to the development of civilization, and what was new in this form of human organization. It also notes the limits of these developments—the many regions that continued living by hunting and gathering as well as the different trajectory that was followed by societies whose people lived by herding animals rather than farming. Chapters 2 and 3 focus on the early civilizations in the river valley centers, in Mesopotamia, Egypt, the Indus valley (India), and the Yellow River valley (China), and also on early civilization centers in the Americas. The similarities suggest why people found these new organizational forms useful and how the forms responded to needs and opportunities within agriculture, but each also had its own flavor and specific history. This distinctiveness helped set in motion enduring differences among the world's civilizations. Chapters 2 and 3 thus also emphasize opportunities to compare the early civilizations. ■

The Neolithic Revolution and the Birth of Civilization

Listen to Chapter 1
on MyHistoryLab

One day about 10,000 years ago, in a rock shelter near the Pecos River, an early human inhabitant of what is today west Texas inserted the bloom stalk of a yucca plant into one of several holes worn into a fire-starting stick and, holding the stalk upright, twirled it between her hands, as depicted in the artist's recreation on this page. After much effort on the part of the young woman, the friction between the spinning stalk and the stick produced wisps of smoke, then sparks, then glowing embers. The woman used the embers to set fire to a small pile of dried yucca leaves that she had gathered. Yucca leaves have thin tendrils that, when dry, catch fire readily. Carefully tended, the leaves could be used to kindle a steady fire that provided not only warmth, but the means for cooking a meal. And, importantly, stalks, fire-sticks, and leaves could easily be carried by migratory groups of early humans.

Read the Document on MyHistoryLab: A Visitor from the Neolithic Age

LEARNING OBJECTIVES

1.1 What were the major concerns and activities of early humans and in what ways might these explain the very slow development of early human societies? p. 9

1.2 Why has sedentary agriculture been so critical to the rise and persistence of civilizations as they are defined in the chapter that follows? p. 14

1.3 In what ways did the rise of towns promote contacts and ongoing linkages between different human communities both within particular regions and across regional boundaries? p. 19

FIGURE **1.1** Crouching against a wall to shelter the first sparks from wind, a Neolithic woman spins a dried yucca stalk against a much-used fire-starter to generate heat that will kindle a fire on the dried plant material she has placed under the fire-starting stick.

👁 Watch the Video Series on MyHistoryLab

Learn about some key topics related to this chapter with the *MyHistoryLab Video Series:* *Key Topics in World History*

Several yucca-based fire-starter kits, some including bows used in the place of hands to turn the yucca stalk, have been found across the American Southwest. These Neolithic (New Stone Age) kits send us a number of messages about early world history. Most obviously, early men and women were tool users. They not only deliberately selected branches, stones, and other natural objects from the environment, they crafted them into weapons, utensils, and tools that could be used to ward off animal and human enemies, hunt, trap, fish, prepare food, and construct shelters. This capacity to fashion tools distinguishes human beings from all other animals. Although a number of other animals, including apes, are tool users, only human beings invent and craft their tools. By this time, humans had known how to make and use fire for thousands of years—another discovery unique to humans. The use of fire for cooking allowed early humans to eat a wider variety of foods, particularly animal protein.

The toolmakers of the American Southwest lived far from eastern Africa, where human beings first evolved. Just decades ago, it was believed that the first humans migrated from northeast Asia into what is now Alaska only 12,000 years ago. Vastly improved archeological techniques have recently revealed that the crossing had been made at least as early as 25,000 B.C.E. and that the migrants spread out quickly, probably traveling both overland and by boat along the Pacific Coast, from Alaska to Chile.

Finally, we know our early ancestors could talk. Human beings had developed what some call the "speech gene" about 70,000 years earlier, vastly improving the species' capacity to communicate, beyond the sounds and gestures common to a number of animal groups. Neolithic humans were what we sometimes call "primitive," but they had already experienced a number of fundamental changes and, in some places, they were poised to introduce some more. ■

The creation of fire-starters and other tools, including weapons, proved critical to the survival of early humans and to the development of ever-larger communities and eventually whole societies. In the chapter that follows we will trace the successive stages of the early material and social development of the human species. We will explore the technological and organizational innovations that made it possible for what became the great majority of humans to move from tiny bands of wandering hunters and gatherers to sedentary village dwellers and then the builders of walled cities with populations in the thousands. More than any other factor, these transformations were made possible by the development of agriculture that increased and made more secure the supply of food by which more and more humans could be sustained.

The domestication of animals and the shift to agriculture were accompanied by major changes in the roles and relationships between men and women and patterns of childrearing. They also led to increasing social stratification, new forms of political organization, increasingly elaborate means of artistic expression, and more lethal ways of waging war. During the millennia of transition farming communities occupied only small pockets of the earth's land area and only rarely ventured out on the sea or large rivers. *Pastoral* peoples who depended on herds of domesticated animals for their livelihood occupied a far greater share of the space where there was a human presence. An uneasy balance between the peoples who followed these two main adaptations to the diverse ecosystems in which humans proved able to survive was a dominant feature of the history of the species and the planet until five or six centuries ago.

| Late Paleolithic | Transition Phase | Neolithic Age | | Metal Age | |
15,000 B.C.E.	10,000 B.C.E.	8000 B.C.E.	6000 B.C.E.	4000 B.C.E.	2000 B.C.E.
18,000–100,000 Central Russian mammoth bone settlements **15,000–12,000** Domestication of dogs **10,500–8000** Natufian settlements	**8500** Domestication of sheep **8500–5000** Development of farming in the Middle East	**7500–6500** Domestication of pigs, goats, cattle **7000** Full-fledged town at Jericho **6250–5400** Çatal Hüyük at its peak	**5600** Beans domesticated **5000–2000** Yangshao culture in north China **5000** Domestication of maize (corn)	**4000–3000** Age of innovation in the Middle East: introduction of writing, metalworking, wheel, plow **3500** Llama domesticated **3500–2350** Civilization of Sumer **c. 3100** Rise of Egyptian civilization **2500–1500** Indus valley civilization in south Asia	2000 Kotosh culture in Peru **c. 1766** Emergence of Shang kingdom in China **1700–1300** Rise of village culture in Mesoamerica **1000–500** Olmec civilization in Mesoamerica **400** Potatoes domesticated

HUMAN LIFE IN THE ERA OF HUNTERS AND GATHERERS

1.1 What were the major concerns and activities of early humans and in what ways might these explain the very slow development of early human societies?

A group of historians currently working on what they call Big History point out that the human experience is only a brief moment in the larger history of the earth itself and the origins of various forms of life. Big History furthers a discussion of when and how the human species emerged and what impact its arrival would have, over time, on the physical environment and on other species. In this approach human history fits into a larger pattern of terrestrial change.

By the late Paleolithic Age (Old Stone Age) in 12,000 B.C.E., humans had evolved in physical appearance and mental capacity to roughly the same level as today. Our species, ***Homo sapiens***, had been competing with increasing success for game and campsites with other humanlike creatures for nearly 100,000 years. *Homo sapiens'* large brain, critical to the survival of all branches of the genus *Homo*, was almost the same size as that of modern humans. As Figure 1.2 shows, the erect posture of Stone Age humans and related humanoids freed their hands. The combination of these free hands with opposable thumbs and a large brain enabled different human species to make and use tools and weapons of increasing sophistication. These implements helped to offset the humans' marked inferiority in body strength and speed to rival predators, such as wolves and wild cats, as well as to many of the creatures that humans hunted. A more developed brain ultimately allowed humans to transform cries and grunts into the patterned sounds that make up language. Language greatly enhanced the possibilities for cooperation and for cohesion within the small bands that were the predominant form of human social organization. By the end of the Paleolithic Age, these advantages had made *Homo sapiens* a species capable of changing its environment.

During the course of human evolution, one other interesting change occurred. In contrast to the great apes and other mammals, human children did not develop mature teeth until well after weaning. For human children to survive, their parents or other adults had to devote a much longer period to providing food. Family structures had to develop accordingly.

Paleolithic Culture

By the late Paleolithic Age, human groups survived by combining hunting and fishing with the gathering of wild fruits, berries, grains, and roots. They had created many tools, such as those shown in Figure 1.3, for these purposes. Tools of wood and bone have perished; surviving stone tools such as these are our main evidence of the technology of this age. Early tools, crafted by species from which humans evolved, have been found at sites well over 2 million years old. These early species made tools by breaking off the edges of stones to create crude points or rough cutting surfaces. By the late Paleolithic Age, their fully human descendants had grown much more adept at working stone. They

Hunting and gathering economies dominated human history until 9,000 B.C.E. These economies helped propel migration over most of the lands on earth.

Homo sapiens The humanoid species that emerged as most successful at the end of the Paleolithic period.

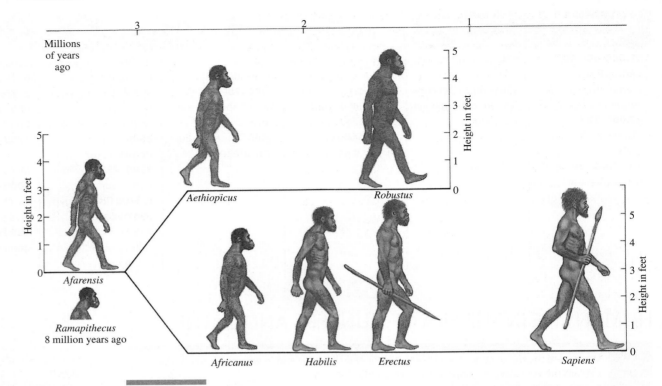

FIGURE **1.2** As this artist's illustration shows, the humanoids' upright posture, which freed their hands, meant that over long periods of time *Homo sapiens* could develop tools and weapons. This meant that they became less fit for life in the tree canopy of forested areas. But their improving eyesight and ability to walk or run ever greater distances proved highly advantageous in the open grassland areas they came to prefer.

preferred to chip and sharpen flakes broken off a larger stone. These chips could be made into knife blades, arrow points, or choppers, which had a wide range of uses, from hunting and warfare to skinning animal carcasses and harvesting wild plants. Well before the Paleolithic—as many as half a million years ago—humans had also mastered fire.

Early human groups also left behind impressive evidence of artistic creativity. The late Paleolithic was a period of particularly intense artistic production. Fine miniature sculpture, beads and other forms of jewelry, and carved bones have been found in abundance at sites dating from this period. But the most striking works that survive from this period are the cave paintings that have been discovered at dwelling sites in areas as diverse as southern France, the plains of Africa south of the Sahara, and the Middle East. Some of these paintings appear to have religious significance. They may have been intended to depict prominent deities or to promote fertility. Paintings at some sites may represent early counting systems or primitive calendars. The art of the Old Stone Age indicates that humans were becoming increasingly interested in leaving lasting images of their activities and concerns.

Paintings and wood or stone sculptures were also crafted to worship and seek the assistance of nature spirits that were the center of the *animistic religions*. Animists believe that the natural world is alive with supernatural forces, which can be concentrated in groves of trees or revered animals or move about the atmosphere. *Shamans* or priests, who were gifted with the ability to communicate with these spirits, were among the first specialists in human societies. Animist beliefs and practices were pervasive in early human societies, and they endure to the present day in some pastoral cultures and among hunter-gathering and shifting cultivating peoples.

The Spread of Human Culture

Migration was essential whenever hunting-and-gathering populations expanded, and it led to the surprisingly early peopling of the world's major land masses. This forms the leading theme of the long first stage of the human experience.

As Map 1.1 illustrates, the possession of fire and tools with which to make clothing and shelters made it possible for different human species to extend the range of their habitation far beyond the areas where they had originated. During the last ice age, which began about 2.5 million years ago and ended in the 12,000s B.C.E., humans first moved northward from Africa into Europe and eastward from the present-day Middle East into central Asia, India, and east Asia. From there, some peoples migrated across a land bridge into the continents we now call North and South America. Rising waters with warmer temperatures eliminated the land bridge and further migration by 10,000 B.C.E. By 12,000 B.C.E., human colonies were found not only in North and South America but also in the south and west of Australia. People reached Australia by boat, but the island chain of Southeast Asia extended much closer to Australia than is now the case, thanks to lower ocean levels and a larger land mass. Thus, by the late Paleolithic Age, groups of the *Homo sapiens* species had colonized all of the continents except Antarctica.

Human Society and Daily Life at the End of the Paleolithic Age

Most human societies in the Paleolithic Age consisted of small groups that migrated regularly in pursuit of game, animals, and wild plants. But recent archeological research has shown that in some places, natural conditions and human ingenuity permitted some groups to establish settlements, where they lived for much of the year and in some cases for generation after generation. These settled communities harvested wild grains that grew in abundance in many areas. After surviving for centuries in this way, some of these communities made the transition to true farming by domesticating plants and animals near their permanent village sites. Others reverted to migration; there was no single pattern.

However successful a particular group proved to be at hunting and gathering, few could support a band larger than 20 to 30 men, women, and children. Dependence on migrating herds of game made these bands **nomads**, many of whom moved back and forth between the same forested and grazing areas year after year. These migration patterns meant that small numbers of humans needed a large land area to support themselves, so human population densities were very low.

Most of us imagine Stone Age peoples living in caves. But recent research suggests that most preferred to live on open ground. The migratory peoples who lived on hilltops or in forest clearings built temporary shelters of skins and leaves or grass thatching. Their flimsy campsites could be readily abandoned when movements of the herd animals they hunted or threats from competing bands prompted migration. Although it is likely that bands developed a sense of territoriality, boundaries were vague, and much conflict focused on rival claims to sources of game and wild foods.

Within each **band**, labor was divided according to gender. Men hunted and fished in riverine or coastal areas. Because they became skilled in the use of weapons in the hunt, it is also likely that men protected the band from animal predators and raids by other human groups. As the cave paintings featured in the Document section suggest, animal hunts were major events in the annual cycle of life in Paleolithic societies. Nearly all able-bodied men participated in the hunting parties, and women and children prepared and preserved the meat. Although women's roles were less adventuresome and aggressive than men's, they were arguably more critical to the survival of the band. Women gathered the foods that provided the basic subsistence of the band and permitted its survival in times when hunting parties were unsuccessful. Women also became adept at using medicinal plants, which were the only means Paleolithic peoples had to treat disease.

Settling Down: Dead Ends and Transitions

Although most humans lived in small hunting-and-gathering bands until well into the **agrarian revolution**, between 8500 and 3500 B.C.E., some prefarming peoples worked out a very different strategy of survival. They devised more intensive hunting-and-gathering patterns that permitted

Read the Document on MyHistoryLab: Marshall Sahlins, "The Original Affluent Society"

FIGURE **1.3** Early human groups developed a variety of stone tools. The tools shown here include weapon points and scrapers for peeling off animal hides or shaping wood.

nomads Cattle- and sheep-herding societies normally found on the fringes of civilized societies; commonly referred to as "barbarian" by civilized societies.

band A level of social organization normally consisting of 20 to 30 people; nomadic hunters and gatherers; labor divided on a gender basis.

agrarian revolution Occurred between 8500 and 3500 B.C.E.; transition from hunting and gathering to sedentary agriculture.

MAP **1.1 The Spread of Human Populations, c. 10,000 B.C.E.** As the map indicates, *Homo sapiens sapiens* first emerged in a single core area in east Africa and then migrated over long periods of time north to the Mediterranean and Europe, east to Asia, and then ultimately across the seas to the Americas and Oceania.

them to establish semipermanent and even permanent settlements and to support larger and more complex forms of social organization. Among the most spectacular Paleolithic settlements are those of central Russia. Apparently, there was an abundance of large but slow woolly mammoths in that region some 20,000 years ago. These animals supplied meat that, when supplemented by wild plant foods gathered in the area, made it possible for local peoples to live in the same place throughout much of the year. Large numbers of mammoth bones found in what were in effect garbage pits at the settlement sites suggest how dependent they were on the mammoths. This reliance is equally vividly demonstrated by the extensive use of the bones of these huge mammals in building dwellings.

Remnants found in food storage pits and other artifacts from the central Russian settlements suggest that these people participated in trading networks with other peoples as far as 500 miles away in the area of the Black Sea. Burial patterns and differing degrees of bodily decoration also indicate clear status differences among the groups that inhabited the settlements. Mammoth bone communities lasted from about 18,000 to 10,000 B.C.E., when they suddenly disappeared for reasons that are still unknown.

Even more sophisticated than the central Russian settlements were those of the **Natufian complex**, which extended over much of present-day Palestine, Israel, Jordan, and Lebanon. Climate changes between 12,000 and 11,000 B.C.E. enabled wild barley and wheat plants to spread over much of this area. When supplemented with nuts and the meat of gazelles and other game, these wild grains were sufficient to support many densely populated settlements on a permanent basis. Between about 10,500 and 8000 B.C.E., the Natufian culture flourished. Population densities reached as high as six to seven times those of other early Neolithic communities. The Natufians developed sophisticated techniques of storing grain, and they devised pestles and grinding slabs to prepare it for meals. They built circular and oval stone dwellings that were occupied year round for centuries.

The evidence from housing layouts, burial sites, jewelry, and other artifacts indicates that, like the mammoth-hunting societies of central Russia, Natufian society was stratified. Clothing appears to have been used to distinguish a person's rank, and grand burial ceremonies marked the death of community chieftains. There is also evidence that Natufian society was **matrilocal** (young men went to live with their wives' families) and **matrilineal** (family descent and inheritance were traced through the female line). The fact that women gathered food crops in the wild may explain the power and influence they enjoyed in Natufian settlements.

Natufian complex Preagricultural culture; located in present-day Israel, Jordan, Lebanon; practiced the collection of naturally present barley and wheat to supplement game; typified by large settlement sites.

matrilocal A culture in which young men upon marriage go to live with the brides' families.

matrilineal Family descent and inheritance traced through the female line.

DOCUMENT

Tales of the Hunt: Paleolithic Cave Paintings as History

THE FIRST HISTORICAL EVENTS RECORDED BY humans were the animal hunts, depicted in remarkably realistic and colorful cave paintings. Because writing would not be devised by any human group for many millennia to come, we cannot be certain of the meanings that those who created the paintings were trying to convey. Some of them may have been done purely for the sake of artistic expression. But others, which clearly depict animals in flight, pursued by human hunters, probably were painted to celebrate and commemorate actual incidents in particularly successful hunting expeditions. Their locations deep in cave complexes and the rather consistent choice of game animals as subject matter suggest that they also served a ritual purpose. Perhaps capturing the images of animals in art was seen as a way of assisting future hunting parties in the wild. In addition, it is possible that those who painted the animal figures hoped to acquire some of the strength and speed of the animals to improve their chances in the hunt and to ward off animals that preyed on the human hunters. Whatever their intentions, those who created these early works of art, such as the one shown here, also created the first conscious historical accounts of the human experience.

Read the Document on MyHistoryLab: The Toolmaker 3300 BCE

In 1940 in Lascaux, France, four boys playing together discovered a long-hidden cave filled with thousands of complex and beautiful Stone Age paintings like this one. Most of the paintings are of animals, some of which were extinct by the time they were painted. No one knows for sure why Stone Age artists painted these pictures, but they remain a powerful reminder of the sophistication of so-called primitive peoples.

QUESTIONS

- Which interpretation of the meanings of the cave paintings outlined here makes the most sense to you? Why?
- How can we use what we know about Paleolithic societies to read these paintings for historical information?

The Natufian strategy for survival did not involve new tools or production techniques. It rested primarily on intensive gathering of wild grains and improvement of storage techniques. But the Natufians' concentration on several grain staples, gazelle meat, and nuts rendered the culture vulnerable. After 9000 B.C.E., the climate of the region where the Natufian settlements were located grew more and more arid. The grains and game on which they depended were reduced or vanished from many locations. One thousand years later, all the Natufian sites had been abandoned.

A Precarious Existence

Until the late Paleolithic, advances in human technology and social organization were remarkably slow compared with the advances that have occurred since about 8000 B.C.E. Millions of years of evolution of the genus *Homo* had produced small numbers of humans, mostly scattered in tiny bands across six continents. Probably no more than 8 million people lived worldwide on the eve of agriculture. On average, the lives of these humans were violent and short. They crouched around their campfires in constant fear of animal predators and human enemies. They were at the mercy of the elements and helpless in the face of injury or disease. They had a few crude tools and weapons; their nomadic existence reflected their dependence on the feeding cycles of migrating animals.

The smaller numbers of human groups that lived in permanent settlements had better shelters, a more secure food supply, and larger communities on which to draw in their relentless struggle for survival. But their lifestyles were precarious; their specialized hunting-and-gathering practices meant that shifts in grazing patterns or the climate could undermine their carefully developed cultures. Late Paleolithic humans had improved greatly on earlier versions of the species. But there was little evidence that within a few thousand years they would radically transform their environments and dominate all other forms of life.

AGRICULTURE AND THE ORIGINS OF CIVILIZATION: THE NEOLITHIC TRANSFORMATIONS

1.2 Why has sedentary agriculture been so critical to the rise and persistence of civilizations?

The Neolithic revolution, between 8500 and 3500 B.C.E., introduced domestication of animals and agriculture. These innovations led to population increases.

There was nothing natural or inevitable about the development of agriculture. Because plant cultivation involves more labor than hunting and gathering, we can assume that Stone Age humans gave up their former ways of life reluctantly and slowly. In fact, peoples such as the Bushmen of southwest Africa still follow them today. But between about 8500 and 3500 B.C.E., increasing numbers of humans shifted to dependence on cultivated crops and domesticated animals for their subsistence. By about 7000 B.C.E., their tools and skills had advanced sufficiently to enable cultivating peoples to support towns with more than 1000 people, such as Jericho in the valley of the Jordan River and Çatal Hüyük (cha-tal HOY-ewk) in present-day Turkey. By 3500 B.C.E., agricultural peoples in the Middle East could support sufficient numbers of non-farmers to give rise to the first civilizations. As this pattern spread to or developed independently in other parts of the world, the character of most human lives and the history of the species were fundamentally transformed. The Big History approach calls attention to what amounts to a long "agricultural period" of the human experience, running from the Neolithic until about 300 years ago.

Because there are no written records of the transition period between 8500 and 3500 B.C.E., we cannot be certain why and how some peoples adopted these new ways of producing food and other necessities of life. Climatic changes associated with the retreat of the glaciers late in the last ice age (from about 12,000 B.C.E.) may have played an important role. These climatic shifts prompted the migration of many big game animals to new pasturelands in northern areas. They also left a dwindling supply of game for human hunters in areas such as the Middle East, where agriculture first arose and many animals were first domesticated. Climatic shifts also led to changes in the distribution and growing patterns of wild grains and other crops on which hunters and gatherers depended.

In addition, it is likely that the shift to sedentary farming was prompted by an increase in human populations in certain areas. This population growth may have been caused by changes in the climate and plant and animal life. It is also possible that population growth occurred because the hunting-and-gathering pattern reached higher levels of productivity. Peoples such as the Natufians found that their human communities could grow significantly as they intensively harvested grains that grew in the wild. As the population grew, more and more attention was given to the grain harvest, which eventually led to the conscious and systematic cultivation of plants and thus the Neolithic transformations in human sustenance and lifestyles.

The Domestication of Plants and Animals

The peoples who first cultivated cereal grains had long observed them growing in the wild and collected their seeds as they gathered other plants for their leaves and roots. In late Paleolithic times, wild barley and wheat grew over large areas in the present-day Middle East. Hunting-and-gathering bands in these areas may have consciously experimented with planting and nurturing seeds taken from the wild, or they may have accidentally discovered the principles of domestication by observing the growth of seeds dropped near their campsites.

However it began, the practice of agriculture caught on only gradually. Archeological evidence suggests that the first agriculturists retained their hunting-and-gathering activities as a hedge against the ever-present threat of starvation. But as Stone Age peoples became more adept at cultivating a growing range of crops, including various fruits, olives, and protein-rich legumes such as peas and beans, the effort they expended on activities outside agriculture diminished.

The earliest farmers probably sowed wild seeds, a practice that cut down on labor but sharply reduced the potential yield. Over the centuries, more and more care was taken to select the best grain for seed and to mix different strains in ways that improved crop yields and resistance to plant diseases. As the time needed to tend growing plants and the dependence on agricultural production increased, some roving bands chose to settle down, and others practiced a mix of hunting and **shifting cultivation** that allowed them to continue to move about.

Several animals may have been domesticated before the discovery of agriculture, and the two processes combined to make up the critical transformation in human culture called the Neolithic revolution. Different animal species were tamed in different ways that reflected both their own natures and the ways in which they interacted with humans. For example, dogs were originally wolves that hunted humans or scavenged at their campsites. As early as 12,000 B.C.E., Stone Age peoples, initially in east Asia, found that wolf pups could be tamed and trained to track and corner game. The strains of dogs that gradually developed proved adept at controlling herd animals such as sheep. Knowledge of dogs spread quickly over almost all inhabited areas—the later migrations to the Americas included Asian dogs—because they were so useful in hunting and herding. Docile and defenseless herds of sheep could be domesticated once their leaders had been captured and tamed. Sheep, goats, and pigs (which also were scavengers at human campsites) were first domesticated in the Middle East between 8500 and 7000 B.C.E. Horned cattle, which could run faster and were better able to defend themselves than wild sheep, were not tamed until about 6500 B.C.E.

Domesticated animals such as cattle and sheep provided New Stone Age humans with additional sources of protein-rich meat and in some cases milk. Animal hides and wool greatly expanded the materials from which clothes, containers, shelters, and crude boats could be crafted. Animal horns and bones could be carved or used for needles and other utensils. Because plows and wheels did not come into use until the Bronze Age, about 4000–3500 B.C.E., when stone tools and weapons gave way to metal ones, most Neolithic peoples made little use of animal power for farming, transportation, or travel. However, there is evidence that peoples in northern areas used tamed reindeer to pull sleds, and those further south used camels to transport goods. More importantly, Neolithic peoples used domesticated herd animals as a steady source of manure to enrich the soil and thus improve the yield of the crops that were gradually becoming the basis of their livelihood.

The domestication of animals, particularly cattle, sheep, horses, and camels, provided humans with another mode, *pastoralism*, of adapting to the environment. In roughly the same era as sedentary agriculture was being developed, groups of humans moved into the grasslands of central Asia and the Middle East, where they bred and tended herds of cattle, sheep, and goats. Domesticated livestock provided them with a steady supply of meat and milk, their staple foods, as well as hides for clothing and housing and bones that could be fashioned into tools and weapons. In some cases, pastoral peoples tamed horses, which allowed them to control larger and larger herds of domesticated animals and to hunt wild animals, such as bison and deer, thus expanding their food supply. On the downside, at least in the early stages of pastoralism and the domestication of animals more generally, contact with humans increased the incidence of disease for all of the species involved. Experts suggest that up to 80 percent of all human diseases came originally from animals. Improvements in food supply and mobility made the tradeoff worthwhile, but agricultural societies and pastoral societies were burdened with new kinds of problems and anxieties as well.

The Spread of the Neolithic Revolution

The greater labor involved in cultivation, and the fact that it did not at first greatly enhance peoples' security or living standards, caused many bands to stay with long-tested subsistence strategies. Through most of the Neolithic Age, sedentary agricultural communities coexisted with more numerous bands of hunters and gatherers, migratory farmers, and hunters and fishers. Long after sedentary agriculture became the basis for the livelihood of the majority of humans, hunters and gatherers and shifting cultivators held out in many areas of the globe. More than any other alternative, **pastoralism** has proved to be the strongest competitor to sedentary agriculture as a way of life throughout most of the world. The nomadic herding way of life has thrived in semiarid areas such as central Asia, the Middle East, the Sudanic belt south of the Sahara desert in Africa, and the savanna zone of east and south Africa and in parts of the Americas and Oceania. These regions could not support dense or large populations, but they have produced independent and hardy

shifting cultivation An intermediate form of ecological adaptation in which temporary forms of cultivation are carried out with little impact on the natural ecology; typical of rainforest cultivators.

Read the Document on MyHistoryLab: David Rindos, from "Symbiosis, Instability, and the Origins and Spread of Agriculture: A New Model"

pastoralism A nomadic agricultural lifestyle dependent on domesticated animal herds that feed on the natural environment; typically more populous than shifting cultivation groups.

peoples. Nomads have developed the military skills needed to challenge more heavily populated agrarian societies. As we shall see, horse-riding nomads who herded sheep or cattle have destroyed powerful kingdoms and laid the foundations for vast empires. The camel nomads of Arabia played critical roles in the rise of Islamic civilization. The cattle-herding peoples of central, east, and south Africa produced some of the most formidable, preindustrial military organizations. Interactions between herding nomads and agricultural peoples have been a major theme in world history until about 500 years ago.

Those who adopted agriculture gained a more stable base for survival and increased in numbers. They also passed on their production techniques to other peoples. The spread of key crops can be traced on Map 1.2. Wheat and barley spread throughout the Middle East and to India. These crops also spread northward to Europe, where oats and rye were added later. From Egypt, the cultivation of grain crops and fibers, such as flax and cotton used for clothing, spread to peoples along the Nile in the interior of Africa, along the north African coast, and across the vast savanna zone south of the Sahara desert.

Agriculture in the African rainforest zone farther south evolved independently in the 2nd millennium B.C.E. and was based on root crops such as cassava and tree crops such as bananas and palm nuts. In northern China during the Neolithic Age, a millet-based agricultural system developed along the Huang-he (hwahng huh) or Yellow River basin. From this core region, it spread in the last millennium B.C.E. east toward the North China Sea and southward toward the Yangzi (YANG-see) basin. A later but independent agricultural revolution based on rice began in mainland southeast Asia sometime before 5000 B.C.E. and slowly spread north toward south China and west toward India and across the islands of southeast Asia. In the Americas, agrarian systems based on maize (corn), manioc, and sweet potatoes arose in Mesoamerica (Mexico and Central America today) and present-day Peru. Long before the arrival of Columbus in the Americas in 1492 C.E., these and other crops had spread through large portions of the continents of the Western Hemisphere, from the temperate woodlands of the North Atlantic coast to the rain forests of the Amazon

Watch the Video on MyHistoryLab: Agricultural Innovations in Ancient Africa (Jonathan T. Reynolds)

MAP **1.2 The Spread of Agriculture** Agriculture appears to have spread in ways similar to human populations, but from a Middle Eastern rather than African epicenter. And in important cases, particularly in the Americas, a wide range of staple crops were known in only some parts of the world until Columbus's voyage in the late-15th century brought together the civilizations of the Americas and Afro-Euroasia.

region. Thus, varying patterns of agricultural production were disseminated on all the inhabited continents except Australia to nearly all the regions of the globe with sufficient rainfall and suitable temperatures.

The Transformation of Material Life

With the development of agriculture, humans began to transform more and more extensively the environments in which they lived. A growing portion of humans became sedentary farmers who cleared the lands around their settlements and controlled the plants that grew and the animals that grazed on them. The greater presence of humans was also apparent in the steadily growing size and numbers of settlements. These were found both in areas that humans had long inhabited and in new regions that farming allowed them to settle. This great increase in the number of sedentary farmers is primarily responsible for the leap in human population during the Neolithic Age. For tens of thousands of years before agriculture was developed, the total number of humans had fluctuated between an estimated 5 and 8 million. By 4000 B.C.E., after four or five millennia of farming, their numbers had risen to 60 or 70 million. Hunting-and-gathering bands managed to subsist in the zones between cultivated areas and continued to fight and trade with sedentary peoples. Areas devoted to pastoralism became even more important. But villages and cultivated fields became the dominant features of human habitation over much of the globe.

The sudden surge in invention and social complexity in the Neolithic Age marks one of the great turning points in human history. Increased reliance on sedentary cultivation led to the development of a wide variety of agricultural tools, such as digging sticks used to break up the soil, axes to clear forested areas, and the plow. Seed selection, planting, fertilization, and weeding techniques improved steadily. By the end of the Neolithic Age, human societies in several areas had devised ways to store rainwater and re-channel river water to irrigate plants. The reservoirs, canals, dikes, and sluices that permitted water storage and control represented another major advance in humans' ability to remake their environment.

More and better tools and permanent settlements gave rise to larger, more elaborate housing and community ritual centers. Houses usually were uniform in construction. Most of the early ones contained the features depicted in Figure 1.4, which shows an archeological reconstruction of a dwelling from the Neolithic Age. Building materials varied greatly by region, but sun-dried bricks, wattle (interwoven branches, usually plastered with mud), and stone structures were associated with early agricultural communities. Seasonal harvests made improved techniques of food storage essential. At first, baskets and leather containers were used. But already in the early Neolithic Age, pottery, which protected stored foods better from moisture and dust, was known to several cultures in the Middle East.

Social Differentiation

The surplus production that agriculture made possible was the key to the social transformations that made up another dimension of the Neolithic revolution. Surpluses meant that farmers could exchange part of their harvest for the specialized services and products of craftspeople such as toolmakers and weavers. Human communities became differentiated by occupations. Full-time political and religious leaders emerged and eventually formed elite classes. But in the Neolithic Age, the specialized production of stone tools, weapons, and pottery was a more important consequence of the development of agriculture than the formation of elites. Originally, each household crafted the tools and weapons it needed, just as it wove its own baskets and produced its own clothing. Over time, however, families or individuals who proved

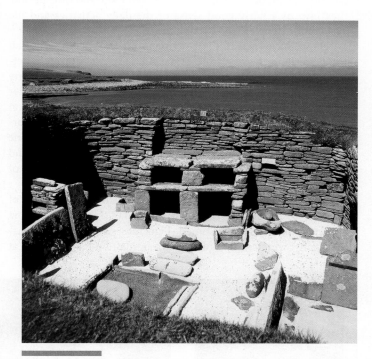

FIGURE **1.4** Houses in early agricultural settlements, such as this one reconstructed at Skara Brae in coastal Scotland, usually included special storage areas for grain, water, and other essentials. Most were centered on clay or stone hearths that were ventilated by a hole in the roof or built into the walls. There were also clearly demarcated and slightly raised sleeping areas, and benches along the walls. More dependable and varied food supplies and sturdy houses greatly enhanced the security and comfort of human groups. These conditions spurred higher birth rates and lowered mortality rates, at least in times when crop yields were high.

particularly skilled in these tasks began to manufacture implements beyond their own needs and to exchange them for grain, milk, or meat.

Villages in certain regions specialized in producing materials that were in demand in other areas. For example, flint, which is extremely hard, was the preferred material for axe blades. Axes were needed for forest clearing, which was essential to the extension of cultivation in much of Europe. The demand was so great that villagers who lived near flint deposits could support themselves by mining the flint or crafting the flint heads and trading, often with peoples who lived far from the sources of production. Such exchanges set precedents for regional specialization and interregional trade.

VISUALIZING THE PAST

Representations of Women in Early Art

THE EARLIEST WRITING SYSTEM WE KNOW of was not introduced until around 3500 B.C.E. in the civilization of Sumer in Mesopotamia (see Chapter 2). Consequently, evidence for piecing together the history of human life in the Paleolithic and Neolithic ages comes mainly from surviving artifacts from campsites and early towns. Stone tools, bits of pottery or cloth, and the remains of Stone Age dwellings can now be dated rather precisely. When combined with other objects from the same site and time period, they give us a fairly good sense of the daily activities and life cycle of the peoples who created them.

As we have seen in the Document on cave paintings, of all the material remains of the Stone Age era, none provide better insights into the social organization and thinking of early humans than works of art. Much of what we know about gender relations, or the status of males and females and the interaction between them, has been interpreted from the study of the different forms of artistic expression of Stone Age peoples. The stone carvings and figurines reproduced here illustrate themes and impressions of women and their roles that recur in the art of many prehistoric cultures.

Some of the earliest rock carvings, such as the Venus of Laussel (c. 25,000 B.C.E.) shown in the far-right image below, depict robust pregnant women. Figurines similar to the Laussel Venus, which was found in the remains of a campsite at St.-Germain-en-Laye in France, are among the most common artifacts of early human cultures. At other early sites, including Çatal Hüyük, women are depicted as goddesses. And at Hacilar, another prehistoric town uncovered in what is today Turkey, they are represented in figurines that may well have served as images of cult veneration and paintings that suggest they may have served as oracles or cult priestesses. As in the Laussel Venus, voluptuous women predominate, and in many of the clay sculptures their roles in reproduction and nurturing are celebrated. But female figures in postures suggesting political authority, such as the woman shown sitting on what may have been a throne with animal heads, have also been found. Many of these statuettes may also have been intended to depict goddesses and have served as objects of worship.

QUESTIONS

- On the basis of the sample provided in these illustrations, which roles in early human society were closely associated with women?
- What do these representations tell us about the extent and sources of power exercised by women in prehistoric times?
- What sort of requests might those who worshiped goddesses have made through their prayers and offerings?

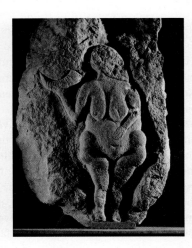

It is difficult to know precisely what impact the shift to agriculture had on the social structure of the communities that made the transition. Social distinctions probably were heightened by occupational differences, but well-defined social stratification, such as that which produces class identity, was nonexistent. Leadership remained largely communal, although village alliances may have existed in some areas. It is likely that property in Neolithic times was held in common by the community, or at least that all households in the community were given access to village lands and water.

By virtue of their key roles as food gatherers in pre-farming cultures, it can be surmised that women played a critical part in the domestication of plants. Nonetheless, their position declined in many agricultural communities. They worked the fields and have continued to work them in most cultures. But men took over tasks involving heavy labor, such as clearing land, hoeing, and plowing. Men monopolized the new tools and weapons devised in the Neolithic Age and later times, and they controlled the vital irrigation systems that developed in most early centers of agriculture. As far as we can tell, men also took the lead in taming, breeding, and raising the large animals associated with both farming and pastoral communities. Thus, although Neolithic art suggests that earth and fertility cults, which focused on feminine deities, retained their appeal (see Visualizing the Past), the social and economic position of women began to decline with the shift to sedentary agriculture.

THE FIRST TOWNS: SEEDBEDS OF CIVILIZATION

1.3   In what ways did the rise of towns promote contacts and ongoing linkages between different human communities both within particular regions and across regional boundaries?

Over time some of the early sedentary communities grew into larger and larger concentrations of human populations with ever more specialized craftspeople and differentiated social groups that we have come to associate with towns, and somewhat later, cities. Two of the earliest of these mega-settlements were at Jericho, in present-day Palestine, and at Çatal Hüyük (kah-THAL HOHY-uhk) in present-day Turkey. With populations of about 2000 and 5000 people, respectively, Jericho and Çatal Hüyük would be seen today as little more than large villages or small towns. But in the perspective of human cultural development, they represented the first stirrings of urban life. Their ruling elites and craft specialists contributed to the introduction in the 4th millennium B.C.E. of critical inventions—such as the wheel, the plow, writing, and the use of bronze—that secured the future of civilized life as the central pattern of human history.

Agriculture generated some surplus that could support other specialist labor. By 7000 B.C.E. cities and crafts that depended on trade emerged in the Middle East.

Jericho

Proximity to the Jordan River and the deep and clear waters of an oasis spring account for repeated human settlement at the place where the town of **Jericho** was built. By 7000 B.C.E., more than 10 acres were occupied by round houses of mud and brick resting on stone foundations. Most early houses had only a single room with mud plaster floors and a domed ceiling, but some houses had as many as three rooms. Entry to these windowless dwellings was provided by a single wood-framed doorway and steps down to the floor of the main room underground. Although there is no evidence that Jericho was fortified in the early stages of its growth, its expanding wealth made the building of walls for protection from external enemies necessary. The town was enclosed by a ditch cut into the rocky soil and a wall almost 12 feet high. The extensive excavation needed for this construction was impressive because the peoples who undertook it had neither picks nor shovels. The stones for the wall were dragged from a riverbed nearly a mile away. These feats suggest a sizable labor force that was well organized and disciplined.

When Jericho was rebuilt in later centuries, the wall reached a height of nearly 15 feet, and the fortifications included a stone tower at least 25 feet high. The area covered by the town increased. Round houses gave way to rectangular ones, entered through larger and more elaborately decorated wooden doorways. Houses were made of improved bricks and provided with plaster hearths and stone mills for grinding grain. They were also furnished with storage baskets and straw mats. Small buildings have been uncovered that were used as religious shrines during the later stages of the town's history.

Although Jericho's economy was based primarily on wheat and barley farming, there is considerable evidence of reliance on hunting and trade. Domesticated goats provided meat and milk, and gazelles and various marsh birds were hunted for their flesh, hides, and feathers. The town was close to large supplies of salt, sulfur, and pitch. These materials, which were in great demand during this

Jericho Early walled urban culture site based on sedentary agriculture; located in modern Israeli-occupied West Bank near Jordan River.

era, were traded for obsidian, a dark, glasslike volcanic rock; semiprecious stones from Anatolia; turquoise from the Sinai; and cowrie shells from the Red Sea.

The ruins excavated at Jericho indicate that the town was governed by a distinct and powerful ruling group, which probably was allied to the keepers of the shrine centers. There were specialized artisans and a small merchant class. In addition to fertility figurines and animal carvings like those found at many other sites, the inhabitants of Jericho sculpted life-sized, highly naturalistic human figures and heads. These sculptures, which may have been used in ancestral cults, give us vivid impressions of the physical features of the people who enjoyed the wealth and security of Jericho.

Çatal Hüyük

Çatal Hüyük Early urban culture based on sedentary agriculture; located in modern southern Turkey; was larger in population than Jericho, had greater degree of social stratification.

The first community at **Çatal Hüyük** in southern Turkey was founded around 7000 B.C.E., somewhat later than the earliest settlements at Jericho. But the town that grew up at this site was a good deal more extensive than that at Jericho, and it contained a larger and more diverse population. Çatal Hüyük was the most advanced human center of the Neolithic Age. At the peak of its power and prosperity, the city occupied 32 acres and contained as many as 6000 people. Its rectangular buildings, which were centers of family life and community interaction, were remarkably uniform and were built of mud-dried bricks. They had windows high in their walls and were entered from holes in their flat roofs. These entryways also served as chimneys. The presence of stored food in early towns such as Çatal Hüyük made the houses tempting targets for nomadic bands or rival settlements. For that reason they were increasingly fortified and, as Figure 1.5 illustrates, often quite ingeniously.

The standardization of housing and construction at Çatal Hüyük suggests an even more imposing ruling group than that found at Jericho. The many religious shrines at the site also indicate the existence of a powerful priesthood. The shrines were built in the same way as ordinary houses, but they contained sanctuaries surrounded by four or five rooms related to the ceremonies of the shrine's cult. The walls of these religious centers were filled with paintings of bulls and carrion eaters, especially vultures, suggesting fertility cults and rites associated with death. The surviving statuary indicates that the chief deity of the Çatal Hüyük peoples was a goddess.

The obvious importance of the cult shrines and the elaborate burial practices of the peoples of Çatal Hüyük reveal the growing role of religion in the lives of Neolithic peoples. The carefully carved sculptures associated with the sanctuaries and the fine jewelry, mirrors, and weapons found buried with the dead attest to the high level of material culture and artistic proficiency of these town dwellers.

Excavations also reveal an economic base that was much broader and richer than that of Jericho. Hunting remained important, but the breeding of goats, sheep, and cattle vastly surpassed that associated with Jericho. Çatal Hüyük's inhabitants consumed a wide range of foods, including several grains, peas, berries, berry wine, and vegetable oils made from nuts. Trade was extensive with the peoples in the surrounding hills and also in places as distant as present-day Syria and the Mediterranean region. Çatal Hüyük was also a major center of production by artisans. Its flint and obsidian weapons, jewelry, and obsidian mirrors were some of the finest produced in the Neolithic Age. The remains of the town's culture leave little doubt that its inhabitants had achieved a civilized level of existence.

View the **Closer Look** on **MyHistoryLab**: Çatal Hüyük

FIGURE **1.5** Excavation of the ancient settlement at Çatal Hüyük, in what is now southern Turkey. Movement within the settlement was mainly across the roofs and terraces of the houses. Because each dwelling had a substantial storeroom for food, the settlement was often the target of attacks by outsiders. The houses were joined together to provide protection from such attacks; when the outside entrances were barricaded, the complex was transformed into a fortress.

THINKING HISTORICALLY

The Idea of Civilization in World Historical Perspective

THE BELIEF THAT THERE ARE FUNDAMENTAL differences between civilized and "barbaric" or "savage" peoples is very ancient and widespread. For thousands of years the Chinese set themselves off from cattle- and sheep-herding peoples of the vast plains to the north and west of China proper, whom they saw as barbarians. To the Chinese, being civilized was cultural, not biological or racial. If barbarians learned the Chinese language and adopted Chinese ways—from the clothes they wore to the food they ate—they were regarded as civilized.

A similar pattern of demarcation and cultural absorption was found among the American Indian peoples of present-day Mexico. Those who settled in the valleys of the mountainous interior, where they built great civilizations, lived in fear of invasions by peoples they regarded as barbarous and called Chichimecs, meaning "sons of the dog." The latter were nomadic hunters and gatherers who periodically moved down from the desert regions of north Mexico into the fertile central valleys in search of game and settlements to pillage. The Aztecs were simply the last, and perhaps the most fierce, of a long line of Chichimec peoples who entered the valleys and conquered the urban-based empires that had developed there. But after the conquerors settled down, they adopted many of the religious beliefs and institutional patterns and much of the material culture of defeated peoples.

The word *civilization* is derived from the Latin word *civilis*, meaning "of the citizens." The term was coined by the Romans. They used it to distinguish between themselves as citizens of a cosmopolitan, urban-based civilization and the "inferior" peoples who lived in the forests and deserts on the fringes of their Mediterranean empire. Centuries earlier, the Greeks, who had contributed much to the rise of Roman civilization, made a similar distinction between themselves and outsiders. Because the languages of the non-Greek peoples to the north of the Greek heartlands sounded like senseless babble to the Greeks, they lumped all the outsiders together as *barbarians*, which meant "those who cannot speak Greek." As in the case of the Chinese and Aztecs, the boundaries between civilized and barbarian for the Greeks and Romans were cultural, not biological. Regardless of the color of one's skin or the shape of one's nose, it was possible for free people to become members of a Greek *polis*—city-state—or to become Roman citizens by adopting Greek or Roman customs and swearing allegiance to the polis or the emperor.

Until the 17th and 18th centuries C.E., the priority given to cultural attributes (e.g., language, dress, manners) as the means by which civilized peoples set themselves off from barbaric ones was rarely challenged. But in those centuries, two major changes occurred among thinkers in western Europe. First, efforts were made not only to define the differences between civilized and barbarian but to identify a series of stages in human development that ranged from the lowest savagery to the highest civilization. Peoples such as the Chinese and the Arabs, who had created great cities, monumental architecture, writing, advanced technology, and large empires, usually won a place along with the Europeans near the top of these ladders of human achievement. Nomadic, cattle- and sheep-herding peoples, such as the Mongols of central Asia, usually were classified as barbarians. Civilized and barbarian peoples were pitted against various sorts of **savages**. These ranged from the hunters and gatherers who inhabited much of North America and Australia to many peoples in Africa and Asia, whom the Europeans believed had not advanced beyond the most primitive stages of social and political development.

> *The word* civilization *is derived from the Latin word* civilis, *meaning "of the citizens."*

The second major shift in Western ideas about civilization began at the end of the 18th century but did not really take hold until a century later. In keeping with a growing emphasis in European thinking and social interaction on racial or biological differences, modes of human social organization and cultural expression were increasingly linked by historians and others to what were alleged to be the innate capacities of each human *race*. Although no one could agree on what a race was or how many races there were, most European writers argued that some races were more inventive, moral, courageous, and artistic—thus more capable of building civilizations—than others. Of course, white (or Caucasian) Europeans were considered by white European authors to be the most capable of all. The hierarchy from savage to civilized took on a color dimension, with white at the top, where the civilized peoples clustered, to yellow, red, brown, and black in descending order.

Some authors, including many prominent historians sought to reserve all the attainments of civilization for whites, or peoples of European stock. As the evolutionary theories of thinkers such as Charles Darwin came into vogue in the late 1800s, race and level of cultural development were seen in the perspective of thousands of years of human change and adaptation rather than as being fixed in time. Nevertheless, this new perspective had little effect on the rankings of different human groups. Civilized whites were simply seen as having evolved much further than backward and barbaric peoples.

The perceived correspondence between race and level of development and the hardening of the boundaries between civilized and "inferior" peoples affected much more than intellectual discourse about the nature and history of human society. These beliefs were used to justify European imperialist expansion, which was seen as a "civilizing mission" aimed at uplifting barbaric and savage peoples across the globe. In the last half of the 19th century, virtually all non-Western peoples came to be

(continued on next page)

dominated by the Europeans, who were confident that they, as representatives of the highest civilization ever created, were best equipped to govern lesser breeds of humans.

In the 21st century much of the intellectual baggage that once gave credibility to the racially embedded hierarchies of civilized and savage peoples has been discarded by most historians and other social scientists. A number of 20th-century developments, including the revolt of colonized peoples and the crimes committed by the Nazis before and during World War II in the name of racial purification, discredited racist thinking. In addition, these ideas have failed because racial supremacists cannot provide convincing proof of innate differences in mental and physical aptitude between various human groups. These trends, as well as research that has resulted in a much more sophisticated understanding of evolution, have led to the abandonment of rigid and self-serving 19th-century ideas about civilization. Historians in particular have increasingly adopted a less Eurocentric or culturally specific definition of civilization that encompasses varied cultures across the globe.

Perhaps the best way to avoid the tendency to define the term with reference to one's own society is to view civilization as we do in this world history as one of several human approaches to social organization rather than attempting to identify specific kinds of cultural achievement (e.g., writing, cities, monumental architecture). All peoples, from small bands of hunters and gatherers to farmers and factory workers, live in societies. All societies produce *cultures:* combinations of the ideas, objects, and patterns of behavior that result from human social interaction. But not all societies and cultures generate the surplus production that permits the levels of specialization, scale, and complexity that distinguish civilizations from other modes of social organization. All peoples are intrinsically capable of building civilizations, but many have lacked the resource base, historical circumstances, or desire to do so.

QUESTIONS

- Identify a society you consider civilized. What criteria did you use to determine that it was civilized?
- Can you apply those criteria to other societies?
- Can you think of societies that might not fit your criteria and yet be civilizations?
- Do the standards that you and others use reflect your own society's norms and achievements rather than neutral, more universal criteria?

---

savages Derogatory term wrongly applied to societies engaged in either hunting and gathering for subsistence or in migratory cultivation; not as stratified and specialized as sedentary and nomadic societies.

The 4th Millennium B.C.E.: Another Watershed

The level of specialization and political organization that developed in early towns, such as Jericho and Çatal Hüyük, proved critical to the invention and dissemination of new tools and production techniques during the 4th millennium B.C.E. The years from 4000 to 3000 B.C.E. saw a second wave of major transformations in human culture in the Middle East and nearby regions. During this transition era, the use of the plow significantly increased crop yields, and wheeled vehicles made it possible to carry more food and other raw materials over greater distances. Both developments meant that even larger populations could be supported and concentrated in particular locales. Although copper had been used for spear and axe heads for millennia, accident and experiment revealed that when copper was mixed with other metals, such as tin, it formed bronze, a harder and more durable material. The bronze tools that were forged from bronze further enhanced agricultural production and contributed to the development of larger and more lethal military forces. Like agriculture earlier, the new technologies—the wheel, the plow, bronze—began to spread in Afro-Eurasia in the centuries after 3500 B.C.E.

As metalworking improved further, better tools and weapons facilitated the rise of more centralized and expansive states. These radically new political units, which were usually centered on fortified towns and cities, greatly increased contacts between farming and nomadic peoples in everything from war and conquest to trade and religious expression. Merchant groups in farming societies also nurtured trading networks that provided perhaps the first enduring linkages between the urban centers of different states and civilizations.

New modes of transportation, state patronage and protection, and a growing inventory of products to exchange made it possible to extend these networks across continents in Afro-Eurasia. Cross-cultural exchanges became ever more complex and vital for the societies that participated in them. The development of writing—first in Mesopotamia and later in India, China, and other centers of agrarian production—greatly improved communications and exchange within both these commercial networks and regional state systems. Writing enhanced the power of the political elites, who directed efforts at imperial expansion. Writing also played a key role in the emergence of each of the transcultural religions that arose in the ancient and classical eras.

The innovative technologies and modes of agrarian production that were at the heart of the Neolithic revolution became the basis for an unparalleled spread and increase of human societies, and made possible the cross-cultural connections and ongoing exchanges that are the focus of world history. Once these processes were in motion, only the most isolated of societies were immune to influences from the outside.

Global Connections and Critical Themes

THE NEOLITHIC REVOLUTION AS THE BASIS FOR WORLD HISTORY

The fundamental transformations in society and culture that we include in the Neolithic revolution were essential to the development of cross-cultural and interregional linkages between formerly dispersed and isolated human groups, and eventually to the rise of world history. The diffusion of agriculture from its initial locations, though gradual, shows how human contacts could spread new ideas and technologies. The spread of foodstuffs initially native to one area across various parts of Asia, Africa, and Europe was another facet of early connections among regions. Nomadic herding groups provided additional contacts, and some developments, like the domestication of dogs, spread both rapidly and widely. The development of sedentary agriculture meant that ever larger numbers of humans could be supported on much smaller amounts of land than was possible for either hunting-and-gathering or pastoral peoples. In the Neolithic transition, farming was also linked to the domestication of animals, such as cattle and sheep, which provided further staple foods for the human diet as well as materials for clothing and modes of transportation.

Pastoralism, which has proved the major alternative to sedentary agriculture through most of recorded history, was much more narrowly dependent on animal husbandry. As a consequence, it has been a good deal more constricted in the options it offered for human social and cultural development. In contrast to pastoralism or hunting and gathering, farming made it possible to concentrate growing numbers of humans in towns and later cities. Because agrarian societies could generate surplus food production, they could also support occupational specialization on the part of groups like full-time blacksmiths, traders, or pottery-makers. Surpluses also facilitated the emergence of non-farming elite groups, like priests or warriors, which governed ever larger and increasingly diverse concentrations of human populations.

Further Readings

World historians have been drawn to Ronald Wright's *A Short History of Progress* (2004), which attempts to show how even the most recent of humanity's struggles can be better understood by examining its origins and early history. Perhaps the fullest account of human prehistory available is Brian Fagan's *People of the Earth* (1998), which includes an extensive bibliography on prehistoric developments in virtually all regions of the world. A considerable literature has developed in recent years on early humans and the critical Neolithic transformations. John Mears's pamphlet on *Agricultural Origins in Global Perspective* (American Historical Association, 2000) provides a concise and authoritative survey of this process in key regions over much of the globe. For other broad overviews that trace the archeological and historical discoveries that made it possible for us to understand these critical processes in the shaping of human history, see Robert J. Wenke's *Patterns in Prehistory* (1984) and C. Wesley Cowan and Patty Jo Watson, eds., *The Origins of Agriculture: An International Perspective* (1992).

For a clear discussion of debates on the Neolithic revolution and references to major authors and works, see Stephen K. Sanderson, *Social Transformations* (1995). Several of these works are of special relevance, despite their sometimes technical language and details, especially Donald O. Henry's *From Foraging to Agriculture* (1989), Douglas Price and James A. Brown, eds., *Prehistoric Hunter-Gatherers: The Emergence of Cultural Complexity* (1986), and Allen W. Johnson and Timothy Earle, *The Evolution of Human Societies: From Foraging to Agriculture* (1987). For the origins of agriculture in the often neglected Americas, see Stuart J. Fiedel, *Prehistory of the Americas* (1992). M. C. and H. B. Quennell's *Everyday Life in the New Stone, Bronze, and Early Iron Ages* (1955) is difficult to top for an imaginative reconstruction of life in the Neolithic Age, although some of it is now dated. The most reliable treatment of technology in this era can be found in volume 1 of C. Singer et al., *A History of Technology* (1954). The most readable introduction to the earliest towns is in James Mellaart's *Earliest Civilizations of the Near East* (1965) and *The Neolithic of the Near East* (1975). Studies focusing on specific nomadic, pastoral societies are listed in the chapters that follow. For an overview of the evolving relationships between humans and domesticated animals, see Jared Diamond, *Gun, Germs and Steel: The Fates of Human Societies* (1997).

On MyHistoryLab

 Study and Review on MyHistoryLab

Critical Thinking Questions

1. What were the key ways in which the human species developed physically, mentally, and socially that has set them off from the rest of life on the planet Earth?

2. What were some of the advantages that eventually allowed sedentary agriculture to replace hunting and gathering?

3. How did the domestication of animals transform existing sedentary agrarian societies and also permit the nomadic pastoral environmental adaptation?

4. In which of these adaptations did women play the most critical roles and enjoy the highest status?

5. How important were town and cities in the early stages of human development?

2

The Rise of Civilization in the Middle East and Africa

((• Listen to **Chapter 2**
on **MyHistoryLab**

How could Mesopotamia and Egypt—societies that were relatively close geographically and that had occasional contact—be so different in their treatment of women?

Early civilization in Mesopotamia emphasized men's control over women. Laws required that women be virgins at marriage and imposed strict punishments on women for sexual misconduct. A clear goal of such laws was to ensure that every man would know that he was the father of his wives' children and could therefore feel comfortable about leaving his property to them. By the third millennium B.C.E., Mesopotamian husbands veiled their wives on marriage. In the Akkadian (ah-KAYD-ee-un) language, the word for this veiling was the same as that for

📖 Read the **Document** on **MyHistoryLab**: Herodotus on the Egyptians

FIGURE **2.1** This detail from Egyptian tomb art shows a husband and wife harvesting grain. As dictated by patriarchal values, the husband takes the lead in the work and the wife follows, but in Egypt, unlike Mesopotamia, men and women were depicted working together.

👁 Watch the Video Series on MyHistoryLab

**Learn about some key topics related to this chapter with the *MyHistoryLab Video Series:
Key Topics in World History***

shutting a door, for the veil was designed to protect the wife's honor just as the walls of the house did. Family honor depended on strict control of women's sexual behavior, whereas for men it rested on the performance of work and (for the upper class) public duties. Widows were the only women allowed to control any property.

In Egypt women were also seen as inferior, and many writers urged men to maintain control of the women in their households, but Egyptian women had a much wider range of permissible activity. Many queens wielded considerable power. Queen Nefertiti (neh-fer-TEE-tee), in the first half of the 14th century B.C.E., was known for her beauty but also for her role in promoting major religious reforms which included the promotion of one of Egypt's many dieties, Aten, over all others. More generally, women and men had equal access to the afterlife: according to Egyptian belief both could become stars in the heavens, which was one way the afterlife was envisaged. Where there were no sons, daughters were responsible for carrying on family religious practices. Unlike almost every other early civilization, including Mesopotamia, Egypt did not practice female infanticide—a practice designed as a form of birth control and an expression of the greater value of sons. ■

Early civilizations—the subject of this chapter—introduced many important changes in human life. They made patriarchal systems more formal, enshrining men's superiority in laws and art as well as government structures. But each early civilization also put its particular stamp on basic aspects of life, as each major society gained distinctive characteristics. Even gender systems varied, depending on particular cultural values and political arrangements. Differences in the ways patriarchy was practiced helped create identities for each civilization. Early travelers would note how women in Egypt seemed to be treated somewhat distinctively, compared to Mesopotamia. Specific gender practices could also be durable, lasting well beyond the early civilization itself. Middle Eastern contexts for women still show traces of approaches first introduced in Mesopotamia.

EARLY CIVILIZATION IN MESOPOTAMIA

2.1 How did ancient Sumer illustrate the key features of civilization as a form of human organization?

> Mesopotamian civilization pioneered basic forms of civilization, from an urban economy to writing. Frequent invasions contributed to distinctive religious belief and political systems.

The cumulative effects of agriculture, followed by the wave of technological changes around 4000 B.C.E., generated civilization as a new organizational form. Sumer's achievements illustrate the elements of civilization as a form of human organization. While not all agricultural economies would ultimately produce civilizations, many did, and the process began in the Middle East. New technologies like the wheel, bronze use, and writing facilitated civilization. Writing, for example, promoted formal bureaucracy and the kind of written records useful for trade. Bronze created more lethal weapons, useful for conquest. It required support for new kinds of specialist manufacturing. Bronze also necessitated longer-distance trade in search of copper and tin. Middle Eastern traders ultimately traveled as far as Britain and Afghanistan seeking resources. Finally, irrigation along great river valleys, vital for greater agricultural productivity, promoted new kinds of organizational structures to coordinate the process and new laws to demarcate property.

7000 B.C.E.	4000 B.C.E.	3000 B.C.E.	2000 B.C.E.	1000 B.C.E.	1 C.E.
7000–4000 Spread of agriculture through most of Middle East **5000** Farming along Nile River **4000** Sumerians settle in Tigris–Euphrates valley	**3500** Early Sumerian alphabet **3100–2700** Initial kingdoms in Mesopotamia and Egypt **3000** Introduction of bronze tools	**2700–2200** Old Kingdom period, Egypt **2600** First great pyramid **2400–2200** Akkadian Empire conquers Sumer **2052–1786** Middle Kingdom period; civilization spreads to Upper Nile with Kingdom of Kush **2000** Phoenician state **2000** *Gilgamesh* epic written	**1800** Babylonian Empire; Hammurabi, 1796–1750 **1700** Hyksos invasion **1600** Minoan civilization (Crete) **1600** Possible settlement of Jews in southeast Mediterranean **1575–1087** New Kingdom period, Egypt **1400–1200** Hittite Empire; use of iron **1250** Moses and Jewish exodus from Egypt **1100** Spread of use of iron **1000–970** Kingdom of Israel under King David **1000** Kush independent kingdom **1000** Indo-European invasion of Greece **1000** Spread of Phoenician settlements in western Mediterranean	**800** Beginning of writing of Bible **730** Kushite rule of Egypt **721** Assyrian invasion conquers northern Israel **665–617** Assyrian Empire **539** Persian Empire	**100 C.E.** Decline of Kush and its capital Meroë **300 C.E.** Rise of Axum (Ethiopia)

The Sumerians

Sumer, the first river valley civilization, used rivers but also feared them. Major floods occurred. Archeologists have found sites where one Sumerian city was built on top of an earlier one, separated by a layer of mud swept over in a flood. Mud tablets containing the first Sumerian "book" tell the story of how the gods decided to wipe out mankind with a flood. Only one man, with his family and animals, was saved. His name was not Noah, but Utnapishtim.

The first civilization arose in the northeastern section of what we now call the Middle East, along the great Tigris and Euphrates rivers that lead to the Persian Gulf (Map 2.1). Between the northern hills and the deserts of the Arabian Peninsula, running from the eastern Mediterranean coast to the plains of the Tigris and Euphrates, lies a large swath of arable land called the Fertile Crescent. The rivers overflow their banks in the spring, depositing fertile soil when they recede. Rainfall is scant, so as population pressure increased as a result of early agriculture, farming communities began to find ways to tame and use the rivers through irrigation ditches. With the improved tools of the Bronze Age, developments in the region were swift. The fertile Tigris–Euphrates region generated large food surpluses, promoting population growth and village expansion as well as increased trade and job specialization. The region was vulnerable in one respect: It was so flat that it was open to invasion.

The **Sumerians** were a people who had migrated into the area from the north about 4000 B.C.E.; they settled in an area of about 700 square miles, where they mixed with other local people in a pattern that has remained characteristic of the region. The Sumerians early developed centers of religion, pilgrimage, and worship. Well before 3000 B.C.E., many of these centers boasted

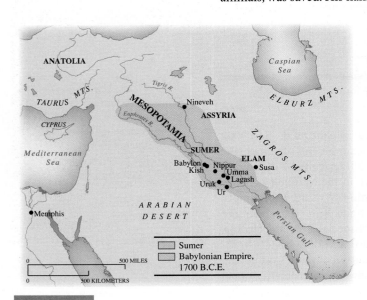

MAP **2.1 Early Sumer.** The civilization fanned out along the Tigris and Euphrates rivers.

elaborately decorated temples built of mud brick. Sumerians were impressed with the power of grim gods who, they believed, ultimately controlled human destiny. It was the Sumerians who introduced the first writing system, capping the developments that created Mesopotamian civilization.

Sumerian Political and Social Organization. Sumerian culture remained intact until about 2000 B.C.E. Its political organization was based on a series of tightly organized **city-states** in which an urban king, who claimed great authority, ruled the agricultural hinterland. In some cases, local councils advised the king. One of the functions of Sumerian city-states was to define boundaries, unlike the less formal territories of precivilized villages in the region. Each city-state helped regulate religion and enforce its duties. It also provided a system of courts for justice. Kings were warriors whose leadership of a trained army in defense and war remained vital in Sumerian politics, where fighting loomed large. Kings and priests controlled vast amounts of land. Slaves, who had been conquered in wars with nearby tribes, worked this land.

Sumerian political and social organization set up traditions that long endured in the region. City-state government established a tradition of regional rule, which sometimes yielded to larger empires but often returned as the principal organizational form. Many successor civilizations also relied on slave labor. The use of slaves and the lack of natural barriers to invasion help explain recurrent warfare, which was needed to supply labor in the form of captured slaves.

The Sumerians, aided by political stability and the use of writing, added to their region's economic prosperity. Farmers learned how to cultivate date trees, onions, and garlic. Oxen were used to pull plows, and donkeys carried goods. Wheeled carts helped transport goods. The Sumerians introduced the use of fertilizer and adopted silver as a means of exchange for buying and selling. Major cities expanded—one city reached a population of over 70,000—with substantial housing units in rows of flat-roofed, mud-brick shops and apartments. More commonly, cities contained as many as 10,000 people. The Sumerians improved the potter's wheel, and the production of pottery expanded. Spurred by the increasing skill level and commercial importance of pottery, men began to take this trade away from women. The Sumerians also invented glass. Trade expanded to the lower Persian Gulf and to the western portion of the Middle East along the Mediterranean. By 2000 B.C.E., the Sumerians had trading contacts with India.

Sumerian Culture and Religion. Writing, the most important invention between the advent of agriculture and the age of the steam engine, was introduced about 3500 B.C.E. The Sumerian invention of writing was probably rather sudden. It was based on new needs for commercial property and political records, including a celebration of the deeds of proud local kings. Writing was preceded by the invention of clay cylinder seals on which little pictures of objects could be recorded. The earliest Sumerian writing evolved from those pictures, baked on clay tablets, which were turned into symbols and gradually transformed into phonetic elements. The early Sumerian alphabet, a set of symbols representing sounds, may have had as many as 2000 symbols derived from the early pictures. Soon writers began to use more abstract symbols to represent sounds, which allowed the Sumerians to reduce the alphabet to about 300 symbols. Figures 2.2 and 2.3 show an example of their writing and its translation.

Sumerian writers used a wedge-shaped stick to impress the symbols on clay tablets. The resulting writing is called **cuneiform**, meaning "wedge shaped," and it was used for several thousand years in the Middle East for many different languages. Cuneiform writing was difficult to learn, so specialized scribes monopolized it. The Sumerians believed that every object in nature should have a separate name to ensure its place in the universe; knowing the name gave a person some power over the object. Writing quickly took on religious purposes, allowing people to impose an abstract order over nature and the social world.

Sumerians People who migrated into Mesopotamia c. 4000 B.C.E.; created first civilization within region; organized area into city-states.

city-state A form of political organization typical of Mesopotamian civilizations; consisted of agricultural hinterlands ruled by an urban-based king.

cuneiform [kyoo-NAY-uh-form] A form of writing developed by the Sumerians using a wedge-shaped stylus and clay tablets.

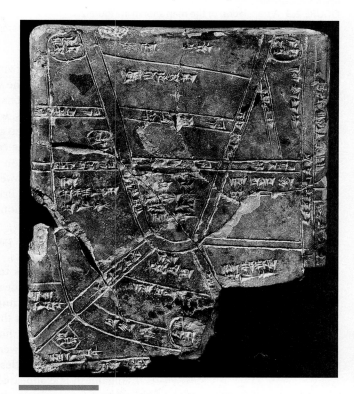

FIGURE **2.2** One of the early uses of writing was to mark property boundaries. This picture shows cuneiform writing on a Mesopotamian map from about 1300 B.C.E. The map focuses on defining the king's estate, with sections for priests and for key gods such as Marduk. In what ways did writing improve property maps?

FIGURE **2.3** A translation of the map shown in Figure 2.2.
(University of Pennsylvania Museum of Archaeology and Anthropology. Neg.#S4-13970)

Epic of Gilgamesh The first literary epic in Western civilization; written down c. 2000 B.C.E.; included story of Great Flood.

ziggurats [ZIG-uh-rat] Massive towers usually associated with Mesopotamian temple complexes.

animism [AH-nuh-mih-zum] A religious outlook that sees gods in many aspects of nature and propitiates them to help control and explain nature; typical of Mesopotamian religions.

By about 2000 B.C.E., the Sumerians wrote down the world's oldest story, the ***Epic of Gilgamesh***, which existed in oral form as early as the 7th millennium B.C.E. Gilgamesh, described as the ruler of a city-state, was the first hero in world literature. This was the epic that also described the great flood. The overall tone of the epic and of Sumerian culture (perhaps reflecting the region's often disastrous floods) was somber. Gilgamesh does great deeds but constantly bumps up against the iron laws of the gods, who ultimately control human destiny.

The heroes, the wise men, like the new moon have their waxing and waning. Men will say, "Who has ever ruled with might and with power like Gilgamesh?" As in the dark month, the month of shadows; so without him there is no light. O Gilgamesh, this was the meaning of your dream. You were given the kingship, such was your destiny; everlasting life was not your destiny. . . . Gilgamesh, why do you search? The life you seek you will never find. When the gods created the world, they made death a part of human fate.

Along with early literature, Sumerian art and science developed steadily. Statues and painted frescoes adorned the temples of the gods, and statues of the gods decorated homes. Sumerians sought to learn more about the movement of the sun and stars, thus founding the science of astronomy. They also wanted to improve their mathematical knowledge. The Sumerian system of numbers, based on units of 12, 60, and 360, is the one we use today in calculations involving circles and hours. Sumerian charts of major constellations have been used for 5000 years in the Middle East and, through later imitation, in India and Europe. In other words, Sumerians and their successors in Mesopotamia created patterns of observation and abstract thought about nature on which many later societies, including our own, still rely.

Religion played a vital role in Sumerian culture and politics. Gods were associated with various forces of nature. At the same time, gods were seen as having human form and many of the more disagreeable human characteristics. Thus, the gods often quarreled and used their power in selfish and childish ways, which made interesting stories but also created a fear that the gods might make life difficult. The gloomy cast of Sumerian religion also included an afterlife of suffering, an original version of the concept of hell. Because gods were believed to regulate natural forces, such as flooding, in a region where nature was often harsh and unpredictable, they were more feared than loved. Priests' power derived from their responsibility for placating the gods through prayers, sacrifices, and magic. Priests became full-time specialists, running the temples and performing the astronomical calculations of the dates for normal flooding, which were needed to manage the irrigation systems.

Each city had a patron god and erected impressive shrines to honor this god and other deities. Massive towers, called **ziggurats**, formed the monumental architecture for this civilization. Prayers and offerings to prevent floods and protect good health were a vital part of Sumerian life. **Animism**—the idea that a divine force lay within natural objects such as rivers, trees, and mountains—was common among agricultural peoples. Sumerians also developed specific religious beliefs about the creation of the earth by the gods from a chaos of water and about divine punishment through floods. These beliefs continue to influence Jewish, Christian, and Muslim cultures, all of which were born much later in the Middle East.

Sumerian activities in trade and war spread widely in the Middle East. Portions of the Gilgamesh tale appeared in later literature such as the Jewish Bible, which developed well to the west of Sumer. Even after Sumer itself collapsed, the Sumerian language was still used in religious schools and temples, showing the power of this early culture and its decidedly religious emphasis.

What Civilization Meant in Sumeria

Sumer's achievements illustrate the elements of civilization, one form of human organization. Some historians offer a bare-bones definition: Civilizations had greater economic surpluses than other forms of society. This was certainly true of Sumer, which boasted a rich agriculture capable of supporting a minority of specialist workers plus priests and government officials.

The initial Mesopotamian civilization also can be used to flesh out a more elaborate definition, which other historians prefer. First, Sumerian civilization generated a clearly defined state, or government, replacing the much more loosely organized communities of previous agricultural societies. Second, civilization involved the creation of cities beyond scattered individual centers such as Jericho. The economy remained fundamentally agricultural, and at least 80 percent of all people still lived in the countryside (as was true in all civilizations until 200 years ago). But the cities were crucial in promoting trade, more specialized manufacture, and the exchange of ideas. At the same time, cities depended on a well-organized regional economy that could provide food for urban areas and on a government capable of running essential services such as a court system to handle disputes.

The Importance of Writing. Writing was another important feature of Sumerian and most other civilizations. While sophisticated societies can develop without writing, the new communication system had various consequences. Societies with writing can organize more elaborate records, including the lists essential for effective taxation. Writing is a precondition for most formal bureaucracies, which depend on standardized communication and the ability to maintain documentation. Societies with writing can record data and build on past discoveries, thus producing a more elaborate intellectual life. For example, it is no accident that, with writing, an early civilization such as Mesopotamia began to generate more formal scientific knowledge. Societies before the development of writing typically depended on poetic sagas to convey their value systems; the poetry was designed to aid in memorization. With writing, the importance of sagas such as the Gilgamesh epic continued, but the diversity of cultural expressions soon increased and other kinds of literature supplemented the long, rhymed epics.

Writing also promoted trade and manufacturing. Sumerian merchants used writing to communicate with their trading partners in places such as India. Written records helped preserve manufacturing knowledge. One of the first recorded uses of Sumerian writing was to transmit a beer recipe.

Writing also created new divisions within the population of early civilizations. Only a small minority of people—priests, scribes, and a few merchants—had time to master writing.

Balance Sheet: Gains and Losses. Civilization is not necessarily progress, and it brings losses as well as gains. Civilization needs careful evaluation, compared to societies where this form of human organization did not develop. As the Middle East moved toward civilization, distinctions based on social class and wealth increased. This was clearly the case in Sumer, where social structure ranged from slaves, who were treated as property, to powerful kings and priests. Civilizations also often create greater inequalities between men and women than noncivilized societies do.

In contrast, noncivilized societies are often well regulated, with interesting, important cultures. Some noncivilized societies, including many Inuit groups, are particularly successful in avoiding anger and aggression in human dealings. In contrast, many civilized societies, including Sumerian society, value aggressive behavior and count warlike qualities as virtues. Civilizations do not even clearly promote human happiness.

It is true, however, that the development of civilization did generate new technological, cultural, and political capacities. In this limited sense, the term **civilization** has meaning and legitimately commands the attention of most historians. Because of the power and splendor civilizations could attain, they tended to spread as other societies came under their influence or deliberately tried to imitate their achievements. However, early civilizations spread slowly because many peoples had no contact with them and because their disadvantages, such as greater social inequality, often seemed repellent.

civilization Societies distinguished by reliance on sedentary agriculture, ability to produce food surpluses, and existence of non-farming elites, as well as merchant and manufacturing groups.

LATER MESOPOTAMIAN CIVILIZATION: A SERIES OF CONQUESTS

A variety of invasions produced a series of empires in Mesopotamia and beyond.

2.2 Why did the Middle East experience so many waves of invasion and conquest?

Later Mesopotamian civilization was recurrently unstable as one ruling people gave way to another invading force. The region's map (see Visualizing the Past) shows the geographic framework for this process. The Sumerians, themselves invaders of the fertile river valleys, ultimately proved unable to withstand pressures from other intruding peoples who began to copy their key achievements.

The Akkadian Empire

Sargon I Ruler of city-state of Akkad; established the first empire in Mesopotamian civilization c. 2400 B.C.E.

Babylonian Empire Unified all of Mespotamia c. 1800 B.C.E.; collapsed due to foreign invasion c. 1600 B.C.E.

Hammurabi (r. 1792–1750 B.C.E.) The most important ruler of the Babylonian empire; responsible for codification of law.

Shortly after 2400 B.C.E., a king from Akkad, a non-Sumerian city in Mesopotamia, conquered the Sumerian city-states and inaugurated the Akkadian Empire. Here one king controlled a fairly large region while maintaining many Sumerian cultural and economic forms. This empire soon sent troops as far as Egypt and Ethiopia. Its first ruler, **Sargon I**, is the first clearly identified individual in world history. He unified the empire and integrated the city-states into a whole. He also added to Sumerian art a new style marked by the theme of royal victory (Figure 2.4). Professional military organization expanded because Sargon maintained a force of 5400 troops. Extensive tax revenues supported his operations. The Akkadians were the first people to use writing for more than commercial and temple records, producing a number of literary works. Sargon's daughter Enheduanna (EHN-hehd-WAHN-uh), high priestess of the gods Nanna and An, left behind the first works of literature whose authorship can be attributed to a specific individual: two hymn cycles praising the gods and temples of Mesopotamia.

The Akkadian Empire lasted only 200 years and then was overthrown by another invading force. By this time, around 2200 B.C.E., kingdoms were springing up in various parts of the Middle East, and new invading groups added to the region's confusion.

The Babylonian Empire

Around 1800 B.C.E., the **Babylonian Empire** arose and again unified much of Mesopotamia. Large cities testified to the wealth and power of this new empire. This Babylonian empire was headed by **Hammurabi**, one of the great rulers of early civilized history. Hammurabi set up an extensive network of officials and judges and maintained a separate priesthood. He also codified the laws of the region to deal with a number of criminal, property, and family issues. At the same time, Sumerian cultural traditions were maintained and elaborated. The famous Hammurabic code thus built on earlier codifications by Sumerian kings. The Document box shows what kinds of problems the code sought to regulate through laws.

Rulers such as Hammurabi claimed great power, often associating themselves with the gods. Artistic monuments celebrated rulers' power in a tradition that has continued ever since (even for rulers not seen as divine).

Babylonian culture did more than celebrate power. A poem expressed the continued pessimism and sobriety of the dominant beliefs: "I look about me and see only evil. My troubles grow and I cannot find justice. I have prayed to the gods and sacrificed, but who can understand the gods in heaven? Who knows what they plan for us? Who has ever been able to understand a god's conduct?"

Finally, Babylonian scientists extended the Sumerian work in astronomy and mathematics. Scholars were able to predict lunar eclipses and trace the paths of some of the planets. Babylonians also worked out useful mathematical tables and an algebraic geometry; they could figure out areas and volumes for many shapes, devise squares, and compound interest. The modern 60-minute hour and 360-degree

FIGURE **2.4** This bronze head of Sargon, founder of the Akkadian dynasty, dates from about 2350 B.C.E. Skilled Mesopotamian craftsmen used their talents to evoke feelings of awe and reverence toward a great leader.

VISUALIZING THE PAST

Mesopotamia in Maps

THE MESOPOTAMIAN CIVILIZATIONS STEADILY EXPANDED FROM their roots in the fertile valley between the Tigris and Euphrates rivers throughout their centuries of existence. Reading the maps can help explain the nature of the civilizations in the region.

This map shows the location of Sumer and two later empires in the Middle East and eastern Mediterranean.

QUESTIONS

- What do these maps suggest about the relationship between Mesopotamian civilizations and the topography of the Middle East?

- Does geography suggest reasons for invasion and political instability in this civilization center?
- Did later empires in the region have the same relationship to river valleys as did the earlier states?
- What were the potential contacts between Mesopotamia and other river valley civilization centers?
- Why has the Middle East been so significant in European, African, and Asian history?

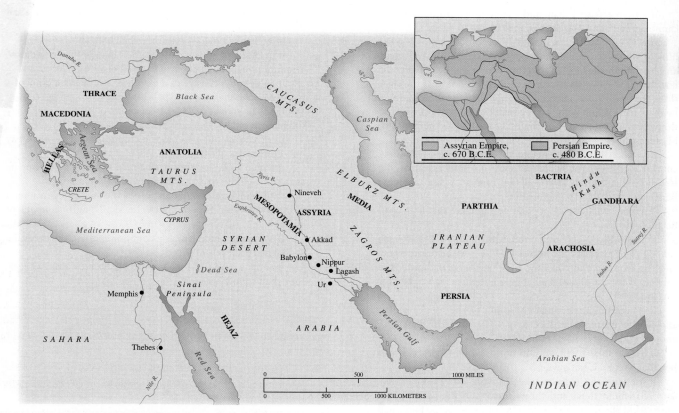

MAP **2.2 Mesopotamia in Maps.** This map shows the location of Sumer and two later empires in the Middle East and eastern Mediterranean.

circle arose from the Babylonian system of measurement applied to earlier Sumerian numbering systems.

Indeed, of all the successors of the Sumerians, the Babylonians constructed the most elaborate culture, although their rule lasted only about 200 years. The Babylonians expanded commerce and a common cultural zone, both based on growing use of cuneiform writing and a shared language.

DOCUMENT

Hammurabi's Law Code

HAMMURABI, AS KING OF BABYLON, UNITED Mesopotamia under his rule from about 1800 to 1750 B.C.E. His law code, the earliest such compilation still in existence, was discovered on a stone slab in Iran in 1901 C.E. Not a systematic presentation, it was a collection of exemplary cases designed to set general standards of justice. The code provides vital insights into the nature of social relations and family structure in this ancient civilization. Examples of the Hammurabic code follow:

…[A]t [this] time [the gods] named me, Hammurabi, the exalted prince, the worshiper of the gods, to cause righteousness to prevail in the land, to destroy the wicked and the evil, to prevent the strong from plundering the weak.

If a man accuse a man, and charge him with murder, but cannot convict him, the accuser shall be put to death.

If a man charge a man with sorcery, but cannot convict him, he who is charged with sorcery shall go to the sacred river, and he shall throw himself into the river; if the river overcome him, his prosecutor shall take to himself his house. If the river show that man to be innocent and he come forth unharmed, he that charged him with sorcery shall be put to death. He who threw himself into the river shall take to himself the house of his ancestor.

If a man, in a case (before the court), offer testimony concerning deeds of violence, and do not establish the testimony that he has given—if that case be a case involving life, that man shall be put to death.

If a man practice robbery and be captured, that man shall be put to death.

If the brigand be not captured, the man who has been robbed shall establish the amount of his loss before the god, and the city and the governor, in whose land or border the robbery was committed, shall compensate him for whatsoever was lost.

If a man points the finger at a nun or the wife of a man and cannot justify it, they shall drag that man before the judges and they shall cut the hair of his forehead.

If a man take a wife and do not draw up a contract with her, that woman is not a wife.

If the wife of a man be taken in lying with another man, they shall bind them and throw them into the water. If the husband of the woman spare the life of his wife, the king shall spare the life of [the man].

If a man forces the (betrothed) wife of a man, who has not known a male and is living in her father's house, and lie in her bosom, and they take him, that man shall be put to death and that woman shall go free.

If a man accuses his wife and she have not been taken in lying with another man, she shall take an oath in the name of God and she shall return to her house.

If the finger have been pointed at the wife of a man because of another man, and she have not been taken in lying with another man, for her husband('s sake) she shall throw herself into the sacred river (i.e., she shall submit to the ordeal).

If a man be taken captive and there be nothing to eat in his house and his wife enter into another house, that woman has no blame.

If a man strikes his father, they shall cut off his hand.

If a man destroys the eye of another man, they shall destroy his eye.

If he breaks a man's bone, they shall break his bone.

If he destroys the eye of a common man or break a bone of a common man, he shall pay one mana of silver.

If he destroys the eye of a man's slave or break a bone of a man's slave, he shall pay one-half his price.

If a man knocks out a tooth of a man of his own rank, they shall knock out his tooth.

If he knocks out a tooth of a common man, he shall pay one-third mana of silver.

If a man smites on the cheek a man who is his superior, he shall receive sixty strokes with an oxtail whip in public.

If the son of a gentleman smites the son of a gentleman of his own rank on the cheek, he shall pay one mana of silver.

If a common man smites a common man on the cheek, he shall pay ten shekels of silver.

If a man's slave smites the son of a gentleman on the cheek, they shall cut off his ear.

QUESTIONS

- What can you tell from the Hammurabic code about the social and family structure of Mesopotamia?
- What is the relationship between law and trade?
- Why did agricultural civilizations such as Babylon insist on harsh punishments for crimes?
- What religious and magical beliefs does the document suggest? Using specific examples, show how interpreting this document for significant historical meaning differs from simply reading it.

During the empire itself, new government strength showed in both the extensive legal system and the opulent public buildings and royal palaces. The rooftop gardens of trees and vines of one king dazzled visitors from the entire region.

The Babylonian empire fell by about 1600 B.C.E. Middle Eastern society had become so prosperous that it was beginning to attract recurrent waves of attack from nomadic peoples pressing in from central Asia, and few geographic barriers impeded the incursions. The invading **Hittite** people, one of the first of the Indo-European groups to enter from central Asia, set up an empire of their own. The Hittites soon yielded, and a series of smaller kingdoms disputed the region for several centuries between about 1200 and 900 B.C.E.

Hittites [HIT-eyet] An Indo-European people who entered Mesopotamia c. 1750 B.C.E.; destroyed the Babylonian empire; swept away c. 1200 B.C.E.

ANCIENT EGYPT

2.3	What were the principal features of the Egyptian state?

Civilization emerged early in northeastern Africa. Egypt generated distinctive approaches to politics and art. Egypt's geography helps explain a different outlook on life. The variation between Egyptian and Mesopotamian gender practices were a key illustration of how these two early civilizations followed different paths.

Egypt, in northeastern Africa, benefited from Mesopotamian trade and technology. The Egyptians developed a different, and more stable, version of civilization.

On Being a God King

Early on, Egypt moved toward a strong kingship. Egyptian kings, called **pharaohs**, were seen as contacts between gods and people, and ultimately as gods themselves. Early kings were seen as manifestations of one god, Horus, and merged into another god, Osiris, after death. Pharaohs were often shown as huge figures in art, towering over their subjects. Their power also showed in the practice of burying servants with a dead pharaoh, so they could help him in the next life. But for all these claims, kings faced limits also. Popular writings often treated them irreverently, which means that it is hard to tell how much ordinary people believed the references to godhood. And priests often controlled the kings, insisting on elaborate rituals to which kings had to conform. Despite the big claims, it was not always clear who ruled—a situation not uncommon in world history.

pharaoh Title of kings of ancient Egypt.

Basic Patterns of Egyptian Society

Unlike Mesopotamia and the Middle East, where a river valley civilization ultimately spread throughout an entire region, Egyptian civilization from its origins to its decline focused on the Nile River and the deserts immediately around it. The Nile's steady flow is marked by predictable flood surges. This also gave a more optimistic cast to Egyptian culture. It could be seen as a source of never-failing bounty to be thankfully received, rather than as a menacing cause of floods, as with Mesopotamian rivers.

Farming had been developed along the Nile by about 5000 B.C.E., but some time before 3200 B.C.E. economic development accelerated, in part because of growing trade with other regions, including Mesopotamia. This acceleration was the basis for the formation of regional kingdoms. Unlike Sumer, Egypt moved fairly directly from precivilization to large government units without passing through a city-state phase, although the first pharaoh (king), **Narmer**, had to conquer a number of petty local kings around 3100 B.C.E. Egypt always had fewer problems with political unity than Mesopotamia did, in part because of the unifying influence of the course of the Nile River. There were also fewer invasions. The vast surrounding deserts acted to limit the kind of attacks that troubled Sumerian civilization. But Egyptian politics tended to be more authoritarian and centralized. Egypt lacked the wider councils and opportunities for interaction that the Mesopotamian city-states developed.

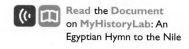

Read the **Document** on **MyHistoryLab:** An Egyptian Hymn to the Nile

Narmer First pharaoh of Egyptian Old Kingdom; ruled c. 3100 B.C.E.

Akhenaton {ah-ken-AH-tehn} (1379–1335 b.c.e.) Egyptian pharaoh of the New Kingdom; attempted to establish a one-god religion, replacing the traditional Egyptian pantheon of gods.

By 3100 B.C.E. Narmer, king of southern Egypt, conquered the northern regional kingdom and created a unified state 600 miles long (Map 2.3). This state was to last 3000 years. Despite some important disruptions, this was an amazing record of stability, even though the greatest vitality of the civilization was exhausted by about 1000 B.C.E. During the 2000-year span in which Egypt displayed its greatest vigor, the society went through three major periods of monarchy (the Old, the Intermediate, and the New Kingdoms), each divided from its successor by a century or two of confusion.

In all its phases, Egyptian civilization was characterized by the strength of the pharaoh. The pharaoh was held to be descended from gods, and he was attributed the power to ensure prosperity and control the rituals that ensured the regular flow of the Nile and the fertility derived from irrigation. Much Egyptian art was devoted to demonstrating the power and sanctity of the pharaoh. An extensive bureaucracy was recruited from the landed nobles and trained in writing and law. Governors were appointed for key regions and were responsible for supervising irrigation and arranging for the great public works that became a hallmark of Egyptian culture. Most Egyptians were peasant farmers who were closely regulated and heavily taxed.

Given the importance of royal rule and the belief that pharaohs were gods, it is not surprising that each of the main periods of Egyptian history was marked by some striking kings. Early in each dynastic period, where a new family line took power, leading pharaohs conquered new territories. Sometimes they pressed up the Nile River into present-day Sudan, and once they even moved up the Mediterranean coast of the Middle East. Late in Egyptian history one pharaoh, **Akhenaton** tried to use his power to install a new one-god religion, replacing the Egyptian pantheon. This was a dramatic assertion of royal authority. As the god spoke only through Akhenaton, it suggested the end of priests' power. However, his effort failed against the powerful priesthood, and the controversy distracted him from military affairs, leading to some difficult wars. Historians debate whether Akhenaton's monotheistic vision was simply a unique development born of one ruler's attempt to consolidate his power or has some larger significance for the evolution of a religious belief.

It was to commemorate their greatness that many pharaohs built the **pyramids** to house themselves and their family and staff after death, commanding work crews of up to 100,000 men to haul and lift the stones. The first great pyramid was built about 2600 B.C.E.; the largest pyramid followed about a century later, taking 20 years to complete and containing 2 million blocks of stone, each weighing 5.5 tons (Figure 2.5). These monuments were triumphs of human coordination, for the Egyptians were not particularly advanced technologically. They even lacked pulleys or other devices to hoist the huge slabs of stone that formed the pyramids. Recent aerial discoveries reveal that early Egyptians built at least one roadway to the stone quarries, but roads were not used during the age of the pyramids. Masses of workers rolled stones over logs and onto Nile barges before assembling the massive monuments on the river's banks.

Some scholars have seen fundamental links between Egypt's stable, centralized politics and its fascination with an orderly death, which gave rise to massive funeral monuments and preservation through mummification. Death rituals suggested a concern with extending organization to the afterlife based on a belief that, through politics, death as well as life could be controlled. A similar connection between strong political structures and careful funeral arrangements developed in Chinese civilization, though with quite different religious beliefs.

MAP **2.3 Egypt, Kush, and Axum, Successive Dynasties.** As Egypt weakened, kingdoms farther up the Nile and deeper into Africa rose in importance.

Egyptian Ideas and Art

Egyptian culture separated itself from Mesopotamia in several ways other than politics and monument building. The Egyptians did not adopt the Sumerian cuneiform alphabet, developing a hieroglyphic alphabet instead. Hieroglyphs, more pictorial than the Sumerian cuneiform, were based on simplified pictures of objects abstracted to represent concepts or sounds. As in Mesopotamia, the writing system was complex, and its use was largely monopolized by the powerful priestly class. Egyptians ultimately developed a new material to write on, papyrus, made from strips of a plant pressed together. This was cheaper to make and to use than clay tablets or animal skins and allowed much more elaborate recordkeeping. Despite the elaborate writing system, Egypt did not generate the same kind of epic literary tradition found in the Middle East.

Egyptian achievements in astronomy were less advanced than those of Mesopotamia. However, the Egyptians were the first people to establish the length of the solar year, which they divided into 12 months, each with three 10-day weeks. The week was the only division of time not based on any natural cycles. The achievement of this calendar suggests Egyptians' concern about predicting the Nile floods and their ability in astronomical observation. The Egyptians also made important strides in medicine, including knowledge of a variety of drugs and some contraceptive devices. The Greeks later learned elements of Egyptian medical knowledge and passed the information on to later Middle Eastern and European civilizations. Geometry was also advanced.

The pillar of Egyptian culture was not science but religion, which was firmly established as the basis of a whole worldview. The Egyptian religion, outside of Akhenaton's unique example, promoted the worship of many gods. Like early religions almost everywhere, it mixed magical ceremonies and beliefs with worship. The Egyptians were concerned with death and preparation for life in another world where—unlike the Mesopotamians—the Egyptians held that a happy, changeless well-being could be achieved. The care shown in preparing tombs and **mummifying** bodies, along with elaborate funeral rituals, particularly for the rulers and bureaucrats, was designed to ensure a satisfactory afterlife, although Egyptians also believed that favorable judgment by a key god, Osiris, was essential. Other Egyptian deities included a creation goddess, similar to other Middle Eastern religious figures later adapted into Christian veneration of the Virgin Mary, and a host of gods represented partially by animal figures. Egyptian art focused heavily on the gods, but earthly and human scenes were portrayed as well in characteristic, stylized forms that lasted without great change for many centuries.

pyramids Monumental architecture typical of Old Kingdom Egypt; used as burial sites for pharaohs.

Read the **Document** on **MyHistoryLab**: Praise of the Scribe's Profession: Egyptian Letter

Read the **Document** on **MyHistoryLab**: Egyptian Folk Tale, c. 2000 B.C.E.

mummification The act of preserving the bodies of the dead; practiced in Egypt to preserve the body for enjoyment of the afterlife.

Continuity and Change

Stability was a hallmark of Egyptian culture. Given the duration of Egyptian civilization, there were surprisingly few basic changes in styles and beliefs. Egypt was fairly isolated, and this isolation helped preserve continuity. Change did occur occasionally. The invasions of Egypt from Palestine near the end of the Old Kingdom period (about 2200 B.C.E.) were distinct exceptions to Egypt's usual self-containment. They were followed by attacks from the Middle East by tribes of Asian origin, which brought a period of division, chaos, and rival royal dynasties. But the unified monarchy was reestablished during the Middle Kingdom period. During this period Egyptian settlements spread southward into what is now the Sudan, toward what later became the African kingdom of Kush (see Map 2.3).

Another period of social unrest and invasion followed, ending in the final great dynastic period, the New Kingdom, about 1570 B.C.E. Trade and other contacts with the Middle East and the eastern Mediterranean, including the island of Crete, gained ground. These contacts spread Egyptian influences, notably in monumental architecture, to other areas. It was during the

FIGURE **2.5** The statue known to the West as the *Sphinx* and to the Arabs as the *Father of Terror* has the head of a man, wearing the royal headdress of ancient Egypt, and the body of a lion. At 200 feet long and 65 feet tall, it was the largest single-stone statue in the ancient world. Exactly who built it and when is unknown, but it is believed to have been constructed as the guardian of the Necropolis at Giza (home of the Great Pyramids) and a symbol of the power of the pharaohs.

THINKING HISTORICALLY

Women in Patriarchal Societies

IN MOST AGRICULTURAL CIVILIZATIONS, WOMEN HAD lower status and potential than in hunting-and-gathering societies. Agricultural civilizations generally were **patriarchal:** They were run by men and based on the assumption that men directed political, economic, and cultural life. Furthermore, as agricultural civilizations developed and became more prosperous and more elaborately organized, the status of women often deteriorated. Historians have struggled to understand the subordination of women given their higher status in the societies that preceded agriculture.

With agriculture individual families became clearly patriarchal. The husband and father made the key decisions, and the wife gave humble obedience to this male authority. Patriarchal family structure rested on men's control of most or all property, starting with land. Marriage was based on property relationships, and it was assumed that marriage, and therefore subordination to men, was the normal condition for women. A revealing symptom of patriarchy in families was the fact that after marrying, a woman usually moved to the orbit (and often the residence) of her husband's family.

Characteristic patriarchal conditions developed in Mesopotamian civilization. Marriages were arranged for women by their parents, and a formal contract was drawn up. Early Sumerians may have given women greater latitude than they enjoyed later on. Their religion attributed considerable power to female sexuality, and their earlier laws gave women important rights so that they could not be treated as outright property. Still, the adultery of a wife was punishable by death, whereas a husband's adultery was treated far more lightly—a double standard characteristic of patriarchalism. Mesopotamian societies after Sumerian times began to emphasize the importance of a woman's virginity at marriage and to require women to wear veils in public to emphasize their modesty. A good portion of Mesopotamian law (such as the Hammurabic code) was devoted to prescriptions for women, ensuring certain basic protections but clearly emphasizing limits and inferiority.

Patriarchal conditions varied from one agricultural civilization to another, however. Egyptian civilization gave women, at least in the upper classes, considerable credit. Artistic works suggest Queen Nefertiti's religious role, for example. Some agricultural societies traced descendants from mothers rather than from fathers. This was true of Jewish law, for example. But even these matrilineal societies held women to be inferior to men; for example, Jewish law insisted that men and women worship separately, with men occupying the central temple space. These variations are important, but they usually operated within a basic framework of patriarchalism. It was around 2000 B.C.E. that an Egyptian writer, Ptah Hotep, put patriarchal beliefs as clearly as anyone in the early civilizations: "If you are a man of note, found for yourself a household, and love your wife at home, as it beseems. Fill her belly, clothe her back. . . . But hold her back from getting the mastery."

Why was patriarchalism so pervasive? As agriculture improved with the use of better techniques, women's labor, although still vital, became less important than it had been in hunting-and-gathering or early agricultural societies. This was particularly true in the upper classes and in cities, where men often took over the most productive work (craft production or political leadership, for example). The inferior position of women in the upper classes, relative to men, usually was more marked than in peasant villages, where women's labor remained essential.

Agriculture also promoted a higher birth rate than in hunting-and-gathering societies, where prolonged breast-feeding provided real birth control. Agricultural societies, needing more family labor, loosened these constraints, with children often born about two years rather than five years apart. This was a key pressure on women's domestic roles.

More generally, agricultural societies were based on concepts of property, beginning with the ways land was organized. Early law codes defined property relationships. It seemed essential in those circumstances for a man to know who his heirs were—that is, to try to make sure that he monopolized the sexual activities of his wife or wives. This situation helps account for the strong legal emphasis on women's sexual fidelity and the tendency to treat women as part of a man's property. Within this framework, it became possible to think of women as inferior and partly ornamental, so that when groups achieved a certain level of wealth, they often tried to demonstrate it by further reducing the status of women. This pattern was very clear in Chinese civilization and operated also in India and later in western Europe. In sum, patriarchalism was a response to economic and property conditions in agricultural civilizations and could deepen over time.

Patriarchalism raises important questions about women themselves. Why did they put up with it? Many women internalized the culture of patriarchalism, holding that it was their job to obey and to serve men and accepting arguments that their aptitudes were inferior to those of men. But patriarchalism did not

A good portion of Mesopotamian law (such as the Hammurabic code) was devoted to prescriptions for women, ensuring certain basic protections but clearly emphasizing limits and inferiority.

(continued on next page)

preclude some important options for women. In many societies, a minority of women could gain expression through religious tasks, such as prayer or service in ceremonies. These could allow them to act independently of family structures. Patriarchal laws defined some rights for women even within marriage, protecting them in theory from the worst abuses. Babylonian law, for example, gave women as well as men the right to divorce under certain conditions when the spouse had not lived up to obligations. Women could also wield informal power in patriarchal societies by their emotional hold over husbands or sons. Such power was indirect, behind the scenes, but a forceful woman might use these means to figure prominently in a society's history. Women also could form networks, if only within a large household. Older women, who commanded the obedience of many daughters-in-law and unmarried daughters, could shape the activities of the family.

Patriarchalism was a commanding theme in most agricultural civilizations from the early centuries onward. Its enforcement, through law and culture, was one means by which societies tried to achieve order. In many agricultural civilizations, patriarchalism dictated that boys, because of their importance in carrying on the family name and the chief economic activities, were more likely to survive. When population excess threatened a family or a community, female infants sometimes were killed as a means of population control.

QUESTIONS

- How do you think most women reared in a patriarchal society would react to their conditions?
- What might cause differences in women's conditions in patriarchal societies?
- Why were upper-class women often more inferior to men in power than peasant women were?

New Kingdom that Egyptians first instituted formal slavery. After about 1150 B.C.E., new waves of invasion, internal conspiracies, and disorganization, including strikes and social protest, brought fairly steady decline.

EGYPT AND MESOPOTAMIA COMPARED

2.4   What were the main differences between Egyptian and Mesopotamian civilizations?

Comparisons in politics, culture, economics, and society suggest that the Egyptian and Mesopotamian civilizations varied substantially because of largely separate origins and environments. The distinction in overall tone was striking, with Egypt more stable and cheerful than Mesopotamia, not only in its beliefs about gods and the afterlife but in the colorful and lively pictures the Egyptians emphasized in their decorative art. The distinction in internal history was also striking: Egyptian civilization was far less marked by disruption than its Mesopotamian counterpart.

Egypt and Mesopotamia differed in many ways thanks to variations in geography, exposure to outside invasion and influence, and different beliefs. Despite trade and war, they did not imitate each other much. Egypt emphasized strong central authority, whereas Mesopotamian politics shifted more often over a substructure of regional city-states. Mesopotamian art focused on less monumental structures and embraced a literary element that Egyptian art lacked. Mesopotamians did not share the Egyptian concern for preparations for the afterlife, which motivated the great tombs and pyramids through which ancient Egypt and some of the pharaohs live on in human memory.

The economies differed as well. Mesopotamia generated more technological improvements because the environment was more difficult to manage than the Nile valley. Trade contacts were more wide ranging, and the Mesopotamians gave considerable attention to a merchant class and commercial law. The differences in ideas about women, and even women's costumes, illustrated separate social systems as well.

Differences were not the whole story, for as river valley civilizations Egypt and Mesopotamia shared important features. Both emphasized social stratification, with a noble, land-owning class on top and masses of peasants and slaves at the bottom. A powerful priestly group also figured in the elite. Although specific achievements in science differed, both civilizations emphasized astronomy and related mathematics and produced durable findings about units of time and measurement. Both

patriarchal Societies in which women defer to men; societies run by men and based on the assumption that men naturally directed political, economic, and cultural life.

By comparing the two first civilizations, we can highlight their differences as well as their important similarities.

Mesopotamia and Egypt changed slowly by more modern standards. Having developed successful political and economic systems, both societies tended strongly toward conservation. Change, when it came, usually was brought by outside forces (natural disasters or invasions).

Finally, both civilizations left important heritages in their regions and adjacent territories. Several smaller civilization centers were launched under the impetus of Mesopotamia and Egypt, and some would produce important innovations of their own by about 1000 B.C.E.

CIVILIZATION CENTERS IN AFRICA AND THE EASTERN MEDITERRANEAN

Egypt and Mesopotamia had contacts outside their core regions. Their outreach influenced the development of important societies in other parts of northeastern Africa, the Middle East, and the eastern Mediterranean.

2.5 Why was Judaism such an important development in the history of religion?

Egypt and Mesopotamia formed regional civilizations, strongly tied to particular river valleys. Trading and military encounters, however, spread cultural and political influences more widely. The results helped spread civilizations to a wider zone, creating additional centers in Africa and in the eastern Mediterranean, some of them with lasting impact.

Kush and Axum: Civilization Spreads in Africa

Kush [kuhsh] An African state that developed along the upper reaches of the Nile c. 1000 B.C.E.; conquered Egypt and ruled it for several centuries.

The kingdom of **Kush** is the first known African state other than Egypt. It sprang up around 2000 B.C.E. along the upper (southern) reaches of the Nile, on the frontiers of Egyptian activity, where Egyptian garrisons were stationed from time to time (see Map 2.4). About 500,000 people lived in

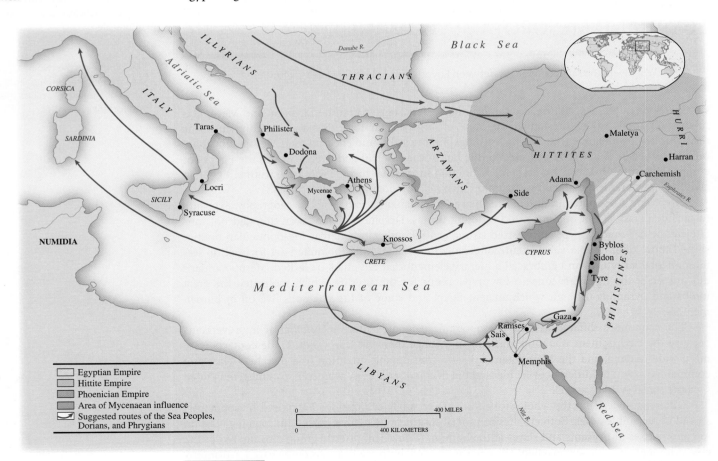

MAP 2.4 The Eastern Mediterranean, c. 1100 B.C.E. By the 12th century B.C.E. many smaller cultures had sprung up around the Mediterranean, such as those of the Mycenaeans and the Hebrews.

what is now Sudan by 2000 B.C.E., growing to a million by 1500—though the kingdom of Kush did not embrace the whole region. Early artistic work illustrates Kush's emergence (Figure 2.6). By 1000 B.C.E. it developed as a strong and independent political unit, although heavily influenced by Egyptian forms. By 730 B.C.E., as Egypt declined, Kush was strong enough to conquer its northern neighbor and rule it for several centuries. When this conquest was ended by Assyrian invasion from the Middle East, the Kushites began to push their frontiers farther south, gaining a more diverse African population and weakening the Egyptian influence. A new capital was established at **Meroë** by the 6th century.

Kushites became skilled in the use of iron and had access to African ore and fuel. The use of iron tools extended the area that could be cultivated. Kushites developed a form of writing derived from Egyptian hieroglyphics that has not yet been fully deciphered. They established several significant cities. Their political organization, similar to Egypt's, emphasized a strong monarchy with elaborate ceremonies based on the belief that the king was a god. Religion was polytheistic, with emphasis on the lion god Apeedemak. Kushite economic influence extended widely in sub-Saharan Africa. They traded extensively with people to the west and through this trade may have spread knowledge of ironmaking to much of the rest of Africa.

The greatest period of the kingdom at Meroë lasted from about 250 B.C.E. to 50 C.E. By this time the kingdom was a channel for African goods—animal skins, ebony, ivory, gold, and slaves—into the Middle East and the Mediterranean. Many monuments were built during those centuries, including huge royal pyramids and an elaborate palace in Meroë, along with fine pottery and jewelry. Meroë began to decline from about 100 C.E. onward and was defeated by a kingdom to the south, **Axum**, about 300 C.E. Prosperity and extensive political and economic activity did not end in this region but extended into the formation of a kingdom in present-day Ethiopia.

The extent of Kush's influence is not entirely clear. Whether African peoples outside the upper Nile region learned much from Kush about political forms is unknown. There was little imitation of its writing, and the region of Kush and Ethiopia would long remain isolated from the wider stream of African history. Nevertheless, the formation of a separate society stretching below the eastern Sahara was an important step in setting the bases for technological and economic change in upper Africa. Although its achievements figure less prominently in later African development, Kush may have done for sub-Saharan Africa what Sumer achieved for the Middle East in setting a wider process of civilization in motion.

Meroë [MEHR-oh-ee] An ancient city of the east bank of the Nile river in modern Sudan; served as the southern capital of the Kushite Kingdom from 800 B.C.E. to 350 C.E.

Axum Kingdom located in Ethiopian highlands; replaced Meroë in first century C.E.; received strong influence from Arabian peninsula; eventually converted to Christianity.

Cultures in the Mediterranean Region

Smaller centers in the Middle East began to spring up after about 1500 B.C.E. (Map 2.4). Although dependent on the larger Mesopotamian culture for many ideas, these centers added important new elements and in some cases extended the hold of civilization westward to the Asian coast of the Mediterranean. They also added to the diversity of the Middle East, creating an array of identities

FIGURE **2.6** This Egyptian wall painting portrays dark-skinned people from the rising kingdom of Kush, who interacted increasingly with Egyptian society and, for several centuries ruled Egypt directly.

that marked the region even under later conquerors, such as the Roman Empire and the sweeping religion of Islam. Several of these smaller cultures proved immensely durable and influenced other parts of the world.

The Hebrews and Monotheism. The most important of the smaller Middle Eastern groups were the Hebrews, who gave the world one of its most influential religions. The Hebrews were a Semitic people (a population group that also includes the Arabs). They were influenced by Babylonian civilization. They may have settled in the southeast corner of the Mediterranean about 1600 B.C.E., probably migrating from Mesopotamia and then developing agriculture. Some may have moved into Egypt, where they were treated as a subject people, although the first clear record of the Hebrews dates only to 1100 B.C.E. According to Jewish tradition, Moses led the Hebrews to Palestine in search of a homeland promised by God in the 13th century B.C.E. This was later held to be the central development in Jewish history.

By 1100 B.C.E. the Jews began to emerge as a people with a self-conscious culture and some political identity (Figure 2.7). At most points, however, the Jewish state was small and weak, retaining independence only when other parts of the Middle East were disorganized. A few Jewish kings unified their people, but at many points the Jews were divided into separate regional states. Most of Palestine came under foreign domination from 722 B.C.E. onward, but the Jews were able to maintain their cultural identity and key religious traditions. A series of dynamic prophets elaborated Jewish beliefs and added to the rich religious literature.

monotheism The exclusive worship of a single god; introduced by the Jews into Western civilization.

The Jews' distinctive achievement was the development of a strong **monotheistic** religion. Early Jewish leaders may have emphasized a particularly strong creator god as the most powerful of many divinities, a hierarchy not common in animism. Such an emphasis encouraged a focus on the father God for prayer and loyalty. According to Mosaic tradition, this divinity, through the prophets, increasingly urged Jews to abandon the worship of all other gods and to receive from God the Torah (a holy law). Keeping this law was enjoined upon all Jews as it made them a holy people under God's special guidance. From this point onward, Jews regarded themselves as a "chosen" people; a community "chosen" to bear witness to God's evolving will on earth. The development of monotheism had a wide significance. In Jewish hands the concept of God became less humanlike and more abstract, a basic change not only in religion but in overall outlook. God had a power and a planning quality far different from the attributes of the traditional gods of the Middle East and Egypt. The gods, particularly in Mesopotamia, were whimsical and capricious; the Jewish god was orderly and just, and people could know what to expect if they adhered to God's rules. The link to ethical conduct and moral behavior was also central. Religion for the Jews was a system of life, not merely a set of rituals and ceremonies. God's laws were clearly spelled out in the Torah and other writings developed between the 9th and 2nd centuries B.C.E. The full impact of this religious transformation on Middle

View the **Closer Look** on **MyHistoryLab:** Tribute from the Land of Punt

FIGURE **2.7** This segment of an Egyptian wall painting depicts a Semitic tribe bringing tribute to the Pharaoh.

Eastern and Mediterranean civilization would come later, when Jewish ideas were taken up by the proselytizing faiths of Christianity and Islam. But the basic concept formed one of the legacies of the twilight period between the first great civilizations and the new cultures that arose in their place.

The impact of Jewish religion beyond the Jewish people was complex. The Jews saw God's guidance in all of human history, not simply their own. Ultimately, all peoples would be led to God. But God's special pact was with the Jews, and little premium was placed on missionary activity or converting others to the faith. This limitation helps explain the intensity and durability of the Jewish faith. It also kept the Jewish people a minority within the Middle East, although at various points the religion was spread somewhat more widely by substantial conversions to Judaism.

The Minoans. About 1600 B.C.E., a civilization developed on the island of Crete. This **Minoan** society traded widely with both Mesopotamia and Egypt and probably acquired many of its civilized characteristics from this exchange. For example, Minoan society copied Egyptian architectural forms and mathematics, although it developed important new artistic styles in the colossal palace built in the capital city, Knossos. The writing system was adapted from Egyptian hieroglyphics. Political structures similar to those of Egypt and the Mesopotamian empires emphasized elaborate bureaucratic controls complete with extensive recordkeeping under a powerful monarch. Minoan navies conquered parts of the Greek mainland; these conquests eventually led to the establishment of the first civilization there. Centered in the kingdom of Mycenae (my-SEE-nee), this early Greek civilization developed a considerable capacity for monumental building and conducted important wars with city-states in the Middle East, including the famous conflict with Troy.

Civilizations in Crete and Greece were overturned by a wave of Indo-European invasions, culminating about 1000 B.C.E. Although the civilization that arose later to form classical Greece had somewhat separate origins, it built extensively on the memories of this first civilized society and on its roots in Egyptian and Mesopotamian achievements.

The Phoenicians. Another distinct society grew up in the Middle East in what is now the nation of Lebanon. Around 2000 B.C.E. a people called the **Phoenicians** settled on the Mediterranean coast. Like the Minoans, they quickly turned to seafaring because their agricultural hinterland was not extensive. The Phoenicians improved on the knowledge they gained through their elaborate trading contacts with the major civilization centers. About 1300 B.C.E. they devised a simplified alphabet of only 22 letters based on the Mesopotamian cuneiform. The Phoenician alphabet served as ancestor to the Greek and Latin lettering systems. The Phoenicians also upgraded the Egyptian numbering system.

However, the Phoenicians were a merchant people, not vested in extensive cultural achievements. They advanced manufacturing techniques in several areas, particularly the production of dyes for cloth. Above all, for commercial purposes, they dispersed and set up colonies at several points along the Mediterranean. They benefited from the weakening of Egypt and the earlier collapse of Minoan society and its Greek successor because there were few competitors for influence in the Mediterranean by 1000 B.C.E. Phoenician sailors moved steadily westward, setting up a major trading city on the coast of north Africa at Carthage and lesser centers in Italy, Spain, and southern France. The Phoenicians even traded along the Atlantic coast of Europe and reached Britain, where they sought tin. By the 6th century B.C.E., Phoenicia collapsed in the wake of the Assyrian invasions of the Middle East, although several of the colonial cities, such as Carthage, long survived.

Minoan [mih-NO-un] A civilization that developed on the island of Crete c. 1600 B.C.E.; capital at the palace complex of Knossos.

Phoenicians [fih-NISH-unz] Seafaring civilization located on the shores of the eastern Mediterranean; established colonies throughout the Mediterranean.

 View the Closer Look on **MyHistoryLab:** Enemies Crossing the Euphrates to Escape Assyrians

THE ISSUE OF HERITAGE

| 2.6 | What were the main legacies of early civilizations in the Middle East and northeast Africa? |

For several centuries after about 1200 B.C.E., a series of invasions and migrations by peoples speaking a language called Indo-European disrupted the civilization of the Middle East. These were hunters and herders. They introduced the use of iron, which soon would establish the basis for a new series of political units and wealthy economies. But for the moment there was some break in developments. The Indo-Europeans played down Mesopotamian and Egyptian beliefs about the divinity

Early civilizations unquestionably created a series of tools that would never have to be reinvented. Historians debate how much influence particular cultures or political patterns would have on societies that later built on the early civilizations. The civilizations were regional, but they involved some wider outreach.

of kings, for example, preferring rulers selected by councils of military leaders. They brought in new religious ideas. They helped bring to a close the river valley civilization phase in the Middle East. Only after 600 B.C.E. would larger civilizations emerge once more, beginning with the Persian Empire.

The accomplishments of the river valley civilizations would continue to have impact, even amid new patterns. The tools of civilization never had to be reinvented in the eastern Mediterranean and north Africa. Basic mathematics and science, the idea of writing, and key technologies persisted, to be used by later societies. Even a few words lasted, like the Sumerian *alsokol*, still visible in English as *alcohol*.

Cultural elements survived as well. The Jewish religion continued to thrive and would later have far wider influence. Musical instruments like harps, drums, and flutes, invented in early Mesopotamian civilization, as well as the development of the seven- and eight-tone scales, would influence the music of Greece and other societies. Egyptian architecture had wide impact, as did ideas of divine kingship.

Clearly, later civilizations in the Mediterranean built on the massive achievements of Mesopotamian and Egyptian societies. Historians debate the range of influence. But there were other formative civilization centers, whose heritage would also loom large in later world history in shaping major societies in Asia.

Global Connections and Critical Themes

THE EARLY CIVILIZATIONS AND THE WORLD

Egypt and Mesopotamia both illustrate changes the advent of civilization introduced in the human experience—for example, the rise of formal states. Comparison shows how the two societies developed different basic patterns. One key difference involved contacts with regions beyond the core boundary of the civilization itself. Neither civilization had massive outreach to a wider world, but each radiated some influence more widely and received much in return. Sumerian trade contacts with India either direct or through intermediaries in the Persian Gulf led to the annual exchange of tons of Sumerian copper for Indian wheat. India also provided fine gemstone necklaces greatly treasured by Sumerian royal households. Later Egyptians imported Indian teak. Interestingly, the early Greeks learned about fermented beverages from the Egyptians and may have returned the favor by sharing with Egypt its advances in the production of wine.

The forces driving these contacts were geographic as well as cultural. Mesopotamia was flat, with few natural barriers to recurrent invasion from the north. Perhaps for this reason, Mesopotamian leaders thought in terms of expansion. Many conquering emperors expanded their territory, although within the Middle East. Thus it was natural that many traders pushed outward, dealing either with merchants to the east or sending expeditions into the Mediterranean and beyond, and also to India. The Middle East's role as active agent in wider contact was clearly being established.

Egypt was not isolated, but it was more self-contained. There was important trade and interaction along the Nile to the south, which brought mutual influences with the peoples of Kush and Ethiopia. Trade and influence also linked Egypt to Mediterranean islands like Crete, south of Greece. A few interactions, finally, occurred with Mesopotamia. But most Egyptians, including the leaders, thought of Egypt as its own world. There was less need or desire to learn of wider horizons. Correspondingly, ancient Egypt played less of a role as intermediary among regions than did Mesopotamia.

Further Readings

Two excellent studies can guide additional work on early civilization in Mesopotamia: C. L. Redman's *The Rise of Civilization: From Early Farmers to Urban Society in the Ancient Near East* (1988) and Marc Van de Mieroop, *King Hammurabi of Babylon: A Biography* (2005). See also Trevor Bryce, *The Trojans and Their Neighbors* (2006); Sarah Iles Johnston, *Ancient Religions* (2007); C. B. F. Walker, *Cuneiform* (1987); G. W. Bowersock, *Mosaics as History: The Near East from Late Antiquity to Islam* (2006); and H. W. F. Saggs, *Babylonians* (1995). Important studies of Egypt include T. G. H. James, *Ancient Egypt: The Land and Its Legacy* (1988); N. C. Grimal, *A History of Ancient Egypt* (1992); Roberto B. Gozzoli, *The writing of History in Ancient Egypt During the First Millennium BC (ca. 1070–180 BC): Trends and Perspectives* (2006); Christiance Cesroches Noblecourt, *Gifts from the Pharaohs: How Egyptian Civilization Shaped the Modern World* (2007); Zahi Hawass, *Tutankhamen and the Golden Age of the Pharaohs* (2005) and *Mountains of the Pharaohs: The Untold Story of the Pyramid Builders* (2006). See also Donald Redford, *Egypt, Canaan, and Israel in Ancient Times* (1995); and David O'Connor, *Ancient Nubia: Egypt's Rival in Africa* (1993); Salima Ikram, *Divine Creatures: Animal Mummies in Ancient Egypt* (2005); John Boardman, *Classical Phoenician Scarabs: A Catalogue and Study* (2003).

For an excellent study of non-Western science beginning with the Egyptians and Mesopotamians, see Dick Teresi, *Lost Discoveries: The Ancient Roots of Modern Science—From the Babylonians to the Maya* (2002). See also Brian Fagan's lavishly illustrated *The Seventy Great Inventions of the Ancient World* (2004). Two books deal with important special topics: M. Silver's *Economic Structures of the Ancient Near East* (1987) and T. Jacobsen's *The Treasures of Darkness: A History of Mesopotamian Religion* (1976). Two studies of Israel are J. Bright, *A History of Israel* (1981), and the first two volumes of W. D. Davies and L. Finkelstein, eds., *The Cambridge History of Judaism* (1984, 1987). For studies of Phoenicia and its role in world history, see N. K. Sanders, *The Sea Peoples* (1985); and M. E. Auber, *The Phoenicians and the West* (1996).

The women of ancient Egypt are addressed in Zahi Hawass, *Silent Images: Women in Pharaonic Egypt* (2000); Barbara S. Lesko, ed., *Women's Earliest Records, from Ancient Egypt to Western Asia* (1989) and Gay Robins, *Women in Ancient Egypt* (1993).

On disruptions in the late Bronze Age, see Trude Dothan and Moshe Dothan, *People of the Sea: The Search for the Philistines* (1992). Martin Bernal's controversial *Black Athena* (1992) seeks to trace ancient African influences on the classical Western world but also can be employed as a window into the use and misuse of history by both Afrocentric and Eurocentric scholars; see also Donald B. Redford's *From Slave to Pharaoh: The Black Experience of Ancient Egypt* (2004). Travel and travel literature has become a major issue in world history. Lionel Casson's *Travel in the Ancient World* (1994) is a well researched and popular study (principally of the Middle East and Mediterranean) that ranges from accounts of tourism (including inns and restaurants) to early postal services.

On MyHistoryLab

 Study and Review on MyHistoryLab

Critical Thinking Questions

1. What types of evidence provide most of our knowledge of the first river valley civilizations? What are the limitations of the evidence?

2. What are some possible causes of the major differences between Mesopotamian and Egyptian civilizations?

3. What were the main characteristics of polytheistic religions in the early civilizations?

4. What was the role of iron in ending the early civilization period in the Middle East and North Africa, and preparing the next stage in the history of civilizations?

3

Asia's First Civilizations: India and China

((•)) Listen to Chapter 3 on MyHistoryLab

LEARNING OBJECTIVES

3.1 What environmental factors were critical to the rise of Harappan civilization in India, and how much of a role do you think climate played in its decline? p. 46

3.2 In what major ways did Indo-European society differ from that of Harappa that preceded it? p. 50

3.3 Why do we know so much more about the early political systems, military organization and religion of China than about India in the Harappan era? p. 53

3.4 What aspects of Shang and Zhou civilization exemplify particular aptitudes for political organization and technological innovation? p. 56

In the late 1850s the British were building railroads through the Indus valley, in what is now Pakistan and northwest India (see Map 3.1). Looking for materials to fill in the rail bed beneath the tracks, British engineers encouraged their Indian construction workers to dig out bricks found in the large dirt mounds of long-abandoned cities in the valley along the route. While on a visit to inspect the railway construction sites in 1856, a British officer named Alexander Cunningham was shown some of the artifacts that had been found among the bricks taken from the mounds. He was particularly intrigued by a number of soapstone seals that were intricately carved with what appeared to be writing in a mysterious script and a variety of human figures and animals, including the bull shown in Figure 3.4. Cunningham was convinced

🔍 **View the Closer Look on MyHistoryLab:** The Walled Mounds of Mohenjodaro

FIGURE **3.1** A water reservoir at an excavated site in Harappan city in present-day Gujarat in India.

👁 Watch the Video Series on MyHistoryLab

Learn about some key topics related to this chapter with the *MyHistoryLab Video Series: Key Topics in World History*

that the seals were of ancient origin and baffled by the writing, which bore little resemblance to that of any of the languages then used in India or anywhere else as far as he was aware. When he was later appointed head of the Indian Archeological Survey, Cunningham ordered the full-scale excavation of what was soon recognized as one of the earliest and in many respects most highly developed of all ancient human civilizations.

Decades of extensive digging at the original site and hundreds of others throughout the Indus valley uncovered a huge complex of cities and villages (see Figure 3.1). The evidence that has been found so far indicates that Harappan civilization, as it came to be called, developed rapidly in the mid-3rd millennium B.C.E. It diverged sharply from the village cultures that preceded it in technology, size, and organization. The civilization was apparently anchored on two capital cities: Harappa, in the north, near one of the five great rivers that flows through the valley, and Mohenjo Daro (moh-HEN-joh-DA-roh), 400 miles to the south, along the banks of the Indus River itself. Recent excavations indicate that there were more than a dozen sites nearly as large, each surrounded by many other urban centers that spread over an area larger than Egypt and Mesopotamia combined.

In East Asia, archeological excavations have provided the basis for a similar reconstruction of the ways in which a complex and populous society developed in ancient China. Like Harappa and other early civilizations in Egypt and Mesopotamia, Chinese civilization had its genesis along a mighty river. South of a great bend in the Huang he (hwahng huh), or Yellow River (see Map 3.2), large farming communities—often protected by high walls of stamped earth—had developed by 4000 B.C.E. And just as Harappan civilization was declining in India in the mid-2nd millennium B.C.E., a nomadic dynasty—the Shang (shahng)—was laying the basis of a kingdom that was powerful enough to demand tribute and exert some degree of control over large numbers of these village communities.

The combination of Shang military prowess and extensive irrigation networks provided the foundations for the longest lived, continuous civilization ever developed. Painstaking archeological work at ancient Chinese sites led to the discovery of a writing system that was initially as puzzling as that found on the seals at sites across the Indus River valley. The Chinese hieroglyphs were carved into animal bones (see Figure 3.2) that had been used by oracles to predict the future—a skill that was particularly prized by the fiercely competitive rulers of the kingdoms that divided up the north China plains. Extensive study of these ancient pictographic inscriptions established that they were the prototypes of the characters that, over time, developed into written Chinese. ∎

In this chapter we will trace the rather different historical trajectories of the first civilizations that developed in south Asia and China. Harappan civilization spread across the vast Indus valley that makes up much of present-day Pakistan and a corner of northwest India. Far to the east, the core areas and institutions of Chinese civilization evolved under first the Shang and then the Zhou dynasties. In these early and formulative centuries, they were surrounded, often invaded, and ruled by neighboring pastoral peoples. The cohabitation and often intermarriage among these herding peoples and the agrarian peoples of the Shang-Zhou core gave rise to a distinct Chinese ethno-linguistic population that would build the great empires and sophisticated sociocultural system that have consistently supported 20 percent of humanity for most of recorded history. By contrast,

400,000 B.C.E.	8000 B.C.E.	4000 B.C.E.	3000 B.C.E.	2000 B.C.E.	1000 B.C.E.
400,000–350,000 Peking Man	**8000–4000** Transition to sedentary agriculture and silk weaving	**4000–2500** Spread of farming and villages in western India	**2600** Emergence of Harappan civilization **2500–2000** Yangshao culture in China **c. 2200** Emergence of Longshan culture in China	**1700–1500** Consolidation of the Shang kingdom **1600–1500** Beginnling of Aryan nomadic migration **1600–1300** Collapse of Harappan civilization **1122–770** Former or western Zhou kings	**770–221** Later or eastern Zhou kings **700** Composition of first of the sacred Vedas **600–500** Age of the Buddha, and Hindu–Buddhist rivalry **550–480** Age of Confucius

Harappan civilization gradually imploded in the same centuries that Shang culture was emerging. Under the pressures of climatic changes and nomadic incursions, Harappan civilization disappeared from world history until the ruins of its cities and towns were excavated in the mid-19th century. The different trajectories of early civilization in both India and China contrast as well with patterns in the Middle East and North Africa, discussed in Chapter 2.

THE INDUS VALLEY AND THE BIRTH OF SOUTH ASIAN CIVILIZATION

3.1 What environmental factors were critical to the rise of Harappan civilization in India, and how much of a role do you think climate played in its decline?

Great torrents of water from the world's highest mountain range, the **Himalayas**, carved out the vast Indus River system, which nurtured the first civilization in the Indian subcontinent (Map 3.1). As the rapidly running mountain streams reached the plains of the Indus valley, they branched out into seven great rivers, of which six remain today. These rivers converge midway down the valley to form the Indus River, which runs for hundreds of miles to the southwest and empties into the Arabian Sea.

The streams that flow from high in the Himalayas are fed by monsoon rains. Rain clouds are carried from the seas surrounding the Indian subcontinent by **monsoons**—seasonal winds—across the lowlands to the mountains, where, cooled and trapped, they release their life-giving waters. These summer, or wet, monsoons, which blow toward central Asia from the sea, are a critical source of moisture for the plains and valleys they cross before they reach the mountains. The streams from the mountains also carry rich soil to the plains, constantly enlarging them and allowing

Between about 2500 and 1600 B.C.E., the two great cities uncovered thus far and numerous towns of Harappan civilization flourished in the Indus River valley. As in the Fertile Crescent, environmental change, natural calamities, and successive nomadic migrations brought about the irretrievable decline of Harappa in the middle centuries of the 2nd millennium B.C.E.

Himalayas Mountain region marking the northern border of the Indian subcontinent; site of the Aryan settlements that formed small kingdoms or warrior republics.

monsoons Seasonal winds crossing the Indian subcontinent and southeast Asia; during summer bring rains.

FIGURE **3.2** The hieroglyphic characters painted on the Chinese oracle bones developed over time into written Chinese.

extensive cultivation and dense human habitation. The Indus is only one of many river systems on the Indian subcontinent formed by melting snow and monsoon rains, but it was the first to nurture a civilization.

The lower Indus plains were a very different place in the 3rd millennium B.C.E. than they are today. Most of the region is now arid and desolate, crisscrossed by dried-up riverbeds. In Harappan times it was green and heavily forested. Game animals and pasturage for domesticated animals were plentiful. Long before the first settlements associated with the Harappan complex appeared, the plains were dotted with farm settlements. By at least 3000 B.C.E., these pre-Harappan peoples cultivated wheat and barley and had developed sophisticated agricultural implements and crop-growing techniques.

The pre-Harappan peoples knew how to make bronze weapons, tools, and mirrors, and they had mastered the art of pottery-making. Recurring motifs, such as bulls and long-horned cattle, on elaborately decorated bowls and storage urns suggest links to early agricultural communities in the Middle East. Pottery designs indicate that fish probably were a major source of food. The long-horned bull was a central image in the Harappan culture and remains important in Indian iconography (the art of pictorial representation). Pre-Harappan peoples in the Indus valley also carved many small figurines of women. These statuettes differ from those found in many other early cultures in the detailed attention given to hairstyles and jewelry.

A Civilization Anchored by Cities in the Indus Valley

Although hundreds of miles apart, Harappa, Mohenjo Daro, and other urban centers were remarkably similar in layout and construction. They were built on a square grid pattern that was divided by main roads into 12 precisely measured segments. Harappa and Mohenjo Daro were surrounded by walls, which extended a mile from east to west and one-half mile from north to south. The buildings and the city walls were usually made of standardized kiln-dried bricks. Coordinated construction on such a massive scale might have meant an effective central government that could organize and supervise the daily tasks of large numbers of laborers.

The existence of a strong ruling class, at least within the major cities, is also indicated by the presence of large, well-fortified citadels in each capital city. These citadels may have served as sanctuaries for the cities' populations in times of attack and as community centers in times of peace. The citadel at Mohenjo Daro included a very large building that may have been a palace. Both citadels

MAP **3.1 India in the Age of Harappa and the Early Aryan Migrations** Although South Asia's first civilization was located in the Indus valley in the northwest, the Aryan invasions from southwest Asia led to extensive settlement in the Ganges valley to the east and to internal migrations that gave rise to the splendid Dravidian civilization in the Deccan and Tamilland further south.

contained what are believed to have been audience and assembly halls or places of worship as well as public bathing tanks. The elaborately decorated bath at Mohenjo Daro was surrounded by a cloister, which opened onto many small rooms that may have housed priests or sheltered bathers. Large granaries near each of the citadels suggest that those who governed the city stored grain for ceremonial purposes, times of shortage, and possibly the regulation of grain production and sale prices.

Although the main avenues were straight and about 30 feet wide, the lanes and paths in the cities' quarters were narrow and twisting. Brick houses of one to three stories were jumbled together in these areas, which must have been densely populated at the height of Harappan civilization. The layout of the houses was strikingly uniform; each consisted of a courtyard surrounded by rooms for sleeping, cooking, and, in the larger homes, receiving visitors. Entrance to the houses was gained through a long passageway from the street, which in combination with few windows may indicate a concern for security. Each home had a bathing area, in which Harappans, like many other peoples in the world then and now, apparently washed standing up by pouring jugs of water over their bodies. Many houses were also equipped with a toilet—perhaps the first ever devised—that was flushed by water from the same jugs and connected by a drainage pipe to a citywide sewage system, which was among the best in the ancient world.

Harappan Culture and Society.   The great cities and many towns of the Harappan complex were supported by a rather advanced agricultural system based on the cultivation of wheat, rye, peas, and possibly rice. Cotton was widely cultivated, and numerous domesticated animals were reared. It is likely that irrigation systems were built to catch and control waters from the monsoon and the rivers and that fish caught in the rivers were a dietary staple. Local goods were carried by riverboats and ox carts, reproduced in clay models like those shown in Figure 3.3.

The cities of Harappa were major trading centers. Jade from China and precious jewels from what later became Burma have been unearthed at various Indus sites. Stone seals produced in the Indus region, such as those shown in Figure 3.4, have been found in the urban ruins of other ancient civilizations such as Sumer in Mesopotamia. In addition to realistic depictions of animals and human figures, the seals contain a complex writing system that no one has ever deciphered. The fact that Harappan merchants used large numbers of the seals to ensure that crates and urns were not opened during transport suggests that trade was highly developed in the Indus valley civilization.

Despite these overseas contacts, Harappan peoples appear to have been conservative and highly resistant to innovations introduced from the outside. They cast tools and weapons in bronze, but most of their implements were inferior to those of Mesopotamian peoples, with whom they had contact. Their weapons were even more primitive and would have left them vulnerable to invasions by peoples more adept at warfare.

Harappan society appears to may have been dominated by a powerful priestly class, which ruled from the citadel of each urban capital. The priests would have derived this control from their role as intermediaries between the Harappan populace and a number of gods and goddesses, who controlled fertility. Several of what are believed to be gods are depicted on seals, such as those in Figure 3.4. One of the recurring figures is a naked male figure with a horned head and a fierce expression. On some of the seals he is pictured in a crossed-legged posture of meditation similar to that later called the lotus position. This suggests that yoga, special techniques for exercise and postures for meditation, may have had its origin in the Harappan era. Numerous figurines of women, also naked except for a great deal of jewelry, have been found. These may have depicted mother goddesses, worshiped by

FIGURE **3.3** This wheeled model clay cart, found during the excavation at Mohenjo Daro, tells us a good deal about the main mode of land transport used in south Asia's first civilization. Similar models have been found in almost all Indus valley settlements, and in some respects they resemble the ox-drawn, nearly solid-wheeled carts still used in parts of India today.

the common people, whereas the horned god was apparently favored by the priests and upper classes. The presence of these seals in Sumer and other urban sites in the Persian Gulf region suggests that large quantities of various commodities were traded in the region spanning Mesopotamia and the Indus River valley.

The obsession with fertility was also reflected in the worship of sacred animals, especially bulls, and in the large quantity of phallic-shaped objects that have been found at Harappan sites. Along with a handful of superbly carved figurines of male notables, statuettes of women, and seal carvings of humped bulls and other animals, these religious objects represent the height of artistic expression for the apparently practical-minded peoples of Harappa. Harappans also excelled at making fine jewelry, a craft that still flourishes in the Indus region today.

The uniformity and rigid ordering of Harappan culture would not have been possible without an extensive administrative class ruling on its own or serving the priests. It is likely that members of this class and possibly wealthy mercantile families lived in the large two- and three-story houses. Size, not decoration, set their dwellings off from those of artisans, laborers, and slaves.

The Slow Demise of Harappan Civilization.
It was once widely accepted that Harappan civilization was the victim of assaults by nomadic invaders eager to claim the rich Indus valley as pastureland for their cattle. A dramatic vision of a wave of "barbarian" invaders smashing Harappans'

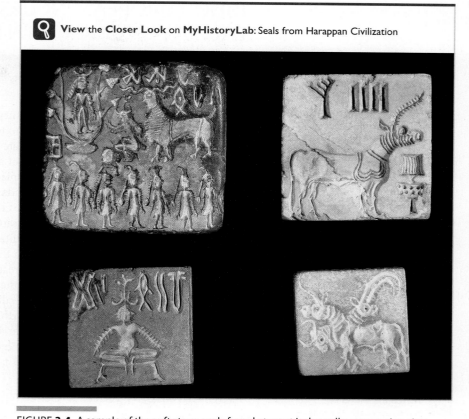

View the **Closer Look** on MyHistoryLab: Seals from Harappan Civilization

FIGURE **3.4** A sample of the soft stone seals found at most Indus valley excavation sites and at trading centers from the Middle East to China. Like some modern languages, such as Arabic, the Harappan script was written and read from right to left. Like Chinese and ancient Egyptian, Harappan writing appears to have been pictographic, but no one has found a consistent pattern that would tell us what the symbols signified.

skulls made for good storytelling perhaps but bad history. Archeological investigations of recent decades have demonstrated that Harappa declined gradually in the mid-2nd millennium B.C.E. But the precise causes of that decline remain highly contested among both historians and archeologists—in part a testament to the paucity of the sort of remains that might provide decisive clues.

It is likely that a combination of factors led to Harappa's demise. There is evidence of severe flooding at Mohenjo Daro and other sites. Short-term natural disasters, including severe earthquakes, may have compounded the adverse effects of long-term climatic changes. Shifts in the monsoon pattern and changes in temperature may have begun the process of desertification that eventually transformed the region into the arid steppe that it has been for most of recorded history. Rapid changes in pottery types suggest sudden waves of migrants into the region. It is possible that the Harappans were too weak militarily to prevent these incoming peoples from settling down or taking over their towns and cities. In many cases these centers of urban life had already been abandoned in response to natural calamities, particularly flooding. A marked decline in the quality of building and town planning suggests that the elites may have lost control over the artisans and laborers.

Some of the migrants were bands of Indo-European herders who entered the Indus region over an extended period of time rather than in militant waves. But the Indo-European pastoralists may have consciously destroyed or neglected the dikes and canals on which the agrarian life of the Harappan peoples had once depended. Cattle breeding would then have replaced crop cultivation, further undermining the economic basis of the civilization. That there was a good deal of violent conflict in this transition cannot be ruled out. Groups of skeletons with smashed skulls or in postures of flight from floods or foreign invaders or internal strife have been found on the stairways at some sites. Thus, environmental changes and related administrative decline may have combined with the effects of nomadic migrations to undermine south Asia's first civilization.

INDO-EUROPEAN INCURSIONS AND EARLY VEDIC SOCIETY IN INDIA

One of the nomadic peoples whose migrations contributed to Harappa's disappearance from history, the Aryans became dominant in south Asia in the last millennia B.C.E. By the last centuries B.C.E., the Aryans had settled down in agrarian societies and kingdoms, which provided the basis for the rise of a splendid new civilization in south Asia and the emergence of two of the great world religions, Hinduism and Buddhism.

Aryans [EH-ree-uhnz] Indo-European nomadic pastoralists who replaced Harappan civilization; militarized society.

Sanskrit The sacred and classical Indian language.

 Watch the Video on MyHistoryLab: The Indo-Europeans in India (Howard Spodek)

3.2   In what major ways did Aryan society differ from that of Harappa that preceded it?

Despite the claims of 19th- and 20th-century racist thinkers, the **Aryans** (Indo-Europeans) were not a race or distinct biological group. The term *Aryan*, often used for the pastoral peoples who filtered into South Asia beginning in the late-Harappan era, is a linguistic one. These people were originally herders who spoke one variant of a group of related Indo-European languages and had formerly lived in the area between the Caspian and Black Seas. For reasons probably related to climatic shifts and conflicts over grazing lands, they began to migrate in large numbers from their homelands in the 3rd and 2nd millennia B.C.E. The first migrations were westward into Asia Minor and eventually Europe. The second waves were eastward toward Iran and the Indus valley.

The Indo-Europeans' mobility and military prowess made it possible for them to prevail over peoples who occupied the lands into which they moved. The remarkable extent of the area affected by their expansion is illustrated by the great variety and prominence of modern languages that belong to the Indo-European family. From the Celtic, Germanic, and Romance languages of western Europe and the Slavic tongues to the east, to the speech of the ancient Persians and modern Iranians and the **Sanskrit**-derived languages of north India, the ancient Indo-European invaders have left a lasting legacy. Despite millennia of separation and differing paths of cultural development on the part of Indo-European groups, the similarities among their widely dispersed languages remain striking. The word for *father*, for example, is *pater* in Latin, *vater* in German, and *pitar* in Sanskrit.

Indo-European Warrior Culture

For the migrating pastoralists, the Indus and the valleys beyond were a paradise of lush, well-watered, and underpopulated grasslands and forests. After spreading across the Indus plains (and either absorbing the Harappan peoples or driving them farther south), the Indo-Europeans moved in waves of small bands to the southeast. There they entered the rich plains and valleys formed by the Ganges River system, which, as Map 3.1 illustrates, surpassed the great Indus complex in area. Like the Indus plains in earlier times, the Ganges region provided the combination of monsoon rains and great river systems that made civilized life possible. The migrating peoples took many centuries to approach the level of civilization achieved by the Harappan peoples. But the potential for agriculture was so obvious that herding bands began to settle down and cultivate lands cleared from the forests in the first centuries after their arrival.

The Indo-Europeans who migrated into South Asia did not develop writing until long after they entered the subcontinent. But we can learn a good deal about their way of life from the hymns they composed for religious-based animal sacrifices, entertainment, and historical chronicles. Transmitted orally for centuries by priests and bards, the hymns were written down in sacred books called the **Vedas** in the 6th century B.C.E.

The Vedic hymns describe the in-migrating pastoralists as a restless and warlike peoples organized at first in tribes and later in small kingdoms. The tribes and kingdoms fought constantly among themselves, often over cattle and pasturelands, and warred with the indigenous peoples. The chief deity of the Aryans was **Indra**, the god of battle and lightning (Figure 3.5). He was described as a colossal, hard-drinking warrior with a huge pot belly. Indra was revered as the smasher of dams and the destroyer of cities. The nomadic peoples were superb horsemen who also used chariots in their wars. Their bows and arrows and metal-tipped spears were a good deal more effective than the weapons of the indigenous peoples. All together the Vedas describe the Indo-Europeans as a rowdy crew who were fond of beer and loved to gamble, race horses, and make war.

Except for the military hardware, early Aryan material culture represented a marked decline from the level reached during the Harappan period. Wood and thatch villages replaced stone and brick cities and towns. There is little evidence of interest in sculpture or painting, and thus it is unlikely that great works of art were produced. However, the Indo-Aryans were extremely fond of music. They played flutes, harps, lutes, and a variety of cymbals and drums, and they delighted in

Vedas Aryan hymns originally transmitted orally but written down in sacred books from the 6th century B.C.E.

Indra Chief deity of the Aryans; depicted as a colossal, hard-drinking warrior.

singing and dancing. If the Vedic hymns are to be believed, they were also much addicted to gambling, particularly dice. One of the few secular early Vedic poems, "The Gambler's Lament," vividly captures the pleasures and pitfalls of the gamblers' den. One passage reminds the tempted youth that

> The dice are armed with hooks and piercing;
> they are deceptive, hot and burning.
> Like children they give and take again,
> they strike back at their conquerors.
> They are sweetened with honey through the magic they
> work on the gambler.

Gambling has been a recurring theme in Indian religious and philosophical discourses throughout history. Allusions to fate as the throw of the dice can be found in philosophical writings. Dice games play pivotal roles in the plots of the great epics that later represented and shaped the civilizations built by the descendants of the early pastoral invaders.

Aryan Society

When they entered the Indian subcontinent, the Indo-European bands were divided into three main social groups: warriors, priests, and commoners. Conflict with and the conquest of indigenous peoples added a fourth group: slaves, or serfs. Although social differences among the first three groups were pronounced, the dividing line between the freeborn Indo-Europeans and the enslaved population was particularly rigid. Apparently, there was also a physical dimension to the sharp division between the free and enslaved. The Indo-Europeans pictured themselves as light-skinned conquerors in a sea of dark-skinned **Dasas**, their name for the indigenous peoples. Attempts were made to prohibit **miscegenation**—sexual relations and procreation—between Indo-Europeans and Dasas. Marriages between the two groups were forbidden. Penalties were prescribed according to the respective ranks of the men and women who had sexual relations.

As the pastoral peoples settled down, social divisions became more complex, with groups such as farmers, merchants, and artisans joining the ruling groups of warriors, priests, and herders. Social distinctions were further complicated by widespread miscegenation. Over the centuries, four broad **varnas** (social classes; lit. colors) developed: priests (Brahmans), warriors (Kshatriyas), merchants (Vaiysa), and farmers (Sudras). Beneath them were the outcaste and untouchable descendants of the Dasas and other non-Indo-European indigenous peoples and migrant groups.

The culture of the pastoral invaders placed great emphasis on physical strength, martial skills, and heroic exploits. Descent and inheritance were **patrilineal**, through the male line. Elder men monopolized authority within the household, although their mothers and wives could influence decisions behind the scenes. At marriage, brides left their own households and families and went to live with those of their husbands. Monogamous marriages were the norm, but **polygamy** (one husband with several wives) and **polyandry** (one wife with several husbands) are recounted in the Aryan epics.

Sizable dowries, or marriage payments, in the form of cattle, food, or precious objects were commonly given to the husband's family. In some cases, a prospective husband paid a bride-price to his future wife's family. This practice suggests that female children had not yet become the economic burden that they have been considered through much of south Asian history. Nonetheless, sons were preferred to daughters because of the men's important family ritual functions and their key roles as warriors and priests. These positions were never held by women, nor were women allowed to be the chieftains of tribal bands or rulers of the kingdoms that developed in the early centuries of Aryan invasions.

Indo-European Religion

The early nomadic migrants were polytheists who worshiped a wide range of deities that physically resembled humans and had human emotions and needs. Similar to those of the ancient Greeks,

Read the **Document** on **MyHistoryLab:** Selections from the Rig Veda

FIGURE **3.5** The Aryan god of war, Indra, was considered king of the cosmos in early times. Later devotees of the religion we now call Hinduism gave Indra a lower status and slimmed down his stomach. But they continued to venerate him as ruler of the skies and the god of rain and thunder. This pattern typifies a tendency in early south Asian religions to identify particular deities with specific natural phenomena and powers.

(Indra, Chief of the Gods, 16th Century. Los Angeles County Museum of Art, Los Angeles, California, USA. Photograph ©2009 Museum Associates/LACMA. Art Resource, NY.)

Dasas Aryan name for indigenous people of Indus valley region; regarded as socially inferior to Indo-Aryans.

miscegenation Practice of interracial marriage or sexual contact; found in virtually all colonial cultures.

varnas Clusters of caste groups in Aryan society; four social castes—Brahmins (priests), warriors, merchants, and peasants; beneath four Aryan castes was a group of socially untouchable Dasas.

patrilineal Family descent and inheritance traced through the male line.

polygamy Marriage practice in which one husband had several wives; practiced in Aryan society.

polyandry Marriage practice in which one woman had several husbands; recounted in Aryan epics.

each Indo-European god and goddess had the power to assist supplicants in a particular aspect of their lives. Thus, there were gods or goddesses to whom devotees offered sacrifices for success in business (the goddess Lakshmi), the means to overcome obstacles in their lives (Ganesha, the elephant-headed god), and the good fortune to conceive children (the god Shiva and a number of female deities). The widespread worship of female deities may well have represented a carryover into Indo-European culture of a prominent aspect of Harappan civilization. Nonetheless, like the human society that worshiped these deities, the Aryan pantheon was dominated by males, particularly gods relating to war, fire, and rain. Religious worship centered on animal sacrifices and ritual offerings of food designed to win specific favors from individual deities. The major function of the Vedic priests was to perform these critical sacrifices, a role that later allowed them to amass great power.

In contrast to their Hindu and Buddhist descendants, there appears to have been little introspection among the early pastoral settlers. The oldest Vedas consist mainly of songs, some quite beautiful, praising the various deities and giving incredibly detailed formulas for sacrifices. There is little speculation on issues that would later preoccupy Indian priests and philosophers, such as the purpose of creation, the fate of the dead, and the nature of the soul. There was no concept of reincarnation (rebirth) or the transmigration of the soul. Much as the ancient Greeks believed, evildoers went to the House of Clay after death, and the virtuous were rewarded in the World of the Fathers. But in an early hymn to Vishvakarman, the creator god, there is a vision of a primal essence and oneness that prefigures later Indian thinking:

> What was the germ primeval which the waters received
> where all the gods were seen together?
> The waters, they received that germ primeval
> wherein the gods were gathered all together.
> It rested set upon the unborn's navel,
> that One wherein abide all things existing.

In a later hymn, this explanation is questioned and the thinker speculates that it is impossible even for the god of creation to know why the universe came into being:

> None knoweth whence creation has arisen;
> And whether he has or has not produced it:
> He who surveys it in the highest heaven,
> He only knows, or haply he may know not.

DOCUMENT

Aryan Poetry in Praise of a War Horse

THE FOLLOWING EARLY VEDIC HYMN EXULTS in the power of a great Aryan war horse.

> Rushing to glory, to the capture of herds,
> Swooping down as a hungry falcon,
> Eager to be first, he darts amid the ranks of the chariots
> Happy as a bridegroom making a garland,
> Spurning the dust and champing at the bit.
> And the victorious steed and faithful,
> His body obedient to his driver in battle,
> Speeding on through the melee,
> Stirs up the dust to fall on his brows.
> And at his deep neigh, like the thunder of heaven,

> The foemen tremble in fear,
> For he fights against thousands, and none can resist him,
> So terrible is his charge.

QUESTIONS

- In what ways does this poem convey the Indo-Europeans' delight in warfare?
- What does it tell us about the way they fought their battles and their attitudes toward the herd animals that were so central to their culture?
- How does it convey the nomads' ideals of manliness, heroism, and loyalty, and what does it say about their attitudes toward death?

Harappa's Fall and Aryan Dominance

During the early centuries of the Indo-European migrations, which began around 1500 B.C.E., civilization disappeared from India. Pastoralism dominated Indian economic life as sedentary agriculture retreated with the fleeing Harappan peoples. A well-defined more centralized elite gave way to feisty chieftains chosen for their popularity among their warrior followers. A complex division of labor and responsibility gave way to highly egalitarian tribal societies that dominated sharply separated subject populations. State control and standardization were replaced by fractious warrior bands and political power was located mainly in local leaders and warrior assemblies.

With the spread of cultivation among the invading tribes and the growth of trade some centuries after the fall of Harappa, the basis for civilization again emerged. The small kingdoms that arose in the foothills of the Himalayas and the upper Ganges plains combined the ingredients that would give rise to India's great classical civilizations. These civilizations produced a succession of wealthy and far-flung empires; gave rise to two major religions, Hinduism and Buddhism, as well as a variety of lesser-known faiths; and produced splendid art, architecture, philosophy, and literature. The new patterns of civilized life that developed in the last centuries B.C.E. diverged widely from those established by the Harappans. Although some Harappan symbols and beliefs were adopted by the Aryans and other invaders, Harappan civilization became little more than a memory.

A BEND IN THE RIVER AND THE BEGINNINGS OF CHINA

3.3	Why do we know so much more about the early political systems, military organization and religion of China than about India in the Harappan era?

Humanlike creatures as well as human beings have lived on the north China plain for hundreds of thousands of years. Peking man, one of the most famous hominids (two-legged primates) had campsites along the Fen River nearly 400,000 years ago, and several Paleolithic sites have been uncovered along the Yellow River where it arcs through the Ordos desert (Map 3.2). From Neolithic times (c. 8500—3500 B.C.E.) cultivating peoples gravitated to the lands that make up the base of the **Ordos bulge**, where conditions were suitable for sedentary agriculture and human settlement.

The region abounded in rich **loess**, a fine-grained, yellow-brown soil deposited by powerful winds from central Asia in prehistoric times. In places, this extremely fertile soil had built up over thousands of millennia to depths of over 300 feet. The Yellow River was named for the peculiar color of the soil that is washed into the river. Rich soil and the abundant supplies of water in areas near the Yellow River and its tributaries made the southern portions of the Ordos bulge and the areas eastward along the north China plain suitable for intensive grain cultivation and dense settlement. In addition, the region was shielded by mountains to the west and south but open to trade and migratory movements from the grasslands of the northwest.

By 4000 B.C.E., human communities supported by sedentary agriculture were spread across the loess zone. These communities developed into two widely spread cultural complexes that laid the basis for the Shang dynasty and Chinese civilization. Both the Yangshao (yang-shoh) culture (c. 2500–2000 B.C.E.) and the Longshan (lahng-shan) culture (c. 2000–1500 B.C.E.) were based on very different mixes of agriculture and hunting. In the Yangshao period, hunting and fishing predominated, supplemented by foods supplied by shifting cultivation. By the Longshan period, the cultivation of grain—millet in particular—was the central preoccupation, and extensive farming made it possible for the inhabitants of the Yellow River region to support large, permanent villages surrounded by walls of stamped earth.

Increasingly elaborate irrigation systems were vital to the expanding agrarian base of society. The shallow bed of the river after it empties onto the plains of north China, and the large quantities of silt it carries, make it particularly treacherous in the spring. The melting snows of the Tibetan plateau and Kunlun mountains turn the river into a raging torrent capable of flooding large portions of the plains. From ancient times, controlling the river by building and maintaining great earthen dikes has been a major preoccupation of peasants—subsistence-oriented farmers—and the ruling classes.

Chinese civilization emerged from the unification of large village communities that had developed along the Yellow River. In the Shang era, which spanned much of the 2nd millennium B.C.E., existing irrigation systems were extended, and a system of writing was devised that has proved a key source of Chinese identity to the present day.

Ordos [OHR-dohs] bulge Located on the Huanghe (Yellow River); region of fertile soil; site of Yangshao and Longshan cultures.

loess [LOH-ehs] Fine-grained soil deposited in Ordos region in China by winds from central Asia; created fertile lands for sedentary agricultural communities.

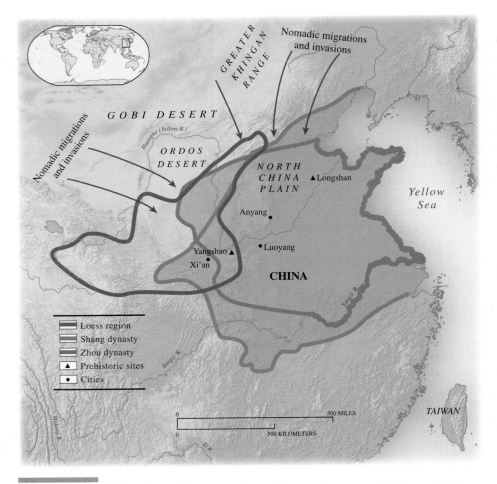

MAP **3.2 China in the Shang and Zhou Eras** As this map of early centers of Chinese civilization depicts dramatically, Chinese peoples occupied only a small portion of the area that would correspond to China from the last centuries B.C.E. to the present day.

These concerns may have given rise to China's first rulers and prompted a high level of community and inter-village cooperation. It is significant that one of the most abused of China's early and semi-mythical leaders was a man named Kun, who proved incapable of controlling a succession of great floods. His son **Yu**, who devised an effective system of flood control, has been revered for millennia as one of the great monarchs of China's mythical golden age. When later thinkers, such as Confucius, searched China's past for leaders whose skill and virtue might be emulated in their own times, men such as Yu came readily to mind.

The Warrior Kings of the Shang Era

Semi-legendary Chinese accounts tell us that Yu, the father of north China's great network of dikes and canals, also founded China's first kingdom, **Xia** (syah). Because no archeological sites connected to Xia have been found, it is possible that the kingdom was the fabrication of later writers. But in the centuries before 1500 B.C.E., numerous small kingdoms had begun to emerge south of the Ordos bulge and east along the north China plain. Most of them were ruled by the nomadic tribal groups that continued to filter into the area from the north and west.

In this region of different ethnic and linguistic groups, a distinctive Chinese culture formed. Key features of this culture included

Yu A possibly mythical Chinese ruler c. 2070 B.C.E.; revered for the construction of an effective system of flood control along the Huanghe valley; founder of the Xia kingdom.

Xia China's first, possibly mythical, kingdom; no archeological sites have been connected to it; ruled by Yu.

Shang First Chinese dynasty for which archeological evidence exists; capital located in Ordos bulge of the Huanghe; flourished 1600 to 1046 B.C.E.

its cooking vessels and cuisine, its reliance on cracked animal bones for divination, its domestication of the silkworm and use of silk fabrics for clothing, and its practice of ancestor worship. The form of ancestor worship also suggests that Chinese culture was already patrilineal.

By 1500 B.C.E., one of the tribes in the Ordos region, the Shang, conquered most of the other tribes and established a kingdom that would lay the foundations of Chinese civilization. Until recent decades we knew little more about the **Shang** than about their Xia predecessors. But extensive excavation of Shang sites at Anyang (ahn-yahng), Zhengzhou (jehng-joh), and elsewhere have given us insights into many aspects of Shang culture and society. In some respects they were very much like the Aryans, who were conquering northern India during this same period. Like the Aryans, the Shang were warlike nomads. They fought on horseback and from chariots with deadly bronze weapons (Figure 3.6). Non-Shang subject peoples provided the foot soldiers that made up the bulk of their armies. Like those of Aryan India and Homeric Greece, Shang battles were wild clashes between massed soldiers that hinged on hand-to-hand combat between a few champions on each side. But unlike the Aryans and ancient Greeks, the Shang warriors were ruled by strong kings, who drew on their vassals' energies and military prowess to build an extensive empire.

The Shang monarch was seen as the intermediary between the supreme being, Shangdi, and ordinary mortals. His kingdom was viewed as the center of the world, and he claimed dominion over all humankind. Shang rulers directed the affairs of state and bore ritual responsibilities for the fertility of their kingdom and the well-being of their subjects. In the springtime, they participated in special ceremonies that included a symbolic mating with female fertility spirits. In times of drought and famine, Shang rulers, or perhaps designated surrogates, were obliged to perform ritual dances

FIGURE **3.6** This beautiful reproduction of a chariot from the Shang era underscores the importance of horses and mobility throughout the ancient Eurasian world. Originally developed by pastoral peoples from the steppes, chariots harnessed horsepower to provide speed and a mobile platform from which archers and spear throwers could strike enemy forces. The chariot was a key weapon of the nomadic invaders who established the Shang empire in north China in the middle centuries of the second millennium B.C.E.

in the nude. The dancer—presumably the surrogate—was later burned alive to placate the spirits whose anger had caused the natural calamities.

Shang Society

Shang monarchs were served by a sizable bureaucracy in the capital city at Anyang and the surrounding areas. But most of the peasant and artisan populations of the kingdom were governed by vassal retainers: subordinate leaders serving the king and great lords and usually bound to them by personal ties. These officials were recruited from the former ruling families and the aristocratic classes of the many subordinate states. The vassals depended on the produce and labor of the commoners in these areas to support their families and military forces. In return for grants of control over varying numbers of peasants, warrior aristocrats collected tribute (usually in the form of agricultural produce), which went to support the monarch and his court. They supplied soldiers for the king's armies in times of war, and they kept the peace and administered justice among the peasants and townspeople.

Shang rulers and their families, servants, and noble retainers lived within walled towns in large compounds that housed **extended families**. These extended families consisted of several generations of the family patriarch's sons and grandsons and their wives. As in Aryan India, family life, at least among the upper classes, was dominated by the elder men in the household. At marriage, a woman went to live with her husband's family. Unswerving obedience was expected of both women and younger men. Within their own households and family spheres, patriarchs and husbands exercised absolute authority. Their commands were carried down the family hierarchy from elder to younger brother and from mother-in-law to young wife.

Judging from later social arrangements in China, the extended family pattern was widespread only among elite groups who had the resources to support large households with many servants. Ordinary peasants, who made up the great majority of the population, lived in modified **nuclear families**: households consisting of husband and wife, their children, and perhaps a grandmother or orphaned cousin. It is likely that peasant families were as male-dominated and patrilocal (the wife living in her husband's village) as those of the elite.

Peasants were in effect the servants of the nobles. By Shang times they were growing a wide range of crops, but their staple foods were millet, wheat, beans, and rice. They cultivated the land in

extended families Consisted of several generations, including the family patriarch's sons and grandsons with their wives and children; typical of Shang China elites.

nuclear families Consisted of husband and wife, their children, and perhaps a grandmother or orphaned cousin; typical of Chinese peasantry.

View the **Closer Look** on **MyHistoryLab**:
A Bronze Axe Head from the Shang Dynasty

FIGURE 3.7 This elaborately decorated bronze vessel from the Shang era shows the sophisticated artistic expression achieved very early in Chinese history. It also demonstrates a high level of metalworking ability, which carried over into Shang weapons and tools. Although the design of these ritual vessels often was abstract, mythical creatures such as dragons and sacred birds were deftly cast in bronzes that remain some of the great treasures of Chinese art.

oracles Shamans or priests in Chinese society who foretold the future through interpretations of animal bones cracked by heat; inscriptions on bones led to Chinese writing.

ideographs Pictographic characters grouped together to create new concepts; typical of Chinese writing.

the village in cooperative work teams using a variety of wooden hoes, spades, and crude plows. They lived in sunken houses of stamped earth and made offerings to local gods of the soil and hearth.

Although the peasants had limited opportunities for social and economic advancement, they were better off than most of the slaves who made up the lowest strata of society in the Shang era. It is likely that many of the artisans were slaves, but some were free and quite prosperous. This latter group probably was engaged in highly skilled crafts, such as weaving silk textiles and casting bronze. Artisan dwellings were located outside the walls of Shang towns, and some were surprisingly large and elaborate.

Shang Culture

Like the elites of many early civilizations, the Shang rulers and nobility were preoccupied with rituals, oracles, and sacrifices. In addition to the fertility functions of the ruler, the entire elite was involved in persuading spirits to provide good crops and large families. Shang artistic expression reached its peak in the ornately carved and expertly cast bronze vessels that were used to make these offerings. Offerings included fine grain, incense, wine, and animals, but Shang records also tell of water festivals at which ritual contests were waged between rival boats, each attempting to sink the other. Those aboard the losing craft drowned when it capsized, and they were offered up to the deities responsible for fertility and good harvests.

War captives and servants were buried with deceased Shang rulers and major officials. Like the pharaohs of ancient Egypt, the kings of Shang went to the otherworld accompanied by their wives, servants, and loyal retainers as well as their favorite horses, hunting dogs, war chariots, and weapons. Ancestral veneration grew into a cult of the royal clan that involved sacrifices of war captives, mass burials, and the construction of tombs for the emperors.

Concern for abundant harvests and victory in war led the Shang elite to put great stock in the predictions of shamans, or priests, who served as **oracles**—sacred people who could prophesy the future. As the bronze vessel in Figure 3.7 shows, much of Shang artistic expression went into producing the ritual objects used by the oracles. Warriors about to go into battle, officials embarking on long journeys, or families negotiating marriage alliances routinely consulted these oracles to ensure that their efforts would turn out well. This reliance on the shamans strongly influenced beliefs and behavior in the Shang era.

The actual procedures followed by the shamans who presided over these rituals gave rise to perhaps the single most important element in Chinese culture—writing. Since pre-Shang times, Chinese oracles had based their predictions on readings taken from animal bones or tortoise shells (see Figure 3.2). A bone or shell was drilled with a hole and seared with a red-hot iron poker. The bone or shell cracked, and the patterns of the cracks were interpreted by a shaman or priest. Over time the practice evolved of inscribing the bones and shells with painted designs that became part of the patterns the shamans read. These designs gradually were standardized and came to form the basis of a written Chinese language.

Like the hieroglyphics of the ancient Egyptians, early Chinese characters were pictographic. Thus, they readily conveyed the ideas they were intended to express. The original character for the sun, for example, was a circle with a dot in the center, the character for a tree was a single tree, and a forest was a set of three trees. Combinations of characters made it possible for the Chinese elite to convey increasingly complex ideas. The character for emperor, for example, combined elements of the **ideographs** for king, heaven, earth, and harmony.

Over time the number of characters increased substantially. By the end of the Shang period, there were an estimated 3000 characters. A well-educated scholar in the modern era would need to master some 8000 characters. The way they are written also changed significantly. Many characters were simplified, and most were stylized so that they have become less pictographic. The bones or bronze vessels on which the characters were originally carved gradually gave way to bamboo slips, silk scrolls, and wooden plates, and they in turn were supplanted in the 1st century C.E. by paper (a critical Chinese invention). Assorted fine brushes and inks were developed to paint the characters, which themselves became a major mode of artistic expression in later periods.

Writing and Chinese Identity

Writing became the key to Chinese identity and the growth of civilization in China. The peoples of the loess region and the north China plain spoke a bewildering variety of languages, often unintelligible from one group to the next. They were surrounded by nomadic herders to the north and shifting cultivators to the south, whose contacts with and movements into the loess zone further complicated the linguistic muddle. But the use of increasingly standardized and sophisticated written characters provided the bond that gave growing numbers of these loess zone peoples a common identity. This sense of identity was felt most keenly by the elite groups, who monopolized the use of the characters, but eventually it filtered down to the cultivating and artisan classes. With the persistence and growth of this identity, the Chinese people entered history for the first time.

THE DECLINE OF THE SHANG AND THE ERA OF ZHOU DOMINANCE

3.4 What aspects of Shang and Zhou civilization exemplify particular aptitudes for political organization and technological innovation?

With the decline of the Shang imperium, a Turkic-speaking nomadic people established a new dynasty, the Zhou, that was the paramount power in north China by the end of the 12th century B.C.E. In the early Zhou era a distinct class of scholar-bureaucrats emerged and Chinese civilization expanded as far south as the valley and vast plains of the Yangzi River.

In the early centuries of their reign, the Zhou rulers exercised more power than their Shang predecessors. Under **Wu**, the military commander who had defeated the Shang, and his brother, the duke of Zhou, the empire was greatly expanded, especially to the east and south. Because the original Zhou capital at **Xi'an** was too far to the west to effectively control these new areas, a second capital was built at **Luoyang** (lwoh-yahng), hundreds of miles to the east (Map 3.2). Wu and other early Zhou rulers governed their vast domains through a hierarchy of vassals, who were controlled to a much greater extent than had been the case under the Shang. Many of the most powerful vassals were relatives, fellow clansmen, or long-standing allies of the Zhou household. Thus, ties of kinship cemented their loyalty and obedience to the Zhou overlords. In turn, the vassals controlled lesser vassals further down the hierarchy, who were often their own subordinates or relatives.

In the early Zhou period, formal oaths of allegiance and regularized fief-granting procedures transformed the Shang vassal system into a more genuine feudal order. Here, as in later political systems of this type, **feudalism** stressed mutual obligation and benefits within the ruling clan. The Zhou rulers granted to their loyal warrior retainers *fiefs*—permission to extract revenue and services from peasant villages. In return, the favored vassals pledged their loyalty to the dynasty in a special ceremony in the ruler's palace. During the ceremony the new fief-holder was given a clump of earth, symbolizing the land and villages granted to him by the monarch. At the same time, a charter of his duties to his ruler and his rights as a fief-holder was presented to the assembled court.

Wu First of the Zhou to be recognized as king, 1122 B.C.E.

Xi'an Along with Luoyang, capital of the Zhou dynasty.

Luoyang Capital of China in the Classical Era.

feudalism The social organization created by exchanging grants of land or fiefs for formal oaths of allegiance and promises of loyal service; typical of Zhou dynasty and European and Japanese "Middle Ages"; greater lords provided protection and aid to lesser lords in return for military service.

Zhou monarchs had virtually no control over the fiefdoms beyond those in the central core regions. If a vassal stopped sending tribute to the capital or refused requests to muster troops for war or laborers for Zhou building projects, he was in effect declaring war and risking annihilation. As long as the Zhou overlords were strong, it was safer, and profitable enough, to pass on revenue to the court and to rally to the Zhou overlord's call to battle. But when the dynasty weakened, the flow of revenue from the vassals' domains dried up and their troops were increasingly used for wars between the feudal lords or in alliances against the Zhou rulers.

Changes in the Social Order

Two developments worked against the continuance of the feudal system. The first was the elaboration of an ideology that the Zhou rulers used to legitimize their rule. When King Wu overthrew the Shang dynasty, he claimed that the Shang had lost the **Mandate of Heaven**, and thus no longer deserved the allegiance of their vassals. The concept of the Mandate of Heaven provided a powerful rationale for the Zhou monarchs to strive to centralize authority. Wu charged that his successful bid for the throne was proof that the Zhou had the moral fiber and leadership potential to inherit the heavenly mandate the Shang had betrayed.

Mandate of Heaven The divine source for political legitimacy of Chinese rulers; established by Zhou to justify overthrow of Shang.

This appeal to a supernatural source of power was a common feature of preindustrial monarchies throughout the world, and it became a pillar of the political system in China. It also meant that

🔍 **View the Closer Look on MyHistoryLab:**
A Jade Scepter from Zhou China

FIGURE **3.8** As this ritual vessel suggests, from very early times but certainly by the Shang era, the Chinese had mastered the art of carving and polishing jade images as well as mirrors, jewelry, and other personal objects. The figure of a woman fashioned here may have represented a slave, but her distinctive facial features and the attention to detail in terms of her dress and hair decoration were to be emulated by Chinese sculptors in the millennia that followed.

shi [shuh] Probably originally priests; transformed into corps of professional bureaucrats because of knowledge of writing during Zhou dynasty in China.

the Zhou had established the principle that supreme political authority was granted by heaven, not by a ruler's vassals or the common people. This claim would greatly enhance the capacity of the Zhou and subsequent royal houses to rule as absolutist and authoritarian monarchs. But it also contained a potentially critical check on their powers, which was to be explored by Chinese social thinkers in the late Zhou era. If a ruler governed by virtue of the Mandate of Heaven, it was possible—as the Shang precedent clearly demonstrated—for a monarch and royal house to fail in their duties and lose the mandate. In that case, it was legitimate for their subjects to overthrow them and replace them with a new imperial house.

The second development working against the persistence of feudalism in China involved the emergence of an alternative to the military retainers who governed most of the empire. During the early Zhou era, the small corps of professional bureaucrats who had once served the Shang rulers began to grow in size and expertise. These administrators, who were the best educated men in the empire, came to be known in the late Zhou period (c. 770–400 B.C.E.) as **shi**, or men of service. Their literacy and willingness to serve as scribes, clerks, advisors, and overseers won them a livelihood as administrators, both at the court and in the palaces of the fief-holders and their subordinate vassals. Some of these aspiring administrators were supported by grants of villages, but others, particularly those at the royal court, were paid regular salaries out of the imperial treasury. The shi performed a wide range of services that could be embarrassingly menial; some even had to cultivate small plots of land to supplement their meager salaries. Increasingly, however, they came to specialize in keeping records; running particular departments, such as public works or war; or organizing palace rituals and ceremonies. There is some evidence that even before the end of the early Zhou era in the mid-8th century B.C.E., the most favored of these administrators had begun to amass considerable influence as advisors to the ruler and powerful nobles.

New Patterns of Life

In the early Zhou era, the conquerors lived separately from the subjugated "black-haired people." This division appears to confirm the supposition that the Zhou were originally Turkic tribespeople with lighter hair and eye coloring than the peoples they found in the loess soil region and along the north China plain. In the twin capitals of Xi'an and Luoyang, the Zhou and their servants lived on one side of the walled city, while peoples of other ethnic groups lived in the other (Figure 3.8).

Zhou vassals lived away from the capitals and resided in walled garrison towns. Each town was laid out on a rectangular grid with two main roads that crossed at a central square. Servants, artisans, and slaves lived in or near the garrison towns. Beyond them stretched the villages and tilled fields of the serfs who made up most of the empire's population. Their staple crops remained millet and wheat, but rice was widely cultivated in the eastern and southern portions of the Zhou domains.

The introduction of better farm implements and the extension of the irrigation system contributed to higher levels of productivity. But much of the increase went to fill the coffers of the lords and the Zhou court rather than to the peasants themselves. The peasants were burdened by their lords' regular demands for labor on road, building, and irrigation projects. They were also obliged to feed and house the lords' retainers when they journeyed from the garrison towns. In times of war, the peasants marched on foot alongside the chariots and cavalry of the lords' army.

As time passed, the lords' demands grew more and more oppressive. A rare insight into the peasants' plight is provided by a poem from the *Book of Odes* that was written in the late Zhou era:

> Big rat, big rat,
> Do not eat my millet!
> Three years I have served you,
> But you will not care for me.
> I am going to leave you
> And go to that happy land;
> Happy land, happy land;

VISUALIZING THE PAST

Mapping the Rise of Civilizations

THE EARLIEST HUMAN CIVILIZATIONS AROSE IN regions with substantial similarities in terms of topography—contours and configuration of the land—and other geographical features. The maps below depict three of these original centers of civilization: Harrapa (Map 3.3) Egypt (Map 3.4), and China (Map 3.5). They illustrate a number of key features of these areas, including mountains, plains, plateaus, deserts, river systems, trading routes, and locations of neighboring nomadic peoples.

Study each of these maps, identifying the key components which all of these early cradles of civilization have in common. Then identify differences between them in terms of physical features, checking these differences against the discussions of the history of these early civilizations in Chapters 2 and 3. Decide the ways in which these differences affected the course of civilized development in each area in ancient times.

QUESTIONS

- What key physical features are shared by the areas where civilizations first developed?
- Which of these are critical for the development of sedentary agriculture in each civilization?
- What roles did the presence of large bodies of water, in the form of rivers or access to the sea, play in the rise and expansion of civilized centers and contacts with other civilized areas?
- What impact did geographical factors and interactions with nomadic peoples have on the long-term persistence or disappearance of civilized life in these different areas?

MAP **3.3 Harappan South Asia** The main entry routes of nomadic migrations and trade to Mesopotamia are shown.

(continued on next page)

Where I will find my place.
Big rat, big rat,
Do not eat my sprouts!
Three years I have served you
But you give me no comfort.
I am going to leave you
And go to those happy fields;
Happy fields, happy fields;
Who there shall long moan?

Peasants at some distance from their lords' garrison towns appear to have been the best off. In fact, communications were so poor in many parts of the empire that local lords were content to leave peasant communities alone if they regularly supplied tribute and gifts on special occasions. The peasants in the outlying villages were, in effect, free farmers. However, the peasant lament just quoted probably more accurately captures the reality of life for most peasants in the Zhou period.

(continued from previous page)

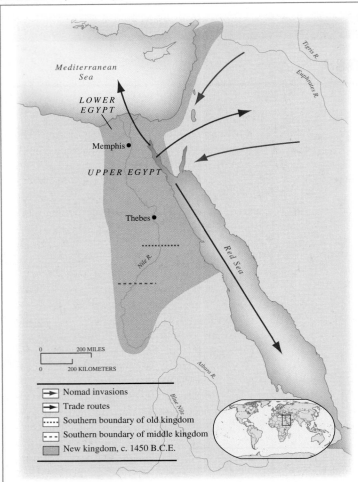

MAP **3.4 Ancient Egypt in the Middle of the Second Millennium**
B.C.E. The map shows the major trading axes and routes of nomadic
invasions.

MAP **3.5 Core Regions of Chinese Civilization** The main direction
on nomadic influx is shown.

Migrations and the Expansion of the Chinese Core

Throughout the centuries of Zhou rule, steady growth occurred in both the area controlled by its vassals and the lands occupied by peoples who identified themselves as Chinese. New agricultural tools and techniques of production stimulated population growth, which in turn led to the extension of cultivation into new areas along the north China plain and then southward along the coast. Periodic nomadic raids and, at times, lasting conquests pushed Chinese peasant migrants to the south and east.

Whatever their reasons for migrating, in the Zhou era hundreds of thousands of Chinese people moved down the Yellow River, into the Shandong peninsula, and then south across the flatlands to first the Huai and later the great Yangzi River basins (see Map 3.5). As they advanced, non-Chinese peoples, who were hunters and gatherers and shifting cultivators, fell back into the hills to the west of the great plains and then to the mountainous region south of the Yangzi. By the end of the Zhou era, Chinese civilization straddled the two great river systems—the Yellow River and the Yangzi—that have been the heart of Chinese civilization for thousands of years. The basin of the Yellow River was securely Chinese, despite the continuing nomadic threat. The Yangzi had barely been reached, but the enormous agricultural potential of the rice-growing, monsoon-watered south had begun to be tapped.

THINKING HISTORICALLY

Nomadic Contacts and the Endurance of Asia's First Civilizations

IN THEIR SIZE, COMPLEXITY, AND LONGEVITY, the first civilizations to develop in south Asia and China match, and in some respects surpass, the earliest civilizations that arose in Mesopotamia and Egypt. But the long-term impact of the Harappan civilization in the Indus basin was strikingly different from that of the Shang and Zhou civilizations in north China. The loess zone and north China plain where the Shang and Zhou empires took hold became the center of a continuous civilization that was to last into the 20th century C.E. and, some historians would argue, to the present day. Although regions farther south, such as the Yangzi basin, would in some time periods enjoy political, economic, and cultural predominance within China, the capital and center of Chinese civilization repeatedly returned to the Yellow River area and the north China plain. By contrast, the Indus valley proved capable of nurturing a civilization that endured for more than a thousand years. But when Harappa collapsed, the plains of the Indus were bypassed in favor of the far more lush and extensive lands in the basin of the Ganges River network to the east. Although the Indus would later serve, for much shorter time spans, as the seat of empires, the core areas of successive Indian civilizations were far to the east and south.

The contrast between the fates of the original geographic centers of Indian and Chinese civilizations is paralleled by the legacies of the civilizations themselves.

The contrast between the fates of the original geographic centers of Indian and Chinese civilizations is paralleled by the legacies of the civilizations themselves. Harappa was destroyed, and it disappeared from history for thousands of years. Although the peoples who built the Indus complex left their mark on subsequent Indian culture, they did not pass on the fundamental patterns of civilized life that they had evolved. Their mother goddess, yoga positions, and the dancing god of fertility endured. Some of their symbols, such as the swastika and the lingam (a phallic image, usually made of stone), were prominent in later artistic and religious traditions. The Harappans' public bathing ponds or tanks remain a central feature of Indian cities, particularly in the south. Their techniques of growing rice and cotton were preserved by cultivating peoples fleeing nomadic incursions and were later taken up by the newly arrived Indo-European migrants.

Nearly everything else was lost. In contrast to the civilizations of Mesopotamia, which fell but were replaced by new civilizations that preserved and built on the achievements of their predecessors, much of what the Harappan peoples had accomplished had to be redone by later civilized peoples. The cities of the Indus civilization were abandoned, and comparable urban centers did not reappear in South Asia for more than a thousand years. The Harappans' remarkably advanced standards for measuring distance and weight ceased to be used. Their system of writing was forgotten, and when rediscovered it was celebrated as an intriguing but very dead language from the past. Harappan skills in community planning, sewage control, and engineering were meaningless to the nomadic peoples who took control of their homelands. The Harappan penchant for standardization and uniformity was profoundly challenged by the brawling, independent-minded warriors who supplanted them as masters of the Indian subcontinent.

In contrast to the civilization of the Indus valley, the original civilization of China has survived nomadic incursions and natural catastrophes and has profoundly influenced the course of Chinese history. Shang irrigation and dike systems and millet and wheat cultivation provided the basis for the innovations and expansion of subsequent dynasties. Shang and Zhou fortified towns and villages surrounded with stamped earth walls have persisted as the predominant patterns of settlement throughout Chinese history. The founders of the Shang and Zhou dynasties have been revered by scholars and peasants alike as philosopher-kings who ought to be emulated by leaders at all levels. The Shang and Zhou worship of heaven and their veneration of ancestors have remained central to Chinese religious belief and practice for thousands of years. The concept of the Mandate of Heaven has been pivotal in Chinese political thinking and organization.

Above all, the system of writing that was originally formulated for Shang oracles developed into the key means of communication between the elites of the many peoples who lived in the core regions of Chinese civilization. The scholar-bureaucrats, who developed this written language and also profited the most from it, soon emerged as the dominant force in Chinese culture and society. Chinese characters provided the basis for the educational system and bureaucracy that were to hold Chinese civilization together through thousands of years of invasions and political crises.

The reasons for the differing legacies of Harappan and early Chinese civilizations are numerous and complex. But critical to the disappearance of the first and the resilience of the second were different patterns of interaction between the sedentary peoples who built early civilizations and the nomadic herders who challenged them. In India, the nomadic threat was remote—perhaps nonexistent—for centuries. The Harappan peoples were deficient in military technology and organization. When combined with

(continued on next page)

(continued from previous page)

natural calamities, the waves of warlike nomads migrating into the Indus region proved too much for the Harappan peoples to resist or absorb. The gap between the nomads' herding culture and the urban, agriculture-based Harappan civilization was too great to be bridged. Conflict between them may well have proved fatal to a civilization long in decline.

By contrast, the loess regions of northern China were open to invasions or migrations on the part of the nomadic herding peoples who lived to the north and west. Peoples from these areas moved almost continuously into the core zones of Chinese civilization. The constant threat posed by the nomads forced the peoples of the north China plain to develop the defenses and military technology needed to thwart nomadic raids or bids for lasting conquest. Contrasting cultures and ways of life strengthened the sense of identity of the cultivating peoples. The obvious nomadic presence prodded these same peoples to unite under strong rulers against the outsiders who did not share Chinese culture. Constant interaction with the nomads led the Shang peoples to develop a culture that was receptive to outside influences, social structures, and political systems. Nomadic energies reinvigorated and enriched the kingdoms of the Shang and the Zhou, in contrast to India, where they proved catastrophic for the isolated and far less adaptable peoples of the Indus valley civilization.

QUESTIONS

- Compare the early civilizations of India and China with those of Sumer and Egypt. Which are more similar in terms of longevity?
- Which factors were critical in the failure of the Indus civilization to persist?
- Which best explain Chinese longevity? Are these the same factors that account for the long life of Egyptian civilization and the shorter time spans of those in Mesopotamia?

 Read the **Document** on **MyHistoryLab:** Excerpt from the Shi Jing (Book of Songs)

Cultural Change in the Early Zhou Period

The Zhou influx into the loess heartland of early China strengthened the dominance of males within the family and in society. Perhaps the key roles played by males in ancestor veneration contributed to their increased authority. The cults of royal and familial ancestors became the centers of religious observance. Human sacrifice ended, but philosophical speculation remained minimal as increasingly elaborate rites and ceremonies developed around the worship of deceased members of the family, clan, and dynasty. Family patriarchs and monarchs monopolized these ceremonies designed to win the blessings of the ancestors or heaven, an abstract realm called **Tian**.

Tian [tyahn] Heaven; an abstract conception in early Chinese religion; possibly the combined spirits of all male ancestors; first appeared during Zhou dynasty.

As in Aryan India, more and more stress was placed on the importance of performing these and other ceremonies flawlessly. An obsession with correctly performed rites led to the elite's more generalized concern with refined manners and proper decorum. The rough nomads had rapidly settled down to enjoy the amenities of the rich and powerful among the civilized.

The End of the Early or Western Zhou

By the 8th century B.C.E., Zhou power was in decline. Its control over its vassals had diminished dramatically, and several of the vassals' domains had grown powerful enough to openly challenge the overlordship of the dynasty. In 771 B.C.E., an allied group of northern nobles attacked Xi'an. The Zhou ruler was killed in battle, and in the months that followed, most of the western portions of the kingdom were lost to leaders of the vassal alliance or to nomadic invaders eager to take advantage of internal divisions among the Chinese. Retainers loyal to the Zhou managed to rescue a young prince and escort him safely to Luoyang. The shift to the eastern capital marks the end of the early or western Zhou era.

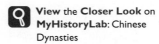 **View** the **Closer Look** on **MyHistoryLab:** Chinese Dynasties

A less powerful eastern Zhou kingdom survived for over five centuries more. The territory it controlled shrank to little beyond the capital and its immediate environs. Zhou vassals warred continuously, using the defense of the royal house to legitimize their attacks and conquests. Over time, successful lords annexed the holdings of defeated neighbors, and several rival kingdoms emerged in place of the fiefdoms that had existed in the early Zhou era. The growing chaos and widespread suffering that resulted prompted a reaction on the part of the shi bureaucrats, a reaction that would produce some of China's greatest thinkers and radically alter the course of Chinese civilization.

Global Connections and Critical Themes

CONTRASTING LEGACIES: HARAPPAN AND EARLY CHINESE CIVILIZATIONS

China, like the early civilizations of Mesopotamia, was one of the great sources of civilizing influences in human history as a whole. The area affected by ideas developed in China was less extensive than that to which the peoples of Mesopotamia gave writing, law, and their other great achievements. But contacts with China provided critical impetus for the development of civilization in Japan, Korea, and Vietnam. Writing and political organization were two areas in which the earliest formulations of Chinese civilization vitally affected other peoples. In later periods, Chinese thought and other modes of cultural expression such as art, architecture, and etiquette also strongly influenced the growth of civilized life throughout east Asia.

China's technological innovations were to have an impact on global civilization comparable to those of early Mesopotamia. Beginning with increasingly sophisticated irrigation systems, the Chinese devised a remarkable share of humankind's basic machines and engineering principles. In the Shang and Zhou eras they also pioneered key processes such as silk manufacturing.

By contrast, because of the processes that saw it virtually disappear from Indian history for thousands of years, Harappan civilization did not have a lasting impact on the human experience as a whole. Traces of the oldest of the civilizations of south Asia, such as yogic practices, have spread worldwide, but more fundamental elements of the civilization, such as its remarkable urban planning and advanced sewage systems, have had no discernable impact on the development of city living in other regions and later times. Despite evidence of extensive commercial links between Harappa and neighboring civilizations in the Middle East, there is little to indicate that the latter were fundamentally altered by imports from the Indus region.

The fact that Harappa proved much more vulnerable than early Chinese civilizations to natural calamities and climate change, as well as the infiltration of large numbers of nomadic herding peoples, goes far to account for the sharply contrasting global legacies of these two core regions of human civilization. Endurance and longevity not only provide more time for a civilized center to disseminate its ideas and material culture, but they also suggest to other peoples that borrowing might enhance their chances to build powerful, wealthy, and enduring civilizations of their own.

Further Readings

For the most authoritative, up-to-date and detailed coverage of all aspects of the Indus civilization, see Gregory L. Possehl, *Indus Age: The Beginnings* (1999); and Mark Kenoyer, *Ancient Cities of the Indus Valley Civilization* (1998). For a sense of the state of archeological research and recent discoveries, see the sometimes technical essays in Possehl, ed., *Harappan Civilization: A Contemporary Perspective* (1982); and N. N. Bhattacharyya, *Ancient Indian History and Civilization: Trends and Perspectives* (1988). Also see Raymond Allchin, *The Archeology of Early Historic South Asia: The Emergence of Cities and States.* (1995); Joan Aruz,, ed. *The Art of the First Cities: The Third Millennium BC from the Mediterranean to the Indus* (2003); and Romilla Thapar's *History of India* (1966; reissued 1991). Interesting works that deal with social life and gender relations in the Vedic period include the textual analyses in Laurie L. Patton, ed., *Jewels of Authority: Women and Textual Tradition in Hindu India* (2002); C. Chakraborty's account of *Common Life in the Rigeveda and Atharvaveda* (1977); and the lively and contentious arguments in *Ancient India* (1969), by D. D. Kosambi. On ancient Indian political systems, see A. C. Pandey, *Government in Ancient India* (2000).

For ancient China, the most current interpretations can be found in the superb essays in Michael Loewe and Edward L. Shaughnessy, eds., *The Cambridge History of Ancient China: From the Origins of Civilization to 221 B.C.* (1999). For earlier accounts that are still readable and informative, see Wolfram Eberhard's *History of China* (1977) and the early portions of Michael Loewe's *Imperial China* (1965). More detailed (and technical) accounts of the formation of China through the early Zhou era include Kwang-chih Chang's *The Archeology of Ancient China* (1977) and *Shang Civilization* (1980); H. G. Creel's *The Origins of Statecraft in Ancient China* (1970); and Ping-ti Ho's *The Cradle of the East* (1975). K. C. Wu's *The Chinese Heritage* (1982) provides the fullest political history of the Shang and early Zhou eras, which can be supplemented by Roger Ames, *The Art of Rulership: A Study of Ancient Chinese Political Thought* (1994). The nomadic impact on the formation of China is treated mainly from the Chinese perspective by Nicola Di Cosmo, *Ancient China and Its Enemies* (2002). Early Chinese cities are explored in Wu Liangyong, *A Brief History of Chinese City Planning* (1985); and early Chinese accomplishments in technology are surveyed in *China: 7000 Years of Discovery* (1983), compiled by the Chinese Scientific and Technological Museum, Beijing.

Critical Thinking Questions

1. Judging by early Chinese and Indian civilizations, what geographical and environmental factors appear to be critical for the emergence of civilizations?

2. What factors account for the greater continuities in civilizational development in China in contrast to the disconnect between the Harappan and Aryan civilizations in India?

3. Which of these civilizations was the most connected with pastoral peoples and other civilized centers through trade and warfare?

I

REVISITING

The Early Period, 2.5 million–600 B.C.E.

CONTACTS AND THEIR LIMITS

No regular contacts among the major population centers developed during the long early phases of human history. Even at the end of the early civilization, no such patterns existed. To be sure, separate developments did not prevent many similar features. In broad outline, early civilizations developed many of the same functions, as they introduced formal governments, writing systems, and significant cities. Agriculture generated common tendencies to establish patriarchal family structures, but these developments occurred spontaneously, the result of similar needs, not because peoples in different regions learned extensively from one another. And, of course, the specifics varied considerably—the system of government and gender relations in Egypt, for example, differed from those in Mesopotamia or China.

Three kinds of contacts did exist during the early phases of human history. Their results were significant, although they were somewhat sporadic. First, local or long-distance trade could spread knowledge of new developments or products. People in one region could learn about innovations in the region next door. Local exchanges of products or symbolic gifts—the latter designed to help keep the peace—served as conduits. Through this kind of interaction, **diffusion** occurred. This was the mechanism through which the knowledge of agriculture gradually spread from the areas where it was first developed to neighboring regions, and ultimately over whole subcontinents. New technologies, like metalworking, spread the same way. So did new foodstuffs: some crops original to Southeast Asia, for example, reached Africa by 1000 C.E. and gradually became staples.

These kinds of diffusion were the most important contacts in early human history. We do not always know the precise processes involved. For example, an Indian Ocean trade system existed by 1000 C.E., involving timber and perfumes; this led to southeast Asian migrations to the island of Madagascar. But we know almost nothing about the specifics of this process. It is also true that some trade contacts, like the Phoenician voyages to southern England to get tin, do not seem to have produced wider diffusion of products or technologies.

A second type of contact resulted from migration and invasion. We have seen that this combination occurred frequently in the Middle East, leading to changes in ruling dynasties, language, and the spread of new technologies. The wheel was almost certainly invented in central Asia, then brought by a migrant group to the Middle East. Migrations and invasions could be extremely disruptive, as when the Indo-Europeans moved into India. But they could also expose immigrants and local populations alike to new knowledge and technologies.

A third kind of contact involved direct trade, diplomatic relations, and military activity between two major early civilization centers. While Mesopotamia and Egypt developed separately for the most part, there were periods of invasion from one direction or another, some trade, and some cultural exchange. Tablets have been found, for example, whose text was written in both cuneiform and hieroglyphics, showing a need for direct translations. Egyptians and Mesopotamians both interacted with parts of Greece, including the island of Crete, which

diffusion The spread of ideas, technology, plants, or other productions of human fabrication across cultures and regions.

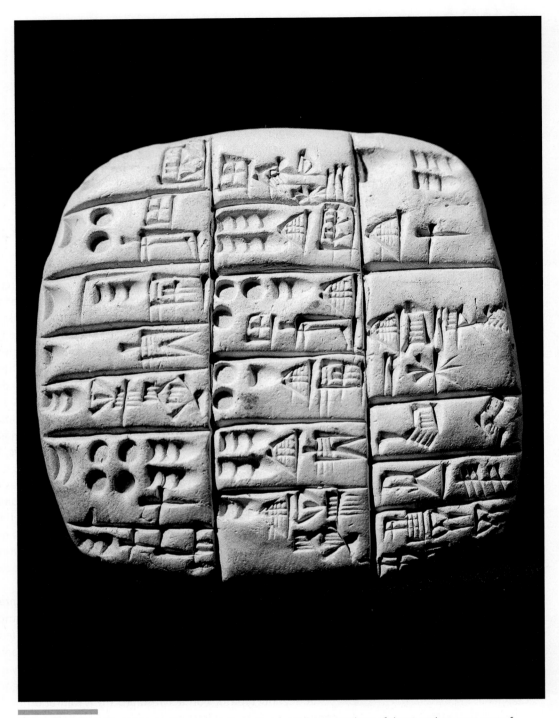

A Sumerian clay tablet with cuneiform characters aimed at tallying numbers of sheep and goats as part of early agriculture.

was therefore able to borrow from both societies. Some trade (although no military contact) occurred between Mesopotamia, China, and the Indus valley. Early civilizations in the Americas were much more isolated.

Contacts brought fundamental changes to the people involved, even in these early periods. Diffusion, particularly, was responsible for basic shifts in economic and therefore social systems. Most contact was sporadic, however, and did not lead to elaborate exchanges of religious or scientific ideas or political institutions. Here, the emphasis on separate patterns of development remains valid.

CRITICAL THEMES

The early period of human history offers a great deal of variety. While the most important developments involved the Neolithic revolution and then the emergence of several early civilizations, it is vital to remember that hunting and gathering societies persisted in many places. Nomadic herding economies dominated several regions as well, presenting yet another pattern.

The substantial separation of major regions also generated huge differences in the timing of key changes. We have seen that there are at least three separate dates for the advent of agriculture, in the Middle East, in East Asia and in the Americas. The initial foundation of civilization also varied with the region. Almost 3000 years separate the Sumerian civilization from the emergence of a complex culture in the Andes. Analysis of the early period requires comparison of patterns across a wide stretch of time.

Regional separations also complicate decisions about when to end the early period, for there was no decisive, sweeping change that affected all of even most of the individual centers. By 600, some of the early civilizations did seem to be losing dynamism. Most obviously, the flourishing period of Olmec civilization had ended, and Harappan civilization had essentially disappeared. New patterns were beginning to emerge in these same areas, with the initial formation of Mayan culture in central America and the religious changes among Aryan peoples in India that would ultimately lead to Hinduism.

In China, the Zhou dynasty, formed around 1100 BCE, continued, though it was after 600 that important cultural innovations took shape, particularly around the philosophy of Confucius. In the Middle East and North Africa, the heyday of the major early empires had passed, with Egypt in partial decline. Again, no single formula captures the variety of situations around 600 BCE.

Two or three changes were, however, on the horizon. Some new centers of activity were beginning to emerge, though they benefited from the legacy of the early civilizations. Mayans built on Olmec achievements. City states arising in and around Greece would use both Egyptian and Mesopotamian heritage. Further, a number of areas were poised to introduce new cultural patterns that would ultimate provide new regional links. China's major philosophies and religions arose in the centuries after 600, and important religious developments were also taking shape in India and Persia. Finally, growing knowledge of iron technology, for tools and weapons, would gradually generate political, military and economic changes in the Middle East, in China and other parts of Asia, and in the Mediterranean world (though not in the clearly separate societies of the Americas). ■

CRITICAL THINKING QUESTIONS

1. Why do some historians argue that the advent of agriculture was an unfortunate development?

2. Why was there no major protest against the emergence of patriarchal gender relations in agricultural societies?

3. Compare Olmec civilization with one of the early civilizations in Asia/North Africa. How do problems of evidence complicate the comparison?

4. What are the advantages and disadvantages of using 600 BCE as an approximate date for ending the early period?

PART II

The Classical Period, 600 B.C.E.–600 C.E.: Uniting Large Regions

A jade funeral suit from the Western Han Dynasty, late 2nd century B.C. Chinese styles spread as the Empire expanded.

PART OUTLINE

THE OVERVIEW

The major development during the classical period of world history was the formation of large regional civilizations in China, India, the Mediterranean, the Middle East, and the Americas. These developments can be seen in the accompanying maps. The map on the top shows the location of the different civilizations in these areas right before the classical period (around 800 B.C.E.); the map on the bottom shows the civilizations that had developed in the same areas around 100 C.E. In China and the Mediterranean, what had been a set of small states—or no states at all—had been replaced by two giant empires. India also developed substantial empires at several key points in the classical centuries. Several new and more extensive civilizations also emerged in the Americas.

Although much of the world remained outside the main areas of civilization, these areas had by far the largest concentrations of population. Furthermore, the influence of these civilizations extended into surrounding regions outside their direct control. Classical civilizations also had important relationships with nomadic groups, mostly from central Asia, who traded with them and periodically attempted invasion. Nevertheless, regions outside the world's main civilizational areas require some separate attention during this long period.

Except for brief interludes, the main civilizations did not share direct borders. Much of the development of each civilization was separate, and the establishment of distinctive cultural and institutional patterns was a key legacy of this period. Nevertheless, trade offered some contacts, as products like silk were carried from east Asia to the Mediterranean. Occasionally, contacts were more direct. Persia and Greece interacted extensively in the 6th and 5th centuries. Later, the conquests of the Greek-trained warrior Alexander the Great resulted in the creation of a short-lived empire that stretched from the Mediterranean into northwestern India. This empire brought into direct contact Mediterranean, Persian, Egyptian, and Indian societies, an encounter that yielded interesting results, some of which are clearly evident in art of the period. For example, a statue sculpted by an Indian artist depicts the beloved Buddha clothed in Greek fashions. This combination of cultural elements, called *syncretism*, is a common result of significant contact between cultures. It can have lasting implications. Syncretism was not the most common feature of the classical period, but its occurrence hinted at what would develop more fully later. Finally, at the end of the period exchanges between India and China intensified.

BIG CONCEPTS

The formation of the classical societies involved several striking features. Each major civilization spread over a large area, so expansion was a key theme. To support expansion, each society worked hard to integrate its new territory. Economic integration was a key issue, as societies from China to the Mediterranean developed internal trade routes and other mechanisms to take advantage of different specialties through commercial expansion. But cultural integration was crucial as well. Intellectual and artistic leaders, sometimes with encouragement from the state, developed core ideas and styles that were then widely disseminated, particularly among elites but with some spillover to wider populations. Finally, each society worked on political and social integration, most obviously through the establishment of unifying empires. Finally, the contacts that did develop among different regions spurred trade and, to some degree, communication. All of these features would affect world history long after the classical period had itself ended.

TRIGGERS FOR CHANGE

Despite the lack of a clear transition, the classical civilizations that began to emerge about 600 B.C.E. were measurably different from their river valley predecessors. While they built on the earlier achievements, they grew noticeably larger in their geographic, cultural, economic, and

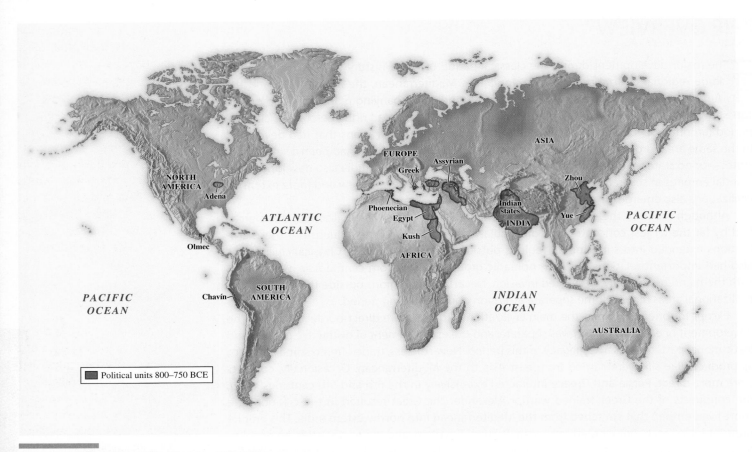

MAP **2.1** **Political Units of the World, c. 800–750** B.C.E.

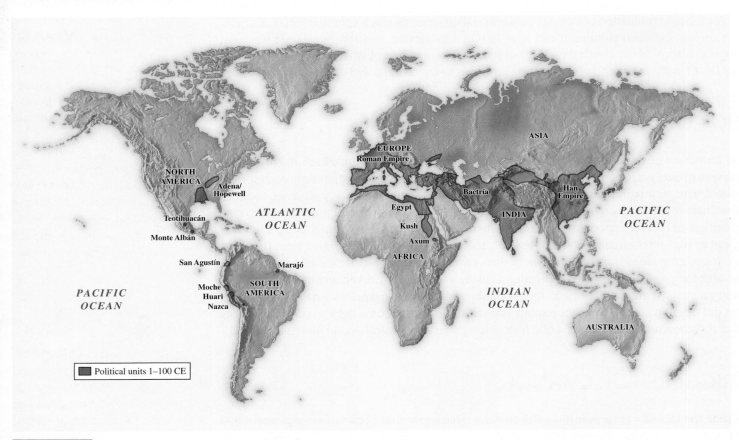

MAP **2.2** **Political Units of the World, c. 1–100** C.E.

political reach. What allowed this greater reach was military conquest, made possible by the spread of iron tools and weapons. New conquests, possible in part because of technological change, led to the further developments intended to integrate larger regions.

Each of the classical societies ultimately declined, and great empires like the Han dynasty in China, the Gupta in India, and the western Roman Empire collapsed altogether. Although these developments did not happen at exactly the same time, together they brought the classical period to a close by 600 C.E.

THE BIG CHANGES

Each of the classical civilizations had its own social structure, religion, political system, system of science, and styles of art. Comparisons of the resulting differences form a vital part of studying the classical period. And the differences left a durable legacy. To take one contemporary example: In the late 20th century the Chinese government proved reasonably effective in mandating drastic changes in birth rates. The Indian government tried and failed to enforce somewhat similar regulations. Many factors accounted for China's success and India's failure in enforcing a population policy, but an important reason was the extent to which people in each country accepted as legitimate a role for government in actively monitoring personal behavior. These differences in attitude can be traced back to the classical period. Civilizational styles set in the classical period hardly predetermined the future, but they had, and continue to have, undeniable influence.

In terms of the classical period itself, the first major change was the development of reasonably well-defined societies that left durable legacies. Each major civilization thus promoted a common cultural system that would legitimate characteristic social and family customs, integrate elites, and provide bonds between ordinary people and leadership groups. This system might involve more than one component. For example, there was outright, although usually peaceful, competition between Buddhism and Hinduism in India. But the generation of powerful beliefs and their spread within each civilization was an important development in the classical period, and one that had lasting impact.

At least periodically, each major civilization conquered additional peoples and areas and created large empires. Although empires were not new in world history, those of the classical period in world history were more powerful and widespread than any that preceded them.

The growth of classical civilizations, with their impressive achievements and monuments, clearly had an impact on surrounding areas. Some trade with neighboring regions was common. India had the widest commercial reach, extending all the way into southeast Asia and west to the Mediterranean, but Rome also traded with parts of Africa and Asia outside its own empire. Even more widely, nomadic peoples were often attracted toward the centers of civilization as immigrants, soldiers, or invaders. Some nomadic peoples facilitated trade between civilizations. These developments were important at the time and had implications for later patterns in world history. For example, cultural and trade contacts often prepared the way for later nomadic migrations into the classical societies.

The achievements of the major classical civilizations inspired awe, at the time and later. Great developments in philosophy, politics, and art in classical civilizations provided the foundations for subsequent civilizations. Confucianism, for example, would influence other Asian societies besides China, and a number of societies, including those in Europe and the Middle East, would build on the achievements of Greek science. It is for this reason that the term *classical* is commonly used to refer to this period.

CONTINUITY

Although the introduction of iron helped usher in the classical period, the period itself did not witness sweeping developments in manufacturing technology. Most peasants continued to use traditional agricultural tools and methods. Rural culture remained somewhat apart from the main cultural innovations, particularly in China and the Mediterranean. Many rural people retained their traditional festivals and polytheistic religious beliefs alongside official religions and philosophies.

Patriarchal arrangements prevailed in each of the major civilizations of the classical period. Each culture had particular ways of defining women's roles and obligations. Comparisons among the classical civilizations are important in this area, for different styles of patriarchy would affect family life and even art, but the basic idea of patriarchal superiority had already been established. The civilizations simply linked the patriarchal system to the particular cultures they developed and emphasized.

Finally, although the classical civilizations all introduced significant innovations beyond their river valley predecessors, they also retained and built on key achievements of the earlier societies. They did not have to reinvent money, the idea of codes of law, or scientific interests such as astronomy. While the classical civilizations left a heritage that powerfully shaped future developments, they also drew upon a heritage established in earlier periods.

IMPACT ON DAILY LIFE: OLD AGE

In all the classical civilizations, the achievement of old age won respect. It was seen, legitimately enough, as a sign of good habits and wisdom. Furthermore, in groups where literacy was uncommon, the elderly could be vital sources of information and cultural memory, which was transmitted in stories that helped shape the identity of families and cultures. Respect for the elderly was a sign of good manners in all the classical societies.

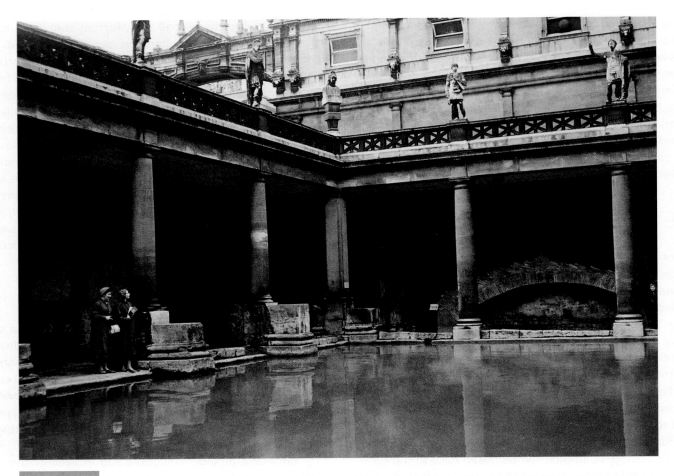

Interior view of the Roman baths, in Bath, England. Roman styles spread to distant parts of the Empire, creating a wide area of partially shared cultures.

600 B.C.E.	500 B.C.E.	250 B.C.E.
600 Zoroastrian religion in Iran **600** Legendary ruler in Japan **551–c. 233** Period of the great Chinese philosophers: Confucius, Laozi, Mencius, Legalists **550** Formation of Persian Empire **c. 542–483** Life of the Buddha	**500–449** Greek wars with Persia **500–450** Beginnings of the Roman republic **470–430** Height of Athenian culture; Socrates and Greek philosophical style **431 ff.** Peloponnesian Wars; decline of Greece **330** Alexander the Great **327–325** Alexander's invasion of the Persian empire **322–185** Mauryan Empire **300–100** Hellenistic Period **300 B.C.E.–900 C.E.** Height of Maya Civilization **264–140** Roman expansion in North Africa (Punic Wars) and eastern Mediterranean	**221** Shi Huangdi proclaimed first emperor of China **202 B.C.E.–9 C.E.** Former Han dynasty; development of horse collar and water mill **200 B.C.E.–200 C.E.** Era of strong Buddhist influence **133 ff.** Decline of the Roman republic **100** Germans begin contact with Rome; Slavs migrate into eastern Europe

But the classical civilizations also differed in their attitudes toward the elderly. Chinese Confucianism placed special emphasis on venerating the elderly. Even older women, if they were mothers (and especially if they were widows and mothers of sons) had considerable status, although officially their sons ran the household.

In Mediterranean cultures there was greater ambivalence concerning older people. The themes of wisdom and respect were visible (although they applied much more clearly to men than to women). But the elderly also were depicted as both greedy and laughable as their capacities declined. Stories made fun of old misers or men who lusted after younger women. In the Mediterranean, more attention was paid to the physical and mental deterioration of older people, and while this sometimes produced sympathy, it could also generate scorn. The Greek dramatist Aeschylus wrote about people "old in their bones, dishonored, cut off," and the Bible offered many accounts of enfeebled, foolish elders. Societies that placed great emphasis on military prowess and youthful beauty could be harsh to people past their prime, and in the Mediterranean, there was no systematic set of beliefs, like Confucianism, to cut through these contradictions.

Did these cultural differences matter in the actual way older people were treated? Here, the evidence is sketchier; we know much more about classical value systems than about the details of daily life. What is clear is that this ambivalence toward the elderly had staying power. Even today, many argue, ambivalence about older people that goes back to Greeks, Romans, and Hebrews affects policy and outlook in the West, while in contrast some east Asian systems write respect for the elderly into their constitutions.

TRENDS AND SOCIETIES

Initial chapters in this section describe developments in each of the major civilizations during the classical period, starting with China in Chapter 4, Persia and Greece in Chapter 5, and India in Chapter 6. Chapter 7 returns to the Mediterranean, to take up the history of Rome. Chapter 8 moves out of the strictly classical orbit to deal with important developments in the Americas, where emerging civilizations had more in common with earlier river valley patterns in Afro-Eurasia than with classical developments. Chapter 9 takes up the spread of agriculture and the roles of nomadic societies in Afro-Eurasia and the Pacific, areas and peoples outside the central orbit of the classical civilizations. Finally, Chapter 10 returns to the main classical centers, dealing with patterns of decline and with concurrent religious innovations, including the rise of Christianity. The story of the decline of each civilization was distinct, but the overall pattern of change had some important common features. ■

1 C.E.	250 C.E.	500 C.E.	750 C.E.
23–220 Later Han dynasty; invention of paper and compass	**300** Decline of Meroë	**476** Last Roman emperor in West	**800–1300** Mississippian culture
27 Augustus founds Roman Empire	**300–400** Yamato claim imperial control of Japan	**527–565** Justinian Eastern emperor	**900** Polynesians to New Zealand
30 Crucifixion of Jesus	**300–700** Rise of Axum; conversion to Christianity	**580 ff.** Spread of Buddhism in Japan	**900–1200** Toltecs
88 Beginning of Han decline	**300–900** Intermediate Horizon period (Andes)	**589–618** Sui dynasty	**1000** Height of kingdom of Ghana, Africa
106 Height of Roman territory	**300–1000** Second wave of Polynesian migrations to Hawaii	**600–647** Harsha's Empire	
180 Beginning of decline of Rome	**312–337** Constantine; formation of Eastern Empire; adoption of Christianity	**618** Tang dynasty	
200–500 Nasca culture (Andes)	**319–540** Gupta Empire	**700 ff.** Spread of Islam; trans-Sahara trade in Africa	
200–700 Mochica culture (Andes)	**400** Chinese script imported		
200–1300 Anasazi in North America	**401 ff.** Large-scale Germanic invasions in Roman Empire		
220 Last Han emperor deposed			

4

Unification and the Consolidation of Civilization in China

Listen to **Chapter 4** on MyHistoryLab

FOCUS QUESTIONS

4.1 Why do you think that the age of warring states that followed the collapse of the Zhou dynasty gave rise to such a remarkable range of major philosophical and religious thinkers from Confucius to Laozi? p. 76

4.2 What were some of the major innovations under the short-lived Qin dynasty that shaped the nature of the Chinese state over the next two millennia? p. 80

4.3 How did the growing strength of social groups, including the scholar-gentry (or shi), merchants, and the military, affect gender and other social relationships and the nature of family life from the Han dynasty onward? p. 84

Late in the 6th century B.C.E., a brilliant middle-aged scholar-philosopher applied for a high post in the bureaucracy of the small kingdom of Lu in northeast China (see Map 4.1). Perhaps because Kong Fuzi—or Confucius as he came to be known centuries later in the West—was widely reputed to be an opinionated and outspoken person, he was denied the position for which he was confident he was well qualified. Angered by this rebuff, Confucius left Lu and took to the road in search of the ideal ruler, who presumably would recognize his talents and offer him employment at a suitable level of distinction at his court.

View the **Map** on **MyHistoryLab**: Historic Sites of Daoism and Confucianism

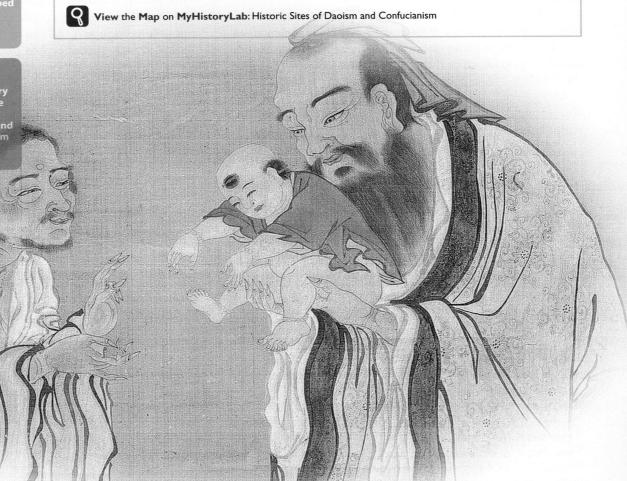

FIGURE **4.1** This 18th-century painting by Wang Shugu vividly illustrates the high esteem in which the philosopher Confucius has been held by the Chinese for over two millennia. Here Confucius is depicted with Laozi, another of China's great thinkers, and the Buddha, an Indian philosopher whose teachings won a widespread following in China. Confucius is clearly the pivotal figure in the painting, while Laozi is depicted as a dignified onlooker. The fact that Buddha is only a baby reflects the artist's sense of the stature of this foreign thinker compared to the two most revered figures of the Chinese intellectual tradition.

👁 Watch the Video Series on MyHistoryLab

Learn about some key topics related to this chapter with the *MyHistoryLab Video Series:
Key Topics in World History*

The China of Confucius's day offered abundant options for a talented political advisor. The declining power of the Zhou kingdom, which had for centuries dominated early Chinese civilization along the Yellow River, opened the way for the rise of a patchwork of rival states. Many of these competing states were ruled by nomadic peoples who had migrated from the north or west. Wars between these upstart forces and the lords of long-established households with imperial pretensions were frequent, banditry was widespread, commerce was threatened, and displaced peasants and warrior bands wandered throughout the countryside. The monarchs of some nomad kingdoms had extensively adopted the distinct culture that had been developing in the Yellow River region since the age of the Shang warrior kings. Nonetheless, Confucius and others in the emerging scholar-gentry—or shi—social strata continued to regard most of the nomads as uncouth, warlike barbarians. Convinced that he was a man with a mission, Confucius undertook a lifelong quest to become the chief advisor to a ruler who possessed the vision and skills to restore centralized control, peace, and order.

One among many wandering scholars in the late Zhou era, Confucius attracted numerous disciples, some of whom became distinguished philosophers in their own right. The master's students preserved, spread, and debated his teachings, and after his death in the early 5th century B.C.E., they compiled his wisdom in what would come to be known as the *Analects*, or collected sayings: hence, "Confucius says . . . ."

Over time, Confucius's political and social philosophy became foundational for one of humanity's greatest and most enduring civilizations (see Figure 4.1). In view of the turmoil in China when Confucian teachings were formulated, it is not surprising that they idealized strong rulers and the consolidation of political power. Confucius advocated rule by a highly educated, exclusively male elite, but one that was deemed responsible for the well-being of all of the subjects of the state. Primarily an ethical rather than a religious system, Confucianism sought to establish norms for all aspects of Chinese life, from relationships within the family that stressed respect for one's elders to the importance of art, music, and elegant calligraphy in the cultivation of scholar-bureaucrats.

Measured in terms of the acquisition of wealth and power, Confucius was a failure. He never found his ideal monarch, or even a suitable post at any of the numerous royal households that jostled for dominance across China. In fact, in the centuries following his death—often appropriately designated as the era of the warring states—political and social disintegration intensified. But the students and disciples of Confucius found a large and enthusiastic audience for his teachings in these troubled times. ■

Later Zhou, c. 550 B.C.E.
Boundaries of principal states, c. 550 B.C.E.
Boundary of Qin Empire, c. 221 B.C.E.
Northern Walls

0   400 MILES
0   400 KILOMETERS

MAP **4.1 The Era of Nomadic Incursions and Warring States** The fragmented state of the core areas of Chinese civilization from the 6th to the 3rd centuries B.C.E. is clearly illustrated on this map of the many states that jostled for power. The map shows the rise of the seminomadic kingdom of Qin in the 3rd century, which both unified politically and greatly enlarged the territory controlled by a mixture of ethnic Chinese and various nomadic peoples.

1200 B.C.E.	600 B.C.E.	400 B.C.E.	200 B.C.E.	1 C.E.	200 C.E.
1122–770 Former or western Zhou kingdom **770–403** Later or eastern Zhou kingdom	**551–c. 233** Period of the "hundred philosophers" (including Confucius, Laozi, Mencius, Xunzi, the Legalists) **403–222** Warring States period	**c. 400–320** Era of Xunzi **221–207** Qin dynasty **221** Shi Huangdi proclaimed first emperor of China **221** Northern walls connected **202–195** Reign of Liu Bang (Gaozu emperor)	**200 B.C.E.–9 C.E.** Former Han dynasty; development of the horse collar, stern-post rudder, and watermill **141–87** Reign of Han Wudi	**23–220** Later Han dynasty; invention of paper and the compass **9–23** Interregnum of Wang Mang	**2nd century** Development of porcelain

Shi Huangdi [shiuh-hwahng-dee] Founder of the brief Qin dynasty in 221 B.C.E.

This chapter focuses on the conditions that gave rise to Confucianism as well as the teachings of rival philosophical systems, such as Legalism, Daoism, and Buddhism. As we shall see, even as late as the end of the 3rd century B.C.E., when Chinese political unity was again restored by the warrior strongman **Shi Huangdi's** kingdom of Qin (chin), Confucian social norms and political prescriptions were eclipsed by more authoritarian alternatives. But with the rise of the Han dynasty after 207 B.C.E., the teachings of Confucius and several of his more prominent followers came to provide the ideological underpinnings of both the Chinese state and society. In subsequent dynasties, the influence of Confucianism waxed and waned, but even after its alleged extinction in the crisis-ridden decades of the 20th century, it has persisted as a major cultural force to the present day. Confucianism has also exerted a pervasive and enduring influence on other societies throughout Asia, from Japan and Korea through central Asia and southward into present-day Vietnam. China's Confucian ideals, scholar-gentry bureaucracy, technological advancements, and prosperous agrarian state captivated major thinkers in Europe and the United States—from Jesuit missionaries to Thomas Jefferson.

PHILOSOPHICAL REMEDIES FOR THE PROLONGED CRISIS OF THE LATER ZHOU

Some of China's greatest thinkers, including Confucius and Laozi, sought to find philosophical remedies for the political and social disorder that resulted from the decline of the Zhou dynasty.

4.1 Why do you think that the age of warring states that followed the collapse of the Zhou dynasty gave rise to such a remarkable range of major philosophical and religious thinkers from Confucius to Laozi?

The warfare that raged throughout China after the Zhou (joh) rulers lost power was a major setback for both the emerging bureaucratic elite and the ordinary people. Military skills and physical prowess were valued over the literary and ceremonial aptitudes of the scholar-administrators, or shi. Local lords whose kingdoms were constantly threatened by their neighbors (see Map 4.1) tended to concentrate power in their own hands. They put little stock in the council of men who stayed behind in the palace while they risked their lives in battle. The military leaders who wore trousers—which were widely adopted following the example of the horse-riding northern nomads—were contemptuous of the courtiers and administrators who wore robes and gowns. In most kingdoms, the power of the old aristocratic families was strengthened. This often occurred at the expense of the bureaucrats, who were reduced to little more than clerks and fawning courtiers of the local strongmen. For example, Confucius grew up in a poor shi family and deeply resented the fact that he had to work at tasks, such as accounting, that were considered demeaning for a young man of his education and abilities. Rituals were neglected, and court etiquette, which had been prized in the early Zhou era, was replaced by the rough manners of nomadic invaders. Many scholar-bureaucrats found themselves without political positions and were forced to work as village schoolteachers and local scribes.

With rulers concentrating on the survival of their kingdoms, most resources were devoted to warfare. Public works, including dikes, canals, and regional granaries, were neglected, and some fell into ruin. Marauding armies stole or destroyed the crops on which the peasants depended. Hard-pressed rulers taxed the farmers heavily and conscripted them to transport military supplies and, increasingly, to fight in the wars of the late Zhou period. Armies spread disease and destruction throughout China. The impact of natural calamities was compounded by the breakdown of public works and social support systems.

Perhaps because most kingdoms depended on outside areas for at least some vital materials (see Map 4.1), such as iron, horses, and salt, trade continued to increase despite political fragmentation and social disruption. The introduction of copper money and the growing acceptance of private property favored the Chinese merchant class. By the end of the Zhou era, traders were growing wealthy by supplying courts, armies, and town populations and investing in land. Wealth and political connections brought these big traders considerable power. For example, a legendary merchant named Zu Gong was said to have saved one kingdom from destruction, strengthened two others, and caused the decline and fall of two more in the course of a single business trip. As trade and production by artisans increased, towns expanded, particularly walled administrative centers. By the last centuries of the Zhou period, China could boast of several urban centers with hundreds of thousands of people. For many centuries to come, no other civilization could support cities of this size.

Confucius and the Restoration of the Shi

Threatened by the great power of the warrior overlords of rival kingdoms and the rising wealth and influence of the mercantile class, the aspiring bureaucrats of the shi social strata found a champion in **Confucius**. He was convinced that a small minority of superior men was destined by their talents and sense of duty to govern and set an example for the common people. In a revolutionary bit of thinking, he argued that these men (women were explicitly excluded) were superior not because of aristocratic birth but because of their education and training. Thus, superior men were made, not born. This meant that even a peasant could aspire to this exalted status. But most of the superior men were drawn from the elite classes, especially the old aristocracy and established shi households.

There was a strong ethical dimension to Confucian thought. Confucius believed that superior men should be given power not to enrich or glorify themselves but to serve society. He stressed that the welfare of the common people must be paramount in the decisions of good emperors and their advisors. Confucius reasoned that in return for their rulers' concern and protection, the common people should respect, support, and acknowledge the superior status of their overlords. Social harmony depended on each person's accepting his or her allotted place and performing the tasks of her or his social station. Obedience and deference were owed to one's superiors and elders, to males from females, and to teachers from students. To Confucius, a good man is one who

> Treats his betters as betters,
> Wears an air of respect,
> Who in serving father and mother
> Knows how to put in his whole strength,
> Who in the service of his prince will lay down his life
> Who in intercourse with friends is true to his word.

Confucius taught that society was held together by personal ties of loyalty and obedience. Five links were stressed: three family links (father and son, elder brother and younger brother, husband and wife), one political link (ruler and subject), and one social link (friend and friend). If these links were honored, Confucius believed, only a minimum of intervention by the state in the lives of its subjects would be necessary.

The Confucian Gentleman

According to Confucius, the superior or educated man was a person of courage who made decisions on his own and then defended them no matter how strong the opposition. Once in positions of power, shi officials were to respect rulers but not be afraid to admonish them for errors

Confucius Also known as Kung Fuzi; major Chinese philosopher born in 6th century B.C.E.; author of *Analects;* philosophy based on need for restoration of order through advice of superior men to be found among the shi.

Read the Document on MyHistoryLab: Confucian political philosophy: An excerpt from Mencius

Mencius [men-shee-us] Also known as Meng Ke; follower of Confucius; stressed consent of the common people.

Legalists Proponents of a political philosophy in 4th century B.C.E. that China's rulers should have absolute power.

Read the Document on MyHistoryLab: Confucius: Selections from the *Analects*

FIGURE **4.2** A portrait of Confucius. Because no contemporary likenesses of Confucius have survived, the artists of each era in China's long history depicted him in ways that reflected the tastes and needs of the elites then in power. Here, for example, Confucius is shown as a kind and wise—even grandfatherly—sage. In less stable and prosperous times, he might be depicted as a stern teacher bent on restoring the moral fiber that the Chinese believed was essential to social harmony.

in judgment or for neglecting the welfare of their subjects. A superior man—a term that became synonymous with membership in the shi class—controlled his emotions. He presented a calm and composed face to rivals, subordinates, and friends. He was well mannered and observed the proper rituals and forms of address and behavior, which varied depending on the social status of the person with whom he was interacting. As the opening story in this chapter illustrates, succeeding generations of Chinese scholars and administrators venerated Confucius as the personification of the well centered, highly accomplished shi gentleman (Figure 4.2).

Above all, the shi gentleman was a generalist rather than a specialist. He strove to be equally accomplished at running a government department, directing the repair of irrigation works, composing poetry, or painting the plum blossoms in his garden. He earned power and status as a moral exemplar, not for performing specific tasks. Confucius thought that with such men in charge of China, war and social strife would be brought under control forever.

The Heirs of Confucius

The most important divisions that arose among the followers of Confucius were between the interpretations of his philosophy elaborated by **Mencius** (Meng Ke) and **Shang Yang**, who lived in the 4th and 3rd centuries B.C.E. Mencius assumed that humans were inclined to be good and thus ought to be ruled in such a way that their goodness could develop to the fullest extent. His egalitarian thinking stressed the consent of the common people as the basis for political power. It provided the philosophical underpinnings for the long-standing Chinese belief that the people had the right to rise up and overthrow incompetent or oppressive rulers.

Shang Yang rejected Mencius's basic assumption. He argued that humans were inclined to be lazy and evil. He concluded that a strong, authoritarian government was necessary to curb their selfish desires and their capacity to harm each other. Shang Yang believed that humans could be improved through strong laws and education, but he did not agree that the people were the ultimate source of political power. The ideas of both thinkers and those of Confucius continued to influence intellectual discourse in China for millennia. But in the short term, the views of Shang Yang, bolstered by the arguments of later political philosophers known as the **Legalists**, were the most influential.

Daoist Alternatives

A very different cure for China's ills in the late Zhou era was offered by the recluse and philosopher **Laozi**. Laozi's life history has been obscured by fantastic legends, including those relating that his mother was pregnant with him for decades and that when he was born he was an old man with a white beard. Whatever his actual background, Laozi developed into a thinker who had little use for government or absolute ethical prescriptions. As a solution for the sufferings brought on by human greed and ambition, Laozi recommended a retreat into nature. Through the contemplation of nature, he believed, the individual could become attuned with the **Dao**: the cosmic force and source of all creation. Laozi stressed nonaction over political power and self-examination over the mastery of others. He taught,

It is wisdom to know others.
It is enlightenment to know one's self.
The conqueror of men is powerful.
The master of himself is stronger.
It is wealth to be content.
It is willful to force one's way on others.

Although much of Laozi's message concerned withdrawal from the world, he could not resist giving advice to those who remained in society, particularly the rulers of China's many kingdoms. He chastised them for enjoying war and the excessive pursuit of pleasure in their palaces while the mass of the population went hungry. He wrote,

> When the court is arrayed in splendor,
> The fields are full of weeds,
> And the granaries are bare.

Laozi exhorted rulers and men of affairs to cultivate the virtues of patience, selflessness, and concern for the welfare of all creatures. He argued that these virtues were consistent with the nature of the Dao. Like Confucius, he believed that wise rulers and honest administrators made for happy and peaceful kingdoms. But Laozi differed from Confucius in his views on how a good ruler was to be nurtured and what qualities he possessed. Unlike Confucius, who viewed a strong state and sound society as the primary goals, Laozi saw them as temporary concerns that were of little relevance to the wise man in search of the hidden meanings of creation and human life.

Like Confucius, Laozi had many disciples in his own lifetime and in later centuries. His poetic sayings were interpreted by these followers in widely varying ways. Some held to his original emphasis on withdrawal from the world, communion with nature, and meditation. Others mixed his ideas with magic, eroticism, and a search for a concoction that would bring immortality to those who drank it. The meditative followers had the greatest appeal to the shi elite and courtiers of later ages. These elite disciples drew on Daoist ideas to enhance their sensitivity to art and the natural world and to satisfy their interest in questions about the supernatural. The masses, on the other hand, were attracted by the magical solutions to everyday problems emphasized by conjurers and charlatans with rather dubious claims to being Laozi's disciples.

Laozi [low-dzuh] Also known as Lao Tsu; major Chinese philosopher in 4th century B.C.E.; recommended retreat from society into nature; individual should seek to become attuned with Dao.

Dao [dow] In Chinese, *the way*. A religious system that stresses contemplation, self-centering, and reverence for the natural world.

DOCUMENT

Teachings of the Rival Chinese Schools

THE BRIEF PASSAGES QUOTED HERE ARE taken from the writings of Confucius, Mencius, Shang Yang, and Laozi. Identify the author of each passage and explain why you believe it was written by the person you chose.

> I take no action and the people are reformed.
> I enjoy peace and people become honest.
> I do nothing and people become rich.
> I have no desires and people return to the good and simple life.

> The gentleman cherishes virtue; the inferior man cherishes possessions.
> The educated man thinks of sanctions; the inferior man thinks of personal favors.

> The nature of man is evil; his goodness is acquired.
> His nature being what it is, man is born, first, with a desire for gain.
> If this desire is followed, strife will result and courtesy will disappear.

> Keep your mouth closed.
> Guard your senses.
> Temper your sharpness.
> Simplify your problems.
> Mask your brightness.
> Be at one with the dust of the earth.
> This is primal union.

> Personal cultivation begins with poetry, is made firm with rules of decorum, and is perfected by music.

> When it is left to follow its natural feelings, human nature will do good. That is why I say it is good. If it becomes evil, it is not the fault of man's original capability.

QUESTIONS
- Which of these ideas are most compatible?
- Which of them could best be called religious?
- Which are most secular?
- Which philosophers propose ideas that are best suited to people who want to build a strong and unified political order?

THE TRIUMPH OF THE QIN AND IMPERIAL UNITY

After centuries of political division and social disorder, a strong new dynasty, the Qin, reunited China at the end of the 3rd century B.C.E. The Qin era brought the foundations of an enduring centralized bureaucracy and major extensions of the northern walls intended to hold the nomads in check.

4.2 What were some of the major innovations under the short-lived Qin dynasty that shaped the nature of the Chinese state over the next two millennia?

Of nomadic origins and located on the northwest fringe of the former Zhou empire (see Map 4.1), the Qin state lagged behind most of its rivals in the fine arts and refined etiquette. But from as early as the 5th century B.C.E., the rulers of Qin had initiated several critical social and political changes that greatly increased their ability to wage war against their snobbish rivals to the east and south. The Qin state had long supported experimentation with bronze and ironworking that had transformed tool- and weapons-making in the Zhou era. To encourage peasants to adopt new tools and more productive cultivation techniques, the Qin freed them from bondage to local lords and allowed them to claim their own land. Over time, these measures substantially increased the resource base on which Qin political ambitions depended. Because freeing the peasants undermined the support of the vassal warriors, who had originally carried out local administration, the Qin attempted to build a regular bureaucracy supported by the dynasty and totally loyal to it. These efforts attracted migrant shi administrators, who were willing to put up with bad manners if well-paying positions were to be had.

Qin power and military prowess were also increased by the many wars the state fought, first to survive and later to conquer the rest of China. The Qin conscripted for military service the peasants it had freed and given land, making its armies larger than those of rival states. The superior bureaucracy of the Qin meant that its forces were better supplied and organized. The nomadic background

MAP **4.2 China from the Later Zhou Era to the Han Era** As this map showing the boundaries of successive Chinese dynasties illustrates, the extent of the early Han empire greatly exceeded even that of the Qin dynasty, which was the first to effectively unify the core regions of Chinese civilization.

of the Qin elite ensured an ample supply of able military leaders. It also made the Qin more receptive to military innovations than many of their adversaries. For example, they were one of the first states to use massed cavalry, which gave their armies mobility. Qin armies were also the first to adopt the crossbow, which came into widespread use in the late Zhou era. Good leadership and free peasants, who may have felt that they had more to fight for than the vassals and serfs of other kingdoms, made the Qin armies famous for their ferocity and speed.

The Legalist Sanction

From at least the 4th century B.C.E., the efforts of Qin rulers to break the power of their vassals were justified by the writings of several statesmen who came to be known collectively as the Legalists. The semilegendary Shang Yang, who served a Qin ruler of the mid-4th century B.C.E., was the founder of the Legalist school of political philosophy. In *The Book of Lord Shang*, he argued that the power of China's rulers should be absolute. Their major objective should be to enhance the strength and wealth of the state. Shang Yang argued that the people existed to serve the state, and he had little to say about the ruler's duty to promote their welfare. He believed that the main responsibility of the state with regard to the people was to enforce strict laws with harsh punishments for offenders. Although the ruler was absolute, even he should not be above the law. To drive this point home, Shang Yang once had the crown prince punished for breaking the law: The cheek of the prince's tutor was tattooed in retribution for the offense.

As Shang Yang discovered at the end of his life, he too was subject to the strict laws. When he fled the court after the death of the ruler who was his patron and protector, the aged statesman sought refuge at a roadside inn. But it was illegal for a traveler to stay at an inn without a permit, which Shang Yang did not have. The innkeeper, who faced death if he did not obey the law, turned out the old man. Shang Yang later led an unsuccessful rebellion, which resulted in his being tied to chariots and ripped apart in punishment.

Shi Huangdi, Emperor of China

The young warrior who took the imperial title of Shi Huangdi, or, the "tiger" of Qin, was extremely receptive to the Legalist approach to government. A man of unbounded ambition, energy, and physical courage, he was also a megalomaniac who did not tolerate the slightest challenge to his rule. Because of complaints from his officials, he once had hundreds of shi buried alive. He harshly punished those who leaked news from the palace. When his grumbling about the overuse of carriages by his courtiers became known throughout the capital, for example, and no one would admit to repeating the offhand remarks he had made in confidence, Shi Huangdi executed all who could have overheard them. When he was told that a chain of hills was blocking the critical wet monsoons, he had the trees on them cut down and their surface dyed red, the color associated with criminals in China.

By 221 B.C.E., Shi Huangdi had completed the work of his predecessors. He had defeated the last rival states which opposed the Qin and had unified China (see Maps 4.1 and 4.2). To strengthen his hold over his vast domain, Shi Huangdi ordered all regional fortresses destroyed and the weapons of local warrior groups collected and melted down. Former states disappeared, and 36 provinces were created in their place. Vassal overlords and regional commanders were replaced by Qin bureaucrats. Surviving princes and aristocrats, as well as very wealthy merchants, were ordered to live in the capital at Xianyang, where Shi Huangdi's huge palace loomed over hundreds of others. The emperor's scribes developed a standard script and coinage, and weights and measures were unified throughout the empire.

Shi Huangdi's greatest passion was for building. His architects joined and expanded the walls that had been built by the northern kingdoms to keep out nomadic invaders, thus extending the long northern walls that were centuries later to form the basis of the famed **Northern Wall**. (Figure 4.3, Maps 4.1 and 4.2). The northern wall and other public works projects, such as canals and roadways, were constructed by millions of forcibly recruited peasant laborers; 700,000 were said to have been used to build the emperor's palace alone. Even Shi Huangdi's death did not put an end to his building projects. In preparing for his own burial, the emperor ordered the construction of a massive tomb at Mount Li, which was not uncovered until 1971. The army of clay soldiers and horses shown in

Read the Document on MyHistoryLab: The Way of the State (475–221 B.C.E)

Northern Wall Chinese defensive fortification intended to keep out the nomadic invaders from the north; initiated during Qin dynasty and reign of Shi Huangdi.

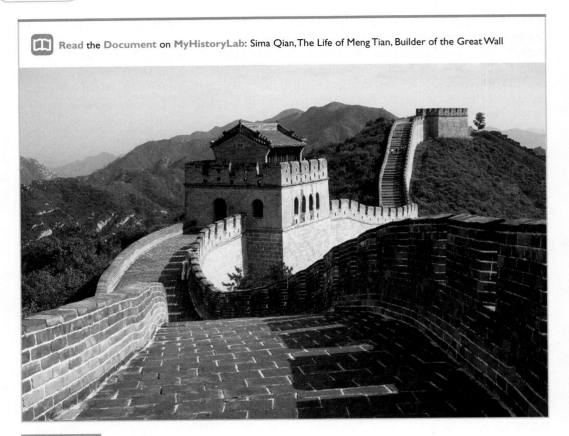

Read the Document on MyHistoryLab: Sima Qian, The Life of Meng Tian, Builder of the Great Wall

FIGURE **4.3** When kept in good repair and supplied with sufficient numbers of soldiers, the high walls and broad battlements of what would become the northern wall were a formidable obstacle for nomads who sought to invade China. The impressive barrier was made by joining and extending several walls that had been built by regional kingdoms in north China before they were conquered by the Qin. Among the most impressive engineering triumphs of the ancient world, the wall ran for more than 1400 miles through and above the north China plain (see Map 4.2). For more than two millennia, the wall, frequently repaired and improved as this photo illustrates, buffered the interaction between Chinese civilization and the nomadic peoples to the west and north of the Yellow River basin. Though impressive the northern wall did not reach its fullest level of development (hence the Great Wall we know today) until the massive renovations and extensions undertaken during the rule of the Ming dynasty in the 15th century.

Figure 4.4, which were buried in the Mount Li tomb with Shi Huangdi, provide a final testament to his megalomania and unchecked demands on his subjects.

The Collapse of a Tyrannical but Pivotal Regime

Read the Document on MyHistoryLab: Li Si and the Legalist Policies of Qin Shihuang (280–208 B.C.E)

Shi Huangdi's building frenzy and the harsh rule of his Legalist administrators aroused resistance throughout the Qin's newly won empire. Even though many of the shi served as administrators in the Qin bureaucracy, they were understandably angered by the repression of any ideas that challenged those of the Legalists. The early efforts at thought control by the Qin ruler culminated in a campaign to burn all but a handful of state-approved books. All works, except an official political history of China, Legalist texts, and works on technology, medicine, and astrology, were to be confiscated by state officials and destroyed. At this time, books were written by hand on bamboo strips that were then bound together. Their high cost and the small numbers of literate elite meant that books were scarce and easily located.

At the same time, the peasants were alienated by the Qin's endless demands for taxes and labor. In fact, Shi Huangdi's appetite for building projects was the immediate cause of the revolt that led to the abrupt collapse of the dynasty in 207 B.C.E., just three years after the emperor's death. The two peasants who began the revolt were conscripted to work on the northern wall

View the **Closer Look** on **MyHistoryLab**: The Terra-Cotta Army of the First Qin Emperor

FIGURE **4.4** Hundreds of these clay warriors were found in the tomb of the first Chinese emperor, Shi Huangdi. Remarkably, each of the warriors has different facial features. Together with the clay horses also found in the tomb, these massed forces are striking evidence of the power of the founder of China's short-lived, first imperial dynasty. They also reflect the emperor's obsession with monumental building projects—a direct cause of the fall of the repressive Qin dynasty within a few years of Shi Huangdi's death.

(see Figure 4.3). On the journey from their village to the construction site, they realized that they could not arrive on time. Because the typical penalty for arriving late for a labor assignment was death, the two men concluded that they had little to lose by rousing others to revolt. Their calls for resistance found a ready audience among the weary peasantry and many of the disaffected shi elite. The revolt spread rapidly, and within months the Qin dynasty was toppled. Shi Huangdi's son was murdered by a band of conspirators, and the emperor's huge palace was burned to the ground.

Although Qin rule over all of China lasted only a matter of decades, its short reign was a turning point in Chinese history. Shi Huangdi not only unified China but governed it with a centralized bureaucracy staffed by salaried officials. This meant that he was not dependent on unsteady and potentially hostile vassals, a dependency that had destroyed earlier dynasties. And despite the regime's repression of non-Legalist thinking, Qin rule also involved strengthening the shi, who increasingly provided the social and political bonds that would hold China together through times of crisis and foreign invasion.

The public works projects of the Qin provided the grid of roads and canals that made it possible for later dynasties to hold far-flung territories together. The construction of the northern wall reinforced the long-standing division between the nomads of central and north Asia and the farmers to the south. Improved communication and a unified currency enabled China's merchants to establish interregional markets and promoted the interdependence of very different geographic areas of the Chinese empire. Although the threat of a return to war and anarchy loomed briefly after the sudden collapse of the Qin, the foundations Shi Huangdi laid for a centralized empire permitted another remarkable leader to establish a far milder and more lasting dynasty in China: the house of Han.

THE HAN DYNASTY AND THE FOUNDATIONS OF CHINA'S CLASSICAL AGE

Harsh rule of the emperor Shi Huangdi and his failure to produce a capable heir led to widespread rebellion after his death and the emergence of a new dynasty, the Han, that would unify China for more than 400 years. The Han era brought the growth of great cities, the expansion of trade and the mercantile classes, and a new surge of inventiveness.

Liu Bang [lyoh-bahng] (247–195 B.C.E.) Founder of the Han dynasty in 202 B.C.E.

4.3 How did the growing strength of social groups, including the scholar-gentry (or *shi*), merchants, and the military, affect gender and other social relationships and the nature of family life from the Han dynasty onward?

The pent-up anger produced by a decade and a half of harsh state demands and repression flared into regional riots and rebellions throughout the former Qin territories. Vassal chiefs fought former Qin bureaucrats for local control, and some dreamed of founding a renewed empire. The unlikely winner of these many-sided contests for power was a man of peasant birth named **Liu Bang**. Liu Bang's early life hardly suggests that he would become the founder of one of China's longest-lived and most illustrious dynasties. In his youth Liu Bang was lazy, uneducated, and jobless. He was best known for his fondness for wine and women, tastes that remained pronounced throughout his life. In the years before the end of the Qin dynasty, Liu Bang, either because he had changed his shiftless ways or through clever maneuvers, had established himself as a village headman. In the confusion that followed the fall of the Qin, he built up a following of soldiers, ex-bureaucrats, and disgruntled peasants.

Liu Bang was not much of a military commander. Legend has it that he lost all the battles he fought for control of China except the last one. But he did have a gift for picking able subordinates and allowing them to exercise their talents. His skill at mediating between quarrelsome followers allowed him to hold his motley armies together while the forces of his enemies dissolved in violent factional fights. In 202 B.C.E., after years of campaigning and negotiation, Liu Bang proclaimed himself the new emperor of China, thus founding the Han dynasty that would rule China, with a brief interruption, for the next 400 years (see Map 4.2).

The Restoration of Imperial Control

For a time it looked as though the new emperor would restore the system of vassalage that had formed the basis for royal administration in the Zhou era. He raised many of his followers to the ranks of the nobility, and he rewarded them, as well as existing lords who had supported his efforts to win the throne, with large estates. However, it soon became clear that even his once-loyal followers were not above using the domains they had been granted to build up independent bases of power that could eventually threaten the dynasty. In addition to this threat, Liu Bang's determination to establish a more centralized imperial administration was promoted by the shi officials who attached themselves to his cause during his struggle for power and after he became emperor. Perhaps because Liu Bang was illiterate, he came to rely heavily on his shi advisors even though he personally despised them. His efforts at bureaucratic centralization focused on enhancing their training and responsibilities.

Liu Bang's moves toward bureaucratic centralization were taken up by several strong and able rulers who succeeded him on the Han throne, most notably Han Wudi (140–87 B.C.E.). First, the larger fiefs granted to the highest nobles were broken up by a royal decree that required the domains of the vassals to be divided between all their sons at the time of their death rather than pass intact to their eldest son. At the same time, regular government appointees, especially regional governors and district magistrates, expanded their authority at the expense of local lords. In the time of Han Wudi, vassals were forbidden to bequeath their domains to heirs they had adopted. When a noble died without legitimate offspring, his estates were confiscated by the central government. Under a variety of pretexts, Han Wudi's administrators also seized the fiefs of many other vassals, who were then relegated to the status of commoners.

Xunzi [shwuhn-dzee] Author of *The Art of War*, a classic book that revolutionized thinking about military organization and the conduct of war.

Xiongnu [shung-noo] A polyglot nomadic group that built an empire in central Asia in the last centuries B.C.E.

Han Expansion

The Han rulers used the impressive military might at their disposal to enlarge the empire and neutralize external threats. The most formidable of the external enemies were the **Xiongnu** nomads (also known as Huns) who lived outside of the northern walls. From the time of the first Han emperor, these skilled horsemen of Mongol descent had raided and looted territories south

THINKING HISTORICALLY

Xunzi and the Shift from Ritual Combat to "Real" War

THE DEVELOPMENT OF CLASSICAL CIVILIZATIONS IN the Middle East, Greece, China, and India greatly advanced the business of making war. Agricultural surpluses made it possible to support specialized fighters and military commanders. Population growth made for larger armies, which needed armor, weapons, and training. Horses, and in some areas camels and elephants, were raised to carry men into battle or pull war chariots. Advances in metalworking meant steadily improving weaponry, and fortification became a major concern for early engineers and architects. Warfare came to involve more soldiers, who fought for longer periods and suffered more casualties. Frontier defenses and military campaigns became primary concerns for those who ruled civilized states.

Despite advances in weaponry and training, at least for warrior elites, warfare in most early civilizations was a combination of ritual and chaos. Wars normally were not fought during harvest times, the winter, or the monsoon season. A ruler was expected to announce his intention to attack a neighboring kingdom well in advance. Before battle, the high priests of each ruler offered sacrifices to the gods. Their readings of various sorts of omens, not strategic considerations, determined the time and place of combat. Battles consisted primarily of formal duels between trained and well-armed warriors in the midst of confused collisions of masses of poorly trained and armed foot soldiers, who were usually slaves or forcibly recruited peasants. Although often fierce, the warriors' duels were regulated by codes of honor and fair play. For example, it was unseemly for a warrior to strike from behind or to strike when his opponent had fallen.

Duels between warrior champions were the set pieces of a battle. As the great epics of early civilizations, such as the Indian *Mahabharata* and the Greek *Iliad* demonstrate, great warriors cut bloody swaths through the ranks of poorly prepared infantry and lesser fighters to get to each other and set up the hand-to-hand combats that normally determined the outcome of battle. The death of a commander, who was often the ruler of the kingdom at war or a renowned champion, usually meant the collapse of his forces and their chaotic flight from the field. Normally, the victorious army did not destroy or capture what remained of the opposing soldiers. The game had been played and won. The winners either retired with their booty to prepare for the next round or began negotiations to set the terms on which the defeated party would submit to their overlordship.

> *"Xunzi argued that war was merely an extension of statecraft. Wars ought not to be games or macho contests for bragging rights; they ought to be fought only for ends that increased the territory, wealth, and power of the state."*

The Shang and early Zhou periods of Chinese history were filled with wars, most of which were fought according to this ritualized pattern. But by the late Zhou period, some commanders and thinkers had become highly critical of the indecisiveness and waste of the endless conflicts between the warring states. In the 4th century B.C.E., Xunzi, an advisor to one of the warring monarchs, responded to these concerns with a treatise, *The Art of War*, a classic of military theory. Xunzi proposed a vision of military conflict very different from the ritualized approach to war.

Xunzi argued that war was merely an extension of statecraft. Wars ought not to be games or macho contests for bragging rights; they ought to be fought only for ends that increased the territory, wealth, and power of the state. With these aims in mind, Xunzi insisted that speed was of the essence in warfare and that long wars burdened the subjects of the warring rulers and bred rebellions. He also urged that target kingdoms be captured swiftly and with as little damage as possible. Xunzi argued that war was a science, which should be the object of extensive study. Rather than brawny warriors, commanders ought to be men well versed in organization, strategy, and tactics. He proposed, and Chinese rulers set up, special schools to train officers in the art of war.

Xunzi's ideas transformed warfare in China. Rulers made every effort short of war to bring down their rivals. Bluffs, spies, threats, and saboteurs were used before armies were sent to war. Both before and after war was actually declared, substantial state resources and large bureaucracies were devoted to building and training armies and supplying them in the field. Sneak attacks were considered fair, and feints and ruses were regularly used by field commanders. Weather conditions and advantageous terrain determined the time and place of battle.

Psychological devices were strongly recommended. For example, techniques were used to make the enemy commanders angry and cause them to make foolish moves that might demoralize their armies. Discipline was needed, rather than individual heroics. This point was driven home by a rulers who had one of his commanders beheaded because the general's troops attacked ahead of schedule, despite the fact that this action was the key to victory. In combat, regular formations replaced mass brawls; soldiers fought as units under the direction of a chain of commanders. Good fighters were still valued, but now as unit leaders rather than accomplished duelists. The main object of battle became the destruction of the enemy's forces as quickly as possible.

(continued on next page)

Shi Huangdi's military and political successes demonstrated how effective warfare reorganized along the lines suggested by Xunzi might be. Halfway across the globe, the Greeks were independently developing comparable patterns of warfare. Ironically, this shift in approaches to warfare between the Greek city-states was occurring at about the same time the compilers of the *Iliad* were celebrating the contests of great heroes such as Achilles and Hector. In roughly the same era as Xunzi and Shi Huangdi, the tightly disciplined formations and training of smaller Greek armies culminated in Alexander the Great's unprecedented conquests.

But these successes did not put an end to ritual warfare between civilized peoples. Although Chinese armies tended to be organized and led according to the prescriptions of Xunzi and other theorists, the chivalric codes and battles centered on the duels of champions persisted. This was particularly true in societies that were dominated by warrior elites, such as those that later developed in India, Japan, Africa, Europe, and Mesoamerica. But conditions in the warring states and the genius of Xunzi had led to a radically new vision of what wars were about and how they were fought. The effects of this vision are still felt by civilized societies.

QUESTIONS

- What were some of the major differences between ritual warfare and the new approach proposed by Xunzi?
- What are the main advantages and drawbacks of each approach?
- If you were an ancient ruler, which would you tell your military commanders to use? Why?

 Read the **Document** on **MyHistoryLab**: Excerpt from *The Art of War* (2nd century B.C.E.).

of the wall. Liu Bang attempted to buy them off by giving them presents and marrying one of his daughters to the highest Xiongnu chieftain. By the time of Han Wudi, it was clear that major expeditions would be necessary to put an end to the Xiongnu incursions. Han Wudi's forces defeated the nomads and annexed their pasturelands to the Han domains.

Han armies also expanded the empire to the east and south. In the east, the northern parts of Korea were conquered in 108 B.C.E. and were ruled by the Chinese for more than 400 years. Conquests in the south extended Chinese civilization into the mountainous interior and down the coast of the South China Sea to present-day Vietnam. The many different ethnic groups who lived in these areas either submitted to Han rule and assimilated to Chinese civilization or, like the various branches of the T'ai-speaking peoples, migrated farther south into what later became Burma, Thailand, and Laos. The southernmost of the peoples who resisted Han rule were subjects of the kingdom the Chinese called Nam Viet. After many attempts, Han armies finally conquered this state in 111 B.C.E, and established control over the Vietnamese people. But in contrast to the other non-Chinese peoples of south China and southeast Asia, the Vietnamese eventually won their independence and were never fully assimilated into Chinese civilization (see Chapter 18).

The Revenge of the Shi

The majority of the shi, who were followers of Confucius and his disciples, deeply resented the favoritism Shi Huangdi showed the Legalists. The fall of the Qin provided them an opportunity to strike back. At the urging of the Confucian school, Liu Bang and his successors banned the works of the Legalists, and members of the school were hounded from the court and in some cases killed. The harsh law codes of the Qin were replaced by the milder edicts of the Han. Legalist ideas were eventually blended into the mix of philosophies and religious beliefs that came to make up China's official ideology.

Confucianism in its varying forms soon became the dominant thought system in Chinese civilization. Its full ascendancy was delayed in the early Han era by the suspicions of rulers, such as Liu Bang, who strongly favored Daoism, and the rivalry of non-Confucian thinkers. But by the end of the 2nd century B.C.E., the shi scholar-officials and the Confucian ideas they championed had won a prominence they would enjoy for much of the next 2000 years. A thorough knowledge of Confucian teachings became essential to employment and promotion in the Han government. This prerequisite for success in Han politics was institutionalized by the founding of an imperial university at the capital at Xi'an in 124 B.C.E. By the end of the Han era there were more than 30,000 students at this state-supported center.

Education, Examinations, and Shi Dominance

Although students at the imperial university were expected to master law and a choice of specialized fields, including history, astronomy, and music, all concentrated on memorizing and interpreting the Confucian classics. These were given even greater emphasis when formal examinations for government positions were established at the beginning of the last century B.C.E. The Chinese examination system marked the beginning of the first professional civil service in human history. At first, exams were confined to the upper levels of government, but local and regional exams were later established to identify and test local talent. Theoretically, any Chinese man could take them. But no one could hope to pass them without a proper education, and education was expensive. This meant that members of established shi families, the old aristocracy, and local landlord households had a clear advantage.

Each elite family supported the brightest of its sons. They were tutored at home as children and then enrolled in local schools, where they mastered the Chinese characters and the Confucian texts. On occasion a particularly bright child from a peasant household was adopted by a shi or landlord family and given the support he needed to do well on the exams and advance in the bureaucracy.

In general, people from the lower classes could not afford a proper education, but several examples are recounted by Chinese historians of enterprising farmers or merchants who rose to high administrative posts. In one instance at the end of the 2nd century B.C.E., a dismissed police official, who had resorted to pig breeding to support himself, in his later years so impressed the emperor with his responses to the examiners' questions that he was eventually given the post of imperial chancellor.

Opportunities for government positions were limited by the fact that only a small percentage of jobs were allotted by competitive examination. Although the Han rulers tried to put an end to hereditary rank, many political positions automatically passed from father to son. Many offices were appointive, and a man's chance of winning an office depended on personal links to the emperor or high officials who distributed the political spoils. Thus, in the Han era, few offices were earned by passing exams. However, the Han system nurtured a revolutionary idea: that administrative office and the exercise of political power ought to depend on personal merit and effort rather than birth alone.

The Emergence of the Scholar-Gentry

The growing influence of the shi in government was also felt in Chinese social life as a whole. In effect, three main social strata came to be recognized by those who wrote the official documents and histories: the literate shi, the ordinary but free subjects, and the underclass, called the "mean people." Within each of these large groupings there were important occupational and status divisions. For example, the shi ranged from the powerful families that served the imperial household to local tutors and petty clerks stationed in frontier provinces. The common people included groups that we would identify as separate social classes. The majority were peasants, but even they varied greatly in wealth and social status. Some controlled large amounts of land, lived in extended family compounds, and tried to provide their sons with the education that would elevate the family to shi status.

Increasingly, local landlord families were linked by marriage or the success of their sons to the shi. This combination gave rise to a new class configuration, the **scholar-gentry**, who superseded the shi. As their dual label suggests, the scholar-gentry upheld their position through both landholdings in the rural areas and political posts in the bureaucracy, which was housed mainly in the towns. Families tended to maintain branches in both areas. Wealth from landholding was used to educate the brightest sons, who increased the family's fortunes by winning lucrative administrative positions. Well-placed family members in the town looked after the interests of their rural elders and cousins in such matters as tax quotas, military protection, and civil litigation. If bandits or nomads raided the area where the rural branch of the family lived, those family members could take refuge with their relatives in town. When towns were attacked by warring armies, the city dwellers fled to the countryside. This double base and mutual support made for remarkable durability. Some families played major roles in Chinese politics and society for centuries. Some lasted for thousands of years—far longer than any imperial dynasty.

In both town and country, scholar-gentry families lived in large walled compounds. These dwellings often had separate buildings for each unit of the extended family. Surviving paintings of gentry homes show that they were multistoried structures with stucco or wooden walls and tiled roofs. Most compounds included an inner garden, where children could play and their elders could

scholar-gentry Chinese class created by the marital linkage of the local land-holding aristocracy with the office-holding shi; superseded shi as governors of China.

chat and enjoy nature. In times of peace, scholar-gentry families lived the good life. Family granaries ensured a ready supply of good food, and household servants took care of tedious chores such as cleaning, cooking, and washing clothes. Male and female members of the family dressed in silks, which commoners, including merchants, were not permitted to wear (at least in public).

When a member of a scholar-gentry household who held an administrative position left the compound for work or a night on the town, he rode in a horse-drawn carriage. Like his clothing, the carriage was of a size and design that indicated his government rank. Both male and female members of the family enjoyed the deference of the common people. Merchants offered them their finest goods, servants scurried to do their bidding, and peasants bowed politely as they passed in their carriages. A commoner who forgot his place could expect to be chided by his peers or roughed up by the toughs that most gentry families employed to look after their safety.

Class and Gender Roles in Han Society

There is considerable evidence that women, particularly those from powerful scholar-gentry households, enjoyed more freedom and status in the Han era than in later periods of Chinese history. Because marriages, especially among the elite, were arranged with family alliances rather than romantic concerns in mind, young men had as little say in the choice of their spouses as women. Although the woman's father paid a dowry to the family of his son-in-law, and she went to her husband's house to live, the young bride usually could rely on her powerful relatives to ensure that she was well treated in her new home. She was often allowed to take along her servants and even a sister as live-in companions. Widowed women were permitted to remarry, and all women participated in family ceremonies. Perhaps most important, women of upper-class families were often tutored in writing, the arts, and music. There were several important female poets in the Han era, and at least one prominent court historian was a woman.

Despite these promising trends, women at all social levels remained subordinated to men. Family households were run by the older men, and although women could inherit, male children normally received the greater share of family property. The following verse from the *Book of Poetry*, which indicates typical responses to the birth into an aristocratic family of a son and a daughter, clearly illustrates the preference for and consequent privileges of males:

> Sons shall be born to him—
> They will be put to sleep on couches;
> They will be clothed in robes;
> They will have scepters to play with;
> Their cry will be loud.
> [Hereafter] they will be resplendent with red knee-covers,
> The [future] king, the princes of the land.

> Daughters shall be born to him—
> They will be put to sleep on the ground;
> They will be clothed in wrappers;
> They will have tiles to play with.
> It will be theirs neither to do wrong nor to do good.
> Only about the liquor and the food will they have to think,
> And to cause no sorrow to their parents.

Political positions were reserved for men, although women could sometimes exert powerful influence from behind the throne. But this backstage control at the court merely confirmed the view of the Confucian scholars that women were unfit for politics. Their attitudes are also bluntly set forth in the *Book of Poetry*:

> A woman with a long tongue
> Is a stepping-stone to disorder.
> Disorder does not come down from Heaven—
> It is produced by women.
> Those from whom come no lessons, no instruction,
> Are women and eunuchs.

Among the scholar-gentry, young married women were subjected to the demands and criticisms of domineering mothers-in-law. This was a lesser problem among the lower classes, where residence in extended households was not common. Nonetheless, women from peasant families were expected to cook, clean house, and work long hours in the fields. Some found social outlets and even a degree of financial independence working in the markets of nearby towns. But all were legally subordinated to their fathers and husbands. At all class levels, women were expected to marry, and whatever their individual talents, their most vital social function remained the bearing of children, preferably boys.

Peasant Life

Ordinary farmers held varying amounts of land, but few produced more than they needed to live and pay taxes. Moderately prosperous farmers sold their surplus to traders or their agents, or in a local market town. Most peasants who had land of their own lived well. But many peasants had too little or no land and were forced to work for landlords in order to earn a meager living. Peasants with plots that were too small to support their families complained to Han officials that they "did not have enough husks and beans to eat and [that] their coarse clothing was not in good condition." Those who worked the land of others as tenants or landless laborers were even more miserable. According to an official description, they "wore the coverings of oxen and horses and ate the food of dogs and pigs."

Key Chinese inventions such as the shoulder collar (which permitted horses to pull greater loads) and the wheelbarrow eased the work of farmers at all levels. Expanded irrigation networks, improved iron tools, and new cropping patterns allowed larger agricultural yields that were consumed mostly by upper-class groups and the town populations. Despite these advances, many of the poorest peasants continued to work the land with very simple tools (see Figure 4.5).

Nonetheless, a strong state and a rapidly increasing peasant population that could improve upon and existing technologies and systems and modes of production and make extensive use of new weapons and tools, led to major environmental transformations. Already a society that had altered the natural world as much or a great deal more than most others, under the Han dynasty the now vast Chinese empire witnessed unprecedented levels of the clearing of forests, the expansion of irrigation and transportation canals, growth in agricultural output, and the harnessing of natural resources for human production.

The existence of farmland in many areas, particularly the south, relieved population pressure and provided frontier outlets where hard-pressed laborers could clear land and start life anew. The losers in this process were the mainly non-Chinese ethnic groups who occupied these areas. Some peasants took to banditry in the rugged hill country or the forested zones that still

FIGURE **4.5** Han relief on a funeral tile found in the Chengdu region in Sichuan (eastern Han dynasty, 25 C.E.–220 C.E.). The hunting scene in a luxuriant landscape in the upper panel is linked with a scene (lower panel) of peasants working in the fields. Such illustrations enable historians to track the development of tool making and weapons making in ancient civilizations such as China. They also make it possible to study patterns of organization in agrarian and artisan production (for which direct evidence is sparse) as well as the leisure activities of officials and the landed elite.

CHAPTER 4 Unification and the Consolidation of Civilization in China   **89**

secret societies Chinese peasant organizations; provided financial support in hard times and physical protection in case of disputes with local aristocracy.

existed in large parts of the Yellow River and Yangzi River basins. Others scraped by as beggars in provincial towns or lived as vagabonds who traveled the roads of the empire in search of temporary employment or vulnerable merchants and country houses to rob. Many more peasants joined **secret societies** with colorful names such as the Red Eyebrows, which provided financial support in times of shortage and physical protection in case of disputes with other farmers or local notables.

The Han Capital at Xi'an

The urban growth that had been one of the most notable social developments in the late Zhou era continued in the Han period. The new capital city at Xi'an took on the basic features of Chinese imperial cities from that time forward. Laid out on a somewhat distorted grid, Xi'an had broad roadways that gave access to and defined the main quarters of the city. Much of the city was protected by long earth and brick walls, with towers and gates at regular intervals. Estimates of Xi'an's population range from about 100,000, which probably count only people living within the walls, to 250,000, which includes people living outside the walls and in neighboring villages.

The emperor lived in an inner walled quarter, which only his family, servants, and closest advisors were permitted to enter. The inner city was an impressive complex of palaces, towers, and decorated gateways. Each palace included audience halls, banquet rooms, large gardens and fish ponds, and luxurious living quarters for the emperor, his wife and **concubines** (women who lived in the palace as secondary wives or sexual partners for the emperors), and their children. To the west of Xi'an, beyond the city walls, a large pleasure garden was laid out for the imperial family. It included one of the earliest known zoos.

concubine A secondary wife, whose status is inferior to that of a ruler or wealthy man's primary wife.

The Forbidden City was surrounded by administrative buildings and the palaces of the most powerful aristocratic and scholar-gentry households. Under later dynasties, this zone became a distinct imperial city within the capital. Some of the imperial palaces and government buildings were made of stone or brick, but many were made of clay covered with brightly colored plaster. Most were roofed with the glazed tiles with upturned edges that would become characteristic of Chinese architecture in the following millennia.

Towns and Traders

The Han capital at Xi'an was only one of many imposing cities in China in this era. It is likely that China was the most urbanized civilization in the world at this time—a fact that tells us much about the productivity of its agricultural sector. There were many towns with more than 10,000 people and several towns, such as Xi'an, with populations in the tens of thousands. Most towns were walled, and many were administrative centers dominated by the multistory residences and offices of imperial officials and scholar-gentry notables. But other towns grew up around mining and manufacturing centers, and many were centers of trade that continued to grow in the Han era.

This growth was greatly advanced by Han military expansion to the west and south. It resulted in the establishment of new overland trade routes into central Asia and south China. Overseas links were also established with what is today northern Vietnam, the rest of southeast Asia, and the rich trading towns of coastal India.

Large mercantile firms controlled these long-distance trading networks. They grew wealthy from the transport and sale of bulk items, such as grain and horses, as well as from supplying the elite classes with exotic luxury items such as incense, fragrant woods, and rhinoceros horn, which when ground into an edible powder was believed to enhance male potency. Merchant families also made great fortunes by lending money and investing in mining, shipbuilding, sheep raising, and less legitimate enterprises such as gambling halls, brothels, and grave robbing.

Although the merchant classes became wealthier and more numerous, they found it increasingly difficult to translate their profits into political power or social status. Fearing their rivalry, the scholar-gentry induced successive Han rulers to issue laws that restricted merchant activities and privileges. Under most Han rulers, for example, merchants could not hold administrative posts, although they often exerted local influence. They were not allowed to own carriages, carry weapons, or wear silk clothing. Scholar-gentry writers consistently ranked merchants below the peasants in terms of their social usefulness, arguing that peasants produced food and essential services, whereas traders lived off the labor of others.

VISUALIZING THE PAST

Capital Designs and Patterns of Political Power

THE DESIGN AND PHYSICAL LAYOUT OF the capital cities of early civilizations can tell us a great deal about the distribution of political power and social status in different centers of the ancient world. In addition, the configurations of these pivotal cities usually manifest religious beliefs and conceptions of the cosmic order in the ways they are oriented and physically constructed. Therefore, plans of the capital centers of ancient civilizations can be read like written texts to help us understand the early history of some of humankind's greatest civilizations. Reproduced here are schematic diagrams of some of the key features of the capital cities of three of the great early civilizations of Eurasia: from Xi'an in Han China, Athens in Greece, and Harappa in India. Study and compare these diagrams for what they tell us about the kinds of elite groups that exercised political power, social stratification, and thinking about the relationship between the supernatural and human rulers in each civilization for which

they served as capitals. In thinking about these issues, you may want to refer to relevant sections in Chapters 3, 4, and 5.

QUESTIONS

- Which social groups were the most powerful politically in each society?

- How prominent was military force in the exercise of power by the elites in each civilization?

- To what extent was political power legitimized by religious figures, ideas, and conceptions of the workings of the cosmos?

- To what degree did the rulers and political elites seek to separate themselves from the subject population, and what evidence could you use to determine this?

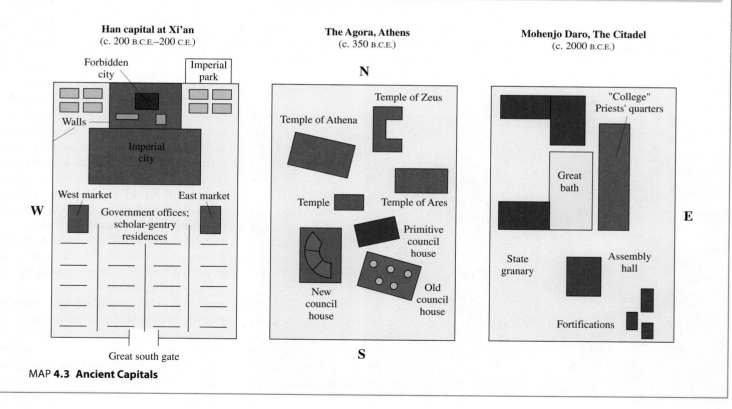

MAP **4.3 Ancient Capitals**

A Genius for Invention and Artisan Production

Long before the Han, the Chinese had displayed a special aptitude for invention and technological innovation. They had built massive irrigation systems, canal networks, and fortifications. They devised cropping techniques that for millennia were some of the most productive known to humanity. In the centuries of Han rule, however, their talent for invention reached new heights, and with it rose the excellence of their artisan production. There is little doubt that China was the most technologically innovative and advanced of all the classical civilizations.

At the level of the elite, the introduction of the brush pen and paper at the end of the 2nd century B.C.E. greatly facilitated the administrative work of the scholar-gentry and advanced their literary and artistic production. The Han Chinese also developed watermills to grind grain and power artisan workshops and rudders and compasses to steer and guide ships (although in the Han era compasses were used primarily for divination; they were not used by sailors until the 9th century C.E.). They devised ingenious mining techniques to allow them to fully exploit the iron and copper resources that had become critical to warfare and domestic production. In the centuries of Han rule, silk making was carried to new levels of refinement, and techniques for making lacquer ware and porcelain were pioneered, which allowed China to remain a leader in ceramics until well into the modern era.

All these advances promoted the growth of the artisan, manufacturing classes. Artisans tended to be clustered in special sectors of Chinese towns, but in some regions villages were devoted almost exclusively to crafts such as pottery making or silk weaving. Skilled artisans were in high demand and probably had a higher living standard than most peasants, although the scholar-gentry accorded them a lower official social status. Again, the ideal and reality did not necessarily correspond, for some members of the artisan classes amassed wealth and were allowed to carry weapons, ride horses, and wear silk clothing.

The Arts and Sciences in the Han Era

Chinese art during the classical period was largely decorative. Careful detail and expert artistry were most valued. Artistic styles often reflected the precision and geometric qualities of the many symbols of Chinese writing, and calligraphy became a highly prized art form. Chinese painting (Figure 4.6) was much less developed than it became under later Chinese dynasties. But the bronzes and ceramic figurines, bowls, and vases produced in this era set a very high standard for later Chinese artists. Important work was also done in jade and ivory carvings and woven silk screens.

acupuncture An ancient Chinese system of medicine that is centered on the insertion of special needles to relieve stress-related pain or ailments.

In the sciences, the Chinese were more drawn to practical experimentation than theorizing. By 444 B.C.E., court astronomers had developed an accurate calendar based on a year of 365.5 days. Later astronomers calculated the movements of the planets Saturn and Jupiter and observed sunspots more than 1500 years before comparable observations were made in Europe. The main purpose of Chinese astronomy was to make celestial phenomena predictable, as part of a wider interest in ensuring harmony between heaven and earth. In astronomy and other areas, Chinese scientists steadily improved their instruments, even inventing a seismograph to register the strength of earthquakes. The Chinese were also active in medical research. They made great strides in diagnosing diseases and prescribing herbal remedies and other drugs to cure them. Recent evidence suggests that physicians in the Han era had begun to explore the principles of **acupuncture**, which remains the most distinctive and one of the most beneficial Chinese contributions to medicine.

FIGURE **4.6** This painting of "The First Emperor of the Han Dynasty Entering Guandang," by Zhao Bozhu, seeks to recapture the pomp and splendor associated with the founder of the Han dynasty, one of the most powerful and long-lived in Chinese history. By the last centuries B.C.E., large, richly attired entourages, which moved about among several palaces and walled cities, were deemed essential for the emperors and regional lords who had become the dominant force in Chinese political life.

Chinese mathematics also stressed the practical. Daoism encouraged some interest in studying the orderly processes of nature, but most research focused on how things work. For example, Chinese scholars studied the mathematics of music in ways that promoted advances in acoustics. They also sought to work out standards for the measurement of distance, volume, and weight. This kind of scientific and mathematical learning won substantial backing from the government and was generally approved by the shi scholar-officials.

Imperial Crisis and Han Restoration

For more than two centuries the Han maintained their hold over a unified Chinese empire. But by the end of the 1st century B.C.E., problems centering on the court threatened to bring an end to Han rule. After Han Wudi, the quality of the emperors declined markedly. Many of his successors neglected the duties of government and, like the monarchs of the late Shang and Zhou, indulged heavily in the pleasures of food, drink, and concubines. As the hold of the emperors over state affairs weakened, the powerful families of their wives sought to take charge of imperial administration. In 6 C.E., the only male heir of the Han dynasty was a small child, giving one of these families, the Wang, the opportunity to seize the throne.

With the initial support of the scholar-gentry and the general populace, an ambitious nephew of the Empress Dowager Wang named **Wang Mang** proclaimed himself emperor in 9 C.E. But Wang Mang's many well-intended reforms rapidly alienated the very groups that had originally supported him. Attempts to exert imperial control over land ownership angered the scholar-gentry. Government monopolies, which sent the price of food and other essentials soaring, led to widespread peasant unrest. In 23 C.E., the hapless Wang Mang was overthrown, and the Han dynasty was restored.

Wang Mang Member of one of the powerful families related to the Han emperors through marriage; temporarily overthrew the Han between 9 and 23 C.E.

The Later Han and Imperial Collapse

The later Han dynasty ruled a unified China for nearly 200 years. For a time the peace and prosperity of the former Han era returned. Internal rebels and nomad invaders were suppressed. The last centuries of the dynasty saw little of the innovation and creativity of the early centuries of Han rule. Inventions were improved, scholars commented on the works of earlier thinkers, the population of the empire continued to grow, and trading networks expanded. But major breakthroughs in government, the arts, and invention would have to wait for centuries and the next great dynasty, the Tang.

Politically, the later Han was a period of steady decline. Han rulers were plagued by struggles between factions at the court, which had been transferred from Xi'an eastward to the city of Luoyang (Map 4.2). Challenges from the families of the emperors' wives continued, but they were complicated by the growing power of the **eunuchs:** men who had been castrated to make them reliable guardians of the emperor's wives and concubines. Although there were often many concubines in residence, they had no official status, and their children normally could not inherit the throne. Some eunuchs were orphans, but many were sons of families who saw their recruitment into the eunuch corps at the palace as a sure way to financial security and political advancement.

eunuchs Castrated males used within the households of Chinese emperors, usually to guard the emperors' concubines; became political counterbalance to powerful marital relatives during Later Han.

Over the years, the number of eunuchs increased, and after the Han dynasty was restored, they gained substantially in power as palace administrators and inner advisors of the later emperors. In the last decades of Han rule, these emperors attempted to use the eunuchs to check the power of their wives' families. The three-way struggles that developed between the scholar-gentry, the families of the rulers' wives, and the eunuchs eventually ripped the court apart.

Divisions at the center of the empire weakened the emperor's ability to stop nomadic incursions and remedy the worsening conditions of the mass of the people. A weak imperial administration meant growing power for landlords and increasing autonomy for regional officials. Local notables pressed the peasantry that worked their lands for more taxes and higher rents. Secret societies spread like wildfire, and peasant uprisings broke out throughout the empire. Military commanders and regional lords seized power and fought against each other for the right to claim the Han throne.

The dynasty was not officially overthrown until 220 C.E., but decades earlier its power had been usurped. The end of the Han meant the return of the warring states and began nearly 400 years of division and turmoil that ended only with the rise of the Sui dynasty at the end of the 6th century C.E. (see Chapter 7).

Global Connections and Critical Themes

CLASSICAL CHINA AND THE WORLD

The short-lived Qin dynasty and four centuries of Han rule established the basic components of the longest-lived civilization in world history. As the achievements of the classical age demonstrate, China had also become one of the most creative and influential civilizations of all human history. The strength of its agrarian base has allowed China to carry about one-fifth of the total human population from the last centuries B.C.E. to the present day. The productivity of its peasants has made it possible for some of the world's largest cities to flourish in China, and nurtured one of history's largest and most creative elites. In China's classical age, the world's largest and for much of history its best-run bureaucracy was established, and civil service exams were invented.

The Chinese also pioneered the development of a whole range of basic technologies that were later disseminated over much of Eurasia and northern Africa. These ranged from paper and compasses, which created new possibilities for human communication and cross-cultural interaction, to water mills, which provided new sources of power and food processing, to porcelain, which elevated dining to unparalleled levels of elegance and opened up exciting possibilities for artistic expression. Over the centuries, beginning in the classical period, Chinese merchants and central Asian nomads disseminated these inventions over much of the globe, and have consequently contributed to technological transformations in societies as diverse as Japan, Rome, the Middle East, and England.

Chinese products had a major influence on the patterns of world trade that developed during the classical period. Fine Chinese silk was highly prized in India, the Middle East, and even the distant Roman Empire. Trade in silk and other luxury products generated a network of roads through central Asia known collectively as the Silk Road. Under the Han, the Chinese government actively encouraged trade with regions to the west. Improved roads, both in China and in the Middle East, also encouraged trade. One Chinese emissary, Zhang Qian, actually traveled to western India. Most trade along the Silk Road was carried by nomadic merchants. Until well after the classical period, no one seems to have traveled all the way from China to the Mediterranean or vice versa. But the trade was lively, spurring the development of sea routes in the Indian Ocean as well. While we do not know the volume of goods involved, the Silk Road trade was important enough to win considerable attention in upper-class and government circles, and it provided an initial framework on which global trading patterns would later be established.

China's role was greater still in the huge swath of territory from central Asia to the Pacific. Over much of central and east Asia, Chinese influence in political thought and organization, approaches to warfare, art and architecture, religion, and social norms was pervasive. For nearly 2000 years, China would serve as the "Middle Kingdom" for the diverse peoples of this vast area—the focus of their trade and the model for their often successful efforts to fashion their own variants of empire, prosperity, and sophistication.

Further Readings

Good introductions to life in China in the classical age can be found in Mark Edwards, *The Early Chinese Empire: Qin and Han* (2007), and Chun-shu Chang, *The Rise of the Chinese Empire* (2007). More detailed accounts of various aspects of the Qin-Han period have been contributed by (among others) Michael Loewe (Former Han Dynasty), Ying-shis Yü, (Foreign Relations), Patricia Ebrey and Sadao Nishijima (Economic and Social History), Robert Kramers (Confucian Thought) and Paul Demiéville (Philosophy and Religion) in Denis Twitchett and Michael Loewe, *Cambridge History of China*, vol. 1 (1986). Two works that deal extensively with the life and reign of Shi Huangdi are Arthur Cotterell's *The First Emperor of China* (1981) and Li Yu-Ning, ed. *The First Emperor of China* (1975).

A brief and clear introduction to Chinese thought is provided by Frederic Mote's *Intellectual Foundations of China* (1971). A much more detailed study that places Chinese thought in a comparative context can be found in Benjamin Schwartz's seminal *The World of Thought in Ancient China* (1983). For Confucius's teachings, see Roger Ames and Henry Rosemon, eds., *The Analects of Confucius* (1998). Michael Loewe's *Everyday Life in Early Imperial China* (1968) is excellent on Han society, as is the more detailed and scholarly work *Han Social Structure* (1972) by T'ung-Tsu Ch'u, which includes extensive quotations from Chinese texts and valuable insights into the position of women, merchants, artisans, and eunuchs. For the scholar-gentry, see Shirley Chan, *The Confucian Shi* (1993). The shifting position of women is the focus of Bret Hinsch's *Women in Early Imperial China* (2002). A detailed survey of the archeological work done on Han sites and what they tell us about Han society is provided by Wang Shongshu's *Han Civilization* (1982). Michèle Pirazzoli-t'serstevens's lavishly illustrated study *The Han Civilization of China* (1982) contains the most comprehensive, up-to-date, and readable overview of Han civilization available. Edmund Capon and William MacQuitty's *Princes of Jade* (1973) is less informative and reliable, but it also contains superb plates and illustrations.

The most authoritative and detailed account of science and technology in the Han and later dynastic periods can be found in Joseph Needham's multivolume *Science and Civilization in China* (1954–). For a more recent and abbreviated survey, see Yingke Deng, *Ancient Chinese Inventors* (2005) Burton Watson's *Courtier and Commoner in Ancient China* (1974), which is a translation of portions of Ban Ku's *History of the Former Han*, includes examples and anecdotes that allow the student to gain a vivid sense of the day-to-day workings of Han society. China's trade and cultural exchanges with neighboring civilizations are treated insightfully in Xinru Liu, *Ancient India and Ancient China: Trade and Religious Exchanges,* AD *1–600* (1988), and John Hill, *Through the Jade Gate to Rome* (2009). On warfare in the early classical period, see Roger Ames, ed., *Sun-Tzu: The Art of Warfare* (1993) and Stephen Turnbull, *The Fighting Ships of the Far East* (2002). For an engaging account of early China's relations with the wider world, see S.A.M. Adshead, *China in World History* (2000).

On MyHistoryLab

 Study and Review on MyHistoryLab

Critical Thinking Questions

1. What were some of the main factors that explain why the Qin dynasty lasted less than two decades while the Han ruled for nearly four centuries?

2. Discuss the most important innovations in methods of governance, technologies, and religious-philosophical systems that were developed in Qin-Han China. How many of them were later adopted or emulated worldwide? Compare and contrast Chinese interactions with nomadic pastoral peoples to the north and west to those with the sedentary-agrarian societies to the east and south across the China Seas and Indian Ocean.

5

Classical Civilizations in the Eastern Mediterranean and Middle East

((• Listen to Chapter 5
on MyHistoryLab

It is one of the most famous stories in history: In 490 B.C.E., the Greeks, under Athenian leaders, defeated a huge Persian army at Marathon. Fear of the Persians had run strong, and news of victory was accordingly sweet. According to legend, a Greek soldier named Pheidippides ran 26 miles to bring the word to Athens. Then, having delivered the message, he collapsed and died. The first modern Olympic Games, in 1896, featured a long-distance endurance race called the "marathon" in memory of that great feat. Pheidippides' run reminds us not only of a great military victory and strong emotion, but of the Greeks' powerful devotion to the public good of the cities they loved.

The Persian invasion of Greece began as a punishment for the revolt of several Greek city-states against Persian rule—a revolt the Persians had easily put down (see Map 5.1). Immediately following the Greek victory at the battle of Marathon, the Persians tried to attack Athens by sea, but the Athenian soldiers had hurried back to defend their city. Vowing revenge, the Persians returned to Asia.

FIGURE **5.1** This famous statue depicts Pheidippides, the Athenian soldier who, according to legend, ran 26 miles to bring his fellow citizens news of victory at the Battle of Marathon and died as he made the announcement. The 26-mile endurance run was named the "marathon" to commemorate Pheidippides's heroic feat.

👁 Watch the Video Series on MyHistoryLab

Learn about some key topics related to this chapter with the *MyHistoryLab Video Series: Key Topics in World History*

A new Persian king, Xerxes, took personal charge of the plan to conquer the Greeks. By 480 B.C.E., he had amassed an army and fleet that outnumbered Greek forces by two to one. Many Greek states held back, assuming the Persians would win this time. Even the Greek priests, trying to foretell the future, urged surrender. To make matters worse, a Greek traitor showed the Persians a mountain pass that, when seized by the Persians, rendered Athens indefensible. Most Athenians were evacuated to an island, where they watched the Persians set fire to their temples on the hill of the Acropolis. But Themistocles, the Athenian leader, realized that the huge Persian navy could not move fast. If it could be led into a narrow strait, where its numbers could not maneuver easily, it could be defeated. Themistocles sent a slave to trick Xerxes, telling him that the Greeks were quarreling among themselves. Thinking that this was their chance to finish off the Greeks, the Persians rowed into the narrow strait of Thermopylae. There, instead of

🔍 **View the Closer Look on MyHistoryLab:** Persepolis: A Royal City

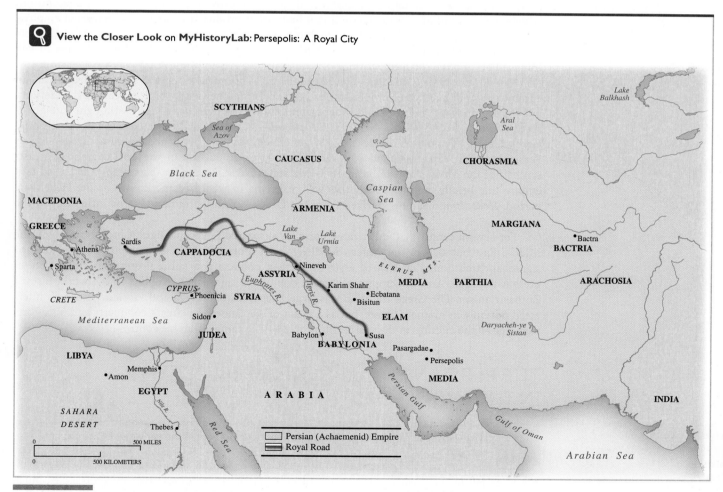

MAP **5.1 The Persian Empire in Its Main Stages** At its height the Persian empire stretched through much of the Middle East to the shores of the Mediterranean, into Egypt, and into the northeast part of the Indian subcontinent.

the divided Greek force they were expecting, they found that every man the Greeks had available was ready to fight them. Xerxes watched the battle from a hill overlooking the strait, where he had thought he would be able to see and reward the bravest of his warriors. Instead he saw his navy virtually destroyed and he fled. ■

History is full of might-have-beens. It is important to consider what would have happened if the normal advantage in military strength had prevailed and the Persians had won and what difference this would have made to world history.

One point is sure. The battle highlighted the developments of not one but two major civilizations in the eastern Mediterranean and Middle East. A massive Persian empire developed, spurred initially by the kind of outside invasion that had earlier produced various Mesopotamian empires. But the Persian Empire grew far larger, illustrating the new capacities of the classical period. Durable political and cultural traditions were established that persisted in and around what is present-day Iran well beyond the classical period.

At the same time, Greek city-states established a presence along the eastern Mediterranean and into parts of southern Europe. Like China and Persia, the Greeks built on earlier civilizations, but they established a strong and independent culture of their own. Greeks thought foreigners' speech sounded funny—like "bar, bar, bar" noises—so they called them barbarians, establishing Greek identity by contrast. Greek society generated less tidy political structures than China or Persia, but their expansion and outreach affected a large portion of western Asia and the eastern half of the Mediterranean basin. As Greek states faded, Alexander the Great forged a military empire that briefly embraced Persia as well, ushering in what became known as the Hellenistic period. *Hellenism*, meaning "derived from the Greek," extended durable Greek influences in the region.

For several centuries, the Persian empire far surpassed Greece in significance, certainly in the Middle East but also in the eastern Mediterranean more generally. The empire also established significant traditions that shaped a strong Persian political and cultural presence, still visible in present-day Iran. And the empire generated one of the significant religions in the world history, Zoroastrianism. The Greek tradition was largely separate, but Greek and Persian influences interacted not only in mutual warfare, but as a result of Alexander the Great's conquests and his efforts to merge all the cultures in the vast territory that briefly came under his control.

THE PERSIAN EMPIRE: A NEW PERSPECTIVE IN THE MIDDLE EAST

The Persians worked quickly to unify their huge empire. They established durable political and cultural traditions in the process.

5.1 Why was the rise of Persia such an important development in the early part of the classical period?

After the fall of the great Egyptian and Hittite empires in the Middle East by 1200 B.C.E., much smaller states predominated. Then new powers stepped in, first the Assyrians and then an influx of Persians. A great conqueror, **Cyrus the Great**, emerged by 550 B.C.E. and established the massive Persian Empire, which ran across the northern Middle East and into northwestern India. The new

500 B.C.E.	400 B.C.E.	300 B.C.E.
500–449 Greek defeat of Persia; spread of Athenian empire **470–430** Athens at its height: Pericles, Phidias, Sophocles, Socrates **431–404** Peloponnesian Wars	**399** Socrates condemned **384–322** Aristotle **359–336** Philip II of Macedon **338–323** Macedonian Empire; Alexander the Great **334** Alexander defeats Persians, end of Persian empire	**300–100** Hellenistic period **250–126** Flourishing of Hellenistic astronomy and mathematics

empire was the clearest successor to the great Mesopotamian states of the past, but it was far larger. Cyrus allowed some parts of the empire to preserve older traditions, such as the use of cuneiform writing, but he introduced important changes as well. In addition to their territorial expansion, the Persians significantly advanced iron technology in the Middle East. In terms of timing and achievements, the rise of Persia neatly illustrates some of the key innovations of the classical period.

Cyrus the Great Established massive Persian empire by 550 B.C.E.; successor state to Mesopotamian empires.

Political Innovations

Persian politics featured several themes that can be compared to the core features of classical China. The first was wide tolerance. The Persian empire embraced a host of languages and cultures, and the early Persian rulers were careful to grant considerable latitude for this diversity. In 539 Cyrus issued a proclamation, sometimes termed the first human rights statement, promising humane treatment and religious freedom to all inhabitants. Second, however, was a strong authoritarian streak. Darius, successor to Cyrus, worked hard to centralize laws and tax collection. The idea of wide participation in politics was rejected (see Figure 5.2). Third, and related to the centralization process, Persian rulers developed a vital infrastructure for the whole empire. A major system of roads reduced travel time, although it still took 90 days to go from one end of the empire to the other. An east–west highway, largely paved, simplified commerce and troop movement from the Indian border to the Mediterranean, and another highway reached Egypt. The Persians established the first regular postal service, and they built a network of inns along their roads to accommodate travelers. These achievements would help connect the Middle East to trade routes coming from central and eastern Asia, a vital step in the growth of new commercial connections.

Zoroastrianism [zôr O as trEE uh niz uhm, zOr-] Animist religion that saw material existence as battle between forces of good and evil; stressed the importance of moral choice; righteous lived on after death in "House of Song"; chief religion of Persian Empire.

Persian emperors, particularly Darius, who worked hard not only to expand but to integrate his vast territories, developed a substantial bureaucracy. This existed alongside an earlier military nobility. The central government introduced several measures to control the activities of officials assigned to distant provinces. Tax collection was carefully regulated, and spies were sent out to make sure regional officials remained loyal to the central government, rather than allying with local political forces.

Persia was also the center of a major new religion. A Persian religious philosopher, Zoroaster (c. 630–550 B.C.E.), revised the polytheistic religious tradition of the Sumerians through the introduction of monotheism. He banned animal sacrifice and the use of intoxicants. He introduced the idea of individual salvation through the free choice of God over the spirit of evil. Zoroaster, and the growing group of Zoroastrian priests (the *Magi*) saw life as a battle between two divine forces: good and evil. **Zoroastrianism** (zohr-oh-AS-tree-uh-NIH-zuhm) emphasized the importance of personal moral choice in picking one side or the other, with a Last Judgment ultimately deciding the eternal fate of each person. The righteous would live on in a heaven, the "House of Song," while the evil would be condemned to eternal pain. Zoroastrianism influenced Persia's later emperors and spread widely in the population as a whole. A Greek

Read the Document on MyHistoryLab: Darius the Great: Ruler of Persia (522 B.C.E.)

FIGURE 5.2 Using ceremonial styles similar to those of earlier Mesopotamia, the Persian Empire celebrated its powerful kings. This wall relief is on the great ceremonial stairway leading to the royal audience hall of Darius and Xerxes.

View the **Closer Look** on **MyHistoryLab**: Zoroastrianism: An Ancient Religion in Modern Times

FIGURE 5.3 Persians established a distinct artistic tradition including fine craftwork, as shown in this chariot.

Read the **Document** on **MyHistoryLab**: The "Cyrus Cylinder"

traveler, Herodotus, noted that the Persian religion was much more spiritual than that of the Greeks, for the Persians did not believe in humanlike gods.

Indeed, the Persian religious influence would prove far greater than that of the Greeks, although Greek culture had wide impact in other respects. Only small groups of Zoroastrians survive in the world today, in Iran and through immigration in a few other places, including the United States. But the religion retained a wide hold for a considerable period of time, and its beliefs—such as the struggle between good and evil—and even terms such as *shaitan* or *Satan* strongly affected Judaism, Christianity, and Islam. Religion did not consume all of Persian cultural energies. An important artistic tradition also emerged with distinctive styles of painting and architecture (Figure 5.3).

Later kings expanded Persian holdings. They were unable to conquer Greece, but they long dominated much of the Middle East, providing an extensive period of peace and prosperity. Conquests also extended into North Africa and the Indian river valley. At its height, Persia embraced at least 14 million people. The population of Persia proper (present-day Iran), at four million people, had doubled under imperial rule (Map 5.1). Ultimately, the Persian Empire was toppled by Alexander the Great, a Greek-educated conqueror. Persian language and culture survived in the northeastern portion of the Middle East, periodically affecting developments in the region as a whole. After the Hellenistic period, a series of Persian empires arose in the northeastern part of the Middle East, competing with Roman holdings and later states.

Persian political institutions strongly impressed Alexander and his successors. Persian art would affect not only the region, but also India and the wider Middle East. Zoroastrianism, one of the major belief systems of the classical period, would ultimately fade in its competition with Islam, but its hold and influences continued well beyond the classical centuries.

THE POLITICAL CHARACTER OF CLASSICAL GREECE

Like the Chinese, Greek civilization placed great emphasis on political life. Greece encouraged various forms of political organization.

5.2   What are the main issues in defining the Greek political legacy?

Slightly before the Persian empire took shape, small Greek political units gradually emerged. A key spur to Greek civilization was a general revival of trade in the eastern Mediterranean. Trade allowed many Greek city-states (including Greek-dominated cities in Greece and Mediterranean Asia, particularly in what is now Turkey) to increase their wealth and their range of contacts. By 700 B.C.E., several Greek centers had trading connections around the Black Sea and in Egypt and southern Italy.

During the 8th century B.C.E., the Greeks adapted the Phoenician alphabet for writing their own language. This alphabet was easier to learn than any previous writing system. The advancement of literacy further stimulated trade by aiding in the exchange of commercial information and enhancing cultural life. At this point two great poems, the ***Iliad*** and the ***Odyssey***, which focused on the legendary Mycenaean war with Troy, were written down, possibly by the poet Homer, to whom they were attributed, or by a larger group of writers gradually formalizing oral tradition. The Homeric achievement set forth definitions of the gods and human nature that profoundly shaped later Greek thinking. A distinctive Greek art also began to emerge, emphasizing the rectangular temple. Greek sculptors, initially relying on Egyptian precedent, moved toward exceptionally lifelike forms (Figure 5.4).

Iliad Greek epic poem attributed to Homer but possibly the work of many authors; defined gods and human nature that shaped Greek mythos.

Odyssey Greek epic poem attributed to Homer but possibly the work of many authors; defined gods and human nature that shaped Greek mythos.

The City-State as a Political Unit

Greek politics took shape in the three centuries after 800 B.C.E. Greek government revolved around the city-state, a regional government centered in a major city, embracing the surrounding agricultural land as well. These units could be tiny or large, like Sparta, one of the key city-states. Athens, the most famous city-state, was about the size of the state of Rhode Island. By the 5th century B.C.E., Athens had a population of roughly 250,000, of whom 100,000 lived in the city proper. The city-state government came naturally to Greece, partly because a mountainous terrain made larger connections difficult (Map 5.2). By 600 B.C.E., nearly 300 independent cities had developed in Greece and surrounding regions. Although the city-state form promoted frequent wars because no single unit predominated, it did encourage a political life of unusual intensity. This explains why the Greek word for city-state government—*polis* (plural *poleis*)—is the origin of our word *politics*.

Early Greek poleis were ruled mainly by land-owning aristocrats, mostly descendants of the Indo-European warrior class who were still responsible for most military activities. Free farmers were also citizens, supporting the government and often participating in periodic assemblies but not ruling directly. Councils played a vital role in the early Greek city-states, even when there was a single king or other ruler.

This system increasingly was challenged from about 700 B.C.E. onward. With the commercial expansion that began in the 8th century, aristocratic rule often was disputed. Some city-states escaped major contests, remaining largely agricultural. Sparta maintained a strong militaristic regime under aristocratic leadership. But in active trading centers, merchants and a growing urban manufacturing group chafed under aristocratic rule. Furthermore, in many areas agriculture itself changed. Landlords began to specialize in growing olives and grapes and in making cooking oil and wines. They began importing cheap grain from colonies in Asia, Egypt, and Sicily to provide basic foodstuffs. These imports squeezed out local independent farmers, widening the gulf between the rich and poor. The ideals of widespread citizenship were contradicted by these developments.

Solon Athenian reformer of the 6th century; established laws that eased burden of debt on farmers, forbade enslavement for debt.

The result by the 6th century B.C.E. was growing social protest, pitting urban groups and dispossessed farmers against the aristocratic elite. Several tyrants emerged, winning popular support against the aristocratic interest. Then reformers, like Solon in 6th century Athens, tried to restore earlier ideals of citizenship while dealing with the new social tensions. **Solon** (SOH-luhn) set up laws that would ease the burden of debts on the farmers by prohibiting slavery for such debts. The idea developed that laws could be written and revised, rather than being passed down unaltered from tradition; here was one source of new political interest and participation.

Other forces pressed for political change. Military activity increasingly involved larger numbers of citizens who formed tightly organized and well-coordinated lines of infantry. Naval forces in the port cities, such as Athens, depended on extensive recruitment of rowers. This development increased the need for strong bonds between citizens within the polis and gave new leverage to nonaristocrats. By 500 B.C.E., participation in public life became a widespread ideal in many poleis; it corresponded to the busy functions that grouped city dwellers together in the marketplace.

The dominant religion also supported this ideal of political unity and involvement. Each

MAP **5.2 The Greek World** Key regions of Greece and its islands, with key colonial cities across the Aegean, in what is now Turkey.

FIGURE **5.4** Vase design was also vital in Greek art. After murdering his wife and children, Hercules, who became the Greeks' greatest mythical hero, was sentenced to perform twelve tasks that would have been impossible for most mortals. This vase depicts the fourth labor of Hercules, in which he was ordered to capture the Erymanthian boar and bring it to his master, Eurystheus. The frightened Eurystheus has hidden in a wine jar.

(Copyright The British Museum)

Pericles Athenian political leader during 5th century B.C.E.; guided development of Athenian Empire; died during early stages of Peloponnesian War.

 Read the **Document** on **MyHistoryLab**: Aristotle, The Creation of the Democracy in Athens

city-state had its own patron god or goddess, and regular rituals called forth prayer and ceremony on behalf of the city's well-being. In 399 B.C.E., the philosopher Socrates was condemned by a jury in Athens for corrupting his students by encouraging skepticism and doubt. Given a choice between exile and death, he chose death. Socrates said the city had been the source of his character and he owed it obedience; better to die than to be apart.

The Rise of Democracy in Athens

After the period of greatest social tension, city-state governments continued to vary. Aristocratic councils returned in many places. Sparta had two kings to check each other, ruling on behalf of the military aristocracy. Generally, however, a democratic tendency gained ground by the 5th century B.C.E., and here Athens proudly took the lead.

Full-blown Athenian democracy, after a few additional reforms about 462 B.C.E., depended on a popular assembly as sovereign authority. All decisions of state emanated from this body or had to be approved by it, and all citizens could debate or propose in assembly meetings. This was direct democracy—the word *democracy* comes from the Greek word for people, *demos*—rather than rule through elected representatives. Because the assembly met frequently, only a minority of citizens had time to attend regularly, and a few leading speakers usually predominated. Citizens also served as jurors in court trials, and every judicial decision could be appealed to a citizen board. Most officials were selected by lot on the grounds that any citizen could serve as an administrator. A few key officials—the generals and imperial treasurers—were elected, usually from the nobility, but the assembly could remove or punish them for faulty service. Terms of office were brief, to encourage popular control.

This was a democracy of a different sort from the version common in the contemporary world. It depended on the small size of the city-state and the intensive participation of its citizens. Furthermore, many adults were excluded from political rights. Women had no rights of political participation. Half of all adult males were not citizens in any sense, being slaves or foreigners. Even at its most democratic, the Athenian government was shaped by considerable aristocratic behind-the-scenes control. The Athenian leader **Pericles** (PEHR-uh-kleez) guided Athens during its decades of greatest glory after the mid-5th century B.C.E. Pericles was an aristocrat who managed to direct affairs year after year through wise manipulation of political groups and his own prestige, even when he did not hold formal office. Many Athenians, and still more Greeks in city-states where democracy did not go as far, persisted in believing that real political virtue lay in aristocratic rule (*aristocracy* was derived from the Greek word *aristos*, or "the best").

Athenian democracy rested far more directly on the public devotion and talent of citizens than modern democracies do. Citizen juries handled trials of officials accused of serving badly. The names of politicians judged to be potential tyrants were scratched on *ostraka*, or pottery fragments. If one name was listed often enough, the person was banished—ostracized—for 10 years.

By the end of the 5th century, when Athens plunged into a devastating war with Sparta, the polis demonstrated some of the weaknesses as well as the strengths of democracy. Ordinary citizens worked hard in the war, but the lower-class citizens, eager for government jobs and booty, often pressed for reckless expeditions that weakened the state in its military efforts and contributed substantially to ultimate defeat.

Greek and Chinese Political Styles Compared

The Greek political approach involved intense emphasis on political virtue and responsibility. Participation in politics was part of the ideal life. This was true in aristocratic states as well as in the less typical democracies. This approach, with its concern for a sound political system, reflected some similarities with the values Confucianism emphasized in China. But in the decentralized atmosphere of Greek politics, a far larger array of political structures was tossed up than was true in China, with its greater emphasis on a single centralized system. Also, the Greeks placed more value on participation (including the idea of citizenship) than on hierarchy and obedience. There was more emphasis on formal preparation of law (a theme the Romans later extended) and far less emphasis on a bureaucracy and bureaucratic codes.

Greek Diplomacy and the Tensions of United Effort

During the four centuries when Greek political forms evolved, many city-states established colonies in other regions, which expanded exposure to Greek political values. Colonies helped relieve population pressure at home. They also provided vital grain supplies while serving as markets for processed products, including wine, cooking oil, and manufactured goods. By the 5th century B.C.E., Greek colonies dotted the Mediterranean coast of present-day Turkey, the entire coastline of the Black Sea, and key points in northern Africa, Italy, southern France, and Spain. Map 5.3 shows the key centers of the Greek colonial empire. By providing new wealth, colonies supported the political and cultural vigor of Greece.

At their best, from 750 to 420 B.C.E., the Greek city-states were capable of considerable coordination. They joined in regular celebrations such as the athletic competitions of the **Olympic Games**, which grouped wrestlers, runners, and other athletes in often bitter (and occasionally rigged) competitions. They supported some common religious organizations, such as the **oracle at Delphi** (DELF-eye) whose predictions and advice were widely sought.

More important was the collaboration that allowed Greece to defend itself against its most pressing outside enemy, the great empire of Persia. Soon after Cyrus the Great created the Persian empire, he turned against wealthy Greek colonies along the Asian side of the Mediterranean and conquered them by about 540 B.C.E. (see Map 5.1). In 499 B.C.E. the conquered Greek cities rebelled against the Persians and were aided by the Athenian navy. The rebellion failed, and the Persian kings (Darius I, then Xerxes) moved against Greece in punishment. In 480 B.C.E., a Persian army of 100,000 troops moved down the Greek peninsula and captured Athens, destroying much of the city. Athenian and Spartan cooperation led to Persian defeats on both land and sea. While Persia continued to dominate the Middle East, Greek independence was preserved. The greatest age of Greek politics and culture followed, including the perfection of Athenian political institutions and the Age of Pericles.

Olympic Games One of the pan-Hellenic rituals observed by all Greek city-states; involved athletic competitions and ritual celebrations.

oracle at Delphi Person representing the god Apollo; allegedly received cryptic messages from the god that had predictive value if the seeker could correctly interpret the communication.

MAP **5.3 Greece and Greek Colonies of the World, c. 431** B.C.E. On the eve of the Peloponnesian War, Greek civilization had spread throughout the eastern Mediterranean.

Delian league Alliance formed by Athens after the Persian Wars; cities contributed to unified treasury on island of Delos to support alliance fleet; later taken over by Athens and became Athenian empire.

In the years after Persia's defeat, Athens began to form an empire of its own. Athenian naval power helped organize an alliance of lesser Greek cities (see Map 5.3). This **Delian League** was headed by an Athenian admiral, and its treasury was controlled by Athens. Increasingly, many cities became completely dependent on Athenian rule without having a voice in policy. The empire provided great resources for Athens, but its wealth complicated Athenian politics. The city included increasing numbers of noncitizens, and the spoils of political office became increasingly attractive and highly contested. Politicians competed to find ways to spend money and curry popular favor. Many Athenians wondered whether authoritarian control of colonies based on military force and heavy tribute payment was compatible with free political life at home. Certainly this type of expansion was different from China's, where integrating most new territory into a single political entity gained great attention. In contrast, city-states, even democracies such as Athens, tended to look on colonies as centers to exploit for wealth and supplies, paying less attention to durable regional linkages.

Athens Versus Sparta

The growing imperial power of Athens attracted competition from Sparta, which had its own alliance system of land-based city-states. Competition in the Greek peninsula increased in the later 5th century B.C.E., with each side fearing that the other might gain a dominant position. Rivalry was heightened by ideological conflicts that some historians have compared with the cold war between the capitalist United States and the communist Soviet Union in the decades after World War II. Sparta stood for the old Greece before its alteration by extensive commerce and massive political change. Aristocratic rule had been transformed into a highly military regime in which boys were trained for battle and girls for the bearing of brave sons. Spartan militarism was designed to control a large force of near-slaves, who did the agricultural work. Use of money was discouraged by minting coins of unwieldy size. Discipline and control were the themes of Spartan society.

Unlike Sparta, Athens encouraged extensive trade and a vibrant, creative culture, and its democracy contrasted with the narrow aristocratic dominance of Sparta. Both sides were aware of their differences and intensely disliked the principles of the rival society. Both also drew allies from like-minded poleis. Sparta had unexpected advantages because its traditional principles were widely admired, even by some aristocratic Athenians. The heavy-handedness of Athens's empire drew hostility from many smaller cities.

Peloponnesian Wars Wars from 431 to 404 B.C.E. between Athens and Sparta for dominance in southern Greece; resulted in Spartan victory but failure to achieve political unification of Greece.

Outright conflict broke out in 431 B.C.E., over rival claims to a colonial city-state. In the resultant **Peloponnesian** (PEL-uh-poh-nee-zhun) **Wars**, the Athenian strategy was to let Sparta invade its countryside while relying on its fleet to maintain supplies and to raid the Spartan coast. But during the second year of the war, a massive plague broke out in Athens, ultimately killing one-third of the population, including Pericles. Grievances rose in Athens, and there was no longer a leader to provide consistent guidance. A victory over Spartan troops brought a chance for peace, but a warlike faction in Athens insisted on continuing the war, seeking to conquer new territory while wasting precious Athenian resources. Self-serving leaders and ordinary people eager for war booty kept the conflict going—a reminder that, at least in the classical world, democracy did not guarantee either peace or good sense. A new attempt to invade Sicily to seek new colonies failed, costing Athens more than 200 ships, 4500 men, and the support of many allies. Finally, in 404 B.C.E., a Spartan general cut off the Athenian food supply. The city had to surrender. Athens was deprived of its remaining ships, and the city walls were torn down. A political age came to an end, not only in Athens but in all of Greece.

THE HELLENISTIC PERIOD

A weak and divided Greece was conquered by the Macedonians, who built an empire under Alexander the Great. Alexander's conquests reached as far as Persia and India, spreading Greek culture across western Asia.

| **5.3** | How did the Hellenistic centuries link Greece and Persia? |

Spartan domination of Greece, after the collapse of Athens, did not work well. Periodic wars against the Persians and among key Greek states dominated the first half of the 4th century. By 355 B.C.E., Greece had returned to a setting of independent, disorganized city-states, many of them exhausted by decades of war and civil strife.

Macedonian Conquest

Into this power vacuum came a new force from the kingdom of **Macedon** (MAS-ih-dohn) on the northern borders of Greece. Macedonian conquests in turn opened a period of three centuries in which Greek culture spread widely in Egypt and far into western Asia. This expansion of Greek influence and culture, but also its interactions with other traditions including Persia's, is called **Hellenism**. Greek city-states persisted in this new Hellenistic world, but they were no longer the dominant forms. In geography, politics, and to an extent culture, a new era opened in the 4th century B.C.E. The roots of the new order lay in the rise of a Macedonian dynasty, which conquered first Greece and then the Persian Empire within two generations.

The kingdom of Macedon, to the north of Greece, was semibarbaric by Greek standards. Its residents spoke Greek, and Macedonian kings had long been interested in Greek culture. When **Philip II** (r. 359–336 B.C.E.) seized power, he strengthened the monarchy within Macedon and then turned his attention to the chaos of Greece. Skilled both as a general and as a diplomat, Philip soon developed a strong army that had more flexible tactics than the standard citizen force of the poleis. By seizing some northern Greek territory, he gained the resources to pay mercenary troops and peasant soldiers. Then he turned to the divided city-states of central Greece.

Despite warnings by insightful leaders, states such as Athens were no longer willing to make major sacrifices for self-defense. Philip also found allies in Greek statesmen who wanted a new unity, even if it was imposed from the outside. Finally, in 338 B.C.E., Philip won a decisive battle, aided by a cavalry charge led by his 18-year-old son Alexander. Macedon now ruled the bulk of Greece, and while the city-states retained their governments with rights of internal administration, Macedonian garrisons ensured tax tributes and loyalty to the new kingdom.

Macedon Kingdom located in northern Greece; originally loosely organized under kings, became centralized under Philip II; served as basis for unification of Greece and later Macedonian Empire.

Hellenism Culture derived from the Greek civilization that flourished between 300 and 100 B.C.E.

Philip II Ruled Macedon from 359 to 336 B.C.E.; founder of centralized kingdom; later conquered rest of Greece, which was subjected to Macedonian authority.

Alexander the Great Successor of Philip II; successfully conquered Persian Empire prior to his death in 323 B.C.E.; attempted to combine Greek and Persian cultures.

Alexander the Great

Philip's death left the next stage of Macedonian expansion to Alexander, who gained power at the age of 20 (Figure 5.5). **Alexander the Great**, eager to continue his father's conquest, turned to the target of the Persian Empire, still vast but now weakly ruled. In 334 B.C.E., Alexander moved into Asia with about 35,000 troops. Daring triumphs brought him control of the Persian side of the Mediterranean coast. Then, in 333 B.C.E., Alexander defeated the main Persian army led by its emperor in Syria (Map 5.4).

Persian efforts to sue for peace were ignored: Alexander wanted the whole empire and more. He moved into Egypt, now a weakened regional state, where he was greeted as pharaoh and son of a god. By 331 B.C.E., he entered Babylon and then seized the vast Persian treasury, as the Greeks and Macedonians gained revenge for the many Persian threats to their homeland. Alexander pressed into India, but he finally had to stop because his men refused to advance: They had won victories against relatively small Indian border states only at great cost and feared a worse fate should they move against the much more formidable Indian states that lay before them.

Alexander planned a dazzling future for his new empire, hoping to merge Greek and Persian institutions and values and add further conquests. He founded many cities bearing his name, including **Alexandria, Egypt**. He spread Macedonian and Greek officials through his vast new Middle Eastern holdings. Alexander also encouraged intermarriage with Persian and other local women, a practice in which he himself set an example. Eager to promote a Hellenistic culture, he founded centers of scholarship in Greek learning, but he also recognized the need to accommodate various traditions in a multinational empire. Whether he could have succeeded in consolidating his unprecedented holdings, given his vision and organizational skills, cannot be known, for he died of a fever in Babylon at the age of 33.

Later Hellenistic States

Alexander's unexpected death quickly brought disunity to the new empire, although not an end to the Hellenistic enterprise. Quarrels among his successors allowed key generals to seize the major provinces as kings. Three major regional dynasties resulted: one

View the Closer Look on MyHistoryLab: Alexander and Darius at the Battle of Issus

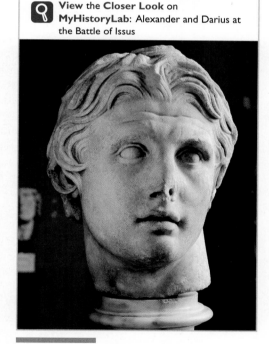

FIGURE **5.5** Alexander came to the throne of Macedonia at the age of 20. Within two years, he had set out to make his mark on the world, accompanied by 35,000 soldiers and an elite group of engineers, architects, scientists, and historians. Alexander the Great, as he came to be called, inspired the love and loyalty of his men by knowing their strengths and weaknesses, praising their courage, arranging games to test their skills, tending the wounded, and holding lavish funerals for the dead. Their conquests spread Greek learning and culture across the Middle East.

Alexandria, Egypt One of the cities founded by and named for Alexander the Great; site of ancient Mediterranean's greatest library; center of literary studies.

Ptolemies One of the regional dynasties that followed the death of Alexander the Great; founded in Egypt; flourished 305 to 30 B.C.E.

Seleucids [si IU sids, -cids] One of the regional dynasties that followed the death of Alexander the Great; founded in Mesopotamia.

Antigonids One of the regional dynasties that followed the death of Alexander the Great; founded in Macedonia and Greece.

in Egypt (the **Ptolemies** (TOHL-uh-meez), which ended with the suicide of the famous queen, Cleopatra, in 31 B.C.E.; another in Mesopotamia (the **Seleucids** (sih-LOO-sihdz)); and one in Macedonia and Greece (the **Antigonids** (an-TIHG-uh-nihdz).

An important but short-lived kingdom, Bactria, in northwestern India (present-day Pakistan), served as an unusual point of cultural exchange in the classical period. Indian artists used Greek themes, portraying even Buddha in Greek costume, and mathematical knowledge was exchanged. Greeks stationed in Bactria sometimes converted to Buddhism or Hinduism, often combining these religions with their earlier beliefs. These religions were not brought back to the Mediterranean, but Indian ideas of personal holiness had some impact on Hellenistic philosophy and may have influenced later religious life, including the rise of Christianity.

The major successor states enjoyed about 125 years of vigor and prosperity. Trade in Greek goods continued to flourish, and all the new kings encouraged commerce. Many Greeks moved toward the government jobs and merchant positions available in the Middle East. However, wealth centered on the city dwellers and the Hellenized upper classes (regardless of whether of Greek origin), while native peasants suffered from high taxes and the lack of adequate land. Internal divisions caused a decline in production, and warfare between the kingdoms weakened the successor states and opened them to outside attack. In the 2nd century B.C.E., Rome moved actively into this vacuum, expanding its own empire.

The two centuries of Hellenism marked the end of the characteristically Greek political style. City-states continued to exist officially, and they maintained some functions even later under

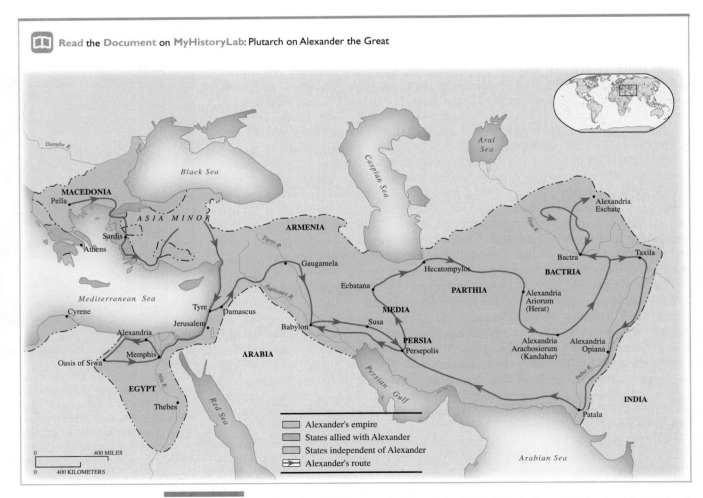

Read the Document on MyHistoryLab: Plutarch on Alexander the Great

MAP **5.4 Alexander's Empire and the Hellenistic World, c. 323** B.C.E. Note the movement through Persia and other parts of the northern Middle East and into the Indian subcontinent and North Africa.

VISUALIZING THE PAST

Political Rituals in Persia

THIS IS A RELIEF FROM THE Audience Hall of the Persian royal Palace in Persepolis, built by Darius I (522–486 B.C.E.). The scene shows court rituals in Persia. Later, when Alexander conquered Persia, he was inclined to install the same rituals, but many of his soldiers objected vigorously, and the whole issue caused great furor in the ranks. It has been speculated, however, that some of these rituals later passed to Europe, where they helped define appropriate behavior in the presence of kings.

QUESTIONS

- What kinds of rituals does this scene suggest, and what kinds of relationships between subjects and the emperor?
- Why, and on what basis, might Greeks object to this kind of behavior toward a ruler?
- Why was Alexander tempted to transfer these rituals to his own court?

Roman control. But they no longer served as intense focal points because of the control exercised by foreign monarchs. Hellenistic politics centered on military empires.

Hellenism promoted wide exchanges. Contacts not only with India but also with the African kingdom of Kush had important effects, including expanded trade and some use of war elephants, the armored tanks of the classical era. Hellenistic leaders also generated innovations, particularly in science. The spread of Greek-derived culture, then, set a new framework for intellectual life in a large and diverse portion of the civilized world, in the Middle East and North Africa as well as in southeastern Europe. This was Hellenism's most lasting legacy.

GREEK AND HELLENISTIC CULTURE

5.4 What was the relationship between Greek religion and Greek philosophy?

> Greek civilization was defined more by its art and philosophy than by politics. It had far less religious impact than did Persia. Hellenistic contributions added to the Greek legacy for later civilizations.

Indo-Europeans brought into Greece beliefs and stories about various gods and goddesses. With time, these developed into a regional religion while also inspiring art and literature. Opportunities to learn from Egypt and the Middle East—Greece sent students directly to Egypt in fields like mathematics—helped generate further work in the sciences and in philosophy.

Religion, Philosophy, and Science

The Greeks did not create a major religion with strong spiritual appeal. In this they differed from Persia, China, and especially India. Greek ideas ultimately influenced great religions, particularly Christianity and to some degree Islam, but this came later. The characteristic Greek religion was derived from belief in the spirits of nature, elevated into a complex set of gods and goddesses who were seen as interfering in human life. Regular ceremonies to the gods had real political importance, and many people sought the gods' aid in foretelling the future or ensuring a good harvest or good health. Stories of the gods' activities provided rich entertainment and could drive home lessons about appropriate moral behavior, including courage and humility.

This religion, passed down from earlier Indo-European experience, cemented community loyalties. Interestingly, the basic Indo-European pantheon of gods was the same as that brought to India, which in both cases assumed human form (see Chapter 6). However, the Greek religion tended toward a human-centered, worldly approach that differed considerably from India's more otherworldly beliefs. Greek stories of the gods and heroes illustrated human qualities, rather like large-scale soap operas; the gods could be jealous, sneaky, lustful, and powerful. In the cultures of both Greece and India, religion helped engender an important literary tradition. The gods provided good stories or served as vehicles for deeper inquiry into human passions and weaknesses. But Greek writers mainly used the gods to explore human nature, not to seek a higher spiritual experience.

The lack of spiritual passion in Greek religion failed to satisfy many ordinary workers and peasants, particularly when times were hard because of political chaos or economic distress. Popular "mystery" religions, which had more exciting rituals and promised greater spiritual insight, often swept through Greece. They offered secret ceremonies, a strong sense of fellowship, and greater focus on divine powers. The mystery religions to some extent paralleled Daoism in providing a contrast to more politically directed religion or philosophy, although none of the mystery religions won the currency or durability of Daoism in China.

Greek religion did not promote systematic thinking about nature or ethics. Hence, from at least the 6th century onward, many Greek thinkers attempted to generate philosophical systems that were separate from a primarily religious base. Their work also reflected the challenge of new contacts with Persian and other Middle Eastern cultural systems. The resultant attempt to understand humankind, society, and nature by rational observation and deduction became one of the hallmarks of Greek and Hellenistic culture.

Many thinkers sought to generate ethical systems on the basis of rational definitions of right and wrong. **Socrates** (SOHK-rah-teez) (b. 465 B.C.E.)—the tutor of Plato, who in turn would teach the philosopher Aristotle—urged people to consider the basis of right action in terms of rational reflection on goals and consequences. In contrast to Zoroastrianism, he thus formulated secular criteria rather than devising rewards and punishments from an otherworldly system. **Aristotle** (AR-ih-STOH-tul), the most important Greek philosopher and the teacher of Alexander the Great, maintained this ethical system by stressing the importance of moderation in human behavior against the instability of political life in Athens and the excesses of the gods.

During the Hellenistic period, other ethical systems were devised. A group called the **Stoics** (STOH-ihks) emphasized an inner moral independence, to be cultivated by strict discipline of the body and personal bravery. These ethical systems were major contributions in their own right, attracting many disciples and generating much literary debate; they were later blended with Christian religious thought.

Greek philosophy devoted much attention to defining appropriate political structures—not surprisingly, given the various Greek constitutional systems. The Athenian philosopher **Plato** (PLAY-toh) in the 5th century B.C.E., devised an ideal government structure in which philosophers would rule. Most Greek political theories stressed the importance of balance between aristocratic principles and some popular contribution. Aristotle also discussed social topics such as slavery and the role and status of women, providing vigorous defenses for the inevitability and usefulness of slavery and for family structures that assumed women's inferiority.

A philosophy separate from official religion, although not necessarily hostile to it, also placed considerable emphasis on the powers of human thought. In Athens, Socrates encouraged his pupils to question received wisdom on the ground that the chief human duty was "the improvement of the soul." Socrates ran afoul of the Athenian government in the aftermath of the Peloponnesian War, for he seemed to be undermining political loyalty with his constant questions. But the Socratic principle of thinking things through by means of skeptical questioning, rather than relying on authority or faith, became a recurrent strand in classical Greek philosophy.

Greek interest in rationality carried over to the underlying order of physical nature. The Greeks were not great scientists compared with the classical Chinese. Few new scientific findings came from Athens, although philosophers such as Aristotle collected large amounts of biological data.

Socrates Athenian philosopher of later 5th century B.C.E.; tutor of Plato; urged rational reflection of moral decisions; condemned to death for corrupting minds of Athenian young.

Aristotle (384–322 B.C.E.) Greek philosopher; teacher of Alexander the Great; espoused knowledge based on observation of phenomena in material world.

Stoics Hellenistic group of philosophers; emphasized inner moral independence cultivated by strict discipline of the body and personal bravery.

Plato Greek philosopher; taught knowledge based on consideration of ideal forms outside the material world; proposed ideal form of government based on abstract principles in which philosophers ruled.

DOCUMENT

The Power of Greek Drama

THIS SECTION CONSISTS OF TWO PASSAGES, one by the great tragedian Aeschylus (525–456 B.C.E.), and one by Athens's leading writer of comedies, Aristophanes (c. 450–385 B.C.E.). Aeschylus' passage, from the play *Libation Bearers*, sees Orestes confront his mother, Clytemnestra, after having killed her lover and suspecting that she killed his father. Clytemnestra has learned what Orestes did and knows what is to come; she asks a slave:

Clytemnestra: Swift! Bring me an axe that can slay. I will know now if I am to win or lose. I stand here on the height of misery.

[Orestes enters with his companion Pylades.]

Orestes: It is you I seek. The other has had his fill. You love him— you shall lie in the same grave.

Clytemnestra: Stop—oh, my son. Look—my breast. Your heavy head dropped on it and you slept, oh, many a time, and your baby mouth where never a tooth was, sucked the milk and so you grew—

Orestes: Oh, Pylades, what shall I do? My mother—Awe holds me. May I spare?

Pylades: Where then Apollo's words and the dread compact? Make all men enemies but not the gods.

Orestes: Good counsel. I obey. You—follow me. I lead you where he lies to kill you there.

Clytemnestra: It seems, my son, that you will kill your mother.

Orestes: Not I. You kill yourself.

Clytemnestra: I am alive—I stand beside my grave. I hear the song of death.

[They go out and the Chorus sings that her fate is just.]

Lift up your head, oh, house. I see the light.

[The palace doors roll back. Orestes stands over the two dead bodies.]

Orestes: I am blameless of the one. He died the death adulterers must die. But she who planned this thing of horror against her husband by whom she had borne beneath her girdle the burden of children—what think you of her? Snake or viper was she? Her very touch would rot a man.

Chorus: Woe—woe—Oh, fearful, deeds!

Orestes: Did she do it or did she not? The proofs you know—the deed and the death. I am victor but vile, polluted.

Chorus: One trouble is here—another comes.

Orestes: Hear me and learn, for I know how it will end. I am borne along a runaway horse. My thoughts are out of bounds. Fear at my heart is leaping up. Before my reason goes—oh, you my friends, I say I killed my mother—yet not without reason—she was vile and she killed my father and God hated her—Look— look—women—there—there—black—all black, and long hair twisting like snakes. Oh, let me go.

Chorus: What fancies trouble you, O son, faithful to your father? Do not fear.

Orestes: No fancies. My mother has sent them. They throng upon me and from their eyes blood drips, blood of hate. You see them not? I—I see them. They drive me. I cannot stay.

[He rushes out.]

Chorus: Oh, where will this frenzy of evil end?

In Aristophanes' play *Plutus*, the author mocks what he sees as the reigning values of Athens. The passage begins with a slave asking his respectable-looking master why they are following a blind man:

Chremylus: I'll tell you why, straight out. Of all my slaves I know that you are the best, most constant—thief. Well—I have been a good, religious man, but always poor—no luck.

Slave: And so you have.

Chremylus: So then I want to ask—not for myself, I've pretty well shot all my arrows now—but for my son, my only son. I prayed that he might change his ways and turn into a scoundrel, wicked, rotten through and through, and so live happily ever after. The god replied, the first man I fell in with to follow.

Slave: Yes—Quite good. Of course, a blind man can see it's better nowadays to be a rotten scoundrel.

[The man in front proves to be Wealth himself, not aware of his power because he is blind. The two others proceed to enlighten him.]

Chremylus: Why everything there is, is just Wealth's slave. The girls, now, if a poor man comes along, will they look at him? But just let a rich one, and he can get a deal more than he wants.

Slave: Oh, not the sweet, good, modest girls. They never would ask a man for money.

Chremylus: No? What then?

Slave: Presents—the kind that cost a lot—that's all.

Chremylus: Well, all the voting's done for Wealth of course. You man our battleships. You own our army. When you're an ally, that side's sure to win. Nobody ever has enough of you. While all things else a man can have too much of—of love.

Slave: Of loaves.

Chremylus: Of literature.

Slave: Of candy.

Chremylus: Of fame.

Slave: Of figs.

Chremylus: Of manliness.

Slave: Of mutton.

QUESTIONS

- What were the purposes of comedy and tragedy in classical Athens?
- How does Aeschylus' passage move toward a starkly tragic view?
- How is a truly tragic situation for a person defined?
- What values might have led an Athenian audience to enjoy a satire such as that by Aristophanes?
- Do the Greek ideas of comedy and tragedy seem different from American definitions today?

In mathematics, Greeks learned from earlier Egyptian findings and often studied in Egypt. The key Greek interest lay in speculation about nature's order. In practice, the Greek concern translated into theories about the motions of the planets and the organization of the elemental principles of earth, fire, air, and water, and into a great interest in mathematics as a means of understanding nature's patterns. Greek and later Hellenistic work in geometry was impressive, featuring the basic theorems of Pythagoras and Euclid's geometry.

Scientists in the Hellenistic period, working mainly in Egypt or the Middle East, made some important contributions, especially in studies of anatomy. Medical writings by Galen were not improved upon in the Western world for many centuries. The Hellenistic astronomer Ptolemy formalized an elaborate theory of the sun's motion around a stationary earth. This new Hellenistic theory contradicted much earlier Middle Eastern astronomy, which had recognized that the earth revolved around the sun. The idea of an earth-centered universe seemed to explain many observed phenomena, including eclipses, and this along with the reputation of Greek science ensured that Ptolemy's theory was long taken as fixed wisdom in Western thought.

Other Hellenistic scientists added more constructively to the observations about planetary motion. Archimedes (c. 287–212 B.C.E.) wrote about mathematics and the measurement of water power. He devised pulley systems to pump out flooded ships and fields and invented novel kinds of fortifications. Other Hellenistic scientists, dissecting the corpses of criminals, made important discoveries about digestion and the vascular system.

Literature and the Visual Arts

Despite the importance of the rationalist tradition, science and mathematics were far less important than art and literature in conveying key cultural values in Greek and Hellenistic culture. The official religion inspired artistic expression and justified the creation of temples, statues, and plays devoted to the glories of the gods. But the human-centered qualities of the Greeks also showed through, as artists emphasized realistic portrayals of the human form and poets and playwrights used the gods as vehicles for pondering the human condition.

All the arts received attention. Music and dance performances were vital parts of religious festivals, but their styles have not been preserved. Far more durable was the Greek interest in drama, for plays took a central role in this culture. Greek dramatists worked on both comedy and tragedy, making a formal division between the two that is still part of the Western tradition. (The Document box illustrates the two approaches.) On the whole, the Greeks placed greatest emphasis on tragedy. Their belief in human reason and balance also involved a sense that these virtues were precarious, so that a person could easily be ensnared in situations of powerful emotion and uncontrollable consequences. The Athenian dramatist **Sophocles**, for example, so insightfully portrayed the psychological flaws of his hero Oedipus that modern psychology long used the term *Oedipus complex* for potentially tragic attachments between a man and his mother. Another Athenian playwright, **Aristophanes**, used similar beliefs in the limitations of human experience to produce comedies poking fun at human nature.

In the visual arts, the emphasis of classical Mediterranean civilization lay in sculpture, architecture, and ceramics. In Athens's brilliant 5th century B.C.E.—the age of Pericles, Socrates, Sophocles, Aristophanes, and many other intensely creative figures—sculptors such as Phidias developed unprecedented skill in realistic portrayals of the human form, from lovely goddesses to muscled warriors and athletes.

Greek architecture from the 8th century B.C.E. onward emphasized monumental construction, square or rectangular in shape, with columned porticoes. As Figure 5.6 shows, the Greeks devised three distinct styles for their massive buildings, each more ornate than the last: the **Doric**, **Ionic**, and **Corinthian**. They invented what Westerners and others in the world today still regard as classical architecture, although the Greeks themselves were influenced by Egyptian and Cretan models. Greece provided abundant stone for ambitious temples, markets, and other public buildings. Many of these structures were filled with products of the sculptors' workshops. They were also brightly

Sophocles (496–406 B.C.E.) Greek writer of tragedies; author of *Oedipus Rex*.

Aristophanes [ar uh stof uh nEEz] (c. 448–380 B.C.E.) Greek writer of the comedies; author of *The Frogs*.

Doric Along with Ionian and Corinthian, distinct style of Greek and Hellenistic architecture; the least ornate of the three styles.

Ionic Along with Doric and Corinthian, distinct style of Greek and Hellenistic architecture; more ornate than Doric but less than Corinthian.

Corinthian Along with Doric and Ionian, distinct style of Greek and Hellenistic architecture; the most ornate of the three styles.

FIGURE **5.6** Over time, the design of Greek columns moved from early Doric simplicity (top left), through the more ornate Ionic (top right), to the highly ornamented Corinthian (bottom).

FIGURE **5.7** Zeus came to power when he overthrew his father, Cronin, and drew lots with his brothers to see who would become the supreme god of the Greeks. He was believed to be noble, wise, and powerful, but neither omnipotent nor omniscient. In fact, he was often tricked by the other gods, and even by mortals. God of the sky and the rain (a precious commodity in arid Greece), he hurled thunderbolts at those who displeased him. In this statue, he was depicted as holding a thunderbolt, now missing.

painted, although over the centuries the paint faded so that later imitators came to think of the classical style as involving plain stone.

Overall, Greek culture, like politics, displayed an interesting tension between masses and elites. Plays and art forms were widely shared (Figure 5.7), and key intellectuals—like Socrates, a stonemason by trade—came from humble beginnings. But Greek philosophy was closed to most ordinary people. In contrast to China, with some popularization of Confucianism, there was no particular effort to persuade ordinary people to participate in the values of the elite.

Hellenistic Culture During and After Alexander

Greek art and sculpture continued to dominate Hellenistic output, and the commercial wealth of the early Hellenistic kingdoms encouraged a vast amount of new building and decoration. Although no new styles emerged, there was some movement toward more sentimental, emotional statuary.

Hellenistic intellectuals concentrated on developing new knowledge in science and mathematics. Alexander and the Hellenistic dynasty in Egypt encouraged this work, and the expansion of cultural exchange in the Mediterranean in the Middle East also favored new research. Hellenistic thinkers thus preserved Greek scientific achievements and added significant new elements. Their work provided most of the scientific learning available to the Western world for almost 2000 years. It also set a durable basis for scientific research in the Middle East and northern Africa. Astronomical charts and maps improved greatly, despite Ptolemy's confusion about the earth as the center of the universe. Geography also improved, and one scientist was able to calculate the circumference of the earth within 200 miles. At the same time, interest in astrology and magic increased.

PATTERNS OF MEDITERRANEAN AND MIDDLE EASTERN SOCIETY

Both Greece and Persia developed new merchant activities and urban life. Greek social structure included aristocrats, independent farmers, traders, and slaves. Family relations emphasized patriarchy but with more ambivalence concerning women than in China.

> **5.5**   Compare the social structures of classical Greece and classical China.

Greek and Persian societies and economies developed under the impact of frequent wars and military expansion. Even more influential was the growth of trade and urban structures, which created vigorous merchant interests and a commercial spirit that would continue to play a significant role in the eastern Mediterranean and Middle East well beyond the classical period.

Economic and Social Structure

Greek and Persian social structures differed in many ways, but they had four key features in common. First, of course, they both relied heavily on agriculture. Both societies had numerous free peasants. Mainland Greece was quite mountainous, which made grain-growing difficult, which encouraged reliance on trade for foodstuffs (The Visualizing the Past box focuses on economic and social aspects of Greek trade). Many Greek city-states established colonies elsewhere in the eastern Mediterranean and even in southern Italy to help provide adequate supplies of grain. In Persia, agricultural surpluses were easier to come by, although they depended on elaborate systems of irrigation, some of which ordinary farmers maintained.

Second, both societies featured a military aristocracy originally derived from conquering invaders—the Persians in the Middle East, the Indo-Europeans in Greece. Aristocrats claimed a considerable role in politics, particularly in Greece, and they also controlled larger agricultural estates. Other social groups, like merchants or, in Persia, the large bureaucratic class, operated alongside the aristocracy, sometimes a bit uneasily.

Third, both Greece and Persia developed a strong merchant class. Greek reliance on seagoing trade was vital. Persia's promotion of the vast road network, and its ability to take advantage of special resources in different parts of the empire, also encouraged the growth of commerce. The Persian empire established a standard for gold coinage that also promoted trade throughout the empire. Urban centers expanded. Athens obviously emphasized urban life. The Persian emperor Darius built a magnificent new capital city in Persepolis, and other cities flourished as well. Some tensions arose. Greek aristocrats tended to scorn trade, and even in Athens many merchants were foreigners, mainly from the Middle East; Sparta, with unusually fertile land, discouraged trade altogether, using large coins that were so unwieldy that they could not be used for daily exchanges. Overall, merchants held a higher standing in much of Greece than in China, but it was less firm than in India or Persia. In the Hellenistic period, however, Greek merchants ranged widely through the Middle East and North Africa, playing a growing role not only in trading but also in cultural exchange.

Finally, both Greece and Persia relied considerably on slavery. Persian slaves included people conquered in battle and also civilians in regions that did not welcome Persian expansion. Some Persians also fell into slavery as a result of debts, in an increasingly commercial society, which they could pay off only by selling their persons. Greek city-states also acquired slaves through the frequent wars. Philosophers like Aristotle produced elaborate justifications of slavery, regarding it as essential to support the wise aristocrats who would guide politics and culture. Greeks and Persians both used slaves widely in domestic service. In Persia, a few slaves even rose high in bureaucratic ranks, serving the state or the priesthood. Greeks also relied on slaves to work the silver mines, vital to Athenian prosperity. Sparta used **helots**, or unfree labor, extensively for agricultural work, as the Indo-European conquerors subjected the local population. Spartan helots outnumbered their masters by nearly 10 to 1; slaves constituted up to a third of the Athenian population. In both Persia and Greece, maintaining slavery required military controls, although many slaves had considerable latitude and a number were freed by their masters.

Both Greece and Persia sponsored considerable manufacturing, with many skilled craft workers. Greece, however, paid less attention to improving manufacturing technology than did China or India. Reliance on slavery was a factor here—in the mines or on agricultural estates, expanding the slave labor force seemed more obvious than considering new equipment. The Greek concern for science as a philosophical system rather than a collection of useful data also played a role. One Hellenistic scholar refused to write a handbook on engineering because "the work of an engineer and everything that ministers to the needs of life is ignoble and vulgar."

On balance, it was the growing emphasis on merchant activity and the importance of slavery—although also its varied forms—that constituted the greatest legacy of Greek and Persian society to the later social development of the region, and to world history more generally.

helots Conquered indigenous population of Spartan city-state; provided agricultural labor for Spartan landowners; only semifree; largest population of Spartan city-state.

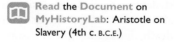
Read the Document on MyHistoryLab: Aristotle on Slavery (4th c. B.C.E.)

Men, Women, and Social Divisions

Both Greek and Persian society emphasized the importance of a tight family structure, with husband and father firmly in control. Women had vital economic functions, particularly in farming and artisan families. A woman with a strong personality could command a major place within a household, and a free woman's responsibility for family possessions was protected by law.

In law and culture, however, women were held inferior. Even the activities of free women were directed toward their husbands' interests. In Greece, the rape of a free woman, although a crime, was a lesser offense than seducing her, because seduction meant winning her affections away from her husband. Families burdened with too many children sometimes put infant girls to death. Pericles stated common beliefs about women when he said, "For a woman not to show more weakness than

THINKING HISTORICALLY

Defining Social History

OVER THE PAST 30 YEARS, HISTORIANS have argued about the proper focus of their work. Should history focus on great achievements by major individuals? Or should social history, with its wider definition of significance, guide our view of the past?

Until fairly recently, many historians wrote as if the principal elements of the past that were worth recapturing involved formal politics—the changes in the structure of the state, the rise and fall of major political leaders, and wars and intellectual life. How the masses of people lived was relevant as it affected taxation levels (and thus what political leaders could do), political protest, and military service. New inventions or big changes in the economic or social system, such as an increase of slavery, could figure in. But the detailed work of the historian focused on charting and explaining what the leading statesmen and thinkers were doing.

Often, the key legacies of a major time period or civilization seem to lie in its dominant political forms, artistic styles, and religious concepts. Thus, in classical Greece, political and intellectual achievements not only commanded great attention at the time, at least in the upper classes, but also contributed greatly to later societies after the Greek and Hellenistic ages had ended. We may well look to Pericles, Socrates, or the great sculptor Phidias for example and inspiration.

Yet modern historical research does not begin or end with the doings of the greatest statesmen and thinkers. The newer field of social history, which has gained momentum in the United States and elsewhere over the past 40 years, increasingly defines a wider agenda. Social historians do not deny the significance of political structures or philosophical systems, but they argue that history also consists of the doings of ordinary people: family activities, death, disease, work, and leisure. For social historians, the past is much larger than was once believed. It includes many groups of people besides the elite: women, peasants and artisans, children and youth. Social historians integrate great ideas with the beliefs of large numbers of people about how the universe worked or what the good life was. They combine attention to political forms with an understanding of the social structures and problems that helped generate these forms.

Think of how these issues apply to classical Greece. Judgments of Greece clearly vary, depending on whether slaves or farmers or aristocrats are the focus. What happens when women's conditions are considered as well as men's?

Social historians do not always have an easy time fleshing out their topics. Ordinary people did not conveniently describe

Social historians do not deny the significance of political structures or philosophical systems, but they argue that history also consists of the doings of ordinary people: family activities, death, disease, work, and leisure.

their beliefs for posterity the way thinkers such as Aristotle and Confucius did. Particularly for early and classical civilizations, when records have been lost and most people were illiterate, it is not easy to characterize work and family values.

Partly for this reason, many world histories until recently focused on formal governments and intellectual history alone. One world historian leaves ordinary people out simply because, in his view, only the groups that produce major milestones are worth attending to; the supporting cast is irrelevant. Another world historian once argued that the lives of ordinary people changed little, at least during the long reign of agriculturally based civilizations, so there is little to know about them in comparison with the obvious ups and downs of governments and artistic styles. Yet social history, for all its complexity, continues to gain ground, determining much of the subject matter of world history, for three major reasons.

First, the history of long-ignored groups and topics helps us understand these same topics in societies today. It is just as important to have a historical perspective on women's roles, and to see how they changed and varied in the past, as it is to understand how Greek leaders were chosen. At certain times, work, women's roles, or family forms may change only gradually, even amid lively political developments. But the reverse may also be true, with women's lives changing rapidly, and there is no question that social historical change can be charted and assessed.

Second, patterns and changes in social history intimately affect the ways governments and intellectuals function, and the reverse is true as well. In classical civilizations, such as China and Greece, a vast gulf often separated wealthy, literate aristocrats or bureaucrats from ordinary peasants or slaves. Yet governments had to be organized in such a way as to keep ordinary people contented or repressed (or they had to contend with protest). Confucianism tried to deal with this issue; Greek city-state governments experimented almost constantly with systems that would preserve a class structure yet provide enough harmony for political life. One key way to grasp a civilization or the causes of change is to talk about how formal institutions and intellectual styles related to the masses of people and the basic structures of life.

Finally, ordinary people and the structures they were involved with could leave legacies, just as intellectual and political leaders did. Later periods or societies would thus build on

(continued on next page)

(continued from previous page)

earlier patterns of work, ways to treat children, or definitions of slavery.

Among the social sciences during the past 30 years, social history has proved to be one of the most fruitful sources of new knowledge and analysis. The result is a redefinition of the past and of the kinds of questions to raise about how societies function.

QUESTIONS

- What are some of the key problems of social history?
- What would a social historian emphasize in discussing the major features of classical Chinese civilization?
- Besides political development and intellectual styles, what would the social historian try to pinpoint in summing up classical Greek and Hellenistic civilization?

is natural to her sex is a great glory, and not to be talked about for good or for evil among men." He also thought that women's bodies showed that they were "failed men." On the other hand, the oppression of women was probably less severe in this civilization than in China, for many Greek women were active in business.

Although Greek culture represented women abundantly as goddesses and as powerful figures in drama, often with revered powers, and celebrated the female form as well as the male form in art, the real cultural status of women was low. Aristotle argued that women provided only an abode for a child developing before birth, claiming that male seed alone contained the full germ of the child. This is why he also thought that women's bodies showed that they were "failed men." Marriages were arranged by a woman's father. Husbands could divorce wives at will, whereas women had to go to court. Adultery was tolerated for men but was grounds for divorce in the case of women. Many upper-class men consorted with slave and noncitizen women more often than with their wives, and there is ample evidence of sexual relations between men and adolescent boys they were mentoring. The traveler Herodotus claimed that some of these Greek customs influenced Persia as well.

Women's daily duties focused on the home. Within upper-class households, women had vital functions, including the supervision of domestic slaves. Men entertained their guests in separate rooms. The training of female children was left to older women in the household. Sometimes women joined together in festivals such as the three-day Thesmophoria in Athens, during which they went to a great encampment to perform rituals designed to promote the fertility of the land.

Conditions for citizen women improved somewhat in the Hellenistic period, as Greek customs mixed with patterns in Middle East and North Africa. Artists and playwrights began to show more interest in women and their conditions. Women in Hellenistic cities appeared more freely in public, and some aristocratic women gained new functions—forming cultural clubs, for example. Several queens exercised great power, often ruling harshly. Cratesiclea, the mother of a Hellenistic king in Sparta, willingly served as a hostage to help form an alliance with a more powerful state. She reputedly said, "Send me away, wherever you think this body of mine will be most useful to Sparta." More widely, Hellenistic women began to take an active role in commerce, although they still could not own property.

A Complex Legacy

Classical Greece, Persia, and their Hellenistic successors lasted for about 600 years. Although major political and social changes took place during this span, some durable characteristics also developed.

Greece's political legacy obviously lay more in the realm of ideas than in enduring political institutions such as China's emperor and bureaucracy, although the next leading Mediterranean city-state, Rome, copied some Greek structures. On the whole, Greek art and philosophy formed the most lasting contributions of this classical civilization. But, partly because they did not generate a major religion, Greek contributions to a durable popular culture were more limited than was true in China or India.

There are two final complexities in dealing with the classical civilizations of the eastern Mediterranean and the Middle East. The first involves the relationship of Greek achievements to contemporary North Americans. Classical Greece is often presented as the first phase of North Americans' own classical past. The framers of the Constitution of the United States were very conscious of Greek precedents. Designers of public buildings in the United States have copied Greek and Roman models. The Western educational tradition has long invited elaborate explorations of the Greco-Roman past as part of the standard intellectual equipment for the educated person.

Yet this important legacy should not obscure the actual Greek record as a classical civilization. Greek ideas did not flow smoothly into a Western tradition (indeed, they had far more initial impact on the Middle East, which was where Greeks tended to look when they thought of spreading their key achievements). Important revivals and modifications had to occur before the Greek approach to science had a fruitful impact on western Europe many centuries later. And democracy did not spread directly from Greece to other societies, although the Greek example was cited by later advocates whose passions had very different sources.

The second complexity involves Persia, an important civilization in its own right. Hellenistic conquests brought Greek cultural influence into Persia. Influences were mutual, however. Hellenistic kings imitated Persian centralization and bureaucracy. Cultural exchange also gave Zoroastrian influences a wider range. This furthered the influence these religious ideas would have on Mediterranean religions, including Judaism, and later, Christianity and Islam. The Jewish book of *Daniel*, for example, may have been influenced by the Zoroastrian idea that righteous humans could have spiritual existence after life.

At the same time, there was no tidy homogenization. Persians continued to see themselves as partially distinct and viewed Alexander's successors as foreigners. Later, more purely Persian kingdoms arose as the Hellenistic states declined. Parthians and then Sasanids revived Persian political institutions and culture in their realms to the east of the Roman Empire's Middle Eastern holdings (see Chapter 11). Under Hellenism and Persia alike, the Middle East enhanced its role as a point of exchange among many different merchants and cultures.

Global Connections and Critical Themes

PERSIA, GREECE, AND THE WORLD

The Persian Empire fostered trade with both Asia and with the eastern Mediterranean. Persian roads and institutions facilitated commerce from Asia to the Mediterranean. Cultural influences spread widely as well. Greeks developed wide contacts also, but more gradually and with some definite prejudices.

Like other classical civilizations, notably China, Greeks had a definite sense of the inferiority of other peoples. Classical Greeks indiscriminately called non-Greeks "barbarians," and some Greek city-states, like Sparta, were quite closed to outside influences. But overall, the Greeks were also a trading and expansionist people. They set up Greek colonies in various parts of the Mediterranean. They traded even more widely, and relied heavily on

foreigners for part of this trade. Greek scholars went to Egypt to further their training in science and mathematics. Some Greeks were immensely curious about other peoples and their habits. The historian and traveler Herodotus (484–425 B.C.E.) talked enthusiastically about customs very different from his own, although he was also capable of believing wild exaggerations about how some people lived.

Greek outreach was extended by Alexander the Great, who did not have such a keen belief in Greek superiority. Alexander forged important new contacts between the eastern Mediterranean, the rest of the Middle East including Persia, and western India. The system did not last, but the interest in setting up stronger links between the eastern Mediterranean and Asia remained an important concern that would be picked up later by the Roman Empire.

Further Readings

The archeology, arts, and culture of ancient Persia are addressed in M. Piotrovsky et al., *Persia: Thirty Centuries of Art & Culture* (2007) and J. Curtis, *Ancient Persia* (1989). On the Persian empire, see J. M. Cook, *The Persian Empire* (1983). Important recent works on Persia include Bruce Lincoln, *Religion, Empire, and Torture: The Case of Achaemenian Persia, with a Postscript on Abu Ghraib* (2007), Oded Lipschits, Oded and Manfred Oeming, eds., *Judah and the Judeans in the Persian Period* (2006); Peter Green, *The Greco-Persian Wars* (1996); Donald Kagan, *The Peloponnesian War* (2003); and John Curtis and Nigel Tallis, eds., *Forgotten Empire: The World of Ancient Persia* (2005). Two good surveys on classical Greece are Stephanie Lynn Budin, *The Ancient Greeks: New Perspectives* (2004) and Nancy Demand's *A History of Ancient Greece* (1996); both have bibliographies. An older study on Greek culture is extremely solid: H. D. F. Kitto's *The Greeks* (1957). Recent works on Hellenism include Shanyn Fiske, *Heretical Hellenism: Women Writers, Ancient Greece, and the Victorian Popular Imagination* (2008); Kathryn Gutzwiller, *A Guide to Hellenistic Literature*, Malden (2007); and Glenn R. Bugh, editor, *The Cambridge Companion to the Hellenistic World* (2006). See also Christian Habicht, *The Hellenistic Monarchies: Selected Papers* (2006); Waldemar Heckel, *Crossroads of History: The Age of Alexander* (2003); and A. B. Bosworth, *The*

Legacy of Alexander: Politics, Warfare, and Propaganda under the Successors (2002).

Works on key special topics are R. Zelnick-Abramovitz, *Not Wholly Free: The Concept of Manumission and the Status of Manumitted Slaves in the Ancient Greek World* (2005) and Oswyn Murray, *Early Greece* (1993). On Greek intellectual life, see Silvia Montiglio, *Wandering in Ancient Greek Culture* (2005); W. Burkert, *Greek Religions* (1985); and G. E. R. Lloyd, *The Revolutions of Wisdom: Studies in the Claims and Practices of Ancient Greek Science* (1987). Particular features of Greek society are treated in Moses Finley, *Slavery in the Ancient World* (1972); Sarah Pomeroy, *Goddesses, Whores, Wives, and Slaves: Women in Classical Antiquity* (1975); R. Just, *Women in Athenian Law and Life* (1988); Yvon Garlan, *Slavery in Ancient Greece* (1988); and Victor Hanson, *The Western Way of War: Infantry Battle in Classical Greece* (1989). On politics, Donald Kagan's *Western Heritage* (1991) deals with a key issue.

An excellent way to approach Greek history is through documents from the period. See Herodotus, *The Histories* (trans. de Selincourt, 1972); M. Crawford, ed., *Sources for Ancient History* (1983); M. R. Lefkowitz and M. B. Fant, eds., *Women's Life in Greece and Rome: A Source Book in Translation* (1982); and Eric W. Robinson, ed., *Ancient Greek Democracy: Readings and Sources* (2004).

Although it deals with a later period, key social features of the region are explored in F. Braudel's classic *The Mediterranean and the Mediterranean World* (2 vols., 1972).

On MyHistoryLab

✔ Study and Review on MyHistoryLab

Critical Thinking Questions

1. How did the Persian Empire illustrate major developments of the classical period?

2. What are the main problems in interpreting the Greek political legacy?

3. Compare the Greek and the Confucian approaches to social inequality.

4. What was the relationship between art and politics in Greek and Hellenistic society?

6

Religious Rivalries and India's Golden Age

)) Listen to Chapter 6
on MyHistoryLab

Of the many enduring expressions of religious devotion in human history, few can match the splendid complexes of temples and monasteries carved from stone into the cliffs at Ajanta and Ellora in the western reaches of the Deccan plateau, which stretches across central India (see Map 6.4). A section of the Ajanta caves is shown in Figure 6.1. More than sixty religious structures were carved into or out of solid rock at the two sites, which are approximately 30 miles apart. These monumental religious edifices were constructed in successive stages from the last centuries B.C.E. through the 8th century C.E. This millennium of history spans an era of momentous change and creativity that in many ways culminated in the Gupta empire, which ruled most of north India from early in the 4th until the mid-6th century C.E.

Q **View the Closer Look on MyHistoryLab:** Gupta Sculpture: Lokanatha

FIGURE **6.1** The cave temples carved out of solid stone at Ajanta in central India provide dramatic evidence of the religious fervor that swept through south Asia in the age of the Buddha and the Hindu revival.

👁 Watch the Video Series on MyHistoryLab

Learn about some key topics related to this chapter with the *MyHistoryLab Video Series: Key Topics in World History*

The art and architecture of Ajanta and Ellora provide dramatic evidence of the intensity of the religious ferment that shaped all aspects of Indian life as a result of the challenges to the existing brahmanical order posed by the emergence of Buddhism and other popular religious alternatives in the 6th and 5th centuries B.C.E. But these monumental buildings, and particularly the exquisite sculptures and paintings they contain, also tell us a great deal about the nature of society, everyday life, and popular culture, as well as the worldview and aspirations of those who lived in what many historians consider India's golden age. The mixture, for example, of Buddhist shrines and monastic quarters and Hindu and Jain cave temples exemplifies the overwhelmingly nonviolent nature of the rivalry between these major religious systems. The blend of religions at Ajanta and Ellora also mirrored the common adoption of rituals, objects of worship, and basic beliefs by the adherents of different Indian religions in this era.

Beyond religious thought and practice, the wall paintings and stone-carved sculptures provide some of the best illustrations we have of everything from Indian ships and styles of dress at different social levels to musical instruments, weapons, and tools for farming and construction. Stone friezes decorating the walls of the shrines and temples illustrate in remarkable detail popular legends of the Buddha's life and path to enlightenment and the rich mythology that developed around the gods and goddesses propitiated by the brahman priests. One of the most celebrated temples, carved out of solid rock to be a free-standing structure, relates in stone carvings numerous episodes from the *Ramayana*, which had become one of the two great epics of Indian civilization by the last centuries B.C.E. ∎

The kings and their consorts, brahman priests and Buddhist monks, workers and temple dancers portrayed in the Ajanta and Ellora cave temples help us to visualize more than a millennium of history that is covered in this chapter, lasting from roughly 700 B.C.E. to 650 C.E., this era saw the rise and fall of some of India's most powerful dynasties. The brahman-dominated society that emerged in the kingdoms Indo-European migrants established in the Gangetic plains was challenged in fundamental ways by the rise of Buddhism in the 6th century B.C.E. Buddhism also played a major role in the emergence of the powerful Maurya dynasty and was in turn weakened by the decline of its empire. The political fragmentation in the centuries after the demise of the Mauryas was mirrored in the intense, although largely peaceful, competition among different schools of Buddhism, Brahmanism, and a wide variety of other religious sects. The patronage of the rulers of the Gupta empire that controlled much of north India from the 4th to the mid-6th centuries C.E. sparked a revival of Brahmanism, which made for an age of remarkable religious effervescence, artistic creativity, and scientific breakthroughs that secured India's enduring stature as one of the core civilizations of the preindustrial world.

THE AGE OF BRAHMAN DOMINANCE

6.1 How did the Brahmans come to dominate the social order over much of the Indian subcontinent by the middle of the first century B.C.E.?

By the last millennium B.C.E., the social order of Aryan-dominated south Asia had become increasingly stratified and controlled by brahman priests, teachers and advisors, and regional warrior elites.

The forces that made for the renewal of civilization in south Asia after the fall of Harappa were initially centered not on the great plains of the Ganges and Indus river systems but in the foothills of the Himalaya Mountains (Map 6.1). Tribes of Indo-European warrior-herders settled in the lush valleys of the cool hills, which provided abundant pasturage for their herds of horses and cattle. The

1600 B.C.E.	1200 B.C.E.	700 B.C.E.	500 B.C.E.
1600–1000 Period of Indo-European migrations **c. 1500** Fall of Harappan civilization	**1200–700** Sacred Vedas composed	**700–c. 550** Era of unrivaled Brahman dominance **c. 542–483** Life of the Buddha	**327–325** Alexander the Great's invasion **322–298** Chandragupta Maurya rules **322–185** Time of the Mauryan Empire

wooded valleys proved easier to clear for farming than the rainforest-covered plains along the Ganges and its tributaries. In the hill regions, single tribes or confederations of tribal groups developed small states—in many ways similar to those in Homeric Greece—that were based on a combination of sedentary agriculture and livestock breeding. The territories of most of these states extended no farther than the hills surrounding a single large valley or several adjoining valley systems. Most of the states were republics ruled collectively by a council of the free warrior elite. Individual leaders were usually called kings, even though their offices and powers more closely resembled those of tribal chieftains. They were elected or removed from office by a vote of the warriors' councils.

The hill republics were well suited to the preservation of traditional nomadic values and lifestyles. Wars between the numerous hill states were frequent, as were feuds and cattle raids. Thus, the warrior elites were kept busy at activities that brought them wealth and honor. The republics nurtured the spirit of independence that had been strong among the migrating Aryan tribes as well as hostility toward those who tried to concentrate political authority in the hands of a single ruler.

The warrior elites were also careful to keep the power of the brahmans in check, and the hill cultures fostered a healthy skepticism toward the priests and the gods they worshiped. In one early hymn the brahmans, chanting their prayers, are compared to croaking frogs gathered about a pond in the rainy season. Given these trends, it is not surprising that the hill regions were major centers of religious reform from the 6th century B.C.E. onward. One of the greatest religious reformers of all time, the Buddha, was from one of these republics, as were the founders of several other, less well known Indian religions such as Jainism.

The Kingdoms of the Gangetic Plain

As Aryan settlement spread in the last millennium B.C.E. from the Indus region and Himalayan foothills to vast plains of the Ganges River system (see Map 6.1), republics and religious skeptics gave way to kings and powerful brahman priests. The hilly regions were divided into a patchwork of rival kingdoms. In the lowland plains, rulers were also drawn from the warrior elite, but they held power in their own right rather than deriving it from selection by warrior councils. Except for their influential brahman advisors, there were no formal checks on the kings' power. Many kings claimed descent from divine ancestors, and their thrones normally were inherited by their sons. All considered themselves to be the supreme war leaders, chief judges, and protectors of the peoples in their domains.

As these roles suggest, the powers and privileges these kings enjoyed were justified by the duties they performed and the services they provided for their subjects. As contemporary writings stress, they were expected to protect their kingdoms from invaders and internal social conflicts. In popular epics and philosophical tracts, rulers were taught to revere the brahmans and follow their advice, to patronize public works, and to rule in ways that promoted the welfare of their people. Ideally, kings were supposed to be

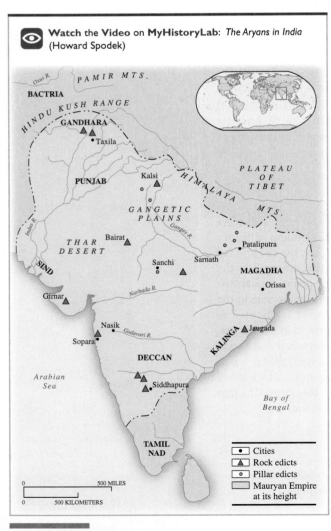

Watch the Video on MyHistoryLab: *The Aryans in India* (Howard Spodek)

Legend:
- Cities
- Rock edicts
- Pillar edicts
- Mauryan Empire at its height

MAP **6.1 India at the Time of Ashoka** Although, as the map shows, the Mauryan monarchs claimed to rule most of present-day south Asia, much of the subcontinent was only loosely controlled.

300 B.C.E.	100 C.E.	300 C.E.
c. 300 Kautilya's *Arthashastra* is written **268–237** Ashoka is emperor of India **200 B.C.E.– 200 C.E.** Period of greatest Buddhist influence **170–165** Yueh-chi invasions **c. 150** Indo-Greek invasions	**1–105** Kushana Empire in the northwest	**319–540** Gupta Empire **405** Fa-hsien's (Fa-xian's) pilgrimage **541** First Hun invasion **606–647** Harsha's empire

hard-working, honest, and accessible to all subjects. Some passages in the ancient texts justify the violent overthrow of evil rulers.

It is highly unlikely that monarchs who lived up to all these ideals would have survived the court intrigues and the assaults of rival rulers that were common in the era of brahman dominance. In fact, the sources from this period suggest a darker side to kingship that may have been closer to the realities of the age. Kings lived in constant fear for their thrones and lives. They were threatened by internal rivals, including their own sons, and by neighboring monarchs. A ruler's survival depended on the extensive use of spies and informers, a strong and loyal palace guard, and his courage and skill as a military commander.

ascetics Persons who had renounced the pleasures of the material world.

Sources of Brahman Power

Although most rulers of the kingdoms on the Ganges plains were members of the warrior elite, brahmans living at the court centers often exercised more real power. Their positions as the educators of the princes who would someday rule and as the chief advisors to the kings themselves made them influential figures in the ruling circles. Like the scholar-gentry in China, their literacy in a society where few could read or write made the brahmans obvious candidates for administrative positions, from heads of bureaucratic departments to judges and tax collectors. In addition, only the brahmans knew how to perform the sacred rituals that were essential to crowning a new king. They alone knew the rites that conferred divine status on a monarch, and without divine status a ruler's legitimacy was in doubt. Once the ruler was installed, brahman astrologers foretold his future and regulated his daily schedule, telling him when to make war or have relations with his wives.

As the brahmans' pivotal role in court ceremonies and prophecy indicates, their power and prestige were linked to their capacity to mediate between the gods and humans. The key function of the priests of the early Aryan invaders was to offer sacrifices to the gods and spirits (Figure 6.2), who often intervened in human affairs. By the 7th and 6th centuries B.C.E., the sacrifices themselves had become more powerful than the gods to whom they were offered. By this time it was widely believed that if the sacrifice was done correctly, the god had no choice but to grant the wish of the petitioner. Thus, a king could ensure victory, a peasant village sufficient rainfall, or a barren woman fertility if the proper ceremony was conducted flawlessly. Only the brahmans were able to perform the ceremony or were allowed to read the sacred texts where the prayers and instructions for various types of sacrifices were set forth.

Only a small percentage of the brahmans in a given kingdom served as advisors at the court or as state administrators. Many were the personal priests or physicians of wealthy high-caste families; most were village priests, schoolteachers, and wandering **ascetics**—persons who had renounced the pleasures of the material world. Some were alchemists, sorcerers, or even charlatans, living off the gullibility of the masses, who believed in their ability to tell fortunes and cast magic spells. But all brahmans, from the palaces of kings to the most remote villages, were privileged beings, exempt from taxes and protected from injury by the harsh punishments imposed on those who dared to assault them. The following passage is from one of the ancient religious texts written by the brahmans. Not surprisingly, it warns that not even kings were considered exempt from the horrible fate that befell those who harmed a brahman.

FIGURE **6.2** Perhaps the most frequently depicted Indian religious image is the god Shiva as the celestial dancer, here portrayed in a south Indian bronze. The position of the god's hands and the objects held in them each represent a different aspect of his power, which may be simultaneously creative and destructive. His left hand closest to his head, for example, is held in the posture of reassurance, and the left hand farthest away holds a drum, which signifies time. His left foot crushes the demon of ignorance, which seems to want to be destroyed by the illustrious god.

Whenever a king, fancying himself mighty, seeks to devour a Brahman, [his] kingdom is broken up.

[Ruin] overflows that kingdom as water swamps a leaky boat;

Calamity smites that country in which a priest is wronged.

Even trees . . . repel, and refuse their shade to, the man who claims a right to the property of a Brahman.

In addition to the power exercised by the brahmans and the services they provided, religion shaped the daily lives of the peoples of south Asia through the ethical prescriptions found in the sacred Vedas. These texts were orally compiled and systematically transmitted by the brahman priests between 1200 and 900 B.C.E. In the last centuries B.C.E., the Vedas were written in Sanskrit, which became the standard and scholarly language of India, akin to Greek and Latin in the West. From the chants and ritual formulas of the early Vedas, the texts were increasingly devoted to religious and philosophical speculation and moral prescriptions. This highly religious culture provided the context for further changes as Indian civilization moved to even greater complexity.

AN ERA OF WIDESPREAD SOCIAL CHANGE

6.2 What were the major forces driving social and cultural change in the late Vedic period and which social groups did these transformations affect the most?

The rise of kings and increasing brahman dominance were only two of the many social changes that occurred as full civilization took shape for the second time in Indian history. Around the court centers of the lowland kings, towns grew up as servant, artisan, and merchant groups catered to the needs of the rulers, their courtiers, and often large numbers of brahman advisors and administrators. Along the Ganges and other rivers, towns developed that were devoted to trade or the specialized manufacture of key products such as pottery, tools, and cotton textiles. With the increase in commerce and specialized production, merchants and artisans became established as distinct social groups. The great wealth of the larger trading houses allowed the merchants to win a prominent place in the Indian social hierarchy, which became both more complex and more rigid in this era.

Another social stratum that assumed major importance in this period was the peasantry. As farming replaced herding as the basis for the economies of the lowland kingdoms, peasants came to make up a large percentage of India's population. Mud-walled farming villages spread across the plains of northern India, although throughout the classical era they continued to be dwarfed in most places by massive rainforests. Irrigation networks and new agricultural tools steadily increased productivity and hence the ability to support ever larger numbers of nonfarming specialists. Most peasants grew staples such as rice, millet, and wheat, but some villages specialized in cotton, plants for dyes such as indigo, and luxury crops such as sugar cane.

The Caste System

The class division in India between warriors, priests, and commoners that made up the tribal social order of the early Aryan invaders had changed radically over the centuries. New social groups, such as merchants and peasants, were added to these broad social categories, and each was subdivided into occupational subgroups, **jatis** or castes, for the purpose of general analysis. These smaller groupings were particular to different regions in south Asia. They were arranged in a hierarchy according to the degree to which the tasks each group performed were considered polluting, particularly at the highest and lowest levels. Those who dealt with human waste or slaughtered animals, for example, were regarded as extremely defiled, whereas scholars and wandering holy men who avoided physical labor and refused to eat animal flesh were revered for their purity.

At the top of the caste pyramid were the brahman, warrior, and merchant groups, who made up only a small minority of the total population. The bulk of the population belonged to peasant and artisan subgroups, which made up most of the central and lower layers of the caste hierarchy. Beneath the peasants and artisans were the **untouchables**, who performed the most despised tasks in Indian society, including removing human waste from towns and villages, sweeping the streets, and tanning

---

With the growth of towns, merchant and artisan social groups became increasingly important economically, but their continuing low social status made them susceptible to religiously based challenges to the existing political, social, and philosophical order.

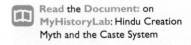 **Read the Document:** on MyHistoryLab: Hindu Creation Myth and the Caste System

jatis The multitude of occupational subgroups into which the Indian caste hierarchy is divided.

untouchables Lowest social caste in Hindu culture; performed tasks that were considered polluting— street sweeping, removal of human waste, and tanning.

THINKING HISTORICALLY

Inequality as a Social Norm

THE INDIAN CASTE SYSTEM IS PERHAPS the most extreme expression of a type of social organization that violates the most revered principles on which modern Western societies are based. Like the Egyptian division between a noble and a commoner and the Greek division between a freeperson and a slave, the caste system rests on the assumption that humans are inherently unequal and that their lot in life is determined by the families and social strata into which they are born. The caste system, like the social systems of all other classical civilizations, presumed that social divisions were fixed and stable and that people ought to be content with the station they had been allotted at birth.

These assumptions directly contradict some of the West's most cherished current beliefs. They run counter to one of the most basic organizing principles of modern Western culture, rooted in a commitment to equality of opportunity. This principle is enshrined in European and American constitutions and legal systems, taught in Western schools and churches, and proclaimed in Western media. The belief in human equality, or at least equality of opportunity, is one of the most important ideas that modern Western civilization has exported to the peoples of Africa, Asia, and Latin America.

The concept of equality rests on two assumptions. The first is that a person's place in society should be determined not by the class or family into which he or she is born but by personal actions and qualities. The second is that the opportunity to rise—or fall—in social status should be open to everyone and protected by law. Some of our most cherished myths reflect these assumptions: that anyone can aspire to be president of the United States, for example, or that an ordinary person has the right to challenge the actions of the politically and economically powerful. Of course, equality is a social ideal rather than something any human society has achieved. No one pretends that all humans are equal in intelligence or talent, and there are important barriers to equality of opportunity.

What is just and natural for modern societies would have been incomprehensible in the classical age, even in the West. In fact, most human societies through most of human history have been organized on assumptions that are much closer to those underlying the Indian caste system than to those underlying modern Western norms. Ancient Egyptians or Greeks, or for that matter medieval Europeans or early modern Chinese, believed that career possibilities, political power, and social privileges should be set by law according to the position of one's family in the social hierarchy. The Indian caste structure was the most complex of the systems by which occupations, resources, and status were allotted.

In nearly all societies, these fixed social hierarchies were upheld by creation myths and religious beliefs that proclaimed their divine origins and the danger of punishment if they were challenged.

But all classical civilizations had similar social mechanisms that determined the obligations and privileges of members of each social stratum.

In some ways, classical Chinese and Greek societies provided exceptions to these general patterns. In China, people from lowly social origins could rise to positions of great status and power, and well-placed families could fall on hard times and lose their gentry status. But "rags-to-riches" success stories were the exception rather than the rule, and mobility between social strata was limited. In fact, Chinese thinkers made much of the distinctions between the scholar-gentry elite and the common people.

Although some of the Greeks, particularly the Athenians, developed the idea of equality for all citizens in a particular city-state, most of the people of these societies were not citizens, and many were slaves. By virtue of their birth, the latter were assigned lives of servitude and drudgery. Democratic participation and the chance to make full use of their talents were limited to the free males of the city-states.

In nearly all societies, these fixed social hierarchies were upheld by creation myths and religious beliefs that proclaimed their divine origins and the danger of punishment if they were challenged. Elite thinkers stressed the importance of the established social order to human peace and well-being; rulers were duty bound to defend it. Few challenged the naturalness of the hierarchy itself; fewer still proposed alternatives to it. Each person was expected to accept his or her place and to concentrate on the duties and obligations of that place rather than worry about rights or personal desires. Males and females alike were required to subordinate their individual yearnings and talents to the needs of their families, clans, communities, or social superiors. In return for a person's acceptance of his or her allotted place in the hierarchy, he or she received material sustenance and a social slot. Of course, these benefits were denied to people who fought the system. They were outcast or exiled, physically punished, imprisoned, or killed.

QUESTIONS
- What arguments did the thinkers of the classical civilizations of Greece, China, and India use to explain and justify the great differences in social status and material wealth?
- How did those who belonged to elite groups justify their much greater status, wealth, and power compared to the peasants, artisans, and servants who made up most of the population?
- Comparing these modes of social organization with the ideals of your own society, what do you see as the advantages and drawbacks of each?

leather hides. The Indians' reverence for cows, which may have been present in Harappan society, and their aversion to dead animals made the latter occupation particularly polluting. Even the untouchables were divided into caste subgroups, with sweepers looking down on manure handlers, who in turn despised leatherworkers.

Over the centuries, the boundaries between caste groups hardened. In addition to occupation, a caste's position in the Indian social hierarchy was distinguished by its diet and by the caste groups with which its members could dine or exchange food. A caste's status also determined the social groups with which its members were allowed to intermarry and whether they were permitted to read the Vedas. Only members of castes belonging to the three highest varnas (Brahmans, warriors, and merchants) were allowed to read the sacred texts. **Rama**, perhaps the greatest Indian cultural hero, was celebrated in the great epic the *Ramayana* for cutting off the head of a peasant holy man who recited hymns from the Vedas while hanging upside down from a tree.

Enforcing Social Divisions

A person was born into a caste group and could not change his or her caste status. Over long periods of time, a caste group could collectively rise or fall in status, but individuals were tied to the fortunes of their caste. Refusal to accept the duties and status of the caste into which one was born could lead to beatings and other forms of physical abuse. If the rebellious person continued to violate caste laws, he or she would be ostracized or outcast. This penalty normally meant certain death because no one, including a member of the outcast's own family, was allowed to pay him or her for labor or offer food, drink, or other services.

In addition to local sanctions, the caste system was upheld by Indian rulers and the belief that it was supernaturally ordained. One of the chief duties of a righteous monarch was to preserve the caste hierarchy and ensure that people at each level carried out the tasks and behaved in the manner appropriate to their rank. Ideally, the caste system allowed a harmonious exchange of products and services at all levels of Indian society. For example, peasants provided food for the brahmans, who saw to their religious and ritual needs, and for the warriors, who defended them from bandits and foreign invaders. Of course, high-caste groups, particularly brahmans and warriors, enjoyed a disproportionate share of wealth and power. But except in times of severe natural calamity or social crisis, even the lowliest untouchables were guaranteed a livelihood, however meager.

The caste position and career determined by a person's birth were called one's **dharma**, or life path, in a particular existence. The concept of **transmigration** of the soul helped to explain why some were given the enviable dharma of a brahman and others were consigned to untouchable status. In the Vedic era, it was widely accepted that a person's soul existed through many human lives and was transferred from one body to another after death. In each of its lives, the soul accumulated varying amounts of merit and demerit, depending on the actions of the person in whose body it dwelled. The sum of these merits and demerits at any given point in time made up one's **karma** (the fruits of one's behavior and actions in previous lives). A soul's karma determined the caste that the soul would be born into in its next **reincarnation**. Thus, a person who was born as a brahman had a soul that had built up a large surplus of merit; a person born as a sweeper was paying the penalty for the sins of his or her past lives.

One of the greatest sins was to violate one's dharma—to refuse the duties and status attached to the caste into which one was born. The only way to ensure a better situation in the next rebirth was to accept one's situation in the present and fully perform the tasks one was allotted. Thus, the concepts of the transmigration of the soul and reincarnation explained the inequities of the caste system and provided a religious rationale for accepting one's place in the caste hierarchy.

The Family and the Changing Status of Women

Some of our best insights into family life and gender relationships in this era are provided by the two great Indian epics, the ***Mahabharata*** and the ***Ramayana***. Although these tales of war, princely honor, love, and social duty were not written down until the last centuries B.C.E., they were related in oral form long before. They suggest that by the middle centuries of the last millennium B.C.E., the extended family was increasingly regarded as the ideal. Those who could support such large households, which normally meant only the highest caste groups, gathered all the male members of a

Rama Major figure in the popular Indian epic *Ramayana*.

dharma [där muh] The caste position and career determined by a person's birth; Hindu culture required that one accept one's social position and perform occupation to the best of one's ability in order to have a better situation in the next life.

transmigration Belief in a number of Indian religious traditions that the souls of living creatures persisted in supernatural realms and returned to inhabit other humans or animals after death.

karma The sum of merits accumulated by a soul at any given point in time; determined the caste to which the soul would be assigned in the next life.

reincarnation The successive attachment of the soul to some animate form according to merits earned in previous lives.

 Read the Document on MyHistoryLab: Transmigration of Souls in the Upanishads (600 B.C.E.).

Mahabharata [muh hä bär uh tuh] Indian epic of war, princely honor, love, and social duty; written down in the last centuries B.C.E.; previously handed down in oral form.

Ramayana One of the great epic tales from classical India; traces adventures of King Rama and his wife, Sita; written 4th to 2nd centuries B.C.E.

given family and their wives and children under the same roof. At times up to four generations, from great-grandparents to their great-grandsons and great-granddaughters, lived together in the same dwelling or family compound.

Although these arrangements offered limited privacy and often led to family quarrels, they also provided a high degree of security and human companionship. Lower-caste groups such as peasants and artisans rarely could afford to support extended households. As a consequence, most Indian families were nuclear families, made up of parents and their children, with perhaps a widowed grandparent sharing their dwelling.

Somewhat contradictory visions of the positions and roles of women emerge from the epics, which suggest that attitudes toward women may have been in flux. On one hand, women were seen as weak, passionate, frivolous, and fond of gossip and slander. Female demons in the *Ramayana* were jealous temptresses and vengeful jilted lovers. Within the family, women remained clearly subordinated to men. Although youths were expected to obey and honor their mothers, parental veneration was focused on the father, to whom complete obedience and loyalty were expected. Wives were instructed to be attentive to their husbands' needs and ready to obey their every command. Rama's wife, Sita, was chosen for her beauty and absolute devotion to her husband. When he was forced into exile in the forest, she followed without question or complaint. When she was carried off to Sri Lanka by the demon Ravanna, Rama raced to defend her honor and his own. Having rescued her after a mighty battle with Ravanna and his evil minions, Rama refused to take her back because he suspected that she may have been raped while in captivity. Only when she proved her virtue by walking unscathed through a fire would he accept her again as his wife. Throughout both epics, the fate of women was controlled by men, be they gods, demons, or mortal humans.

On the other hand, some passages in the epics and other sources from this period indicate that in certain ways women had greater freedom and opportunities for self-expression than was true in the last centuries B.C.E. Women in the epics often were depicted as strong-willed and cunning. Sita and Draupadi, who was the wife of the five Pandava brothers—the great heroes of the *Mahabharata*—displayed remarkable courage and strength of character during their ordeals. Contemporary sources mention women who were renowned scholars of the sacred Vedic texts, which later they were not even permitted to read. Women in this era also made their mark as teachers, poets, musicians, and artists, although the last two activities were not highly esteemed. Like their brothers, girls from high-caste families were allowed to undergo the special ceremonies that celebrated their twice-born or exalted status—an honor boys continued to enjoy after it gradually died out for young women. Women were even famed for their skills in the martial arts, as the amazon (female warrior) palace guards of several monarchs demonstrated.

Read the Document on MyHistoryLab: Excerpt from the *Ramayana*

The End of an Era

Roughly 1000 years after the first Aryan tribes entered India, a new civilization had come into being that was different in many ways from the Harappan complex it replaced. Sedentary agriculture was well established and was productive enough to support a variety of specialized elites, true cities, extensive trade, and nonagrarian artisan manufacturers. In the caste system, the Indians had developed perhaps the most complex scheme of social stratification and labor division in human history. They had also made notable accomplishments in philosophical and religious speculation and artistic creativity. Although most of the artworks were done in wood and thus have perished over time, the profound thought of the age has been transmitted through the ages in extensive Sanskrit texts such as the Vedas and the great Indian epics. Some of the most sublime speculation about the supernatural and the meanings of human existence is contained in the portions of the *Mahabharata* called the *Bhagavad Gita*, or "Song Divine." In the following passage, the god Krishna counsels Arjuna (AHR-joo-nuh), one of the great warriors of the epic, as he prepares for battle.

> To action alone hast thou a right and never at all to its fruit; let not the fruits of action be thy motive; neither let there be in thee any attachment to inaction.
>
> Fixed in yoga, do thy work, O winner of wealth [Arjuna], abandoning attachment, with an even mind in success and failure, for evenness of mind is called yoga. . . .
>
> The wise who have united their intelligence [with the Divine], renouncing the fruits which their action yields and freed from the bonds of birth, reach the sorrowless state.

However, these great achievements of the brahmanic age were only a prelude to the religious, philosophical, and artistic creativity that occurred in south Asia in the last centuries B.C.E. The absolute and increasingly self-serving dominance of the brahmans, the succession of petty wars between the kings they advised, and the religious bankruptcy displayed by the sacrificial cults all prompted major challenges. These challenges and the brahman responses to them both remade and enriched Indian civilization in the millennium between 500 B.C.E. and 500 C.E.

RELIGIOUS FERMENT AND THE RISE OF BUDDHISM

The rise of the Buddha and other dissenting religious teachers posed major challenges to the caste-based, brahman-dominated order that had developed in the millennium after the Aryan migrations into India.

6.3 From what social groups did Buddhism gain most of its support and why?

By the late 6th century B.C.E., numerous challenges to the brahmanical order emerged in the teachings and practices of a diverse range of religious figures, many of whom were holy men who wandered in the hills and forests and lived on the fringes of Indian society. Some of these outsiders questioned the brahmans' dominance and the value of the sacrifices on which it ultimately rested, and they proposed alternatives to the caste system as the basis for India's social order. They also posed questions about the nature of the universe and the goals of life that the Vedic thinkers had debated for centuries, and they often came up with very different answers. Some experimented with new techniques of meditation and self-mortification; others promoted new religions that would free the masses from what were viewed as the oppressive teachings of the brahmans. One holy man and thinker, the Buddha, did all of these things and in the process made the most globally influential religious and philosophical breakthroughs of an age of remarkable intellectual ferment.

The Making of a Religious Teacher

Accounts of the Buddha's life are so cluttered with myths and miracles that it is difficult to know what kind of man he actually was and what sort of message he originally preached. We are fairly certain that he lived from the mid-6th century to the second decade of the 5th century B.C.E. He was born into one of the warrior clans of the hill states south of the Himalayas (see Map 6.1), where, as we have seen, the rule of kings and the hold of the brahmans was weak. Buddhist traditions hold that he was the son of the local ruler who was haunted by a prophecy made by a religious seer at the time of the Buddha's birth. The seer predicted that the child would someday refuse his father's throne and become a wandering *ascetic*.

To prevent this, the king confined his son to the palace grounds and provided him with every imaginable human pleasure and comfort. But as he approached manhood, the prince grew curious about the world beyond the palace gardens and walls. With the aid of a trusted servant, the Buddha ventured forth into the nearby countryside, where he encountered for the first time illness, old age, death, and a wandering ascetic. Unsettled by these encounters with human suffering, the prince became moody and withdrawn. Finally, as the holy man had predicted, he renounced all claims to succeed his father as king and set off with a group of wandering ascetics to meditate and ponder the many questions posed by his discoveries beyond the palace walls.

gurus Originally referred to as brahmans who served as teachers for the princes of the imperial court of the Guptas.

In the wilderness, the Buddha experimented with the many ways Indian **gurus**, or religious teachers, had devised to reach a higher understanding of the nature of humanity and the supernatural world. He did yogic exercises, fasted almost to death, chanted sacred prayers for days on end, and conversed with every seer he encountered. Discouraged by his failure to find the answer to the questions that had driven him to take up the life of a wandering ascetic, and exhausted by the self-punishment he had inflicted, the Buddha collapsed, legend has it, under a huge tree. Saved from death by the care of a young woman, the Buddha turned to meditation in his search for understanding. Ultimately, by disciplining his mind and body, he achieved enlightenment, which rested on his discovery of what Buddhists came to call the Four Noble Truths.

The central issue for the Buddha was the problem of suffering, which he believed all living things experience because all living things and the objects to which they are attached are impermanent. The moment we are born we begin to die, he reasoned. People whom one loves or befriends may turn indifferent or hostile or simply move away; love and friendship are inevitably ended by death. The goals to which humans devote their lives, such as fame and wealth, are empty and, once attained, can easily be lost. These attachments to the illusory and impermanent things of the world are the source of suffering.

One can escape suffering only by ceasing to desire the things of the world and realizing that even one's sense of self is part of the illusion. This realization, or enlightenment, can be achieved by following the eight-step process that includes right action, thinking, and meditation. Once enlightenment has been attained, the individual is released from suffering because she or he is free from desire and attachment. He or she has attained **nirvana**—not heaven in the Christian sense, but simply an eternal state of tranquility.

nirvana The Buddhist state of enlightenment, a state of tranquility.

Having attained enlightenment, the Buddha, because of his great compassion for all living creatures, set out to spread his message to all humanity (and, Buddhist legends relate, to the creatures of the forest). He became the most successful of the numerous seers and gurus who traveled through the hill and lowland kingdoms in this era, some of whom challenged the teachings of the brahmans and offered alternative modes of worship and paths to salvation. The Buddha soon gained a large following, which ranged from exalted monarchs to humble sweepers and included both men and women. As he feared, his followers turned his teachings into an organized religion. What had probably begun as a starkly pessimistic and antiworldly vision of existence, without gods or the promise of an everlasting paradise, became one of the great salvationist faiths of all human history.

The Emergence of Buddhism as a Religion

After his death the Buddha was worshiped as a deity—often in the form of lifelike sculptures. His most faithful disciples became monks who devoted their lives to spreading his message and achieving nirvana. They held conferences in which they tried to compile authoritative collections of his teachings and the traditions concerning his life. Not surprisingly, disagreements over points of doctrine and meaning arose at these sessions. These disputes led to the formation of rival schools of monks, who vied with each other, the brahmans, and other sects to build a popular following.

Over time, the rival schools created elaborate philosophical systems. But in their efforts to attract a broader following, the monks stressed more accessible aspects of what had become a new religion. They offered miraculous tales of the Buddha's life, which included traditions that his mother had been a virgin and that he had been visited by revered scholars from afar soon after his birth. In the popular mind, nirvana became equated with heaven. Graphic visions of heavenly pleasures and the tortures of hell became central features of popular Buddhism. The Buddha was worshiped as a savior who returned periodically to help the faithful find the way to heaven. Although within the monastic communities Buddhist monks continued their emphasis on meditation and the achievement of nirvana, laypeople were encouraged to perform good deeds that would earn enough merit for their souls to go to one of the Buddhist heavens after death.

The Buddhist Challenge

Many philosopher-ascetics criticized the religious beliefs and caste system that the brahmans had established. But none was as successful at winning converts as the Buddha and the many monastic orders committed to his teachings. The monks and monastic organizations provided a viable alternative to the brahman priesthood as centers of scholarship, education, and religious ritual, and often directly opposed the beliefs that the brahmans championed. Although the Buddha retained the ideas of karma and reincarnation, he rejected the Vedas as divinely inspired teachings that ought to be accepted as the ultimate authority on all issues. He ridiculed the powers the brahmans claimed for their sacrifices and the gods for whom they were intended. He favored introspection and self-mastery over ritual. In so doing, he struck at the very heart of the brahmans' social and religious dominance.

The Buddha rejected the lifestyles of both the brahmans who had become addicted to worldly power and the brahman ascetics who practiced extreme forms of bodily mortification. He tried to do away with the caste system, an aim that gave his teachings great appeal among the untouchables and other groups. The Buddha also accepted women as his followers and taught that they were capable of attaining nirvana. These opportunities were institutionalized in Buddhist monastic organizations, which normally included provisions for communities of nuns. The evidence we have suggests that monastic life became a fulfilling career for women in many parts of India. This outlet proved doubly meaningful in an era when educational and other occupational opportunities for women were declining, and upper-caste women in particular were increasingly confined to the home.

The Greek Interlude

The intellectual and social ferment that swept northern India in the 6th century B.C.E. was intensified by political upheavals touched off by the invasion of northwestern India by Alexander the Great. This was an important, although not unique, case of direct contact between two core civilization areas during the classical period. In 327 B.C.E. Alexander's armies crossed the Hindu Kush into India, thus beginning his last major campaign of conquest. Although his incursions began well, the ultimate retreat of his armies clearly demonstrated that his rapidly built empire was overextended and Indian forces among the most formidable he faced in his many campaigns. Initially, his greatly outnumbered armies won a series of battles against the peoples living in the upper Indus valley. As in his Persian campaigns, Alexander's well-trained troops proved more than a match for the war chariots, archers, and cavalry of his Indian adversaries. Once the surprise wore off, his veteran soldiers also proved able to cope with the war elephants that had frightened their horses in early battles.

Victory stirred Alexander's passion for further conquests. But his soldiers, weary of endless battles and fearful of the stiffening resistance of Indian princes in what seemed to them an exotic and very distant land, refused to go farther east. After much debate, Alexander agreed to lead his forces out of India. Those who survived an epic march through the desert wastes to the north and west of the Indus river returned to Persia in 324 B.C.E. Alexander's death a year later left his Indian conquests to be fought over by the commanders who divided up his empire.

Although several Greek rulers controlled territory in India's northwest for decades after Alexander's invasion, the impact of his campaign was largely indirect. It stimulated trade and cultural exchange between India and the Mediterranean region. Of particular importance were the flow of Greek astronomical and mathematical ideas to India and the impact of Indian thinking on religious movements in the Mediterranean. Greek Stoicism and the mystery religions that swept the eastern Mediterranean in the centuries around the birth of Christ owe much to Indian philosophical influences. In the arts, the combination of Indian and Greek styles led to an Indo-Greek school of sculpture that was both distinctive and influential in shaping approaches to the depiction of the Buddha. Indian motifs were blended with Greek physical features and artistic techniques.

THE RISE AND DECLINE OF THE MAURYAS

6.4 | What changes in religious practices and brahman interaction with other Indian social groups were most critical to the Brahmanical revival and the beginnings of the decline of Buddhism in South Asia?

Appropriately, the most lasting effects of Alexander's invasion were military and political. The defeats suffered by the kingdoms in the northwest created a political vacuum that was soon filled by the ablest of the regional lords, **Chandragupta Maurya** (322–298 B.C.E.). Despite some initial setbacks, Chandragupta, whose original base was on the Ganges plain in the vicinity of the present-day state of Bihar, embarked on a sustained campaign to build a great empire. After conquering much of the northwest and driving the Greek successors of Alexander out of India, his armies began to conquer the kingdoms of the Ganges plain that would later form the heartland of the **Mauryan** (MAHR-yuhn) empire (see Map 6.1).

As Chandragupta's empire grew, the folksy atmosphere of earlier localized court centers gave way to a new imperial style. He reigned from an elaborately carved and decorated palace set in large and well-tended gardens. Adopting the Persian example, Chandragupta proclaimed himself an absolute emperor and on state occasions sat on a high throne above hundreds of his splendidly attired courtiers. He was guarded by a special corps of amazons, and elaborate precautions were taken to safeguard his life. The food Chandragupta ate was first tasted by servants to ensure that it was not poisonous. There were hollow pillars in which to hide palace spies, secret passages to enable the king to move about the palace undetected, and an obligatory bath and frisking for all who entered. Chandragupta built a standing army that Greek writers estimated (overly generously) at 500,000, and he tried with some success to replace regional lords with his own administrators.

With the support of the powerful Mauryan ruler Ashoka, from the 3rd century B.C.E. Buddhism appeared destined to become the preeminent philosophy and main arbiter of social relations in a rapidly changing Indian civilization.

Chandragupta Maurya [chun druh gUp tuh mour EE uh] (r. 322–298 B.C.E.) Founder of Maurya dynasty; established first empire in Indian subcontinent; first centralized government since Harappan civilization.

Mauryan Dynasty established in Indian subcontinent in 4th century B.C.E. following invasion by Alexander the Great.

Arthashastra [är thä shäs trä] Political treatise written during reign of Chandragupta Maurya; advocated use of spies and assassins, bribery, and scientific forms of warfare.

All of these safeguards were consistent with the recommendations set forth in a treatise on statecraft, the *Arthashastra*, that dominated political thinking during Chandragupta's reign and in the centuries that followed. The *Arthashastra* bore a much greater resemblance to Xunzi's *Art of War* than to Plato's *Republic*. Attributed to **Kautilya**, an astute advisor to Chandragupta Maurya, the work is actually a compilation over many generations of the political theory and practical advice of several authors. In great detail, Kautilya and his fellow political strategists described the techniques a ruler must use to attain and hold power. Spies disguised as beggars, barbers, and even holy men should be stationed everywhere in a king's own domains and those of his enemies. Crime and internal dissent must be punished harshly. The authors of the *Arthashastra* sanctioned the removal of rival rulers by bribery and assassination (for which specially trained prizefighters were recommended) and by using traitors to undermine resistance in neighboring kingdoms. Like Xunzi in China, they scorned the notion of chivalrous warfare.

With such advice, it is little wonder that Chandragupta and his successors rapidly conquered a vast empire that included all of south Asia but the southern tip (Map 6.1). Chandragupta's son and successor, Bindusara, extended the Mauryan Empire to the east along the Ganges plains and far to the south of the subcontinent. Little is known about Bindusara, but he was apparently a highly cultured man. He once requested wine, figs, and a philosopher as presents from one of the Greek rulers in western Asia. He received the wine and figs, but not the philosopher because, as the ruler informed him, the Greeks did not trade in philosophers. Bindusara's son, **Ashoka**, completed the conquests begun by his father and grandfather, and in his long reign from 268 to 232 B.C.E., northern India enjoyed unprecedented political unity, prosperity, and cultural splendor.

Ashoka's Conversion and the Flowering of Buddhism in the Mauryan Age

In the early years of his rule, Ashoka showed little of the wisdom and tolerance that set off his reign as one of the great periods in Indian history. He won his throne only after a bloody struggle in which he eliminated several brothers. According to contemporary Buddhist sources, which are intent on depicting Ashoka before his conversion in the worst possible light, he was both bad-tempered and impetuous. One often-cited example of Ashoka's brutal excesses was his insistence that a woman from his harem be put to death for telling him that he was ugly. He also delighted in conquest, at least until he witnessed the horrible sufferings that were caused by his conquest of Orissa in eastern India. That experience, and regret for his earlier brutality, led to his conversion to Buddhism.

From the time of his conversion onward, Ashoka strove to serve his people and promote their welfare. He ceased to enlarge his domains by conquest, used his revenues to build roads, hospitals, and rest houses, and sought to reduce the slaughter of animals in his kingdom by encouraging vegetarianism. His attempts to curb the slaughter of cows, either for sacrifices or for food, were particularly important. These efforts, in conjunction with a long-standing reverence for cattle that reached back to the Harappan era, contributed to the sacred status that this animal long ago attained in Indian civilization. Because Ashoka's edicts were aimed at restricting animal sacrifices, they aroused the anxiety of the brahmans, who saw them as a threat to the rituals that were vital to their dominance in Indian society.

The influence of Buddhism on Ashoka's personal life spilled over into his state policy. Drawing on the Buddhist concept of a righteous world ruler spreading peace and good government, Ashoka attempted to build an imperial bureaucracy that would enforce his laws and sanctions against war and animal slaughter. Although his efforts to establish meaningful

Kautilya (350–275 B.C.E.) Political advisor to Chandragupta Maurya; one of the authors of *Arthashastra*; believed in the scientific application of warfare.

 Read the **Document** on MyHistoryLab: Kautilya, from *Arthashastra*, "The Duties of Government Superintendents"

Ashoka [uh sO kuh] (r. 273–232 B.C.E.) Grandson of Chandragupta Maurya; completed conquests of Indian subcontinent; converted to Buddhism and sponsored spread of new religion throughout his empire.

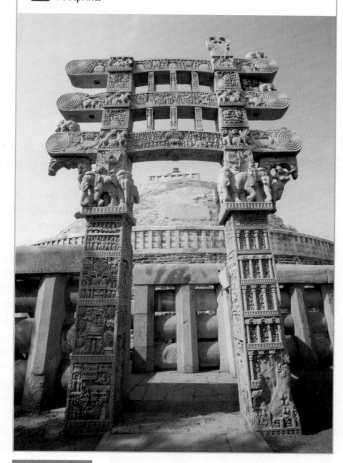

View the **Closer Look** on MyHistoryLab: The Buddha's Footprints

FIGURE 6.3 The great Buddhist stupa at Sanchi in central India. Stupas were built to house relics of the Buddha, and they became major sites of pilgrimage. The intricate carved gates and railing surrounding the stupa related incidents from the Buddha's life or displayed symbols associated with his teachings. The great dome that covered the dirt mound that formed the core of the stupa often was painted white, and it struck approaching pilgrims as a great cloud floating on the horizon.

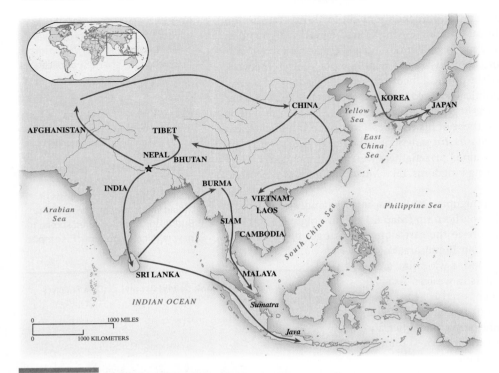

MAP **6.2 The Spread of Buddhism in Asia, 400** B.C.E.–**600** C.E. In less than two centuries wandering missionaries had carried the Buddhist faith from central Asia to Sri Lanka and into China and Japan.

View the **Closer Look** on MyHistoryLab: Lion Capital of Ashoka at Sarnath

FIGURE **6.4** Two of the four lions that originally sat atop the Ashoka column at Sarnath, in present-day Uttar Pradesh, India (this view of the sculpture obscures the other two lions). This sculpture, now housed at the Sarnath Museum, was carved from a single sandstone block. Ashoka used the lions as the emblem of his rule.

control by a centralized administration met with some success, they also aroused opposition. The brahmans, resenting their displacement as political advisors and administrators by Ashoka's bureaucrats, tried to stir up local resistance. Warrior families that had once ruled the small states also sought to retain control over local politics. They waited for signs of dynastic weakness in the hope of reviving their lost kingdoms.

Imperial Patronage and Social Change

Several social groups gained from Ashoka's attempts to recast Indian society in a Buddhist mold. Seeing in Buddhism an advantageous alternative to the caste system, merchants and artisans supported Ashoka's efforts. They generously patronized orders of Buddhist monks, which increased greatly in wealth and membership. Women also had good reasons to support the Buddhist alternative. Their position within the family was strengthened under Buddhist law. In addition, the monastic life gave them opportunities for achievement and self-expression as nuns, scholars, and artists.

One of the chief signs of the Buddhist surge under Ashoka and his successors was the spread of great monastery complexes throughout the subcontinent. Most of the monasteries were made of wood and thus were lost in fires or destroyed by later invaders. But the Buddhist architectural legacy was preserved in the great stone shrines, or **stupas**, that were built to house pieces of bone or hair and personal possessions that were said to be relics of the Buddha (Figure 6.3). Most of the freestanding stupas were covered mounds of dirt surrounded by intricately carved stone gateways and fences. In many ways more technically impressive were the shrines and monasteries, such as those at Ajanta pictured and discussed at the beginning of the chapter, crafted out of solid rock.

Another major effect of Ashoka's dedication to Buddhism resulted from his efforts to spread the faith beyond the Indian subcontinent (Figure 6.4). He sent missions, including one led by one of his sons, to Sri Lanka to the south and to the Himalayan kingdoms and the steppes of central Asia to the north. Establishing Buddhism in each region was critical because converted rulers and monks in these areas were instrumental in spreading the religion to much of the rest of Asia. From Sri Lanka, Buddhism was carried to Burma, Java, and many other parts of southeast Asia. From Nepal and central Asia, it was carried into Tibet, China, and the rest of east Asia (Map 6.2).

Ashoka's Death and the Decline of the Mauryas

Ashoka's bold experiments in religious and social change and the empire that he and his forebears had established did not long survive his death. Weaker rulers followed him to the throne. The empire was first divided between rival claimants within the Maurya household and then pulled apart by internal strife and local lords who attempted to reestablish the many kingdoms that had been absorbed into the empire. By 185 B.C.E., the Mauryan Empire had disappeared. Political fragmentation returned to the subcontinent, and new warrior invaders compounded the rapidly growing divisions. Although some of these conquerors built substantial empires and were devoted to the continued spread of Buddhism, none of them could match Ashoka in power and resolution.

 Read the **Document** on **MyHistoryLab:** Emperor Asoka, from the *Edicts of Asoka*

BRAHMANICAL RECOVERY AND THE SPLENDORS OF THE GUPTA AGE

stupas Stone shrines built to house pieces of bone or hair and personal possessions said to be relics of the Buddha; preserved Buddhist architectural forms.

6.5 Why are the Maurya and Gupta dynasties considered a golden age in the history of Indian civilization?

Even in the centuries immediately after the fall of the Mauryan dynasty, when the influence of Buddhism in Indian society was at its height, patterns had developed that rendered it vulnerable to a brahman counteroffensive. Over time, Buddhist monks became more and more concentrated in huge monasteries. Increasingly isolated from village and urban life, the monks grew obsessed with fine points of philosophy that often had little or no relevance to ordinary believers. Because Buddhism in India had not developed a sequence of family and life-cycle rituals or folk festivals, the monks had little occasion to interact with the people. They focused their services more and more on wealthy patrons, whose donations supported the monasteries. This support made the daily rounds to collect alms unnecessary for the monks in many areas and led to luxurious lifestyles and lax discipline at some of the more prominent Buddhist centers.

While the Buddhist monks became more remote from the Indian populace, the brahmans strove to make changes in belief and worship that would make **Hinduism** more appealing to ordinary people. They played down the need for grand and expensive sacrifices and stressed the importance of personal worship and small, everyday offerings of food and prayers to the gods. Increasing emphasis was placed on intense devotion to gods, who were seen as manifestations of one divine essence. The most important of these gods included **Shiva** (see Figure 6.2 on page 121) and **Vishnu** and their female consorts Kali and Lakshmi. Certain gods were especially revered by particular occupational groups, such as Ganesh, the elephant-headed, pot-bellied deity who was favored by merchants.

Temples sprang up to house the multitude of statues that were the focus for popular worship of the gods. Devotional cults were open to people at all caste levels, sometimes including the untouchables. Women also were allowed to participate, at times, as cult poets and singers. In addition, the brahmans multiplied or enriched special festivals and rites of passage, such as child-naming celebrations, weddings, and funerals. These occasions enlarged the role the brahmans played in the everyday life of the Indian people. Over centuries, revived Hinduism simply absorbed salvationist Buddhism. The brahmans treated the Buddha as another god of the Hindu pantheon and allowed their followers to worship him as one of the worldly forms of the preserver god Vishnu.

At the elite level, brahman philosophers and gurus placed increasing emphasis on the sophisticated and sublime philosophical ideas associated with the later books of the Vedas, the *Upanishads.* Not heaven or hell but the release of the soul from the endless cycle of rebirths was stressed in these teachings. Moderate asceticism and meditation were the means by which this release was achieved. In contrast to the Buddha, who preached that the soul itself was an illusion, the orthodox Hindu schools taught that the soul was real and its ultimate purpose was to fuse with the universal divine essence from which it had come. The world was *maya*, or illusion, only because it was wrongly perceived by most humans. Those who had achieved realization and release understood that the world was an extension of a single reality that encompassed everything.

In addition to monastic weaknesses and brahman reforms, Buddhism in India was weakened by economic changes that altered the social circumstances that had favored the new religion. Most critical was the decline of the Rome–China trading axis with the fall of the Han Empire in the 3rd century C.E. Not only did this undermine the position of the merchant groups that had been major patrons of Buddhism, but it also made large-scale traders more and more dependent on local kings and warrior households, which remained the chief allies of the brahmans.

The damage done to Buddhism by the diminished support of the mercantile classes was compounded by the collapse of the Mauryan and later Buddhist empires, which had been the monastic

The loss of patronage on the part of the powerful Mauryan dynasty proved a major setback for Buddhism in its largely peaceful rivalry with Brahmanism. This trend in turn paved the way for the rise of the Gupta dynasty and the consolidation of the religious systems and social hierarchies that Western scholars later viewed as a coherent Hindu religious and social order.

Hinduism The name given to the mixture of forms of religious expression that became the predominant religion of India from last centuries B.C.E. Hinduism developed from the blending of sublime philosophical thinking, popular polythesistic cults, and mysticism.

Shiva Hindu god of destruction and reproduction; worshiped as the personification of cosmic forces of change.

Vishnu The brahminical, later Hindu, god of sacrifice; widely worshiped.

Upanishads. [oo-PAHN-uh-shadz] Later books of the Vedas; contained sophisticated and sublime philosophical ideas; utilized by brahmans to restore religious authority.

VISUALIZING THE PAST

The Pattern of Trade in the Ancient Eurasian World

THE PERIOD OF MAURYAN RULE COINCIDED with a great expansion in trade between the main centers of civilization in Eurasia and Africa. In the centuries that followed, a permanent system of exchange developed that extended from Rome and the Mediterranean Sea to China and Japan. The trading networks that made up this system included both those established between ports connected by ships and sea routes and those consisting of overland exchanges transmitted along the chain of trading centers that crossed central Asia and the Sudanic region of Africa. By the last

centuries B.C.E., this far-flung trading system included much of the world as it was known to the peoples of the Eastern Hemisphere.

Some products produced at one end of the system, such as Chinese silks and porcelains, were carried the entire length of the network to be sold in markets at the other edge, in Rome, for example. As a general rule, products carried over these great distances tended to be high-priced luxury goods such as spices and precious jewels. But most of the exchanges, particularly in bulk goods such as metal ores or foodstuffs, were between adjoining

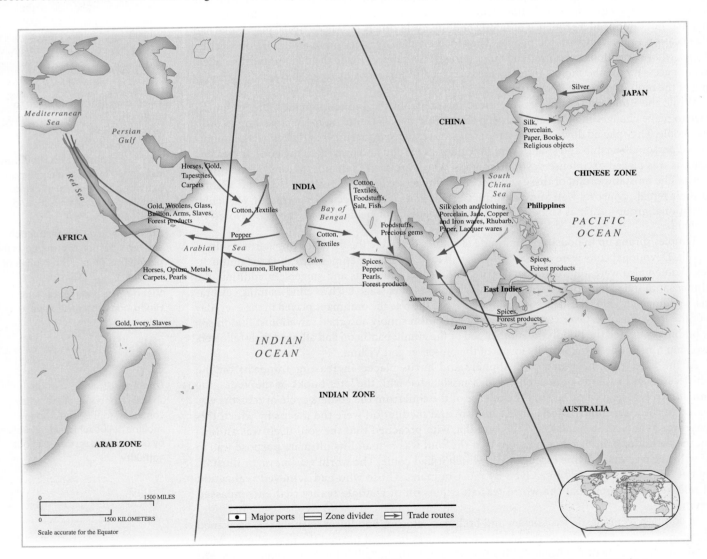

MAP **6.3 Eurasian and African Trading Goods and Routes, c. 300 B.C.E. to 300 C.E.** As the map illustrates, a vibrant oceanic trading system was in place across the Afro-Eurasian continents by the last centuries B.C.E., and the Indian subcontinent was central as a producer and consumer in this vast network of contact and exchange.

(continued on next page)

regions. The ports of western India, for example, carried on a brisk trade with those in the Red Sea and Persian Gulf, while trading centers in southeast Asia supplied China with forest products and other raw materials in exchange for the many items manufactured by China's highly skilled artisans. Although some merchants and sailors, particularly the Chinese and Arabs, could be found in ports far from their homelands, most confined their activities within regional orbits, such as the Arabian Sea, the Persian Gulf, or the South China Sea.

Map 6.3 provides an overview of this great trading network in the age of the classical civilizations, roughly the 3rd century B.C.E. to the 3rd century C.E. It shows the main centers of production, the goods exported overland and overseas, and the main directions of trade in these products.

QUESTIONS

- Which civilizations or areas in the global trading network were the main centers for the production of finished products, such as cloth and pottery?
- What major centers supplied raw materials, such as forest products or foods? Why were luxury goods likely to be transported the greatest distances?
- Why were bulk goods, especially foods, usually shipped only short distances, if at all?
- Besides trade goods, what other things might be transmitted through the trading networks?

orders' supreme source of patronage. Their eventual replacement by the **Guptas**, who were enthusiastic supporters of the brahmans and Hinduism, all but sealed the fate of Buddhism in India. Its demise was gradual and only occasionally hastened by violent persecution. But centuries of rule by the Guptas in north India and Hindu kingdoms in the south left only pockets of Buddhist strength, which decayed over time.

Guptas Dynasty that succeeded the Kushans, one of the Buddhist dynasties that emerged after the fall of the Mauryas in the 3rd century C.E.; built empire that extended to all but the southern regions of Indian subcontinent; less centralized than Mauryan Empire.

The Gupta Empire

In the last decades of the 3rd century C.E., a family of wealthy landholders in the eastern Ganges plains infiltrated the court of the local ruler and seized his throne. Through a succession of clever alliances and timely military victories, the Gupta family built an empire that by the end of the 4th century C.E. extended across most of northern India (Map 6.4). The Guptas' domains were not nearly as extensive as those of the Mauryas, and they had far less control over the regional lords and villages than the Mauryas had, particularly under Ashoka. The Gupta rulers never tried to build a genuine bureaucracy or regulate affairs at the local level. Their empire was in fact a massive tributary edifice in which former kings were left to rule in the name of the Guptas, and regional warrior elites were autonomous governors of all but the empire's heartlands in the Ganges basin.

The Guptas were content to be acknowledged as supreme overlords and to draw tribute from the many vassals under their rule. Weak control from the center meant that local lords periodically revolted or squabbled among themselves. Although internal warfare continued, it was at a lower level than in the centuries after the fall of the Mauryas. Until the 5th century, foreign invaders were kept beyond the Himalayas and internal conflicts were short and localized. Gupta dominance brought more than two and a half centuries of peace and prosperity to much of north India.

A Hindu Renaissance

From the outset, the Guptas had been staunch defenders of Hinduism and patrons of the brahmans. With the family's rise to power, the brahmans' roles as sanctifiers of and advisors to kings were fully restored. Buddhist monks were increasingly confined to their monasteries, which, lacking the patronage of the imperial court, had to depend on wealthy local merchants or landowners for support. The brahmans' roles as gurus, or teachers, for the princes of the imperial court and the sons of local notables also became

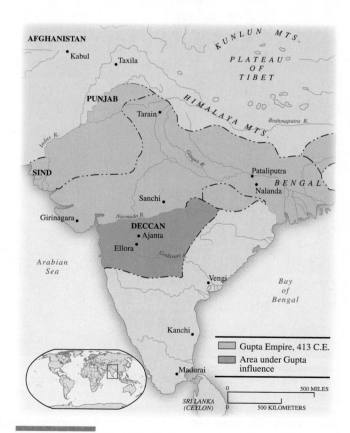

MAP **6.4 The Gupta Empire** Not only was the territory claimed by the Gupta dynasty a good deal smaller than the empire of their Mauryan predecessors, even the area controlled was ruled to a far greater extent by local lords than the Gupta emperors.

Signet Ring of Rakshasa One of the great Sanskrit dramas produced in the Gupta period; dramatized authority of brahmans.

entrenched. Brahmans regained the aura of mystery and supernatural power that they had enjoyed in the Vedic age. In the **Signet Ring of Rakshasa** (rahk-SHAH-sah), one of the great dramas produced in the Gupta epoch, King Chandragupta prostrates himself at the feet of his teacher and advisor, Chanyaka (chahn-YAK-ah). The ruler lavishes presents on brahmans linked to the court and relies on their stratagems to thwart his adversaries. With their power base and sources of patronage restored, brahman priests, poets, scholars, and patrons of the arts became the driving force behind an era of splendid achievement in literature, music, art, architecture, and the natural sciences.

The most dramatic expressions of the Hindu resurgence were the great temples that rose above the rapidly growing urban centers, both within the Gupta domains and in the independent kingdoms in the far south (Figure 6.5). In many cases the temples provided the impetus for urban growth. Merchants, artisans, servants, and laborers migrated to the towns where the temples were located to serve the growing numbers of pilgrims who journeyed to the sacred sites. The intricately carved stone gateways and sanctuary towers proclaimed the majesty of the Hindu gods and goddesses. In eastern and South India, the temple towers teemed with sculptures of deities and friezes of their exploits; with animals, which were often the vehicles or manifestations of major gods or goddesses; and with humans engaged in all manner of activities, including sexual intercourse.

Hindu art stressed symbolism rather than the accurate representation that was so highly valued by the ancient Greeks. The sculpture and the god or goddess it depicted stood for something else, including creation (Brahma), destruction (Shiva), fertility (Lakshmi), and death (Kali as Durga). In fact, the temple complexes as a whole were massive **mandalas** (MUN-duh-luhs), or cosmic diagrams, measured precisely and laid out according to established conventions.

mandalas Cosmic diagrams; part of the Hindu belief system.

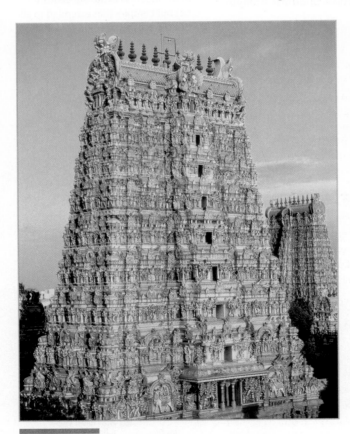

FIGURE **6.5** Like medieval cathedrals and Islamic mosques, great temples like this one attest to the intense faith and devotion associated with the Hindu resurgence of the early centuries c.e. Meenakshi Temple, shown here, is eleven stories tall and entirely covered with intricate sculptures. The temple forms the core of Madura, one of the oldest cities in India, whose streets were built in concentric rectangles around the temple, symbolizing the structure of the cosmos.

Achievements in Literature and the Sciences

Although written languages had developed in India before the rise of the Gupta dynasty, the Gupta reign initiated one of the great ages of Indian literary achievement. In the Gupta period and the centuries that followed, many of the great classics of Sanskrit, the sacred and classical Indian language, and Tamil, one of the major languages of the south, were written. The poet Kalidasa (kah-lee-DAH-sah), who is acknowledged as the greatest Sanskrit author, lived in a period when Gupta power was at its height. In the "Cloud Messenger" and numerous other poems, he provided vivid pictures of life in the Gupta age. In the following passage, for example, the clouds bringing the monsoon rains pass over a town where, the poet exclaims,

> Your body will grow fat with the smoke of incense from open windows where women dress their hair.
>   You will be greeted by palace peacocks, dancing to welcome you, their friend.
>   If your heart is weary from travel you may pass the night above mansions fragrant with flowers
>   Whose pavements are marked with red dye from the feet of lovely women.

In addition to poetry and drama, Hindu scholars in the classical era wrote treatises on the nature of time, space, and causality. These works contain arguments that have much in common with the findings of modern science on many issues. In fact, the era of the Hindu revival was a time of great Indian achievement in mathematics and the sciences. In addition to advances in geometry and algebra that were made independently of the work in these fields by the Greeks, Indian thinkers calculated the circumference of the globe and the value of pi (π) with remarkable accuracy. They also used the concept of zero, devised decimals, and, most critically, formulated the system of numbers that virtually all human societies use today. We in the "West" call these "Arabic" numerals because it was through Arab merchants and scholars that they came to be known and used in Europe from the 10th century c.e. onward. In the Gupta age and afterward, the

Indians also made major breakthroughs in medicine. They developed hospitals, surgical techniques, and sophisticated treatments for a variety of illnesses.

INTENSIFYING CASTE AND GENDER INEQUITIES AND GUPTA DECLINE

6.6 Why and by what was Buddhism eventually eclipsed in India even as it spread through much of the rest of Asia?

As the brahmans recovered their social dominance, the caste hierarchy they had long promoted became the backbone of the Indian social system. Caste divisions grew even more complex and came to vary significantly between different areas in the subcontinent. Styles of dress increasingly distinguished members of each varna, and the restrictions on untouchables and other low-caste groups grew harsher and more pervasive. In some areas, for example, untouchables traveling on roadways had to clap sticks together or shout to warn high-caste groups that they were in danger of being polluted. If a brahman or merchant was seen approaching, the untouchable was required to leave the road and pass by through the fields at a distance. The untouchables were not allowed to use any wells but their own or to worship in the temples used by other caste groups. Their living quarters were segregated from the rest of the towns and rural villages.

Women at all caste levels suffered a further reduction of their status and restriction of career outlets. They were no longer allowed to read the sacred Vedas, although a few remained prominent in the devotional cults. Hindu law declared that women were legally minors, subject to the supervision and protection of their fathers, husbands, and (if widowed) sons. Except for their personal clothing and jewelry, women were not allowed to inherit property. The fact that family fortunes could pass only from father to son and that large dowries were required to arrange marriages with suitable spouses meant that girls were increasingly seen as an economic liability. In some regions where dowry amounts were highly inflated, female infants were killed to save families from financial ruin.

Women were tied to the home, their lives run by men. As the passage quoted in the Document box indicates, a young woman was raised to defer to her husband and to respond to his every wish. Marriages were primarily a means of establishing alliances between families. They were arranged with the groom having little say and the bride none. Child marriages were not uncommon among the upper castes. Young girls left the familiar surroundings of their own homes to live with their husbands' families. In their new households, they were at the mercy of their mothers-in-law, who could be caring and reassuring but, if the literature from this and later periods is any gauge, were very often bossy and critical. A young girl's place in the new household depended almost wholly on her ability to bear sons, who would care for her in old age. A woman whose husband died before she bore him a son was doomed to a lonely life in the remote corners of the family compound. Even widows who bore sons were not to be envied. They were not allowed to remarry or go out alone lest they defile the memory of their deceased husbands.

Other than marriage, few avenues were open to women. A single woman was regarded as an economic liability and a blot on her family's honor. As the Buddhist monasteries shrank in numbers and size, the possibility of becoming a nun diminished. Only by becoming a courtesan, accomplished in all the arts including sexual intercourse, could a woman establish some degree of independence. Courtesans, who are sometimes celebrated in the literature of this period, could become well educated, acquire wealth, and find outlets for their talents. They were far above the despised common prostitutes in status, but they could not hope to have social respectability or raise families of their own. Unlike married women, whose husbands were duty bound to support them, courtesans depended on the tastes and whims of men, who dominated all aspects of interaction between the sexes in the Gupta age.

The Pleasures of an Elite Life

Although women were limited in career options and largely confined to the home, life for those of the upper castes had its rewards, at least once a woman had established her place in her husband's family by having sons. Well-to-do families lived in large compounds set in gardens filled with flowering

The surge in creativity in the arts and sciences that came with the restoration under the Guptas of the brahmans' influence was offset to some extent by the growing rigidity of the caste system and the increase in control that males, particularly household heads, were able to exert over women at all social levels.

Read the Document on MyHistoryLab: Cast(e)aways? Women in Classical India (200 C.E., 6th c. C.E.)

plants and colorful birds. They were waited on by servants and entertained at periodic festivals and in their own compounds by swings, games such as chess and pachisi (both of which the Indians invented), and wandering musicians. They dressed in silks and fine cottons and enjoyed one of the world's great cuisines. When they ventured away from the family compound, the very wealthy were carried in litters borne by servants and given the place of honor to which their caste entitled them.

Men from the upper castes were particularly privileged. They were expected to experience the four stages of the ideal Hindu life that were firmly established in this era for men only. In their youth they were to work hard as students, but many diversions and pleasures were available to the fashionable sons of well-to-do families. Many of these pastimes are described in the famous ***Kamasutra*** (kah-muh-SOO-truh) by Vatsayana (vaht-seh-YAH-neh), who lived in the Gupta era. Although often dismissed as little more than a glorified sex manual, Vatsayana's work contains detailed instructions on virtually all aspects of the good life for the wealthy young man. There are recommendations for grooming and hygiene, discussions of good etiquette in various situations, advice on the best way to select a wife, and, of course, instructions in making love to either a witty and knowledgeable courtesan or one's future wife. There was a double standard: Young men were expected to come to marriage knowledgeable in the ways of love, but young women who were not virgins were disgraced and unmarriageable.

The student was expected in the second stage of life to become a householder and, ideally, a faithful husband. Preserving or adding to the family fortune was a major task in this phase of life, and bearing sons to perform one's funeral rites and continue the family line was essential. At some point in middle age, the householder was supposed to bid farewell to his family and go off to the forest to join the hermits in meditation. In his final years, the upper-caste man was expected to enter the fourth stage of life by becoming a wandering holy man, completely dependent on the charity of others. Few men actually advanced beyond the householder stage. But the fact that the sequence had become the social ideal in the Gupta age indicates that religion and society could readily accommodate scholarship and worldly pursuits, bodily denial, and meditation as valid paths to self-fulfillment.

Kamasutra Written by Vatsayana during Gupta era; offered instructions on all aspects of life for higher-caste males, including grooming, hygiene, etiquette, selection of wives, and lovemaking.

DOCUMENT

A Guardian's Farewell Speech to a Young Woman About to Be Married

ONE OF THE GREAT PLAYS WRITTEN during the Hindu revival of the early centuries C.E. was Shakuntala, by Kalidasa. The play is a Cinderella-style tale about a beautiful young woman, Shakuntala, who is loved by a king, and the travails she must endure before they are happily united. In the following exchange, as Shakuntala sets out to join her husband at his palace, she is instructed by her guardians (the hermits Kashyapa and Gautami) on the proper behavior for a young wife, in a manner that recalls the famous speech by Polonius to his son, Laertes, in Shakespeare's *Hamlet*.

Kashyapa: Now you Shakuntala. Respect your superiors,
Be friendly toward the ladies of the palace.
Never be angry with your husband, no matter what happens.
Be polite with the maids;
In everything be humble.
These qualities make a woman; those without them are black sheep in their families.
What is your opinion, Gautami?

Gautami: A bride needs nothing more. Remember his advice, Shakuntala.

Shakuntala: How will I ever manage in the palace? I feel so lost. I belong here, Father.

Kashyapa: Don't worry, my child; you are privileged.
You will be his great wife;
He is noble and great.
You will give him a son, as the East gives us light.
The pain of separation will then pass.

QUESTIONS
- What does this conversation tell you about gender relationships and marriage in classical India?
- What does it say about attitudes toward women?
- How do these relationships and attitudes compare with those found in China and Greece in this era?
- How do they compare with those in our own society?

Lifestyles of the Ordinary People

For most Indian peasants, artisans, and sweepers at the lower levels of the caste system, the delights of upper-caste youths or the life of a wandering holy man were unattainable. Most Indians lived lives of hard work, if not sheer drudgery. Most knew no deference from others but rather spent their lives bowing to and serving their caste superiors. At the lower-caste levels, women were somewhat freer in their ability to move about the town and countryside and buy and sell in the local marketplace. But they had no servants to perform their many household chores and had to do backbreaking farming tasks, such as weeding fields or transplanting rice.

There were, of course, small pleasures. Even low-caste groups could attend temple festivals, watch dances (Figure 6.6), and dramatics performed in the open air, and risk their meager wages in dice games or betting on roosters specially bred to fight with each other. In an age when India was one of the most fertile and productive regions on the earth, it is probable that all but the untouchables lived as well as ordinary people did anywhere in the world.

The Indian economy continued to grow in the Gupta period, despite the decline of long-distance trade with China and Rome. Leadership in international commerce increasingly shifted to the trading cities on the east and west coasts and the southern seaports. Strong trading links were maintained with kingdoms in Sri Lanka and throughout southeast Asia, which were strongly influenced by Indian cultural exports. In fact, India became the pivot of the great Indian Ocean trading network that stretched from the Red Sea and Persian Gulf in the west to the South China Sea in the east—a position it maintained until the age of European overseas expansion from the 16th century C.E. By the time of the Guptas, India was known as a land of great wealth as well as the home of many religions. A Chinese Buddhist, Fa-hsien, on a pilgrimage to India, exclaimed, "The people are many and happy. They do not have to register their households with the police. There is no death penalty. Religious sects have houses of charity where rooms, couches, beds, food, and drink are supplied to travelers."

FIGURE **6.6** Stylized sculptures depicting young women from the Hindu temple at Khajuraho in eastern India. These figures represent a standardized form of feminine beauty in south Asian culture: large breasts, small waist, and ornate jewelry. The profusion of jewelry was already in evidence in the Harappan figurines that are believed in many cases to be goddesses. The stylized physical features may have reflected the well-conditioned figures of female dancers. In the Gupta era these highly trained professionals were a prominent feature of major court centers and large temple complexes, such as the one at Khajuraho.

Gupta Decline and a Return to Political Fragmentation

For nearly 250 years, the Guptas managed to hold together the collection of vassal kingdoms that they passed off as an empire. Signs of future danger appeared in the northwest with the first of the probes across the Himalayas by the nomadic Huns from central Asia in the early 5th century C.E. Preoccupied by the growing threat on their northern frontier, the later Gupta rulers failed to crush resistance from their vassals and challenges from states to the south of the Gupta domains. By the middle of the century, Gupta efforts to hold back repeated assaults by greater and greater numbers of Hun invaders were faltering. With the death of **Skanda Gupta** (SKAHN-deh GOOP-the), the last of the truly able Gupta monarchs, a flood of nomadic invaders broke into the empire. Their pillaging and widely dispersed assaults finished off what remained of Gupta military might, and the empire dissolved into a patchwork of local kingdoms and warring states. From the mid-7th century until the establishment of the Delhi Sultanate (DEHL-ee SUHL-tehn-ate) in the early 13th century, northern India was divided and vulnerable to outside invasions.

Skanda Gupta Last of the able rulers of the Gupta dynasty; following his late 5th-century reign, the empire dissolved under the pressure of nomadic invasions.

Global Connections and Critical Themes

INDIA AND THE WIDER WORLD

The 6th and 5th centuries B.C.E. were a time of great social turmoil and philosophical speculation throughout Eurasia. In China, Confucius and Laozi proposed very different views of the proper organization of human society and purposes of life. In Persia, Zoroaster founded a new religion, while in Palestine the prophets Ezekiel and Isaiah strove to improve the Hebrews' understanding of their single, almighty God. In Greece, the writings of Thales and Pythagoras laid the basis for unprecedented advances in philosophy, the sciences, and mathematics. India too was caught up in this transcontinental trend of social experimentation and intellectual probing. No classical civilization was more open to outside influences than that of the Indian subcontinent. And none was more central to cross-cultural exchanges in the centuries that ushered in what we have come to label the Common Era (C.E.) of world history.

The brahman-dominated, caste-ordered civilization that flourished at the end of the Vedic era and later under the Guptas produced some of humanity's most sublime art and philosophy; important breakthroughs in mathematics, the sciences, and technology; prosperous urban centers; and a population that has been second in size only to that of China through much of human history. The period dominated by the Mauryas in between saw the spread of Buddhism, one of a handful of truly world religions. In this era and the age of the Guptas that followed, Buddhism was but one of numerous components of Indian civilization that were exported to China and east Asia, across the steppes of central Asia, throughout most of southeast Asia, and as far west as the Mediterranean.

In mainland and island southeast Asia, the impact of Indian civilization was especially critical. Indian merchants played a key role in trade with these regions, and other influences followed. Indian religions and epics, art and architecture, and concepts of kingship sparked the rise of centralized states and complex societies that culminated in great civilizations, such as those centered at Angkor Wat (AHNG-kohr what) in Cambodia and the kingdom of Majapahit (mah-jeh-PAH-hiht) in central Java. In the Mediterranean Indian influences were felt in areas as diverse as artistic techniques, philosophies such as Stoicism, and religious ideas that significantly affected Christianity. Central to all of these developments was the fact that in the centuries that witnessed the flowering of Indian civilization under the Mauryas and Guptas, the coastal areas of the Indian subcontinent became, and would remain for millennia, one of the core areas of an ever-expanding trading network that would eventually encompass most of the Eastern Hemisphere. Indian manufactured goods, such as cotton textiles and bronze statuary, soon became some of the most coveted commodities in this system of exchange. Indian merchants and sailors would carry them throughout the Indian Ocean and to the emporiums of the Silk Road that dominated overland trade beyond the Himalaya Mountains. Indian religions, artwork, scientific discoveries, and epic literature came to enrich, and at times spur major transformations in, civilizations over much of the known world.

Further Readings

Perhaps the most readable introductions to life and society in India's classical age can be found in A. L. Basham's *The Wonder That Was India* (1963) and Jeannine Auboyer's *Daily Life in Ancient India* (2002 reprint ed.). The works of Romilla Thapar, especially *Ashoka and the Decline of the Mauryas* (1997) and *Early India: From the Origins to AD 1300* (2003), are the best on the political history of the era. Her broader *A History of India*, Vol. 1 (1991 reprint), and more recent *Cultural Pasts: Essays in Early Indian History* (2000) are very detailed and quite technical—certainly a challenge for the beginner. On the Guptas the most comprehensive recent work is Ashvini Agrawal's *Rise and Fall of the Imperial Guptas* (1989). Fine narrative histories of all aspects of Indian civilization in this period can be found in the appropriate chapters of *The History and Culture of the Indian People* (1964), edited by R. C. Majumdar, A. K. Majumdar, and D. K. Ghose. Some of the best works on the position of women and social life more generally include Pandharinath Prabhu's *Hindu Social Organization* (1940), L. K. Tripathi, *Position and Status of Women in Ancient India* (1988), and S. Tharu & K. Lalita, eds., *Women Writing in India 600 to the Present* (1991). On the development of the caste system, see B. R. Kamble, *Caste and Philosophy in Pre-Buddhist India* (1979). A wide range of other aspects of ancient Indian culture is covered in the fine essays in A. L. Basham's *A Cultural History of India* (1975).

Superb introductions to various branches of Indian religious and philosophical thinking, with well-selected portions of the appropriate texts, can be found in S. Radhakrishnan and Charles Moore, eds., *A Source Book in Indian Philosophy* (1967); and Ainslee Embree, ed., *Sources of Indian Tradition*, Vol. 1, *From the Beginning to 1800* (2nd ed., 1988). Of the many books on Buddhism, Trevor Ling's *The Buddha* (1973) is one of the more accessible, but needs to be supplemented with recent research, many of the findings of which are explored in Jonathan S. Walters, *Finding Buddhists in Global History* (1998). The spread of Indian culture to southeast Asia in this period is covered in the classic work by G. Coedés, *The Indianized States of Southeast Asia* (1964), and more recently in G.C. Pande's *India's Interaction with Southeast Asia* (2006).

S. Radhakrishnan's *Hindu View of Life* (1927) provides a useful insider's view of Hindu religious beliefs and social organization. Heinrich Zimmer's *Philosophies of India* (1956), although somewhat dated, remains a good place to begin exploring the riches and diversity of Indian mythology and religious thinking. Susan Huntington's *The Art of Ancient India* (1985) offers a stimulating and very accessible discussion of the art of this period. Benjamin Rowland's *The Art and Architecture of India* (1970), which includes Southeast Asia, remains the most comprehensive work available in English on Indian art overall; J. C. Harle's *Gupta Sculpture* (1974) provides an introduction to some of the glories of the Gupta age. For a taste of Indian literature in the classical period, there are English translations of the *Ramayana* and the *Mahabharata* and P. Lal's fine translations of *Great Sanskrit Plays* (1957).

Critical Thinking Questions

1. What factors were responsible for the political divisions and short-life spans of the few imperial dynasties that emerged in classical India? What, by contrast, in Chinese civilization made possible the succession of powerful dynasties that unified and exerted significant control over most of China in this era?

2. What aspects of India's geography, social system, and economy account for the dominant role it played in the Indian Ocean trading system and the advantages and profits Indians enjoyed in commerce with distant civilizations, particularly the Roman Empire?

3. Why were Indian religions, especially Hinduism and Buddhism, as well as Indian myths, epics, and art forms so readily diffused throughout southeast, central and east Asia as well as Greece and the eastern Mediterranean?

7

Rome and Its Empire

((•)) Listen to Chapter 7
on MyHistoryLab

The heralded Roman legions are among the most famous fighting forces in world history. The Roman army began as a citizen army, fighting for a republic that had recently freed itself from outside control. Its initial spirit derived from the enthusiasm for defending one's own land or pushing back immediate enemies. As Rome expanded, however, citizen enthusiasm for military service declined: It was hard to be away from home so much. So the army gradually became more professional, offering inducements such as the granting of citizenship for service.

The army was well trained and well equipped. Each soldier had protective breastplates and headgear as well as a long and short sword, one for each hand. Discipline was tight; deserters

🔍 **View the Closer Look on MyHistoryLab**: Spoils from Jerusalem on the Arch of Titus in Rome

FIGURE **7.1** A stone relief from Rome's Arch of Titus, a monument celebrating the achievements of the Emperor Titus, most notably, the defeat of the Jews who had revolted against the Roman occupation of Judea. This relief depicts Roman soldiers carrying away loot, including a menorah, taken during the destruction of the Temple of Jerusalem in 70 C.E.

were put to death. The word *decimation* comes from the practice of identifying cowardly or disloyal groups of soldiers: One-tenth of their number—the term comes from the Roman word for ten—was selected by lot, and the other soldiers had to stone them to death. Soldiers were schooled never to give up. In contrast to Greek phalanxes, the infantry in the Roman legions lined up in three columns, making breakthroughs less likely—but service in the front line could be correspondingly deadly. And military service was no small commitment. As the army professionalized, stints lasted for 20 years, with an additional four years in reserves.

Still, until Rome's declining years, the volunteers poured in. Would-be soldiers sent in letters of recommendation and tried to find patrons to get them a place. Many were fleeing poverty. Many were attracted to citizenship or to other benefits, including small grants of land that were awarded to those who served in the army. As time went on, the army's legions received special insignia, including eagle emblems, which were a source of pride and identity.

What was most impressive, however, in drawing recruits and then motivating the army itself, was the tight comradeship the army established. Modern sociologists have shown that what really keeps troops going in battle is their loyalty to their immediate comrades. Rome had no sociologists, but it knew the importance of tight social ties. Troops were called to order in their groups, with trumpets blaring out signals. When it was time to move out from camp, a general's crier asked each group, in its own language, whether it was ready to go to war. The troops responded with loud shouts, "We are ready," raising their right hands. One observer noted that "a kind of martial fury" seized them well before actual battle began. After major victories, parades in front of adoring Roman crowds and public monuments commemorating the campaign could solidify the loyalty of the soldiers.

At the height of the army's power, the Roman legions contained 160,000 troops, and there were many additional border guards. Later in the empire, the army began to deteriorate. Its loyalty to Rome became questionable, its drawing power was reduced, and ultimately, it cost more than a declining economy could afford. For centuries, however, as Rome moved from small republic to giant empire, the military, with its organization and fighting zeal, served as a backbone to a complex society. ■

The army, and its achievements and evolution, connect directly to the larger history of Rome. The earliest phases of Roman history occurred while Greece and then Alexander and his successors held center stage to the east. It was during the 5th century B.C.E. that a new city-state near the middle of the Italian peninsula began to define a separate existence. Soon Rome took on the trappings of a regional civilization, complete with its own language and an alphabet derived from the Greek letters. Roman influence in Italy gradually expanded, making the Italian peninsula a focus of activity in the western Mediterranean. In the process, Rome picked up additional trappings of Greek culture, extending Mediterranean civilization to the west, in Europe and north Africa alike.

The emergence of Rome, and particularly its empire, invites comparison with developments in classical China—a number of similarities and differences emerge. Both contrast with the more frequently divided and localized political experience in Greece and India. Rome, however, did not generate as powerful a cultural identity as China managed, in part because it depended so heavily on Greek examples that were on the whole more creative and original.

Roman expansion began early. In the 3rd century B.C.E., Rome twice defeated the north African city-state of Carthage. These wars not only made Rome supreme in the west but also involved it in the affairs of the declining Hellenistic kingdoms. By the mid-2nd century B.C.E., Rome ruled Greece and the eastern Mediterranean directly, although it never penetrated fully into the Middle East's heartland.

500 B.C.E.	300 B.C.E.	100 B.C.E.	1 C.E.	100 C.E.	200 C.E.
500–450 Beginnings of Roman republic; Twelve Tables of Law **400** Rome completes control of central Italy	**264–146** Punic Wars **167** Rome begins conquest in eastern Mediterranean **146–133** Decline of Roman republic **133–121** Gracchus brothers' reform attempts **107 ff.** Increasing power of generals **106–43** Cicero	**70–19** Vergil **46** Julius Caesar dictator **44** Assassination of Caesar **27** Augustus Caesar; rise of Roman Empire	**c. 30** Crucifixion of Jesus **35** Paul converts to Christianity	**101–106** Under Trajan, Roman Empire reaches its greatest size **180** Death of Emperor Marcus Aurelius; beginning of decline of Empire	**313** Constantine legalizes Christianity **476** Fall of Rome

The Romans' massive empire flourished for four centuries and then limped through another 250 years in decline, an achievement in political organization and durability that the Greeks had never attained. Consequently, the fall of the Roman empire, in 476 C.E., was far more dramatic than the more gradual evolution of Greece and the Hellenistic world.

Finally, the Roman empire served as a seedbed for one of the great religious changes in world history: the advent of Christianity. Christianity did not spring directly from the mainstream principles of Greco-Roman civilization, but it did use many of these principles selectively. In its spread and in its church structure, it depended directly on what Rome had achieved.

Rome's development calls attention to political and military issues and achievements above all. Social and economic changes were significant as well, as the Romans worked hard at economic integration of the Mediterranean. Military expansion seemed necessary in part to nourish the social system, as well as supporting the political structure of the later republic and empire. Cultural activities were interesting but decidedly less original, until the emergence of Christianity began to alter the philosophical and artistic, as well as religious, structure of much of the region.

THE DEVELOPMENT OF ROME'S REPUBLIC

7.1   What were the causes of Roman expansion?

The people of Rome were Indo-Europeans who migrated to Italy beginning about 1000 B.C.E. They gradually adopted agriculture and, by about 800 B.C.E., gained some contact with Greek settlements farther south. Rome was ruled for a time by the **Etruscans**, who provided powerful kings and organized tightly knit armies skilled in the use of horses and war chariots. The Etruscans imposed a strong government, but about 510 B.C.E., the local Roman aristocracy rebelled and gradually devised a constitution carefully crafted to avoid tyrannical control. The Romans developed a *republic*—a state without a king—because they had found monarchy contrary to the public good *(res publica)*. By this time the Romans had also adapted the Greek alphabet to form their own Latin alphabet, which remains in use throughout western Europe and the Americas today.

The Early Republic

The constitution of the early **Roman republic** favored the aristocracy. Aristocrats staffed the powerful **Senate**, which advised on policy and selected magistrates (Figure 7.2). But lower-class citizens gained some voice. As in Greece, citizenship gave some people definite legal and political rights. In about 450 B.C.E., a law code was written to protect the property holdings of ordinary people and facilitate commerce. Soon, the ordinary citizens, or **plebeians**, won the right to elect their own representatives, the **tribunes**. However, it was the Senate that continued to serve as the center of Roman political life.

During the republic, Rome established balanced political institutions, providing aristocratic leadership and some popular control. From the beginning, Rome engaged in territorial expansion.

Etruscans Culture that ruled Rome prior to republic; ruled through powerful kings and well-organized armies; expelled by Romans c. 510 B.C.E.

 View the Map on MyHistoryLab: Italy before the Roman Empire, ca. 900–509 B.C.E.

Roman republic The balanced constitution of Rome from c. 510 to 47 B.C.E.; featured an aristocratic Senate, a panel of magistrates, and several popular assemblies.

The two chief executives, or **consuls**, were elected by an annual assembly in which the wealthy predominated. This basic political structure successfully balanced various interests but resembled many Greek city-states in depending heavily on the aristocratic voice. It lasted for several centuries as Rome moved from a small local state to the center of a growing empire.

The early Roman economy also resembled that of Greece about three centuries before. Aristocrats controlled large estates, but there were many grain-growing farmers, who were also independent citizens capable of military service. By introducing early the idea of written law (which placed some check on arbitrary aristocratic actions) and by allowing popular assemblies and elected officials to give some voice alongside the aristocratic Senate, the Roman republic constructed more explicit balances than most of the early Greek city-states had done. More than the Greeks, the Romans emphasized patron-client (**clientage**) relationships by which landlords would aid and protect lesser citizens in return for loyalty and work.

Rome's diplomatic and military directions departed even more markedly from the patterns of the early Greek poleis because there were fewer social tensions to distract the government and because no successful city-state rivals managed to restrain the dynamic newcomer.

The Expansion of Rome

Rome initially developed its solid army based on the service of citizen-farmers. Roman leaders often chose to be portrayed in military dress, for the army quickly gained a role beyond the most immediate self-defense. Rome was not as sheltered from outside attack by natural boundaries as many of the Greek poleis had been. It faced challenges from other areas in Italy, including a league of city-states to the north. Rome dealt with these challenges, from 496 B.C.E. onward, through a combination of alliances and military attacks. By about 400 B.C.E. it had gained control over the whole of central Italy. A second wave of expansion, toward the southern end of the peninsula, began about 360 B.C.E., gradually winning over rival tribes by means of superior military organization and tight control over allied states.

Scholars have debated why Rome became so expansionist. Some point to a general greed and aggressiveness, others to the specific political system in which consuls had only a year in office in which to gain glory through military victories. Romans themselves usually argued that they were acting in self-defense, and certainly each acquisition prompted new argument for further expansion to protect the territory against attack. Ultimately, other motives developed, such as the quest for slaves, that made continued expansion essential.

The Roman military legions were supported by the rich agricultural economy of central Italy, which provided an abundant population base, and each wave of expansion increased the military and economic resources available. Once established, Roman rule proved flexible, although it provoked some resentment. Beginning in 338 B.C.E., Rome began to grant elites in some conquered areas Roman citizenship, which reduced the likelihood of rebellion. In other cases, Rome allowed local governments to persist. Only in a few cases did colonies depend only on garrisons of Roman soldiers to keep order, although civilian and military settlements did extend the reach of Roman culture.

Expansion into southern Italy made Rome a rival of the former Phoenician colony **Carthage** for control of the western Mediterranean. Carthage, located in northern Africa in the modern nation of Tunisia, had a substantial navy and was quick to see the threat from Roman control over Sicily. A series of **Punic Wars** (*Punic* from the Roman word for *Phoenician*) began in 264 B.C.E. Rome developed its own navy for the first time; both Carthage and Rome generated new allies and colonies in Spain as competition escalated. During the Second Punic War the great Carthaginian general **Hannibal** brought a large army to Italy, including 50 war elephants. But gradually the Romans wore Carthage down. In the Third Punic War (146 B.C.E.) the Romans decided to kill or enslave every inhabitant of Carthage. Insisting "Carthage must be destroyed," Romans also spread salt around the city so nothing could grow. Rome now had a significant overseas empire, including much of Spain and substantial parts of northern Africa held either outright or through allied states.

Senate Assembly of Roman aristocrats; advised on policy within the republic; one of the early elements of the Roman constitution.

plebeians Ordinary citizens; originally those Roman families that could not trace their relationship to one of the major Roman clans.

tribunes Plebeian representatives in the Roman republic; elected in the Councilium Plebis Tributum on an annual basis.

consuls Two chief executives or magistrates of the Roman republic; elected by an annual assembly dominated by aristocracy.

clientage The social relationship whereby wealthy Roman landholders offered protection and financial aid to lesser citizens in return for political support and labor.

Read the Document on MyHistoryLab: Livy, The Rape of Lucretia and the Origins of the Republic

FIGURE **7.2** Marcus Junius Brutus (c. 85–42 B.C.E.) was a Roman political leader who became the protégé of Julius Caesar. When Caesar declared himself dictator, Brutus turned against him and was one of the chief architects of and participants in the dramatic assassination carried out by a number of Roman senators on the Ides of March, 44 B.C.E.

Carthage Originally a Phoenician colony in northern Africa; became a major port and commercial power in the western Mediterranean; fought the Punic Wars with Rome for dominance of the western Mediterranean.

Punic Wars Fought between Rome and Carthage to establish dominance in the western Mediterranean; won by Rome after three separate conflicts.

Hannibal Great Carthaginian general during Second Punic War; successfully invaded Italy but failed to conquer Rome; finally defeated at Battle of Zama.

As Map 7.1 demonstrates, Rome's growing power also drew the new empire toward the eastern Mediterranean, partly to defeat Carthaginian allies such as Macedon and partly because rival states in the region appealed for help. The collapse of the Hellenistic kingdoms left a vacuum of power in this region that Rome was called to fill. From 167 B.C.E. onward the Romans began to conquer Macedonia and Greece, and they soon set up a protectorate over the Asian coast of the Mediterranean as well as Egypt.

The Results of Expansion

The republic was often brutal in its treatment of the areas conquered outside Italy. Opponents of Roman rule in Greece were punished severely; much wealth and many prisoners were seized. The conquest of Spain during the 2nd century B.C.E. produced repeated atrocities. Imperial expansion changed Roman society and politics, to the dismay of traditionalists. New trade and wealth enriched the upper classes, creating larger gaps between rich and poor and making it increasingly difficult to manage Rome's balanced constitution. Aristocrats exploited many farmers who could not compete with cheap grains imported from Sicily and later northern Africa. Central Italy, like Greece before it, turned into a grape and olive region, highly commercial and organized mainly in large estates. Adding to social complexity was the rise of an important business class, which also helped the state to collect taxes. Slavery also increased as a result of military conquests. Many slaves worked in households

MAP **7.1 The Expansion of the Roman Republic, 133** B.C.E. By the end of the Punic Wars, Rome dominated much of the Mediterranean world.

or craft production, even tutoring Roman children, but bands of slaves were used in mining and on the great agricultural estates. Scholars generally believe that at least 2 million people passed through slavery in Italy during the 2nd and 1st centuries B.C.E.

The Crisis of the Republic

What was happening around Rome closely resembled earlier patterns in Greece, where social and economic tensions produced political unrest. But the Roman crisis was in many ways greater because the expanding empire created so many new opportunities for the upper classes to gain new lands and increase their supply of slaves. Dispossessed farmers flooded into the city of Rome. This began a process that would push the city's population past 1 million, much of it consisting of poor, irregularly employed laborers. The result of these changes was a deep class conflict between popular leaders and aristocrats during the final decades of the republic. In this setting many ambitious leaders in both camps, including successful army generals, maneuvered for personal advantage.

In 133 B.C.E., a new tribune, **Tiberius Gracchus**, tried to limit the size of large estates, with the government redistributing some land to the poor. The Senate opposed the plan, and Tiberius was assassinated by conservatives. During the following decades, **Gaius Gracchus**, Tiberius' brother, introduced land reforms and made a special attempt to appeal to both the rising business class and the urban poor. Gracchus also proposed extending Roman citizenship to more of the Italian people, but the Roman masses selfishly opposed this dilution of their authority. The Senate decreed that Gracchus was to be put to death; a servant helped him fall on his sword. Political rivalries and violence continued.

The republic became little more than a battleground for opposing ambitions. In 107 B.C.E., a successful army general, **Marius**, who had put down a rebellion in one of Rome's client kingdoms in northern Africa, became consul. Marius began using paid volunteers from the lower classes for his army, creating a permanent military group with great political potential through their ability to coerce the Senate. In 77 B.C.E., another general, Pompey, came to the fore. Like his predecessors, he enhanced his power by winning new conquests, first in Spain and then in the Middle East. His success, plus renewed civil war at home, prompted the Senate to give him special powers. A middle-class political leader, **Cicero**, eloquently pleaded for a return to republican balance, arguing against the generals and demagogues who tried to win popular support through emotional appeals and promises, but he was not heeded.

Pompey then joined with other generals, including **Julius Caesar**, to form a new government that could override the Senate. Caesar, who won considerable support from the Roman lower classes, pursued his own goals by winning new territory across the Alps in Gaul (present-day France). He then defied Pompey and the Senate by bringing his troops back to Italy and taking over the government in 49 B.C.E. Effectively, Caesar's victory in the ensuing civil war ended the republic.

Caesar made few formal changes in government institutions. The Senate, which was packed with Caesar's men, still existed and debated, but its acts were a sham because of Caesar's control of the army. Caesar brought more Italians and other provincials into politics at the expense of old Roman families. Made dictator for 10 years and then for life, Caesar named many new officials and judges and introduced important reforms, such as a more scientific calendar that formed the basis for the one we use today. Caesar was suspected of wanting to set up a monarchy, and he was assassinated by traditionalist senators in 44 B.C.E.

Caesar's death led to 13 more years of civil war; his cause was defended by his grandnephew and adopted son Octavian, who fought the armies of the Senate. Octavian soon took the name *Caesar*, which would come to mean emperor. In a series of wars, particularly in Egypt and the Middle East, Octavian finally won out. His last opponents, Mark Antony and his wife, Cleopatra, queen of Egypt, committed suicide in 31 B.C.E, ending the civil strife and making Octavian absolute master of Rome and the entire Mediterranean world. Octavian then crafted a new set of institutions that would be suited to Rome's vast territory while not unduly offending the republican traditions still cherished by many citizens. He created an outright empire, with himself as first emperor under the name **Augustus Caesar**. This empire was a success as Rome, unlike the earlier Greek poleis, made a successful transition to a new form of government.

Gracchus, Tiberius (163–132 B.C.E.) Along with Gaius Gracchus, tribune who attempted to introduce land and citizenship reform within the Roman republic; assassinated by conservatives.

Gracchus, Gaius (154–121 B.C.E.) Tribune who, along with Tiberius Gracchus, attempted to introduce land and citizenship reform within the Roman republic; killed on the command of the Senate.

 Read the **Document** on **MyHistoryLab:** Appian of Alexandria, "War, Slaves, and Land Reform: Tiberius Gracchus" (ca. 150 CE)

Marius (157–86 B.C.E.) Successful Roman general who introduced the concept of using paid volunteers in his army rather than citizen conscripts; created military force with personal loyalties to commander.

Cicero (106–43 B.C.E.) Conservative Roman senator; Stoic philosopher; one of great orators of his day; killed in reaction to assassination of Julius Caesar.

Caesar, Julius Roman general responsible for conquest of Gaul; brought army back to Rome and overthrew republic; assassinated in 44 B.C.E. by conservative senators.

Augustus Caesar (63 B.C.E.–14 C.E.) Name given to Octavian following his defeat of Mark Antony and Cleopatra; first emperor of Rome.

Rome

Rome began as a small village in the 9th century B.C.E., on the Tiber River and near the Mediterranean coast. Its location benefited from trade along the western side of the Italian peninsula. The city itself was built out from several hills, and by the third century was the leading city in the whole peninsula. The expansion of slave-operated farms by the second century B.C.E. drove a rapid expansion of the city's population. City walls, some of which still stand, had to be frequently extended to accommodate the growth in size. Housing was often in short supply, and substantial apartment buildings were crowded with tenants. As in all the cities of agricultural societies, craft shops combined production and sales, with the producers living on the premises, while open-air markets dispensed food from the countryside.

By the time of the Roman Empire the city was the largest in the world, with a population estimated at between one and two million. Augustus and other emperors sponsored massive new buildings—it was said of Augustus that he found a city of brick and left a city of marble. The government also had to subsidize food for this huge agglomeration, paying directly for 25% of all grain supplies and covering the costs by taxes on people throughout the Empire. Plagues and other challenges began to reduce the city's population from the second century C.E. onward, and periodic "barbarian" invasions furthered the process of decline. But Rome preserved great luster, which accounts for the ultimate decision to locate the Catholic papacy there.

ROMAN CULTURE

Roman culture embraced Greek and Hellenistic styles, creating a common cultural framework for elites throughout the Mediterranean basin.

7.2   What was the relationship of Greek and Roman culture?

Greek artistic styles and literary influence increasingly shaped Roman upper-class life, from the 2nd century B.C.E. into the days of the empire, although as the Document box reveals, the result was a raging cultural controversy over what Roman values should be. Many aristocratic families were educated by Greek slaves, who as tutors had considerable independence and in a few cases produced important literary and historical works of their own. Imitation of Greece was aided by the similarity between Roman and Greek religions in which essentially the same gods and goddesses merely had different names.

The Range of Roman Art

Vergil (70–19 B.C.E.) One of greatest of Roman poets during "Golden Age" of Latin literature; patronized by Augustus; author of *Aeneid*.

Rome began to develop an important literature by the time of the late republic, although its literary creativity was less impressive than that of the Greeks. The Roman poet **Vergil** picked up the Greek epic tradition and linked Roman history and mythology with the great stories of the *Iliad* and the *Odyssey* in his work the *Aeneid*. Roman poets and biographers also were active, shaping the Latin language and providing stylistic models. Roman sculptors worked mainly in the Greek tradition, producing busts of great men and statues and scenes of heroic grandeur. Rome also developed active painters, who produced lively (and sometimes pornographic) decorations for the houses of the wealthy.

Greek influence and the practical issues of politics in an increasingly complex society prompted creativity in many other areas, although science advanced little beyond the compilation of Greek material into textbooks. Roman leaders valued skill in oratory, and they advanced discussions of the arts of rhetoric. Ethical philosophy received much attention. Hellenistic schools, including Stoicism, won many converts because Roman leaders were eager to develop arguments for moral behavior that had strong logical support. Writers such as Cicero discussed the joys and sorrows of human life, urging moderation and a dedication to the public good.

Roman architecture benefited as the city's wealth grew. Again, Greek styles provided primary inspiration, with the Romans preferring more ornate designs for columns and arches, as Figure 7.3 illustrates. But Rome added its own genius to Greek architecture, mainly through engineering advances that allowed larger structures to be built. Huge stadiums, public baths, temples, massive aqueducts to carry water to cities, great stretches of paved road, and huge port facilities began to appear in the later republic. Urban Romans, both men and women, delighted in bath pavilions that

DOCUMENT

Rome and a Values Crisis

ROME'S INCREASING CONTACT WITH THE EASTERN Mediterranean, particularly Greece, brought important debates about culture. Many conservatives deplored Greek learning and argued that it would corrupt Roman virtue. Cicero, a leading politician in the Senate and a major Latin writer, here defends Greek literature, using Hellenistic justifications of beauty and utility. Cicero played a major role in popularizing Greek culture during the 1st century B.C.E. His comments also reflect the concerns that Greek culture inspired a source of change.

Do you think that I could find inspiration for my daily speeches on so manifold a variety of topics, did I not cultivate my mind with study, or that my mind could endure so great a strain, did not study provide it with relaxation? I am a votary of literature, and make the confession unashamed; shame belongs rather to the bookish recluse, who knows not how to apply his reading to the good of his fellows, or to manifest its fruits to the eyes of all. But what shame should be mine, gentlemen, who have made it a rule of my life for all these years never to allow the sweets of a cloistered ease or the seductions of pleasure or the enticements of repose to prevent me from aiding any man in the hour of his need? How then can I justly be blamed or censured, if it shall be found that I have devoted to literature a portion of my leisure hours no longer than others without blame devote to the pursuit of material gain, to the celebration of festivals or games, to pleasure and the repose of mind and body, to protracted banqueting, or perhaps to the gaming-board or to ball-playing? I have the better right to indulgence herein, because my devotion to letters strengthens my oratorical powers, and these, such as they are, have never failed my friends in their hour of peril. Yet insignificant though these powers may seem to be, I fully realize from what source I draw all that is highest in them. Had I not persuaded myself from my youth up, thanks to the moral lessons derived from a wide reading, that nothing is to be greatly sought after in this life save glory and honour, and that in their quest all bodily pains and all dangers of death or exile should be lightly accounted, I should never have borne for the safety of you all the brunt of many a bitter encounter, or bared my breast to the daily onsets of abandoned persons. All literature, all philosophy, all history, abounds with incentives to noble action, incentives which would be buried in black darkness were the light of the written word not flashed upon them. How many pictures of high endeavor the great authors of Greece and Rome have drawn for our use, and bequeathed to us, not only for our contemplation, but for our emulation!

These I have held ever before my vision throughout my public career, and have guided the workings of my brain and my soul by meditating upon patterns of excellence.

But let us for the moment waive these solid advantages; let us assume that entertainment is the sole end of reading; even so, I think you would hold that no mental employment is so broadening to the sympathies or so enlightening to the understanding. Other pursuits belong not to all times, all ages, all conditions; but this gives stimulus to our youth and diversion to our old age; this adds a charm to success, and offers a haven of consolation to failure. In the home it delights, in the world it hampers not. Through the night watches, on all our journeying, and in our hours of country ease, it is an unfailing companion.

If anyone thinks that the glory won by the writing of Greek verse is naturally less than that accorded to the poet who writes in Latin, he is entirely in the wrong. Greek literature is read in nearly every nation under heaven, while the vogue of Latin is confined to its own boundaries, and they are, we must grant, narrow. Seeing, therefore, that the activities of our race know no barrier save the limits of the round earth, we ought to be ambitious that whithersoever our arms have penetrated there also our fame and glory should extend; for the reason that literature exalts the nation whose high deeds it sings, and at the same time there can be no doubt that those who stake their lives to fight in honour's cause find therein a lofty incentive to peril and endeavor. We read that Alexander the Great carried in his train numbers of epic poets and historians. And yet, standing before the tomb of Achilles at Sigeum, he exclaimed, "Fortunate youth, to have found in Homer an herald of thy valor!" Well might he so exclaim, for had the *Iliad* never existed, the same mound which covered Achilles' bones would also have overwhelmed his memory.

QUESTIONS

- What kind of objections to Greek learning is Cicero arguing against?
- Which of his arguments had the most lasting appeal to those who were reshaping Roman culture?
- Can you think of similar debates about foreign culture in other times and places in history?
- How would you use this document to reconstruct the debate Cicero was participating in and why it seemed important?

Source: Cicero, *Pro Archia Poeta*. Translated by N. H. Watts. Loeb Classical Library. Cicero, *Pro Archia* (Harvard University Press, 1965), 12–14, 16, 23–24.

FIGURE **7.3** This is an artist's recreation of the Forum in imperial times. The use of decorative styles that originated in classical Greece was a central feature of Roman architecture, but as the empire grew, buildings became steadily more massive. Larger columns and greater heights reflected the Roman taste for the monumental. Ultimately, Roman architects also developed the capacity to build domed structures—a feat of engineering.

(Hypothetical reconstruction of the Roman Forum in Imperial Times. Southern part. Watercolor. Soprintendenza alle Antichita, Rome, Italy/Scala/Art Resource, NY.)

Read the Document on MyHistoryLab: Vitruvius, "On Symmetry" from *The Ten Books on Architecture*

Horace Poet who adapted Greek poetic meters to the Latin language; author of lyrical poetry laudatory of the empire; patronized by Augustus.

featured pools of hot and cold water, often in ornate surroundings. Baths, along with stadiums, began to appear not only in Rome but in cities throughout the empire, as a means of displaying power and attracting Roman colonists. Roman ability to construct elaborate arches, which allowed buildings to carry great structural weight, was unsurpassed anywhere in the world. Under Augustus, statues, fountains, and temples to the gods spread through Rome, making the city the showcase of the new empire, with a population of 1 million. Massive monuments, in styles adapted from the Greeks, were built from England in the north to the desert fringes of northern Africa, from Spain to present-day Hungary and Romania, and down the Middle Eastern coast of the Mediterranean.

Of course, not all Roman architecture was of such splendor. Many plebeians in Rome and other cities lived in *insulae*, crowded, unstable apartment buildings. After a fire in 64 C.E., new measures were introduced to make the insulae more comfortable and fire-resistant. The buildings now had to abide by maximum height limits and to be constructed at least partially from fireproof stone, not just wood. The government made more efforts to maintain the public water system, so that water was accessible to all.

Major Themes in Roman Literature

Prosperity and greater stability during the reign of Augustus and his successors brought growing attention to other cultural activities. Many writers praised the new imperial house, but poets such as **Horace** combined this loyalty with humor and creative skill in adapting Greek poetic meters to the Latin language. Horace, initially a republican, shifted his support to Augustus; his odes were lyrical poems, many of them praising the emperor and his family.

Vergil's great epic poem the *Aeneid* was dedicated to the glories of Augustus and his empire:

Now fix your sight, and stand intent, to see your Roman race, and Julian progeny.
There mighty Caesar waits his vital hour,
Impatient for the world, and grasps his promised power.
Africa and India shall his power obey . . .
But Rome! 'tis thine alone, with awful sway,
To rule mankind, and make the world obey,
Disposing peace and war, thy own majestic way.

After the cultural surge of the late republic and early empire, which was spurred by the assimilation of Greek forms, Roman cultural activity declined somewhat. Intellectual life continued, but it stressed preservation, imitation, textbook summaries, and education of the upper classes. Well before the empire began to deteriorate politically, mainstream literary and artistic vitality began to decline. Only the new religious inspiration of Christianity generated new uses for Latin and Greek literary skill, philosophy, and art.

HOW ROME RULED ITS EMPIRE

Augustus and his successors built the Roman Empire on a strong military, tolerance, and an effective legal code.

7.3 How did the Roman empire survive so many inept rulers?

The legacy of Rome included its republican institutions, elements of its culture, but also the structure and achievements of its empire. By the time of Octavian, Rome governed a population almost as large as that of China, but its organizing principles were somewhat different from those of its Chinese counterpart.

Rome's rule of its growing empire rested heavily on tolerance. The empire depended far less on an extensive bureaucracy than its Chinese counterpart. Local governments, including the old Greek city-states, gained autonomy as the harsh colonial policies of the republic were revised. Some whole kingdoms, as in parts of northern Africa, were preserved, although they were required to obey Roman foreign policy and obtain permission for any new succession to the throne. This policy of tolerance greatly facilitated Roman control, for an elaborate bureaucratic apparatus was not needed. Only much later, in different circumstances, did lack of centralization prove to be a disadvantage. At the same time, Rome maintained small military garrisons in most areas and large outposts in newly conquered or threatened regions. Army generals doubled as provincial governors in such cases, which allowed them to build regional power, even to the point of challenging the emperor back in Rome. In only a few cases, such as the forced dissolution of the independent Jewish state in 63 C.E. after a major local rebellion, did the Romans take over distant areas completely.

Augustus and His Successors

In building an imperial government after his final victory in 31 B.C.E., Octavian talked sincerely about the validity of republican virtues and the importance of discipline and family virtues. He also retained many of the agencies of the republic, including the Senate, while weakening most of them by installing his own supporters, who were in full control. Symbolizing the transition, in 27 B.C.E. the Senate voted to grant Octavian the title *Augustus*, a word often applied to gods and appropriate to an office that dominated the state. The emperor thus controlled the apparatus of government, making major appointments and military decisions and establishing new laws and policies.

Augustus set about consolidating his new regime by instituting moral reforms, banning mystery religions, and insisting on adherence to traditional Roman ceremonies. He revised the law to strengthen family stability while encouraging people to have children by ruling that women with at least three children could gain new rights. Augustus launched an ambitious new building program in Rome, which brought new jobs to the Roman masses and new entertainments as well. Augustus also tried to regularize control over the provinces. He relied heavily on his army of 250,000 men, including the fabled Roman legions, giving them abundant rewards for long service and loyalty. He maintained the earlier policy of allowing local autonomy to accompany military strength while encouraging the development of Romanized colonies in many provinces, particularly in northern Africa and western Europe.

The empire Augustus created maintained its basic organizational structure for about two centuries. Incompetent emperors were common in this period, in part because no clear lines of succession were established. Effectively, the army controlled basic power, which worked well when a strong emperor held the army's loyalty but badly when an emperor lost command of the troops. Succession battles among rival generals were common. By 96 C.E., emperors began to reduce these problems by adopting their own successors. This practice yielded a series of five good emperors who brought Rome to its greatest power. The best of the early emperors tried to maintain Augustus's careful balance between real authority and the appearance of respect for political tradition and law. For example, Emperor Claudius wanted to marry his niece, which was illegal. He might have ignored the law, but instead he changed it so that any Roman man could marry a niece.

Government and Expansion

The Roman imperial state maintained a fairly standard set of functions. Regulation of commerce was essential to the Roman state's efforts to ensure vital stocks of grain from Egypt, Sicily, and northern Africa. A large official staff was needed to oversee food supplies and prices for huge cities such as Rome. Public works in the form of roads and harbors facilitated military transport as well as commerce, and government-sponsored amenities such as public baths and stadiums attracted public loyalty and helped recruit Roman settlers for such distant provinces as Britain. The building of aqueducts to carry water to cities was another major state activity. All these public works and regulations took substantial tax revenues.

Government-supported religious ceremonies continued, but there was little attempt to impose this religion on all subjects, and various other religions, including the worship of the Egyptian goddess Isis, usually were tolerated. Only Jews and, later, Christians found the state's claim to primary loyalty unacceptable, and only they drew Roman reprisals. The Roman government tolerated Jewish monotheism but reacted fiercely to Jewish revolt. Even the later Roman emperors, who promoted the idea that the emperor was a god, normally were tolerant of other religions, inconsistently attacking Christianity because of the Christians' refusal to place the state first in their devotion.

View the **Closer Look** on **MyHistoryLab**: A Roman Warship

Trajan Roman emperor from 101 to 106 C.E.; instituted more aggressive imperial foreign policy resulting in expansion of empire to its greatest limits.

Expansion continued during the early empire. The emperor **Trajan** adopted an aggressive foreign policy in 101–106 C.E. The boundaries of the empire were pressed to the greatest extent ever; fortifications were built in northern England and along the Rhine and Danube rivers, signaling the inclusion of much of western Europe in the new geography of Mediterranean civilization. The empire also reached deeper into the Middle East, with new provinces in Armenia, Assyria, and Mesopotamia (Map 7.2). Trajan declared war on a powerful Persian empire, called Parthia, but internal unrest prevented him from victory, and he had to pull back. From this point onward, struggles with the Persians—including the Sassanian Empire that replaced Parthia—frequently challenged Roman leaders. More generally, the expense of maintaining the vast boundaries placed growing burdens on the imperial economy. A turn from expansion to defense, though probably inevitable, led to a voluntary withdrawal under Trajan's successor, Hadrian, west of the Euphrates.

By 180 C.E., the empire had reached a pinnacle of power that would quickly, although gradually, turn to descent. Foreign policy became defensive, building walls and trying to finance border garrisons to keep invaders out. The later Roman empire, although still capable of impressive achievements, was enmeshed in a pattern of slow decline, which in turn was part of the general collapse of the classical world.

Roman Law

Emperors continued the policies of the late republic in making citizenship possible for some people in various parts of the Empire. Although most people never became citizens, the citizenship network did provide rewards and helped solidify imperial rule.

Rome's greatest political contribution lay in its legal system. Although local laws applied to many areas of the empire, Roman law provided a general system, open to citizens in any part of the empire. The law also facilitated commerce. Roman jurists carefully thought through general principles, building one of the most extensive legal systems anywhere in the world.

The law focused heavily on protecting private property and family stability. It let the state determine fairness in some areas that had previously been open to decisions by families and landlords. A minority of people throughout the empire were allowed citizenship and full access to this law.

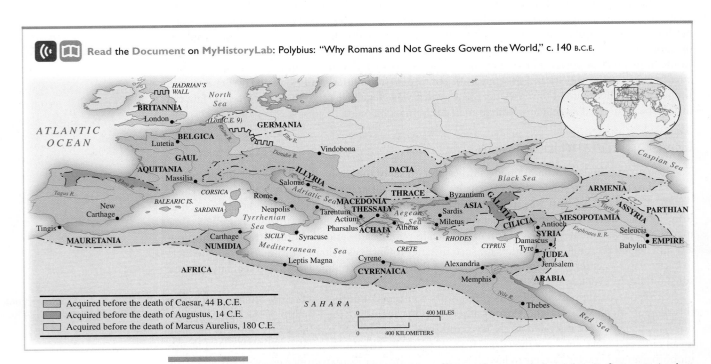

Read the Document on MyHistoryLab: Polybius: "Why Romans and Not Greeks Govern the World," c. 140 B.C.E.

MAP **7.2 The Roman Empire from Augustus to 180 C.E.** The empire expanded greatly in its first centuries, but such far-flung colonies proved impossible to maintain, both militarily and economically. How do the size and location of the empire compare with the earlier expansion of the republic?

VISUALIZING THE PAST

Religions in Rome

THE TEMPLE OF HORUS IN EDFU, Egypt, served as an architectural model for the Temple of Isis in Rome. The date of the Temple of Isis is not known, but Emperor Domitian added embellishments to the structure in 95 C.E. The Roman temple was the same length as its counterpart in Edfu, and the Egyptian style was mixed with some Roman elements, including statues, fountains, and representations of the Nile and Tiber rivers.

Temple of Horus in Edfu, Egypt.

QUESTIONS

- Why would an emperor not only tolerate but patronize a temple devoted to an Egyptian goddess?
- What does the temple suggest about Rome's religious policy?
- Does cultural assimilation tend to be mutual for both the conqueror and the conquered in an empire?

Paul, a key figure in early Christianity and born a Jew, was proud of being a Roman citizen. Principles of Roman law would be revived in other societies later on.

Useful law, plus regional tolerance and some access to citizenship, promoted loyalty and allowed Rome to maintain its empire in considerable peace for several centuries. This achievement was more impressive than the initial conquests.

Paul (3–67) One of the first Christian missionaries; moved away from insistence that adherents of the new religion follow Jewish law; use of Greek as language of the church.

THE EVOLUTION OF ROME'S ECONOMIC AND SOCIAL STRUCTURE

7.4 How did the Roman economy take advantage of regional specializations around the Mediterranean?

As earlier in the Greek city-states, a class of merchants expanded during the final centuries of the republic. Many merchants were foreigners, for Romans did not take well to seafaring and built clumsy boats that hugged the shores. Traders from Greece and the Middle East played a vital role. But a native business group expanded as well, and its prestige was higher than that of its counterpart in classical Greece had been. Merchants gained political voice in the Roman Senate in the later days of the republic, although they never matched aristocratic prestige. Rome and other imperial cities also developed large artisan and shopkeeper groups and a large, sometimes troubling, propertyless lower class.

Rome's family structure resembled that of the other major classical civilizations. Family structure was firmly patriarchal. Early Roman law stipulated that "the husband is the judge of his wife. If she commits a fault, he punishes her; if she has drunk wine, he condemns her; if she has been guilty of adultery, he kills her." Later, however, husbands' power was modified by the need for approval by a family court including members of both families. Here was a key contribution of Roman law. If divorced because of adultery, a Roman woman lost one-third of her property and had to wear a special garment that set her apart like a prostitute. The oppression of women was less severe in Rome than in Greece and China, however. As wives and mothers, many aristocratic Roman women wielded political power, if only through their husbands. Women freely appeared in public and attended major entertainments; some were educated, although rarely as well as men in the same class. However, inequality between men and women increased again in the empire's final stages.

Roman society, initially composed mainly of aristocrats and free farmers, became steadily more complex. Growing reliance on slavery marked Rome's society and economy.

7.1 7.2 7.3 7.4 7.5 7.6

Slavery in Rome

Social inequality increased fairly steadily from the later republic onward. The spread of Roman slavery contributed further to the decline of free farmers and to the unusual militarism of Rome in the late republic and early empire. Slave revolts, although not common, required a military presence. Displaced Italian farmers increasingly sought a longer-term career in the military, where they could earn pay and have some chance to acquire property as veterans. Most obviously, military expansion was a vital source of additional slaves, for the Roman slave population did not reproduce itself. This was an obvious contrast to China and India, where an expansionist foreign policy was not a central issue in labor supply.

Not surprisingly, slavery brought tension to the Roman world, both between slaves and their masters and between different segments of the free population. For example, in 61 c.e., the city prefect of Rome was murdered by one of his slaves. Custom dictated that every one of the 400 slaves in the household be executed in retribution, although to keep order the emperor had to line soldiers along the entire route on which the condemned slaves passed.

Roman slavery must be interpreted subtly, however. Being a slave was not necessarily the worst condition possible. Some people sought slavery as a way to get into a richer household or even to escape the countryside for the city. Many would have agreed that being a free rural worker was often worse than being a slave. Partly this reflected widespread poverty; economic security could seem preferable to freedom. It also reflected the variable conditions of slavery. Many slaves, again particularly in cities, had great latitude and interesting work. Many could buy or gain freedom. As in other forms of historical inequality, it is important not to impose contemporary standards on the complexity of the past.

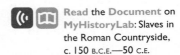

Read the Document on MyHistoryLab: Slaves in the Roman Countryside, c. 150 B.C.E.—50 C.E.

But slavery itself could change, and it had social as well as personal consequences in Rome. As Roman agriculture became increasingly commercialized from the 2nd century B.C.E. onward, slavery spread steadily. Many new slaves were used for manual labor, and large supplies of these slaves were brought in from Spain and later Britain, Germany, the Slavic lands of the northern Balkans, and Africa. Slaves worked the mines and quarries under brutal conditions. They also increasingly staffed the large estates, along with some paid laborers and tenant farmers. Far more than in earlier Greece, the Roman economy became dependent on slave labor; grain supplies and other agricultural products relied on this labor to an extent that was unusual in the classical world.

Finally, the extensive use of slaves at Rome's high point helps explain the stagnant production technology in manufacturing and agriculture. The Romans displayed real engineering genius in their buildings, roads, and city design, but they paid little attention to techniques of food supply or manufacturing. Estate agriculture and government organization of ports and markets, not production methods, took center stage, with abundant slave labor as a vital component. A few engine designs were sketched, but merely as exercises; there was no interest in building or using them. Some manufacturing operations used waterwheels for power, and there is evidence that these spread in the 2nd century c.e. Still, there were few new inventions.

A further result was an ongoing lag behind the economies of India and China in sophisticated manufacturing. The Roman upper classes eagerly bought silks and other processed goods that came from Asia, arriving at the Mediterranean by the overland Silk Road through the Middle East. In return, the Romans offered exotic African animals, skins, and gold, not products they made.

Rome's Economic Structure

The empire was not joined in a single economic and social pattern. The social arrangements characteristic of Italy were not uniform through the Roman Empire. The environmental impact of Rome's agricultural needs varied as well.

Rome established vigorous cities in Spain, France, and England and populated them with the families of soldiers, who married local women, and with colonists. Only gradually and incompletely, however, did estate agriculture spread to Europe north of the Mediterranean. Many local farmers continued to practice subsistence agriculture and even hunting. The gap between new, Romanized cities and the rural people, who were usually ignorant of Latin as well as illiterate, was often wide. In parts of northern Africa, Romans urged a ruthless policy of economic exploitation. Peasants in Egypt and in other parts of northern Africa were pressed to produce grain for sale in the Italian

THINKING HISTORICALLY

The Classical Civilizations in Comparative Perspective

THE THREE GREAT CLASSICAL CIVILIZATIONS LEND themselves to a variety of comparisons. The general tone of each differed from the others, ranging from India's otherworldly strain to China's emphasis on government centralization, although it is important to note the varieties of activities and interests and the changes that occurred in each of the three societies. Basic comparisons include several striking similarities. Each classical society developed empires. Each relied primarily on an agricultural economy. Greco-Roman interest in secular culture bears some resemblance to Confucian emphasis in China, although in each case religious currents remained as well. But Greco-Roman political values and institutions differed from the Confucian emphasis on deference and bureaucratic training. Greek definitions of science contrasted with those of India and China, particularly in the emphasis on theory. Several focal points can be used for comparison.

Each classical civilization emphasized a clear social hierarchy, with substantial distance between elites and the majority of people who did the manual and menial work. This vital similarity between the civilizations reflected common tensions between complex leadership demands and lifestyles and the limited economic resources of the agricultural economy. Groups at the top of the social hierarchy judged that they had to control lower groups carefully to ensure their own prosperity. Each classical society generated ideologies that explained and justified the great social divisions. Philosophers and religious leaders devoted great attention to this subject.

Within this common framework, however, there were obvious differences. Groups at the top of the social pyramid reflected different value systems. The priests in India, the bureaucrats in China, and the aristocrats in Greece and the Roman republic predominated. The status of merchants varied despite the vital role commerce played in all three civilizations.

Opportunities for mobility varied also. India's caste system allowed movement within castes, if wealth was acquired, but little overall mobility. This was the most rigid classical social structure because it tied people to their basic social and occupational position by birth. China's bureaucratic system allowed a very small number of talented people from below to rise on the basis of education, but most bureaucrats continued to come from the landed aristocracy. Mediterranean society, with its aristocratic emphasis, limited opportunities to rise to the top, but the importance of acquired wealth (particularly in Rome) gave some nonaristocrats important economic and political opportunities. Cicero, for example, came from a merchant family. Various classes also shared some political power in city-state assemblies; the idea of

> *Each classical civilization distinctively defined the position of the lowest orders.*

citizens holding basic political rights across class lines was unusual in classical civilizations.

Each classical civilization distinctively defined the position of the lowest orders. India's untouchables performed duties culturally evaluated as demeaning but often vital. So did China's "mean people," who included actors. As Greece and then Rome expanded, they relied heavily on the legal and physical compulsions of slavery to provide menial service and demanding labor. Greece and Rome gave unusual voice to farmers when they maintained their own property but tended to scorn manual labor itself, a view that helped justify slavery. Confucianism urged deference but offered praise for peasant work.

Finally, each classical civilization developed a different cultural glue to help hold its social hierarchy together. Greece and Rome left much of the task of managing the social hierarchy to local authorities; community bonds, as in the city-states, were meant to pull different groups into a sense of common purpose. They also relied on military force and clear legal statements that defined rights according to station. Force and legal inequalities played important roles in China and India as well, but there were additional inducements. India's Hinduism helped justify and sustain the hierarchy by promising rewards through reincarnation for those who submitted to their place in any given existence. Chinese Confucianism urged general cultural values of obedience and self-restraint, creating some agreement—despite varied religions and philosophies—on the legitimacy of social ranks by defining how gentlemen and commoners should behave. Chinese and Indian social structures lasted longer than those of Greece and Rome.

In no case did the social cement work perfectly; social unrest surfaced in all the classical civilizations, as in major slave rebellions in the Roman countryside or peasant uprisings in China. At the same time, the rigidity of classical social structures gave many common people some leeway. Elites viewed the masses as being so different from themselves that they did not try to revamp all their beliefs or community institutions.

QUESTIONS

- Why did the classical civilizations seem to need radical social inequalities?
- What was the relationship between wealth and social position in each classical civilization?
- If India used religion to compensate for social inequalities, what did China and the Mediterranean use?

markets, and large estates quickly predominated. Ultimately, production pressure had devastating environmental results in this region, as desert conditions expanded. Another distinctive region was the portion of the empire in Greece and western Asia, where more active commerce and larger merchant groups maintained pre-Roman traditions and wielded greater wealth than existed in much of the western empire.

Pressing the Environment

Rome's economy had serious environmental consequences. In Rome itself, the burning of wood for heat but also for manufacturing created serious problems of air pollution. The accumulation of garbage was also a serious issue. Widespread use of lead, in wine production and for tableware, created extensive poisoning that, some have argued, contributed to imperial decline.

At least as serious was deforestation and inroads on natural vegetation. Trees were cut down for fuel and for construction materials, but above all to expand agriculture. Eager to promote more food production, in 111 B.C.E. the republic decreed that anyone could keep up to 20 acres of public land if they brought it into cultivation. Deforestation, particularly on hillsides, promoted erosion and loss of topsoil. Widespread grazing by herds of sheep and goats also cut into grasslands, again promoting erosion. And sheer overfarming, particularly in grain growing regions like North Africa, reduced the fertility of soil and gradually reduced productivity. Here too, historians have speculated that the results may have promoted the empire's ultimate decline.

Because of the divisions of classical Mediterranean society, by region as well as class and gender, no easy generalizations about overall social achievement can be made. An 18th-century English historian characterized the high point of the Roman Empire before 180 C.E. as the period in human history "during which the condition of the human race was most happy or prosperous." This is doubtful, given the technological accomplishments of China and India. And certainly many slaves, women, and poor farmers might have disagreed, even in the Mediterranean world itself. Furthermore, Mediterranean society, like most classical civilizations, was massively split between upper-class and urban populations and the rural majority. Many farmers continued to work largely as their ancestors had, with similar tools and similar poverty, untouched by the doings of the great or the bustle of the cities, except when wars swept over their lands.

THE ORIGINS OF CHRISTIANITY

> Christianity, ultimately one of the world's great religions, benefited from the Roman Empire but also contested many of its values.

7.5 What was the relationship between Christianity and the Roman state?

In the initial decades of the Roman Empire, at the eastern end of the Mediterranean, a new religion, Christianity, emerged. Much of the impetus for this new religion rested in issues in the Jewish religion, including a long-standing belief in the coming of a Messiah and rigidities that had developed in the Jewish priesthood. Regardless of whether Christianity was created by God, as Christians believe, the early stages of the religion focused on cleansing the Jewish religion of stiff ritualism and rigid leadership, which resulted from the orthodox community's efforts to preserve Judaism in the face of Roman oppression. It had little to do with Roman culture at first. Christianity arose in a remote province and appealed particularly to poor people.

Life and Death of Jesus

Jesus of Nazareth Prophet and teacher among the Jews; believed by Christians to be the Messiah; executed c. 30 C.E.

Christianity originated with **Jesus of Nazareth**, a Jewish prophet and teacher who was regarded as the son of God by his disciples (Figure 7.4). Jesus preached in Israel during the time of Augustus, urging a purification of the Jewish religion that would free Israel and establish the kingdom of God on earth. He urged a moral code based on love, charity, and humility, and he asked the faithful to follow his lessons, abandoning worldly concerns. Many disciples believed that a final judgment day was coming on which God would reward the righteous with immortality and condemn sinners to everlasting hell.

Jesus won many followers among the poor. He also roused suspicion among the upper classes and the leaders of the Jewish religion. These people helped persuade the Roman governor, already concerned about unrest among the Jews, that Jesus was a dangerous agitator. As a result, Jesus was put to death, crucified along with common criminals, about 30 C.E. His followers believed that he was resurrected on the third day after his death, proof that he was the son of God. This belief helped the further spread of the religion among Jewish communities in the Middle East, both within the Roman Empire and beyond. As they realized that the Messiah was not immediately returning to earth to set up the Kingdom of God, the disciples of Jesus began to fan out, particularly around the eastern Mediterranean, to spread the new religious message.

Initially, converts were Jewish by birth and followed the basic Jewish law. However, their belief that Christ was divine as well as human roused hostility among other Jews. When one early convert, Stephen, was stoned to death for blasphemy, many disciples left Israel and traveled throughout western Asia.

Christianity Gains Converts and Religious Structure

Gradually over the next 250 years, Christianity won many converts (Map 7.3). By the 4th century C.E., about 10 percent of the residents of the Roman Empire were Christian, and the new religion had also made converts elsewhere in the Middle East and in **Ethiopia**. As it spread, Christianity connected increasingly with larger themes in Roman history. With its appeal to the poor, Christianity was well positioned to reflect social grievances in an empire of increasing inequality. Slaves, dispossessed farmers, and poor city dwellers found hope in a religion that promised rewards after death. Christianity also answered

FIGURE **7.4** This mosaic from the city of Ravenna depicts the Last Supper, which took place on the night before Jesus was crucified. According to Christian belief, at this supper Jesus broke bread and drank wine with his disciples, teaching them the ritual of the Eucharist. Mosaic designs like this one were common in Roman buildings, often inlaid into floors and depicting both secular and religious scenes. The mosaic tradition continued in the Eastern Empire, mainly used there to depict Christian figures, becoming ever more elegant and richly detailed.

cultural and spiritual needs—especially but not exclusively among the poor—left unmet by mainstream Roman religion and culture. Roman values had stressed political goals and ethics suitable for life in this world. They did not join peoples of the empire in more spiritual loyalties, and they did not offer many emotionally satisfying rituals.

As the empire consolidated, reducing direct political participation, a number of highly emotional religions spread from the Middle East and Egypt. These religions offered rituals charged with excitement and mystery. Worship of divinities such as Mithra and Isis, derived from earlier belief systems, attracted some Romans with rites of sacrifice and a strong sense of religious community. Christianity, although far more than a mystery religion, had some of these qualities and won converts on this basis as well. Christianity gained ground in part because of features of Roman political and cultural life.

The spread of Christianity also benefited from some of the positive qualities of Rome's empire. Political stability and communication over a wide area aided missionary efforts, and the Roman example helped inspire the government forms of the growing Christian church. At the same time, separate church institutions were essential, since that state seemed unreliable for Christians—a key contrast to Islam later on. Early Christian communities regulated themselves, but with expansion more formal government was introduced, with **bishops** playing a role like that of Rome's provincial governors. Bishops headed churches in regional centers and supervised the activities of other churches in the area. Bishops in politically powerful cities, including Rome, gained particular authority.

Roman principles also helped move what initially had been a religion among Jews to a genuinely cosmopolitan stance. Under the leadership of PAUL, converted to Christianity about 35 C.E., Christian missionaries began to move away from insisting that adherents of the new religion must follow Jewish law. Rather, in the spirit of Rome and Hellenism, the new faith was seen as universal, open to all regardless of whether they followed Jewish practices in diet, male circumcision, and so on.

Paul's conversion to Christianity proved vital. Paul was Jewish, but he had been born in a Greek city and was familiar with Greco-Roman culture. He helped explain basic Christian beliefs in terms

Ethiopia A Christian kingdom that developed in the highlands of eastern Africa under the dynasty of King Lalibela; retained Christianity in the face of Muslim expansion elsewhere in Africa.

bishops Headed Christian churches and regional centers and supervised the activities of other churches within the jurisdictional area.

Read the Comparative Case Study on MyHistoryLab: The Roman and Christian Views of the Good Life

THE SPREAD OF CHRISTIANITY BY 300 C.E.

- Christians: 50% or more of population by 300 c.e.
- Christians: 30%–50% or more of population by 300 c.e.
- Paul's travels
- ■ Christian communities in the first century c.e.

MAP **7.3 Origins and Early Spread of Christianity, to 4th–5th Century** Christian conversions fanned out from the religion's birthplace in the Middle East. Most movement occurred within the Roman Empire, but some spilled beyond.

Greeks and Romans could grasp, and he preached in Greece and Italy as well as the Middle East. Paul created Christian theology as a set of intellectual principles that followed from, but generalized, the message of Jesus. Paul also modified certain initial Christian impulses. Jesus drew a large number of women followers, but Paul stressed women's subordination to men and the dangers of sexuality. It was Paul's emphasis on Christianity as a universal religion, requiring abandonment of other religious beliefs, and his related use of Greek—the dominant language of the day throughout the eastern Mediterranean—that particularly transformed the new faith.

Relations with the Roman Empire

Gradually, Christian theological leaders made further contact with Greco-Roman intellectual life. They began to develop a body of Christian writings beyond the Bible messages written by Jesus' disciples. By the 4th century C.E., Christian writings became the most creative cultural expressions in the Roman Empire, as theologians explained issues in the new religion and related it to Greek philosophy and Roman ethics. Ironically, as the Roman Empire was in most respects declining, Christianity produced an outpouring of complex thought and often elegant use of language. The *Confessions* of **Augustine** were thoroughly Christian but reflected Latin classical style and Greek philosophical concepts. Christianity thus not only redirected Roman culture but also preserved many earlier literary and philosophical achievements.

Adherents of the new religion did clash with Roman authorities. Christians, who like Jews put their duties to God first, would not honor the emperor as a god. They also seemed to reject the authority of the state in other spheres. Several early emperors, including Nero, persecuted Christians, killing some and driving their worship underground. Persecution was not constant, however, which helps explain why the religion continued to spread. It resumed only in the 3rd century, when several

Augustine (Saint) Influential church father and theologian (354–430 C.E.); born in Africa and ultimately bishop of Hippo in Africa; champion of Christian doctrine against various heresies and very important in the long-term development of Christian thought on such issues as predestination.

emperors tried to use religious conformity and new claims to divinity as a way of cementing loyalty to a declining state. Roman beliefs, including periodic tolerance, helped shape a Christian view that the state had a legitimately separate but subordinate sphere; western Christians often cited Christ as saying, "Render unto Caesar that which is Caesar's, and unto God that which is God's."

The full story of early Christianity goes beyond the history of Rome, and we will turn to it again in Chapter 10. Christianity had more to do with opening a new era in the history of the Mediterranean region than with shaping the later Roman Empire. Yet important connections did exist that explain features of Christianity and later Roman history.

THE DECLINE OF ROME

7.6 What were the principal political and economic challenges as the Roman Empire began to decline?

Rome declined gradually after 180 C.E., losing territory and confronting new economic problems.

Well before Christianity became a major factor in Mediterranean life, the Roman Empire began to show significant signs of decay. Its political and social framework became increasingly vulnerable. The army increasingly controlled the selection of emperors, some of whom were murdered when they did not please their sponsors. In one stretch of time, 235–284 C.E., all but three emperors either died in civil wars or were assassinated. More broadly, defending the borders of the empire and maintaining government proved increasingly costly, and tax revenues began to decline. Further expansion of the empire became impossible after 117 C.E. because the government could not afford the troops needed to keep order in more distant provinces and because pressures from border groups, particularly the Germanic tribes in central Europe, began to increase. Yet without expansion, the necessary rewards for the armies became more difficult to obtain. Other economic disruptions followed from regional changes. The Italian economy, for example, began to suffer by the 3rd century C.E. as Spanish- and French-grown wine cut into local profits, reducing prosperity and tax revenues at the empire's core. Disruptions of this sort forced new, more subsistence-oriented economic arrangements. Slavery declined. More estates turned into local economic and political units rather than commercial operations as connections that had cemented the empire began to come apart. The empire also suffered from devastating epidemics, possibly the result of contacts with unfamiliar diseases from south Asia, that killed off much of the population.

The Classical Mediterranean Heritage

By preserving and extending Greek culture and political ideas, and adding its own achievements in law and empire and in monumental architecture, Rome helped create a lasting heritage from the classical Mediterranean world. The great achievement of course was sheer expansion, from the Atlantic Ocean deep into the Middle East. This meant that the Greco-Roman heritage would have wide geographic impact, for centuries to come.

In the Middle East, Rome's geography differed from that of the earlier Hellenistic empire. Rome conquered the eastern shore of the Mediterranean and penetrated far eastward, in the northern part of the region, into Armenia. However, the Romans never conquered the revived Persian Empire, which had arisen as Alexander the Great's holdings divided after his death. Rome thus helped preserve and solidify many Greek ideas and values, also extending them westward in both southern Europe and north Africa. Important divisions, however, revived in the Middle East, with important distinctions from the Mediterranean zone.

At the same time, however, the Mediterranean heritage was not passed on smoothly. The capacity to unite the Mediterranean world was lost entirely after Rome's decline. Rome and Greece were remembered with the same reverence as classical China or India. But their legacy was more selective, and its transmission proved more complex as Rome's imperial structure faltered.

Global Connections and Critical Themes

ROME AND THE WORLD

During the early centuries of Rome's development, its leaders were quite conscious of a wider Mediterranean world. Rome's expansion reflected this awareness of powerful competitors, including Carthage in North Africa. Roman leaders were also alert to the influence of Greek culture in the eastern Mediterranean. Some feared elaborate Greek art and lifestyles as a distraction from the simple virtues of the Roman republic, but even more were drawn to the benefit of further incorporating Greek culture. The movement toward the east brought Rome into interaction with many Middle Eastern peoples, as far as Persia.

At the height of the empire, Rome seemed to have created its own world. There was trade on the fringes of the empire. On the northern border in Europe, Germanic tribes learned about the empire through trade and occasional fighting. This helped some decide, ultimately, that they wanted to move into the empire directly. Trade also occurred with other parts of Africa, particularly in the northeast, including Ethiopia. Wealthy Romans were also quite aware of luxury goods from Asia, particularly Chinese silks, although they knew little of China itself. The goods were brought to the Mediterranean by nomadic merchants. Some Roman merchants visited India in search of trading opportunities. Roman emperors sponsored some of these expeditions, using their control over Egypt to launch fleets into the Red Sea and, thence, to the Indian Ocean; several Indian rulers sent missions to Rome to encourage trade. Overall, the attraction of Asian luxury goods threatened some drain of wealth from the empire itself. But the major focus in Rome was internal development in a territory that clearly surpassed any empire ever established in the area. Tolerant of local diversities, Romans also built the same kinds of monuments and amenities in Asia, Africa, and Europe—a testimony to their confidence in the universal appeal of their own culture and to their sense that there was little to learn beyond their own borders.

Further Readings

Three solid surveys with bibliographies are K. Christ, *The Romans: An Introduction to Their History and Civilization* (1984); M. Grant, *The World of Rome* (1990); and Everitt, *Anthony Cicero: The Life and Times of Rome's Greatest Politician* (2003). Excellent analyses of the basic features of Roman cultural and social life are M. Grant, *A Social History of Greece and Rome* (1992); Matthew Roller, *Dining Posture in Ancient Rome: Bodies, Values and Status* (2006); and P. Garnsey and R. Saller, *The Roman Empire: Economy, Society and Culture* (1987). See also R. MacMullen, *Roman Social Relations 50 B.C. to A.D. 284* (1981). A bold quantitative study is R. Duncan-Jones, *The Economy of the Roman Empire* (1982). J. Andreau offers close study of *Banking and Business in the Roman World* (1999). On slavery, see S. R. Joshel, *Slavery in the Roman World* (2010); K. Hopkins, *Conquerors and Slaves, Slaves and Masters in the Roman Empire* (1987); and K. R. Bradley and W. Philips Jr., *Slavery from Roman Times to the Early Transatlantic Trade* (1985). On women, see Eve D'Ambra, *Roman Women* (2007); Kristina Milnor, *Gender, Domesticity, and the Age of Augustus: Inventing Private Life* (2005); Suzanne Dixon, *The Roman Family* (1992); J. F. Gardner, *Women in Roman Law and Society* (1986); and Elaine Fanthum and others, *Women in the Classical World: Image and Text* (1994). Florence DuPont's *Daily Life in Ancient Rome* (1999 ed.) examines Roman ideas of space and time and of honor as well as family relations and social divisions. See also David Potter, ed., *A Companion to the Roman Empire* (2006); Mark Graham, *News and Frontier Consciousness in the Late Roman Empire* (2006); L. Casson, *Everyday Life in Ancient Rome* (1998).

For war, politics and diplomacy, see Peter Connolly, *Greece and Rome at War* (1998); Harold James, *The Roman Predicament: How the Rules of International Order Create the Politics of Empire* (2006); Dennis Kehoe, *Law and the Rural Economy in the Roman Empire* (2007); Y. Garlan, *War in the Ancient World* (1975); and E. N. Luttwak, *The Grand Strategy of the Roman Empire* (1976). See also K. J. Holkeskamp and H. Heitmann-Gordon, *Reconstructing the Roman Republic* (2010); Susan Raven, *Rome in Africa* (1993); Hans Pohlsander, *The Emperor Constantine* (2004); Stephen Dyson, *The Creation of the Roman Frontier* (1985); and Andrew Lintott, *The Constitution of the Roman Republic* (2003).

Collections of source materials include M. Crawford, ed., *Sources for Ancient History* (1983); and C. Fornara, *Translated Documents of Greece and Rome* (1977). J. Boardman, J. Griffin, and O. Murray, *The Oxford History of the Roman World* (1990) and T. Cornell and J. Mathews, *Atlas of the Roman World* (1982) are useful reference guides to Roman civilization.

The rise and spread of Christianity are treated in two outstanding studies: R. MacMullen's *Christianizing the Roman Empire* (1984) and Peter Brown's *The World of Late Antiquity, A.D. 150–750* (1971). More recently, see C. M. Conway, *Behold the Man: Jesus and Greco-Roman Masculinity* (2008); James B. Rives, *Religion in the Roman Empire* (2007); David L. Dungan, *Constantine's Bible: Politics and the Making of the New Testament* (2007); James W. Ermatinger, *Daily Life of Christians in Ancient Rome* (2007); and Mark Edwards, *Constantine and Christiandom* (2003).

Critical Thinking Questions

1. Compare the Roman empire with the Chinese empire under the Han dynasty.

2. Why did some people deliberately seek to become slaves in the Roman empire?

3. What caused the changes in Roman policy toward Christianity?

4. What were the main contributions of Rome to Middle Eastern and to African history?

5. Can Greece, Hellenistic society, and Rome be treated as phases of a more durable Mediterranean civilization, or is separate treatment essential?

8

The Peoples and Civilizations of the Americas

(((Listen to Chapter 8
on MyHistoryLab

He was called Lord Hanab Pacal (HAN-ahb pah-KAHL). He was ruler of a powerful city-state, builder of a dynasty and an empire. He came to the throne as a boy, and when he was finally laid to rest at the age of 80, his name was admired—or feared—throughout southern Mexico and Central America. Deep in the forest of Chiapas, Mexico, where almost 10 feet of rain falls each year, his ruined city rises in the foothills overlooking the floodplain toward the Gulf of Mexico. Even today, its beautifully crafted limestone buildings and monuments capture the imagination and demand admiration.

Long shrouded in mystery, the history of the Maya is now better known because of recent advances in understanding their written language. We now know that on March 26, 615,

FIGURE **8.1** The funeral trappings of the great Maya ruler Pacal, who ruled Palenque from 615–683 C.E. and who made that city one of the great powers of the Maya world. At burial, Pacal's face was covered with a jade mask, and his body was adorned with jewelry and other precious objects. His elaborate tomb was not discovered until the 20th century.

👁 Watch the Video Series on MyHistoryLab

Learn about some key topics related to this chapter with the *MyHistoryLab Video Series: Key Topics in World History*

12-year-old Hanab Pacal became ruler of the city-state we know as Palenque (pah-LEHNG-kay). His accession to the double-headed jaguar throne and his crowning with the plumed headdress of rule was attended with elaborate public ceremonies and ritual sacrifices. He had inherited the throne from his mother, Lady Zac-Kuk, which was itself extraordinary, since Maya women did not usually rule, and he had a strong sense of his own supernatural status because he equated his mother with the mythological mother of the gods.

Palenque had been invaded and defeated by neighboring states in the years before he took the throne, and Hanab Pacal dedicated himself to restoring its stability. The boy became a ruler of great power and accomplishments. Through wars and alliances, he extended the power of Palenque over most of its neighbors. He also became a patron of the arts and fostered the building of a number of palaces and temples, including the Temple of Inscriptions, which would one day hold his tomb. There, in 683, his body was laid with ceremonial care, his face covered with a mosaic jade mask (Figure 8.1). A large stone slab, engraved to show his rebirth as the god of maize, was placed over his sarcophagus (Figure 8.2). The tomb was sealed and hidden beneath the temple floor. The walls of the temple were later inscribed with one of the longest Maya texts, a dynastic history in which Hanab Pacal was tied to the past and future of time.

Eventually Palenque again suffered defeats by its rivals, and the city was abandoned sometime around 900 C.E. The forest advanced again, thick vegetation enveloped the walls, and the splendor and power of the great king and his final resting place were lost to memory, as was much of the story of this civilization. Only rumors of lost cities and a few claims by scholars gave any clue to this lost and forgotten past.

It was not until 1839 that a young and adventurous American named John Lloyd Stephens, accompanied by Frederick Catherwood, an English artist, set out to explore reports of ancient cities buried in the rainforest of Central America. Stephens was an experienced traveler who had seen Egypt and parts of the Middle East, and he wished to examine once and for all the idea that something like the civilizations of the Old World might have existed in the Americas. Many people were skeptical; they simply could not believe that Native Americans had achieved anything like the civilizations of the classical world.

Stephens and Catherwood explored, surveyed, and recorded in their drawings and reports a number of ruins lost in the forest and underbrush. The monuments, pyramids, and temples of Palenque and other cities were described in rich detail by Stephens. Today we know these places were cities of the Maya civilization. The book published by the two young explorers, *Incidents of Travel in Central America*, revealed for the first time to a large public the vanished glories of a forgotten past, and it changed forever the way in which the Americas were seen as part of world history. Stephens was convinced of the skills and capacities of the builders: "Savages," he said, "did not build these places." He captured the story and the enigma of American civilization: "Here were the remains of a cultivated, polished, and peculiar people, who had passed through all the stages incident to the rise and fall of nations."

We have continued to uncover the past of these ancient American civilizations. The hidden tomb of Hanab Pacal was discovered in 1947 by a Mexican archeologist, although the inscriptions recounting Pacal's exploits were not fully deciphered until the 1980s.

FIGURE **8.2** At burial, Pacal's body was placed in a large stone sarcophagus whose cover was decorated with a scene showing Pacal at the moment of his death. It shows his fall into the underworld, down the Tree of Life—a Maya symbol of the axis of the world. The elaborate Temple of Inscriptions, where his tomb was found, was decorated with carvings that emphasized the continuity of power from Pacal to his son and successor.

40,000 B.C.E.	9000 B.C.E.	5000 B.C.E.
40,000–8000 Earliest migration from Asia **9500** Earliest evidence of human occupation	**9000–7000** Clovis and Folsom style weapons and tools in North America **7000** Evidence of agriculture; Guitarrero cave in Peru	**5000** Plant domestication becoming widespread **4000** Maize domesticated in Mexico **c. 3000–1500** Evidence of cotton cultivation, metallurgy, ceramics **2000 B.C.E.–500 C.E.** Early cultures in southwestern United States **2000** Pottery in use in Mesoamerica **1800–1200** Ceremonial centers in the highlands of southern Mexico **1500–800** Olmec civilization flourishes

Today the discoveries continue, but we now have a general idea of the development of these ancient American societies in the context of world history. ◼

Although there were some parallels with developments in Asia and North Africa, what took place in the Americas seems to have had no connection to the classical world we have examined thus far. American separateness was vital to making the achievements of civilization all the more impressive, but it also constrained them. Separateness meant that American chronology had only accidental connections with the classical civilizations. It was based instead on regional interchanges, and like Old World civilizations, it encountered similar problems of internal deterioration and outside attack. Civilization in the New World moved to its own rhythm. Crucial developments in American civilization occurred during the classical period of world history, but our exploration of the history of the Americas in this chapter extends before and after the 1000 B.C.E.–500 C.E. span. With few large domesticated animals, the Americas drew on a different resource base than Europe, Asia, or Africa, but the Americas also developed a number of plants that yielded a higher caloric output than those of Asia or Europe. Many civilizations in America lacked elements like metallurgy or writing that were found in the early civilizations of the Old World and so the American civilizations suggest alternative patterns and paths of development.

The history of the Western Hemisphere is part of the greater story of human development, and the cultures and civilizations of the Americas bear marked similarities to those of the Old World. But there were also important differences in the pace of development and the level of technology that ultimately placed the inhabitants of the Americas at a disadvantage. By the time Europeans arrived in the early 16th century, they encountered great empires, such as that of the Aztecs, whose technology had changed little in 1000 years and was in some ways similar to the technology of the ancient Near East.

ORIGINS OF AMERICAN SOCIETIES

During the last ice age, peoples from Asia entered the Americas. These ancient hunters eventually created diverse societies, and with the development of agriculture in Mesoamerica and Peru, they formed civilizations organized as chiefdoms, states, and sometimes empires.

8.1   What are the parallels and differences between the developments of civilizations of The Americas and those of the Middle East and Africa?

For more than a century, archeologists believed that peoples from Asia, moving during the period of the last ice age when the level of the oceans fell, were probably the first inhabitants of America. They argued that *Homo sapiens* in Europe and Asia had moved onto the northern steppes and tundra by about 20,000 B.C.E. From there, these people moved across the land bridge that formed in the present Bering Strait between Siberia and Alaska. Hunters followed the mammoths, mastodons, and other large game across this route. Then a rise in the world's temperature about 10,000 years ago caused the ice to melt and eventually raised the level of the oceans, and the land migrations from northern Asia stopped. The last migrations by the ancestors of the Inuits (IHN-yoo-ihts) (Eskimos) probably were made across the polar ice or in boats, another method that other earlier migrants to America

1000 B.C.E.	1 C.E.	500 C.E.	1000 C.E.
900 Maya civilization beginnings; classic period in Mesoamerica **850–250** Early Horizon; Chavín culture flourishes **300 B.C.E.–900 C.E.** Height of Maya civilization **200 B.C.E.–500 C.E.** Nazca culture	**1–650** Teotihuacan flourishes in central Mexico **100–600** Mound builders of Adena **c. 100–700** Hopewell culture **200–700** Mochica culture **200–1300** Anasazi culture in Southwest **300–900** Intermediate Horizon in Peru **300–900** Tihuanaco **400–800** Monte Alban flourishes in Oaxaca	**600–1000** Huari state **800–1300** Mississippian culture flourishes **900–1500** Postclassic era **900–1500** Maya cities under Mexican influence flourish in Yucatan **900–1200** Toltec empire in central Mexico	**1200–1400** Chimu state **1350** Rise of the Aztecs

had probably used. These migrations took place between 20,000 B.C.E. and 8000 B.C.E. The earliest definite archeological evidence of people in the Americas dated from about 9500 B.C.E., but many recent discoveries and a reevaluation of previously collected evidence from the Pacific coast of the United States, Chile, and Brazil have now led many scholars to conclude that occupation was much older than was previously thought, perhaps beginning as early as 40,000 B.C.E. The Americas appear to have been settled by a variety of peoples. The skeletal remains of some of the earliest inhabitants do not appear to be north Asian; they bear physical similarities to other groups like the Caucasians, Polynesians, and the Australasians. In other words, the ancestors of the Native Americans, sometimes called Paleo-Indians, came from a variety of physical backgrounds. The remains of a man found in Kennewick, Washington, who died over 9000 years ago, seem similar to the ancient Ainu of Japan. The fact that all Indians of South America are of blood type O, whereas type B predominates today in Asia, indicates that the migration may have occurred before the present genetic makeup of Asian populations emerged. Studies of DNA evidence have led some scholars to believe that most Native Americans descend from a single, small population group in Asia, suggesting that other groups died out, but these findings are still in question.

Still, all the genetic evidence indicates a large degree of common ancestry and a relative isolation from other human populations. The variations between Indians can be attributed to adaptations and localized natural selection. American Indian languages also indicate growing diversity. These languages seem to have developed from a few parent stocks into a variety of languages. Such findings are controversial and open to question. Another question is how long it took for the American continents to be occupied. But what is clear is that the settlement of the Americas was a complex process that we still do not fully understand.

The Ancient Hunters

Stone spearheads document the presence of hunting bands in the Americas. By about 11,000 years ago, stone tools and simple spear points associated with these early hunters were widely dispersed over North America.

As the climate became drier and warmer, the ice began to melt. The great mammal herds diminished and some species disappeared. The ancient Americans seem to have been particularly successful hunters, and it has been argued that the disappearance of such animals as the mammoth, the ancient horse, the camel, and the giant anteater was caused, at least in part, by overhunting. After all, the climate changed in Eurasia as well, but nowhere else in the world did the number of mammals that became extinct equal that in the Americas, especially North America. Still, changes in mean temperatures, especially between seasons, may have been particularly hard on the young of large mammal species and led to their decline.

Little is known about the society of these early ice age hunters. They probably lived in small groups or bands of 20 to 25 people, following the game in a seasonal pattern. Kinship provided the basis of social organization, and there was little specialization or hierarchy in society. Age and gender were the main determinants of an individual's roles and contributions to the group.

The Question of Outside Contacts

The possibility of later contacts with the Americas across the Pacific or the Atlantic continues to fascinate archeologists and cause heated debate. Definite mysteries and gaps in the history of pre-Columbian cultures remain unresolved. Artistic motifs and styles in the Americas similar to those of Shang China and southeast Asia seem to indicate contact. Plants such as cotton and bottle gourds seem to be of Old World origin, and their presence in the Americas suggests spread by human agents. Although many scholars admit the possibility of sporadic transoceanic contacts with Chinese, Phoenicians, Africans, Polynesians, and others, the evidence is still mostly circumstantial. No identifiable Old World object has ever been positively identified in a pre-Columbian archeological site, and if Phoenicians or Chinese introduced pottery or writing to the Americas, why they failed to introduce the wheel or bronze at the same time remains a puzzle.

Biological and archeological records indicate that the peopling of the Americas took place long before the beginnings of agriculture in the Old World, and that with the disappearance of the Bering land bridge, this population lived in isolation from the rest of humankind. Most scholars believe that the peoples of the Americas developed their cultures independently of the Old World. Still, occasional contacts were possible, and ideas and material things certainly may have been introduced from elsewhere into American Indian cultures.

Independent development and isolation also had some negative results when Native American populations came into contact with the peoples of Europe, Africa, and Asia. Their lack of the wheel, the plow, and iron put American Indians at a disadvantage. Dogs, turkeys, and guinea pigs were domesticated, but with the exception of llamas in the Andes, the lack of large mammals such as cattle and horses was also a disadvantage in terms of diet, transportation, and power. With the exception of a limited area in the high Andes, pastoralism, so important in the Old World, was not a way of life in the Americas. Most importantly, the isolation of American populations from the disease environment of the larger Old World populations left the inhabitants of the Americas with no immunities to several diseases of Asia, Europe, and Africa. This vulnerability proved disastrous after permanent contact was established.

The Archaic Cultures

By about 9000 B.C.E., small bands of hunters were widely dispersed over the American continents. Changes in climate with the ending of the last ice age may lie behind changes in diet and ways of life. The culture of these early, or **archaic**, populations adapted to the changing environment. People made baskets and used stone grinding tools to prepare the roots and plants they collected for food. As the seacoasts stabilized between 5000 and 4000 B.C.E., populations concentrated around lagoons and river mouths to exploit fish and shellfish.

There is evidence from highland Peru of cultivation as early as 7000 B.C.E., and by 5000 B.C.E. plant domestication had taken place in many regions in the Americas. The introduction of agriculture, the American version of the Neolithic revolution, was not as complete and drastic a change as we once thought, and many peoples continued to practice hunting and gathering along with some cultivation. In many places, farmers and hunter-gatherers eventually lived in close contact with each other as a result of social choices and different adaptations to environments.

Eventually, agriculture was practiced all over the Americas, from the woodlands of eastern North America to the tropical forests of the Amazon basin. American Indians eventually cultivated more than 100 different crops, including peppers, squash, tomatoes, and the grains amaranth and quinoa. Some crops, particularly maize, potatoes, and manioc, became essential sources of food for dense populations. As in Asia earlier, agriculture restricted human behavior and the patterns of human action; as American societies depended increasingly on agriculture, a process was set in motion that resulted in the development of complex social, economic, and political systems.

By about 4000 B.C.E., the domestication of **maize** from a wild grass had taken place in central Mexico. Along with it came the cultivation of peppers, squash, and beans. These expanded and more dependable food resources resulted in population growth. Maize cultivation spread far and wide. By 2000 B.C.E., peoples in Peru grew it along with the potato and other crops native to that region. Maize spread northward to the area of the present southern United States, and by about 1000 C.E., maize was grown by groups such as the Iroquois in Canada.

archaic cultures Hunting-and-gathering groups dispersed over the American continents by 9000 B.C.E.

maize One of the staple crops of sedentary agriculturists in the Americas; domesticated by 4000 B.C.E. in central Mexico.

In the tropical forests of the Orinoco and Amazon basins, people had developed an agriculture based on varieties of **manioc**, or cassava, a root that could be made into flour. The introduction of maize in areas that had depended on manioc probably resulted in population growth and the rise of more complex societies. Potatoes were the staple in highland South America, and manioc was the principal crop of the lowlands of South America and the islands of the Caribbean, but maize spread in all directions and was often grown in those areas along with other staples. In **Mesoamerica**, the area from north central Mexico to Nicaragua, maize dominated the diet of agricultural peoples.

It seems clear that in most cases, agriculture allowed societies to achieve the surplus production and complexity needed to develop the elements usually associated with civilization. With the adoption of agriculture and a sedentary way of life, the process of civilization was set in motion in the Americas.

manioc One of staple crops of sedentary agriculturists in the Americas; principal crop of peoples of the lowlands of South America and the islands of the Caribbean.

Mesoamerica Mexico and Central America; along with Peru, site of development of sedentary agriculture in Western hemisphere.

Types of American Indian Societies

In the regions of Mesoamerica and the Peruvian orbit, including the coastal areas of Ecuador and Peru and the Andean highlands (Map 8.1), civilizations developed based on intensive agriculture and including most of the features usually associated with Old World civilizations. In both areas, several cycles of cultural advancement and sometimes of empire building took place. Artistic styles flourished and declined, and states rose and fell over thousands of years.

Some scholars suggest that the area between these cultural hearths, including present-day Panama and Colombia, also contained advanced societies with great cultural achievements (especially in metallurgy and goldworking) that differed only in that they did not build large stone buildings. Thus, the whole region from central Mexico to Chile formed a continuous core of American civilizations. On the edges of this core, by influence and imitation, other Indian peoples adopted features of these civilizations, but we should also note that recent archeological findings from the Amazon region suggest that some of the cultural spread may have gone in the other direction and that the lowlands also were areas of great ingenuity and early development.

Many differences and variations existed among American cultures, but there were also similarities in organization, subsistence, technology, and belief that made them more like one another than any one of them was to the civilizations of the Old World. To some extent we can distinguish between ancient American societies on the basis of their economic and political organization. Sedentary agriculture, and with it population density, was a key. Hunter-gatherers continued to occupy large portions of the continents, divided into small bands and moving seasonally to take advantage of the resources. These peoples sometimes were organized in larger tribes and might recognize a chief, but generally their societies were organized around family groups or clans, and there was little hierarchy or specialization of skills. With some exceptions, the material culture of these people tended to be simple.

Peoples who had made a partial transition to agriculture lived in larger and more complex societies. Here the village of 100 or 200 rather than the band of 25 was more common. Men often continued to hunt or make war, but women tilled the fields. Agricultural techniques tended to be simple and often necessitated periodic migration when soils were depleted. The villages of these tribes of semisedentary farmers and hunters have been found on the Brazilian coast and in the woodlands of eastern North America.

It was among peoples who had adopted sedentary agriculture that the complex societies emerged most clearly, for it was here that surplus production was most firmly established. These populations could reach the millions. Men shifted into agriculture, forming a peasant base for a hierarchical society that might have included classes of nobles, merchants, and priests. Strong states and even empires could result, and the extraction of tribute from subject peoples and redistribution by central authority formed the basis of rule.

Chiefdoms and States

To some extent, the large imperial states with highly developed religious and political systems and monumental architecture (societies we call civilizations) were variants of a common pattern, the chiefdom. From the Amazon to the Mississippi valley, hereditary chieftains ruled from central towns over a large territory, including smaller towns and villages that paid tribute to the ruler. The governed

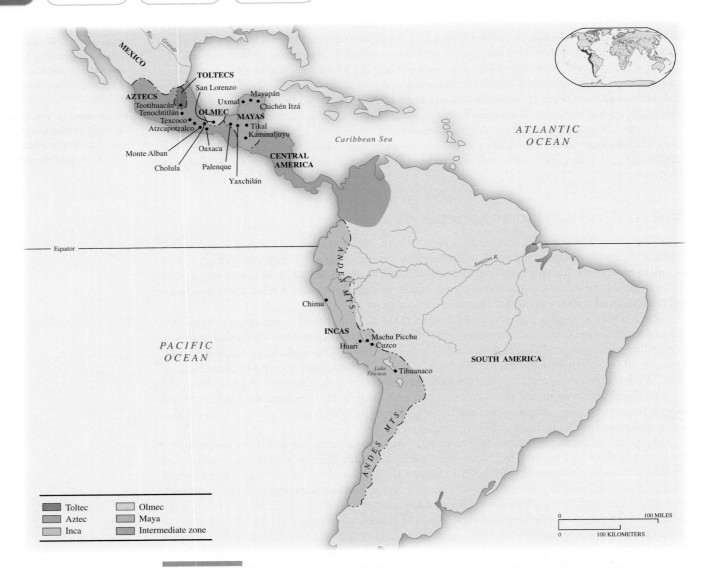

MAP **8.1 Civilizations of Central and South America** Three cultural "hearths" are represented: Mesoamerica, extending from north-central Mexico to Nicaragua; the Andean region in South America, and the Intermediate zone of modern-day Colombia and Panama which shared many characteristics with the other zones but did not build in stone.

populations sometimes numbered in the tens of thousands. The predominant town often had a ceremonial function, with large temples and a priest class. Beautiful pottery and other goods indicate specialization of labor.

Many chiefdoms had a social hierarchy with classes of nobles and commoners. It is sometimes argued that in the state-building societies, ceremonial centers became true cities and social classes replaced clan or family relations. The scale of society differed, but in terms of social organization, ceremonies, and warfare, there were many similarities between the large states and chiefdoms. In South America and southeastern North America these chiefdoms flourished, but since they often did not build in stone, archeology has revealed less about them. Cahokia (near modern St. Louis), for example, was an important town of the Mississippian culture (c. 1050–1200 C.E.). It had great earthen mounds covering an area of 5 square miles, and probably supported a population of more than 30,000—as large as the great cities of the Maya civilization (Figure 8.3).

Read the Document on **MyHistoryLab:** Two Nineteenth-Century Archaeologists Provide the First Scientific Description of the Indian Mounds of the Mississippi Valley

FIGURE **8.3** Cahokia was a large walled city that may have had 30,000 residents. Located near the confluence of the Missouri, Illinois, and Mississippi rivers, Cahokia was inhabited for more than 300 years. Its people built enormous earthen mounds on top of which their leaders built great wooden houses that have not survived the centuries. These structures rivaled in size the great buildings of Mesoamerica. The city was slowly abandoned after 1200.

SPREAD OF CIVILIZATION IN MESOAMERICA

8.2 What role did astronomy and the calendar system play in Native American civilizations and why?

Geographically, the region of Mesoamerica is a complex patchwork of zones that is also divided vertically into cooler highlands, tropical lowlands and coasts, and an intermediate temperate zone (Map 8.2). These climatic variations created different possibilities for human exploitation. They also created a basis for trade as peoples attempted to acquire goods not available locally. Much trade flowed from the tropical lowlands to the cooler central plateau.

Beginning about 5000 B.C.E., an increasing use of plant foods eventually led to the domestication of certain plants. People grew beans, peppers, avocados, squash, and eventually maize. Later innovations such as pottery took place about 2000 B.C.E. When the Shang dynasty ruled in China, permanent sedentary villages based to some extent on agriculture were first beginning to appear in Mesoamerica. These were small, modest settlements without much hierarchy or social differentiation and an apparent lack of craft specialization. But the number of these archaic villages proliferated, and population densities rose.

The Olmec Mystery

Quite suddenly, a new phenomenon appeared. On the southeastern coast of Mesoamerica (Veracruz and Tabasco), without much evidence of gradual development in the archeological record, a cultural tradition emerged that included irrigated agriculture, monumental sculpture, urbanism, an elaborate

The Olmec civilization spread certain elements of culture over the Mesoamerican region and was followed by an era of great cultural achievement at Teotihuacan and especially in the Maya city-states. The reasons for the collapse of these civilizations are only partially understood.

MAP **8.2 Mesoamerican Settlements** Distinct cultural zones developed, but many elements from language to religious ideas and technology were shared between zones. In different eras cultural elements were diffused from central Mexico southward to Yucatan and Central America and northward toward the American southwest. Scholars debate whether the diffusions indicate military and political expansion.

religion, and the beginnings of calendar and writing systems. We call these people **Olmec**, but their origins remain unknown. Their impressive settlements, drainage systems, temple complexes, and ability to move stones weighing tons attest to a high degree of social organization and artistic skill. The major Olmec sites at San Lorenzo (1200–900 B.C.E.) and La Venta (900–500 B.C.E.) are in the wet tropical forests of the Gulf coast of eastern Mexico, but Olmec objects and art style spread to the drier highlands of central Mexico and toward the Pacific coast to the south.

The Olmecs have been called the mother civilization of Mesoamerica. They grew maize, especially along the rivers, and it provided the basis for a state ruled by a hereditary elite in which the ceremonialism of a complex religion dominated life. About the time that Tutankhamen ruled in Egypt, the Olmec civilization flourished in Mesoamerica.

The Olmecs remain an enigma. Some of their monumental sculptures are great stone heads made from basalt rocks weighing tons that were moved many miles without the use of the wheel. Some of these seem to have African features (Figure 8.4); others appear to be representations of humans with feline attributes. The Olmecs were great carvers of jade, and they traded or conquered to obtain it. They developed a vigesimal numerical system (based on 20) and a calendar that combined a 365-day year with a 260-day ritual cycle. This system became the basis of all Mesoamerican calendars. What language the Olmecs spoke and what became of their civilization remain unknown. The major cities were eventually abandoned or destroyed, but the reasons for the decline are unclear. Some scholars believe that they were the ancestors of the great Maya civilization that followed.

During this preclassic period (c. 2000–300 B.C.E.), other civilizations were developing elsewhere in Mesoamerica. Olmec objects and, probably, Olmec influence and religious ideas spread into many areas of the highlands and lowlands, such as the Zapotec ceremonial center at **Monte Alban** (MOHN-teh ahl-BAN) in Oaxaca (wah-HAH-kah), creating the first generalized culture in the region. Farther to the south, some early Maya centers began to appear. In the central valley of Mexico, Olmec artistic influence could be seen in expanding communities.

Much of what we know about these cultures must be interpreted from their architecture and art and the symbols they contain. Art, especially public art, was both decorative and functional. It defined the place of the individual in society and the universe. It had political and religious functions; in the Americas, as in many civilizations, these aspects usually were united. The interpretation of artistic styles and symbols presents a variety of problems in the absence of written sources. The spread of Olmec symbols is a good example of the problem. Did the use of these symbols by other peoples in distant places indicate trade networks, missionary activity, colonies, conquest, or simply aesthetic appreciation? We do not know, but clearly Olmec influence was widely felt throughout the region.

View the Closer Look on MyHistoryLab:
The Basalt Olmec Heads

FIGURE **8.4** The origins of the Olmecs remain shrouded in mystery. Some of their enormous stone sculptures seem to have distinctively African features that indicate possible transatlantic contact. Similar features also have been found in early Khmer art from Southeast Asia.

The Classic Era of Mesoamerican Civilization

After the Olmec initiative, the period from about 150 to 900 C.E. was a great age of cultural achievement in Mesoamerica. Archeologists refer to it as the *classic* period, and during it great civilizations flourished in many places. The two main centers of civilization were the high central valley of Mexico and the more humid tropical lands of southern Mexico, Yucatan, and Guatemala.

The Valley of Mexico: Teotihuacan. In central Mexico, the city of **Teotihuacan** (tay-oh-tee-wah-KAHN), near modern Mexico City, emerged as an enormous urban center with important religious functions. It was supported by intensive agriculture in the surrounding region and probably by crops planted around the great lakes that dominated the central valley of Mexico. The city developed slowly, but by the first centuries C.E. it was flourishing. Teotihuacan's enormous temple pyramids rival those of ancient Egypt and suggest a large state apparatus with the power to mobilize many workers. Population estimates for this city, which covered 9 square miles, are as high as 200,000. This would make it greater than the cities of ancient Egypt or Mesopotamia and probably second only to ancient Rome of the cities of classical antiquity.

Certain trades and ethnic groups had their own residential districts, and there is much evidence of wide social distinctions between the priests, nobles, and common people. The many gods of Mesoamerica, still worshiped when the Europeans arrived in the 16th century, were already honored at Teotihuacan. The god of rain, the feathered serpent, the goddess of corn, and the goddess of waters all appear in the murals and decorations of the palaces and temples. In fact, almost all Teotihuacan art seems to have been religious.

The influence of Teotihuacan extended as far south as the Maya states in Guatemala, and tribute probably was exacted from many regions. Teotihuacan objects, such as pottery and finely worked obsidian, and Teotihuacan artistic styles are found in many other areas. Teotihuacan influence was strong at Monte Alban in Oaxaca. Images of warriors dressed in the style of Teotihuacan can be found far to the south in the Maya region, and their presence there may indicate increasing militarization of Teotihuacan.

Teotihuacan represented a political empire or a dominant cultural and ideological style that spread over much of central Mexico and beyond. The lack of battle scenes on the walls of Teotihuacan has led some scholars to believe that the dominance of Teotihuacan led to a long period of peace maintained by the authority and power of the great city. Internally, the fact that the later buildings tend to be secular palaces rather than temple pyramids may indicate a shift in power from religious to civil authority. By the 8th century C.E. the city was in decline, and it was finally abandoned after attacks probably from nomadic raiders from the north. But for centuries thereafter, the memory of Teotihuacan lived on among the peoples of Mesoamerica as a golden age of cultural achievements.

The Classic Maya. Between about 300 and 900 C.E., at roughly the same time that Teotihuacan dominated the central plateau, the **Maya** peoples were developing Mesoamerican civilization to its highest point in southern Mexico and Central America. While the Tang dynasty ruled China, Charlemagne created his domain in Europe, and Islam spread its influence from Spain to India after the classical period had ended in the Old World, this great civilization flourished in the American tropics. The American classic period, launched as the Old World classical civilizations were coming to an end, lasted well into the next period of world history. We can use the Maya as an example of the classic period in Mesoamerican development: Although their civilization was distinctive, it was based on some principles common to the area.

The Maya culture extended over a broad region that now includes parts of five different countries: Mexico, Guatemala, Belize, Honduras, and El Salvador. It included several related languages, and it had considerable regional variation, as can be seen in its art styles. The whole region shared a common culture that included monumental architecture, a written language, a calendar and mathematical system, a highly developed religion, and concepts of statecraft and social organization. Using only stone tools in an area of dense forests, plagued by insects and poor soils, as many as 50 city-states flourished.

How did the large urban-religious centers, such as Tikal, Copán, Quirigua, and Palenque, with populations between 30,000 and 80,000, support themselves? **Slash-and-burn agriculture**, practiced today in the region, was not enough. The classic Maya used several agricultural systems. Evidence of irrigation, swamp drainage, and a system of artificially constructed ridged fields at river mouths (where intensive agriculture was practiced) seems to explain the Mayan ability to support large urban centers and a total population of perhaps 5 million. Although some authorities still believe that the

Olmec culture Cultural tradition that arose at San Lorenzo and La Venta in Mexico c. 1200 B.C.E.; featured irrigated agriculture, urbanism, elaborate religion, beginnings of calendrical and writing systems.

Monte Alban Chief center of Zapotec culture in southern Mexico during preclassic period; contemporary with Olmec culture; based on irrigated agriculture and calendrical and writing systems.

Teotihuacan [tay-oh-tee-wah-KAHN] Site of classic culture in central Mexico; urban center with important religious functions; supported by intensive agriculture in surrounding regions; population of as much as 200,000.

View the **Closer Look** on **MyHistoryLab**: The Pyramid of the Sun in Teotihuacan

Maya Classic culture emerging in southern Mexico and Central America contemporary with Teotihuacan; extended over broad region; featured monumental architecture, written language, calendrical and mathematical systems, highly developed religion.

slash-and-burn agriculture A system of cultivation typical of shifting cultivators; forest floors cleared by fire are then planted.

Maya centers were ceremonial and were occupied primarily by rulers, artisans, and an elite, it seems clear that populations were concentrated in and around these centers. The Maya cities vary in size and layout, but almost all include large pyramids surmounted by temples, complexes of masonry buildings that served administrative or religious purposes, elite residences, a ritual ball court, and often a series of altars and memorial pillars. These memorial monuments, or **stelae**, were erected to commemorate triumphs and events in the lives of the Maya rulers or to mark ceremonial occasions. The stelae usually were dated and were inscribed with a hieroglyphic script. A complex calendar and a sophisticated writing system were two of the greatest Maya achievements.

stelae Large memorial pillars erected to commemorate triumphs and events in the lives of rulers or other ceremonial occasions.

Religion, Writing, and Society. The calendar system and sophisticated astronomical observations were made possible by a vigesimal system of mathematics (that is, based on 20). The Maya knew the concept of zero and used it in conjunction with the concept of place value or position. With elegant simplicity and with signs for only 1, 5, and 0, they could make complex calculations. As among all the Mesoamerican peoples, the Maya calendar was based on a concept of recurring cycles of different length. The Maya had a sacred cycle of 260 days divided into months of 20 days each, within which there was a cycle of 13 numbers. This ritual calendar meshed with a solar calendar of 365 days, or 18 months of 20 days each, with 5 "dead" or inauspicious days at the end of the year. The two calendars operated simultaneously, so any day had two names, but the particular combination of those two days recurred only once every 52 years. Thus, among the Maya and most Mesoamericans, cycles of 52 years were sacred.

The classic Maya differed from their neighbors in that they also kept a **long count**, or a system of dating from a fixed date in the past. This date, 3114 B.C.E. by the Christian calendar, probably marked the beginning of a great cycle of 5200 years since the creation of the world. Like other Mesoamericans and the ancient Peruvians, the Maya believed in great cycles of creation and destruction of the universe. The long count enabled the Maya to date events with precision. The earliest recorded Maya date that survives is the equivalent of 292 C.E., and the last to appear on a classic Maya object would be 928 C.E. The Maya fascination with cycles of destruction and creation has intrigued the modern world; a misreading of Maya astronomy and legends led to many theories that the world would end in 2012. A second great Maya accomplishment was the creation of a writing system. The Maya wrote on stone monuments, murals, and ceramics and in books of folded bark paper and deerskin, only four of which survive. Scribes were honored and held an important place in society. Although we still cannot fully decipher many inscriptions, recent advances now permit the reading of many texts. The Maya written language, like Chinese and Sumerian, was a logographic system, which combined phonetic and semantic elements. With this system and about 287 symbols, the Maya recorded complex ideas. The few surviving books are religious and astronomical texts, and many inscriptions on ceramics deal with the cult of the dead and the complex Maya cosmology, but hundreds of the inscriptions refer to the reign of kings, their victories, their accomplishments, and their lineages.

long count Mayan system of dating from a fixed date in the past, 3114 B.C.E.; marked the beginning of a great cycle of 5200 years; allowed precision dating of events in Mayan history.

The Maya had a complex religious system with many deities, but there was a basic Mesoamerican concept of dualism—male and female, good and bad, day and night. This idea, similar to that found in some Asian religions, emphasized the unity of all things. Each god had a parallel female consort or feminine form and often an underworld equivalent as well. In addition, there were patron deities of various occupations and classes. The number of gods and goddesses in the inscriptions seems overwhelming, but they should be understood as manifestations of a more limited set of supernatural forces, much like the various incarnations of the Hindu gods.

 Read the Document: From the Popol Vuh: The Great Mythological Book of the Ancient Maya [ca. 1550]

From the historical inscriptions we know that the major Maya centers were the cores of city-states, which controlled outlying territories. There was constant warfare, and rulers such as Pacal of Palenque expanded their territories by conquest. The rulers exercised civil and probably religious power, and an elite aided their rule and performed administrative functions. A class of scribes, or perhaps priests, tended to the cult of the state and specialized in the complex calendar observations and calculations. The ruler and the scribes organized and participated in rituals of self-mutilation and human sacrifice that among the Maya, as in much of Mesoamerica, were an important aspect of religion. Also, as a form of both worship and sport, the Maya, like other Mesoamerican peoples, wagered on and played ritual **ball games** on specially constructed courts in which players moved a ball with their hips or elbows. The stakes were high. Losers might forfeit their possessions or their lives.

ball games Ritual elements of many American cultures; played on formal courts; religious significance required that losing teams pay a penalty of forfeiture of goods or their lives.

Builders, potters, scribes, sculptors, and painters worked in the cities for the glory of the gods and the rulers. However, most people were peasant farmers whose labor supported the elaborate ritual and political lives of the elite. Captives were enslaved. Patrilineal families probably formed the basis of social life, as they did among the Maya of later days, but the elite traced their families through both fathers and mothers. Elite women often are represented in dynastic monuments in positions of importance. State marriages were important, and elite women retained many rights. Among the common people, women were responsible for food preparation and domestic duties, including the production of fine cloth on small looms. The division of tasks by gender probably was supported by religious belief and custom.

Classic Collapse

Between about 700 and 900 C.E., the Mesoamerican world was shaken by the rapid decline of the great cultural centers. The reasons for this collapse are not fully understood, but it was widespread. In the central plateau, Teotihuacan was destroyed about 650 C.E. by outside invaders, probably nomadic hunters from the north, perhaps with the help of some of the groups under the dominance of Teotihuacan. The city may have already been in decline because of increasing problems with agriculture.

The most mysterious aspect of the collapse was the abandonment of the Maya cities. During the 8th century C.E., Maya rulers stopped erecting commemorative stelae and large buildings, and population sizes dwindled. By 900 C.E., most of the major Maya centers had been deserted. Scholars do not agree whether this process was the result of ecological problems and climatic change, agricultural exhaustion, internal revolt, or foreign pressure. The collapse took place at different times in different places and seems to have been the result of several processes, of which increasing warfare was either a cause or a symptom. The warfare may be related to the decline of Teotihuacan and the attempt of Maya city-states to control old trade routes.

The primary explanation for the Maya collapse is agricultural exhaustion. The Mayan ability to create a civilization in the dense rain forest of the Peten in Guatemala and in the Chiapas lowlands was based on a highly productive agricultural system. By the 8th century, the limits of that system, given the size and density of population, may have been reached. Tikal had an estimated density of more than 300 people per square mile. Maintaining the great population centers was an increasing burden. Epidemic disease has also been suggested as a cause of the collapse, perhaps indicating some unrecorded contact with the Old World. Others believe that the peasants simply refused to bear the burdens of serving and feeding the political and religious elite and that internal rebellion led to the end of the ruling dynasties and their cities.

The cultural achievements of the classic period were not attained again. Long-count dating ended, the stelae cult ceased, and the quality of ceramics and architectural accomplishments declined. But as the great Maya centers of the southern lowlands and highlands were abandoned or declined, Maya cities in the Yucatan and in the Guatemala highlands expanded and carried on some of the traditions, also receiving much cultural influence from central Mexico. Mexicanized ruling families established themselves at **Chichén Itzá** and other towns in Yucatan. The northern Maya area accommodated these influences and created a new synthesis of Maya and central Mexican culture. In the great southern Maya cities, such as Tikal and Palenque, the rain forest soon overran the temples and palaces.

After 1000 C.E., the **Nahuatl**-speaking **Toltecs**, one of the new groups that occupied the central plateau after the fall of Teotihuacan, established political control over a large territory and eventually extended their influence into Maya territory. Their genius seems to have been military, and much of their culture was derived from classic traditions. From their capital at Tula in central Mexico, Toltec influence and trade may have spread as far as the American Southwest, where the cliff-dwelling Anasazi (ah-nuh-SAH-zee) people, the ancestors of the Pueblo Indians discussed later in this chapter, produced beautiful ceramics and cultivated maize in the desert valleys. In Yucatan, the ruling families claimed descent from Toltec invaders. Even when the Toltec empire fell, about 1200 C.E., the cultural traditions of Mesoamerica did not die, for imperial states and civilization do not necessarily go together. Eventually, however, a new power, the **Aztecs**, rose in the central plateau of Mexico. The Aztecs initiated yet another cycle of expansion based on the deep-rooted ways of life and thought of Mesoamerica.

Chichén Itzá [chee-CHEHN-eet-she] Originally a Mayan city; conquered by Toltecs c. 1000 and ruled by Toltec dynasties; architecture featured pyramid of Feathered Serpent (Quetzalcoatl).

Nahuatl [NAH-wahtl] Language spoken by the Toltecs and Aztecs.

Toltecs [TOHL-tehks] Nomadic peoples from beyond the northern frontier of the sedentary agricultural area in Mesoamerica; established capital of Tula following migration into central Mesoamerican plateau.

Aztecs The Mexica; one of the nomadic tribes that used political anarchy after fall of Toltecs to penetrate into the sedentary agricultural zone of Mesoamerican plateau; established empire after 1325 around shores of Lake Texcoco.

solar cycle Calendrical system based on solar year; typical of all civilizations; variations of solar calendars in Western civilization are Julian and Gregorian calendars; Mayas also constructed solar calendar.

lunar cycle One of the principal means of establishing a calendar; based on cycles of moon; differed from solar cycles and failed to provide accurate guide to round of the seasons; required constant revision or intercalation.

DOCUMENT

Deciphering the Maya Glyphs

OF ALL THE PEOPLES OF ANCIENT America, the Maya developed the most complex system of writing to record their history, religion, philosophy, and politics. Maya hieroglyphs have baffled and fascinated researchers since the 1820s, when the first steps toward deciphering the rich glyphs and symbols of Maya monuments, ceramics, and the few surviving Maya books were made. This process continues, and although we are not yet able to read all the surviving texts, those that have been deciphered have changed our view of Maya society and its underlying beliefs.

One of the problems of decipherment was a false start. In the 16th century, a Spanish bishop of Yucatan, Diego de Landa, burned many books in an attempt to stamp out Maya religion. Landa's attempt to describe the Maya writing, based on his questioning of Indian informants, was badly flawed. Landa thought the glyphs were letters, not syllables, so his description confused scholars. Despite his deficiencies, however, Landa provided the only guide available for many years. Unlike the decipherment of Egyptian hieroglyphs, no text with Maya and some other known language side by side exists, so the problem of reading the Maya glyphs remains difficult.

The first modern advances were made in reading Maya numbers and identifying glyphs for the months in the calendar cycle. By the 1940s, scholars could read the dates rather well, and because so many inscriptions and the four remaining books seemed to be numerical and related to the calendar, most specialists believed that the Maya writing was primarily about the calendar system and that the Maya were obsessed with time. Many things complicated the reading of the other glyphs, such as the fact that scholars were not sure which one of the various Maya languages that survives was the language of the inscriptions. In 1952 a young Russian researcher argued that the Maya glyphs combined signs that stood for whole words with others that represented sounds or syllables. In this, the Maya script was like ancient Egyptian and cuneiform writings. Although the theory was not fully accepted at first, it has proved to be accurate.

A major breakthrough took place in 1960, when art historian Tatiana Proskouriakoff noted that on certain sets of monuments the earliest and last dates were never more than 62 years apart, and that the first date was always accompanied by one certain glyph and the next always by another. She recognized that the images on the monuments were not gods or mythical figures, but kings, and that the first glyph

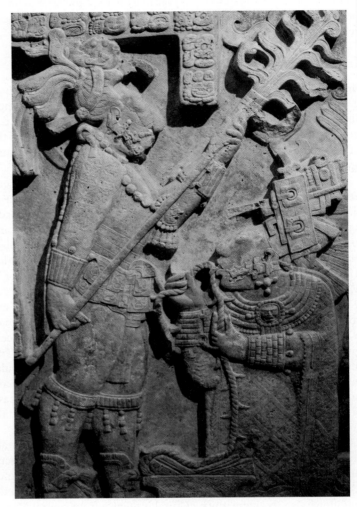

FIGURE **8.5** This relief from the Maya palace complex at Yaxchilan shows a kneeling woman pulling a rope barbed with thorns across her tongue to draw blood. Her husband, a king named Shield-Jaguar, holds a torch above her head. The king's hair is adorned with the shrunken head of a sacrificial victim.

indicated birth and the second accession. Sixty-two years was consistent with a human lifespan. With this approach, scholars have figured out the names of the rulers and their families and something about the dynastic history of a number of Maya cities.

(continued on next page)

(continued from previous page)

Scholars now understand that despite regional variations, the texts were written in a language widely understood throughout the Maya region. The glyphs combine syllables, symbols, emblems, and ideas in what is basically a complex phonetic system. Now that we are able to read numbers, dates, place or city emblems, and a few nouns and verbs, a new window has been opened on the ancient Maya.

QUESTIONS

- What do the elaborate ritual life and sumptuous clothing suggest about the nature of Maya society?
- Do the complex calendar and writing system indicate widespread literacy or the power of an elite class that controlled this esoteric knowledge?
- Does the role of writing in Mesoamerican civilization seem similar to that in ancient Egypt, Sumer, and China?

THINKING HISTORICALLY

Different Times for Different Peoples

IN THIS PRESENTATION OF THE INDIGENOUS civilizations of the Americas that were often concerned with time, it is appropriate to examine the importance of time and its measurement in world history. The calendar and timekeeping are so much a part of everyday life that we often think of these measures only as aspects of the natural order. We divide the day into 24 hours of 60 minutes each, and the year into 12 months or 365 days, without much reflection on the meaning or origins of these divisions. Our lives are guided by the clock and marked by its division into working hours, doctor's appointments, class periods, and TV time slots, all of which reflect not only a widely accepted system of measurement but also an ideology of time and its value.

The marking and division of time is a complex matter with cultural, political, and even biological aspects. The concept and meaning of time have varied greatly from culture to culture and have changed historically within cultures. The leaders of both the French Revolution of 1789 and the Russian Revolution of 1917 created new calendar systems to represent what they hoped were the beginnings of new historical ages. Calendar systems and time measurement reflect ideas about politics and history as well as perceptions of the natural world.

Observing the cyclical motion of the heavens was the key for constructing a yearly calendar by which agriculture could be regulated and religious cycles could be set. Early peoples observed the recurring patterns of the stars and planets. Clearly observed stages of the moon guided the ancient Babylonians, but because the annual cycle of the moon differed from the **solar cycle**, the lunar calendar was not an accurate guide to the seasons. The **lunar cycle** calendar constantly needed adjustment, or intercalation, which added extra days or months so that the seasons

Both the ancient Hindus and the Maya calculated great cycles of thousands of years as part of a divine plan.

would occur in the same place in the cycle in each calendar year. Despite its difficulties, the lunar calendar was adopted by the Hebrews. It is still in use by Jews and is also the basis of the Muslim calendar.

The ancient Egyptians were the first to use a solar year, and as early as 4000 B.C.E. they had devised a calendar of 12 months of 30 days each, to which they added five days of celebration at the start of each year. (The Maya and other peoples of Mesoamerica had a similar solution but added their five days at the end of the year.) The Egyptian solar calendar, although not exact and also needing periodic adjustments, was the basis for the Roman Empire's Julian calendar, established by Julius Caesar in 45 B.C.E. This calendar was modified and improved in the Gregorian calendar, instituted by Pope Gregory XIII in the late 16th century and adopted slowly throughout Europe.

Other peoples and civilizations also worked out calendar systems based on observation of the heavens, and these in turn were related to concepts about time and history. The Maya peoples were acute observers of the heavens. They built observatories and wrote treatises on the movement of the stars and planets. Like other Mesoamerican peoples, they used two calendars simultaneously: a 260-day ritual calendar and a 365-day solar calendar. The days of the two lined up only every 52 years, creating a cyclical view of time divided into 52-year cycles. Thus for the ancient peoples of Mesoamerica, as in India and Sumer, time was cyclical. The events of history fit into recurring patterns that might reveal a divine purpose or plan but did not lead in any particular direction. Both the ancient Hindus and the Maya calculated great cycles of thousands of years as part of a divine plan.

The ancient Chinese were concerned with measuring time, and water clocks were used during the Shang period, about

(continued on next page)

(continued from previous page)

1500 B.C.E. By the 11th century, Su Sung, a court official, had designed for the emperor an elaborate clock regulated by the flow of water. But Chinese interest in mechanical clocks did not continue, and time did not figure prominently in Chinese philosophical thought or in the lives of most people. A new emperor often introduced a new calendar, for control of the calendar was viewed as an attribute of power. The Chinese concept of history was marked by belief in a divine mandate that was given to each dynasty and then withdrawn when it failed in its duties and obligations. Thus, time and history were redefined as each dynasty attempted to fulfill this Mandate of Heaven.

For the ancient Hebrews, whose ideas on this subject were later taken up by Christians and Muslims, history was not cyclical but linear: It moved toward an end, the revelation of God's will. The present was influenced by the past and the future. It has been suggested that a concept of the future and of progress depends on a linear view of time and history.

Before the 19th century, the vast majority of the world's people, including the peasants of the most technologically advanced societies, measured time by the cycle of work and daily tasks: when the cows had to be milked, how much time until dinner, how many hours of daylight remained. These natural rhythms kept work and life close together, and there was little concern for time as a separate thing that could be precisely measured and counted, lost, or gained. The day might be divided by the hours of daily prayer or by the duration of a task, but exact time was of little importance.

Although the Chinese had experimented with clocks, and other cultures had used sundials, candles, and water clocks to measure the passage of time, synchronizing these instruments was difficult. Clocks were curiosities and vehicles for artistic expression, more likely to be found in royal collections than in private homes. In 807 C.E., for example, Europeans marveled at a mechanical water clock sent as a gift by the Muslim leader Haroun al-Rashid to Charlemagne. But despite such wonders, the inaccurate instruments of antiquity were of limited use.

It was in Europe that time measurement was transformed. Perhaps the deficiencies of sundials and water clocks in the cloudy and frosty climates of northern Europe led to the perfection of the mechanical clock. The cause simply could have been Europe's growing interest in machines.

Between the 14th and 17th centuries, the measurement of time experienced a profound but gradual transformation. Church and town clocks appeared in the major urban centers, and clocks began to appear in private homes, especially after the introduction of pendulum clocks in about 1660. By the end of the 17th century, pocket watches based on balance springs made accurate timekeeping a personal matter, and the aristocrats, master artisans, and merchants of Europe began to live their lives by the clock. When Catholic missionaries arrived in China in the 17th century, the Chinese were amazed by the complexity and accuracy of the clocks they brought. Some authors see Europe's fascination with time and perfection of the clock as a symbol of changes in attitudes about labor and nature. Moreover, accurate clocks were precise machines and symbolized the development of technology that accompanied the Scientific Revolution of the 17th century and then the Industrial Revolution of the 18th century.

The "revolution in time," as historian David Landes calls it, was related to changes in work discipline needed in the new industries, where synchronizing tasks in a factory called for precision and a sense of time different from that of rural labor. Such coordination had already begun to appear in activities such as shipbuilding and on sugar plantations. Time became something that workers sold and employers bought, and the concept of productivity measured by the amount of work done in a specific amount of time became a basic part of the industrial work ethic. The shift was difficult, however. Older working patterns were slow to change, and industrialists complained that workers still honored "Saint Monday" by not showing up for work on that day, or that they preferred to work not by the hour but by the job. Early industrial workers were not eager to become captives of the machine and the clock.

Preindustrial habits and attitudes of work persisted in most of the world outside of Europe in the 19th century. Most people still lived with a rhythm of intense labor at some times of the year and less work at others, and they thought in terms of the job and not by the amount of time it took to do it. European travelers to Asia, Africa, the Pacific, and the Americas commented on the natives' lack of punctuality, the natural or religious rhythms of their life, their inability to measure time, and often their seeming disregard for it. The myth of the lazy native was being born. The clock became a measure of what Europeans and North Americans valued and what set them apart. When an English missionary in southern Africa wrote in his diary, "Today we have unpacked our clock and we seem a little more civilized," he summarized a great deal of modern world history.

QUESTIONS

- Why did measuring time become important in the early civilizations of Egypt, the Near East, and China?
- How did concepts of time reflect a view of history?
- What are the implications of the technological changes in keeping time?

THE PEOPLES TO THE NORTH

8.3 What possible evidence is there of contacts between Mesoamerica and societies further to the north and those in South America?

Archeologists have distinguished various stages of archaic culture, from Alaska to northern Mexico, among the ancestors of the North American Indians. We cannot deal in detail with the many cultural traditions that evolved from those cultures of the archaic period, but two broad regions in North America merit special attention because of the complex, sedentary agricultural societies that developed there: the eastern woodlands of what are now the southern United States and the arid Southwest.

The Mound Builders

In the valleys of the Mississippi and Ohio rivers, people began to practice agriculture by 2000 B.C.E. By 700 B.C.E. a society that combined hunting and agriculture had begun to emerge. In southern Ohio and neighboring areas, these peoples built large earthen constructions and mounds. Some of the mounds were defensive, and others served as places for burials. These burials contain pottery, pipes (indicating the use of tobacco), jewelry, and copper objects that indicate long-distance trade from as far away as Michigan. This culture may have been spread by migrants or by trade contacts to other places, such as New York State and Maryland, where it lasted as late as 700 C.E. In Ohio and southern Illinois, however, it was already being replaced by a more complex culture.

The **Hopewell culture** (c. 200–500 C.E.) introduced new levels of scale and complexity. Elaborate mounds, some of great size and often organized into groups, were characteristic of this mound-building culture. Some of the mounds, such as Serpent Mound in Ohio, were built as effigies, or representations, of animals. Burials contained jewelry, personal items, weapons, and religious symbols of copper, quartz, galena, and mica. Conch shells and shark teeth indicate long-distance trade with peoples of the Gulf coast, and other materials were brought from as far away as the Rocky Mountains. Hopewell artisans worked in stone and clay and produced beautiful pottery, pipes, and effigies, luxury items seemingly designed for the cult of the dead. By about 400 C.E., large-scale construction of mounds had ceased in the main centers of Hopewell culture, and the trade network had begun to break down.

After about 400 years, the Hopewell culture was succeeded by a new complex that spread throughout the Mississippi valley. Between 800 and 1300 C.E., very large towns and ceremonial centers, such as Moundville (Alabama) and Cahokia (Illinois), flourished throughout the southeastern region. Mound building here was not only for burials or effigies but also for fortification and large pyramid platforms. Cahokia had one temple mound about 100 feet high, containing more than 2 million cubic feet of earth. Large populations and smaller towns lived around these Mississippian centers. For example, at least 50 communities appear to have been under Cahokia's influence. Except for the absence of stone architecture, Cahokia seemed to parallel the urban development of Mesoamerica.

The rich variety and excellent quality of artifacts indicate social divisions within this society, but we know little about its social organization. The best clues come from the 18th-century observations of the Natchez Indians, who carried on the Mississippian tradition. They were organized as a powerful chiefdom under a ruler known as the Great Sun, who ruled a society composed of four distinct social classes, the lowest of which were called the stinkards. The Natchez were the last remnants of a culture that had mostly disappeared by 1400 C.E.

One explanation for the rise of **Mississippian culture** was the introduction of new strains of maize from Mesoamerica and its adoption of maize, bean, and squash cultivation. Mississippians depended more fully on agriculture than their Hopewell and earlier predecessors. Mississippian populations were larger than those of previous cultures, and the search for new agricultural lands seems to have been a motive for political expansion. The large towns and urban centers, temple complexes, pyramid mounds, religious symbols, and crops appear to reflect a strong Mesoamerican influence, but no identifiable Mesoamerican artifacts have been found in Mississippian sites.

The Desert Peoples

Across the American Southwest a different cultural tradition developed with great local variation. By about 300 B.C.E., settled communities developed in this region, living first in pit houses partially beneath the ground and later in stone structures. Irrigation was used to grow maize, beans, and other

To the north of Mesoamerica, complex cultures developed, often based on agriculture. The extent of their contact with Mesoamerica is not clear, but in the Mississippi basin and the American Southwest, the ancestors of the later Indian peoples formed complex societies with large populations.

Hopewell culture A North American mound-building culture; lasted from c. 200 to 500 C.E.

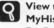

View the **Image** on **MyHistoryLab**: Snake and Egg Earthwork Ohio

Mississippian culture Last of the mound-building cultures of North America; flourished between 800 and 1300 C.E.; featured large towns and ceremonial centers; lacked stone architecture of Central America.

crops, and ball courts and temple mounds that appeared by 600 C.E. suggest the influence of Meso-american cultures. Distinctive pottery developed in each cultural region, and there seems to have been trade between these areas and with Mexico. In southern New Mexico by about 1000 C.E., multiroom stone dwellings were being used.

Perhaps the most famous southwestern regional tradition is that of the **Anasazi** (Navajo for "the ancient ones"), who lived in the Four Corners region of New Mexico, Arizona, Colorado, and Utah. Settled in the region from about 200 B.C.E., they began to live in large, multistory adobe and stone dwellings by 700 C.E. Apparently, pressure from hostile neighbors caused them to build these dwellings in protected canyons or in cliffs, where access is difficult. The existing cliff-dwelling ruins at Mesa Verde and Canyon de Chelly are excellent examples of Anasazi settlements (Figure 8.6). A characteristic feature of these villages and towns is the circular pit, or **kiva** (KEE-vuh), used for religious meetings by the men of the community. This structure is still used today by the Pueblo Indians of the region.

Kivas are also found in another type of Anasazi settlement. The ruins of about 125 towns in New Mexico's Chaco Canyon and the surrounding areas are remarkable for their planning and the care of their stone and adobe construction. Many of these towns were connected by an extensive system of what seem to be roads or ritual lines, which linked the city to celestial or natural phenomena. The Anasazi produced excellent pottery without the potter's wheel, and they had trading contacts with Mesoamerica, where the turquoise of their region was traded for items such as parrots, valued for their feathers.

A long period of drought in the late 13th century seems to explain the decline of the Anasazi and other southwestern peoples. and may also have affected Cahokia and the Mississippian settlements. These agrarian societies were particularly vulnerable to rapid climatic change. In the Southwest,

Anasazi "The ancient ones"; culture located in southwestern United States; flourished from 200 to 1200 C.E.; featured large multistory adobe and stone buildings built in protected canyons or cliffs.

kiva Circular pit in Anasazi and other communities used for religious meetings by the men in the society.

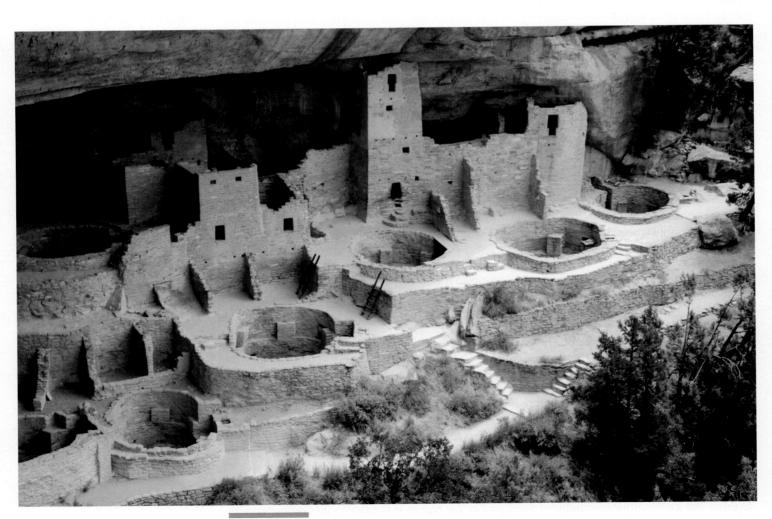

FIGURE **8.6** Anasazi dwelling at Mesa Verde.

perhaps the technology in managing water resources was unable to keep pace with a drought that lasted for hundreds of years. Anasazi decline, followed by pressure from nomads such as the Navajo and Apache, eventually led to the abandonment of the towns, but many scholars believe that the traditions of the Anasazi have continued in the culture of the modern Hopi and other Pueblo Indians of the American Southwest.

The contacts with Mesoamerican civilization are clearer among the ancient peoples of the southwestern United States than in the eastern woodlands. However, both regions demonstrate the spread of many aspects of civilization and the development of settled agricultural societies throughout the Americas.

THE ANDEAN WORLD

8.4 What similarities and differences were there between Mesoamerica and South America?

The Andean world presented a peculiar geography of complex microregions with extreme changes in altitude and temperature (Map 8.3). The narrow, arid strip on the western coast, cut by a few rivers that flow to the Pacific, gives way quickly to the high Andes, where some peaks rise to more than 15,000 feet. Between the two major chains of the Andes lie high valleys and steppes, or **puna**, that form the highlands, or altiplano. On these cool uplands (usually above 10,000 feet), the land is level and there is adequate water. Here potatoes and maize could be grown, and the puna provided good grazing for **llamas** and **alpacas**, the "sheep of the Andes." Andean populations were concentrated here or down on the arid coast in the river valleys that made irrigation possible. On the eastern slopes of the Andes, large rivers run down into the tropical rain forest concentrated at the basins of the Amazon and La Plata rivers. This is the humid **montaña**, where tropical fruits and coca leaf grow.

This rugged topography imposed limitations and created opportunities for civilization to develop. The arid coastal valleys had to be irrigated, and this spurred population growth and social complexity. In the highlands, irrigation and terracing increased the food supply in regions where the amount of arable land was limited. Populations were concentrated in the fertile valleys but were separated from one another by steep mountains. Trade and communication were difficult. It took large, well-organized projects to build roads, bridges, and agricultural terraces. The reasons for state building were good. The warfare, military images, and trophy heads seen in much ancient Peruvian art represent a world of limited resources and competition.

In the Andean world, sharp vertical changes created microclimates within short distances. Peoples and even individual communities or families strove to control the different ecological zones where different kinds of crops could be raised. A community might live in the altiplano, growing potatoes and quinoa (an Andean grain), but could also have fields in the lower valleys to grow maize, pastures miles away at a higher elevation for the llamas, and even an outer colony in the montaña to provide cotton, coca, and other tropical products. In fact, access to a variety of these ecological zones by colonization, occupation, conquest, or trade seems to have been a constant feature in Andean life, which determined pre-Columbian patterns of settlement and influenced the historical development of the Andean world.

Early Developments and the Rise of Chavín

Much of early Andean history alternates between periods of decentralization, in which various local or regional centers developed distinctive cultures, and periods in which one of these centers spread its control over very large areas, establishing a cultural horizon under centralized authority. Between 3000 and 2000 B.C.E., permanent agricultural villages were established in the Andean highlands and on the arid Pacific coast. Maize was introduced from Mesoamerica and was grown along with indigenous crops such as the potato. Pottery appeared by about 2700 B.C.E., first on the north coast in present-day Ecuador and then in the highlands of central Peru. This early pottery, called Valdivia ware, indicates advanced techniques of production. It is remarkably similar to Japanese Jomon-period (3rd millennium B.C.E.) ceramics, and this has led some scholars to suggest trans-Pacific contact by Japanese fishers. Whatever the origins of pottery in the region, the presence of sedentary agriculture, ceramics, weaving, and permanent villages marked a level of productivity that was soon followed

In South America, periods of broadly shared culture were followed by eras of regional diversity. The civilization of Chavín spread along the Peruvian coast, created a horizon of widely shared culture; it was followed by vibrant regional cultures such as Nazca and Moche and then by the highland states of Huari and Tihuanaco.

puna High valleys and steppes lying between the two major chains of the Andes mountains; site of South American agricultural origins, also only location of pastoralism in Americas.

llamas Along with alpacas, domesticated animals of the Americas; basis for only form of nomadic pastoralism in the New World until European importation of larger animals in 15th century C.E.

alpacas Along with llamas, domesticated animals of the Americas; basis for only form of nomadic pastoralism in the New World until European importation of larger animals in 15th century C.E.

montaña Located on eastern slopes of Andes mountains; location of cultivation and gathering of tropical fruits and coca leaf.

MAP **8.3 Andean Societies** Note the development of civilization centers on the coast and in the highlands.

View the Closer Look on
MyHistoryLab: The Raimondi
Stela at Chavín de Huantar

by evidence of political organization. Early sites, such as El Paraiso on the Peruvian coast, contain monumental buildings of great size, but we know little of the societies that built them.

Between 1800 and 200 B.C.E., ceremonial centers with large stone buildings were constructed in the highlands and on the coast. Pottery was now widely distributed, the llama had been domesticated, and agriculture had become more complex, with evidence of simple irrigation at some places. The most important of these centers was Chavín de Huantar (SHAH-van deh WAHN-tahr) (850–250 B.C.E.) in the Peruvian highlands. Chavín contained several large temple platforms and adobe and stone buildings. Its artisans worked in ceramics, textiles, and gold. **Chavín culture** was characterized by artistic motifs that were spread widely through much of the Andean region and seem to represent a cult or a system of religious beliefs. Jaguars, snakes, birds of prey, and humans with feline characteristics were used as decorations, often along with scenes of war and violence. Many of these elements were characteristic of the tropical forest regions to the east, but in its architectural design, Chavín used features associated with early developments of the coastal regions.

The Chavín artistic style was so widely diffused that archeologists call this epoch a **horizon**, a period when a broad central authority seems to have integrated a widely dispersed region. In truth, we do not know whether conquest, trade, or missionary activity spread the religion of Chavín, nor do we know the religion's origins, but a strong argument has been made that Chavín developed the use of pack trains of llamas, each carrying a burden of up to 130 pounds, thus suggesting that trade was a major aspect of its expansion. Its artistic style does have some remarkable similarities with Olmec art in Mesoamerica. Some archeologists point out certain tropical features in both and suggest the Amazonian lowlands as a possible point of origin for both traditions.

The evidence of warfare in early Peruvian agricultural societies may indicate a general process. With the development of intensive agriculture and a limited amount of arable land, it became necessary to organize irrigation and create political authority and eventually states that could mobilize to protect or expand the available land.

Regional Cultures and a New Horizon

By 300 B.C.E., Chavín was in decline, and whatever unity the widely spread Chavín style indicated was lost. The Andean world became characterized by regional centers, each with its own cultural and artistic traditions. This was a period without political unity, but it produced some of the Andean world's finest art. Irrigated agriculture that produced a wide variety of crops, the domestication of llamas and related animals, dense populations, and hierarchical societies could be found in many places. Some societies, such as those in Nazca (NAHZ-kah) on the south coast and Moche to the north, produced remarkable pottery and weaving.

Nazca weaving reached a high point for the Americas. Discovery in the 1920s of a group of richly dressed mummies at Paracas (pah-RAH-kahs), near Nazca, revealed the artistic accomplishments of these ancient weavers. More than 100 colors were used, and many weaving techniques and cloth types were produced; the designs often were abstract. The plain near Nazca is also the scene of great figures of various animals, which cover many hundreds of feet and can be seen only from the air. There are also great straight lines or paths that cut across the plain and seem to be oriented toward distant mountains or celestial points. Why these lines and designs were drawn is unknown.

The **Mochica state** (200–700 C.E.), in the Moche valley and on the coast to the north of Chavín, mobilized workers to construct great clay brick temples, residences, and platforms. Artisans produced gold and silver jewelry and copper tools. The potter's art reached a high point; scenes on Mochica ceramics depict rulers receiving tribute and executing prisoners. Nobles, priests, farmers, soldiers, and slaves are also portrayed in remarkably lifelike ways; many vessels are clearly portraits of individual members of the elite. The Mochica also produced a great number of pottery vessels showing a variety of explicit sexual acts. These scenes are almost always in a domestic setting and indicate descriptions of everyday life rather than ritual unions.

Moche expanded its control by conquest. Mochica art contains many representations of war, prisoners, and the taking of heads as trophies. There is also archeological evidence of hilltop forts and military posts. Politically, Moche and the other regional states seem to have been military states or chiefdoms, supported by extensive irrigated agriculture and often at war.

Some idea of life in Moche society was spectacularly revealed with the discovery in 1988 of the tomb of a warrior-priest. Buried with servants and his dog, this nobleman that archaeologists call the Lord of Sipán was covered with gold, silver, and copper ornaments, fine cloth, and jewelry (Figure 8.7). The scenes on these objects and on the pottery buried with him include depictions of captive prisoners, ritual sacrifice, and warfare. This spectacular archaeological discovery of an untouched burial chamber revealed the art and skill of Moche craftsmen, but also the social divisions and privileged status of the elites of Moche society.

This pattern of regional development continued until about 300 c.e., when two large centers, **Tihuanaco** on the shores of Lake Titicaca (TIH-tih-KAH-kuh) and **Huari** farther to the north in southern Peru, began to emerge as large states. As with the earlier case of Chavín, the religious symbols and artistic style associated with these centers spread widely through the Andean world, creating perhaps a second or intermediate horizon (c. 300–900 c.e.) roughly contemporary with the classic Maya and Teotihuacan in Mesoamerica.

Tihuanaco was an urban ceremonial center with a population of perhaps 40,000, with another 75,000 settled in other urban centers. Recent archeological work has revealed an extensive system of raised fields, irrigated by canals, that could produce high yields. Tihuanaco's inhabitants probably spoke Aymara (eye-mah-RAH), the language of the southern Andes that is spoken today in Bolivia. The art style of Tihuanaco and the representations of its gods, especially the Staff God, spread all over the southern Andean zone.

In typical Andean fashion, Tihuanaco extended its political control through colonies as far away as Chile and the eastern Andean slopes in order to ensure access to fish, coca, and tropical plants, the products of different ecological zones. Huari may have begun as a colony of Tihuanaco, but it eventually exercised wide influence over much of the north Andean zone, an influence spread along its system of roads. The period of its control was short, but the urban area of Huari eventually covered more than six square miles.

The intermediate horizon, represented by Tihuanaco and Huari, came to an end in the 9th century c.e., about the same time as the end of the classic period in Mesoamerica. Whether these two processes were connected remains unknown. With the decline of these expansive cultures in Peru, another period of regional development followed as different peoples, especially those along the coast, tried to establish control over their neighbors. The **Chimu state** on the north coast eventually controlled more than 600 miles of the coastal zone.

The Chimu state, founded about 800 c.e., was still expanding when it fell to the Incas in 1465. During this period other small states had formed. In the highlands various ethnic groups were struggling for control of their neighbors. One of these, a group of Quechua-speaking clans, or **ayllus**, took control of the highlands around Cuzco and began to expand, especially after 1400 c.e. These were the **Incas**, who were creating a new horizon of centralized control and cultural influence over the various ethnic and linguistic groups of the Andean world from Ecuador to Chile when the Europeans arrived in 1532.

Andean Lifeways

Although it is difficult to reconstruct much of the social and political organization of early Andean societies on the basis of archeological evidence, by using later observations from Inca times along with archeological materials, we can identify some characteristic features. We have already spoken of verticality, or the control of several economic niches at different altitudes, as a principle of Andean

FIGURE **8.7** A figurative nose ornament of a warrior priest buried in the Moche royal tomb of the Lord of Sipán, Peru.

Chavín culture Appeared in highlands of Andes between 1800 and 1200 b.c.e.; typified by ceremonial centers with large stone buildings; greatest ceremonial center was Chavín de Huantar; characterized by artistic motifs.

horizon Archeological term for a period when a broad central authority seems to have integrated a widely dispersed region.

Mochica state [MOH-chay] Flourished in Andes north of Chavín culture in the Moche valley between 200 and 700 c.e.; featured great clay-brick temples; created military chiefdom supported by extensive irrigated agriculture.

Tihuanaco [TEE-uh-wah-NAH-koh] Along with Huari, large center for regional chiefdoms between 300 and 900 c.e.; located in southern Peru; featured large ceremonial center supported by extensive irrigated agriculture; established widely diffused religious and artistic symbols spread all over Andean zone.

Huari [WAH-ree] Along with Tihuanaco, large center for regional chiefdoms between 300 and 900 c.e.; located in southern Peru; featured large ceremonial center supported by extensive irrigated agriculture; established widely diffused religious and artistic symbols spread all over Andean zone.

Chimu state [chee-MOO] Regional Andean chiefdom that flourished from 800 to 1465 C.E.; fell to Incas.

ayllu [eye-LUHS] Households in Andean societies that recognized some form of kinship; traced descent from some common, sometimes mythical ancestor.

life. This control and the related self-sufficiency sometimes were the objective of states, but they were also the goal of families and communities. Kin groups were another constant of the Andean world.

Andean peoples were divided into ethnic groups and spoke several languages, although Aymara came to predominate in the Bolivian highlands, and the Incas later spread Quechua (KEECH-wah) from the central Andes to the coast and north to Ecuador. Despite ethnic and linguistic differences, communities generally were composed of households, which together recognized some form of kinship. Members of a kinship unit, or ayllu, traced their descent from a common, sometimes mythical ancestor, and they referred to other members of the ayllu as brother and sister. People usually married

VISUALIZING THE PAST

Ancient Agriculture

THE ANCIENT PEOPLES OF THE AMERICAS devised complex systems of irrigation, combining their knowledge of agriculture and hydrology to produce high yields in areas of drought, frost, or difficult soil that even today present great challenges to agriculture. Some of the projects were enormous, involving miles of canals and ditches. In the lowlands of Bolivia and in arid coastal Peru, there is evidence of ridged fields in which irrigation apparently supported dense populations. At Tihuanaco, near the shores of Lake Titicaca in the Andes, canals were dug, and the mud from them was used to fertilize the fields alongside. Estimates are that productivity in such fields was as much as seven times greater than in nonirrigated fields. Similar systems were developed

elsewhere in the Americas. The ingenuity and importance of irrigation for many American Indian civilizations seems clear.

QUESTIONS

- What are the implications of such systems for social and political organization?
- Are states necessary to create such projects?
- What are the demographic implications and their consequences?
- Does the existence of such systems throughout the Americas indicate diffusion or parallel development?

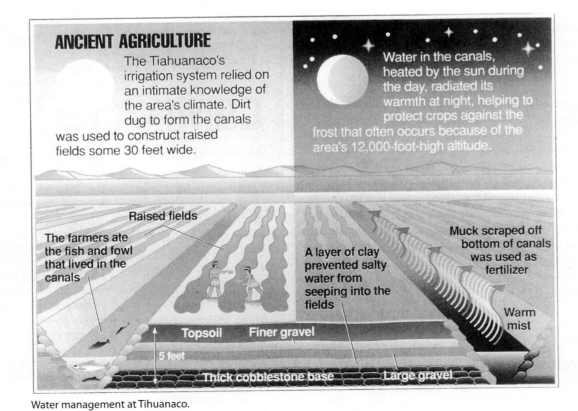

Water management at Tihuanaco.

within their ayllu. The ayllu assigned land and access to herds and water to each household. But rights and access were not equal for every household or family within an ayllu. Ayllus often were divided into halves, which might have different functions or roles. The peoples of the highland civilizations shared this form of organization with many tribes of the Amazonian forests.

There were also community leaders who had privileges of dress and access to resources. Groups of ayllus sharing a similar dialect, customs, and dress were bound together into ethnic groups, and sometimes several of these were forged into a state. The ties of kinship were used to mobilize the community for cooperative labor and war. The ayllu was a basic organization, and kinship provided an understanding of cooperation and conflict from the village to the empire. Some authors suggest that even in the large states, conflicts were more often between ayllus or groups of ayllus than between secondary social classes.

The principle of reciprocity that lay beneath the cooperative organization of the ayllu-infused Andean social life. Reciprocal obligations existed at many levels: between men and women within the family, between households within the ayllu, and between the leaders or **curacas**, who were expected to represent the interests of the ayllu. Eventually, in theory at least, reciprocity also existed between communities and a large state such as Huari, which in return for labor and tribute was expected to provide access to goods or to mobilize large projects, such as irrigation or terracing, that would benefit the community. Reciprocity also underlay religious belief. Andean peoples lived in a world where sacred spirits and powers, or **huacas**, were apparent in caves, mountains, rocks, rivers, and other natural phenomena. Worship of the huacas and of the mummies of ancestors (which were also considered holy and part of Andean religious life), at least from the Nazca period, was a matter of reciprocal exchange as well.

Inca Group of clans centered at Cuzco that were able to create empire incorporating various Andean cultures; term also used for leader of empire.

curacas [koo-RAH-kahs] Ayllu chiefs with privileges of dress and access to resources; community leaders among Andean societies.

huacas [WAH-kahs] Sacred spirits and powers that resided or appeared in caves, mountains, rocks, rivers, and other natural phenomena; typical of Andean societies.

Global Connections and Critical Themes

AMERICAN CIVILIZATIONS AND THE WORLD

There are striking parallels in the cultural development and the chronology of the two major areas of civilization in the Americas. This may be a result of convergence—that is, people in different places often work out similar solutions to the same problems—but there also seems to have been a great deal of contact between these regions over a long period of time. Much of this contact probably was indirect, funneled through the intermediate areas of Colombia and Panama, where large-scale chiefdoms based on intensive cultivation flourished. Their societies were hierarchical, and their crafts, especially metallurgy, were highly developed and widely traded. South American gold artifacts turn up in offerings at Mayan shrines in Yucatan. Through such intermediate societies, contact between Mesoamerica and the Andean world may have been made. There are other examples of cultural spread and contact. The ritual ball game that was played for sport and worship on special courts throughout Mesoamerica and the Maya area has been found as far away as the American Southwest and even among the peoples of the Caribbean islands.

American Indian peoples and civilizations shared much, but there were differences as well. The Peruvian cultures developed metallurgy to a greater degree than other cultures in the Americas and eventually produced bronze tools. The puna supported herds of llamas and permitted a form of pastoralism unknown in Meso-america. Unlike the Maya, the ancient peoples of the Andes never invented a writing system. Still, in many ways the civilizations of the Americas had more in common with each other than with those of the Old World, and that fact probably indicates their shared origins and their contacts over thousands of years.

It should be clear that there is much we do not know about the history of the Western Hemisphere. The long history of civilization in the New World, the strength of the languages, traditions, and beliefs of the American Indians, and the crops domesticated by their ancestors all affected the history of these continents. But in terms of global connections, the Americas remained relatively isolated from the developments in the rest of the world after the arrival and dispersion of the Paleo-Indians. The long isolation of the Americas from the populations, and therefore from the diseases, of the Old World, and the inability of the Americas to share in the technological advances of the Old World proved disastrous after the first contact with Europeans. Ultimately however, the resilience of Indian cultures as well as their achievements in agriculture and social organization, shaped the societies of the Americas in many ways.

Further Readings

An excellent survey of the early history of the Americas is Stuart Fiedel's *Prehistory of the Americas* (1987), Richard E. W. Adams, *Ancient Civilizations of the New World* (1997) provides an excellent overview. Charles C. Mann, *1491* (2005) is written for the general reader but incorporates recent scientific evidence on prehistory.

On the early history of Peru, Richard L. Burger, *Chavin and the Origins of Andean Civilization* (1992), is a good starting point while Michael Mosley, *The Incas and Their Ancestors* (1992) provides an authoritative introduction. Nigel Davies, *The Ancient Kingdoms of Mexico* (1983), offers a broad overview that combines archeology, art history, and history.

One of the best books on the Maya is Stephen Houston and Takeshi Inomata, *The Classic Maya* (2009) that covers the major aspects of classic Maya culture and is especially good on the debates among scholars. An excellent survey is Arthur Demarest, *Ancient Maya. The Rise and Fall of a Rainforest Civilization* (2004). Mary Ellen Miller, *Maya Art and Architecture* (1999), provides an excellent survey. On deciphering the Maya glyphs and the new history they are revealing, see Linda Schele and David Freidel, *A Forest of Kings: The Untold Story of the Ancient Maya* (1990); Michael Coe, *Breaking the Maya Code* (1992) tells how it was done. A popular interpretation of the advances in the field is seen in David Drew, *The Lost Chronicles of the Maya Kings* (1999), and a book that explains the calendar system and the industry of its modern misinterpretation is Matthew Restall and Amara Solari, *2012 and the End of the World* (2011).

Two good introductions to the ancient cultures of North America are Brian Fagan, *Ancient North America* (1995) and George G. Gumerman, ed., *The Anasazi in a Changing Environment* (1988). George S. Stuart's *America's Ancient Cities* (1988) uses a good text and excellent photos to emphasize the continuity between the peoples of North America and Mesoamerica. Timothy Pauketat and Thomas Emerson, *Cahokia: Domination and Ideology in the Mississippian World* (1997) is an excellent introduction to North American developments. On the impact of climate change on early North American indigenous peoples, see William Foster, *Climate and Cultural Change in North America, AD 900-1600* (2012).

A fine example of a scholarly monograph that demonstrates exciting discoveries about the ancient Americas and does not center on great cities and lost civilizations is Anna C. Roosevelt's *Parmana: Prehistoric Maize and Manioc Subsistence Along the Amazon and Orinoco* (1980). Finally, the *Cambridge History of Native Peoples of the Americas*, 3 vols. in six parts (1996–2000), is the best general history available.

On MyHistoryLab

 Study and Review on MyHistoryLab

Critical Thinking Questions

1. What were the principal differences between Mesoamerican and Andean societies?

2. How did geography and environment influence the development of civilizations in the two regions?

3. What were the effects of a relative lack of large domestic animals on Native American civilizations, and what were its implications on social organization and labor?

4. What is the role of written language in the development of civilizations? Is it always necessary?

The Spread of Civilizations and the Movement of Peoples

Far up the Nile, above the sixth cataract, beyond the borders of ancient Egypt, even beyond the land of the Nubians, who themselves had created dynasties that ruled for a while as the pharaohs of Egypt, there was a kingdom in the highlands of Ethiopia called Axum. The influences of the great civilizations like Egypt often reach far beyond their borders, and from Egypt in the 4th century C.E., Christianity had spread by way of missionary activity and trade up the Nile. The local population of Axum had mixed with peoples that came from Eritrea and had migrated from southern Arabia. Axum had challenged and then defeated the Nubian kingdom of Meroë, and by the third century C.E., it was flourishing—in part because of its commerce. Axum's port city of Adulis on the Red Sea, famous for trade in gold, ivory, jewelry, and textiles, welcomed Byzantine, Persian, Italian, and Indian traders from the Mediterranean and the Arabian seas.

((Listen to Chapter 9 on MyHistoryLab

LEARNING OBJECTIVES

How had sub-Saharan Africa linked to other parts of the world before and during the Classical Period? p. 186 — **9.1**

What were the most important migration waves into Europe by the Classical Period? p. 195 — **9.2**

Why and how did Japan reach out to China during the Classical Period? p. 201 — **9.3**

What were the distinctive features of Polynesian migration and expansion? p. 205 — **9.4**

FIGURE 9.1 Both Ethiopian Christianity and Ethiopian nationality draw on their continuity with aspects of the Old Testament. The *Kebra Negast*, Ethiopia's national epic, recounts the marriage of the biblical King Solomon and the Queen of Sheba and her return to Ethiopia with their son Menilek. He became the founder of the dynasty that ruled Ethiopia until the end of the 20th century. This modern illustration of that story is done in the artistic style that developed in Ethiopian monasteries.

👁 Watch the Video Series on MyHistoryLab

Learn about some key topics related to this chapter with the *MyHistoryLab Video Series:*
Key Topics in World History

At the court of King Ezana, the ruler of Axum, the products of Egypt, the Middle East, India and Arabia were all available and the influences of these diverse cultures could be felt. By the 2nd century C.E., Axum had outstripped Meroë and become a power in its own right, its influence extending from Sudan to Yemen.

Here legend joins history. Around 350 C.E. King Ezana converted to Christianity. A Byzantine historian claimed that a Greek merchant ship returning from India was captured on the African coast and its Christian merchant and crew killed. Two young boys survived and were taken as servants to the court of Axum. One of them, Frumentius, eventually became the tutor to young Prince Ezana, heir to the throne. The bond between Frumentius and the prince was strong and his influence grew. Frumentius sponsored increasing contacts with the world of Christianity. His efforts eventually led to his appointment as bishop of Ethiopia by the Christian authorities in Alexandria, and his most important convert was the king.

Axum, the forerunner of modern Ethiopia, became a Christian kingdom in the heart of Africa. The people of Axum developed a flourishing Christian society with impressive churches, monasteries, large stone commemorative columns, and a distinctive Semitic written language called "Ge'ez," which was used for ceremonial life, although Greek was also understood at the royal palace. The Bible was translated, and the Axumites sought to establish their ties to the biblical past by claiming that the queen of Sheba, the mysterious and beautiful monarch who had married King Solomon, was really a ruler of Axum, and that when she returned to her country she had with her Solomon's son, David, who later became Menelik I, the first ruler of Ethiopia. Later with the spread of Islam in the 8th century, Christian Ethiopia became relatively isolated from contacts with the rest of the Christian world, but it fiercely maintained its religion and its independence. Frumentius

7000 B.C.E.	1000 B.C.E.	500 B.C.E.
7000–3000 Desiccation of the Sahara	**1000 ff.** Germans spread through Germany, displacing Celts	**100** Germans in southern Germany, on Roman borders
c. 5000 Early migrations and settlement of Japan	**800 B.C.E.–1000 C.E.** Migration of Bantu speakers throughout sub-Saharan Africa	
3200 Unification of Upper and Lower Egypt	**7th–3rd centuries** Scythian state in southern Russia	
3000–2000 Jomon culture	**750–666** Kings of Meroë rule Egypt	
3000–1000 Spread of agriculture south of the Sahara	**600 B.C.E.–1000 C.E.** Iron diffused throughout Africa	
2000 ff. Germanic peoples settle in Scandinavia (present-day Denmark)	**600** Legendary Emperor Jimmu establishes state in Japan	
1500–500 Beginnings of Polynesian migrations; Lapita pottery found in Fiji, Tonga, Samoa		
1500–300 Horses introduced to Africa by way of Egypt		

became a Christian saint and is remembered as the Apostle of Ethiopia and "the Father of Peace." Although the English historian of Rome Charles Gibbon said that Axum, once cut off "slept for a thousand years," in truth it laid the foundations of Christianity in Ethiopia. ■

The story of Axum highlights the themes of cultural diffusion, migrations, and cross-cultural trade, all of which have played central roles in world history and in the contact between the centers of civilization and the rest of the world. The movements of peoples, goods, ideas, and cultural patterns have all shaped the patterns of world history. We have concentrated thus far on the centers of civilization and their internal developments in the classical societies of the Old World and the emerging civilizations in the Americas. In this chapter we explore the connections between the established centers and the rest of the world's peoples. The major civilizations have been expansive, and their innovations and cultures have influenced their neighbors and sometimes peoples who lived far away. Although scholars still debate the issue, many believe that important early breakthroughs, such as agriculture, the domestication of animals, pottery, and metallurgy, were not repeatedly reinvented across the globe but rather were spread by contacts and migration. For example, agriculture may have been "invented" more than once, but most people learned about it by contact with those who already practiced it.

How do cultures spread? At times, as with Rome, conquest has been the means of imposing ideas, language, and institutions. Roman culture and law were carried to the far ends of the empire by the conquering Roman legions. In other places, long-distance traders have carried ideas as well as goods, and as in the case of Axum, sometimes missionary activity and local trade have been the channels through which peoples learned of one another's ways. Thus the ship, the caravan, ideas, and the sword have all been instruments of cultural diffusion.

The history of Rome after the empire was invaded demonstrates another possibility, for it is not always conquerors who spread their culture; sometimes it is the conquered. In late Rome, as in pre-Columbian Mesoamerica and China, the "barbarian" conquerors absorbed the culture of a defeated civilization and adopted its ways. The result was a new fusion of cultural elements. In other places, trade or missionary activity spread civilization. In this chapter, for example, our discussion of early Japanese society will demonstrate the peaceful spread of Chinese culture and its transformation in Japan, a process in which Buddhism played a major role.

This chapter examines five areas of the world—sub-Saharan Africa, central Asia, northern Europe, Japan, and the Pacific islands—which at the time their cultures took shape were not civilization

1 C.E.	500 C.E.	1000 C.E.
c. 55–112 Tacitus writes about Germans	**580s** Buddhism adopted as the religion of the Yamato domains, Japan	**1000** Ghana at height of its power
100 ff. Improvements in German political organization, rise of local kings, movement of some Germans into Roman Empire	**679** Bulgars (Turkic people) migrate to Balkans, become largely Slavicized, set up first Slavic kingdom in Balkans	**1076** Ghana conquered by Almoravids
100 ff. Increasing movement of Slavs into eastern Europe	**700–800** Islam sweeps across north Africa	**1100–1300** Series of voyages from Hawaii to Tahiti
100 Rise of kingdom of Axum	**800–1100** Growth of the trans-Sahara gold trade	
100–200 Camels introduced to Africa from Asia	**900** New Zealand settled	
300 Meroë declines	**985** King of Gao converts to Islam	
300–400 Yamato clan establishes imperial control in Japan		
300–700 Conversion to Christianity of Nubian kingdoms in Axum		
300–1000 Polynesian migrations; settlement of Hawaii and Easter Island		
4th century Germans pressed by Huns		
401 ff. Larger Germanic invasions of Roman Empire		
400 Chinese script introduced		

centers. Nevertheless, the peoples of these areas were influenced by developments or innovations in those centers or, in the case of the Pacific islands, by earlier cultural developments on the Asian mainland. Central Asia provides its own special case, as a seedbed for major nomadic societies that interacted with civilizations through trade, migration, and invasion. In each case, we will see how ideas, techniques, and material objects were adapted to new environments and different social circumstances so that the spread of civilization and the contact of cultures usually were creative processes, not simply a matter of copying.

It may at first seem strange to discuss peoples as different as the Polynesians, the Germanic tribes, the Slavs, the Japanese, and the early sub-Saharan Africans together. But the processes of migration, cultural spread, and cultural development are the basis for our discussion. Moreover, unlike earlier chapters, in which the chronological limits have been fairly precise, our discussion here ranges more broadly over time, because the pace and rhythm of cultural spread varied greatly in these widely separated parts of the world. The story of how these peoples began to develop their distinctive cultures, often in contact with centers of civilization, should be our focus, rather than a limited time frame. Finally, this chapter also introduces some peoples whose role in world history later became particularly important.

THE SPREAD OF CIVILIZATION IN AFRICA

9.1 How had sub-Saharan Africa linked to other parts of the world before and during the Classical Period?

Africa is a vast continent, almost 12 million square miles, which is about three times the size of the United States. Most of it lies in the tropics, and although we often think of Africa in terms of its rainforests, less than 10 percent of the continent is covered by tropical forests. Much of the African surface is covered by savannas, or open grasslands, and by arid plains and deserts. Large rivers—the Congo, the Nile, the Zambezi, and the Niger—begin in the interior of the continent and flow to the sea over great falls and cataracts that mark the passage from plateau to coast. These falls have historically made movement from the coast to the interior difficult, but the great river systems have also provided the African interior with communication routes.

Africa was the scene of human beginnings. Even before the appearance of *Homo sapiens* (the ancestors of modern human beings) about 300,000 years ago, other hominid species, such as *Homo erectus*, had moved outward from Africa to Asia and Europe. In Chapter 2 we discussed the remarkable civilization of Egypt in the Nile valley and its extension to the upper Nile kingdoms of Kush and Ethiopia. In this chapter, we will examine the spread of elements of civilization to other areas of Africa.

Despite the false image of Africa as the dark and isolated continent, it was often in contact with other areas of the world. Technology, crops, ideas, and material goods from Asia and Europe stimulated social and cultural innovations. Moreover, the contacts were not always in one direction; there is much evidence that not only early humans but also certain languages, crops, and political and cultural influences spread outward to Europe and Asia from Africa.

Climatic change altered the appearance of the African continent and seems to have set a whole series of historical processes in motion. That change centers on the **Sahara**, which during the Late Stone Age (6000–500 B.C.E.) received 10 to 50 times as much rain as it does today (Map 9.1). Archeological evidence indicates that several peoples inhabited the area of the Sahara during this period, including the ancestors of the modern-day Berbers and Tuaregs of north Africa, who speak languages related to ancient Egyptian, and the ancestors of the Negro peoples of sub-Saharan Africa, some of whom also spoke these Afro-Asiatic languages. About 9000 years ago, these conditions began to change as temperatures in the Sahara rose and rainfall became erratic. By about 3000 B.C.E., much of the area was desert. This process continues today.

As the Sahara became less habitable, the populations moved north toward the Mediterranean coast and south into the area of the dry **sahel**, or fringe, and especially onto the grassy savannas suitable for agriculture and grazing that stretch across Africa from the mouth of the Senegal River on the west coast to Lake Chad and the upper Nile valley. This broad region, the Sudan, became a center of cultural development after about 300 B.C.E. The movement of peoples into the Sudan and toward the Nile valley and the Mediterranean set the stage for major developments in the later history of Africa.

Climatic changes and foreign influences set a series of cultural changes in motion in Africa. The migration of Bantu-speaking peoples and the spread of agriculture and ironworking were followed by the growth of kingdoms such as Axum in Ethiopia and Ghana in the western Sudan which represented the development of African civilizations.

Sahara Desert running across northern Africa; separates the Mediterranean coast from southern Africa.

sahel The extensive grassland belt at the southern edge of the Sahara; a point of exchange between the forests to the south and northern Africa.

Areas of Rainfall: Around 10,000 B.C.E. to 7000 B.C.E

Around 7000 B.C.E. to Present

MAP **9.1 Africa: Variations in Climate** Lying on the equator, Africa is not subject to severe fluctuations in temperature, but there are a wide variety of environments on the continent from tropical rainforest (8 percent) and desert (40 percent) to mountains and grasslands. Climates and rainfall patterns have changed over time. The Sahara region became a desert due to climatic change as rainfall shifted southward.

Agriculture, Livestock, and Iron

Agriculture may have developed independently in Africa, but many scholars believe that the spread of agriculture and iron throughout Africa is evidence of the continent's links to centers of civilization in the Near East and the Mediterranean world. The drying of the Sahara had pushed many peoples to the south into sub-Saharan Africa. These were the ancestors of the Negro peoples. They settled at first in scattered hunting-and-gathering bands, although fishers lived near lakes and rivers. Agriculture seems to have reached these peoples from the Near East because the first domesticated crops were millet and sorghum, whose origins are not African but west Asian. The route of agricultural distribution may have gone through Egypt or Ethiopia, which long had contacts across the Red Sea with the Arabian peninsula. There is evidence of agriculture before 3000 B.C.E. Also, in Africa, unlike other areas, herding may have preceded cultivation. These developments may be the result of climatic change, a long wet period from 12,000 to 7500 years ago when North Africa received much more moisture than before.

Once the idea of planting spread, Africans began to develop their own crops, such as certain varieties of rice, and continued to be receptive to new imports. African crops were domesticated in a band that extends from Ethiopia across the southern Sudan to west Africa. Later, other crops such as bananas were introduced from southeast Asia. In the 16th century C.E., American crops, such as maize and manioc, spread throughout Africa.

Livestock also came from outside Africa. Cattle, goats, and domestic sheep were introduced from Asia. Horses apparently were introduced to Africa from west Asia by the Hyksos (HIHK-soos) invaders of Egypt (1780–1560 B.C.E.) and then spread across the Sudan to west Africa. Rock paintings in the Sahara show the use of horses and chariots to traverse the desert, and by 300–200 B.C.E., trade routes extended across the desert. Horses became the symbol of kingly authority and a basis of military power in some states that developed large cavalry regiments. One observer claimed that in the 14th century B.C.E., the later west African empire of Mali could field 10,000 riders. The obvious power and utility of the horse might have led to even wider use, but as with other new technologies

tsetse fly [tsee-tsee] Flourished in wet lowlands; carried sleeping sickness that severely limited pastoralism in western and central Africa.

transhumant A form of pastoralism common to the Mediterranean basin and the Sahara; involves moving from one region to another according to the season.

Nok Culture featuring highly developed art style flourishing between 500 B.C.E. and 200 C.E.; located in forests of central Nigeria.

Yoruba City-states developed in northern Nigeria c. 1200 C.E.; Ife featured artistic style possibly related to earlier Nok culture; agricultural societies supported by peasantry and dominated by ruling family and aristocracy.

 View the Closer Look on **MyHistoryLab:** Nigerian Sculpture: the Clay Heads from the Nok Culture

Bantu Originated in eastern Nigeria in west Africa; migrated into central and southern Africa using rivers—particularly the Congo Basin; village dwellers who depended on agriculture and fishing.

and cultural elements, the physical environment was a limiting factor. The horse was widely adopted in the west African grasslands, but in humid tropical forests and brush where the **tsetse fly** thrived, raising livestock became almost impossible. The tsetse fly carried "sleeping sickness," or trypanoso-miasis, to which horses, cattle, and humans are susceptible. Cavalry campaigns were impossible in the rainy season, when the range of the flies increased. This tiny but tenacious foe brought African cavalries to a halt.

Environment created both limits and opportunities, but the balance between them was sometimes changed by new elements. The introduction of the camel from Asia about the 1st century C.E. was an important innovation. Its ability to thrive in harsh desert conditions and to carry large loads cheaply made it an effective and efficient means of transportation. The camel transformed the desert from a barrier into a still difficult but more accessible route of trade and communication.

Livestock provided a living to peoples in the arid portions of the savanna belt and the Sahara and allowed a **transhumant**, or seasonally moving, way of life to flourish in certain inhospitable regions. In some areas, it appears that livestock and agriculture arrived about the same time.

While some scholars believe that Africans developed the making of iron independently, many believe that ironworking came from west Asia, although by routes somewhat different from those of agriculture. In most of Africa, societies moved directly from a technology of stone to iron without passing through the intermediate stage of copper or bronze, although some early copper metallurgy sites have been found in west Africa. Iron had been worked in the Near East and Anatolia for at least a thousand years before it began to penetrate into sub-Saharan Africa. The Phoenicians carried the knowledge of iron smelting to their colonies, such as Carthage in north Africa, by the 8th century B.C.E., and from there to their trading ports along the coast of Morocco. By sea down the coast or by land across the Sahara, this knowledge penetrated into the forests and savannas of west Africa during the last millennium B.C.E., or at roughly the same time that ironmaking was reaching western Europe. Evidence of ironmaking has been found in Nigeria, Ghana, and Mali, and iron implements seem to have slowly replaced stone ones at several sites. This technological shift caused profound changes in the complexity of African societies. Iron represented power. In west Africa, the blacksmith who made tools and weapons had an important place in society, often with special religious powers and functions. Those who knew the secrets of ironmaking gained ritual and sometimes political power.

Ironmaking seems to have traveled from the Red Sea into Ethiopia and east Africa and down the Nile from Egypt into the Sudan, where large African states such as Meroë were in close contact with dynastic Egypt. By the 1st century C.E., iron was known in sub-Saharan Africa, and within about a thousand years, it had reached the southern end of the continent. Iron tools and weapons increased the efficiency of both agriculture and war. In the later stages of this story, after about 1200 C.E., the adoption of agriculture and the use of iron tools and weapons were roughly simultaneous.

Unlike the peoples of the Americas, for whom metallurgy was a very late and limited development, Africans had iron from an early date, developing ingenious furnaces to produce the high heat (1100 degrees Fahrenheit) needed for production. The **Nok** culture, which flourished in northern Nigeria from around 800 B.C.E. to 200 C.E., was characterized by the use of iron as well as impressive sculptures. It was probably the cultural tradition on which later artistic traditions in that region drew. Bronzeworking was also known to Africans, and by 1000 C.E. remarkably lifelike bronze sculptures were cast at the city-state of Ife in Nigeria by the **Yoruba** people. Ife became a kind of cultural and ritual capital in the region, a recognition of its historical importance and cultural leadership.

The Bantu Dispersal

The spread of agriculture and later of iron was accompanied by a great movement of people who may have carried these innovations. These **Bantu** peoples probably originated in eastern Nigeria in west Africa. Their migration may have been set in motion by an increase in population caused by a movement into their homelands of peoples fleeing the drying of the Sahara (Map 9.2). They spoke proto-Bantu (*Bantu* means "the people"), which is the parent tongue of many related languages still spoken throughout sub-Saharan Africa. In fact, about 90 percent of the languages south of a line from the Bight of Benin on the west coast to Somalia on the east coast are part of the Bantu family.

Why and how these peoples spread out into central and southern Africa remains a mystery, but archeologists believe that at some stages their iron weapons allowed them to conquer hunting-and-gathering societies, which still used stone implements. Still, the process is uncertain, and peaceful migration—or simply rapid demographic growth—may have also caused the Bantu expansion.

The migrations moved first to the central Sudan and then into the forests of west and central Africa. The rivers, especially the Congo basin, provided the means of movement. The migration was long, gradual, and intermittent. Moving outward from central Africa, Bantu peoples arrived at the east coast, where they met cattle-raising peoples of a different linguistic tradition. By the 12th century, the Bantu speakers pushed south of the Zambezi River into modern Zimbabwe and eventually into southern Africa.

From the study of the related Bantu languages, it is possible to learn something about the original culture of the proto-Bantu speakers. The early Bantu depended on agriculture and fishing. They grew sorghum and raised goats and perhaps cattle. Later they also raised bananas, which came to Africa from southeast Asia. They were village dwellers who organized their societies around kinship ties. Leadership of the villages probably was in the hands of a council of elders. The spirits of the natural world played a large role in the lives of these peoples. They looked to their ancestors to help deal with those spirits, and they depended on village religious specialists to deal with calamity and to combat witchcraft, which they feared greatly.

People's lives and societies changed during the course of the migrations. Long-distance trade in pottery, metals, canoes, and crafts developed in some regions. In many places ritual forms of kingship reinforced by elaborate ceremonies replaced older systems of authority based on age or kinship. Cultural life flourished in forms as diverse as great oral epics, polyphonic music, and sophisticated wood sculpture. These societies gave birth to wisdom, too. Consider this poem of the Yoruba peoples of Nigeria about children:

MAP **9.2 Bantu Migrations** In a long and uneven process, speakers of Bantu languages from a homeland in Nigeria spread out over much of sub-Saharan Africa. In some places that migration seems to have been accompanied by the diffusion of ironmaking and ceramics, but not everywhere. There are now about 450 languages identified as part of the Bantu linguistic family.

> A child is like a rare bird.
> A child is like a precious coral.
> A child is like brass.
> You cannot buy a child on the market.
> Not for all the money in the world.
> The child you can buy for money is a slave. . . .
> Only a child gives us joy.
> One must not rejoice too soon over a child.
> Only the one who is buried by his child,
> Is the one who has truly borne a child.

Source: Ulli Beier and Bakare Gbadamosi, "Praise of a Child," in *Poems from Africa*, ed. Samuel W. Allen (New York: Thomas Y. Crowell, 1973).

In about a thousand years the Bantu-speaking peoples expanded over much of the continent, spreading their languages and cultures among the existing populations, absorbing those original peoples and being absorbed by them. By the 13th century C.E., cattle-raising, iron-using Bantu peoples had approached the southern end of the continent. Winter rains prevented sorghum from growing beyond that point, and their progress stopped. Earlier inhabitants, the Khoisan (KOH-ee-sahn) speakers, remained farther to the south. By that time, Africa's major features were in place. A few purely hunting peoples remained, such as the **Pygmies** of central Africa, but their way of life was different from that of most Africans. Agricultural and herding societies with ironworking knowledge could be found throughout sub-Saharan Africa. Although pockets of peoples still speaking non-Bantu languages existed, such as the Khoi-Khoi and San of southern Africa, and in east Africa the influence of Ethiopian culture was still strong, Bantu languages predominated in southern and central Africa and marked the trail of one of the world's great migrations.

Pygmies One of few pure hunting societies left in Africa following Bantu migration.

Africa, Civilization, and the Wider World

The development of Egyptian civilization paralleled developments in the Fertile Crescent, but many aspects of Egyptian life, such as ideas about religion and kingship, strongly resembled those of other African societies. There is much debate on whether the Egyptian idea of the king as a divine being with special powers over natural phenomena (an idea also found in some west African kingdoms) came from the common origins of both or whether these concepts spread from Egypt to the Sudan

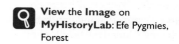

View the **Image** on **MyHistoryLab**: Efe Pygmies, Forest

and other areas of Africa. There are other striking parallels, such as brother–sister marriage among rulers and certain rituals when a ruler takes office, that seem to tie the cultures of sub-Saharan Africa to Egypt. Whatever the African origins of Egyptian civilization, there is no doubt of extensive contact between Egypt and peoples living southward along the Nile valley in the Sudan and northern Ethiopia.

Axum: A Christian Kingdom. We discussed the Egyptian contacts with Kush in Chapter 2 and the fact that the Kushites and their capitals were influenced by Egyptian culture. For a short period, from 751 B.C.E. until the invasion of Egypt by the Assyrians in 666 B.C.E., the kings of Meroë also ruled as pharaohs of Egypt. Meroë had the mineral ores and fuels needed to produce iron on a large scale. That technology, and its extensive trade with Egypt and the Mediterranean, allowed Meroë to flourish. But Meroë was not alone. Other town-based societies also existed in the region of the eastern Sudan and Ethiopia.

The kingdom of Axum surpassed Meroë in importance around the 1st century C.E. Axum introduced another cultural stream into the history of Africa. It seems to have received strong influences and settlers from the Arabian peninsula. It also traded with Alexandrian Egypt and eventually with Rome, Byzantium, and India. Those contacts led to a fusion of cultural elements. By about 200 C.E., Axum was involved in military and political affairs across the Red Sea in Yemen on the Arabian peninsula. By the mid-3rd century C.E., Axum had defeated Meroë and emerged as the dominant power in the horn of Africa. The history of Axum underlines the cross-fertilization of cultures across the Red Sea.

All this indicates considerable influence and contact between this African kingdom and the outside world well before the arrival of Islam. The civilization of Axum became the basis for much of the distinctive culture of Christian Ethiopia in the centuries that followed. Here, as along the Mediterranean coast of Africa, where Phoenician, Greek, and Roman settlements were established, or up the Nile valley, the ideas, techniques, material goods, and artistic styles as is shown in Figure 9.2 from the Mediterranean and western Asia mixed with African peoples and practices.

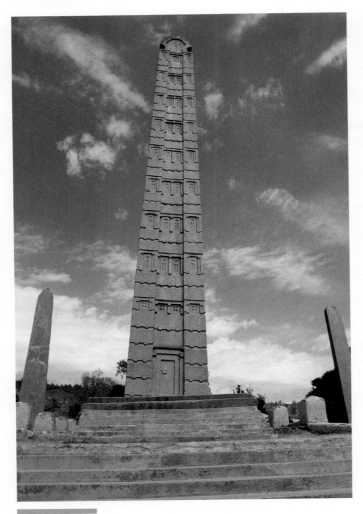

FIGURE **9.2** Commemorative stelae at Axum, used to mark the burial site of the kings, were erected in pre-Christian days. The largest, shown here, is more than 75 feet tall.

Golden Ghana: A Trading State. An area of grassy savanna extends across the Sudan into West Africa, and the defeated leaders of Meroë apparently moved westward into the Sudan and reestablished themselves at Darfur and Kordofan in the 4th century C.E. Their influence may have extended even farther west. Several accounts and myths associated with royal families and ancient kingdoms in west Africa point to Egypt, Arabia, and even Persia as the original home of the founders. But in west Africa there is also evidence of long-term contact with the Mediterranean world directly across the Sahara. These long-distance external influences were paralleled by an extended period of internal development among the peoples of west Africa such as the Yoruba, Mande, and Fulbe.

The peoples of the savanna took advantage of their location to serve as intermediaries between the southern gold-producing forest zone in the region of the Niger and Senegal river valleys and the markets of north Africa. Trading salt for gold to the peoples of the forest and then sending the gold north along established caravan routes that crossed the Sahara, several states like Gao and Ghana took form before the 8th century C.E. as intermediaries in the trans-Sahara trade (Map 9.3).

Trans-Sahara commerce was the basis for the growth of the empire of **Ghana**, which lay squarely on the trade route. This was a trading state created by the west African Soninke peoples. Early Arab chroniclers wrote that in Ghana, 20 kings had ruled before the time of Muhammad, which was a way of saying that the kingdom was an ancient one. When Arab visitors began to write about Ghana and other **Sudanic states** in the 9th century C.E., these states were already well-established kingdoms. Their position was a result of their advantageous geographic position and a joint heritage of internal development and external influences and trade. The external influences increased with the arrival of

📖 Read the Document on MyHistoryLab: Ghana and Its People in the Mid-Eleventh Century

Ghana First great sub-Saharan state; created by Soninke people; by 9th century C.E. a major source of gold in the Mediterranean world.

Sudanic states Kingdoms that developed during the height of Ghana's power in the region; based at Takrur on the Senegal River to the west and Gao on the Niger River to the east; included Mali and Songhay.

DOCUMENT

Myths of Origin

LEGENDS AND MYTHS HAVE LONG FASCINATED anthropologists, literary scholars, and folklorists because they offer an opportunity to see how various peoples have explained the universe and themselves within it. Noted French anthropologist Claude Lévi-Strauss believed that all myths were built around certain basic structures of human thought and that those structures could be revealed by the comparative study of myths. He also argued that for some cultures, such as those of South American Indians, myths with their essentially recurring structures were the primary means of explaining life, while in other cultures, such as those of western Europe and China, a sense of change and history came to predominate in these explanations. Recent scholarship has begun to question the separation of myth and history and has begun to look at the possible historical context and content of myths.

In this chapter, we have examined several peoples whose origins are shrouded in mystery and about whom many questions remain unanswered. The following excerpts provide these peoples' explanations of their own origins or those of their world.

A BANTU MYTH OF MIGRATION

A series of origin epics and tales among the Luba peoples, who lived in central Africa to the east of the Kongo kingdom, were collected in the 20th century. The concept of splitting off from an existing village and settling in new territory is part of many African origin myths.

> In the country of the east, on the right bank of the Lualaba River, there once was a man and a woman. Their names mean respectively "he who builds many houses," and "she who makes much pottery." They lived in ignorance of each other. Guided by the sound of chopping, the man discovered the woman, who was preparing firewood. They lived for a long time under the same roof, sleeping in separate beds. The copulation of a pair of jackals gave them the idea of sleeping together. They brought forth twins of opposite sex, who became inseparable companions. One day the twins found a locality that was exceptionally rich in fish. They finally obtained permission from their parents to leave the village and devote themselves entirely to fishing. In their turn, they brought forth twins, who lived in the same incestuous manner, far from their parents. This new generation took up trapping. So pairs of twins, moving each generation a little farther westward, populated the country.

Source: Luc de Heusch, *The Drunken King or the Origin of the State* (Bloomington: Indiana University Press, 1982), pp. 11–12.

A GERMANIC MYTH: THE BIRTH OF THE GODS

This tale from the rich Norse mythology deals with the birth of the gods. Drawn from the songs and sagas of the Germanic peoples, these stories were part of an oral literature until about the 12th century, when they were committed to writing.

> In the beginning of the ages there lived a cow, whose breath was sweet and whose milk was bitter. The cow was called Audhumla and she lived by herself in a frosty, misty plain, where there was nothing to be seen but heaps of snow and ice. A giant named Ymir came out of the dark north and lay down on the ice near Audhumla. "You must let me drink of your milk," said the giant to the cow; and though her milk was bitter, he liked it well. The cow saw a few grains of salt sprinkled over the ice, so she licked the salt and breathed with her sweet breath. Then long golden locks rose out of the ice, and the southern day shone on them, making them bright and glittering. The giant frowned but the cow continued to lick the salt, and after three licks an entire man arose—a hero strong and beautiful.
>
> When the giant looked full in the face of that beautiful man, he hated him with all his heart and he took a terrible oath that he would never cease fighting until either he or Bur, the hero, should lie dead on the ground. He kept this vow.
>
> Afterwards when the sons of the hero began to grow up, the giant and his sons fought against them too, and were very near conquering them many times. There was one of the sons of these heroes, called Odin, who after many combats did at last slay the great old giant Ymir, and pierced his body with a keen spear. The blood poured forth in a torrent and drowned all the hideous brood, except for one who fled.
>
> After this, Odin gathered around him his sons, brothers, and cousins and spoke to them thus:
>
> "Heroes, we have won a great victory; our enemies are dead, or have fled. We cannot stay any longer here where there is nothing evil for us to fight against." The heroes looked around them at the words of Odin. They spoke out with one voice, "It is well spoken, Odin; we will follow you."
>
> "Southward," answered Odin, "heat lies, and northward night. From the dim east the sun begins his journey westward home."
>
> "Westward home!" they shouted all.
>
> Odin rode in the midst of them, and they all paid to him reverence and homage as to a king and father. On his right hand rode Thor, Odin's strong, warlike, eldest son. On his left hand rode Baldur, the most beautiful of his children. After him came Tyr, the Brave; the silent Vidar; and many more mighty lords and heroes; and then came a shell chariot, in which sat Frigga, the wife of Odin, with all her daughters, friends, and maids.

Source: Adapted from A. Keary and E. Keary, *The Heroes of Asgard: Tales from Scandinavian Mythology* (New York: Macmillan, 1909), pp. 1–4.

THE BIRTH OF JAPAN

According to Japanese legend, the Lord of Heaven sent two young gods, Izanagi and his consort, Izanami, to subdue chaos and create beauty after the earth had been created. Descending on a carriage

(Continued on next page)

(continued from previous page)

of clouds, Izanagi took the divine spear given to him by the Lord of Heaven and, stirring the fog, created a beautiful island in the midst of the sea. But the island was too small for goodness to grow. Izanagi and Izanami were married and built a shrine.

When Izanagi and his wife came out of the shrine, they stood transfixed. Before them stretched the long, curving shore of a vast island, and on the far horizon were the shapes of others. In great joy the two set out to view their new domains. From island to island they went, marveling at each new land; and when they had traveled them all, they found that there were eight, and to them they gave these names in the order of their birth; first the island of Shikoku, followed by Kyushu, Oki and Sado which [each] were born as twins, Tsushima, and finally Iki. Together they were called the country of the eight great islands, and as time passed they became known as Japan.

More and more islands appeared, and every day Izanagi traveled the land and sea watching over them. Sometimes Izanami went with him, but serving in the shrine took much of her time and she found the long journeys exhausting.

"My dear husband, there is nothing I wish to do more than to live here with you in peace and contentment. But now that so many islands have been born I pray that we too may bear children for our help and delight."

Her prayers were answered and in the years that followed many children were born to them. The first was the Sea Spirit, the next a Mountain Spirit, and then in succession, the spirits of fields, trees, rivers, and all natural things. Under their care and guidance the islands grew more and more verdant and beautiful. Soon the seasons were born, and the breaths of the winds and rains brought their changing cycles to the mountains and fields. Everywhere the forests grew thick and dense, and in the groves flocks of birds gathered and sang. Crops and harvests multiplied and flowers and bushes bloomed in profusion.

Izanagi and his wife lived in utmost contentment among their family, and when a daughter was born to them, who was the goddess of the Sun, their joy was unbounded. She was the most beautiful and radiant being. . . . Everywhere she went she filled the darkest air with light and brilliance. Her they named Amaterasu.

Source: Helen McAlpine and William McAlpine, *Japanese Tales and Legends* (London: Oxford University Press, 1958), pp. 13–14.

A POLYNESIAN CREATION STORY

In this tale from Tahiti, Tangaroa, the ancestor of all the gods and the creator of Havaiki, the birthplace of the land, the gods, the chiefs, and humanity, creates the world. This version of the story was collected in Tahiti in 1822.

For a long time Tangaroa lived within his shell. It was round like an egg and in the lasting darkness it revolved in the void. There

was no sun, there was no moon, there was no land nor mountain, all was moving in the void. There was no man, no fowl, no dog, no living thing; there was no water, salt or fresh.

At the end of a great time Tangaroa flicked his shell, and it cracked and fell apart. Then, Tangaroa stepped forth and stood upon that shell and called:

"Who is above there? Who is below there?"

No voice replied. He called again:

"Who is in front there? Who is behind there?"

Still no voice answered. Only Tangaroa's voice was heard; there was no other.

Then Tangaroa said, "O rock, crawl here!"

But no rock was to crawl to him.

He therefore said, "O sand, crawl here!"

There was no sand to crawl to him. And Tangaroa became angry because he was not obeyed. He therefore overturned his shell and raised it up to form a dome for the sky, and he named it Rumia, that is, Overturned.

After a time great Tangaroa, wearied from confinement, stepped out from another shell that covered him; and he took this shell for rock and sand. But his anger was not finished, and so he took his backbone for a mountain range and his ribs for the ridges that ascend. He took his innards for the broad floating clouds and his flesh for the fatness of the earth, and his arms and legs for the strength of the earth. . . . Of his feathers he made trees and shrubs and plants to clothe the land.

And the blood of Tangaroa became hot, and it floated away to make the redness of the sky, and also rainbows. All that is red is made from Tangaroa's blood.

Tangaroa called forth gods. It was only later that he called forth man [people], when Tu was with him.

As Tangaroa had shells, so everything has a shell. The sky is a shell, which is endless space, where the gods placed the sun, the moon, the constellations, and the other stars.

The land is a shell to the stones and the water, and to the plants that spring from it. The shell of a man is woman, since it is from her that he comes forth. And a woman's shell is woman, since it is from her that she comes forth.

No one can name the shells of all the things that are in the world.

Source: Anthony Alpers, *Legends of the South Seas* (New York: Thomas Crowell, 1970), pp. 51–54.

QUESTIONS

- Do myths seem to encode history, or are they an alternative way to explain the past?
- What are the roles of men and women in the myths recorded here and what do they indicate about these early societies?
- Do the origin myths of the civilizations such as China, Greece, and Rome differ greatly from those recorded here?

Islam. In 985 C.E., the king of Gao converted to Islam and set in motion a series of conversions among the elite of the west African states. Conversion of the masses proceeded more slowly.

The ancient kingdom of Ghana (not to be confused with the modern nation of Ghana) lay mostly within the boundaries of the present-day Republic of Mali. It traded for salt, cloth, and manufactured goods from north Africa and the Mediterranean in return for gold. Ghana's power depended on its location and control over subject states and provinces, especially gold-producing regions in the forest

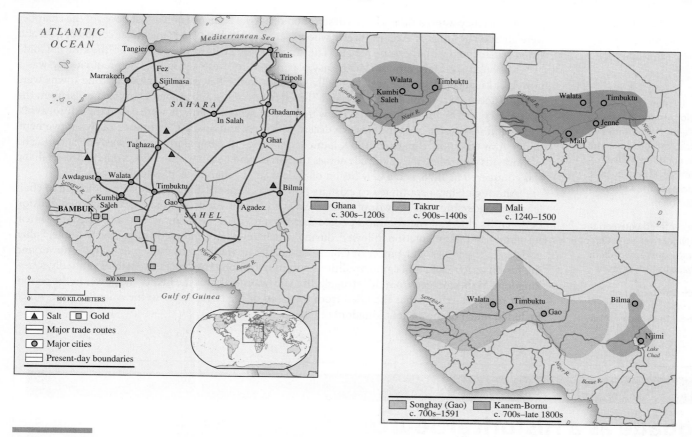

MAP **9.3 West African States** The western Sahara region became crisscrossed by trade routes over which gold, slaves, and salt were moved into the Mediterranean world. In the sahel along the margins of the Sahara, a series of large states emerged whose merchants controlled those routes and whose power derived from their strategic location. The arrival of camels in the 4th century C.E. allowed these states to solidify their control of the desert trade routes.

zones to the south. In 1067 C.E., al-Bakri, a scholar from Muslim Spain, described Ghana's splendor and power.

> . . . [The king] sits in audience or to hear grievances against officials in a domed pavilion around which stand ten horses covered with gold-embroidered materials. Behind the king stand ten pages holding shields and swords decorated with gold, and on his right are the sons of the (vassal) kings of his country wearing splendid garments and their hair plaited with gold.

Source: Hopkins, *Corpus of Early Arabic Sources for West African History* (Cambridge University Press, 1981), pp. 79–81.

At that time, the capital of Ghana, **Kumbi Saleh** appears to have been divided into two cities about six miles apart. One was occupied by the king and his court, surrounded by the dwellings of the people. This city also contained buildings for worship and shrines to the local deities. The other was inhabited by long-distance Muslim traders, religious leaders, and scholars. Its mosques and houses were built in the style of the mud-walled architecture of north Africa. Together, the population of these cities may have reached 20,000.

Tax revenues from the gold and salt trades increased the kingdom's wealth. Historian al-Bakri reported that Ghana could field an army of 200,000 men. Even if we allow for exaggeration, it should be noted that the Normans invaded England at about this time with fewer than 5000 men. Al-Bakri's account describes the existence of a powerful and well-organized kingdom dominated by the royal family and a group of elite retainers, whose strength rested on control of the trade and on the tribute collected from neighboring peoples.

The image of Ghana in contemporary Arab sources was one of fabled wealth. The account of al-Bakri stated that the king had a monopoly on all gold nuggets found, but the people could gather as much

Kumbi Saleh [KUHM-bee sah-LEH] Capital of empire of Ghana; divided into two adjoining cities—one for the king, court, and indigenous people, one for the merchants, scholars, and religious leaders; flourished 750–1240.

gold dust as they wanted for trade. His description of a royal audience noted that doors of the chamber were guarded by "dogs of excellent breed, who never leave the king's seat; they wear collars of gold and silver, ornamented with the same metals." The king was known as Kaya-Maghan, or "the king of Gold."

Although a certain amount of fantasy was mixed in these accounts, Ghana obviously was a powerful kingdom. Its influence eventually spread into the Sahara, and major trading towns were brought under its control. The Berber and Tuareg tribes of the Sahara had converted to Islam in the 7th century, and by the 11th century a new movement, whose followers were called the **Almoravids**, had begun to sweep across the western desert, Morocco, and Spain. One branch of this movement, under Abu Bakr ibn Umar (d. 1087), launched a series of campaigns in the western Sudan. The Almoravids controlled the gold trade across the Sahara and began to move toward its sources. Ghana was conquered in 1076, and a new fusion of Sudanic and Saharan peoples took place.

Although Ghana continued to exist, its power was weakened, and other states emerged to challenge its leadership. The growth of Islam weakened the kingdom and may have deepened division between its elite and the common people. Former provinces broke away, and a period of political instability and fragmentation followed, during which new states emerged among the Soninke, Fulbe, and Malinke peoples. The power of Ghana ended, but its tradition of trade and military power and the fusion of African and Islamic traditions continued among the successor states. Eventually, a new kingdom, **Mali**, emerged from this struggle. In many ways Mali was the heir to the power in the region, and it ruled a territory that extended from the bend of the Niger River to the Atlantic coast, which included much of the ancient kingdom of Ghana.

Almoravids [al muh räv udz] A puritanical reformist movement among the Islamic Berber tribes of northern Africa; controlled gold trade across Sahara; conquered Ghana in 1076; moved southward against African kingdoms of the savanna and westward into Spain.

Mali Empire centered between the Senegal and Niger rivers; creation of Malinke peoples; broke away from control of Ghana in 13th century.

 Read the Document on MyHistoryLab: Al-Umari Describes Mansa Musa of Mali

THINKING HISTORICALLY

Language as a Historical Source

HISTORIANS CONSTANTLY SEARCH FOR NEW WAYS to understand the past. For much of the early history of the world, we must depend on the archeological record. Cultures leave their traces not only in pottery, weapons, temples, and mummies but also in language, written or not. Language is a guide to the thought patterns of a people and to their society and institutions. Moreover, language is a guide to its speakers' historical relationships to others. The development of historical linguistics has greatly furthered our understanding of the past and has provided a set of theories and techniques that have become indispensable aids to the study of both preliterate and literate societies. The Bantu migration is a case in point.

The early study of languages was motivated by recognition of the close relationship between thought and language and the relationship between the structure of thought and language and the overall culture of a people. Early students of language, such as the French thinker Condillac, who wrote in the mid-18th century, believed that "each language expresses the character of the people that speak it." However, linguistic insights sometimes were influenced by cultural bias. Some later linguists shared the opinion of the learned Wilhelm von Humboldt, who wrote in his essay "On Language" (1836) that some languages were "more perfect" and better suited to the "mental cultivation of mankind." Not surprisingly, he believed that the Indo-European languages like his own German

The study of languages can tell us much about the values, social structure, and material life of peoples in the past.

best fit that definition. By the 20th century the early work of people such as von Humboldt had laid the foundation for the modern study of historical linguistics.

The great migration of the Indo-European peoples from central Asia into India and western Europe, the movement of the Bantu peoples throughout southern Africa, and the spread of the Polynesians across the Pacific are among the world's greatest migrations. Much of what can be said in all three cases—and in the study of the early settlement of the Americas—is based on a study of the vocabulary, structure, and spread of languages.

The study of language as a historical record is based on some fundamental ideas. Languages change over time, as any reading of Chaucer or Shakespeare immediately reveals. As they change, they may diverge from related languages. Languages with strong similarities in structure and vocabulary that cannot be explained by borrowing or contacts are considered part of the same family, and it is assumed that sometime in the past an original language was the parent of all the languages in that family. As groups of people separated, their language changed and diverged. Further separation resulted in further divergence, so that over time a large number of related languages could result from the original language. The proto-Indo-European language was the parent of Sanskrit, Persian, and Latin, but Latin later split into French, Italian, Rumanian, Portuguese,

(continued on next page)

and other related languages. By looking at structural and vocabulary similarities, we can establish linguistic subgroups and their relationship to each other as well as to the parent language. The study of the 300 to 600 (experts disagree) Bantu languages spoken today by more than 400 million people across much of the African continent is a case in point. From the comparative study of their vocabulary, we can tell much about their original cultures, but how can language be used to chart their history?

It can be assumed that the more diversity between languages, the more time has elapsed since their separation from each other. For a while, some linguists thought that if they could establish the rate at which linguistic changes took place, they could calculate the time that had elapsed since one language and its speakers separated from another. On the basis of 100 or 200 basic words, they attempted to calculate the percentage of change or loss from one language to another. This technique, called glottochronology, is no longer popular because it is clear that languages do not change at a constant rate of speed, and such change depends on many factors. Still, rates of change in written languages can be studied, and when used in conjunction with archeology, language can provide further historical evidence.

It is simple enough to see that the similarity of words in languages (barring random coincidence or words borrowed directly from a foreign language) can indicate a common origin. *Mother* in English, *mater* in Latin, and *mata* in Hindi all point to their common Indo-European origin. The word for *eye* in Tahiti was *mata*, in Hawaii *maka*, and among the New Zealand Maori *mata*; these similarities point to their common heritage as Polynesian languages. Despite the similar sounds involved in these two sets, the meanings indicate that we are dealing with two different language families.

Although historical linguistics has developed various methods for establishing these relationships, explaining the divergence or the reason for the separation of the peoples that speak the languages is another story. Without the help of archeology, oral traditions, or written records, historical linguistics cannot describe the course of change.

The study of languages can tell us much about the values, social structure, and material life of peoples in the past. A language with 12 adjectives to describe the color of the sea between the speaker and the horizon, or another language that has 20 ways of describing the color of a llama's coat, indicates the importance of those things to the people involved. A language that has no word for private property or nobility probably lacked those concepts. The grammar and pronunciation of a language can be independent of the physical world of its speakers, but the vocabulary cannot. It reflects what people knew and thought about. It can be assumed that if all the languages that split off from a parent tongue have the same word for iron, dog, cattle, or canoe, then the original speakers must have had these things. This kind of reasoning lies behind much of what we can say about the early Polynesians, the Bantu, and the Indo-Europeans. For example, by studying the distribution of words in various Polynesian languages, linguists have argued that even though we do not know the original home of the Polynesians, the original speakers of the parent language were inhabitants of some mountainous tropical island or islands in the western Pacific, and they grew taro, yams, bananas, and sugar cane before their expansion and dispersal.

Putting the linguistic evidence together with the historical record is challenging. When that record is available, as in the case of Aztec and Roman expansion, we can see that language change and spread sometimes are the result of intentional policy rather than undirected change.

Historical linguistics also concerns itself with variations and subdivisions within languages, or dialects, and with their geographic distribution. What is the difference between a dialect and a language? Linguists argue on this point, but some unknown skeptic once said, "A language is a dialect with an army behind it." That comment should focus our attention on the social and historical reasons for the predominance of some languages. It also underlines the necessary relationship between linguistics and other methods of knowing the past as tools that should be used together whenever possible.

QUESTIONS

- In what ways are language and literacy expressions of social or political power?

- What are some ways in which changes in our own language indicate broad historical changes?

- Is there a problem in using language as historical evidence because spoken language often differs from written language?

NOMADIC SOCIETIES AND INDO-EUROPEAN MIGRATIONS

9.2   What were the most important migration waves into Europe by the Classical Period?

In the vast expanse of territory that stretched from the steppes of the Ukraine across the center of Asia to the northern borders of China lived a variety of nomadic, herding peoples whose way of life revolved around their animals. These were peoples who practiced pastoralism, moving their herds seasonally, and living in close relation to their animals (Figure 9.3). Whether these **pastoral nomads** tended camels in the Sahara, or reindeer on the tundra of northern Russia, or sheep and horses in central Asia, their way of life had many similarities. They tended to live in small clans that could come

As agriculture had developed in several key centers, herding economies took shape in areas like central Asia, and some of these peoples later pushed into Europe. Political organization in northern Europe developed some significant features but—outside of Rome's boundaries—lagged behind the kingdoms of sub-Saharan Africa.

FIGURE **9.3** This 18th-century painting shows Kazak nomads bringing tribute horses to the emperor of China. Such tribute payments often were used by nomadic peoples to acknowledge their subordination to or alliances with strong dynasties in the civilized core regions, such as China. But splendid presents also were given by kings and emperors to nomad leaders. These exchanges of gifts also were used, particularly by the Chinese, to establish broader, more regular trading relationships.

pastoral nomads An intermediate form of ecological adaptation dependant on domesticated animal herds that feed on the natural environment; typically more populous than shifting cultivation groups.

together as tribes, migrating year after year in regular patterns to feed and water their flocks or herds, influenced by climate, rainfall, and distance. Wealth and status were often directly measured by the size and quality of the herd or by military prowess, for the nomadic way of life was hard and it placed great value on the virtues of courage and strength.

These were societies that jealously guarded their pastures or water holes but made hospitality a virtue, a necessity for travelers in the vast expenses of the deserts or plains where the nomads lived. The loyalties of extended families were essential, and the ability to lead often combined a dynamic or charismatic personality, personal courage, and the support of kinsmen. Women often had more varied roles than was true in the settled civilizations, including service in marketing goods. The arts of the nomads often made use of the products of their herds or flocks—woolen carpets, leather tents, tools made of horn—and incorporated their animals in their decorative designs.

Nomadic peoples had long lived in a relation of both attraction and rejection with the centers of civilization. They raided the sedentary populations of towns and villages, drawn by their surplus food and richer material culture, but were sometimes also employed by the settled societies that sought to exploit the military prowess of the nomads. Nomads also facilitated long-distance trade, including the traffic along the Silk Road from western China to the Middle East. The civilizations of China, Byzantium, Persia, and Rome all lived in a close and ambiguous relation with the nomads on their borders. Sometimes the nomads captured or destroyed empires and civilizations and created their own successor states, as the Hyksos did in Egypt in the 2nd millennium B.C.E. or the Aryans did in India in the 1st millennium B.C.E. But, while the nomads could conquer the centers of civilization as the Mongols, Hittites, and Turks were later to do, they usually had to adopt the institutions, social arrangements, and economic practices of the settled peoples. Most of history has been lived and made by the sedentary agrarian peoples and the city dwellers they supported, but the dynamic interplay with the nomads has often affected the course of civilized history and sometimes dominated it.

While various peoples like the Turks and Mongols lived this way of life, the first nomadic peoples about whom we know a good deal are the Indo-European tribes of the mid-2nd millennium B.C.E. For more than a thousand years thereafter, these horse nomads threatened the early civilizations of the Middle East and the Indus plains. Some Indo-European peoples, such as the Hittites and Hyksos, also established their own empires and centers of civilization, while others, such as the early Greeks, settled in the lands to which they migrated. As late as the last centuries B.C.E., these settled groups still struggled to fight off the incursions of later Indo-European migrants such as the Scythians, who invaded Europe and Asia Minor, or the Aryans who menaced Harappan civilization in India. Another group that became important in the age of the classic civilizations were the Xiongnu (later known in Europe as the Huns). They devastated China beginning in the 4th century B.C.E. and then centuries later toppled the Gupta Empire in India and smashed into the crumbling Roman Empire.

The original homeland of the Indo-Europeans was probably the area of the Dnieper River north of the Black and Caspian seas. Linguistic evidence indicates that they were herders and farmers. Although they first used their horses to pull chariots and carts, eventually they became riders. By about 3000 B.C.E. Indo-European peoples had moved into Anatolia and were moving eastward toward India. From the ancient homeland also came the populations that occupied Europe.

The Celts and the Germans

Celtic peoples spoke an Indo-European language. The **Celts** formed Europe's first culture, which stretched from Spain northward and into the British Isles. They were organized in small regional kingdoms with fierce warrior leaders, and they mixed agricultural and hunting economies. They had no cities and no writing, and their most impressive buildings were crude stone forts and arrays of stone set up to honor the gods of nature (Figure 9.4). The Romans considered the Celtic peoples barbarians. As Rome expanded its empire into Gaul, Spain, and Britain, various Celtic peoples came under Roman influence. A population of Romanized Celts developed in villages and towns across western Europe.

Germanic peoples populated much of the northwestern portion of the European continent. Their culture and institutions in many ways resembled those of the Celts (whom they had in some regions displaced). Certainly, to Roman observers, the Germanic tribes north of the empire's boundaries were undistinguished barbarians, pure and simple. As the Roman historian Tacitus wrote, "Who, indeed, would leave Asia, Africa, or Italy to seek Germany, with its desert scenery, its harsh climate, its sullen manners and aspect?" He might have added "and its warlike people," for by Tacitus' time the Romans had already developed a wary respect for the German warriors.

Tacitus had other comments on the Germans, although at times he emphasized their virtues as a way of criticizing what he considered Rome's moral degeneracy. The strength and bravery of the German warriors impressed him. He pointed out that warriors were pledged to support their chiefs and that the chiefs led by example and tried to outdo their men in battle. The size of a chief's retinue was a measure of his power and distinction, and men strove to gain a place in such a following.

Women, the elderly, and slaves did agriculture and all household tasks. Women were thought to have an element of holiness and the gift of prophecy. Their advice was sought and respected. Men and women married rather late, and usually a bride-price was paid to the woman. This included oxen, a horse, and arms, which symbolized the union of the couple and their shared responsibilities. Women were supposed to pass these gifts on to their children. Strong matrilineal ties existed, and the relationship between a man and his sisters' sons was particularly strong. The married state was respected, adultery was rare, and infanticide was not practiced. In a criticism of the Rome of his day, Tacitus said, "Good morality is more effective in Germany than good laws are elsewhere."

But Tacitus also commented on the rude material life of the Germans, their lack of cities, their simple dwellings, their lack of writing, and their constant fighting. Judgments of this sort accurately reflected the fact that the peoples of northwestern Europe had not formulated a civilization. However, they overlooked several important achievements and changes among some groups, such as the Germanic tribes, that accelerated during the final centuries of the classical era. Like the Celts, the Germanic peoples typically mixed agriculture and hunting, and they also herded cattle in a nomadic pattern. Among many Germans, however, agriculture steadily improved in the 1st centuries C.E. There were also marked improvements in iron use and the manufacture of cloth and other items. Some of these improvements resulted from knowledge of Roman skills, which spread beyond the empire's boundaries.

Read the Document on MyHistoryLab: Ammianus Marcellinus on the Huns

Celts Inhabited most of Britain and Ireland; organized in small regional kingdoms; featured mixed agricultural and hunting economies; replaced in most places by Germans.

FIGURE **9.4** Stonehenge, in England, was built over a period of 2000 years, beginning about 3000 B.C.E. Some of the stones weigh as much as 90,000 pounds, and thousands of people must have labored to erect these monuments. There are many theories about who built Stonehenge and why, but its story remains largely unknown.

Völkerwanderungen [fôlk er van der Un gen] Movement of Germanic peoples southward into the Roman Empire; resulted from population growth, pressure of Asian groups on eastern flanks of Germanic regions.

 Read the **Document** on MyHistoryLab: Germania (1st c. C.E.) Tacitus

Political cohesion among some German groups improved by the 3rd and 4th centuries C.E. Like many traditionally nomadic peoples, the Germans had long been organized in decentralized tribes of a few thousand members each, and even the tribes were loosely organized, with individual family groups settling most disputes. A tribe might have a king or an assembly of warrior chiefs; in either case, vigorous discussion of any policy issue among all fighting men was essential. Group loyalty and a certain amount of political equality were important parts of this tradition and would affect European institutions in the centuries after the classical era. After about 200 C.E., some German tribes merged into larger units as they learned to copy Roman military structure somewhat and were forced by Roman pressure to improve their organizational ability. The power of individual kings increased as they ruled large confederations of tribes.

Thus, even apart from the Germans who filtered into the Roman Empire or joined its armies, integrating portions of Roman civilization directly, there were important changes in the Germanic lands during the classical era, with improvements in agriculture, trade, manufacture, and politics. However, Germanic culture seems to have changed little outside Rome's boundaries. The German religion, like that of the Bantu, was animistic, worshiping the spirits of nature. Horses were the most common sacrifice.

The Germans made their first clear mark in world history as growing bands began to move southward into the Roman Empire, ultimately probing into Italy, Spain, and north Africa (Map 9.4). Their movement, the ***Völkerwanderungen***, resulted from population growth in their own lands, the nomadic tradition, Rome's attractiveness and growing weakness, and invasions by Asian groups on the eastern flanks of the Germanic region. German pressure within the Roman Empire played a major role in toppling it.

Saxon migration 409 C.E.
Burgundians migration 436–443 C.E.
Franks migration 486 C.E.
Visigoths migration 376–462 C.E.
Slavic peoples, c.400–c.600 C.E.

SAXONS
FRANKS
BURGUNDIANS
SLAVS
VISIGOTHS

400 MILES
400 KILOMETERS

MAP **9.4 Germanic and Slavic Peoples on the Move, 375–450 C.E.** During the final century of the Roman Empire in the west, extensive migrations occurred that altered the map of European peoples. Germanic tribes moved into many parts of the Empire in the West, while Slavic peoples migrated into various sections of eastern and southeastern Europe.

Growing cohesion among some Germanic groups had an influence beyond the pressures on Rome. It helped prepare larger areas of Europe for the gradual development of civilization in the centuries after Rome's fall. This new civilization reflected many Roman legacies and a strong Christian influence, but it also built on some Germanic elements. Even as Rome fell, in fact, a new Germanic center was taking shape in Scandinavia that would have wide influence in the following centuries. Far from Roman influence, Scandinavian populations were growing, and political confederations were being formed by the 5th century. This would soon lead to invasions and trade throughout much of the Mediterranean world.

The Slavs in Eastern Europe

While developments among various Germanic peoples held the stage in northwestern Europe, a somewhat similar pattern of precivilizational advance emerged in various parts of eastern Europe, with some influence from the Hellenistic kingdoms and then the eastern portions of the Roman Empire. As early as 3000 B.C.E., agriculture had been established in the southern part of what is now Russia, spreading from the Middle East. Bronze tools were also introduced, and then a wave of Indo-European invasions, about 1000 B.C.E., brought iron. Several new invasions from central Asia followed, and a loosely organized Scythian state controlled the region from the 7th to the 3rd centuries B.C.E. The Scythians were nomadic warriors, but agriculture continued to flourish in the plain north of the Black Sea. Scythian rule was followed by an invasion by a people known as the Sarmatians, some of whose descendants live in the central Caucasus region of Russia today. Under both Scythians and Sarmatians, Greek and Persian trade and cultural influence, including artistic styles, spread into this region.

Slavs An Indo-European group in Russia and the Balkans that ultimately dominated much of eastern Europe from the Balkans northward.

By the final centuries of the classical era, Slavic peoples were increasingly migrating into Russia and other parts of eastern Europe. Some **Slavs** had been in this region before, and the origin of these people is disputed. What is known is that the Slavic people were an Indo-European group, that they had become increasingly noticeable in Russia and the Balkans by the time of the early Roman Empire, and that they would ultimately dominate much of eastern Europe from the Balkans northward. Slavic political organization may have been a bit less developed than Germanic, but by the 5th century C.E. some regional kingdoms had been formed, notably in Bulgaria. Agriculture and manufacturing, including skilled ironwork, gained ground steadily, and (in advance of the Germanic northwest) some trading cities had been formed.

As with the Germans to the west, it would be premature to refer to a civilization of eastern Europe beyond the Mediterranean zone at the time of Rome's fall, and the Slavic peoples were severely disrupted by invasions from central Asia as the Huns and others cut across their lands. Nevertheless, an increasingly prosperous agricultural economy and rudiments of political organization beyond the tribal level characterized parts of the Slavic world toward the end of the classical era and foreshadowed more important developments.

VISUALIZING THE PAST

Varieties of Human Adaptation and the Potential for Civilization

PERHAPS THE BEST WAY TO UNDERSTAND and compare various human adaptations to environmental conditions is to relate them to the two extreme types of adaptation that ecologists call the *niche* and the *holding* patterns. In the first instance, the human group works its way into the environment in which it lives, rather than transforming that environment. Like the plants and animals with which they share a particular ecosystem, these peoples simply occupy one of many niches available in the overall ecosystem. Their activities have a minimal impact on the other niches or the life forms that occupy them. In the most extreme manifestations of the niche pattern, exhibited by rainforest peoples of Central and South America, southeast Asia, and Africa, small human groups, *forest farmers*, hunt game and gather fruits and vegetables in the jungle without altering the forest environment. These peoples move continuously through large areas of the forest, ingeniously tapping the many sources of plant and animal food.

Before the Industrial Revolution, *sedentary wet-rice agriculture*, which depended on elaborate irrigation systems, was the most developed form of the holding approach to ecological adaptation. Peoples who practice this approach extensively transform the natural environments in which they live. Wet-rice farmers, for example, clear forests, haul away stones, and plow grasses and weeds to prepare large tracts of land for cultivation.

They dig ditches to carry water to the rice fields, which are surrounded by dikes to hold the water in during the growing season. In addition, they clear fields and forests to support domesticated animals. Thus, the original vegetation and animal life are supplanted by domesticated plants and livestock. The domesticated plants are arranged in patterns determined by human needs rather than natural processes. They are protected from wild animals by fences and shelters, and wild plants are removed. Areas near the rice fields are also transformed by the construction of human dwellings, shrines, and granaries, which are combined to form villages and sometimes grow into cities.

Between the niche pattern and the holding pattern, several intermediate forms of human adaptation have developed. One of the most important of these in terms of the numbers of humans supported by it is *dry farming* of grain crops such as wheat, rye, barley, and millet. Although the environment is not as extensively transformed by dry farming as by wet-rice agriculture, both involve building permanent villages, raising livestock, and building systems of food storage and transportation.

Shifting cultivation (or *slash-and-burn* farming), concentrated in the rainforests of both the Eastern and Western Hemispheres, is an adaptation that is much closer to the niche pattern than either form of sedentary agriculture. Shifting cultivators burn off the jungle undergrowth but leave the large trees and the cover they provide to protect the fragile tropical soils. Using the ashes created by their fires as a natural fertilizer, shifting farmers cultivate the area cleared on the forest floor. The foods grown in this manner form the staples of their diet, which are supplemented by meat, wild berries, and other forest plants. After working a particular clearing for a year or two, shifting farmers move to another patch in the forest, where they again begin the burning-cultivating sequence.

Pastoral nomadism is a second major alternative between hunting and gathering and sedentary agriculture. Although nomadic groups differ in the kinds of animals they herd and

(continued on next page)

whether they ride horses or camels or work their herds on foot, their pattern of adaptation to their natural environment is similar. Like the shifting cultivators, nomads do not seek to transform their natural environments in major ways. In the steppe and savanna grasslands where they live in the winter and spring, they introduce large herds of domesticated livestock. Their herds harvest the plant cover in these areas. The nomads also set up temporary camps of tents or wagons near their herds. When the hot, dry summer arrives, the nomads break camp and move with their herds to riverine or hilly areas where there is enough water and plant life to sustain their livestock.

QUESTIONS

- Which forms of human adaptation are the most likely to produce civilizations as we have defined them in Chapter 1, and why?
- In which areas will it be possible to build highly centralized political systems with considerable state control of local populations, and why?
- What would a people gain by choosing the holding pattern and developing a civilization?
- What might they lose by giving up a nomadic or shifting-cultivating way of life?

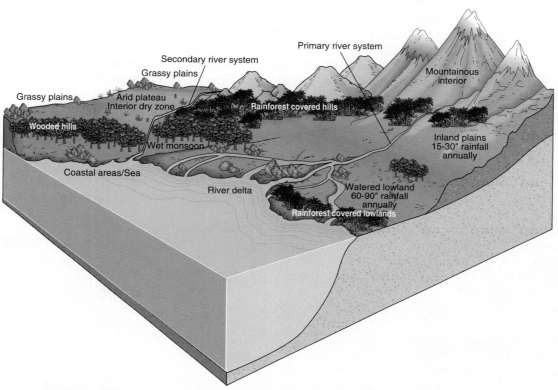

The Variety of Ecosystems This composite map contains examples of the different sorts of ecosystems in which each of these adaptations (wet-rice agriculture, hunting and gathering, dry farming, shifting cultivation, and pastoralism) has developed. After matching ecosystems with patterns of adaptation, discuss the questions in this section.

THE SPREAD OF CHINESE CIVILIZATION TO JAPAN

9.3 | Why and how did Japan reach out to China during the Classical Period?

The Japanese developed a unique civilization from a blend of their own culture and a selective importation and conscious refashioning of Chinese influences. Not conquering armies, but merchants and traveling monks—and eventually Japanese students who studied in China—were the most important agents by which elements of Chinese culture were transmitted across the sea. Especially in the early

The transmission of key elements in Chinese culture to the offshore islands that came to make up Japan is one of the most important examples of the spread of civilization from a central core area to neighboring or overseas peoples. In the first centuries C.E., the peoples of Japan imported ideas, institutions, and techniques of production from the Chinese mainland, which were gradually adapted to the sophisticated culture they had already developed.

centuries of borrowing, from the 1st to the 5th centuries C.E., interchange between China and Japan was largely indirect. It was mediated by the peoples and kingdoms of Korea, who had adapted key aspects of Chinese civilization to their own cultures somewhat earlier than the Japanese.

In contrast to the Vietnamese, who were ruled by the Chinese for nearly a millennium, and the peoples of south China, who were eventually absorbed by Chinese civilization, the Japanese initiated and controlled the process of cultural borrowing from China. Despite a willingness to acknowledge the cultural superiority of the Chinese Middle Kingdom, the Japanese retained political independence throughout the centuries of intense borrowing. Consequently, they could be more selective in their adoption of Chinese ideas than most of the other peoples influenced by China.

Natural Setting and the Peopling of the Islands

The four main islands that make up the homeland of the Japanese people rise abruptly and dramatically from the Pacific Ocean along the northeast coast of Asia (Map 9.5). Formed by volcanic eruptions that still occur periodically, the islands are dominated by mountains and rugged hills. Only a small portion of their surface area is level and extensive enough for the cultivation of wet rice, which from prehistoric times has been the staple of the Japanese diet. Thus, from the time of the earliest settlements, the Japanese have occupied mainly the coastal plains, especially in the south central portions of the largest island, **Honshu**, which remain the most heavily populated areas of the islands today.

Honshu Largest of the Japanese islands; most heavily populated.

Although poor in natural resources, the islands are difficult to match in their combination of temperate climate and subtle natural beauty that instilled in the Japanese people a refined aesthetic sensibility and sensitivity to the natural world reflected in their religion, art, and architecture. At the same time, the islands' limited resource base nurtured a disciplined, hard-working population that was regulated by strict legal codes and ruled through much of the islands' history by warrior elites.

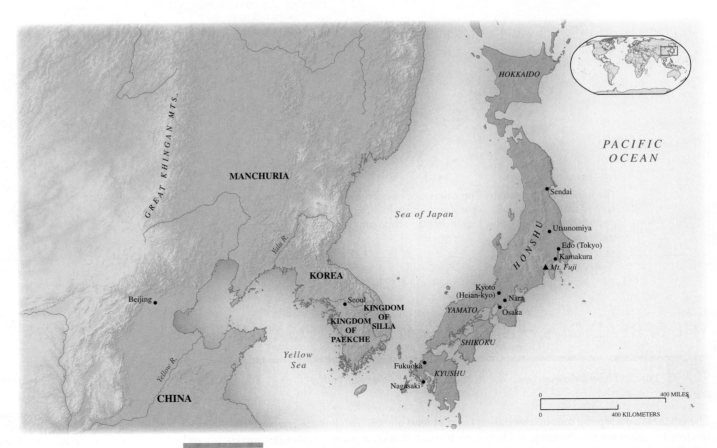

MAP **9.5 East Asia at the End of the Classical Period** Despite significant borrowing from China, by the end of the classical era quite distinct cultures had emerged in both Japan and Korea.

Archeological evidence suggests that as early as 5000 B.C.E., the ancestors of the Japanese people had begun to migrate to the islands. Drawn from numerous east Asian ethnic groups, the migrants came in small bands and periodically in larger waves over many centuries. One of these waves of migrants produced the **Jomon culture** in the 3rd millennium B.C.E. The Jomon were a hunting-and-gathering people who lived in pits dug in the ground. They produced a distinctive pottery whose cordlike decoration gave the people their name.

Most of the new settlers crossed to the islands from the Korean peninsula and Manchuria (Map 9.6). Because they were isolated from political upheavals and social transformations occurring on the mainland, by the first centuries C.E. the diverse migrant streams had blended into a homogenous population with a distinctive Japanese language, culture, and physical appearance. By then they had driven the Ainu, who had settled the islands before them, into northern Honshu and Hokkaido. Over the past two millennia, the Japanese have gradually displaced or absorbed nearly all the remaining Ainu, building a strong sense of cultural and ethnic identity.

Indigenous Culture and Society

Long before Chinese cultural influences began to shape Japanese historical development, the indigenous peoples of the islands had taken significant steps toward creating a civilization of their own. In the last centuries B.C.E., migrants from the mainland introduced wet-rice agriculture and ironworking into Japan. In this period, which is known as the **Yayoi epoch**, the Japanese also produced wheel-turned pottery and very sophisticated bronzeware, including elaborately decorated bells that were sometimes four or five feet high.

Until the early 5th century C.E., most of the Japanese population was divided into hundreds of clans, each dominated by a small warrior aristocracy. The clan elites drew their support from the peasantry, which made up over 90 percent of the population of the islands. They were also served by slaves, who like their counterparts in China were only a small minority of the Japanese people. Early visitors from the mainland noted the rigid social distinctions, including different sorts of tattoos and other body markings, that separated the warrior elite from the mass of the people. They also remarked on the strong position of women in early Japanese culture, in marked contrast to their clear subordination in China. Early Japanese households appear to have been matriarchal—that is, dominated by childbearing women. Women also played key roles as shamans, who were central to Japanese religious ceremonies and worship, as leaders of some of the clans, and later as empresses.

The importance of women in early Japanese culture is also indicated by their legends about the creation of the world. The sun goddess, **Amaterasu**, played a central role, and her worship became the central element in the **Shinto** religion developed by the island peoples. Shinto devotees worshiped many gods and spirits associated with the natural world. Some of these deities were identified with objects, such as huge trees or mountains such as the famous Mount Fuji. Others were linked to animals that were believed to possess special powers. Gods and spirits were believed to be capable of doing good or evil to humans. To ensure that they brought blessings rather than misfortune, the Japanese made offerings of food and prayers to the gods and nature spirits at special shrines that were built of unfinished wood and were notable for their simple lines and lack of ornamentation. They gave rise to a unique Shinto style of Japanese architecture, which persists to the present day and has had a great impact on architecture in the modern world (Figure 9.5).

In the 4th and 5th centuries C.E., when one of the clans, the **Yamato**, gained power over the others, an imperial cult developed around the sun goddess and Shinto worship. A central shrine was established at Ise near the Honshu political heartland of early Japanese history, and the priest-chief heads of the Yamato clan claimed descent from the sun goddess herself. Building on this powerful source of legitimacy, the Yamato brought most of the lowland plains of the southern islands under their control through alliances and conquest. By the late 4th century C.E., their sway also extended to southern Korea. This overseas extension of the Yamato domains brought

Jomon culture [JOH-muhn] Created by early migrants to Japan after 3000 B.C.E.; hunting-and-gathering people, produced a distinctive pottery form.

Yayoi epoch [yay-YOH-ee] Last centuries B.C.E. in Japan; featured introduction of wet-rice cultivation, ironworking; produced wheel-turned pottery and sophisticated bronzeware.

Amaterasu [ä mä te Rä sU] Sun goddess of the Shinto religion.

Shinto Religion of early Japanese culture; devotees worshiped numerous gods and spirits associated with the natural world; offers of food and prayers made to gods and nature spirits.

Yamato Japanese clan that gained increasing dominance in the 4th and 5th centuries C.E.; created imperial cult around Amaterasu and Shinto; brought most of the lowland plains of the southern islands under control.

MAP **9.6 The Rise of Japanese Civilization** Japanese civilization expanded in the classical era from the central plains of the largest island, Honshu, driving earlier inhabitants, the Ainu, to the north and eventually the island of Hokkaido, where most of their remaining descendants reside today.

intensified contacts with Chinese civilization, then about to enter one of its most illustrious phases. The combination of these contacts and the Yamatos' successful campaigns to unify the Japanese people led to profound transformations in Japanese society and culture in the centuries that followed.

The Chinese Model and the Remaking of Japan

The introduction of the Chinese script in the 4th century C.E. was a major turning point in Japanese cultural development. Writing with the Chinese characters, which were adapted only with great difficulty to the Japanese language, made it possible for the Yamato to begin to build a real bureaucracy and thus more firmly establish their control over vassal clan heads and the peasantry. The use of the Chinese written language also meant that the Japanese could learn from Chinese texts on all manner of subjects, from science and philosophy to art and religion. These works, as well as Chinese scribes to make additional copies and interpret them, were imported from the 5th century onward. Later, Japanese students and scholars who were fluent in Chinese were sent to China to acquire new learning firsthand.

From the mid-6th century, the Buddhist religion became a pivotal factor in the transmission of Chinese influence to Japan. In the period of chaos that followed the fall of the Han dynasty in the early 3rd century C.E., Buddhism was widely adopted by the distressed populace of China and the rulers of the warring kingdoms that succeeded the Han. The pervasive influence of the religion in China in this era and the powerful position of Buddhist monks at the courts of Chinese rulers gave great impetus to its spread to Korea and Japan. In the mid-6th century, a Korean ruler sent Buddhist images and scriptures as presents to the Japanese emperor and urged him to adopt the religion and convert his subjects to it. After considerable debate and even open strife among the families serving the imperial household over the advantages and dangers of introducing Buddhism into Japan, it was officially adopted as the religion of the Yamato domains in the late 580s.

From that time onward, Japanese rulers tried to propagate the new religion among their subjects. Warrior aristocrats and peasants converted to the new beliefs, but without giving up their long-standing reverence for Shinto spirits and deities. Thus, Shintoism and Buddhism developed side by side as twin pillars of state and society in Japan. The Japanese elite supported the efforts of Buddhist monks to spread their faith, and the monks in turn served as advisors to the emperor and regional lords. In their teachings of Buddhism, the monks stressed scriptural passages and Buddhist ethical prescriptions that supported rule by a strong monarch and a centralized state.

Although converts from aristocratic Japanese families studied the complex beliefs of Buddhist philosophy and practiced its highly developed meditation techniques, to the illiterate mass of the Japanese people Buddhism was little more than a magical cult. Buddhist monks provided colorful rituals that enriched the peasants' monotonous lives and charms to ward off sickness or evil spirits, but the common people knew little of Buddhist teachings beyond highly mythologized versions of the Buddha's life.

Political and Social Change

Beginning in the early 7th century, the Yamato rulers styled themselves the "emperors of the rising sun" in official letters to (one imagines) the somewhat dismayed Chinese "emperors of the setting sun." Inspired by Chinese examples, they established councils and government departments and tried to introduce genuine bureaucratic control at the local level. At **Nara** and later **Heian** (Kyoto), the Japanese emperors laid out courts and capital cities patterned after the ancient imperial centers of China. The Yamato rulers strove to build a peasant conscript army and impose legal codes and a landholding system similar to those in China.

In the centuries after the introduction of Buddhism, Chinese influences were felt in virtually all spheres of Japanese society. Alongside the traditional warrior elite, a class of monks and scholars developed that for several centuries exercised power at the imperial court. Trade with China and Korea and improved communication within Japan enriched existing merchant groups and led to their emergence

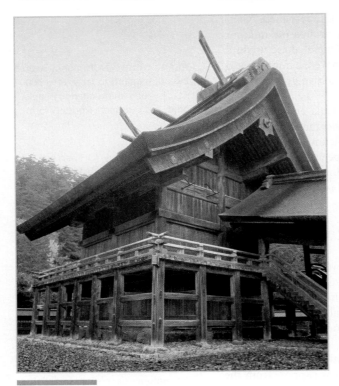

FIGURE **9.5** The simplicity and woodland setting of this shrine at Izumo, Japan, are characteristic of Shinto architecture, which was designed to reflect reverence for and harmony with nature.

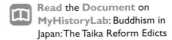

Read the Document on MyHistoryLab: Buddhism in Japan: The Taika Reform Edicts

Nara Along with Heian, capital of the Yamato emperors; patterned after ancient imperial centers of China; never fully populated.

Heian [hay-yan] Capital city of Japan under the Yamato emperors, later called Kyoto; built in order to escape influence of Buddhist monks; patterned after ancient imperial centers of China; never fully populated.

as a distinct class. New tools and techniques imported from the mainland increased the output of Japanese farmers and made possible a great expansion of the islands' previously marginal mining industry.

The introduction into Japan of the patriarchal and patrilineal family, which had long been dominant in China, presented a major challenge to traditional Japanese approaches to gender roles and relationships. For several centuries, the position of women within the family remained strong, and the ideal of wives and lovers who were accomplished in literature and the arts was preserved by the courtly elites at the imperial capitals of Nara and Heian. But the adoption of Chinese law codes eroded the control that Japanese women had over their own children and eventually reduced their overall social status. These changes were reflected in the spread of polygamy among the Japanese aristocracy. From the early 9th century, the changes were even more evident in the elite's refusal to allow women from the imperial family to rule in their own right, as they had periodically in the early centuries of Japanese history. Japanese women, like those in China and India, were increasingly subordinated to their fathers and husbands. As in China and India, entry into religious orders or successful careers as courtesans were nearly the only alternatives to careers as subordinated wives and mothers.

Chinese Influence and Japanese Resistance

Contacts with China and innovations based on the Chinese model were pushed from the 4th century C.E. onward by those at the top of Japanese society. Japanese rulers and their chief advisors were motivated mainly by the desire to increase the power of the state to control the warrior nobles and to extract resources from the peasantry. Buddhist ethics and Confucian legal codes enhanced the rulers' legitimacy, Chinese rituals gave a new dignity and luster to court routines, and the growth of a Chinese-style bureaucracy provided the means for creating the first genuine state in Japanese history. Because the Japanese remained politically independent from China, their rulers could convincingly argue that the adoption of Chinese ways was voluntary and carefully controlled. Only imports that would strengthen the Japanese state or contribute to the well-being of the Japanese populace need be accepted. Chinese ideas and institutions could be reworked to suit conditions in Japan and fit the needs of the Japanese people. Selective borrowing from their ancient and advanced Chinese neighbors, the innovators argued, allowed the Japanese to become fully civilized without destroying their own culture and identity.

Because Japanese rulers lacked the resources of the Chinese emperors and worked with a society that differed greatly in scale and organization, many of their efforts to imitate Chinese patterns failed. The bloated bureaucracies that resulted from the imitation of China were a growing burden for the peasants who had to support them. Efforts to establish local control and reorganize landholding along Chinese lines foundered because of the opposition of regional lords and their retainers. The warrior elite also frustrated the attempt to make soldiers of the peasantry. Conscripts in Japan in this era were little more than forced laborers. Many of the imported Chinese legal injunctions bore little relation to social conditions in Japan and were not enforced. The impressive capital cities laid out by the emperors' architects remained half-built and underpopulated, even at the height of the early dynasties' power.

Japan could not simply be made in China's image. From the outset, the introduction of writing, Buddhism, and other imports from China had given rise to concerns about preserving Japan's own culture. At times, as in the 580s and the mid-7th century, controversy over foreign influences became a central element in violent struggles between the aristocratic families closest to the throne. But until the 8th century each struggle was won by the forces favoring continuing imports from abroad and the further transformation of Japan along Chinese lines.

THE SCATTERED SOCIETIES OF POLYNESIA

9.4   What were the distinctive features of Polynesian migration and expansion?

Peoples from Asia navigated across the vast expanse of the Pacific. On islands such as Hawaii and New Zealand, they created complex societies, mostly in isolation from the rest of humankind.

The peoples of the far Pacific, who had left the Asian mainland before the rise of classical China and India, were unaffected by the spread of Chinese and Indian civilization. They had brought with them the cultural features of late Neolithic Asia, and in isolation they had developed these features on the islands of the vast Pacific.

Certainly one of the great epics of human achievement for which we have only fragmentary evidence is the peopling of the islands of the Pacific Ocean. The image of the prows of their great outrigger canoes cutting through the waves of the vast Pacific Ocean to reach uninhabited islands grips our imagination. The distance across the Pacific from southeast Asia to Central America is some 12,000 miles, and the waters of that ocean are dotted with thousands of islands (Map 9.7). These islands vary in size from tiny atolls formed by coral reefs, to large "high" islands with volcanic peaks and lush valleys, to the great continent of Australia. Most of these islands lie in the tropics, although some, like New Zealand, do not. They are inhabited by a variety of peoples whose physical appearance, language, and culture are quite different but whose origins for the most part seem to be in Asia.

The remarkable story of the Polynesians can serve as a case study of the spread of culture by long-distance maritime migration in the Pacific. Here we are not dealing with the spread from a great center of civilization but with the migration of peoples and their adaptation to new challenges in isolation.

Between roughly 1500 B.C.E. and 1000 C.E., almost all the major islands west of New Guinea were visited, and many were settled, by the ancestors of the peoples we call Polynesians. They left no written records, so we must depend on the evidence of archeology and linguistics, their own oral traditions, and the observations of Europeans who first contacted them to reconstruct the history of their societies.

Linguistic evidence is a starting point. The Polynesians speak about 30 related languages from a family of languages called **Austronesian**, which is also found in the Philippines, Indonesia, and southeast Asia. The Austronesians were clearly peoples from Asia, but they were not the first migrants in the Pacific. By the time of their expansion about 4000 years ago, New Guinea and Australia had already long been settled (probably since 38,000 B.C.E.) by dark-skinned peoples who spoke languages unrelated to Austronesian. New DNA analyses may provide other clues. Recent studies indicate that the pre-Chinese peoples of Taiwan are the closest relatives to the Polynesian peoples of New Zealand.

Austronesian Family of 30 related languages found in the Philippines, Indonesia, and southeast Asia; people of this linguistic group migrated throughout the Pacific.

The Great Migration

Groups of these Austronesians, speaking a language ancestral to the Polynesian languages, began to expand eastward from Melanesia to Fiji, Tonga, and Samoa. By the time of this expansion, these people practiced agriculture, growing yams, taro (a tuber), and other crops; raised dogs, pigs, and chickens; and had already developed a variety of complex fishing techniques. Archeologists can identify their scattered settlements by a distinctive type of pottery called *Lapita*, with stamped decorations, and by polished stone adzes, fishhooks, and other implements.

From Tonga and Samoa these peoples began to spread eastward to **Polynesia** proper. Polynesia includes the islands contained in a rough imaginary triangle whose points lie at Hawaii to the north, New Zealand to the south, and Easter Island far to the east. Another group of these peoples seems to have moved westward, eventually settling on the island of Madagascar off the African coast.

On the widely dispersed islands of the Pacific, each culture and language began to adapt and evolve differently and thus to diverge from the ancestral Polynesian forms. Some constants in the shared heritage of the ancestral Polynesian culture remained, however. For example, in the 18th century, English explorer Captain James Cook was surprised to find that the words he had learned from the Tahitians were understandable to the Hawaiians, although almost 2500 miles separated those two island groups. Also, a Tahitian named Tupia served Captain Cook effectively as a translator when he contacted the **Maori** of New Zealand.

Basic principles of economy and social organization could also be found throughout Polynesia, especially on the larger islands. From small groups of original colonists, island populations grew in size and density. By the late 18th century, the island populations totaled 700,000. Although potterymaking was abandoned or forgotten, in

Polynesia Islands contained in a rough triangle whose points lie in Hawaii, New Zealand, and Easter Island.

Maori Residents of New Zealand; migrated to New Zealand from Society Islands as early as 8th century C.E.

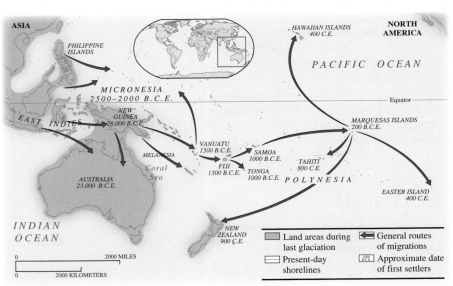

MAP **9.7 The Spread of Polynesian Peoples** The tremendous ocean navigation ability of the Polynesians is suggested by this map showing their expansion from Indonesia and the Philippines across the Pacific Ocean to New Zealand, Easter Island, and Hawaii. Across the expanse of ocean they created a variety of societies but some basic elements of their language and culture were broadly shared.

many places agriculture became increasingly complex and intensive. Stratified societies with powerful chiefdoms based on lineage characterized many Polynesian islands, and in some places, such as Hawaii, they became extremely hierarchical. Chiefs were able to mobilize their followers for ceremonial and public architecture or for wars and interisland raiding. Ritual and religion oriented many aspects of life and served as the basis of the chiefs' power.

The Voyagers of the Pacific

How did these ancient Polynesians discover and occupy the islands of the vast Pacific? The Polynesians knew how to make a variety of seaworthy vessels, but for long-distance voyaging, they used great double canoes, or **pahi** (Figure 9.6). These vessels usually carried a platform between the two hulls on which shelter could be given to people, animals, and plants. With large triangular sails, these vessels, some of which were 60 to 100 feet long, were capable of long voyages at sea and could travel more than 120 miles a day in good weather. They could sail windward, against the winds and tides of the Pacific, which tend to move from east to west.

Naturally, navigation was a problem. Some scholars have held that the voyages were accidental—boats were blown off course, which led to the occupation of new islands—but Polynesian traditions and the continuing ability of some Pacific islanders to navigate long distances by observing the stars, wave patterns, and other techniques support the idea that voyages of colonization were planned. Moreover, sometimes they were two-way. For example, Hawaiian traditions commemorate the arrival of Tahitian chiefs who made voyages to and from Hawaii for about 200 years (1100–1300 C.E.). In 1976, to establish the possibility of such voyaging, the *Hokulé*, a reconstructed double canoe based on traditional proportions and using only traditional navigational techniques, was sailed from Hawaii to Tahiti in about 35 days.

Much of the Polynesians' voyaging seems to have been sporadic, as groups pushed by war, population pressure, famine, or a spirit of exploration followed a chief or navigator into the unknown. In the 18th century, when the Europeans arrived, such long-range voyaging was rarely practiced. By that time, however, the Polynesians had explored and colonized almost every habitable island in the vast Pacific.

pahi Double canoes used for long-distance voyaging; carried a platform between canoes for passengers or cargo.

Kamehameha I [kä mAY hä mAY hä, kuh mAY uh mAY uh] (1758–1819) Fought series of wars backed by British weapons and advisors resulting in unified Hawaiian kingdom by 1810; as king he promoted economic change by encouraging Western merchants to establish export trade in Hawaiian goods.

Ancient Hawaii

We can use the widely separated large islands of New Zealand and Hawaii as examples of Polynesian societies that developed in isolation in response to particular environmental conditions. Hawaii includes eight major islands in a chain about 300 miles long. The volcanic nature of the islands and the tropical climate created an environment of great beauty and majesty that impressed the early inhabitants. The islands probably were settled in at least two migratory waves beginning about 300 C.E. There, early Polynesian culture was adapted and elaborated in isolation over a long period of time. The islands had good soil, and the population grew large, reaching about 200,000 people by the time of European contact in the 1700s. Towns and cities were absent, and houses, here as elsewhere in Polynesia, were scattered along the coast and in valleys leading to the higher interior. A number of chiefly families competed for control of the islands. It was not until after European contact that King **Kamehameha I** united all the islands under his control in 1810.

FIGURE **9.6** Large double-hulled Polynesian canoes were used for the long voyages of discovery that sometimes covered more than a thousand miles. The Polynesian mariners were great navigators who explored the far reaches of the Pacific Ocean. (© 2009 Herb Kawainui Kane.)

ali'i [ah-LEE-ee] High chiefs of Hawaiian society who claimed descent from the gods and rested their claims on their ability to recite in great detail their lineages.

mana Power of Hawaiian ali'i; emanated from their lineages and enabled them to extract labor or tribute from their subjects.

kapu [kah-POO] Complex set of social regulations in Hawaii that forbade certain activities and regulated social discourse.

Of all the Polynesian societies, Hawaii became the most hierarchical. The high chiefs, or **ali'i** claimed descent from the gods. In some cases, marriage to their sisters ensured the purity of the chiefly family. Their power, authority, and sacredness, or **mana**, came from their lineages and enabled them to extract labor or tribute from their subjects or even take their land. Feathered capes and helmets as well as tattoos distinguished the chiefs. The ali'i were revered and feared. A Hawaiian proverb held that "The chief is a shark that swims on land." A class of lesser nobility and subchiefs of their relatives supported the rule of the ali'i.

Society rested on the commoners but most of the land was controlled by nobles who viewed the commoners almost as a separate people. As elsewhere in Polynesia, the land was divided into sections that usually reached from the ocean to the top of mountain ridges. This division promoted sustainability, as landholders cultivated starches, principally taro, in the mountain valleys, while drawing upon large man-made coastal fisheries for protein. In Hawaii, this combination of agriculture and aquaculture was so efficiently managed as to help support a population of about 300,000.

Hawaiian society was intensely agricultural, and the community's control of land was a central aspect of social and political relations. Within the hierarchy, commoners were viewed almost as a separate people or at least as a people lacking in lineage. Their lives were constrained and limited by a complex set of **kapu** (*tapu* in Tahiti), or taboos, which forbade certain activities and regulated social discourse. It was kapu for women to eat certain foods, to enter the house of a chief, to eat together with men, to view certain ceremonies limited to the chiefs, or even to cast a shadow on a chief. Violations could lead to death. The number of kapu surrounding a chief was a measure of his status and his sanctity, as much a sign of his position in his society as material goods might be in our society.

Many aspects of life were ritualized. The many gods were honored at ceremonial centers whose precincts were sacred. Ritual feasting and hula, or dancing, accompanied many ceremonies. Human and other sacrifices were offered to Ku, the god of war, and to the other deities. Lono, the god of fertility and agricultural rebirth, held special importance to the Hawaiians. The great Makahiki festival of thanksgiving, which lasted for four months and at which the chiefs received their tribute from the commoners, was celebrated in honor of the annual return of Lono. During this time war was kapu, hulas were danced, and sexual activity was engaged in frequently in the hope of stimulating fertility. In fact, lovemaking was an art and a preoccupation of the Hawaiians, with important religious, kinship, and political meanings.

Of the various Polynesian societies, Hawaii can be seen as the most successful in terms of its political and social complexity, economic foundations, art and material culture, and religion. With a Neolithic technology, the Hawaiians created a complex culture on their islands. Although they lacked a written language, their legends and oral histories, which could trace the genealogies of chiefly families back to the original canoes of the first migrants, were remarkable achievements that formed and preserved their culture.

The New Zealand Landfall and the Development of Maori Culture

Perhaps as early as the 8th century C.E., the crews of canoes or rafts from the Society Islands and other parts of eastern Polynesia had sailed thousands of miles to the southwest and by chance discovered the two large islands that today make up New Zealand. Over the centuries additional bands of seafarers reached the islands, where they embarked on a struggle to survive in an environment that was colder and harsher than their home islands in Polynesia. Their success is evidenced by the large numbers of Maori—perhaps as many as 200,000 people descended from the Polynesian seafarers—who lived in the islands when the Europeans first came to stay in the late 18th century.

The "land of the long white clouds," or Aotearoa as the Polynesians referred to the mist-covered islands of New Zealand, had few edible plants beyond berries and fern roots. There were no native land mammals except bats and various kinds of **moa**, or large, wingless birds, soon overhunted to extinction. Fishing and the introduction by later migrants of many of the staple crops of Polynesia, including the sweet potato, taro, and yam, filled the dietary gap left by the disappearance of the moa.

moa Large, wingless birds native to New Zealand; hunted to extinction by early settlers; extinction established need to develop new sources of protein.

The moderate climate and rich soils of the north island rendered it more suitable for settlement than the cold and desolate south island, which stretched beneath the 40th parallel toward the South Pole. Consequently, Maori tribes numbering in the thousands warred over control of the forests and croplands on the north island. Long before the arrival of the Europeans, tribal territories with clearly defined boundaries had been established throughout most of the north island.

Maori Culture and Society. Each Maori tribe was divided into subgroups called **hapu**, the primary unit of identity and community. The Maori lived in extended families in large, elaborately carved wooden houses. All the land the Maori farmed for their subsistence was owned by the hapu village and allotted by a communal council to each of the extended families for its support.

hapu Primary social unit of Maori society in New Zealand; divisions of tribes consisting of extended families; land allotted to extended families in common.

Each hapu was led by a male chief, who was not a specialized political leader but rather a particularly skillful warrior. Chieftainships were hereditary, although weak leaders were soon displaced by more able warriors. Despite the magical aura associated with the hapu and tribal chieftains, their actual power was limited by village and tribal councils made up of the free men of a given group. Virtually all hapu communities also included slaves, usually prisoners of war or their descendants.

Although they had a strong voice within the family, women were clearly subordinated to men. Male dominance was evidenced by the monopoly they enjoyed with regard to positions of leadership and to highly prestigious activities such as making war and woodcarving.

Maori society could not support full-time specialists, but many kinds of religious and craft experts were recognized. Priests were of several kinds, varying according to social status and functions. The most esteemed were the chiefs, who were also trained as priests. The chief-priest presided over communal ceremonies and knew the special prayers to protect the tribe or hapu. The Maori world was alive with spirits, gods, and goddesses who intervened constantly in human affairs. At the other end of the social scale were shamans, who specialized in healing and served as the mediums by which gods and spirits made their desires known to humans.

A War-Oriented Society. In addition to priests, Maori society had a wide variety of experts, ranging from those who built canoes to woodcarvers and tattoo specialists. The most important experts, however, were those with skills relating to making war. Maori society was obsessed with war. During the appropriate season, tribes and hapus fought regularly with their neighbors or distant confederations. Young men proved their worth as warriors, and leaders could not long maintain their positions without demonstrating their martial prowess. Much of the time and energy of Maori men was devoted to planning campaigns against neighboring tribes or building the intricate hilltop fortresses found throughout the north island. Although the loss of life in Maori wars was low by European standards, their combats were fierce. Hand-to-hand fighting with spears and exquisitely carved war clubs was the preferred mode of combat. Successful ambushes and surprise attacks were highly admired. The priest-leader of a hapu or tribe would cut out the heart of the first enemy killed in battle and offer it to the gods of his people. Enemy casualties sometimes were eaten, and enemy prisoners were enslaved.

On the Threshold of Civilization. Polynesian seafarers had accomplished much in the harsh but beautiful environment of their New Zealand landfall. Mainly on the basis of imported crops, they had developed a fairly steady and productive agricultural system. Although they did not work metals, their material culture was quite impressive. In woodworking and decoration, in particular, they surpassed the Polynesian societies from which their ancestors had come. They had also developed a wonderfully rich oral tradition, which placed a premium on oratorical skills and produced a complex and fascinating collection of myths and legends. Although divided and politically decentralized, the Maori had developed closely knit and well organized communities within the hapu and the tribe.

Their isolation and limited resources prevented the Maori from achieving the full occupational specialization that, as we have seen, was critical to the advance to true civilization elsewhere. Isolation limited Maori technological advances and their resistance to disease. These limits rendered them vulnerable to peoples such as the Europeans, who had more sophisticated tools and weapons and transmitted diseases that decimated the tribes of New Zealand. Although their skills in war and their adaptability allowed the Maori to survive in the long run, they could do little to prevent the disintegration of their culture and the destruction of much of the world they had known before the coming of the Europeans.

Global Connections and Critical Themes

THE EMERGING CULTURES

Two important features were shared by the societies that formed on the fringes of the major core of world civilizations during the classical period and slightly beyond. First, as they adopted or imported agriculture, they were able to form more structured political units and develop a more complex social hierarchy. Second, each of the emerging societies exhibited important characteristics from its own past. These characteristics carried forward into the history of these regions, even as other influences were encountered. Expansions and contacts established during the classical period would lead directly to further developments in the next world history period.

Most of the fringe societies obviously participated in a new range of contacts, either through migration into greater interaction with an established civilization or, as with Japan, through deliberate imitation. Nomadic peoples more generally also enhanced contacts, bringing new influences through trade, migration, or invasion.

The four emerging areas also displayed one vital difference in addition to specific characteristics in art, language, and the like. Three of the areas—northern and eastern Europe, Japan, and sub-Saharan Africa—were in contact with more established civilization centers, at least to some extent. Polynesia stood apart by its early separation from Asia. This resulted in an impressive set of independent achievements as Polynesian society advanced and spread, but also in important constraints, most obviously in technology. In other words, the availability of outside influence can explain important differences between societies.

Further development of contacts with more established centers for the Japanese, the Slavs, Celts, and Germans, and the Sudanic kingdoms of Africa depended on changes in the classical civilizations themselves. The decline of the great classical empires after the 2nd century C.E., then the new influences that helped reestablish vigorous societies in the same areas, had a vital spillover effect in northern Europe and Asia and in sub-Saharan Africa. This fact returns us to the classical centers, as they declined but also brought forth dynamic new forces capable of transforming wide stretches of the Old World.

Further Readings

The general process of cultural migration and the problems of interpreting archeological and linguistic evidence are among the subjects addressed in Pat Manning's *Migration and World History* (2004) and Irving Rouse's *Migrations in Prehistory* (1986), which includes excellent chapters on the Japanese and the Polynesians. Manning's *Migration in Modern World History, 1500–2000*, a CD-ROM (2000), is an invaluable resource for migration generally as well as for later eras.

The history, society, and geography of Africa are all treated in an informative way in Paul Bohannan and Philip Curtin, *Africa and the Africans* (1995). A very good introduction to and synthesis of Africa's ancient past are provided in Christopher Ehret, *The Civilizations of Africa* (2002); Joseph Harris, *Africans and Their History* (1998); James Newman, *The Peopling of Africa: A Geographic Interpretation* (1995); and John Ilife, *The Africans: The History of a Continent* (1995). Philip Curtin et al., eds., *African History: From Earliest Times to Independence* (1995), contains excellent chapters on various regions. Stuart Munro-Hay, *Aksum. An African Civilization of Late Antiquity* (1991) incorporates archaeological and numismatic evidence. Some of the basic texts from Axum translated into English are available in Stanley Burstein, *Ancient African Civilizations: Kush and Axum* (1997). Nehemia Levitzion and Jay Spaulding, *Medieval West Africa: Views from Arab Scholars and Merchants* (2003) provides basic sources in translation.

New work on the Indo-Europeans is found in J. P. Mallory, *In Search of the Indo-Europeans* (1989) and L. L. Cavalli-Sforza, *The Great Human Diasporas* (1995). Justine Davis Randers-Pehrson, *Barbarians and Romans: The Birth Struggle of Europe*, A.D. 400–700 (1983), gives a broad overview of the Germans and Slavs during this period. Tacitus' classic on the Germans is easily available in the translation by H. Mattingly, *The Agricola and the Germania* (1970).

Conrad Schirokauer's *A Brief History of Japanese Civilization* (1993) emphasizes Japan's cultural traditions. The fullest, but somewhat dated, account of early Japanese cultural development available in English is included in G. B. Sansom, *A History of Japan to 1334* (1961). Useful introductions to the early period can also be found in Mikiso Hane, *Pre-Modern Japan: An Historical Survey* (1990); E. O. Reischauer and Alfred M. Craig, *Japan: Story of a Nation* (1989); and (especially for political developments) John W. Hall, *Japan from Prehistory to Modern Times* (1970). The best introductions to society and culture in the early period are provided by G. B. Sansom, *Japan: A Short Cultural History* (1986); and H. Paul Varley, *Japanese Culture: A Short History* (2000).

Patrick Kirch and Jean-Louis Rallu, eds., *The Growth and Collapse of Pacific Island Societies* (2007) is based on recent archaeological findings. Tim Bayliss-Smith et al., *Islands, Islanders and the World* (1988), studies the impact of the Polynesian environment on its history. That approach also figures prominently in Jared Diamond, *Collapse* (2005), in his discussion of Easter Island. Kirch's *Gods and Fishhooks* (1985) explores the archeology of Hawaii. Marshall Sahlins, *Islands in History* (1985), has become a classic interpretation of Hawaiian culture at the moment of contact with Europe. Ann Salmond, *Aphrodite's Island. The European Discovery of Tahiti* (2009) recounts the contact in that Polynesian island. Janet Davidson's *Prehistory of New Zealand* (1987) and Davidson and D. C. Starzecka's *Maori Art and Culture* (1998) are authoritative studies of early Maori life. H. G. Robley's *Maori Tattooing* (2004) discusses this still-surviving Maori tradition. Classic accounts of Maori society and customs include Te Rangi Hiroa (Peter Buck), *The Coming of the Maori* (1949), and the works of Elsdon Best, especially *Some Aspects of Maori Myth and Religion* (1923). Patricia Ledyard's *The Tongan Past* (1999) is an accessible history of one of the world's oldest surviving monarchial traditions. William Mariner's experiences as the adopted son of a Tongan prince in 1806, recounted in *Tonga: Mariner's Account* (1991), holds a well-deserved place in the literature of cultural contact. Nicholas Thomas, *In Oceania. Visions, Artifacts, Histories* (1997).

Critical Thinking Questions

1. Discuss the causes of two of the following migrations: Bantu speakers throughout most of sub-Saharan Africa, the invasions by nomadic herders from Central Asia into China and Europe, and the spread of Polynesians through parts of the Pacific.

2. Compare the ways the China, India, and Rome spread aspects of their economic systems and cultures to neighboring peoples.

3. Why and how did peoples in Japan and Axum borrow from older civilization centers?

4. Compare the interactions of Germanic tribes with Rome to interactions between Japan and China.

10

The End of the Classical Era: World History in Transition, 200–700 C.E.

((Listen to Chapter 10
on MyHistoryLab

LEARNING OBJECTIVES

10.1 What were the main differences in the process of decline in classical China and in classical India? p. 214

10.2 What were the causes of decline in the Roman Empire? p. 218

10.3 How did the organization of Christianity reflect its complex relationships with the Roman Empire? p. 223

At the highpoint of the classical period, with the Han and Roman empires in full swing, the Indian Ocean provided a network of important contacts. The major civilizations did not depend on long-distance trade: Rome, China, and India were economically and culturally self-sufficient. But Roman fleets and Chinese ships regularly sailed the ocean, along with more local Persian, Arab, and Indonesian merchants. The Roman government actually arranged for archers on their convoys to beat back local pirates. Rome wanted spices and textiles from the region. The Chinese wanted exotic goods as well—one Han emperor sent a mission to India to acquire a rhinoceros.

Some types of cultural exchange also occurred in the Indian Ocean region, although historians are not sure how much. For example, Buddhism had established a number of institutions,

FIGURE **10.1** In the 12th-century Sicilian mosaic at left, Christ's head is surrounded by a halo, representing his holiness, and he is holding up his hand in a sign of blessing. The Buddha was also commonly depicted, as in the 6th-century Afghan painting at right, with a halo and with his hand raised in a sign of blessing. Scholars ponder whether these symbols of sacredness could have arisen independently in two very different cultures.

👁 Watch the Video Series on MyHistoryLab

**Learn about some key topics related to this chapter with the *MyHistoryLab Video Series:
Key Topics in World History***

rituals, and symbols prior to the rise of Christianity. These included the halo (technically, the nimbus) used in artistic representations of saints, the very idea of saints, monasteries, holy water, the five-chained censer to burn incense, and the hand blessing (Figure 10.1). Christianity would later develop versions of these same practices. Had these elements of Buddhism become familiar to early Christians as a result of trade (and some Buddhist missions to Persia)? We simply do not know, but the coincidences are striking. There was also movement in the other direction. Early Christians from the Middle East established at least one church for their community in India, and later Christian missionaries—including, according to legend, the apostle Thomas—went to India as well. Again, we do not know, although there is a tomb designated for Saint Thomas in southern India.

Trade and some cultural exchange raise a final question: What would happen when the decline of Rome and Han China opened the region to other initiatives? Trading opportunities still existed, but they now invited other participants. India was the first beneficiary. The Gupta Empire persisted for a century or more after Rome foundered. Indian merchants fanned out from the Persian Gulf to southeast Asia, as the Guptas encouraged business. Indian elites valued gold highly, which motivated much of their trade with southeast Asia. In return, they could offer fine cotton cloth. Indian prosperity reached new levels, and many new temples were built as one result. Indian influence helped expand Hinduism and, to a greater degree, Buddhism into southeast Asia.

The Gupta dynasty finally fell. Indian trading activity continued for a time, but there were new opportunities for Persians and Greeks (from the Eastern Roman empire) to rekindle competition for trade in the Indian Ocean. China would begin to reassert itself as well. When the dust settled from the long crisis of the classical world, the Indian Ocean was open to new claimants for trade supremacy. It would be the Arabs, previously confined to lesser commercial roles, including piracy, who would first meet this postclassical challenge. ∎

This chapter returns to a primary focus on the centers of classical civilization in Eurasia and north Africa. The end of the classical era is defined by changes in Asia, north Africa, and the Mediterranean, not the whole world. Nevertheless, the fading of the great classical empires had consequences beyond their borders. The resulting change in civilization boundaries unleashed new forces that affected sub-Saharan Africa, northern Europe, and other parts of Asia.

Three issues predominate. First, why did these civilizations decline? Invasions were an important cause. Nomadic forces accustomed to fighting on horseback had an advantage over the armies of the classical civilizations. But in their prime, the empires would have been able to turn the invaders back—so what else was going on? Second, why did different regions see different patterns of decline, with different results? And third, what was the significance of these developments—not just for the end of one period, but for the beginning of another? The rapid spread of world religions, as the empires faded, provides a vital part of the answer.

 Watch the **Video** on **MyHistoryLab**: Symbiosis: The Exchange of Languages, Goods, and Ideas in Central Asia (Al Andrea)

100 C.E.	200 C.E.	300 C.E.	400 C.E.	500 C.E.	600 C.E.
88 Beginning of Han decline **180 ff.** Beginning of Rome's decline; population decline **184** Daoist Yellow Turban rebellion	**220** Last Han emperor deposed; Time of Troubles begins; nomadic invasions in North China **231** First Germanic invasions of Roman Empire **284–305** Reign of Diocletian emperor	**300–700** Spread of Buddhism **312–337** Reign of Constantine; establishment of Eastern Roman Empire; toleration of Christianity **330–379** Basil organizes Eastern monasticism **354–430** Life of Augustine	**400–500** Decline of Buddhism in India; evolution of popular Hinduism **401 ff.** Increased Germanic invasions **410** Rome sacked by Visigoths under Alaric **450** Hun invasions begin **476** Last Roman emperor in West deposed **480–547** Life of Benedict, founder of Western monasticism	**527–565** Reign of Justinian, Eastern emperor **c. 540** Collapse of Gupta dynasty **589–618** Sui dynasty	**618** Tang dynasty **606–647** Loose empire under Harsha in India **610** Beginning of Islam **657 ff.** Rajput (regional princes) dominant in India; periodic clashes with Islamic armies in northwest

UPHEAVALS IN EASTERN AND SOUTHERN ASIA

10.1 What were the main differences in the process of decline in classical China and in classical India?

The Han dynasty declined first, opening a period of significant change in China. Gupta India was the last classical empire to decline, with definite but more limited results in south Asia than in China.

Symptoms of classical decline first appeared in China. After the reign of Wudi, the Han dynasty briefly faltered, then seemed to recover, and by about 80 C.E. the central government was about as effective and the economy about as prosperous as before. The Chinese launched a new expansion campaign in central Asia. After about 88 C.E., however, the quality of the emperors began to decline. Most reigns were short and full of plotting; empresses and officials joined the fray (see Chapter 4). This set the stage for more fundamental problems.

Decline and Fall in Han China

The deteriorations of the late Han dynasty operated on several levels. Assassinations of and by bureaucrats competing for power at the top occurred on several occasions. At a basic level, conditions among the peasantry began to deteriorate. Large landowners, always powerful under the Han, grew more so, avoiding taxes and forming private armies. Taxes on peasants increased, and many farmers were forced into serfdom, where they had to provide labor and turn over much of their own produce to the landlords. Social protest increased.

Yellow Turbans Chinese Daoists who launched a revolt in 184 C.E. in China promising a golden age to be brought about by divine magic.

Peasant unrest culminated in a great revolutionary effort led by the Daoists in 184 C.E. Leaders called the **Yellow Turbans** promised a golden age to be brought about by divine magic. Han generals suppressed this rebellion but set themselves up as regional rulers, a clear sign of the collapse of the central state. The last Han emperor was deposed in 220 C.E. China was divided into three kingdoms for several decades, but finally even these began to collapse. For several centuries, China was ruled by the land-owning class, operating beyond the control of formal government. Southern and northern China also pulled apart, with the south maintaining higher levels of economic growth and continuing to absorb tribal peoples into Chinese culture.

No firm dynasties could be established in this 350-year period, although there were short-lived regimes in the south. Northern China was pressed by invasions from central Asia. Nomadic peoples had been incorporated into Chinese armies, much as later Roman rulers tried to use Germanic troops, but as the government deteriorated, the nomads broke loose and began to invade the Middle Kingdom. Several nomad-dominated states were formed, but none lasted long. Internal warfare became endemic in this unusually long breakdown in Chinese stability.

Into this chaos came the new fascination with Buddhism, which offered spiritual solace in response to political uncertainty and economic distress. Also, like Christianity in Europe, it provided cultural cohesion at a time when political links had broken down. Imported from India—the only case until modern times when China borrowed a major idea from abroad—and disseminated by silk merchants and missionaries, Buddhism spread among both the Chinese and the nomadic warriors, helping gradually to mold a common culture in which Chinese ingredients predominated. Buddhist influence also brought to China a new impetus for art and sculpture, altering the established styles and themes.

Buddhism came under periodic attack by Daoist regional rulers, but the faith reached throughout China by the 5th century C.E., and it spread rapidly for many decades (Map 10.1). Buddhist monasteries for women as well as men gained ground. Many Chinese monks made pilgrimages to India, and Buddhist literature and philosophy spread widely. Chinese Buddhists blended practices from many Indian Buddhist sects, using meditation, prayers, and devotional exercises. The Document section shows what benefits Chinese converts might expect from their new religion. The Chinese imposed some of their own values on Buddhism as well. For instance, they insisted on the importance of forming families so that the ancestral line could be preserved. Typically, as a result, only second sons became Buddhist monks, and first sons maintained the family responsibilities. Buddhists were also pressed into political loyalty, paying taxes to the government and submitting to government regulations on the formation of monasteries.

Buddhism had a fascinating impact on women in China among families who converted. On the face of things, Buddhism should have disrupted China's firm belief in patriarchal power, because Buddhists believed that women had souls along with men. Indeed, some individual women in China won great attention because of their spiritual accomplishments. But Chinese culture generated changes in Buddhism within the empire. Buddhist phrases like "husband supports wife" were changed to "husband controls his wife," while "the wife comforts the husband"—another Buddhist phrase from India—became "the wife reveres her husband." Finally, many men valued pious Buddhist wives, because they might benefit the family's salvation and because Buddhist activity could keep their wives busy, calm, and out of mischief. Buddhism could be meaningful to Chinese women, but it did not really challenge patriarchy. A biography of one Buddhist wife put it this way: "At times of crisis she could be tranquil and satisfied with her fate, not letting outside things agitate her mind."

The growing Buddhist influence also had an impact on Daoism, forcing greater formalization of Daoist doctrine and more efforts to reach the common people. Many Chinese found great similarities between the two faiths, although Buddhism continued to have the advantage of offering a clearer doctrine of personal salvation—the chance of holy life after death—and a firmer set of personal ethics. Daoist leaders developed a variety of practices, including meditation and dietary restrictions, that might bring immortality. Popular Daoism, mixing Daoist beliefs with an animistic pantheon of many gods, tended to hold that good or evil done in this life would be compensated by heavens or hells hereafter. Popular Daoism also provided priests and shamans who practiced faith healing to cure disease. These ramifications of Daoism appealed to the Chinese peasantry, lasting in some parts of eastern Asia even today.

Confucianism lost ground during this confused period in Chinese history, eclipsed by the more otherworldly interests. But the legacy of Chinese institutions and secular beliefs did not disappear, and as nomadic invaders were partly converted to Chinese ways, the opportunity for political revival reemerged toward the end of the 6th century. A series of strong rulers in the north drove out nomadic bands and then merged, under a general of Chinese-Turkish background, into a new **Sui** dynasty. Under this brief dynasty, northern China was united and south China was reconquered. The government built new canals and repaired the Great Wall. Attempts to expand into Korea and central Asia brought financial collapse, along with new rebellions, and only in 618 C.E. was the more durable **Tang** dynasty established. The time of troubles had ended. New artistic works reflected renewed political integration (Figure 10.2).

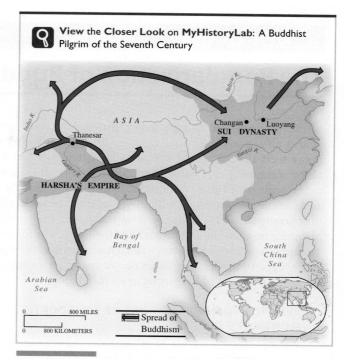

View the **Closer Look** on **MyHistoryLab:** A Buddhist Pilgrim of the Seventh Century

MAP **10.1 Asia, c. 600** C.E. Buddhism spread from India to China and other parts of Asia at the end of the classical era.

Sui [sway] Dynasty that succeeded the Han in China; emerged from strong rulers in northern China; united all of northern China and reconquered southern China.

Tang Dynasty that succeeded the Sui in 618 C.E.; more stable than previous dynasty.

DOCUMENT

The Popularization of Buddhism

CHINESE BUDDHISM, UNLIKE MOST CHINESE BELIEFS, spread among all regions and social groups. Although it divided into many sects that disagreed over details of theology and rituals by commenting on earlier Buddhist scriptures (the Sutras), many ordinary Chinese believers cared little for such details and were more concerned with direct spiritual benefits. Often they arranged to have Buddhist sermons copied, as a means of obtaining merit, while adding a note of their own. The following passages come from such notes, written mainly in the 6th century. They suggest the various reasons people might go through the challenging process of converting to a new religion.

RECORDED ON THE 15TH DAY OF THE FOURTH MONTH OF 531.

The Buddhist lay disciple Yuan Rong—having lived in this degenerate era for many years, fearful for his life, and yearning for home—now makes a donation of a thousand silver coins to the Three Jewels [the Buddha, the Law, and the Monastic Order]. This donation is made in the name of the Celestial King Vaisravana. In addition, he makes a donation of a thousand to ransom himself and his wife and children [from their earthly existence], a thousand more to ransom his servants, and a thousand more to ransom his domestic animals. This money is to be used for copying sutras. It is accompanied by the prayer that the Celestial King may attain Buddhahood; that the disciple's family, servants, and animals may be blessed with long life, may attain enlightenment, and may all be permitted to return to the capital.

DATED THE 29TH DAY OF THE FOURTH MONTH OF 550.

Happiness is not fortuitous: pray for it and it will respond. Results are not born of thin air: pay heed to causes and results will follow. This explains how the Buddhist disciple and nun Daorong—because her conduct in her previous life was not correct—came to be born in her present form, a woman, vile and unclean.

Now if she does not honor the awesome decree of Buddha, how can future consequences be favorable for her? Therefore, having cut down her expenditures on food and clothing, she reverently has had the Nirvana Sutra copied once. She prays that those who read it carefully will be exalted in mind to the highest realms and that those who communicate its meaning will cause others to be so enlightened.

She also prays that in her present existence she will have no further sickness or suffering, that her parents in seven other incarnations (who have already died or will die in the future) and her present family and close relatives may experience joy in the four realms [earth, water, fire, and air], and that whatever they seek may indeed come to pass. Finally, she prays that all those endowed with knowledge may be included within this prayer.

RECORDED ON THE 28TH DAY OF THE FIFTH MONTH OF 583.

The Army Superintendent, Song Shao, having suffered the heavy sorrow of losing both his father and mother, made a vow on their behalf to read one section each of [many] sutras. He prays that the spirits of his parents will someday reach the Pure Land [paradise] and will thus be forever freed from the three unhappy states of existence and the eight calamities and that they may eternally listen to the Buddha's teachings.

He also prays that the members of his family, both great and small, may find happiness at will, that blessings may daily rain down upon them while hardships disperse like clouds. He prays that the imperial highways may be open and free of bandits, that the state may be preserved from pestilence, that wind and rain may obey their proper seasons, and that all suffering creatures may quickly find release. May all these prayers be granted!

The preceding incantation has been translated and circulated.

If this incantation is recited 7, 14, or 21 times daily (after having cleansed the mouth in the morning with a willow twig, having scattered flowers and incense before the image of Buddha, having knelt and joined the palms of the hands), the four grave sins, the five wicked acts, and all other transgressions will be wiped away. The present body will not be afflicted by untimely calamities; one will at last be born into the realm of immeasurably long life; and reincarnation in the female form will be escaped forever.

Now, the Sanskrit text has been reexamined and the Indian Vinaya monk Buddhasangha and other monks have been consulted; thus we know that the awesome power of this incantation is beyond comprehension. If it is recited 100 times in the evening and again at noon, it will destroy the four grave sins and five wicked acts. It will pluck out the very roots of sin and will ensure rebirth in the Western Regions. If, with sincerity of spirit, one is able to complete 200,000 recitations, perfect intelligence will be born and there will be no relapses. If 300,000 recitations are completed, one will see Amita Buddha face to face and will certainly be reborn into the Pure Land of tranquility and bliss.

Copied by the disciple of pure faith Sun Szu-chung on the 8th day of the fourth month of 720.

QUESTIONS

- Why did Buddhism spread widely in China by the 6th century?
- How did popular Buddhism compare with original Buddhist teachings (see Chapter 6)?
- How did Chinese Buddhists define holy life?
- How do these documents suggest some of the troubles China faced after the collapse of the Han dynasty?

The decline and fall of the Han had thus disrupted Chinese civilization and opened it to new religious influences. But old values survived as well. Even the competing landlords retained some training in Confucianism and with that training the idea of a united empire. With its greater cultural homogeneity established in the classical era, China differed markedly from the Mediterranean, where Christianity and Islam came close to displacing older philosophical concerns while challenging earlier political loyalties. Many nomadic invaders imitated Chinese styles and thus encouraged the revival of older political habits.

The End of the Guptas: Decline in India

The decline of classical civilization in India was less drastic than the collapse of Han China in that India had not depended so heavily on political structures to hold its civilization together. Yet the Gupta collapse left durable traces in later Indian history, as political unity became more difficult to achieve. The high point of Gupta rule came under Chandragupta II early in the 5th century, but his immediate successors managed to remain prosperous. India about 450 C.E. probably was the most stable and peaceful area in the world. However, in 440 C.E., the nomadic Huns began a series of invasions that gradually reduced the empire's strength. The Gupta pattern of somewhat decentralized rule, whereby vassal princes were treated as partial allies rather than subject to direct central administration, made response to invasion more difficult. The Huns controlled much of northwestern India—the typical invasion route of the subcontinent—by 500 C.E. By this time, the quality of Gupta kings was also diminishing, and this added to the problem (see Chapter 6). It was a regional prince, **Harsha** Vardharna, not the Guptas themselves, who broke the hold of the Huns in the northwest about 530 C.E., and the Guptas were too weak to restore their claims. The dynasty collapsed entirely about 550 C.E.

A few echoes of Gupta splendor were heard during the 7th century. Harsha, a descendant of the Guptas through his grandmother, established a loose empire across northern India between 616 and 657. But he died without heirs, and his empire broke up again. From this point onward, until a better-organized series of outside invasions began, northern India was politically divided. Regional dynasties occasionally were powerful, but few lasted very long. A section of northern India was invaded by Tang Chinese-led Tibetan troops, who captured a young Indian prince and took him back to the Chinese capital in 648. This was the first and, until our own era, the only military clash between China and India. The northern regional princes, collectively called the **Rajput** emphasized military prowess. Although there were many local wars, few political events had great significance.

In this localized framework, Indian culture continued to evolve. Buddhism declined steadily in India. The Guptas had preferred Hinduism, and the Hun invaders disliked the otherworldly tone of Buddhism as well. Military-minded princes had little sympathy for the Buddhist principles of calm and contemplation. Hindu beliefs gained ground, converting the Hun leaders, among other groups. Within Hinduism, worship of a mother goddess, **Devi**, spread widely, which encouraged a new popular emotionalism in religious ritual. In essence, India partially redefined its core culture by emphasizing the Hindu strain more clearly while relying heavily on cultural cohesion at a time when political life became more difficult. The reassertion of Hinduism also promoted the caste system, now

View the **Closer Look** on **MyHistoryLab**: A Tang Painting of the Goddess of Mercy

FIGURE **10.2** Stone relief from the tomb of the Tang emperor Taizong (7th century), showing one of his warhorses attended by a bearded "barbarian" groom. How does this relief suggest the barbarian threat was being handled after China's crisis period had ended?

(Relief of Emperor T'ai Tsung's Horse, "Autumn Dew." The University Museum, University of Pennsylvania.)

Harsha Ruler who followed Guptas in India; briefly constructed a loose empire in northern India between 616 and 657 C.E.

Rajput [RAHJ-poot] Regional princes in western India; emphasized military control of their regions.

Devi Mother goddess within Hinduism; widely spread following collapse of Guptas; encouraged new emotionalism in religious ritual.

Read the Document on MyHistoryLab: From the Periplus of the Erythraean Sea: Travel and Trade in the Indian Ocean

MAP 10.2 Indian Ocean Trading Routes in the Classical Period These routes show the surprising range of trading contacts with India at their center, from Persia, the Roman Empire and Africa in the west to various parts of southeast and eastern Asia to the east.

spreading to southern India. The number and complexity of jati (JAH-tee), or castes, increased as invaders were assimilated into the system, but the basic principles remained.

India's economic activity also remained strong, although in periods of outright invasion there were new hardships. Here too, Indian civilization did not collapse to the extent of Han China or the western Mediterranean. Indeed, the decades after the fall of the Guptas saw new outreach in trade and even some conquest by southern Tamil kingdoms, which were trying to establish firmer strongholds along the Indian Ocean in southeast Asia (Map 10.2).

Although Indian civilization largely maintained its position, albeit with a more diverse political lineup, another threat came after 600 C.E. from the new Middle Eastern religion of **Islam** (see Chapters 11 and 12). At first, India's contacts with this new force were limited. Arab armies, fighting under the banner of Islam, reached India's northwestern frontier during the 7th century, and although there was initially little outright conquest, Islam won some converts in the north. By the 8th century, Islamic competition also began to hit India's international economic position. Arab traders soon took control of the Indian Ocean from Tamil merchants and reduced India's commercial strength.

THE DECLINE AND FALL OF THE ROMAN EMPIRE

> The decline of the Roman Empire, in between the Han and Gupta declines, was particularly severe.

10.2 What were the causes of decline in the Roman Empire?

Signs of decay at various levels began to emerge in the Roman Empire in the late 2nd century. Population size declined as birth rates no longer kept pace with mortality rates, and it became more difficult to recruit effective armies. Political signs included the greater brutality and arbitrariness of many later Roman emperors—victims, according to one commentator at the time, of "lustful and cruel habits." Tax collection became increasingly difficult as residents of the empire fell on hard times. The governor of Egypt complained that "the once numerous inhabitants of the aforesaid villages have now been reduced to a few, because some have fled in poverty and others have died . . . and for this reason we are in danger owing to impoverishment of having to abandon the tax-collectorship."

Islam Major world religion having its origins in 610 C.E. in the Arabian peninsula; meaning literally submission; based on prophecy of Muhammad.

Wide-Ranging Signs of Decline

Above all there were the human symptoms. Inscriptions on Roman tombstones increasingly ended with the motto "I was not, I was, I am not, I have no more desires," suggesting despair. As the structures of the empire deteriorated, meaning in life became harder to find, and this mood made efforts at structural revival more difficult. The signs of change in the quality of political and economic life began to emerge after about 180 C.E., at which point the empire's geographic expansion had slightly receded from its high point. Unlike Han China or Gupta India, the Roman Empire had depended extensively on expansion, not only to provide prestige but to recruit the necessary slaves. With the empire's boundaries now pushed to the limits it could support, Rome had to restructure its labor policies on the great commercial estates and in the mines. This restructuring reduced economic vitality and market production.

Initially more pressing were the internal issues of politics and population. Government leadership became a problem. Growing political confusion, including disputes over how emperors should be appointed, produced a series of weak rulers and many battles over succession to the throne. Intervention of the army in the selection of emperors, as the army became an increasingly separate institution, complicated political life and contributed to the worsening of rule.

Causes of Roman Decline

The decline of the Roman state raises the question of human agency: When things go badly in a society, are weak leaders an accident, causing growing disarray, or do larger trends cause the selection of inferior rulers? Still more important in this decline was a series of plagues that swept over the empire at the end of the 2nd century C.E. These plagues decimated the population and severely disrupted economic life. Some authorities argue that Rome's urban population also suffered lead poisoning from the pipes leading from the aqueducts, which further weakened people and reduced their numbers. Lower population added to the problems of finding labor. With recruitment of troops becoming more difficult, the empire had to hire Germanic soldiers to guard its frontiers. The need to pay troops added to the demands on the state's budget, just as declining production cut into tax revenues and the absence of new conquests cut into other rewards for soldiers. Environmental deterioration in north Africa reduced grain supply and hurt the Roman tax base; overuse had reduced soil fertility and advanced desertification.

This may be the key to the process of decline: a set of general problems, including a cycle of plagues that could not be prevented, resulting in a spiral that steadily worsened, particularly as the selection of emperors deteriorated. But there is another side to Rome's downfall, although whether it was a cause or result of the initial difficulties is hard to say. Rome's upper classes became steadily more pleasure-seeking and individualistic, turning away from the concepts of civil duty that had characterized the republic and early empire. Cultural life decayed. Aside from some truly creative Christian writers, the fathers of Western theology, there was very little sparkle to the art or literature of the later empire. The Romans wrote textbooks about rhetoric instead of displaying rhetorical talent in actual political life; they wrote simple compendiums about animals or geometry that barely captured the essentials of what earlier intellectuals had known, and they often added superstitious beliefs that previous generations would have scorned. This cultural decline was not clearly caused by disease or economic collapse; it began in some ways before these larger problems hit. Something was happening to the Roman elite, perhaps because of the deadening hand of authoritarian political rule, perhaps because of a new commitment to luxuries and sensual indulgence. Military service became less attractive to the upper class, which forced the recruitment of paid soldiers from groups such as the Germanic tribes along the northern borders of the empire (Figure 10.3).

View the **Closer Look** on **MyHistoryLab:** Tetrarchy: The Division of the Roman Empire under Diocletian

FIGURE **10.3** This plaque portrays the Roman general Stilicho with his wife, Serena, and their son. Stilicho's energy and ability allowed him to become Master of Soldiers and Consul of Rome. But the facts that his father had been a Vandal and that he himself was not a Christian made him vulnerable to the rumors spread by his enemies, who said that he was intriguing against the interests of the empire and intended to place his own son on the throne. In 408 he was imprisoned and his son, Eucherius, was murdered.

The Process of Roman Decline

As the quality of imperial rule declined and as life became more dangerous and economic survival more precarious, many farmers clustered around the protection of large landlords, surrendering full control of their plots of land, hoping for military and judicial protection. The decentralization of political and economic authority, which was greatest in the western, or European, portions of the empire, foreshadowed the manorial system of Europe in the Middle Ages. The estate system gave great political power to the landlords and could provide some local stability. But it weakened the emperor's power and tended to drive the economy away from the elaborate trade patterns of Mediterranean civilization in its heyday. Many estates attempted to produce almost everything needed on the spot. Trade and production declined further, causing tax revenues to drop and cities to shrink. The empire was locked in a vicious circle in which the responses to initial deterioration merely lessened the chances of recovery.

Diocletian Roman emperor from 284 to 305 C.E.; restored later empire by improved administration and tax collection.

Constantine Roman emperor from 312 to 337 C.E.; established second capital at Constantinople; attempted to use religious force of Christianity to unify empire spiritually.

 Read the Document on MyHistoryLab: Eusebius of Caesarea, selections from *Life of Constantine*

Some later emperors tried to reverse the flow. **Diocletian**, who ruled from 284 to 305 C.E., tightened up the administration of the empire and tried to improve tax collection. Regulation of the dwindling economy increased. Diocletian also tried to monopolize political loyalty, increasing the pressure to worship the emperor as god. This was what prompted him to persecute Christians with particular viciousness, for they would not give Caesar preference over their god. The emperor **Constantine**, who ruled from 312 to 337, tried other experiments. He set up a second capital city, Constantinople, to regulate the eastern half of the empire more efficiently. He tried to use the religious force of Christianity to unify the empire spiritually, extending toleration and adopting it as his own faith. These measures were not without result. The eastern empire, ruled from Constantinople (formerly the Greek colony of Byzantium, now the Turkish city of Istanbul), remained an effective political and economic unit. Christianity spread under official sponsorship, although some new problems were attached to success.

But none of these measures revived the empire as a whole. Human agency could have real impact, setting new forces in motion, but it could not reverse basic trends. Division merely made the weakness of the western half worse. Attempts to regulate the economy reduced economic initiative and lowered production; ultimately, tax revenues declined once again. The army deteriorated further. When the Germanic invasions began in earnest in the 400s, there was little resistance. Many peasants, burdened

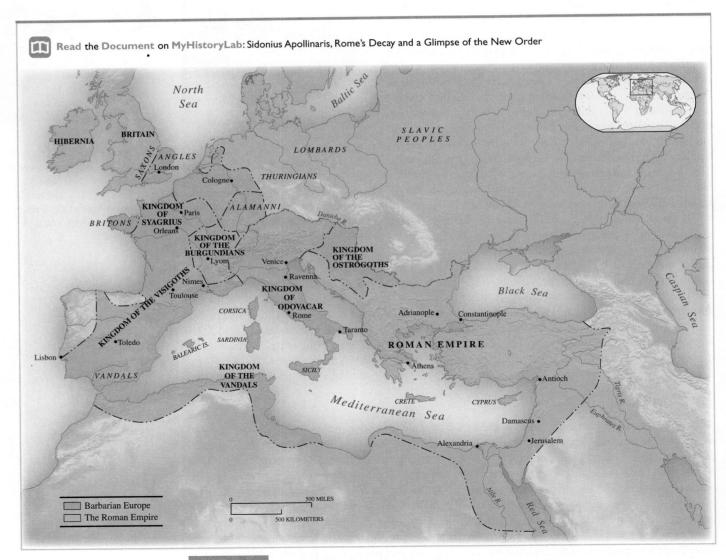

Read the Document on MyHistoryLab: Sidonius Apollinaris, Rome's Decay and a Glimpse of the New Order

- Barbarian Europe
- The Roman Empire

MAP **10.3 Germanic Kingdoms After the Invasions** Nomadic tribes converged mainly on the western part of the Roman Empire, invading Rome and its European outposts. Was this the cause or the result of the fact that the western portion of the empire was weaker than the eastern?

by the social and economic pressures of the decaying empire, actually welcomed the barbarians. A priest noted, "In all districts taken over by the Germans, there is one desire among all the Romans, that they should never again find it necessary to pass under Roman jurisdiction." German kingdoms were set up in many parts of the empire by 425, and the last Roman emperor in the West was displaced in 476 (Map 10.3). The Germanic invaders numbered, at most, 5 percent of the population of the empire, but so great was the earlier decline that this small, uncoordinated force put an end to one of the world's great political structures.

Attila the Hun

In Europe, the most famous invader was Attila the Hun, who lived from 406 to 453. Attila led the nomadic Huns, fighting with great fierceness. He organized a loose kingdom that ran from Germany to China. Known by Christians as the "scourge of God," Attila invaded what is now France in 451. Both Romans and Germanic tribes resisted him. An end run into Italy brought him to Rome, where the pope pleaded with him to spare the city—to no avail. Attila highlighted and contributed to Rome's collapse. His own kingdom fell after his death. But his success called attention to the importance of cavalry in warfare, something the Greeks and Romans, with their preference for infantry, had largely ignored.

Patterns of Decline?

The fall of Rome echoes some of the same questions that apply to China and India. Do civilizations inevitably fall, or at least undergo cycles of decline? When the collapse involves outside invading forces, does one look primarily at internal decay? Germanic or central Asian invaders had a few military advantages. Their reliance on hunting and herding gave them some skills, including excellent equestrian skills in the case of the Huns, that allowed them to overrun more populous peasant settlements where people were unaccustomed to battle. From their contacts on the Roman borders, the Germans had also learned new organizational methods that made them a more formidable force. But there is no question that in their glory days, the professional armies of Rome or Han China could have contained the invaders; it was internal weakness that allowed the invaders to have such disruptive effects. Rome seemed headed for downfall even before the Germanic intruders dealt the final blows. At the same time, the luxurious living of the upper classes and the impressive reputation of the classical empires helped lure the invaders in.

Results of the Fall of Rome

The collapse of Rome echoed through the later history of Europe and the Middle East. Rome's fall split the unity of the Mediterranean lands that had been won through Hellenistic culture and then the Roman Empire itself. This was one sign that the end of the Roman Empire was more serious than the displacement of the last classical dynasties in India and China. Greece and Rome, unlike China, had not produced the shared political culture and bureaucratic traditions that could allow revival after a period of chaos. Nor had Mediterranean civilization, for all its vitality, generated a common religion that reached deeply enough, or satisfied enough needs, to maintain unity amid political fragmentation,

FIGURE 10.4 The Chora Church in Istanbul, Turkey, is one of the finest Byzantine churches still in existence. Its interior is covered with exquisite mosaics and frescos depicting biblical scenes. For almost 500 years, while the church was used as a mosque, these great works of art were covered by a layer of plaster due to Islam's prohibition against images. After World War II, the art was restored and the building opened to the public as a museum.

as in India. Such religions reached the Mediterranean world as Rome fell, but they came too late to save the empire, and they produced a deep rift between Christian and Muslim that has not been healed to this day.

In effect, the fall of Rome divided the Mediterranean world into three zones, the starting point of three distinct civilizations that developed in later centuries. In the northeastern part of the empire, centered in Constantinople, the empire in a sense did not fall. Classical civilization was more deeply entrenched there than in some of the western European portions of the empire, and there were fewer pressures from invaders (Figure 10.4). Emperors continued to rule Greece, other parts of southeast Europe, and the northern Middle East. This eastern empire, later known as the **Byzantine empire**, was a product of the Hellenistic era and late imperial Rome, and it demonstrated great survival power (see Chapter 14).

Byzantine empire Eastern half of Roman Empire following collapse of western half of old empire; retained Mediterranean culture, particularly Greek; later lost Palestine, Syria, and Egypt to Islam; capital at Constantinople.

THINKING HISTORICALLY

The Problem of Decline and Fall

EXPLAINING THE DECLINE OF CIVILIZATIONS HAS fascinated observers since civilizations began to decline. As Rome's vitality ebbed, many writers tried to figure out what was going on. Christian theologians such as Augustine wrote massive tomes to prove that Christianity was not to blame; some non-Christian philosophers argued that the religion's otherworldly emphasis had sapped Rome's strength. Both Christian and pagan writers worried that the cause of Rome's collapse was immorality, a loss of the virtues of self-denial and devotion to the common good that had made Rome great in the first place. Many of these arguments have been taken up by world historians in more recent times. In the 18th century, Edward Gibbon, a British philosopher-historian, returned to the attack on Christianity, holding that it contradicted key Roman qualities of military valor and civic devotion and so brought the empire's fall. Several 20th-century historians argued that Rome's moral decline—the growing self-indulgence and pleasure-seeking of the aristocracy and the urban masses—led the people to accept forms of government in which they no longer participated. This argument is interesting because it corresponds to some undeniable changes in the culture of the later Roman Empire. It also has won attention because of anxieties contemporary Westerners have about their own society: too materialistic, too devoted to sexual indulgence, too dominated by the tastes of the masses. Perceived similarities with the failing Roman Empire play a significant role in current concerns about moral decline.

Another approach to the problem of decline argues that it is almost inevitable. Civilizations, like individual humans, go through a period of vigor and reach the mature height of their powers but then begin to lose their grip and deteriorate. At the civilization level, this means that government officials focus on protecting their position rather than seeking new ways to

Another approach to the problem of decline argues that it is almost inevitable.

do things; that upper classes become soft and selfish; and that territories expand farther than a society can control, leaving supply routes and defenses overextended and vulnerable to attack. An American diplomatic historian, Paul Kennedy, has argued that this last process of overextension, which reduces internal economic vitality through its sheer costliness, occurred not only in Rome but in 19th-century Britain and most recently in the United States and Russia.

World history certainly lends itself to a search for patterns in the life cycles of civilizations. But it also generates some warnings. Civilization decline does not occur in the same ways in all cases. The result is not necessarily the death of a civilization but rather a period of regrouping, after which the civilization may reemerge with new combinations of tradition and innovation. Rome's fall, after all, was unusual at the end of the classical era and really occurred only in the western portion of the empire. Eastern Rome remained highly civilized and successful. China and India, although not unchanged by the decline of the great classical empires, did not perish as civilizations. So the question of decline must be phrased carefully, with awareness of the diverse examples world history yields.

QUESTIONS

- How great a role did moral decline play in the collapse of the classical empires?
- What historical "laws" accurately describe what happened not only in Rome but in Gupta India and Han China?
- Why can it be argued that the eastern part of the Roman Empire did not decline?
- Why was Rome more vulnerable than India, and why was western Rome more vulnerable than the eastern Mediterranean?

The second zone that devolved from Rome's fall was more seriously disrupted, although more in political terms than in economic or cultural terms. This zone consisted of north Africa and the southeastern shores of the Mediterranean. The eastern empire held its ground briefly but then pulled back. Several regional kingdoms briefly succeeded the empire. Although Christianity spread in the area—indeed, one of the greatest Christian theologians, Augustine, was a bishop in north Africa—it was not as uniformly triumphant as in the Byzantine empire or western Europe. Furthermore, differing beliefs and doctrines soon split north African Christianity from the larger branches, producing most notably the Coptic church in Egypt, which still survives as a Christian minority in that country, and another branch in Ethiopia. Soon much of north Africa was filled with the still newer doctrines of Islam and a new Arab empire.

Finally, there was the western part of the empire: Italy, Spain, and points north. Here is where Rome's fall not only shattered unities but reduced the level of civilization itself. Crude, regional Germanic kingdoms grew in parts of Italy, France, and elsewhere. The only clearly vital force in this region was not Roman tradition but the spread of Christianity. Even Christianity could not sustain sophisticated literature, art, or even theology, however. In Rome's collapse, cities and commercial activity also declined.

THE DEVELOPMENT AND SPREAD OF WORLD RELIGIONS

10.3 | How did the organization of Christianity reflect its complex relationships with the Roman Empire?

As with the period of chaos in China, Rome's decline encouraged vital new religious influences, in this case to societies around the Mediterranean. Christianity moved westward from its original center in the Middle East, just as in Asia Buddhism was spreading east from India. Although initially less significant than Buddhism in terms of numbers of converts, Christianity ultimately became one of the two largest world faiths. It played a direct role in forming the postclassical civilizations of eastern and western Europe.

The newly expanding religions (including Islam soon afterward) all emphasized intense devotion and piety, stressing the importance of spiritual concerns beyond the daily cares of life. All three offered the hope of a better existence after this life ended, and all responded to new political instability and to the growing poverty of many people in various parts of the classical world. All, finally, promoted active missionary efforts, seeking to spread their ideas of religious truth across cultural and political boundaries.

> World religions are those religions capable of spreading across political and cultural boundaries. Although both Buddhism and Christianity had started earlier—Buddhism indeed much earlier—the religions spread more rapidly as the empires faded.

Christianity and Buddhism Compared

Christianity resembled Buddhism in important ways. It could stress the unimportance of things of this world, urging a focus on spiritual destiny and divinity. Not surprisingly, Christianity, like Buddhism, produced an important monastic movement, in which people seeking holiness came together in groups to live a spiritual life and serve their religion. Christianity resembled the version of Buddhism that spread to China (and later Korea and Japan) by stressing the possibility of an afterlife and the role holy leaders could play in helping to attain it.

The Chinese version of Buddhism, called **Mahayana**, or the Greater Vehicle, placed considerable emphasis on Buddha as god or savior. Statues of the Buddha as god violated the earlier Buddhist hostility to religious images, but they emphasized the religion as a channel of salvation (Figure 10.5). Well-organized temples, with priests and rituals, also helped bring religious solace to ordinary people in east Asia. The idea developed also that Buddhist holy men, or **bodhisattvas** built up such spiritual merit that their prayers, even after death, could aid people and allow them to achieve some holiness. These were people who had achieved enlightenment, thereby breaking the cycle of reincarnation, but chose to return to earth to help others do the same thing. Christianity in many respects moved in similar directions. It also came to emphasize salvation, with well-organized rituals. Religious images, though contrary to Jewish beliefs against idol worship, helped focus popular belief in most versions of Christianity. Holy men and women, sometimes granted the title **saints** after their deaths, were

Mahayana Chinese version of Buddhism; placed considerable emphasis on Buddha as god or savior.

bodhisattvas [boh-dih-SAHT-vuh] Buddhist holy men and women; built up spiritual merits during their lifetimes; prayers even after death could aid people to achieve reflected holiness.

saints Holy men and women, often martyrs, who were revered in Christianity as models of Christian lifestyles; built up treasury of merit that could be tapped by more ordinary Christians.

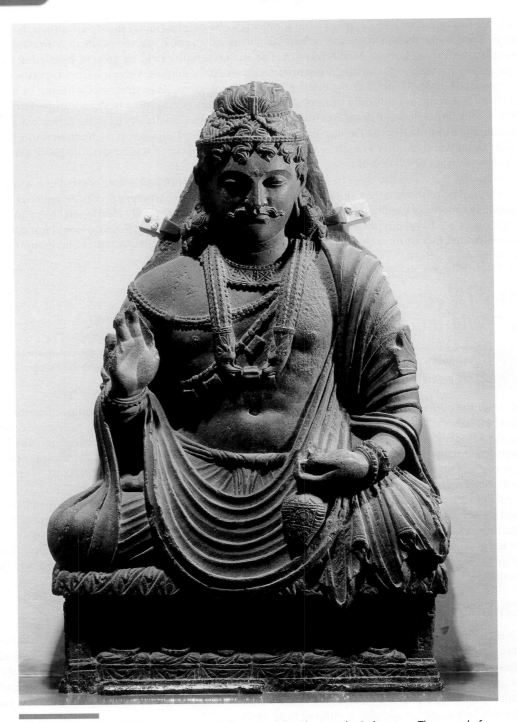

FIGURE **10.5** This sculpture of Maitreya, the future Buddha, dates to the 3rd century. The spread of Buddhism produced major new themes in Chinese art, many of which focused on stylized figures of the Buddha himself. The Buddha became an object of worship in this process, with statues great and small conveying his majesty.

revered because their spiritual attainments could lend merit to the strivings of more ordinary people. The broad similarities between Christianity and the evolving Buddhism of east Asia remind us of the common processes at work as new religions spread amid the ruins of great empires.

Yet Christianity had a flavor of its own. More than any of the forms of Buddhism, it emphasized church organization and structure, copying the example of the Roman Empire. It also placed greater value on missionary activity and widespread conversions, believing that error must be actively opposed in God's name. More perhaps than any other major religion—certainly more than the contemplative and tolerant Buddhism—Christianity stressed its possession of exclusive truth and its intolerance of competing beliefs. Such fierce confidence was not the least of the reasons for the new religion's success.

Early Christianity

Christianity began as part of a Jewish reform movement. Initially, there seems to have been no intent to found a new religion. After Jesus' crucifixion, the disciples expected his imminent return and with it the end of the world. Only gradually, when the Second Coming did not happen, did the disciples begin to fan out and, through preaching, pick up supporters in various parts of the Roman Empire.

The message of Jesus and his disciples seemed clear. There was a single God who loved humankind despite earthly sin. A virtuous life should be dedicated to the worship of God and fellowship with other believers. Worldly concerns were secondary, and a life of poverty might be most conducive to holiness. God sent Jesus, called Christ (from the Greek word *Christos*, "God's anointed"), to preach his holy word and, through his sacrifice, to prepare for the possibility of an afterlife of heavenly communion with God. Belief, good works, and discipline of fleshly concerns would lead toward heaven; rituals, such as commemorating Christ's Last Supper with wine and bread, would promote the same goal.

This message spread at an opportune time. The official religion of the Greeks and Romans had long seemed rather sterile, particularly to many of the poor. The Christian emphasis on the beauty of poverty and the spiritual equality of all people, plus the fervor of the early Christians and the satisfying rituals they provided, gained growing attention. The wide reach of the Roman Empire made it easy for Christian missionaries to travel through Europe and the Middle East and spread the new word. Then, when conditions began to deteriorate in the empire, the solace of this otherworldly religion won even more converts.

Paul of Tarsus (c. 10–67 C.E.) was a key Christian leader. Initially a Jewish rabbi, he was hostile to Christians as heretics. But on a journey to try to round up the Christians in Damascus, a vision of Jesus came to him. He became an ardent Christian missionary and contributed to several adjustments in Christian doctrine. He spent his last years in jail, first in Roman-ruled Jerusalem, then in Rome, because of the official opposition to Christianity.

The adjustments made by early Christian leaders drew even more converts. Under the guidance of Paul, Christians began to see themselves as part of a new religion rather than a Jewish reform movement, and they welcomed non-Jewish converts. Paul also encouraged more formal organization in the new church, with local groups selecting elders to govern them; soon, a single leader, or bishop, was appointed for each major city. This structure paralleled the provincial government of the empire. Finally, Christian doctrine became increasingly well organized as the writings of several disciples and others were collected into what became the New Testament of the Christian Bible.

Christianity Gains Ground

During the first three centuries after Christ, Christianity did not advance entirely smoothly. The new religion faced periodic persecution from the normally tolerant imperial government. Even so, by the time Constantine converted to the religion, Christianity had won perhaps 10 percent of the empire's population. One convert was Constantine's mother, who visited the Holy Land and founded many churches there. Constantine's favor brought some new troubles to Christianity as the state began to interfere in matters of doctrine.

Nevertheless, it became much easier to spread Christianity with official backing. Christian writers began to claim that both church and empire were works of God. At the same time, continued deterioration of the empire added to the motives to join this successful new church. In the eastern Mediterranean, where imperial rule remained strong, state control of the church became a way of life and an important motive, for certain people, for adopting Christianity in the first place. A pagan prefect of Constantinople, Cyrus of Panopolis, facing the disapproval of an imperial official in the mid-5th century, could save himself only by converting and becoming a Christian bishop. But in the west, where conditions were far more chaotic, bishops had a freer hand.

A centralized church organization under the leadership of the bishop of Rome, called the **pope** from the Latin word *papa*, or father, gave the Western church unusual strength and independence. By the time Rome collapsed, Christianity had thus demonstrated immense spiritual power and a solid

pope Bishop of Rome; head of the Christian Church in western Europe.

organization, although it differed from east to west. The new church faced several controversies over doctrine but managed to promote certain standard beliefs. A key tenet was a complex doctrine of the Trinity, which held that the one God had three persons, the Father, the Son (Christ), and the Holy Ghost (God as present in human spiritual experience). In 325 C.E., the church **Council of Nicaea** (Council of nye-SEE-uh), under imperial sponsorship, met to debate a doctrine known as Arianism, which argued that Christ was divine but not of the same nature as God the Father. Ruling against Arianism, the resultant Nicene Creed insisted on the shared divinity of all three parts of the Trinity. An important but complex decision, it showed how important unified doctrine was to Christianity, in contrast to the greater toleration of diversity in Hinduism and Buddhism. Experience in fighting heresies promoted the Christian interest in defending a single belief and strengthened its resistance to any competing doctrine or faith.

In its founding but also in its consolidation, Christianity was aided by strong individual leadership, although it can be debated how much this leadership caused religious success and how much it flowed from the religion's appeal. For example, Pope Leo I (d. 461) most clearly established the papacy as the supreme authority in western Europe. Born a Roman aristocrat, he faced the rapid collapse of the empire, negotiating with German rulers to save the city of Rome and using their backing to assert his authority over church leaders in France and elsewhere. Leo competed with the patriarch of Alexandria for spiritual primacy in Christianity, centralizing the Western church and standardizing its rituals, prayers, and doctrine.

Early Christianity also produced an important formal theology through formative writers such as Augustine. This theology blended many elements of classical philosophy with Christian belief and helped the church gain respectability among intellectuals. Theologians such as Augustine grappled with such problems as freedom of the will: If God is all-powerful, can mere human beings have free will? And if not, how can human beings be justly punished for sin? By working out these issues in elaborate doctrine, the early theologians, or church fathers, provided an important role for formal, rational thought in a religion that continued to emphasize the primary importance of faith.

Like all successful religions, Christianity combined several appeals. It offered deep devotion to an all-powerful God. Christianity also developed its own complex and fascinating intellectual system. Mystical holy men and women flourished under Christian banners, particularly in the Middle East. In the West, soon after the empire's collapse, this impulse was partially disciplined through the institution of monasticism, which gained ground in Italy under **Benedict of Nursia** early in the 6th century. Benedict started a monastery to demonstrate the true holy life to Italian peasants in a region still (to Benedict's horror) worshiping the sun god Apollo. The Benedictine rule, which soon spread to many other monasteries and convents, urged a disciplined life, with prayer and spiritual development alternating with hard work in agriculture and study. Monastic movements also developed in the eastern empire, in Greece and Turkey, and in Egypt. Eastern monasticism was organized by Saint Basil in the 4th century.

Thus, Christianity tried to encourage but also to discipline intense piety and to avoid a complete gulf between the lives of saintly men and women and the spiritual concerns of ordinary people. Christianity's success and organizational strength obviously appealed to political leaders. But the new religion never became the creature of the upper classes alone, because its message of ritual and salvation continued to draw the poor. Like Hinduism in India, Christianity provided some religious unity among different social groups. It even held special interest for women. Christianity did not preach equality between men and women, but it did preach the equal importance of women's and men's souls, and unlike many other faiths, it encouraged men and women to worship together.

Christianity promoted a new culture among its converts (Figure 10.6). The rituals, the otherworldly emphasis, and the interest in spiritual equality were very different from the central themes of classical Mediterranean civilization. Christianity modified classical beliefs in the central importance

Council of Nicaea Christian council that met in 325 C.E. to determine orthodoxy with respect to the Trinity; insisted on divinity of all persons of the Trinity.

Read the Document on MyHistoryLab: Pope Leo I on Bishop Hilary of Arles

Benedict of Nursia Founder of monasticism in what had been the western half of the Roman Empire; established Benedictine Rule in the 6th century; paralleled development of Basil's rules in Byzantine Empire.

FIGURE **10.6** People of European background are accustomed to seeing the Madonna and child depicted as looking much like them. As this 10th-century Byzantine image demonstrates, Christians from other parts of the world developed different imagery for the major figures of their religion.

of the state and political loyalties. Although Christians accepted the state, they did not put it first. Christianity also worked against other classical institutions, such as slavery, in the name of brotherhood (although later Christians accepted slavery in other contexts). Western monasticism may have fostered a greater respectability for disciplined work than had been current in the aristocratic ethic of Mediterranean civilization.

Christianity preserved important classical values in addition to the interest in solid organization and some of the themes of classical philosophy. Church buildings in western Europe retained Roman

Read the Document on MyHistoryLab: From the Rule of St. Benedict (6th c.) (Excerpt) by St. Benedict of Nursia

VISUALIZING THE PAST

Religious Geography

THE DISTRIBUTION OF THE WORLD'S MAJOR religions calls for knowledge both of numerical data and geography. Map 10.4 and this table, using contemporary data, also suggest which aspects of the world's religious distribution were beginning to solidify at the end of the late classical period and which aspects depended on developments yet to come.

QUESTIONS

- Where are the greatest concentrations of the four major religions today?
- Which aspects of modern religious geography follow from the patterns of religious dissemination under way by the end of the classical period?
- Which cannot be explained by these late classical developments?

RELIGIONS AND THEIR DISTRIBUTION IN THE WORLD TODAY

Religion	Distribution*
Christianity	2 billion
Islam	1.3 billion
Hinduism	900 million
Buddhism	360 million
Shintoism	4 million
Daoism and other Chinese traditional religions	225 million
Judaism	14 million
Non-religious	850 million

*Figures for several religions have been reduced over the past 50 years by the impact of communism in Eastern Europe and parts of Asia.

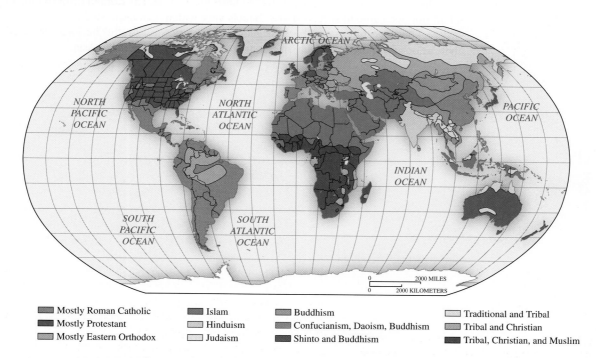

Mostly Roman Catholic | Islam | Buddhism | Traditional and Tribal
Mostly Protestant | Hinduism | Confucianism, Daoism, Buddhism | Tribal and Christian
Mostly Eastern Orthodox | Judaism | Shinto and Buddhism | Tribal, Christian, and Muslim

MAP **10.4 Major Religions of the Modern World** This map shows the contemporary geography of the major religions, including areas of considerable mixture like Africa.

architectural styles, although often with greater simplicity, if only because of the poverty of the later empire and the Germanic states. Latin remained the language of the church in the West, Greek the language of most Christians in the eastern Mediterranean. Monasticism played a very valuable role in preserving classical as well as Christian learning through the patient librarianship of the monks.

The New Religious Map

The centuries after the rise of Christianity, the spread of Buddhism, and the inception of Islam (610 C.E.) saw the conversion of most of the civilized world to one or another of the great faiths. This produced a religious map that in Europe, Asia, and parts of Africa did not change greatly until our own time. The spread of the great religions caused many people in many different societies to shift their beliefs away from traditional ideas about a host of divine spirits in nature to concentration on a single divine force and on new hopes for an afterlife. Buddhism, Christianity, and Islam, plus Hinduism in a few parts of southeast Asia, provided shared beliefs that could transcend divided, bickering political units. They could indeed draw allegiance and funding away from politics. The three most widespread religions raised new social questions, because they all stressed a basic spiritual equality. The great religions could even facilitate international trade because they did not depend on local customs but on an ever-present God or divine order throughout the world; in turn, successful trade could help spread the religions. A new force was at work in world history.

In the Wake of Decline and Fall

By 600 C.E., the major civilizations looked very different from the classical world at its height, and many of the differences have never been erased. The results of classical decline went beyond the striking shifts in religious allegiance. Some areas, however, changed far more than others. China was unique in its ability to recapture so many classical ingredients. China and India shared an ability to maintain substantial cultural cohesion, based on widespread beliefs as well as restored politics in China's case. Today, Indian and Chinese civilizations are in essentially the same places where they had taken root by late classical times, and until quite recently, they still abundantly reflected the classical heritage: India in the caste system and an otherworldly cultural tone, China in Confucian beliefs and a fascination with a strong, bureaucratic state.

The case was quite different in the Mediterranean zone. The Roman Empire split, in part because it had not been able to spread shared beliefs very widely. Classical Mediterranean civilization left a very real heritage, but in part because geographic unity was lost, this heritage was used by successor civilizations far more selectively than was true in eastern or southern Asia.

Global Connections and Critical Themes

THE LATE CLASSICAL PERIOD AND THE WORLD

During most of the classical period, key developments often focused within civilizations. We have seen that there were wider contacts. Each civilization radiated trade and other influences to a larger region; thus India had contacts with other parts of south-southeast Asia, and China with Korea and Vietnam. Trade along the Silk Road through central Asia, conducted mainly by nomadic merchants, was another key connection, as were the exchanges in the Indian Ocean.

As the classical civilizations began to fail, contacts in some ways accelerated—but they also encountered new difficulties. Overland travel between China and Rome became more dangerous, because government protection faltered in both empires. This placed a new premium on using shipping connections, particularly in the Indian Ocean. On the other hand, traders, missionaries, and of course nomadic invaders began to reach out in new ways, as borders became more porous. The end of the classical period thus witnessed important new cultural exchanges across regions. These included the spread of Buddhism from India to China and to other parts of east Asia, and the spread of Christianity beyond the Roman Empire into parts of northeast Africa and into Armenia. These developments set new bases for connections among various societies in Afro-Eurasia.

Further Readings

The fall of the Roman Empire has generated rich and interesting debate: See E. Gibbon and H. Mueller, *The Decline and Fall of the Roman Empire* (2009); Simon Swain and Mark Edwards, eds., *Approaching Late Antiquity: The Transformation from Early to Late Empire* (2004); James W. Ermatinger, *The Decline and Fall of the Roman Empire* (2004); Bryan Ward-Perkins, *The Fall of Rome and the End of Civilization* (2005). On barbarian attacks, J. H. G. W. Liebeschuetz, *Decline and Change in Late Antiquity: Religion, Barbarians and Their Historiography* (2006); Simon MacDowall, *Adrianopole, AD 378: The Goths Crush Rome's Legions* (2005); Peter Heather, *The Fall of the Roman Empire: A New History of Rome and the Barbarians* (2007); and Stephen Mitchell, *A History of the Later Roman Empire, AD 284–641* (2007).

For interpretation and discussion of earlier views, see A. H. M. Jones, *The Decline of the Ancient World* (1966); J. Vogt, *The Decline of Rome* (1965); and F. W. Walbank, *The Awful Revolution: The Decline of the Roman Empire in the West* (1960). On India and China in decline, worthwhile sources include R. Tharpar, *Early History of India* (2004); R. C. Majumdar, ed., *The Classical Age* (1966); Raymond Dawson, *Imperial China* (1972); and J. A. Harrison, *The Chinese Empire* (1972). See also J. R. Fairbank and E. O. Reischauer, *China: Tradition and Transformation* (1989), a fine survey with good postclassical coverage.

On the role of disease in imperial decline, W. McNeill's *Plagues and Peoples* (1977) is provocative and useful. Speculations on the causes of the rise and fall of civilizations, including those of the classical world, are addressed in Jared Diamond, *Guns, Germs, and Steel: The Fate of Human Societies* (1997); Christopher Chase-Dunn and Thomas D. Hall, *Rise and Demise: Comparing World Systems* (1997); Walter Goffart, *Barbarian Tides: The Migration Age and the Later Roman Empire* (2006); Michael Whitby, *Rome at War, AD 293–696* (2003); Joseph A. Tainter, *The Collapse of Complex Societies* (1988); and Norman Yoffee and George L. Cowgill, eds., *The Collapse of Ancient States and Civilizations* (1991).

For the rise and spread of world faiths, see Ann Heirman and Stephan Peter Bumbacher, eds., *The Spread of Buddhism* (2007); and Frederick Denny, *Atlas of the World's Religions* (2007). A good overview is Geoffrey Parinder, ed., *World Religions* (1971); see also Lewis M. Hopfe, *Religions of the World* (1997); and Jamail Ragi al Farugi, ed., *Historical Atlas of the Religions of the World* (1974). On Hinduism, see N. C. Chandhuri's *Hinduism: A Religion to Live By* (1979). Two good studies of Buddhism are N. Ross Reat, *Buddhism: A History* (1994) and A. F. Wright, *Buddhism in Chinese History* (1959). Christianity's spread is the subject of E.E. Cairns, *Christianity through the Centuries* (2009); S. Renko, *Pagan Rome and the Early Christians* (1986); and M. Hengel, *Acts and the History of Earliest Christianity* (1986). Important special topics are covered in J. Bowker, *Problems of Suffering in Religions of the World* (1975), a fascinating comparative effort; A. Sharma, ed., *Women in World Religions* (1987); and on Christianity, B. Witherington, *Women in the Earliest Churches* (1988). An important study of civilization contacts in this period and later is Jerry Bentley's *Old World Encounters: Cross-Cultural Exchanges and Contacts in Pre-Modern Times* (1993).

Critical Thinking Questions

1. What were the main differences in the process of decline in the four major cases: China, India, eastern Mediterranean, western Mediterranean?

2. What are some possible debates over the causes of decline at the end of the classical period?

3. What was the relationship of religious change to the process of political and economic decline?

4. What were the major adaptations of Buddhism as it spread to China? What were the main adaptations of Christianity in the later Roman Empire?

5. Compare the principal features of Buddhism and Christianity as world religions.

REVISITING
The Classical Period, 600 C.E.–600 C.E.: Uniting Large Regions

CONTACTS AND THEIR LIMITS

In contrast to the early river valley civilizations, which had no regular interregional exchange system (save possibly in the Indian Ocean), reasonably systematic contacts developed during the classical period linking China, India, the Middle East, and the Mediterranean. Some goods were shipped along sea routes in the Indian Ocean, reaching as far as Egypt via the Red Sea. Important overland routes—the routes historians have labeled collectively as the Silk Road—brought goods from western China through central Asia to the Middle East, where they could also be trans-shipped to the Mediterranean. Important systems connected south Indian merchants and some Hindu and Buddhist missionaries to various parts of southeast Asia. Ethiopians in northeastern Africa traded actively with both the Mediterranean and the Middle East.

A few decades ago archeologists, excavating the ruins of Roman Pompeii, found an ivory carving of a woman made at Taxila in what is now northwestern Pakistan. This find confirmed the

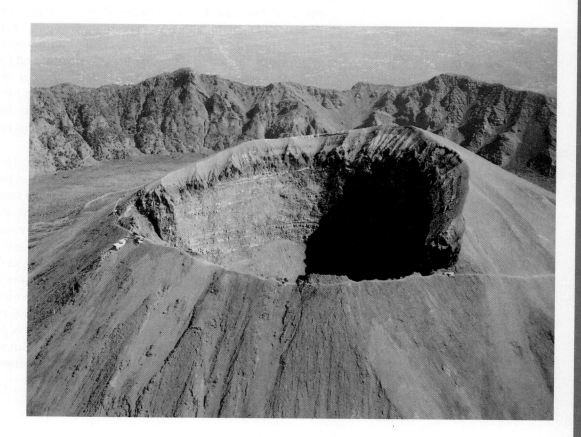

The enormous crater of Mount Vesuvius in Italy that erupted in 70 B.C.E., burying the town of Pompeii. Pompeii's ruins, later excavated, would be part of the Roman heritage to the modern world.

importance of trade links between Rome and south Asia. Taxila had been part of the Hellenistic orbit established by Alexander the Great, and exchanges with the Mediterranean continued thereafter. Taxila was also a major center along the Silk Road, serving as a link not only to the Mediterranean but also to east and southeast Asia. New levels of long-distance commerce gave many elites an active taste for goods, like silk, produced in distant places.

Improvements in technology, particularly for the fuller use of draft animals, began to contribute to transportation, along with the important road systems constructed by leaders in Persia, China, and the Mediterranean. After about 200 B.C.E., for example, the Chinese improved the harnesses used for horses, developing straps that would not choke the horse. These horse collars facilitated trade within China, but also on the routes to central Asia; ultimately, but only centuries later, knowledge of the horse collar would also reach Europe. More widely important was the growing use of saddles, with major developments from about 500 B.C.E. onward. The first saddle knob seems to have been introduced in China around 200. Bareback riding continued, but increasingly saddles provided both greater comfort and maneuverability, in turn increasing the utility of horses for travel and military purposes alike. Not only horses, but camels and donkeys played crucial roles in overland exchange.

Contacts had some wider effects, beyond trade itself. Knowledge of south Asian crops like cotton and rice spread to the Middle East, altering agricultural patterns there. We have seen that diseases also spread, particularly from south Asia, affecting population patterns in the Mediterranean and China as part of classical decline.

Besides the trade routes, two major episodes occurred that involved direct contact between different civilizations. Alexander the Great's conquests brought Greek culture into interaction with those of Persia and India, as well as with Egypt. We have seen that Indian artists imitated Greek styles in their own work. Greeks and Indians both gained new mathematical knowledge (although it is intriguing that the Greeks did not adopt Indian numbering, which, later transmitted to Europe by the Arabs, proved much superior to Greek and Roman numbering systems). Indian missionaries to the Middle East, although failing to establish Buddhism, may have influenced ethical thought in the later Roman Empire and, through this, Christianity.

Interest in Asian goods also motivated Rome, although with less wide-ranging results. Once they controlled Egypt, the Romans established regular Indian Ocean expeditions from the Red Sea. Small groups of Roman merchants, located in India in particular, demonstrated a desire for more direct access to Indian spices, particularly pepper, and Chinese silks also helped motivate frequent wars with empires in Persia, although the Romans often fared badly and were unable to break through to the sources of the goods they valued. China, for its part, established regular diplomatic relations with empires in Persia, largely to further direct trade. None of these interesting interactions, however, seems to have had significant results in terms of institutional or cultural exchange.

The second major contact, toward the end of the classical period, involved China's fascination with Indian Buddhism. Chinese knowledge of Buddhism initially spread as a result of Chinese merchant ventures into India; later, religious students were sent directly. This was the only major case of successful outside influence on Chinese culture until very recent times.

These developments were exceedingly important. They also had serious limits. Interregional trade was certainly vital to some of the trading hubs in central Asia, such as Samarkand, but it had relatively little economic importance to societies like China. It was nothing compared to the growth of production for China's internal trade. There is no uncontested evidence that anyone traveled all the way from Rome to China, and Roman knowledge of China (as well as Chinese knowledge of Rome) was extremely hazy. There was trade, but no interaction between Chinese and Roman culture or technology. The two cases of direct exchange between civilizations described above are fascinating but they also stand out as unusual. And the lasting effects of the Hellenistic experience in northwestern India are questionable. Even in art, after about two

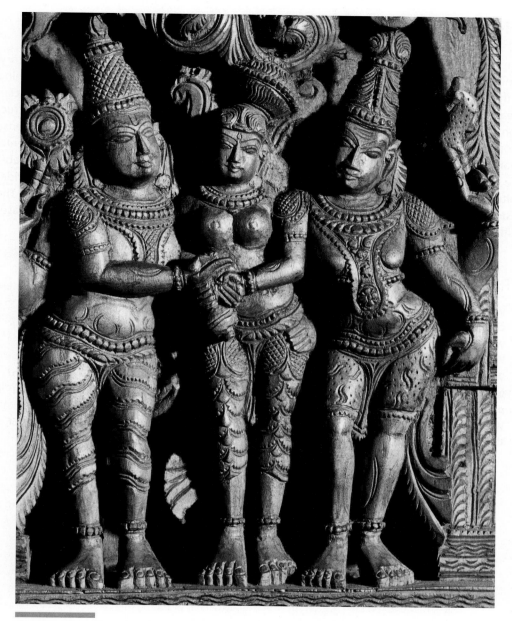

Three Hindu goddesses appear in an intricate carving on a temple in India. Hindu art remains an active element in Indian culture.

centuries, Mediterranean influence seems to have disappeared, and stylistic differences once again became apparent.

So, while contacts advanced significantly in this period, the primary framework for the major societies remained internal. The classical civilizations developed largely separately. The most important kinds of contacts occurred *within* the civilizations, not among them: the careful, sometimes tense mixing of the northern Chinese with the people in the newer territories in the south; the partial extension of Greek culture to the western Mediterranean and portions of the Middle East and north Africa; the spread of Hinduism and the caste system southward on the Indian subcontinent. These contacts were vital to the formation of larger civilizational areas, which was the fundamental feature of the classical period. Clearly, far more energy went into this process than into interregional linkages at this stage in world history.

CRITICAL THEMES

The classical period added important dimensions to a number of central themes in world history. A number of social systems gained greater organization and also cultural support, beginning with the Indian caste system but extending also to Mediterranean slavery and the Confucian ideas about social order in China. State building won new attention, particularly in the construction of empires, although here too regional differences require careful comparison. More intense economic activity, including pressures applied by political leaders, contributed to environmental changes, as deforestation expanded and certain regions were overfarmed. Ultimately, probably the most important single thematic category in the period involved the elaboration of wider cultural systems—the new religions and philosophies and their links to artistic production. The systems were important at the time and proved to have tremendous durability, in many cases outlasting the classical societies themselves. ▪

CRITICAL THINKING QUESTIONS

1. What were the main differences between the classical period and the previous period of early civilizations? What were some of the causes of change?

2. What kinds of sources help us understand gender relationships during the classical period? What kinds of additional evidence would be desirable?

3. What were the main causes of the success of Confucianism as a cultural system in classical China?

4. What were the primary limitations on contacts among the main civilization areas in the classical period?

5. What were the main similarities and differences in patterns of decline, in the main civilizations of the classical period?

The Postclassical Period, 600–1450: New Faith and New Commerce

Hagia Sophia, Istanbul, Turkey. The great cathedral symbolized the growing importance of religion.

PART OUTLINE

THE OVERVIEW: THE WORLD MAP CHANGES

The big changes in the period 600–1450 did not involve political boundaries. They involved the spread of the major world religions—Buddhism, Christianity, and Islam—across political and cultural borders and the development of new, more regular systems of trade that connected much of Asia, Africa, and Europe.

In some ways, an age characterized by faith and trade may seem contradictory. Indeed, many religious leaders looked down on merchants as likely to be seduced from a life of piety by the lure of wealth. But in fact the spread of trade often helped disseminate religion, and confidence in a divine order helped merchants to take risks.

The maps included here show the surge of Buddhism, Christianity, and Islam from their initial centers and the expansion of Afro-Eurasian trade around the same period. While Buddhism and Christianity started well before this period, they gained new vigor as the classical empires collapsed. Islam, which spread most rapidly, was entirely new. All three religions involved active missionary efforts. All periodically benefited from government sponsorship and sometimes from military pressure as well. For example, conquerors might impose higher taxes on those they conquered who did not convert to the conquerors' religion, or they might forcibly expel "nonbelievers" from the territory. Through a combination of persuasion and pressure, many millions of people changed their beliefs about the world around them and about the goals of life. The religious beliefs they adopted during the postclassical period established the dominant religious frameworks that still prevail in Asia, Europe, and parts of Africa today.

During the postclassical period, systematic international trade developed that went far beyond the carrying capacity of the old Silk Road. The Indian Ocean and the Mediterranean Sea were the hubs of this trade, which brought northwestern Europe, west Africa, Japan, and other regions into the existing east–west trade routes between China and Egypt. Gradually and tentatively, these connections among societies (rather than separate developments within societies) began to shape world history in important ways.

Mystical conversation between Sufic sheikhs. Sufi mysticism became an important element in Islam's missionary efforts.

Big Concepts

Along with, and partly because of, religious change, three Big Concepts help organize the understanding of the postclassical period. First, transregional communication and exchange networks expanded with important new routes added. Missionary activity and new seafaring technologies both contributed to this. Second, forms of state organization diversified, with centralized empires now juxtaposed to a variety of looser political structures. Third, several societies—headed by China—increased their productive capacity, with social consequences extending to the emergence of new urban centers and the experimentation with different forms of labor.

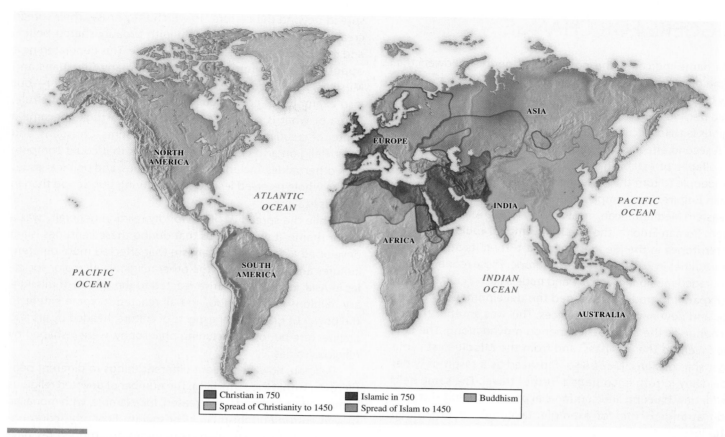

Spread of Buddhism, Christianity, and Islam to c. 1450

Main Routes of Afro-Eurasian Trade, c. 1250

TRIGGERS FOR CHANGE

As its name indicates, the postclassical period followed the decline of the great classical empires. As areas that had previously been under the control of these empires experienced economic decline and increasing disorder, people turned toward religious faith for security, reassurance, and guidance.

A second effect of the decline of the classical empires was the collapse of established boundaries, which caused ambitious people to turn their attention to new areas. The fall of the Roman Empire, for example, opened up new opportunities in the eastern Mediterranean, most notably for the Arabs. When the Eastern Roman Empire (the Byzantine Empire) could not regain lost territories in the Mediterranean, it turned its attention to opportunities in Russia and eastern Europe. These reorientations encouraged missionary activity and trade alike.

Expanding trade encouraged the development of better ships and new navigational devices. This was another trigger for change as the postclassical period moved along. The Chinese invented the compass, and from the Middle East came better ship designs. Maps also improved as a result of wider trade. They in turn encouraged further travel. The same held true for new banking and commercial practices: Long-distance credit arrangements, for example, facilitated international exchange.

THE BIG CHANGES

Religion and commerce were the engines of change in the postclassical period. Changes in their own right, they were the causes of many other changes. Buddhism, Christianity, and Islam were the religions that showed the greatest capacity to spread beyond the cultures in which they arose. Their spread created larger groups of people with broadly shared beliefs and religious institutions than ever before. This generated new opportunities for mutual intolerance—many Christians and Muslims, particularly, developed disdain for each other—but also examples of constructive tolerance. Under Islamic rule, Iberia or what is present day Spain and Portugal, became a center of creative interaction among Muslims, Christians, and Jews. Religion also created new loyalties that could compete with other values, including political values, and political issues on the whole received less attention during this period than in the classical era.

While the spread of otherworldly religion generally was a major theme, it was obvious that during these centuries Islam developed a particular dynamism that affected more different cultures and peoples than the other religions. All major societies in Asia, Europe, and Africa reacted to the spread of missionary religions in this period, and all reacted to some extent to the power of Islam. Other aspects of culture, headed by art and architecture but often including philosophy, were reshaped by religious values.

Religion, however, meant different things to different people, even within the same faith. The number of devoted religious communities and leaders increased, for example, with monastic movements in Buddhism and Christianity. Economic contributions to religious institutions sometimes outstripped tax payments to governments. But many people combined religion with other interests, including commercial life. And most peoples combined new religions with older values and styles.

Key comparisons, obviously, follow from the spread of world religions and the changing religious map. What were the main similarities and differences among the missionary religions? How did each major society in Africa, Asia, and Europe react to new religious opportunities?

500 C.E.	600 C.E.	700 C.E.	800 C.E.	900 C.E.
527–565 Justinian, Eastern Roman (Byzantine) Emperor **570–632** Muhammad **589–618** Sui dynasty (China)	**610–613** Origins of Islam **618–907** Tang dynasty (China) **634–750** Arab Expansion in Middle East; spread of Islam in North Africa **661–750** Ummayad Caliphate **668** Korea becomes independent from China	**711** First Islamic incursions into India **718** Byzantines defeat Arab attack on Constantinople **750** Abbasid caliphate founded **777** Independent Islamic kingdoms begin in North Africa and Iberia	**800–814** Charlemagne's Empire in western Europe **c. 855** Russian kingdom around Kiev **864** Cyril and Methodius missionaries in eastern Europe **878** Last Japanese embassy to China	**960–1127** Song dynasty (China) **968** Tula established by Toltecs (Mesoamerica) **980–1015** Christian Conversion of Vladimir I of Russia

THE TRANSREGIONAL NETWORK

The development of regular trade created a series of interlocking trade routes that joined key parts of Asia, Africa, and Europe. These built on connections developed in the classical period, but they were more elaborate. The Arabs opened the period with new activities in the Indian Ocean, reaching from the Middle East to south and southeast Asia and to China; fairly soon, clusters of Arab traders located even in Chinese port cities. The Byzantine Empire also linked into this trade. As a result, goods like silks, porcelains, and wine traded among elite customers throughout these core regions.

But new routes linked additional regions into the network. Sub-Saharan West Africa traded overland to North Africa, and thence to the Middle East, thanks in part to improvements in the use of camels. Another route, on Africa's Indian Ocean coast, relied on regular shipping from present-day Tanzania north to the Middle East. Overland traders, using rivers in part, worked from Scandinavia down to Constantinople and the Arab centers, a third north-south route. A bit later, merchants used coastal shipping or overland and river trade to move from northwestern Europe into the Mediterranean and contacts with Arab commerce. Japan, finally, began a regular exchange with Korea and China. On the whole, the more distant regions provided less-processed goods in world trade, including gold, exotic animals, forest products, and spices.

Trade facilitated other kinds of exchanges—including, of course, missionary religions. It brought knowledge of new technologies. A number of Chinese inventions, first paper (when Islamic troops captured some papermakers in western China), then printing and explosives spread to the Middle East and on to Europe. Early in the postclassical period, this exchange was very slow (although faster than in previous centuries), but it became more rapid as time went on. At the end of the postclassical period, key Chinese inventions like printing and explosives moved westward more swiftly.

Ideas spread as well. Thanks to trade, Indian mathematics, including the numbering system, spread to the Middle East. Then Arab mathematics, blending earlier Greek and Indian achievements with Arab innovations, reached Western Europe (where people thought Arabs had invented the numbering system). Food exchange was another key development, sometimes helping to create a hint of consumer culture dependent on transregional exchange. A taste for tea developed widely in Asia. Granulated sugar, developed earlier in India and easily manufactured and transported, had already reached Persia. Arabs learned about it during their initial conquests, and spread awareness to places like North Africa and Spain. Europeans encountered it in turn—with the first English-language mention of sugar dating from 1099. The spread of disease accelerated as well. In the 14th century a new epidemic of bubonic plague—the "Black Death"—moved from China through the Middle East to Europe, killing up to a third of the population in many areas.

The interregional trade of the postclassical era was not what we think of as a global economy today. Fewer societies were involved, and the volume and range of trade were far lower. However, despite downsides like disease, the wide exchanges of the postclassical era had major effects, including new opportunities for imitation. Societies newer to interregional trade quickly realized that they could use their new contacts to copy more advanced forms, not only in technology but also in culture. The result was a major, often quite explicit, effort at borrowing that added up to another innovation in the period as a whole.

Wider patterns of trade facilitated a new breed of long-distance travelers, particularly by the final centuries of the postclassical period. These included merchants and missionaries who went from one part of Asia to another, or through the Indian Ocean basin, or into Africa or eastern Europe from centers elsewhere.

1000 c.e.	1100 c.e.	1200 c.e.	1300 c.e.	1400 c.e.
1000 Ghana Empire at its height (West Africa)	**c. 1100** Invention of explosive powder (China)	**1200** Rise of empire of Mali (West Africa)	**1320s** Europeans first use cannons in war	**1400** End of Polynesian expeditions
1054 Schism between Eastern and Western Christianity	**1150** Disintegration of Toltec Empire	**1206** Delhi sultanate in India	**1320–1340** Bubonic plague breaks out in Gobi desert and spreads to other parts of Asia and west to the Mediterranean and Europe.	**1405–1433** Chinese trading expeditions
1055 Seljuk Turks control Abbasid caliphate	**1150–1350** Spread of Gothic style; scholasticism in western Europe	**1231–1392** Mongols rule Korea		**1439** Portugal captures Azores Islands
1066 Norman conquest of England; rise of feudal monarchy in western Europe	**1185–1333** Kamakura Shogunate (Japan)	**1236** Capture of Baghdad by Mongols; end of Abbasid caliphate	**1325** Rise of Aztec Empire (Mesoamerica)	**1453** Turks capture Constantinople; end of Byzantine Empire
1096–1099 First Christian Crusade to Palestine		**1260** Death of Sundiata	**1338–1453** Hundred Years' War in Europe	**1471–1493** Peak of Inca Empire
		1265 First English parliament	**1350** Rise of Incas (Andes)	
		1279–1368 Mongol Empire in China	**1392–1910** Yi dynasty (Korea)	
		1290s Islam begins to spread to southeast Asia		

Travel reflected new contacts, with motives ranging from religious pilgrimage to simple delight in adventure, but travelers' accounts also helped motivate still further ventures. Extensive knowledge of Arabic was a key facilitator of contacts, serving as something of a first-world language. At an extreme, contacts could even lead to broader visions of a better world: a Chinese observer in the 14th century proclaimed (with a great deal of exaggeration), "civilization had spread everywhere, and no more barriers existed. . . . Brotherhood among peoples has certainly reached a new plane."

We live today in a period of rapidly intensifying contacts among all the world's major societies, and the process is increasingly referred to as globalization. Globalization has many new features, starting with dramatic communications technologies like the Internet. We increasingly realize, however, that contemporary globalization was prepared by previous periods in which interactions among major regions expanded. The postclassical period marked a major separation between earlier eras, in which contacts among different regions were slow or occasional, into a situation in which trade, travel and exchange created significant new, often routinized, influences on the ways individual societies developed. Defining the relationship between the systems of interaction in the postclassical period and later patterns provides a key way to map the process of change in world history.

The transcontinental network itself compelled many societies in Afro-Eurasia to decide on how to organize their participation in trade and exchange, and how to take advantage of the opportunities involved. No society responded in exactly the same way—comparing responses is an obvious assignment in analyzing the postclassical period—and some societies changed their responses over time. The spread of world religions, which created huge new areas of shared faith, but also new divisions among the religions themselves, contributed to but also complicated the evolution of the transcontinental network.

CONTINUITY AND LIMITATIONS

Change, including the formation of the transcontinental network, inevitably affected different societies to different degrees. Continuities combined with change. Even though the classical empires had collapsed, the successes of classical civilization encouraged many people to maintain or retrieve classical forms. China eagerly revived the structures of its classical age, including the empire, the bureaucracy, and Confucianism. It was touched by Islam and Buddhism, but ultimately it limited the influence of outside religions. China was not a changeless society—its growing participation in interregional trade proved its capacity to take advantage of new opportunities—but continuity remained extremely important.

The Middle East underwent great change as a result of the rise of Islam, but it also maintained continuities. Hellenistic science interacted with Islam, leading to important philosophical discussions of the relationship between science and faith. Earlier practices, such as the veiling of women in the cities, were revived. Although Islam opposed the enslavement of fellow Muslims, slavery continued to be a major component of social and labor systems over much of Afro-Eurasia, another sign of the hold of earlier traditions in the region.

Continuities also showed in the blending of traditional forms with the missionary religions. Christian architecture long used Greco-Roman styles. Buddhism adapted to Chinese values, for example, by placing more emphasis on the family loyalties of women. And there were sweeping innovations in social structures or even political forms during the postclassical centuries. The expansion of a merchant class affected social structure, but landlords remained dominant in most societies and peasants made up the bulk of the population. In key areas slavery or (in India) the caste system also maintained or revived older social institutions. Large political units developed in a few places, but outside of China and the Byzantine Empire, polities were mainly loosely organized.

Finally, major areas were still outside the system shaped by world religions and interregional trade. Most notably, the Americas and Pacific Oceania, although scenes of significant developments, operated on separate dynamics and had few if any contacts with the rest of the world.

IMPACT ON DAILY LIFE: WOMEN

The postclassical period saw an intriguing tension that affected conditions for women in many parts of Afro-Eurasia. On the one hand, the major religions all insisted that women were spiritually equal to men—that they had souls or shared in the divine essence. This was a huge innovation. And religious change was not a matter of ideals alone. Buddhist leaders in Japan argued for women's importance. Islam established new rights for women, including property ownership. Buddhism and Christianity both established religious communities for women, giving them not only new forms of expression but also new leadership roles. As these religions spread, many women gained new positions and modes of expression through religious life. On the other hand, the condition of women also deteriorated during this period. Many scholars have argued that growing trade and urban prosperity reduced women's role in political and economic life and created conditions in which upper-class women were treated as ornaments. So, although religion provided new outlets for women, the spiritual focus might also distract them from other issues such as newer gender inequalities.

Other changes were less favorable to women. Footbinding— the clearest attempt to make women more purely ornamental— spread in China. In India the practice of sati, in which some widows threw themselves on their husbands' funeral pyres to demonstrate their grief, spread somewhat, mainly within the highest castes. As Islamic society matured in the Middle East, women were increasingly secluded and excluded from active roles in public life. But in other Islamic societies, especially in Africa and southeast Asia, this was less true. At the same time, most historians conclude that the condition of women in western Europe had deteriorated by the later postclassical period, as judged, for example, by their greater exclusion from most skilled urban crafts. Thus, the postclassical period was an important one in women's history. New religions were important to many women, but new customs also limited opportunities for women to a greater degree than in the classical era. In much of the world, at least the vestiges of these limitations survive to the present day.

TRENDS AND SOCIETIES IN THE EARLY MODERN PERIOD

Chapters 11 and 12 examine the surge of Islam, first in the Middle East and then in other parts of Asia. Chapter 13 describes the expansion of trade and civilization in sub-Saharan Africa, which had various facets, but the link to Islam and the Islamic trading system was crucial. Two dynamics developed in Europe; each had contacts (both creative and hostile) with Islam and certainly with interregional trade. In eastern Europe, as detailed in Chapter 14, Byzantine culture took root, while a newer society emerged in western Europe, as described in Chapter 15. Chapter 16 describes the major cultures that developed in the Americas and the contacts among them. Chapters 17 and 18 address developments in China and the expansion of Chinese influence in Japan, Korea, and Vietnam—key parts of the network of interregional trade.

The last two centuries of the postclassical period, as Arab power declined, saw important new developments. Chapter 19 describes the Mongol conquests in the 13th and 14th centuries that, for a time, revolutionized the political map of Asia and parts of Europe, accelerating and redefining interregional trade and other exchanges. The decline of the Mongols, and the end of a brief Chinese experiment in leading world trade, left the world poised for further innovation. Chapter 20 describes a transitional moment and the complex factors that would alter world balance yet again. ∎

11

The First Global Civilization: The Rise and Spread of Islam

(((Listen to **Chapter 11**
on **MyHistoryLab**

LEARNING OBJECTIVES

11.1 What were the major ways in which the city of Mecca interacted with the bedouin tribes that lived in the desert areas around it? p. 244

11.2 Which aspects of Muhammad's religious message do you think accounted for its powerful appeal to both urban dwellers and nomadic peoples in Arabia and beyond? p. 249

11.3 What were the key factors that made possible the rapid Arab conquests in the Middle East, Central Asia, and North Africa? p. 252

11.4 In what ways was the Islamic religion a faith that elevated the status and opportunities of women, and what were the constraints on this process? p. 260

In any ranking of the greatest survivors in world history, 'Abd al-Rahman I would have to be near or at the top of the list. The grandson of the last distinguished caliph (leader of the Muslim faithful) of the Umayyad dynasty, he had barely survived the vengeful slaughter of the many male descendants of that first house of Muslim rulers by the warriors of the 'Abbasid coalition that had seized power in 749. After narrowly escaping capture and beheading on his estate on the upper Euphrates River, 'Abd al-Rahman, dodging 'Abbasid pursuers and bounty hunters alike, fled through Syria and Palestine and across north Africa. After a half decade as fugitive, he

Q **View** the **Closer Look** on **MyHistoryLab**: The Congregational Mosque

FIGURE **11.1** The graceful "horseshoe" arches of the Great Mosque at Córdoba in southern Spain provide a striking example of the sophistication and beauty of the arts and architecture produced by the fusion of Muslim, Jewish, and Christian cultural traditions in Islamic Iberia from the 8th to the 15th centuries.

finally found uneasy sanctuary in Morocco at the western end of the lands to which Islam had spread to that point in time. In 755, the 24-year-old crossed the narrow Straits of Gibraltar that separated north Africa from the Iberian peninsula. Rallying to his cause several hundred Syrians, whose homelands had been the mainstay of the vanquished Umayyad dynasty and who had joined in earlier Arab-Berber campaigns to conquer the peninsula, 'Abd al-Rahman began his quest to become master of Iberia.

Despite continuing resistance by rivals and rebels from within and invasions plotted by Abbasid rulers in distant Baghdad, 'Abd al-Rahman steadily consolidated his control over Iberia. His early victories, particularly the capture of Córdoba in 756, secured his position as the paramount lord on the peninsula within years of his arrival. In the following decades as the capital of a flourishing Muslim kingdom, Córdoba grew rapidly into one of the most cosmopolitan and celebrated cities in the Mediterranean world. Córdoba boasted well-paved and well-lit streets, houses with running water, one of the world's finest universities, and a library with over 400,000 volumes at a time when the largest collections in Christian Europe contained a few thousand at best. But Córdoba's crowning glory was its great mosque. It was famed for its hundreds of splendid marble columns topped by ornate horseshoe arches and its elaborately decorated vaulted ceilings, shown in Figure 11.1. But even more remarkable than its distinctive architecture and decoration were the ways in which the mosque encapsulated the exceptional synergy generated by cooperation among and the blending of the diverse peoples and cultures that came together in Islamic Spain.

Like the development of Muslim civilization more generally, the construction of the great mosque of Córdoba owed much to earlier and even contemporary rival civilizations. It was built on the ruins of a Christian church, and many of the pillars that supported the signature horseshoe arches were taken from Roman ruins. And although the influence of Syrian-style Islamic architecture is apparent, the mosque's bell tower and thick walls decorated with geometric stone carvings shared key features with the Romanesque churches then found throughout Latin Christendom. Much of the mosque's stonework, and especially its intricate mosaics, were crafted by Christian Orthodox artisans from Constantinople, and its architects, laborers, and overseers were drawn from Arab and Berber Muslim migrants as well as the majority Christian population of Iberia.

The cross-cultural influences and interethnic and religious cooperation that played such vital roles in the construction of the grand mosque of Córdoba were also prominent features of Muslim Iberian society as a whole. Under the Muslims the peninsula became a key locus for the transmission of ideas, technology, and material culture between the Middle East, north Africa, and Europe. Arab and Berber migrants brought paper (originally invented, as we have seen, in China) and refined steel working to al-Andalus (the Arab name for Iberia), and their descendants carried leather working skills back to Morocco and the broader Muslim world. Muslim migrants to Iberia also introduced sophisticated irrigation systems and a wide variety of staple foods and plants, including oranges, sugar cane, and cotton.

Jews and Christians, as "people of the book," were allowed in Iberia as in the rest of the Muslim world to worship openly, to regulate their everyday lives according to their own laws, and to collaborate with Muslims in trade, scholarship, and the arts. Arab and Jewish scholars in Córdoba, Seville, and other urban centers, for example, were renowned throughout the Mediterranean for their translations of classic Greek texts. By the tenth and eleventh centuries, their collaboration had become pivotal for the recovery in Latin Christendom of the writings of the great Greek

600 C.E.	620 C.E.	640 C.E.	660 C.E.	680 C.E.
c. 570 Birth of the prophet Muhammad **597–626** Wars between the Byzantine and Sasanian (Persian) empires **610** Muhammad's first revelations **613** Muhammad begins to preach the new faith	**622** Muhammad's flight (hijra) from Mecca to Medina **624–627** Wars between the followers of Muhammad and the Quraysh of Mecca **628** Muslim–Meccan Truce **630** Muhammad enters Mecca in triumph **632** Death of Muhammad **632–634** Rule of Caliph Abu Bakr **633–634** Ridda Wars in Arabia **634–643** Early Muslim conquests in the Byzantine Empire **634–644** Rule of Caliph Umar **637** Arab invasion and destruction of Sasanian Empire	**644–656** Rule of Caliph Uthman **656–661** Rule of Caliph Ali; first civil war	**661–680** Mu'awiya **661–750** Umayyad caliphate	**680** Death of Ali's son Husayn at Karbala **680–692** Second civil war **744–750** Third civil war; Abbasid revolt **750** Abbasid caliphate begins

philosopher and scientist Aristotle in such critical areas as astronomy, mathematics, geography, and meteorology. Muslim Spain was a key source of the tradition of wandering minstrels or troubadours, who carried music, fables, and the notion of romantic love northward into Christian Europe. It was also a land where upper-class, educated Muslim, Christian, and Jewish women flourished as poets, musicians, scribes, and university students. ■

In the chapter that follows we shall see that in many ways Muslim Iberia was a microcosm—albeit a very forward-looking one—of much of the Islamic world in its early centuries. Although spread initially mainly by nomadic camel-herding peoples of Arabia, Islam was from its inception a religion of the towns and trade. Muhammad himself was a successful caravan leader before he began to receive the divine revelations that transformed him into the founder of one of the great world religions. As in Iberia, conversion to Islam as it spread from Arabia was generally peaceful and voluntary, and in the early decades the faithful were, if anything, reluctant to recruit new believers. Even after the new faith came to undergird vast and expansive empires, such as those fashioned by the Umayyads and Abbasids, adherents of other religions based on divinely inspired scriptures—from the Jews and Christians to the Hindus—prayed and practiced their rituals openly, and their communities very often flourished economically. As was the case in Iberia, many of the most brilliant contributions of early Islamic civilization came from the openness of Arabs to borrowing from the ancient civilizations that surrounded the Arab heartlands. The Arabs' absorption and then innovations on the sciences, arts, and technologies of Greece, Rome, Byzantium, Persia, Egypt, India, and China were essential to the rise of the first genuinely global civilization in human history.

DESERT AND TOWN: THE HARSH ENVIRONMENT OF THE PRE-ISLAMIC ARABIAN WORLD

> Before the rise of Islam, Arabia was a peripheral desert wasteland whose once great trading cities had fallen on hard times. The sparse population of the Arabian peninsula was divided into rival tribes and clans that worshiped local gods.

11.1 What were the major ways in which the city of Mecca interacted with the bedouin tribes that lived in the desert areas around it?

The Arabian Peninsula (Map 11.1) was a very unlikely birthplace for the first global civilization. Much of the area is covered by some of the most inhospitable desert in the world. An early traveler wrote of the region,

MAP **11.1 Arabia and Surrounding Areas Before and During the Time of Muhammad** Although much of Arabia was separated by vast deserts from surrounding classical civilizations, as the map shows it maintained contact by sea in the west and south and through camel caravans into Palestine and Syria.

All about us is an iron wilderness; a bare and black shining beach of heated volcanic stones . . . a vast bed and banks of rusty and basaltic bluish rocks . . . stubborn as heavy matter, as iron and sounding like bell metal; lying out eternally under the sand-driving desert wind.

In the scrub zones on the edges of the empty quarters, or uninhabitable desert zones, a wide variety of **bedouin** or nomadic, cultures had developed over the centuries, based on camel and goat herding. In oases like that pictured in Figure 11.2, which dotted the dry landscape, towns and agriculture flourished on a limited scale. Only in the coastal regions of the far south had extensive agriculture, sizable cities, and regional kingdoms developed in ancient times. Over much of the rest of the peninsula, the camel nomads, organized in tribes and clans, were dominant. Yet in the rocky

Bedouin [BEHD-oo-ihn] Nomadic pastoralists of the Arabian peninsula; culture based on camel and goat nomadism; early converts to Islam.

FIGURE **11.2** With their supply of water, shade, and date palms, oases like this one in Egypt have long been key centers of permanent settlement and trade in the desert. Major towns usually grew around the underground springs and wells or small rivers that fed the oases. Travelers' and traders' caravans stopped at the oases to water their camels and horses and to rest and eat after their arduous treks through the desert. As points of concentration of wealth, food, and precious water, oases were tempting targets for raids by bedouin bands.

regions adjacent to the Red Sea, several trading towns had developed that played pivotal roles in the emergence of Islam.

Although the urban roots of Islam have often been stressed by writers on Muslim civilization, the bedouin world in which the religion arose shaped the career of its prophet, his teachings, and the spread of the new beliefs. In fact, key towns such as Mecca and Medina were largely extensions of the tribal culture of the camel nomads. Their populations were linked by kinship to bedouin peoples. For example, Mecca had been founded by bedouins and at the time of Muhammad was ruled by former bedouin clans. The safety of the trade routes on which the towns depended was in the hands of the nomadic tribes that lived along the vulnerable caravan routes to the north and south. In addition, the town dwellers' social organization, which focused on clan and family, and their culture—including language and religion—were much like those of the nomads.

Clan Identity, Clan Rivalries, and the Cycle of Vengeance

The harsh desert and scrub environment of Arabia gave rise to forms of social organization and a lifestyle that were similar to those of other nomadic peoples. Bedouin herders lived in kin-related clan groups in highly mobile tent encampments. Clans, in turn, were clustered in larger tribal groupings, but these were rarely congregated together and then only in times of war or severe crisis. The struggle for subsistence in the unforgiving Arabian environment resulted in a strong dependence on and loyalty to one's family and clan. Survival depended on cooperation with and support from kin. To be cut off from them or expelled from the clan encampment was in most cases fatal. The use of watering places and grazing lands, which were essential to maintaining the herds on which bedouin life depended, was regulated by clan councils. But there could be wide disparities of wealth and status within clan groups and between clans of the same tribe. Although normally elected by councils of elder advisors, the **shaykhs**, or leaders of the tribes and clans, were almost always men with large herds, several wives, many children, and numerous retainers. The shaykhs' dictates were enforced by bands of free warriors whose families made up a majority of a given clan group. Beneath the warriors were slave families, often the remnants of rival clans defeated in war, who served the shaykhs or the clan as a whole.

Clan cohesion was reinforced by fierce inter-clan rivalries and struggles to control vital pasturelands and watering places. If the warriors from one clan found those from another clan drawing water from one of their wells, they were likely to kill them. Wars often broke out as a result of one clan's encroaching on the pasture areas of another clan. In a culture in which one's honor depended on respect for one's clan, the flimsiest pretexts could lead to inter-clan violence. For instance, an insult to a warrior in a market town, the theft of a prize stallion, or one clan's defeat in a horse race by another clan could end in battles between clan groups. All the men of a given clan joined in these fights, which normally were won by the side that could field several champions who were famed for their strength and skill with spears or bows and arrows.

These battles were fought according to a code of chivalry that was quite common in early cultures. Although battles usually were small in terms of the numbers involved, they were hard-fought and often bloody affairs. Almost invariably the battles either initiated or perpetuated clan feuds, which could continue for hundreds of years. The deaths of the warriors of one clan required that revenge be taken on the clan that had killed them. Their deaths led in turn to reprisals. This constant infighting weakened the bedouins in relation to the neighboring peoples and empires and allowed them to be manipulated and set against each other.

Towns and Long-Distance Trade

Although bedouin herders occupied most of the habitable portions of Arabia, farmers and town dwellers carved out small communities in the western and southern parts of the peninsula in the classical era. Foreign invasions and the inroads of bedouin peoples had all but destroyed these civilizations centuries before the birth of Muhammad. But a number of cities had developed farther north as links in the transcontinental trading system that stretched from the Mediterranean to east Asia. The most important of these cities was **Mecca**, located in the mountainous region along the Red Sea on the western coast of Arabia (Map 11.1). The town had been founded by the **Umayyad** clan of the **Quraysh** bedouin tribe, and members of the clan dominated its politics and commercial economy.

The wealth and status of Mecca and its merchant elite were enhanced by the fact that the city was the site of the **Ka'ba**, one of the most revered religious shrines in pre-Islamic Arabia. Not only did the shrine attract pilgrims and customers for Mecca's bazaars, but at certain times of the year it was the focus of an obligatory truce in the inter-clan feuds. Freed from fears of assault by rival groups, merchants and bedouins flocked to the town to trade, exchange gossip, and taste the delights of city life.

Northeast of Mecca was a town named Yathrib (Map 11.1) that later came to be known as **Medina**, or the city of the prophet Muhammad. Like most of the other towns in the peninsula, Medina was established in an oasis. Wells and springs made sedentary agriculture possible. In addition to wheat and other staples, Medina's inhabitants grew date palms, whose fruit and seeds (which were fed to camels) they traded to the bedouins. Medina was also engaged, although on a much smaller scale than Mecca, in the long-distance caravan trade that passed through Arabia. In contrast to Umayyad-dominated Mecca, control in Medina was contested by two bedouin and three Jewish clans. Their quarrels left the city a poor second to Mecca as a center of trade, and these divisions proved critical to the survival of the prophet Muhammad and the Islamic faith.

shaykhs [shAYks] Leaders of tribes and clans within bedouin society; usually men with large herds, several wives, and many children.

Mecca City located in mountainous region along Red Sea in Arabian peninsula; founded by Umayyad clan of Quraysh; site of Ka'ba; original home of Muhammad; location of chief religious pilgrimage point in Islam.

Umayyad [oo-MY-yad] Clan of Quraysh that dominated politics and commercial economy of Mecca; clan established a dynasty under this title as rulers of Islam, 661 to 750.

Quraysh [koo-RAYSH] Tribe of bedouins that controlled Mecca in 7th century C.E.

Ka'ba Most revered religious shrine in pre-Islamic Arabia; located in Mecca; focus of obligatory annual truce among bedouin tribes; later incorporated as important shrine in Islam.

Medina Also known as Yathrib; town located northeast of Mecca; grew date palms whose fruit was sold to bedouins; became refuge for Muhammad following flight from Mecca (hijra).

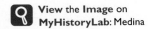

View the Image on
MyHistoryLab: Medina

Marriage and Family in Pre-Islamic Arabia

Although the evidence is scant, there are several indications that women in pre-Islamic Arabian bedouin culture enjoyed greater freedom and higher status than those who lived in neighboring civilized centers, such as the Byzantine and Sasanian empires that then dominated the Middle East (Map 11.1). Women played key economic roles, from milking camels and weaving cloth to raising children. Because the men of the clan were often on the move, many tribes traced descent through the mother rather than the father. In some tribes, both men and women were allowed multiple marriage partners. To seal a marriage contract, the man was required to pay a bride-price to his prospective wife's family, rather than the woman's father sending a dowry or gift to the prospective husband. Unlike the women (especially those of elite status) in neighboring Syria and Persia, women in pre-Islamic Arabia were not secluded and did not wear veils. Their advice was highly regarded in clan and tribal councils, and they often composed poems that were the focus of bedouin cultural life in the pre-Islamic era.

Despite these career outlets, women were not by any means considered equal to men. They could not gain glory as warriors, the most prized occupation of the bedouins, and often they were little more than drudge laborers. Their status depended on the custom of individual clans and tribes rather than on legal codes. As a result, it varied widely from one clan or family to the next. Customary practices of property control, inheritance, and divorce heavily favored men. In the urban environment of trading centers such as Mecca, the rise of a mercantile elite and social stratification appear to have set back the position of women on the whole. The more stable family life of the towns led to the practice of tracing descent through the male line, and while men continued to practice polygamy, women were expected to be monogamous.

Poets and Neglected Gods

Because of the isolation of Arabia in the pre-Islamic age and the harshness and poverty of the natural environment, Arab material culture was not highly developed. Except in the far south, there was little art or architecture of worth. Even Mecca made little impression on the cosmopolitan merchants who passed through the city in caravans from the fabled cities of the ancient civilizations farther north. The main focus of bedouin cultural creativity in the pre-Islamic era was poetry, which was composed and transmitted orally because there was as yet no written language. Clan and tribal bards narrated poems that told of their kinsmen's heroics in war and the clan's great deeds. Some poets were said to have magical powers or to be possessed by demons. More than any other source, poems provide a vision of life and society in pre-Islamic Arabia. They tell of lovers spurned and passion consummated, war and vendettas, loyalty and generosity.

Allah The Arab term for the high god in pre-Islamic Arabia that was adopted by the followers of Muhammad and the Islamic faith.

Bedouin religion was for most clans a blend of animism and polytheism, or the worship of many gods and goddesses. Some tribes, such as the Quraysh, recognized a supreme god named Allah. But they seldom prayed or sacrificed to **Allah**, concentrating instead on less abstract spirits who seemed more relevant to their daily lives. Both spirits and gods (for example, the moon god, Hubal) tended to be associated with night, a cool period when dew covered the earth, which had been parched by the blaze of the desert sun. Likewise, the worship of nature spirits focused on sacred caves, pure springs, and groves of trees—places where the bedouins could take shelter from the heat and wind. Religion appears to have had little to do with ethics. Rather, standards of morality and proper behavior were rooted in tribal customs and unwritten codes of honor.

How seriously the bedouins took their gods is also a matter of some doubt. Their lukewarm adherence is illustrated by the famous tale of a bedouin warrior who had set out to avenge his father's death at the hands of a rival clan. He stopped at an oracle along the way to seek advice by drawing arrows that indicated various courses of action he might take. Three times he drew arrows that advised him to abandon his quest for revenge. Infuriated by this counsel, he hurled the arrows at the idol of the oracle and exclaimed, "Accursed one! Had it been thy father who was murdered, thou would not have forbidden my avenging him."

THE LIFE OF MUHAMMAD AND THE GENESIS OF ISLAM

11.2   Which aspects of Muhammad's religious message do you think accounted for its powerful appeal to both urban dwellers and nomadic peoples in Arabia and beyond?

> In the 7th century the revelations of the prophet Muhammad provided the basis for the emergence of a new religion—Islam—in the Arabian peninsula. Although initially an Arab religion, in both beliefs and practices, Islam contained a powerful appeal that eventually made it one of the great world religions.

By the 6th century C.E., camel nomads were dominant throughout much of Arabia. The civilized centers to the south were in ruins, and trading centers such as Mecca and Medina depended on alliances with neighboring bedouin tribes to keep the caravan routes open. The constricted world of clan and kin, nomadic camp, blood feud, and local gods persisted despite the lure of the empires and cosmopolitan urban centers that stretched in a great arc to the north and east of the Arabian peninsula (see Map 11.1).

But pressures for change were mounting. Both the Byzantine and **Sasanian empires** struggled to assert greater control over the nomadic tribes of the peninsula. In addition, Arab peoples migrated into Mesopotamia and other areas to the north, where they came increasingly under foreign influence. From these regions, the influence of established monotheistic religions, especially Judaism and Christianity, entered Arabia. These new currents gave rise to a number of Arab prophets who urged the bedouin tribes to renounce idol worship and rely on a single, almighty god. The prophet **Muhammad** and the new religion that his revelations inspired in the early decades of the 7th century responded both to these influences flowing into Arabia and to related social dislocations that were disrupting Arab life.

The hardships of Muhammad's early life underscore the importance of clan ties in the Arabian world. He was born around 570 C.E. into a prominent clan of the Quraysh tribe, the Banu Hashim, in a bedouin encampment where he spent the first six years of his life. Because his father died before he was born, Muhammad was raised by his father's relatives. The loss of his father was compounded by the death of Muhammad's mother shortly after he went to live with her some years later. Despite these early losses, Muhammad had the good fortune to be born into a respected clan and powerful tribe. His paternal uncle, Abu Talib, was particularly fond of the boy and served as his protector and supporter through much of his early life. Muhammad's grandfather, who like other leading members of the clan was engaged in commerce, educated the young man in the ways of the merchant. With Abu Talib, Muhammad made his first caravan journey to Syria, where on this and later trips he met adherents of the Christian and Jewish faiths, whose beliefs and practices had a great impact on his teachings.

In his adolescence, Muhammad took up residence in Mecca. By his early 20s he was working as a trader for **Khadijah**, the widow of a wealthy merchant, whom he married some years later. His life as a merchant in Mecca and on the caravan routes exposed Muhammad to the world beyond Arabia and probably made him acutely aware of the clan rivalries that had divided the peoples of the region for millennia. He would also have become increasingly concerned about new forces undermining solidarity within the clans. The growth of the towns and trade had enriched some clan families and left others behind, often in poverty. It had also introduced a new source of tension between clan and tribal groupings because some clans, such as the Umayyads, grew rich on the profits from commerce, whereas others maintained their herding lifestyle.

As a trader and traveler, Muhammad would almost certainly have been aware of the new religious currents that were sweeping Arabia and surrounding areas in the early 7th century. Particularly notable among these was the spread of monotheistic ideas and a growing dissatisfaction with the old gods that had been venerated by the bedouin peoples. In Muhammad's time, several prophets had arisen, proclaiming a new faith for the Arabs.

Although socially prominent, economically well off, and widely admired for his trading skills and trustworthiness, Muhammad grew increasingly distracted and dissatisfied with a life focused on material gain. He spent increasing amounts of time in meditation in the hills and wilderness that surrounded Mecca. In 610 or earlier, he received the first of many revelations, which his followers believe Allah transmitted to him through the angel Gabriel. These revelations were later written in Arabic and collected in the **Qur'an**. The teachings and injunctions of the Qur'an formed the basis of the new religion that Muhammad began to preach to his clan and the people of Mecca.

Sasanian empires The dynasty that ruled Persia (contemporary Iran) in the centuries before the rise of Muhammad and the early decades of Islamic expansion.

Muhammad Prophet of Islam; born c. 570 to Banu Hashim clan of Quraysh tribe in Mecca; raised by father's family; received revelations from Allah in 610 C.E. and thereafter; died in 632.

Khadijah [kah-DEE-juh] (555–619) First wife of the prophet Muhammad, who had worked for her as a trader.

Qur'an [kuh-RAHN] Recitations of revelations received by Muhammad; holy book of Islam.

Read the Document on MyHistoryLab: The Holy Qur'an (7th c. c.e.)

Persecution, Flight, and Victory

At first Muhammad's following was small, consisting mainly of his wife, several members of his clan, and some servants and slaves. As his message was clarified with successive revelations, the circle of the faithful grew so that the Umayyad notables who dominated Meccan life saw him as a threat to their own wealth and power. Above all, the new faith threatened to supplant the gods of the Ka'ba, whose shrines had done so much to establish the city as a center of commerce and bedouin interchange. Although he was protected for a time by his own clan, Muhammad was increasingly threatened by the Umayyads, who plotted with other clans to murder him. It was clear that Muhammad must flee Mecca, but where was he to find refuge? Muhammad's reputation as a skillful and fair negotiator prepared the way for his successful flight from Umayyad persecution. The quarrels between the clans in the nearby city of Medina had set off increasingly violent clashes, and the oasis community was on the verge of civil war. Leaders of the bedouin clans in Medina sent a delegation to invite Muhammad, who was related to them on his mother's side, to mediate their disputes and put an end to the strife that had plagued the town.

Clever ruses and the courage of his clansman **Ali**, who at one point took Muhammad's place and thus risked becoming the target of assassins, secured in 622 the safe passage of Muhammad and a small band of followers from Mecca to Medina. His *hijra* (HIH-jruh), or flight to Medina, marks the first year of the Islamic calendar. In Medina he was given a hero's welcome. He soon justified this warm reception by deftly settling the quarrels between the bedouin clans of the town. His wisdom and skill as a political leader won him new followers, who joined those who had accompanied him from Mecca as the core believers of the new faith.

In the eyes of the Umayyad notables, Muhammad's successes made him a greater threat than ever. Not only was he preaching a faith that rivaled their own, but his leadership was strengthening Mecca's competitor, Medina. Muslim raids on Meccan caravans provided yet another source of danger. Determined to put an end to these threats, the Quraysh launched a series of attacks in the mid-620s on Muhammad and his followers in Medina. These attacks led to several battles. In these clashes, Muhammad proved an able leader and courageous fighter.

The ultimate victory for Muhammad and his followers was signaled by a treaty with the Quraysh in 628, which included a provision granting the Muslims permission to visit the shrine at Ka'ba in Mecca during the season of truce. By then Muhammad's community had won many bedouin allies, and more than 10,000 converts accompanied him on his triumphal return to his hometown in 629. After proving the power of Allah, the single god he proclaimed, by smashing the idols of the shrine, Muhammad gradually won over the Umayyads and most of the other inhabitants of Mecca to the new faith.

Ali (c. 599–661) Cousin and son-in-law of Muhammad; one of orthodox caliphs; focus for Shi'a.

Arabs and Islam

Although Islam was soon to become one of the great world religions, the beliefs and practices of the prophet Muhammad were initially adopted only by the Arab town dwellers and bedouins among whom he had grown up. There is a striking parallel here with early Christianity, which focused on Jewish converts. The new religion preached by Muhammad had much to offer the divided peoples of Arabia. It gave them a form of monotheism that belonged to no single tribe and transcended clan and class divisions. It provided a religion that was distinctly Arab in origin and yet the equal of the monotheistic faiths held by the Christians and Jews, who lived in the midst of the bedouin tribes. If anything, the monotheism preached by Muhammad was even more uncompromising than that of the Christians because it allowed no intermediaries between the individual and God. God was one; there were no saints, and angels were nothing more than messengers. In addition, there were no priests in the Christian or Jewish sense of the term.

Islam offered the possibility of an end to the vendettas and feuds that had so long divided the peoples of Arabia and had undermined their attempts to throw off the domination of neighboring empires. The **umma**, or community of the faithful, transcended old tribal boundaries, and it made possible a degree of political unity undreamed of before Muhammad's time. The new religion provided a single and supernaturally sanctioned source of authority and discipline. With unity, the skills and energies that the bedouins had once channeled toward warring with each other were turned outward in a burst of conquest that is perhaps unmatched in human history in its speed and extent. From vassals, borderland warriors, or contemptible "savages" of the desert waste, the Arab bedouins were transformed into the conquerors and rulers of much of the Middle Eastern world.

umma Community of the faithful within Islam; transcended old tribal boundaries to create degree of political unity.

The new religion also provided an ethical system that did much to heal the deep social rifts within Arabian society. Islam stressed the dignity of all believers and their equality in the eyes of Allah. It promoted a moral code that stressed the responsibility of the well-to-do and strong for the poor and weak, the aged and infirm. Payment of the **zakat**, a tax for charity, was obligatory in the new faith. In both his revelations and his personal behavior, Muhammad enjoined his followers to be kind and generous to their dependents, including slaves. He forbade the rich to exploit the poor through exorbitant rents or rates of interest for loans.

zakat Tax for charity; obligatory for all Muslims.

The prophet's teachings and the revelations of the Qur'an soon were incorporated into an extensive body of law that regulated all aspects of the lives of the Muslim faithful. Held accountable before Islamic law on earth, they lived in a manner that would prepare them for the Last Judgment, which in Islam, as in Christianity, would determine their fate in eternity. A stern but compassionate God and a strict but socially minded body of law set impressive standards for the social interaction between adherents of the new faith.

Universal Elements in Islam

Although only Arabs embraced the religion of Islam in its early years, from the outset it contained beliefs and practices that would give it a strong appeal to peoples at virtually all stages of social development and in widely varying cultural settings. Some of these beliefs—Islam's uncompromising monotheism, highly developed legal codes, egalitarianism, and strong sense of community—were the same as the attributes that had won it support among the peoples of Arabia. Its potential as a world religion was enhanced by the fact that most of the attributes of Islam were to some degree anticipated by the other Semitic religions, particularly Judaism and Christianity, with which Muhammad had contact for much of his life. He accepted the validity of the earlier divine revelations that had given rise to the Jewish and Christian faiths. He taught that the revelations he had received were a refinement of these earlier ones and that they were the last divine instructions for human behavior and worship.

View the **Closer Look** on **MyHistoryLab**:The Ka'ba in Mecca

FIGURE **11.3** The Ka'ba in Mecca, with masses of pilgrims. Each year tens of millions of the Muslim faithful from all around the world make the journey to the holy sites of Arabia. The rituals performed by pilgrims at Mecca and Medina are key religious duties for all who can afford to travel to the holy cities.

five pillars The obligatory religious duties of all Muslims; confession of faith, prayer, fasting during Ramadan, zakat, and hajj.

Ramadan Islamic month of religious observance requiring fasting from dawn to sunset.

hajj A Muslim's pilgrimage to the holy city of Mecca, to worship Allah at the Ka'ba.

In addition to the beliefs and practices that have given Islam a universal appeal, its **five pillars**, principles that must be accepted and followed by all believers, provided the basis for an underlying religious unity. (1) The confession of faith was simple and powerful: "There is no God but Allah, and Muhammad is his Prophet." The injunctions (2) to pray, facing the holy city of Mecca, five times a day and (3) to fast during the month of **Ramadan**, enhanced community solidarity and allowed the faithful to demonstrate their fervor. (4) The zakat, or tithe for charity, also strengthened community cohesion and won converts from those seeking an ethical code that stressed social responsibility and the unity of all believers. (5) The **hajj**, or pilgrimage to the holy city of Mecca, to worship Allah at the Ka'ba, shown in Figure 11.3, drew together the faithful from Morocco to China. No injunction did more to give Islam a universal character.

THE ARAB EMPIRE OF THE UMAYYADS

Despite a time of crisis after the death of the prophet Muhammad in 632 C.E., the Muslim community held together. Eventually, Muhammad's old adversaries, the Umayya clan, seized leadership of the Muslim faithful and began a sequence of stunning conquests throughout the Middle East and north Africa.

11.3 What were the key factors that account for the rapid Arab conquests in the Middle East and Central Asia and North Africa?

Many of the bedouin tribes that had converted to Islam renounced the new faith in the months after Muhammad's death, and his remaining followers quarreled over who should succeed him. Although these quarrels were never fully resolved, the community managed to find new leaders who directed a series of campaigns to force those who had abandoned Islam to return to the fold. Having united most of Arabia under the Islamic banner by 633, Muslim military commanders began to mount serious expeditions beyond the peninsula, where only probing attacks had occurred during the lifetime of the prophet and in the period of tribal warfare after his death. The courage, military prowess, and religious zeal of the warriors of Islam, and the weaknesses of the empires that bordered on Arabia, resulted in stunning conquests in Mesopotamia, north Africa, and Persia, which dominated the next two decades of Islamic history. The empire built from these conquests was Arab rather than Islamic. Most of it was ruled by a small Arab warrior elite, led by the Umayyads and other prominent clans. These groups had little desire to convert the subject populations, either Arab or otherwise, to the new religion.

Consolidation and Division in the Islamic Community

The leadership crisis brought on by Muhammad's death in 632 was compounded by the fact that he had not appointed a successor or even established a procedure by which a new leader would be chosen. Opinion within the Muslim community was deeply divided as to who should succeed him. In this moment of extreme danger, a strong leader who could hold the Islamic community together was urgently needed. On the afternoon Muhammad died, one of the clans that remained committed to the new faith called a meeting to select a leader who would be designated as the **caliph**, the political and religious successor to Muhammad. Several choices were possible, and a deadlock between the clans appeared likely—a deadlock that would almost certainly have been fatal to a community threatened by enemies on all sides.

caliph The political and religious successor to Muhammad.

Read the **Document** on MyHistoryLab: Al-Tabari and Ibn Hisham, from "The Founding of the Caliphate"

Abu Bakr [ah-BOO BA-kuhr] The first caliph or leader of the Muslim faithful elected after Muhammad's death in 632. Renown for his knowledge of the nomadic tribes who then dominated the Islamic community.

One of the main candidates, Ali, the cousin and son-in-law of Muhammad, was passed over because he was considered too young to assume a position of such great responsibility. This decision later proved to be a major source of division in the Islamic community. But in 632, it appeared that a difficult reconciliation had been won by the choice of one of Muhammad's earliest followers and closest friends, **Abu Bakr** (ah-BOO BA-kuhr) (caliph from 632 to 634). In addition to his courage, warmth, and wisdom, Abu Bakr was well versed in the genealogical histories of the bedouin tribes, which meant that he knew which tribes could be turned against each other and which ones could be enticed into alliances. Initially, at least, his mandate was very limited. He received no financial support from the Muslim community. Thus, he had to continue his previous occupation as a merchant on a part-time basis, and he only loosely controlled the military commanders.

Ridda Wars Wars that followed Muhammad's death in 632; resulted in defeat of rival prophets and some of larger clans; restored unity of Islam.

These commanders turned out to be very able. After turning back attacks on Mecca, the Islamic faithful routed one after another of the bedouin tribes. The defeat of rival prophets and some of the larger clans in what were known as the **Ridda Wars** soon brought about the return of the Arabian tribes to the Islamic fold. Emboldened by the proven skills of his generals and the swelling ranks of the Muslim faithful, Abu Bakr oversaw raids to the north of Arabia into the sedentary zones in present-day Iraq and Syria and westward into Egypt (Map 11.1).

The unified bedouin forces had originally intended to raid for booty and then retreat back into the desert. But their initial probes revealed the vulnerability of the Byzantine and Persian empires, which dominated or ruled the territories into which the Muslim warriors rode. The invaders were also encouraged by the growing support of the Arab bedouin peoples who had been migrating into the Fertile Crescent for centuries. These peoples had long served as the vassals and frontier guardians of the Byzantine and Persian empires. Now they joined their brethren in a combined assault on both of them.

Motives for Arab Conquests

The Arab warriors were driven by many forces. The unity provided by the Islamic faith gave them a new sense of common cause and strength. United, they could stand up to the non-Arab rulers who had so long played them against each other and despised them as unwashed and backward barbarians from the desert wastelands. It is also probable that the early leaders of the community saw the wars of conquest as a good way to release the pent-up energies of the martial bedouin tribes they now sought to lead (see Figure 11.4). Above all, the bedouin warriors were drawn to the campaigns of expansion by the promise of a share in the booty to be won in the rich farmlands raided and the tribute that could be exacted from towns that came under Arab rule. As an early Arab writer observed, the bedouins forsook their life as desert nomads not out of a promise of religious rewards, but because of a "yearning after bread and dates."

The chance to glorify their new religion may have been a motive for the Arab conquests, but they were not driven by a desire to win converts to it. In fact, other than fellow bedouin tribes of Arab descent, the invaders had good reason to avoid mass conversions. Not only would Arab warriors have to share the booty of their military expeditions with ever larger numbers if converts were made, but Muslims were exempted from some of the more lucrative taxes levied on Christian, Jewish, and other non-Muslim groups. Thus, the vision of **jihads**, or holy wars launched to forcibly spread the Muslim faith, which has long been associated with Islam in the Christian West, misrepresents the forces behind the early Arab expansion.

jihads [jih-HAHDs] Struggles; often used for wars in defense of the faith, but also a term to indicate personal quests for religious understanding.

Weaknesses of the Adversary Empires

Of the two great empires that had once fought for dominance in the Fertile Crescent transit zone, the Sasanian Empire of Persia proved the more vulnerable. Power in the extensive Sasanian domains was formally concentrated in the hands of an autocratic emperor. By the time of the Arab explosion, the emperor was manipulated by a landed, aristocratic class that harshly exploited the farmers who made up most of the population of the empire. Zoroastrianism, the official religion of the emperor, lacked popular roots. By contrast, the religion of a visionary reformer named Mazdak, which had won considerable support among the peasants, had been brutally suppressed by the Sasanian rulers in the period before the rise of Islam.

At first, the Sasanian commanders had contempt for the Arab invaders and set out against them with poorly prepared forces. By the time the seriousness of the Islamic threat was made clear by decisive Arab victories in the Fertile Crescent region and the defection of the Arab tribes on the frontier,

FIGURE 11.4 This illustration from an account of the Muslim conquest of Sicily in the 9th century c.e. is one of the earliest known artistic renderings of an Arab army at war. The camp, the armored warriors, and the siege in progress help us to envision the Muslim forces that built the first great Arab empire under the early caliphs in the 7th century c.e.

Muslim warriors had broken into the Sasanian heartland. Further Muslim victories brought about the rapid collapse of the vast empire. The Sasanian rulers and their forces retreated eastward in the face of the Muslim advance. The capital was taken, armies were destroyed, and generals were slain. When in 651 the last of the Sasanian rulers was assassinated, Muslim victory and the destruction of the empire were ensured.

Despite an equally impressive string of Muslim victories in the provinces of their empire, the Byzantines proved a stronger adversary (see Chapter 14). However, their ability to resist the Muslim onslaught was impeded by both the defection of their own frontier Arabs and the support the Muslim invaders received from the Christians of Syria and Egypt. Members of the Christian sects dominant in these areas, such as the **Copts** and **Nestorians**, had long resented the rule of the Orthodox Byzantines, who taxed them heavily and openly persecuted them as heretics. When it became clear that the Muslims would not only tolerate the Christians but tax them less heavily than the Byzantines did, these Christian groups rallied to the Arabs.

Weakened from within and exhausted by the long wars fought with Persia in the decades before the Arab explosion, the Byzantines reeled from the Arab assaults. Syria, western Iraq, and Palestine were quickly taken by the Arab invaders, and by 640 a series of probes had been made into Egypt, one of the richest provinces of the empire (Map 11.2). In the early 640s, the ancient center of learning and commerce, Alexandria, was taken, most of Egypt was occupied, and Arab armies extended their conquests into Libya to the west. Perhaps even more astounding from the point of view of the Byzantines, by the mid-640s the desert bedouins were putting together war fleets that increasingly challenged the long-standing Byzantine mastery of the Mediterranean. The rise of Muslim naval supremacy in the eastern end of the Mediterranean sealed the loss of Byzantium's rich provinces in Syria and Egypt. It also opened the way to further Muslim conquests in north Africa, the Mediterranean islands, and even southern Italy (Map 11.2 and Figure 11.4). For a time the Byzantines managed to rally their forces and stave off further inroads into their Balkan and Asia Minor heartlands. But the early triumphs of

Copts Christian sect of Egypt; tended to support Islamic invasions of this area in preference to Byzantine rule.

Nestorians A Christian sect found in Asia; tended to support Islamic invasions of this area in preference to Byzantine rule; cut off from Europe by Muslim invasions.

MAP **11.2 The Expansion of Islamic Civilization, 622–750** Whether by land or sea, Islamic civilization expanded by both conquest and trade, while the Muslim faith was spread mainly peacefully along ancient trading routes, often by sufi holymen.

the Arab invaders had greatly reduced the strength of the Byzantine Empire. Although it survived for centuries, it was henceforth a kingdom under siege.

The Problem of Succession and the Sunni–Shi'a Split

The stunning successes of Muslim armies and the sudden rise of an Arab empire diverted attention, for a time at least, from continuing divisions within the community. Although these divisions were often generations old and the result of personal animosities, resentments had also begun to build over how the booty from the conquests should be divided among the tribal groups that made up the Islamic community. In 656, just over two decades after the death of the prophet, the growing tensions broke into open violence. The spark that began the conflict was the murder of the third caliph, **Uthman**, by mutinous warriors returning from Egypt. His death was the signal for the supporters of Ali to proclaim him as caliph. Uthman's unpopularity among many of the tribes, particularly those from Medina and the prophet's earliest followers, arose in part from the fact that he was the first caliph to be chosen from Muhammad's early enemies, the Umayyad clan. Already angered by Uthman's murder, the Umayyads rejected Ali's claims and swore revenge when he failed to punish Uthman's assassins. Warfare erupted between the two factions.

Ali was a renowned warrior and experienced commander, and his deeply committed supporters soon gained the upper hand. After his victory at the Battle of the Camel in late 656, most of the Arab garrisons shifted to his side against the Umayyads, whose supporters were concentrated in the province of Syria and the holy city of Mecca. Just as Ali was on the verge of defeating the Umayyad forces at the **Battle of Siffin** in 657, he was won over by a plea for mediation. His decision to accept mediation was fatal to his cause. Some of his most fervent supporters renounced his leadership and had to be suppressed violently. While representatives of both parties tried unsuccessfully to work out a compromise, the Umayyads regrouped their forces and added Egypt to the provinces backing their claims. In 660, **Mu'awiya**, the new leader of the Umayyads, was proclaimed caliph in Jerusalem, directly challenging Ali's position. A year later, Ali was assassinated, and his son Hasan was pressured by the Umayyads into renouncing his claims to the caliphate.

In the decades after the prophet's death, the question of succession generated deep divisions in the Muslim community. The split between the **Sunnis**, who backed the Umayyads, and the **Shi'a**, or supporters of Ali, remains to this day the most fundamental in the Islamic world. Hostility between these two branches of the Islamic faithful was heightened in the years after Ali's death by the continuing struggle between the Umayyads and Ali's second son, Husayn. After being abandoned by the clans in southern Iraq, who had promised to rise in a revolt supporting his claims against the Umayyads, Husayn and a small party were overwhelmed and killed at **Karbala** in 680. From that point on, the Shi'a mounted sustained resistance to the Umayyad caliphate.

Over the centuries, factional disputes about who had the right to succeed Muhammad, with the Shi'a recognizing none of the early caliphs except Ali, have been compounded by differences in belief, ritual, and law that have steadily widened the gap between Sunnis and Shi'a. These divisions have been further complicated by the formation of splinter sects within the Shi'a community in particular, beginning with those who defected from Ali when he agreed to arbitration.

The Umayyad Imperium

After a pause to settle internal disputes over succession, the remarkable sequence of Arab conquest was renewed in the last half of the 7th century. Muslim armies broke into central Asia, inaugurating a rivalry with Buddhism in the region that continues to the present day (Map 11.2). By the early 8th century, the southern prong of this advance had reached into northwest India. Far to the west, Arab armies swept across north Africa and crossed the Straits of Gibraltar to conquer Spain and threaten France. Although the Muslim advance into western Europe was blocked by the hard-fought victory of Charles Martel and the Franks at Poitiers in 732, the Arabs did not fully retreat beyond the Pyrenees into Spain until decades later. Muslim warriors and sailors dominated much of the Mediterranean, a position that was solidified by the conquest of key islands such as Crete, Sicily, and Sardinia in the early decades of the 9th century. By the early 700s, the Umayyads ruled an empire that extended from Spain in the west to the steppes of central Asia in the east. Not since the Romans had there been an empire to match it; never had an empire of its size been built so rapidly.

Uthman Third caliph and member of Umayyad clan; murdered by mutinous warriors returning from Egypt; death set off civil war in Islam between followers of Ali and the Umayyad clan.

Battle of Siffin Fought in 657 between forces of Ali and Umayyads; settled by negotiation that led to fragmentation of Ali's party.

Mu'awiya [moo-UH-wee-uh] (602–680) Leader of Umayyad clan; first Umayyad caliph following civil war with Ali.

Sunnis Political and theological division within Islam; supported the Umayyads.

Shi'a Also known as Shi'ites; political and theological division within Islam; followers of Ali.

Karbala Site of defeat and death of Husayn, son of Ali; marked beginning of Shi'a resistance to Umayyad caliphate.

Damascus Syrian city that was capital of Umayyad caliphate.

Although Mecca remained the holy city of Islam, under the Umayyads the political center of community shifted to **Damascus** in Syria, where the Umayyads chose to live after the murder of Uthman. From Damascus a succession of Umayyad caliphs strove to build a bureaucracy that would bind together the vast domains they claimed to rule. The empire was very much an Arab conquest state. Except in the Arabian peninsula and in parts of the Fertile Crescent, a small Arab and Muslim aristocracy ruled over peoples who were neither Arab nor Muslim. Only Muslim Arabs were first-class citizens of this great empire. They made up the core of the army and imperial administration, and only they received a share of the booty derived from the ongoing conquests. They could be taxed only for charity. The Umayyads sought to keep the Muslim warrior elite concentrated in garrison towns and separated from the local population. It was hoped that isolation would keep them from assimilating to the subjugated cultures, because intermarriage meant conversion and the loss of taxable subjects.

Converts and "People of the Book"

mawali Non-Arab converts to Islam.

jizya [JIHZ-yuh] Head tax paid by all nonbelievers in Islamic territories.

dhimmi [DIH-mee] Literally "people of the book"; applied as inclusive term to Jews and Christians in Islamic territories; later extended to Zoroastrians and even Hindus.

Umayyad attempts to block extensive interaction between the Muslim warrior elite and their non-Muslim subjects had little chance of succeeding. The citified bedouin tribes were soon interacting intensively with the local populations of the conquered areas and intermarrying with them. Equally critical, increasing numbers of these peoples were voluntarily converting to Islam, despite the fact that conversion did little to advance them socially or politically in the Umayyad period. In this era Muslim converts, **mawali**, still had to pay property taxes and in some cases the **jizya**, or head tax, levied on nonbelievers. They received no share of the booty and found it difficult, if not impossible, to get important positions in the army or bureaucracy. They were not even considered full members of the umma but were accepted only as clients of the powerful Arab clans.

As a result, the number of conversions in the Umayyad era was low. By far the greater portion of the population of the empire were the **dhimmi**, or "people of the book." As the name suggests, it was originally applied to Christians and Jews who shared the Bible with the Muslims. As Islamic conquests spread to other peoples, such as the Zoroastrians of Persia and the Hindus of India, the designation *dhimmi* was necessarily stretched to accommodate the majority groups within these areas of the empire. As the early illustration of Jewish worship in Muslim Spain in Figure 11.5 shows, the Muslim overlords generally tolerated the religions of dhimmi. Although they had to pay the jizya and both commercial and property taxes, their communities and legal systems were left intact, and they were allowed to worship as they pleased. This approach made it a good deal easier for these peoples to accept Arab rule, particularly because many had been oppressed by their pre-Muslim overlords.

FIGURE **11.5** Jews worshiping in a synagogue. As dhimmi, or "people of the book," Jews were allowed to build impressive synagogues and worship freely throughout the Muslim world. Jewish merchant families amassed great wealth, often in partnership with Muslims, and Jewish scholars were revered from Spain to Baghdad for their many contributions to learning.

Family and Gender Roles in the Umayyad Age

Broader social changes within the Arab and widening Islamic community were accompanied by significant shifts in the position of women, both within the family and in society at large. In the first centuries of Arab expansion, the greatly strengthened position of women under Islam prevailed over the seclusion and subordination that were characteristic features of women's lives through much of the rest of the pre-Islamic Middle East. Muhammad's teachings and the dictates of the Qur'an stressed the moral and ethical dimensions of marriage. The kindness and concern the prophet displayed for his own wives and daughters did much to strengthen the bonds between husband and wife and the nuclear family in the Islamic community.

Muhammad encouraged marriage as a replacement for the casual and often commercial sexual liaisons that had been widespread in pre-Islamic Arabia. He vehemently denounced adultery on the part of both husbands and wives, and he forbade female infanticide, which apparently had been widely practiced in Arabia in pre-Islamic times. Men were allowed to marry up to four wives. But the Qur'an forbade multiple marriages if the husband could not support more than one wife or treat all of his wives equally. Women could not take more than one husband. But Muhammad gave his own daughters a say as to whom they would marry and greatly strengthened the legal rights of women in inheritance and divorce. He insisted that the bride-price paid by the husband's family be given to his future wife rather than to her father.

The prophet's teachings proclaimed the equality of men and women before God and in Islamic worship. Women, most notably his wife Khadijah, were some of Muhammad's earliest and bravest followers. In the battle with the Meccans, women accompanied the forces on both sides, and a woman was the first martyr for the new faith. Many of the **hadiths**, or traditions of the prophet, which have played such a critical role in Islamic law and ritual, were recorded by women. In addition, Muhammad's wives and daughters played an important role in compiling the Qur'an.

hadiths [huh-DEETHs] Traditions of the prophet Muhammad.

Although women were not allowed to lead prayers, they played an active role in the politics of the early community. Muhammad's widow, Aisha, actively promoted the claims of the Umayyad party against Ali, while Zainab, Ali's daughter, went into battle with the ill-fated Husayn. Through much of the Umayyad period, little is heard of veiled Arab women, and women appear to have pursued a wide range of occupations, including scholarship, law, and commerce. Perhaps one of Zainab's nieces best epitomizes the independent-mindedness of Muslim women in the early Islamic era. When chided for going about without a veil, she replied that Allah in his wisdom had chosen to give her a beautiful face and that she intended to make sure that it was seen in public so that all might appreciate his grace.

Umayyad Decline and Fall

The ever-increasing size of the royal harem was just one manifestation of the Umayyad caliphs' growing addiction to luxury and soft living. Their legitimacy had been disputed by various Muslim factions since their seizure of the caliphate. But the Umayyads further alienated the Muslim faithful as they became more aloof in the early 8th century and retreated from the dirty business of war into their pleasure gardens and marble palaces. Their abandonment of the frugal, simple lifestyle followed by Muhammad and the earliest caliphs—including Abu Bakr, who made a trip to the market the day after he was selected to succeed the prophet—enraged the dissenting sects and sparked revolts throughout the empire. The uprising that proved fatal to the short-lived dynasty began among the frontier warriors who had fought and settled in distant Iran.

By the mid-8th century, more than 50,000 warriors had settled near the oasis town of Merv in the eastern Iranian borderlands of the empire (Figure 11.6). Many of them had married local women, and over time they had come to identify with the region and to resent the dictates of governors sent from distant Damascus. The warrior settlers were also angered by the fact that they were rarely given the share of the booty, which was now officially tallied in the account books of the royal treasury, they had earned by fighting the wars of expansion and

FIGURE **11.6** Muslim worshippers in modern Pakistan. Whether in a nearby mosque or in their homes and shops, Muslims are required to pray five times a day, facing the holy city of Mecca. Those congregating in a mosque, as in this photo, are oriented to Mecca by the qibla wall, which is marked by a highly ornamented inset that indicates the direction of the holy city. Men congregate in the open spaces in the center of and outside the mosque, while women pray in areas on the sides or in the back or, sometimes, in balconies above that are screened off by pillars or carved panels from the areas where the men worship.

THINKING HISTORICALLY

Civilization and Gender Relationships

WITHIN A CENTURY OF MUHAMMAD'S DEATH, the strong position women had enjoyed as a result of the teachings and example of the prophet had begun to erode. We do not fully understand all the forces that account for this decline. Ambiguities in the Qur'an and other early sources—especially the hadith, or traditions of the prophet—provide part of the answer. These sources indicate that, in both his domestic and public life, Muhammad was concerned about good treatment for women and defined certain rights, for example, to property. But early records also stipulate women's inferiority to men in key legal rights (differential punishments for adultery were a case in point). And, like their Christian counterparts, Islamic thinkers argued that women were more likely than men to be sinners. But more critical were the beliefs and practices of the urbanized, sedentary peoples in the areas the Arabs conquered and where many of them settled from the mid-7th century onward.

The example of these ancient and long-civilized peoples increasingly influenced the Arab bearers of Islam. They developed a taste for city life and the superior material and artistic culture of the peoples they ruled. In terms of gender roles, most of these influences weakened the position of women. We have seen this apparent connection between increasing political centralization and urbanization and the declining position of women in many of the ancient and classical civilizations treated thus far. In China, India, Greece, and the Middle East, women enjoyed broader occupational options and a stronger voice within the family, and in society as a whole, before the emergence of centralized polities and highly stratified social systems. In each case, the rise of what we have called civilizations strengthened paternal control within the family, inheritance through the male line, and male domination of positions of power and the most lucrative occupations. Women in these societies became more and more subjected to men—their fathers and brothers, husbands and sons—and more and more confined to the roles of homemakers and bearers of children. Women's legal rights were reduced, often sharply. In many civilizations, various ways were devised to shut women off from the world.

As we have seen, women played active and highly valued roles in the bedouin tribes of pre-Islamic Arabia. Particularly in towns such as Mecca, they experienced considerable freedom in terms of sexual and marriage partners, occupational choices (within the limited range available in an isolated pastoral society), and opportunities to influence clan decisions. The position of Muhammad's first wife, Khadijah, is instructive. Her position as a wealthy widow in charge of a thriving trading enterprise

Islamic law preserved for women property, inheritance, divorce, and remarriage rights that often were denied in other civilized societies.

reveals that women were able to remarry and to own and inherit property. They could also pursue careers, even after their husbands died. Khadijah employed Muhammad. After he had successfully worked for her for some time, she asked him to marry her, which apparently neither surprised nor scandalized her family or Meccan society. It is also noteworthy that Khadijah was 15 years older than Muhammad, who was 25 at the time of their betrothal.

The impact of the bedouin pattern of gender roles and relationships is also clear in the teachings and personal behavior of Muhammad. Islam did much to legalize the strong but by no means equal status of women. In addition, it gave greater uniformity to their position from one tribe, town, or region to the next. For a century or two after the prophet's death, women in the Islamic world enjoyed unprecedented opportunities for education, religious expression, and social fulfillment. Then the influences of the cultures into which the Arabs had expanded began to take hold. The practices of veiling and female seclusion that were long followed by the non-Arab dwellers of Syria and Persia were increasingly adopted by or imposed upon Muslim women. Confined more and more to the home, women saw their occupational options decrease, and men served as their go-betweens in legal and commercial matters.

Ironically, given the earlier status of women, such as Khadijah, the erosion of the position of women was especially pronounced among those who lived in the cities that became the focus of Islamic civilization. Upper-class women, in particular, felt growing restrictions on their movement and activities. In the great residences that sprang up in the wealthy administrative centers and trading towns of the Middle East, the women's quarters were separate from the rest of the household and set off by high walls and gardens. In the palaces of Islamic rulers and provincial governors, this separation was marked by the development of the *harem*, or forbidden area. In the harem, the notables' wives and concubines lived in seclusion. They were constantly guarded by the watchful eyes and sharp swords of corps of eunuchs, men castrated specifically to qualify them for the task.

When upper-class women went into the city, they were veiled from head to toe and often were carried in covered sedan chairs by servants who guarded them from the glances of the townsmen and travelers. In their homes, upper-class women were spared the drudgery of domestic chores by large numbers of female slaves. If we are to judge from stories such as those related in the *Arabian Nights* (from which excerpts are included in the Document feature on page 264), female slaves and servants were largely at the mercy

(continued on next page)

of their male masters. Although the veiling, seclusion, and other practices that limited the physical and occupational mobility of women also spread to the lower urban classes and rural areas, they were never as strictly observed there as in urban, upper-class households. Women from poorer families had to work to survive. Thus, they had to go out, "veiled but often unchaperoned," to the market or to work as domestic servants. Lower-class women also worked hard at home, not just at housekeeping but at weaving, rug-making, and other crafts that supplemented the family income. In rural areas and in towns distant from the main urban centers, veiling and confinement were observed less strictly. Peasant women worked the family or local landlord's fields, planted their own gardens, and tended the livestock.

Because of Islamic religion and law, in all locales and at all class levels the position of women in the Middle East never deteriorated to the same extent as in India, China, and many other civilized centers. Because of the need to read the Qur'an, women continued to be educated, family resources permitting, even if they rarely were able to use their learning for scholarship or artistic expression. Islamic law preserved for women property, inheritance, divorce, and remarriage rights that often were denied in other civilized societies. Thus, the strong position women had enjoyed in bedouin cultures, and that in many respects had been built into Islam, was never entirely undone by the customs and practices Muslims encountered as they came to rule the civilized centers in the rest of the Middle East.

The fact that the position of women has also been strong in other cultural areas where authority is decentralized and social organization not highly stratified, such as those in west Africa (see Chapter 13), suggests that at least in certain stages of its development, civilization works against the interests of women. Women in decentralized societies have often been able to own their own property, to engage in key economic activities, and to play important roles in religious ceremonies. The positions and status they have achieved in decentralized societies, such as those in early Arabia or much of sub-Saharan Africa and southeast Asia, suggest factors that may help explain the greater balance in gender roles and power in less centralized societies. The very immediate connection between women and agriculture and stock-raising, which are central to survival in these societies, may also account for the greater respect accorded them and for their often prominent roles in fertility rituals and religious cults. Whatever the explanation, until the present era, higher degrees of centralization and social stratification—both characteristic features of civilized societies—have almost always favored men in the allotment of power and career opportunities.

QUESTIONS

- Compare the position of upper-class women in classical Indian, Chinese, Greek, and Roman societies with regard to their ability to hold property, opportunity to pursue careers outside the home, rights in marriage and divorce, and level of education. In which of these societies were women better off, and why?

- Were differences in the position of women at lower-class levels similar between these societies?

- In what ways were women better off in decentralized pastoral or forest-farming societies?

- What advantages have they enjoyed in highly urbanized and more centralized civilizations?

---

defending the frontiers. They were contemptuous of the Umayyads and the Damascus elite, whom they saw as corrupt and decadent. In the early 740s, an attempt by Umayyad palace officials to introduce new troops into the Merv area touched off a revolt that soon spread over much of the eastern portions of the empire (Map 11.2).

Marching under the black banners of the **Abbasid** party, which traced its descent from Muhammad's uncle, al-Abbas, the frontier warriors openly challenged Umayyad armies by 747. Deftly forging alliances with dissident groups that resisted the Umayyads throughout the empire, their leader, Abu al-Abbas, the great-great-grandson of the prophet's uncle, led his forces from victory to victory. Among his most important allies were the Shi'a, who, as we have seen, had rejected Umayyad authority from the time of Ali. Also critical were the mawali, or non-Arab converts to Islam. The mawali felt that under Umayyad rule they had never been recognized as fully Muslim. In supporting the Abbasids, the mawali hoped to attain full acceptance in the community of believers.

Abbasid [uh bas id, ab uh sid] Dynasty that succeeded the Umayyads as caliphs within Islam; came to power in 750 C.E.,

This diverse collection of Muslim rebels made short work of what remained of the Umayyad imperium. Persia and then Iraq fell to the rebels. In 750, the Abbasid forces met an army led by the Umayyad caliph himself in the massive **Battle of the River Zab** near the Tigris. The Abbasid victory opened the way for the conquest of Syria and the capture of the Umayyad capital.

Battle of the River Zab Victory of Abbasids over Umayyads; resulted in conquest of Syria and capture of Umayyad capital.

Wanting to eliminate the Umayyad family altogether to prevent recurring challenges to his rule, Abu al-Abbas invited many members of the clan to what was styled as a reconciliation banquet. As the Umayyads were enjoying the feast, guards covered them with carpets and they were slaughtered by Abbas's troops. An effort was then made to hunt down and kill all the remaining members of the family throughout the empire. Most were slain, but, as we have seen, the grandson of a former caliph fled to Spain and founded there what later became the Umayyad caliphate of Córdoba, which lived on for centuries after the rest of the Umayyads' empire had disappeared (see Map 11.3 and Figure 11.1).

📖 **Read** the **Document** on **MyHistoryLab:** Harun al-Rashid and the Zenith of the Caliphate

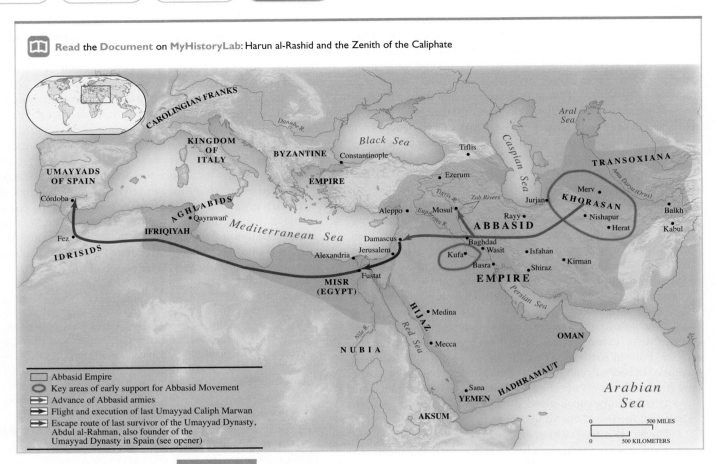

MAP 11.3 Emergence of the Abbasid Dynasty Frontier warriors from Khorasan far from the Umayyad capital at Damascus built a military force that overthrew the Umayyads between 747 and 750 C.E.

FROM ARAB TO ISLAMIC EMPIRE: THE EARLY ABBASID ERA

> Under the Abbasids, who succeeded the Umayyads, Islam became a universal religion that spread across much of north Africa and Euro-Asia. With its capital at Baghdad, Islamic civilization flourished under the Abbasids, even as their empire began to fragment into regional power centers.

Baghdad Capital of Abbasid dynasty located in Iraq near ancient Persian capital of Ctesiphon.

11.4   In what ways was the Islamic religion a faith that elevated the status and opportunities of women, and what were the constraints on this process?

The rough treatment the Umayyad clan had received at the hands of the victorious Abbasids should have forewarned their Shi'a and mawali allies of what was to come. But the Shi'a and other dissenting groups continued the support that allowed the Abbasids to level all other centers of political rivalry. Gradually, the Abbasids rejected many of their old allies, becoming more and more righteous in their defense of Sunni Islam and increasingly less tolerant of what they called the heretical views of the various sects of Shi'ism. With the Umayyads all but eliminated and their allies brutally suppressed, the way was clear for the Abbasids to build a centralized, absolutist imperial order.

The fact that they chose to build their new capital, **Baghdad**, in Iraq near the ancient Persian capital of Ctesiphon was a clear sign of things to come. Soon the Abbasid caliphs were perched on jewel-encrusted thrones, reminiscent of those of the ancient Persian emperors, gazing down on the great gatherings of courtiers and petitioners who bowed before them in their gilt and marble audience halls. The caliphs' palaces and harems expanded to keep pace with their claims to absolute power over the Islamic faithful as well as the non-Muslim subjects of their vast empire.

The ever-expanding corps of bureaucrats, servants, and slaves who strove to translate Abbasid political claims into reality lived and worked within the circular walls of the new capital at Baghdad.

The bureaucratization of the Islamic Empire was reflected above all in the growing power of the **wazir**, or chief administrator and head of the caliph's inner councils. It was also embodied in a more sinister way in the fearful guise of the royal executioner, who stood close to the throne in the public audiences of the Abbasid rulers. The wazirs oversaw the building of an administrative infrastructure that allowed the Abbasids to project their demands for tribute to the most distant provinces of the empire. Sheer size, poor communications, and collusion between Abbasid officials and local notables meant that the farther the town or village was from the capital, the less effectively royal commands were carried out. But for more than a century, the Abbasid regime was fairly effective at collecting revenue from its subject peoples and preserving law and order over much of the empire.

Islamic Conversion and Mawali Acceptance

The Abbasid era saw the full integration of new converts, both Arab and non-Arab, into the Islamic community. In the last decades of the Umayyad period, there was a growing acceptance of the mawali, or non-Arab Muslims, as equals. There were also efforts to win new converts to the faith, particularly among Arab peoples outside the Arabian peninsula. In the Abbasid era, when the practice of dividing booty between the believers had long been discarded, mass conversions to Islam were encouraged for all peoples of the empire, from the Berbers of north Africa to the Persians and Turkic peoples of central Asia. Converts were admitted on an equal footing with the first generations of believers, and over time the distinction between mawali and the earlier converts all but disappeared.

Most converts were won over peacefully through the great appeal of Islamic beliefs and the advantages they enjoyed over non-Muslim peoples in the empire. Not only were converts exempt from paying the head tax, but they had greater opportunities to get advanced schooling and launch careers as administrators, traders, or judges. No group demonstrated the new opportunities open to converts as dramatically as the Persians, who, in part through their bureaucratic skills, soon came to dominate the upper levels of imperial administration. In fact, as the Abbasid rulers became more dissolute and less interested in affairs of state, several powerful Persian families close to the throne became the real locus of power in the imperial system.

Town and Country: Commercial Boom and Agrarian Expansion

The rise of the mawali was paralleled in the Abbasid era by the growth in wealth and social status of the merchant and landlord classes of the empire. The Abbasid age was a time of great urban expansion that was linked to a revival of the Afro-Eurasian trading network, which had declined with the fall of the Han dynasty in China in the early 3rd century C.E. and the slow collapse of the Roman Empire in the 4th and 5th centuries. The Abbasid domains in the west and the great Tang and Song empires in the east became the pivots of the revived commercial system.

From the western Mediterranean to the South China Sea, Arab **dhows**, or sailing vessels with lateen (triangular) sails, which later influenced European ship design, carried the goods of one civilized core to be exchanged with those of another. Muslim merchants often formed joint ventures with Christians and Jews. Because each merchant had a different Sabbath, the firm could do business all week. Merchants grew rich by supplying the cities of the empire with provisions. Mercantile concerns also took charge of the long-distance trade that specialized in luxury products for the elite classes. The great profits from trade were reinvested in new commercial enterprises, the purchase of land, and the construction of the great mansions that dominated the central quarters of the political and commercial hubs of the empire. Some wealth also went to charity, as required by the Qur'an. A good deal of the wealth was spent on building and running mosques and religious schools, baths, and rest houses for weary travelers (Figure 11.7). Large donations were

wazir [wuh-ZEER] Chief administrative official under the Abbasid caliphate; initially recruited from Persian provinces of empire.

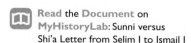
Read the Document on MyHistoryLab: Sunni versus Shi'a Letter from Selim I to Ismail I

dhows Arab sailing vessels with triangular or lateen sails; strongly influenced European ship design.

Read the Document on MyHistoryLab: Baghdad: City of Wonders

FIGURE **11.7** The rulers and nobility of the Abbasid capital in Baghdad frequented baths like that shown in this Persian miniature painting. Here the caliph, Haroun al-Rashid, receives a haircut while servants prepare the steam rooms. At the baths, the Abbasid elite could relax, exchange gossip, and enjoy expert massages. (British Library, London.)

VISUALIZING THE PAST

The Mosque as a Symbol of Islamic Civilization

FROM ONE END OF THE ISLAMIC world to the other, Muslim towns and cities can be readily identified by the domes and minarets of the mosques where the faithful are called to prayer five times daily. The illustrations included here trace the development of the mosque and the refinement of mosque architecture, the crowning glory of Islamic material culture, during the early centuries of Muslim expansion. As you look at these pictures and follow the development of the mosque, consider what the functions of the mosque and the evolving style of mosque architecture can tell us about Muslim beliefs and values and the impact of earlier religions, such as Judaism and Christianity, on Islam.

Given the low level of material culture in pre-Islamic Arabia, it is not surprising that the earliest prayer houses were simple in design and construction. In fact, these first mosques were laid out along the lines suggested by Muhammad's own house. They were square enclosures with a shaded porch on one side, a columned shelter on the other, and an open courtyard in between. The outer perimeter of the earliest mosques was made of reed mats, but soon more permanent stone walls surrounded the courtyard and prayer areas. After Mecca was taken and the Ka'ba became the central shrine of the new faith, each mosque was oriented to the qibla, or Mecca wall, which always faced in the direction of the holy city.

In the last years of the prophet, his chair was located so that the faithful could see and hear him during prayer sessions. During the time of the first caliphs, the raised area became the place from

Pulpit (minbar) from which the Friday sermons are delivered throughout the Muslim world.

which sermons were delivered. From the mid-8th century, this space evolved into a genuine pulpit (*minbar* in Arabic). Somewhat earlier, the practice of building a special and often elaborately decorated niche in the qibla had developed.

Over time, mosques became more elaborate. Very often the remains of Greek or Roman temples or abandoned Christian churches formed the core of major mosques, or the ruins of these structures were mined for stone for mosque construction. In the larger cities, the courtyards of the great mosques were surrounded by columns and arches, and eventually they were enclosed by great domes such as that at the Dome of the Rock in Jerusalem.

Domes and minarets of the Shah Mosque at Isfahan, Iran.

(continued on next page)

(continued from previous page)

Drawing of the early mosque design.

Al-Aqsa Mosque (or Dome of the Rock) in Jerusalem, the third holiest site in Islam.

The first minarets, or towers from which the faithful were called to prayer, were added in the early 8th century and soon became a key feature of the mosque complex. As mosques grew larger and more architecturally refined, elaborate decoration in brightly colored ceramic tiles, semiprecious stones, and gold and silver filigree adorned their sides and domes. Because human and animal images were forbidden, geometric designs, passages from the Qur'an in swirling Arabic, and flower and plant motifs were favored. Nowhere were these decorations more splendid than in the mosques of Persia. Thus, in the early centuries of Islam, these great houses of worship became the focal points of Islamic cities, key places of community worship and socialization, and, with the schools that were often attached, vital intellectual and educational centers of the Islamic world.

QUESTIONS

- What do the design and decoration of Muslim mosques tell us about the Islamic view of a supreme being and the relationship between Allah and humans?
- Discuss the Christian and Jewish influences you detect in mosque design and the pattern of religious worship conducted there. What do you think is the significance of the lavish application of color and the frequent use of floral and plant motifs and Arabic verses from the Qur'an in the decoration of mosques through much of the Muslim world?

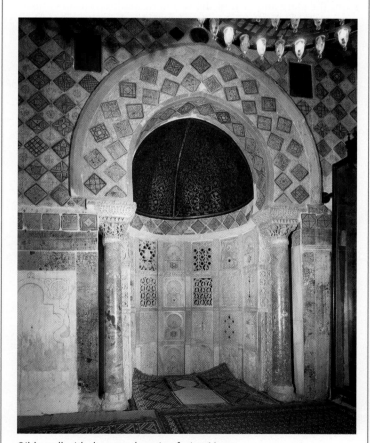

Qibla wall with decorated section facing Mecca.

also made to hospitals, which in the numbers of their patients and the quality of their medical care surpassed those of any other civilization of that time.

The growth of Abbasid cities was also fed by a great increase in handicraft production. Both government-run and privately owned workshops expanded or were established to produce a wide range of products, from necessities such as furniture and carpets to luxury items such as glassware, jewelry, and tapestries. Although the artisans often were poorly paid and some worked in great

DOCUMENT

The Thousand and One Nights as a Mirror of Elite Society in the Abbasid Era

THE LUXURIOUS LIFESTYLE OF THE ABBASID rulers and their courtiers reflected the new wealth of the political and commercial elites of the Islamic Empire. At the same time, it intensified sectarian and social divisions in the Islamic community. As the compilation of folktales from many parts of the empire titled *The Thousand and One Nights* testifies, life for much of the elite in Baghdad and other major urban centers was luxurious and oriented to the delights of the flesh. Caliphs and wealthy merchants lived in palatial residences of stone and marble, complete with gurgling fountains and elaborate gardens, which served as retreats from the glare and heat of the southern Mediterranean climate. In the Abbasid palaces, luxurious living and ostentation soared to fantastic heights. In the Hall of the Tree, for example, there was a huge artificial tree, made entirely of gold and silver and filled with gold mechanical birds that chirped to keep the caliph in good cheer.

Because the tales were just that—tall tales—there is some exaggeration of the wealth, romantic exploits, and sexual excesses of the world depicted. But for some members of the elite classes, the luxuries, frivolities, and vices of the Abbasid age were very real. The following passages are taken from an English translation of *The Thousand and One Nights*. Each is selected to reveal a different facet of high society in the Abbasid era. The first, which describes the sumptuous interior of a mansion in Baghdad, indicates that conspicuous material consumption existed far beyond the palace.

> They reached a spacious ground-floor hall, built with admirable skill and beautified with all manner of colors and carvings, with upper balconies and groined [sharply curved] arches and galleries and cupboards and recesses whose curtains hung before them. In the midst stood a great basin full of water surrounding a fine fountain, and at the upper end on the raised dais was a couch of juniper wood set with gems and pearls, with a canopy-like mosquito curtain of red satin-silk looped up with pearls as big as filberts [hazelnuts] and bigger.

In another tale, a fallen prince details the proper upbringing and education for a person of substance:

> I am a king, son of a king, and was brought up like a prince. I learned intoning the Koran [Qur'an] according [to] the seven schools and I read all manner [of] books, and held disputations on their contents with the doctors and men of science. Moreover, I studied star lore and the fair sayings of poets, and I exercised myself in all branches of learning until I surpassed the people of my time. My skill in calligraphy [writing, in this case Arabic and perhaps Persian] exceeded that of all of the scribes, and my fame was bruited abroad over all climes and cities, and all the kings learned to know my name.

In the following passage, a stylishly dressed woman from the elite classes is described in great detail:

> There stood before him an honorable woman in a mantilla [veil] of Mosul silk broidered with gold and bordered with brocade [a rich cloth with a raised design, often of gold or silver]. Her walking shoes were also [broidered] with gold, and her hair floated in long plaits. She raised her face veil . . . showing two black eyes fringed with jetty lashes, whose glances were soft and languishing and whose perfect beauty was ever blandishing.

The woman leads a porter to a marketplace, which again reflects the opulence accessible to the rich and powerful of Abbasid society:

> She stopped at the fruiter's shop and bought from him Shami apples and Osmani quinces and Omani peaches, and cucumbers of Nile growth, and Egyptian limes and Sultani oranges and citrons, besides Aleppine jasmine, scented myrtle berries, Damascene nenuphars [water lilies], flower of privit and camomile, blood-red anemones, violets, and pomegranate bloom, eglantine [wild rose], and narcissus, and set the whole in the porter's crate.

QUESTIONS

- What objects are key symbols of wealth in Abbasid society?
- What attainments are highly valued for upper-class men?
- What do they tell us about occupations and talents that brought high status in Abbasid society, and how do they compare with career aspirations in our own?
- In comparison, what attributes of women are stressed in these passages?

workshops, they were not slaves or drudge laborers. They owned their own tools and were often highly valued for their skills. The most accomplished of the artisans formed guildlike organizations, which negotiated wages and working conditions with the merchants and supported their members in times of financial difficulty or personal crisis.

In towns and the countryside, much of the unskilled labor was left to slaves, often attached to prominent families as domestic servants. Large numbers of slaves also served the caliphs and their highest advisors. It was possible for the more clever and ambitious slaves to rise to positions of great power, and many eventually were granted their freedom or were able to buy it. Less fortunate were the slaves forced into lives of hard labor under the overseer's whip on rural estates and government projects, such as those devoted to draining marshlands, or into a lifetime of labor in the nightmare conditions of the great salt mines in southern Iraq. Most of these drudge laborers were non-Muslims captured on slaving raids in east Africa.

In the countryside, a wealthy and deeply entrenched landed elite called the **ayan** emerged in the early decades of Abbasid rule. Many of these landlords had been long established. Others were new-comers: Arab soldiers who invested their share of the booty in land, or merchants and administrators who funneled their profits and kickbacks into sizeable estates. In many regions, most peasants did not own the land they worked. They occupied it as tenants, sharecroppers, or migrant laborers who were required to give the greater portion of the crops they harvested to the estate owners.

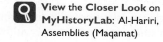

View the **Closer Look** on **MyHistoryLab**: Al-Hariri, Assemblies (Maqamat)

ayan [ä yän] The wealthy landed elite that emerged in the early decades of Abbasid rule.

The First Flowering of Islamic Learning

In the first phase of Abbasid rule, the Islamic contribution to human artistic expression focused on the great mosques, such as those featured in the Visualizing the Past box, and great palaces. In addition to advances in religious, legal, and philosophical discourse, learning in the Muslim domains focused on the sciences and mathematics. In the early Abbasid period, the main tasks were recovering and preserving the learning of the ancient civilizations of the Mediterranean and Middle East. Beyond the works of Plato, for example, much of Greek learning had been lost to the peoples of western Europe. Thanks to Muslim and Jewish scholars, the priceless writings of the Greeks on key subjects such as medicine, algebra, geometry, astronomy, anatomy, and ethics were saved, recopied in Arabic, and dispersed throughout the empire. From Spain, Greek writings found their way into Christendom. Among the authors rescued in this manner were Aristotle, Galen, Hippocrates, Ptolemy, and Euclid.

In addition, scholars working in Arabic transmitted ideas that paralleled the rise of Arab traders and merchants as the carriers of goods and inventions. For example, Muslim invaders of south Asia soon learned of the Indian system of numbers. From India they were carried by Muslim scholars and merchants to the Middle Eastern centers of Islamic civilization. Eventually, the Indian numerical system was transmitted across the Mediterranean to Italy and from there to northern Europe. Along with Greek and Arab mathematics, Indian numbers later proved critical to the early modern Scientific Revolution in western Europe.

Global Connections and Critical Themes

EARLY ISLAM AND THE WORLD

The rise of Islamic civilization from the 7th to 9th centuries C.E. was a stunning development without precedent in human history. Not only had the largely nomadic peoples from an Arabian backwater built one of the greatest empires of the preindustrial world, they had laid the basis for the first truly global civilization if one excludes the Americas, which were unknown to the peoples of the Eastern Hemisphere. Building on earlier religious traditions, especially Christianity and Judaism, Arab culture had nurtured Islam, one of the great universal religions of humankind. The mosques, the prayer rituals and pilgrimages of the faithful, and the influence of Islamic law proclaimed the pervasive effects of this new creed in societies from Spain to eastern Indonesia and from central Asia to the savannas of west Africa.

The Arab commitment to trade and merchant activity was crucial in setting up wider connections among Asia, Africa, and Europe, with the Middle East as the hub. The region's earlier roles in commerce, in and between the Indian Ocean and Mediterranean Sea, expanded greatly.

In the arts and sciences, the Muslims initially relied heavily on the achievements of the classical civilizations of Greece and Mesopotamia. But the work of preserving and combining the discoveries of earlier peoples soon led to reformulation and innovation. As in religion and politics, Muslim peoples were soon making important contributions to learning, invention, and artistic creativity. These were carried by their armies and religious teachers to other civilizations in Europe, Africa, and Asia.

Never before had a civilization spanned so many different cultures and combined such a patchwork of linguistic groups, religions, and ethnic types. Never before had a single civilization mediated so successfully between the other centers of civilized life. Never had a civilized lifestyle so deeply affected so many of the nomadic cultures that surrounded the pools of sedentary agriculture and urban life. Ironically, the contacts Islamic mediation made possible between the civilized cores of the Eastern Hemisphere contributed much to the transformations in technology and organization that increasingly tilted the balance of power against the Muslim peoples. But those reversals were still far in the future. In the short run, Islamic conversion and contact ushered in an age of unparalleled nomadic intervention in and dominance over global history.

Further Readings

There are many accounts of Muhammad's life and the rise of Islam. The most readable is Karen Armstrong's *Muhammad: A Biography of the Prophet* (1992). A sense of the very different interpretations that have been offered to explain these pivotal developments in global history can be gained by comparing W. Montgomery Watt, *Muhammad: Prophet and Statesman* (1961); Tor Andrae, *Muhammad: The Man and His Faith* (1960); Maxime Rodinson, *Mohammad* (1971); and the more recent revisionist (and somewhat less accessible) writings of Elizabeth Crone and Michael Cook.

Despite its title, H. A. R. Gibb's *Mohammedism* (1962) remains a useful introduction to Islam as a religion. John Esposito's *Islam: The Straight Path* (1991) and Karen Armstrong's *Islam: A Short History* (2000) also provide good and updated overviews of the faith. On early Islamic expansion and civilization through the first centuries of the Abbasid caliphate, see G. E. von Grunebaum's *Classical Islam* (1970) and M. A. Shaban's *Islamic History: An Interpretation* (1971) and *The Abbasid Revolution* (1970). On nearly all of these topics, it is difficult to surpass Marshall G. S. Hodgson's brilliant analysis, *The Venture of Islam*, vol. 1 (1974), but some grounding in the history and beliefs of the Muslims is recommended before one attempts this sweeping and provocative work. More accessible, dated in some respects, but still authoritative and highly interpretive is Philip Hitti's *History of the Arabs* (1967 ed.), which can be supplemented by his very engaging *Makers of Arab History* (1968). More encyclopedic and benefiting from recent research, the surveys of Ira M. Lapidus, *A History of Islamic Societies* (1988) and Albert Hourani, *A History of the Arab Peoples* (1991) provide useful overviews.

On early Islamic society generally, see M. M. Ahsan, *Social Life Under the Abbasids* (1979). On women in Islam specifically, there is a superb essay by Guity Nashat, "Women in the Middle East, 8000 B.C.–A.D. 1800," in the collection titled *Restoring Women to History* (1988), published by the Organization of American Historians. See also the relevant portions of the essays in Lois Beck and Nikki Keddi, eds., *Women in the Muslim World* (1978); and the early chapters of Leila Ahmed, *Women and Gender in Islam* (1992). For a broad treatment of the roles and position of women in ancient civilizations more generally, see Sarah and Brady Hughes, *Women in Ancient Global History* (1998). For insights into Islamic culture and civilization from a literary perspective, a good place to begin is Eric Schroeder's delightful *Muhammad's People: A Tale by Anthology* (1955) and N. J. Dawood's translation of *Tales from the Thousand and One Nights* (1954). Of the many works on Muslim art and architecture Robert Hillenbrand's recent *Islamic Art and Architecture* (1999) is engaging, well researched, and lavishly illustrated. K. A. Creswell's *Early Muslim Architecture*, 2 vols. (1932–1940), and the more recent Markus Hattstein and Peter Delius, eds., *Islam: Art and Architecture* (2000), provide even greater detail and ample illustrations.

Critical Thinking Questions

1. What were the most important social bonds and status relationships in pre-Islamic society in Arabia and how did they contribute to survival in the harsh desert environment?

2. What are the five pillars of the Islamic faith and how do they make for a strong sense of identity and community within the Islamic *umma*?

3. What were the major factors that led to the Sunni—Shi'a split in the Muslim Arab community?

4. What were the major motives for converting to Islam when the *umma* opened up to non-Muslims in the Abbasid era?

Abbasid Decline and the Spread of Islamic Civilization to South and Southeast Asia

((• Listen to Chapter 12
on MyHistoryLab

LEARNING OBJECTIVES

Of all of the factors that contributed to the spread of Islamic civilization in the millennium after the prophet Muhammad received his divine revelations in the early 7th century c.e., perhaps none was as crucial—yet neglected—as the rather modest sailing vessels that plied the waters of the Red Sea and Persian Gulf. Most commonly known as *dhows* (see Chapter 11, p. 261), but appearing in numerous variations with different names and found from the Mediterranean Sea to the Indian Ocean, these ships were probably first developed along the Nile River. Compared to the great junks of China, or even many of the less-imposing trading ships in the Indian Ocean in the classical age, dhows were rather small vessels. They normally had one or two masts and planked, wooden hulls that resembled modern yachts in shape, with pointed bows and square

FIGURE 12.1 Arab traders made the most of seasonal winds, sailing dhows like this one to Africa and Asia in winter and returning home during the summer months. Dhows were small but sturdy, graceful, and highly maneuverable sailing vessels. They that carried Arab traders, Sufi holy men, and warriors from the Middle East across the Mediterranean, the Red Sea and Persian Gulf, and throughout the vast Indian Ocean trading system.

⊙ Watch the Video Series on MyHistoryLab

Learn about some key topics related to this chapter with the *MyHistoryLab Video Series: Key Topics in World History*

sterns (Figure 12.1). The dhows' hull design contributed to their swiftness and maneuverability, but it was the configuration of their sails that have made them one of the most popular and enduring of the world's ships for two millennia. Dhows were propelled by one or two large, triangular **lateen** sails that attached to the masts by long booms or yard arms, which extended diagonally high across both the fore and aft portions of the ship.

Although their relatively shallow hulls meant that dhows could not match junks or bulkier merchant ships in cargo capacity, their slender shape gave them a considerable advantage over most other ships in speed. Their triangular sails meant that they could tack against the wind, which was very difficult in the best of conditions for square-rigged ships. Most often, however, those who sailed dhows followed a seasonal pattern set by the direction of the monsoon winds that alternated between flows to the sea or land according to the time of the year in the India Ocean and adjacent waterways. Although galleys like those of classical Greece and Rome were widely used by Arabs in the Mediterranean, from Spain to China tens of thousands of dhows were the main carriers of Muslim commerce. And along with merchants and their trade goods, many of the same ships conveyed Sufis or Muslim holy men to regions as far-flung as India, Java and Malaya, and the Philippine Islands.

Seaworthy ships like the dhows were essential to the remarkable spread of the Islamic faith and the civilizations it gave rise to in this era. In contrast to the expansion of Muslim empires, which was largely carried out by Arab armies traveling over land, lasting mass conversions of conquered peoples to the religion of Islam were mainly due to the efforts of Sufis and other spiritual leaders. These missionaries of the Islamic faith traveled by caravan into central Asia and across the Sahara or traversed the seas in sturdy dhows. In either case, those who went out to win converts to Islam also disseminated broader products of Muslim culture. These included the Arabic language; advanced technologies, such as water pumps and windmills; Muslim science, law, and philosophy; and Islamic art and architecture.

Despite their speed and dexterity, dhows did not make great warships, either before or after gunpowder was introduced into sea warfare. They were too small to provide a suitable firing platform for regular cannon, and they could not carry enough soldiers to grapple, board, and overwhelm the crews of enemy ships. Like most of the ships that sailed the seas of the Middle East, east Africa, and Asia, dhows were built for trade and not war. Designs for that purpose served the peoples of the Indian Ocean and adjoining seas well until the last years of the 15th century. But with the arrival of well-armed Portuguese fleets after 1498, neither the dhows nor any of the ships in Asia west of the South China Sea could hold back expansionist Christian warriors and seafarers. These aspiring empire builders were eager to tap into the wealth, knowledge, and technological acumen of Islamic and Chinese culture zones far more advanced in most areas of human endeavor than their own. ■

lateen Triangular sails attached to the masts of dhows by long booms, or yard arms, which extended diagonally high across the fore and aft of the ship.

Even as Muslim traders and Sufi holymen spread Islam across a great swath of Afro-Euroasia from north Africa in the west to the Philippines in the east, the Abbasid empire was crumbling from within. In many of the areas newly won to the faith, rival dynasties arose to challenge Abbasid power. These new polities and the Abbasids themselves were in turn threatened by the invasions of nomadic peoples launched by successive waves of Turkish-speakers and the Mongols from central Asia as well as Berber jihadists from Saharan Africa. Ironically, as the political hold of various Muslim rulers weakened, Islamic civilization reached new heights of creativity.

700 C.E.	800 C.E.	900 C.E.	1000 C.E.	1200 C.E.
661–750 Umayyad caliphate (Damascus) **711–713** First Muslim raids into India **750** Establishment of the Abbasid caliphate (Baghdad) **775–785** Reign of al-Mahdi **777** Independent dynasty established in Algeria **786–809** Reign of al-Rashid **788** Independent dynasty established in Morocco	**800** Independent dynasty established in Tunisia **809** First war of succession between Abbasid princes **813–833** Reign of al-Ma'mun; first mercenary forces recruited 865–925 Life of al-Razi, physician and scientist	**945** Persian Buyids capture Baghdad; caliphs become puppet rulers **973–1050** Life of al-Biruni, scientist **998** Beginning of Ghazni raids into western India	**c. 1020** Death of Firdawsi, author of the *Shah-Nama* **1055** Seljuk Turks overthrow Buyids, control caliphate **1096–1099** First Christian Crusade in Palestine **1058–1111** Life of al-Ghazali, philosopher and scientist **1038–1123** Life of Omar Khayyam, scientist and poet	**1206** Establishment of the Delhi sultanate in India **1258** Fall of Baghdad to Mongols; end of Abbasid caliphate **1290s** Beginning of the spread of Islam in southeast Asia **1291** Fall of Acre; last crusader stronghold in Middle East

As we shall see in this chapter, the Abbasid age was a time of remarkable achievements in architecture and the fine arts, in literature and philosophy, and in mathematics and the sciences. Many of these developments were enriched by the wealth, knowledge, and products exchanged among the many regions of an ever-expanding Muslim world and the non-Muslim peoples contacted in border regions from Europe to China. From the 10th to the 14th centuries, Muslim mystics, traders, and at times warriors carried the faith of Muhammad across much of the known world. In this chapter we will focus on this process in south and southeast Asia. In those that follow, north and west Africa and central Asia will be the focus of our inquiry.

THE ISLAMIC HEARTLANDS IN THE MIDDLE AND LATE ABBASID ERAS

12.1   What were the major sources contributing to the decline of the Abbasid dynasty?

The vast Abbasid empire (Map 12.1) gradually disintegrated between the 9th and 13th centuries C.E. Political decline and recurring social turmoil were fed both by the emergence of rival centers of power and the inroads of nomadic peoples attracted to the rich and fertile regions where Muslim urban life and power were centered.

al-Mahdi [al-mä dEE] (r. 775–785) Third of the Abbasid caliphs; attempted but failed to reconcile moderates among Shi'a to Abbasid dynasty; failed to resolve problem of succession.

Harun al-Rashid   One of the great Islamic rulers of the Abbasid era.

As early as the reign of the third Abbasid caliph, **al-Mahdi** (r. 775–785), the courtly excesses and political divisions that eventually contributed to the decline of the empire were apparent. Al-Mahdi's efforts to reconcile the moderates among the Shi'a opposition to Abbasid rule ended in failure. This meant that Shi'a revolts and assassination attempts against Abbasid officials would plague the dynasty to the end of its days. Al-Mahdi also abandoned the frugal ways of his predecessor. In the brief span of his reign, he cultivated a taste for luxury and monumental building and surrounded himself with a multitude of dependent wives, concubines, and courtiers. These habits would prove to be an ever-greater financial drain in the reigns of later caliphs.

Perhaps most critically, al-Mahdi failed to solve the vexing problem of succession. Not only did he waver between which of his older sons would succeed him, but he allowed his wives and concubines, the mothers of different candidates, to become involved in the palace intrigues that became a standard feature of the transfer of power from one caliph to the next. Although a full-scale civil war was avoided after al-Mahdi's death, within a year his eldest son and successor was poisoned. That act cleared the way for one of the most famous and enduring of the Abbasid caliphs, **Harun al-Rashid** (r. 786–809), to ascend the throne.

Imperial Extravagance and Succession Disputes

Emissaries sent in the early 9th century to Baghdad from Charlemagne (Map 12.1), then the most powerful monarch in Christian Europe, provide ample evidence that Harun al-Rashid shared his father's taste for sumptuous living. Harun al-Rashid dazzled the Christians with the splendor of

MAP **12.1 The Abbasid Empire at Its Peak**

Baghdad's mosques, palaces, and treasure troves, which is reflected in the painting of nightlife in a palace in Figure 12.2. He also sent them back to Charlemagne with presents, including an intricate water clock and an elephant, which were literally worth a king's ransom.

The luxury and intrigue of Harun's court have also been immortalized by the tales of *The Thousand and One Nights* (see the Document in Chapter 11), set in the Baghdad of his day. The plots and maneuvers of the courtesans, eunuchs, and royal ministers related in the tales suggest yet another source of dynastic weakness. Partly because he was only 23 at the time of his accession to the throne, Harun became heavily dependent, particularly in the early years of his reign, on a family of Persian advisors. Although he eventually resisted their influence, the growth of the power of royal advisors at the expense of the caliphs became a clear trend in succeeding reigns. In fact, from the mid-9th century onward, most caliphs were pawns in the power struggles between different factions at the court.

Harun al-Rashid's death prompted the first of several full-scale civil wars over succession. In itself, the precedent set by the struggle for the throne was deeply damaging. But it had an additional consequence that would all but end the real power of the caliphs. The first civil war convinced the sons of al-Ma'mun (813–833), the winner, to build personal armies in anticipation of the fight for the throne that would break out when their father died. One of the sons, the victor in the next round of succession struggles, recruited a "bodyguard" of some 4000 slaves, mostly Turkic-speaking nomads from central Asia. On becoming caliph, he increased this mercenary force to more than 70,000.

Not surprisingly, this impressive army soon became a power center in its own right. In 846 slave mercenaries murdered the reigning caliph and placed one of his sons on the throne. In the next decade, four more caliphs were assassinated or poisoned by the mercenary forces. From this time onward, the leaders of the slave mercenary armies were often the real power behind the Abbasid throne and were major players in the struggles for control of the capital and empire. The mercenaries also became a major force for violent social unrest. They were often the catalyst for the food riots that broke out periodically when the price of everyday staples rose too sharply because of shortages or price gouging in Baghdad and other urban centers.

Imperial Breakdown and Agrarian Disorder

In the last decades of the 9th century, the dynasty brought the slave armies under control for a time, but at a great cost. Constant civil violence drained the treasury and alienated the subjects of the Abbasids. A further strain was placed on the empire's dwindling revenues by some caliphs' attempts to escape the turmoil of Baghdad by establishing new capitals near the original one. The construction of palaces, mosques, and public works for each of these new imperial centers added to the already exorbitant costs of maintaining the court and imperial administration. Of course, the expense fell heavily on the already hard-pressed peasantry of the central provinces of the empire, where some imperial control remained. The need to support growing numbers of mercenary troops also increased the revenue demands on the peasantry.

Spiraling taxation and outright pillaging led to the destruction or abandonment of many villages in the richest provinces of the empire. The great irrigation works that had for centuries been essential to agricultural production in the fertile Tigris–Euphrates basin fell into disrepair, and in some areas they collapsed entirely. Some peasants perished through flood, famine, or violent assault; others fled to wilderness areas beyond the reach of the Abbasid tax collectors or to neighboring kingdoms. Some formed bandit gangs or joined the crowds of vagabonds that trudged the highways and camped in the towns of the imperial heartland. In many cases, dissident religious groups, such as the various Shi'a sects, instigated peasant uprisings. Shi'a participation meant that these movements sought not only to correct the official abuses that had occurred under the Abbasid regime but to destroy the dynasty itself.

The Declining Position of Women in the Family and Society

The harem and the veil became the twin emblems of women's increasing subjugation to men and confinement to the home in the Abbasid era. Although the seclusion of women had been practiced by some Middle Eastern peoples since ancient times, the harem was a creation of the Abbasid court. The wives and the concubines of the Abbasid caliphs were restricted to the forbidden quarters of the imperial palace. Many of the concubines were slaves, who could win their freedom and gain power by bearing healthy sons for the rulers. The growing wealth of the Abbasid elite created a great demand for female and male slaves, who were found by the tens of thousands in Baghdad and other large cities. Most of these urban slaves continued to perform domestic services in the homes of the wealthy. One of the 10th-century caliphs is reputed to have had 11,000 eunuchs among his slave corps; another is said to have kept 4000 slave concubines.

Most of the slaves had been captured or purchased in the non-Muslim regions surrounding the empire, including the Balkans, central Asia, and Sudanic Africa. They were sold in the slave markets found in all of the larger towns of the Abbasid realm. Female and male slaves were prized for both their beauty and their intelligence. Some of the best-educated men and women in the empire were slaves. Consequently, caliphs and high officials often spent more time with their clever and talented slave concubines than with their less-educated wives. Slave concubines and servants often had more personal liberty than freeborn wives. Slave women could go to the market, and they did not have to wear the veils and robes that were required for free women in public places.

Although women from the lower classes farmed, wove clothing and rugs, or raised silkworms to help support their families, rich women were allowed almost no career outlets beyond the home. Often married at puberty (legally set at age 9), women were raised to devote their lives to running a household and serving their husbands. But at the highest levels of society, wives and concubines

FIGURE 12.2 The richness and vitality of urban life in the Islamic world in the Abbasid age and later eras are wonderfully captured in this 16th-century Persian illustration from the *Khamsah* (Five Poems) of Nizami. The miniature painting gives us a bird's-eye view of a typical night in one of the great palaces of Baghdad. The multiple scenes vividly capture the bustle and high artistry of the splendidly decorated rooms and gardens, from a group of musicians serenading a man who is presumably the lord of the mansion, to kitchen servants buying food and preparing to serve it to the lord and his guests.

(Attributed to Mir Sayyid 'Ali "Nighttime in a Palace." Folio from a Manuscript, c. 1539–1543. Harvard Art Museum, Arthur M. Sackler Museum, Gift of John Goelet, formerly in the collection of Louis J. Cartier, 1958.76. Katya Kallsen © President and Fellows of Harvard College.)

cajoled their husbands and plotted with eunuchs and royal advisors to advance the interests of their sons and win for them the ruler's backing for succession to the throne. Despite these brief incursions into power politics, by the end of the Abbasid era, the freedom and influence—both within the family and in the wider world—that women had enjoyed in the first centuries of Islamic expansion had been severely curtailed.

Nomadic Incursions and the Eclipse of Caliphal Power

Preoccupied by struggles in the capital and central provinces, the caliphs and their advisors were powerless to prevent further losses of territory in the outer reaches of the empire. In addition, areas as close to the capital as Egypt and Syria broke away from Abbasid rule (Map 12.1). More alarmingly, by the mid-10th century, independent kingdoms that had formed in areas that were once provinces of the empire were moving to supplant the Abbasids as lords of the Islamic world. In 945, the armies of one of these regional splinter dynasties, the **Buyids** of Persia, invaded the heartlands of the Abbasid empire and captured Baghdad. From this point onward, the caliphs were little more than puppets controlled by families such as the Buyids. Buyid leaders took the title of *sultan* ("victorious" in Arabic), which came to designate Muslim rulers, especially in the West.

The Buyids controlled the caliph and the court, but they could not prevent the further disintegration of the empire. In just over a century, the Buyids' control over the caliphate was broken, and they were supplanted in 1055 by another group of nomadic invaders from central Asia via Persia, the **Seljuk Turks**. For the next two centuries, Turkic military leaders ruled the remaining portions of the Abbasid empire in the name of caliphs, who were usually of Arab or Persian extraction. The Seljuks were staunch Sunnis, and they moved quickly to purge the Shi'a officials who had risen to power under the Buyids and to rid the caliph's domains of the Shi'a influences the Buyids had tried to promote. For a time, the Seljuk military machine was also able to restore political initiative to the much-reduced caliphate. Seljuk victories ended the threat of conquest by a rival Shi'a dynasty centered in Egypt. They also humbled the Byzantines, who had hoped to take advantage of Muslim divisions to regain some of their long-lost lands. The Byzantines' crushing defeat also opened the way to the settlement of Asia Minor, or Anatolia, by nomadic peoples of Turkic origins, some of whom would soon begin to lay the foundations of the Ottoman Empire.

The Impact of the Christian Crusades

Soon after seizing power, the Seljuks faced a very different challenge to Islamic civilization. It came from Christian crusaders, knights from western Europe (see Chapter 15) who were determined to capture the portions of the Islamic world that made up the Holy Land of biblical times. Muslim political divisions and the element of surprise made the first of the crusaders' assaults, between 1096 and 1099, by far the most successful. Much of the Holy Land was captured and divided into Christian kingdoms. In June 1099, the main objective of the Crusade, Jerusalem, was taken, and its Muslim and Jewish inhabitants were massacred by the rampaging Christian knights.

For nearly two centuries, the Europeans, who eventually mounted eight **Crusades** that varied widely in strength and success, maintained their precarious hold on the eastern Mediterranean region. But they posed little threat to the more powerful Muslim princes, whose disregard for the Christians was demonstrated by the fact that they continued to quarrel among themselves despite the intruders' aggressions. When united under a strong leader, as they were under Salah-ud-Din (known as **Saladin** in Christian Europe) in the last decades of the 12th century, the Muslims rapidly reconquered most of the crusader outposts. Saladin's death in 1193 and the subsequent breakup of his kingdom gave the remaining Christian citadels some respite. But the last of the crusader kingdoms was lost with the fall of Acre in 1291.

Undoubtedly, the impact of the Crusades was much greater on the Christians who launched them than on the Muslim peoples who had to fend them off. Because there had long been so much contact between western Europe and the Islamic world through trade and through the Muslim kingdoms in Spain and southern Italy, it is difficult to be sure which influences to attribute specifically to the Crusades. But the crusaders' firsthand experiences in the eastern Mediterranean certainly intensified European borrowing from the Muslim world that had been going on for centuries. Muslim weapons, such as the famous damascene swords (named after the city of Damascus), were highly prized and sometimes copied by the Europeans, who were always eager to improve on their methods of making war. Muslim techniques of building fortifications were adopted by many Christian rulers, as can be

Buyids [BOO-yihds] Regional splinter dynasty of the mid-10th century; invaded and captured Baghdad; ruled Abbasid Empire under title of sultan; retained Abbasids as figureheads.

Seljuk Turks [SEHL-jook Turks] Nomadic invaders from central Asia via Persia; staunch Sunnis; ruled in name of Abbasid caliphs from mid-11th century.

Crusades Series of military adventures initially launched by western Christians to free Holy Land from Muslims; temporarily succeeded in capturing Jerusalem and establishing Christian kingdoms; later used for other purposes such as commercial wars and extermination of heresy.

Saladin Muslim leader in the last decades of the 12th century; reconquered most of the crusader outposts for Islam.

 Read the **Document** on MyHistoryLab: A Muslim View of the Crusades: Behâ-ed-Din, Richard I Massacres Prisoners after Taking Acre, 1191

seen in the castles built in Normandy and coastal England by William the Conqueror and his successors in the 11th and 12th centuries. Richard the Lionheart's legendary preference for Muslim over Christian physicians was but one sign of the Europeans' avid centuries-old interest in the superior scientific learning of Muslim peoples.

From Muslims and Jews in Spain, Sicily, Egypt, and the Middle East, the Europeans recovered much of the Greek learning that had been lost to northern Europe during the waves of nomadic invasions after the fall of Rome. They also mastered Arabic (properly Indian) numerals and the decimal system, and they benefited from the great advances Arab and Persian thinkers had made in mathematics and many of the sciences. The European demand for Middle Eastern rugs and textiles is demonstrated by the Oriental rugs and tapestries that adorned the homes of the European upper classes in Renaissance and early modern paintings. It is also reflected in European (and our own) names for different kinds of cloth, such as *fustian*, *taffeta*, *muslin*, and *damask*, which are derived from Persian terms or the names of Muslim cities where the cloth was produced and sold.

Ibn Khaldun [i buhn kal dUn, KHUn] (1332–1406) A Muslim historian; developed concept that dynasties of nomadic conquerors had a cycle of three generations—strong, weak, dissolute.

DOCUMENT

Ibn Khaldun on the Rise and Decline of Empires

ALTHOUGH HE LIVED IN THE CENTURY after the Abbasid caliphate was destroyed in 1258, **Ibn Khaldun** was very much a product of the far-flung Islamic civilization that the Abbasids had consolidated and expanded. He was also one of the greatest historians and social commentators of all time. After extensive travels in the Islamic world, he served as a political advisor at several of the courts of Muslim rulers in north Africa. With the support of a royal patron, Ibn Khaldun wrote a universal history that began with a very long philosophical preface called *The Muqaddimah*. Among the subjects he treated at length were the causes of the rise and fall of dynasties. The shifting fortunes of the dynasties he knew well in his native north Africa, as well as the fate of the Abbasids and earlier Muslim regimes, informed his attempts to find persistent patterns in the complex political history of the Islamic world. The following passages are from one of the most celebrated sections of *The Muqaddimah* on the natural life span of political regimes.

We have stated that the duration of the life of a dynasty does not as a rule extend beyond three generations. The first generation retains the desert qualities, desert toughness, and desert savagery. [Its members are used to] privation and to sharing their glory [with each other]; they are brave and rapacious. Therefore, the strength of group feeling continues to be preserved among them. They are sharp and greatly feared. People submit to them.

Under the influence of royal authority and a life of ease, the second generation changes from the desert attitude to sedentary culture, from privation to luxury and plenty, from a state in which everybody shared in the glory to one in which one man claims all the glory for himself while the others are too lazy to strive for [glory], and from proud superiority to humble subservience. Thus, the vigor of group feeling is broken to some extent. People become used to lowliness and obedience. But many of [the old virtues] remain in them, because they had direct personal contact with the first generation and its conditions.

The third generation, then, has [completely] forgotten the period of desert life and toughness, as if it had never existed. They have lost [the taste for] group feeling, because they are dominated by force. Luxury reaches its peak among them, because they are so much given to a life of prosperity and ease. They become dependent on the dynasty and are like women and children who need to be defended [by someone else]. Group feeling disappears completely. People forget to protect and defend themselves and to press their claims. With their emblems, apparel, horseback riding, and [fighting] skill, they deceive people and give them the wrong impression. For the most part, they are more cowardly than women upon their backs. When someone comes and demands something from them, they cannot repel him. The ruler, then, has need of other, brave people for his support. He takes many clients and followers. They help the dynasty to some degree, until God permits it to be destroyed, and it goes with everything it stands for.

Three generations last one hundred and twenty years. As a rule, dynasties do not last longer than that many years, a few more, a few less, save when, by chance, no one appears to attack [the dynasty]. When senility becomes preponderant [in a dynasty], there may be no claimant [for its power, and then nothing will happen] but if there should be one, he will encounter no one capable of repelling him. If the time is up [the end of the dynasty] cannot be postponed for a single hour, no more than it can be accelerated.

QUESTIONS

- What does this passage reveal about Ibn Khaldun's views of the contrasts between nomads and urban dwellers?
- Why does he see the former as a source of military power and political strength?
- What forces undermine dynasties in later generations?
- How well do these patterns correspond to the history of the Umayyad and Abbasid dynasties we have been studying?

Muslim influences affected both the elite and popular cultures of much of western Europe in this period. These included Persian and Arabic words, games such as chess, chivalric ideals and troubadour ballads, as well as foods such as dates, coffee, and yogurt. Some of these imports, namely the songs of the troubadours, can be traced directly to the contacts the crusaders made in the Holy Land. But most were part of a process of exchange that extended over centuries, and was largely a one-way process. Although Arab traders imported some manufactures, such as glass and cloth, and raw materials from Europe, Muslim peoples in this era showed little interest in the learning or institutions of the West. Nevertheless, the Italian merchant communities, which remained after the political and military power of the crusaders had been extinguished in the Middle East, contributed a good deal more to these ongoing interchanges than all the forays of Christian knights.

AN AGE OF LEARNING AND ARTISTIC REFINEMENTS

12.2 Discuss the major advances in the arts and sciences that occurred in the Islamic world in the late-Abbasid period.

> Paradoxically, even as the political power of the Abbasids declined, Islamic civilization reached new heights of achievement and entered into a phase of renewed expansion.

Although town life became more dangerous, the rapid growth and increasing prosperity that characterized the first centuries of Muslim expansion continued until late in the Abbasid era. Despite the declining revenue base of the caliphate and deteriorating conditions in the countryside, there was a great expansion of the professional classes, particularly doctors, scholars, and legal and religious experts (Figure 12.3). Muslim, Jewish, and in some areas Christian entrepreneurs amassed great fortunes supplying the cities of the empire with staples such as grain and barley, essentials such as cotton and woolen textiles for clothing, and luxury items such as precious gems, citrus fruits, and sugar cane. Long-distance trade between the Middle East and Mediterranean Europe and between coastal India and southeast Asia, in addition to the overland caravan trade with China, flourished through much of the Abbasid era (Map 12.2).

Among the chief beneficiaries of the sustained urban prosperity were artists and artisans, who continued the formidable achievements in architecture and the crafts that had begun in the Umayyad period. Mosques and palaces grew larger and more ornate in most parts of the empire. Even in outlying areas, such as Córdoban Spain, Muslim engineers and architects created some of the great architectural treasures of all time. The tapestries and rugs of Muslim peoples, most famously the Persians, were in great demand from Europe to China. To this day, Muslim rugs have rarely been matched for their exquisite designs, their vivid colors, and the skill with which they are woven. Muslim artisans also produced fine bronzes and superb ceramics.

The Full Flowering of Persian Literature

As Persian wives, concubines, advisors, bureaucrats, and (after the mid-10th century) Persian caliphs came to play central roles in imperial politics, Persian gradually replaced Arabic as the primary written language at the Abbasid court. Arabic remained the language of religion, law, and the natural sciences. Persian was favored by Arabs, Turks, and Muslims of Persian descent as the language of literary expression, administration, and scholarship. In Baghdad and major cities throughout the Abbasid empire and in neighboring kingdoms, Persian was the chief language of "high culture," the language of polite exchanges between courtiers as well as of history, poetic musings, and mystical revelations.

Written in a modified Arabic script and drawing selectively on Arabic vocabulary, the Persian of the Abbasid age was a supple language as beautiful to look at when drafted by a skilled calligrapher as it was to read aloud. Catch phrases ("A jug of wine, a loaf of bread, and Thou") from the *Rubaiyat* (ROO-bee-AHT) of Omar Khayyam (OH-mahr keye-YAHM) are certainly the pieces of Persian literature best known in the West. But other writers from this period surpassed Khayyam in profundity of thought and elegance of style. Perhaps the single most important work was the lengthy epic poem ***Shah-Nama*** (Book of Kings), written by Firdawsi in the late 10th and early 11th centuries. The work relates the history of Persia from the beginnings of time to the Islamic conquests, and it abounds in dramatic details of battles, intrigues, and illicit love affairs. Firdawsi's Persian has been extolled for

Shah-Nama Written by Firdawsi in late 10th and early 11th centuries; relates history of Persia from creation to the Islamic conquests.

FIGURE **12.3** The subtlety and depth attained by Muslim civilizations in the far-flung regions in which they were found is illustrated by this 17th-century watercolor painting titled *A Discourse between Muslim Sages.* The meditative figures, with scholarly books before them, surrounded by grass and trees, captures the commitment to learning and refined aesthetic sense that was cultivated by members of the elite classes throughout the Islamic world.

📖 **Read** the **Document** on **MyHistoryLab**: The Rubaiyat (11th c. CE) Omar Khayyam

ulama Orthodox religious scholars within Islam; pressed for a more conservative and restrictive theology; increasingly opposed to non-Islamic ideas and scientific thinking.

al-Ghazali [al Gaz-AHL-ee] (1058–1111) Brilliant Islamic theologian; struggled to fuse Greek and Qur'anic traditions; not entirely accepted by ulama.

🔍 **View** the **Image** on **MyHistoryLab**: Islamic science and alchemy: page from "The Lanterns of Wisdom and the Keys of Mercy"

its grand, musical virtuosity, and portions of the *Shah-Nama* and other Persian works were read aloud to musical accompaniment. Brilliantly illustrated manuscripts of Firdawsi's epic history are among the most exquisite works of Islamic art.

In addition to historical epics, Persian writers in the Abbasid era wrote on many subjects, from doomed love affairs and statecraft to accounts of distant travels and mystical striving for communion with the divine. One of the great poets of the age, Sa'di, fuses an everyday incident with a religious one in the following relation of a single moment in his own life:

> Often I am minded, from the days of my childhood,
> How once I went out with my father on a festival;
> In fun I grew preoccupied with all the folk about,
> Losing touch with my father in the popular confusion;
> In terror and bewilderment I raised up a cry,
> Then suddenly my father boxed my ears:
> "You bold-eyed child, how many times, now,
> Have I told you not to lose hold of my skirt?"
> A tiny child cannot walk out alone,
> For it is difficult to take a way not seen;
> You too, poor friend, are but a child upon endeavour's way:
> Go, seize the skirts of those who know the way!

This blend of the mystical and commonplace was widely adopted in the literature of this period. It is epitomized in the *Rubaiyat*, whose author is much more concerned with finding meaning in life and a path to union with the divine than with extolling the delights of picnics in the garden with beautiful women.

Achievements in the Sciences

From preserving and compiling the learning of the ancient civilizations they had conquered in the early centuries of expansion, Muslim peoples—and the Jewish scholars who lived peacefully in Muslim lands—increasingly became creators and inventors in their own right. For several centuries, which spanned much of the period of Abbasid rule, Islamic civilization outstripped all others in scientific discoveries, new techniques of investigation, and new technologies. The many Muslim accomplishments in these areas include major corrections to the algebraic and geometric theories of the ancient Greeks and great advances in the use of basic concepts of trigonometry: the sine, cosine, and tangent.

Two discoveries in chemistry that were fundamental to all later investigation were the creation of the objective experiment and al-Razi's scheme of classifying all material substances into three categories: animal, vegetable, and mineral. The sophistication of Muslim scientific techniques is indicated by the fact that in the 11th century, al-Biruni was able to calculate the specific weight of 18 major minerals. This sophistication was also manifested in astronomical instruments such as those in Figure 12.4, developed through cooperation between Muslim scholars and skilled artisans. Their astronomical tables and maps of the stars were in great demand among scholars of other civilizations, including those of Europe and China.

As these breakthroughs suggest, much of the Muslims' work in scientific investigation had very practical applications. This practical bent was even greater in other fields. For example, Muslim cities such as Cairo boasted some of the best hospitals in the world. Doctors and pharmacists had to follow a regular course of study and pass a formal examination before they were allowed to practice. Muslim scientists did important work on optics and bladder ailments. Muslim traders introduced into the Islamic world and Europe many basic machines and techniques—namely, papermaking, silk-weaving, and ceramic firing—that had been devised earlier in China. In addition, Muslim scholars made some of the world's best maps, which were copied by geographers from Portugal to Poland.

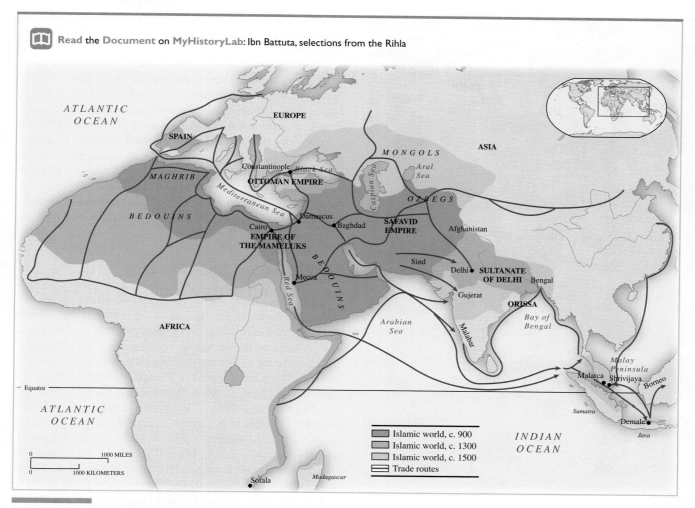

Read the Document on MyHistoryLab: Ibn Battuta, selections from the Rihla

MAP **12.2 The Spread of Islam, 10th–16th Centuries** Arrows indicate the routes by which Islam spread to south, and southeast and Central Asia, Asia Minor and the Balkans, and Sudanic Africa.

Religious Trends and the New Push for Expansion

The contradictory trends in Islamic civilization—social strife and political divisions versus expanded trading links and intellectual creativity—were strongly reflected in patterns of religious development in the later centuries of the caliphate. On one hand, a resurgence of mysticism injected Islam with a new vibrancy. On the other, orthodox religious scholars, such as the **ulama**, grew increasingly suspicious of and hostile to non-Islamic ideas and scientific thinking. The Crusades had promoted the latter trend. This was particularly true regarding Muslim borrowing from ancient Greek learning, which the ulama associated with the aggressive civilizations of Christian Europe. Many orthodox scholars suspected that the questioning that characterized the Greek tradition would undermine the absolute authority of the Qur'an. They insisted that the Qur'an was the final, perfect, and complete revelation of an all-knowing divinity. Brilliant thinkers such as **al-Ghazali** perhaps the greatest Islamic theologian, struggled to fuse the Greek and Qur'anic traditions. Their ideas were often rejected by orthodox scholars.

Much of the religious vitality in Islam in the later Abbasid period was centered on the Sufist movement. In its various guises, including both Sunni and Shi'a manifestations, Sufism was a reaction against the impersonal and abstract divinity that many ulama scholars argued was the true god of the Qur'an. Like the Indian mystics, the Sufis—whose title was derived from the woolen robes they wore—and their followers tried to see beyond what they believed to be the illusory existence of everyday life and to delight in the presence of Allah in the world. True to the strict monotheism of Islam, most Sufis insisted on a clear distinction between Allah and

Mongols Central Asian nomadic peoples; smashed Turko-Persian kingdoms; captured Baghdad in 1258 and killed last Abbasid caliph.

Chinggis Khan [JEHNG-gihs KAHN] Born in 1170s in decades following death of Kabul Khan; elected khagan of all Mongol tribes in 1206; responsible for conquest of northern kingdoms of China, territories as far west as the Abbasid regions; died in 1227, prior to conquest of most of Islamic world.

Hulegu [hoo-LAY-goo] (1217–1265) Ruler of the Ilkhan khanate; grandson of Chinggis Khan; responsible for capture and destruction of Baghdad in 1257.

 Read the Document on MyHistoryLab: Science and Mathematics: Al-Ghazzali, "On the Separation of Mathematics and Religion"

FIGURE **12.4** This 15th-century Persian miniature of a group of Arab scientists testing and working with a wide variety of navigational instruments conveys a strong sense of the premium placed on scientific investigation in the Muslim world in the Abbasid age and the centuries thereafter. Muslim prototypes inspired European artisans, cartographers, and scientists to develop instruments and maps, which were essential to European overseas expansion from the 14th century onward.

Mamluks Muslim slave warriors; established a dynasty in Egypt; defeated the Mongols at Ain Jalut in 1260 and halted Mongol advance.

 Read the Document on MyHistoryLab: Rabi'a al-'Adawiyya, "Brothers, my peace is in my aloneness."

From the 7th century onward, Muslim invaders, traders, and migrants carried the Islamic faith and Islamic civilization to the vast south Asian subcontinent. Muslim conquests and conversions provoked a variety of Hindu responses and attempts by some followers of both religions to reconcile their differences.

humans. But in some Sufist teachings, Allah permeated the universe in ways that appeared to compromise his transcendent status.

Some Sufis gained reputations as great healers and workers of miracles; others led militant bands that tried to spread Islam to nonbelievers. Some Sufis used asceticism or bodily denial to find Allah; others used meditation, songs, drugs, or ecstatic dancing, which gave the famous whirling dervishes their name. Sufis also pursued scientific investigations as well as writing major works on ethics and political philosophy. The more accomplished Sufis built up a sizable following, and the movement as a whole was a central factor in the continuing expansion of the Muslim religion and Islamic civilization in the later centuries of the Abbasid caliphate.

New Waves of Nomadic Invasions and the End of the Caliphate

As we have seen, in the 10th and 11th centuries the Abbasid domains were divided by ever growing numbers of rival successor states. In the early 13th century, a new threat arose at the eastern edge of the original Abbasid domains. Another central Asian nomadic people, the **Mongols**, united by their great commander, **Chinggis Khan**, first raided in the 1220s and then smashed the Turko-Persian kingdoms that had developed in the regions to the east of Baghdad. Chinggis Khan died before the heartlands of the Muslim world were invaded, but his grandson, **Hulegu**, renewed the Mongol assault on the rich centers of Islamic civilization in the 1250s. In 1258, the Abbasid capital at Baghdad was taken by the Mongols, and much of it was sacked. The 37th and last Abbasid caliph was put to death by the Mongols. They then continued westward until they were finally defeated by the **Mamluks**, or Turkic slaves, who then ruled Egypt.

Baghdad never recovered from the Mongol attacks. In 1401, it suffered a second capture and another round of pillaging by the even fiercer forces of Timur or Tamerlane, another Turkic conqueror from Central Asia. Baghdad shrank for centuries from the status of one of the great cities of the world to a provincial backwater. It was gradually supplanted by Cairo to the west and then Istanbul to the north.

THE COMING OF ISLAM TO SOUTH ASIA

12.3 How did Hindu religious leaders and organizations counter the considerable appeal of Sufi missionaries and their efforts to win converts in south and southeast Asia from the 10th through the 16th centuries?

All through the millennia when a succession of civilizations from Harappa to the brahmanic empire of the Guptas developed in south Asia, foreigners had entered India in waves of nomadic invaders or as small bands of displaced peoples seeking refuge. Invariably, those who chose to remain were assimilated into the civilizations they encountered in the lowland areas. They converted to the Hindu or Buddhist religion, found a place in the caste hierarchy, and adopted the dress, foods, and lifestyles of the farming and city-dwelling peoples of the many regions of the subcontinent. This capacity to absorb peoples moving into the area resulted from the strength and flexibility of India's civilizations and from the fact that India's peoples usually enjoyed a higher level of material culture than migrant groups entering the subcontinent. As a result, the persistent failure of Indian rulers to unite against aggressors meant periodic disruptions and localized destruction but not fundamental challenges to the existing order. All of this changed with the arrival of the Muslims in the last years of the 7th century C.E. (Map 12.2).

With the coming of the Muslims, the peoples of India encountered for the first time a large-scale influx of bearers of an outside civilization as sophisticated, if not as ancient, as their own. They were also confronted by a religious system that was in many ways the very opposite of the ones they had nurtured. Hinduism, the predominant Indian religion at that time, was open, tolerant, and inclusive of widely varying forms of religious devotion, from idol worship to meditation in search of union with the spiritual source of all creation. Islam was doctrinaire, proselytizing, and committed to the exclusive worship of a single, transcendent god.

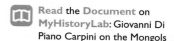
Read the Document on MyHistoryLab: Giovanni Di Piano Carpini on the Mongols

VISUALIZING THE PAST

The Pattern of Islam's Global Expansions

THE TABLE SHOWS THE PRESENT-DAY DISTRIBUTION of Muslims in key countries from Africa to Asia. It indicates the total number of Muslims in each of the countries listed, the percentage of Muslims in the total population of that area, and the numbers and percentages of other religious groups. The table also indicates the manner in which Islam was spread to each of these areas and the key agents of that diffusion. After using the table to compare the patterns of Islamization in different areas, answer the questions that follow.

QUESTIONS

- Which areas have the highest absolute numbers of Muslims in the present day?
- Is this distribution what you would have expected, or is it surprising?
- What were the main ways that Islam was transmitted to most areas?
- What does this say about the popular notion that Islam was historically a militant religion spread primarily by forcible conversion?
- Do the statistics suggest that Islam is able to coexist with other faiths?

COMPARATIVE STATISTICS OF MODERN STATES WITH A SIZABLE MUSLIM POPULATION

	Total Population (2000 est.)	Total Number of Muslims	Percentage of Muslims	Total Number of Non-Muslims	Percentages of Other Religious Groups	Principal Agents/Modes of Conversion
Nigeria	114 million	57 million	50	57 million	40–Christian; 10–Other (African religions)	Trading Contacts Sufi Missionaries
Egypt	67 million	63 million	94	4 million	4–Christian 2–Other	Arab Migration Conquest Voluntary Mass Conversion
Iraq	22.5 million	21.8 million	97: Shi'a: 60–65; Sunni: 32–37	700,000	3–Other (Zoroastrian, Christian, Jewish)	Arab Migration Conquest Voluntary Mass Conversion
Iran	65 million	64.35 million	99: Shi'a: 89; Sunni: 10	650,000	1—Other (Zoroastrian, Bahai, Christian, Jewish)	Arab Conquest Migration Voluntary Mass Conversion
Pakistan	138 million	133.85 million	97: Shi'a 20; Sunni: 77	4.15 million	3–Other (Hindu, Christian, Buddhist)	Sufi Missionaries Voluntary Mass Conversion
India	1.001 billion	140.1 million	14	860.9 million	80–Hindu; 6–Other (Buddhist, Sikh, Christian, Jain)	Sufi Missionaries Trading Contacts Conquest Voluntary Mass Conversion
Indonesia	216 million	188 million	87	28 million	6–Protestant; 7–Other (Catholic Buddhist, etc.)	Sufi Missionaries Trading Contacts
The Phillipines	79.5 million	4 million	5	75.5 million	83–Catholic; 9–Protestant; 3–Other	Trading contacts Sufi Missionaries
Morocco	30 million	29.7 million	99	300,000	1–Other	Voluntary Mass Conversion Sufi Missionaries Conquest

NOTE: Numbers based on information from Wiesenfeld and Famighetti et al., eds., *The World Almanac and Book of Facts 2000* (Mahwah, NJ: World Almanac Books).

Socially, Islam was highly egalitarian, proclaiming all believers equal in the sight of God. In sharp contrast, Hindu beliefs validated the caste hierarchy. The latter rested on the acceptance of inborn differences between individuals and groups and the widely varying levels of material wealth, status, and religious purity these differences were believed to produce. Thus, the faith of the invading Muslims was religiously more rigid than that of the absorptive and adaptive Hindus. But the caste-based social system of India was much more compartmentalized and closed than the society of the Muslim invaders, with their emphasis on mobility and the community of believers.

Because growing numbers of Muslim warriors, traders, Sufi mystics, and ordinary farmers and herders entered south Asia and settled there, extensive interaction between invaders and the indigenous peoples was inevitable. In the early centuries of the Muslim influx, conflict, often violent, predominated. But there was also a good deal of trade and even religious interchange between them. As time passed, peaceful (if often wary) interaction became the norm. Muslim rulers employed large numbers of Hindus to govern the largely non-Muslim populations they conquered; mosques and temples dominated different quarters within Indian cities. In addition, Hindu and Muslim mystics strove to find areas of agreement between their two faiths. Nonetheless, tensions remained, and periodically they erupted into communal rioting or warfare between Hindu and Muslim rulers.

Muhammad ibn Qasim [moh-HAM-ihd ihbn HAH-sihm] (661–750) Arab general; conquered Sind in India; declared the region and the Indus valley to be part of Umayyad Empire.

Political Divisions and the First Muslim Invasions

The first and least enduring Muslim intrusion, which came in 711, resulted indirectly from the peaceful trading contacts that had initially brought Muslims into contact with Indian civilization. Since ancient times, Arab seafarers and traders had been major carriers in the vast trading network that stretched from Italy in the Mediterranean to the South China Sea. After converting to Islam, these traders continued to visit the ports of India, particularly those on the western coast. An attack by pirates sailing from Sind in western India (Map 12.3) on ships owned by some of these Arab traders prompted the viceroy of the eastern provinces of the Umayyad Empire to launch a punitive expedition against the king of Sind. An able Arab general, **Muhammad ibn Qasim** who was only 17 years old when the campaign began, led more than 10,000 horse- and camel-mounted warriors into Sind to avenge the assault on Arab shipping. After victories in several fiercely fought battles, Muhammad ibn Qasim declared the region, as well as the Indus valley to the northeast, provinces of the Umayyad empire.

In these early centuries, the coming of Islam brought little change for most inhabitants of the Indian subcontinent. In fact, in many areas, local leaders and the populace surrendered towns and districts willingly to the conquerors because they promised lighter taxation and greater religious tolerance. The Arab overlords decided to treat both Hindus and Buddhists as protected "people of the book,"

MAP **12.3 Early Islam in India** Beginning with raids into the Indus Valley in the 8th century c.e., Muslim armies invaded and established a succession of dynasties centered on Delhi in north-central India.

View the **Closer Look** on
MyHistoryLab: "Qutb Minar"

despite the fact that their faiths had no connection to the Bible, the book in question. This meant that although they were obliged to pay special taxes, non-Muslims, like Jews and Christians, enjoyed the freedom to worship as they pleased.

As in other areas conquered by the Arabs, most of the local officials and notables retained their positions, which did much to reconcile them to Muslim rule. The status and privileges of the brahman castes were respected. Nearly all Arabs, who made up only a tiny minority of the population, lived in cities or special garrison towns. Because little effort was expended in converting the peoples of the conquered areas, they remained overwhelmingly Hindu or Buddhist.

Indian Influences on Islamic Civilization

Although the impact of Islam on the Indian subcontinent in this period was limited, the Arab foothold in Sind provided contacts by which Indian learning was transmitted to the Muslim heartlands in the Middle East. As a result, Islamic civilization was enriched by the skills and discoveries of yet another great civilization. Of particular importance was Indian scientific learning, which rivaled that of the Greeks as the most advanced of the ancient world. Hindu mathematicians and astronomers traveled to Baghdad after the Abbasids came to power in the mid-8th century. Their works on algebra and geometry were translated into Arabic, and their instruments for celestial observation were copied and improved by Arab astronomers.

Most critically, Arab thinkers in all fields began to use the numerals that Hindu scholars had devised centuries earlier. Because these numbers were passed on to the Europeans through contacts with the Arabs in the early Middle Ages, we call them Arabic numerals today, but they originated in India. Because of the linkages between civilized centers established by the spread of Islam, this system of numerical notation has proved central to two scientific revolutions. The first in the Middle East was discussed earlier in this chapter. The second, discussed in Chapter 22, occurred in Europe some centuries later. From the 16th century to the present, it has brought fundamental transformations to Europe and much of the rest of the world.

In addition to science and mathematics, Indian treatises on subjects ranging from medicine to music were translated and studied by Arab scholars. Indian physicians were brought to Baghdad to run the well-endowed hospitals that the Christian crusaders found a source of wonderment and a cause for envy. On several occasions, Indian doctors were able to cure Arab rulers and officials whom Greek physicians had pronounced beyond help. Indian works on statecraft, alchemy, and palmistry were translated into Arabic, and it is believed that some of the tales in the *Arabian Nights* were based on ancient Indian stories. Indian musical instruments and melodies made their way into the repertoires of Arab performers, and the Indian game of chess became a favorite of both royalty and ordinary townspeople.

Arabs who emigrated to Sind and other Muslim-ruled areas often adopted Indian dress and hairstyles, ate Indian foods, and rode on elephants just as the Hindu *rajas* (kings) did. As Figure 12.5 illustrates, the conquerors also adopted Indian building styles and artistic motifs. In this era, additional Arab colonies were established in other coastal areas, such as Malabar to the south and Bengal in the east (Map 12.3). These trading enclaves later provided the staging areas from which Islam was transmitted to island and mainland southeast Asia.

From Booty to Empire: The Second Wave of Muslim Invasions

After the initial conquests by Muhammad ibn Qasim's armies, little territory was added to the Muslim foothold on the subcontinent. In fact, disputes between the Arabs occupying Sind and their quarrels

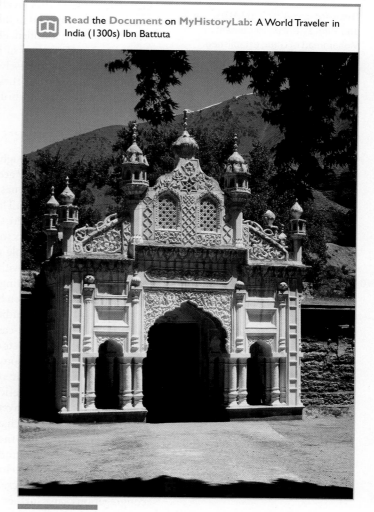

Read the **Document** on **MyHistoryLab**: A World Traveler in India (1300s) Ibn Battuta

FIGURE 12.5 The Shahi mosque, surrounded by the Hindu Kush mountains in northwestern Pakistan, is a superb example of the blending of Islamic and Hindu architectural forms, building materials, and artistic motifs.

with first the Umayyad and later the Abbasid caliphs gradually weakened the Muslim hold on the area. This was reflected in the reconquest of parts of the lower Indus valley by Hindu rulers. But the gradual Muslim retreat was dramatically reversed by a new series of military invasions, this time launched by a Turkish slave dynasty that in 962 had seized power in Afghanistan to the north of the Indus valley. The third ruler of this dynasty, **Mahmud of Ghazni**, led a series of expeditions that began nearly two centuries of Muslim raiding and conquest in northern India. Drawn by the legendary wealth of the subcontinent and a zeal to spread the Muslim faith, Mahmud repeatedly raided northwest India in the first decades of the 11th century. He defeated one confederation of Hindu princes after another, and he drove deeper and deeper into the subcontinent in the quest of ever richer temples to loot.

The raids mounted by Mahmud of Ghazni and his successors gave way in the last decades of the 12th century to sustained campaigns aimed at seizing political control in north India. The key figure in this transition was a tenacious military commander of Persian extraction, **Muhammad of Ghur**. After barely surviving several severe defeats at the hands of Hindu rulers, Muhammad put together a string of military victories that brought the Indus valley and much of north central India under his control. In the following years, Muhammad's conquests were extended along the Gangetic plain as far as Bengal, and into west and central India, by several of his most gifted subordinate commanders. After Muhammad was assassinated in 1206, **Qutb-ud-din Aibak**, one of his slave lieutenants, seized power.

Significantly, the capital of the new Muslim empire was at Delhi along the Jumna River on the Gangetic plain. Delhi's location in the very center of northern India graphically proclaimed that a Muslim dynasty rooted in the subcontinent itself, not an extension of a Middle Eastern central Asian empire, had been founded. For the next 300 years, a succession of dynasties ruled much of north and central India. Alternately of Persian, Afghan, Turkic, and mixed descent, the rulers of these imperial houses proclaimed themselves the *sultans of Delhi* (literally, princes of the heartland). They fought each other, Mongol and Turkic invaders, and the indigenous Hindu princes for control of the Indus and Gangetic heartlands of Indian civilization.

Patterns of Conversion

Although the Muslims fought their way into India, their interaction with the indigenous peoples soon came to be dominated by accommodation and peaceful exchanges. Over the centuries when much of the north was ruled by dynasties centered at Delhi, sizable Muslim communities developed in different areas of the subcontinent. The largest of these were in Bengal to the east and in the northwestern areas of the Indus valley that were the points of entry for most of the Muslim peoples who migrated into India.

Few of these converts were won forcibly. The main carriers of the new faith often were merchants, who played a growing role in both coastal and inland trade, but were most especially Sufi mystics. The latter shared much with Indian gurus and wandering ascetics in both style and message. Belief in their magical and healing powers enhanced the Sufis' stature and increased their following. Their mosques and schools often became centers of regional political power. Sufis organized their devotees in militias to fend off bandits or rival princes, oversaw the clearing of forests for farming and settlement, and welcomed low-caste and outcaste Hindu groups into Islam. After their deaths, the tombs of Sufi mystics became objects of veneration for Indian Muslims as well as Hindu and Buddhist pilgrims.

Most of the indigenous converts, who came to form a majority of the Muslims living in India, were drawn from specific regions and social groups. Surprisingly small numbers of converts were found in the Indo-Gangetic centers of Muslim political power, a fact that suggests the very limited importance of forced conversions. Most Indians who converted to Islam were from Buddhist or low-caste groups. In areas such as western India and Bengal, where Buddhism had survived as a popular religion until the era of the Muslim invasions, esoteric rituals and corrupt practices had debased Buddhist teachings and undermined the morale of the monastic orders.

This decline was accelerated by Muslim raids on Buddhist temples and monasteries, which provided vulnerable and lucrative targets for the early invaders. Without monastic supervision, local congregations sank further into orgies and experiments with magic. All of these trends opposed the Buddha's social concerns and religious message. Disorganized and misdirected, Indian Buddhism was no match for the confident and vigorous new religion the Muslim invaders carried into the subcontinent. This was particularly true when those who were spreading the new faith had the charisma and organizing skills of the Sufi mystics.

Buddhists probably made up the majority of Indians who converted to Islam. But untouchables and low-caste Hindus, as well as tribal peoples who were animists worshiping spirits found in the natural world, were also attracted to the more egalitarian social arrangements promoted by the new faith. As was the case in earlier centuries with the Buddhists, group conversions were essential because those who remained in the Hindu caste system would have little to do with those who had changed religions. Some conversions resulted from the desire of Hindus or Buddhists to escape the head tax the Muslim rulers levied on unbelievers. They were prompted by intermarriage between local peoples and Muslim migrants. Muslim migrants also swelled the size of the Islamic community in the subcontinent. This was particularly true in periods of crisis in central Asia. In the 13th and 14th centuries, for example, Turkic, Persian, and Afghan peoples retreated to the comparative safety of India in the face of the Mongol and Timurid conquests that are examined in detail in Chapter 19.

Patterns of Accommodation

Although Islam won many converts in certain areas and communities, it initially made little impression on the Hindu population as a whole. Despite military reverses and the imposition of Muslim political rule over large areas of the subcontinent, high-caste Hindus in particular saw the invaders as the bearers of an upstart religion and as polluting outcastes. Al-Biruni, one of the chief chroniclers of the Muslim conquests, complained openly about the prevailing Indian disdain for the newcomers:

> The Hindus believe that there is no country but theirs, no nation like theirs, no kings like theirs, no religion like theirs, no science like theirs. They are haughty, foolishly vain, self-conceited and stolid.

Many Hindus were willing to take positions as administrators in the bureaucracies of Muslim overlords or as soldiers in their armies and to trade with Muslim merchants. But they remained socially aloof from their conquerors. Separate living quarters were established everywhere Muslim communities developed. Genuine friendships between members of high-caste groups and Muslims were rare, and sexual liaisons between them were severely restricted.

During the early centuries of the Muslim influx, the Hindus were convinced that like so many of the peoples who had entered the subcontinent in the preceding millennia, the Muslims would soon be absorbed by the superior religions and more sophisticated cultures of India. Many signs pointed to that outcome. Hindus staffed the bureaucracies and made up a good portion of the armies of Muslim rulers. In addition, Muslim princes adopted regal styles and practices that were Hindu-inspired and contrary to the Qur'an. Some Muslim rulers proclaimed themselves to be of divine descent, and others minted coins decorated with Hindu images such as Nandi, the bull associated with a major Hindu god, Shiva.

More broadly, Muslim communities became socially divided along caste lines. Recently arrived Muslims generally were on top of the hierarchies that developed, and even they were divided depending on whether they were Arab, Turk, or Persian. High-caste Hindu converts came next, followed by "clean" artisan and merchant groups. Lower-caste and untouchable converts remained at the bottom of the social hierarchy. This may help to explain why conversions in these groups were not as numerous as one would expect given the original egalitarian thrust of Islam. Muslims also adopted Indian foods and styles of dress and took to chewing *pan*, or limestone wrapped with betel leaves.

The Muslim influx had unfortunate consequences for women in both Muslim and Hindu communities. The invaders increasingly adopted the practice of marrying women at the earlier ages favored by the Hindus and the prohibitions against the remarriage of widows found especially at the high-caste levels of Indian society. Some high-caste Muslim groups even performed the ritual of *sati*, the burning of widows on the same funeral pyres as their deceased husbands, which was found among some high-caste Hindu groups.

Islamic Challenge and Hindu Revival

Despite a significant degree of acculturation to Hindu lifestyles and social organization, Muslim migrants to the subcontinent held to their own distinctive religious beliefs and rituals. The Hindus found Islam impossible to absorb and soon realized that they were confronted by an actively proselytizing religion with great appeal to large segments of the Indian population. Partly in response to

THINKING HISTORICALLY

Conversion and Accommodation in the Spread of World Religions

ALTHOUGH NOT ALL GREAT CIVILIZATIONS HAVE produced world religions, the two tend to be closely associated throughout human history. World religions are those that spread across many cultures and societies, forge links between civilized centers, and bring civilized lifestyles to nomadic pastoral or shifting cultivating peoples. Religions with these characteristics appeared before the rise of Islam. As we have seen, India alone produced two of these faiths in ancient times: Hinduism, which spread to parts of southeast and central Asia, and Buddhism, which spread even more widely in the Asian world. At the other end of the Eastern Hemisphere, Christianity spread throughout the Mediterranean region before claiming northern and western Europe as its core area. Judaism spread not because it won converts in non-Jewish cultures but because the Jewish people were driven from their homeland by Roman persecution and scattered throughout the Middle East, north Africa, and Europe.

Because religious conversion affects all aspects of life, from the way one looks at the universe to more mundane decisions about whom to marry or how to treat others, a world religion must be broad and flexible enough to accommodate the existing culture of potential converts. At the same time, its core beliefs and practices must be well enough defined to allow its followers to maintain a clear sense of common identity despite their great differences in culture and society. These beliefs and practices must be sufficiently profound and sophisticated to convince potential converts that their own cultures can be enriched and their lives improved by adopting the new religion.

In most instances, until the 16th century, when Christianity spread through the Western Hemisphere, no world religion could match Islam in the extent to which it spread across the globe and in the diversity of peoples and cultures that identified themselves as Muslims. Given its uncompromising monotheism, very definite doctrines, and elaborate rituals and principles of social organization, Islam's success at winning converts from very different cultural backgrounds is surprising at first glance. This is particularly true if it is compared with the much more flexible beliefs and ceremonial patterns of earlier world religions such as Buddhism and Hinduism. However, closer examination reveals that Islamic beliefs and social practices, as written in the Qur'an and interpreted by the ulama, proved quite flexible and adaptable when the religion was introduced into new, non-Islamic cultures.

The fact that Islam won converts overwhelmingly through peaceful contacts between long-distance traders and the

The fact that Islam won converts overwhelmingly through peaceful contacts between long-distance traders and the preaching and organizational skills of Sufis exemplifies this capacity for accommodation.

preaching and organizational skills of Sufis exemplifies this capacity for accommodation. Those adopting the new religion did not do so cause they were pressured or forced to convert but because they saw Islam as a way to enhance their understanding of the supernatural, enrich their ceremonial expression, improve the quality of their social interaction, and establish ongoing links to a transcultural community beyond their local world.

Because Islam was adopted rather than imposed, those who converted had a good deal to say about how much of their own cultures they would change and which aspects of Islam they would emphasize or accept. Certain beliefs and practices were obligatory for all true believers: the worship of a single god, adherence to the prophet Muhammad and the divine revelations he received as recorded in the Qur'an, and the observance of the five pillars of the faith. But even these were subject to reinterpretation. In virtually all cultures to which it spread, Islamic monotheism supplanted but did not eradicate the animistic veneration of nature spirits or person and place deities. Allah was acknowledged as the most powerful supernatural force, but people continued to make offerings to spirits that could heal, bring fertility, protect their homes, or punish their enemies. In such areas as Africa and western China, where the veneration of ancestral spirits was a key aspect of religious life, the spirits were retained not as powers in themselves but as emissaries to Allah. In cultures such as those found in India and southeast Asia, Islamic doctrines were recast in a heavily mystical, even magical mode.

The flexibility of Islam was exhibited in the social as well as the religious sphere. In Islamic southeast Asia and in sub-Saharan Africa, the position of women remained a good deal stronger in critical areas, such as occupation and family law, than it had become in the Middle East and India. In both regions, the male-centric features of Islam that had grown more pronounced through centuries of accommodation in ancient Middle Eastern and Persian cultures were played down. As Islam was adapted to societies where women had traditionally enjoyed more influence, both within the extended family and in occupations such as farming, marketing, and craft production. Even the caste system of India, which in principle is opposed to the strong egalitarian strain in Islam, developed among Muslim groups that migrated into the subcontinent and survived in indigenous south Asian communities that converted to Islam.

(continued on next page)

(continued from previous page)

Beyond basic forms of social organization and interaction, Islam accommodated diverse aspects of the societies into which it spread. For example, the African solar calendar, which was essential for coordinating the planting cycle, was retained along with the Muslim lunar calendar. In India, Hindu-Buddhist symbols of kingship were appropriated by Muslim rulers and acknowledged by both their Hindu and Muslim subjects. In island southeast Asia, exquisitely forged knives, called *krises*, which were believed to have magical powers, were among the most treasured possessions of local rulers both before and after they converted to Islam.

There was always the danger that accommodation could go too far: that in winning converts, Islamic principles would be so watered down and remolded that they no longer resembled or actually contradicted the teachings of the Qur'an. Sects that came to worship Muhammad or his nephew Ali as godlike, for example, clearly violated fundamental Muslim principles. This danger

was a key source of the periodic movements for purification and revival that have been a notable feature of nearly all Islamic societies, particularly those on the fringes of the Islamic world. But even these movements, which were built around the insistence that the Muslim faith had been corrupted by alien ideas and practices and that a return to Islamic fundamentals was needed, were invariably cast in the modes of cultural expression of the peoples who rallied to them.

QUESTIONS

- Can you think of ways in which world religions, such as Christianity, Hinduism, and Buddhism, changed to accommodate the cultures and societies to which they spread?
- Do these religions strike you as more or less flexible than Islam?
- Why?

this challenge, the Hindus placed greater emphasis on the devotional cults of gods and goddesses that earlier had proved so effective in neutralizing the challenge of Buddhism.

Membership in these **bhaktic cults** was open to all, including women and untouchables. In fact, some of the most celebrated writers of religious poetry and songs of worship were women, such as **Mira Bai**. Saints from low-caste origins were revered by warriors and brahmans as well as by farmers, merchants, and outcastes. One of the most remarkable of these mystics was a Muslim weaver named **Kabir**. In plain and direct verse, Kabir played down the significance of religious differences and proclaimed that all faiths could provide a path to spiritual fulfillment. He asked,

> O servant, where do thou seek Me?
> Lo! I am beside thee.
> I am neither in temple nor in mosque:
> Neither am I in rites and ceremonies, nor in Yoga and
>   renunciation.

Because many songs and poems, such as those by Mira Bai and Kabir, were composed in regional languages, such as Bengali, Marathi, and Tamil, they were more accessible to the common people and became prominent expressions of popular culture in many areas.

Bhakti mystics and gurus stressed the importance of a strong emotional bond between the devotee and the god or goddess who was the object of veneration. Chants, dances, and in some instances drugs were used to reach the state of spiritual intoxication that was the key to individual salvation. Once one had achieved the state of ecstasy that came through intense emotional attachment to a god or goddess, all past sins were removed and caste distinctions were rendered meaningless. The most widely worshiped deities were the gods Shiva and Vishnu, the latter particularly in the guise of Krishna the goat herder depicted in the folk painting in Figure 12.6. The goddess Kali was also venerated in a number of different manifestations. By increasing popular involvement in Hindu worship and by enriching and extending the modes of prayer and ritual, the bhakti movement may have done much to stem the flow of converts to Islam, particularly among low-caste groups.

FIGURE 12.6 This Indian miniature painting of milkmaids serving the Hindu god Krishna reflects the highly personalized devotional worship that was characteristic of the bhakti movement. The eroticism in the milkmaids' songs, in praise of Krishna's great beauty, reveals a blending of sacred and secular, carnal and spiritual that is a recurring motif in Hindu worship and art.

bhaktic cults [BAHK-teek] Hindu groups dedicated to gods and goddesses; stressed the importance of strong emotional bonds between devotees and the god or goddess who was the object of their veneration; most widely worshipped gods were Shiva and Vishnu.

Mira Bai [MIHR-uh Bay] (1498–1547) Celebrated Hindu writer of religious poetry; reflected openness of bhaktic cults to women.

Kabir (1440–1518) Muslim mystic; played down the importance of ritual differences between Hinduism and Islam.

Stand-Off: The Muslim Presence in India at the End of the Sultanate Period

The attempts of mystics such as Kabir to minimize the differences between Hindu and Islamic beliefs and worship won over only small numbers of the followers of either faith. They were also strongly repudiated by the guardians of orthodoxy in each religious community. Sensing the long-term threat to Hinduism posed by Muslim political dominance and conversion efforts, the brahmans denounced the Muslims as infidel destroyers of Hindu temples and polluted meat-eaters. Later Hindu mystics, such as the 15th-century holy man Chaitanya, composed songs that focused on love for Hindu deities and set out to convince Indian Muslims to renounce Islam in favor of Hinduism.

For their part, Muslim ulama, or religious experts, grew increasingly aware of the dangers Hinduism posed for Islam. Attempts to fuse the two faiths were rejected on the grounds that although Hindus might argue that specific rituals and beliefs were not essential, they were fundamental for Islam. If one played down the teachings of the Qur'an, prayer, and the pilgrimage, one was no longer a true Muslim. Thus, contrary to the teachings of Kabir and like-minded mystics, the ulama and even some Sufi saints stressed the teachings of Islam that separated it from Hinduism. They worked to promote unity within the Indian Muslim community and to strengthen its contacts with Muslims in neighboring lands and the Middle Eastern centers of the faith.

After centuries of invasion and migration, a large Muslim community had been established in the Indian subcontinent. Converts had been won, political control had been established throughout much of the area, and strong links had been forged with Muslims in other lands such as Persia and Afghanistan. But non-Muslims, particularly Hindus, remained the overwhelming majority of the population of the vast and diverse lands south of the Himalayas. Unlike the Zoroastrians in Persia or the animistic peoples of north Africa and the Sudan, most Indians showed little inclination to convert to the religion of the Muslim conquerors. After centuries of Muslim political dominance and missionary activity, south Asia remained one of the least converted and integrated of all the areas Muhammad's message had reached.

THE SPREAD OF ISLAM TO SOUTHEAST ASIA

From the 13th century, traders and Sufi mystics spread Islam to island southeast Asia. As was the case in India, conversion was generally peaceful, and Islamic teachings and rituals were mixed with the animist, Hindu, and Buddhist religions long established in Malaya, Java, and other areas.

12.4 Beyond the Sufis, who were the major agents and what were the motivations for conversions to the Islamic religion in South and South Asia in this same era?

From a world history perspective, island southeast Asia had long been mainly a middle ground. It was the zone where the Chinese segment of the great Euro-Asian trading complex met the Indian Ocean trading zone to the west. At ports on the coast of the Malayan peninsula, east Sumatra, and somewhat later north Java, goods from China were transferred from east Asian vessels to Arab or Indian ships. In these same ports, products from as far west as Rome were loaded into the emptied Chinese ships to be carried to east Asia. By the 7th and 8th centuries C.E., sailors and ships from areas of southeast Asia, particularly Sumatra and Malaya, had become active in the seaborne trade of the region. Southeast Asian products had also become important exports to China, India, and the Mediterranean region. Many of these products were luxury items, such as aromatic woods from the rain forests of Borneo and Sumatra and spices such as cloves, nutmeg, and mace from the far end of the Indonesian archipelago. These trading links were to prove even more critical to the expansion of Islam in southeast Asia than they had earlier been to the spread of Buddhism and Hinduism.

From the 8th century onward, the coastal trade of India came increasingly to be controlled by Muslims from such regions as Gujarat in western India and various parts of south India. As a result, elements of Islamic culture began to filter into island southeast Asia. But only in the 13th century, after the collapse of the far-flung trading empire of **Shrivijaya**, centered on the Strait of Malacca between Malaya and the northeast of Sumatra (Map 12.4), was the way open for the widespread introduction of Islam. Indian traders, Muslim or otherwise, were welcome to trade in the chain of ports controlled by Shrivijaya. But because the rulers and officials of Shrivijaya were devout Buddhists, there was little incentive for the traders and sailors of southeast Asian ports to convert to Islam, the religion of growing numbers of the merchants and sailors from India. With the fall of Shrivijaya, incentives increased for the establishment of Muslim trading centers and efforts to preach the faith to the coastal peoples.

Shrivijaya [SHREE-vih-JAY-uh] Trading empire centered on Malacca Straits between Malaya and Sumatra; controlled trade of empire; Buddhist government resistant to Muslim missionaries; fall opened up southeastern Asia to Muslim conversion.

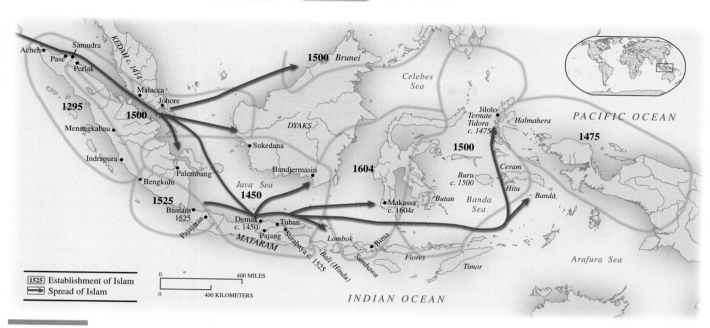

MAP **12.4 The Spread of Islam in Southeast Asia** Traders and Islamic mystics were the main agents responsible for the rapid spread of Islam throughout island southeast Asia.

Trading Contacts and Conversion

As in most of the areas to which Islam spread, peaceful contacts and voluntary conversion were far more important than conquest and force in spreading the faith in southeast Asia. Throughout the islands of the region, trading contacts paved the way for conversion. Muslim merchants and sailors introduced local peoples to the ideas and rituals of the new faith and impressed on them how much of the known world had already been converted. Muslim ships also carried Sufis to various parts of southeast Asia, where they played as vital a role in conversion as they had in India. The first areas to be won to Islam in the late 13th century were several small port centers on the northern coast of Sumatra. From these ports, the religion spread in the centuries that followed across the Strait of Malacca to Malaya.

On the mainland, the key to widespread conversion was the powerful trading city of **Malacca**, whose smaller trading empire had replaced the fallen Shrivijaya. From Malacca, Islam spread along the coasts of Malaya to east Sumatra and to the trading center of **Demak** on the north coast of Java. From Demak, the most powerful of the trading states on north Java, the Muslim faith spread to other Javanese ports. After a long struggle with a Hindu-Buddhist kingdom in the interior, the rest of the island was eventually converted. From Demak, Islam was also carried to the Celebes and the Spice Islands in the eastern archipelago, and from the latter to Mindanao in the southern Philippines.

This progress of Islamic conversion shows that port cities in coastal areas were particularly receptive to the new faith. Here trading links were critical. Once one of the key cities in a trading cluster converted, it was in the best interest of others to follow suit to enhance personal ties and provide a common basis in Muslim law to regulate business deals. Conversion to Islam also linked these centers, culturally as well as economically, to the merchants and ports of India, the Middle East, and the Mediterranean.

Islam made slow progress in areas such as central Java, where Hindu–Buddhist dynasties contested its spread. But the fact that the earlier conversion to these Indian religions had been confined mainly to the ruling elites in Java and other island areas left openings for mass conversions to Islam that the Sufis eventually exploited. The island of Bali, where Hinduism had taken deep root at the popular level, remained largely impervious to the spread of Islam. The same was true of most of mainland southeast Asia, where centuries before the coming of Islam, Buddhism had spread from India and Ceylon and won the fervent adherence of both the ruling elites and the peasant masses.

Malacca Portuguese factory or fortified trade town located on the tip of the Malayan peninsula; traditionally a center for trade among the southeastern Asian islands.

Demak Most powerful of the trading states on north coast of Java; converted to Islam and served as point of dissemination to other ports.

Sufi Mystics and the Nature of Southeast Asian Islam

Because Islam was spread in many areas by Sufis from South Asia, it was often infused with mystical strains and incorporated animist, Hindu, and Buddhist elements. Just as they had in the Middle East and India, the Sufis who spread Islam in southeast Asia varied widely in personality and approach. Most were believed by those who followed them to have magical powers, and nearly all Sufis established mosque and school centers from which they traveled in neighboring regions to preach the faith.

In winning converts, the Sufis were willing to allow the inhabitants of island southeast Asia to retain pre-Islamic beliefs and practices that orthodox scholars would have found contrary to Islamic doctrine. Pre-Islamic customary law remained important in regulating social interaction, whereas Islamic law was confined to specific sorts of agreements and exchanges. Women retained a much stronger position, both within the family and in society, than they had in the Middle East and India. For example, trading in local and regional markets continued to be dominated by small-scale female buyers and sellers. In such areas as western Sumatra, lineage and inheritance continued to be traced through the female line after the coming of Islam, despite its tendency to promote male dominance and descent. Perhaps most tellingly, pre-Muslim religious beliefs and rituals were incorporated into Muslim ceremonies. Indigenous cultural staples, such as the brilliant Javanese puppet shadow plays that were based on the Indian epics of the brahmanic age, were refined, and they became even more central to popular and elite beliefs and practices than they had been in the pre-Muslim era.

Global Connections and Critical Themes

ISLAM: A BRIDGE BETWEEN WORLDS

Although problems of political control and succession continued to plague the kingdoms and empires that divided the Muslim world, the central position of Islamic civilization in global history was solidified during the centuries of Abbasid rule. Its role as the go-between for the more ancient civilizations of the Eastern Hemisphere grew as Arab trading networks expanded into new areas. More than ever, it enriched the lives of nomadic peoples, from the Turks and Mongols of central Asia to the Berbers of north Africa and the camel herders of the savanna regions south of the Sahara. Equally critically, Islam's original contributions to the growth and refinement of civilized life greatly increased. From its great cities and universities and the accomplishments generated in the fine arts, sciences, and literature to its vibrant religious and philosophical life, Islam pioneered patterns of organization and thinking that would affect the development of human societies in major ways for centuries to come.

For more than five centuries, the spread of Islam played a central role in the rise, extension, or transformation of civilization in much of the Afro-Asian world. The Islamic world also became a great conduit for the exchange of ideas, plants and medicines, commercial goods, and inventions both between centers of urban and agrarian life and between these core regions of civilization and the areas dominated by nomadic peoples that still encompassed much of the globe.

In the midst of all this achievement, however, there were tendencies that would put the Muslim peoples at a growing disadvantage, particularly in relation to their long-standing European rivals. Muslim divisions would leave openings for political expansion that the Europeans would eagerly exploit, beginning with the island southeast Asian extremities of the Islamic world and then moving across India. The growing orthodoxy and intolerance of many of the ulama, as well as the Muslim belief that the vast Islamic world contained all requirements for civilized life, caused Muslim peoples to grow less receptive to outside influences and innovations. These tendencies became increasingly pronounced at precisely the time when their Christian rivals were entering a period of unprecedented curiosity, experimentation, and exploration of the world beyond their own heartlands.

Further Readings

M. A. Shaban's *Islamic History: An Interpretation*, 2 vols. (1971), contains the most readable and thematic survey of early Islam, concentrating on the Abbasid period. Although Philip Hitti's monumental *History of the Arabs* (1967) and J. J. Saunders' *A History of Medieval Islam* (1965) are now somewhat dated, they contain much valuable information and some fine insights into Arab history. Also useful are the works of G. E. von Gruenenbaum, especially *Classical Islam* (1970), which covers the Abbasid era. On changes in Islamic religion and the makeup of the Muslim community, Marshall Hodgson's *Venture of Islam*, vol. 2 (1974), is indispensable, but it should not be tackled by the beginner. *The Cambridge History of Islam*, 2 vols. (1970); Ira Lapidus, *A History of Islamic Societies* (1988); and Albert Hourani, *A History of the Islamic Peoples* (1991), are excellent reference works for the political events of the Abbasid era and Muslim achievements in various fields. D. M. Dunlop's *Arab Civilization to A.D. 1500* (1971) also contains detailed essays on Islamic culture as well as an article on the accomplishments of Muslim women in this era.

On social history, B. F. Musallam's *Sex and Society in Islam* (1983) has material on the Abbasid period, and some of the more prominent works on urban life include Ira Lapidus's *Muslim Cities in the Later Middle Ages* (1984 ed.), Nezar al-Sayyid's *Cities and Caliphs* (1991), and Albert Hourani and S. M. Stern, eds., *The Islamic City* (1970). Two essential works on the spread of Islam to India are S. M. Ikram, *Muslim Civilization in India* (1964); and Aziz Ahmad, *Studies in Islamic Culture in the Indian Environment* (1964). For the role of the Sufis in Islamic conversion, Richard Eaton's *Sufis of Bijapur* (1978) and *The Rise of Islam and the Bengal Frontier* (1993) are particularly revealing. The best introduction to the pattern of Islamic conversion in southeast Asia is H. J. de Graaf's essay in *The Cambridge History of Islam*, vol. 2 (1976). Toby Huff's *The Rise of Early Modern Science: Islam, China, and the West* (1993) is a stimulating account of the ways in which science and technology were transmitted between these key centers of the Eastern Hemisphere and the effects of these exchanges on global history. On the exchanges among Islamic and other Eurasian civilizations more generally, see R.M. Savory, ed., *Introduction to Islamic Civilization* (1976).

On MyHistoryLab

Study and Review on MyHistoryLab

Critical Thinking Questions

1. To what extent did Islam constitute the world's first global civilization?

2. What were the major reasons for the Sunni-Shi'a split in the Islamic *umma*?

3. What were the main motives for converting to Islam when full membership in the *umma* was opened to non-Arabs in the Abbasid Era?

4. In what ways did Muhammad's example and the teachings of the Quran make for improvements in the lives of women and what were the limits to these advances?

13

African Civilizations and the Spread of Islam

((• Listen to **Chapter 13**
on **MyHistoryLab**

LEARNING OBJECTIVES

13.1 Why did the Sudanic states develop in the sahel and what advantages did they have? p. 291

13.2 How did African societies accommodate Islam and what was the effect of its spread across Africa? p. 295

13.3 How integrated into international commerce were the cities of East Africa, and why? p. 301

13.4 What kinds of political organization developed in central and southern Africa? p. 303

In 1324, a great caravan of more than a hundred camels, many slaves, and a multitude of retainers crossed the arid Sahara desert and wended its way into Cairo, on the banks of the Nile. Mansa Musa, lord of the African empire of Mali, was making the *hajj*, the pilgrimage to Mecca, distributing gold with an open hand. The wealth and prodigality of the young king dazzled all who witnessed it, his polished manners and command of Arabic impressed those who met him, and his fame spread throughout the Islamic world and beyond. The chronicler al-Omari, who visited Cairo a dozen years later, reported that people still spoke of the entourage of the young king that had spent so much gold in the markets and had given so much as gifts and alms that

📖 Read the **Document** on **MyHistoryLab**: Al-Umari describes Mansa Musa of Mali

FIGURE **13.1** In 1324, Mansa Musa, King of Mali, made a pilgrimage to Mecca that brought the attention of the Muslim world to the wealth of his kingdom. A Jewish cartographer in Spain, Abraham Cresques, depicted the trip more than 50 years later in the map shown above. Mansa Musa is depicted at the bottom right with a golden scepter and crown, symbolizing his royal power, and an enormous gold nugget, symbolizing his country's wealth.

◉ Watch the Video Series on MyHistoryLab

Learn about some key topics related to this chapter with the *MyHistoryLab Video Series: Key Topics in World History*

the price of gold actually declined due to its ample supply. Other great caravans had made the trek from Mali across the desert before and some came after, but none had been so magnificent. Mansa Musa's caravan symbolized the wealthy potential of Africa, but even by the time he made his trip, west African gold was already well known in the world economy and Africa was already involved in contacts of vaious kinds with other areas of the world.

Mali, the kingdom of this great lord, fascinated the Muslim observers in Cairo, Damascus, and Fez. Like the earlier kingdom of Ghana, Mali was another state of the savannah country, between the desert and the forests of west Africa. Formed by the Malinke peoples, its access to gold and control of the caravan routes had promoted its rise, and its powerful army had created an empire that extended over much of the savannah from the Niger to the Senegal River. Its ruling families had converted to Islam, but the famous and cosmopolitan Moroccan traveler Abdallah Ibn Batuta, who visited Mali not long after Mansa Musa's pilgrimage, found the local customs and food less refined than those of the elegant courts to which he was accustomed and some of the practices shocking. Yet much was recognizable to him as well. Mali was an African kingdom that had become an extension of the Islamic world, and its success was tied to the trade routes that linked it to the Mediterranean and the Middle East. ■

The history of Mali underlines the fact that Africa below the Sahara was never totally isolated from the centers of civilization in Egypt, west Asia, or the Mediterranean, but for long periods the contacts were difficult and intermittent. This chapter will examine the increasing impact of a growing international network on Africa roughly in the period between 800 and 1600 C.E. Chief among those influences was the arrival of Islam, which transformed many aspects of life in some African societies and brought them through trade, politics, and cultural exchange into increasing contact. But, we must also recognize that the African societies influenced by Islam often maintained their own traditions and that other African societies remained little touched by Islam and continued to develop along their own trajectories.

African civilizations built somewhat less clearly on prior societies than did other postclassical civilizations. Some earlier themes, such as the Bantu migration and the formation of large states in the western Sudan, persisted. Overall, sub-Saharan Africa remained a varied and distinctive setting; parts of it, like the port cities of the East African coast, were drawn into new contacts with the growing world network, but much of it retained a certain isolation or cultural autonomy. The spread of universal faiths like Islam and Christianity was an important aspect of African history in this period, but much of central and southern Africa still flourished relatively unaffected by these outside influences.

AFRICAN SOCIETIES: DIVERSITY AND SIMILARITIES

> **13.1** Why did the Sudanic states develop in the sahel and what advantages did they have?

Like most continents, Africa is so vast and its societies so diverse that it is almost impossible to generalize about them. Differences in geography, language, religion, politics, and other aspects of life contributed to Africa's lack of political unity over long periods of time. Unlike in many parts of Asia, Europe, and north Africa, neither universal states nor universal religions characterized the history of sub-Saharan Africa. Yet universal religions, first Christianity and later Islam, did find adherents in Africa and sometimes contributed to the formation of large states and empires.

> African societies developed diverse forms, from stateless societies organized around kinship or age sets to large centralized states, and within this diversity were many shared aspects of language and beliefs. Universalistic faiths penetrated the continent and served as the basis for important cultural developments in Nubia and Ethiopia.

100 C.E.	600 C.E.	1000 C.E.	1200 C.E.	1400 C.E.
100–200 Camels introduced for trade in the Sahara **300** Origins of the kingdom of Ghana	**600–700** Islam spreads across North Africa	**1000** Ghana at height of its power **1100** Almoravid movement in the Sahara	**1200** Rise of the empire of Mali **1260** Death of Sundiata; earliest stone buildings at Zimbabwe; Lalibela rules in Ethiopia; Yoruba culture flourishes at Ile-Ife **1300** Mali at its height; Kanem empire is a rival **1324** Pilgrimage of Mansa Musa	**1400** Flourishing of cities of Timbuktu and Jenne; Ethiopian Christian kingdom; Swahili cities flourish on east African coast **1417, 1431** Last Chinese trade voyages to east Africa **1500** Songhay empire flourishes; Benin at height of power

Societies With and Without States

stateless societies African societies organized around kinship or other forms of obligation and lacking the concentration of political power and authority associated with states.

Some African societies had rulers who exercised control through a hierarchy of officials in what can be called states, but others were **stateless societies**, organized around kinship or other forms of obligation and lacking the concentration of political power and authority we normally associate with the state. Sometimes the stateless societies were larger and more extensive than the neighboring states. Stateless societies had forms of government, but the authority and power normally exercised by a ruler and his court in a kingdom could be held instead by a council of families or by the community, with no need to tax the population to support the ruler, the bureaucrats, the army, or the nobles, as was usually the case in state-building societies. Stateless societies had little concentration of authority, and it affected only a small part of the peoples' lives. In these societies, government was rarely a full-time occupation and there was no political class. Such societies often were less hierarchical and more egalitarian.

Other alternatives to formal government were possible. Among peoples of the west African forest, secret societies of men and women controlled customs and beliefs and were able to limit the authority of rulers. Especially among peoples who had sharp rivalries between lineages or family groupings, secret societies developed that cut across the lineage divisions. Members' allegiance to these groups transcended their lineage ties. The secret societies settled village disputes. They acted to maintain stability within the community, and they served as an alternative to the authority of state institutions.

Throughout Africa many stateless societies thrived, perhaps aided by the fact that internal social pressures or disputes often could be resolved by allowing dissidents to leave and establish a new village in the sparsely populated continent. Still, stateless societies found it difficult to resist external pressures, mobilize for warfare, organize large building projects, or create stable conditions for continuous long-distance trade with other peoples. All these needs or goals contributed to the formation of states in sub-Saharan Africa.

State-building took place under a variety of conditions. For example, west Africa experienced both the cultural influence of Islam and its own internal developments. The formation of some powerful states, such as Mali and Songhay, depended more on military power and dynastic alliances than on ethnic or cultural unity. In this development and in the process of state formation itself, Africa paralleled the roughly contemporaneous developments of western Europe. The growth of city-states with strong merchant communities in west Africa and on the Indian Ocean coast bore certain similarities to the urban developments of Italy and Germany in this period. However, disparities between the technologies and ideologies of Europeans and Africans also created differences in the ways these societies developed. That was made clear with the arrival of Europeans—the Portuguese—in the 15th century whose contact drew Africans increasingly into the world economy in ways that transformed African development in the following centuries.

Common Elements in African Societies

Even amid the diversity of African cultures, certain similarities in language, thought, and religion provided some underlying unities. The spread of the Bantu-speaking peoples provided a linguistic base across much of Africa, so that even though specific languages differed, structure and vocabulary allowed some mutual understanding between neighboring Bantu speakers.

The same might be said of the animistic religion that characterized much of Africa. From its earliest beginnings it was a belief that a soul or spirit existed in every object, even if it was inanimate. In a future state this soul or spirit would exist as part of an immaterial soul. The spirit, therefore, was thought to be universal. Africans, like Europeans, believed that some evil, disasters, and illnesses were produced by witchcraft. Specialists were needed to combat the power of evil and eliminate the witches. This led in many societies to the existence of a class of diviners or priests who guided religious practice and helped protect the community. Above all, African religion provided a cosmology—a view of how the universe worked—and a guide to ethics and behavior.

Many African peoples shared an underlying belief in a creator deity whose power and action were expressed through spirits or lesser gods and through the founding ancestors of the group. The ancestors often were viewed as the first settlers and thus the "owners" of the land or the local resources. Through them, the fertility of the land, game, people, and herds could be ensured. Among some groups, working the land took on religious significance, so the land itself had a meaning beyond its economic usefulness.

Religion, economics, and history were thus closely intertwined. The family, lineage, or clan around which many African societies were organized also had an important role in dealing with the gods. Deceased ancestors often were a direct link between their living relatives and the spirit world. Veneration of the ancestors and gods was part of the same system of belief. Such a system was strongly linked to specific places and people. It showed remarkable resiliency even in the face of contact with monotheistic religions such as Islam and Christianity.

The economies of Africa are harder to describe in general terms than some basic aspects of politics and culture. North Africa, fully involved in the Mediterranean and Arab economic world, stands clearly apart. Sub-Saharan Africa varied greatly from one region to the next. In many areas, settled agriculture and skilled ironwork had been established before or advanced rapidly during the post-classical period. Specialization encouraged active local and regional trade, the basis for many lively markets and the many large cities that grew in both the structured states and the decentralized areas. The bustle and gaiety of market life were important ingredients of African society, and women as well as men participated actively. Professional merchants, in many cases in hereditary kinship groupings, often controlled trade. Participation in international trade increased in many regions in this period, mainly with the Islamic world and often through Arab traders.

Finally, one of the least known aspects of early African societies is the size and dynamics of their populations. This is true not only of Africa but of much of the world. Archeological evidence, travelers' reports, and educated guesses are used to estimate the population of early African societies, but in truth, our knowledge of how Africa fits into the general trends of the world population is very slight. By 1500, Africa may have had 30 to 60 million inhabitants.

The Arrival of Islam in North Africa

Africa north of the Sahara had long been part of the world of classical antiquity, where Phoenicians, Greeks, Romans, and Vandals traded, settled, built, battled, and destroyed. The Greek city of Cyrene (c. 600 B.C.E.) in modern Libya and the great Phoenician outpost at Carthage (founded c. 814 B.C.E.) in Tunisia attest to the part north Africa played in the classical world. After the age of the pharaohs, Egypt (conquered by Alexander in 331 B.C.E.) had become an important part of the Greek world and then later a key province in the Roman Empire, valued especially for its grain. Toward the end of the Roman Empire, Christianity had taken a firm hold in Mediterranean Africa, but in the warring between the Vandals and the Byzantines in north Africa in the 5th and 6th centuries C.E., great disruption had taken place. During that period, the Berber peoples of the Sahara had raided the coastal cities. As we have seen with Egypt, north Africa was linked across the Sahara to the rest of Africa in many ways. With the rise of Islam, those ties became even closer.

Ifriqiya [IHF-rih-kee-uh] The Arabic term for eastern north Africa.

Maghrib [MAH-gribb] The Arabic word for western north Africa.

Between 640 and 700 C.E., the followers of Muhammad swept across north Africa from Suez to Morocco's Atlantic shore. By 670 C.E., Muslims ruled Tunisia, or **Ifriqiya**—what the Romans had called Africa. (The Arabs originally used this word as the name for eastern north Africa and **Maghrib** for lands to the west.) By 711, Arab and Berber armies had crossed into Spain. Only their defeat in France by Charles Martel at Poitiers in 732 brought the Muslim advance in the West to a halt. The message of Islam found fertile ground among the populations of north Africa. Conversion took place rapidly within a certain political unity provided by the Abbasid dynasty. This unity eventually broke down, and north Africa divided into several separate states and competing groups.

In opposition to the states dominated by the Arab rulers, the peoples of the desert, the Berbers, formed states of their own at places such as Fez in Morocco and at Sijilimasa, the old city of the trans-Saharan caravan trade. By the 11th century, under pressure from new Muslim invaders, a great puritanical reformist movement, whose followers were called the Almoravids (ahl-MOHR-uh-vihdz), grew among the desert Berbers of the western Sahara. Launched on the course of a *jihad*—a holy war waged to purify, spread, or protect the faith—the Almoravids moved south against the African kingdoms of the savanna and west into Spain. In 1130 another reformist group, the **Almohadis**, followed the same pattern. These north African and Spanish developments were an essential background to the penetration of Islam into sub-Saharan Africa.

Almohadis [AHL-moh-HAH-dees] A reformist movement among the Islamic Berbers of northern Africa; later than the Almoravids; penetrated into sub-Saharan Africa.

Islam offered many attractions within Africa. Its fundamental teaching that all Muslims are equal within the community of believers made the acceptance of conquerors and new rulers easier. The Islamic tradition of uniting the powers of the state and religion in the person of the ruler or caliph appealed to some African kings as a way of reinforcing their authority. The concept that all members of the umma, or community of believers, were equal put the newly converted Berbers and later Africans on an equal footing with the Arabs, at least in law. Despite these egalitarian and somewhat utopian ideas within Islam, practices differed considerably at local levels. Social stratification remained important in Islamicized societies, and ethnic distinctions also divided the believers. Despite certain teachings on the equality between men and women, the fine for killing a man was twice that for killing a woman. The disparity between law and practice—between equality before God and inequality within the world—sometimes led to utopian reform movements. Groups such as the Almohadis are characteristic within Islamic history, often developing in peripheral areas and dedicated to purifying society by returning to the original teachings of Muhammad.

The Christian Kingdoms: Nubia and Ethiopia

Islam was not the first universalistic religion to take root in Africa, and the wave of Arab conquests across northern Africa had left behind it islands of Christianity. Christian converts had been made in Egypt and Ethiopia even before the conversion of the Roman Empire in the 4th century C.E. In addition to the Christian kingdom of Axum, Christian communities thrived in Egypt and Nubia, farther up the Nile. The Christians of Egypt, the Copts, developed a rich tradition in contact with Byzantium, translating the gospels and other religious literature from Greek to Coptic, their own tongue, which was based on the language of ancient Egypt. On doctrinal and political issues, they eventually split from the Byzantine connection. When Egypt was conquered by Arab armies and then converted to Islam, the Copts were able to maintain their faith; Muslim rulers recognized them as followers of a revealed religion and thus entitled to a certain tolerance. The Coptic influence had already spread up the Nile into Nubia, the ancient land of Kush. Muslim attempts to penetrate Nubia were met with such stiff resistance in the 9th century that the Christian descendants of ancient Kush were left as independent Christian kingdoms until the 13th century.

The Ethiopian kingdom that grew from Axum was perhaps the most important African Christian outpost. Cut off from Christian Byzantium by the Muslim conquest of Egypt and the Red Sea coast, surrounded by pagan neighbors, and probably influenced by pagan and Jewish immigrants from Yemen, the Christian kingdom turned inward. Its people occupied the Ethiopian highlands, living in fortified towns and supporting themselves with agriculture on terraced hillsides. Eventually, through a process of warfare, conversion, and compromise with non-Christian neighbors, a new dynasty emerged, which under King Lalibela (d. 1221) sponsored a remarkable building project in which 11 great churches were sculpted from the rock in the town that bore his name (Figure 13.2).

In the 13th and 14th centuries, an Ethiopian Christian state emerged under a dynasty that traced its origins back to the biblical marriage of Solomon and Sheba. Using the Ge'ez language of Axum as a

FIGURE **13.2** This extraordinary 13th-century church, *Bet Giorgis*, represents the power of early Christianity in Ethiopia. It was one of a great complex of eleven churches that King Lalibela believed God had commanded him to build. Dedicated to St. George, the patron saint of Ethiopia, it was cut out of the bedrock of the earth. Its roof, in the shape of an enormous cross, lies at ground level. Although it is surrounded by impassable walls and can be reached only by way of an underground tunnel carved in stone, it is still used for worship today.

religious language and Amharic as the common speech, this state maintained its brand of Christianity in isolation while facing constant pressure from its increasingly Muslim neighbors.

The struggle between the Christian state in the Ethiopian highlands and the Muslim peoples in Somalia and on the Red Sea coast shaped much of the history of the region and continues to do so today. When one of these Muslim states, with help from the Ottoman Turks, threatened the Ethiopian kingdom, a Portuguese expedition arrived in 1542 at Massawa on the Red Sea and turned the tide in favor of its Christian allies. Portuguese attempts thereafter to bring Ethiopian Christianity into the Roman Catholic church failed, and Ethiopia remained isolated, Christian, and fiercely independent.

KINGDOMS OF THE GRASSLANDS

13.2 How did African societies accommodate Islam and what was the effect of its spread across Africa?

In the sahel grasslands, several powerful states emerged that combined Islamic religion and culture with local practices. The kingdoms of Mali and Songhay and the Hausa states were African adaptations of Islam and its fusion with African traditions.

As the Islamic wave spread across north Africa, it sent ripples across the Sahara, not in the form of invading armies but at first in the merchants and travelers who trod the dusty and ancient caravan routes toward the savanna. Africa had three important "coasts" of contact: the Atlantic, the Indian Ocean, and the savanna on the southern rim of the Sahara.

On the edge of the desert, where several resource zones came together, African states such as Ghana had already formed by the 8th century by exchanging gold from the forests of west Africa for salt or dates from the Sahara or for goods from Mediterranean north Africa. Camels, which had been introduced from Asia to the Sahara between the 1st and 5th centuries C.E., had greatly improved the possibilities of trade, but these animals, which thrived in arid and semiarid environments, could not live in the humid forest zones because of disease. Thus, the sahel, the extensive grassland belt at the southern edge of the Sahara, became a point of exchange between the forests to the south and north Africa—an active border area where ideas, trade, and people from the Sahara and beyond arrived in increasing numbers. Along the sahel, several African states developed between the trading cities, taking advantage of their position as intermediaries in the trade. But their location on the open plains of the dry sahel also meant that these states were subject to attack and periodic droughts.

Founded probably in the 3rd century C.E., Ghana rose to power by taxing the salt and gold exchanged within its borders. By the 10th century, its rulers had converted to Islam, and Ghana was at the height of its power. At a time when William the Conqueror could muster perhaps 5000 troops for his invasion of England, Muslim accounts reported that the king of Ghana could field an army many times that size. Eventually, however, Almoravid armies invaded Ghana from north Africa in 1076. The kingdom survived, but its power declined. By the beginning of the 13th century, new states had risen in the savanna to take Ghana's place of leadership.

Sudanic States

There were several Sudanic kingdoms, and even during the height of Ghana's power, neighboring and competing states persisted, such as Takrur on the Senegal River to the west and Gao (on the Niger River) to the east. Before we deal with the most important kingdoms that followed Ghana, it is useful to review some of the elements these states had in common.

The Sudanic states often had a patriarch or council of elders of a particular family or group of lineages as leaders. Usually these states had a territorial core area in which the people were of the same linguistic or ethnic background, but their power extended over subordinate communities. These were conquest states, which drew on the taxes, tribute, and military support of the subordinate areas, lineages, and villages. The effective control of subordinate societies and the legal or informal control of their sovereignty are the usual definition of empires. The Sudanic states of Ghana, Mali, and Songhay fit that definition (Map 13.1).

The rulers of these states were considered sacred and were surrounded by rituals that separated them from their subjects. With the conversion of the rulers of Ghana and Takrur after the 10th century, Islam was used to reinforce indigenous ideas of kingship, so that Islam became something of a royal cult. Much of the population never converted, and the Islamicized ruling families also drew on their traditional powers to fortify their rule.

Several savanna states rose among the various peoples in the Sudan. We can trace the development and culture of two of the most important, Mali and Songhay, as examples of the fusion of Islamic and indigenous African cultures within the context of trade and military expansion.

The Empire of Mali and Sundiata, the "Lion Prince"

The empire of Mali, centered between the Senegal and Niger rivers, was the creation of the Malinke peoples, who in the 13th century broke away from the control of Ghana, which was by then in decline. In Mali the old forms of kingship were reinforced by Islam. As in many of the Sudanic states, the rulers supported Islam by building mosques, attending public prayers, and supporting preachers. In return, sermons to the faithful emphasized obedience and support of the king. Mali became a model of these Islamicized Sudanic kingdoms. The economic basis of society in the Mali Empire was agriculture. This was combined with an active tradition of trade in many products, although like Ghana, Mali also depended on its access to gold-producing areas to the south. Malinke merchants, or **juula**, formed small partnerships and groups to carry out trade throughout the area. They spread beyond the borders of the empire and throughout much of west Africa.

 Read the **Document** on MyHistoryLab: Ghana and Its People in the Mid-Eleventh Century

juula [JOO-luh] Malinke merchants; formed small partnerships to carry out trade throughout Mali Empire; eventually spread throughout much of west Africa.

Watch the **Video** on MyHistoryLab: West African States

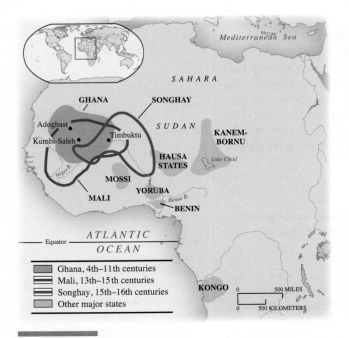

MAP **13.1 Empires of the Western Sudan**

The beginning of Malinke (also called Mandinka or Mandingo) expansion is attributed to **Sundiata** (sometimes written Sunjata), a brilliant leader whose exploits were celebrated in a great oral tradition. The **griots**, professional oral historians who also served as keepers of traditions and advisors to kings, began their epic histories of Mali with Sundiata, the "Lion Prince."

> Listen then sons of Mali, children of the black people, listen to my word, for I am going to tell you of Sundiata, the father of the Bright Country, of the savanna land, the ancestor of those who draw the bow, the master of a hundred vanquished kings. . . . He was great among kings, he was peerless among men; he was beloved of God because he was the last of the great conquerors.

After a difficult childhood, Sundiata emerged from a period of interfamily and regional fighting to create a unified state. Oral histories ascribed to him the creation of the basic rules and relationships of Malinke society and the outline of the government of the empire of Mali. He became the mansa, or emperor. It was said that Sundiata "divided up the world," which meant that he was considered the originator of social arrangements. Sixteen clans of free people were entitled to bear arms and carry the bow and quiver of arrows as the symbol of their status, five clans were devoted to religious duties, and four clans were specialists such as blacksmiths and griots. Such clan arrangements were traditional among the peoples of the savanna and had existed in ancient Ghana, but now Sundiata was credited with their origins. Although he created the political institutions of rule that allowed for great regional and ethnic differences in the federated provinces, he also stationed garrisons to maintain loyalty and security. Travel was secure and crime was severely punished, as **Ibn Battuta** (1304–1368 C.E.), the Arab traveler, reported: "Of all peoples," he said, "the Blacks are those who most hate injustice, and their emperor pardons none who is guilty of it." The security of travelers and their goods was an essential element in a state where commerce played so important a role.

Sundiata died about 1260, but his successors expanded the borders of Mali until it controlled most of the Niger valley almost to the Atlantic coast. A sumptuous court was established and hosted a large number of traders. Mali grew wealthy from the trade. Perhaps the most famous of Sundiata's successors was Mansa Kankan Musa (c. 1312–1337), whose pilgrimage to Mecca in 1324 brought the attention of the Muslim world to Mali, as was described in the beginning of this chapter. Mansa Musa's trip had other consequences as well. From Mecca he brought back poet and architect Ishak al-Sahili, who came from Muslim Spain. The architect directed the building of several important mosques, and eventually a distinctive form of Sudanic architecture developed that made use of beaten clay. This can still be seen in the great mosque of Jenne.

City Dwellers and Villagers

The cities of the western Sudan began to resemble those of north Africa, but with a distinctive local architectural style. The towns were commercial and often included craft specialists and a resident foreign merchant community. The military expansion of states such as Ghana, Mali, and later Songhay contributed to their commercial success because the power of the state protected traders. A cosmopolitan court life developed as merchants and scholars were attracted by the power and protection of Mali. Malinke traders ranged across the Sudan and exploited their position as intermediaries. Cities of commercial exchange flourished, such as Jenne and **Timbuktu**, which lay just off the flood plain on the great bend in the Niger River. Timbuktu was reported to have a population of 50,000, and by the 14th century, its great Sankore mosque contained a library and an associated university where scholars, jurists, and Muslim theologians studied. The book was the symbol of civilization in the Islamic world, and it was said that the book trade in Timbuktu was the most lucrative business.

For most people in the empire of Mali and the other Sudanic states, life was not centered on the royal court, the great mosque, or long-distance trade but rather on the agricultural cycle and the village. Making a living from the land was the preoccupation of most people, and about 80 percent of the villagers lived by farming. This was a difficult life. The soils of the savanna were sandy and shallow. Plows were rarely used. The villagers were people of the hoe who looked to the skies in the spring for the first rains to start their planting. Rice in the river valleys, millet, sorghums, some wheat, fruits, and vegetables provided the basis of daily life in the village and supplied the caravan trade. Even large farms rarely exceeded 10 acres, and most were much smaller. Clearing land often was done communally, accompanied by feasts and competition, but the farms belonged to families and were worked

Sundiata The "Lion Prince"; a member of the Keita clan; created a unified state that became the Mali Empire; died about 1260.

griots [grEE O, grEE O, grEE ot] Professional oral historians who served as keepers of traditions and advisors to kings within the Mali Empire.

Ibn Battuta (b. 1304) Arab traveler who described African societies and cultures in his travel records.

Timbuktu Port city of Mali; located just off the flood plain on the great bend in the Niger River; population of 50,000; contained a library and university.

 Read the **Document** on MyHistoryLab: Leo Africanus Describes Timbuktu

DOCUMENT

The Great Oral Tradition and the Epic of Sundiata

ORAL TRADITIONS TAKE VARIOUS FORMS. SOME are simply the shared stories of a family or people, but in many west African societies, the mastery of oral traditions is a skill practiced by *griots*. Although today's griots are professional musicians and bards, historically they held important places at the courts of west African kingdoms. The epic of Sundiata, the great ruler of Mali, has been passed down orally for centuries. In the following excerpts from a version collected among the Malinke people of Guinea by the African scholar D. T. Niane, the role of the griot and the advantages of oral traditions are outlined.

> We are now coming to the great moments in the life of Sundiata. The exile will end and another sun will rise. It is the sun of Sundiata. Griots know the history of kings and kingdoms and that is why they are the best counsellors of kings. Every king wants to have a singer to perpetuate his memory, for it is the griot who rescues the memories of kings from oblivion, as men have short memories. Kings have prescribed destinies just like men, and seers who probe the future know it. They have knowledge of the future, whereas we griots are depositories of the knowledge of the past. But whoever knows the history of a country can read its future.
>
> Other peoples use writing to record the past, but this invention has killed the faculty of memory among them. They do not feel the past any more, for writing lacks the warmth of the human voice. With them everybody thinks he knows, whereas learning should be a secret. The prophets did not write and their words have been all the more vivid as a result. What paltry learning is that which is concealed in dumb books!

The following excerpt describes the preparation for a major battle fought by Sundiata against the forces of Soumaoro, king of the Sossos, who had taken control of Mali and who is called an evil sorcerer in the epic. Note the interweaving of proverbs, the presence of aspects of Muslim and animist religion, the celebration of Sundiata's prowess, the recurring references to iron, and the high value placed on the cavalry, the key to military power in the savanna. Note how the story of Alexander the Great inspires this "African Alexander."

> Every man to his own land! If it is foretold that your destiny should be fulfilled in such and such a land, men can do nothing against it. Mansa Tounkara could not keep Sundiata back because the destiny of Songolon's son was bound up with that of Mali. Neither the jealousy of a cruel stepmother, nor her wickedness could alter for a moment the course of great destiny.

> The snake, man's enemy, is not long-lived, yet the serpent that lives hidden will surely die old. Djata (Sundiata) was strong enough now to face his enemies. At the age of eighteen he had the stateliness of the lion and the strength of the buffalo. His voice carried authority, his eyes were live coals, his arm was iron, he was the husband of power.
>
> Moussa Tounkara, king of Mema, gave Sundiata half of his army. The most valiant came forward of their own free will to follow Sundiata in the great adventure. The cavalry of Mema, which he had fashioned himself, formed his iron squadron. Sundiata, dressed in the Muslim fashion of Mema, left the town at the head of his small but redoubtable army. The whole population sent their best wishes with him. He was surrounded by five messengers from Mali, and Manding Bory [Sundiata's brother] rode proudly at his side. The horsemen of Mema formed behind Djata a bristling iron squadron. The troop took the direction of Wagadou, for Djata did not have enough troops to confront Soumaoro directly, and so the king of Mema advised him to go to Wagadou and take half the men of the king, Soumaba Cissé. A swift messenger had been sent there and so the king of Wagadou came out in person to meet Sundiata and his troops. He gave Sundiata half of his cavalry and blessed the weapons. Then Manding Bory said to his brother, "Djata, do you think yourself able to face Soumaoro now?"
>
> "No matter how small a forest may be, you can always find there sufficient fibers to tie up a man. Numbers mean nothing; it is worth that counts. With my cavalry I shall clear myself a path to Mali."
>
> Djata gave out his orders. They would head south, skirting Soumaoro's kingdom. The first objective to be reached was Tabon, the iron-gated town in the midst of the mountains, for Sundiata had promised Fran Kamara that he would pass Tabon before returning to Mali. He hoped to find that his childhood companion had become king. It was a forced march and during the halts the divines, Singbin Mara Cissé and Mandjan Bérété, related to Sundiata the history of Alexander the Great and several other heroes, but of all of them Sundiata preferred Alexander, the king of gold and silver, who crossed the world from west to east. He wanted to outdo his prototype both in the extent of his territory and in the wealth of his treasury.

QUESTIONS
- Can oral traditions be used like other sources?
- Even if they are not entirely true, do they have historical value?
- Judging from this epic, how did people of the Sudan define the qualities of a king?
- What aspects of the epic reveal contacts between this part of Africa and the wider world?

by them. A man with two wives and several unmarried sons could work more land than a man with one wife and a smaller family. Polygamy, the practice of having multiple wives, was common in the region, and it remains so today.

Given the difficulties of the soil, the periodic droughts, insect pests, storage problems, and the limitations of technology, the farmers of the Sudanic states—by the methods of careful cultivation, crop rotation, and in places such as Timbuktu, the use of irrigation—were able to provide for their people the basic foods that supported them and the imperial states on which they were based. The hoe and the bow became symbols of the common people of the savanna states.

The Songhay Kingdom

As the power of Mali began to wane, a successor state from within the old empire was already beginning to emerge. The people of **Songhay** dominated the middle areas of the Niger valley. Traditionally, the society of Songhay was made up of "masters of the soil," that is, farmers, herders, and "masters of the waters," or fishers. Songhay had begun to form in the 7th century as an independent kingdom, perhaps under a Berber dynasty. By 1010, a capital was established at Gao on the Niger River, and the rulers had become Muslims, although the majority of the population remained pagan. Dominated by Mali for a while, by the 1370s Songhay had established its independence again and began to thrive as new sources of gold from the west African forests began to pass through its territory. Gao became a large city with a resident foreign merchant community and several mosques. Under a dynamic leader, Sunni Ali (r. 1464–1492), the empire of Songhay was forged.

Sunni Ali was a great tactical commander and a ruthless leader. His cavalry expanded the borders and seized the traditional trading cities of Timbuktu and Jenne. The middle Niger valley fell under his control, and he developed a system of provincial administration to mobilize recruits for the army and rule the far-flung conquests. Although apparently a Muslim, he met any challenge to his authority even when it came from the Muslim scholars of Timbuktu, whom he persecuted. A line of Muslim rulers who took the military title *askia* succeeded him. These rulers, especially **Muhammad the Great**, extended the boundaries of the empire so that by the mid-16th century Songhay dominated the central Sudan.

Life in the Songhay Empire followed many of the patterns established in the previous savanna states. The fusion of Islamic and pagan populations and traditions continued. Muslim clerics and jurists sometimes were upset by the pagan beliefs and practices that continued among the population, and even more by the local interpretation of Islamic law. They wanted to impose a strict interpretation of the law of Islam and were shocked that men and women mixed freely in the markets and streets, that women went unveiled.

Songhay remained the dominant power in the region until the end of the 16th century. In 1591, a Muslim army from Morocco, equipped with muskets, crossed the Sahara and defeated the vastly larger forces of Songhay. This sign of weakness stimulated internal revolts against the ruling family, and eventually the parts of the old empire broke away.

The demise of the Songhay imperial structure did not mean the end of the political and cultural tradition of the western Sudan. Other states that combined Muslim and pagan traditions rose among the **Hausa** peoples of northern Nigeria, based on cities such as Kano and Katsina. The earliest Muslim ruler of Kano took control in the late 14th century and turned the city into a center of Muslim learning. In Kano and other Hausa cities of the region, an urbanized royal court in a fortified capital ruled over the animistic villages, where the majority of the population lived. With powerful cavalry forces these states extended their rule and protected their active trade in salt, grains, and cloth. Although these later Islamicized African states tended to be small and their goals were local, they reproduced many of the social, political, and religious forms of the great empires of the grasslands.

Beyond the Sudan, Muslim penetration came in various forms. Merchants became established in most of the major trading cities, and religious communities developed in each of these, often associated with particular families. Networks of trade and contact were established widely over the region as merchants and groups of pastoralists established their outposts in the area of Guinea. Muslim traders, herders, warriors, and religious leaders became important minorities in these segmented African societies, composed of elite families, occupational groups, free people, and slaves. Intermarriage often

Songhay [sohng-HEYE] Successor state to Mali; dominated middle reaches of Niger valley; formed as independent kingdom under a Berber dynasty; capital at Gao; reached imperial status under Sunni Ali (r. 1464–1492).

Muhammad the Great Extended the boundaries of the Songhay Empire; Islamic ruler of the mid-16th century.

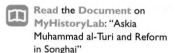
Read the **Document** on **MyHistoryLab**: "Askia Muhammad al-Turi and Reform in Songhai"

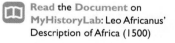
Read the **Document** on **MyHistoryLab**: Leo Africanus' Description of Africa (1500)

Hausa Peoples of northern Nigeria; formed states following the demise of Songhay Empire that combined Muslim and pagan traditions.

took place, but Muslim influence varied widely from region to region. Nevertheless, families of traders and lineages that became known as specialists in Muslim law spread widely through the region, so that by the 18th century Muslim minorities were scattered widely throughout west Africa, even in areas where no Islamicized state had emerged.

Political and Social Life in the Sudanic States

We can generalize from these brief descriptions of Mali and Songhay about the nature of the Sudanic states. The village communities, clans, and various ethnic groups continued to organize many aspects of life in the savanna. The development of unified states provided an overarching structure that allowed the various groups and communities to coexist. The large states usually represented the political aims and power of a particular group and often of a dominant family. Many states pointed to the immigrant origins of the ruling families, and in reality the movement and fusion of populations were constant features in the Sudan. Islam provided a universalistic faith that served the interests of many groups. Common religion and law provided solidarity and trust to the merchants who lived in the cities and whose caravans brought goods to and from the savanna. The ruling families used Islamic titles, such as *emir* or *caliph*, to reinforce their authority, and they surrounded themselves with literate Muslim advisors and scribes, who aided in government administration. The Muslim concept of a ruler who united civil and religious authority reinforced traditional ideas of kingship. It is also important to note that in Africa, as elsewhere in the world, the formation of states heightened social differences and made these societies more hierarchical.

In all the Sudanic states, Islam was fused with the existing traditions and beliefs. Rulership and authority were still based on the ability to intercede with local spirits, and although Sundiata and Sunni Ali were nominally Muslim, they did not ignore the traditional basis of their rule. For this reason, Islam in these early stages in the Sudan tended to accommodate pagan practice and belief. Large proportions of the populations of Mali and Songhay never converted to Islam, and those who did convert often maintained many of the old beliefs as well.

We can see this fusion of traditions clearly in the position of women. Several Sudanic societies were matrilineal, and some recognized the role of women within the lines of kinship, contrary to the normal patrilineal customs inscribed in the **Sharia**, or Islamic law. As in the case of Songhay, north African visitors to the Sudan were shocked by the easy familiarity between men and women and the freedom enjoyed by women.

Finally, slavery and the slave trade between black Africa and the rest of the Islamic world had a major impact on women and children in these societies. Various forms of slavery and dependent labor had existed in Africa before Islam was introduced. Although we know little about slavery in central Africa in this period, slavery had been a marginal aspect of the Sudanic states. Africans had been enslaved by others before, and Nubian (African) slaves had been known in the classical world, but with the Muslim conquests of north Africa and commercial penetration to the south, slavery became a more widely diffused phenomenon, and a slave trade in Africans developed on a new scale.

In theory, Muslims viewed slavery as a stage in the process of conversion—a way of preparing pagans to become Muslims—but in reality, conversion did not guarantee freedom. Slaves in the Islamic world were used in a variety of occupations, as domestic servants and laborers, but they were also used as soldiers and administrators who, having no local ties and affiliations, were considered to be dependent on and thus trustworthy by their masters. Slaves were also used as eunuchs and concubines, hence the emphasis on enslaving women and children. The trade caravans from the sahel across the Sahara often transported slaves as well as gold, and as we shall see, other slave trade routes developed from the African interior to the east African coast.

Frequently the children of slave mothers were freed and integrated into Muslim society. Although this custom was positive in one sense, it also meant a constant demand for more slaves to replace those freed. Estimates of the volume of the trans-Saharan slave trade vary widely. One scholar places the total at 4.8 million, with another 2.4 million sent to the Muslim ports on the Indian Ocean coast. Actual figures may have been considerably lower, but the trade extended over 700 years and affected a large area. It was one more way in which Islamic civilization changed sub-Saharan Africa.

Sharia [shä rEE ä] Islamic law; defined among other things the patrilineal nature of Islamic inheritance.

The Architecture of Faith

THE SPREAD OF ISLAM EVENTUALLY CREATED spiritual, commercial, and cultural bonds between west Africa and the Middle East and especially north Africa and Spain. The process of Islam's expansion and its local adaptation is apparent in the distinctive architectural style of west African mosques. Built usually of clay, incorporating wood beams for support and decoration, with a *mirab* tower and an open courtyard, these places of worship created spaces of simple elegance with local materials that reflect ethnic and regional differences. West African mosques vary considerably from the traditional patterns of the Middle East and south Asia. Mosques, like the simple buildings among the Dogon people or the elaborate Sankoré mosque at Timbuktu begun in 1324 by Mansa Musa and later the center of a university, reflect the integration of Islam into African life.

QUESTIONS

- The architectural styles of west African mosques differ from the classic models of the Middle East. In what way does that suggest that Islam's entry to the region was gradual and transmitted by merchants and traders?
- In what ways do the mosques of West Africa reflect local conditions and practices?
- What functions beside prayer did mosques play and how did their construction tie west Africa to a wider world?

Dogon village mosque in Kani-Kombole, Mali, west Africa.

Domed Middle Eastern mosques shown in the skyline of Yazd, Iran.

THE SWAHILI COAST OF EAST AFRICA

13.3   How integrated into international commerce were the cities of East Africa, and why?

While the kingdoms of west Africa came under the influence of Islam from across the Sahara, another center of Islamic civilization was developing on the seaboard and offshore islands of Africa's Indian Ocean coast (Map 13.2). Along that coast, extending south from the horn of Africa to modern-day Mozambique, a string of Islamicized trading cities developed that reflected their cosmopolitan contacts with trading partners from Arabia, Persia, India, and China. Islam provided the residents of these towns a universal set of ethics and beliefs that made their maritime contacts easier, but in east Africa, as in the savanna kingdoms of west Africa, Islamization was slow to reach the general population. When it did, the result often was a compromise between indigenous ways and the new faith.

A string of Islamicized African ports tied to the trade across the Indian Ocean dotted the east African coast. Although these cities were Islamicized, African customs and the Bantu Swahili language remained so strong that they represented a cultural fusion, mostly limited to the coast.

The Coastal Trading Ports

View the Closer Look on MyHistoryLab: Malindi Mosque

Zenj [zehnj] Arabic term for the east African coast.

A 1st-century Greek account of the Indian Ocean, *The Periplus of the Erythraean Sea*, mentioned some ports in east Africa but was vague about whether the inhabitants were Africans or immigrants from the Arabian peninsula. From that century to the 10th century, the wave of Bantu migration had clearly reached the east African interior. Bantu-speaking herders in the north and farmers in the south mixed with older populations in the region. Other peoples were also moving to the African coast.

Contact across the Indian Ocean dated back to at least the 2nd century B.C.E. From Indonesia or Malaya, seaborne immigrants settled on the large island of Madagascar and from there introduced foods such as bananas and coconuts to the African coast. These were widely adopted and spread rapidly along the coast and into central Africa. Small coastal villages of fishers and farmers, making rough pottery and working iron, dotted this coast. By the 8th and 9th centuries, Muslim visitors and refugees from Oman and the Persian Gulf had established themselves at some of these villages, attracted by the possibilities of trade with the land of **Zenj** (zehnj), the Arabic term for the east African coast.

By the 13th century, a string of urbanized east African trading ports had developed along the coast. These towns shared the common Bantu-based and Arabic-influenced Swahili (which means "coastal") language and other cultural traits, although they were governed by separate Muslim ruling families. Towns such as Mogadishu, Mombasa, Malindi, Kilwa, Pate, and Zanzibar eventually contained mosques, tombs, and palaces of cut stone and coral. Ivory, gold, iron, slaves, and exotic animals were exported from these ports in exchange for silks from Persia and porcelain from China for the ruling Muslim families. The Arab traveler Ibn Batuta was impressed with the beauty and refinement of these towns. He described Kilwa as "one of the most beautiful and well constructed towns in the world" and was also impressed by the pomp and luxury of its ruler. Kilwa's advantage was its access to the gold coming from the interior and the fact that it was the furthest point south from which the ships sailing from India could hope to return in a single monsoon season.

From the 13th to the 15th centuries, Kilwa flourished in the context of international trade, but it was not alone; about 30 of these port towns eventually dotted the coast. They were tied to each other by an active coastal commerce and, in a few places, to the interior by a caravan trade, although it was usually Africans who brought the goods to the coast. Some Chinese ports sent goods directly to Africa in the 13th century, and as late as 1417 and 1431, large, state-sponsored expeditions sailing directly from China stopped at the east African coast to load ivory, gold, and rare woods. The Chinese discontinued such contact after 1431, and goods from China came to the coast thereafter in the ships of Arab or Indian traders.

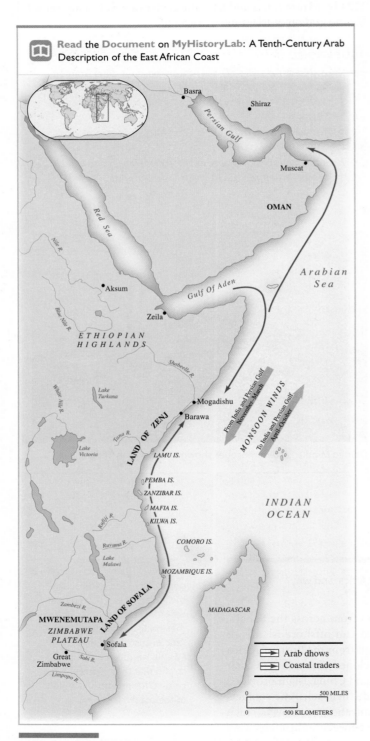

Read the Document on MyHistoryLab: A Tenth-Century Arab Description of the East African Coast

MAP 13.2 The Swahili Coast; African Monsoon Routes and Major Trade Routes

The Mixture of Cultures on the Swahili Coast

The Islamic influence in these towns promoted long-distance commerce. The 13th century was a period of great Islamic expansion, and as that faith spread eastward to India and Indonesia, it provided a religious bond of trust and law that facilitated trade throughout ports of the Indian Ocean. The ruling families in the east African trading ports built mosques and palaces; the mosque at Mogadishu was begun in 1231. Many of these ruling families claimed to be descendants of immigrants from Shiraz in Persia—a claim intended to legitimize their position and orthodoxy. In fact, some evidence indicates that the original Muslim families had emigrated to the Somali coast and from there to other towns farther south. The institutions and forms of the Muslim world operated in these cities. Whereas the rulers and merchants tended to be Muslim, the majority of the population on the east African coast, and perhaps even in the towns themselves, retained their previous beliefs and culture.

African culture remained strong throughout the area. The Swahili language was essentially a Bantu language containing a large number of Arabic words, although many of these words were not incorporated until the 16th century. The language was written in an Arabic script some time before the 13th century; the ruling families could also converse in Arabic. Islam itself penetrated very little into the interior among the hunters, pastoralists, and farmers. Even the areas of the coast near the trading towns remained largely unaffected. In the towns, the mud and thatch houses of the non-Muslim common peoples surrounded the stone and coral buildings of the Muslim elite. Islamization was to some extent class-based. Still, a culture developed that fused Islamic and traditional elements. For example, family lineage was traced both through the maternal line, which controlled property (the traditional African practice), and through the paternal line, as was the Muslim custom. Swahili culture was a dynamic hybrid, and the Swahili people spread their language and culture along the coast of east Africa.

By the time the Portuguese arrived on this coast around 1500, the Swahili culture was widely diffused. Kilwa was no longer the predominant city, and the focus of trade had shifted to Malindi and Mombasa on the Kenya coast, but the commerce across the Indian Ocean continued. Eventually, the Portuguese raided Kilwa and Mombasa in an attempt to take control of trade. Their outpost on Mozambique and their control of Sofala put much of the gold trade in their hands. Although the Portuguese built a major outpost at Fort Jesus in Mombasa in 1592, they were never able to control the trade on the northern Swahili coast. The east African patterns, as established by 1500, persisted even more than those of the Sudanic kingdoms. In some areas like the Swahili coast and the West African savanna, Islam became a dominant cultural force. In other areas such as the forest region of West Africa, Muslims remained a minority, and in other areas like the central African forests Islam hardly penetrated at all.

 Read the **Document** on MyHistoryLab: Hans Mayr, Account of Francisco d'Almeida's attack on Kilwa and Mombasa

PEOPLES OF THE FOREST AND PLAINS

13.4 What kinds of political organization developed in central and southern Africa?

As important as the Islamic impact was on the societies of the savanna and the east African coast, other African peoples in the continent's interior and in the forests of west Africa were following their own trajectories of development. We must emphasize that African societies were diverse. By 1000 C.E., most of these societies were based on a varied agriculture, sometimes combined with herding, and most societies used iron tools and weapons. Many were still organized in small village communities. In various places, however, states had formed. Some of them began to resolve the problems of integrating large territories under a single government and ruling subject peoples. Whereas Egypt, Kush, and Ethiopia had developed writing and other areas borrowed the Arabic script, many sub-Saharan African societies were preliterate and transmitted their knowledge, skills, and traditions by oral methods and direct instruction. The presence or absence of writing has often been used as a measure of civilization by Western observers, but as in pre-Columbian Peru, various African societies made great strides in the arts, building, and statecraft, sometimes in the context of highly urbanized settings, without a system of writing.

Across central Africa, kingdoms developed that were supported by complex agrarian societies capable of great artistic achievements. At Benin, in the Kongo, in the Yoruba city-states, and at Great Zimbabwe, royal authority—often considered divinely inspired—led to the creation of powerful states.

Artists and Kings: Yoruba and Benin

In the forests of central Nigeria, terra-cotta objects of a realistic and highly stylized form have been discovered near the village of Nok. These objects, most of which date from about 500 B.C.E. to 200 C.E., reveal considerable artistic skill. The inhabitants of ancient Nok and its region practiced agriculture and used iron tools. They remain something of a mystery, but it appears that their artistic traditions spread widely through the forest areas and influenced other peoples. Nevertheless, there is a long gap in the historical and archeological record between the Nok sculptures and the renewed flourishing of artistic traditions in the region after about 1000 C.E.

Among the Yoruba-speaking peoples of Nigeria, at the city of Ile-Ife (eel-EE-fuh), remarkable terra-cotta and bronze portrait heads of past rulers were produced in the period after 1200 C.E. The lifelike quality of these portraits and the skill of their execution place them among the greatest achievements of African art (Figure 13.3). The artists of Ile-Ife also worked in wood and ivory. Much of the art seems to be associated with kings and the authority of kingship. Ile-Ife, like other Yoruba states, seems to have been an agricultural society supported by a peasantry and dominated by a ruling family and an aristocracy. Ile-Ife was considered by many peoples in the region to be the original cultural center, and many of them traced their own beginnings to it.

Yoruba origins are obscure. Ile-Ife was seen as the holiest city of the Yoruba, their place of birth. Another legend maintained by the royal historians was that Oduduwa, a son of the king of Mecca, migrated from the east and settled in Yoruba. Modern historians have suggested that the real origins were perhaps Meroë and Nubia, or at least in the savanna south of the Sahara. In any case, the Yoruba spoke a non-Bantu language of the west African Kwa family and recognized a certain affinity between themselves and neighboring peoples, such as the Hausa, who spoke Afro-Asian languages.

The Yoruba were organized in small city-states, each controlling a radius of perhaps 50 miles. The Yoruba were highly urbanized, although many of the town inhabitants farmed in the surrounding countryside. These city-states developed under the strong authority of regional kings, who were considered divine. A vast royal court that included secondary wives, musicians, magicians, and bodyguards of soldier-slaves surrounded the king. His rule was not absolute, however. We can use the example of the Yoruba state of Oyo, which had emerged by the 14th century. Its king, the alafin, controlled subject peoples through "princes" in the provinces, drawn from local lineages, who were allowed to exercise traditional rule as long as they continued to pay tribute to Oyo. In the capital, a council of state, made up of nobles from the seven city districts, advised the ruler and limited his power, and the Ogboni, or secret society of religious and political leaders, reviewed decisions of the king and the council. The union of civil and supernatural powers in the person of the ruler was the basis of power. The highly urbanized nature of Yoruba society and the flourishing of artisan traditions within these towns bear some similarity to those of the city-states of medieval Italy or Germany.

Patterns similar to those in the Yoruba city-states could be found among Edo peoples to the east of Yoruba. A large city-state called **Benin** was formed sometime in the 14th century. Under Ewuare the Great (r. 1440–1473), Benin's control extended from the Niger River to the coast near modern Lagos. Benin City was described by early European visitors in the 16th century as a city of great population and broad avenues. The oba, or ruler, lived in a large royal compound surrounded by a great entourage, and his authority was buttressed by ritual and ceremony.

FIGURE **13.3** In the 13th and 14th centuries, Ile-Ife artists worked in terra-cotta as well as bronze and produced skilled individual portraits like this one.

(The Brooklyn Museum of Art)

Benin Powerful city-state (in present-day Nigeria) which came into contact with the Portuguese in 1485 but remained relatively free of European influence; important commercial and political entity until the 19th century.

THINKING HISTORICALLY

Two Transitions in the History of World Population

AFRICA AND THE ANCIENT AMERICAS ARE two regions that make clear the difficulty of establishing the past size and structure of populations. Estimates based on fragmentary sources, the amount of available resources, and analysis of agricultural or hunting techniques have been used as rough guesses about population size. The results often are inadequate or controversial, but historians believe that the question is important. **Demography**, the study of population, has increasingly become a valued tool of historical inquiry. Clearly, unless we know the size, density, age structure, health, and reproductive capacity of a population, it is difficult to understand many aspects of its society, politics, and economy. In the contemporary world, most nations conduct periodic censuses to assess the present situation of their populations and to plan for the future. Before the mid-18th century, when census-taking became a regular procedure, population estimates and counts were sporadic and usually inaccurate. Estimating populations in the past, especially in nonliterate societies, is a highly speculative exercise in which archeological evidence and estimates of productive capacity of agricultural practices and technology are used. The earliest date

(continued on next page)

(continued from previous page)

for a population estimate with a margin of error less than 20 percent is probably 1750.

The history of human population can be divided into two basic periods: a long era—almost all of human history—of very slow growth and a very short period—about 275 years from 1750 to the present—of very rapid growth. For most of this history, the human population was very small and grew very slowly. Before agriculture was developed, the hunting-and-gathering economies of the world's populations supported 5 to 10 million people, if modern studies of such populations can be used as a guide. After about 8000 B.C.E., when plants and animals were domesticated, there was a first demographic transition as population began to increase more rapidly but still at a modest level. Agriculture provided a more secure and larger food supply, but population concentration in villages and towns may have made people more susceptible to disease and thus reduced their numbers. Other historians believe that the settled agricultural life also led to intensified warfare (because of the struggle for land and water) and increasing social stratification within societies.

Still, the Neolithic revolution and the development of agriculture stimulated population growth. It was the first major transition in the history of world population. One estimate, based on Roman and Chinese population counts and some informed guesses about the rest of the world, is an annual growth rate of about 0.36 per million. By 1 C.E., the world population may have been about 300 million people. It increased between 1 C.E. and 1750 C.E. to about 500 million people. We should bear in mind that during this period of general increase, there were always areas that suffered decline, sometimes drastic, because of wars, epidemics, or natural catastrophes. The disastrous decline of American Indian populations after contact with Europeans, caused by disease, conquest, and social disruption, is a case in point. The effect of the slave trade on Africa, although still debated, is another. Sharp population changes usually resulted in profound social and cultural adjustments. Some scholars argue that the slave trade had just such an impact on social and political patterns in Africa.

A second and extremely important transition took place between the mid-17th and the mid-18th centuries. Initially based on new food resources, this transition often is associated with the Industrial Revolution, when new sources of energy were harnessed. The growth rate greatly increased during this period in the countries most affected. Between 1750 and 1800, the world population grew at a rate of more than 4 percent a year to more than a billion people. By the mid-20th century, the world growth rate had tripled, and by 2012 world population had risen to more than 7 billion.

This **demographic transition** took place first in Europe and is still more characteristic of the developed world. Most premodern agrarian economies were characterized by a balance between the annual number of births and deaths; both were high. Life expectancy usually was less than 35 years, and the high mortality was compensated by high fertility; that is, women had many children. Improvements in medicine, hygiene, diet, and the general standard of living contributed to a decrease in mortality in the 18th century. This allowed populations to begin to grow at a faster rate. By the 19th century in most of western Europe, the decline in mortality was followed by a decline in fertility brought about by contraception. In some countries such as France, these two transitions took place at about the same time, so population growth was limited. In much of Europe, however, the decline in fertility lagged behind the decrease in mortality, so there was a period of rapid population growth. Until the 1920s, population growth in western Europe and the United States was higher than in the rest of the world, especially in the less industrialized countries. In recent times, that situation has been reversed.

Some demographers believe that demographic transition is part of the process of shifting from a basically agrarian society to an industrial, urbanized one and that the improvements in medicine, technology, and higher standards of living will necessarily result in a change to a modern demographic structure. They believe that a decreasing need for children as part of the family economic unit, laws against child labor, and state intervention in family planning will eventually lower the world birth rate and decrease the pressure of population on economic growth. This assumption remains to be proved, and responses may vary greatly from one region of the world to another because of economic conditions and cultural attitudes about proper family size.

> *At present, the world's population is growing because of a moderate rate of growth in the industrialized nations and a high rate in the developing countries.*

Finally, we should also note that responses to demographic transition can vary greatly according to historical conditions. In the 18th and 19th centuries, Europe resolved the problem of population growth with an enormous wave of emigration to the Americas, Australia, and various colonies around the globe. Present-day political circumstances make this solution less possible, although the new waves of migration in the global economy may indicate that the process is continuing.

Still, it is clear that a demographic transition has begun to take place in the developing world of Latin America, Africa, and Asia. Mortality has dropped very rapidly since 1950 because of modern medical technology, and life expectancy has doubled. To cite a single example, in Sri Lanka the mortality rate was almost cut in half between 1945 and 1952 simply by eliminating malarial mosquitoes. Fertility has declined in many places in Asia and Latin America, but in Africa, where children continue to have an important economic and social role in the extended family, it remains high. It is difficult to project what demographic transitions will take place in these areas of the world. However, all countries are faced with the problem of balancing their population's growth against the ability of the society to feed and provide an adequate standard of living to the people.

(continued on next page)

(continued from previous page)

At present, the world's population is growing because of a moderate rate of growth in the industrialized nations and a high rate in the developing countries. In the 1970s, demographer Ansley Coale pointed out that the rate of growth, about 2 percent a year, is 100 times greater than it had been for most of human history. At this rate the world's population would be multiplied by 1000 every 350 years. The results of such growth would be disastrous. Coale concluded that the present period of growth is transitory. Some people who are concerned with rapid population growth believe that the solution is to limit population growth in the developing nations by state intervention, like China's one child per family policy or through incentives to have smaller families and education about birth control. Others believe that a redistribution of resources from rich nations to poor nations would alleviate the human misery created by population pressure and eventually lead to political and social conditions that would contribute to a gradual lowering of the birth rates. Clearly, demographic questions must always be set in political, economic, and social contexts.

QUESTIONS

- Why do nations differ in their need to control population growth?
- Why has the rate of population growth varied in different areas of the world?
- Is overpopulation essentially a biological, social, or political problem?

---

demography The study of population.

demographic transition Shift to low birth rate, low infant death rate, stable population; first emerged in western Europe and United States in late 19th century.

That authority was also the theme of the magnificent artistic output in ivory and cast bronze that became characteristic of Benin. Tradition had it that Iguegha (eh-GUAY-gah), an artisan in bronze casting, was sent from Ile-Ife to introduce the techniques of making bronze sculptures. Benin then developed its own distinctive style, less naturalistic than that of Ile-Ife but no less impressive. Celebration of the powers and majesty of the royal lineage as well as objects for the rituals surrounding kingship were the subjects of much of this art. When the first Europeans, the Portuguese, visited Benin in the 1480s, they were impressed by the power of the ruler and the extent of his territory. Similarly, the artists of Benin were impressed with the Portuguese, and Benin bronzes and ivories began to include representations of Portuguese soldiers and other themes that reflected the contact with outsiders (Figure 13.4).

Central African Kingdoms

South of the rain forest that stretched across Africa almost to Lake Victoria lay a broad expanse of savanna and plain, cut by several large rivers such as the Kwango and the Zambezi. From their original home in Nigeria, the Bantu peoples had spread into the southern reaches of the rainforest along the Congo River, then southward onto the southern savannas, and eventually to the east coast. By the 5th century C.E., Bantu farmers and fishers had reached beyond the Zambezi, and by the 13th century they were approaching the southern end of the continent. Mostly beyond the influence of Islam, many of these central African peoples had begun their own process of state formation by about 1000 C.E., replacing the pattern of kinship-based societies with forms of political authority based on kingship. Whether the idea of kingship developed in one place and was diffused elsewhere or had multiple origins is unknown, but the older system based on seniority within the kinship group was replaced with rule based on the control of territory and the parallel development of rituals that reinforced the ruler's power. Several important kingdoms developed. In Katanga, the Luba peoples modified the older system of village headmen to a form of divine kinship in which the ruler and his relatives were thought to have a special power that ensured fertility of people and crops; thus, only the royal lineage was fit to rule. A sort of bureaucracy grew to administer the state, but it was hereditary, so that brothers or male children succeeded to the position. In a way, this system was a half step toward more modern concepts of bureaucracy, but it provided a way to integrate large numbers of people in a large political unit.

Kongo Kingdom, based on agriculture, formed on lower Congo River by late 15th century; capital at Mbanza Kongo; ruled by hereditary monarchy.

The Kingdoms of Kongo and Mwene Mutapa

Beginning about the 13th century, another kingdom was forming on the lower Congo River. By the late 15th century this kingdom, **Kongo**, was flourishing. On a firm agricultural base, its people also developed the skills of weaving, pottery, blacksmithing, and carving. Individual artisans, skilled in the working of wood, copper, and iron, were highly esteemed. There was a sharp division of labor between men and women. Men took responsibility for clearing the forest and scrub, producing palm oil and palm wine, building houses, hunting, and long-distance trade. Women took charge of cultivation in all its aspects, the care of domestic animals, and household duties. On the seacoast, women made salt from seawater, and they also collected the seashells that served as currency in the Kongo kingdom. The population was distributed in small family-based villages and in towns. The area around the capital, Mbanza Kongo, had a population of 60,000 to 100,000 by the early 16th century.

The kingship of the Kongo was hereditary but local chieftainships were not, and this gave the central authority power to control subordinates. In a way, the Kongo kingdom was a confederation of smaller states brought under the control of the manikongo, or king, and by the 15th century it was divided into eight major provinces. The word *mani* means "blacksmith," and it demonstrated the importance of iron and the art of working it in its association with political and ritual power.

Farther to the east, another large Bantu confederation developed among the farming and cattle-herding Shona-speaking peoples in the region between the Zambezi and Limpopo rivers. Beginning in the 9th century C.E., migrants from the west began to build royal courts in stone, to which later immigrants added more polished constructions. There were many of these zimbabwe, or stone house, sites (about 200 have been found) that housed local rulers and subchiefs, but the largest site, called **Great Zimbabwe**, was truly impressive (Figure 13.5). It was the center of the kingdom and had a religious importance, associated with the bird of God, an eagle that served as a link between the world and the spirits. The symbol of the bird of God is found at the ruins of Great Zimbabwe and throughout the area of its control. Great Zimbabwe (not to be confused with the modern nation of Zimbabwe) included several structures, some with strong stone walls 15 feet thick and 30 feet high, a large conical tower, and extensive cut-stone architecture made without the use of mortar to join the bricks together. Observers in the 19th century suspected that Phoenicians or Arabs had built these structures, mostly because their prejudices prevented them from believing that Africans were capable of erecting such buildings, but archeologists have established that a Bantu kingdom had begun construction in stone by the 11th century C.E. and had done its most sophisticated building in the 14th and 15th centuries.

By the 15th century, a centralized state ruled from Great Zimbabwe had begun to form. It controlled a large portion of the interior of southeast Africa all the way to the Indian Ocean. Under a king who took the title *Mwene Mutapa* (which the Portuguese later pronounced "Monomotapa"), this kingdom experienced a short period of rapid expansion in the late 15th and 16th centuries. Its dominance over the sources of gold in the interior eventually gave it great advantages in commerce, which it developed with the Arab port of Sofala on the coast. Evidence of this trade is found in the glass beads and porcelain unearthed by archeologists at Great Zimbabwe. By the 16th century, internal divisions and rebellion had split the kingdom apart, and perhaps an emphasis on cattle as a symbol of wealth led to soil exhaustion. Control of the gold fields still provided a source of power and trade. Representatives of the Mwene Mutapa called at the east-coast ports to buy Indian textiles, and their regal bearing and fine iron weapons impressed the first Europeans who saw them. As late as the 19th century, a much smaller kingdom of Mwene Mutapa survived in the interior and provided some leadership against European encroachment, but pastoralism had come to play a central role in the lives of the Shona people who descended from the great tradition.

FIGURE **13.4** Bronze plaque of Oba and retainers. African rulers often negotiated with the Portuguese on equal terms and incorporated them into local political and commercial networks. In this plaque, the presence of Portuguese retainers—the helmeted figures armed with muskets on each side of the main figure's head—were marks of the Oba's power.

Great Zimbabwe Bantu confederation of Shona-speaking peoples located between Zambezi and Limpopo rivers; developed after 9th century; featured royal courts built of stone; created centralized state by 15th century; king took title of Mwene Mutapa.

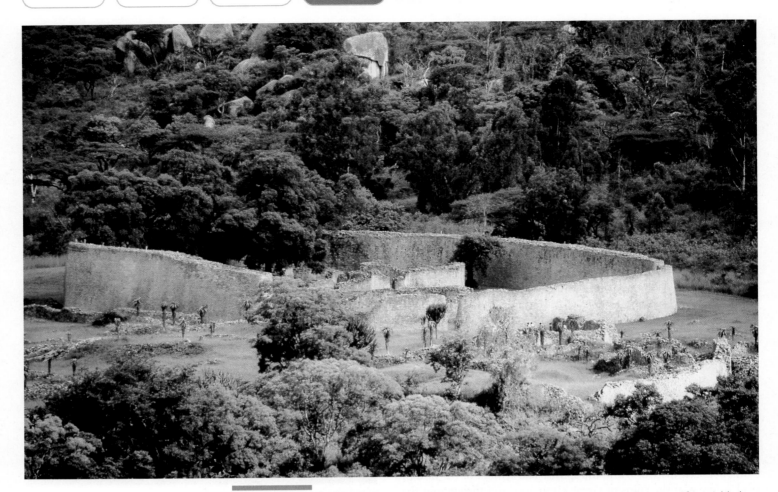

FIGURE **13.5** Great Zimbabwe was one of several stone settlement complexes in southeastern Africa. Added to at different times, it served as the royal court of the kingdom. In their search for traces of the non-African people they believed "must" have built these massive stone structures, European explorers and treasure-seekers stripped the site of layers of artifacts that might have told more of the story of Great Zimbabwe.

Global Connections and Critical Themes

INTERNAL DEVELOPMENT AND GLOBAL CONTACTS

This chapter has concentrated on the Sudanic states and the Swahili coast, where the impact of Islam was the most profound and where, because of the existence of written sources, it is somewhat easier to reconstruct the region's history. Sub-Saharan Africa had never been totally isolated from the Mediterranean world or other outside contacts, but the spread of Islam obviously brought large areas of Africa into more intensive contact with the global community, even though Africa remained something of an Islamic frontier. Still, the fusion of Islamic and indigenous African cultures created a synthesis that restructured the life of many Africans. Sudanic kingdoms and the Swahili coast participated in extensive borrowing and interactions with north Africa and the Middle East, similar to imitation efforts by several other societies in the postclassical period. Islamic contacts were also heavily involved in the growing integration of several parts of sub-Saharan Africa with global trade.

Although the arrival of Islam in Africa in the period from 800 to 1500 was clearly a major event, it would be wrong to see Africa's history in this period exclusively in terms of the Islamic impact. Great Zimbabwe and the Kongo kingdom, to cite only two examples, represented the development of Bantu concepts of kingship and state-building independently of trends taking place elsewhere on the continent. Similar processes and accomplishments could also be seen in Benin and among the Yoruba of west Africa. Meanwhile in Ethiopia, east Africa, and the eastern Sudan, the impact of Christianity and the pre-Islamic Mediterranean world had been long felt. The dynamic relationship between the impact of the civilizations and peoples external to Africa and the processes of development within the continent itself was a major theme in Africa's history.

Developments in Africa had their own special characteristics, and of course quite varied patterns emerged. The Sudanic kingdoms, however, warrant particular comparison with several other regions during the postclassical period. They showed the capacity to organize large, although fairly loosely structured, states.

They expanded trade and cultural contacts with other civilization centers, particularly of course in North Africa and the Middle East. They imitated aspects of their contact societies, though quite selectively. They clearly formed a vital part of the expansion of transregional trade, while constructing their own reactions to the other great theme of the period, the spread of world religions.

By the late 15th century, when the first Europeans, the Portuguese, began to arrive on the west and east coasts of Africa, in many places they found well-developed, powerful kingdoms that were able to deal with the Portuguese as equals. This was even truer in the parts of Africa that had come under the influence of Islam and through it had established links with other areas of Muslim civilization. In this period, Africa had increasingly become part of the general cultural trends of the wider world. Moreover, the intensified export trade in ivory, slaves, and especially gold from Africa drew Africans, even those far from the centers of trade, into a widening network of global relations. With the arrival of Europeans in sub-Saharan Africa in the late 15th century, the pace and intensity of the cultural and commercial contacts became even greater, and many African societies faced new and profound challenges.

Further Readings

Several books are also useful in relation to this chapter. The period covered is summarized in Robert O. Collins and James M. Burns, *A History of Sub-Saharan Africa* (2007). Essential reading on central Africa is Jan Vansina, *Paths in the Rainforests* (1990) and his *How Societies Are Born: Governance in West Central Africa* (2004). A general introduction to the grassland empires of the western Sudan is presented in David Conrad, *Empires of Medieval West Africa* (2005), while John Hunwick, *Timbuktu and the Songhay Empire* (2003) presents a translation of one of the great chronicles. On the Swahili coast, see A. Mazrui and I. Shariff, *The Swahili: Idiom and Identity of an African People* (1994) which emphasizes language; and R. L. Pouwells, *Horn and Crescent: Cultural Change and Traditional Islam on the East African Coast, 800–1900, 2nd ed. (2002)* John Middleton, *The World of the Swahili* (1992) Mark Horton and John Middleton, *The Swahili: The Social Landscape of a Mercantile Society* (2000), and Chapurukha Kusimba, *The Rise and Fall of Swahili City States* (1999) are all good introductions to the topic. On Ethiopia see Harold Marcus, *A History of Ethiopia* (1994). Stuart Munro-Hay, *The Quest for the Ark of the Covenant* (2005) delves into the Judaic and Christian origins of Ethiopia. A very good survey of the early history of Africa with interesting comments on the Nok culture is Susan Keech McIntosh and Roderick J. McIntosh's "From Stone to Metal: New Perspectives on the Later Prehistory of West Africa," *Journal of World History* 2, no. 1 (1988): 89–133. Graham Connah, *Forgotten Africa: An Introduction to Its Archaeology* (2004) reveals recent findings in that field. J. F. Ade Ajayi and Michael Crowder's *History of West Africa*, 2 vols. (1987), contains excellent review chapters by specialists. N. Levtzion's *Ancient Ghana and Mali* (1973) is still the best short introduction to these kingdoms of the sahel, but more recent are *On Islam*, David Robinson, *Muslim Societies in African History* (2004), and the essays collected in Nehemia Levtzion and Randall Pouwels, eds., *The History of Islam in Africa* (2000) are excellent starting points.

Two good books on the Kongo kingdom are Anne Hilton's *The Kingdom of the Kongo* (1992), which shows how African systems of thought accommodated the arrival of Europeans and their culture, and Georges Balandier's older *Daily Life in the Kingdom of the Kongo* (1969), which makes good use of travelers' reports and other documents to give a rounded picture of Kongo society. Joseph Vogel, *Great Zimbabwe: The Iron Age in South Central Africa* (2004) is a good starting point; David Birmingham and Phyllis Martin's *History of Central Africa*, 2 vols. (1983), is an excellent regional history.

Two multivolume general histories of Africa that provide synthetic articles by leading scholars on many of the topics discussed in this chapter are *The Cambridge History of Africa*, 8 vols. (1975–1986); and the UNESCO *General History of Africa*, 7 vols. to date (1981–).

Some important source materials on African history for this period include three translations of the Mande epic *Sundiata*: David C. Conrad and Djanta Tassey Conde's *Sunjata: A West African Epic of the Mande Peoples* (2004); D. T. Niane's *Sundiata: An Epic of Old Mali* (1986); and Bamba Suso and Banna Kanute, *Sunjata: Gambian Versions of the Mande Epic* (2000). Other sources include G. R. Crone, ed., *The Voyages of Cadamosto*, 2nd series, vol. 80 (1937), which deals with Mali, Cape Verde, Senegal, and Benin; Maylin Newitt, ed., *The Portuguese in West Africa 1415–1670* (2010) and Ross Dunn's indispensable edition of *The Adventures of Ibn Batuta: A Muslim Traveler of the 14th Century* (1990). Arab sources are translated in Nehemia Levtzion and Jay Spaulding, *Medieval West Africa: Views from Arab Scholars and Merchants* (2003).

On MyHistoryLab

 Study and Review on MyHistoryLab

Critical Thinking Questions

1. What were the products of Africa that attracted international trade and what did Africans want in return?

2. How did the expansion of Islam affect African societies?

3. Compare the advantages and disadvantages of stateless societies and those with monarchies or other forms of hereditary rule.

14

Civilization in Eastern Europe: Byzantium and Orthodox Europe

((• Listen to Chapter 14
on MyHistoryLab

Late in the 10th century, Vladimir, king of a Russian state centered in the city of Kiev, faced an important decision. What major religion should he choose—not only for himself, but for his people? Some Christian activity had been brought in from the Byzantine Empire to the south, and Vladimir's grandmother had converted, but the majority of Russians were traditional polytheists.

Vladimir's decision raised two issues. First, why decide? Why not adhere to tradition? Most of the societies around Russia were part of the growing surge of world religions—religions that appealed to people of many cultures. Vladimir likely thought that his kingdom's growing trade and military activity would be complemented by a religion that had wider appeal than that of the traditional Russian gods. Vladimir was also defending his rule against internal strife and external attack: A successful move to impose a new religion would bolster his authority.

FIGURE 14.1 This 15th-century miniature shows Russia's King Vladimir I being baptized in Cherson in the year 988.

Second, decide on what? Placed as Russia was, Vladimir had knowledge of Islam, Judaism, Western Catholicism, and Byzantine, or Orthodox, Christianity. Legend has it that he rejected Judaism because it was not associated with a strong state. He rejected Catholicism (gaining ground in neighboring Poland) because he wanted no interference from the pope. He rejected Islam because of its prohibition of alcohol: "for drink is the joy of the Russian."

In truth, the decision was probably easy. The Byzantine Empire was Russia's prosperous neighbor, a leading trading partner and sometime military ally. Vladimir was eager to marry the sister of the Byzantine emperor—according to another legend, the emperor was reluctant to give his sister in marriage to what he considered a backward warrior, but Vladimir captured a major Byzantine city and refused to give it back until the emperor relented. Choosing Orthodox Christianity would be a part of this larger relationship with Byzantium. ■

Vladimir's decision was unquestionably important. Additional Byzantine influences, from art and literature to manners, began to shape Russian culture. Christianity was extended eastward, changing the boundaries between Christianity and Islam. The Russian state did gain new prestige and used religion to help unify its far-flung populace. At the same time, Vladimir's choice separated the kingdom from Roman Catholic western Europe, helping to create what would become a long-standing cultural division between eastern and western Europe. The implications of this separation continue to affect world affairs, even as other parts of eastern and western Europe are uniting.

CIVILIZATION IN EASTERN EUROPE

14.1 What was the relationship between the Byzantine Empire and the earlier Roman Empire and what were the main similarities and differences?

> The power of the Byzantine empire and the spread of Orthodox Christianity long surpassed the global influence of Christian Western Europe.

During the postclassical period two major Christian civilizations took shape in Europe. Both developed close relations with the Islamic world, and both played major roles in long distance trade. One, centered on the papacy in Rome, encompassed Western Europe, but the other radiated out from Constantinople. Both civilizations came to illustrate the diversification of state forms that was characteristic of the post classical period.

The Power of the Byzantine Empire

The Byzantine empire maintained high levels of political, economic, and cultural activity during much of the period from 600 to 1450 C.E. It controlled an important but fluctuating swath of territory in the Balkans, the northern Middle East, and the eastern Mediterranean. Its leaders saw themselves as latter-day Roman emperors, and their government was in many ways a direct continuation of the eastern portion of the late Roman empire.

The real significance of the Byzantine empire goes well beyond its ability to keep Rome's memory alive. The empire lasted for almost a thousand years, between Rome's collapse in the West and the final overthrow of the regime by Turkish invaders. The empire's capital, Constantinople, was one of the truly great cities of the world, certainly the most opulent and important city in Europe in this

100 c.e.	600 c.e.	800 c.e.	1000 c.e.	1200 c.e.	1400 c.e.
330s Constantinople becomes capital of eastern Roman empire **527–565** Reign of Justinian	**650s** Slavic migrations into eastern Europe **718** Arab attack on Constantinople defeated	**855** Rurik king of Kievan Russia (according to legend) **864** Beginning of Christian missionary work of Cyril and Methodius in Slavic lands **870** First kingdom in what is now Czech and Slovak republics **896** Magyars settle in Hungary **c. 960** Emergence of Polish state **980–1015** Conversion of Russia to Christianity	**1018** Byzantine defeat of Bulgarian kingdom **1019–1054** Reign of Yaroslav, king of Rus' **1054** Schism between Eastern and Western Christianity **1100–1453** Byzantine decline; under growing attack by Ottomans	**1203–1204** Fourth Crusade, Westerners sack Constantinople **1237–1241** Mongols (Tatars) capture Russia	**1453** Ottoman Turks capture Constantinople; end of Byzantine empire **1480** Expulsion of Tatars from Russia

period. From Constantinople radiated one of the two major branches of Christianity: the Orthodox Christian churches that became dominant throughout most of eastern Europe.

Like the other great civilizations of the period, the Byzantine empire spread its cultural and political influence to parts of the world that had not previously been controlled by any major civilization. Just as Muslim influence helped shape civilization in parts of Africa south of the Sahara, the Byzantines began to shape civilization in the Balkans and western Russia (present-day Ukraine and Belarus as well as western Russia proper).

The empire also served as a major agent in interregional trade. It had active exchanges with the Arab world and with other parts of Asia. The empire even imported techniques of silk production from China, which reduced its dependence on foreign trade for this commodity but showed its connection to larger fashion standards. Constantinople served as a hub for goods brought in from east central Europe and Russia, to be exchanged for Arab and Byzantine products. In various ways, the empire played a key role in extending the range of contacts as part of the formation of the transcontinental network.

There were many commonalities between developments in eastern and in western Europe. In both cases, civilization spread northward partly because of the missionary appeal of the Christian religion. In both cases, polytheism gave way to monotheism, although important compromises were made, particularly at the popular level. In both cases, more northerly political units, such as Russia, Poland, Germany, and France, struggled for political definition without being able to rival the political sophistication of the more advanced societies in Asia and north Africa or in Byzantium itself. In both cases, new trading activities brought northern regions into contact with the major centers of world commerce, including Constantinople. In both cases, newly civilized areas looked back to the Greco-Roman past, as well as to Christianity, for cultural inspiration, using some of the same political ideas and artistic styles.

Yet with all these shared ingredients, the civilizations that expanded in the east and developed in the west operated largely on separate tracks. They produced different versions of Christianity that were culturally as well as organizationally separate, even hostile. The civilizations had little mutual contact. Until late in this period, commercial patterns in both cases ran south to north rather than east to west. During most of the postclassical millennium, major portions of eastern Europe were significantly more advanced than western Europe in political sophistication, cultural range, and economic vitality. Byzantium long surpassed the West in its involvement with interregional trade.

When the two civilizations did meet, in this period and later, they met as distant cousins, related but not close kin.

THE BYZANTINE EMPIRE

14.2 How does the Byzantine Empire fit the theme of state building and expansion?

The Byzantine empire in some senses began in the 4th century C.E., when the Romans set up their eastern capital in Constantinople. This city quickly became the most vigorous center of the otherwise fading imperial structure. Emperor Constantine constructed a host of elegant buildings, including Christian churches, in his new city, which was built on the foundations of a previously modest town called Byzantium. Soon, separate eastern emperors ruled from the new metropolis, even before the western portion of the empire fell to the Germanic invaders. They warded off invading Huns and other intruders while enjoying a solid tax base in the peasant agriculture of the eastern Mediterranean. Constantinople was responsible for the Balkan peninsula, the northern Middle East, the Mediterranean coast, and north Africa. Although for several centuries Latin was the court language of the eastern empire, Greek was the common tongue, and after Emperor Justinian in the 6th century, it became the official language as well. Indeed, in the eyes of the easterners, Latin became an inferior, barbaric means of communication. Knowledge of Greek enabled the scholars of the eastern empire to read freely in the ancient Athenian philosophical and literary classics and in the Hellenistic writings and scientific treatises.

The new empire benefited from the high levels of commerce long present in the eastern Mediterranean. New blood was drawn into administration and trade as Hellenized Egyptians and Syrians, long excluded from Roman administration, moved to Constantinople and entered the expanding bureaucracy of the Byzantine rulers. The empire faced many foreign enemies, although the pressure was less severe than that provided by the Germanic tribes in the West. It responded by recruiting armies in the Middle East itself, not by relying on barbarian troops. Complex administration around a remote emperor, who was surrounded by elaborate ceremonies, increasingly defined the empire's political style.

Justinian's Achievements

The early history of the Byzantine empire was marked by a recurrent threat of invasion. Eastern emperors, relying on their local military base plus able generalship by upper-class Greeks, beat off attacks by the Sassanian empire in Persia and by Germanic invaders. Then, in 533 C.E., with the empire's borders reasonably secure, a new emperor, Justinian, tried to reconquer western territory in a last futile effort to restore an empire like that of Rome (see Map 14.1). He was somber, autocratic, and prone to grandiose ideas. A contemporary historian named Procopius described him as "at once villainous and amenable; as people say colloquially, a moron. He was never truthful with anyone, but always guileful in what he said and did, yet easily hoodwinked by any who wanted to deceive him." The emperor was also heavily influenced by his power-hungry wife Theodora, a courtesan connected with Constantinople's horse-racing world. Theodora stiffened Justinian's resolve in response to popular unrest and pushed the plans for expansion.

Justinian's positive contributions to the Byzantine empire lay in rebuilding Constantinople, ravaged by earlier riots against high taxes, and systematizing the Roman legal code. Extending later Roman architecture, with its addition of domes to earlier classical styles, Justinian's builders created many new structures, the most inspiring of which was the huge new church, the **Hagia Sophia**, long one of the wonders of the Christian world. (The great church would later become a mosque and is now a museum.) This was an achievement in engineering as well as architecture, for no one had previously been able to build the supports needed for a dome of its size. Justinian's codification of Roman law reached a goal that earlier emperors had sought but not achieved, summing up and reconciling many prior edicts and decisions. Unified law not only reduced confusion but also united and organized the new empire, paralleling the state's bureaucracy. Updated by later emperors, the code ultimately helped spread Roman legal principles in various parts of Europe.

The Byzantine empire was shaped by the decline of the Roman empire and the rise of the Arabs. The empire weathered many attacks and flourished for several centuries, playing a major role in Asian and European trade.

Hagia Sophia [hä juh sä FEE uh] New church constructed in Constantinople during reign of Justinian.

View the Image on **MyHistoryLab**: Emperor Justinian

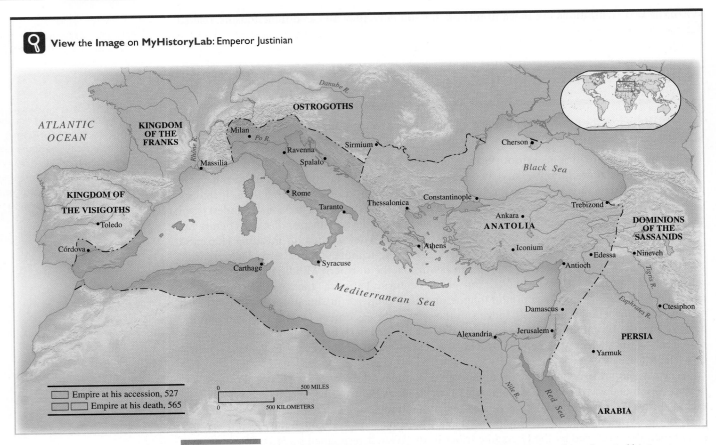

MAP **14.1 The Byzantine Empire Under Justinian** Justinian's ambitious expansion exhausted his treasury, and the empire had lost all its holdings outside the northeastern Mediterranean within 50 years after his death.

FIGURE **14.2** Dazzling mosaics from the early period of the Byzantine empire illustrate some of the highest achievements of Byzantine religious art. This mosaic features a rather militant Christ the Redeemer.

Justinian's military exploits had more ambiguous results. The emperor wanted to recapture the old Roman Empire itself. With the aid of a brilliant general, **Belisarius**, new gains were made in north Africa and Italy. Justinian's forces made their temporary capital, Ravenna, a key artistic center, embellished by some of the most beautiful Christian mosaics known anywhere in the world (Figure 14.2). But the major Italian holdings were short-lived, unable to withstand Germanic pressure, and north African territory was soon besieged as well.

Furthermore, Justinian's westward ambitions had weakened the empire in its own sphere. Persian forces attacked in the northern Middle East, while new Slavic groups, moving into the Balkans, pressed on another front (Map 14.1). Justinian finally managed to create a new line of defense and even pushed Persian forces back again, but some Middle Eastern territory was lost. Furthermore, all these wars, offensive and defensive alike, created new tax pressures on the government, and these triggered several popular revolts while forcing Justinian to exertions that contributed to his death in 565 C.E.

Arab Pressure and the Empire's Defenses

After some setbacks, Justinian's successors began to concentrate on defending the eastern empire itself. Persian advances in the northern Middle East were reversed in the 7th century, and the population was forcibly reconverted to Christianity. The resultant empire, centered in the southern Balkans and the western and central portions of present-day Turkey, was a far cry from

Rome's greatness. However, it was sufficient to amplify a rich Hellenistic culture and blend it more fully with Christianity while advancing Roman achievements in engineering and military tactics as well as law.

The Byzantine empire was also strong enough to withstand the great new threat of the 7th century, the surge of the Arab Muslims, although not without massive losses. By the mid-7th century, the Arabs had built a fleet that challenged Byzantine naval supremacy in the eastern Mediterranean while repeatedly attacking Constantinople. They quickly swallowed the empire's remaining provinces along the eastern seaboard of the Mediterranean and soon cut into the northern Middle Eastern heartland as well. Arab cultural and commercial influence also affected patterns of life in Constantinople. Byzantine territory was cut back to about half the size of the earlier eastern Roman empire.

The Byzantine empire held out nevertheless. A major siege of the capital in 717–718 C.E. was beaten back, partly because of a new weapon, a kind of napalm called **Greek fire** (a petroleum, quicklime, and sulfur mixture) that devastated Arab ships. The Arab threat was never removed entirely. Furthermore, wars with the Muslims had added new economic burdens to the empire. Invasions and taxation weakened the position of small farmers and resulted in greater aristocratic estates plus new power for aristocratic generals. The free rural population that had served the empire during its early centuries—providing military recruits and paying the bulk of the taxes—was forced into greater dependence on aristocratic landowners, often losing their land outright. Recurrent peasant risings occurred; one in 932, interestingly, involved a peasant leader posing as an aristocrat defending the people against the state.

These social changes, from the 10th century onward, weakened state revenues and military recruitment. But the empire hung on, supported in part by successful commercial activity including foreign trade. Politically, greater emphasis was given to organizing the army and navy. After the greatest Arab onslaughts had been faced, the empire was run by a dizzying series of weak and strong

Belisarius (c. 505–565) One of Justinian's most important military commanders during period of reconquest of western Europe; commanded in north Africa and Italy.

Greek fire Byzantine weapon consisting of mixture of chemicals that ignited when exposed to water; utilized to drive back the Arab fleets that attacked Constantinople.

VISUALIZING THE PAST

Women and Power in Byzantium

THIS MOSAIC, DEVELOPED BETWEEN 1034–1042, PORTRAYS the Empress Zoë, her consort, and Christ (in the center). Zoë would later rule jointly with her sister Theodora, despite their earlier struggle for power.

QUESTIONS

- What evidence does this mosaic provide about the political relationship between Zoë and her husband?
- What does it suggest about the relationship between church and state in Byzantium and about ways religion might be used to bolster political power?
- (Interpreting the haloes is a good start in answering this question.) What sense of history and religion made it reasonable to show Christ between two 11th-century people?

Istanbul, St. Sophia, Mosaic in the South Tribune: Christ with the Empress Zoë, who is presenting him with a scroll listing her donations to the church, and her consort, Monomachus, who is offering him a purse containing gold coins.

Bulgaria Slavic kingdom established in northern portions of Balkan peninsula; constant source of pressure on Byzantine empire; defeated by Emperor Basil II in 1014.

View the **Closer Look** on **MyHistoryLab**: A Holy Emperor: Basil II

icon An icon is an artistic representation, usually of a religious figure.

emperors. Periods of vigor alternated with seeming decay. Arab pressure continued. Conquest of the island of Crete in the 9th century allowed the Muslims to harass Byzantine shipping in the Mediterranean for several centuries. Slavic kingdoms, especially **Bulgaria**, periodically pressed Byzantine territory in the Balkans, although at times military success and marriage alliances brought Byzantine control over the feisty Bulgarian kingdom. Thus, while a Bulgarian king in the 10th century took the title of *tsar*, a Slavic version of the word *Caesar*, steady Byzantine pressure through war eroded the regional kingdom. In the 11th century, the Byzantine emperor Basil II, known as *Bulgaroktonos*, or slayer of the Bulgarians, used the empire's wealth to bribe many Bulgarian nobles and generals. He defeated the Bulgarian army in 1014, blinding as many as 15,000 captive soldiers. The sight of this tragedy brought on the Bulgarian king's death. Bulgaria became part of the empire, its aristocracy settling in Constantinople and merging with the leading Greek families.

Briefly, at the end of the 10th century, the Byzantine emperor may have been the most powerful monarch on earth, with a capital city whose rich buildings and abundant popular entertainments awed visitors from western Europe and elsewhere.

Byzantine Society and Politics

The Byzantine political system had remarkable similarities to the earlier patterns in China, both serving as important examples of state building. The emperor was held to be ordained by God, head of church as well as state. He appointed church bishops and passed religious as well as secular laws. The power of the state over the church was a key feature of Orthodox Christianity, in contrast to patterns in Western Europe. Elaborate court rituals symbolized the ideals of a divinely inspired, all-powerful ruler, although they often immobilized rulers and inhibited innovative policy.

At key points, women held the imperial throne while maintaining the ceremonial power of the office. The experiences of Empress Theodora (981–1056), namesake of Justinian's powerful wife, illustrate the complex nature of Byzantine politics and the whims of fate that affected women rulers. Daughter of an emperor, Theodora was strong and austere; she refused to marry the imperial heir, who then wed her sister Zoë. Zoë was afraid of Theodora's influence and had her confined to a convent. A popular rebellion against the new emperor installed Theodora and Zoë jointly (and one assumes uneasily) as empresses. Later, Theodora managed to check unruly nobles and limit bureaucratic corruption, although her severe retaliation against personal enemies brought criticism.

Supplementing the centralized imperial authority was one of history's most elaborate bureaucracies. Trained in Greek classics, philosophy, and science in a secular school system that paralleled church education for the priesthood, Byzantine bureaucrats could be recruited from all social classes. As in China, aristocrats predominated, but talent also counted among this elite of highly educated scholars. Bureaucrats were specialized into various offices, and officials close to the emperor were mainly eunuchs. Provincial governors were appointed from the center and were charged with keeping tabs on military authorities. An elaborate system of spies helped preserve loyalty while creating intense distrust even among friends. It is small wonder that the word *byzantine* came to refer to complex institutional arrangements. Careful military organization arose as well. Byzantine rulers adapted the later Roman system by recruiting troops locally and rewarding them with grants of land in return for their military service. The land could not be sold, but sons inherited its administration in return for continued military responsibility. Many outsiders, particularly Slavs and Armenian Christians, were recruited for the army in this way. Increasingly, hereditary military leaders assumed regional power, displacing more traditional and better-educated aristocrats. One emperor, Michael II, was a product of this system and was notorious for his hatred of Greek education and his overall personal ignorance. On the other hand, the military system had obvious advantages in protecting a state recurrently under attack from Muslims of various sorts—Persians, Arabs, and later Turks—as well as nomadic intruders from central Asia. Until the 15th century, the Byzantine empire effectively blocked the path to Europe for most of these groups.

Socially and economically, the empire depended on Constantinople's control over the countryside, with the bureaucracy regulating trade and controlling food prices. Food prices were kept artificially low, to content the numerous urban lower classes, in a system supported largely by taxes on the hard-pressed peasantry. Other cities were modest in size—for example, Athens dwindled—because the focus was on the capital city and its food needs. The empire developed a far-flung trading network with Asia to the east and Russia and Scandinavia to the north. Silk production expanded in the empire, and various luxury products, including cloth, carpets, and spices, were sent north. This gave the empire a favorable trading position with less sophisticated lands. Only China produced luxury goods of comparable quality. The empire also traded actively with India, the Arabs, and east Asia while receiving simpler products from western Europe and Africa. At the same time, the large merchant class never gained significant political power, in part because of the elaborate network of government controls. In this, Byzantium again resembled China and differed notably from the looser social and political networks of the West, where merchants were gaining greater voice.

Byzantine cultural life centered on the secular traditions of Hellenism, so important in the education of bureaucrats, and on the evolving traditions of Eastern, or Orthodox, Christianity. The Byzantine strength lay in preserving and commenting on past forms more than in developing new ones. Art and architecture were exceptions; a distinct Byzantine style developed fairly early. The adaptation of Roman domed buildings, the elaboration of powerful and richly colored religious mosaics, and a tradition of **icon** paintings—paintings of saints and other religious figures, often richly ornamented—expressed this artistic impulse and its marriage with Christianity. The icons' blue-and-gold backgrounds set with richly dressed religious figures were meant to represent the unchanging brilliance of heaven.

View the **Closer Look** on **MyHistoryLab**: Hagia Sophia

FIGURE **14.3** A view of the interior of the Hagia Sophia, or St. Sophia—the Church of Holy Wisdom—in what is today the city of Istanbul. This magnificent church was built 532–537 C.E. under the reign of the Emperor Justinian.

THE SPLIT BETWEEN EASTERN AND WESTERN CHRISTIANITY

14.3 Why did the two major regional versions of Christianity part? How significant was the split?

> Growing divisions opened up between the two main branches of Christianity. The impact of these divisions increased when the Byzantine empire began to decline.

Byzantine culture and politics, as well as the empire's economic orientation toward Asia and northeastern Europe, helped explain the growing break between its eastern version of Christianity and the western version headed by the pope in Rome. There were many milestones in this rift. Different rituals developed as the Western church translated the Greek Bible into Latin in the 4th century. Later, Byzantine emperors deeply resented papal attempts to loosen state control over the Eastern church to make it conform more fully to their own idea of church–state relations. Contact between the two branches of Christianity trailed off, although neither the Eastern nor Western church cared to make a definitive break. The Eastern church acknowledged the pope as first among equals, but papal directives had no hold in the Byzantine church, where state control loomed larger. Religious art conveyed different styles and beliefs, as Figures 14.4 and 14.5 suggest. Even monastic movements operated according to different rules.

The Schism

Then, in 1054, an ambitious church patriarch in Constantinople raised a host of issues, including a quarrel over what kind of bread to use for the celebration of Christ's last supper in the church liturgy. The bread quarrel was an old one, relating to ritual use of bread in Christ's day, and whether communion bread must be baked without yeast. The patriarch also attacked the Roman Catholic practice, developed some centuries earlier, of insisting on celibacy for its priests; Eastern Orthodox priests could marry. Delegations of the two churches discussed these disputes, but this led only to new bitterness. The Roman pope finally excommunicated the patriarch and his followers, banishing them from

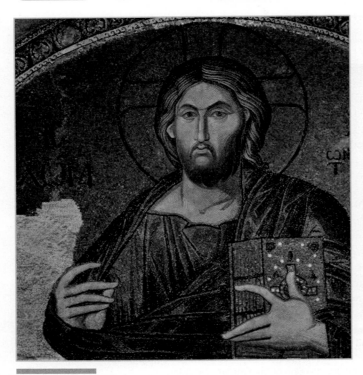

FIGURE **14.4** Just as theologians through the centuries have worked to understand Christ's message, so too have artists struggled to capture his image. This powerful mosaic of Christ at the Church of Chora in Istanbul was created in the first part of the 14th century. Notice the difference between this image and the images of Christ common in Western Christianity, which place more emphasis on suffering and less on divine majesty.

FIGURE **14.5** The Byzantine empire developed a distinctively stylized religious art, adapted from earlier Roman painting styles and conveying the solemnity of the holy figures of the faith. This illustration from a 14th-century manuscript features the holy women at the sepulchre of Christ.

Christian fellowship and the sacraments. The patriarch responded by excommunicating all Roman Catholics. Thus, the split, or schism, between the Roman Catholic church and Eastern Orthodoxy—the Byzantine or Greek, as well as the Russian Orthodox, Serbian Orthodox, and others—became formal and has endured to this day. A late-12th-century church patriarch in Constantinople even argued that Muslim rule would be preferable to that of the pope: "For if I am subject to the Muslim, at least he will not force me to share his faith. But if I have to be under the Frankish rule and united with the Roman Church, I may have to separate myself from God."

The split between the Eastern and Western churches fell short of complete divorce. A common Christianity with many shared or revived classical traditions and frequent commercial and cultural contacts continued to enliven the relationship between the two European civilizations. The division did reflect the different patterns of development the two civilizations followed during the postclassical millennium. Not only separate artistic forms and rituals, but also different ideas about the role of scholarship separated the two regions—with eastern Europe developing a less elaborate philosophical tradition in relation to religion. Differences in the role of the state in religious affairs may have contributed not just to divisions at this time, but to later distinctions in governments' claims to power between the two main European regions.

The Empire's Decline

Shortly after the split between the Eastern and Western churches, the Byzantine empire entered a long period of decline (Map 14.2). Turkish invaders who had converted to Islam in central Asia began to press on its eastern borders, having already gained increasing influence in the Muslim caliphate. In the late 11th century, Turkish troops, the Seljuks, seized almost all the Asiatic provinces of the empire, thus cutting off the most prosperous sources of tax revenue and the territories that had supplied most of the empire's food. The Byzantine emperor lost the battle of Manzikert in 1071, his larger army was annihilated, and the empire never recovered. It staggered along for another four centuries, but its doom, at least as a significant power, was sealed. The creation of new, independent Slavic kingdoms in the Balkans, such as Serbia, showed the empire's diminished power.

Eastern emperors appealed to Western leaders for help against the Turks, but their requests were largely ignored. Although the requests helped motivate Western Crusades to the Holy Land, this did not help the Byzantines. At the same time, Italian cities, blessed with powerful navies, gained increasing advantages in Constantinople, such as special trading privileges—a sign of the shift in power between East and West. Byzantium's role in world trade now attracted Western—particularly, Italian—appetites. One Crusade, in 1204, ostensibly set up to conquer the Holy Land from the Muslims, actually turned against Byzantium. Led by greedy Venetian merchants, the Crusade attacked and conquered Constantinople, briefly unseating the emperor and weakening the whole imperial structure. But the West was not yet powerful enough to hold this ground, and a small Byzantine empire was restored, able through careful diplomacy to survive for another two centuries.

Turkish settlements pressed ever closer to Constantinople in the northern Middle East—in the area that is now Turkey—and finally, in 1453, a Turkish sultan brought a powerful army, equipped with artillery purchased from Hungary, against the city, which fell after two months. By 1461, the Turks had conquered remaining pockets of Byzantine control, including most of the Balkans, bringing Islamic power farther into eastern Europe than ever before. The great eastern empire was no more.

Read the Document on MyHistoryLab: Chronicle of the Fourth Crusade (12th–13th c.) Geoffrey de Villhardouin

Read the Document on MyHistoryLab: Nestor-Iskander on the Fall of Constantinople (1450s)

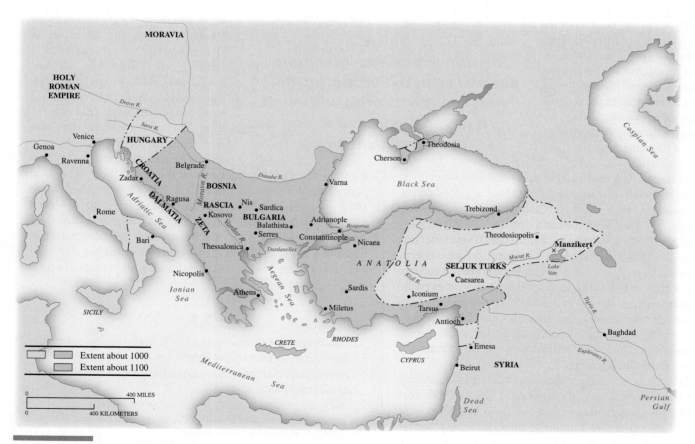

MAP **14.2 The Byzantine Empire, 1000–1100** The Byzantine empire went from a major to a minor power in the period portrayed on this map. After the Turkish defeat at Manzikert in 1071, the Byzantines maintained effective control of only a small fringe of Anatolia. In the Balkans, new Serbian, Bulgarian, and Hungarian states grew powerful, despite the Byzantines' claim to control of the region.

The fall of Byzantium was one of the great events in world history, and we will deal with its impact in several later chapters. It was a vital event because the Byzantine empire had been so durable and important, anchoring a vital corner of the Mediterranean and an important segment of world trade even amid the rapid surge of Islam. The empire's commercial contacts and its ability to preserve and spread classical and Christian learning made it a vital unit throughout the postclassical period. After its demise, its legacy continued to affect other societies, including the new Ottoman empire.

THINKING HISTORICALLY

Eastern and Western Europe: The Problem of Boundaries

THE PROBLEM OF BOUNDARIES BETWEEN CIVILIZATIONS and even between states has long attracted the attention of scholars. The continuing evolution of nation states and their often self-serving desire to define themselves within larger civilizational boundaries greatly complicates the task of deciding where one civilization ends and another begins.

Defining the territory of the two related civilizations that developed in Europe is particularly difficult. A number of states sat, and still sit, on the borders of the two civilizations, sharing some characteristics of each. Furthermore, political disputes and nationalist attachments, fierce in this border territory of east central Europe during the past two centuries, make territorial definitions an emotional issue. So the question of defining Europe's civilizations is a particularly thorny case of a larger problem.

If a civilization is defined simply by its mainstream culture, then eastern and western Europe in the postclassical period divide logically according to Orthodox and Catholic territories (and use of the Cyrillic and Greek or of the Latin alphabet). By this reckoning, Poland, the Czech areas, and the Baltic states (these latter did not convert to Catholicism until the 14th century) are western, and Hungary is largely so. South Slavs are mainly but not entirely Orthodox. Russia and Ukraine are decidedly Orthodox in tradition. Religion matters. Poland and other Catholic regions have long maintained much more active ties with western Europe than Russia has. At the end of the postclassical period, a Czech religious dissenter, Jan Hus, even foreshadowed the later Protestant Reformation in his attacks on the Catholic church.

Politically, the case is more complicated. Poland, Hungary, and Lithuania formed large regional kingdoms at various times during and after the postclassical period. But these kingdoms were very loosely organized, much more so than the feudal monarchies that were developing in western Europe. Exceptionally large

> *Russian expansion later pulled parts of eastern Europe, including Poland, into its orbit, although it never eliminated strong cultural identities.*

aristocracies in Poland and Hungary (by western or by Russian standards) helped limit these states.

Trade patterns also did not closely unite Poland or Hungary with western Europe until much later, when the two regions were clearly different in economic structure. Also, Polish and Hungarian societies often shared more features with Russia than with western Europe.

Russian expansion later pulled parts of eastern Europe, including Poland, into its orbit, although it never eliminated strong cultural identities. It is also important to remember that borders can change. The Mongol invasions that swept through Russia also conquered Poland and Hungary, but the armies did not stay there. Part of the Ukraine was also free from direct Mongol control, which helped differentiate it from Russia proper. For two centuries, at the end of the postclassical period, the divisions within eastern Europe intensified. Since 1989, many eastern European countries have again achieved full independence from Russia, and they want to claim their distinctive pasts. Not an easy border area to characterize in terms of a single civilization, east central Europe has also been a victim of many conquests interspersed with periods of proud independence.

QUESTIONS
- What were the main characteristics of Russian civilization as it first emerged in the postclassical period?
- In what ways did Poland, Hungary, and the Czech lands differ from these characteristics?
- Are there other civilization border areas, in the postclassical period or later, that are similarly difficult to define because of their position between two other areas?

THE SPREAD OF CIVILIZATION IN EASTERN EUROPE

14.4 What were the main commonalities among the societies that developed in eastern Europe during the postclassical period?

Long before the Byzantine decline after the 11th century, the empire had been the source of a new northward surge of Christianity. Orthodox missionaries sent from Constantinople busily converted most people in the Balkans to their version of Christianity, and some other trappings of Byzantine culture came in their wake. In 864, the Byzantine government sent the missionaries **Cyril** and **Methodius** to the territory that is now the Czech and Slovak republics. Here the venture failed, in that Roman Catholic missionaries were more successful. But Cyril and Methodius continued their efforts in the Balkans and in southern Russia, where their ability to speak the Slavic language greatly aided their efforts. The two missionaries devised a written script for this language, derived from Greek letters; to this day, the Slavic alphabet is known as Cyrillic. Thus, the possibility of literature and some literacy developed in eastern Europe along with Christianity, well beyond the political borders of Byzantium. Byzantine missionaries were quite willing to have local languages used in church services—another contrast with western Catholicism, which insisted on church Latin.

The East Central Borderlands

Eastern missionaries did not monopolize the borderlands of eastern Europe. Roman Catholicism and the Latin alphabet prevailed not only in the Czech area but also in most of Hungary (which was taken over in the 9th century by a Turkic people, the Magyars) and in Poland. Much of this region would long be an area of competition between eastern and western political and intellectual models. During the centuries after the conversion to Christianity, this stretch of eastern Europe north of the Balkans was organized in a series of regional monarchies, loosely governed amid a powerful, land-owning aristocracy. The kingdoms of Poland, Bohemia, and Lithuania easily surpassed most western kingdoms in territory. This was also a moderately active area for trade and industry. For example, ironworking was more developed than in the West until the 12th century.

Eastern Europe during these centuries also received an important influx of Jews, who were migrating away from the Middle East but also fleeing intolerance in western Europe. Poland gained the largest single concentration of Jews. Eastern Europe's Jews, largely barred from agriculture and often resented by the Christian majority, gained strength in local commerce while maintaining their own religious and cultural traditions. A strong emphasis on extensive education and literacy, although primarily for males, distinguished Jewish culture not only from the rest of eastern Europe but also from most other societies in the world at this time.

THE EMERGENCE OF KIEVAN RUS'

14.5 What kinds of imitation affected Russia's development in the postclassical period?

Russia shared many features with the rest of northeastern Europe before the 15th century. As in much of eastern Europe, the centuries of Byzantine influence were an important formative period that would influence later developments, even as Russia became more important. Slavic peoples had moved into the sweeping plains of Russia and eastern Europe from an Asian homeland during the time of the Roman Empire (Map 14.3). They mixed with and incorporated some earlier inhabitants and some additional invaders, such as the Bulgarians, who adopted Slavic language and customs. The Slavs already used iron, and they extended agriculture in the rich soils of what is now Ukraine and western Russia. The Slavs maintained an animist religion with gods for the sun, thunder, wind, and fire. The early Russians also had a rich tradition of folk music and oral legends, and they developed some very loose regional kingdoms.

> Christian missionaries, new trade routes, and Byzantine military activity affected much of eastern Europe. Within this context, the Kievan Rus' formed the core of Russian culture and politics.

Cyril (827–869) Along with Methodius, missionary sent by Byzantine government to eastern Europe and the Balkans; converted southern Russia and Balkans to Orthodox Christianity; responsible for creation of written script for Slavic known as Cyrillic.

Methodius (826–885) Along with Cyril, missionary sent by Byzantine government to eastern Europe and the Balkans; converted southern Russia and Balkans to Orthodox Christianity; responsible for creation of written script for Slavic known as Cyrillic.

> Russia gradually emerged through its role in trade, growing political claims, and the decision to participate in Christianity.

Read the Document on MyHistoryLab: Ibn Fadlan's Account of the Rus'

MAP **14.3** **East European Kingdoms and Slavic Expansion c. 1000** Beginning around the 5th century c.e., the Slavs moved in all directions from their lands around the Pripet River in what is today Ukraine and Belarus. Their migrations took them from the Baltic Sea to the Oder River and down to the Adriatic and Aegean seas. The arrival of the Hungarians in the 9th and 10th centuries prevented the Slavs from unifying. The arrival of the Hungarians in the 9th and 10th centuries complicated the Slavic holdings, tending to separate Russians and Slavs in the Balkans. Still, the various Salvic peoples dominated a vast territory in eastern Europe.

New Patterns of Trade

Kiev Trade city in southern Russia established by Scandinavian traders in 9th century; became focal point for kingdom of Russia that flourished to 12th century.

Rurik Legendary Scandinavian, regarded as founder of the first kingdom of Russia based in Kiev in 855 c.e.

During the 6th and 7th centuries, traders from Scandinavia began to work through the Slavic lands, moving along the great rivers of western Russia, which run south to north, particularly the Dnieper (DNEE-puhr). Map 14.3 shows the route that led from Scandinavia to Byzantium, and the Russian territory that began to coalesce around it. Through this route the Norse traders were able to reach the Byzantine empire, and a regular, flourishing trade developed between Scandinavia and Constantinople. Luxury products from Byzantium and the Arab world traveled north in return for furs and other crude products. The Scandinavian traders, militarily superior to the Slavs, gradually set up some governments along their trade route, particularly in the city of **Kiev**. A monarchy emerged, and according to legend a man named **Rurik**, a native of Denmark, became the first prince of what came to be called **Kievan Rus'** (KEE-eh-vehn ROOS) about 855 C.E. This principality, though still loosely organized through alliances with regional, landed aristocrats, flourished until the 12th century. It was at this time that the word *Russia* was coined, possibly from a Greek word for "red," for the hair color of many of the Norse traders.

Contacts between Kievan Rus' and Byzantium extended steadily. Kiev, centrally located, became a prosperous trading center, and from there many Russians visited Constantinople. This was the context in which Prince **Vladimir I**, a Rurik descendant who ruled from 980 to 1015, took the step of converting to Christianity, not only in his own name but on behalf of all his people. Having made his decision, Vladimir organized mass baptisms for his subjects, forcing conversions by military pressure. Early church leaders were imported from Byzantium, and they helped train a literate Russian priesthood. As in Byzantium, the king characteristically controlled major appointments, and a separate **Russian Orthodox** church soon developed.

As Kievan Rus' became Christian, it was the largest single state in Europe, although highly decentralized. Rurik's descendants managed for some time to avoid damaging battles over succession to the throne. Following Byzantine example, they issued a formal law code that reduced the severity of traditional punishments and replaced community vendettas with state-run courts, at least in principle. The last of the great Kievan princes, **Yaroslav**, issued the legal codification while building many churches and arranging the translation of religious literature from Greek to Slavic.

Kievan Rus' The predecessor to modern Russia; a medieval state that existed from the end of the 9th to the middle of the 13th century; its territory spanned parts of modern Belarus, Ukraine, and Russia.

Vladimir I Ruler of Russian kingdom of Kiev from 980 to 1015; converted kingdom to Christianity.

 View the Closer Look on **MyHistoryLab:** The Baptism of Vladimir

Russian Orthodoxy Russian form of Christianity imported from Byzantine empire and combined with local religion; king characteristically controlled major appointments.

Yaroslav (978–1054) Last of great Kievan monarchs; issued legal codification based on formal codes developed in Byzantium.

DOCUMENT

Russia Turns to Christianity

THIS DOCUMENT FROM A MONK'S CHRONICLE, describing King Vladimir's conversion policy, indicates what was officially believed about the power of Russian princes, Russian social structure, and the relationship between Christianity and earlier animism. These official claims are important, but they may not reflect the whole reality of this important transition in Russia history. Here is a classic case of the need to understand a particular mindset and genre of writing, to understand why particular explanations are offered without accepting their reality.

For at this time the Russes were ignorant pagans. The devil rejoiced thereat, for he did not know that his ruin was approaching. He was so eager to destroy the Christian people, yet he was expelled by the true cross even from these very lands.... Vladimir was visited by Bulgars of the Mohammedan faith.... [He] listened to them for he was fond of women and indulgence, regarding which he heard with pleasure. But ... abstinence from pork and wine were disagreeable to him. "Drinking," said he, "is the joy of the Russes. We cannot exist without that pleasure." [Russian envoys sent to Constantinople were astonished by the beauty of the churches and the chanting], and in their wonder praised the Greek ceremonial....

[Later, Vladimir was suffering from blindness; a Byzantine bishop baptized him] and as the bishop laid his hand upon him, he straightway recovered his sight. Upon experiencing this miraculous cure, Vladimir glorified God, saying, "I have now perceived the one true God." When his followers beheld this miracle, many of them were also baptized.... Thereafter Vladimir sent heralds throughout the whole city to proclaim

that if any inhabitant, rich or poor, did not betake himself to the river [for mass baptism] he would risk the Prince's displeasure. When the people heard these words, they wept for joy and exclaimed in their enthusiasm, "If this were not good, the Prince and his nobles would not have accepted it." ... There was joy in heaven and upon earth to behold so many souls saved. But the devil groaned, lamenting, "Woe is me. How am I driven out hence ... my reign in these regions is at an end." ...

He [Vladimir] ordered that wooden churches should be built and established where [pagan] idols have previously stood. He founded the Church of Saint Basil on the hill where the idol of Perun and the other images had been set, and where the prince and the people had offered their sacrifices. He began to found churches, to assign priests throughout the cities and towns, and to bring people in for baptism from all towns and villages. He began to take the children of the best families and send them for instruction from books.

QUESTIONS

- In what ways might the account be simplistic in describing royal powers and popular response?
- What explanations does this religious chronicler offer for the conversion of Russians to Christianity?
- Which of the explanations are most likely, and which are the results of some kind of bias?
- What kind of church–state relationship did this kind of conversion predict?

Institutions and Culture in Kievan Rus'

Kievan Rus' borrowed much from Byzantium, but it was in no position to replicate major institutions such as the bureaucracy or an elaborate educational system. Major princes were attracted to Byzantine ceremonials and luxury and to the concept (if not yet the reality) that a central ruler should have wide powers. Many characteristics of Orthodox Christianity gradually penetrated Russian culture. Fervent devotion to the power of God and to many eastern saints helped organize worship. Churches were ornate, filled with icons and the sweet smell of incense. A monastic movement developed that stressed prayer and charity. Traditional practices, such as polygamy, gradually yielded to the Christian practice of monogamy. The emphasis on almsgiving long described the sense of obligation felt by wealthy Russians toward the poor.

The Russian literature that developed, which used the Cyrillic alphabet, featured chronicles that described a mixture of religious and royal events and showered praises on the saints and the power of God. Disasters were seen as expressions of the just wrath of God against human wickedness, and success in war followed from the aid of God and the saints in the name of Russia and the Orthodox faith. This tone also was common in western Christian writing during these centuries, but in Kievan Rus' it monopolized formal culture; a distinct philosophical or scientific current did not emerge in the postclassical period.

Russian and Ukrainian art focused on the religious also, with icon painting and illuminated religious manuscripts becoming a Kievan specialty. Orthodox churches, built in the form of a cross surmounted by a dome, similarly aped Byzantine models, although the building materials often were wood rather than stone. Domed structures adapted Byzantine themes to Russian conditions, in what proved to be a durable regional style. Religious art and music were rivaled by popular entertainments in the oral tradition, which combined music, street performances, and some theater. The Russian church unsuccessfully tried to suppress these forms, regarding them as pagan.

Just as Russia's religious culture developed separately from western Europe's, Russian social and economic patterns took distinctive shape. Russian peasants were fairly free farmers, although an aristocratic landlord class existed. Russian aristocrats, called **boyars**, had less political power than their counterparts in western Europe, although the Kievan princes had to negotiate with them.

boyars Russian aristocrats; possessed less political power than did their counterparts in western Europe.

For all its distinctiveness, Russia was not unaware of other parts of Europe. The greatest ruler of the period, Yaroslav the Wise (1019–1054), used marriages to create ties. He arranged over 30 marriages with central European royalty, including 11 with Germany, pressing six Russian princes to take German wives while inducing five German nobles to accept Russian brides. Even here, however, Yaroslav kept his main focus on Byzantium, promoting Byzantine styles in the great cathedral of Kiev and using Byzantine example as the basis for Russia's first law code.

Kiev

Kiev (or Kyiv, in Ukrainian) was the leading city of Kievan Rus', a key center for north–south trade from Scandinavia to the Middle East. Novgorod was its only main competitor along this route. The city had been founded earlier, on the site of scattered Slavic settlements. The kings who began to carve out the first Russian state adopted the city as their capital. The location was good: The main part of the city could be built on a substantial hill—as with many European cities at the time, defense against raids was a key concern. Along with city walls, a hilltop location helped. But at the base of the hill flowed the Dneiper River, a substantial artery that would facilitate trade.

Kiev quickly became a religious center. In 988, Vladimir required a mass baptism of the city's citizens in the local river, converting them to Christianity. During the following two centuries, Kiev witnessed a massive amount of church building, including the great cathedral of Saint Sophia and also a major monastery complex in the caves of Lavra. As was true of most Christian cities in the postclassical period, Kiev was dominated by religious architecture. By 1200 the city boasted 400 churches, or approximately one per 130 inhabitants, obviously a massive investment.

The city also contained eight markets, however, and an array of economic activities. In 1200 the city was the largest in Europe, with 50,000 people—by comparison, London had but 20,000 at the same point. Travelers called the city a "charming gem," and one German visitor compared it to Constantinople. But the comparison was in fact misleading: The cities of Europe outside the Byzantine empire remained tiny by Asian standards; Constantinople itself had 350,000 people at this point.

Kiev hit hard times after 1200. It was raided many times by turbulent Russian princes, and then it fell to Mongol attack. Recovery would come slowly.

Kievan Decline

The Kievan principality began to fade in the 12th century. Rival princes set up regional governments, and the royal family often squabbled over succession to the throne. Invaders from Asia whittled at Russian territory. The rapid decline of Byzantium reduced Russian trade and wealth, for the kingdom had always depended heavily on the greater prosperity and sophisticated manufacturing of its southern neighbor. The final blow in this first chapter of Russian history came in 1237–1238 and 1240–1241, when two invasions by Mongols from central Asia moved through Russia and into other parts of eastern Europe (see Chapter 9). The initial Mongol intent was to add the whole of Europe to their growing empire. The Mongols easily captured the major Russian cities, but they did not penetrate much farther west because of political difficulties in their Asian homeland. Called **Tatars** in the Russian tradition (from a Turkish word), the invaders were quickly despised but also feared—"the accursed raw-eating Tatars," as one chronicle put it.

For over two centuries much of Russia remained under Tatar control. This control further separated the dynamic of Russian history from that of western Europe. Russian literature languished under Tatar supervision. Trade lapsed in western Russia, and the vigorous north–south commerce of the Kievan period never returned. At the same time, loose Tatar supervision did not destroy Russian Christianity or a native Russian aristocratic class. As long as tribute was paid, Tatar overlords left day-to-day Russian affairs alone. Thus, when Tatar control was finally forced out in the second half of the 15th century, a Russian cultural and political tradition could reemerge, serving as a partial basis for the further, fuller development of Russian society.

Russian leaders retained an active memory of the glories of Byzantium. When Constantinople fell to the Turks in 1453, just as Russia was beginning to assert its independence from the Tatars, it was logical to claim that the mantle of east European leadership had fallen on Russia. A monk, currying favor, wrote the Russian king in 1511 that whereas heresy had destroyed the first Roman Empire and the Turks had cut down the second, Byzantium—a "third, new Rome" under the king's "mighty rule"—"sends out the Orthodox Christian faith to the ends of the earth and shines more brightly than the sun." According to the monk, "Two Romes have fallen, but the third stands, and there will be no fourth." This sense of an eastern Christian mission, inspiring a Russian resurgence, was just one result of this complicated formative period in the emergence of a separate European civilization in the Slavic lands.

Tatars Mongols; captured Russian cities and largely destroyed Kievan state in 1236; left Russian Orthodoxy and aristocracy intact.

The End of an Era in Eastern Europe

With Byzantium and Russia both under siege, eastern European civilization fell on hard times at the end of the postclassical era. These difficulties confirmed the largely separate trajectories of western and eastern Europe. Western Europe remained free from outside control and, despite some new problems, maintained a clearer vigor in politics, economy, and culture. When eastern Europe did reemerge, it was at some disadvantage to western Europe in terms of power and economic and cultural sophistication—a very different balance from that of the glory days of Byzantium and the vigor of Kievan Russia.

Tatar invasion and Byzantine collapse were profoundly disruptive. Key features of Kievan social structure disappeared in the later development of imperial Russia. Yet continuity was not entirely lost. Not only Christianity but also eastern European assumptions about political rulers and church–state relations and the pride in a lively artistic culture served as organizing threads when Russia and other Slavic societies turned to rebuilding.

Global Connections and Critical Themes

EASTERN EUROPE AND THE WORLD

The Byzantine empire and eastern Europe more generally participated actively in forging new economic connections. Byzantine trade was a central part of the transregional trading network, bringing links to Arab traders and wider opportunities in Asia as well as the Mediterranean. Kievan Rus' channeled trade from the Baltic to Constantinople, helping to link northern Europe to the larger network as well. The number of Arab coins formed along the trade routes, all the way to Scandinavia, indicates the key links.

Eastern Europe served also as a stage for major cultural change and connection. The spread of Christianity, but the rivalry between the two main versions of Christianity, were important at the time and subsequently.

State building was another obvious feature. The Byzantine state was carefully organized, in part because of military challenges in the region. Russian and other Slavic leaders were aware of the Byzantine example, but the kingdoms they created were more loosely organized.

The vitality of eastern Europe unquestionably declined during the final centuries of the postclassical era, in part because of new weaknesses in the Byzantine Empire. Under the Mongol conquest, Russia became more isolated, raising questions about what kind of contacts it would seek when, by the 15th century, it began to regain greater independence of action.

Further Readings

Recent overviews include John Rosser, *The A to Z of Byzantium* (2006); Averil Cameron, *The Byzantines* (2006); Judith Herrin, *Byzantium: The Surprising Life of a Medieval Empire* (2008); and Cyril Mango, ed., *The Oxford History of Byzantium* (2002). On early Byzantium, see Peter Sarris, *Economy and Society in the Age of Justinian* (2006), and James Allan Evans, *The Emperor Justinian and the Byzantine Empire* (2005). Byzantine Christianity is studied in G. Every, *The Byzantine Patriarchate, 451–1204* (1978) and J. M. Hussey and Andrew Louth, *The Orthodox Church in the Byzantine Empire* (2010); Derek Krueger, ed., *Byzantine Christianity* (2006); and S. Runciman, *The Byzantine Theocracy* (1977); see also D. M. Nicol, *Church and Society in the Last Centuries of Byzantium* (1979). On culture, see William Brumfield, ed., *Christianity and the Arts in Russia* (1991); Helen Evans and William Wixom, *The Glory of Byzantium: Art and Culture of the Middle Byzantine Era A.D. 843–1261* (1997); and E. Kitzinger, *Byzantine Art in the Making* (1977). Byzantine relations with the West are the main topic in H. J. Magoulias, *Byzantine Christianity: Emperor, Church and the West* (1982). On Byzantine influence in eastern Europe, D. Obolensky, *The Byzantine Commonwealth: Eastern Europe, 500–1453* (1971), remains an excellent analysis. See also Lynda Garland, ed., *Byzantine Women: Varieties of Experience 800–1200* (2006) and A. P. Kazhdan and A. W. Epstein, *Changes in Byzantine Culture in the Eleventh and Twelfth Centuries* (1985).

On Russian history, the best survey is Nicholas Riasanovsky, *A History of Russia* (1992), which has a good bibliography. See also Alfred Rambaud, *The History of Russia: From the Earliest Times to 1877* (2006); Maureen Perrie, ed., *The Cambridge History of Russia* (2006); David G. Rowley, *Exploring Russia's Past: Narrative, Sources, Images* (2006); Judith Martin, *Medieval Russia, 980–1584* (2007); and Serhii Plokhy, *The Origins of the Slavic Nations: Pre-modern Identities in Russia, Ukraine, and Belarus* (2006). Natalia Pushkareva and Eve Levin's survey *Women in Russian History: From the Tenth to the Twentieth Century* (1997) examines the place of women in early Russian history. Books dealing with early Russian culture include Mary Charmot, *Russian Painting and Sculpture* (1963); N. P. Kondakov, *The Russian Icon* (1927); J. H. Billington, *The Icon and the Axe: An Interpretive History of Russian Culture* (1966); and Arthur Voyce, *The Art and Architecture of Medieval Russia* (1967). Vladimir Volkoff, *Vladimir the Russian Viking, 960–1015* (1985), offers a unique glimpse of early Russia. Two collections are also very helpful on early Russian history: Thomas Riha, ed., *Readings in Russian Civilization*, vol. 1, *Russia Before Peter the Great, 900–1700* (1970); and especially S. A. Zenkovsky, ed. and trans., *Medieval Russia's Epics, Chronicles and Tales* (1963). The impact of the Mongols on the shaping of Russian history is examined in Robert Marshall, *Storm from the East: From Genghis Khan to Khubilai Khan* (1993), and in an older but still serviceable work, M. N. Thompson, *The Mongols and Russia* (1966).

On MyHistoryLab

 Study and Review on MyHistoryLab

Critical Thinking Questions

1. How does comparison help identify key features of eastern Europe? What were the main differences and similarities between Orthodox and Catholic (Western) Christianity?

2. How does Russian development compare with other major cases of imitation and contact during the postclassical centuries—for example, with Japanese borrowings from China?

3. What were the main changes and continuities, in the eastern Mediterranean, between patterns during the Roman empire and patterns in the postclassical period?

4. With a focus on causation, what are some of the explanations for the growing weakness of the Byzantine empire in the centuries before 1450?

A New Civilization Emerges in Western Europe

15

((• Listen to Chapter 15
on MyHistoryLab

Sometimes an individual life displays the complexities of a larger society. Godric—ultimately, Saint Godric—was a 12th-century Englishman (Figure 15.1). His father was an ordinary farmer, but he early developed greater ambition. Godric started as a peddler and, according to his biographer, quickly learned how to turn a profit on cheap items. He was physically strong, and a hard worker—necessary qualities for a life of trade and travel. He soon turned to urban commerce, which was beginning to increase rapidly during the 1100s. He participated in seagoing trade with other parts of Britain and with the European continent, and clearly made a good living, acquiring a number of ships.

LEARNING OBJECTIVES

15.1 What were the main stages of change in western Europe, from the early postclassical centuries to 1450, and what were the characteristic western political forms in each main stage? p. 329

15.2 What were the main cultural issues that west European intellectuals grappled with during the postclassical centuries? p. 340

15.3 How did growing trade fit the basic social structure of western Europe? p. 343

15.4 What were the basic shifts in west European characteristics at the end of the postclassical period? Was the region declining? p. 346

FIGURE **15.1** Having experienced many close calls with the weather during his years at sea, St. Godric was troubled on stormy nights for the rest of his life, thinking of the peril of sailors. He is best remembered for his extraordinary affinity for wild animals. He protected hunted animals and is said to have allowed snakes to warm themselves at his fire.

◉ Watch the Video Series on MyHistoryLab

Learn about some key topics related to this chapter with the *MyHistoryLab Video Series: Key Topics in World History*

But he was not entirely at peace with himself. His biographer, a clergyman named Reginald of Durham, is eager to emphasize Godric's consistent Christianity. So he portrays him as content with a simple life even amid his riches, and quickly attracted to the saints and a life of God. He argues that Godric's sea voyages, undoubtedly risky, helped the future saint realize the importance of divine aid—and surely religion did often provide a sense of security to venturesome merchants. Finally, however, a purely material life did not seem sufficient.

Godric began visiting saints' shrines with increasing frequency. He began to be disturbed by the high living—feasting and drinking—of some of his merchant colleagues. He also found that some of them stole outright. He attempted to correct them but was rebuffed. Ashamed of his own materialism (and possibly of some misdeeds of his own), he went on a pilgrimage to Rome. After that, with his parents' blessing, he decided to give himself entirely to a religious life. He sold all of his goods, gave the proceeds to the poor, and spent the rest of his life wandering as a religious hermit.

Few Europeans lived lives as polarized as that of Godric, but many, particularly in growing cities, felt some tension between commercial change and religious commitment. Could someone interested in making money keep a primary devotion to God? Some, as Godric discovered, would choose commerce. Others opted for religion. Still others worked for some combination. While few made Godric's dramatic ultimate choice, many merchants gave abundantly to the splendid churches of the cities, and not a few made deathbed renunciations of their commercial pasts. ■

The postclassical period was a great age of faith in western Europe, and Christianity provided the most obvious unifying factor in the new geography of western European civilization. Christian missionary efforts led most western Europeans to convert from polytheistic faiths in the initial postclassical centuries. But there were other key developments as well, including Europe's growing participation in trade and in wider interregional contacts. Not surprisingly, it was not always easy, even for individuals, to put the pieces together.

The postclassical period in western Europe began with the fall of the Roman Empire and lasted until the 15th century. The period is known as the **Middle Ages** in European history (the adjective form is *medieval*). The period featured gradual recovery from the shock of Rome's collapse. At the same time, the forms of civilization spread northward, beyond the Roman orbit, covering the whole of western Europe. Key characteristics of western European civilization emerged from these dynamic processes.

Medieval western Europe participated in the network of expanding contacts among major societies in Asia, Europe, and parts of Africa. New tools introduced by invaders from Asia, including a new kind of plow, helped spur medieval agriculture from the 10th century onward. New crops from Africa, including new varieties of wheat, increased food production. The revival of trade in the Mediterranean, bringing contacts with the Arabs, yielded other technological gains, such as the first European paper factory. Medieval culture was at least as powerfully shaped by connections with the wider world. By the 11th and 12th centuries, contact with the Byzantines and the Arabs had taught Western scholars new lessons in mathematics, science, and philosophy. The medieval West unquestionably took more from the emerging world network than it contributed, but it was also challenged by its international position to seek new world roles.

Middle Ages The period in western European history from the decline and fall of the Roman Empire until the 15th century.

500 C.E.	800 C.E.	1000 C.E.	1150 C.E.	1300 C.E.	1450 C.E.
500–900 Recovery period after Rome's fall; Christian missionaries work in northern Europe **732** Franks defeat Muslims in France	**800–814** Charlemagne's empire **900–1000** Spread of new plows; use of horses in agriculture and transport **962** Germanic kings revive Roman empire	**1018** Beginning of Christian reconquest of Spain **1066** Norman conquest of England, strong feudal monarchy **1070–1141** Peter Abelard **1073–1085** Gregory VII, reform pope **1096–1270** Crusades	**1150–1300** Gothic style spreads **1180** University of Paris **1200–1274** Thomas Aquinas and flowering of scholasticism **1215** Magna Carta **1226–1270** Louis IX of France **1265** First English parliament	**1303** Seizure of papacy by French king **1338–1453** Hundred Years' War **1348–1380** Black Death (bubonic plague)	**1469** Formation of single Spanish monarchy

STAGES OF POSTCLASSICAL DEVELOPMENT

15.1 What were the main stages of change in western Europe, from the early postclassical centuries to 1450, and what were the characteristic western political forms in each main stage?

> Postclassical western Europe was hard hit by the Roman collapse. However, after about 900, agriculture and trade revived, while political development advanced under the influence of feudalism and the Catholic church.

From about 550 C.E. until about 900, western Europe suffered from a number of problems. Rome continued to serve as the center of the growing Catholic church, in turn the most powerful institution in the West. But Italy was divided politically. Spain, another key region of the Roman Empire in the West, lay in the hands of the Muslims through much of the Middle Ages. A vibrant intellectual and economic life was focused there, and it would have an important influence on western developments later on, but it was for the time being out of the western mainstream. The center of the postclassical West lay in France, the Low Countries, and southern and western Germany, with England increasingly drawn in—areas where civilization, as a form of human organization, was new.

Frequent invasions reflected and prolonged the West's weakness, making it difficult to develop durable government or economic forms. Raids by the seagoing **Vikings** from Scandinavia periodically disrupted life from Ireland to Sicily. With weak states and little more than subsistence agriculture, it was small wonder that intellectual activity declined. The few who could read and write were concentrated in the hierarchy and the monasteries of the Catholic church, where they kept learning alive. But they could do little more than copy older manuscripts, including those of the great Christian thinkers of the later Roman Empire. By their own admission, they could not understand much of the philosophy involved, and they often apologized for their inability to write good Latin. Western Europe was still shaped by elements of the Roman heritage, but the connection was disrupted.

The Manorial System: Obligations and Allegiances

Between Rome's fall and the 10th century, effective political organization was largely local, although Germanic kings ruled some territories, such as a portion of what is France today. **Manorialism** was the system of economic and political relations between landlords and their peasant laborers. Understanding manorialism is a vital step in assessing social structures in many open cultural societies.

In European manorialism, most people were **serfs**, living on self-sufficient agricultural estates called manors. Serfs were agricultural workers who received some protection, including the administration of justice, from the landlords; in return, they were obligated to turn over part of their goods and to remain on the land. The manorial system had originated in the later Roman Empire. It was strengthened by the decline of trade and the lack of larger political structures. Serfs needed the military forces the landlords could muster for their security. Without much market economy to stimulate production and specialization, these same landlords used the serfs' produce and labor to support their own modest establishments.

Vikings Seagoing Scandinavian raiders from Sweden, Denmark, and Norway who disrupted coastal areas of western Europe from the 8th to the 11th centuries.

 Watch the **Video** on **MyHistoryLab:** Vikings (Aberth)

manorialism System that described economic and political relations between landlords and their peasant laborers during the Middle Ages; involved a hierarchy of reciprocal obligations that exchanged labor or rents for access to land.

serfs Peasant agricultural laborers within the manorial system of the Middle Ages.

 Read the **Document** on MyHistoryLab: On Feudal Obligations, "Mutual Duties of Vassals and Lords" (1020) Fulbert of Chartres

moldboard Heavy plow introduced in northern Europe during the Middle Ages; permitted deeper cultivation of heavier soils; a technological innovation of the medieval agricultural system.

three-field system System of agricultural cultivation by 9th century in western Europe; included one-third in spring grains, one-third fallow.

Life for most serfs was difficult. Agricultural equipment was limited, and production was low. The available plows, copied from Mediterranean models, were too light to work the heavy soils of France and Germany effectively. In the 9th century a better plow, the **moldboard** (a curved iron plate), was introduced that allowed deeper turning of the soil. Most Western peasants early in the postclassical period also left half their land uncultivated each year to restore nutrients. This again limited productivity, although by the 9th century a new **three-field system** improved the situation. Here, only a third of the land was left unplanted each year, to regain fertility.

The obligations of the manorial system bore as heavily on most serfs as did the technological limitations. Serfs had to give their lord part of their crops in return for grazing their animals on his land or milling their grain. They also provided many days of labor repairing the lord's castle or working the lands under his control. Serfs were not slaves: They could not be bought or sold, and they retained essential ownership of their houses and lands as long as they kept up with their obligations. They could also pass their property rights on through inheritance. Nevertheless, life remained hard, particularly in the early postclassical centuries. Some serfs escaped landlord control, creating a host of wanderers who added to the disorder of the early Middle Ages.

The Church: Political and Spiritual Power

During the centuries of recovery after the Roman empire's collapse in the 6th century, the Catholic church was the only extensive example of solid organization. Here was a crucial contrast with the state's dominance over religion in the Byzantine empire. In theory, and to an extent in fact, the church copied the government of the Roman empire to administer Christendom. The pope in Rome was the top authority. Regional churches were headed by bishops, who were supposed to owe allegiance to the church's central authority; bishops, in turn, appointed and to some degree supervised local priests. The popes did not always appoint the bishops, for monarchs and local lords often claimed this right, but they did send directives and receive information. The popes also regulated doctrine, beating back several heresies that threatened a unified Christian faith. Moreover, they sponsored extensive missionary activity. Papal missionaries converted the English to Christianity. They brought the religion to northern and eastern Germany, beyond the borders of the previous Roman empire, and, by the 10th century, to Scandinavia. They were active in the border regions of eastern Europe (see Chapter 9), sometimes competing directly with Orthodox missionaries.

Clovis Early Frankish king; converted Franks to Christianity c. 496; allowed establishment of Frankish kingdom.

The interest of early Germanic kings in Christianity was a sign of the political as well as spiritual power of the church. A warrior chieftain, **Clovis**, converted to Christianity about 496 C.E. to gain greater prestige over local rivals, who were still pagan. This authority, in turn, gave him a vague dominion over the Franks, a Germanic tribe located in much of what is France today. Conversion of this sort also strengthened beliefs by Western religious leaders, particularly the popes, that they had a legitimate authority separate from and superior to the political sphere. As Figure 15.2 suggests, religious commitments continued to expand to many people.

The church also developed an important chain of monasteries during the centuries immediately after Rome's fall. Western monasteries helped discipline the intense spirituality felt by some individual Christians, people who wanted to devote themselves to prayer and religious discipline and escape the limits of ordinary material life. The most important set of monastic rules was developed by Benedict of Nursia (in Italy) in the 6th century; the spread of Benedictine monasteries promoted Christian unity in western Europe. Monasteries also served ordinary people as examples of a holy life, adding to the spiritual focus that formed part of the fabric of medieval society. Many monasteries helped improve the cultivation of the land at a time when agricultural techniques were at a low ebb. Monasteries also provided some education and promoted literacy.

FIGURE **15.2** *Last Judgment: Apocalypse of Reichenau.* This picture was part of materials to be read in religious services in the 11th century in Germany. At the bottom, the dead are rising from their tombs for the Last Judgment, summoned by angels escorted by the winds. The picture illustrates the goals Christians were urged to make paramount, focusing on life after death.

VISUALIZING THE PAST

Peasant Labor

THIS SCENE, FROM AN ILLUMINATED (ILLUSTRATED) manuscript of the 15th century, shows peasant labor and tools in France, near a stylized great palace.

QUESTIONS

- What kind of social and gender structure does the picture suggest?
- What kinds of tools were used in farming, and how productive would they be?
- The picture should be compared to earlier medieval representations, such as the representation of Charlemagne's coronation: What were the trends in medieval artistic styles, in terms of dealing with human figures and nature?

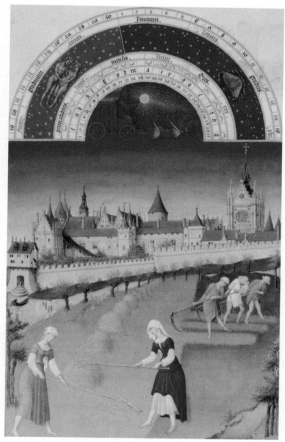

Peasants at labor.

Charlemagne and His Successors

One significant development occurred during the early postclassical centuries in the more strictly political sphere. The royal house of the Franks grew in strength during the 8th century. A new family, the **Carolingians**, took over this monarchy, which was based in northern France, Belgium, and western Germany. One founder of the Carolingian line, **Charles Martel**, or "Charles the Hammer," was responsible for defeating the Muslims in the battle of Tours in 732, although his victory had more to do with Arab exhaustion and an overextended invasion force than Carolingian strength. This defeat helped confine the Muslims to Spain and, along with the Byzantine defeat of the Arabs in the same period, preserved Europe for Christianity.

A later Carolingian ruler in this same royal line, Charles the Great, or **Charlemagne**, established a substantial empire in France and Germany around the year 800 (see Map 15.1). Briefly, it looked as if a new Roman empire might revive in the West; indeed, Charlemagne's successors in Germany continued to use the title of emperor (see Figure 15.3). Charlemagne helped to restore some church-based education in western Europe, and the level of intellectual activity began a slow recovery, in part because of these efforts. When Charlemagne died in 814, however, this empire did not long survive him. Rather, it was split into three portions as inheritance for his three grandsons: the outlines of modern France, Germany, and a middle strip consisting of the Low Countries, Switzerland, and

 Read the **Document** on MyHistoryLab: Description of Cluny

Carolingians Royal house of Franks after 8th century until their replacement in 10th century.

Charles Martel (686–741) Carolingian monarch of Franks; responsible for defeating Muslims in battle of Tours in 732; ended Muslim threat to western Europe.

Charlemagne [SHAR-luh-mayn] Charles the Great; Carolingian monarch who established substantial empire in France and Germany c. 800.

MAP **15.1 Charlemagne's Empire and Successor States** Charlemagne gathered a wide section of western Europe under his sway, but the empire was divided among his three grandsons after his death.

northern Italy (Map 15.1). Several of Charlemagne's successors, with nicknames such as "the Bald" and "the Fat," were not great leaders even in their regional kingdoms.

From this point onward, the essential political history of western Europe consisted of the gradual emergence of regional monarchies; a durable empire proved impossible, given competing loyalties and the absence of a strong bureaucracy. The regional decentralization and frequent warfare contrasted with political patterns in China, the Arab caliphate, and the Byzantine Empire. Western Europe proved to have strong cultural unity, initially centered in Catholic Christianity, but with pronounced political divisions. No single language united this civilization, any more than did a single government. Intellectuals and the church officials used Latin, but during the Middle Ages separate spoken languages evolved, usually merging Germanic and Latin elements. These separate languages, such as French and English, in turn helped form the basis of halting national identities when political and cultural boundaries roughly coincided, which is what began to happen in key cases after the 9th century.

The royal houses of several lands gained new visibility soon after Charlemagne's empire split. At first, the rulers who reigned over Germany and northern Italy were in the strongest position. It was they who claimed the title *emperor*, beginning around the 10th century. Later they called themselves **Holy Roman emperors**, merging Christian and classical claims. By this time, however, their rule had become increasingly hollow, precisely because they relied too much on their imperial claims and did not build a solid monarchy from regional foundations. Local lords often went

Holy Roman emperors Emperors in northern Italy and Germany following split of Charlemagne's empire; claimed title of emperor c. 10th century; failed to develop centralized monarchy in Germany.

their own way in Germany, while Italy was marked by the emergence of vibrant city states. For most of western Europe, however, the future lay elsewhere, with the rise of monarchies in individual states—states that ultimately would become nations.

New Economic and Urban Vigor

By 900, a series of developments began to introduce new sources of strength into Western society that ultimately had clear political and cultural repercussions. New agricultural techniques developed from contacts with eastern Europe and with Asian raiders into central Europe. The new mold-board plow and the three-field system were crucial gains; so was a new horse collar that allowed horses to be yoked without choking. The use of horse collars and stirrups also confirmed the military dominance of the lords, who monopolized fighting on horseback. The European nobility became defined by land ownership and military power. But better plows helped the ordinary people by allowing deeper working of heavy soil and the opening of new land. Monasteries also promoted better agricultural methods (in contrast to the less worldly orientation of monks in eastern Europe). During the 10th century, Viking raids began to taper off, partly because regional governments became stronger (sometimes when the Vikings themselves took over, as in the French province of Normandy) and partly because the Vikings, now Christianized, began to settle down. Greater regional political stability and improved agriculture promoted population growth, an important fact of Western history from the 10th through the 13th centuries.

Population growth encouraged further economic innovation. More people created new markets. There was a wedge here for growing trade, which in turn encouraged towns to expand, another source of demand. Landlords and serfs alike began to look to lands that had not previously been converted to agriculture. Whole regions, such as northeastern Germany, became colonized by eager farmers, and new centers sprang up throughout settled regions such as France. To woo labor to the new farms, landlords typically had to loosen the bonds of serfdom and require less outright labor service, sometimes simply charging a money rent. Harsh serfdom still existed, but most serfs gained greater independence, and some free peasants emerged. Contacts with other countries brought knowledge of new crops, such as durum wheat (from north Africa), the vital ingredient for pasta, and alfalfa (from Persia). The pace of economic life created a less rigid social structure, and more commercial, market-oriented economic motives began to coexist with earlier military and Christian ideals.

The growth of towns reflected the new vigor of western Europe's agriculture. In parts of Italy and the Low Countries, where trade and urban manufacturing were especially brisk, urban populations soared to almost 20 percent of the total by the 13th century. Overall, the townspeople made up about 5 percent of the West's population—a significant figure, although still below the often 15 percent levels of the advanced Asian civilizations. Few European cities approached a population level of 100,000 people (in contrast, China had 52 larger cities), but the rise of modest regional centers was an important development. Literacy spread in the urban atmosphere, spurring the popular languages; professional entertainers introduced new songs as well as dazzling tricks such as fire-eating and bear-baiting; urban interests spurred new forms of religious life, including city-based monastic orders dedicated to teaching or hospital work. Merchant activity and craft production expanded.

Read the **Document** on MyHistoryLab: Life of Charlemagne (early 9th c.) Einhard

FIGURE 15.3 The pope's coronation of the emperor Charlemagne was a vital precedent for the idea that church approval was essential for a legitimate state in western Europe. In fact, however, Charlemagne's power greatly exceeded the pope's.

(Coronation of Charlemagne at St. Peter's by Pope Leo III. Grandes Chroniques de France, fol. 106r. Musee Goya, Castres, France. Giraudon/Art Resource, NY.)

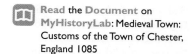

Read the **Document** on MyHistoryLab: Medieval Town: Customs of the Town of Chester, England 1085

Europe's economic and urban surge helped feed formal cultural life, which had already gained somewhat under Charlemagne's encouragement. By the 9th and 10th centuries, schools began to form around important cathedrals, training children who were destined for church careers. By the 11th century, there was enough demand for educated personnel to sustain the first universities. Italy offered universities to train students in medicine and law; the legal faculties profited from a growing revival in knowledge of Roman law, and medicine benefited from new learning imported from the Arabs and from revived Greek and Hellenistic science. By the 12th century, a more characteristic university was forming in Paris. It specialized in training clergy, with theology as the culminating subject but with faculties in other subjects as well. The Parisian example inspired universities in England (Oxford and Cambridge), Germany, and elsewhere. Solid educational institutions, although destined for only a small minority of Europe's population, supported increasingly diverse and sophisticated efforts in philosophy and theology. At the same time, medieval art and architecture reached a new high point, spurred by the same prosperity.

Feudal Monarchies and Political Advances

Prosperity also promoted political change, influenced by structures established in more unstable times. From the 6th century onward, the key political and military relationships in western Europe had evolved in a system called feudalism. Feudal relationships linked military elites, mostly landlords, who could afford the horses and iron weaponry necessary to fight. Greater lords provided protection and aid to lesser lords, called **vassals**; vassals in turn owed their lords military service, some goods or payments, and advice. Early feudalism after Rome's fall was very local; many landlords had armed bands of five or ten local vassals, easily converted into raiding parties. But feudal relationships could be extended to cover larger regions and even whole kingdoms. Charlemagne's empire boosted this more stable version of feudalism. He could not afford to pay his own bureaucracy, so he rewarded most of his military leaders with estates, which they quickly converted into family property in return for pledges of loyalty and service. Many German duchies were created by powerful lords with their own armies of vassals, ostensibly deferring to the Holy Roman emperor. On the whole, European feudalism inhibited the development of strong central states, but it also gradually reduced purely local warfare.

vassals Members of the military elite who received land or a benefice from a feudal lord in return for military service and loyalty.

Furthermore, kings could use feudalism to build their own power. Kings of France began to win growing authority, from the 10th century onward, under the Capetian royal family. At first they mainly exploited their position as regional feudal lords in the area around Paris. They controlled many serf-stocked manors directly, and they held most other local landlords as vassals. More attentive administration of this regional base produced better revenues and armies. The kings also formed feudal links with great lords in other parts of France, often through marriage alliances, gradually bringing more territory under their control. They experimented with the beginnings of bureaucratic administration by separating their personal accounts from government accounts, thus developing a small degree of specialization among the officials who served them. Later Capetian kings sent out officials to aid in regional administration.

The growth of a strong feudal monarchy in France took several centuries. By the early 14th century, the process of cautious centralization had gone so far in France that a king could claim rights to make the church pay taxes (an issue that caused great conflict). The king could mint money and employ some professional soldiers apart from the feudal armies that still did most of the fighting.

Feudal monarchy in England was introduced more abruptly. The Duke of Normandy, of Viking descent, who had already built a strong feudal domain in his French province, invaded England in 1066. The duke, now known as **William the Conqueror**, extended his tight feudal system to his new kingdom. He tied the great lords of England to his royal court by bonds of loyalty, giving them estates in return for their military service. But he also used some royal officials, called sheriffs, to help supervise the administration of justice throughout the kingdom. In essence, he and his successors merged feudal principles with a slightly more centralized approach, including more standardized national law codes issued by the royal court.

William the Conqueror Invaded England from Normandy in 1066; extended tight feudal system to England; established administrative system based on sheriffs; established centralized monarchy.

The growth of feudal monarchy unknowingly duplicated measures taken much earlier in other societies, such as China. Developing an explicit bureaucracy, with some specialized functions, and sending emissaries to outlying provinces are examples. In Europe, kings often chose urban business or professional people to staff their fledgling bureaucracies, because unlike the feudal nobles, they would be loyal to the ruler who appointed them. Government functions expanded modestly, as kings tried to tax subjects directly and hire a small professional army to supplement feudal forces.

Limited Government

Stronger monarchies did not develop evenly throughout Europe. The West remained politically divided and diverse. Germany and Italy, although nominally controlled by the Holy Roman emperor, were actually split into regional states run by feudal lords and city-states. The pope directly ruled the territory of central Italy. The Low Countries, a vigorous trade and manufacturing region, remained divided into regional units. Equally important were the limitations over the most successful feudal monarchies. Political centralization remained far short of Chinese levels. The power of the church continued to limit political claims, for the state was not supposed to intrude on matters of faith except in carrying out decisions of the popes or bishops.

Feudalism created a second limitation, for aristocrats still had a powerful independent voice and often their own military forces. The growth of the monarchy cut into aristocratic power, but this led to new statements of the limits of kings. In 1215, the unpopular English King John faced opposition to his taxation measures from an alliance of nobles, townspeople, and church officials. Defeated in his war with France and then forced down by the leading English lords, John was compelled to sign the Great Charter, or **Magna Carta**, which confirmed feudal rights against monarchical claims. John promised to observe restraint in his dealings with the nobles and the church, agreeing, for example, not to institute new taxes without the lords' permission or to appoint bishops without the church's permission. The Magna Carta showed how feudalism could generate claims of rights against the power of a king.

Late in the 13th century, this same feudal balance led to the creation of **parliaments** as bodies representing not individual voters but privileged groups such as the nobles and the church. (Even earlier, in 1000, the regional kingdom of Catalonia created a parliament.) The first full English parliament convened in 1265, with the House of Lords representing the nobles and the church hierarchy, and the Commons made up of elected representatives from wealthy citizens of the towns. As with the Magna Carta, the parliament institutionalized the feudal principle that monarchs should consult with their vassals. In particular, parliaments gained the right to rule on any proposed changes in taxation; through this power, they could also advise the crown on other policy issues. Although the parliamentary tradition became strongest in England, similar institutions arose in France, Spain, Scandinavia, and several of the regional governments in Germany. Here too, parliaments represented the key **three estates**: church, nobles, and urban leaders. They were not widely elected.

Feudal limited government was not modern limited government. People had rights according to the estate into which they were born; nobles transmitted membership in their estate to their children. There was no general concept of citizenship and certainly no democracy. Still, by creating the medieval version of representative institutions, Western feudal monarchy produced the beginnings of a distinctive political tradition. This tradition differed from the political results of Japanese feudalism, which emphasized group loyalty more than checks on central power.

Even with feudal checks, European monarchs developed more capacity for central administration during the later Middle Ages (see Map 15.2). The results clearly were uneven and by Asian standards still woefully limited. European rulers also continued to see war as a key purpose. Local battles gave way to larger wars, such as the conflicts between the proud rulers of France and England. In the 14th century, a long battle began—the **Hundred Years' War**, between the national monarchies of France and England—over territories the English king controlled in France and over feudal rights versus the emerging claims of national states.

The West's Expansionist Impulse

During the period of political development and economic advance, western Europe began to show its muscle beyond its initial postclassical borders (Map 15.2). Population growth spurred the expansionist impulse, as did the memory of Rome's lost greatness and the righteous zeal provided by Christianity. Germanic knights and agricultural settlers poured into sparsely settled areas in what is now eastern Germany and Poland, changing the population balance and clearing large areas of forest. A different kind of expansionist surge occurred in Spain. Small Christian states remained in northern Spain by the 10th century, and they gradually began to attack the Muslim government that held most of the peninsula. The "reconquest" escalated by the 11th century, as Christian forces, swelled by feudal warriors from various areas, pushed into central Spain, conquering the great Muslim center of Toledo. Full expulsion of Muslim rulers occurred only at the end of the Middle Ages in 1492, but the trend

Magna Carta Great Charter issued by King John of England in 1215; confirmed feudal rights against monarchical claims; represented principle of mutual limits and obligations between rulers and feudal aristocracy.

 Read the **Document** on **MyHistoryLab**: The Magna Carta, 1215

parliaments Bodies representing privileged groups; institutionalized feudal principle that rulers should consult with their vassals; found in England, Spain, Germany, and France.

three estates The three social groups considered most powerful in Western countries: church, nobles, and urban leaders.

Hundred Years' War Conflict between England and France from 1337 to 1453; fought over lands England possessed in France and feudal rights versus the emerging claims of national states.

MAP 15.2 Western Europe Toward the End of the Middle Ages, c. 1360 c.e. Near the end of the postclassical period, strong monarchies had consolidated their holdings, and boundaries between states were coming into sharper focus.

Urban II Called for First Crusade in 1095; appealed to Christians to mount military assault to free the Holy Land from the Muslims.

of the Christian offensive was clear even earlier. During the 15th century, regional Spanish monarchies fused through the marriage of Ferdinand and Isabella, which provided the political muscle to complete the Christian "reconquesta."

At Europe's other extreme, Viking voyagers had pushed out into the northern Atlantic, establishing settlements in Iceland. By the 11th century, other voyages had pushed to Greenland and the Hudson Bay area in what is now Canada, where short-lived outposts were created. By the 13th century, Spanish and Italian seafarers entered the Atlantic from the Mediterranean, although without much initial result except several lost expeditions.

The most dramatic expansionist move involved the great Crusades against the Muslim control of the Holy Land. Pope **Urban II** called for the First Crusade in 1095, appealing to the piety of the West's rulers and common people. Crusaders were promised full forgiveness of sins if they died in battle, ensuring their entry to heaven, which obviously enhanced the religious motivations involved. The idea of attacking Islam had great appeal, as Figure 15.4 suggests. The attraction of winning spoils from the rich Arab lands added to the inducement, as did the thirst for excitement among the West's feudal warriors. Internal wars were declining in Europe, and the military values of feudalism sought outlets elsewhere. Three great armies, with tens of thousands of crusaders from various parts of the West, assembled in Constantinople in 1097, much to the distress of the Byzantine government. The Western crusaders moved toward Jerusalem, winning it from the Turkish armies that held the area by that time. For almost a century, western knights ruled the "kingdom of Jerusalem," losing it to a great Muslim general, Saladin, during the 12th century.

DOCUMENT

European Travel: A Monk Visits Jerusalem

WILLIBALD, AN ENGLISH MONK, JOURNEYED TO Jerusalem between 721 and 727 c.e. His account was written down by a German nun.

In Syria

Willibald's party had now grown to eight in number, and they became an object of suspicion to the Muslims, who, seeing that they were strangers, seized them and threw them into prison, because they knew not of what country they were, and supposed them to be spies. They carried them as prisoners before a certain rich old man, that he might examine them; and

he inquired whence they came and the object of their mission; whereupon they related to him the true cause of their journey. The old man replied, "I have often seen men of the parts of the earth whence these come, traveling hither; they seek no harm, but desire to fulfil their law." And upon that they went to the palace, to obtain leave to proceed to Jerusalem.

While they were in prison it happened, by a manifest intervention of Devine Providence, that a merchant residing there was desirous, as an act of charity, and for the salvation of his soul, to purchase their deliverance, that they might pursue

(continued on next page)

their way, but he was not allowed to carry his generous design into effect; nevertheless he sent them daily their meals, and on Wednesdays and Saturdays sent his son to them in prison, who took them out to the bath, and brought them back again. And on Sunday he took them to church through the market, that they might see the shops, and whatever they seemed to take a liking to he afterwards bought for them at his own expense. The townsmen used then to come there to look at them, because they were young and handsome, and clad in good garments.

Then, while they were still remaining in prison, a man, who was a native of Spain, came and spoke with them, and inquired earnestly who they were and from whence they came, and they told him the object of their pilgrimage. This Spaniard had a brother in the kind's palace, who was chamberlain to the king of the Muslims. . . . When [Willibald and the Spaniard] came before the king, and told him the case, he asked whence the prisoners came. And they said, "These men come from the west country, where the sun sets; and we know of no land beyond them, but water only." And the king replied, "Why ought we to punish them? they have not sinned against us: – give them leave, and let them go." And even the fine of four deniers, which the other prisoners had to pay, was remitted to them . . . .

JERUSALEM AND BETHLEHEM

On their arrival at Jerusalem, they first visited the spot where the holy cross was found, where there is now a church which is called the Place of Calvary, and which was formerly outside of Jerusalem; but when St. Helena found the cross, the place was taken into the circuit of the city. Three wooden crosses stand in this place, on the outside of the wall of the church, in memory of our Lord's cross and of those of the other persons crucified at the same time.

He next came to the place where the angel appeared to the shepherds, and thence to Bethlehem, where our Lord was born, distant seven miles from Jerusalem.

[Later, heading home they] reached Constantinople. Here repose in one altar the three saints, Andres, Timothy, and Luke the evangelist; and the sepulcher of John Chrysostome is before the altar where the priest stands when he performs mass. Willibald remained there two years, and was lodged in the church, so that he might behold daily where the saints reposed.

QUESTIONS

- What relationships between Christians and Muslims does this passage suggest, for the postclassical period?
- Why would a Spaniard play a special role in Willibald's Middle Eastern experience?
- What were Willibald's motives for travel?
- What kind of larger results did this sort of travel have, in post-classical world history?

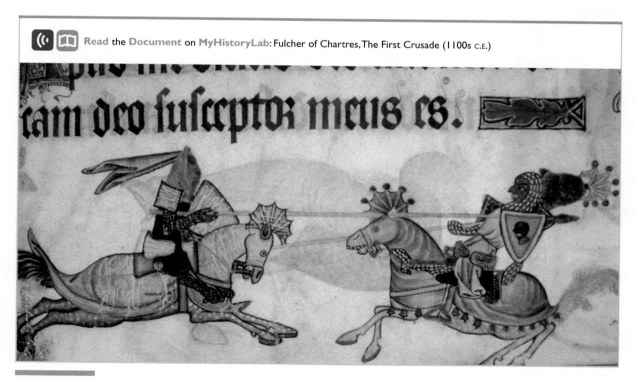

Read the Document on MyHistoryLab: Fulcher of Chartres, The First Crusade (1100s C.E.)

cain deo fufceptor meus es.

FIGURE **15.4** This imaginary duel between the noble Christian champion King Richard of England and the Muslim leader Saladin clearly shows the difference between "good guys" and "bad guys." Although many actual crusaders respected Saladin as a skilled military leader, in Europe he was condemned as an infidel.

Several later Crusades attempted to win back the Holy Land, but many later efforts turned toward other goals or toward pure farce. The Third Crusade at the end of the 12th century led to the death of the German emperor and the imprisonment of the English king, although it did produce a brief truce with Saladin that facilitated Christian pilgrims' visits to Jerusalem. The Fourth Crusade was manipulated by merchants in Venice, who turned it into an attack on their commercial rivals in Constantinople.

The Crusades did not demonstrate a new western superiority in the wider world, despite brief successes. In the Middle East, they generated only a passing episode. But in expressing a combination of religious zeal and growing commercial and military vigor on the part of the knights and merchants who organized the largest efforts, the Crusades unquestionably showed the aggressive spirit of the western Middle Ages at their height. They also helped expose the West to new cultural and economic influences from the Middle East, where European invaders were impressed by urban standards of living. This was a major spur to further change, including a greater thirst for goods, like spices, available only through international trade. Simply visiting the thriving urban center of Constantinople during the Crusades could open European eyes to new possibilities. One crusader exclaimed, "Oh, what a great and beautiful city is Constantinople! How many churches and palaces it contains, fashioned with wonderful skill! Their tradesmen at all times bring by boat all the necessities of man."

Religious Reform and Evolution

Gregory VII Pope during the 11th century who attempted to free church from interference of feudal lords; quarreled with Holy Roman Emperor Henry IV over practice of lay investiture.

investiture Practice of state appointment of bishops; Pope Gregory VII attempted to ban the practice of lay investiture, leading to war with Holy Roman Emperor Henry IV.

As medieval society developed, the Catholic church went through several periods of decline and renewal. At times, church officials and the leading monastic groups became preoccupied with their land holdings and their political interests. The church was a wealthy institution; it was tempting for many priests and monks to behave like ordinary feudal lords in pursuit of greater worldly power. Several reform movements fought this secularism, such as the 13th-century flowering that created orders such as the Franciscans, devoted to poverty and service in Europe's bustling cities. Saint Clare of Assisi (1194–1253) exemplified this new spirit of purity and dedication to the church (Figure 15.5). She was deeply influenced by Saint Francis, also from Assisi, who had converted to a life of piety and preaching in 1205 and who founded a new monastic order. Clare refused to marry, as her parents wanted, but rather founded a women's Franciscan order (later known as the Order of Saint Clare, or the Poor Clares) with Francis's backing. Like many women in Europe, Clare found in monasticism a vital means of personal expression. In 1958 Pope Pius XII declared her the patron saint of television, for during her last illness she miraculously heard and saw on the wall of her room a Christmas mass being performed on the other side of Assisi.

In addition to monastic leaders, reform-minded popes, such as **Gregory VII** (r. 1073–1085), tried to purify the church and free it from interference by feudal lords. One technique was insistence on the particularly holy character of the priesthood. Reformers stipulated that all priests remain unmarried, to separate the priesthood from the ordinary world of the flesh. Gregory also tried to free the church from any trace of state control. He quarreled vigorously with Holy Roman Emperor Henry IV over the practice of state appointment, or **investiture**, of bishops in Germany. Ultimately, by excommunicating the emperor from the church, Gregory won his point. The emperor appealed to the pope for forgiveness on his knees in the snow of a northern Italian winter, and the investiture controversy ended, apparently in the church's favor. Gregory and several later popes made clear their beliefs that the church not only was to be free from state interference but was superior to the state in its function as a direct channel of God's word. While governments still influenced religious affairs, a network of church courts developed to rule on matters of religious law and to bring heretics to trial and occasionally to execution. This was the origin of recurrent Western beliefs in church–state separation.

FIGURE **15.5** On the night of March 20, 1212, the Count of Sasso-Rosso's 18-year-old daughter, Clare, stole away from her father's house to dedicate herself to a life of poverty and holiness. She resisted all attempts by her father to bring her home and by the church to persuade her to accept some income as a guarantee against starvation for her order, which depended entirely on the begging of local friars for its daily bread. Clare was named abbess of a convent just three years later, and she never again left its grounds. Her sisters, her mother, and an aunt followed her into the order. She was canonized Saint Clare of Assisi in 1255.

The High Middle Ages

The postclassical version of Western civilization reached its high mark in the 12th and 13th centuries. Fed by the growing dynamism of western Europe's population, agriculture, and cities, the High Middle Ages were characterized by a series of creative tensions. Feudal

THINKING HISTORICALLY

Western Civilization

IN RECENT YEARS, HISTORIANS HAVE BEEN critically examining the term "Western civilization," which is sometimes (wrongly) taken as self-evident.

The concept of "the West" or "western civilization" was actively used in the 20th-century cold war with the Soviet Union, yet it is hard to define. We have seen that the classical Mediterranean world did not directly identify a "Western" civilization, and this classical heritage was used most selectively by postclassical western Europe. Further, the consistent absence of political unity in western Europe complicates any definition of common structures.

Western Europeans could not have identified Western civilization in the postclassical period, but they would have recognized the concept of Christendom, along with some difference between their version of this religion and that of eastern Europe.

> *Defining Western civilization is also complicated . . . because Western leaders copied so much from other societies.*

The first definition of this civilization was primarily religious, although artistic forms associated with religion also figured in this definition. Regional cultures varied, of course, and there was no linguistic unity, but cultural developments in one area—for example, the creation of universities, which started in Italy—surfaced elsewhere fairly quickly. Supplementing culture were some reasonably common social structures—like manors and guilds—and trade patterns that increasingly joined northern and much of southern Europe. The resulting civilization was by no means as coherent as Chinese civilization; many of its members detested each other, like the English and French, who were often in conflict and sometimes engaged in name-calling (the English were "les goddams," because they swore so much, and the French were "frogs" because of what they ate). Until very recently, Europeans thought in terms of distinctive national histories, not European ones. But it is possible to define some common features that differed from those of neighboring civilizations. Even as the civilization began to change, late in the postclassical period, it preserved some common directions. Debate continues about the balance between the Western and more purely national features.

Defining Western civilization is also complicated in the postclassical period because Western leaders copied so much from other societies. They eagerly learned of new technologies from Asia. They benefited from Arab mathematics and philosophy, and they imitated Muslim commercial law on how to treat tradespeople from outside the locality. But even in imitating, most Europeans were keenly conscious of their distinctiveness as Christians. They sometimes resented the societies they copied from. Toward the end of the Middle Ages, as Europeans began to seek a new role in the world at large, the openness to imitation also began to decline, as part of the further definition of a Western or European identity.

QUESTIONS

- Was there a Western civilization before the postclassical period? What were the defining features of Western civilization by the end of the postclassical period?
- How does the definition of Western civilization today compare to that of the postclassical period?

---

political structures, derived from local and personal allegiances, were balanced by emerging central monarchies. The unquestionable authority of the church and the cultural dominance of Christianity jostled with the intellectual vitality and diversity that formed part of university life. A social order and economy, based primarily on agriculture and the labor of serfs, now had to come to terms with important cities, merchants, and some new opportunities even for ordinary farmers.

WESTERN CULTURE IN THE POSTCLASSICAL ERA

15.2 What were the main cultural issues that West European intellectuals grappled with during the postclassical centuries?

> Christian culture dominated European philosophy and art, but it generated both change and some conflict.

During the centuries before about 1000, a small number of clergy continued the efforts of preserving and interpreting past wisdom, particularly the writings of church fathers such as Augustine, but also the work of some non-Christian Latin authors. During Charlemagne's time, a favorite practice was to gather quotations from ancient writers around key subjects. Interest in classical principles of rhetoric, particularly logic, reflected the concern for coherent organization; Aristotle, known to the Middle Ages as *the* philosopher, was valued because of his clear exposition of rational thought.

Theology: Assimilating Faith and Reason

From 1000 onward, a series of outstanding clerics advanced the logical exposition of philosophy and theology to new levels. They stressed the importance of absolute faith in God's word, but they believed that human reason could move toward an understanding of some aspects of religion and the natural order as well. Thus, according to several theologians, it was possible to prove the existence of God. Fascination with logic led some intellectuals to a certain zeal in pointing out inconsistencies in past wisdom, even in the writings of the church fathers. In the 12th century, **Peter Abelard** in Paris wrote a treatise called *Yes and No* in which he showed several logical contradictions in established interpretations of doctrine. Although Abelard protested his faith, saying, "I would not be an Aristotle if this were to part me from Christ," he clearly took an impish delight in suggesting skepticism. Here was a fascinating case of an individual's role in history. Abelard was clearly working in an established logical tradition, but his personality helped move the tradition to a new critical level. At the same time, his defiant attitudes may have drawn more attack than a softer approach would have done, which had consequences too.

The logical-rationalist current in western philosophy was hardly unopposed. A powerful monk, **Bernard of Clairvaux**, successfully challenged Abelard. Bernard, an intellectual of a different sort, stressed the importance of mystical union with God, attainable even on this earth in brief blissful glimpses, rather than rationalist endeavor. Bernard believed that reason was dangerous and that God's truth must be received through faith alone.

The debates over how and whether to combine the classical Mediterranean philosophical and scientific tradition with revealed religious faith reflected the earlier debates among Arab intellectuals during the 10th and 11th centuries. Both Christianity and Islam relied heavily on faith in a revealed word, through the Bible or Qur'an, respectively, but some intellectuals in both cultures strained to include other approaches.

Combining rational philosophy and Christian faith was the dominant intellectual theme in the postclassical West, showing the need to come to terms with both Christian and classical heritages, and with Middle Eastern learning as well. This combination of rational philosophy and Christian faith also posed formidable and fascinating problems. By the 12th century, the zeal for this kind of knowledge produced several distinctive results. It explained the intellectual vitality of most of the emerging universities, where students flocked to hear the latest debates by leading theologians. Higher education certainly benefited students through resulting job opportunities; for example, trained lawyers could hope for advancement in the growing bureaucracies of church or state. In contrast to China's institutions, however, the new universities were not directly tied into a single bureaucratic system, and the excitement they engendered during the Middle Ages was not just opportunistic. A large number of students, from the whole of western Europe, sought out the mixture of spiritual and rational understanding that leading thinkers were trying to work out.

The postclassical intellectual drive also motivated a growing interest in knowledge newly imported from the classical past and from the Arab world, and this knowledge fed the highest achievements of medieval learning. By the 12th century, Western scholars were reading vast amounts of material translated from Greek in centers in the Byzantine Empire, Italy, and Muslim Spain. They gained familiarity with the bulk of ancient Greek and Hellenistic philosophy and science. They also read translations of Arab and Jewish learning, particularly the works in which Middle Eastern scholars had wrestled with the problems of mixing human reasoning with truths gained by faith.

With much fuller knowledge of Aristotelian and Hellenistic science, plus the work of Arab rationalists such as Ibn-Rushd (IH-buhn RUSHT) (known in the West as Averroës (uh-VEHR-oh-eez), Western philosopher-theologians in the 13th century proceeded to the final great synthesis of medieval learning. The leading figure was **Thomas Aquinas**, the Italian-born monk who taught at the University of Paris. Aquinas maintained the basic belief that faith came first, but he greatly expanded the scope given to reason. Through reason alone, humans could know much of the natural order,

---

Abelard, Peter (1079–1142) Author of *Yes and No;* university scholar who applied logic to problems of theology; demonstrated logical contradictions within established doctrine.

Bernard of Clairvaux [klehr-VOH] (1090–1153) Emphasized role of faith in preference to logic; stressed importance of mystical union with God; successfully challenged Abelard and had him driven from the universities.

 Read the Document on MyHistoryLab: Professor Abelard Confronts Bernard of Clairvaux, c. 1140

Aquinas, Thomas [Thomas ah-KWY-nuhs] (1225–1274) Creator of one of the great syntheses of medieval learning; taught at University of Paris; author of several *Summas;* believed that through reason it was possible to know much about natural order, moral law, and nature of God.

moral law, and the nature of God. Aquinas had complete confidence that all essential knowledge could be organized coherently, and he produced a host of *Summas*, or highest works, that used careful logic to eliminate all possible objections to truth as revealed by reason and faith. Essentially, this work restated in Christian terms the Greek efforts to seek a rationality in nature that would correspond to the rational capacities of the human mind. To be sure, a few philosophers carried the interest in logic to absurd degrees. After the 13th century, **scholasticism**—as the dominant medieval philosophical approach was called because of its base in the schools—sometimes degenerated into silly debates such as the one about how many angels could dance on the head of a pin. But at its height, and particularly with Aquinas, scholasticism demonstrated an unusual confidence in the logical orderliness of knowledge and in human ability to know.

Medieval philosophy did not encourage a great deal of new scientific work. The emphasis on mastering past learning and organizing it logically could lead to overemphasis on previous discoveries rather than empirical research. Thus, university-trained doctors stressed memorization of Galen, the Hellenistic authority, rather than systematic practical experience. Toward the end of the 13th century, a current of practical science developed. In Oxford, members of the clergy, such as Roger Bacon, did experimental work with optics, pursuing research done earlier by Muslim scholars. An important by-product of this interest was the invention of eyeglasses. During the 14th and 15th centuries, experimenters also advanced knowledge in chemistry and astronomy. This early work set the stage for the flourishing of Western science.

scholasticism Dominant medieval philosophical approach; so called because of its base in the schools or universities; based on use of logic to resolve theological problems.

Popular Religion

Far less is known about popular beliefs than about formal intellectual life in the Middle Ages. Christian devotion undoubtedly ran deep and may well have increased with time among many ordinary people. At least in the early medieval centuries, many people diligently followed Christian rituals yet seemed unaware of how many of their actions might contradict Christian morality. For example, Raoul de Cambrai, hero of a French epic written down in the late 12th century but orally transmitted earlier, sets fire to a convent filled with nuns, then asks a servant to bring him some food. The servant berates him for burning the convent, then reminds him that it is Lent, a time of fasting and repentance before Easter. Raoul denies that his deed was unjust, for the nuns deserved it for insulting his knights, but admits that he had forgotten Lent and goes off to distract himself from his hunger by playing chess.

Regardless of whether day-to-day morality improved, popular means of expressing religious devotion expanded over time. The rise of cities saw the formation of lay groups to develop spirituality and express their love of God. The content of popular belief evolved as well. Enthusiasm for the veneration of Mary, the mother of Jesus, expanded by the 12th century, showing a desire to stress the merciful side of Christianity, rather than the supposed sternness of God the Father, and new hopes for assistance in gaining salvation. The worship of various saints showed a similar desire for intermediaries between humanity and God. At the same time, ordinary people continued to believe in various magical rituals, and they celebrated essentially pagan festivals, which often involved much dancing and merriment. They blended their version of Christianity with great earthiness and spontaneity, some of which was conveyed by late medieval authors such as English writer Geoffrey Chaucer.

Religious Themes in Art and Literature

Religious art was another cultural area in which the medieval West came to excel, as was the case in other societies where religious enthusiasm ran strong, such as the Islamic Middle East or Hindu India. Like philosophy, medieval art and architecture were intended to serve the glory of God. Western painters used religious subjects almost exclusively. Painting mainly on wooden panels, artists in most parts of western Europe depicted Christ's birth and suffering and the lives of the saints, using stiff, stylized figures. By the 14th and 15th centuries, artists improved their ability to render natural scenes realistically and portrayed a host of images of medieval life as backdrops to their religious subjects. Stained-glass designs and scenes for churches were another important artistic expression.

Medieval architecture initially followed Roman models, particularly in church building, using a rectangular, or Romanesque, style sometimes surmounted by domes. During the 11th century, however, a new style took hold that was far more original, although it benefited from knowledge of Muslim design plus advances in structural engineering in the West itself. **Gothic** architects built soaring church spires and tall arched windows, as Figure 15.6 illustrates. Although their work focused on creating churches and great cathedrals, some civic buildings and palaces also picked up the Gothic motif. It is not far-fetched to see the Gothic style as representative of western postclassical culture more generally. Its spiritual orientation showed in the towers cast up to the heavens. It built also on growing technical skills and deep popular devotion, expressed in the money collected to build the huge monuments and the patient labor needed for construction that often lasted many decades. The originality of Gothic styles reflected the growing Western ability to find suitable new means of expression, just as use of Gothic styles in the later Western world showed the ongoing power of medieval models.

Medieval literature and music reflected strong religious interests. Most Latin writing dealt with points of philosophy, law, or political theory. However, alongside writing in Latin came the development of a growing literature in the spoken languages, or vernaculars, of western Europe. The pattern was not unlike that of India a few centuries earlier after the fall of the Gupta empire, when Sanskrit served as a scholarly language but increasing power was given to popular languages such as Hindi. Vernacular literature helped develop separate European languages and focused largely on secular themes. Several oral sagas, dealing with the deeds of great knights and mythic figures in the past, were written down. From this tradition came the first known writing in early English, *Beowulf*, and in French, *The Song of Roland*. Late in the Middle Ages, a number of writers created adventure stories, comic tales, and poetry in the vernacular tongues, such as Chaucer's *Canterbury Tales*. Much of their work, and also plays written for performance in the growing cities, reflected the tension between Christian values and a desire to portray the richness and coarseness of life on earth. Chaucer's narrative shows a fascination with bawdy behavior, a willingness to poke fun at the hypocrisy of many Christians, and an ability to capture some of the tragedies of human existence. In France, a long poem called *The Romance of the Rose* used vivid sexual imagery, and the poet Villon wrote, in largely secular terms, of the terror and poignancy of death.

Also using vernacular language, a series of courtly poets, or troubadours, based particularly in southern France in the 14th century, wrote hymns to the love that could flourish between men and women. Although their verses stressed platonic devotion rather than sexual love and paid homage to courtly ceremonies and polite behavior, their concern with love was the first sign of a new valuation of this emotional experience in the Western tradition.

In sum, medieval intellectual and artistic life created a host of important themes. Religion was the centerpiece, but it did not preclude a growing range of interests, from science to romantic poetry. Medieval culture was a rich intellectual achievement in its own right. It also set in motion a series of developments—in rationalist philosophy, science, artistic representations of nature, and vernacular literature—that would be building blocks for later Western thought and art.

Gothic An architectural style that developed during the Middle Ages in western Europe; featured pointed arches and flying buttresses as external supports on main walls.

FIGURE **15.6** The cathedral of Notre-Dame (Our Lady) at Amiens, France, is a grand example of gothic architecture, which flourished during the later Middle Ages in western Europe. The cathedral, which dwarfs the surrounding buildings, was built between 1220 and 1402 and was the tallest building in Europe at the time of its completion.

CHANGING ECONOMIC AND SOCIAL FORMS
IN THE POSTCLASSICAL CENTURIES

15.3 How did growing trade fit the basic social structure of western Europe?

> While merchant capitalism gained ground in western Europe, other economic values predominated.

Although culture provided the most obvious cement for Western society during the Middle Ages, economic activity and social structure also developed common features. Here too, the postclassical West demonstrated impressive powers of innovation, for classical patterns had little hold. As trade revived by the 10th century, the West became a common commercial zone. Most regions produced primarily for local consumption, as was true in agricultural societies generally. But Italian merchants actively sought cloth manufactured in the Low Countries (present-day Belgium and the Netherlands), and merchants in many areas traded for wool produced in England or timber supplies and furs brought from Scandinavia and the Baltic lands. Great ports and trading fairs, particularly in the Low Countries and northern France, served as centers for Western exchange as well as markets for a few exotic products such as spices brought in from other civilizations (Map 15.3).

Western Europe also saw a clear expansion in productive capacity during much of the postclassical period, with gains in agriculture supporting some growth in urban manufacturing. Their achievements here did not rival those of east Asia, where the production gains and social consequences were more

MAP 15.3 Leading Trade Routes Within Western and Central Europe and to the Mediterranean

substantial, but they did contribute important changes including a growing capacity to participate in transregional trade.

New Strains in Rural Life

The improvements in agriculture after 900 C.E. brought important new ingredients to rural life. Some peasants were able to shake off the most severe constraints of manorialism, becoming almost free farmers with only a few obligations to their landlords, although rigid manorialism remained in place in many areas. Noble landlords still served mainly military functions, for ownership of a horse and armor were prerequisites for fighting until the end of the medieval period. Although most nobles shunned the taint of commerce—like aristocrats in many societies, they found too much money-grubbing demeaning—they did use trade to improve their standard of living and adopt more polished habits. The courtly literature of the late Middle Ages reflected this new style of life.

As many lords sought improved conditions, they were often tempted to press their serfs to pay higher rents and taxes, even as serfs were gaining a new sense of freedom and control over their own land. From the late Middle Ages until the 19th century, this tension produced a recurrent series of peasant–landlord battles in Western society. Peasants sought what they viewed as their natural and traditional right to the land, free and clear. They talked of Christian equality, turning such phrases as "When Adam delved and Eve span, Who was then a gentleman?" A more complex economy clearly brought new social strains, similar to the recurrent wave of popular unrest in China or the rural uprisings in the Middle East, where religion helped prompt egalitarian sentiments as well. The gap between lord and peasant was the crucial social inequality in Europe, but it was open to change and it generated some egalitarian ideas in response.

On the whole, the lives of western peasants improved between 900 and 1300. Landlord controls were less tight than they had become in other societies, such as the Middle East. Western agriculture was not yet particularly advanced technologically (compared with east Asia, for example), but it had improved notably over early medieval levels.

Growth of Trade and Banking

Gains in agriculture promoted larger changes in medieval economic life. Urban growth allowed more specialized manufacturing and commercial activities, which in turn promoted still greater trade. Spearheaded by Italian businesspeople, banking was introduced to the West to facilitate the long-distance exchange of money and goods (Figure 15.7). The use of money spread steadily, to the dismay of many Christian moralists and many ordinary people who preferred the more direct, personal ways of traditional society. The largest trading and banking operations, not only in Italy but in southern Germany, the Low Countries, France, and Britain, were clearly capitalistic. Big merchants invested funds in trading ships and the goods they carried, hoping to make large profits on this capital. Profitmaking was not judged kindly by Christian thinkers such as Thomas Aquinas, who urged that all prices should be "just," reflecting only the labor put into the goods.

Rising trade took several forms. There were exchanges between western Europe and other parts of the known world. Wealthy Europeans developed a taste for some of the luxury goods and spices of Asia. The latter were not used merely to flavor food but were vital in preserving perishable items such as meat. Spice extracts also had great medicinal value. The Crusades played a role in bringing these products to wider attention. A Mediterranean trade redeveloped, mainly in the hands of Italian merchants, in which European cloth and some other products were exchanged for the more polished goods of the East. Commerce within Europe involved exchanges of timber and grain from the north for cloth and metal products manufactured in Italy and the Low Countries. At first an exporter of raw wool, England developed some manufactured goods for exchange by the later Middle Ages. Commercial alliances developed. Cities in northern Germany and southern Scandinavia grouped together in the **Hanseatic League** to encourage trade. With growing banking facilities, it became possible to organize commercial transactions throughout much of western Europe. Bankers, including many Jewish businesspeople, were valued for their service in lending money to monarchs and the papacy.

The growth of trade and banking in the Middle Ages served as the origin of **capitalism** in Western civilization. The greater Italian and German bankers, the long-distance merchants of the Hanseatic cities, were clearly capitalistic in their willingness to invest in trading ventures with the expectation of profit. Given the dangers of trade by land and sea, the risks in these investments were

Hanseatic League An organization of cities in northern Germany and southern Scandinavia for the purpose of establishing a commercial alliance.

capitalism Economic system based on profit-seeking, private ownership, and investment.

substantial, but profits of 100 percent or more were possible. In many cities, such as London, groups of powerful merchants banded together to invest in international trade, each buying shares in the venture and profiting or losing accordingly.

Individual merchants could amass—and lose—great fortunes. Jacques Coeur (JAHK KUR) (c. 1395–1456), one of Europe's most extraordinary merchants, demonstrated the opportunities and risks of new forms of trade. Son of a furrier, he married the daughter of a royal official and served as a tax official until he was caught minting coins with less valuable metals. He then founded a trading company that competed with Italians and Spaniards in dealing with the Middle East. He visited Damascus to buy spices, setting up a regular trade in rugs, Chinese silk, and Indonesian spices and sugar. He also became financial advisor and supplier to the French king and was ennobled. With the largest fleet ever owned by a French subject, Coeur surrounded himself with splendor, even arranging with the pope for his 16-year-old son to become an archbishop. But he had enemies, many of them nobles in debt to him, and they turned the king against him. Tortured, he admitted to various crimes, including supplying weapons to Muslims. His property was confiscated, but adventurer to the last, he died on a Greek island while serving in a papal fleet against the Turks.

By world standards this was not a totally unprecedented merchant spirit. European traders were still less venturesome and less wealthy than some of their Muslim counterparts. Nor was Western society as tolerant of merchants as Muslim or Indian societies were. Yet Western commercial endeavors clearly were growing. Because Western governments were weak, with few economic functions, merchants had a freer hand than in many other civilizations. Many of the growing cities were ruled by commercial leagues. Monarchs liked to encourage the cities as a counterbalance to the power of the landed aristocracy, and in the later Middle Ages and beyond, traders and kings typically were allied. However, aside from taxing merchants and using them as sources of loans, royal governments did not interfere much with trading activities. Merchants even developed their own codes of commercial law, administered by city courts. Thus, the rising merchant class was staking out an unusually powerful and independent role in European society.

Capitalism was not yet typical of the Western economy, even aside from the moral qualms fostered by the Christian tradition. Most peasants and landlords had not become enmeshed in the market system. In the cities, the dominant economic ethic stressed group protection, not

FIGURE **15.7** This 14th-century miniature shows views of a banking house. People might keep money in banks, seek loans, or arrange transactions with merchants in faraway centers of trade.

profitmaking. The characteristic institution was not the international trading firm but the merchant or artisan guild. **Guilds** grouped people in the same business or trade in a single city, sometimes with loose links to similar guilds in other cities. These organizations were new in western Europe, although they resembled guilds in various parts of Asia but with greater independence from the state. They stressed security and mutual control. Merchant guilds thus attempted to give all members a share in any endeavor. If a ship pulled in loaded with wool, the clothiers' guild of the city insisted that all members participate in the purchase so that no one member would monopolize the profits.

Artisan guilds were made up of the people in the cities who actually made cloth, bread, jewelry, or furniture. These guilds tried to limit their membership so that all members would have work. They regulated apprenticeships to guarantee good training but also to ensure that no member would employ too many apprentices and so gain undue wealth. They discouraged new methods because security and a rough equality, not maximum individual profit, were the goals; here was their alternative to the capitalistic approach. Guilds also tried to guarantee quality so that consumers would not have to worry about shoddy quality on the part of some unscrupulous profit-seeker. Guilds played an important political and social role in the cities, giving their members recognized status and often a voice in city government. Their statutes were in turn upheld by municipal law and often backed by the royal government as well.

guilds Sworn associations of people in the same business or craft in a single city; stressed security and mutual control; limited membership, regulated apprenticeship, guaranteed good workmanship; often established franchise within cities.

Despite the traditionalism of the guilds, manufacturing and commercial methods improved in medieval Europe, although the region still lagged well behind Asia in ironmaking and textile manufacture. In a few areas, such as clockmaking—which involved both sophisticated technology and a concern for precise time initially linked to the schedule of church services—European artisans led the world. Furthermore, some manufacturing spilled beyond the bounds of guild control. Particularly in the Low Countries and parts of Italy, groups of manufacturing workers were employed by capitalists to produce for a wide market. Their techniques were simple, and they worked in their own homes, often alternating manufacturing labor with agriculture. Their work was guided not by the motives of the guilds but by the inducements of merchant capitalists, who provided them with raw materials and then paid them for their production.

Thus, by the later Middle Ages, western Europe's economy and society embraced many contradictory groups and principles. Commercial and capitalist elements jostled against the slower pace of economic life in the countryside and even against the dominant group protectionism of most urban guilds. Most people remained peasants, but a minority had escaped to the cities, where they found more excitement, along with increased danger and higher rates of disease. Medieval tradition held that a serf who managed to live in the city for a year and a day became a free person. A few prosperous capitalists flourished, but most people operated according to very different economic values, directed toward group welfare rather than individual profit. This was neither a static society nor an early model of a modern commercial society. It had its own flavor and its own tensions—the fruit of several centuries of economic and social change.

Limited Sphere for Women

The increasing complexity of medieval social and economic life may have had one final effect, which is familiar from patterns in other agricultural societies: new limits on the conditions of women. Women's work remained vital in most families. The Christian emphasis on the equality of all souls and the practical importance of women's monastic groups in providing an alternative to marriage continued to have distinctive effects on women's lives in Western society. The veneration of Mary and other female religious figures gave women real cultural prestige, counterbalancing the biblical emphasis on Eve as the source of human sin. In some respects, women in the West had higher status than their sisters under Islam: They were less segregated in religious services (although they could not lead them) and were less confined to the household. Still, women's voice in the family may have declined in the Middle Ages.

Urban women often played important roles in local commerce and even operated some craft guilds, but they found themselves increasingly hemmed in by male-dominated organizations. In contrast to Islam, women were not assured of property rights. By the late Middle Ages, a literature arose that stressed women's roles as the assistants and comforters to men, listing supplemental household tasks and docile virtues as women's distinctive sphere. Patriarchal structures seemed to be taking deeper root.

THE DECLINE OF THE MEDIEVAL SYNTHESIS

Key characteristics of western Europe began to shift after 1300, with new problems of overpopulation and disease.

15.4   What were the basic shifts in west European characteristics at the end of the postclassical period? Was the region declining?

A major war engulfed France and England during the 14th and 15th centuries, and this proved to be both symptom and cause of larger difficulties. The Hundred Years' War, which sputtered into the mid-15th century, lasted even longer than its name and initially went very badly for France—a sign of new weakness in the French monarchy. As the war dragged on, kings reduced their reliance on the prancing forces of the nobility in favor of paid armies of their own. New military methods challenged the key monopoly of the feudal lords, as ordinary paid archers learned how to unseat armored knights with powerful bows and arrows and with crossbows (Figure 15.8). The war ended with a French victory, sparked in part by the heroic leadership of the inspired peasant woman Joan of Arc, but both its devastation and the antifeudal innovations it encouraged suggested a time of change.

Concurrently, from about 1300 onward, key sources of Western vitality threatened to disappear. Medieval agriculture could no longer keep pace with population growth: The readily available new lands had been used up, and there were no major new technological gains to compensate. The result included severe famines and a decline in population levels until the end of the century. A devastating series of plagues that persisted for several centuries, beginning with the **Black Death** in 1348, further reduced Europe's population (Figure 15.9). Plague came from Asia and the Middle East, due to trade contacts, but the results were devastating. New social disputes arose, heightening some of the tensions noted earlier between peasants and landlords, artisans and their employees. Not until the 16th century would the West begin to work out a new social structure.

The West's economy did not go into a tailspin. In some respects, as in manufacturing and mining technology, progress may even have accelerated. The 150 to 200 years after 1300 form in Western history a transition period in which the features of the Middle Ages began to blur while new problems and developments began to take center stage. Western civilization was not in a spiral of decline, but the postclassical version of this civilization was.

Signs of Strain

The decline of medieval society involved increasing challenges to several typical medieval institutions. During the 14th century, the ruling class of medieval society, the land-owning aristocracy, began to show signs of confusion. It had long staked its claim to power on its control of land and its military prowess, but its skill in warfare was now open to question. The growth of professional armies and new weaponry such as cannon and gunpowder made traditional fighting methods, including fortified castles, increasingly irrelevant. The aristocracy did not simply disappear, however. Rather, the nobility chose to emphasize a rich ceremonial style of life, featuring tournaments in which military expertise could be turned into competitive games. The idea of chivalry—carefully controlled, polite behavior, including behavior toward women—gained ground. The upper class became more cultivated. We have seen similar transformations in the earlier Chinese and Muslim aristocracy. Yet at this transitional point in Europe, some of the elaborate ceremonies of chivalry seemed rather hollow, even a bit silly—a sign that medieval values were losing hold without being replaced by a new set of purposes.

Another key area involved decisive shifts in the balance between church and state that had characterized medieval life. For several decades in the aftermath of the taxation disputes in the early 14th century, French kings wielded great influence on the papacy, which they relocated from Rome to Avignon, a town surrounded by French territory. Then rival claimants to the papacy confused the issue further. Ultimately, a single pope was returned to Rome, but the church was clearly weakened. Moreover, the church began to lose some of its grip on western religious life. Church leaders were so preoccupied with their political involvement that they tended to neglect the spiritual side. Religion was not declining; indeed, signs of intense popular piety continued to blossom, and new religious groups formed in the towns. But devotion became partially separated from the institution of the church. One result, again beginning in the 14th century, was a series of popular heresies, with leaders in places such as England and Bohemia (the present-day Czech Republic) preaching against the hierarchical apparatus of the church in favor of direct popular experience of God. Another result was an important new series of mystics, many of them women, who claimed direct, highly emotional contacts with God.

A third area in which medievalism faded was the breakdown of the intellectual and even artistic synthesis. After the work of Aquinas, church officials became less tolerant of intellectual daring, and they even declared some of Aquinas's writings heretical. The earlier blend of rationalism and religion no longer seemed feasible. Ultimately, this turned some thinkers away from religion, but this daring

FIGURE **15.8** The Siege of Paris, pictured here, took place in 1465, after the French nobility rose up against King Louis XI, whose treatment of them had left them angry and ambitious to reestablish their independence from the Crown. Calling themselves the League of Public Good, they marched on Paris, but the fighting there was indecisive and gave Louis the chance to regroup. The uprising was ended by treaty two months later. This incident was a revealing clash between feudal values and new royal ambition.

Black Death Plague that struck Europe in 14th century; significantly reduced Europe's population; affected social structure.

View the **Closer Look** on **MyHistoryLab**: Black Death: A Burial Scene

FIGURE **15.9** This painting shows survivors at Tournai placing plague victims in coffins before mass burial became the only way to keep up with the deaths. The Black Death, which killed up to a quarter of the population of Europe in just 20 years, devastated medieval society.

development took time. In art, growing interest in realistic portrayals of nature, although fruitful, suggested the beginnings of a shift away from medieval artistic standards. Religious figures became less stylized as painters grew more interested in human features for their own sake. The various constraints on forms of postclassical culture prompted many Western intellectuals to look for different emphases. In Italy most clearly, new kinds of literature and art took shape that differed from the styles and subjects of the postclassical centuries.

The Postclassical West and Its Heritage

Medieval Europe had several faces. The term *Middle Ages* implies a lull between the glories of Rome and the glitter of more modern Europe. There is some truth to this, for medieval Europe did grapple with backwardness and vulnerability.

But the Middle Ages were also a period of growing dynamism. Particularly after 900 C.E., gains in population, trade and cities, and intellectual activity created a vigorous period in European history. Key developments set a tone that would last even after the specifically medieval centuries had ended. Universities and Gothic art (often intertwined, as in the many American campuses that revived the

Gothic style for their buildings) were an enduring legacy to Western society. Distinctive ideas about government, building on Christian and feudal traditions, constituted another medieval contribution.

The medieval period was also a special moment in the relationship between Europe and the regions around it. Opportunities to advance by imitation were particularly striking, from technology to science to trade and consumption. Even the medieval university may have had Arab origins in the higher schools of the Muslim world. Europe was able to develop new contacts, but it did not reach the technological or urban levels of the leading Asian societies.

Medieval Europe warrants a particular comparison with other areas in which civilization was partially new during the postclassical period and where change and imitation proceeded rapidly. Divided political rule in Europe resembled conditions in west Africa and Japan (the only other feudal society in the period). The imitation process can be compared among Europe, Africa, Japan, and Russia. But the Crusades revealed a distinctive expansionist spirit in Europe that also warrants attention, suggesting a more aggressive interest in the wider world than the other emerging societies were demonstrating.

Global Connections and Critical Themes

MEDIEVAL EUROPE AND THE WORLD

During the Middle Ages, western Europe developed something of a love–hate relationship with the world around it. In the early Middle Ages, Europe seemed at the mercy of invasions, from the Vikings in the north or various nomadic groups pushing in from central Asia. European leaders were also keenly aware of the power of Islam, which controlled most of the Mediterranean, including Spain. Most Europeans saw Islam as a dangerously false religion and an obvious threat.

At the same time, there was much to be learned from this wider world. During the Middle Ages, Europeans actively copied a host of features from Islam, from law to science and art. They imported products and technologies from Asia. This process of imitation accelerated during the centuries of Mongol control, when European traders and travelers eagerly pushed into eastern Asia. A key question for Europe at the end of the Middle Ages involved how to gain greater control over the benefits that came from world contacts, while reducing the sense of threat. Partly through weakness, partly because of the advantages that Europeans learned from contact, the new civilization developed active growing sense of global awareness. Europe itself did not, however, become a major attraction for people in other societies, except for some of the raiders who helped keep the region off balance during the early part of the period. Neither European manufacturing nor culture was widely appealing, outside the region itself.

Further Readings

For the Middle Ages generally, Joseph Strayer's *Western Europe in the Middle Ages* (1982) is a fine survey. More recent works include Judith Bennett, *Medieval Europe: A Short History* (2010); Charles H. Parker and Jerry H. Bentley, eds., *Between the Middle Ages and Modernity: Individual and Community in the Early Modern World* (2007); Eric H. Mielants, *The Origins of Capitalism and the "Rise of the West"* (2007); and David Power, ed., *The Central Middle Ages: Europe 950–1320* (2006). Key topics are covered in Peter Reid, *Medieval Warfare: Triumph and Domination in the Wars of the Middle Ages* (2007); Huw Pryce and John Watts, eds., *Power and Identity in the Middle Ages* (2007); Isabel Davis, *Writing Masculinity in the Later Middle Ages* (2007); R. S. Lopez, *The Commercial Revolution of the Middle Ages, 950–1350* (1976); and C. H. Lawrence, *Medieval Monasticism: Forms of Religious Life in Western Europe in the Middle Ages* (1984). National histories are important for the period, particularly on political life; see J. W. Baldwin, *The Government of Philip Augustus: Foundations of French Royal Power in the Middle Ages* (1986); G. Barraclough, *The Origins of Modern Germany* (1984); Michael Alexander, *Medievalism: The Middle Ages in Modern England* (2007); and Christopher Dyer, *An Age of Transition?: Economy and Society in England in the Later Middle Ages* (2005). R. Barlett, *The Making of Medieval Europe* (1992), suggests that Western civilization was the product of cross-cultural fertilization.

Social history has dominated much recent research on the period. See P. Ariès and G. Duby, eds., *A History of Private Life*, vol. 2 (1984) and Barbara Hanawalt, *The Ties That Bound: Peasant Families in Medieval England* (1986), for important orientation in this area. David Herlihy's *Medieval Households* (1985) is a vital contribution, as is J. Chapelot and R. Fossier's *The Village and House in the Middle Ages* (1985). Margaret Schaus, *Women and Gender in Medieval Europe: An Encyclopedia* (2006) and J. Kirshner and S. F. Wemple, eds., *Women of the Medieval World* (1985), are good collections. On tensions in popular religion, see Lisa M. Bitel and Felice Lifshitz, *Gender and Christianity in Medieval Europe: New Perspectives* (2010); C. Bynum, *Jesus as Mother: Studies in the Spirituality of the High Middle Ages* (1982); and L. Little, *Religious Poverty and the Profit Economy in Medieval Europe* (1978). A highly readable account of medieval life is E. Leroy Ladurie, *Montaillou: The Promised Land of Error* (1979).

Several excellent studies take up the theme of technological change: J. Gimpel, *The Medieval Machine: The Industrial Revolution of the Middle Ages* (1977); Lynn White Jr., *Medieval Technology and Social Change* (1962); and David Landes, *Revolution in Time: Clocks* and the Making of the Modern World (1985). On environmental impact, see Roland Bechmann, *Trees and Man: The Forest in the Middle Ages* (1990).

On intellectual and artistic life, E. Gilson's *History of Christian Philosophy in the Middle Ages* (1954) is a brilliant sketch, and his *Reason and Revelation* (1956) focuses on key intellectual issues of the age. S. C. Ferruolo's *The Origins of the University* (1985)

and N. Pevsner's *An Outline of European Architecture* (1963) deal with other important features; see also H. Berman's *Law and Revolution: The Formation of the Western Legal Tradition* (1983). On contacts, see Khalil Semaan, *Islam and the Medieval West: Aspects of Intercultural Relations* (1980). An intriguing classic, focused primarily on culture, is J. Huizinga, *The Waning of the Middle Ages* (1973).

On MyHistoryLab

 Study and Review on MyHistoryLab

Critical Thinking Questions

1. How do developments in European agricultural reflect the importance of new technology?

2. What were the main differences between early European capitalism and the economic ethic of the guilds?

3. How did the consequences of the Crusades compare to the initial causes?

4. What are the distinctive features of feudalism as a political system? How does the feudal system help explain patterns of political change in postclassical Europe?

5. Looking at both eastern and western Europe, what were some of the main reasons many additional people converted to Christianity in the postclassical period?

6. How did western Europe compare with sub-Saharan Africa as a participant in postclassical transregional trade? What were its comparative strengths and weaknesses?

The Americas on the Eve of Invasion

 Listen to Chapter 16
on MyHistoryLab

If you climbed the steep stairway to the temple at its summit and looked out from atop the great pyramid at its center, you could see that the splendid city of Tenochtitlan, capital of the Aztec Empire, rose from two islands in a large lake (Figure 16.1). All around its shores were densely settled towns and cities surrounded by cultivated fields. Canoes constantly traversed the lake and entered the city through a maze of canals, large crowds trod across the causeways that linked the city and its markets to the shores, and in some marshy areas, complex farming on "floating gardens" kept thousands of peasants at work. The Mexica or Tenocha people (sometimes called the Aztecs) who built the city considered it the "foundation of Heaven." For them it was a sacred space as well as a thriving metropolis and the heart of their empire.

LEARNING OBJECTIVES

What were the main features of the Toltec and Aztec empires? p. 353	**16.1**
What were the principal strengths and constraints of the Aztec economy? p. 358	**16.2**
What were the principal causes of the expansion of the Inca empire? p. 362	**16.3**
What were the characteristic economic forms of American groups outside the two great imperial territories? p. 368	**16.4**

FIGURE **16.1** The great Aztec city-state of Tenochtitlan was established on an island in the midst of a large lake. Connected to the shores by causeways, supplied with fresh water by an aqueduct, it housed a population estimated to be over 150,000. Early Spanish observers compared its canals to Venice and were fascinated by its markets and gardens. To the Aztecs it was the center of political and spiritual power, or as they called it, "the foundation of heaven."

👁 Watch the Video Series on MyHistoryLab

Learn about some key topics related to this chapter with the *MyHistoryLab Video Series:* *Key Topics in World History*

When the first Europeans saw Tenochtitlan in 1520, the city had a population of over 150,000 and covered about 5 square miles, making it as large as contemporary Seville or Paris. The first Europeans who saw it were amazed. Some of them compared the city and its canals to Venice. Hernán Cortés, the Spanish captain who first entered the city, reported "the stone masonry and the woodwork are equally good; they could not be bettered anywhere." His companion, the foot soldier Bernal Díaz del Castillo, a man usually given to plain speech, could not hide his admiration:

> Gazing on such wonderful sights, we did not know what to say, or whether what appeared before us was real, for on one side, on the land, there were great cities, and in the lake ever many more, and the lake was crowded with canoes, and in the causeway were many bridges at intervals, and in front of us stood the great city of Mexico.

Díaz del Castillo went on to describe the palaces and temples, the two-storied homes of the nobles, the stuccoed buildings hung with garlands of flowers, the smell of the cedar wood beams, the zoo, the aviary, the rooftop gardens, and the bustling markets filled with everything from chocolate to elaborate textiles and from parrot feathers to precious stones and slaves. The hum of the crowd in the great market, he said, could be heard miles away. Of course, there was much about the city that he did not understand, such as the fact that each city ward was controlled by a kin group that cared for its temples, shrines, and palaces. Later, he came to understand that the purpose of temples was for ceremonies of human sacrifice, which he found appalling, but his overall impression was one of admiration and wonder.

Tenochtitlan, clearly a great urban center, was the largest of about 50 such city-states that dotted central and southern Mexico. They were the heirs of the long development of civilization in the Americas, a process that seems to have taken place in relative isolation from the other centers of world history. ■

Indians Misnomer created by Columbus referring to indigenous peoples of New World; implies social and ethnic commonality among Native Americans that did not exist; still used to apply to Native Americans.

By 1500, the Americas were densely populated in many places by peoples long indigenous to the New World. These peoples were later called **Indians**. That term of course, is derived from a mistake Columbus made when he thought he had reached the Indies, what Europeans called India and the lands beyond, but the label is also misleading because it implies a common identity among the peoples of the Americas that did not exist until after the arrival of Europeans. *Indian* as a term to describe all the peoples of the Americas could have a meaning only when there were non-Indians from which to distinguish them. Still, the term has been used for so long—and is still in use by many Native Americans today—that we will continue to use it along with the term *Native Americans* to describe the early peoples of the Americas.

As should already be clear, there were many different peoples with a vast array of cultural achievements. The variety of cultural patterns and ways of life of pre-Columbian civilizations makes it impossible to discuss each in detail here, but we can focus on a few areas where major civilizations developed, based on earlier achievements. By concentrating on these regions, we can demonstrate the continuity of civilization in the Americas. This chapter examines in some detail Mesoamerica, especially central Mexico, and the Andean heartland. In both these areas great imperial states were in place when European expansion brought them into direct contact with the Old World. Discussed

900 C.E.	1150 C.E.	1300 C.E.	1450 C.E.
900 End of intermediate horizon and decline of Tihuanaco and Huari **900–1465** Chimor Empire based on Chan-Chan on north coast of Peru **968** Tula established by Toltecs **1000** Toltec conquest of Chichén Itzá and influence in Yucatan	**1150** Fall of Tula, disintegration of Toltec Empire **1200–1500** Mississippian culture flourishes	**1325** Aztecs established in central Mexico; Tenochtitlan founded **1350** Incas established in Cuzco area **1434** Creation of triple alliance **1434–1471** Great expansion under Inca Pachacuti **1434–1472** Rule of Nezhualcoyotl at Texcoco **1438** Incas dominate Cuzco and southern highlands **1440–1469** Reign of Moctezuma I	**1471–1493** Inca Topac Yupanqui increases areas under control **1493–1527** Huayna Capac expands into Ecuador; his death results in civil war **1502–1520** Reign of Moctezuma II

in less detail are a few areas influenced by the centers of civilization—and some whose development seems to have been independent of them—to provide an overview of the Americas on the eve of invasion.

POSTCLASSIC MESOAMERICA, 1000–1500 C.E.

16.1   What were the main features of the Toltec and Aztec empires?

With the collapse of Teotihuacan (tay-oh-tee-wah-KAHN) in central Mexico and the abandonment of the classical Maya cities in the 8th century C.E., Mesoamerica experienced significant political and cultural change. In central Mexico, nomadic peoples from the north took advantage of the political vacuum to move into the richer lands. Among these peoples were the Toltecs, who established a capital at Tula about 968. **Toltec culture** adopted many features from the sedentary peoples and added a strongly militaristic ethic. This included the cult of sacrifice and war that is often portrayed in Toltec art. Later Mesoamerican peoples, such as the Aztecs, had some historical memory of the Toltecs and thought of them as the givers of civilization. However, the archeological record indicates that Toltec accomplishments often were fused or confused with those of Teotihuacan in the memory of the Toltecs' successors.

> The Toltecs and later the Aztecs were the chief civilizations that followed the fall of Teotihuacan and the abandonment of the classic Maya cities in the 8th century C.E. These new civilizations built on the accomplishments of their predecessors but rarely surpassed them except in political and military organization.

The Toltec Heritage

Among the legends that survived about the Toltecs were those of **Topiltzin**, a Toltec leader and apparently a priest dedicated to the god **Quetzalcoatl** (the Feathered Serpent) who later became confused with the god himself in the legends. Apparently, Topiltzin, a religious reformer, was involved in a struggle for priestly or political power with another faction. When he lost, Topiltzin and his followers went into exile, promising to return in the future to claim his throne on the same date, within the cyclical calendar system. Supposedly, Topiltzin and his followers sailed for Yucatan; there is much evidence of Toltec influence in that region. The legend of Topiltzin/Quetzalcoatl was well known to the Aztecs and may have influenced their response when the Europeans arrived.

The Toltecs created an empire that extended over much of central Mexico, and their influence spread from their capital, Tula, to areas as far away as Guatemala (Figure 16.2). About 1000 C.E., Chichén Itzá (chee-CHEHN-eet-she) in Yucatan was conquered by Toltec warriors, and it and several other cities were ruled for a long time by central Mexican dynasties or by Maya rulers under Toltec influence.

Toltec influence spread northward as well. Obsidian was mined in northern Mexico, and the Toltecs may have traded for turquoise in the American Southwest. It has been suggested that the great Anasazi adobe town at Chaco Canyon in New Mexico was abandoned when the Toltec empire fell and the trade in local turquoise ended.

Toltec culture Succeeded Teotihuacan culture in central Mexico; strongly militaristic ethic including human sacrifice; influenced large territory after 1000 C.E.; declined after 1200 C.E.

 View the **Closer Look** on **MyHistoryLab:** The Pyramid of the Sun in Teotihuacan

Topiltzin [toh-PEYEL-tzihn] Religious leader and reformer of the Toltecs in 10th century; dedicated to god Quetzalcoatl; after losing struggle for power, went into exile in the Yucatan peninsula.

Quetzalcoatl [keht-zahl-KOH-ah-tuhl] Toltec deity; Feathered Serpent; adopted by Aztecs as a major god.

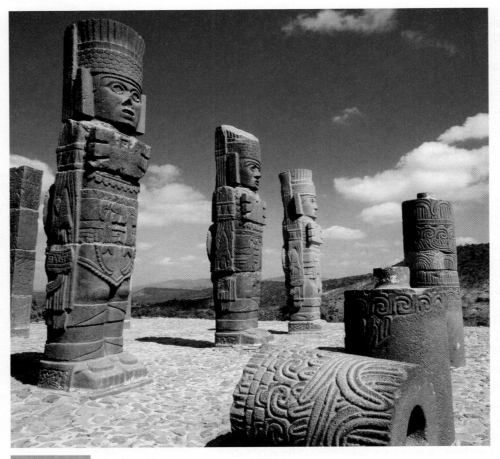

FIGURE **16.2** Toltec political and cultural influence spread from its capital at Tula in northern Mexico to places as far south as Chichén Itzá in Yucatan. The colossal statues of warriors shown here served as columns that supported the roof of a great temple.

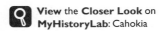
View the Closer Look on MyHistoryLab: Cahokia

How far eastward Toltec influence spread is a matter of dispute. Was there contact between Mesoamerica and the elaborate culture and concentrated towns of the Hopewell peoples of the Ohio and Mississippi valleys? Scholars disagree. Eventually, in the lower Mississippi valley from about 700 C.E., elements of Hopewell culture seem to have been enriched by external contact, perhaps with Mexico. This Mississippian culture, which flourished between 1200 and 1500 C.E., was based on maize and bean agriculture that probably spread from Mexico. Towns, usually located along rivers, had stepped temples made of earth, and sometimes large burial mounds. Some of the burial sites include well-produced pottery and other goods, and some burials seem to have been accompanied by ritual executions or sacrifices of servants or wives. This indicates social stratification in the society. Cahokia, near East St. Louis, Illinois, covered 5 square miles and may have had more than 30,000 people in and around its center. Its largest earthen pyramid, now called Monk's Mound, covers 15 acres and is comparable in size to the largest pyramids of the classic period in Mexico. Many of these cultural features seem to suggest contact with Mesoamerica.

The Aztec Rise to Power

The Toltec empire lasted until about 1150, when it apparently was destroyed by nomadic invaders from the north, who also seem to have sacked Tula about that time. The center of population and political power in central Mexico shifted to the valley of Mexico and especially to the shores of the large chain of lakes in that basin. These provided a rich aquatic environment. The shores of the lakes were dotted with settlements and towns and supported a dense population. Of the approximately 3000 square miles in the basin of the valley, about 400 square miles were under water. The lakes became the cultural heartland and population center of Mexico in the postclassic period. In the unstable world of post-Toltec Mesoamerica, various peoples and cities jockeyed for control of the lakes. The winners of this struggle, the Aztecs—or, as they called themselves, the *Mexica*—eventually built a great empire, but when they first emerged on the historical scene, they were the most unlikely candidates for power.

The Aztec rise to power and formation of an imperial state was as spectacular as it was rapid. According to some of their legends, the Mexica had once inhabited the central valley and had known agriculture and the "civilized" life but had lived in exile to the north in a place called Aztlan (AZT-lahn) (from whence we get the name *Aztec*). This may be an exaggeration by people who wanted to lay claim to a distinguished heritage. Other sources indicate that the Aztecs were simply one of the nomadic tribes that used the political anarchy, after the fall of the Toltecs, to penetrate the area of sedentary agricultural peoples. Like the ancient Egyptians, the Aztecs rewrote history to suit their purposes.

What seems clear is that the Aztecs were a group of about 10,000 people who migrated to the shores of Lake Texcoco (Map 16.1) in the central valley of Mexico around 1325. After the fall of the Toltec empire, the central valley was inhabited by a mixture of peoples: Chichimec migrants from the northwest and various groups of sedentary farmers. In this period, the area around the lake was dominated by several tribes or peoples organized into city-states. Much like medieval Europe, this was a world of political maneuvers and state marriages, competing powers and shifting alliances. These political units claimed authority on the basis of their military power and their connections to Toltec culture. Many of these peoples spoke Nahuatl (NAH-wahtl), the language the Toltecs had spoken. The Aztecs also spoke this language, a fact that made their rise to power and their eventual claims to legitimacy more acceptable.

An intrusive and militant group, the Aztecs were distrusted and disliked by the dominant powers of the area, but their fighting skills could be put to use, and this made them attractive as mercenaries or allies. For about a century the Aztecs wandered around the shores of the lake, being allowed to settle for a while and then driven out by more powerful neighbors.

In a period of warfare, the Aztecs had a reputation as tough warriors and fanatical followers of their gods, to whom they offered human sacrifices. This reputation made them both valued and feared. Their own legends held that their wanderings would end when they saw an eagle perched on a cactus with a serpent in its beak. Supposedly, this sign was seen on a marshy island in Lake Texcoco, and there, on that island and one nearby, the Mexica settled. The city of **Tenochtitlan** was founded about 1325.

From this secure base the Aztecs began to take a more active role in regional politics. Serving as mercenaries and then as allies brought prosperity to the Aztecs, especially to their ruler and the warrior nobles, who took lands and tribute from conquered towns. By 1428, the Aztecs had emerged as an independent power. In 1434, Tenochtitlan created an alliance with two other city-states that controlled much of the central plateau. In reality, Tenochtitlan and the Aztecs dominated their allies and controlled the major share of the tribute and lands taken.

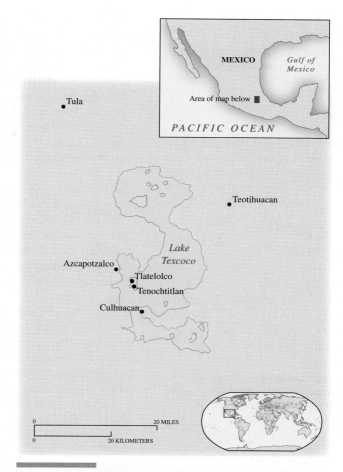

MAP **16.1 Central Mexico and Lake Texcoco** An aquatic environment at the heart of the Aztec empire.

The Aztec Social Contract

Aztec domination extended from the Tarascan frontier about a hundred miles north of present-day Mexico City southward to the Maya area. Subject peoples were forced to pay tribute, surrender lands, and sometimes do military service for the growing Aztec empire.

Aztec society had changed in the process of expansion and conquest. From a loose association of clans, the Mexica had become a stratified society under the authority of a supreme ruler. The histories were rewritten and the Mexica were described as a people chosen to serve the gods. Human sacrifice, long a part of Mesoamerican religion, greatly expanded into an enormous cult in which the military class played a central role as suppliers of war captives to be used as sacrificial victims. A few territories were left unconquered so that periodic "flower wars" could be staged in which both sides could obtain captives for sacrifice. Whatever the religious motivations of this cult, the Aztec rulers manipulated it as an effective means of political terror. By the time of Moctezuma II, (1502–1520) the Aztec state was dominated by a king who represented civil power and served as a representative of the gods on earth. The cult of human sacrifice and conquest was united with the political power of the ruler and the nobility.

Tenochtitlan [teh-nahk-teet-LAHN] Founded c. 1325 on marshy island in Lake Texcoco; became center of Aztec power; joined with Tlacopan and Texcoco in 1434 to form a triple alliance that controlled most of central plateau of Mesoamerica.

Religion and the Ideology of Conquest

Aztec religion incorporated many features that had long been part of the Mesoamerican belief system. Religion was a vast, uniting, and sometimes oppressive force in which little distinction was made between the world of the gods and the natural world. The traditional deities of Mesoamerica—the gods of rain, fire, water, corn, the sky, and the sun, many of whom had been worshiped as far back as the time of Teotihuacan—were venerated among the Aztecs. There were at least 128 major deities, but there seemed to be many more: As in popular Hinduism each deity had a male and female form, because a basic duality was recognized in all things. Moreover, gods might have different manifestations, somewhat like the avatars of the Hindu deities. Each god had at least five aspects, each associated with one of the cardinal directions and the center. Certain gods were thought to be the patrons of specific cities, ethnic groups, or occupations.

Tlaloc [tlah-LOHK] Major god of Aztecs; associated with fertility and the agricultural cycle; god of rain.

Huitzilopochtli [WEE-tsuh-loh-POHKT-lee] Aztec tribal patron god; central figure of cult of human sacrifice and warfare; identified with old sun god.

Nezhualcoyotl [nehz-uh-WAHL-koh-YOH-tihl] Leading Aztec king of the 15th century.

The gods were supported by a round of yearly festivals and ceremonies that involved feasting and dancing along with penance and sacrifice. This complex array of deities can be organized into three major themes or cults. The first were the gods of fertility and the agricultural cycle, such as **Tlaloc**, the god of rain (called *Chac* by the Maya), and the gods and goddesses of water, maize, and fertility. A second group centered on the creator deities, the great gods and goddesses who had brought the universe into being. The story of their actions played a central role in Aztec cosmography. Much Aztec abstract and philosophical thought was devoted to the theme of creation. Finally, the cult of warfare and sacrifice built on the preexisting Mesoamerican traditions that had been expanding since Toltec times and, under the militaristic Aztec state, became the cult of the state. **Huitzilopochtli**, the Aztec tribal patron, became the central figure of this cult.

The Aztecs revered the great traditional deities—such as Tlaloc and Quetzalcoatl, the ancient god of civilization—so holy to the Toltecs, but their own tribal deity, Huitzilopochtli, was paramount. The Aztecs identified him with the old sun god, and they saw him as a warrior in the daytime sky fighting to give life and warmth to the world against the forces of the night. To carry out that struggle, the sun needed strength, and just as the gods had sacrificed themselves for humankind, the nourishment the gods needed most was that which was most precious: human life in the form of hearts and blood. The great temple of Tenochtitlan was dedicated to both Huitzilopochtli and Tlaloc. The tribal deity of the Aztecs and the ancient agricultural god of the sedentary peoples of Mesoamerica were thus united.

In fact, although human sacrifice had long been a part of Mesoamerican religion, it expanded considerably in the postclassic period of militarism. Warrior cults and the militaristic images of jaguars and eagles devouring human hearts were characteristic of Toltec art. The Aztecs simply took an existing tendency and carried it further. Both the types and frequency of sacrifice increased, and a whole symbolism and ritual, which included ritual cannibalism, developed as part of the cult (Figure 16.3). How much of Aztec sacrifice was the result of religious conviction and how much was a tactic of terror and political control by the rulers and priests is still open to debate.

FIGURE **16.3** Human sacrifice was practiced by many Mesoamerican peoples, but the Aztecs apparently expanded its practice for political and religious reasons. This image shows Aztec priests cutting out their victims' hearts and then rolling the bodies down the steps of the pyramid.
(Ms. Magliabechiano: sacrificio umano azteco. Biblioteca Nazionale Firenze. Scala/Art Resource, NY.)

Beneath the surface of this polytheism, there was also a sense of spiritual unity. **Nezhualcoyotl**, the king of Texcoco, wrote hymns to the "lord of the close vicinity," an invisible creative force that supported all the gods. Yet his conception of a kind of monotheism, much like that of Pharaoh Akhenaton in Egypt, appears to have been too abstract and never gained great popularity.

Although the bloody aspects of Aztec religion have gained much attention, we must also realize that the Aztecs concerned themselves with many of the same great religious and spiritual questions that have preoccupied other civilizations: Is there life after death? What is the meaning of life? What does it mean to live a good life? Do the gods really exist?

Nezhualcoyotl, whose poetry survived in oral form and was written down in the 16th century, wondered about life after death:

Do flowers go to the land of the dead?
In the Beyond, are we dead or do we
    still live?
Where is the source of light, since that
    which gives life hides itself?

As in the Vedas of ancient India, he also wondered about the existence of the gods:

> Are you real, are you fixed?
> Only You dominate all things
> The Giver of Life.
> Is this true?
> Perhaps, as they say, it is not true.

Aztec religious art and poetry are filled with images of flowers, birds, and song, all of which the Aztecs greatly admired, as well as human hearts and blood, the "precious water" needed to sustain the gods. This mixture of images makes the symbolism of Aztec religion difficult for modern observers to appreciate.

Aztec religion depended on a complex mythology that explained the birth and history of the gods and their relationship to peoples, and on a religious symbolism that infused all aspects of life. As we have seen, the Mesoamerican calendar system was religious, and many ceremonies coincided with particular points in the calendar cycle (Figure 16.4). Moreover, the Aztecs also believed in a cyclical view of history, and that the world had been destroyed four times before and would be destroyed again. Thus, there was a certain fatalism in Aztec thought and a premonition that eventually the sacrifices would be insufficient and the gods would again bring catastrophe.

FIGURE **16.4** This Aztec stone calendar is about 12 feet across and 4 feet thick, and it weighs about 24 tons. It was unearthed accidentally by construction crews in Mexico City in 1790.

Feeding the People: The Economy of the Empire

Feeding the great population of Tenochtitlan and the Aztec confederation in general depended on traditional forms of agriculture and on innovations developed by the Aztecs. Lands of conquered peoples often were appropriated, and food sometimes was demanded as tribute. In and around the lake, however, the Aztecs adopted an ingenious system of irrigated agriculture by building **chinampas** for agriculture. These were beds of aquatic weeds, mud, and earth that had been placed in frames made of cane and rooted to the lake floor. They formed artificial floating islands about 17 feet long and 100 to 330 feet wide. This narrow construction allowed the water to reach all the plants, and willow trees were also planted at intervals to give shade and help fix the roots. Much of the land of Tenochtitlan itself was chinampa in origin, and in the southern end of the lake, more than 20,000 acres of chinampas were constructed. The yield from chinampa agriculture was high: Four corn crops a year were possible. Apparently, this system of irrigated agriculture had been used in preclassic days, but a rise in the level of the lakes had made it impossible to continue. After 1200, however, lowering water levels once again stimulated chinampa construction, which the Aztecs carried out on a grand scale.

chinampas Beds of aquatic weeds, mud, and earth placed in frames made of cane and rooted in lakes to create "floating islands"; system of irrigated agriculture utilized by Aztecs.

Production by the Aztec peasantry and tribute provided the basic foods. In each Aztec community, the local clan apportioned the lands, some of which were also set aside for support of the temples and the state. In addition, individual nobles might have private estates, which were worked by servants or slaves from conquered peoples. Each community had periodic markets—according to various cycles in the calendar system, such as every 5 and 13 days—in which a wide variety of goods were exchanged. Cacao beans and gold dust sometimes were used as currency, but much trade was done as barter. The great market at Tlatelolco (TLAT-ehl-UHL-koh) operated daily and was controlled by the special merchant class, or **pochteca**, which specialized in long-distance trade in luxury items such as plumes of tropical birds and cacao. The markets were highly regulated and under the control of inspectors and special judges. Despite the importance of markets, this was not a market economy as we usually understand it.

pochteca [pahk-TEHK-uh] Special merchant class in Aztec society; specialized in long-distance trade in luxury items.

The state controlled the use and distribution of many commodities and redistributed the vast amounts of tribute received from subordinate peoples. Tribute levels were assigned according to whether the subject peoples had accepted Aztec rule or had fought against it. Those who surrendered paid less. Tribute payments, such as food, slaves, and sacrificial victims, served political and economic ends. More than 120,000 mantles of cotton cloth alone were collected as tribute each year and sent to Tenochtitlan. The Aztec state redistributed these goods. After the original conquests, it rewarded its nobility richly, and the commoners received far less.

AZTEC SOCIETY IN TRANSITION

Aztec society became more hierarchical as the empire grew and social classes with different functions developed, although the older organization based on clans and kinship groups never disappeared. Tribute was drawn from subject peoples, but Aztec society confronted technological barriers that made it difficult to maintain the large population of central Mexico.

16.2   What were the principal strengths and constraints of the Aztec economy?

Like all societies, Aztec society experienced changes over time. The Mexica were one of a number of peoples who spoke the Nahuatl language and occupied the region of central Mexico. From their humble origins as hunters and gatherers they emerged as a dominant power, and their rise created opportunities for some groups and a loss of status for others within their society. Eventually, they held sway over the 50 or so political units of the central valley of Mexico. Expansion by warfare privileged the warriors, and the religious basis for expansion made the priests and the cults of the temples a force in society. No ruler could govern without the support of these sectors of society, a support obtained and preserved by giving out rewards and benefits. But such policies transformed the nature of Aztec society.

A Widening Social Gulf

calpulli [kal-PUHL-lee] Clans in Aztec society, later expanded to include residential groups that distributed land and provided labor and warriors.

During their wanderings, the Aztecs had been divided into seven **calpulli**, or clans, a form of organization that they later expanded and adapted to their imperial position. The calpulli were no longer only kinship groups but also residential groupings, which might include neighbors, allies, and dependants. Much of Aztec local life was based on the calpulli, which performed important functions such as distributing land to heads of households, organizing labor gangs and military units in times of war, and maintaining a temple and school. Calpulli were governed by councils of family heads, but not all families were equal, nor were all calpulli of equal status.

The calpulli obviously had been the ancient and basic building block of Aztec society. In the origins of Aztec society every person, noble, and commoner had belonged to a calpulli but as Aztec power increased, the calpulli had been transformed, and other forms of social stratification had emerged. As the empire expanded, a class of nobility emerged, based on certain privileged families in the most distinguished calpulli. Originating from the lineages that headed calpulli and from marriages, military achievements, or service to the state, this group of nobles accumulated high offices, private lands, and other advantages. The most prominent families in the calpulli, those who had dominated leadership roles and formed a kind of local nobility, eventually were overshadowed by the military and administrative nobility of the Aztec state.

Although some commoners might be promoted to noble status, most nobles were born into the class. Nobles controlled the priesthood and the military leadership. In fact, the military was organized into various ranks based on experience and success in taking captives (Figure 16.5). Military virtues were linked to the cult of sacrifice and infused the whole society; they became the justification for the nobility's status. The "flowery death," or death while taking prisoners for the sacrificial knife, was the fitting end to a noble life and ensured eternity in the highest heaven—a reward also promised to women who died in childbirth. The military was highly ritualized. There were orders of warriors: The Jaguar and Eagle "Knights" and other groups each had a distinctive uniform and ritual and fought together as units. Banners, cloaks, and other insignia marked off the military ranks.

The social gulf that separated the nobility, or *pipiltin* from the commoners was widening as the empire grew. Egalitarian principles that may have existed in Aztec life disappeared, as happened among the warring Germanic tribes of early medieval Europe. Social distinctions were made apparent by the use of and restrictions on clothing, hairstyles, uniforms, and other symbols of rank. The imperial family became the most distinguished of the pipiltin families.

As the nobility broke free from their old calpulli and acquired private lands, a new class of workers almost like serfs was created to serve as laborers on these lands. Unlike the commoners attached to the land-controlling calpulli, these workers did not control land and worked at the will of others. Their status was low, but it was still above that of the slaves, who might have been war captives, criminals, or people who had sold themselves into bondage to escape hunger. Finally, there were other social groups. The scribes, artisans, and healers all were part of an intermediate group that was especially important in the larger cities. The long-distance merchants formed a sort of calpulli with their own patron gods, privileges, and internal divisions. They sometimes served as spies or agents for the Aztec military, but they were subject to restrictions that hindered their entry into or rivalry with the nobility.

It is possible to see an emerging conflict between the nobility and the commoners and to interpret this as a class struggle, but some specialists emphasize that to interpret Aztec society on that basis is to impose Western concepts on a different reality. Corporate bodies such as the calpulli, temple maintenance associations, and occupational groups cut across class and remained important in Aztec life. Competition between corporate groups often was more apparent and more violent than competition between social classes.

Overcoming Technological Constraints

Membership in society was thus defined by participation in various wider groups, such as the calpulli or a specific social class. It was also defined by gender roles. Aztec women assumed a variety of roles. Peasant women helped in the fields, but their primary domain was the household, where child-rearing and cooking took up much time. Above all, weaving skill was highly regarded. The responsibility for training young girls fell on the older women. Marriages often were arranged between lineages, and virginity at marriage was highly regarded for young women. Polygamy existed among the nobility, but the peasants were monogamous. Aztec women could inherit property and pass it to their heirs. The rights of Aztec women seem to have been fully recognized, but in political and social life their role, although complementary to that of men, remained subordinate.

FIGURE **16.5** In the militarized society of the Aztec empire, warriors were organized into regiments and groups distinguished by their uniforms. They gained rank and respect by capturing enemies for sacrifice. Note the symbolic gripping of the defeated captives' hair as a sign of military success.

 Read the Document on MyHistoryLab: The Midwife Addresses the Woman Who Has Died in Childbirth—Anonymous

The technology of the Americas limited social development in a variety of ways. Here we can see a significant difference between the lives of women in Mesoamerica and in the Mediterranean world. In the maize-based economies of Mesoamerica, women spent six hours a day grinding corn by hand on stone boards, or *metates*, to prepare the household's food. Although similar hand techniques were used in ancient Egypt, they were eventually replaced by animal- or water-powered mills that turned wheat into flour. The miller or baker of Rome or medieval Europe could do the work of hundreds of women. Maize was among the simplest and most productive cereals to grow but among the most time-consuming to prepare. Without the wheel or suitable animals for power, the Indian civilizations were unable to free women from the 30 to 40 hours a week that went into preparing the basic food.

Finally, we must consider the size of the population of the Aztec state. Estimates have varied widely, from as little as 1.5 million to more than 25 million, but there is considerable evidence that population density was high, resulting in a total population that was far greater than previously

DOCUMENT

Aztec Women and Men

IN THE MID-16TH CENTURY, BERNARDINO DE Sahagún, a Spanish missionary, prepared an extraordinary encyclopedia of Aztec culture. His purpose was to gather this information to learn the customs and beliefs of the Indians and their language in order to better convert them. Although Sahagún hated the Indian religion, he came to admire many aspects of their culture. His *Florentine Codex: The General History of the Things of New Spain* is one of the first ethnographies and a remarkable compendium of Aztec culture. Sahagún used many Indian informants to tell him about the days before the European arrival, and even though this work dates from the postconquest era, it contains much useful information about earlier Aztec life.

In the following excerpts, the proper behavior for people in different roles in Aztec society are described by the Aztecs themselves.

FATHER

One's father is the source of lineage. He is the sincere one. One's father is diligent, solicitous, compassionate, sympathetic, a careful administrator of his household. He rears, he teaches others, he advises, he admonishes one. He is exemplary; he leads a model life. He stores up for himself; he stores up for others. He cares for his assets; he saves for others. He is thrifty; he saves for the future, teaches thrift. He regulates, distributes with care, establishes order.

The bad father is incompassionate, negligent, unreliable. He is unfeeling . . . a shirker, a loafer, a sullen worker.

MOTHER

One's mother has children; she suckles them. Sincere, vigilant, agile, she is an energetic worker—diligent, watchful, solicitous, full of anxiety. She teaches people; she is attentive to them. She caresses, she serves others; she is apprehensive for their welfare; she is careful, thrifty—constantly at work.

The bad mother is evil, dull, stupid, sleepy, lazy. She is a squanderer, a petty thief, a deceiver, a fraud. Unreliable, she is one who loses things through neglect or anger, who heeds no one. She is disrespectful, inconsiderate, disregarding, careless. She shows the way to disobedience; she expounds nonconformity.

THE RULERS

The ruler is a shelter—fierce, revered, famous, esteemed, well-reputed, renowned.

The good ruler is a protector: one who carries his subjects in his arms, who unites them, who brings them together. He rules, he takes responsibilities, assumes burdens. He carries his subjects in his cape; he bears them in his arms. He governs; he is obeyed. To him as a shelter, as refuge, there is recourse. . . .

The bad ruler is a wild beast, a demon of the air, an ocelot, a wolf—infamous, avoided, detested as a respecter of nothing. He terrifies with his gaze; he makes the earth rumble; he implants; he spreads fear. He is wished dead.

THE NOBLE

The noble has a mother, a father. He resembles his parents. The good noble is obedient, cooperative, a follower of his parents' ways, a discreet worker; attentive, willing. He follows the ways of his parents; he resembles his father; he becomes his father's successor; he assumes his lot.

One of noble lineage is a follower of the exemplary life, a taker of the good example of others, a seeker, a follower of the exemplary life. He speaks eloquently; he is soft-spoken, virtuous, deserving of gratitude. He is noble of heart, gentle of word, discreet, well-reared, well-taught. He is moderate, energetic, inquiring, inquisitive. He scratches the earth with a thorn. He is one who fasts, who starves his entrails, who parches his lips. He provides nourishment to others. He sustains one, he serves food, he provides comfort. He is a concealer [of himself], a belittler of himself. He magnifies and praises others. He is a mourner for the dead, a doer of penances, a gracious speaker, devout, godly, desirable, wanted, memorable.

The bad noble is ungrateful and forgetful, a debaser, a disparager of things, contemptuous of others, arrogant, bragging. He creates disorder, glories over his lineage, extols his own virtues.

THE MATURE COMMON WOMAN

The good mature woman is candid. She is resolute, firm of heart, constant—not to be dismayed; brave like a man; vigorous, resolute, persevering—not one to falter. She is long-suffering; she accepts reprimands calmly—endures things like a man. She becomes firm—takes courage. She is intent. She gives of herself. She goes in humility. She exerts herself.

The bad woman is thin, tottering, weak—an inconstant companion, unfriendly. She annoys others, chagrins them, shames, oppresses one. She becomes impatient; she loses hope, becomes embarrassed—chagrined. Evil is her life; she lives in shame.

THE WEAVER OF DESIGNS

She concerns herself with using thread, works with thread. The good weaver of designs is skilled—a maker of varicolored capes, an outliner of designs, a blender of colors, a joiner of pieces, a matcher of pieces, a person of good memory. She does things dexterously. She weaves designs. She selects. She weaves tightly. She forms borders. She forms the neck. . . .

The bad weaver of designs is untrained—silly, foolish, unobservant, unskilled of hand, ignorant, stupid. She tangles the thread, she harms her work—she spoils it.

(continued on next page)

THE PHYSICIAN

The physician is a knower of herbs, of roots, of trees, of stones; she is experienced in these. She is one who conducts examinations; she is a woman of experience, of trust, of professional skill: a counselor.

The good physician is a restorer, a provider of health, a relaxer—one who makes people feel well, who envelops one in ashes. She cures people; she provides them health; she lances them; she bleeds them . . . pierces them with an obsidian lancet.

QUESTIONS

- In what ways do the expectations for men and women differ in Aztec society?
- To what extent do the roles for men and women in Aztec society differ from our own?
- Did the Aztecs value the same characteristics as our own and other historical societies?

suspected. Some historical demographers estimate that the population of central Mexico under Aztec control reached over 20 million, excluding the Maya areas. This underlines the extraordinary ability of the Aztec state to intimidate and control such vast numbers of people.

A Tribute Empire

Each city-state was ruled by a speaker chosen from the nobility. The Great Speaker, the ruler of Tenochtitlan, was first among supposed equals. He was in effect the emperor, with great private wealth and public power, and was increasingly considered a living god. His court was magnificent and surrounded with elaborate rituals. Those who approached him could not look him in the eye and were required to throw dirt upon their heads as a sign of humility. In theory he was elected, but his election was really a choice between siblings of the same royal family. The prime minister held a position of tremendous power and usually was a close relative of the ruler. There was a governing council; in theory, the rulers of the other cities in the alliance also had a say in government, but in reality most power was in the hands of the Aztec ruler and his chief advisor.

During the century of greatest Aztec expansion after 1426, a social and political transformation had taken place. The position and nature of the old calpulli clans had changed radically, and a newly powerful nobility with a deified and nearly absolute ruler had emerged. The ancient cult of military virtues had been elevated to a supreme position as the religion of the state, and the double purpose of securing tribute for the state and obtaining victims for Huitzilopochtli drove further Aztec conquests.

The empire was never integrated, and local rulers often stayed in place to act as tribute collectors for the Aztec overlords. In many ways the Aztec empire was simply an expansion of long-existing Mesoamerican concepts and institutions of government, and it was not unlike the subject city-states over which it gained control. These city-states, in turn, were often left unchanged if they recognized Aztec supremacy and met their obligations of labor and tribute. Tribute payments served both an economic and a political function, concentrating power and wealth in the Aztec capital. Archeologists at the recent excavations of the Great Temple beneath the center of Mexico City have been impressed by the large number of offerings and objects that came from the farthest ends of the empire and beyond. At the frontiers, neighboring states such as that of the Tarascans of Michoacan in West Central Mexico preserved their freedom, while within the empire enclaves of independent kingdoms such as Tlaxcala (tlaks-KAHL-uh) maintained a fierce opposition to the Aztecs. There were many revolts against Aztec rule or a particular tribute burden, which the Aztecs often put down ruthlessly.

In general, the Aztec system was a success because it aimed at exerting political domination and not necessarily direct administrative or territorial control. In the long run, however, the increasing social stresses created by the rise of the nobles and the system of terror and tribute imposed on subject peoples were internal weaknesses that contributed to the Aztec empire's collapse.

The Aztecs were a continuation of the long process of civilization in Mesoamerica. The civilizations of the classic era did not simply disappear in central Mexico or among the Maya in Yucatan and Central America, but they were reinterpreted and adapted to new political and social realities. When Europeans arrived in Mexico, they assumed that what they found was the culmination of Indian civilization, when in fact it was the militarized afterglow of earlier achievements.

TWANTINSUYU: WORLD OF THE INCAS

After about 1300 C.E., the Inca empire emerged in the highlands of Peru and eventually spread its control over the whole region by integrating many ethnic groups into an extensive imperial state.

16.3 What were the principal causes of the expansion of the Inca empire?

Almost at the same time that the Aztecs extended their control over much of Mesoamerica, a great imperial state was rising in the Andean highlands, and it eventually became an empire some 3000 miles in extent (Map 16.2). The Inca empire incorporated many aspects of previous Andean cultures but fused them together in new ways. With a genius for state organization and bureaucratic control over peoples of different cultures and languages, it achieved a level of integration and domination previously unknown in the Americas.

Throughout the Andean cultural hearth, after the breakup of the large "intermediate horizon" states of Tihuanaco and Huari (c. 550–1000 C.E.), several smaller regional states continued to exercise some power. Unlike the breakdown of power that took place in postclassic Mesoamerica, in the Andean zone many large states continued to be important. Some states in the Andean highlands on the broad open areas near Lake Titicaca and the states along rivers on the north coast, such as those in the Moche valley, remained centers of agricultural activity and population density. This was a period of war between rival local chiefdoms and small states and in some ways was an Andean parallel to the post-Toltec militaristic era in Mesoamerica. Of these states, the coastal kingdom of Chimor, centered on its capital of Chan-Chan, emerged as the most powerful. Between 900 and its conquest by the Incas in 1465, it gained control of most of the north coast of Peru.

Pachacuti [PACH-uh-KOO-tee] Ruler of Inca society from 1438 to 1471; launched a series of military campaigns that gave Incas control of the region from Cuzco to the shores of Lake Titicaca.

ayllus [EYEL-lehs] Households in Andean societies that recognized some form of kinship; traced descent from some common, sometimes mythical ancestor.

The Inca Rise to Power

While Chimor spread its control over 600 miles of the coast, in the southern Andean highlands, where there were few large urban areas, ethnic groups and small states struggled over the legacy of Tihuanaco. Among these groups were several related Quechua-speaking clans, or **ayllus**, living near Cuzco, an area that had been under the influence of Huari but had not been particularly important. Their own legends stated that 10 related clans emerged from caves in the region and were taken to Cuzco by a mythical leader. Wherever their origins, by about 1350 C.E. they lived in and around Cuzco, and by 1438 they had defeated their hostile neighbors in the area. At this point under their ruler, or *inca*, **Pachacuti** (r. 1438–1471), they launched a series of military alliances and campaigns that brought them control of the whole area from Cuzco to the shores of Lake Titicaca.

Over the next 60 years, Inca armies were constantly on the march, extending control over a vast territory. Pachacuti's son and successor, Topac Yupanqui (TOH-pak YUH-pan-KEE), conquered the northern coastal kingdom of Chimor by seizing its irrigation system, and he extended Inca control into the southern area of what is now Ecuador. At the other end of the empire, Inca armies reached the Maule River in Chile against stiff resistance from the Araucanian Indians. The next ruler, Huayna Capac (WEYE-nah kah-PAHK) (r. 1493–1527), consolidated these conquests and suppressed rebellions on the frontiers. By the time of his death, the Inca Empire—or, as they called it, **Twantinsuyu**—stretched from what is now Colombia to Chile and eastward across Lake Titicaca and Bolivia to northern Argentina. Between 9 and 13 million people of different ethnic backgrounds and languages came under Inca rule, a remarkable feat, given the extent of the empire and the technology available for transportation and communication.

Inca Empire
- To 1438
- To 1471
- To 1493
- To 1527

MAP **16.2 Inca Expansion** Each ruler expanded the empire in a series of campaigns to increase wealth and political control.

Conquest and Religion

What impelled the Inca conquest and expansion? The usual desire for economic gain and political power that we have seen in other empires is one possible explanation, but there may be others more in keeping with Inca culture and ideology. The cult of the ancestors was extremely important in Inca belief. Deceased rulers were mummified and then treated as intermediaries

VISUALIZING THE PAST

Archeological Evidence of Political Practices

THE INCA SYSTEM OF SPLIT INHERITANCE probably originated in the Chimu kingdom. Chimu king lists recorded 10 rulers' names. Excavations at Chan-Chan, the Chimu capital, have revealed 10 large walled structures. Archeologists believe that each of these palatial compounds was a different king's residence and that each became a mausoleum for his mummy upon his death.

QUESTIONS

- To what extent does such evidence indicate the composite nature of Inca culture?
- What are some of the possible problems of archeological interpretation?
- To what extent can material remains be used to explain or illustrate social phenomena?

Chan-Chan covered more than 2 square miles. It contained palace compounds, storehouses, residences, markets, and other structures.

City of Chan-Chan.

with the gods, paraded in public during festivals, offered food and gifts, and consulted on important matters by special oracles. From the Chimor kingdom the Incas adopted the practice of royal **split inheritance**, whereby all the political power and titles of the ruler went to his successor but all his palaces, wealth, land, and possessions remained in the hands of his male descendants, who used them to support the cult of the dead Inca's mummy for eternity. To ensure his own cult and place for eternity, each new Inca needed to secure land and wealth, and these normally came as part of new conquests. In effect, the greater the number of past rulers, the greater the number of royal courts to support, and the greater the demand for labor, lands, and tribute. This system created a self-perpetuating need for expansion, tied directly to ancestor worship and the cult of the royal mummies, as well as tensions between the various royal lineages. The cult of the dead weighed heavily on the living.

Twantinsuyu [twahn-tihn-SOO-yoo] Word for Inca empire; region from present-day Colombia to Chile and eastward to northern Argentina.

split inheritance Inca practice of descent; all titles and political power went to successor, but wealth and land remained in hands of male descendants for support of cult of dead Inca's mummy.

Inca political and social life was infused with religious meaning. Like the Aztecs, the Incas held the sun to be the highest deity and considered the Inca to be the sun's representative on earth. The magnificent **Temple of the Sun** in Cuzco was the center of the state religion, and in its confines the mummies of the past Incas were kept. The cult of the sun was spread throughout the empire, but the Incas did not prohibit the worship of local gods.

Other deities were also worshiped as part of the state religion. Viracocha (vee-reh-KOH-chuh), a creator god, was a favorite of Inca Pachacuti and remained important. Popular belief was based on a profound animism that endowed many natural phenomena with spiritual power. Mountains, stones, rivers, caves, tombs, and temples were considered *huacas*, or holy shrines. At these places, prayers were offered and animals, goods, and humans were sacrificed. In the Cuzco area, imaginary lines running from the Temple of the Sun organized the huacas into groups for which certain ayllus took responsibility. The temples were served by many priests and women dedicated to preparing cloth and food for sacrifice. The temple priests were responsible mainly for the great festivals and celebrations and for the divinations on which state actions often depended.

Temple of the Sun Inca religious center located at Cuzco; center of state religion; held mummies of past Incas.

The Techniques of Inca Imperial Rule

The Inca were able to control their vast empire by using techniques and practices that ensured cooperation or subordination. The empire was ruled by the Inca, who was considered almost a god. He ruled from his court at Cuzco, which was also the site of the major temple; the high priest usually was a close relative. Twantinsuyu was divided into four great provinces, each under a governor, and then divided again. The Incas developed a state bureaucracy in which almost all nobles played a role. Although some chroniclers spoke of a state organization based on decimal units of 10,000, 1000, 100, and smaller numbers of households to mobilize taxes and labor, recent research reveals that many local practices and variations were allowed to continue under Inca rule. Local rulers, or *curacas*, were allowed to maintain their positions and were given privileges by the Inca in return for their loyalty. The curacas were exempt from tribute obligations and usually received labor or produce from those under their control. For insurance, the sons of conquered chieftains were taken to Cuzco for their education.

tambos Way stations used by Incas as inns and storehouses; supply centers for Inca armies on the move; relay points for system of runners used to carry messages.

mita Labor extracted for lands assigned to the state and the religion; all communities were expected to contribute; an essential aspect of Inca imperial control.

The Incas intentionally spread the Quechua (KEHCH-uh-wah) language as a means of integrating the empire. The Incas also made extensive use of colonists. Sometimes Quechua-speakers from Cuzco were settled in a newly won area to provide an example and a garrison. On other occasions, the Incas moved a conquered population to a new home. Throughout the empire, a complex system of roads was built, with bridges and causeways when needed (Map 16.3). Along these roads, way stations, or **tambos**, were placed about a day's walk apart to serve as inns, storehouses, and supply centers for Inca armies on the move. Tambos also served as relay points for the system of runners who carried messages throughout the empire. The Inca probably maintained more than 10,000 tambos.

The Inca empire extracted land and labor from subject populations. Conquered peoples were enlisted in the Inca armies under Inca officers and were rewarded with goods from new conquests. Subject peoples received access to goods not previously available to them, and the Inca state undertook large building and irrigation projects that formerly would have been impossible. In return, the Incas demanded loyalty and tribute. The state claimed all resources and redistributed them. The Incas divided conquered areas into lands for the people, lands for the state, and lands for the sun—that is, for religion and the support of priests. Also, some nobles held private estates.

With few exceptions the Incas, unlike the Aztecs, did not demand tribute in kind but rather exacted labor on the lands assigned to the state and the religion. Communities were expected to take turns working on state and church lands and sometimes on building projects or in mining. These labor turns, or **mita**, were an essential aspect of Inca control. In addition, the Inca required women to weave high-quality cloth for the court and for religious

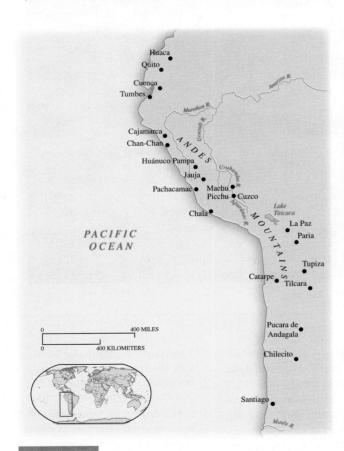

MAP **16.3 The Ancient Cities of Peru** The Inca system of roads, with its series of tambos, linked major towns and cities and allowed rapid communication and troop movement.

THINKING HISTORICALLY

The "Troubling" Civilizations of the Americas

FROM THE FIRST ENCOUNTER WITH THE peoples of the Americas, European concepts and judgments about civilization, barbarism, morality, power, politics, and justice were constantly called into question. The American Indian societies had many religious ideas and practices that shocked Christian observers, and aspects of their social and familial arrangements clashed with European sensibilities. Those sensibilities often were influenced by religious and political considerations. Many of those who most condemned human sacrifice, polygamy, or the despotism of Indian rulers were also those who tried to justify European conquest and control, mass violence, and theft on a continental scale. Other European voices also were heard. Not long after the Spanish conquests in the 16th century, defenders of Indian rights came forward to argue that despite certain "unfortunate" habits, Indian civilization was no less to be admired than that of the ancient (and pagan) Romans and Greeks.

For Western civilization, evaluating and judging non-Western or past societies has always been a complex business that has mixed elements of morality, politics, religion, and self-perception along with the record of what is observed or considered to be reality. That complexity is probably just as true for Chinese, Persian, or any culture trying to understand another. Still, Western society seems to have been particularly troubled by the American civilizations, with their peculiar combination of Neolithic technology and imperial organization. At times this has led to abhorrence and rejection—as of Aztec sacrifice—but at other times it has led to a kind of utopian romanticism in which the accomplishments of the Indian past are used as a critique of the present and a political program for the future.

The existence of **Inca socialism** is a case in point. Some early Spanish authors portrayed Inca rule as despotic, but others saw it as a kind of utopia. Shortly after the conquest of Peru, Garcilaso de la Vega, the son of a Spaniard and an Indian noblewoman, wrote a glowing history of his mother's people in which he presented an image of the Inca empire as a carefully organized system in which every community contributed to the whole, and the state regulated the distribution of resources on the basis of need and reciprocity. There was some truth in this view, but it ignored some aspects of exploitation as well. In the 20th century, Peruvian socialists, faced with underdevelopment and social inequality in their country, used this utopian view of Inca society as a possible model for their own future. Their interpretation and that of historians who later wrote of Inca socialism tended to ignore the hierarchy in the Inca empire and the fact that the state extracted labor and goods from the subject communities to support the

Perhaps nothing challenges our appreciation of the American civilizations more than the extensive evidence of ritual torture and human sacrifice.

nobles, who held extensive power. The utopian view of the Incas was no less political than the despotic view. Perhaps the lesson here is that what we see in the past often depends on what we think about the present or what we want for the future.

But if Inca socialism and despotism have fascinated students of the past, Aztec religion has caught the imagination of historians and the general public. It causes us to ask how a civilization as advanced as this could engage in a practice so cruel and, to us, so morally reprehensible. Perhaps nothing challenges our appreciation of the American civilizations more than the extensive evidence of ritual torture and human sacrifice, which among the Aztecs reached staggering proportions. On some occasions thousands of people were slain, usually by having their hearts ripped out.

First, we must put these practices in perspective. Cruelty and violence can be found in many cultures, and to a world that has seen genocide, mass killings, and atomic warfare, the Aztec practices are not so different from what our own age has seen. Certain customs in many past civilizations and present cultures seem to us strange, cruel, and immoral. We find Aztec human sacrifice particularly abhorrent, but such practices also were found among the ancient Canaanites and the Celtic peoples, and the Old Testament story of Abraham and Isaac, although its message is against such sacrifice, reflects a practice known in the ancient Near East. Human sacrifice was practiced in pre-Christian Scandinavia and ancient India. Although by the time of Confucius human sacrifice of wives and retainers at the burial of a ruler was no longer practiced in China, the custom had been known. Sati, the Hindu ritual suicide of the widow on the funeral pyre of her husband, existed in India in the 19th century, although admittedly it may have been exaggerated by the British colonial authorities. The Aztecs certainly were not alone in taking human life as a religious rite. Whatever our moral judgments about such customs, it remains the historian's responsibility to understand them in the context of their own culture and time.

How have historians tried to explain or understand Aztec human sacrifice? Some defenders of Aztec culture have seen it as a limited phenomenon, greatly exaggerated by the Spanish for political purposes. Many scholars have seen it as a religious act central to the Aztec belief that humans must sacrifice that which was most precious to them—life—to receive the sun, rain, and other blessings of the gods that make life possible. Others have viewed Aztec practice as the intentional manipulation and expansion of a widespread phenomenon that had long existed among many American peoples. In other words, the Aztec rulers, priests,

(continued on next page)

(continued from previous page)

and nobility used the cult of war and large-scale human sacrifice for political purposes, to terrorize their neighbors and subdue the lower classes. Another possible explanation is demographic. If central Mexico was as densely populated as we believe, then the sacrifices may have been a kind of population control.

Other interpretations have been even more startling. Anthropologist Marvin Harris has suggested that Aztec sacrifice, accompanied by ritual cannibalism, was a response to a lack of protein. He argued that in the Old World, human sacrifice was replaced by animal sacrifice, but in Mesoamerica, which lacked cattle and sheep, that transformation never took place. Harris called the Aztec empire a "cannibal kingdom." Other scholars have strongly objected to Harris's interpretation of the evidence, which gave little attention to the ritual aspects of these acts. Still, human sacrifice shades all assessments of Aztec civilization.

These debates ultimately raise important questions about the role of moral judgments in historical analysis and the way in which our vision of the past is influenced by our own political, moral, ethical, and social programs. We cannot and perhaps should not abandon those programs, but we must always try to understand other times and other peoples in their own terms.

QUESTIONS
- What special features of Aztec civilization must be explained?
- Are they really distinctive?
- What explanations are most persuasive in terms of historical sensitivity and contemporary standards?
- What features of 21st-century society are similar to those of Aztec civilization and will later need to be explained?

Inca socialism A view created by Spanish authors to describe Inca society as a type of utopia; image of the Inca empire as a carefully organized system in which every community collectively contributed to the whole.

purposes. The Incas provided the wool, but each household was required to produce cloth. Woven cloth, a great Andean art form, had political and religious significance. Some women were taken as concubines for the Inca; others were selected as servants at the temples, the so-called Virgins of the Sun. In all this, the Inca had an overall imperial system but remained sensitive to local variations, so that its application accommodated regional and ethnic differences.

In theory, each community aimed at self-sufficiency and depended on the state for goods it could not acquire easily. The ayllus of each community controlled the land, and the vast majority of the men were peasants and herders. Women worked in the fields, wove cloth, and cared for the household (Figure 16.6). Roles and obligations were gender-specific and, at least in theory, equal and interdependent. Andean peoples recognized parallel descent, so that property rights within the ayllus and among the nobility passed in both the male and female lines. Women passed rights and property to daughters, men to sons. Whether in pre-Inca times women may have served as leaders of ayllus is open to question, but under the Incas this seems to have been uncommon. The Inca emphasis on military virtues reinforced the inequality of men and women.

The concept of close cooperation between men and women was also reflected in the Inca view of the cosmos. Gods and goddesses were worshiped by men and women, but women felt a particular affinity for the moon and the goddesses of the earth and corn: the fertility deities. The Inca queen, the Inca's senior wife (usually also a sister of the Inca), was seen as a link to the moon. Queen and sister of the sun, she represented imperial authority to all women. But despite an ideology of gender equality, Inca practice created a gender hierarchy that paralleled the dominance of the Inca state over subject peoples. This fact is supported, and the power of the empire over local ethnic groups is demonstrated, by the Incas' ability to select the most beautiful young women to serve the temples or be given to the Inca.

The integration of imperial policy with regional and ethnic diversity was a political achievement. Ethnic headmen were left in place, but over them were administrators drawn from the Inca nobility in Cuzco. Reciprocity and hierarchy continued to characterize Andean groups as they came under Inca rule; reciprocity between the state and the local community was simply an added level. The Inca state could provide roads, irrigation projects, and hard-to-get goods. For example, maize usually was grown on irrigated land and was particularly important as a ritual crop. State-sponsored irrigation added to its cultivation. The Inca state manipulated the idea of reciprocity to extract labor power, and it dealt harshly with resistance and revolt. In addition to the ayllu peasantry, there was also a class of people, the **yanas**, who were removed from their ayllus and served permanently as servants, artisans, or workers for the Inca or the nobility.

yanas A class of people within Inca society removed from their ayllus to serve permanently as servants, artisans, or workers for the Inca or the Inca nobility.

Members of the Inca nobility were greatly privileged, and those related to the Inca himself held the highest positions. The nobility were all drawn from the 10 royal ayllus. In addition, the residents of Cuzco were given noble status to enable them to serve in high bureaucratic posts. The nobles were distinguished by dress and custom. Only they were entitled to wear the large ear spools that enlarged the ears and caused the Spaniards to later call them *orejones*, or "big ears." Noticeably absent in most of the Inca empire was a distinct merchant class. Unlike in Mesoamerica, where long-distance trade was so important, the Incas' emphasis on self-sufficiency and state regulation of production and surplus limited trade. Only in the northern areas of the empire, in the chiefdoms of Ecuador, the last region brought under Inca control, did a specialized class of traders exist.

The Inca imperial system, which controlled an area of almost 3000 miles, was a stunning achievement of statecraft, but like all other empires it lasted only as long as it could control its subject populations and its own mechanisms of government. A system of royal multiple marriages as a way of forging alliances created rival claimants for power and the possibility of civil war. That is exactly what happened in the 1520s, just before the Europeans arrived. When the Spanish first arrived in Peru, they saw an empire weakened by civil strife.

Inca Cultural Achievements

The Incas drew on the artistic traditions of their Andean predecessors and the skills of subject peoples. Beautiful pottery and cloth were produced in specialized workshops. Inca metalworking was among the most advanced in the Americas, and Inca artisans worked gold and silver with great skill. The Incas also used copper and some bronze for weapons and tools. Like the Mesoamerican peoples, the Incas made no practical use of the wheel, but unlike them, they had no system of writing. However, the Incas did use a system of knotted strings, or **quipu**, to record numerical and perhaps other information. It worked like an abacus, and with it the Incas took censuses and kept financial records. The Incas had a passion for numerical order, and the population was divided into decimal units from which population, military enlistment, and work details could be calculated. The existence of so many traits associated with civilization in the Old World combined with the absence of a system of writing among the Incas illustrates the variations of human development and the dangers of becoming too attached to certain cultural characteristics or features in defining civilizations.

The Incas' genius was best displayed in their land and water management, extensive road system, statecraft, and architecture and public buildings. They developed ingenious agricultural terraces on the steep slopes of the Andes, using a complex technology of irrigation to water their crops. The empire was linked together by almost 2500 miles of roads, many of which included rope suspension bridges over mountain gorges and rivers. Inca stonecutting was remarkably accurate; the best buildings were built of large fitted stones without the use of mortar. Some of these buildings were immense. These structures, the large agricultural terraces and irrigation projects, and the extensive system of roads were among the Incas' greatest achievements, displaying their technical ability as well as their ability to mobilize large amounts of labor.

Comparing Incas and Aztecs

The Inca and the Aztec cultures were based on a long development of civilization that preceded them. Although in some areas of artistic and intellectual achievement earlier peoples had surpassed their accomplishments, both cultures represented the success of imperial and military organization. Both empires were based on intensive agriculture organized by a state that accumulated surplus production and then controlled the circulation of goods and their redistribution to groups or social classes, although the well-developed merchant class of Mesoamerica was mostly absent in the Inca realm. In both states, older kinship-based institutions, the ayllu and the calpulli, were transformed by the emergence of a social hierarchy in which the nobility was increasingly predominant. In both areas, these nobles also were the personnel of the state, so that the state organization was almost an image of society.

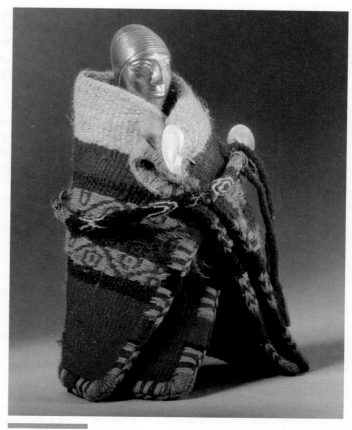

FIGURE 16.6 This Inca sculpture, made of gold, portrays one of the mamaconas, or "chosen women," who served as concubines to the Inca emperors. The wool of her cloak is woven in a classic Inca design.

quipu [KEE-poo] System of knotted strings utilized by the Incas in place of a writing system; could contain numerical and other types of information for censuses and financial records.

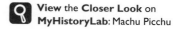

View the **Closer Look** on **MyHistoryLab**: Machu Picchu

Although the Incas tried to create an overarching political state and to integrate their empire as a unit (the Aztecs did less in this regard), both empires recognized local ethnic groups and political leaders and allowed variation from one group or region to another as long as Inca or Aztec sovereignty was recognized and tribute paid. Both the Aztecs and the Incas, like the Spaniards who followed them, found that their military power was less effective against nomadic peoples who lived on their frontiers. Essentially, the empires were created by the conquest of sedentary agricultural peoples and the extraction of tribute and labor from them.

We cannot overlook the great differences between Mesoamerica and the Andean region in terms of climate and geography or the differences between the Inca and Aztec civilizations. Trade and markets were far more developed in the Aztec empire and earlier in Mesoamerica in general than in the Andean world. There were differences in metallurgy, writing systems, and social definition and hierarchy. But within the context of world civilizations, it is probably best to view these two empires and the cultural areas they represent as variations of similar patterns and processes, of which sedentary agriculture is the most important. Basic similarities underlying the variations can also be seen in systems of belief and cosmology and in social structure. Whether similar origins, direct or indirect contact between the areas, or parallel development in Mesoamerica and the Andean area explains the similarity is unknown. But the American Indian civilizations shared much with each other; that factor and their isolation from external cultural and biological influences gave them their peculiar character and their vulnerability. At the same time, their ability to survive the shock of conquest and contribute to the formation of societies after conquest demonstrates much of their strength. Long after the Aztec and Inca empires had ceased to exist, the peoples of the Andes and Mexico continued to draw on these cultural traditions.

THE OTHER PEOPLES OF THE AMERICAS

The civilizations of Mesoamerica and the Andes, were high points of a Native American cultural achievement. However, the Americas continued to be occupied by a variety of peoples who lived in different ways, ranging from highly complex sedentary agricultural empires to simple kin-based bands of hunters and gatherers.

16.4   What were the characteristic economic forms of American groups outside the two great imperial territories?

Rather than seeing a division between "primitive" and "civilized" peoples in the Americas, it is more useful to consider gradations of material culture and social complexity. Groups such as the Incas had many things in common with the tribal peoples of the Amazon basin, such as the division into clans or halves—that is, a division of villages or communities into two major groupings with mutually agreed-upon roles and obligations. Moreover, as we have seen, the diversity of ancient America forces us to reconsider ideas of human development based on Old World examples. Social complexity, for example, was not necessarily dependent on agriculture. In the Americas, some groups of fishers and hunters and gatherers, such as the peoples of the northwest coast of the United States and British Columbia, developed complex hierarchical societies. For those who see control of water for agriculture as the starting point for political authority and the state, such societies as the Pimas of Colorado and some of the chiefdoms of South America, who practiced irrigated agriculture but did not develop states, also provide exceptions to theories based on Old World evidence. Finally, archaeological finds in the Amazon now suggest that pottery and agriculture may have developed there even before it did in the Andean region.

How Many People?

A major issue that has fascinated students of the Americas for centuries is the question of population size. For years after the European conquests, many observers discounted the early descriptions of large and dense Indian populations as the exaggeration of conquerors and missionaries who wanted to make their own exploits seem more impressive. In the early 20th century, the most repeated estimate of Native American population about 1492 was 8.4 million (4 million in Mexico, 2 million in Peru, and 2.4 million in the rest of the hemisphere). Since that time, new archeological discoveries, a better understanding of the impact of disease on indigenous populations, new historical and demographic studies, and improved estimates of agricultural techniques and productivity have led to major revisions. Estimates still vary widely, and some have gone as high as 112 million at the time of contact. Most scholars agree that Mesoamerica and the Andes supported the largest populations. Table 16.1 summarizes one of the most careful estimates, which places the total figure at more than 67 million, although a Native American demographer has increased this figure to 72 million. Other scholars are still unconvinced by these estimates.

These figures should be considered in a global context. In 1500, the population of the rest of the world was probably about 500 million, of which China and India each had 75 to 150 million people and Europe had 60 to 70 million, a figure roughly equivalent to the population of the Americas (Table 16.2). If the modern estimates are valid, the peoples of the Americas clearly made up a major segment of humanity.

Differing Cultural Patterns

Although it is impossible to summarize the variety of cultural patterns and lifeways that existed in the Americas on the eve of contact with Europeans, we can describe the major patterns outside the main civilization areas. Northern South America and part of Central America were an intermediate area that shared many features with the Andes and some with Mesoamerica and perhaps served as a point of cultural and material exchange between the two regions. In fact, with the exception of monumental architecture, the intermediate zone chieftainships resembled the sedentary agriculture states in many ways.

Similar kinds of chieftainships based on sedentary agriculture were found elsewhere in the Americas. There is strong evidence of large chieftainships along the Amazon, where the rich aquatic environment supported complex and perhaps hierarchical societies. The island Arawaks or Tainos encountered by Columbus on the Caribbean island of Hispaniola were farmers organized in a hierarchical society and divided into chiefdoms. These Indian chiefdom-level societies strongly resemble the societies of Polynesia. On the bigger Caribbean islands, such as Hispaniola and Puerto Rico, chieftainships ruled over dense populations, which lived primarily on the root crop called manioc.

Agriculture was spread widely throughout the Americas by 1500. Some peoples, such as those of the eastern North American woodlands and the coast of Brazil, combined agriculture with hunting and fishing. Techniques such as slash-and-burn farming led to the periodic movement of villages when production declined. Social organization in these societies often remained without strong class divisions, craft specializations, or the demographic density of people who practiced permanent, intensive agriculture. Unlike Europe, Asia, and Africa, the Americas lacked nomadic herders. However, throughout the Americas, from Tierra del Fuego to the Canadian forests, some people lived in small, mobile, kin-based groups of hunters and gatherers. Their material culture was simple and their societies were more egalitarian.

Nowhere is Native American diversity more apparent than in North America. In that vast continent, by 1500, perhaps as many as 200 languages were spoken, and a variety of cultures reflected Indian adaptation to different ecological situations. By that time, most concentrated towns of the Mississippian mound-builder cultures had been abandoned, and only a few groups in southeastern North America still maintained the social hierarchy and religious ideas of those earlier cultures. In the Southwest, descendants of the Anasazi and other cliff dwellers had taken up residence in the adobe pueblos mostly along the Rio Grande (Figure 16.7), where they practiced terracing and irrigation to support their agriculture. Their rich religious life, their artistic ceramic and weaving traditions, and their agricultural base reflected their own historical traditions.

Elsewhere in North America, most groups were hunters and gatherers or, like the Iroquois of the northeast or the Natchez of the southeast, combined those activities with some agriculture. Sometimes an environment was so rich that complex social organization and artistic specialization could develop without an agricultural base. This was the case among the Indians of the northwest coast, who depended on the rich resources of the sea. In other cases, technology was a limiting factor. The tough prairie grasses could not be farmed easily without metal plows, nor could the buffalo be hunted effectively before Europeans introduced the horse. Thus, the Great Plains were only sparsely occupied.

TABLE 16.1 Population Estimate for the Western Hemisphere, 1492

Area	Population (thousands)
North America	4,400
Mexico	21,400
Central America	5,650
Caribbean	5,850
Andes	11,500
Lowland South America	18,500
Total	67,300

SOURCES: William M. Deneven, *The Native Population of the Americas in 1492* (1976), 289–292; John D. Durand, "Historical Estimates of World Population," *Population and Development Review* 3 (1957): 253–296; Russell Thornton, *American Indian Holocaust and Survival* (1987).

TABLE 16.2 World Population, c. 1500

Area	Population (thousands)
China	100,000–150,000
Indian subcontinent	75,000–150,000
Southwest Asia	20,000–30,000
Japan	15,000–20,000
Rest of Asia (except Russia)	15,000–30,000
Europe (except Russia)	60,000–70,000
Russia (USSR)	10,000–18,000
Northern Africa	6,000–12,000
Rest of Africa	30,000–60,000
Oceania	1,000–2,000
Americas	57,000–72,000
Total	389,000–614,000

SOURCES: William M. Deneven, *The Native Population of the Americas in 1492* (1976), 289–292; John D. Durand, "Historical Estimates of World Population," *Population and Development Review* 3 (1957): 253–296; Russell Thornton, *American Indian Holocaust and Survival* (1987).

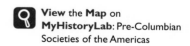
View the Map on MyHistoryLab: Pre-Columbian Societies of the Americas

FIGURE **16.7** Taos Pueblo, in the foothills of what is now New Mexico. The pueblos of the Rio Grande Valley were based on agriculture and the concentration of population in urban areas. This reflected a number of the traditions of the older Native American cultures of the southwestern United States.

Finally, we should note that although there was great variation among the Indian cultures, some aspects stood in contrast to contemporary societies in Europe and Asia. With the exception of the state systems of Mesoamerica and the Andes, most Indian societies were strongly kin-based. Communal action and ownership of resources, such as land and hunting grounds, were emphasized, and material wealth often was disregarded or placed in a ritual or religious context. It was not that these societies were necessarily egalitarian but rather that ranking usually was not based on wealth. Although often subordinate, women in some societies held important political and social roles and usually played a central role in crop production. Indians tended to view themselves as part of the ecological system and not in control of it, balancing their hunting or farming with existing resources. These attitudes stood in marked contrast to those of many contemporary European and Asian civilizations.

American Diversity in World Context

By the end of the 15th century, two great imperial systems had risen to dominate the two major centers of civilization in Mesoamerica and the Andes. Both empires were built on the achievements of their predecessors, and both reflected a militaristic phase in their area's development. These empires proved to be fragile, weakened by internal strains and the conflicts that any imperial system creates but also limited by their technological inferiority.

The Aztec and Inca empires were one end of a continuum of cultures that went from the most simple to the most complex. The Americas contained a broad range of societies, from great civilizations with millions of people to small bands of hunters. In many of these societies, religion played a dominant role in defining the relationship between people and their environment and between the individual and society. How these societies would have developed and what course the American civilizations might have taken in continued isolation remain interesting and unanswerable questions. The first European observers were simultaneously shocked by the "primitive" tribespeople and astounded by the wealth and accomplishments of civilizations such as that of the Aztecs. Europeans generally saw the Indians as curiously backward. In comparison with Europe and Asia, the Americas did seem strange—more like ancient Babylon or Egypt than contemporary China or Europe—except that without the wheel, large domesticated animals, the plow, and to a large extent metal tools and written languages, even that comparison is misleading. The isolation of the Americas had remained important in physical and cultural terms, but that isolation came to an end in 1492, with disastrous results.

Global Connections

THE AMERICAS AND THE WORLD

Conditions in the Americas before 1492 reveal the importance of global connections in Afro-Eurasia and the absence of such connections in the Americas. American isolation from effective global connections is exhibited by the absence of key technologies, like ironworking and the wheel, that would have been easily transmitted had contacts been available. American isolation shows in the absence of the standard range of domesticated animals. It would show, tragically, in the absence of any immunity to some of the common contagious diseases of Afro-Eurasia.

The absence of several features that had become normal in Afro-Eurasia must be stated carefully. It should not detract from the impressive economic, cultural, and political achievements of the key American Indian civilizations, including their ability (particularly in Mesoamerica) to sustain dense populations. It should not obscure the heritage of these societies to later patterns in the Americas. The comparative distinctions that resulted from lack of wider contact would count only when the Americas were forced into new global connections after 1492—but then they mattered greatly.

Further Readings

Charles C. Mann, *1491* (2005) provides a well-written overview of many aspects of Native American cultures and accomplishments. Mary Miller, *Art of Mesoamerica: From Olmec to Aztec* (2006) surveys evidence from archaeology and art history. Friedrich Katz's *The Ancient Civilizations of the Americas*, 2nd revised ed. (1997), provides the best overall survey that compares Mesoamerica and Peru. It traces the rise of civilization in both areas. Michael Coe et al., *Atlas of Ancient America* (1986), include excellent maps, illustrations, and an intelligent and comprehensive text.

The literature on the Aztecs continues to grow rapidly. Bernardino de Sahagún's *Florentine Codex: The General History of the Things of New Spain*, ed. and trans. Charles Dibble and Arthur J. O. Anderson, 12 vols. (1950–1968), is a fundamental source that most scholars still use as a starting point. Good overviews are provided by Frances Berdan's *The Aztecs of Central Mexico: An Imperial Society*, 2nd ed. (2005) and Michael E. Smith, *The* Aztecs (2012), Miguel Leon-Portilla's *Fifteen Aztec Poets* (1992) deals with religion and philosophy in a sympathetic way while David Carrasco, *Religions of Mesoamerica: Cosmovision and Ceremonial Centers* (1990) tries to integrate archaeology into an understanding of the Mesoamerican cosmology. Elizabeth Boone, *Stories in Red and Black: Pictorial Histories of the Aztecs and Mixtecs* (2000) discusses with writing systems while Ross Hassig, *Aztec Warfare* (1988), examines their military organization, and Inga Clendinnen, *The Cost of Courage in Aztec Society* (2010), provides thoughtful essays on their philosophy of war. Susan D. Gillespie, *The Aztec Kings* (1989), views Aztec history in terms of myth. Manuel Aguilar-Moreno, *Handbook to Life in the Aztec World* (2006), is a useful encyclopedia on many aspects of Aztec culture.

On Peru, a good overview through solid scholarly articles is provided in Richard W. Keatinge, ed., *Peruvian Prehistory* (1988). The article on Inca archeology by Craig Morris is especially helpful. Also useful is Michael Moseley, *The Incas and Their Ancestors* (1992). Art and archeology are the focus of Rebecca Stone Miller, *Art of the Andes from Chavín to Inca* (1995). María Rostoworowski de Diez Canseco, *History of the Inca Realm* (1996), integrates historical and archeological sources, while Juan de Betanzos, *Narrative of the Incas* (1996), makes a classic available to modern readers. Terence D'altroy, *The Incas* (2002), integrates anthropology and archaeology. John Murra's classic *The Economic Organization of the Inca State* (1980) has influenced much thinking about the Incas. J. Hyslop's *The Inca Road System* (1984) examines the building and function of the road network. The work of Gary Urton, *The History of a Myth: Pacariqtambo and the Origin of the Inka* (1990), and Frank Salomon, *The Code Keepers* (2004), on the quipus show how ethnohistory is deepening our understanding of Inca society. Interesting social history is now being done. Irene Silverblatt's *Moon, Sun, and Witches: Gender Ideologies and Class in Inca and Colonial Peru* (1987) is a controversial book on the position of women before, during, and after the Inca rise to power. Brian S. Bauer, *The Development of the Inca State* (1996), offers a new interpretation of government and rule.

In Geoffrey W. Conrad and Arthur A. Demerest's *Religion and Empire: The Dynamics of Aztec and Inca Expansionism* (1984), two archeologists compare the political systems of the two empires and the motivations for expansion. The authors find more similarities than differences. On the native peoples who lived north of Mesoamerica there is an extensive literature. Colin G. Calloway, *One Vast Winter Count* (2003), provides an excellent and up-to-date overview while Linda Cordell, *Ancient Pueblo Peoples* (1994), and George Miner, *The Moundbuilders: Ancient Peoples of Eastern North America* (2004), provide more detail. Carroll L. Riley, *Becoming Aztlan: Mesoamerican Influence in the Greater Southwest, AD 1200–1500* (2005) weighs the evidence on the possible ties between Mesoamerica and the Anasazi and other groups. Timothy R. Pauketat, *Cahokia. Ancient America's Great City on the Mississippi* (2009), is a good starting point on Mississippian cultures that suggests inspiration from Mesoamerica. Finally, on the question of the populations of the Americas, see Noble D. Cook, *Born to Die* (1998), which tries to establish the populations when post-1492 contact took place.

Critical Thinking Questions

1. What were the strengths and weaknesses of the Aztec empire?

2. What were the main similarities and differences between the Aztec and Inca empires?

3. What are the key issues involved in trying to understand Aztec religious practices?

4. What were the most important differences between Central American and Andean civilizations; and the major societies of Africa, Asia and Europe during the postclassical period?

Reunification and Renaissance in Chinese Civilization: The Era of the Tang and Song Dynasties

17

Listen to Chapter 17 on MyHistoryLab

Under the aegis of two of its most celebrated dynasties, the Tang and the Song, which ruled from the early 7th century to the late 13th century c.e., Chinese society advanced in virtually all areas of human endeavor as far as any to that time. It was the largest (both in population and territory) and most prosperous empire on earth. Nowhere during these centuries were China's remarkable achievements so obvious as in the great cities found throughout the empire (see Figure 17.1), several of which exceeded a million people, surpassing those of any other civilization of the age. Although it was not the largest city, Hangzhou (hohng-joh), the capital of the Song rulers, was renowned for its beauty and sophistication.

LEARNING OBJECTIVES

17.1 What were the key factors in the Sui-Tang era that made for the restoration of a strong, unified Chinese empire after centuries of division and turmoil? p. 374

17.2 Why did Buddhism become such a dominant force in the political and sociocultural life of China in the early Tang period and who led the campaigns to rein in the wealth and influence of the Buddhist monastic orders? p. 381

17.3 What innovations and socioeconomic developments account for the widespread prosperity of Chinese civilization in the Tang-Song era and what were the main social effects of those developments? p. 385

FIGURE **17.1** This cityscape of the Song city of Bian Liang (Kaifeng), painted by Zhang Zeduan, conveys the energy and prosperity that characterized Chinese urban life in the Tang-Song eras. Like Hangzhou, Bian Liang's graceful bridges, bustling river markets, and spacious parks attracted many visitors, especially at times of festival celebrations like that depicted here.

◉ Watch the Video Series on MyHistoryLab

**Learn about some key topics related to this chapter with the *MyHistoryLab Video Series:*
*Key Topics in World History***

Located between a large lake and a river in the Yangzi delta (Map 17.1), Hangzhou was criss-crossed by canals and bridges. The city's location near the Yangzi and the coast of the East China Sea allowed its traders and artisans to prosper through the sale of goods and the manufacture of products from materials drawn from throughout China as well as overseas. By late Song times, Hangzhou had more than a million and a half residents and was famed for its wealth, cleanliness, and the number and variety of diversions it offered.

A visitor to Hangzhou could wander through its ten great marketplaces, each stocked with products from much of the known world. The less consumption-minded visitor could enjoy the city's many parks and delightful gardens or go boating on the Western Lake. There the pleasure craft of the rich mingled with special barges for gaming, dining, or listening to Hangzhou's famous "singing-girls." In the late afternoon, one could visit the bath houses that were found throughout the city. At these establishments, one could also get a massage and sip a cup of tea or rice wine.

In the evening, one might dine at one of the city's many fine restaurants, which specialized in the varied and delicious cuisines of the different regions of China. After dinner, there were a variety of entertainments from which to choose. One could take in the pleasure parks, where acrobats, jugglers, and actors performed for the passing crowds. Other options included the city's ornate tea houses, an opera performance by the lake, or a viewing of landscape paintings by artists from the city's famed academy. Having spent such a day, it would be hard for a visitor to disagree with Marco Polo (a native from another beautiful city of canals, Venice) that Hangzhou was "the most noble city and the best that is in the world." ∎

Although enjoyed mainly by elite social groups, the good life in cities like Hangzhou was made possible by the large, well-educated bureaucracy that had governed China for centuries. As we will see in this chapter, centralized control and a strong military brought long periods of peace, during which the ruling elites promoted technological innovation, agrarian expansion, and commercial enterprise at both home and overseas. Despite increasing pressure from nomadic invaders from west and north from the 11th century onward, these trends persisted. Well into the modern era, China went on to produce some of the great art of humankind and remained one of the world's most prosperous societies.

REBUILDING THE IMPERIAL EDIFICE IN THE SUI-TANG ERA

17.1	What were the key factors in the Sui-Tang era that made for the restoration of a strong, unified Chinese empire after centuries of division and turmoil?

The emergence of the Sui dynasty at the end of the 6th century C.E. signaled a return to strong dynastic control in China. In the Tang era that followed, a Confucian revival enhanced the position of the scholar-gentry administrators and provided the ideological basis for a return to highly centralized rule under an imperial dynasty.

The initial rise of the Sui dynasty in the early 580s appeared to be just another factional struggle of the sort that had occurred repeatedly in the splinter states fighting for control of China in the centuries after the fall of the Han. Yang Jian, a member of a prominent north Chinese noble family that had long been active in these contests, struck a marriage alliance between his daughter and the ruler of the northern Zhou empire (Map 17.1). The Zhou monarch had recently defeated several rival rulers and united much of the north China plain. After much intrigue, Yang Jian seized the throne of his son-in-law and proclaimed himself emperor. Although Yang Jian was Chinese, he secured his power base by

200 C.E.	600 C.E.	800 C.E.	950 C.E.	1100 C.E.	1250 C.E.
220 End of the Han dynasty **220–589** Era of the Six Dynasties; political discord in China; time of great Buddhist influence **589–618** Sui dynasty; building of the Grand Canal	**618–626** Gaozu emperor **618–907** Tang dynasty **627–649** Tang Taizong emperor **688** Korean conquest; vassal state of Silla **690–705** Empress Wu; Buddhist influence in China peaks **712–756** Xuanzong emperor	**840s** Period of Buddhist persecution **907** End of the Tang dynasty	**960–1279** Song dynasty; Neo-Confucian revival **c. 1050** Invention of block printing with movable type **1067–1085** Shenzong emperor; reforms of Wang Anshi	**c. 1100** Invention of gunpowder **1115** Jurchen (Jin) kingdom in north China **1119** First reference to use of compass for sea navigation **1127–1279** Southern Song dynasty	**1279–1368** Mongol (Yuan) dynasty rules all China

winning the support of neighboring nomadic military commanders. He did this by reconfirming their titles and showing little desire to favor the Confucian scholar-gentry class at their expense. With their support, Yang Jian, who took the title Wendi (or Literary Emperor), extended his rule across north China. In 589 Wendi's armies attacked and conquered the weak and divided Chen kingdom, which had long ruled much of the south. With his victory over the Chen, Wendi reunited the traditional core areas of Chinese civilization for the first time in over three and a half centuries (Map 17.2).

Yangdi Second member of Sui dynasty; murdered his father to gain throne; restored Confucian examination system; responsible for construction of Chinese canal system; assassinated in 618.

Wendi won widespread support by lowering taxes and establishing granaries throughout his domains. Bins for storing grain were built in all of the large cities and in each village of the empire to ensure that there would be a reserve food supply in case floods or drought destroyed the peasants' crops and threatened the people with famine. Large landholders and poor peasants alike were taxed a portion of their crop to keep the granaries filled. Beyond warding off famine, the surplus grain was brought to market in times of food shortages to hold down the price of the people's staple food.

Sui Excesses and Collapse

The foundations Wendi laid for political unification and economic prosperity were at first strengthened even further by his son, **Yangdi**, who murdered his father to reach the throne. Yangdi extended his father's conquests and drove back the nomadic intruders who threatened the northern frontiers of the empire. He established a milder legal code and devoted resources to upgrading Confucian education. Yangdi also sought to restore the examination system for regulating entry into the bureaucracy. These legal and educational reforms were part of a broader policy of promoting the scholar-gentry in the imperial administration. But their advancement often worked to the detriment of the great aristocratic families and nomadic military commanders.

MAP 17.1 China During the Age of Division After the collapse of the Han dynasty, China fragmented into warring kingdoms for nearly 400 years. The deep divisions of this period were captured by its designation in Chinese histories as the era of the Six Dynasties.

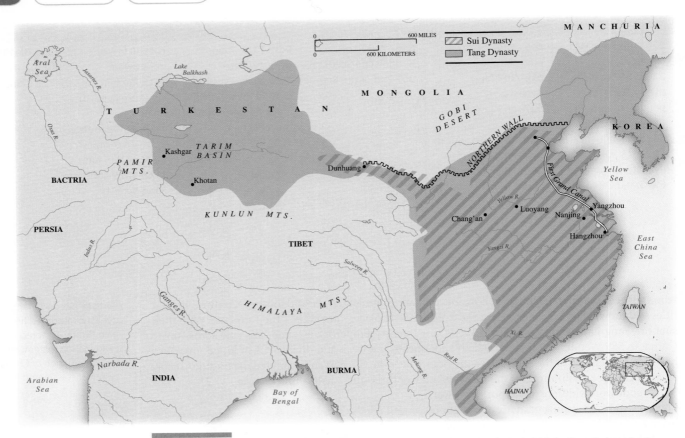

MAP **17.2 The Sui Dynasty and the Tang Dynasty** The short-lived Sui dynasty laid the foundations for the expansive Tang. Under the latter the Chinese empire was restored on a scale not known since the Han era.

Yangdi was overly fond of luxury and extravagant construction projects. He forcibly conscripted hundreds of thousands of peasants to build palaces, a new capital city at Luoyang (lwoh-yahng) (Map 17.1), and a series of great canals to link the various parts of his empire. His demands on the people seemed limitless. In his new capital, Yangdi had an extensive game park laid out. Because there was not enough forest on the site chosen, tens of thousands of laborers were forced to dig up huge trees in the nearby hills and cart them miles to be replanted in the artificial mounds that tens of thousands of other laborers had built.

Even before work on his many construction projects was completed, Yangdi led his exhausted and angry subjects into a series of unsuccessful wars to bring Korea back under Chinese rule. His failures in the Korean campaigns between 611 and 614, and the near-fatal reverse he suffered in central Asia at the hands of Turkic nomads in 615, set in motion widespread revolts throughout the empire. Provincial governors declared themselves independent rulers, bandit gangs raided at will, and nomadic peoples again seized large sections of the north China plain. Faced with a crumbling empire, the increasingly deranged emperor retreated to his pleasure palaces in the city of Hangzhou on the Yangzi River to the south. When Yangdi was assassinated by his own ministers in 618, it looked as if China would return to the state of political division and social turmoil it had endured in the preceding centuries.

The Emergence of the Tang and the Restoration of the Empire

Li Yuan [lee wahn] (566–635) Also known as Duke of Tang; minister for Yangdi; took over empire following assassination of Yangdi; first emperor of Tang dynasty; took imperial title of Gaozu.

The dissolution of the imperial order was averted by the military skills and political savvy of one of Yangdi's officials, **Li Yuan**, the Duke of Tang. Of noble and mixed Chinese-nomadic origins, Li Yuan was for many years a loyal supporter of the Sui ruler. In fact, on one occasion Li Yuan rescued Yangdi, whose forces had been trapped by a far larger force of Turkic cavalry in a small fort that was part of the Great Wall defenses. But as Yangdi grew more and more irrational and unrest spread from one end of the empire to another, Li Yuan was convinced by his sons and allies that only rebellion could save his family and the empire. From the many-sided struggle for the throne that followed Yangdi's death and continued until 623, Li Yuan emerged the victor. Together with his second son, Tang Taizong (tahng teye-zohng), in whose favor he abdicated in 626, Li Yuan laid the basis for the golden age of the Tang.

Tang armies conquered deep into central Asia as far as present-day Afghanistan. These victories meant that many of the nomadic peoples who had dominated China in the Six Dynasties era had to submit to Tang rule. Tang emperors also completed the repairs begun by the Sui and earlier dynasties on the northern walls and created frontier armies. Partly recruited from Turkic nomadic peoples, these frontier forces gradually became the most potent military units in the empire. The sons of Turkic tribal leaders were sent to the capital as hostages to guarantee the good behavior of the tribe in question. At the Tang capital, they were also educated in Chinese ways in the hope of their eventual assimilation into Chinese culture.

The empire was also extended to parts of Tibet in the west, the Red River valley homeland of the Vietnamese in the south (see Chapter 13), and Manchuria in the north (Map 17.2). In the Tang period, the Yangzi River basin and much of the south were fully integrated with north China for the first time since the Han. In 668, under the emperor Gaozong, Korea was overrun by Chinese armies, and a vassal kingdom called Silla was established that long remained loyal to the Tang. In a matter of decades, the Tang had built an empire that was far larger than even that of the early Han empire whose boundaries in many directions extended beyond the borders of present-day China.

Rebuilding the World's Largest and Most Pervasive Bureaucracy

Crucial for the restoration of Chinese unity were the efforts of the early Tang monarchs to rebuild and expand the imperial bureaucracy. A revived scholar-gentry elite and reworked Confucian ideology played central roles in the process. From the time of the second Sui emperor, Yangdi, the fortunes of the scholar-gentry had begun to improve. This trend continued under the early Tang emperors, who desperately needed loyal and well-educated officials to govern the vast empire they had put together in a matter of decades. The Tang rulers also used the scholar-gentry bureaucrats to offset the power of the aristocracy. As the aristocratic families' control over court life and administration declined, their role in Chinese history was reduced. From the Tang era onward, political power in China was shared by a succession of imperial families and the bureaucrats of the civil service system. Members of the hereditary aristocracy continued to occupy administrative positions, but the scholar-gentry class staffed most of the posts in the secretariats and executive ministries that oversaw a huge bureaucracy.

This bureaucracy reached from the imperial palace down to the subprefecture, or district level, which was roughly equivalent to an American county. One secretariat drafted imperial decrees; a second monitored the reports of regional and provincial officials and the petitions of local notables. The executive department, which was divided into six ministries—including war, justice, and public works—ran the empire on a day-to-day basis. In addition, there was a powerful Bureau of Censors whose chief task was to keep track of officials at all levels and report their misdeeds or failings. Finally, there was a very large staff to run the imperial household, including the palaces in the new capital at **Chang'an** and the residences of the princes of the imperial line and other dignitaries.

Read the Document on MyHistoryLab: Tang Daizong on The Art of Government

Chang'an [chahng-an] Capital of Tang dynasty; population of 2 million, larger than any other city in the world at that time.

Institutionalizing Meritocracy: The Growing Importance of the Examination System

Like Yangdi, the Tang emperors patronized academies to train state officials and educate them in the Confucian classics, which were thought to teach moral and organizational principles essential to effective administrators. In the Tang era, and under the Song dynasty that followed, the numbers of the educated scholar-gentry rose far above those in the Han era. In the Tang and Song periods, the examination system was greatly expanded, and the pattern of advancement in the civil service was much more regularized. This meant that in the political realm more than any previous political system (and those yet to come for centuries), the Chinese connected merit as measured by tested skills with authority and status. Several different kinds of examinations were administered by the **Ministry of Rites** to students from government schools or to those recommended by distinguished scholars.

Ministry of Rites Administered examinations to students from Chinese government schools or those recommended by distinguished scholars.

The highest offices could be gained only by those who were able to pass exams on the philosophical or legal classics at the highest imperial or metropolitan level. Those who passed the latter earned the title of **jinshi**. Their names were announced throughout the empire, and their families' positions were secured by the prospect of high office that was opened up by their success. Overnight they were transformed into dignitaries whom even their former friends and fellow students addressed formally and treated with deference. Success in exams at all levels won candidates special social status. This meant that they earned the right to wear certain types of clothing and were exempt from corporal punishment. They gained access to the higher level of material comfort and the refined pleasures that were enjoyed by members of the scholar-gentry elite, some of whom are shown at play in Figure 17.2.

Even though a much higher proportion of Tang bureaucrats won their positions through success in civil service examinations than had been the case in the Han era, birth and family connections continued to be important in securing high office. Some of these relationships are clearly illustrated by the petitioner's letter printed in the Document feature. Established bureaucrats not only ensured that their sons and cousins got into the imperial academies but could pull strings to see that even failed candidates from their families received government posts. Ethnic and regional ties also played a role in staffing bureaucratic departments. This meant that although bright commoners could rise to upper-level positions in the bureaucracy, the central administration was overwhelmingly dominated by a small number of established families. Sons followed fathers in positions of power and influence, and prominent households bought a disproportionate share of the places available in the imperial academies. Many positions were reserved for members of the old aristocracy and the low-ranking sons and grandsons of lesser wives and concubines belonging to the imperial household. Merit and ambition counted for something, but birth and family influence often counted for a good deal more.

Read the **Document** on **MyHistoryLab**: An Essay Question from the Chinese Imperial Examination System

FIGURE **17.2** As shown in this ink drawing of Chinese philosophers of the Song dynasty, board games and musical recitals were highly esteemed leisure activities for the scholar-gentry class. Members of the scholar-gentry elite might also attend poetry reading or writing parties, travel to mountains to meditate amid scenic splendors, or paint the blossoming plum trees in their gardens. As in their work, members of this highly educated elite admired those who at leisure pursued a diverse array of activities.

(Handscroll "Gathering of Philosophers." The Metropolitan Museum of Art, New York, NY, U.S.A. Image copyright © The Metropolitan Museum of Art/Art Resource, NY.)

State and Religion in the Tang and Song Eras

Increasing state patronage for Confucian learning threatened not only the old aristocratic families but also the Buddhist monastic orders, which had become a major force in Chinese life in the Six Dynasties era. These tensions represent a well-documented instance of the longstanding (and still globally widespread) problem of delineating the boundaries between established religions and state systems. Many of the rulers in the pre-Tang era, particularly those from nomadic origins, were devout Buddhists and strong patrons of the Buddhist establishment. In the centuries after the fall of the Han, Buddhist sects proliferated in China. The most popular were those founded by Chinese monks, in part because they soon took on distinctively Chinese qualities. Among the masses, the salvationist **pure land** strain of Mahayana Buddhism won widespread conversions because it seemed to provide a refuge from an age of war and turmoil. Members of the elite classes, on the other hand, were more attracted to the **Chan** variant of Buddhism, or **Zen**, as it is known in Japan and the West. With its stress on meditation and the appreciation of natural and artistic beauty, Zen had great appeal for the educated classes of China.

The goal of those who followed Chan was to come to know the ultimate wisdom, and thus find release from the cycle of rebirth, through introspective meditation. The nature of this level of consciousness often was expressed in poetic metaphors and riddles, such as those in the following lines from an 8th century C.E. treatise called the *Hymn to Wisdom*:

> The power of wisdom is infinite.
> It is like moonlight reflected in a thousand waves; it can see, hear, understand, and know.
> It can do all these and yet is always empty and tranquil.

pure land Buddhism Emphasized salvationist aspects of Chinese Buddhism; popular among masses of Chinese society.

Chan Buddhism Known as Zen in Japan; stressed meditation and appreciation of natural and artistic beauty; popular with members of elite Chinese society.

Zen Buddhism Known as Chan Buddhism in China; stressed meditation and the appreciation of natural and artistic beauty.

 View the **Closer Look** on **MyHistoryLab**: A Tang Painting of the Goddess of Mercy

DOCUMENT

Ties That Bind: Paths to Power

THE FOLLOWING LETTER WAS INCLUDED IN a short story by Tang author Niu Su. It was sent by a local functionary named Wu Bao to a high official to whom Wu hoped to attach himself and thus win advancement in the imperial bureaucracy. What can this letter tell us about the ways in which the Chinese bureaucracy worked in the Tang and Song eras?

To my great good fortune, we share the same native place, and your renown for wise counsel is well known to me. Although, through gross neglect, I have omitted to prostrate myself before you, my heart has always been filled with admiration and respect. You are the nephew of the Prime Minister, and have made use of your outstanding talents in his service. In consequence of this, your high ability has been rewarded with a commission. General Li is highly qualified both as a civil and a military official, and he has been put in full command of the expedition [to put down "barbarian" rebellions in the southern parts of the empire]. In his hands he unites mighty forces, and he cannot fail to bring these petty brigands to order. By the alliance of the General's heroic valor and your own talent and ability, your armies' task of subjugation will be the work of a day. I, in my youth, devoted myself to study.

Reaching manhood, I paid close attention to the [Confucian] classics. But in talent I do not compare with other men, and so far I have held office only as an officer of the guard. I languish in this out-of-the-way corner beyond the Jian

[mountains], close to the haunts of the barbarians. My native place is thousands of miles away, and many passes and rivers lie between. What is more, my term of office here is completed, and I cannot tell when I shall receive my next appointment. So lacking in talent, I fear I am but poorly fitted to be selected for an official post; far less can I entertain the hope of some meager salary. I can only retire, when old age comes, to some rustic retreat, and "turn aside to die in a ditch." I have heard by devious ways of your readiness to help those in distress. If you will not overlook a man from your native place, be quick to bestow your special favour on me, so that I may render you service "as a humble groom." Grant me some small salary, and a share however slight in your deeds of merit. If by your boundless favor I could take part in this triumphal progress, even as a member of the rear-most company, the day would live engraved on my memory.

QUESTIONS

- What techniques does Wu use to win the high official's favor?
- How does Wu expect the official to help him?
- What does he promise in return?
- Does birth or merit appear to be more important in his appeals?
- What dangers to the imperial system are contained in the sorts of ties that Wu argues bind him to the high official?

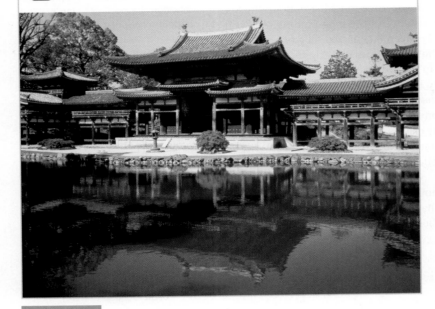

FIGURE **17.3** Tang era architecture at the Phoenix Pavilion in Japan. Some of the most characteristic features of this splendid style of construction are its steeply sloping tiled roofs with upturned corners, the extensive use of fine wood in the floors, walls, and ceilings, and the sliding panels that covered doors and windows in inclement weather and opened up the temples or monasteries to the natural world on pleasant days.

Empress Wu Tang ruler 690–705 C.E. in China; supported Buddhist establishment; tried to elevate Buddhism to state religion; had multistory statues of Buddha created.

Being empty means having no appearance.
Being tranquil means not having been created.
One will then not be bound by good and evil, or be
     seized by quietness or disturbance.
One will not be wearied by birth and death or rejoice
     in Nirvana.

The combination of royal patronage and widespread conversion at both the elite and mass levels made Buddhism a strong social, economic, and political force by the time of the Tang unification. The early Tang rulers continued to patronize Buddhism while trying to promote education in the Confucian classics. Emperors such as Taizong endowed monasteries, built in the style of those pictured in Figure 17.3. They also sent emissaries to India to collect texts and relics and commissioned Buddhist paintings and statuary. However, no Tang ruler matched **Empress Wu** (r. 690–705) in supporting the Buddhist establishment. At one point she tried to elevate Buddhism to the status of a state religion.

Empress Wu also commissioned many Buddhist paintings and sculptures. The sculptures are noteworthy for their colossal size. She had statues of the Buddha, which were as much as two and three stories high, carved from stone or cast in bronze. Some of these statues, such as those pictured in Figure 17.4, were carved out of the rock in the great caves near her capital at Luoyang; for cast figures at other locations, Wu had huge pagodas built. With this sort of support, it is not surprising that Buddhism flourished in the early

FIGURE **17.4** At sites such as Longmen near the Tang capital of Luoyang on the Yellow River and Yunkang far to the north, massive statues of the Buddha were carved out of rocky cliffsides beginning in the 6th century C.E. Before the age of Buddhist predominance, sculpture had not been highly developed in China, and the art at these centers was strongly influenced by that of central and even west Asia. Known more for their sheer size than for artistic refinement, the huge Buddhas of sites such as Longmen attest to the high level of skill the Chinese had attained in stone- and metalworking.

centuries of Tang rule. By the mid-9th century, there were nearly 50,000 monasteries and hundreds of thousands of Buddhist monks and nuns in China.

The Anti-Buddhist Backlash

Buddhist successes aroused the envy of Confucian and Daoist rivals. Some of these notables attacked the religion as alien, even though the faith followed by most of the Chinese was very different from that originally preached by the Buddha or that practiced in India and southeast Asia. Daoist monks tried to counter Buddhism's appeals to the masses by stressing their own magical and predictive powers. Most damaging to the fortunes of Buddhism was the growing campaign of Confucian scholar-administrators to convince the Tang rulers that the large Buddhist monastic establishment posed a fundamental economic challenge to the imperial order. Because monastic lands and resources were not taxed, the Tang regime lost huge amounts of revenue as a result of imperial grants or the gifts of wealthy families to Buddhist monasteries. The state was also denied labor power because it could neither tax nor conscript peasants who worked on monastic estates.

By the mid-9th century, state fears of Buddhist wealth and power led to measures to limit the flow of land and resources to the monastic orders. Under Emperor **Wuzong** (r. 841–847), these restrictions grew into open persecution of Buddhism. Thousands of monasteries and Buddhist shrines were destroyed, and hundreds of thousands of monks and nuns were forced to abandon their monastic orders and return to civilian lives. They and the slaves and peasants who worked their lands were again subject to taxation, and monastery lands were parceled out to taxpaying landlords and peasant smallholders.

Although Chinese Buddhism survived this and other bouts of repression, it was weakened. Never again would the Buddhist monastic orders have the political influence and wealth they had enjoyed in the first centuries of Tang rule. The great age of Buddhist painting and cave sculptures gave way to art dominated by Daoist and Confucian subjects and styles in the late Tang and the Song dynastic era that followed. The Zen and pure land sects of Buddhism continued to attract adherents, with those of the latter numbering in the millions. But Confucianism emerged as the central ideology of Chinese civilization for most of the period from the 9th to the early 20th century. Buddhism left its mark on the arts, the Chinese language, and Chinese thinking about things such as heaven, charity, and law, but it ceased to be a dominant influence. Buddhism's fate in China contrasts sharply with its ongoing and pivotal impact on the civilizations of mainland southeast Asia, Tibet, and parts of central Asia, where it continued to spread in the centuries of Tang-Song rule.

Wuzong Chinese emperor of Tang dynasty who openly persecuted Buddhism by destroying monasteries in 840s; reduced influence of Chinese Buddhism in favor of Confucian ideology.

TANG DECLINE AND THE RISE OF THE SONG

17.2   Why did Buddhism become such a dominant force in the political and sociocultural life of China in the early Tang period and who led the campaigns to rein in the wealth and influence of the Buddhist monastic orders?

The motives behind the mid-9th-century Tang assault on the Buddhist monastic order were symptomatic of a general weakening of imperial control that had begun almost a century earlier. After the controversial but strong rule between 690 and 705 by Empress Wu, who actually tried to establish a new dynasty, a second attempt to control the throne was made by a highborn woman who had married into the imperial family. Backed by her powerful relatives and a group of prominent courtiers, Empress Wei poisoned her husband, the son of Empress Wu, and placed her own small child on the throne. But Empress Wei's attempt to seize power was thwarted by another prince, who led a palace revolt that ended with the destruction of Wei and her supporters. The early decades of the long reign of this prince, who became the **Xuanzong** emperor (r. 713–756), marked the peak of Tang power and the high point of Chinese civilization under the dynasty.

Initially, Xuanzong took a strong interest in political and economic reforms, which were pushed by the very capable officials he appointed to high positions. But increasingly, his interest in running the vast empire waned. More and more he devoted himself to patronizing the arts and enjoying the pleasures available within the confines of the imperial city. These diversions included music, which he played himself and also had performed by the many musicians he patronized. Thousands of concubines vied in the imperial apartments for the attention of the monarch. After the death of his second

Beset by internal rebellions and nomadic incursions, the Tang gave way to the Song in the early 10th century. Although the Song domains were smaller than those of the Tang, the Confucian revival flourished under the successor dynasty.

Xuanzong [shwant-song] Leading Chinese emperor of the Tang dynasty who reigned from 713 to 755, although he encouraged overexpansion.

 Read the **Document** on MyHistoryLab: Ibn Wahab, An Arab merchant visits Tang China

FIGURE 17.5 This painting of Yang Guifei gives a vivid impression of the opulence and refinement of Chinese court life in the late Tang era. Here a very well-dressed Yang Guifei is helped by some of her servants onto a well-fed horse, presumably for a trot through the palace grounds. Two fan-bearers stand ready to accompany the now-powerful concubine on her sedate ride while other attendants prepare to lead the horse through the confined space of the royal enclosure.

Yang Guifei [yäng gwä fä] (719–756) Royal concubine during reign of Xuanzong; introduction of her relatives into royal administration led to revolt.

Zhao Kuangyin [jaoo kwän yin] (r. 960–976) Founder of Song dynasty; originally a general following fall of Tang; took title of Taizu; failed to overcome northern Liao dynasty that remained independent.

wife, the aged and lonely emperor became infatuated with **Yang Guifei**, a beautiful young woman from the harem of one of the imperial princes (Figure 17.5).

Their relationship was one of the most famous and illstarred romances in all of Chinese history. But it was only one of the more fateful of a multitude of interventions by powerful women at the courts of emperors and kings throughout Afro-Euroasia. Xuanzong promenaded in the imperial gardens and gave flute lessons to Yang. Soon she was raised to the status of royal concubine, and she used her new power to pack the upper levels of the government with her greedy relatives. They and Yang assumed an ever-greater role in court politics. The arrogance and excessive ambition of Yang Guifei and her family angered members of the rival cliques at court, who took every opportunity to turn Yang's excesses into a cause for popular unrest. Xuanzong's long neglect of state affairs resulted in economic distress, which fed this discontent. It also led to chronic military weaknesses, which left the government unable to deal with the disorders effectively. The deepening crisis came to a head in 755 when one of the emperor's main military leaders, a general of nomadic origins named An Lushan, led a widely supported revolt with the aim of founding a new dynasty to supplant the Tang.

Although the revolt was crushed and the Tang dynasty preserved, victory was won at a very high cost. Early in the rebellion, Xuanzong's retreating and demoralized troops mutinied, first killing several members of the Yang family and then forcing the emperor to have Yang Guifei executed. Xuanzong lived on for a time, but his grief and disillusionment rendered him incapable of continuing as emperor. None of the Tang monarchs who followed him could compare with the able leaders that the dynasty had consistently produced in the first century and a half of its rule.

Equally critical, to defeat the rebels the Tang had sought alliances with nomadic peoples living on the northern borders of the empire. They had also delegated resources and political power to regional commanders who remained loyal to the dynasty. As had happened so often in the past, in the late 8th and 9th centuries the nomads used political divisions within China to gain entry into and eventually assert control over large areas of the north China plain. At the same time, many of the allied provincial governors became in effect independent rulers. They collected their own taxes, passing little or none on to the imperial treasury. These regional lords raised their own armies and bequeathed their titles to their sons without asking for permission from the Tang court. Worsening economic conditions led to a succession of revolts in the 9th century, some of which were popular uprisings led by peasants.

The Founding of the Song Dynasty

By the end of the 9th century little remained of the once-glorious Tang Empire. By 907, when the last emperor of the Tang dynasty was forced to resign, China appeared to be entering another phase of nomadic dominance, political division, and social strife. In 960, however, a military commander emerged to reunite China under a single dynasty. **Zhao Kuangyin** had established a far-flung reputation as one of the most honest and able of the generals of the last of the Five Dynasties that had struggled to control north China after the fall of the Tang. Although a fearless warrior, Zhao was a scholarly man who collected books rather than booty while out campaigning. Amid the continuing struggles for control in the north, Zhao's subordinates and regular troops insisted that he proclaim himself emperor. In the next few years Zhao, renamed Emperor Taizu, routed all his rivals except one, thus founding the Song dynasty that was to rule most of China for the next three centuries.

The one rival Taizu could not overcome was the northern **Liao dynasty**, which had been founded in 907 by the nomadic **Khitan** peoples from Manchuria. This failure set a precedent for weakness on the part of the Song rulers in dealing with the nomadic peoples of the north. This shortcoming plagued the dynasty from its earliest years to its eventual destruction by the Mongols in the late 13th century. Beginning in 1004, the Song were forced by military defeats at the hands of the Khitans to sign a series of humiliating treaties with their smaller but more militarily adept northern neighbors. These treaties committed the Song to paying a very heavy tribute to the Liao dynasty to keep it from raiding and possibly conquering the Song domains. The Khitans, who had been highly *Sinified*, or influenced by Chinese culture, during a century of rule in north China, seemed content with this arrangement. They clearly saw the Song empire as culturally superior—an area from which they could learn much in statecraft, the arts, and economic organization.

Liao [lyow] **dynasty** Founded in 907 by nomadic Khitan peoples from Manchuria; maintained independence from Song dynasty in China.

Khitans [kiht-ahn] Nomadic peoples of Manchuria; militarily superior to Song dynasty China but influenced by Chinese culture; forced humiliating treaties on Song China in 11th century.

Song Politics: Settling for Partial Restoration

A comparison of the boundaries of the early Song Empire (Map 17.3) with that of the Tang domains (Map 17.2) reveals that the Song never matched its predecessor in political or military strength. The weakness of the Song resulted in part from imperial policies that were designed to ward off the conditions that had destroyed the Tang dynasty. From the outset, the military was subordinated to the civilian administrators of the scholar-gentry class. Only civil officials were allowed to be governors, thereby removing the temptation of regional military commanders to seize power. In addition, military commanders were rotated to prevent them from building up a power base in the areas where they were stationed.

At the same time, the early Song rulers strongly promoted the interests of the Confucian scholar-gentry, who touted themselves as the key bulwark against the revival of warlord influence. Officials' salaries were increased, and many perks—including additional servants and payments of luxury goods such as silk and wine—made government posts more lucrative. The civil service exams were fully routinized. They were given every three years at three levels: district, provincial, and imperial. Song examiners passed a far higher percentage of those taking the exams than the Tang examiners had, and these successful candidates were much more likely to receive an official post than their counterparts in the Tang era. As a result, the bureaucracy soon became bloated with well-paid officials who often had little to do. In this way, the ascendancy of the scholar-gentry class over its aristocratic and Buddhist rivals was fully secured in the Song era.

MAP **17.3 China in the Song and Southern Song Dynastic Periods** A comparison of the territory controlled during the two phases of the Song dynasty clearly indicates both the growing power and pressure of nomadic peoples from the north and the weakened state of the Song rulers of China.

The Revival of Confucian Thought

The great influence of the scholar-gentry in the Song era was mirrored in the revival of Confucian ideas and values that dominated intellectual life. Many scholars tried to recover long-neglected texts and decipher ancient inscriptions. New academies devoted to the study of the classical texts were founded, and impressive libraries were established. The new schools of philosophy propounded rival interpretations of the teachings of Confucius and other ancient thinkers. They also sought to prove the superiority of indigenous thought systems, such as Confucianism and Daoism, over imported ones, especially Buddhism.

Zhu Xi [ju shEE] (1130–1200) Most prominent of neo-Confucian scholars during the Song dynasty in China; stressed importance of applying philosophical principles to everyday life and action.

The most prominent thinkers of the era, such as **Zhu Xi**, stressed the importance of applying philosophical principles to everyday life and action. These **neo-Confucians**, or revivers of what they believed to be ancient Confucian teachings, argued that cultivating personal morality was the highest goal for humans. They argued that virtue could be attained through knowledge gained by book learning and personal observation as well as through contact with men of wisdom and high morality. In these ways, the basically good nature of humans could be cultivated, and superior men, fit to govern and teach others, could be developed. Neo-Confucian thinking had a great impact on Chinese intellectual life during the eras of all the dynasties that followed the Song. Its hostility to foreign philosophical systems, such as Buddhism, made Chinese rulers and bureaucrats less receptive to outside ideas and influences than they had been earlier. The neo-Confucian emphasis on tradition and hostility to foreign influences was one of a number of forces that eventually stifled innovation and critical thinking among the Chinese elite.

neo-Confucians Revived ancient Confucian teachings in Song era China; great impact on the dynasties that followed; their emphasis on tradition and hostility to foreign systems made Chinese rulers and bureaucrats less receptive to outside ideas and influences.

The neo-Confucian emphasis on rank, obligation, deference, and traditional rituals reinforced class, age, and gender distinctions, particularly as they were expressed in occupational roles. Great importance was given to upholding the authority of the patriarch of the Chinese household, who was compared to the male emperor of the Chinese people as a whole. If men and women kept to their place and performed the tasks of their age and social rank, the neo-Confucians argued, there would be social harmony and prosperity. If problems arose, the best solutions could be found in examples drawn from the past. They believed that historical experience was the best guide for navigating the uncertain terrain of the future.

Roots of Decline: Attempts at Reform

The means by which the Song emperors had secured their control over China undermined their empire in the long run. The weakness they showed in the face of the Khitan challenge encouraged other nomadic peoples to carve out kingdoms on the northern borders of the Song domains. By the mid-11th century, **Tangut** tribes, originally from Tibet, had established a kingdom named **Xi Xia** to the southwest of the Khitan kingdom of Liao (Map 17.3). The tribute that the Song had to pay these peoples for protection of their northern borders was a great drain on the resources of the empire and a growing burden for the Chinese peasantry. Equally burdensome was the cost of the army—numbering nearly 1 million soldiers by the mid-11th century—that the Song had to maintain to guard against invasion from the north. But the very size of the army was a striking measure of the productivity and organizational ability of Chinese civilization. It dwarfed its counterparts in other civilizations from Japan to western Europe.

Tangut Rulers of Xi Xia kingdom of northwest China; one of regional kingdoms during period of southern Song; conquered by Mongols in 1226.

Xi Xia [shee-shyah] Kingdom of Tangut people, north of Song kingdom, in mid-11th century; collected tribute that drained Song resources and burdened Chinese peasantry.

The emphasis on civil administration and the scholar-gentry and the growing disdain among the Song elite for the military also took their toll. Although Song armies were large, their commanders rarely were the most able men available. In addition, funds needed to upgrade weapons or repair fortifications often were diverted to the scholarly pursuits and entertainments of the court and gentry. At the court and among the ruling classes, painting and poetry were cultivated, while the horseback riding and hunting that had preoccupied earlier rulers and their courtiers went out of fashion.

Wang Anshi Confucian scholar and chief minister of a Song emperor in 1070s; introduced sweeping reforms based on Legalists; advocated greater state intervention in society.

In the 1070s and early 1080s, **Wang Anshi**, the chief minister of the Song Shenzong emperor, tried to ward off the impending collapse of the dynasty by introducing sweeping reforms. A celebrated Confucian scholar, Wang ran the government on the basis of the Legalist assumption that an energetic and interventionist state could greatly increase the resources and strength of the dynasty. For 20 years, in the face of strong opposition from the conservative ministers who controlled most of the administration, Wang tried to correct the grave defects in the imperial order. He introduced cheap loans and government-assisted irrigation projects to encourage agricultural expansion. He taxed the landlord and scholarly classes, who had regularly exempted themselves from military service. Wang used the increased revenue to establish well-trained mercenary forces to replace armies that had formerly been conscripted from the untrained and unwilling peasantry. Wang even tried to reorganize university education and reorient the examination system. His reforms stressed analytical thinking rather than the rote memorization of the classics that had long been the key to success among the scholar-gentry.

Reaction and Disaster: The Flight to the South

Unfortunately, Wang's ability to propose and enact reforms depended on continuing support from the Shenzong emperor. In 1085 that emperor died, and his successor favored the conservative cliques that had long opposed Wang's changes. The neo-Confucians came to power, ended reform, and reversed many of Wang's initiatives. As a result, economic conditions continued to deteriorate, and peasant unrest grew throughout the empire. Facing banditry and rebellion from within, an unprepared military proved no match for the increasing threat from beyond the northern borders of the empire. In 1115, a new nomadic contender, the **Jurchens**, overthrew the Liao dynasty of the Khitans and established the **Jin** kingdom north of the Song empire (Map 17.3). After successful invasions of Song territory, the Jurchens annexed most of the Yellow River basin to their Jin kingdom. These conquests forced the Song to flee to the south. With the Yangzi River basin as their anchor and their capital transferred to Hangzhou, the Song dynasty survived for another century and a half. Politically, the **Southern Song** dynasty (1167–1279) was little more than a rump state carved out of the much larger domains ruled by the Tang and northern-based Song. Culturally, its brief reign was to be one of the most glorious in Chinese history—perhaps in the history of humankind.

Jurchens [YUHR-chehns] Founders of the Jin kingdom that succeeded the Liao in northern China; annexed most of the Yellow River basin and forced Song to flee to south.

Jin Kingdom north of the Song Empire; established by Jurchens in 1115 after overthrowing Liao dynasty; ended 1234.

Southern Song Rump state of Song dynasty from 1127 to 1279; carved out of the much larger domains ruled by the Tang and northern Song; culturally one of the most glorious reigns in Chinese history.

TANG AND SONG PROSPERITY: THE BASIS OF A GOLDEN AGE

17.3 What innovations and socioeconomic developments account for the widespread prosperity of Chinese civilization in the Tang-Song era and what were the main social effects of those developments?

The attention given to canal building by the Sui emperors and the Tang rulers who followed them was driven by a major shift in the population balance within Chinese civilization. The **Grand Canal**, which Yangdi risked his throne to have built, was designed to link the original centers of Chinese civilization on the north China plain with the Yangzi River basin more than 500 miles to the south (see Maps 17.1 and 17.2). Because the great river systems that were essential to China's agrarian base ran from west to east—from the mountains of central Asia to the sea—the movement of people and goods in that direction was much easier than from north to south.

Although no major geographic barriers separated the millet-growing areas of northern China from the rice-producing Yangzi basin, overland travel was slow and difficult. The transport of bulk goods such as millet and rice was prohibitively expensive. The great increase of the Chinese population in the southern regions in the later Han and Six Dynasties periods made it necessary to improve communications between north and south once the two regions were joined by the Sui conquests. Not only did more and more of the emperor's subjects live in the southern regions, but the Yangzi basin and other rice-growing areas in the south were fast becoming the major food-producing areas of the empire. By late Tang and early Song times, the south had surpassed the north in both crop production and population.

Yangdi's Grand Canal was intended to facilitate control over the southern regions by courts, bureaucracies, and armies centered in ancient imperial centers such as Chang'an and Luoyang in the north. The canal made it possible to transport to the capital revenue collected in the form of grain from the fertile southern regions and to transfer food from the south to districts threatened by drought and famine in the north. No wonder that Yangdi was obsessed with canal construction. By the time the Grand Canal was finished, more than a million forced laborers had worked, and many had died, on its locks and embankments. The completed canal system was an engineering achievement every bit as impressive as the northern wall. Most stretches of the canal, which was nearly 1200 miles long, were 40 paces wide, and imperial highways lined with willow trees ran along the banks on both sides.

The Tang and Song eras were a time of major shifts in the population balance within China, new patterns of trade and commerce, renewed urban expansion, novel forms of artistic and literary expression, and a series of technological innovations.

Grand Canal Built in 7th century during reign of Yangdi during Sui dynasty; designed to link the original centers of Chinese civilization on the north China plain with the Yangtze river basin to the south; nearly 1200 miles long.

A New Phase of Intercontinental Commercial Expansion by Land and Sea

Tang conquests in central Asia and the building of the canal system did much to promote commercial expansion in the Tang and Song eras. The extension of Tang control deep into central Asia meant that the overland silk routes between China and Persia were reopened and protected. This intensified international contacts in the postclassical period. Tang control promoted exchanges between China and Buddhist centers in the nomadic lands of central Asia as well as with the Islamic world farther west. Horses, Persian rugs, and tapestries passed to China along these routes, while fine silk textiles, porcelain, and paper were exported to the centers of Islamic civilization. As in the Han era, China exported mainly manufactured goods to overseas areas, such as southeast Asia, while importing mainly luxury products such as aromatic woods and spices.

In late Tang and Song times, Chinese merchants and sailors increasingly carried Chinese trade overseas instead of being content to let foreign seafarers come to them. Along with the dhows of the Arabs, Chinese **junks** were the best ships in the world in this period. They were equipped with water-tight bulkheads, sternpost rudders, oars, sails, compasses, bamboo fenders, and gunpowder-propelled rockets for self-defense. With such vessels, Chinese sailors and merchants became the dominant force in the Asian seas east of the Malayan peninsula.

The heightened role of commerce and the money economy in Chinese life was readily apparent in the market quarters found in all cities and major towns (Figure 17.1). These were filled with shops and stalls that sold products drawn from local farms, regional centers of artisan production, and trade centers as distant as the Mediterranean. The Tang and Song governments supervised the hours and marketing methods in these centers, and merchants specializing in products of the same kind banded together in guilds to promote their interests with local officials and to regulate competition.

This expansion in scale was accompanied by a growing sophistication in commercial organization and forms of credit available in China. In the following millennium these innovations in instruments for economic exchange transformed domestic marketing and international commerce worldwide. The proportion of exchanges involved in the money economy expanded greatly, and deposit shops, an early form of the bank, were found in many parts of the empire. The first use of paper money also occurred in the Tang era. Merchants deposited their profits in their hometowns before setting out on trading caravans to distant cities. They were given credit vouchers, or what the Chinese called **flying money**, which they could then present for reimbursement at the appropriate office in the city of destination. This arrangement greatly reduced the danger of robbery on the often perilous journeys merchants made from one market center to another. In the early 11th century, the government began to issue paper money when an economic crisis made it clear that the private merchant banks could no longer handle the demand for the new currency.

The expansion of commerce and artisan production was complemented by a surge in urban growth in the Tang and Song eras. At nearly 2 million, the population of the Tang capital and its suburbs at Chang'an was far larger than that of any other city in the world at the time. The imperial city, an inner citadel within the walls of Chang'an, was divided into a highly restricted zone dominated by the palace and audience halls and a section crowded with the offices of the ministries and secretariats of the imperial government. Near the imperial city but outside Chang'an's walls, elaborate gardens and a hunting park were laid out for the amusement of the emperors and favored courtiers. The spread of commerce and the increasing population also fed urban growth in the rest of China. In the north and especially the south, old cities mushroomed as suburbs spread in all directions from the original city walls. Towns grew rapidly into cities, and the proportion of the empire's population living in urban centers grew steadily. The number of people living in large cities in China, which may have been as high as 10 percent, was also far greater than that found in any civilization until after the Industrial Revolution.

Expanding Agrarian Production and Life in the Country

The movement of the population southward to the fertile valleys of the Yangzi and other river systems was part of a larger process of agrarian expansion in the Tang and Song period. The expansion of Chinese settlement and agricultural production was promoted by the rulers of both dynasties. Their officials actively encouraged peasant groups to migrate to uncultivated areas or those occupied by shifting cultivators or peoples of non-Chinese descent. The state also supported military garrisons

junks Chinese ships equipped with watertight bulkheads, sternpost rudders, compasses, and bamboo fenders; dominant force in Asian seas east of the Malayan peninsula.

flying money Chinese credit instrument that provided credit vouchers to merchants to be redeemed at the end of the voyage; reduced danger of robbery; early form of currency.

in these areas to protect the new settlements and to complete the task of subduing non-Chinese peoples. State-regulated irrigation and embankment systems advanced agrarian expansion. For example, the great canals made it possible for peasants who grew specialized crops, such as tea, or those who cultivated silkworms to market their produce over much of the empire.

The introduction of new seeds, such as the famed Champa rice from Vietnam; better use of human, animal, and silt manures; more thorough soil preparation and weeding; and multiple cropping and improved water control techniques increased the yields of peasant holdings. Inventions such as the wheelbarrow eased the plowing, planting, weeding, and harvesting tasks that occupied much of the time of most Chinese people. The engraving shown in Figure 17.6 gives us a glimpse of rural scenes that were reproduced hundreds of thousands of times across China all through the Tang and Song centuries and much of the millennium that followed.

The rulers of both the Sui and Tang dynasties had adopted policies aimed at breaking up the great estates of the old aristocracy and distributing land more equitably among the free peasant households of the empire. These policies were designed in part to reduce or eliminate the threat that the powerful aristocracy posed for the new dynasties. They were also intended to bolster the position of the ordinary peasants, whose labors and well-being had long been viewed by Confucian scholars as essential to a prosperous and stable social order. To a point, these agrarian measures succeeded. For a time the numbers of the free peasantry increased, and the average holding size in many areas rose. The fortunes of many of the old aristocratic families also declined, thus removing many of them as independent centers of power. They were supplanted gradually in the rural areas by the gentry side of the scholar-gentry combination that dominated the imperial bureaucracy.

The extended-family households of the gentry that were found in rural settlements in the Han era increased in size and elegance in the Tang and Song. The widespread use of the graceful curved roofs, with upturned corners that one associates with Chinese civilization, dates from the Tang period. By imperial decree, curved roofs were reserved for people of high rank, including the scholar-gentry families. With intricately carved and painted roof timbers topped with glazed tiles of yellow or green, the great dwellings of the gentry left no doubt about the status and power of the families who lived in them. At the same time, their muted colors, wood and bamboo construction, and simple lines blended beautifully with nearby gardens and groves of trees.

FIGURE **17.6** The farming methods developed in the Song era are illustrated by this 17th-century engraving. Note the overseer, protected by an umbrella from the hot sun. Improved productivity, particularly of staple crops such as irrigated rice, meant that China's long-held advantages over other civilizations in terms of the population it could support increased in this era. By the early 14th century, as much as a quarter of humanity may have lived in the Chinese empire.

(© The Trustees of the British Museum/Art Resource, NY.)

Family and Society in the Tang and Song Eras

Chinese family organization at various class levels in the Tang and Song centuries closely resembled that found in earlier periods. Nonetheless, the position of women showed signs of improving under the Tang and early Song eras, and then deteriorated steadily in the late Song. As in the classical age, extended-family households were preferred, but normally they could be afforded only by the upper classes. The male-dominated hierarchy promoted by Confucius and other early thinkers held sway at all class levels. In the Tang period, the authority of elders and males within the family was buttressed by laws that prescribed beheading as a punishment for children who struck their parents or grandparents in anger, and two and one-half years of hard labor for younger brothers or sisters who hit their older siblings.

Over the centuries, a very elaborate process of forging marriage alliances developed. Professional go-betweens, almost always women, helped both families to negotiate such prickly issues as matching young men and women and the amount of the dowry to be paid to the husband's family. Brides and grooms in China, in contrast to those in India, were generally about the same age, probably because of the Confucian reluctance to mix generations.

Both within the family and in society at large, women remained clearly subordinate to men. But some evidence suggests that at least for women of the upper classes in urban areas, the opportunities for personal expression increased in the Tang and early Song. As the example of the empresses Wu and Wei and the concubine Yang Guifei make clear, Tang women could wield considerable power at the highest levels of Chinese society. That they also enjoyed access to a broad range of activities, if not career possibilities, is indicated by a surviving pottery figure from the early Tang period of a young woman playing polo.

Tang and Song law allowed divorce by mutual consent of both husband and wife. There were also laws prohibiting a husband from setting aside his wife if her parents were dead or if he had been poor when they were married and later became rich. These suggest that Chinese wives had more defenses against capricious behavior by their husbands than was the case in India at this time. A remarkable degree of independence is also indicated by the practice, reported in late Song times, of wealthy women in large cities such as Hangzhou taking lovers (or what were politely called "complimentary husbands") with the knowledge of their husbands.

The Neo-Confucian Assertion of Male Dominance

Evidence of the independence and legal rights enjoyed by a small minority of women in the Tang and Song eras is all but overwhelmed by the worsening condition of Chinese women in general. The assertion of male dominance was especially pronounced in the thinking of the neo-Confucian philosophers, who, as we have seen, became a major force in the later Song period. The neo-Confucians stressed the woman's role as homemaker and mother, particularly as the bearer of sons to continue the patrilineal family line. They advocated confining women and emphasized the importance of virginity for young brides, fidelity for wives, and chastity for widows. Like their counterparts in India, widows were discouraged from remarrying.

At the same time, men were permitted to have premarital sex without scandal, to take concubines if they could afford them, and to remarry if one or more of their wives died. The neo-Confucians attacked the Buddhists for promoting career alternatives for women, such as scholarship and the monastic life, at the expense of marriage and raising a family. They drafted laws that favored men in inheritance, divorce, and familial interaction. They also excluded women from the sort of education that would allow them to enter the civil service and rise to positions of political power. Footbinding epitomized the extent to which elite women's possibilities for self-fulfillment had been constricted by the later Song period.

View the **Closer Look** on **MyHistoryLab**: Erotic Deformity: Chinese Foot-binding

Invention, Artistic Creativity, and China's Global Impact

Perhaps even more than for political and economic transformations, the Tang and Song eras are remembered as a time of remarkable Chinese accomplishments in science, technology, literature, and the fine arts. Major technological breakthroughs and scientific discoveries were made under each dynasty. Some of them, particularly those involving the invention of new tools, production techniques, and weapons, gradually spread to other civilizations and fundamentally changed the course of human development. Until recent centuries, the arts and literature of China were not well known beyond its borders. Their impact was confined mainly to areas such as central Asia, Japan, and Vietnam, where Chinese imports had long been a major impetus for cultural change. But the poetry and short stories of the Tang and the landscape paintings of the Song are some of the most splendid artistic creations of all human history.

As we have seen, new agricultural tools and innovations such as banks and paper money contributed a great deal to economic growth and social prosperity in the Tang and Song eras. In this respect, the engineering feats of the period are particularly noteworthy. In addition to building the Grand

VISUALIZING THE PAST

Footbinding as a Marker of Male Dominance

NO ASPECT OF GENDER RELATIONS EXEMPLIFIES the degree to which women in the Tang-Song era were constricted in terms of career choices and subordinated to males as dramatically as **footbinding**. This practice may have had its origins in the delight one of the Tang emperors took in the tiny feet of his favorite dancing girls or, as has been recently argued, the fashion preference of elite women for small feet. Whatever its rationales, by the later Song era, upper-class men had developed a preference for small feet for women. This preference gradually spread to some groups further down on the social scale, including the well-to-do peasantry.

In response to male demands, on which the successful negotiation of a young woman's marriage contract might hinge, mothers began to bind the feet of their daughters as early as age five or six. The young girl's toes were turned under and bound with silk, which was wound more tightly as she grew, as shown by the accompanying photo. By the time she reached marriageable age, a young woman's feet had been transformed into the "lotus petal" or "golden lily" shapes that were presumably preferred by prospective husbands.

Bound feet were a constant source of pain for the rest of a woman's life, and they greatly limited her mobility by making it very difficult to walk even short distances. Limited mobility made it easier for husbands to confine their wives to the family compound. It also meant that women could not engage in occupations except ones that could be pursued within the extended family household, such as textile production. For this reason, the lower classes, whose households often depended on women's labor in the fields, markets, or homes of the wealthy to make ends meet, were slow to adopt the practice. But once it was in fashion among the scholar-gentry and other elite classes, footbinding became vital to winning a husband. In part, because a good marriage for their daughters was the primary goal of Chinese mothers, the practice was usually unquestioningly passed from one generation of women to the next.

As this photograph vividly illustrates, mature women with bound feet needed special footware since they depended heavily on the very thick heel that resulted from footbinding for support when standing and walking. Little of the sole of the foot touched the ground, and toes were fused together to make a pointed foot.

- Why would it be much more difficult for the laboring classes of the towns and ordinary peasant families to adopt footbinding?

- How did the structure of the family, the nature of women's extra-family links, and the sorts of pressures that could be brought to bear make it nearly impossible for women in well-to-do households to resist the imposition of the footbinding procedures?

- Beyond their lack of military training, why might the practice of footbinding make them much more vulnerable than men, especially in times of social unrest and civil war?

QUESTIONS

- In what ways did the rise of the practice of footbinding reflect the level of prosperity achieved by China's upper classes in the Tang-Song eras and the neo-Confucian conviction that women belonged in the domestic sphere?

Canal, Tang and Song engineers made great advances in building dikes and dams and regulating the flow of water in complex irrigation systems. They also devised ingenious new ways to build bridges, long a major focus of engineering efforts in a land dominated by mountains and waterways. From arched and segmented to trussed and suspension, most of the basic bridge types known to humans were pioneered in China.

footbinding Practice in Chinese society of mutilating women's feet in order to make them smaller; produced pain and restricted women's movement; made it easier to confine women to the household.

One of the most important of the many technological advances made in the Tang era, the invention of explosive powder, at first had little impact on warfare. For centuries, the Chinese used these potent chemical mixtures mainly for fireworks, which delighted emperors and the masses alike. By the late Song, however, explosive powder was widely used by the imperial armies in a variety of grenades and bombs that were hurled at the enemy by catapults. Song armies and warships also were equipped with naphtha flamethrowers, poisonous gases, and rocket launchers. These projectiles were perhaps the most effective weapons the dynasty used in its losing struggle to check nomadic incursions. On the domestic scene, chairs modeled on those found in India were introduced into the household, the habit of drinking tea swept the empire, coal was used for fuel for the first time, and the first kite soared into the heavens.

Although the number of major inventions in the Song era was lower than in the Tang, several were pivotal for the future of all civilizations. Compasses, which had been used since the last centuries B.C.E. by Chinese military commanders and magicians, were applied to sea navigation for the first time in the Song period. The abacus, the ancestor of the modern calculator, was introduced to help merchants count their profits and tax collectors keep track of revenues. In the mid-11th century, a remarkable artisan named Bi Sheng devised the technique of printing with movable type. Although block printing had been perfected in China in the preceding centuries, the use of movable type was a great advance in the production of written records and scholarly books. Combined with paper, which the Chinese had invented in the Han period, printing made it possible for them to attain a level of literacy that excelled that of any preindustrial civilization.

Scholarly Refinement and Artistic Accomplishment

The reinvigorated scholar-gentry elite was responsible for much of the artistic and literary creativity of the Tang and Song eras. Buddhist art and architecture had been heavily patronized by the court, prosperous merchants, and wealthy monasteries in the Tang period. But scholar-administrators and Confucian teachers wrote much of the literature for which the Tang is best remembered. They also painted the landscapes that were the most sublime cultural productions of the Song era. Confucian thinkers valued skillful writing and painting, and educated people were expected to practice these arts. The Chinese educational establishment was geared to turning out generalists rather than the specialists who are so revered in our own society. A well-educated man dabbled with varying degrees of success in many fields. After a hard day at the Ministry of Public Works, a truly accomplished official was expected to spend the evening composing songs on his lute, admiring a new painting or creating his own, or sipping rice wine while composing a poem to the harvest moon. Thus, talented and often well-trained amateurs wrote most of the poems, composed much of the music, and painted the landscapes for which the Tang and Song eras are renowned (Figure 17.7).

As the Confucian scholar-gentry supplanted the Buddhists as the major producers of art and literature, devotional objects and religious homilies gave way to a growing fixation on everyday life and the delights of the natural world. Much of the short story literature was focused on the lives of the common people, popular beliefs in witchcraft and demons, ill-fated romances, and even detective stories about brutal murders. Tang poetry moved from early verses that dwelt on the "pleasant breezes that envelope[d] the emperor's chair" to a seemingly endless variety of ways of celebrating the natural world. No one was better at the latter than the most famous poet of the Tang era, **Li Bo**. His poems, like those of the great Persian authors, blend images of the everyday world with philosophical musings:

Li Bo (701–762) Most famous poet of the Tang era; blended images of the mundane world with philosophical musings. The name is alternately spelled Li Po and Li Bai.

> The rain was over, green covered the land.
> One last cloudlet melted away in the clear sky.
> The east wind came home with the spring
> Bearing blossoms to sprout on the branches.
> Flowers are fading now and time will end.
> All mortal men perceive it and their sighs are deep.
> But I will turn to the sacred hills
> And learn from Tao [Dao] and from magic how to fly.

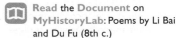
Read the Document on MyHistoryLab: Poems by Li Bai and Du Fu (8th c.)

This intense interest in nature came to full artistic fruition in the landscape paintings of the Song era. Most of them were produced by the cultivated men of the scholar-gentry class, and they pulled together diverse aspects of Chinese civilization. The brushes and techniques used were similar

THINKING HISTORICALLY

Artistic Expression and Social Values

STUDYING ARTISTIC CREATIVITY IS ONE OF the most effective ways of probing the beliefs and values of a civilization. In some cases in which the civilization in question did not develop writing, or at least writing that we can now decipher, art and architecture provide much of the evidence by which we can learn about the attitudes and lifestyles of vanished peoples. Some of the most notable examples include the ancient Indus civilization of South Asia and many of the high civilizations of the Americas and sub-Saharan Africa. Even in civilizations for which written records have survived, we can learn a good deal about social structure by discovering who produced the art and for whom it was created, about technology by studying artistic techniques and materials, and about worldviews by exploring the messages the art was intended to convey. In comparing some of the major forms of artistic expression of the great civilizations, we can also identify underlying similarities and differences in the values by which the peoples who developed them organized their societies and responded to the natural and supernatural worlds.

> [T]he artistic creativity of China's political elite underscores the importance of the preference for civil over military leaders in Chinese society.

The fact that members of the ruling political elite produced most of the landscape paintings of the Song era is unusual in the history of civilization. The sculptures that adorned the temples of India and the statues, paintings, and stained glass that graced the cathedrals of medieval Europe were created mainly by specialized and highly trained artisans whose skills were passed down over many generations. By contrast, the Song artists were often amateurs who painted in their leisure time. Even the most talented, who won enough patronage to devote themselves to painting full time, began as Confucian scholars and very often administrators. It is not just the amateur and "master of all fields" ideals that are remarkable here but the fact that so much art was produced by the men who also ran the country. In most of the other civilizations we have studied, political life has been dominated by warrior and priestly classes, not artistic scholar-bureaucrats like those who governed China.

Even in civilizations such as those of medieval Europe and Islam, where priests and religious teachers produced fine art in the form of manuscript illuminations, the people involved seldom had political responsibilities or power. Thus, the artistic creativity of China's political elite underscores the importance of the preference for civil over military leaders in Chinese society. It also tells us a good deal about the qualities the Chinese associated with a truly civilized and superior person—a person who was deemed worthy to rule the Middle Kingdom.

Song landscapes expressed the reactions and ideals of individual people, whom we can identify by the distinctive seals with which they stamped their paintings. The paintings clearly were intended for the pleasure and edification of the Chinese educated classes, not for museum viewing or mass consumption. Landscape painting reinforced the identity and values of the scholarly elite across the vast spaces of the Chinese empire as well as across time. In a famous incident, the Confucian philosopher Zhu Xi remarked on the nobility and loyalty that he saw so clearly in the calligraphy of scholars from the Warring States era.

This individualism and elitism in Chinese art can be contrasted with the anonymous creation of sculptures and religious paintings in Hindu and Buddhist civilizations and medieval Europe or the mosaic decorations of the mosques of Islam. In each of these other civilizations, artistic works that adorned temples, cathedrals, and mosques were intended for a mass audience. The moral instruction for the scholarly few that was contained in the Song landscapes had a very different purpose than the religious sculptures or mosaics of other civilizations. The sculptures and mosaics were created to convey a religious message, to remind the viewers of a key event in the life of Christ or the Buddha, or to impress upon them the horrors of hell or the delights of heaven.

Thus, the highest art forms, linked to a common religion, bridged the gulf between elites and the masses in Hindu, Buddhist, Christian, and Muslim civilizations. Imported Buddhist art forms performed this function in some periods in Chinese history. But the more enduring Confucian-Daoist artistic creativity, best exemplified by landscape painting, accentuated the differences that separated the educated scholar-gentry and the common people.

QUESTIONS

- What do you think the small size of the people in Chinese landscape paintings can tell us about Chinese views on the relationship between humans and the natural world?
- Can you think of American or European politicians who have created great works of art?
- Do we expect this sort of creativity from our elected officials?
- If not, what does this tell us about the values of our own civilization?

FIGURE **17.7** The simplicity of composition, the use of empty space, and the emphasis on nature are all characteristic of Chinese landscape painting at its height in the Song era. The colors used tended to be muted; often only brown or black ink was used. Most artists stamped their work with signature seals, like the red ones in this image, and poems describing scenes related to those in the painting floated in the empty space at the top or sides.

(Ma Yuan, Chinese, 1190–1235 "Bare Willows and Distant Mountains." Photograph © 2010 Museum of Fine Arts, Boston. Special Chinese and Japanese Fund, 14.61)

to those used in writing the Chinese language, which itself was regarded as a high art form. The paintings were symbolic, intended to teach moral lessons or explore philosophical ideas. The objects depicted were not only beautiful in themselves but stood for larger concepts: A crane and a pine tree, for example, represented longevity; bamboo shoots were associated with the scholar-gentry class; and a dragon could call to mind any number of things, including the emperor, the cosmos, or life-giving rain.

There was an abstract quality to the paintings that gives them a special appeal in the present day. The artists were not concerned with depicting nature accurately but rather with creating a highly personal vision of natural beauty. A premium was placed on subtlety and suggestion. For example, the winner of an imperial contest painted a lone monk drawing water from an icy stream to depict the subject announced by the emperor: a monastery hidden deep in the mountains during the winter. Song landscapes often were painted on scrolls that could be read as the viewer unfolded them bit by bit. Most were accompanied by a poem, sometimes composed by the painter, which complemented the subject matter and was aimed at explaining the artist's ideas.

Global Connections and Critical Themes

CHINA'S WORLD ROLE

The postclassical period in world history saw a vital consolidation of Chinese civilization. Although fewer fundamental changes occurred in China than those experienced in eastern and Western Europe, the Americas, and certainly the Middle East, Chinese civilization developed in important new ways. Some of these innovations, especially the technological ones, soon affected the wider world. China also consolidated its own orbit of more intense influence in eastern Asia through ongoing exchanges with central Asia, Japan, Korea, Vietnam, and elsewhere in southeast Asia. Although more isolated than the Islamic empires and India, China nevertheless contributed vitally to other regions as it flourished under two vigorous dynasties, the Tang and the Song.

From the Tang era until the 18th century, the Chinese economy was one of the world's most advanced in terms of market networks, volume of overseas trade, productivity per land area, and the sophistication of its tools and techniques of craft production. Production of luxury goods, from silks to fine ceramics, attracted traders from abroad and delighted upper-class consumers in distant lands. As a key source of both manufactured goods and cultivated consumables, such as tea and rhubarb, China contributed in major ways to the expanding Afro-Eurasian commercial system. Chinese inventions such as paper, printing, and gunpowder were also widely disseminated and fundamentally changed the course of development in all other human civilizations. Until the 18th century, the imperial dynasties of China had political power and economic resources unmatched by those of any other civilization.

By retreating to the south, the Song rulers managed to survive the assaults of the nomads from the north. But as the dynasty weakened, enduring patterns of nomadic incursions resurfaced and built to the apex of pastoral military and political expansion under the Mongols. The Song emperors could not retreat far enough to escape the onslaught of the most brilliant nomadic commander of them all, Chinggis Khan, who directed perhaps the most powerful military machine the world had seen up to that time. The Song rulers bought time by paying tribute to the Mongol Khan and making alliances with him against their common enemies. But a later Mongol leader, Kubilai Khan, launched a sustained effort to conquer the southern refuge of the Song dynasty, which was completed by 1279.

Further Readings

In addition to the general histories of China suggested in Chapter 4, several important works cover the Tang and Song eras. The recent and magisterial history of *Imperial China, 900–1800* (1999) by F. W. Mote is a superb place to start, and the volume, edited by Denis Twitchett, devoted to the Tang and Song in the *Cambridge History of China* is an essential reference work. There are detailed works on the founding of the Tang dynasty by C. P. Fitzgerald (1970) and Woodbridge Bingham (1940), but these should be read in conjunction with the more recent *Mirror to the Son of Heaven* (1974), which provides valuable correctives to the interpretations of these earlier authors. Useful insights into political and cultural life in the Tang era can be gleaned from the specialized essays in the volume *Perspectives on the Tang* (1973), edited by Arthur Wright and Denis Twitchett. On social patterns in the Tang era, see Charles Benn, *Daily Life in Traditional China: The Tang Dynasty* (2002). Until recently, the most accessible work on society and politics in the Song era was Jacques Gernet, *Daily Life in China on the Eve of the Mongol Invasion, 1250–1276* (1962), which is highly entertaining and informative. On the great social and economic transitions of the Song era, Mark Elvin, *The Pattern of the Chinese Past* (1973), is insightful, provocative, and controversial. These standard accounts can now be supplemented by P. B. Ebry, *The Aristocratic Families of Early Imperial China* (1978); Heng Chye Kiang, *Cities of Aristocrats and Bureaucrats: The Development of Medieval Chinese Cities* (1999); and D. McMullen, *State and Scholars in T'ang China* (1988). Bret Hinsch, *Women in Early Imperial China* (2002), provides a useful introduction to this subject, which is closely examined in Kathryn Bernhardt, *Women and Property in China, 960–1949* (1999), and Bettine Birge, *Women, Property and Confucian Reaction in Sung and Yüan China, 960–1368* (2002).

Of the numerous works on Chinese art and painting, perhaps the best place to start is with the standard work by Mai-mai Sze, *The Way of Chinese Painting* (1956), which quotes extensively from Chinese manuals. Of more recent works, the general survey by Laurence Sickman and Alexander Soper, as well as James Cahill's study of landscape painting, stand out. And they can be supplemented by Alfreda Murch's recent study of *Poetry and Painting in Song China* (2000). A wonderful sampler of Li Bo's poetry can be found in a volume titled *Bright Moon, Perching Bird* (1987), edited by J. P. Seaton and James Cryer.

On MyHistoryLab

 Study and Review on MyHistoryLab

Critical Thinking Questions

1. In what major ways did the relations between the Chinese and the nomadic peoples to the north and west in Central Asia shape the fortunes of Chinese dynasties in the Sui-Song eras?

2. How did the scholar-gentry become such a dominant force in Chinese politics and society from the early Tang through the Song periods?

3. How do the production, subject matter, and intended audiences of Chinese art differ from those in the Buddhist, Muslim, and Christian societies we have studied in other great civilized centers?

18

The Spread of Chinese Civilization: Japan, Korea, and Vietnam

Listen to Chapter 18 on MyHistoryLab

LEARNING OBJECTIVES

18.1 What were the key aspects of Chinese culture and organization that the Japanese imported in the early imperial era? p. 396

18.2 Why did Japan's imperial order break down beginning in the ninth century and what sort of political and social system replaced it? p. 400

18.3 What were the results of Korea's links to China? p. 405

18.4 What were the main differences in Vietnamese-Chinese relations from those in Korea and Japan? p. 408

Following a centuries-old protocol, a distinguished Vietnamese official named Ly Van Phúc entered the Chinese imperial capital at Beijing at the head of an embassy that had come to pay tribute to the Chinese ruler. Well versed in Confucian ways, Phúc was at home in the crowded streets of the great city. Because Chinese and other Asian potentates (often with good reason) regarded embassies as little more than fronts for spies, Phúc and his entourage were visiting rather than preparing to take up residence in the capital. The Vietnamese had been assigned a hostel near the Forbidden City, which housed the magnificent imperial palace where, in an elaborate ceremony, Phúc would pay homage to the Daoguang emperor (Figure 18.1).

Read the Document on MyHistoryLab: Guidelines for Tributary Missions, Qing Dynasty, 1764

FIGURE **18.1** At the height of the power and prosperity of the Qing dynasty, the emperor Qianlong, who ruled for more than 60 years, receives tribute from "the ten thousand countries" in one of his imposing palace complexes. Participation in the tribute ceremony, which had become essential for all countries—including Japan, Korea, and Vietnam—that wished to trade with China, had been established as early as the Tang dynasty in the 7th century C.E.

394

👁 Watch the Video Series on MyHistoryLab

**Learn about some key topics related to this chapter with the *MyHistoryLab Video Series:
Key Topics in World History***

As Phúc and his countrymen approached the quarters to which they had been officially assigned, they were confronted by a placard on the building that identified it as "The Vietnamese Barbarians' Hostel." Deeply humiliated and struggling to contain his anger, Phúc ordered his companions not to enter but rather prepare an improvised campsite in the middle of the street. After commanding two of his companions to destroy the sign, he sat down and composed a strongly worded treatise entitled "On Distinguishing Barbarians." Demonstrating his admirable proficiency in Chinese calligraphy, he wrote to the Daoguang emperor, describing the insult that—whether out of ignorance or intent—the emperor's officials had directed toward the Vietnamese.

Phúc reminded the Chinese emperor (who was of Manchu descent, and thus just a few generations away from barbarian status in the Chinese view) that the Vietnamese had nurtured Chinese culture for millennia. Phúc pointed out that, like the Chinese emperor himself, the Vietnamese royal family and officials were fluent in Chinese, honored Confucian principles of governance and social organization, and organized their educational system around the classic works of Chinese civilization. As soon as it was composed, the essay was presented to Chinese officials to be delivered to the emperor. It is not certain that the very polite reprimand actually reached that exalted personage, but Vietnamese accounts of the incident expressed great satisfaction that the Chinese were most apologetic. Apparently, they even admitted their gratitude that the mistaken use of "barbarian" had been challenged and was corrected. ■

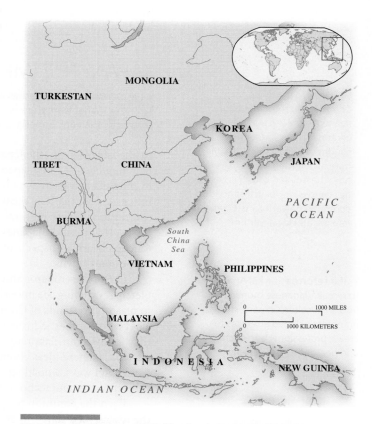

MAP **18.1 Key Centers of Civilization in East Asia in the First Millennium** c.e. Despite steady expansion over much of East Asia from the end of the last millennium b.c.e. through the first millennium c.e., the Chinese were not able to absorb three large areas on their periphery—Korea, Japan and Vietnam—into their civilization.

Both the reverence for Chinese civilization and the decided ambivalence regarding the extent of its influence illustrated by the Phúc incident capture key features of centuries of interaction between China and other societies across much of central and southeast Asia. In earlier chapters we dealt in some depth with the persisting and dynamic exchanges between the Chinese and the nomadic peoples of central and northeast Asia. A similar pattern of attraction and resistance runs through the centuries when Chinese influence contributed in vital ways to the rise of complex and sophisticated societies in Japan, Korea, and Vietnam. For two millennia, China has been the premier civilization of East Asia and surrounding areas—the seedbed of technological innovation; a model for social, military, and political organization; a persisting influence on philosophical and religious thinking; and a major locus of commercial exchange (see Map 18.1).

As Phúc's obvious pride in his mastery of the Chinese language, history, and manners strikingly reveals, these influences have been particularly pervasive in agrarian-based societies, such as those that developed in neighboring Japan, Korea, and Vietnam. But Phúc's sensitivity to insults to his people and culture and his vigorous response also reflect an underlying wariness of Chinese domination that was displayed by all three of these societies. Korea and Vietnam were ruled directly by China for centuries and frequently rose in violent rebellions aimed at asserting their political independence. Japanese elites were often deeply divided about which and how much Chinese influence to introduce, and

200 B.C.E.	600 C.E.	800 C.E.	1000 C.E.	1200 C.E.	1400 C.E.
206 B.C.E.–220 C.E. Reign of Han dynasty in China **111** Vietnam conquered by China **109** Choson (Korea) conquered by China **39 C.E.** Trung sisters revolt in Vietnam **222–589** Era of Division in China **589–618** Sui dynasty in China	**618–907** Tang dynasty in China **646** Taika reforms in Japan **668** Korea wins independence from Tang conquerors **668–918** Silla kingdom in Korea **710–784** Imperial Japanese capital at Nara **794** Japanese capital shifts to Heian (Kyoto)	**838** Last Japanese embassy to China **857–1160** Period of Fujiwara dominance in Japan **918–1392** Koryo dynasty in Korea **939** Vietnam wins independence from China **960–1279** Song dynasty in China **980–1009** Le dynasty in Vietnam	**1160–1185** Taira clan dominant in Japan **1180–1185** Gempei Wars in Japan **1185–1333** Kamakura Shogunate in Japan	**1231–1392** Mongol rule in Korea **1279–1368** Mongol rule in China **1392–1910** Yi dynasty in Korea	**1467–1477** Onin War in Japan **1500** Nguyen dynasty in central/south Vietnam founded **1539–1787** Trinh dynasty in Red River area (Vietnam) **1600** Founding of the Tokugawa Shogunate in Japan

Japanese peasants and merchants often balked at integrating Chinese imports—whether ideas or new ways of growing rice or making war—into their daily lives.

In all three cases, the tensions between the desire to emulate and borrow from China and the determination to preserve their distinctive languages, social customs, and other cultural forms profoundly shaped the nature of the highly civilized societies that developed in Japan, Korea, and Vietnam. As Phúc's confrontation with Chinese officialdom in the mid-19th century suggests, these tensions continued to shape social and political dynamics throughout east Asia well into the modern era.

JAPAN: THE IMPERIAL AGE

18.1 | What were the key aspects of Chinese culture and organization that the Japanese imported in the early imperial era?

> Chinese influence on Japan peaked in the 7th and 8th centuries as Japanese rulers sought to build a Chinese-style bureaucracy and society. Over time the isolated court centers at Nara and later Heian lost political control to powerful aristocratic families and local warlords.

By the late 600s C.E., the Japanese court at Nara (Map 18.2) was awash in imports from China, which had long been seen by Japan and China's other neighbors as the most advanced society in east Asia in pursuits as varied as politics, intellectual production, and material culture. Indigenous cultural influences, particularly those linked to Shinto views of the natural and supernatural world, remained central to Japanese cultural development. But in the Taika (645–710), Nara (710–784), and Heian (794–1185) periods, Japanese borrowing from China—although selective—peaked. This borrowing touched nearly all aspects of Japanese life, particularly at the level of the elites and among the people of the court towns.

> **Taika reforms** [tai kä] Attempt to remake Japanese monarch into an absolute Chinese-style emperor; included attempts to create professional bureaucracy and peasant conscript army.

In 646 the emperor and his advisors introduced the far-reaching **Taika reforms**, aimed at completely revamping the imperial administration along Chinese lines. Japanese court scholars struggled to master thousands of Chinese characters, which bore little relationship to the language they spoke. They wrote dynastic histories patterned after those commissioned by the emperors of China, and they followed an elaborate court etiquette that somewhat uneasily combined Chinese protocol with ancient Japanese ideas about politeness and decorum. The Japanese aristocracy struggled to master Confucian ways, worshiped in Chinese-style temples, and admired Buddhist art that was Chinese in subject matter and technique.

Even the common people were affected by the steady flow of influence from the mainland. In the towns, they stared in awe at the great Buddhist temples and bowed to passing aristocrats trying to present themselves as Confucian scholars. The peasants turned to Buddhist monks for cures when they were sick or to Buddhist magic when they needed a change of luck. They had begun to mesh the worship of Buddhist deities with that of the ancient *kami*, or nature spirits, of Japan.

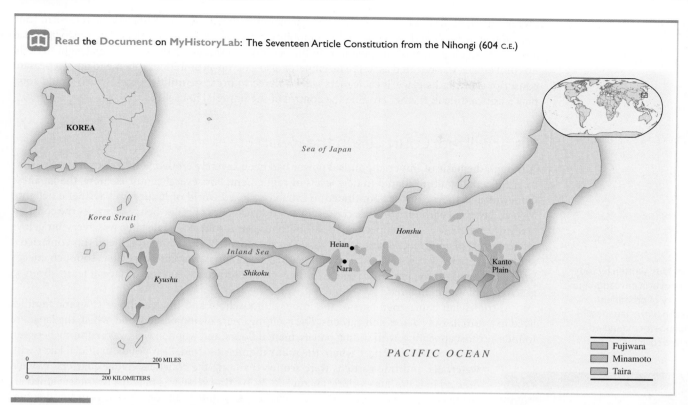

Read the **Document** on **MyHistoryLab**: The Seventeen Article Constitution from the Nihongi (604 C.E.)

MAP **18.2 Japan in the Imperial and Warlord Periods** Power in warlord era was concentrated in the region of the Kanto plain, which was the main rice granary of the islands and thus able to support a relatively dense population.

Crisis at Nara and the Shift to Heian (Kyoto)

If they had succeeded, the Taika reforms of 646 would have represented the culmination of centuries of Japanese borrowing from China. The central objectives of the proposed changes were to remake the Japanese monarch into an absolutist Chinese-style emperor (even to the point of adding "Son of Heaven" to the Japanese ruler's many titles). The reforms also were intended to create a genuine professional bureaucracy and peasant conscript army in Japan to match those of Han and Tang China. But the changes necessary for these goals to be achieved were frustrated by the resistance of the aristocratic families and the Buddhist monastic orders, who dominated both the emperor and the capital as a whole.

A century after the reforms were introduced, the Buddhist monks in particular had grown so bold and powerful that the court and aristocracy lived in fear of street demonstrations by "rowdy monks" and of the escalating demands of the heads of the monastic orders. Their influence even threatened to engulf the throne in the 760s, when a clever Buddhist prelate worked his way into the inner circle of the empress Koken. His schemes to marry her and become emperor were uncovered and foiled. But it was clear to the emperor's advisors that measures had to be taken to ensure that women could never rule Japan and to check the growing influence of the monastic orders at court.

In 794 the emperor Kammu established a new capital city at Heian (hay-yan) (Map 18.2), which was later called Kyoto. Buddhists were forbidden to build monasteries in the new capital. But to get around this restriction, the monks established monasteries in the hills surrounding Heian, and they soon reemerged as a potent force at court as royal advisors.

In addition to trying to control the Buddhist monks, the emperor abandoned all pretense of continuing the Taika reforms, which had long been stalled by aristocratic and popular opposition. He fully restored the great aristocratic families, whose power the reforms had been intended to curb. The elaborate system of ranks into which the aristocrats were divided (patterned after that in China)

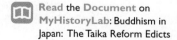 Read the **Document** on **MyHistoryLab**: Buddhism in Japan: The Taika Reform Edicts

was maintained. But like the Koreans, the Japanese broke with Chinese precedent in determining rank solely by birth and by allowing little mobility between the various orders. The aristocrats had already taken over most of the positions in the central government. Now, their formal right to build up rural estates was restored as well. The emperor also gave up an ambitious scheme to build a peasant conscript army. In its place, local leaders were ordered to organize militia forces, which would soon play a critical role in further eroding the control of the imperial household.

Ultracivilized: Court Life in the Heian Era

Although the basis of imperial political power had been severely eroded within decades of the shift to Heian, court culture soared to new levels of refinement. For several centuries more, the Japanese emperors and their courtiers continued to inhabit a closed world of luxury and aesthetic delights. Men and women of the aristocratic classes followed strict codes of polite behavior, under the constant scrutiny of their peers and superiors. In this hothouse atmosphere, social status was everything, love affairs were a major preoccupation, and gossip was rampant. By our standards, life in this constricted and very artificial world was false and suffocating. Yet rarely in human history has so much energy been so focused on the pursuit of beauty or has social interaction—on the surface at least—been so gracious and well mannered.

Tale of Genji, The Written by Lady Murasaki; first novel in any language; relates life history of prominent and amorous son of the Japanese emperor; evidence for mannered style of Japanese society.

At the Heian court, members of the imperial household and the leading aristocratic families lived in a complex of palaces and gardens. The buildings were of unpainted wood, which the Japanese found the most appealing, with sliding panels, matted floors, and wooden walkways running between the separate residences where the many dignitaries lived. Fish ponds, artificial lakes with waterfalls, and fine gardens were scattered among the courtiers' living quarters. Women dressed in elaborate clothing (Figure 18.2). Writing verse was perhaps the most valued art at the court. The poems were often written on painted fans or scented paper, and sometimes they were sent in little boats down the streams that ran through the palace grounds. The verse was brief and full of allusions to Chinese and Japanese classical writings. In the following couplet, a young courtier expresses his disappointment at being denied access to a pretty young woman:

> Having come upon an evening blossom
> The mist is loath to go with the morning sun.

Partly to accommodate the need for literary expression of this type, the written script the Japanese had borrowed from the Chinese was simplified, making it more compatible with spoken Japanese. One result of these changes was an outpouring of poetic and literary works that were more and more distinctively Japanese. The most celebrated of these was Lady Murasaki's *The Tale of Genji*. None of the works on court life captured its charm and its underlying tensions and sadness as wonderfully as Lady Murasaki's classic, which was the first novel in any language (Figure 18.3). In the story, she relates the life history of a prominent and amorous son of the emperor and the fate of his descendants. As the story makes clear, Genji's life is almost wholly devoted to the pursuit of aesthetic enjoyment, whether in affairs with beautiful women or in musical entertainments in a garden scented with blooming flowers. Uncouth commoners and distasteful things, such as dirt, cheap pottery, and rough popular entertainments, are to be avoided at all costs. When her rivals at the court want to insult Genji's mother, for example, they leave spoiled fruit in the passages where she or her maidservants must pass. An encounter with a shriveled piece of fruit contributes to the illness that leads to her premature death.

FIGURE **18.2** From this artist's impression of the elaborate dress and studied pose of a Heian courtier, one gains a vivid sense of the formality and attention to aesthetic pleasures that dominated the lives of the Japanese elite in this era. As the focus upon a woman in the painting suggests, the intense world of the Heian court provided a tiny minority of Japanese women with outlets for expressing emotion and creativity that have been denied to most women through much of civilized history.

Everyone who matters in Genji's world is obsessed with the social conventions that govern everything, from which gown is proper for a given ceremony to the composition of a suitable poem to woo a potential lover or win the emperor's favor. Although women rivaled men as poets, artists, and musicians and in their pervasive cultivation of aesthetic pleasure, it was unseemly for them to openly pursue lovers. Nonetheless, as Lady Murasaki's poignant novel makes clear, some women did court prospective lovers with great guile and passion. It was not uncommon for a high-born woman to spurn a suitor and humiliate him in front of her maidservants.

In addition to novels such as Lady Murasaki's, some of the most elegant poetry in the Japanese language was written in this era. Again, it is sparing in words but rich in imagery and allusions to the natural world:

> This perfectly still
> Spring Day bathed in the soft light
> From the spread-out sky,
> Why do the cherry blossoms so restlessly scatter down?
> Although I am sure
> That he will not be coming
> In the evening light
> When the locusts shrilly call
> I go to the door and wait.

As the female authorship of this poem and *The Tale of Genji* clearly illustrate, women at the Heian court were expected to be as poised and cultured as men. Because they were less involved, however, with Chinese cultural imports (presumed to be a superior male preserve), they actually, for a time, played an unusually creative role in Japanese productions. They wrote poems, played flutes or stringed instruments in informal concerts, and participated in elaborate schemes to snub or disgrace rivals. Like their counterparts in China and the Islamic world, they also became involved in palace intrigues and power struggles.

The Decline of Imperial Power

While the emperor and his courtiers admired the plum blossoms and the newest fashions in court dress, some of the aristocratic families at court were busy running the rapidly shrinking imperial bureaucracy. By the mid-9th century, one of these families, the **Fujiwara**, exercised exceptional influence over imperial affairs. Not only did they pack the upper administration with family members and shape imperial policy, but they also increasingly married Fujiwaras into the imperial family. By the middle of the 10th century, one aged Fujiwara chief minister had seen four of his daughters married to emperors.

Families such as the Fujiwara used the wealth and influence of their high office to build up large estates that provided a stable financial base for their growing power. Especially in the vicinity of the capital, they had to compete in these purchases with the Buddhist monasteries. But both could work together in the steady campaign to whittle down imperial control and increase their own. As the lands under their control expanded, both the monks and the court nobility greatly increased the number of peasants and artisans they in effect ruled. Cooperation between monastic orders and court aristocrats was promoted by the introduction of the secret texts and ceremonies of esoteric Buddhism in this period. These teachings and techniques to achieve salvation through prayers and meditation, which were focused by mystical diagrams and special hand positions, were the rage among the Heian elite. As aristocrats and monks steadily built up their own power in the capital, however, they failed to reckon with the growing power of the local lords.

The Rise of the Provincial Warrior Elites

The pursuit of landed estates that increasingly preoccupied the court aristocracy was also taken up by elite families in the provinces. Some of these families had aristocratic origins, but most had risen to power as landowners, estate managers, or local state officials. These families came to control land and labor and to deny these resources to the court. They gradually carved out little kingdoms, ruled by "house" governments, in various parts of the islands. They dominated their mini-states within the larger Japanese realm from small fortresses surrounded by wooden or earthen walls and moat-like ditches. The local lord and his retainers were housed within the fortress, constantly on the alert for an attack by a neighboring lord or the forces of one of the powerful families at court. Granaries for storing the rice provided by local peasants, blacksmith forges and stables, wells for water, and even armories made the fortresses self-contained worlds.

📖 **Read** the **Document** on **MyHistoryLab:** Murasaki Shikibu, selections from *The Tale of Genji*

FIGURE 18.3 This painting illustrating one of the episodes in Lady Murasaki's *The Tale of Genji* captures the inward-looking character of court life that gradually cut the emperor and his entourage off from the warriors, townspeople, and peasants they ruled. The growing isolation of the court provided opportunities for regional lords with a more military orientation and more effective links to the population as a whole to seize effective control of Japan.

Fujiwara Japanese aristocratic family in mid-9th century; exercised exceptional influence over imperial affairs; aided in decline of imperial power.

bushi Regional warrior leaders in Japan; ruled small kingdoms from fortresses; administered the law, supervised public works projects, and collected revenues; built up private armies.

samurai Mounted troops of Japanese warrior leaders (bushi); loyal to local lords, not the emperor.

Within the mini-states ruled from the forts, the warrior leaders, or **bushi**, administered law, supervised public works projects, and collected revenue—mainly for themselves, not the court. The failure of the court's plans to build conscript armies also allowed the bushi to build up their own armies. These soon became the most effective military forces in the land. The troops who served the bushi came to be called **samurai**. They were loyal to the local lords, not to the court or high aristocratic officials, even though they were increasingly called in to protect the emperor and his retainers and to keep the peace in the capital. As the imperial government's control over the country weakened in the 11th and 12th centuries, bandits freely roamed the countryside and the streets of the capital. Buddhist monasteries employed armed toughs to protect them and attack rival sects. In this atmosphere of rampant crime and civil strife, the court and high officials hired provincial lords and their samurai retainers to serve as bodyguards and to protect their palaces and mansions from robbery and arson.

These trends proved critical to the emergence of a warrior class. Counting on peasant dependants to supply them with food and other necessities, the bushi and samurai devoted their lives to hunting, riding, archery practice, and other activities that sharpened their martial skills. Until the 12th century, the main weapons of the mounted warriors were powerful longbows and spears, although they also carried straight swords. From the 12th century on, they increasingly relied on the superbly forged, curved steel swords that we commonly associate with the Japanese samurai. The bushi and the samurai warriors who served them rode into battles that increasingly hinged on the duels of great champions. These combats represented heroic warfare in the extreme. The time and location of battles were elaborately negotiated beforehand, and each side tried to demonstrate the justice of its cause and the treachery of its enemies. Before charging into battle, Japanese warriors proudly proclaimed their family lineage and its notable military exploits to their adversaries, who often missed the details because they were shouting back their own.

A warrior code developed that stressed family honor and death rather than retreat or defeat. Beaten or disgraced warriors turned to ritual suicide to prove their courage and restore their family's honor. They called this practice **seppuku**, which meant disembowelment. But it has come to be known in the West by the more vulgar expression *hara-kiri*, or belly splitting. Battles were chaotic—lots of shouting and clashing but few fatalities—and were won or lost depending on the performance of the champions on each side. Although a full chivalric code did not develop until some centuries later, Japan was steadily moving toward a feudal order that was remarkably similar to that developing in western Europe in this same postclassical period.

seppuku Ritual suicide or disembowelment in Japan; commonly known in West as hara-kiri; demonstrated courage and a means to restore family honor.

The rise of the samurai frustrated all hopes of creating a free peasantry. In fact, Japanese peasants were reduced in the next centuries to the status of serfs, bound to the land they worked and treated as the property of the local lord. They were also separated by rigid class barriers from the warrior elite, which was physically set off by its different ways of dressing and by prohibitions against the peasants carrying swords or riding horses. In their growing poverty and powerlessness, the peasants turned to popular Buddhism in the form of the salvationist pure land sect. The teachings of the pure land offered the promise of bliss in heaven for those who lived upright lives on earth. Colorful figures, such as the dancing monk Kuya, were intended to make Buddhist teachings comprehensible and appealing to both the peasantry and the artisans, who were concentrated in the fortress towns. Buddhist shrines and images became popular destinations for pilgrimages and objects of veneration.

THE ERA OF WARRIOR DOMINANCE

From the 12th century onward, Japanese history was increasingly dominated by civil wars between shifting factions of the court aristocracy and local warlords, which ended only with the rise of the Tokugawa warlord family in the early 1600s. Chinese influence declined steadily in this era, but despite strife and social dislocation, the arts and literature flourished in Japan.

18.2   Why did Japan's imperial order break down beginning in the ninth century and what sort of political and social system replaced it?

As the power of the provincial lords grew, that of the imperial household and court aristocracy declined. Powerful families at the court, such as the Fujiwara, increasingly depended on alliances with regional lords to support them in disputes with their rivals. By the 11th and 12th centuries, the provincial families had begun to pack the court bureaucracy and compete for power. By the mid-12th century, competition turned to open feuding between the most powerful of these families, the **Taira** and the **Minamoto**. For a time, the Taira gained the upper hand by controlling the emperor and dominating at court. But when rivalry turned to open warfare in the early 1180s, the Minamoto commanders and their powerful network of alliances with provincial lords in various parts of the country proved superior to the leaders or allies the Taira could muster. More importantly, the Tairas' concentration of their power-grabbing efforts in the capital led to the breakdown of critical links with rural notables, who often sided with the Minamoto in the factional struggles.

The Declining Influence of China

As the power of the imperial house weakened, the relevance of Chinese precedents and institutions diminished for the Japanese. Pretensions to a heavenly mandate and centralized power became ludicrous; the emergence of a scholar-gentry elite was stifled by the reassertion of aristocratic power and prerogatives. Grand designs for an imperial bureaucracy never materialized. Buddhism was increasingly transformed by both aristocrats and peasants into a distinctively Japanese religion. With the decline of the Tang and a return to decades of political uncertainty and social turmoil in China, the Chinese model seemed even less relevant to the Japanese. As early as 838, the Japanese court decided to discontinue its embassies to the much-reduced Tang court. Japanese monks and traders still made the dangerous sea crossing to China, but the emperor's advisors no longer deemed official visits and groveling before the Son of Heaven to be worth all the bother.

For five years, the **Gempei Wars** raged in the heartland of the main island of Honshu (Map 18.2). This conflict brought great suffering to the peasantry, whose farmlands were ravaged. At the same time, they were compelled to fight against each other. Often large numbers of poorly trained peasants were cut down by the better-armed, professional samurai warriors, who met these hapless rivals in the course of their seemingly endless ritual combats. By 1185, the Taira house faction had been destroyed. The Minamoto then established the **bakufu** (which literally means "tent"), or military government. The Minamoto capital was located at Kamakura in their base area on the Kanto plain, far to the east of the old court center at Heian (Map 18.2). The emperor and his court were preserved, but real power now rested with the Minamoto and their samurai retainers. The feudal age in Japan had begun.

The Breakdown of Bakufu Dominance and the Age of the Warlords

Yoritomo, the leader of the victorious Minamoto, gravely weakened the Kamakura regime because of his obsessive fear of being overthrown by members of his own family. Close relatives, including his brother Yoshitsune, whose courage and military genius had much to do with the Minamoto triumph over the Taira, were murdered or driven into exile. Fear of spies lent an element of paranoia to elite life under the first of the Kamakura **shoguns**, which was the title taken by the military overlords of the bakufu. Although Yoritomo's rule went unchallenged, the measures he adopted to protect his throne left him without an able heir. His death and the weakness of those who succeeded him led to a scramble on the part of the bushi lords to build up their own power and enlarge their domains. The **Hojo**, one of the warrior families that had long been closely allied to the Minamoto, soon dominated the Kamakura regime, although they were content to leave the Minamoto as the formal rulers. Thus, a curious and confusing three-tiered system arose. Real power rested in the Hojo family, who manipulated the Minamoto shoguns, who in turn claimed to rule in the name of the emperor who lived at Kyoto.

In the early 14th century, the situation became even murkier when the head of one of the branches of the Minamoto family, **Ashikaga Takuaji**, led a revolt of the bushi that overthrew the Kamakura regime and established the **Ashikaga Shogunate** (1336–1573) in its place. Because the emperor at the time of Ashikaga's seizure of power refused to recognize the usurper and tried to revive imperial power, he was driven from Kyoto to the mountain town of Yoshino. There, with the support of several warlords, the exiled emperor and his heirs fought against the Ashikaga faction and the puppet emperors they placed on the throne at Kyoto for much of the rest of the 14th century.

Although the Ashikaga were finally successful in destroying the rival Yoshino center of imperial authority, the long period of civil strife seriously undermined whatever authority the emperor had left as well as that of the shogunate. The bushi vassals of the warring factions were free to crush local rivals and to seize the lands of the peasantry, the old aristocracy, and competing warlords. As the power of the bushi warlords grew, the court aristocracy, which was impoverished by its inability to defend its estates, was nearly wiped out. The lands the warlords acquired were parceled out to their

Taira [teye-ruh] Powerful Japanese family in 11th and 12th centuries; competed with Minamoto family; defeated after Gempei Wars.

Minamoto Defeated the rival Taira family in Gempei Wars and established military government (bakufu) in 12th-century Japan.

Gempei Wars [gehm-pay] Waged for five years from 1180, on Honshu between Taira and Minamoto families; resulted in destruction of Taira.

bakufu Military government established by the Minamoto following the Gempei Wars; centered at Kamakura; retained emperor, but real power resided in military government and samurai.

shoguns Military leaders of the bakufu (military governments in Japan).

Hojo Warrior family closely allied with Minamoto; dominated Kamakura regime and manipulated Minamoto rulers who claimed to rule in name of Japanese emperor at Kyoto.

Ashikaga Takuaji [ah-she-kah-gah tahk-oo-ah-jee] Member of the Minamoto family; overthrew the Kamakura regime and established the Ashikaga Shogunate from 1336–1573; drove emperor from Kyoto to Yoshino.

Ashikaga Shogunate [ah-she-kah-gah shoh-guh-nayt] Replaced the Kamakura regime in Japan; ruled from 1336 to 1573; destroyed rival Yoshino center of imperial authority.

THINKING HISTORICALLY

Comparing Feudalisms

IN ONE SENSE, THE EXISTENCE OF feudalism is easily explained. Many societies generated only weak central government structures simply because they lacked the resources, shared political values, and bureaucratic experience to develop alternatives. China under the Zhou dynasty is sometimes called feudal. The Russian kings from Rurik onward exercised only loose control over powerful landlords. Kings in the divine monarchy systems of sub-Saharan Africa, which flourished from about the 9th to the 19th century in various parts of the continent, similarly relied on deals and compromises with local and regional leaders. Indeed, African historians have often noted that kingdoms such as Ghana and Mali were ruled about as effectively as were Western monarchies during the Middle Ages.

A comparison of this sort reminds us that feudal systems were in many ways early, less sophisticated versions of political societies that were gradually moving from purely local toward more centralized organization. Indeed, almost all civilizations have experienced long periods of semi-centralized rule. In all such cases, including feudal ones, the claims of central authorities are not matched by effective power. Regional leaders have armies of their own and do much of the effective administration of their localities. Kings have to make deals with such leaders, relying on personal negotiation and pledges of mutual respect, marriage alliances, negotiation, and a willingness to give the local princes free rein in practice.

The feudal systems that arose in the West and Japan differed in some respects from the many other decentralized systems they resemble. These differences make it desirable not to call all such systems feudal, thus diluting an extremely useful term beyond recognition. For example, Russia was often decentralized and often saw its rulers, whatever their grandiose claims, make concessions to regional nobles because the tsars depended on the loyalty and service of these subordinate lords. But Russia never developed a genuinely feudal political hierarchy, which is one of the features that distinguished it from the West. The same holds true for Zhou China or even the Sudanic empires of Africa.

Japan and the medieval West developed feudal systems grounded in a set of political values that embraced, however imperfectly, most of the participants in the system. The most important of these participants were the aristocratic lords, who effectively controlled the mass of the peasants. The idea of mutual ties and obligations, and the rituals and institutions that expressed them, went beyond the more casual local deals and compromises characteristic of ancient China or medieval and early modern Russia.

In both western Europe and Japan, feudalism was highly militaristic. Both the medieval West and Japan went through long centuries of unusually frequent and bitter internal warfare, based in large part on feudal loyalties and rivalries. Although this warfare was more confined to the warrior-landlord class in Europe than in Japan, in both instances feudalism summed up a host of elite military virtues that long impeded the development of more stable, centralized government. These values included physical courage, personal or family alliances, loyalty, ritualized combat, and often contempt for non-warrior groups such as peasants and merchants.

The military aura of feudalism survived the feudal era in both cases. It left Japan with serious problems in controlling its samurai class after the worst periods of internal conflict had passed in the early 17th century. In the West, the warrior ethic of feudalism persisted in the prominent belief that a central purpose of the state was to make war, thereby providing opportunities for military leaders to demonstrate their prowess. But the legacy of feudalism was not simply military. For example, the idea of personal ties between leaders or among elite groups as a foundation for political activity continued to affect political life and institutions, both in the West and in Japan, long after the feudal period ended.

The characteristics of feudalism in Japan and in the West were not identical. Western feudalism emphasized contractual ideas more strongly than did Japanese. Although mutual ties were acknowledged by members of the European warrior elite, feudal loyalties were sealed by negotiated contracts, in which the parties involved obtained explicit assurances of the advantages each would receive from the alliance. Japanese feudalism relied more heavily on group and individual loyalties, which were not confirmed by contractual agreements. Probably for this reason, the clearest ongoing legacy of feudalism in the West proved to be parliamentary institutions, where individual aristocrats (as well as townspeople and clergy) could join to defend their explicitly defined legal interests against the central monarch. (Western feudalism also helped encourage the emergence of lawyers, who have never played a comparable role in Japan.) In Japan, the legacy of feudalism involved a less institutionalized group consciousness. This approach encouraged individuals to function as part of collective decision-making teams that ultimately could be linked to the state.

> *[T]he idea of personal ties between leaders or among elite groups as a foundation for political activity continued to affect political life and institutions, both in the West and in Japan, long after the feudal period ended.*

(continued on next page)

(continued from previous page)

Can the common fact of a feudal heritage be used to explain another similarity between the West and Japan that emerged clearly in the 20th century? Both societies have been unusually successful in industrial development. Both have also proven adept at running capitalist economies. It is certainly tempting to point to feudalism, the medieval feature the two societies uniquely shared, as a partial explanation for these otherwise unexpected 19th- and 20th-century resemblances. The feudal legacy may also help to account for less positive aspects of western European and Japanese development in these centuries, especially their propensity for imperialist expansion and the fact that they frequently resorted to war to solve conflicts with foreign powers. In the case of Japan and Germany, recent historians have established intriguing connections between the persistence of feudalism late into the early modern era and the rise of right-wing militarist regimes in the 1930s.

When the Japanese talent for group cohesion is identified so strikingly as an ingredient in 20th-century economic success, or when Western nations win political stability through use of parliamentary forms, it surely seems legitimate to point to some persistent threads that run through the experience of the two societies. Whether the common experience of feudalism is a basis for later economic dynamism is a matter for speculation. However, it need not be excluded from a list of provocative uses of comparative analysis simply because the links are challenging.

QUESTIONS

- Do you think the characteristics of feudalism help explain the later success of Western and Japanese societies? If so, in what ways? If not, why not?

- Which aspects of feudalism do you think had the greatest effect on these outcomes?

- What other factors should be taken into account if we want to fully analyze these trends?

---

samurai retainers, who in turn pledged their loyalty and were expected to provide military support whenever their lord called on them.

The collapse of centralized authority was sharply accelerated by the outbreak of full-scale civil war, which raged from 1467 to 1477. Rival heirs to the Ashikaga Shogunate called on the warlord chiefs to support their claims. Samurai flocked to rival headquarters in different sections of Kyoto, where feuding soon broke into all-out warfare. Within a matter of years, the old imperial capital had been reduced to rubble and weed-choked fields. While the shogunate self-destructed in the capital, the provincial lords continued to amass power and plot new coalitions to destroy their enemies. Japan was divided into nearly 300 little kingdoms, whose warlord rulers were called **daimyos** rather than bushi.

daimyos [daim-yo] Warlord rulers of 300 small states following civil war and disruption of Ashikaga Shogunate; holdings consolidated into unified and bounded mini-states.

Toward Barbarism? Military Division and Social Change

Although the rituals became more elaborate, the armor heavier, and the swords more superbly forged, the chivalrous qualities of the bushi era deteriorated noticeably in the 15th and 16th centuries. In the place of mud-walled forts, there arose the massive wood and stone castles, such as that at Himeji pictured in Figure 18.4. These imposing structures dominated the Japanese landscape in the centuries that followed. Spying, sneak attacks, ruses, and timely betrayals became the order of the day. The pattern of warfare was fundamentally transformed as large numbers of peasants armed with pikes became a critical component of daimyo armies. Battles hinged less and less on the outcome of samurai combat. Victory depended on the size and organization of a warlord's forces and on how effectively his commanders used them in the field.

The badly trained and poorly fed peasant forces became a major source of the growing misery of the

 View the **Closer Look** on **MyHistoryLab**: Edo Castle, Tokyo, Japan

FIGURE 18.4 Himeji Castle was one of the most formidable of the many fortresses that became focal points of much of the Japanese landscape in the era dominated by the samurai warriors. Although the inner buildings were often made of wood, these more vulnerable structures were defended by walls and long, fortified passageways made of stone. Like those of medieval Europe, each castle had wells and granaries for the storage of food that allowed its defenders to withstand long sieges by the forces of rival warlords.

common people. As they marched about the countryside to fight the incessant wars of their overlords, they looted and pillaged. The peasantry in different areas sporadically rose up in hopeless but often ferocious revolts, which fed the trend toward brutality and destruction. It is no wonder that contemporary accounts of the era, as well as those written in later centuries, are dominated by a sense of pessimism and foreboding, a conviction that Japan was reverting from civilized life to barbarism.

Despite the chaos and suffering of the warlord period, there was much economic and cultural growth. Most of the daimyo clearly recognized the need to build up their petty states if they were to survive in the long run. The more able daimyo tried to stabilize village life within their domains by introducing regular tax collection, supporting the construction of irrigation systems and other public works, and building strong rural communities. Incentives were offered to encourage the settlement of unoccupied areas. New tools, the greater use of draft animals, and new crops—especially soybeans—contributed to the well-being of the peasantry in the better-run domains. Peasants were also encouraged to produce items such as silk, hemp, paper, dyes, and vegetable oils, which were highly marketable and thus potential sources of household income. Daimyos vied with each other to attract merchants to their growing castle towns. Soon a new and wealthy commercial class emerged as purveyors of goods for the military elite and intermediaries in trade between Japan and overseas areas, especially China. As in medieval Europe, guild organizations for artisans and merchants were strong in this era. They helped provide social solidarity and group protection in a time of political breakdown and insecurity.

Evidence reveals that the growth of commerce and the handicraft industries gave some Japanese women opportunities to avoid the sharp drop in status that most experienced in the age of the warring daimyos. Women in merchant and artisan families apparently exercised a fair degree of independence. This was reflected in their participation in guild organizations and business management and by the fact that their positions were sometimes inherited by their daughters. But the status of women in the emerging commercial classes contrasted sharply with that of women in the warrior elites. In earlier centuries, the wives and daughters of the provincial bushi households learned to ride and to use a bow and arrow, and they often joined in the hunt. By the 14th and 15th centuries, however, the trend among the daimyo families toward primogeniture, or limiting inheritance to the eldest son, dealt a heavy blow to women of the elite classes. The wives and daughters of warrior households, who had hitherto shared in the division of the family estate, now received little or no land or income.

Disinheritance was part of a larger pattern that saw women increasingly treated as defenseless appendages of their warrior fathers or husbands. They were given in marriage to cement alliances between warrior households and reared to anticipate their warrior husband's every desire. They were also taught to slay themselves rather than dishonor the family line by being raped by illicit suitors or enemy soldiers. Japanese women of all classes lost the role of the celebrant in village religious ceremonies and were replaced in Japanese theatrical performances by men specially trained to impersonate women.

FIGURE **18.5** Patronage of landscape painting and the other fine arts in Japan allowed artistic expression to survive in the long centuries of political division and civil war. In paintings such as the one pictured here, Chinese aesthetic preferences and techniques were strong. In fact, Japanese artists consciously imitated the monochrome (one-colored) paintings of Song China, which they regarded as the apex of the genre. Japanese artists not only concentrated on the same themes, such as landscapes with tiny human figures, but imitated the brushstrokes that they believed had been used by the Song masters.

(Shen Zhou (Chinese 1427–1509), "Poet on a Mountain Top." The Nelson-Atkins Museum of Art, Kansas City, Missouri. Purchase: Nelson Trust, 46-51/2. Photo: Robert Newcombe.)

Artistic Solace for a Troubled Age

Fears that the constant wars between the swaggering samurai might drag Japan back to barbarism were somewhat mollified by continuing cultivation of the arts. Zen Buddhism, which because of its stress on simplicity and discipline had a special appeal to the warrior elite, played a critical role in securing the place of the arts in an era of strife and destruction. Zen monasteries provided key points of renewed diplomatic and trade contacts with China, which in turn led to a revival of Chinese influence in Japan, at least at the cultural level. Although much painting of the era imitated earlier Chinese work of the Song period, the monochrome ink sketches of Japanese artists were both brilliant and original. Also notable were screen and scroll paintings, such as the one in Figure 18.5, that capture the natural beauty of Japan; others provide us with invaluable glimpses into Japanese life in this period. Zen sensibilities are also prominent in some of the splendid architectural works of this period, including the Golden and Silver Pavilions that Ashikaga shoguns had built in Kyoto (Figure 18.6). Each pavilion was designed to blend into the natural setting in which it was placed to create a pleasing shelter that would foster contemplation and meditation.

This contemplative mood is also evident in the design of some of the more famous gardens of this era. One of these, at the Ryoanji Temple, consisted entirely of islands of volcanic rock set amid white pebbles, which were periodically raked into varying patterns. The influence of Shintoism and Zen Buddhism on such gardens, and the related Japanese ability to find great beauty in the rough and simple, were also present in the tea ceremony that developed in the era of warrior dominance. The graceful gestures, elaborate rituals, and subtly shaped and glazed pots and cups associated with the service of tea on special occasions all lent themselves to composure and introspection. These arts and aesthetic sensibilities were cultivated through centuries of warfare. They continued during the "long peace" of the Tokugawa shogunate that marked the last phase of the feudal period that persisted until the late-19th century.

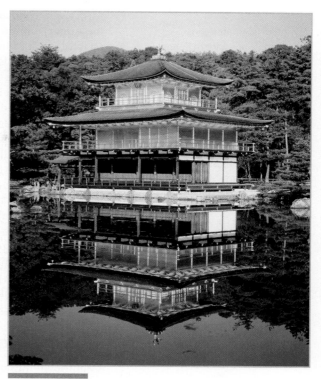

FIGURE **18.6** The Golden Pavilion (or Kinkakuji) is one of the great architectural treasures of the age of the warring houses in Japan. Built on a small lake near Kyoto in the 15th century, the wooden, tile-roofed structure reflects the Zen and Shinto stress on simplicity typical of almost all Japanese artistic production in the centuries of the warring states. Its gold-painted exterior and the reflecting pond enhance these sensibilities.

KOREA: BETWEEN CHINA AND JAPAN

18.3   What were the results of Korea's links to China?

Because the Korean peninsula is an extension of the Chinese mainland, and because, historically, Korean kingdoms were dwarfed by their giant neighbor to the west, most observers have treated Korea as little more than an appendage of China. But lumping Korea together with China overlooks the fact that the peninsula was ruled by indigenous dynasties through most of its history, even though these dynasties often paid tribute to the reigning Chinese emperor. At an even more basic level, the peoples who occupied the Korean peninsula represented a different ethnic blend than those who, centuries earlier, had come to identify themselves as Chinese. The Koreans descended from the hunting and herding peoples of eastern Siberia and Manchuria rather than the Mongolian- and Turkic-speaking tribes to the west. By the 4th century B.C.E., the peoples who moved into the Korean peninsula had begun to acquire sedentary farming and metalworking techniques from the Chinese.

From this point onward, the Koreans played a role in the dynastic struggles that preoccupied the peoples of the north China plain. In 109 B.C.E., the earliest Korean kingdom, **Choson**, was conquered by the Han emperor Wudi. Thereafter, parts of Korea were colonized by Chinese settlers, who remained for nearly four centuries. These colonies soon became a channel by which Chinese influences began to filter into Korean culture in the critical centuries of its early development. A small Japanese enclave in the southeast of the peninsula provided contact with the islands as well, although cultural influences in this era ran overwhelmingly eastward, from China to Korea and then on to Japan.

Of all the areas to which the Chinese formula for civilized development spread, Korea was the most profoundly influenced for the longest period of time. Despite repeated Chinese interventions, the Korean people developed a separate identity that was expressed in distinctive forms of dress, cuisine, and a unique social class system.

Choson [choh-suhn] Earliest Korean kingdom; conquered by Han armies in 109 B.C.E.

Koguryo [koh-goor-yoo] Tribal people of northern Korea; established an independent kingdom in the northern half of the peninsula in 37 B.C.E.; began a process of Sinification.

Silla Independent Korean kingdom in southeastern part of peninsula; defeated Koguryo along with their Chinese Tang allies; submitted as a vassal of the Tang emperor and agreed to tribute payment; ruled united Korea by 668.

Paekche [pah-EHK-chee] Independent Korean kingdom in southwestern part of peninsula; defeated by rival Silla kingdom and its Chinese Tang allies in 7th century.

Sinification Extensive adoption of Chinese culture in other regions; typical of Korea, Japan, and Vietnam.

Despite conquest and colonization under the Han, the tribal peoples of the peninsula, particularly the **Koguryo** in the north, soon resisted Chinese rule. As Chinese control weakened, the Koguryo established an independent state in the northern half of the peninsula that was soon at war with two southern rivals, **Silla** and **Paekche** (Map 18.3). Contacts between the splinter kingdoms that ruled north China after the fall of the Han and the Koguryo kingdom resulted in the first wave of **Sinification**—that is, the extensive adoption of Chinese culture—in Korea. As was the case in Japan, Buddhism supplied the key links between Korea and the successors of the Han dynasty in northeast China. Korean rulers patronized Buddhist artists and financed the building of monasteries and pagodas. Korean scholars traveled to China, and a select few made the long journey to the source of the Buddhist faith, India.

In addition to Sinified variants of Buddhism, Chinese writing was introduced, even though the spoken Korean language was as ill-suited for adaptation to the Chinese characters as the Japanese language had also been. The Koguryo monarch imposed a unified law code patterned after that of Han China. He established universities, where Korean youths struggled to master the Confucian classics and their teachers wrote histories of China rather than their own land. To expand his power and improve revenue collection, the Koguryo ruler also tried to put together a Chinese-style bureaucracy. But the noble families who supported him had little use for a project that posed such an obvious threat to their own power. Without their support, the monarch did not have the resources for such an ambitious undertaking. Thus, full implementation of these policies had to wait for a more powerful dynasty to emerge some centuries later.

Tang Alliances and the Conquest of Korea

Centuries of warfare between the three Korean kingdoms weakened each without giving paramount power in the peninsula to any. Internal strife also left Korea vulnerable to further attacks from the outside. In addition to the unsuccessful campaigns of the Sui (see Chapter 17), the founders of the more lasting Tang dynasty included Korea in the territories they staked out for their empire. But it was several decades before one of them could finally mount a successful invasion. The stubborn warriors of the Koguryo kingdom bore the brunt of the Tang assaults, just as they had borne those of the Sui rulers. Finally, Tang strategists hit on the idea of taking advantage of Korean divisions to bring the troublesome region into line. Striking an alliance with the rulers of the Silla kingdom to the southeast, they destroyed the Paekche kingdom and then defeated the Koguryo. Thus, the Chinese finally put an end to the long-lived dynasty that had played such a key role in Korea's early development.

The Chinese conquerors soon began to quarrel with their Silla allies over how to divide the spoils. When the Silla proved able to fight the larger Chinese forces in the peninsula to a standstill and revolts broke out in the former Paekche and Koguryo territories already conquered, the Tang decided it was time to strike a deal. In return for regular tribute payments and the Silla monarch's submission as a vassal of the Tang emperor, the Chinese withdrew their armies in 668. In so doing, they left the Silla the independent rulers of a united Korea. Despite brief lapses, the Koreans maintained this independence and roughly the same boundaries established by the Silla until the occupation of their land by the Japanese in the early 20th century.

MAP **18.3 The Korean Peninsula During the Three Kingdoms Era** The Chinese were often able to play off the rival kingdoms that dominated Korea's early history against each other and thereby exert great influence on the political and social development of the country.

Sinification: The Tributary Link

Under the Silla monarchs, who ruled from 668 until the late 9th century, and the **Koryo** dynasty (918–1392) that followed, Chinese influences peaked and Korean culture achieved its first full flowering. The Silla rulers consciously strove to turn their kingdom into a miniature of the Tang empire. They regularly sent embassies and tribute to the Tang court, where Korean scholars collected Chinese texts and noted the latest fashions in court dress and etiquette. The Koreans' regular attendance on the Chinese emperors was a key sign of their prominent and enduring participation in the Chinese tribute system. At various times, the participants in the system included nomads from central and north Asia, the Tibetans, many of the kingdoms of southeast Asia, and the emperors of Japan. None of these participants were more committed to the tributary arrangements than the Koreans. Rather than try to conquer the Koreans and other surrounding peoples, most Chinese emperors were content to receive their embassies. These emissaries offered tribute in the form of splendid gifts and acknowledged the superiority of the Son of Heaven by their willingness to kowtow to him (kowtowing involved a series of ritual bows in which the supplicant prostrated himself before the throne).

To most of the peoples involved, this seemed a small price to pay for the benefits they received from the Middle Kingdom. Not only did submission and tribute guarantee continuing peace with the Chinese, but it brought far richer gifts than the tribute bearers offered to the Chinese ruler. In addition, the tributary system provided privileged access to Chinese learning, art, and manufactured goods. Tribute missions normally included merchants, whose ability to buy up Chinese manufactures and sell their own goods in the lucrative Chinese market hinged on their country's participation in the Chinese system. Missions from heavily Sinified areas, such as Japan, Korea, and Vietnam, also included contingents of scholars. They studied at Chinese academies or Buddhist monasteries and busily purchased Chinese scrolls and works of art to fill the libraries and embellish the palaces back home. Thus, the tribute system became the major channel of trade and intercultural exchange between China and its neighbors.

The Sinification of Korean Elite Culture

The Silla rulers rebuilt their capital at Kumsong on the Kyongju plain to look like its Tang counterpart. The streets were laid out on a regular grid; there were central markets, parks, lakes, and a separate district to house the imperial family. Fleeing the tedium of the backward rural areas and provincial capitals, the aristocratic families who surrounded the throne and dominated imperial government crowded their mansions into the areas around the imperial palace. With their large extended families and hundreds of slaves and hangers-on, they made up a large portion of the capital's population. Some aristocrats studied in Chinese schools, and a minority even submitted to the rigors of the Confucian examination system introduced under the Silla rulers. Most of the aristocracy opted for the artistic pursuits and entertainments available in the capital. They could do so because most positions in the government continued to be occupied by members of the aristocratic families by virtue of their birth and family connections rather than their knowledge of the Confucian classics.

 Read the Document on MyHistoryLab: Preface to The Ten Diagrams of Sage Learning (1568) Yi Hwang (T'oegye)

Partly out of self-interest, the Korean elite continued to favor Buddhism over Confucianism, which was much more strongly associated with Chinese culture. They and the Korean royal family lavishly endowed monasteries and patronized works of religious art, which became major forms of Korean cultural creativity. The capital at Kumsong soon became crowded with Buddhist temples, which usually were made of wood. Buddhist monks were constantly in attendance on the ruler as well as on members of the royal family and the more powerful aristocratic households. But the schools of Buddhism that caught on among the elite were Chinese. Korean artwork and monastic design reproduced, sometimes splendidly, Chinese prototypes. Even the location of monasteries and pagodas in high places followed Chinese ideas about the need to mollify local spirits and balance supernatural forces.

Sometimes the Koreans borrowed from the Chinese and then outdid their teachers. Most notable in this regard was the pottery produced in the Silla and Koryo eras. The Koreans first learned the techniques of porcelain manufacture from the Chinese. But in the pale green-glazed celadon bowls and vases of the late Silla and Koryo, they created masterworks that even Chinese connoisseurs admired and collected. They also pioneered in making oxide glazes that were used to make the black- and rust-colored stoneware (pictured in Figure 18.7), which was characteristic of this era.

Another endeavor in which the Koreans improved on the Chinese was in the art of printing. As we have seen, the Chinese were the first to develop wood block and, later, movable metal-type printing. But after the latter was introduced into Korea, local artisans came upon an ingenious way to hold the metal type in place in the long registers in which it was assembled for printing. Using honey as a sort of glue, they were able to fix the type

FIGURE **18.7** Although all of the major civilized centers of east Asia produced refined ceramics, perhaps nowhere was this art as highly developed as in Korea. As the simple, yet elegant, pitcher in this photo illustrates, Korean pottery was initially crafted for household use. That which has survived from earlier periods of Korean history has become sought after by collectors of fine arts and is prominently displayed in museums.

(The Bridgeman Art Library/Detroit Institute of Arts.)

temporarily and yet disassemble it when a particular task was finished. Until the Koreans devised this technique, the Chinese had found that the metal type wore down very fast and was difficult to stabilize in the registers.

Civilization for the Few

With the exception of Buddhist sects such as the pure land that had strong appeal for the ordinary people, imports from China in this and later eras were all but monopolized by the tiny elite. The aristocratic families were divided into several ranks that neither intermarried nor socialized with each other, much less the rest of the population. They not only filled most of the posts in the Korean bureaucracy but also dominated the social and economic life of the entire kingdom. Much of Korea's trade with the Chinese and Japanese was devoted to providing these aristocrats with the fancy clothing, special teas, scrolls, and artwork that occupied such an important place in their idle lives. In return, Korea exported mainly raw materials, such as forest products and metals especially copper, which was mined by near-slaves who lived in horrendous conditions.

Members of the royal family and the aristocratic households often financed artisan production for export or to supply the court. In addition, some backed mercantile expeditions and even engaged extensively in money lending. All of this limited the activities of artisans and traders. The former were usually considered low in status and were poorly paid for their talents and labor. The latter were so weak that they did not really form a distinct class.

The aristocrats were the only people who really counted for anything in Korean society. The classes beneath them were oriented to their service. These included government functionaries, who were recognized as a separate social category. More numerous were the commoners, who were mainly peasants, and near-slaves, who were known as the "low born" and ranged from miners and artisans to servants and entertainers. Buddhist festivals periodically relieved the drudgery and monotony of the lives of the common people, and Buddhist salvationist teachings gave them hope for bliss in the afterlife.

Koryo Collapse, Dynastic Renewal

Yi Korean dynasty that succeeded Koryo dynasty following period of Mongol invasions; established in 1392; ruled Korea to 1910; restored aristocratic dominance and Chinese influence.

Periodically, the common people and the low born found their lot too much to bear and rose up against a ruling class that was obviously much more devoted to pursuing its own pleasures than to their well-being. Most of these uprisings were local affairs and were ruthlessly repressed by armies of the ruling class. But collectively they weakened both the Silla and Koryo regimes, and in combination with quarrels between the aristocratic households and outside invasions, they contributed to the fall of both dynasties. In the absence of real alternatives, the aristocratic families managed to survive these crises and elevated one of their number to the royal throne. After nearly a century and a half of conflict and turmoil triggered by the Mongol invasion in 1231, the **Yi** dynasty was established in 1392. Remarkably, it ruled Korea until 1910. Although there were some modifications, the Yi quickly restored the aristocratic dominance and links to China that had predominated under their predecessors. Of all of the peoples who received higher civilization from China, none were as content to live in the shadow of the Middle Kingdom as the Koreans.

BETWEEN CHINA AND SOUTHEAST ASIA: THE MAKING OF VIETNAM

At the end of the 2nd century B.C.E., the Han dynasty conquered the kingdom of the Nam Viet, thus beginning an effort to absorb the Vietnamese people into Chinese civilization that would span a thousand years. Although they benefited greatly from borrowings from China, the Vietnamese had a distinct identity that provided the basis for a series of rebellions and eventually produced an independent kingdom with expansionist designs against neighboring southeast Asian peoples.

18.4 What were the main differences in Vietnamese-Chinese relations from those in Korea and Japan?

The preconquest culture of the Vietnamese gave them a strong sense of themselves as a distinct people with a common heritage that they did not want to see overwhelmed by an expanding China. The Viets were well aware of the benefits they derived from the superior technology, modes of political organization, and ideas they received from China. But their gratitude was tempered by their fear of losing their own identity and becoming just another part of China's massive civilization.

Ironically, the Viets first appear in recorded history as a group of "southern barbarians" mentioned by Chinese scholars in accounts of Qin raids in south China in the 220s B.C.E. At that time, their kingdom, which the Chinese called Nam Viet, meaning "people in the south," extended along the southern coastal area of what is now China (Map 18.4). The initial raids by Qin forces left little lasting Chinese presence. But they probably gave a boost to the lively trade that had been conducted between the Viets and the peoples of south China for centuries. In exchange for silk manufactured by the Chinese, the Viets traded ivory, tortoise shells, pearls, peacock feathers, aromatic woods, and other exotic products drawn from the sea and tropical forests. Some decades after the Qin raids, the Viet rulers defeated the feudal lords who controlled the Red River valley and brought their lands under the control of the Viet kingdom. In the centuries that followed, the Viets intermarried and blended with the Mon-Khmer- and Tai-speaking peoples who occupied the Red River area. This proved to be a crucial step in the formation of the Vietnamese as a distinct ethnic group.

As the Viets' willingness to intermarry with ethnic groups such as the **Khmers** (today's Cambodians) and the Tais suggests (Map 18.4), before their conquest by the Han Chinese, their culture had many features characteristic of southeast Asia. Their spoken language was not related to Chinese. They enjoyed a strong tradition of village autonomy, physically symbolized by the bamboo hedges that surround northern Vietnamese villages to the present day. The Vietnamese favored the nuclear family to the extended household preferred by the Chinese, and they never developed the clan networks that have been such a prominent feature of south Chinese society. Vietnamese women have historically had greater freedom and more influence, both within the family and in society at large, than their Chinese counterparts. They were, for example, the dominant force in both local and large urban markets and the trading system more generally.

Vietnamese customs and cultural forms also differed very significantly from Chinese. The Vietnamese dressed very differently. For example, women preferred long skirts to the black pants that non-elite women wore in China. The Vietnamese delighted in the cockfight, a typical southeast Asian pastime; they chewed betel nut, which the Chinese found disgusting; and they blackened their teeth, which the Chinese considered equally repulsive. In the centuries when they were dominated by the Chinese politically, the Vietnamese managed to preserve most of these features of their society. They also became much more fervently attached at the grassroots level to Buddhism, and they developed art and literature, especially poetry, that was refined and distinct from that of the Chinese.

MAP **18.4 South China and Vietnam on the Eve of the Han Conquest** As this map illustrates, Nam Viet, which formed the original core of Vietnam, could be seen as a logical extension of China and was long ruled as the southern province of Chinese empires.

Khmers [kuh-MEHRs] Indianized rivals of the Vietnamese; moved into Mekong River delta region at time of Vietnamese drive to the south.

Conquest and Sinification

As the Han rulers who succeeded the Qin tried to incorporate south China into their empire, they came into conflict with the Viets. The Han emperor initially settled for the Viet ruler's admission of his vassal status and periodic payments of tribute. But by 111 B.C.E., the Han thought it best to conquer the feisty Viets outright and to govern them directly using Chinese officials. The Red River area was garrisoned by Chinese troops, and Chinese administrators set to work co-opting the local lords and encouraging them to adopt Chinese culture. Because the Viet elite realized that they had a great deal to learn from their powerful neighbors to the north, they cooperated with the agents of the new regime. Sensing that they had found another barbarian people ripe for assimilation, the Chinese eagerly introduced essential elements of their own culture into the southern lands.

In the centuries after the Chinese conquest, the Vietnamese elite was drawn into the bureaucratic machine that the Han emperors and the shi (bureaucrats) had developed to hold together the empire won by the Qin. They attended Chinese-style schools, where they wrote in the Chinese script and read and memorized the classical Chinese texts of Confucius and Mencius. They took exams to qualify for administrative posts, whose responsibilities and privileges were defined by Chinese precedents. They introduced Chinese cropping techniques and irrigation technology, which soon made Vietnamese agriculture the most productive in southeast Asia. This meant that Vietnamese society, like that of China, could support larger numbers of people. The result was the high population density characteristic of the Red River valley and the lowland coastal areas to the south.

The Vietnamese also found that Chinese political and military organization gave them a decisive edge over the peoples to the west and south, who had adopted Indian patterns of kingship and warfare, and with whom they increasingly clashed over the control of lands to settle and cultivate. Over time, the Vietnamese elite also adopted the extended family model and took to venerating their ancestors in the Confucian manner. Their Chinese overlords had every reason to assume that the Vietnamese "barbarians" were well on their way to becoming civilized—that is, like the Chinese themselves.

Roots of Resistance

Sporadic revolts led by members of the Vietnamese aristocracy, and the failure of Chinese cultural imports to make much of an impression on the Vietnamese peasantry, ultimately frustrated Chinese hopes for assimilating the Viets. Although they had learned much from the Chinese, the Vietnamese lords chafed under their rule, in part because the Chinese often found it difficult to conceal their disdain for local customs in what they considered a backward and unhealthy outpost of the empire. Vietnamese literature attests to the less than reverent attitudes felt by Vietnamese collaborators toward Chinese learning and culture. In the following poem, a teacher mocks himself and doubts his usefulness to the students he serves:

> I bear the title "Disciple of Confucius."
> Why bother with blockheads, wearing such a label?
> I dress like a museum piece:
> I speak only in learned quotations (poetry and prose);
> Long since dried out, I still strut like a peacock;
> Failed in my exams, I've been dropped like a shrivelled root.
> Doctorate, M.A.: all out of reach,
> So why not teach school, and beat the devil out of my students.

Elsewhere in Vietnamese writings, self-doubt and mockery turn to rage and a fierce determination to resist Chinese dominance, whatever the cost. The following sentiments of a Vietnamese caught up in resistance to the reimposition of rule from China by the Mongols in the 13th century provide a dramatic case in point:

> I myself often forget to eat at mealtime, and in the middle of the night I wake up and caress my pillow. My intestines hurt me incessantly, as if they had been cut off, and tears flow abundantly from my eyes. My only grief is that I have not yet succeeded in hacking apart the enemy's body, peeling off his skin, swallowing his liver, drinking his blood.

The intensity and ferocity of this passage give some sense of why the Chinese failed to assimilate the Vietnamese. They also failed because the peasantry rallied again and again to the call of their own lords to rise up and drive off the alien rulers. The most famous of these early uprisings, which broke out in 39 c.e., was led by the **Trung sisters**, who were children of a deposed local leader. Their role as rebel leaders underscores the stronger position of women in Vietnamese society, in contrast to the Chinese, and their persisting importance in Vietnamese protest movements and resistance to foreign invaders.

Trung sisters Leaders of one of the frequent peasant rebellions in Vietnam against Chinese rule; revolt broke out in 39 c.e.; demonstrates importance of Vietnamese women in indigenous society.

Vietnamese women were understandably hostile to the Confucian codes and family system that would have confined them to the household and subjected them to male authority figures. We do not know whether this resentment figured in the Trung sisters' decision to revolt. But poetry written in later centuries by female authors leaves little doubt about the reactions of Vietnamese women to Confucian norms or male dominance. One of the most famous of these writers, Ho Xuan Huong (hoo shwahn wahng), flouts Confucian decorum in the following ribald verse and mocks her male suitors:

> Careful, careful where are you going:
> You group of know-nothings!
> Come here and let your older sister teach you to write poems.
> Young bees whose stingers itch rub them in wilted flowers.
> Young goats who have nothing to do with their horns butt them against sparse shrubbery.

In another poem, "Sharing a Husband," Huong ridicules those who advocate polygamy, a practice favored by any self-respecting Confucian:

> One wife is covered by a quilted blanket, while one wife is left in the cold.
> Cursed be this fate of sharing a common husband. Seldom do you have an occasion to possess your husband,

Not even twice in one month.
You toil and endure hardships in order to earn your steamed rice, and then the rice is cold and
    tasteless. It is like renting your services for hire, and then receiving no wages.
How is it that I have turned out this way,
I would rather suffer the fate of remaining unmarried and living alone by myself.

Winning Independence and Continuing Chinese Influences

In addition to a strong sense of identity and motives for resistance that crossed class and gender barriers, the Vietnamese struggle for independence was assisted by the fragility of the links that bound them to China. Great distances and mountain barriers created nightmare conditions for Chinese administrators responsible for supplying military expeditions to in the far south. Only small numbers of Chinese—mostly bureaucrats, soldiers, and merchants—lived in the Red River area, and few of them did so permanently. Most critically, Chinese control over the distant Vietnamese depended on the strength of the ruling dynasties in China. The Vietnamese were quick to take advantage of political turmoil and nomadic incursions in northern China to assert their independence. After failing to completely free themselves on several occasions, they mounted a massive rebellion during the period of chaos in China after the fall of the Tang dynasty in 907.

By 939 the Vietnamese had won political independence from their northern neighbors. Although both the Mongol and Ming rulers of China later tried to reassert control, both efforts ended in humiliating retreats. From 939 until the conquests by the French in the 19th century, the Vietnamese were masters of their own land.

Although the Chinese political hold was broken, Chinese cultural exports continued to play central roles in Vietnamese society. A succession of Vietnamese dynasties beginning with the Le (980–1009), which became the source of legitimacy for the rest, built Chinese-style palaces, as in Figure 18.8, in the midst of forbidden cities patterned after those in Chang'an and Beijing. They ruled through a bureaucracy that was a much smaller copy of the Chinese administrative system, with secretariats, six main ministries, and a bureau of censors to keep graft and corruption in check. Civil service exams were reintroduced, and an administrative elite schooled in the Confucian classics sought the emperor's favor and commanded deference from the common people.

But the Vietnamese equivalent of the Chinese scholar-gentry never enjoyed as much power. For one thing, their control at the local level was much less secure than that of their Chinese counterparts. Much more than those in China, local Vietnamese officials tended to identify with the peasantry rather than with the court and higher administrators. To a much greater degree, they looked out for the interests of the peasants and served as leaders in village uprisings against the ruling dynasty when its demands on the common people became too oppressive.

The power of the scholar-bureaucrats in Vietnam was also limited in the reign of many dynasties by competition from well-educated Buddhist monks. Buddhists had much stronger links with the Vietnamese peasantry than the monastic orders had in China, which meant that the Buddhists had a good deal more popular support in their struggles with the Confucian scholars. The high esteem in which women were held in Buddhist teachings and institutions also

FIGURE **18.8** As this view of the moat and part of the palace of the Vietnamese emperors at Hue illustrates, Chinese taste and architectural styles strongly influenced the construction and decoration of the Vietnamese court. Not only were the upturned, tiled roofs and long galleries built in deliberate imitation of prototypes in Chang'an or Beijing, but they were set amid moats, ponds, and gardens patterned after those that Vietnamese envoys had seen in China. Despite this imitation, however, Vietnamese rulers were more accessible to their subjects, and their palaces and capital city made little impression on Chinese visitors, who disparaged the informality and lack of grandeur at the Hue court.

VISUALIZING THE PAST

What Their Portraits Tell Us: Gatekeeper Elites and the Persistence of Civilizations

SOME DECADES AGO, A DISTINGUISHED HISTORIAN of pre-modern China called the scholar-gentry elite the gatekeepers of Chinese civilization. In his usage, gatekeepers are pivotal elite groups that have emerged in all civilizations and proved critical to their persistence over time. Although they usually shared power with other social groups and often did not rule in their own right, gatekeepers played vital roles in shaping the dominant social values and worldviews of the most human cultures. In everything from the positions they occupied to their manners and fashions in dress, gatekeepers defined the norms and served as role models for much of the rest of society. Some gatekeeper elites, such as the scholar-gentry in China and the brahmans in India, promoted norms and ideals in written treatises on good government or the proper social order. Other gatekeepers, such as the samurai of Japan and the Aztec warriors of Tenochtitlan, embodied these ideals in their public personas and military enterprises, which at times were immortalized in songs, legends, and epics.

The illustrations shown here provide portraits of people belonging to gatekeeper elites from four of the civilizations we have considered in depth thus far. Because each of these portraits was produced by artists from the same society as the gatekeeper elite depicted here, we can assume that the portraits capture the values, symbols of legitimacy, and demeanor that these people intended to project to the viewer. Carefully examine each of these portraits, paying special attention to clothing, poses adopted, objects included in the portraits, backgrounds selected, and activities depicted.

For historical background of the civilizations that each exemplifies, see the relevant sections of Chapters 15, 16, 17, and 18.

Compare each of the portraits to the others, and then answer the questions that follow.

QUESTIONS

- What do the dress, poses, and settings of each of these portraits tell you about the values, ideals, and worldviews that each gatekeeper elite group is intended to represent?
- With which elite groups did they share power?
- How did they legitimize their power and privileges and to what degree is this reflected in the portraits?
- What are comparable gatekeeper elite groups in the contemporary United States?

Bankers and merchants from western Europe.

A samurai warrior.   Warrior ranks from the Aztec empire.

(continued on next page)

(continued from previous page)

Chinese scholars enjoying their leisure time.

(Handscroll "Gathering of Philosophers." The Metropolitan Museum of Art, New York, NY, U.S.A. Image copyright © The Metropolitan Museum of Art/Art Resource, NY.)

enhanced the popularity of the monks in Vietnam. Thus, competing centers of power and influence prevented most Vietnamese dynasties from enjoying the authority of their Chinese counterparts.

The Vietnamese Drive to the South

However watered down, the Chinese legacy gave the Vietnamese great advantages in the struggles within Indochina that became a major preoccupation of independent Vietnamese rulers. The Vietnamese refused to move into the malarial highlands that fringed the Red River area and rose abruptly from the coastal plains farther south. This meant that their main adversaries were the **Chams** and Khmers, who occupied the lowland areas to the south that the Vietnamese sought to settle themselves (Map 18.4). The Vietnamese launched periodic expeditions to retaliate for raids on their villages by the peoples in the hills. They also regularly traded with the hill dwellers for forest products. But the Vietnamese tried to minimize cultural exchange with these hunters and shifting cultivators, whom they saw as "nude savages."

As they moved out in the only direction left to them—south along the narrow plain between the mountains and the sea—the Vietnamese made good use of the larger population and superior bureaucratic and military organization that the Chinese connection had fostered. From the 11th to the 18th century, they fought a long series of generally successful wars against the Chams, an Indianized people living in the lowland areas along the coast. Eventually most of the Chams were driven into the highlands, where their descendants—in much smaller numbers—live to the present day. Having beaten the Chams and settled on their former croplands, the Vietnamese next clashed with the Khmers, who had begun to move into the Mekong delta region during the centuries of the Vietnamese drive south. Again, Indianized armies proved no match for the Chinese-modeled military forces and weapons of the Vietnamese. By the time the French arrived in force in the Mekong area in the late 18th century, the Vietnamese had occupied much of the upper delta and were beginning to push into territory that today belongs to Cambodia.

Expansion and Division

As Vietnamese armies and peasant colonists moved farther and farther from the capital at Hanoi, the dynasties centered there found it increasingly difficult to control the commanders and peasants fighting and living in the frontier areas. As the southerners intermarried with and adopted some of the customs of the Chams and Khmers, differences in culture and attitude developed between them

Chams Indianized rivals of the Vietnamese; driven into the highlands by the successful Vietnamese drive to the south.

DOCUMENT

Literature as a Mirror of the Exchanges Among Asian Centers of Civilization

THE FOLLOWING PASSAGES FROM LADY MURASAKI's classic Japanese account of court life, *The Tale of Genji* (Houghton-Mifflin, 1929 edition), and from perhaps the most popular and beloved work of Vietnamese literature, Nguyen Du's *The Tale of Kieu* (New Haven: Yale University Press, 1983 edition), are superb examples of the important and far-reaching exchanges between the civilizations of south and east Asia. Not surprisingly, Chinese influences, including many allusions to Chinese writings and historical events, are paramount, but Buddhist (hence originally Indian) themes are pervasive in both works. There is also evidence in one of these passages of significant exchanges between the satellite civilizations of China.

. . . Kieu sensed a girl was standing by.
And whispered she: "Your karma's still undone:
How could you shirk your debt of grief to life"
You're still to bear the fortune of a rose [woman]:
you wish to quite but heaven won't allow."

. . . . the picture of Kuei-fei, skillful though the painter might be, was but the work of a brush, and had no living fragrance. And though the poet tells us that Kuei-fei's grace was that of "the hibiscus of the Royal Lake or the willows of the Wei-yang Palace," the lady in the picture was all paint and powder and had a simpering Chinesified air.

Now all is lost; for since she [the nun] cannot at every moment be praying for strength, there creeps into her mind the sinful thought that she did ill to become a nun and so often does she commit this sin that even Buddha must think her wickeder now than she was before she took her vows. . . . But if the *karma* of their past lives should chance to be strongly weighted against a parting, she will be found and captured before she has taken her final vows.

He said: "You've won wide fame as lutanist:
like Chung Tzu-ch'i I've longed to hear you play."
. . . then she [Kieu] played.

An air, *The Battlefield of Han and Ch'u*,
made one hear bronze and iron clash and clang.
The Ssu-ma tune, *A Phoenix Seeks His Mate*,
sounded so sad, the moan of grief itself.
Here was Chi K'ang's famed masterpiece, Kuang-ling—
was it a stream that flowed, a cloud that roamed?
Crossing the Border-gate—here was Chao-chün,
half lonesome for her lord, half sick for home.

She [a woman who was attracted to one of Genji's friends] sent me marvelous letters written in a very far-fetched epistolary style and entirely in Chinese characters; in return for which I felt bound to visit her, and by making her my teacher I managed to learn how to write Chinese poems. . . . Let her but be one to whom the *karma* of our past lives draws us in natural sympathy, what matter if now and again her ignorance distresses us? Come to that, even men seem to me to get along very well without much learning.

When evil strikes, you must bow to circumstance.
As you must weigh and choose between your love
and filial duty, which will turn the scale?
She [Kieu] put aside all vows of love and troth—
A child first pays the debts of birth and care.
Resolved on what to do, she said: "Hands off—
I'll sell myself and Father I'll redeem."

QUESTIONS

■ From these passages, can you identify Chinese precedents in terms of place names and historical personages, allusions to Chinese literary works, and attitudes toward gender or social organization that can be traced to Chinese models?

■ Can you detect passages that convey Buddhist ideas about the nature of the world and human existence?

■ Are additional Indian influences suggested?

■ Are there ideas that are distinctively Japanese or Vietnamese, or are the authors totally caught up in Chinese precedents?

Nguyen [nhuwin] Rival Vietnamese dynasty that arose in southern Vietnam to challenge traditional dynasty of Trinh in north at Hanoi; kingdom centered on Red and Mekong rivers; capital at Hue.

Trinh Dynasty that ruled in north Vietnam at Hanoi, 1533 to 1772; rivals of Nguyen family in south.

and the northerners. Although both continued to identify themselves as Vietnamese, the northerners (much like their counterparts in the United States) came to see the Vietnamese who settled in the frontier south as less energetic and slower in speech and movement. As the hold of the Hanoi-based dynasties over the southern regions weakened, regional military commanders grew less and less responsive to orders from the north and slower in sending taxes to the court. Bickering turned to violent clashes, and by the end of the 16th century a rival dynasty, the **Nguyen**, had emerged to challenge the claims of legitimacy of the **Trinh** family that ruled the north.

The territories of the Nguyen at this time were centered on the narrow plains that connected the two great rice bowls of present-day Vietnam along the Red and Mekong rivers. Their capital was at Hue (Map 18.4), far north of the Mekong delta region that in this period had scarcely been settled by the Vietnamese. For the next two centuries, these rival houses fought for the right to rule Vietnam.

Neither accepted the division of Vietnam as permanent; each sought to unite all of the Vietnamese people under a single monarch. This long struggle not only absorbed much of the Vietnamese energies but also prevented them from recognizing the growing external threat to their homeland. For the first time in history, the danger came not from the Chinese giant to the north but from a distant land and religion about which the Vietnamese knew and cared nothing—France and the conversion-minded Roman Catholic church.

Global Connections and Critical Themes

IN THE ORBIT OF CHINA: THE EAST ASIAN CORNER OF THE GLOBAL SYSTEM

The first millennium C.E. was a pivotal epoch in the history of the peoples of east Asia. The spread of ideas, organizational models, and material culture from a common Chinese center spawned the rise of three distinct patterns of civilized development in Japan, Korea, and Vietnam. In contrast to the lands of the nomadic peoples who had long been in contact with China from the north and west, each of these regions contained fertile and well-watered lowland areas that were suited to sedentary cultivation, which was essential to the spread of the Chinese pattern of civilized development. In fact, each provided an ideal environment for the cultivation of wet rice, which was increasingly replacing millet and other grains as the staple of China.

Common elements of Chinese culture, from modes of writing and bureaucratic organization to religious teachings and art, were transmitted to each of these three areas. In all three cases, Chinese imports, with the important exception of popular Buddhism, were all but monopolized by court and provincial elite groups, the former prominent in Japan and Korea, the latter in Vietnam. In all three cases, Chinese thought patterns and modes of social organization were actively and willingly cultivated by these local elites, who knew that they were the key to a higher level of development.

One of the great world religions, Buddhism, played key roles in the transmission of Chinese civilization and the development of all three of these "satellite" societies. Because Buddhism originated in India, the layers of cross-cultural interaction in these processes are all the more complex and profound. In each case, ideas and rituals originating in India were filtered through Chinese society and culture before being passed on to Japan, Korea, and Vietnam. Buddhism also provided a critical link between the civilizations developing in Korea and Japan.

In some phases of their borrowing from China, Japan, Korea, and Vietnam shared prominent aspects of political organization, social development, and intellectual creativity. But the differing ways in which Chinese influences were transmitted to each of these very different societies resulted in very different long-term outcomes. The various combinations of Chinese-derived and indigenous elements produced distinctive variations on a common pattern of civilized life. In Korea, the period of direct Chinese rule was brief, but China's physical presence and military power were all too apparent. Thus, the need for symbolic political submission was obvious and the desire for long-term cultural dependence firmly implanted. In Vietnam, where Chinese conquest and control lasted more than a thousand years, a hard-fought struggle for political independence gave way to a growing attachment to Chinese culture as a counterbalance to the Indian influences that had brought civilization to the southeast Asian rivals of the Vietnamese.

In Japan, where all attempts by Chinese dynasties to assert direct control had failed, Chinese culture was emulated by the courtly elite that first brought civilization to the islands. But the rise of a rival aristocratic class, which was based in the provinces and championed military values that were fundamentally opposed to Chinese Confucianism, led to the gradual limitation of Chinese influence in Japan and the reassertion of Japanese traditional ways. Japanese political patterns, in particular, formed a marked contrast with the predominance of rule by a centralized bureaucracy in China. Nonetheless, in Japan as in the rest of east Asia, China remained the epitome of civilized development; Chinese ways were the standard by which all peoples in this far-flung region were judged.

Despite different patterns, the power of the Chinese model had one other important result for Korea, Japan, and to a large extent Vietnam. Contacts with other parts of the world were slight to nonexistent, because there was no sense that any other place had examples worth emulating. The intensity of interactions within the east Asian region generated tendencies toward isolation from the world beyond.

Further Readings

There are many good secondary works on early Japanese and Vietnamese history. Some older but accessible works on Korea are William Heathorn's *History of Korea* (1971), which gives some attention to the arts, and Hatada Takashi's *A History of Korea* (1969). The best new short introduction to the history of Korea is C. J. Eckert, *Korea Old and New: A History* (1980). K. B. Lee, *A New History of Korea* (1984), trans. E. Wagner et al., is quite comprehensive,

while L. Kendall, *Shahmans, Housewives, and Other Restless Spirits: Women in Korean Ritual Life* (1985), offers a fresh perspective on Korean social history. The best introductory works on Japanese history and culture are the writings of E. Reischauer, especially his sections in J. K. Fairbank et al., *East Asia: The Modern Transformation* (1999); J. W. Hall's *Japan from Prehistory to Modern Times* (1970), and Mikisio Hane's superb overview, *Japan: A Historical Survey* (1972). H. Paul Varley, *Japanese Culture: A Short History* (1973), has fine sections on the arts, religion, and literature of the warlord era.

Also good on this period are Peter Duus, *Japanese Feudalism* (1969); H. Paul Varley, Ivan Morris, and Nobuko Morris, *Samurai* (1970); and George Sansom, *A History of Japan*, vols. 1 and 2 (1958, 1960).

For an understanding of the Chinese impact on Vietnam, there is no better place to begin than Alexander Woodside, *Vietnam and the Chinese Model* (1971). The best works on the earliest period in Vietnamese history are translations of the writings of French scholar

Georges Coedes and the superspecialized *Birth of Vietnam* (1983) by Keith Taylor. Thomas Hodgkin's survey of Vietnamese history is highly readable and makes extensive use of Vietnamese literature. Troung Buu Lam's edited volume, *Patterns of Vietnamese Response to Foreign Intervention* (1967) and the Genji and Kieu tales cited in the Document feature of this chapter provide wonderful ways for the student to get inside Japanese and Vietnamese culture.

On MyHistoryLab

 Study and Review on MyHistoryLab

Critical Thinking Questions

1. Compare and contrast the ways in which Japan, Korea, and Vietnam interacted with China.

2. How much control did each satellite civilization have over the extent to which it borrowed from China and what factors shaped that process and the longer-term acceptance or rejection of Chinese influences?

3. What were the underlying commonalities that bound these four culture areas together and made East Asia a distinctive center of global civilization over the millennia?

4. In what ways were art and literature key elements in this East Asia cultural complex?

5. Is it more accurate to think of a common East Asian civilization by the postclassical period or to look at Japanese, Korean, and Vietnamese societies as separate cases with some interactions with China?

6. Did the spread of Chinese values to other East Asian societies suggest any particular relationship between East Asia and other parts of the world?

The Last Great Nomadic Challenges: From Chinggis Khan to Timur

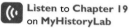
Listen to Chapter 19
on MyHistoryLab

The Mongol retribution came so swiftly and was so ferocious that it completely demoralized Muhammad Shah, the ruler of Khwarazm, whose arrogance brought death and destruction to his kingdom on an appalling scale. Muhammad Shah had scoffed at Chinggis Khan's demand for retribution for the plunder and slaughter of a Mongol caravan that had entered Khwarazm in 1218 (Map 19.1). Chinggis Khan had personally dispatched the caravan as a signal that he wished to establish political and commercial relations with Khwarazm. Having in effect declared war on the Mongols by ignoring their demands for just recompense, Muhammad Shah compounded his folly by quarreling with the caliph of Baghdad, who consequently had little inclination to come to his rescue.

LEARNING OBJECTIVES

What can the struggles Chinggis Khan faced in his youth and early career tell us about the organization and values of Mongol society? p. 419	**19.1**
What were the key components that made for the remarkable success of the Mongol war machine? p. 425	**19.2**
Compare the impact of Mongol conquest and rule in the Muslim Middle East, Russia, and China: On which area was there a greater impact, to what extent did the Mongol interlude alter the historical trajectory of each these major culture areas, and what were the similarities and differences in terms of the nature of and effects of Mongol invasions and rule? p. 429	**19.3**

FIGURE **19.1** A 14th-century miniature painting from Rashid al-Din's *History of the World* depicts Mongol cavalry charging into battle against retreating Persians. The speed and endurance of Mongol cavalry made it difficult for routed foes to retreat and live to fight another day. As the painting suggests, surrender or death were often the only options for those overrun by Mongol units.

(Bibliotheque Nationale de France.)

◉ Watch the Video Series on MyHistoryLab

Learn about some key topics related to this chapter with the *MyHistoryLab Video Series:*
Key Topics in World History

Caught off guard by the Mongol assault that drove deep into his empire from several directions, Muhammad Shah was at first immobilized with fear, and then in full flight, leaving his hapless subjects to fend for themselves. Columns of battle-hardened Mongol cavalry besieged, then stormed, one after another of the legendary cities that were the glory of Khwarazm. Bukhara was taken in early 1220 after its Turkish garrison was eliminated; several months later, most of the inhabitants of Samarkand, who had initially attempted to resist the invaders, were massacred. The Mongols inundated Gurganj, the former capital of Khwarazm, by opening the flood gates of a nearby river. And the ancient citadel of Bamian, where Chinggis Khan's much-loved grandson was killed by a defender's arrow, was obliterated and given the name "accursed city."

Over time the mass slaughters (often dramatized by references to pyramids of skulls) and the destruction of Khwarazm's ancient cities became defining features in accounts of the sudden emergence of the nomadic Mongols as conquerors of much of Eurasia. Until quite recently, most histories have depicted these and similar Mongol conquests as savage assaults by backward and barbaric peoples on ancient and highly developed centers of human civilization. But even the Khwarazm campaign, which was certainly one of the most violent launched by Mongol forces, provides ample illustration of another side to the Mongol imperium. Traditionally, the Mongols' contributions to cross-cultural exchange and human advance have been neglected by historians. But in many of the cities of Khwarazm, where the population resisted and was killed wholesale, skilled artisans were spared in the thousands. Some of these were sent to the Mongol capital at Karakorum. Others carried their skills throughout the empire, and both manufacturing and commerce soon thrived under the aegis of Mongol rule.

The century and a half of Mongol dominance also saw a revitalization of commerce and urban life in places like Bukara and Samarkand, along the Silk Road—the great trading network that had, for millennia, linked China and East Asia with the Middle East, India, and Europe (see the Visualizing the Past feature). Without question, the price of Muhammad Shah's treachery and the resistance that opened the way to this renewal was high—perhaps intolerably so—but it is important to take fully into account the constructive aftermath of Mongol expansionism in Khwarazm and other regions. ■

As we shall see in this chapter, the Mongols very often exhibited great curiosity and openness toward the peoples and cultures that they conquered. And perhaps none of them exemplified these qualities more than the founder of the Mongol empire, Chinggis Khan himself, who sought to attract philosophers and religious scholars from throughout Eurasia to his capital at Karakorum. He delighted in questioning them and debating the merits and drawbacks of different belief systems. In Samarkand and other cities where Muslim scholars and

MAP 19.1 The Transcontinental Empire of Chinggis Khan Easily the largest empire built before the Industrial Revolution, the Mongol imperium linked most of the great Eurasian centers of civilization.

900 C.E.	1100 C.E.	1200 C.E.	1250 C.E.	1300 C.E.
907–1118 Khitan conquest of north China **1037–1194** Seljuk Turks dominate the Middle East	**1115–1234** Jurchens (Jin dynasty) rule north China **1126** Song dynasty flees to south China **1130–c. 1250** Almohads rule north Africa and Spain	**1206** Temujin takes the name of Chinggis Khan; Mongol state founded **1215** First Mongol attacks on north China; Beijing captured **1219–1223** First Mongol invasions of Russia and Islamic world **1227** Death of Chinggis Khan; Ogedei named successor **1234** Mongols take all of north China; end of Jin dynasty **1235–1279** Mongol conquest of south China; end of southern Song dynasty **1236–1240** Mongol conquest of Russia **1240–1241** Mongol invasion of western Europe	**1253** Mongol victory over Seljuk Turks; rise of Ottoman Turks in Middle East **1258** Mongol destruction of Baghdad **1260** Mamluk (slave) rulers of Egypt defeat Mongols at Ain Jalut; end of drive west **1260–1294** Reign of Kubilai Khan in China **1271–1295** Journey of Marco Polo to central Asia, China, and southeast Asia **1271–1368** Reign of the Yuan (Mongol) dynasty in China **1274–1280** Failed Mongol invasions of Japan **1290s** First true guns used in China	**1336–1405** Life of Timur **mid-14th century** Spread of Black Death in Eurasia

mosque attendants refused to encourage resistance, they were usually left unharmed and permitted to attend to the spiritual and physical needs of the survivors. In the aftermath of the Mongol invasions, this privileging of religious leaders was reflected in a broader tolerance on the part of these nomadic overlords for the diverse faiths and ethnic groups that had come under their rule.

As we will argue in this chapter, although the Mongols were indeed fierce fighters and capable of terrible acts of retribution against those who dared to defy them, their conquests brought much more than death and devastation. At the peak of their power, the domains of the Mongol *khans* made up a vast realm in which once-hostile peoples lived together in peace and most religions were tolerated. From the khanate of Persia in the west to the empire of the fabled Kubilai Khan in the east, the law code promulgated by Chinggis Khan gave order to human interaction. Like the far less warlike Islamic expansion that preceded it, the Mongol explosion laid the foundations for human interaction on a global scale, extending and intensifying the world network that had been building since the classical age.

THE TRANSCONTINENTAL EMPIRE OF CHINGGIS KHAN

19.1 What can the struggles Chinggis Khan faced in his youth and early career tell us about the organization and values of Mongol society?

In the early 13th century, long-standing obstacles to Mongol expansion were overcome, primarily because of the leadership of Chinggis Khan. The Mongols and allied nomadic groups built an empire that stretched from the Middle East to the China Sea.

In most ways, the Mongols epitomized nomadic society and culture. Their survival depended on the well-being of the herds of goats and sheep they drove from one pasture area to another according to the cycle of the seasons. Their staple foods were the meat and milk products provided by their herds, supplemented in most cases by grain and vegetables gained through trade with sedentary farming peoples. They also traded hides and dairy products for jewelry, weapons, and cloth made in urban centers. They dressed in sheepskins, made boots from tanned sheep hides, and lived in round felt tents made of wool sheared from their animals (Figure 19.2). The tough little ponies they rode to round up their herds, hunt wild animals, and make war were equally essential to their way of life. Mongol

Read the Document on MyHistoryLab: Excerpt from William of Rubruck's Account of the Mongols

FIGURE **19.2** This sketch shows a Mongol household on the move. The Mongols depended on sheep for food, clothing, and shelter, and they rode both horses and camels. As the drawing shows, they also used oxen to transport their housing for seasonal or longer-term migrations. The Mongols mounted their tents and other goods on enormous wagons so heavy that large teams of oxen were required to pull them. This combination of animal transport and comfortable but movable shelters made the Mongols one of the most mobile preindustrial societies.

boys and girls could ride as soon as they were able to walk. Mongol warriors could ride for days on end, sleeping and eating in the saddle.

Like the early Arabs and other nomadic peoples we have encountered, the basic unit of Mongol society was the tribe, which was divided into kin-related clans whose members camped and herded together on a regular basis. When threatened by external enemies or preparing for raids on other nomads or invasions of sedentary areas, clans and tribes could be combined in great confederations. Depending on the skills of their leaders, these confederations could be held together for months or even years. But when the threat had passed or the raiding was done, clans and tribes drifted back to their own pasturelands and campsites. At all organizational levels, leaders were elected by the free men of the group. Although women exercised influence within the family and had the right to be heard in tribal councils, men dominated leadership positions.

Courage in battle, usually evidenced by bravery in the hunt, and the ability to forge alliances and attract dependents were vital leadership skills. A strong leader could quickly build up a large following of chiefs from other clans and tribal groups. If the leader grew old and feeble or suffered severe reverses, his subordinates would quickly abandon him. He expected this to happen, and the subordinates felt no remorse. Their survival and that of their dependents hinged on attaching themselves to a strong tribal leader.

The Making of a Great Warrior: The Early Career of Chinggis Khan

Since the early millennia of recorded history, nomadic peoples speaking Mongolian languages had enjoyed moments of power and had actually carved out regional kingdoms in north China in the 4th and 10th centuries C.E. In the early 12th century, Chinggis Khan's (JEHNG-gihs kahn) great-grandfather, Kabul Khan, led a Mongol alliance that had won glory by defeating an army sent against them by the Jin kingdom of north China. Soon after this victory, Kabul Khan became ill and died. His successors could neither defeat their nomadic enemies nor hold the Mongol alliance together. Divided and beaten, the Mongols fell on hard times.

Chinggis Khan, who as a youth was named Temujin, was born in the 1170s into one of the splinter clans that fought for survival in the decades after the death of Kabul Khan. Temujin's father was an able leader who built up a decent following and negotiated a promise of marriage between his eldest son and the daughter of a stronger Mongol chief. According to Mongol accounts, just when the family fortunes seemed to be on the upswing, Temujin's father was poisoned by the agents of a rival nomadic group. Suddenly, Temujin, who was still a teenager, was thrust into a position of leadership. But most of the chiefs who had attached themselves to his father refused to follow a mere boy, whose prospects of survival appeared to be slim.

In the months that followed, Temujin's much-reduced encampment was threatened and finally attacked by a rival tribe. He was taken prisoner in 1182, locked into a wooden collar, and led in humiliation to the camp of his enemies. After a daring midnight escape, Temujin rejoined his mother and brothers and found refuge for his tiny band of followers deep in the mountains. Facing extermination, Temujin did what any sensible nomad leader would have done: He and his people joined the camp of a more powerful Mongol chieftain who had once been aided by Temujin's father. With the support of this powerful leader, Temujin avenged the insults of the clan that had enslaved him and another that had taken advantage of his weakness to raid his camp for horses and women.

These successes and Temujin's growing reputation as a warrior and military commander soon won him allies and clan chiefs eager to attach themselves to a leader with a promising future (Figure 19.3). Within a decade, the youthful Temujin had defeated his Mongol rivals and routed the forces sent to crush him by other nomadic peoples. In 1206, at a **kuriltai**, or meeting of all of the Mongol chieftains, Temujin— renamed Chinggis Khan—was elected the **khagan**, or supreme ruler, of the Mongol tribes. United under a strong leader, the Mongols prepared to launch a massive assault on an unsuspecting world.

kuriltai [KURL-tuh] Meeting of all Mongol chieftains at which the supreme ruler of all tribes was selected.

khagan [KAH-gahn] Title of the supreme ruler of the Mongol tribes.

tumens Basic fighting units of the Mongol forces; consisted of 10,000 cavalrymen; each unit was further divided into units of 1000, 100, and 10.

Building the Mongol War Machine

The men of the Mongol tribes that had elevated Chinggis Khan to leadership were natural warriors. Trained from youth not only to ride but also to hunt and fight, they were physically tough, mobile, and accustomed to killing and death. They wielded a variety of weapons, including lances, hatchets, and iron maces. None of their weapons was as devastating as their powerful short bows. A Mongol warrior could fire a quiver of arrows with stunning accuracy without breaking the stride of his horse. He could hit enemy soldiers as distant as 350 yards (the range for the roughly contemporary English longbow was 250 yards) while ducking under the belly of his pony, or leaning over the horse's rump. The fact that the Mongol armies were entirely cavalry meant that they moved so rapidly that their advances alone could be demoralizing to enemy forces.

To a people whose very lifestyle bred mobility, physical courage, and a love of combat, Chinggis Khan and his many able subordinate commanders brought organization, discipline, and unity of command. The old quarrels and vendettas between clans and tribes were overridden by loyalty to the khagan. Thus, energies once devoted to infighting were now directed toward conquest and the forcible exaction of tribute, both in areas controlled by other nomadic groups and in the civilized centers that fringed the steppes on all sides. The Mongol forces were divided into armies made up of basic fighting units called **tumens**, each consisting of 10,000 warriors. Each tumen was further divided into units of 1000, 100, and 10 warriors. Commanders at each level were responsible for training, arming, and disciplining the cavalrymen under their charge. The tumens were also divided into heavy cavalry, which carried lances and wore some metal armor, and light cavalry, which relied primarily on the bow and arrow and leather helmets and body covering. Even more lightly armed were the scouting parties that rode ahead of Mongol armies and, using flags and special signal fires, kept the main force informed of the enemy's movements.

Read the Document on MyHistoryLab: On Chinghis Khan (1270s) Marco Polo

FIGURE **19.3** In this miniature from a Persian history, Chinggis Khan is shown acknowledging the submission of a rival prince. Although he conquered a vast empire, Chinggis Khan did not live long enough to build a regular bureaucracy to govern it. His rule was dependent on vassal chieftains such as the one shown in the painting, whose loyalty in turn depended on the maintenance of Mongol military might. When the military strength of the Mongol empire began to decline, subject princes soon rose up to establish the independence of their domains.

Chinggis Khan also created a separate messenger force whose bodies were tightly bandaged to allow them to remain in the saddle for days, switching from horse to horse to carry urgent messages between the khagan and his commanders. Military discipline had long been secured by personal ties between commanders and ordinary soldiers. Mongol values, which made courage in battle a prerequisite for male self-esteem, were buttressed by a formal code that dictated the immediate execution of a warrior who deserted his unit. Chinggis Khan's swift executions left little doubt about the fate of traitors to his own cause or turncoats who abandoned enemy commanders in his favor. His generosity to brave foes was also legendary. The most famous of the latter, a man named Jebe, nicknamed the Arrow, won the khagan's affection and high posts in the Mongol armies by standing his ground after his troops had been routed and fearlessly shooting Chinggis Khan's horse out from under him.

A special unit supplied Mongol armies with excellent maps of the areas they were to invade. These were drawn largely according to the information supplied by Chinggis Khan's extensive network of spies and informers. New weapons, including a variety of flaming and exploding arrows, gunpowder projectiles, and later bronze cannons, were also devised for the Mongol forces. By the time Chinggis Khan's armies rode east and west in search of plunder and conquest in the second decade of the 13th century, they were among the best armed and trained and the most experienced, disciplined, and mobile soldiers in the world.

Conquest: The Mongol Empire Under Chinggis Khan

When he was proclaimed the khagan in 1206, Temujin probably was not yet 40 years old. At that point, he was the supreme ruler of nearly one-half million Mongols and the overlord of 1 to 2 million more nomads who had been defeated by his armies or had allied themselves with this promising young commander. But Chinggis Khan had much greater ambitions. He once said that his greatest pleasure in life was making war, defeating enemies, forcing "their beloved [to] weep, riding on their horses, embracing their wives and daughters." He came to see himself and his sons as men marked for a special destiny: warriors born to conquer the known world. In 1207, he set out to fulfill this ambition. His first campaigns humbled the Tangut (TANG-uht) kingdom of Xi Xia (shee-shyah) in northwest China (Map 19.1), whose ruler was forced to declare himself a vassal of the khagan and pay a hefty tribute. Next, the Mongol armies attacked the much more powerful Jin empire, which the Manchu-related Jurchens (YUHR-chehns) had established a century earlier in north China.

In these campaigns, the Mongol armies were confronted for the first time with large, fortified cities whose inhabitants assumed that they could easily withstand the assaults of these uncouth nomads from the steppes. Indeed, the Mongol invaders were thwarted at first by the intricate defensive works that the Chinese had perfected over the centuries to deter nomadic incursions. But the adaptive Mongols, with the help of captured Chinese artisans and military commanders, soon devised a whole arsenal of siege weapons. These included battering rams, catapults that hurled rocks and explosive balls, and bamboo rockets that spread fire and fear in besieged towns.

Chinggis Khan and the early Mongol commanders had little regard for these towns, whose inhabitants they saw as soft. Therefore, when they met resistance, the Mongols adopted a policy of terrifying retribution. Although the Mongols often spared the lives of famous scholars, whom they employed as advisors, and artisans with particularly useful skills, towns that fought back were usually sacked once they had been taken. The townspeople were slaughtered or sold into slavery; their homes, palaces, mosques, and temples were reduced to rubble. Towns that surrendered without a fight were usually spared this fate, although they were required to pay tribute to their Mongol conquerors as the price of their deliverance.

The First Assault on the Islamic World

Once they had established a foothold in north China and solidified their empire in the steppes, the Mongol armies moved westward against the Kara Khitai (KAH-rah KIHT-uh) empire, which had been established by a Mongolian-speaking people a century earlier (Map 19.1). Having overwhelmed and annexed the Kara Khitai by 1219, and, as we have seen, provoked by Muhammad Shah, Chinggis Khan led his armies in the conquest of the Khwarazm (kwahr-ahzm) empire further west. Again and again, the Mongols used their favorite battle tactic in these encounters. Cavalry were sent to attack the enemy's main force. Feigning defeat, the cavalry retreated, drawing the opposing forces out of formation in the hope of a chance to slaughter the fleeing Mongols. Once the enemy's pursuing horsemen

DOCUMENT

A European Assessment of the Virtues and Vices of the Mongols

AS WE HAVE SEEN, MUCH OF what we know about the history of nomadic peoples is based on the records and reactions of observers from sedentary cultures that were often their mortal enemies. Some of the most famous observers were those, including Marco Polo, who visited the vast Mongol domains at the height of the khans' power in the 12th and 13th centuries. Many tried to assess the strengths and weaknesses of these people, who were suddenly having such a great impact on the history of much of the known world. One of the most insightful of these observers was a Franciscan friar named Giovanni de Piano Carpini. In 1245, Pope Innocent IV sent Piano Carpini as an envoy to the "Great Khan" to protest the recent assaults by his Mongol forces on Christian Europe. The pope's protest had little effect on the Mongol decision to strike elsewhere in the following years. But Piano Carpini's extensive travels produced one of the most detailed accounts of Mongol society and culture to be written in the mid-13th century. As the following passages suggest, like other visitors from sedentary areas, he gave the Mongols a very mixed review:

The aforesaid men (namely the Tartars) obey their lords more than anyone else in the world, whether clergymen or laymen, and they respect them greatly and do not easily lie to them. The Tartars seldom argue to the point of insult, and there are no wars, quarrels, injuries or murders among them.

Each man respects his fellow and they are friendly to each other, and though food is scare among them, there is still enough to share . . . . When riding horses they tolerate great cold and heat. Nor are the men touchy; they do not appear jealous of their neighbors, and it seems that none are envious. No man turns another away, but instead helps him and supports him as much as possible.

The Tartars are prouder than other men and despise everyone else; indeed it is as through they held outsiders for nothing whether noble or base born . . . . The Tartars become quite angry with other men, are indignant by nature and lie to all outsiders; almost no truth is found among them. At first they are very mild, but in the end they sting like a scorpion. The Tartars are subtle and treacherous and, if they can, they get around everything by cunning.

The men are filthy with regard to their clothing, food and other things . . . . Drunkenness is honorable among the Tartars . . . . They are very jealous and greedy, demanding of favors, tenacious of what they have and stingy givers, and they think nothing of killing foreigners. In short, because their evil habits are so numerous they can hardly be set down.

QUESTIONS

- What might the qualities of the Mongols that Piano Carpini emphasizes tell us about his own society and its values or shortcomings?
- In what respects are the Mongol virtues he extols linked to the achievements of Chinggis Khan and the stunning Mongol wars of conquest?
- To what extent would they be typical of nomadic societies more generally?
- Why might his account of Mongol vices be simply dismissed as sour grapes resulting from European defeats?

had spread themselves over the countryside, the main force of Mongol heavy cavalry, until then concealed, attacked them in a devastating pincer formation. And the great cities of adversary powers fell to the new siege weapons and tactics the Mongols had perfected in their north China campaigns.

Within two years, his once flourishing cities in ruin and his kingdom in Mongol hands, Muhammad Shah, having retreated across his empire, died on a desolate island in the Caspian Sea. In addition to greatly enlarging his domains, Chinggis Khan's victories meant that he could bring tens of thousands of Turkic horsemen into his armies. By 1227, the year of his death, the Mongols ruled an empire that stretched from eastern Persia to the North China Sea.

Long Distance Trade and Cross-Cultural Exchange: Life under the Mongol Imperium

Despite their aggressiveness as warriors and the destruction they could unleash on those who resisted their demands for submission and tribute, the Mongols were remarkably astute and tolerant rulers. Chinggis Khan himself set the standard. He was a complex man, capable of gloating over the ruin of his enemies but also open to new ideas and committed to building a world where the diverse peoples of his empire could live together in peace. Although illiterate, Chinggis Khan was neither the ignorant savage nor the cultureless vandal often depicted in the accounts of civilized writers—usually those who had never met him. Once the conquered peoples had been subdued, he took a keen interest in their arts and learning, although he refused to live in their cities. Instead, he established a new capital at **Karakorum** on the steppes and summoned the wise and clever from all parts of the empire to the lavish palace of tents with gilded pillars where he lived with his wives and closest advisors.

At Karakorum, Chinggis Khan consulted with Confucian scholars about how to rule China, with Muslim engineers about how to build siege weapons and improve trade with the lands farther west, and with Daoist holy men, whom he hoped could give him an elixir that would make him immortal. Although he himself followed the *shamanistic* (focused on nature spirits) beliefs of his ancestors, all religions were tolerated in his empire. An administrative framework that drew on the advice and talents of both Muslim and Chinese bureaucrats was created. A script was devised for the Mongolian language to facilitate recordkeeping and the standardization of laws. Chinggis Khan's legal code was enforced by specially designated policemen. Much of the code was aimed at ending the divisions and quarrels that had so long plagued the Mongols and other nomadic peoples. Grazing lands were allotted to specific tribes, and harsh penalties were established for rustling livestock or stealing horses.

The Mongol conquests brought peace to much of Asia that in some areas persisted for generations. In the towns of the empire, handicraft production and scholarship flourished and artistic creativity was allowed free expression. Secure trade routes made for prosperous merchants and wealthy, cosmopolitan cities. One Muslim historian wrote of the peoples within the Mongol empire that they "enjoyed such a peace that a man might have journeyed from the land of sunrise to the land of sunset with a golden platter upon his head without suffering the least violence from anyone." Paradoxically, Mongol expansion, which sedentary chroniclers condemned as a "barbarian" orgy of violence and destruction, also became a major force for economic and social development and the enhancement of civilized life. But there was also a downside, the movement of merchants and commercial goods also facilitated the spread of disease. In fact, some historians believe that the infamous intercontinental wave of bubonic plague that came to be known as the Black Death was carried from China by the fleas on rats nesting in the saddle bags of Mongol cavalrymen across central Asia to the Black Sea and from there by ships to the Mediterranean and Europe.

The Death of Chinggis Khan and the Division of the Empire

In 1226, his wars to the west won, Chinggis Khan turned east with an army of 180,000 warriors to complete the conquest of China that he regretted having left unfinished more than a decade earlier. After routing a much larger Tangut (TANG-uht) army in a battle fought on the frozen waters of the Yellow River, the Mongol armies overran the kingdom of Xi Xia, plundering, burning, and mercilessly hunting down Tangut survivors. As his forces closed in on the Tangut capital and last refuge, Chinggis Khan, who had been injured in a skirmish some months earlier, fell grievously ill. After lecturing his sons on the dangers of quarreling among themselves for the spoils of the empire, the khagan died in August 1227.

With one last outburst of wrath, this time directed against death itself, the Mongols carried his body back to Mongolia for burial. The Mongol forces escorting the funeral procession hunted down and killed every human and animal in its path. The vast pasturelands the Mongols now controlled were divided between Chinggis Khan's three remaining sons and **Batu**, a grandson and heir of the khagan's recently deceased son, Jochi. Towns and cultivated areas such as those in north China and parts of Persia were considered the common property of the Mongol ruling family. A kuriltai was convened at Karakorum, the Mongol capital, to select a successor to the great conqueror. In accordance with Chinggis Khan's preference, **Ogedei**, his third son, was elected khagan. Although not as capable a military leader as his brothers or nephews, Ogedei was a crafty diplomat and deft manipulator. As it turned out, these skills were much needed to keep the ambitious heads of the vast provinces of the empire from each other's throats.

For nearly a decade, Ogedei directed Mongol energies into further campaigns and conquests. The areas targeted by this new round of Mongol expansion paid the price for peace within the Mongol empire. The fate of the most important victims—Russia and Eastern Europe, the Islamic heartlands, and China—will be the focus of most of the rest of this chapter.

Karakorum Capital of the Mongol empire under Chinggis Khan, 1162 to 1227.

Batu [BAH-too] Ruler of Golden Horde; one of Chinggis Khan's grandsons; responsible for invasion of Russia beginning in 1236.

Ogedei [OHGD-dih] (1186–1241) Third son of Chinggis Khan; succeeded Chinggis Khan as khagan of the Mongols following his father's death.

THE MONGOL DRIVE TO THE WEST

19.2 What were the key components that made for the remarkable success of the Mongol war machine?

Russia and Europe were added to the Mongols' agenda for world conquest. Subjugating these regions became the project of the armies of the **Golden Horde**, named after the golden tent of the early khans of the western sector of the Mongol Empire. The territories of the Golden Horde made up one of the four great **khanates** into which the Mongol Empire was divided at the time of Chinggis Khan's death (Map 19.2). Under the rule of Chinggis Khan's grandson Batu, Mongol armies began an invasion of Russia in 1236. In a very real sense, the assault on Russia was a side campaign, a chance to fine-tune the war machine and win a little booty on the way to Western Europe.

As we saw in Chapter 14, in the first half of the 13th century when the Mongol warriors first descended, Russia had been divided into numerous petty kingdoms, centered on trading cities such as Novgorod and Kiev (see Map 14.3). By this time, Kiev, which originally dominated much of central Russia, had been in decline for some time. As a result, there was no paramount power to rally Russian forces against the invaders. Despite the warnings of those who had witnessed the crushing defeats suffered by the Georgians in the early 1220s, the princes of Russia refused to cooperate. They preferred to fight alone, and they were routed individually.

In 1236, Batu led a Mongol force of more than 120,000 cavalrymen into the Russian heartlands. From 1237 to 1238 and later in 1240, these Tatars, or Tartars (meaning people from hell), as the Russians called them, carried out the only successful winter invasions in Russian history. In fact, the Mongols preferred to fight in the winter. The frozen earth provided good footing for their horses, and frozen rivers gave them access to their enemies. One after another, the Mongol armies defeated the often much larger forces of local nomadic groups and Russian princes. Cities such as Ryazan, Moscow, and Vladimir, which resisted the Mongol command to surrender, were destroyed; their inhabitants were slaughtered or led into slavery. As a contemporary Russian chronicler observed, "No eye remained to weep for the dead." Just as it seemed that all of Russia would be ravaged by the Mongols, whom the Russians compared to locusts, Batu's armies withdrew. The largest cities, Novgorod and Kiev, appeared to have been spared. Russian priests thanked God; the Mongol commanders blamed the spring thaw, which slowed the Mongol horsemen and raised the risk of defeat in the treacherous mud.

The Mongols returned in force in the winter of 1240. In this second campaign, even the great walled city of Kiev, which had reached a population of more than 100,000 by the end of the 12th century, fell. Enraged by Kievan resistance—its ruler had ordered the Mongol envoys thrown from the city walls—the Mongols reduced the greatest city in Russia to a smoldering ruin. The cathedral of Saint Sophia was spared, but the rest of the city was looted and destroyed, and its inhabitants were smoked out and slaughtered. Novgorod braced itself for the Mongol onslaught. Again, according to the Russian chroniclers, it was "miraculously" spared. In fact, it was saved largely because of the willingness of its prince, Alexander Nevsky, to submit, at least temporarily, to Mongol demands. In addition, the Mongol armies were eager to move on to the main event: the invasion of Western Europe, which they perceived as a far richer but equally vulnerable region.

Russia in Bondage

The crushing victories of Batu's armies initiated nearly two and a half centuries of Mongol dominance in Russia. Russian princes were forced to submit as vassals of the khan of the Golden Horde and to pay tribute. Mongol demands fell particularly heavily on the Russian peasantry, who had to give their crops and labor to both their own princes and the Mongol overlords. Impoverished and ever fearful of the lightning raids of Mongol marauders, the peasants fled to remote areas or became, in effect, the serfs (see Chapter 14) of the Russian ruling class in return for protection. Some Russian towns made profits on the increased trade made possible by the Mongol links. Sometimes the gains exceeded the tribute they paid to the Golden Horde. No town benefited from the Mongol presence more than Moscow. Badly plundered and partially burned in the early Mongol assaults, the city was gradually rebuilt, and its ruling princes steadily swallowed up nearby towns and surrounding villages. After 1328, Moscow also profited from its status as the tribute collector for the Mongol khans. Its princes

Mongol commanders launched raids into Georgia and across the Russian steppe that set the stage for their conquest of the vulnerable Christian lands to the west.

Golden Horde One of the four subdivisions of the Mongol empire after Chinggis Khan's death, originally ruled by his grandson Batu; territory covered much of what is today south central Russia.

khanates [KAHN-ayts] Four regional Mongol kingdoms that arose following the death of Chinggis Khan.

📖 Read the Document on MyHistoryLab: The Mongols: An Excerpt from the Novgorod Chronicle, 1315

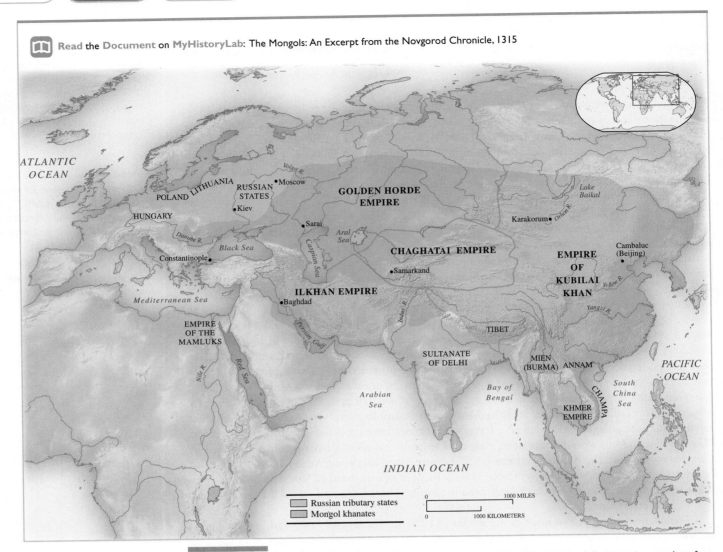

MAP **19.2 The Four Khanates of the Divided Mongol Empire** Sheer distances and slow-moving modes of transportation made it difficult to hold together the vast domains conquered by Chinggis Khan and his immediate successors.

not only used their position to fill their own coffers but also annexed other towns as punishment for falling behind on tribute payments.

As Moscow grew in strength, the power of the Golden Horde declined. Mongol religious toleration benefited both the Orthodox Church and Moscow. The choice of Moscow as the seat of the Orthodox leaders brought new sources of wealth to its princes and buttressed its claims to be Russia's leading city. In 1380, those claims got an additional boost when the princes of Moscow shifted from being tribute collectors to being the defenders of Russia. In alliance with other Russian vassals, they raised an army that defeated the forces of the Golden Horde at the **Battle of Kulikova**. Their victory and the devastating blows Timur's attacks dealt the Golden Horde two decades later effectively broke the Mongol hold over Russia.

Although much of the Mongols' impact was negative, their conquest was a turning point in Russian history in several ways. In addition to their importance to Moscow and the Orthodox Church, Mongol contacts led to changes in Russian military organization and tactics and in the political style of Russian rulers. Claims that the Tatars were responsible for Russian despotism, either tsarist or Stalinist, are clearly overstated. Still, the Mongol example may have influenced the desire of Russian princes to centralize their control and reduce the limitations placed on their power by the landed nobility, clergy, and wealthy merchants. By far the greatest effects of Mongol rule were those resulting

Battle of Kulikova Russian army victory over the forces of the Golden Horde; helped break Mongol hold over Russia.

from Russia's isolation from Christian lands farther west. On one hand, the Mongols protected a divided and weak Russia from the attacks of much more powerful kingdoms such as Poland, Lithuania, and Hungary (Map 19.2). On the other hand, in the period of Mongol rule, Russia was cut off from key transformations in western Europe that were inspired by the Renaissance and led ultimately to the Reformation.

Mongol Incursions and the Retreat from Europe

Until news of the Mongol campaigns in Russia reached European peoples such as the Germans, Poles, and Hungarians farther west, Christian leaders had been quite pleased by the rise of a new military power in central Asia. Rumors and reports from Christians living in the area, chafing under what they saw as persecution by their Muslim overlords, convinced many in western Europe that the Mongol khan was none other than **Prester John**. Prester John was the name given to a mythical rich and powerful Christian monarch whose kingdom had supposedly been cut off from Europe by the Muslim conquests of the 7th and 8th centuries. Sometimes located in Africa, sometimes in central Asia, Prester John loomed large in the European imagination as a potential ally who could strike the Muslim enemy from the rear and join up with European Christians to destroy their common adversary. The Mongol assault on the Muslim Khwarazm empire appeared to confirm the speculation that Chinggis Khan was indeed Prester John.

The assault on Christian, although Orthodox, Russia made it clear that the Mongol armies were neither the legions of Prester John nor more partial to Christians than to any other people who stood in their way. The rulers of Europe were nevertheless slow to realize the magnitude of the threat the Mongols posed to western Christendom. When Mongol envoys, one of whom was an Englishman, arrived at the court of King Bela of Hungary demanding that he surrender a group of nomads who had fled to his domains after being beaten by the Mongols in Russia, the king contemptuously dismissed them. King Bela also rebuffed Batu's demand that he submit to Mongol rule. The Hungarian monarch reasoned that he was the ruler of a powerful kingdom, whereas the Mongols were just another ragtag band of nomads in search of easy plunder. His refusal to negotiate provided the Mongols with a pretext to invade. Their ambition remained the conquest and pillage of all western Europe. That this goal was clearly attainable was demonstrated by the sound drubbing they gave to the Hungarians in 1240 and later to a mixed force of Christian knights led by the Polish ruler, King Henry of Silesia.

These victories left the Mongols free to raid and pillage from the Adriatic Sea region in the south to Poland and the German states of the north. It also left the rest of Europe open to Mongol conquest. Just as the kings and clergy of the western portions of Christendom were beginning to fear the worst, the Mongol forces disappeared. The death of the khagan Ogedei, in the distant Mongol capital at Karakorum, forced Batu to withdraw in preparation for the struggle for succession. The campaign for the conquest of Europe was never resumed. Perhaps Batu was satisfied with the huge empire of the Golden Horde that he ruled from his splendid new capital at Sarai on the Volga River in what is southern Russia today. Most certainly the Mongols had found richer lands to plunder in the following decades in the Muslim empires of the Middle East. Whatever the reason, Europe was spared the full fury of the Mongol assault. Of the civilizations that fringed the steppe homelands of the Mongols, only India was as fortunate.

The Mongol Assault on the Islamic Heartland

After the Mongol conquest of the Khwarazm empire, it was only a matter of time before they struck westward against the far wealthier Muslim empires of Mesopotamia and North Africa (see Map 12.2 and Map 19.2). The conquest of these areas became the main project of Hulegu, another grandson of Chinggis Khan and the ruler of the Ilkhan portions of the Mongol empire. As we saw in Chapter 12, one of the key results of Hulegu's assaults on the Muslim heartlands was the capture and destruction of Baghdad in 1258 (Figure 19.4). The murder of the Abbasid caliph, one of some 800,000 people who were reported to have been killed in Mongol retribution for the city's resistance, ended the dynasty that had ruled the core regions of the Islamic world since the mid-8th century. A major Mongol victory over the Seljuk Turks in 1243 also proved critical to the subsequent history of the region. It opened up Asia Minor (present-day Turkey) to conquest by a different Turkic-speaking people, the Ottomans, who would eventually become the next great power in the Islamic heartlands.

Prester John In legends popular from 12th to 17th century, a mythical Christian monarch whose kingdom was cut off from Europe by Muslim conquests; Chinggis Khan was originally believed to be this mythical ruler.

VISUALIZING THE PAST

The Mongol Empire as a Bridge Between Civilizations

CHINGGIS KHAN AND HIS SUCCESSORS ACTIVELY promoted the growth of trade and travelers by protecting the caravans that made their way across the ancient Asian silk routes. The Mongols also established rest stations for weary merchants and fortified outposts for those harassed by bandits. These measures transformed the Mongol imperium into a massive conduit between the civilizations of Europe, the Middle East, and the rest of Asia. The map illustrates a wide variety of marketable goods and inventions, as well as the agents and objects of several religions, between areas within the empire and along its lengthy borders. Study these patterns and then answer the questions that follow.

QUESTIONS

- Discuss some of the major ways in which the Mongol empire facilitated exchanges and interaction between civilizations and culture areas. What were the main centers of different kinds of products?
- What were the main directions in which ideas, goods, and new inventions flowed?
- Based on the discussions in the preceding chapters, who were some of the key agents of these exchanges?
- Why were the networks of exchange established by the Mongols so short-lived?

MAP **19.3 The Mongol Empire and the Global Exchange Network**

Baibars [bl bars] (1223–1277) Commander of Mamluk forces at Ain Jalut in 1260; originally enslaved by Mongols and sold to Egyptians.

Berke [ber kuh] (r. 1257–1266) A ruler of the Golden Horde; converted to Islam; his threat to Hulegu combined with the growing power of Mamluks in Egypt forestalled further Mongol conquests in the Middle East.

Given the fate of Baghdad, it is understandable that Muslim historians treated the coming of the Mongols as one of the great catastrophes in the history of Islam. The murder of the caliph and his family left the faithful without a central authority. The sack of Baghdad and many other cities from central Asia to the shores of the Mediterranean devastated the focal points of Islamic civilization. One contemporary Muslim chronicler, Ibn al-Athir, found the violence the Mongols had done to his people so horrific that he apologized to his readers for recounting it and wished that he had not been born to see it. He lamented,

In just one year they seized the most populous, the most beautiful, and the best cultivated part of the earth whose inhabitants excelled in character and urbanity. In the countries that have not yet been overrun by them, everyone spends the night afraid that they may yet appear there, too. . . . Thus, Islam and the Muslims were struck, at that time by a disaster such as no people had experienced before.

Given these reverses, one can imagine the relief the peoples of the Muslim world felt when the Mongols were finally defeated in 1260 by the armies of the Mamluk, or slave, dynasty of Egypt. Ironically, **Baibars**, the commander of the Egyptian forces, and many of his lieutenants had been enslaved by the Mongols some years earlier and sold in Egypt, where they rose to power through military service. The Muslim victory was won with the rare cooperation of the Christians, who allowed Baibars's forces to cross unopposed through their much diminished crusader territories in Palestine. Christian support demonstrated how far the former crusader states had gone in accommodating their more powerful Muslim neighbors.

Hulegu was in central Asia, engaged in yet another succession struggle, when the battle occurred. Upon his return, he was forced to reconsider his plans for conquest of the entire Muslim world. The Mamluks were deeply entrenched and growing stronger; Hulegu was threatened by his cousin **Berke**, the new khan of the Golden Horde to the north, who had converted to Islam. After openly clashing with Berke and learning of Baibars's overtures for an alliance with the Golden Horde, Hulegu decided to settle for the kingdom he already ruled, which stretched from the frontiers of Byzantium to the Amu Darya (Oxus) River in central Asia (Map 19.2).

THE MONGOL INTERLUDE IN CHINESE HISTORY

19.3 Compare the impact of Mongol conquest and rule in the Muslim Middle East, Russia, and China: On which area was there a greater impact, to what extent did the Mongol interlude alter the historical trajectory of each these major culture areas, and what were the similarities and differences in terms of the nature of and effects of Mongol invasions and rule?

Soon after Ogedei was elected as the great khan, the Mongol advance into China was resumed. Having conquered the Xi Xia and Jin empires, the Mongol commanders turned to what remained of the Song Empire in south China (Maps 19.1 and 19.2). In the campaigns against the Song, the Mongol forces were directed by **Kubilai Khan** (Figure 19.5). Kubilai was one of the grandsons of Chinggis Khan, and he would play a pivotal role in Chinese history for the next half century. Even under a decadent dynasty that had long neglected its defenses, south China was one of the toughest areas for the Mongols to conquer. From 1235 to 1279, the Mongols were constantly on the march; they fought battle after battle and besieged seemingly innumerable, well-fortified Chinese cities. In 1260, Kubilai assumed the title of the great khan, much to the chagrin of his cousins who ruled other parts of the empire. A decade later, in 1271, on the recommendation of Chinese advisors, he changed the name of his Mongol regime to a Chinese-language dynastic title, the **Yuan**. Although he was still nearly a decade away from fully defeating the last-ditch efforts of Confucian bureaucrats and Chinese generals to save the Song dynasty, Kubilai ruled most of China. He now set about the task of establishing more permanent Mongol control.

As the different regions of China came under Mongol rule, Kubilai passed many laws to preserve the distinction between Mongol and Chinese. He forbade Chinese scholars to learn the Mongol script, which was used for records and correspondence at the upper levels of the imperial government. Mongols were forbidden to marry ethnic Chinese, and only women from nomadic families were selected for the imperial harem. Even friendships between the two peoples were discouraged, and Mongol

View the Closer Look on MyHistoryLab: A Mongol Passport

FIGURE **19.4** The Abbasid capital at Baghdad had long been in decline when the Mongols besieged it in 1258. The Mongols' sack of the city put an end to all pretenses that Baghdad was still the center of the Muslim world. The Mongol assault on Baghdad also revealed how vulnerable even cities with high and extensive walls were to the artillery and other siege weapons that the Mongols and Chinese had pioneered. In the centuries that followed, major innovations in fortifications, many introduced first in Europe, were made to counter the introduction of gunpowder and the new siege cannons.

(The Mongols under their chief Hülegü conquering Baghdad in 1258. From Rashid al-Din's "Jami' al-Tawarikh" (Compendium of Chronicles). Illuminated manuscript page, 14th c.e. Inv. Diez A Fol.70, image 7. Bildarchiv Preussischer/Art Resource, NY. Photo: Ruth Schacht. Oriental Division.)

After decades of hard campaigning in the mid-13th century, the Mongols gained control of the greatest prize of all, China, which they ruled for a century. Although the Chinese capacity to assimilate nomadic conquerors was evident from the outset, the Mongols managed to retain a distinct culture and social separateness.

Read the Document on MyHistoryLab: Marco Polo on Chinese Society under the Mongol Rule (1270s)

FIGURE **19.5** This portrait of Kubilai Khan, by far the most important Mongol ruler of China, emphasizes his Mongol physical features, beard and hair styles, and dress. But Kubilai was determined to "civilize" his Mongol followers according to Chinese standards. Not only did he himself adopt a Chinese lifestyle, but he had his son educated by the best Confucian scholars to be a proper Chinese emperor. Kubilai also became a major patron of the Chinese arts and a promoter of Chinese culture.

Kubilai Khan [KOO-bluh KAHN] (1215–1294) Grandson of Chinggis Khan; commander of Mongol forces responsible for conquest of China; became khagan in 1260; established Sinicized Mongol Yuan dynasty in China in 1271.

Dadu Present-day Beijing; so-called when Kubilai Khan ruled China.

Chabi [CHAH-bee] Influential wife of Kubilai Khan; promoted interests of Buddhists in China; indicative of refusal of Mongol women to adopt restrictive social conventions of Chinese; died c. 1281.

military forces remained separate from the Chinese. Mongol religious ceremonies and customs were retained, and a tent encampment in the traditional Mongol style was set up in the imperial city even though Kubilai usually lived in a Chinese-style palace.

Despite his measures to ensure that the conquering Mongol minority was not completely absorbed by the culture of the defeated, Kubilai Khan had long been fascinated by Chinese civilization. Even before beginning the conquest of the Song Empire, he had surrounded himself with Chinese advisors, some Buddhist, others Daoist or Confucian. His capital at **Dadu** in the north (present-day Beijing) was built on the site occupied by earlier dynasties, and he introduced Chinese rituals and classical music into his own court. Kubilai also put the empire on the Chinese calendar and offered sacrifices to his ancestors at a special temple in the imperial city. But he rebuffed the pleas of his Confucian advisors to reestablish the civil service exams, which had been discontinued by the Jin rulers.

In the Yuan era, a new social structure was established in China, with the Mongols on top and their central Asian nomadic and Muslim allies right below them in the hierarchy. These two groups occupied most offices at the highest levels of the bureaucracy. Beneath them came the ethnic Chinese and then the minority peoples of the south. Thus, ethnic Chinese from both north and south ran the Yuan bureaucracy at the regional and local levels, but they could exercise power at the top only as advisors to the Mongols or other nomadic officials. At all levels, their activities were scrutinized by Mongol functionaries from an enlarged and much strengthened censors' bureau.

Gender Roles and the Convergence of Mongol and Chinese Culture

Mongol women remained aloof from Chinese culture—at least Chinese culture in its Confucian guise. They refused to adopt the practice of footbinding, which so limited the activities of Chinese women. They retained their rights to property and control within the household as well as the freedom to move about the town and countryside. No more striking evidence of their independence can be found than contemporary accounts of Mongol women riding to the hunt, both with their husbands and at the head of their own hunting parties. The daughter of one of Kubilai's cousins went to war, and she refused to marry until one of her many suitors was able to throw her in a wrestling match.

The persisting influence of Mongol women after the Mongols settled down in China is exemplified by **Chabi**, the wife of Kubilai Khan (Figure 19.6). She was one of Kubilai's most important confidants on political and diplomatic matters, and she promoted Buddhist interests in the highest circles of government. Chabi played a critical role in fostering policies aimed at reconciling the majority ethnic Chinese population of the empire to Mongol rule. She convinced Kubilai that the harsh treatment of the survivors of the defeated Song imperial family would only anger the peoples of north China and make them more difficult to rule. On another occasion, she demonstrated that she shared Kubilai's respect for Chinese culture by frustrating a plan to turn cultivated lands near the capital into pasturelands for the Mongols' ponies. Thus, the imperial couple was a good match of astute political skills and cosmopolitanism, tempered by respect for their own traditions and a determination to preserve those they found the most valuable.

The Mongol era was too brief and the number of influential Mongol women far too small to reverse the trends that for centuries had been lowering the position of women in Chinese society. As neo-Confucianism gained ground under Kubilai's successors, the arguments for confining women multiplied. Ultimately, even women of the Mongol ruling class saw their freedom and power reduced.

Mongol Tolerance and Foreign Cultural Influence

Like Chinggis Khan and other Mongol overlords, Kubilai and Chabi had unbounded curiosity and very cosmopolitan tastes. Their generous patronage drew scholars, artists, artisans, and office-seekers from many lands to the splendid Yuan court. Some of the most favored came from Muslim kingdoms to the east that had come under Mongol rule. Muslims were included in the second highest social grouping, just beneath the Mongols themselves. Persians and Turks were admitted to the inner circle of Kubilai's administrators and advisors. Muslims designed and supervised the building of his Chinese-style imperial city and proposed new systems for more efficient tax collection. Persian astronomers imported more advanced Middle Eastern instruments for celestial observations, corrected the Chinese calendar, and made some of the most accurate maps the Chinese had ever seen. Muslim doctors ran the imperial hospitals and added translations of 36 volumes on Muslim medicine to the imperial library.

In addition to the Muslims, Kubilai welcomed travelers and emissaries from many foreign lands to his court. Like his grandfather, Kubilai had a strong interest in all religions and insisted on toleration in his domains. Buddhists, Nestorian Christians, Daoists, and Latin Christians made their way to his court. The most renowned of the latter were members of the Polo family from Venice in northern Italy, who traveled extensively in the Mongol empire in the middle of the 13th century. Marco Polo's account of Kubilai Khan's court and empire, where Polo lived and served as an administrator for 17 years, is perhaps the most famous travel account written by a European (Figure 19.7). Polo accepted fantastic tales of grotesque and strange customs, and he may have taken parts of his account from other sources. Still, his descriptions of the palaces, cities, and wealth of Kubilai's empire enhanced European interest in Asia and helped to inspire efforts by navigators, such as Columbus, to find a sea route to these fabled lands.

Social Policies and Scholar-Gentry Resistance

Kubilai's efforts to promote Mongol adaptation to Chinese culture were overshadowed in the long run by measures to preserve Mongol separateness. The ethnic Chinese who made up the vast majority of his subjects, particularly in the south, were never really reconciled to Mongol rule. Despite Kubilai's cultivation of Confucian rituals and his extensive employment of Chinese bureaucrats, most of the scholar-gentry saw the Mongol overlord and his successors as uncouth barbarians whose policies endangered Chinese traditions. As it was intended to do, Kubilai's refusal to reinstate the examination route to administrative office prevented Confucian scholars from dominating politics. The favoritism he showed Mongol and other foreign officials further alienated the scholar-gentry.

To add insult to injury, Kubilai went to great lengths to bolster the position of the artisan classes, who had never enjoyed high standing, and the merchants, whom the Confucian thinkers had long dismissed as parasites. From the outset the Mongols had shown great regard for artisans and because of their useful skills had often spared them while killing their fellow city dwellers. During the Yuan period in China, merchants also prospered and commerce boomed, partly because of Mongol efforts to improve transportation and expand the supply of paper money. With amazing speed for a people who had no prior experience with seafaring, the Mongols developed a substantial navy, which played a major role in the conquest of the Song empire. After the conquest of China was completed, the great Mongol war fleets were used to put down pirates, who threatened river and overseas commerce. Toward the end of Kubilai's reign, the navy also launched a number of overseas expeditions of exploration and conquest, which led to attacks on Japan and a brief reoccupation of Vietnam.

FIGURE **19.6** A portrait of Chabi, the energetic and influential wife of Kubilai Khan. Kubilai's determination to adopt Chinese culture without being overwhelmed by it was bolstered by the advice and example of Chabi. Displaying the independent-mindedness and political savvy of many Mongol women, Chabi gave Kubilai critical advice on how to counter the schemes of his ambitious brother and how to handle the potentially hostile scholar-gentry elite and peasantry that came to be ruled by Mongol overlords.

Read the Document on MyHistoryLab: Marco Polo at the Court of Kublai Khan, c. 1300

Ironically, despite the Mongols' suspicion of cities and sedentary lifestyles, both flourished in the Yuan era. The urban expansion begun under the Tang and Song dynasties continued, and the Mongol elite soon became addicted to the diversions of urban life. Traditional Chinese artistic endeavors, such as poetry and essay writing, languished under the Mongols in comparison with their flowering in the Tang and Song eras. But popular entertainments, particularly musical dramas, flourished. Perhaps the most famous Chinese dramatic work, **Romance of the West Chamber**, was written in the Yuan period. Dozens of major playwrights wrote for the court, the rising merchant classes, and the Mongol elite. Actors and actresses, who had long been relegated by the Confucian scholars to the despised status of "mean people," achieved celebrity and social esteem. All of this rankled the scholar-gentry, who waited for the chance to restore Confucian decorum and what they believed to be the proper social hierarchy for a civilized people.

Initially, at least, Kubilai Khan pursued policies toward one social group, the peasants that the scholarly class would have heartily approved. He forbade Mongol cavalrymen from turning croplands into pasture and restored the granary system for famine relief that had been badly neglected in the late Song. Kubilai also sought to reduce

Read the Document on MyHistoryLab: Mongols and Trade on the Silk Roads

FIGURE **19.7** This 15th-century manuscript illumination depicts Marco Polo and his uncle offering homage to the Great Khan. The Polos were Venetian merchants, and Marco's elders had already traveled extensively in Asia in the decade before they set off with Marco. Marco had a great facility with languages, which served him well in his journeys through Asia by land and sea. On his way home in the mid-1290s, he related his many adventures to a writer of romances while both were prisoners of the Genoese, who were fierce rivals of the Venetians. Eventually published under the title *Description of the World*, Polo's account became one of a handful of definitive sources on the world beyond Europe for the explorers of the coming age of overseas expansion.
(Paris, Bibliotheque Nationale, Ms. 2810.)

Romance of the West Chamber
Chinese drama written during the Yuan period; indicative of the continued literary vitality of China during Mongol rule.

peasant tax and forced-labor burdens, partly by redirecting peasant payments from local nonofficial tax farmers directly to government officials. He and his advisors also developed a revolutionary plan to establish elementary education in the villages. Although the level of learning they envisioned was rudimentary, such a project, if it had been enacted, would have been a major challenge to the educational system centered on the elite that long had dominated Chinese civilization.

The Fall of the House of Yuan

Historians often remark on the seeming contradiction between the military prowess of the Mongol conquerors and the short life of the dynasty they established in China. Kubilai Khan's long reign encompassed a good portion of the nine decades in which the Mongols ruled all of China. Already by the end of his reign, the dynasty was showing signs of weakening. Song loyalists raised revolts in the south, and popular hostility toward the foreign overlords was expressed more and more openly. The Mongol aura of military invincibility was badly tarnished by Kubilai's rebuffs at the hands of the military lords of Japan and the failure of the expeditions that he sent to punish them, first in 1274 and again in a much larger effort in 1280. The defeats suffered by Mongol forces engaged in similar expeditions to Vietnam and Java during this same period further undermined the Mongols' standing.

Kubilai's dissolute lifestyle in his later years, partly brought on by the death of his most beloved wife, Chabi, and five years later the death of his favorite son, led to a general softening of the Mongol ruling class as a whole. Kubilai's successors lacked his capacity for leadership and cared little for the tedium of day-to-day administrative tasks. Many of the Muslim and Chinese functionaries to whom they entrusted the imperial finances enriched themselves through graft and corruption. This greatly angered the hard-pressed peasantry, who bore the burden of rising taxes and demands for forced

THINKING HISTORICALLY

The Global Eclipse of the Nomadic Warrior Culture

AS THE SHOCK WAVES OF THE Mongol and Timurid explosions amply demonstrate, nomadic incursions into the civilized cores have had an impact on global history that far exceeds what one would expect, given the small numbers of nomadic peoples and the limited resources of the regions they inhabited. From the time of the great Indo-European migrations in the 3rd and 2nd millennia B.C.E. through the classical and postclassical eras, nomadic peoples periodically emerged from their steppe, prairie, and desert fringe homelands to invade, often build empires, and settle in the sedentary zones of Eurasia, Africa, and the Americas. Their intrusions have significantly changed political history by destroying existing polities and even, as in the case of Assyria, whole civilizations. They have also generated major population movements, sparked social upheavals, and facilitated critical cultural and economic exchanges across civilizations. As the Mongols' stunning successes in the 13th century illustrate, the ability of nomadic peoples to break through the defenses of the much more populous civilized zones and to establish control over much richer and more sophisticated peoples arose primarily from the nomads' advantages in waging war.

With the introduction early in the 17th century of light, mobile field artillery into the armies of the warring states of central and western Europe, the nomads' retreat began.

A reservoir of battle-ready warriors and mobility have proved to be the keys to success for expansion-minded nomads. Harsh environments and ongoing intertribal and interclan conflicts for survival within them produced tough, resourceful fighters who could live off the land on the march and who saw combat as an integral part of their lives. The horses and camels on which pastoral peoples in Eurasia and Sudanic Africa relied gave them a degree of mobility that confounded the sedentary peoples who tried to ward off their incursions. The mounted warriors of nomadic armies had the advantages of speed, surprise, and superior intelligence, gathered by mounted patrols. The most successful nomadic invaders, such as the Mongols, also were willing to experiment with and adapt to technological innovations. Some of these, such as the stirrup and various sorts of harnesses, were devised by the nomads themselves. Others, such as gunpowder and the siege engines—both Muslim and Chinese—that the Mongols used to smash the defenses of walled towns were borrowed from sedentary peoples and adapted to the nomads' fighting styles.

Aside from the military advantages of the nomads' lifestyles and social organization, their successes in war owed much to the weaknesses of their adversaries in the sedentary, civilized zones. Even in the best circumstances, the great empires that provided the main defense for agricultural peoples against nomadic incursions were diverse and overextended polities. Imperial control and protection diminished steadily as one moved away from the capital and core provinces. Imperial boundaries were usually fluid, and the outer provinces were vulnerable to nomadic raids and conquest.

Classical and postclassical empires, such as the Egyptian and Han and the Abbasid, Byzantine, and Song, enjoyed great advantages over the nomads in terms of the populations and resources they controlled. But their armies, almost without exception, were too slow, too low on firepower, and too poorly trained to resist large and well-organized forces of nomadic intruders. In times of dynastic strength in the sedentary zones, well-defended fortress systems and ingenious weapons—such as the crossbow, which the peasant conscripts could master fairly easily—were quite effective against nomadic incursions. Nonetheless, even the strongest dynasties depended heavily on protection payments to nomad leaders and the divisions between the nomadic peoples on their borders for their security. Even the strongest sedentary empires were shaken periodically by nomadic raids into the outer provinces. When the empires weakened or when large numbers of nomads were united under able leaders, such as the prophet Muhammad and his successors or Chinggis Khan, nomadic assaults made a shambles of sedentary armies and fortifications.

In many ways, the Mongol and Timurid explosions represented the apex of nomadic power and influence on world history. After these remarkable interludes, age-old patterns of interaction between nomads and town-dwelling peoples were transformed. These transformations resulted in the growing ability of sedentary peoples to first resist and then dominate nomadic peoples, and they mark a watershed in the history of the human community. Some of the causes of the shift were immediate and specific. The most critical of these was the devastation wrought by the Black Death on the nomads of central Asia in the 14th century. Although the epidemic was catastrophic for large portions of the civilized zones as well, it dealt the sparse nomadic populations a blow from which they took centuries to recover.

In the centuries after the Mongol conquests, the rulers of sedentary states found increasingly effective ways to centralize their political power and mobilize the labor and resources of their domains for war. The rulers of China and the empires of the Islamic belt made some improvements, but the sovereigns of the emerging states of western Europe surpassed all others in this regard. Stronger control and better organization allowed a

(continued on next page)

growing share of steadily increasing national wealth to be channeled toward military ends. The competing rulers of Europe also invested heavily in technological innovations with military applications, from improved metalworking techniques and radical innovations in fortress construction to more potent gunpowder and firearms. From the 15th and 16th centuries, the discipline and training of European armies also improved. With pikes, muskets, exacting drill in the use of firearms, and trained commanders, European armies were more than a match for the massed nomad cavalry that had so long terrorized sedentary peoples.

With the introduction early in the 17th century of light, mobile field artillery into the armies of the warring states of central and western Europe, the nomads' retreat began. States such as Russia, which had centralized power on the western European model, as well as the Ottoman Empire in the eastern Mediterranean and the Qing in China, which had shared many of the armament advances of the Europeans, moved steadily into the steppe and desert heartlands of the horse and camel nomads. Each followed a conscious policy of settling part of its rapidly growing peasant population in the areas taken from the nomads. Thus, nomadic populations not only were brought under the direct rule of sedentary empires but saw their pasturelands plowed and planted wherever the soil and water supply permitted.

These trends suggest that the nomadic war machine had been in decline long before the new wave of innovation that ushered in the Industrial Revolution in the 18th century. But that process sealed its fate. Railways and repeating rifles allowed sedentary peoples to penetrate even the most wild and remote nomadic refuges and subdue even the most determined and fierce nomadic warriors, from the Plains Indians of North America to the bedouin of the Sahara and Arabia. The periodic nomadic incursions into the sedentary zones, which had recurred for millennia, had come to an end.

QUESTIONS

- What are some of the major ways in which nomadic peoples and their periodic expansions have affected global history?
- Which of their movements and conquests do you think were the most important?
- Why were the Mongols able to build a much greater empire than any previous nomadic contender?
- Why did the Mongol Empire collapse so rapidly, and what does its fall tell us about the underlying weaknesses of the nomadic war machine?

White Lotus Society Secret religious society dedicated to overthrow of Yuan dynasty in China; typical of peasant resistance to Mongol rule.

Zhu Yuanzhang The given name of the Hongwu emperor, the founder of the Ming dynasty.

Ming dynasty Succeeded Mongol Yuan dynasty in China in 1368; lasted until 1644; initially mounted huge trade expeditions to southern Asia and elsewhere, but later concentrated efforts on internal development within China.

Timur-i Lang Also known as Tamerlane; leader of Turkic nomads; beginning in 1360s from base at Samarkand, launched series of attacks in Persia, the Fertile Crescent, India, and southern Russia; empire disintegrated after his death in 1405.

📖 **Read the Document on MyHistoryLab:** A Contemporary Describes Timur

labor. The scholar-gentry played on this discontent by calling on the people to rise up and overthrow the "barbarian" usurpers.

By the 1350s, the signs of dynastic decline were apparent. Banditry and piracy were widespread, and the government's forces were too weak to curb them. Famine hit many regions and spawned local uprisings, which engulfed large portions of the empire. Secret religious sects, such as the **White Lotus Society**, were dedicated to overthrowing the dynasty. Their leaders' claims that they had magical powers to heal their followers and confound their enemies helped encourage further peasant resistance against the Mongols. As in the past, rebel leaders quarreled and fought with each other. For a time, chaos reigned as the Yuan regime dissolved, and the Mongols who could escape the fury of the mob retreated into central Asia. The restoration of peace and order came from an unexpected quarter. Rather than a regional military commander or an aristocratic lord, a man from a poor peasant family, **Zhu Yuanzhang**, emerged to found the **Ming dynasty**, which ruled China for most of the next three centuries.

Aftershock: The Brief Ride of Timur, the Last of the Great Nomadic Conquerors

Just as the peoples of Europe and Asia had begun to recover from the upheavals caused by Mongol expansion, a second nomadic outburst from central Asia plunged them again into fear and despair. This time the nomads in question were Turks, not Mongols, and their leader, **Timur-i Lang** (Timur the Lame, or Tamerlane) was from a noble land-owning clan, not a tribal, herding background. Timur's personality was complex. On one hand, he was a highly cultured person who delighted in the fine arts, lush gardens, and splendid architecture and who could spend days conversing with great scholars, such as Muslim historian Ibn Khaldun (see the Document feature in Chapter 12). On the other, he was a ruthless conqueror, apparently indifferent to human suffering and capable of commanding his troops to commit atrocities on a scale that would not be matched in the human experience until the 20th century. Beginning in the 1360s, his armies moved out from his base at Samarkand to conquests in Persia, the Fertile Crescent, India, and southern Russia.

Although his empire did not begin to compare with that of the Mongols in size, he outdid them in the ferocity of his campaigns. In fact, Timur is remembered for little more than barbaric destruction:

His armies built pyramids of skulls with the heads of those they killed. Tens of thousands of people were slaughtered after they took the city of Aleppo in Asia Minor, and thousands of prisoners were massacred as a warning to the citizens of Delhi, in north India, not to resist his armies. In the face of this wanton slaughter, the fact that he spared artisans and scientists to embellish his capital city at Samarkand counts for little. Unlike that of the Mongols, his rule brought neither increased trade and cross-cultural exchanges nor internal peace. Fortunately, his reign was as brief as it was violent. After his death in 1405, his empire was pulled apart by his warring commanders and old enemies anxious for revenge. With his passing, the last great challenge of the steppe nomads to the civilizations of Eurasia came to an end.

Global Connections and Critical Themes

THE MONGOL LINKAGES

From the first explosion of Mongol military might from the steppes of central Asia in the early 13th century to the death of Timur in 1405, the nomads of central Asia made a stunning return to center stage in world history. Mongol invasions ended or interrupted many of the great empires of the postclassical period and also extended the world network that had increasingly defined the period. Under Chinggis Khan, the Mongols and their many nomadic neighbors were forged into the mightiest war machine the world had ever seen. With stunning rapidity the Mongols conquered central Asia, northern China, and eastern Persia (Map 19.1). Under Chinggis Khan's sons and grandsons, the rest of China, Tibet, Persia, Iraq, much of Asia Minor, and all of southern Russia were added to the vast Mongol imperium.

Although much of what the Mongols did was destructive, their forays into Europe, China, and the Muslim heartlands brought some lasting changes that were often transformative and at times beneficial. They taught new ways of making war and impressed on their Turkic and European enemies the effectiveness of gunpowder. Mongol conquests facilitated trade between the civilizations at each end of Eurasia, making possible the exchange of foods, tools, and ideas on an unprecedented scale. The revived routes brought great wealth to traders, such as those from north Italy, who set up outposts in the eastern Mediterranean, along the Black Sea coast, and as far east as the Caspian Sea.

The Mongol framework for Asian-European interactions, although short-lived, also facilitated other exchanges. It opened China to influences from Arab and Persian lands, and even to contacts with Europe. These connections came to full fruition in the centuries of indigenous Chinese revival that followed under the Ming dynasty. Europeans gained new knowledge of Chinese products and technologies that they would soon adapt back home. Explosive powder and printing were the most important examples. Regions more remote from the Mongols, such as Africa, lacked this kind of stimulus. Even the collapse of the Mongol network had an impact. Many societies had an interest in maintaining contacts, although China grew more wary of outsiders. But the Mongol decline made land-based travel more dangerous, which quickly turned attention toward sea routes. Thus, the legacy of the Mongol period was both complex and durable.

Perhaps the greatest long-term impact of the Mongol drive to the west was indirect and unintended. In recent years, a growing number of historians have become convinced that the Mongol conquests played a key role in transmitting the fleas that carried bubonic plague from south China and central Asia to Europe and the Middle East. The fleas may have hitched a ride on the livestock the Mongols drove into the new pasturelands won by their conquests or on the rats that nibbled the grain transported by merchants along the trading routes the Mongol rulers had reestablished between east and west. Whatever the exact connection, the Mongol armies unknowingly paved the way for the spread of the dreaded Black Death across the steppes to much of China, to the Islamic heartlands, and from there to most of Europe in the mid-14th century. In so doing, they unleashed possibly the most fatal epidemic in all human history. It led to mortality rates higher than 50 percent in some areas of Europe and the Middle East, and forced economic and social adjustments wherever it spread. This accidental but devastating side effect of the Mongol conquests influenced the course of civilized development in Europe, Asia, and north Africa for centuries.

Further Readings

A substantial literature has developed on the Mongol interlude in global history. The most readable and reliable biography of Chinggis Khan is René Grousset, *Conqueror of the World* (1966). Grousset has also written a broader history of central Asia, *The Empire of the Steppes* (1970). Peter Brent's more recent *The Mongol Empire* (1976) provides an updated overview and wonderful illustrations. Berthold Spuler, *History of the Mongols* (1968), supplies a wide variety of firsthand accounts of the Mongols. Timothy May's *The Mongol Art of War: Chinggis Khan and the Mongol Military System* (2000) shows that the Mongol armies had much in common with modern forces.

For the Mongols' impact on global history, see David Morgan, *The Mongols* (2006); Peter Jackson, *The Mongols and the West* (2005); and especially Thomas Allsen, *Culture and Conquest in Mongol Eurasia* (2001). Robert S. Marshall, *Storm from the East: From Genghis Khan to Khubilai Khan* (1993), and Charles J. Halperin,

Russia and the Golden Horde: The Mongol Impact on Medieval Russian History (1985), examine the Mongol impact on Russia. While George Vernadsky, *The Mongols in Russia* (1953), remains the standard work on that subject, some of its views are now contested. Morris Rossabi, *Kubilai Khan: His Life and Times* (1988), is by far the best work on the Mongols in China. George James Chambers, *The Devil's Horsemen* (1979), and Denis Sinor, *History of Hungary* (1957), contain good accounts of the Mongol incursions into eastern and central Europe. T. Allsen, *Mongol Imperialism* (1987), is the best account of the rise and structure of the empires built by Chinggis Khan and his successors. The fullest and most accessible

summary of the links between Mongol expansion and the spread of the Black Death can be found in William H. McNeill, *Plagues and Peoples* (1976).

Recent works examining the broader interactions between agricultural and pastoral societies in Eurasia include Thomas J. Barfield, *The Perilous Frontier* (1992); Donald Ostrowski, *Muscovy and the Mongols: Cross-Cultural Influences on the Steppe Frontier, 1304–1589* (1998); Andrew Bell-Fialkoff, *The Role of Migration in the History of the Eurasian Steppe* (2000); and Nicola Di Cosmo, *Ancient China and Its Enemies: The Rise of Nomadic Power in East Asian History* (2004).

On MyHistoryLab

 ✓ Study and Review on MyHistoryLab

Critical Thinking Questions

1. Discuss the ways in which the Mongol imperium enhanced contacts, particularly between China and the Islamic world. Which areas received the most benefit from these exchanges?

2. Why was the era of Mongol dominance so short-lived and what were some of the consequences of its disintegration?

3. What were the main effects of the Mongol period on world history? What are some of the ways that recent historical studies have forced us to rethink the nature and impact of the Mongol interlude in world history, and the roles played by nomadic peoples more generally?

The World in 1450:
Changing Balance of World Power

Listen to Chapter 20
on MyHistoryLab

The compass is a simple enough device—something you can make yourself with an iron needle and a magnet. Yet it was also a revolutionary device, allowing sailors (and now, airplane pilots) to maintain a sense of direction no matter how dark, stormy, foggy, or unfamiliar the environment.

Although there has been debate about the origins of the compass, the instrument was clearly developed first by the Chinese. Chinese scientists may have had some knowledge of magnetic principles as early as the 1st century. Actual compasses may have been developed during the Tang dynasty. They undoubtedly originated from the discovery of naturally magnetized iron, or lodestone, that could then be used to fashion a needle that would point north. Some believe that the Chinese first used compasses in the practice of *feng shui*, which was a set of design principles by which people could align their living quarters with the forces of nature.

LEARNING OBJECTIVES

What were the most important changes in the Middle East between the 13th and the 15th centuries? p. 439	20.1
What caused the Chinese decision to abandon major expeditions? p. 440	20.2
What are the main issues in explaining new outreach from western Europe? What are the principal interpretations? p. 442	20.3
How do patterns in the Americas and Polynesia reflect their isolation from main transregional trade networks? p. 448	20.4

FIGURE **20.1** Chinese oceangoing ship from expeditions in the 16th century. This was a smaller ship than those used earlier in the great voyages of the early 15th century, whose end opened opportunities for other international traders. But the Chinese maintained active commerce even after this, particularly in maintaining contacts established in the postclassical period with the Philippines and with southeast Asia.

👁 Watch the Video Series on MyHistoryLab

Learn about some key topics related to this chapter with the *MyHistoryLab Video Series:*
Key Topics in World History

Compasses for navigation had been introduced by 1100. They were part of a growing Chinese effort to make contact with sources of spices and teas in southeast Asia. Prior to that point, Chinese seagoing had been confined to coastlines, but now it became much more venturesome. Wide-ranging Chinese expeditions introduced the compass to seafarers throughout the Indian Ocean, including Arab merchants, by the 12th century. Europeans are first known to have used the compass in 1187. Europeans may have invented the compass separately, but it is far more likely that they learned about its use as a result of contacts with Arabs or Asians.

The compass was fundamental to ambitious seagoing expeditions, like the great Chinese voyages through the Indian Ocean. Along with observation of the sun and stars, the compass provided the guidance for Columbus's travels to the Americas. It changed the shape of world history by facilitating dramatic new contacts and exchanges. By the 13th century, various seagoing peoples—Malaysians, for example, as well as Europeans—were introducing improvements in the compass, making it easier to read and more stable at sea. Italian navigators introduced the compass card, which involved placing the needle over a set of indicators. Knowledge of the compass reached Scandinavia by 1300, a further step in the long process of dissemination. ■

In 1400 the world was undergoing a profound transition. This chapter highlights the main features of that process. The principal focus is the shifting balance among civilizations in Asia, Africa, and Europe and how these power shifts changed the nature of international contact.

This period of transition began with the decline of Arab strength—symbolized by the fall of the last Arab caliphate in 1258—and the disruptions that Mongol incursions caused elsewhere in Asia and eastern Europe. These developments created new opportunities in the Afro-Eurasian network that had been established during the postclassical centuries, initially under Arab sponsorship. Various candidates emerged to take a new international leadership role, including, for a short time, Ming China. The Chinese expeditions showed the importance transregional contacts had acquired. The end of the expeditions, however, opened the way for new alignments. Within the Middle East itself, Arab and then Mongol decline created new opportunities for Turkish conquerors and migrants. In 1453 the Ottoman Turks captured Constantinople, effectively completing the destruction of the Byzantine empire and creating a new Islamic political power. The Ottomans quickly established control around much of the Black Sea, including the Balkans, and began to push southward into Arab lands.

📖 Read the Document on MyHistoryLab: Kritovoulos on the Fall of Constantinople (1450s)

While the Ottomans would play some role in transregional trade, ultimately the most dynamic new contender for leadership ultimately proved to be western Europe; the conditions that propelled Western civilization into this new position around 1400 are the second key theme of this chapter. The West was not yet a major power; it did not replace the Arabs or Chinese as international leaders quickly or easily. The first stages of the rise of the West were accompanied by important changes in Western civilization itself, which were beginning to take shape by 1400. At this point, Italy, Spain, and Portugal took the lead in western European outreach, a lead that they would hold for about two centuries.

It is also vital to note changes in societies outside the international network, in the Americas and Polynesia. New difficulties in the great American empires, in particular, would reduce their ability to respond to the challenge of contact with Europeans after 1492.

Focusing on new frameworks for international contacts, this chapter inevitably deals with the question of why individual societies reacted differently to key forces. Comparison is essential. Western Europe's response, for example, should be compared to reactions at the same time in regions like Japan or sub-Saharan Africa.

1250 C.E.	1300 C.E.	1350 C.E.	1400 C.E.	1450 C.E.
1258 Mongol conquest of Baghdad; fall of Abbasid caliphate **c. 1266–1337** Life of Giotto **1275–1292** Marco Polo in China **1290–1317** Famines in Europe **1291** First Italian expedition seeks route to Indies	**1304–1374** Life of Petrarch; development of Italian Renaissance **1320s** Spread of bubonic plague (Black Death) in Gobi desert **1320s** First European use of cannon in warfare **1330s** Black Death reaches China **1347** Black Death reaches Sicily **1348** Peak of Black Death in Middle East **1348–1375** Black Death spreads in Europe and Russia	**1368** Mongols expelled from China; Ming dynasty	**1400** End of Polynesian migrations **1405–1433** Chinese trading expeditions **1439** Portugal takes over Azores; increasing expeditions into Atlantic and along northwest African coast	**1453** Ottomans capture Constantinople, fall of Byzantine Empire **1469** Union of Aragon and Castile; rise of Spanish monarchy

Amid variations and great change, the transitions around 1450 highlighted one important continuity as well: the importance of the level of contacts that had developed through the formation of the transcontinental network. A variety of societies in Africa, Asia, and Europe depended on far-flung trade relations, and when one exchange network collapsed—as with the decline in travel security overland when the Mongol empires faded—another system quickly moved into place. Not only trade, but continued exchanges of technology and ideas continued to mark Afro-Eurasian relationships during the 15th century.

KEY CHANGES IN THE MIDDLE EAST

20.1   What were the most important changes in the Middle East between the 13th and the 15th centuries?

In 1200, the Middle East was still dominated by two powerful empires, the Byzantine in the northwest and the Islamic caliphate through much of the Middle Eastern heartland. By 1400, this structure was in disarray. The Byzantine empire still existed, but it was in rapid decline, pressed by invading Ottoman Turks. The Turkish capture of the imperial capital, Constantinople, in 1453 effectively ended the empire. Two centuries earlier, the caliphate, long sapped by increasing reliance on foreign troops and advisors, including the Turks, had fallen to Mongol invasion. Division in the Middle East, and among Arab peoples, took new forms.

The new world order that was beginning to emerge by 1400 first involved major reshuffling in the Middle East and north Africa.

Social and Cultural Change in the Middle East

Culture shifted, along with politics, in this crucial region. An earlier tension in philosophy and the arts yielded to the predominance of the Islamic faith. The new piety associated with the rising Sufi movement, discussed in Chapter 12, contributed to a new religious emphasis. In literature, attention to secular themes, such as the joys of feasting and hunting, gave way to more strictly religious ideas. In philosophy, the rationalistic current encountered new attack. In Muslim Spain, philosopher Ibn Rushd (IH-buhn RUSHT) (Averroës) (uh-VEHR-oh-eez), espoused Greek rationalism, but his efforts were largely ignored in the Middle East. In fact, European scholars were more heavily influenced by his work. In the Middle East proper, a more typical philosopher, Al-Ghazali, in a book revealingly titled *The Destruction of the Philosophers*, now claimed to use Aristotle's logic to show that it was impossible to discover religious truth by human reason. Many Sufi scholars wrote excitedly of their mystical contacts with God and the stages of their religious passion. Islamic science continued, but its role diminished.

 Read the **Document** on **MyHistoryLab**: Ibn Rushd (Averröes) (12th c.)

Changes in society and the economy were as telling as the shifts in politics and intellectual life. As the authority of the caliphate declined, landlords seized power over the peasantry. As a result, from about 1100 onward, Middle Eastern peasants increasingly lost their freedom, becoming serfs on large estates, providing the labor and produce landlords now sought. This loss was not the peasants' alone, for agricultural productivity suffered as a result. Landlords turned to sucking what they could from their estates rather than trying to develop a more vital agriculture. Tax revenues declined, and Arab and other Middle Eastern traders began to lose ground. Few Arab coins have been found in Europe dating from later than 1100. European merchants began to control their own turf and challenge the Arabs in other parts of the Mediterranean, gaining increasing initiative in this vital trading area.

Arab decline was gradual and incomplete. It cannot be compared with the dramatic fall of the Roman empire many centuries before. A more subtle model is needed. The reduced dynamism in trade did not take the Arabs out of major world markets, for example. Indeed, Middle Eastern commerce rebounded somewhat by 1400.

Finally, the political fragmentation of the Arab world did not produce prolonged confusion in the Middle East. The emerging Ottoman Turkish state soon mastered many of the lands of the old caliphate as well as the Byzantine corner, expanding into southeastern Europe. The new empire gave renewed vitality to Islamic politics, and it would soon be joined by two other Islamic empires, too, in Persia and India. (See Chapter 26 for the development of the new Ottoman Empire.) It is important to realize that the empire was far more powerful, politically and militarily, than the caliphate had been for many centuries. It was thus more challenging to observers in neighboring civilizations such as western Europe.

THE STRUCTURE OF TRANSREGIONAL TRADE

20.2   What caused the Chinese decision to abandon major expeditions?

Even the rise of the Ottoman empire did not restore the full international vigor that the Islamic caliphate wielded had at the height of its powers. The empire did not become the sole hub of an international network, as the caliphate had been a few centuries before. By the 15th century, merchants from many societies were competing for roles in transregional trade. In the Mediterranean, European, and particularly Italian, merchants were increasingly active; even North African pilgrims to Mecca often booked space on Italian ships. In the Indian Ocean, merchants from India and southeast Asia, most of them Muslims, rivaled Arab activity.

The big issue in the 15th century, however, involved the aftermath of the Mongol era. For 150 years, the interlocking Mongol states had facilitated overland trade between China, the Middle East, and Europe. Essentially, this Mongol system replaced earlier Arab leadership in facilitating transregional trade. But Mongol defeat in China, late in the 14th century, and new pressure on Mongol rulers in Russia and elsewhere unraveled this system. Overland travel become more difficult and dangerous without Mongol political protection. Trade and its motivations did not diminish in importance, but inevitably new emphasis focused on seagoing routes, particularly in the Indian Ocean. Two societies, first China and then Europe, sought to take advantage of the new opportunities involved.

Chinese Outreach and Reconsideration

For a brief time China asserted new leadership in international trade. This activity reflected earlier gains in Chinese shipping, and China's longstanding focus on manufacturing for export. Rebellions in China drove out the deeply resented Mongol overlords in 1368. A rebel leader from a peasant family, Zhu Yuanzhang (joo wan-jang), seized the Mongol capital of Beijing and proclaimed a new Ming— meaning "brilliant"—dynasty that was to last until 1644. The dynasty began with a burst of unusual expansionism. The initial Ming rulers pressed to secure the borders of the Middle Kingdom. This meant pushing the Mongols far to the north, to the plains of what is now Mongolia. It meant reestablishing influence over neighboring governments and winning tribute payments from states in Korea, Vietnam, and Tibet, reviving much of the east Asian regional structure set up by the Tang dynasty. Far more unusual was a new policy, adopted soon after 1400, of mounting huge, state-sponsored trading expeditions to southern Asia and beyond.

A first fleet sailed in 1405 to India, with 62 ships carrying 28,000 men. Later voyages reached the Middle East and the eastern coast of Africa, bringing chinaware and copper coinage in exchange for local goods. Chinese shipping at its height consisted of 2700 coastal vessels, 400 armed naval ships, and at least as many long-distance ships. Nine great treasure ships, the most sophisticated in the world at the time, explored the Indian Ocean, the Persian Gulf, and the Red Sea, establishing regular trade all along the way.

Between 1405 and their termination in 1433, these expeditions were commanded by the admiral **Zheng He**. A Muslim from western China, Zheng He was well suited to deal with Muslims in southeast Asia on the Indian Ocean trade route. Zheng He was also a eunuch, castrated for service at the royal court. China's Ming emperors retained a large harem of wives to ensure succession, and eunuchs were needed to guard them without threat of sexual rivalry; many gained bureaucratic powers well beyond this service. Zheng He's expeditions usually hugged the coastline, but he had an improved compass and excellent maps as well as huge vessels that contained ample supplies—even gardens—as well as goods for trade. His fleets must have impressed, even terrified, the local rulers around the Indian Ocean, many of whom paid tribute to the emperor. For even though Zheng He brought gifts, he also had well-armed troops on his expeditions. Several missions visited China from the Middle East and Africa. From Africa also came ostriches, zebras, and giraffes for the imperial zoo; the latter became the unicorns of Chinese fable. But Zheng He was resented by the Confucian bureaucrats, who refused even to write much about him in their chronicles.

There is no question that the course of world history might have been changed dramatically had the Chinese thrust continued, for the tiny European expeditions that began to creep down the western coast of Africa at about the same time would have been no match for this combination of merchant and military organization. Indeed, historians wonder if one expedition might have rounded Africa to at least glimpse the Atlantic. But China's emperors called the expeditions to a halt in 1433. The bureaucrats had long opposed the new trade policy, out of rivalry with other officials such as Zheng He, but there were deeper reasons as well. The costs seemed unacceptable, given the continuing expenses of the campaigns against the Mongols and establishing a luxurious new capital city in Beijing. A new emperor also wanted to differentiate his policies from those of his predecessor.

This was a crucial shift. It reflected a preference for traditional expenditures rather than distant foreign involvements. Chinese merchant activity continued to be extensive in southeast Asia. Chinese trading groups established permanent settlements in the Philippines, Malaysia, and Indonesia, where they added to the cultural diversity of the area and maintained a disproportionate role in local and regional trading activities into the 20th century. And manufacturing levels remained high. Nonetheless, China's chance to become a dominant world trading power was lost, at least for several centuries.

One result, today, is an interesting challenge to interpretation. To Western eyes, accustomed to judging a society's dynamism by its ability to reach out and gain new territories or trade positions, China's decision may seem hard to understand—the precursor to decline. But to the Chinese, it was the ambitious expeditionary flurry that was unusual, not its end. Its leaders were suspicious of any policy that would unduly elevate commercial activity as opposed to rule by the scholar-gentry. Ming emperors consolidated their rule over the empire's vast territory. Internal economic development continued as well, with no need for foreign products save for goods from southeast Asia. Moreover, Chinese products continued to be highly valued in the world market. Industry expanded, with growth in the production of textiles and porcelain; ongoing trade with southeast Asia enriched the port cities; agricultural production and population increased. The end of the expeditions had no immediate downsides for China itself.

The shift in Chinese policy unintentionally cleared the way for another, in most ways less organized civilization to work toward a new international position. With the Arabs in partial eclipse and with China retreating from its brief initiative, hesitant Western expansionism, ventured before 1400, began to take on new significance. Within a century, Western explorers and traders had launched an attempt to seize international trading dominance and had expanded the international network to include parts of the Americas for the first time.

Zheng He [jehng huh] Chinese Muslim admiral who commanded series of Indian Ocean, Persian Gulf, and Red Sea trade expeditions under third Ming emperor, Yunglo, between 1405 and 1433.

 Read the **Document** on MyHistoryLab: A Ming Naval Expedition (15th c.)

 View the **Map** on MyHistoryLab: Voyages of Zheng He

THE RISE OF THE WEST

20.3 What are the main issues in explaining new outreach from western Europe? What are the principal interpretations?

The West's gradual emergence into larger world contacts during the 15th century was surprising in many respects. Westerners remained awed by the powerful bureaucracies and opulent treasuries of empires in the traditional civilization centers such as Constantinople. Furthermore, the West was changing in some painful ways. Key features of medieval culture and society were being questioned by 1400. The church, which had long been one of the organizing institutions of Western civilization, was under new attack. Medieval philosophy had passed its creative phase. Warrior aristocrats, long a key leadership group in feudal society, softened their style of life, preferring court rituals and jousting tournaments and adopting military armor so cumbersome that real fighting was difficult.

Even more strikingly, the lives and economic activities of ordinary Europeans were in disarray. This was a time of crisis, and Europe's expanding world role could not reverse the fundamental challenges to its internal economic and demographic structure. Europeans began to suffer from recurrent famine after 1300 because population outstripped the food supply and no new food production techniques were discovered. Famine reduced disease resistance, making Europe more vulnerable to the bubonic plagues that spread from Asia.

Bubonic plague, or Black Death, surfaced in various parts of Asia in the 14th century. In China it reduced the population by nearly 30 percent by 1400. Following trade routes, it then spread into India and the Middle East, causing thousands of deaths per day in the larger cities. The plague's worst European impact occurred between 1348 and 1375, by which time 30 million people, one-third of Europe's population, died. The resulting economic dislocation produced bitter strikes and peasant uprisings.

Sources of Dynamism: Medieval Vitality

How, in this context, could the West be poised for a new global role? The answer to that question is complex. A number of different interpretations deserve attention, although some might be blended. First, several key advances of medieval society were not really reversed by the troubles of the decades around 1400. For example, the strengthening of feudal monarchy provided more effective national or regional governments for much of the West. The Hundred Years War between Britain and France stimulated innovations in military organization, including nonaristocratic soldiers recruited and paid directly by the royal government, that enhanced central political power. Strong regional monarchies took hold in parts of Spain and in Portugal as Christian leaders drove back the Muslim rulers of this region. The growth of cities and urban economies continued to spur the commercial side of Western society. Even the church had made its peace with such key principles of capitalism as profit-seeking. Technology continued to advance, particularly in ironwork—used for bells and weapons—and timekeeping.

In short, explaining the new Western vigor involves an understanding that some of the gains the West achieved during the postclassical period continued even as certain characteristic medieval forms wavered.

Imitation and Commercial Problems

Two additional factors affected western Europe's international position, one a clear plus, the other a growing problem. New opportunities for imitation were an obvious advantage. The Mongol empire established in Asia and eastern Europe in the late 13th and early 14th centuries provided new access to Asian knowledge and technology. Political stability and an openness to foreign visitors by the great khans helped Westerners learn of Asian technologies, ranging from printing to the compass and explosive powder. Western Europe had ideal access in the Mongol period. It was not disrupted by the Mongols, as eastern Europe and so many parts of Asia were, but it was in active contact, unlike sub-Saharan Africa. Internal European warfare and merchant zeal made western Europe an eager learner, for the Asian technologies promised to respond to both military and commercial needs.

The second international factor was the intensification of European problems in the existing world market and international arena. From the Crusades onward, Western elites had become used to increasing consumption of Asian luxury products, including spices such as cinnamon and nutmeg,

Western expansion had many causes. It must be seen as the result of growing problems as well as new strengths.

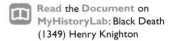

Read the Document on MyHistoryLab: Black Death (1349) Henry Knighton

VISUALIZING THE PAST

Population Trends

PERCENTAGES OR PROPORTIONS OF TOTAL WORLD POPULATION

Continents	1000	1700	1800	1900	1975
Europe	12.2	19.6	19.7	24.0	16.3
Asia	62.9	67.6	69.3	59.8	59.2
Africa	11.2	10.0	7.8	6.8	9.9
Americas	13.4	2.1	2.7	8.9	14.0
Oceania	0.4	0.4	0.3	0.3	0.6

(Column header "Years" spans 1000–1975)

SOURCE: Adapted from Dennis H. Wrong, ed., *Population and Society* (1977).

QUESTIONS

The following population charts show relationships in population size, and comparative trends in population size, among the major inhabited regions of the world. Population pressure did not drive European expansion in the 15th century, because population was falling temporarily, but there were longer-term trends, from the year 1000, that might have encouraged the expansionist effort. The chart allows comparison, showing what regions experienced the greatest changes in population levels between 1000 and 1800. What might have caused these changes? Finally, the chart extends comparisons into the later 20th century.

Reading population statistics provides vital information, but it also raises questions, including ones about causation, which numbers alone cannot answer. What other data would be most helpful to put these figures in appropriate world history contexts? Which figures are more revealing: absolute numbers or percentages? Why?

POPULATION LEVELS (MILLIONS)

Continents	1000	1700	1800	1900	1975
Europe	36	120	180	390	635
Asia (includes Middle East)	185	415	625	970	2300
Africa	33	61	70	110	385
Americas	39	13	24	145	545
Oceania (includes Australia)	1.5	2.25	2.5	6.75	23
Totals	294.5	611.25	901.5	1621.75	3888

(Column header "Years" spans 1000–1975)

NOTE: Earlier figures are only estimates; they are fairly accurate indicators of relative size.

SOURCE: Adapted from Dennis H. Wrong, ed., *Population and Society* (1977).

silks, sugar, perfumes, and jewels. In exchange for the luxury items, Europeans mainly had cruder goods to offer: wool, tin, copper, honey, and salt. The value of European exports almost never equaled the value of what was imported from Asia. The resulting unfavorable balance of trade had to be made up in gold, but western Europe had only a limited gold supply. By 1400, the constant drain to Asia was creating a gold famine that threatened the whole European economy with collapse.

Furthermore, there were legitimate fears of a new Muslim threat. The Ottoman empire was taking shape, and Europeans began to fear a new Muslim surge. Even before this, the Muslim capture of the last crusader stronghold (the city of Acre in the Middle East) in 1291 gave Muslim traders, particularly Egyptians, new opportunities to act as intermediaries in the Asian trade, for there were no western-controlled ports left in the eastern Mediterranean. One response to this was a series of conquests by the city-state of Venice along the eastern coast of the Adriatic. A more important response was to begin exploring alternative routes to Asia that would bypass the Middle East and the feared and hated Muslim realms.

In sum: One explanation for Europe's new activity would emphasize the gains made in the later postclassical centuries, particularly in terms of urban and commercial growth, despite population setbacks. These gains could now be combined with new technologies learned from Asia—especially weaponry. The final ingredient was the realization that innovations were essential to meet balance of payments problems and concern about reliance on Muslim traders.

DOCUMENT

Bubonic Plague

THE SPREAD OF THE PLAGUE IN the 14th century, affecting major parts of Asia, the Middle East and Egypt, and Europe, was one of the great devastations in world history. Muslim and Christian observers described the plague and reactions to it. Ibn al-Wardi was a Muslim scholar who died of the plague in 1349; Jean de Venette was a monk who died in 1368.

IBN AL-WARDI

God is my security in every adversity. My sufficiency is in God alone. Is not God sufficient protection for His servant? Oh God, pray for our master, Muhammad, and give him peace. Save us for his sake from the attacks of the plague and give us shelter.

The plague frightened and killed. It began in the land of darkness. Oh, what a visitor! It has been current for fifteen years. China was not preserved from it nor could the strongest fortress hinder it. The plague afflicted the Indians of India. It weighted upon the Sind. It seized with its hand and ensnared even the lands of the Uzbeks. The plague destroyed mankind in Cairo. Its eye was cast upon Egypt, and behold, the people were wide-awake. It stilled all movement in Alexandria. The plague did its work like a silkworm. . . .

Then, the plague turned to Upper Egypt. It, also, sent forth its storm to Barqah. The plague attacked Gaza, and it shook ʿAsqalān severely. The plague oppressed Acre. The scourge came to Jerusalem and paid the *zakāt* [with the souls of men]. It overtook those people who fled to the al-ʿAqsā Mosque, which stands beside the Dome of the Rock. If the door of mercy had not been opened, the end of the world would have occurred in a moment. It then hastened its pace and attacked the entire maritime plain. The plague trapped Sidon and descended unexpectedly upon Beirut, cunningly.

This plague is for the Muslims a martyrdom and a reward, and for the disbelievers a punishment and a rebuke. When the Muslim endures misfortune, then patience is his worship. It has been established by our Prophet: God bless him and give him peace, that the plague-stricken are martyrs. This noble tradition is true and assures martyrdom. And this secret should be pleasing to the true believer. If someone says it causes infection and destruction, say: God creates and recreates. If the liar disputes the matter of infection and tries to find an explanation, I say that the Prophet, on him be peace, said: who infected the first? If we acknowledge the plague's devastation of the people, it is the will of the Chosen Doer. So it happened again and again. . . .

Among the benefits . . . is the removal of one's hopes and the improvement of his earthly works. It awakens men from their indifference for the provisioning of their final journey.

Nothing prevented us from running away from the plague except our devotion to the noble tradition. Come then, seek the aid of God Almighty for raising the plague, for He is the best helper. Oh God, we call You better than anyone did before. We call You to raise from us the pestilence and plague. We do not take refuge in its removal other than with You. We do not depend on our good health against the Plague but on you. We seek your protection, oh Lord of creation, from the blows of this stick.

JEAN DE VENETTE

This sickness or pestilence was called an epidemic by the doctors. Nothing like the great numbers who died in the years 1348 and 1349 has been heard of or seen or read of in times past. This plague and disease came from *ymaginatione* or association and contagion, for if a well man visited the sick he only rarely avoided the risk of death. Wherefore in many towns timid priests withdrew, leaving the exercise of their ministry to such of the religious as were more daring. . . . A very great number of the saintly sisters of the Hôtel-Dieu who, not fearing to die, nursed the sick in all sweetness and humility, with no thought of honor, a number too often renewed by death, rest in peace with Christ, as we may piously believe.

Some said that this pestilence was caused by infection of the air and waters, since there was at this time no famine nor lack of food supplies, but on the contrary great abundance. As a result of this theory of infected water and air as the source of the plague the Jews were suddenly and violently charged with infecting wells and water and corrupting the air. The whole world rose up against them cruelly on this account. In Germany and other parts of the world where Jews lived, they were massacred and slaughtered by Christians, and many thousands were burned everywhere, indiscriminately. . . .

But woe is me! the world was not changed for the better but for the worse. . . . For men were more avaricious and grasping than before, even though they had far greater possessions. They were more covetous and disturbed each other more frequently with suits, brawls, disputes and pleas. Nor by the mortality resulting from this terrible plague inflicted by God was peace between kings and lords established. And this fact was very remarkable. Although there was an abundance of all goods, yet everything was twice as dear, whether it were utensils, victuals, or merchandise, hired helpers or peasants and serfs, except for some hereditary domains which remained abundantly stocked with everything. Charity began to cool, and iniquity with ignorance and sin to abound, for few could be found in the good towns and castles who knew how or were willing to instruct children in the rudiments of grammar. . . .

QUESTIONS

- How did Christian and Muslim reactions compare?
- Did the reactions suggest that the plague might have different results in the Middle East and in Europe?
- How did the plague relate to other major developments toward the end of the postclassical period?

De Venette from Richard A. Newhall, ed., *The Chronicle of Jean de Venette*, pp. 51–2, *Records of Civilization, Sources and Studied*, No. 50. Copyright © 1953 Columbia University Press. Ibn al-Wardi from Michael Dols, "Ibn Al-Wardi's Risalha al-Naba, A translation of major sources for the history of the black death in the Middle East," in Dickran Kouymijian, ed., *Near Eastern Numismatics, Iconography, Epigraphy and History: Studies in Honor of George C. Miles*, Beirut, University of Beirut, 1974, pp. 443–55.

This explanation may not be entirely adequate, and it certainly is not the explanation preferred by most European historians. They turn—sometimes exclusively—to another set of factors: developments within Europe that would then spill outward.

Secular Directions in the Italian Renaissance

Significant changes in Europe, away from characteristic postclassical patterns, started in Italy. Medieval forms had never fully taken hold here. Cities were livelier and more independent, and institutions like feudalism did not gain ground. In 1400, Italy was in the midst of a vital cultural and political movement known as the **Renaissance**, or rebirth—referring to revival of styles and themes from classical Greece and Rome. The early phases of the Renaissance stressed more secular subjects in literature and art. Religious art remained dominant but used more realistic portrayals of people and nature, and some nonreligious themes surfaced outright (Figure 20.2). The doings of human beings deserved attention for their own sake, in the Renaissance view, not as they reflected a divine plan. Artists and writers became more openly ambitious for personal reputation and glory. Italy was the center of initial Renaissance culture because it had more contact with Roman tradition than did the rest of Europe and because by the 14th century it led the West in banking and trade.

Renaissance [REHN-uh-sahns] Cultural and political movement in western Europe; began in Italy c. 1400; rested on urban vitality and expanding commerce; featured a literature and art with distinctly more secular priorities than those of the Middle Ages.

Renaissance Culture

Although it had political and commercial roots in Italian cities, the Renaissance was first and foremost a cultural movement, launched in Florence and manifesting itself in literature and various arts (Figure 20.3). The Renaissance focused on a new interest in stylistic grace and a concern for practical ethics and codes of behavior for urban gentlemen. One leading 14th-century writer, **Francesco Petrarch**, not only took pride in his city and his age but explored the glories of personal achievement with new confidence.

Petrarch, Francesco [PEE-trahrk] (1304–1374) One of the major literary figures of the Western Renaissance; an Italian author and humanist.

FIGURE **20.2** Europe's new spirit amid old values. Dante, Italian writer of the 14th century, holds a copy of his great work, the *Divine Comedy*, with both religious (souls tormented in hell) and Renaissance (the solid, classical-style urban buildings of the city of Florence) symbolism greeting him. The painting was designed by Domenico di Michelina for the cathedral of Florence in 1465.

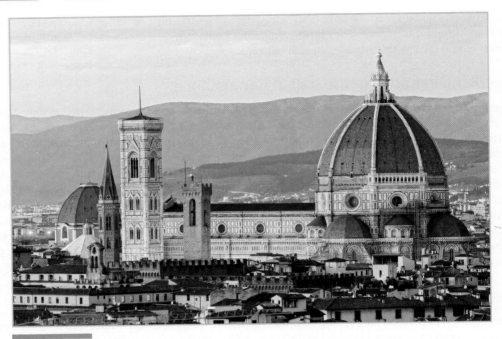

FIGURE **20.3** Although the nave of Florence Cathedral was completed in the fourteenth century, it was not until the fifteenth century that architect Filippo Brunelleschi was able to solve the engineering challenge presented by the plan for the massive dome. In order to eliminate the need for temporary wooden scaffolding during construction, Brunelleschi used a skeleton of eight large ribs alternated with eight pairs of thinner ribs, all tied together by nine sets of horizontal ties, all of which would be able to support the workers as the dome was raised.

Innovation flourished in the visual arts and music as well. The subject matter of art moved toward nature and people, including cityscapes and portraits of the rich and powerful, whether the themes were religious or secular. Florentine painter Giotto (gee-YAW-toh), led the way, departing from medieval formalism and stiffness. While still a young apprentice to the painter Cimabue (chee-mah-BOO-eh), Giotto painted a fly on the nose of one of Cimabue's portrait subjects, and it was so realistic that Cimabue repeatedly tried to swat it off before going back to work on the canvas. Other painters, beginning later in the 14th century, started to introduce perspective while using new colors and other materials. In architecture, favor shifted away from the Gothic to a classicism derived from the styles of Greece and Rome. Vivid, realistic statues complemented the new palaces and public buildings.

The impact of the early Renaissance must not be exaggerated. It had little influence outside of Italy. Even in Italy, it focused on high culture, not popular culture, and on the arts; there was little initial interest in science. And although it built on distinctive political and economic forms, it was not a full break from medieval tendencies.

Nevertheless, these new cultural currents were an important innovation in Western history. The full ramifications of the Renaissance feed into the next period of both world and Western history (see Chapter 22). The movement was only getting started by 1400. However, the wide range of Italian commerce and shipping proved to be one of the building blocks of European outreach. By the 15th century, ships, particularly from the western Italian city of Genoa, which was less well placed than Venice for eastern Mediterranean trade and the resultant links to Asia, were ready for new roles. Ambitious city-state governments encouraged new ventures, eager to collect more tax money and promote commerce as one of their explicit functions. A general "Renaissance spirit" could also spur innovation. Whereas people such as Petrarch defined human ambition mainly in cultural terms, other urban and commercial leaders, including seafarers such as Genoa's Christopher Columbus, might apply some of the same confidence and desire for personal glory to different areas, such as exploration or conquest.

The Iberian Spirit of Religious Mission

Along with Italy, a key center for change by the 14th century was the Iberian peninsula, where Christian military leaders had for several centuries been pressing back the boundaries of the Muslim state in Spain. Soon after 1400, major regional monarchies had been established in the provinces of **Castile** and **Aragon**, which would be united through royal marriage in 1469.

Even before the marriage between Ferdinand and Isabella, Spanish and Portuguese rulers had developed a vigorous military and religious agenda. They supported effective armies, including infantry and feudal cavalry. And they believed that government had a mission to promote Christianity by converting or expelling Arabs and Jews and by maintaining doctrinal purity within the church. Close links between church and state, portrayed in art, provided revenues and officials for the royal government. In return, the government supported church courts in their efforts to enforce moral and doctrinal purity. Later in the 15th century, this interaction led to the reestablishment of the church-run courts of the Inquisition in Spain, designed to enforce religious orthodoxy. In other words, Spain and Portugal were developing effective new governments with a special sense of religious mission and religious support. These changes promoted the West's expansion into wider world contacts.

The First Phases of Western Expansion

As early as 1291, two Italian brothers, the **Vivaldis** from Genoa, sailed with two galleys through the Straits of Gibraltar, seeking a western route to the "Indies," the spice-producing areas of south and southeast Asia. They were never heard from again. Although they were precursors of a major western thrust into the southern Atlantic, it is not even entirely clear what they meant by the "Indies." Early in the 14th century, other explorers from Genoa rediscovered the Canary Islands, in the Atlantic, populated by a hunting-and-gathering people. These islands had been known vaguely since classical times but had never been explored by Europeans. Genoese sailors also visited the Madeiras and probably reached the more distant Azores by 1351. Soon after this, ships from northeastern Spain, based in the port of Barcelona, sailed along the African coast as far south as present-day Sierra Leone.

Until 1430, technological barriers prevented further exploration for alternative routes. Without adequate navigation instruments, Europeans could not risk wider ventures into the Atlantic. They also needed better ships than the shallow-drafted, oar-propelled Mediterranean galleys. However, efforts were under way to develop an oceangoing sailing vessel. At the same time, the crucial navigational problems were met by the compass and the astrolabe, used to determine latitude at sea by reckoning from the stars. Contacts with Arab merchants and with the Chinese provided knowledge of these devices. European mapmaking, improving steadily during the 14th century, was another key innovation. Because of these advances, as well as mistaken geographic assumptions shown on the map in Figure 20.4, Europeans were ready in the decades after 1400 to undertake voyages impossible just a century before. In 1498, the Portuguese explorer **Vasco da Gama** was the first European to reach India by sea, preparing Portuguese entry into the Indian Ocean (Figure 20.5).

Castile and Aragon Regional kingdoms of the Iberian Peninsula; pressed reconquest of peninsula from Muslims and ultimately united under the Spanish monarchy.

Vivaldis Two Genoese brothers who attempted to find a western route to the "Indies"; disappeared in 1291; precursors of thrust into southern Atlantic.

da Gama, Vasco Portuguese captain who sailed for India in 1497; established early Portuguese dominance in Indian Ocean.

Henry the Navigator Portuguese prince responsible for direction of series of expeditions along the African coast in the 15th century; marked beginning of western European expansion.

FIGURE **20.4** Columbus is supposed to have had a copy of this world map in Spain. The map, dating from about 1489, shows the Old World as Europeans were increasingly coming to know it. Note how reachable India looked to Europeans using this map—although, of course, they had to go around Africa.

Read the Document on MyHistoryLab: Excerpt from the Travel Journal of Vasco da Gama

FIGURE **20.5** This 18th-century engraving portrays Vasco da Gama's audience with the Indian ruler of Calicut in 1498. This picture was painted well after the fact. What kind of comparison does it suggest between European and Indian societies?

Read the Document on MyHistoryLab: Voyage from Lisbon

Colonial Patterns

Even as these wider-ranging voyages began, westerners, led by the Spanish and Portuguese, had begun to take advantage of the new lands they had already discovered. A driving force behind both the further expeditions and the efforts to make already discovered areas economically profitable was Prince Henry of Portugal, known as **Henry the Navigator**. A student of astronomy and nautical science, Henry sponsored about a third of Portuguese voyages of exploration before his death in 1460. His mixture of motivations—scientific and intellectual curiosity, desire to spread the name of Christ to unfamiliar lands, and financial interest—reflected some of the key forces in late postclassical Europe.

Portugal by 1439 had taken control of the Azores and had granted land to colonists. Soon Spaniards and Portuguese had conquered and colonized the Madeiras and Canaries, bringing in western plants, animals, weapons, and diseases. The result was something of a laboratory for the larger European colonialism that would soon take shape, particularly in the Americas. European colonists quickly set up large agricultural estates designed to produce cash crops that could be sold on the European market. First they introduced sugar, an item once imported from Asia but now available in growing quantities from western-controlled sources. Ultimately, other crops such as cotton and tobacco were also introduced to the Atlantic islands. To produce these market crops, the new colonists brought in slaves from northwestern Africa, mainly in Portuguese ships—the first examples of a new, commercial version of slavery and the first sign that western expansion could have serious impact on other societies as well.

These developments about 1400 remained modest, even in their consequences for Africa. They illustrate mainly how quickly Western conquerors decided what to do with lands and peoples newly in their grasp. The ventures were successful enough to motivate more extensive probes into the southern Atlantic as soon as technology permitted. Indeed, voyages of exploration down the coast of Africa and across the Atlantic began to occur as the island colonies were being fully settled.

Finally, these early ventures summed up the swirl of forces that were beginning to reshape the West's role in the world: inferiorities and fears, particularly with regard to the Muslims; economic pressure from an inferior but eager position in world trade; new energies of Renaissance merchants and Iberian rulers. In final analysis, what is the best explanation for why Europe began to reach out in new ways?

OUTSIDE THE WORLD NETWORK

Tensions in key societies in the Americas and Oceania made them vulnerable to conquest.

20.4 How did patterns in the Americas and Polynesia reflect their isolation from main transregional trade networks?

Developments in the Americas and Polynesia were not affected by the new international exchange. During the next period of world history, these regions all were pulled into a new level of international contact, but a world balance sheet in 1400 must emphasize their separateness.

At the same time, several of the societies outside the international network were experiencing some new problems during the 15th century that would leave them vulnerable to outside interference thereafter. Such problems included new political strains in the leading American civilizations and a fragmentation of the principal island groups in Polynesian culture.

Political Issues in the Americas

As we discussed in Chapter 16, the Aztec and Inca empires ran into increasing difficulties not long after 1400. Aztec exploitation of subject peoples for gold, slaves, and religious sacrifices roused great resentment. What would have happened to the Aztec empire if the Spaniards had not intervened after 1500 is not clear, but it is obvious that disunity created opportunities for outside intervention that might not have existed otherwise. The Inca system, although far less brutal than that of the Aztecs, provided ongoing tension between central leadership and local initiative. This complicated effective control of the vast expanse of the Inca domains. Here too, overextension made change likely by the 1500s—indeed, the empire was already receding somewhat—even without European intervention. At the same time, other cultures were developing in parts of the Americas that might well have been candidates for new political leadership, if American history had proceeded in isolation or if European intervention had been less sweeping.

Expansion, Migration, and Conquest in Polynesia

A second culture that was later pulled into the expanding world network involved Polynesia. Here, as in the Americas, important changes took place during the postclassical era but with no relationship to developments in societies elsewhere in the world. The key Polynesian theme from the 7th century to 1400 was expansion, spurts of migration, and conquest that implanted Polynesian culture well beyond the initial base in islands such as Tahiti, Samoa, and Fiji (Map 20.1).

One channel of migration pointed northward to the islands of Hawaii. The first Polynesians reached these previously uninhabited islands before the 7th century, traveling in great war canoes. The canoes carried all that was needed to settle on new lands, including pigs. These were to wreak some havoc on native flora and fauna in Hawaii, but at the same time Hawaiians created a land use system incorporating coastal fisheries, mid-mountain vegetable crops, and highland hunting that supported a sustainable lifestyle for centuries.

From the 7th century until about 1300 or 1400, recurrent contacts remained between the Hawaiian Islands and the larger Society Islands group, allowing periodic new migration. From about 1400 until the arrival of European explorers in 1778, Hawaiian society was cut off even from Polynesia.

Polynesians in Hawaii spread widely across the islands in agricultural clusters and fishing villages amid the volcanic mountains. Hawaiians were inventive in using local vegetation, weaving fabrics as well as making materials and fishing nets from grass. Politically, Hawaii was organized into regional kingdoms, which were highly warlike. Society was structured into a caste system with priests and nobles at the top, who reserved many lands for their exclusive use. Commoners were viewed almost as a separate people, barred from certain activities.

Thus, with a Neolithic technology and no use of metals, the Hawaiians created a complex culture on their islands. Without a written language, their legends and oral histories, tracing the genealogies of chiefly families back to the original war canoes, provided a shared set of stories and values.

Isolated Achievements by the Maori

Another group of Polynesians migrated thousands of miles to the southwest of the Society Islands, perhaps as early as the 8th century, when canoe or raft crews discovered the two large islands that today make up New Zealand. The original numbers of people were small but were supplemented over the centuries that followed by additional migrations from the Polynesian home islands. The Polynesians in New Zealand, called the Maori, successfully adapted to an environment considerably colder and harsher than that of the home islands. They developed the most elaborate of all Polynesian art and produced an expanding population that may have reached 200,000 people by the 18th century, primarily on the northern of the two islands. As in Hawaii, tribal military leaders and priests held great power in Maori society; each tribe also included a group of slaves drawn from prisoners of war and their descendants.

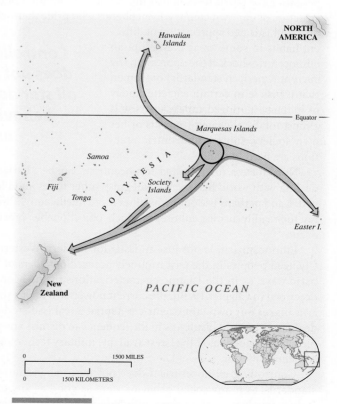

MAP **20.1 Polynesian Expansion** Starting in the 7th century, the Polynesians expanded north and south of their starting point in the Society Islands.

All these achievements were accomplished in total isolation from the rest of the world and, particularly after 1400, substantial isolation of each major island grouping from the rest of the Polynesian complex. Polynesians would be the last of the major isolated cultures to encounter the larger world currents brought forcefully by European explorers in the 18th century. When this encounter did come, it produced the same effects that it had in the Americas: vulnerability to disease, weakness in the face of superior weaponry and technology, and cultural disintegration.

THINKING HISTORICALLY

The Problem of Ethnocentrism

MANY CULTURES ENCOURAGE AN ETHNOCENTRIC OUTLOOK, and the culture of the West is certainly one of them. Ethnocentrism creates problems in interpreting world history. The dictionary definition of *ethnocentrism* is "a habitual disposition to judge foreign peoples or groups by the standards and practices of one's own culture or ethnic group"—and often finding them inferior. Most of us take pride in many of our own institutions and values, and it is tempting to move from this pride to a disapproval of other peoples when they clearly do not share our behaviors and beliefs. Many Americans have a difficult time understanding how other peoples have failed to establish the stable democratic political structure of our own country. Even liberals who pride themselves on a sophisticated appreciation of different habits in some areas may adopt an ethnocentric shock at the oppression (by current American standards) of women that is visible in certain societies today or in the past. Indeed, unless a person is almost totally alienated from his or her own society, some ethnocentric reactions are hard to avoid.

Nevertheless, unexamined ethnocentrism can be a barrier in dealing with world history. We will grasp other times and places better, and perhaps use our own values more intelligently, if we do not too readily dismiss cultures in which "objectionable" practices occur.

Ethnocentrism is not just an issue for modern Westerners. Civilized peoples in the past routinely accused outsiders of barbaric ways, as in the Islamic characterizations of the Mongols described in Chapter 19. But the current power of Western standards makes our own ethnocentric potential a real issue today in dealing with world history, as in the tendency to dismiss any people who did not exploit the latest available military technology as somehow inferior.

Controlling ethnocentrism does not mean abandoning all standards, as if any social behavior were as good as any other. It does involve a certain open-mindedness and sophistication. Reducing distracting levels of ethnocentrism can be aided by some specific procedures. It is important to realize that few

Controlling ethnocentrism does not mean abandoning all standards, as if any social behavior were as good as any other.

cultures behave irrationally over long periods of time. They may differ from our taste, but their patterns respond to valid causes and problems. Our own values are not without complexity. We sometimes believe things about our own society that are not as true as we want, or in judging other societies, we forget about drawbacks in our own surroundings. Perspective on our own habits, including awareness of how other cultures might judge us, helps us restrain our ethnocentrism.

However, ethnocentrism may become a particularly strong impulse in dealing with some of the changes in world history taking shape about 1400. The West was gaining strength. Because many Americans identify with Western civilization, it is tempting to downplay some of the subtleties and disadvantages of this process or to exaggerate the extent to which the West began to organize world history more generally.

The balance of power among civilizations was beginning to shift about 1400, and it is legitimate—not simply ethnocentric—to note that the West's rise was one of the leading forces of this change. It is unnecessary to ignore the many other patterns continuing or emerging—including new vigor in several other societies—or to gloss over the motives and results that the West's rise entailed. The rise of the West was not just "good." It did not result simply from a triumph of progressive values. At the same time, avoiding ethnocentric impulses in evaluating this crucial transition period in world history does not require an anti-Western approach. Balance and perspective are essential—easy to say, not always easy to achieve.

QUESTIONS

- Why can ethnocentrism complicate interpretations of world history?
- How can one balance disapproval and understanding in dealing with practices such as female infanticide?
- What are some nonethnocentric ways to interpret initial European expansion?

Adding Up the Changes

It is tempting to see some sort of master plan in the various changes that began to occur around 1400. People who emphasize an ethnocentric approach to world history, stressing some inherent superiorities in Western values, might be tempted to simplify the factors involved. However, a series of complex coincidences provides a more accurate explanation, as in other cases in which the framework of world history changed substantially. Independent developments in the Americas and elsewhere figured in, as did crucial policy decisions in places such as China. Each of the separate steps can be explained, but their combination was partly accidental.

Several elements of the world history transition deserve particular attention. Technology played a role, as opportunities to copy Asian developments were supplemented by European initiative, particularly in gunnery and ship design. The role of individuals, such as Prince Henry, must be compared with the impact of more general forces, such as Europe's international trade woes.

The overall result of change affected even societies where existing patterns persisted. Sub-Saharan Africa, for example, was not experiencing great political or cultural shifts around 1400. Regional kingdoms fluctuated: The empire of Mali fell to regional rivals, but another Muslim kingdom, Songhay, soon arose in its stead, flourishing between 1464 and 1591. African political and religious themes persisted for several centuries, but the context for African history was shifting. The decline of the Arabs reduced the vitality of Africa's key traditional contact with the international network, although African merchants remained comfortable in dealing with North Africa and the Middle East. In contrast to the Europeans, Africans had no exchange with the Mongols. Even as Africa enjoyed substantial continuity, its power balance with western Europe was beginning to change, and this became a source of further change.

Global Connections and Critical Themes

1450 AND THE WORLD

The end of the postclassical period saw both change and continuity in the contacts that affected so many societies in Asia, Africa, and Europe. Change came in the procession of societies that served as active agents for contacts. Muslim traders and missionaries from the Middle East continued to be active, particularly in the Indian Ocean and in dealing with Africa. But the period of Mongol consolidation had introduced a new set of contacts, many of them land-based and involving Asia and Europe. Mongol overlords turned out to be delighted to encounter different ideas and to use officials from many different places and cultures. Mongol decline returned attention to sea-based contacts, particularly in the Indian Ocean. This was where, for a brief time, China took an unusually active stance. The Mongol era left other impacts as well: Japan, proud of its avoidance of Mongol occupation in contrast to China, began to think in terms of greater self-sufficiency, less reliance on imitation. Russian leaders, initially around Moscow, began to gain greater independence from Mongol control; their chief goal involved further expansions of territory and they paid attention to other contacts. Overall, at a time of many regional changes the question of roles in global contacts was a vital one, and by 1450 it was in flux.

The key continuity involved the interest and dependence of many societies on interregional trade and other contacts. African merchants and leaders continued to rely heavily on interactions with the Middle East. Western Europe's involvement in contacts was intensifying. Southeast Asia was increasingly drawn in, not only to trade but also to Muslim missionary efforts. The Middle East, India, and China continued to assume the availability of goods and merchant activities beyond their own borders. The diverse advantages of Afro-Eurasian contacts were widely realized, even amid changes in trade routes and regional initiatives.

The decades around the mid-15th century both reflected and intensified the transcontinental network. On the one hand, it was clear that the level of intercontinental connections developed in the postclassical period allowed increasingly rapid imitation, in areas like technology. This gave once-backward societies, like western Europe, a chance to accelerate their economic and military development. The networks also brought sufficient advantages, in access to luxury consumer goods, that the decline of one trade system—for example, the overland Mongol routes—quickly brought forward other societies eager to develop an alternative framework—the Chinese, then the Europeans. This process, from the Mongols onward, quickened the pace of contact, from ambitious travelers like Ibn Battuta (IH-buhn BAH-too-tuh) and Marco Polo, to imaginative merchants and explorers. The stage was set for a next phase in the globalization process, in which the whole world would, for the first time, be directly involved.

Further Readings

On the world network, see Jerry Bentley, *Old World Encounters: Cross Cultural Contacts and Exchanges in Pre-Modern Times* (1993). Crucial changes in the Middle East are covered in F. Babinger, *Mehmed the Conqueror and His Times* (1978), on the Ottoman leader who captured Constantinople; and Bernard Lewis, *The Arabs in History* (1958), which offers a brisk interpretation of Arab decline. See also H. Islamoglu-Inan, ed., *The Ottoman Empire and the World Economy* (1987). On China, see D. Wu, *Footprints of foreign explorers on the Silk Road* (2006); and Charles O. Hucker, *The Ming Dynasty: Its Origins and Evolving Institutions* (1978).

An important, highly readable interpretation of the West's rise in a world context is C. Cipolla, *Guns, Sails, and Empires: Technological Innovation and the Early Phases of European Expansion, 1400–1700* (1985). See also John M. Hobson, *The Eastern Origins of Western Civilization* (2004); and K. Ciggaar and M. Metcalf, eds., *East and West in the Medieval Eastern Mediterranean* (2006). An important interpretation of new Western interests is S. W. Mintz, *Sweetness and Power: The Place of Sugar in Modern History* (1985).

On the Black Death and economic dislocation, see M. W. Dols, *The Black Death in the Middle East* (1977); W. H. McNeill, *Plagues and Peoples* (1976); and the very readable B. Tuchman, *A Distant Mirror: The Calamitous 14th Century* (1979). A provocative study of relevant western outlook is P. Ariès, *The Hour of Our Death* (1981).

J. Huizinga, *The Waning of the Middle Ages* (1973), deals with the decline of medieval forms in Europe. See also Gerald MacLean, ed., *Re-Orienting the Renaissance: Cultural Exchanges with the East* (2005). The early Renaissance is treated in D. Hay, *The Italian Renaissance* (1977); see also Walter Pater, *The Renaissance: Studies in Art and Poetry* (2011); Gary Fergusan, *Queer (re)readings of the French Renaissance* (2008); C. Hibbert, *Florence: The Biography of a City* (1993). For more cultural emphasis, see Guido Ruggiero, *Machiavelli in Love: Sex, Self, and Society in the Italian Renaissance* (2007); Manfredo Tafuri, *Interpreting the Renaissance: Princes, Cities, Architects* (2006); John Jeffries Martin, ed., *The Renaissance: Italy and Abroad* (2003); Richard Mackenney, *Renaissances: The Cultures of Italy c. 1300–c. 1600* (2005); and C. Trinkhaus, *The Scope of Renaissance Humanism* (1983). On Spain, see F. Braudel, *The Mediterranean and the Mediterranean World*, 2 vols. (1978); and E. Paris, *The End of Days* (1995), on Spanish Jews and the Inquisition. On expansion in general, see Robert Bartlett, *The Making of Europe: Conquest, Colonization, and Cultural Change* (1993).

An excellent overview of the period is Janet L. Abu-Lughod's *Before European Hegemony: The World System* A.D. *1250–1350* (1989).

On MyHistoryLab

 Study and Review on MyHistoryLab

Critical Thinking Questions

1. What were the consequences of the fall of the Byzantine empire? Was this a short-term or long-term change in world history?

2. What was new about Renaissance culture? Is it possible to use a cultural change of this sort to explain innovations in trade and exploration?

3. What caused the main differences between developments in West Africa and those in western Europe during the 14th and 15th centuries?

4. Should China have maintained its commitment to great expeditions?

5. What distinctive features of Polynesian society reflected lack of contact with other major centers?

PART

III

REVISITING

The Postclassical Period, 600–1450: New Faith and New Commerce

CONTACTS AND THEIR LIMITS

Expansion of economic systems and increasing interaction reflected crucial changes in the postclassical period. They were supported by technological shifts, particularly in shipbuilding and navigational devices, and also by expansion of manufacturing and some key improvements in agriculture. They involved many merchant families, who would send relatives to distant outposts to help facilitate exchange.

New contacts form a key part of the postclassical period. Contacts were not economic alone. Missionary exchanges as well as trade brought about new connections among people in Asia, Africa, and Europe. Southeast Asia, for example, began to contribute spice production to transcontinental trade. In turn, by the end of the postclassical period, merchants and missionaries were importing Islam into this region.

Many world historians now argue that, because of the new patterns of contact, the basic dynamic of world history was reshaped around 1000 C.E. Before that point, most societies had separate patterns of activity, and contacts with other cultures were somewhat superficial, with a few luxury goods exchanged. After that point, contact became the name of the game, and a growing number of societies vigorously sought new connections.

A key aspect of the postclassical period involved explicit efforts at imitation, another result of contact. Trade and sometimes missionary connections brought outlying parts of the Afro-Eurasian world into interaction with regions that had complex cultural, manufacturing, and urban systems. Not surprisingly, many of these societies decided to copy—selectively—in order to advance. Japan copied China; Russia copied the Byzantines; western Europe and parts of Africa borrowed widely (although differently) from Arab society. Mostly, societies imitated one another's technology and cultural forms (such as alphabets). It proved harder to copy political structures, and several ambitious efforts (particularly in Japan and western Europe) failed. Peoples in the Americas had contact with one another, but they remained isolated from Afro-Eurasia. The same was true in Polynesia. Here were important exceptions to the patterns of exchange elsewhere.

While contacts increased, they hardly homogenized Afro-Eurasia. Societies on the peripheries, like western Europe or Russia, simply lacked the manufacturing sophistication or urban wealth required to fully imitate the leading centers of Asia. In other instances, explicit decisions were made to reject foreign influences. After a brief period of enthusiasm for Chinese political institutions, for example, Japanese leaders decided they did not want to imitate some aspects of Chinese society—for example, its bureaucracy. Despite ongoing trade and important new interactions with Islam, the majority of Indians remained Hindu and lived according to its distinctive caste system. And of course Europeans, while imitating some aspects of Islamic society, had no desire for religious change—unless it involved imposing their religion on Muslims. Religion, indeed, could create new barriers among people.

453

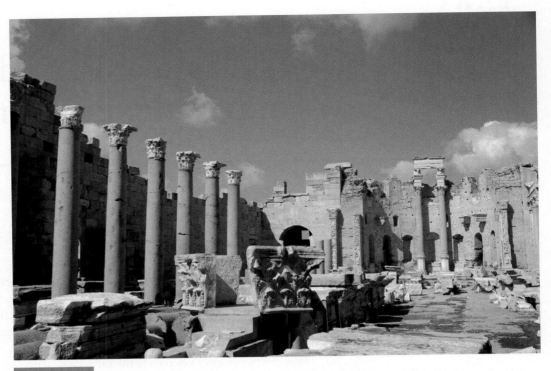

The ruins of Leptis Magna, one of the three great early Roman cities, which gave Tripolitania its name. Leptis was an elaborate city with baths and ornate buildings; it was also the center of African trade.

Long-distance travel increased in the postclassical centuries. Ibn Battuta, a north African, traveled almost 80,000 miles in his lifetime, visiting various parts of Africa and Asia as well as islands in the Indian Ocean. Toward the end of this period, several western Europeans traveled widely, as did some Chinese. Greater travel was a testimony to the power of world trade and the new religious map—Ibn Battuta, for example, journeyed mainly within the Islamic world, which gave him plenty of scope.

While travel reflected and encouraged contact, it also brought people to the limits of tolerance. While he praised the piety of his hosts in sub-Saharan Africa, Ibn Battuta was appalled by the freedom that women there enjoyed. This was not his view of a fully Muslim society. European travelers to China, at the end of the period, might hope to convert the Chinese or to imitate some of their achievements—in technology, for example—but they had a strong sense of the profound differences between European and Chinese culture.

CRITICAL THEMES

New patterns of contact and changes in the religious map dominated world history during the postclassical centuries. They sometimes supported each other, when missionary and merchant expansion went hand in hand, as was often the case with Islam. But they could also create new tensions: What were merchants to do when they had to deal with people of another religion? Cultural developments and interactions can be compared with patterns of trade, but the relationships could be complex.

On the whole, social changes in the period were less significant than economic and cultural shifts. The slave trade into the Middle East and the extension of India's caste system built on earlier precedent. A number of societies deepened patriarchal gender relations, as in Chinese footbinding. Social implications of the major religions were not always translated into practice, although there was some impact.

Ibn Battuta, in Egypt. Ibn Battuta's wide travels utilized and encouraged a growing pattern of contacts.

Political developments reflected great diversity. This was a vital period for state building in areas like Japan, Russia, and West Africa. It is important to compare some of the more decentralized systems, including European and Japanese feudalism, with each other, but also to the more elaborate political forms of China, the Arab caliphate, and the Byzantine empire. This was also a period of frequent warfare. Most conflict occurred among units within regions—like western Europe, or sub-Saharan Africa. But there were a few larger military efforts, most notably the Arab military burst in the centuries after 600 and then the great Mongol conquests. A number of technological innovations accompanied warfare, such as the European crossbow and particularly the Chinese use of explosive powder.

Buddhist prayer on a scroll—earliest known printed work, 868 c.e. The image depicts the frontispiece to the world's earliest dated printed book, the Chinese translation of the Buddhist text the "Diamond Sutra." This consists of a scroll, over 16 feet long, made up of a long series of printed pages. Printed in China in 868 c.e., it was found in the Dunhuang Caves in 1907, in the northwestern province of Gansu.

All the major societies of Afro-Eurasia reacted to the key forces of the age, including the expansion of one or more of the world religions, but of course they reacted diversely; comparison remains essential. Even religious change usually offered some accommodations to older cultural patterns. Overall rates of change also varied. Some societies displayed more continuity with earlier traditions than did others.

Finally, it is vital to remember the continuing divisions in world geography during the post-classical period. Interactions in Afro-Eurasia contrast with the separate, although often impressive, trajectories of the Americas and Oceania. Deep divides in technology, animal use, and disease reflected this complexity. ■

CRITICAL THINKING QUESTIONS

1. Pick two societies, one that changed a lot between 600 and 1450 and another that displayed more continuity. How do you compare rates of change in these two cases? What caused one society to change more than the other?

2. Should developments between 1250 and 1450 be counted as part of the postclassical period, or should they be treated as a separate period? Explain your decision.

3. What kinds of change did the rise of Islam cause? What were the major ways the world was different in 1450 from what it had been in 600, because of Islam?

4. What similarities did the "Abrahamic" religions (Judaism, Christianity, and Islam) share? How did these religions differ from Buddhism?

5. What kinds of evidence are most helpful in analyzing the impact of Islam on women?

The Early Modern Period, 1450–1750: The World Shrinks

Explorer Vasco de Gama kneels before the king under a Portuguese flag while his ship waits in the distance. European ventures in trade and exploration helped define a new world history period.

PART OUTLINE

THE OVERVIEW: THE WORLD MAP CHANGES

These maps depict two of the big changes in world history that occurred between 1450 and 1750. Over these centuries, a number of new empires came into being, replacing smaller political units characteristic of the preceding postclassical period. Several European countries acquired overseas empires, a clear first in world history. Equally important, new land-based empires arose in Asia and eastern Europe. The Russian and Ottoman empires extended over both European and Asian territory, while the new Mughal empire ruled much of the Indian subcontinent.

The second big change involved trade routes. In 1450, transregional trade focused on exchanges among Asia, Africa, and Europe across some overland routes, but also via seaways in the Indian Ocean and the Mediterranean Sea. By 1750, oceangoing routes across the Pacific and particularly the Atlantic had become increasingly important, although the Indian Ocean sea routes remained significant. For the first time, the Americas and, soon, Pacific Oceania were caught up in global exchanges, with results not only in these regions but for the rest of the world as well.

Change, of course, is never complete. Even as world geography shifted fundamentally, some political features persisted during the three Early Modern centuries. Trade routes also maintained some holdovers from the past.

Big Concepts

Three themes predominated during the Early Modern period. First, contacts with the Americas ushered in a vital series of biological exchanges—of diseases, crops, animals, and people. This Columbian Exchange led to major population shifts in many different parts of the world. It also had environmental impact, particularly in the Americas. Second, obviously, the transregional trade network was redefined, becoming global. Levels of trade increased, with major impact on economies from China to Africa to the Americas. Shipping technology improved once again, and naval contacts were transformed with the use of ships' cannon. Third, partly because of the use of guns, the various new empires formed. Several European powers staked claims in the Americas, but also in certain coastal regions and island groups in Asia. New Islamic empires were joined by the rise of Russia and also renewed political energy in China.

The Early Modern period saw important social changes, particularly in the establishment of Atlantic slavery and an intensification of serfdom in several key regions. Exploitation of labor increased in many societies, responding to new pressures to produce for global trade and also to population changes. Gender relations shifted in several societies, though there were no global patterns.

Finally, the Early Modern period did not experience systematic cultural change. Important developments occurred, but these must be explored in individual societies or through particular sets of contacts. Precisely because economic exchanges were expanding, many societies proved eager to defend a separate cultural identity.

TRIGGERS FOR CHANGE

Several developments sparked the beginning of the Early Modern period, distinguishing it from the postclassical period that preceded it. The first was the revival of empire building. A striking example of this development involved the Ottoman Turks, who conquered Constantinople, the capital of the Byzantine empire. Soon the Ottomans extended their rule over most Byzantine territories and beyond, putting a Muslim power in charge of one of the great Christian cities and territories of the past. Worried Christian leaders elsewhere in the world turned to new activities to compensate for the loss of influence and territory. The second development visible by 1450—the steady progression of explorations by Europeans along the Atlantic coast of Africa—was motivated in part by the desire to find ways to trade with east Asia that would circumvent the centers of Islamic power. New European outreach would soon have wider effects.

Model of the slave ship *Brookes*, showing plan view of slave positions. The Atlantic slave trade had major effects in four continents.

Major Political Units of the World, c. 1450

Legend:
- Major Political Units, c.1450
- The Silk Road } routes opened during the "Mongol Peace" c. 1250–1350
- Other Route
- Arab Trade Routes
- Chinese Trade Routes
- Genoese Trade Routes
- Main Hanseatic Trade Routes
- Venetian Trade Routes
- Other Trade Routes

Major Political Units of the World, c. 1750

Legend:
- Major Political Units, c.1750
- Portuguese Trade Routes
- Spanish Trade Routes
- Dutch Trade Routes
- Other Trade Routes

New military technologies constituted the third development that played a vital role in defining the new framework for this period. European mariners began to use compasses and other navigational devices, first introduced by the Chinese and Arabs. Europeans also learned how to design better sailing ships. The most important new military technology was the growing use of guns and gunpowder, another Chinese invention now adapted by Europeans and others. New guns played a vital role in the creation of new empires both on land and overseas. Guns also affected political patterns within Africa, Japan, and Europe, although with less sweeping results.

Larger, sturdier ships, armed with cannon and featuring greater shipping capacity, sailed the new trade routes across the Atlantic and Pacific oceans. Europeans exercised disproportionate dominance over these routes, and they employed the new military technologies in establishing their new overseas empires.

THE BIG CHANGES

The changes in world empires and trade routes depicted on the maps on page 459 and the effects of new naval and military technologies highlight the distinctive features of the Early Modern period. Every major society reacted differently, depending on world position and existing tradition. In general, however, these developments led to the three broad changes: (a) the forging of a new global economy and through this the unfolding of an initial phase of globalization; (b) new biological exchanges of food, animals, and people; and (c) the new importance of large political units and their diplomatic and military interactions.

A New Global Economy and Proto-Globalization

International trade increased, for the first time including the Americas in the exchange. This was a major step in bringing the various regions of the world closer together and exposing them more widely to international influences. The result was a process called proto-globalization—a foretaste of the fuller range of contacts now called globalization but (hence the term *proto*) in a more preliminary sense.

Globalization involves intense and varied interactions among regions that help shape human lives; proto-globalization in this period helped set this process in motion. Several changes separated proto-globalization from the transcontinental network that had emerged in the postclassical period— although world trade still relied on some of the exchanges developed earlier, such as trade between East Africa and the Middle East. Most obviously, commerce was now global, including all major parts of the world and not just the three continents of Africa, Asia, and Europe. The intensity of contacts increased as well: Trade, and production for trade, now involved more people, more effort, and it began to help shape political and social systems as well as commercial ones. Business forms changed. Major European powers now created new merchant companies, formed to organize trade with distant parts of the Americas, Asia, and Africa. These companies introduced more impersonal management structures. They depended less on kinship relations that had been true of Muslim trade during the postclassical period.

Migration across oceans, some of it forced, was a new phenomenon as well. New consumer tastes developed in several

1300 c.e.	1400 c.e.	1500 c.e.	1550 c.e.
1281 Founding of Ottoman dynasty **1350s** Ottoman invasion of southeastern Europe **1368** Ming dynasty in China **1390** Ming restrictions in overseas trade	**1405–1433** Chinese expedition period **1434–1498** Portuguese expeditions down west African coast **1441** Beginning of European slave trade in Africa **1453** Ottoman conquest of Constantinople **1480** Moscow region free of Mongol control **1492** Columbus expeditions **1498–1499** Vasco da Gama expedition opens seas to Asia	**1500–1600** Europe's commercial revolution **1501–1510** Safavid conquest of Iran **1509** Spanish colonies on American mainland **1510–1511** Portugal conquers Goa (India), Malacca (Malaysia) **1517–1541** Protestant Reformation (Europe) **1519–1521** Magellan circumnavigates globe **1519–1524** Cortes conquers Mexico **1520–1566** Suleiman the Magnificent (Ottoman) **1526** Babur conquest in northern India (Mughal) **1533** Pizarro wins Peru **1548** Portuguese government in Brazil	**1552** Russia begins expansion in central Asia and western Siberia **1570** Portuguese colony of Angola (Africa) **1571** Ottoman naval defeat of Lepanto **1590** Hideyoshi unifies Japan **1591** Fall of Songhay (Africa)

societies that depended on goods imported from distant areas, going well beyond patterns in the earlier transcontinental network. Here, clearly, was an important step toward fuller globalization.

There was, however, still a gap between proto-globalization and the global patterns we see today. The new technologies that would revolutionize global travel and communication were still in the future. Trade contacts were important, but they had not yet reached contemporary levels. There were no internationally shared games or political standards, in contrast to the surge of cultural and political globalization that would emerge later on. Like contemporary globalization, proto-globalization brought both advantages and disadvantages, depending on the groups and regions involved. Those who profited from the new system would ultimately help prepare additional kinds of global connections.

Biological Exchange

The inclusion of the Americas global trade set in motion a number of biological exchanges of enormous consequence. Overall population leveled but also regional population balances were redefined. Foods from the Americas, like corn and the potato, began to be grown in Asia and, later, Europe. Combined with local improvements in agriculture, these new foods resulted in population increases. Europeans introduced new diseases into the Americas and Pacific island territories, decimating the native populations. Population loss encouraged new migrations, particularly from Europe and Africa, into the Americas. The massive African slave trade was in part a response to a labor shortage in the Americas. New animals, like the horse, greatly altered life in the Americas. These biological exchanges, called the "Columbian Exchange," altered many relationships among populations. New foods helped generate population increase worldwide, trumping the devastation wrought by new diseases. But new diseases and unprecedented levels of death were agonizing realities for many regions.

New Empires

The gunpowder empires formed large political units. Building and maintaining these new political structures required huge energies and huge expenses. New land-based empires in India, the Middle East, southeastern Europe, and Russia challenged political traditions in their imperial territories, while Spain, Portugal, France, England, and the Netherlands exerted pressure on their new overseas holdings.

The new empires also formed what would later be called "multinational" units, embracing different cultural and ethnic groups. The solidity of the multinational approach would be an important world history issue for the future.

The three main developments—the new global economy, the biological exchange, and the emergence of new empires—involved considerable shifts in world power. The world position of western Europe increased most obviously. Russia gained a new role as well. New masters ruled over many parts of the Americas, while portions of Africa found themselves immersed in novel orbits. Systematic patterns of inequality began to characterize some of the societies that supplied foods and raw materials to western Europe. Europe

1600 C.E.	1650 C.E.	1700 C.E.	1750 C.E.
1600 Dutch and British merchants begin activity in India	**1652** Dutch colony South Africa	**1713** New Bourbon dynasty, Spain	**1756–1763** Seven Years War
1600–1690 Scientific Revolution (Europe)	**1658–1707** Aurangzeb reign, beginning of Mughal decline	**1722** Fall of Safavid dynasty (Iran)	**1763** Britain acquires "New France"
1603 Tokugawa shogunate	**1682–1699** Turks driven from Hungary	**1759–1788** Reforms of Latin American colonial administration	**1764** British East India Company controls Bengal (India)
1607 First British colonies in North America	**1689–1725** Peter the Great (Russia)		**1770s** European–Bantu conflicts in southern Africa
1608 First French North American colonies			**1772–1795** Partition of Poland
1637 Russian pioneers to Pacific			**1775–1783** American Revolution
1640s Japan moves into isolation			**1781** Indian revolts in New Grenada and Peru (Latin America)
1641 Dutch colonies in Indonesia			**1792** Slave uprising in Haiti
1642–1727 Isaac Newton			
1644 Qing dynasty, China			

became wealthier and ever more powerful as it supplied processed goods and commercial services to these same regions. But several Asian societies, although less active in foreign trade, benefited from the new economy as well. China, the world's manufacturing leader, earned the greatest share of the silver exported from the Americas, brought by European merchants eager for Chinese goods. But India prospered also, until a major readjustment in the 18th century reduced Indian independence.

It is crucial to understand the complex balance among world regions during the Early Modern period. Western gains were important, but initiatives from several other societies helped shape both regional and global relationships.

CONTINUITY

Change is never complete. Even as world geography shifted, some political features persisted during the three centuries of the Early Modern period. Some existing trade routes continued to be important avenues of global exchange.

Many societies reacted to the big changes of the Early Modern period by preserving key features of their past. No sweeping, global cultural change occurred during this era. Although the spread of world religions was no longer a dominant theme, continued Islamic and Buddhist outreach affected parts of Asia and southeastern Europe, while the spread of Christianity to the Americas was a major development. Notable cultural innovations took place within individual societies, such as the new influence of science in western Europe or the rise of Japanese Confucianism. But cultural stability described much of the world, and global contacts did not overturn regional culture patterns.

No systematic changes occurred in gender relations in the Early Modern period. The new African slave trade affected gender balances on both sides of the Atlantic. More men than women were seized in Africa; as a result, the lack of adequate numbers of husbands encouraged African polygamy. New ideas sparked some debate over women's conditions in western Europe, although there was little real change. Relations between men and women in most other societies adhered to established patriarchal patterns.

Aside from the new developments in the military sphere, there were no technological breakthroughs until after 1750. Many societies participated only gradually in the use of guns and gunnery. Manufacturing techniques changed modestly, and little change took place in agriculture beyond the foodstuffs.

While political change, signaled by the rise of empires, was more general, several societies emphasized continuity in this realm as well. China prided itself on reviving and then maintaining its system of government. Many African societies preserved earlier traditions of divine kinship.

IMPACT ON DAILY LIFE: WORK

Changes of the Early Modern period profoundly affected ordinary people in many parts of the world. Indians in the Americas died by the thousands as European and African immigrants brought diseases like smallpox and measles. Europeans used silver to pay for desirable Chinese goods. Flush with new wealth, the Chinese government began to require that taxes be paid in silver, thus compelling ordinary Chinese to find new ways to obtain money. Often such efforts were unsuccessful, and as a result many Chinese fell ever deeper into poverty. Millions of Africans were seized from their homes and subjected to a terrifying and often deadly passage to the Americas. Those who managed to survive the voyage discovered that they were now compelled to live out their lives as slaves.

The most general social change during the Early Modern period was the growing pressure to work harder. The Early Modern world was increasingly commercial and crowded. Population increases in some regions demanded more from workers to help sustain larger families and villages. Many manufacturers and landowners tried to force their workers to increase their pace. The new forms of race-based slavery in the Americas placed greater emphasis on production. In western Europe, for example, Protestantism preached a work ethic that convinced many people that labor was a way to demonstrate God's grace.

People of all ages responded to the pressure to work harder. Child labor increased in many regions. Many European children were pressed into service as indentured laborers; for example, whole groups of orphans might be transported to work sites. By the 18th century, London orphans might be sent to work in new English factories or to North America as indentured servants. Even in old age, adults had to work if they wanted to survive. Master artisans, from makers of porcelain in China to gunsmiths in Europe, tried to compel their workers and apprentices to turn out more product. The pressure to work harder and longer was a personal side to the systemic changes that were reshaping the world.

The name commonly given to this period—Early Modern—captures complexity. The period is more recognizably modern than its predecessor. The renewed emphasis on political structures may strike a modern chord as well. But if modern, this was still early: Many features, including the continued dominance of traditional agriculture even in the most advanced economies, make it clear that there were still many changes to come in world history after 1750.

TRENDS AND SOCIETIES IN THE EARLY MODERN PERIOD

The chapters that follow examine the differing reactions to the major developments and changes of the Early Modern period. Chapter 21 offers an overview of the new global trading patterns that followed from the changes in naval technology and warfare. New trading opportunities and colonial expansion were closely related to significant changes within western Europe, the subject of Chapter 22. Chapters 23 and 24 return to the larger Atlantic world. The Early Modern era was a formative period for a new society in Latin America, born of interactions among native populations, Europeans, and Africans. Chapter 25 deals with Russia, one of the great new land-based empires of the period. Russian expansion affected not only eastern Europe, but also various parts of Asia, and complex interactions developed with western Europe as well.

Chapter 26, on the new Muslim states in the Middle East and southern Asia, concentrates on the emergence of other gunpowder empires. East Asia responded in its own, largely successful way to the new world economy. In these areas internal dynamics had more to do with developments that occurred between 1450 and 1750.

Each of the chapters in this part deals with reactions to world trade, biological exchange, and new pressures on labor. Each also highlights the diversity of patterns emerging in different parts of the world, depending on cultural orientation and shifts in positions of world power. ■

The World Economy

((•)) Listen to **Chapter 21**
on MyHistoryLab

How did silver mined by conscripted South American Indians change China's tax system? Silver quickly became the global currency of the Early Modern period. Production and use of silver show the power of the new **world economy** emerging after 1500. Silver had long been valued, of course, but new sources of production made it a commonly traded commodity. Japanese mines raised their output, trading with Europe and China. But it was European discoveries of silver in the Americas that really turned the tide. Mexican silver mines were important, but the big find, in the mid-16th century, was at Potosi, in Bolivia, where there was an enormous vein of ore (Figure 21.1). Desperate for labor, the Spanish revived *mita*—the Inca system of drafting workers for short stints. By 1600 there were 150,000 miners at Potosi, more than a third of them conscripted through the mita system.

FIGURE **21.1** This engraving of the Potosi silver mine in 1590 shows a cut-away view of a mountain. Inside, Native American miners work by torchlight.

Latin American silver was a godsend to Europeans. The Spanish crown kept a fifth of the silver its colonies produced, and this was its chief gain from the American colonies. Silver allowed Spain to build massive armies and grand new public buildings. But most of the silver sent to Europe passed through Spain to merchants elsewhere. They, in turn, used silver primarily to buy Asian goods that had long been sought, such as Indian spices and Chinese porcelain and silk. The Spanish also sent considerable silver to the Philippines, where it was traded for Chinese products sent to elites in the Americas and Europe. Silver greased the wheels of international commerce, allowing Europeans to buy Asian imports that could not otherwise have been afforded.

China and India were the largest recipients of New World silver—a clear sign of Asia's dynamism in the new world economy. Silver encouraged economic growth in Asia. It began to replace paper money. Merchants required silver even for purchases of common items like food. The Ming dynasty required periodic tax payments in silver. This reduced the number of tax collections (because each payment was now more valuable)—a reform known as "one whip of the lash." Silver imports helped sustain a standard of living in China that, into the early 19th century, was superior to that of western Europe.

But there were also worries. Many Chinese observers thought that silver was creating a wider gap between rich and poor, and they pointed out that the poor had to struggle to find the silver needed to pay their taxes. A few Europeans mused about expending so much effort to obtain silver that would only be swallowed up in Asia, but most agreed that the new consumer goods were well worth the trouble. A very few Europeans, but undoubtedly lots of ordinary Latin Americans, worried about the harsh working conditions in the mines. ■

world economy Established by Europeans by the 16th century; based on control of seas, including the Atlantic and Pacific; created international exchange of foods, diseases, and manufactured products.

This chapter deals with the consequences of some key developments long celebrated in American school texts: the voyages of Columbus and other explorers and the empires built by European conquerors and missionaries. The result was a power shift in world affairs, but another set of crucial developments in world history also resulted: the redefinition of interchanges among major societies in the world.

The story is not, however, simply the familiar one. European countries did play a disproportionate role in causing global change, particularly the huge shifts affecting the Americas and Africa. But African and Asian contributions were active as well.

THE WEST'S FIRST OUTREACH: MARITIME POWER

21.1   Why was Western Europe able to gain a new role in world trade during the centuries after 1450?

Various European leaders, particularly merchants but also some princes and clergy, had become increasingly aware of the larger world around them since 1100. The Crusades brought knowledge of the Islamic world's superior economy and the goods that could be imported from Asia. The Mongol empire, which sped up exchanges between the civilizations of Asia, also spurred European interest. The fall of the khans in China disrupted this interchange, as China became once again a land of mystery to Europeans. Europe's upper classes had by this time become accustomed to imported products

European merchant fleets seized control of key international trading routes. Initial Spanish and Portuguese leadership was challenged by growing efforts from Britain, France, and Holland.

1400 C.E.	1500 C.E.	1600 C.E.	1700 C.E.
1394–1460 Life of Prince Henry the Navigator	**1509** First Spanish colonies on Latin American mainland	**1607** First permanent British colony in Virginia	**1744** French–British wars in India
1433 China ends its great expeditions	**1514** Portuguese expedition to Indonesia	**1608** First French colonies in Canada; England gains first trading concession in India	**1756–1763** Seven Years War in Europe, India, and North America
1434 Portugal extends expeditions along west African coast	**1519–1521** Magellan circumnavigates the globe	**1641** Dutch begin conquests of Java (Indonesia)	**1763** British acquire New France
1488 Portuguese round Cape of Good Hope	**1534** First French explorations in Canada	**1652** Dutch launch colony in southern Africa	**1775–1783** American Revolution
1492 Columbus's first expedition	**1542** Portuguese reach Japan		**1756** "Black hole" of Calcutta
1497–1498 Vasco da Gama sails to India	**1562** Britain begins its slave trade		**1764** East India Company controls Bengal
	1571 Ottoman fleet defeated in Battle of Lepanto		
	1588 British defeat Spanish Armada		
	1597 Japan begins isolation policy		

from southeast Asia and India, particularly spices. These goods were transported to the Middle East in Arab ships, then brought overland, where they were loaded again onto vessels (mainly from Genoa and Venice, in Italy) for the Mediterranean trade.

Europeans entered into this era of growing contacts with several disadvantages. They remained ignorant of the wider world. Viking adventurers from Scandinavia had crossed the Atlantic in the 10th century, reaching Greenland and then North America, which they named Vinland. However, they quickly lost interest beyond establishing settlements on Greenland and Iceland, in part because they encountered indigenous warriors whose weaponry was good enough to cause them serious problems. Many Europeans were also fearful of distant voyages lest they fall off the world's edge.

As Europeans launched a more consistent effort at expansion from 1291 onward, they were pressed by new problems: fear of the strength of the emerging Ottoman empire and the lack of gold to pay for Asian imports. Initial settlements in island groups in the south Atlantic fed their hopes for further gains. However, the first expeditions were limited by the small, oar-propelled ships used in the Mediterranean trade, which could not travel far into the oceans.

New Technology: A Key to Power

During the 15th century, a series of technological improvements began to change the equation. Europeans developed deep-draft, round-hulled sailing ships for the Atlantic, capable of carrying heavy armaments. They were using and improving the compass. Mapmaking and other navigational devices improved as well. New combinations of sails, introduced on ships like the Portuguese caravel, allowed European ships to take advantage of different wind directions. Along with better ships' hulls, these innovations allowed European ships to navigate in mid-ocean, no longer dependent on coastal waters, hence not only regular trips across the Atlantic and the Pacific, but greater speed and flexibility even in the Indian Ocean.

Finally, European knowledge of explosives, another Chinese invention, was adapted into gunnery. European metalwork, steadily advancing in sophistication, allowed Western metalsmiths to devise the first guns and cannons. Although not very accurate, these weapons were awesome by the standards of the time (and terrifying to many Europeans, who had reason to fear the new destructive power of their own armies and navies). The West began to forge a military advantage over all other civilizations of the world, at first primarily on the seas—an advantage it would retain into the 20th century. With an unprecedented ability to kill and intimidate from a distance, western Europe was ready for its big push.

Portugal and Spain Lead the Pack

The specific initiative came from the small kingdom of Portugal, whose Atlantic location made it well suited for new initiatives. Portugal's rulers were drawn by the excitement of discovery, the harm they might cause to the Muslim world, and a thirst for wealth—a potent mix. A Portuguese prince, Henry the Navigator (Figure 21.2), organized a series of expeditions along the African coast and also outward to islands such as the Azores. Beginning in 1434 the Portuguese began to press down the African coast, each expedition going a little farther than its predecessor. They brought back slaves, spices such as pepper, and many stories of gold hoards they had not yet been able to find.

Later in the 15th century, Portuguese sailors ventured around the **Cape of Good Hope** in an attempt to find India, where direct contact would give Europeans easier access to luxury cloths and spices. They rounded the cape in 1488, but weary sailors forced the expedition back before it could reach India. Then, after news of Columbus's discovery of America for Spain in 1492, Portugal redoubled its efforts, hoping to stave off the new Spanish competition. Vasco da Gama's fleet of four ships reached India in 1498, with the aid of a Hindu pilot picked up in east Africa. The Portuguese mistakenly believed that the Indians were Christians, for they thought the Hindu temples were churches. They faced the hostility of Muslim merchants, who had long dominated trade in this part of the world, and they brought only crude goods for sale, like iron pots. But fortunately they had some gold as well. They managed to return with a small load of spices. A later trip involved more violence, as Europeans substituted force for their lack of attractive items for world trade. Da Gama used ships' guns to intimidate, and his forces killed or tortured many Indian merchants to set an example.

Da Gama's success set in motion an annual series of Portuguese voyages to the Indian Ocean, outlined in Map 21.1. One expedition, blown off course, reached Brazil, where it proclaimed Portuguese sovereignty. Portugal began to set up forts on the African coast and also in India—the forerunners of such Portuguese colonies as Mozambique, in east Africa, and Goa, in India. By 1514 the Portuguese had reached the islands of Indonesia, the center of spice production, and China. In 1542 one Portuguese expedition arrived in Japan, where a missionary effort was launched that met with some success for several decades.

FIGURE **21.2** Prince Henry the Navigator financed annual expeditions down the western coast of Africa in an effort to find a sea route to the Indies, establish trade with Africa, and find the fabled Christian kingdom of Prester John.

Meanwhile, only a short time after the Portuguese quest began, the Spanish reached out with even greater force. Here also was a country only reconquered from Muslim rule, full of missionary zeal and a desire for riches. The Spanish had traveled into the Atlantic during the 14th century. Then in 1492, the same year that the final Muslim fortress was captured in Spain, the Italian navigator **Christopher Columbus**, operating in the name of the newly united Spanish monarchy, set sail for a westward route to India, convinced that the round earth would make his quest possible. As is well known, he failed, reaching the Americas instead and mistakenly naming their inhabitants "Indians" (Figure 21.3). Although Columbus believed to his death that he had sailed to India, later Spanish explorers realized that they had voyaged to a region where Europeans, Africans, and Asians had not traveled previously. One expedition, headed by Amerigo Vespucci, gave the New World its name. Spain, eager to claim this new land, won papal approval for Spanish dominion over most of what is now Latin America, although a later treaty awarded Brazil to Portugal.

Finally, a Spanish expedition under **Ferdinand Magellan** set sail westward in 1519, passing the southern tip of South America and sailing across the Pacific, reaching the Indonesian islands in 1521 after incredible hardships. It was on the basis of this voyage, the first trip around the world, that Spain claimed the Philippines, which it held until 1898.

Portugal emerged from this first round of exploration with coastal holdings in parts of Africa and in the Indian port of Goa, a lease on the Chinese port of Macao, short-lived interests in trade with Japan, and finally, the claim on Brazil. Spain asserted its hold on the Philippines, various Pacific islands, and the bulk of the Americas. During the 16th century, the Spanish backed up these claims by military expeditions to Mexico and South America. The Spanish also held Florida and sent expeditions northward from Mexico into California and other parts of what later became the southwestern United States.

Cape of Good Hope Southern tip of Africa; first circumnavigated in 1488 by Portuguese in search of direct route to India.

Columbus, Christopher Genoese captain in service of king and queen of Castile and Aragon; successfully sailed to New World and returned in 1492; initiated European discoveries in Americas.

 Read the **Document** on **MyHistoryLab**: Christopher Columbus, journal excerpt and letter

Magellan, Ferdinand (1480–1521) Spanish captain who in 1519 initiated first circumnavigation of the globe; died during the voyage; allowed Spain to claim Philippines.

Read the Document on MyHistoryLab: Voyage from Lisbon to the Island of São Thomé (1540)

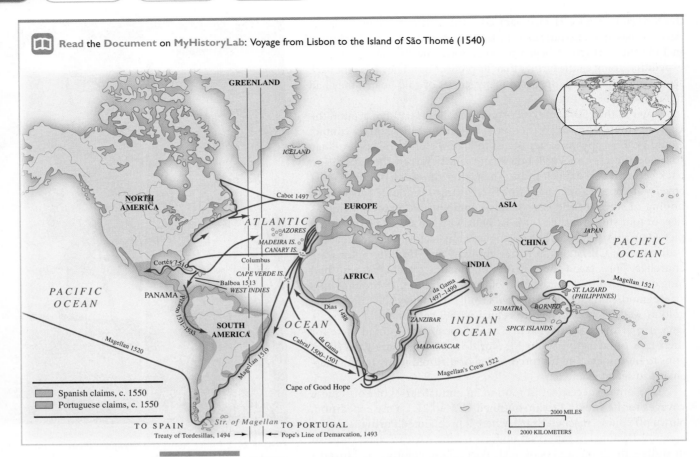

MAP **21.1 Spain and Portugal: Explorations and Colonies** In the early years of exploration, Spanish and Portuguese voyagers surveyed much of the coast of South America and some choice ports in Africa and Asia.

Northern European Expeditions

Later in the 16th century, the lead in exploration passed to northern Europe, as newly strong monarchies, such as France and England, got into the act and zealous Protestants in Britain and Holland strove to rival Catholic gains (Map 21.2). In part this shift in dynamism occurred because Spain and Portugal were busy digesting the gains they had already made; in part it was because northern Europeans, particularly the Dutch and the British, improved the design of oceanic vessels, producing lighter, faster ships than those of their Catholic adversaries. Britain won a historic sea battle with Spain in 1588, routing the massive Spanish Armada. From this point onward, the British, the Dutch, and to some extent the French vied for dominance on the seas, although in the Americas they aimed mainly northward because they could not challenge the Spanish and Portuguese colonies. Only in the sugar-rich West Indies did northern Europe seize islands initially claimed by Spain.

The new adventurers, like their Spanish and Portuguese predecessors, appreciated the economic potential of such voyages. Britain and Holland, now Protestant countries, emphasized religious interests less than European Catholics did at this point. Two 16th-century English explorers, trying to find an Arctic route to China, were told to keep an eye out for any native populations en route, for such people would provide a perfect market for warm English woolens. And if the territory was unpopulated, it might be put to use as a source of fish for Britain. A quest for profit had become a dominant policy motive.

French explorers crossed the Atlantic first in 1534, reaching Canada, which they claimed. In the 17th century, various expeditions pressed down from Canada into the Great Lakes region and the Mississippi valley.

View the **Closer Look** on **MyHistoryLab**: An Early European Image of Native Americans

FIGURE **21.3** This 1505 woodcut is one of the first known European portrayals of Native Americans. It was done by an unknown German artist who had never been to America but based his drawing on the testimony of those who had. The accompanying text reported: "The people are thus naked, handsome, brown. . . . They also eat each other . . . and hang the flesh of them in the smoke. They become a hundred and fifty years of age, and have no government."

The British also turned their attention to North America, starting with a brief expedition as early as 1497. The English hoped to discover a northwest passage to spice-rich India, but they accomplished little beyond exploration of the Hudson Bay area of Canada during the 16th century. England's serious work began in the 17th century, with the colonization of the east coast of North America. Holland also had holdings in North America and, for a time, in Brazil.

The Dutch entered the picture after winning independence from Spain, and Holland quickly became a major competitor with Portugal in southeast Asia. The Dutch sent many sailors and ships to the region, ousting the Portuguese from the Indonesian islands by the early 17th century. Voyagers from the Netherlands explored the coast of Australia, although without much immediate result. Finally, toward the mid-17th century, Holland established a settlement on the southern tip of Africa, mainly to provide a relay station for its ships bound for the East Indies.

The Netherlands, Britain, and France all chartered great joint-stock trading companies, such as the **Dutch East India Company**. These companies were given government monopolies of trade in the regions designated, but they were not rigorously supervised by their own states. They had rights to raise armies and coin money on their own. Thus, semiprivate companies, amassing great commercial fortunes, long acted almost like independent governments in the regions they claimed. For some time, a Dutch trading company effectively ruled the island of Taiwan off the coast of China. The **British East India Company** played a similar role in parts of India during much of the 18th century. The companies in North America traded actively in furs.

No matter where in Europe they came from, explorers and their crews faced many hardships at sea. The work was tiring and uncertain, with voyages lasting many months or years, and diseases such as scurvy were rampant. One expedition accepted only bachelors for its crew because married men would miss their families too much. A sailor on another trip complained that "he was tired of being always tired, that he would rather die once than many times, and that they might as well shut their eyes and let the ship go to the bottom."

Dutch East India Company Joint stock company that obtained government monopoly over trade in Asia; acted as virtually independent government in regions it claimed.

British East India Company Joint stock company that obtained government monopoly over trade in India; acted as virtually independent government in regions it claimed.

 Read the **Document** on MyHistoryLab: Jan van Linschoten on Dutch business in the Indian Ocean

THINKING HISTORICALLY

Causation and the West's Expansion

BECAUSE OF THEIR INTEREST IN SOCIAL change, historians inevitably deal with causation. What prompted the fall of Rome? Why did Islam spread so widely? What factors explain why most agricultural civilizations developed patriarchal family structures?

Historical causation differs from the kinds of causation many scientists test. When experiments or observations can be repeated, scientists can gain a fairly precise understanding of the factors that produce a phenomenon: Remove an ingredient, for example, and the product changes. Historical causation is more complex. Major developments may resemble each other, but they never happen the same way twice. Definitive proof that factor *X* explains 40 percent of the spread of Buddhism in east Asia is impossible. This is why historians often disagree about causation. But if precision is impossible, high probability is not. We can get a fairly good sense of why things happen, and sloppy causation claims can be disproved. Furthermore, probing causation helps us explore a phenomenon itself. We know more about the nature of Western expansion in the 15th and 16th centuries if we discuss what caused it.

Some historians and other social scientists look to a single kind of cause as the explanation of a variety of circumstances. Some anthropologists are cultural determinists. They judge that a basic set of cultural factors, usually assumed to be very durable, causes the ongoing differences between societies: Chinese and Greeks, on average, respond differently to emotional stimuli because of their different cultural conditioning. More common is a technological or economic determinism. Some historians see technological change as setting other changes in motion. Others, including Marxists, argue that economic arrangements—how the economy is structured and what groups control it—produce at least the basic framework for innovations. At another pole, some historians used to claim "great men" as the prime movers in history. The causes of change thus became Chinggis Khan or Asoka, with no need to look much further.

Various approaches to causation have been applied to the West's explorations and colonial conquests in the Early Modern period. There is room for a "great man" analysis. Many descriptive accounts that dwell on explorers and conquerors (Vasco da Gama and Cortés, for example) and on leaders who sponsored them (such as Henry the Navigator) suggest that the key cause of the West's new role stemmed from the daring and vision of exceptional individuals.

Cultural causation can also be invoked. Somehow, Europe's expansion must relate to the wonders of innovation introduced by the Renaissance. A partial link with Christian culture is even

[S]ome historians used to claim "great men" as the prime movers in history.

easier to prove, for a missionary spirit quickly supplemented the efforts of early explorers, leading to more voyages and settlements in Asia and the Americas. Catholic powers took a lead here; Protestant countries like Holland and Britain were less interested in missionary efforts at this point.

Political causation enters in, if not in causing the initial surge, at least in confirming it. Starting in the 16th century, rivalries between the nation-states motivated a continuing quest for new trade routes and colonies.

There is also room for a simpler, technologically determinist approach. In this view, Europe's gains came from a handful of new inventions. Benefiting from knowledge of advances in China and the Middle East, Europeans introduced naval cannons. Along with steady improvements in navigation and ship design, new techniques explain why Europe gained as it did. Except in the Americas, where they had larger technical and organizational advantages, Europeans advanced in areas they could reach by sea and dominate by ships' guns—port cities, islands, and trade routes—and not elsewhere. Put simply, Europe gained because of these few technological edges.

Like all determinisms, however, this technological approach raises as many questions as it answers. Why were Europeans so ready to adopt new inventions? (What caused the cause?) Why did other societies that were aware of Europe's innovations, such as China, deliberately decide not to imitate Western naval techniques? Here a separate culture determined a reaction different from that of the West, as the Chinese learned how to benefit from world trade in distinctive ways. Technology and culture went hand in hand. Clearly, some combined causal framework is needed in this case.

We cannot expect uniform agreement on a precise ordering of causation. However, we can expect fruitful debate—the kind of debate that has already moved our understanding beyond surface causes, such as the powerful personalities of a few people, to a grasp of more underlying contexts.

QUESTIONS

- If you had to choose a single determinism (cultural, technological, or economic) as basic to social change, which one would you pick? Why?
- In what ways might the professed motives of Western explorers and colonists have differed from their real motives?
- Would they necessarily have been aware of the discrepancy?

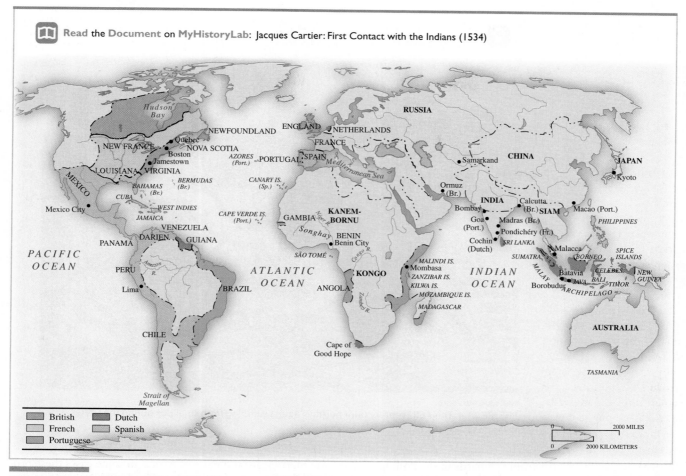

Read the Document on MyHistoryLab: Jacques Cartier: First Contact with the Indians (1534)

Legend:
- British
- French
- Portuguese
- Dutch
- Spanish

2000 MILES

2000 KILOMETERS

MAP 21.2 French, British, and Dutch Holdings, c. 1700 During the 17th century, northwestern Europe took the initiative in explorations, venturing into North America and seeking convenient trading stations elsewhere.

THE COLUMBIAN EXCHANGE OF DISEASE AND FOOD

21.2 What were the principal regional results of the Columbian Exchange?

Europe's new initiatives added to existing transregional trade patterns. The range and significance of exchange began to increase steadily—a key manifestation of proto-globalization. Simply including the Americas, making exchanges truly global affected almost all major regions.

The impact of wider exchange became visible quickly. The extension of contacts across the Atlantic spread disease (see Chapter 23). The greatest victims were millions of Native Americans who had not previously been exposed to Afro-Eurasian diseases such as smallpox and measles and who therefore had no natural immunities (Figure 21.4). During the 16th and 17th centuries, they died in huge numbers. Overall, in North and South America, more than half the native population would die; some estimates run as high as 80 percent. Whole island populations in the West Indies were wiped out. This was a major blow to earlier civilizations in the Americas as well as an opportunity for Europeans to forge a partially new population of their own citizens and slaves imported from Africa. The devastation occurred over a 150-year period, although in some areas it was more rapid. When Europeans later made contact with Polynesians and Pacific Coast peoples in the 18th century, the same dreadful pattern played out, again undermining vibrant cultures.

Other exchanges were less dire. New World crops were spread rapidly via Western merchants. American corn and sweet potatoes were taken up widely in China (where merchants learned of them

Europe's new maritime strength and new trade patterns generated wider changes, developing from the 1490s onward. One was the Columbian Exchange of foods, diseases, and people. New global economic inequalities and new overseas empires also emerged.

View the **Closer Look** on MyHistoryLab: Columbian Exchange

FIGURE **21.4** This 16th-century print portrays Aztecs suffering from smallpox during the Cortés invasion (1518–1519).

from Spaniards in the Philippines), the Mediterranean, and parts of Africa. In some cases these productive new crops, along with local agricultural improvements, triggered large population increases. For example, China began to experience long-term population growth in the 17th century, and new crops played a key role. When Europeans introduced the potato around 1700, major population upheaval occurred there as well.

Indeed, food played a key role in the world system created during the Early Modern period. About 30 percent of the foods consumed in the world today come from plants of American origin. Corn became a staple in the African diet. Europeans, ironically, were more conservative. Rumors spread that American foods spread disease. It took more than a century for the potato to gain ground, but fried potatoes (French fries) were being sold on the streets of Paris by the 1680s.

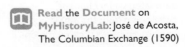

Read the Document on MyHistoryLab: José de Acosta, The Columbian Exchange (1590)

Animal husbandry became more similar across the world as European and Asian animals, such as horses and cattle, were introduced to the New World. The spread of basic products and diseases formed an important backdrop to world history from the 16th century on, with varying effects on population structures in diverse regions.

Environment and Labor

The Columbian Exchange had substantial environmental impact. Europeans ignored the environmental experience of local populations in the Americas, bent on introducing European products and expanding output. Introduction of sheep, for example, devastated local vegetation in many parts of the Americas, because of their close grazing, with increased soil erosion an obvious result. Deforestation increased in many regions, either because of population increase or, in the Americas, the desire to expand exports. By 1700 25 percent of the world's forests had been cut down, and by 1850 the percentage had risen to 50. In Latin America alone, forest clearances increased five-fold between 1650 and 1750. Hunting and fishing expanded. Many species lost ground in parts of North America thanks to the fur trade. Beginning with Spanish expeditions in the 16th century, new forms of deep-sea whaling developed, and in general extensive fishing in the North Atlantic—in part to provide cheap food for slaves—began to cut into supplies, particularly of common species like cod.

New trading opportunities and population changes generated new, or partially new, labor systems. Faced with market demand for products like sugar, now introduced to the Americas, but short of local workers thanks to disease, Europeans actively sought alternatives. Experiments with indentured servitude—with workers brought from Europe under tight contracts that controlled their labor for many years—had some success, but failed to recruit sufficient labor. The slave trade, quickly developed with Africa, proved a more important response, with millions ultimately forcibly shipped across the Atlantic. Atlantic slavery, however, was no mere imitation of earlier slave systems. Not only were greater numbers involved, but plantation owners actively strove to increase discipline and production (see Chapter 24). The Columbian Exchange thus played a major role in the general global effort to increase human labor during the Early Modern period.

TOWARD A WORLD ECONOMY

21.3 What new kinds of regional economic inequality emerged during the period?

Europeans did not displace all Asian shipping from the coastal waters of China and Japan, nor did they completely monopolize the Indian Ocean (see Chapter 27). Along the east African coast, while a few European bases were established, Muslim traders remained active, and commerce continued to move toward the Middle East. Generally, however, western Europe dominated a growing percentage of oceanic shipping, even using war ships to muscle in on trade between other societies, as between India and southeast Asia. This greatly increased Europe's overall profits, and disproportionate control by the great merchant companies increased the European ability to determine the framework for international trade. In the eastern Mediterranean, for example, a Spanish-directed fleet defeated the navy of the Ottoman empire in the battle of **Lepanto** in 1571. With this setback, any hope of successful Muslim rivalry against European naval power ended. The Turks rebuilt their fleet and continued their activity in the eastern Mediterranean, but they could not challenge the Europeans on the larger international routes.

Although western Europe did not conquer much inland territory in Africa or Asia, it did seek a limited network of secure harbors. Led by Spain and Portugal, then followed by the various northern powers, European ports spread along the west coast of Africa, several parts of the Indian subcontinent, and the islands of southeast Asia by the 17th century. Even in China, where unusually strong governments limited the Europeans' ability to seize harbors outright, the Portuguese won effective control over the island port of Macao. European-controlled ports served as areas for contact with overland traders (usually local merchants) and provided access to inland goods not directly within the reach of the West.

Where direct control was not feasible, European influence led to the formation of special western enclaves in existing cities. This was the pattern in the Ottoman empire, where Western merchants were permitted to form limited self-governing communities alongside other foreign merchants within Constantinople, and in Russia, where Western shipping agents set up first in Moscow and then in St. Petersburg. Elements of this system even emerged in Japan after a firm isolationist policy was launched about 1600, as Dutch traders were given special access to the port of Nagasaki, a privilege shared by and formerly enjoyed only by Chinese merchants. The point was obvious: International trade gained growing importance in supplementing regional economies. Because western Europe now ran began to play a larger role in trans-regional trace, its merchants often gained some new access, though Chinese traders were still dominant in most East Asian markets.

Imbalances in World Trade

The most active competition in world trade emerged between European nations themselves. Spain briefly dominated, thanks to its imports of silver from the Americas. But it lacked a good banking system and could not support a full commercial surge. England, France, and Holland, where merchants had firmer status, soon pulled in the lion's share of profits from world trade. Western Europe quickly expanded its manufacturing operations, so that it could export expensive finished goods, such as guns and cloth, in return for unprocessed goods, such as silver and sugar, traded by other societies. Here was another margin for profit.

Europe developed a network of overseas colonies, particularly in the Americas but also in a few parts of Africa and Asia. By the 18th century, growing European inroads in India marked a decisive change in south Asia.

Lepanto Naval battle between the Spanish and the Ottoman empire resulting in a Spanish victory in 1571.

core nations Nations, usually European, that enjoyed profit from world economy; controlled international banking and commercial services such as shipping; exported manufactured goods for raw materials.

mercantilism Economic theory that stressed governments' promotion of limitation of imports from other nations and internal economies in order to improve tax revenues; popular during 17th and 18th centuries in Europe.

The dominant **core nations** in the new world system supplemented their growing economic prowess by self-serving political policies. The doctrines of **mercantilism**, which urged that a nation-state not import goods from outside its own empire but sell exports as widely as possible in its own ships, both reflected and encouraged the new world system. Tariff policies discouraged manufacturing in colonial areas and stimulated home-based manufacturing.

Beyond western Europe lay areas that were increasingly enmeshed in the world economy but as dependents to the core nations. These areas produced low-cost goods: precious metals and cash crops such as sugar, spice, tobacco, and later cotton. Human labor was a vital item of exchange. Parts of sub-Saharan Africa entered the new world economy mainly as suppliers of slaves. The earlier west African patterns of trade across the Sahara yielded to a dominant focus on the Atlantic and therefore to activities organized by Western shippers. In return for slaves and unprocessed goods, Europeans traded their manufactured items, including guns, while profiting from their control of commercial and shipping services.

A System of International Inequality

The new world economic relationships proved highly durable. Most of the areas established as dependent by the 17th century still carry some special burdens in world trade today. In dependent areas such as Latin America and the slave-supplying parts of Africa, not all people were mired in poverty. African slave traders and princes who taxed the trade might grow rich. In Latin America the silver mines and commercial estates required regional merchants and farmers to supply food. Furthermore, many peasants in Latin America and even more in Africa were not yet involved in a market economy at all—whether regional or international—but rather produced for local subsistence with traditional motives and methods. However, significant minorities were involved in production for the world market. Also, most African and Latin American merchants and landlords did not fully control their own terms of trade. They might prosper, but their wealth did not stimulate much local manufacturing or general economic advance. Rather, they tended to import European-made goods, including (in the case of American planters) art objects and luxury items.

Coercive labor systems spread. Because dependent economies relied on cheap production of unprocessed goods, there was a tendency to build a system of forced labor that would cost little even

VISUALIZING THE PAST

West Indian Slaveholding

THE FOLLOWING TABLE DESCRIBES THE RISE of the plantation system, and attendant slaveholding, on the British West Indian island of Antigua, where sugar growing for export gained increasing hold. Trends of the sort indicated in this table raise further analytical issues about cause and effect. What might have caused the main changes in Antigua's estate system? What do the trends suggest about the European demand for sugar and about production methods used to meet this demand?

What impact would the trends have had on slaves themselves? Laws in the British Caribbean soon began to enforce the estate system, exempting masters from murder charges when slaves died from beatings administered as punishment and fining groups such as the Quakers for daring to bring slaves to religious meetings. How do the statistical trends help explain the imposition of new laws of this sort?

	1688	1706	1767
Slaveholders	16	30	65
Planters with 20+ slaves	6	16	46
Planters with 100+ slaves	0	4	22
Slaves	332	1,150	5,610
Acreage	5,811	5,660	12,350

QUESTIONS
- What trends in the social and economic structure of this part of Antigua during the 18th century do these figures suggest?
- Did the estate economy become more or less labor intensive, given the acreage involved and the comparative growth rates of owner and slave populations?
- What do the trends suggest about the nature of the European-born or European-derived elite of Antigua?

when the overall labor supply was precarious. In the Americas, given the population loss from disease, this led to the massive importation of African slaves as well as the more limited use of indentured servants. Also, for many Native Americans and **mestizos** (people of mixed European and Native American blood), systems of estate management developed that demanded large amounts of labor. More limited examples of estate agriculture, with peasants forced into labor without the legal freedom to leave, arose for spice production in the Dutch East Indies and, by the 18th century, in British-dominated agricultural operations in India.

How Much World in the World Economy?

Asia, although not sponsoring the most active merchant ventures, participated strongly, and often profitably, in the world economy. The Chinese government, having renounced large-scale international trade of its own early in the 15th century, deliberately avoided involvement with international trade on someone else's terms. It did copy some firearms manufacturing from the Europeans, but at a fairly low level. Beyond this it depended on extensive government regulation, backed up by a coastal navy, to keep European activities in check. Most of the limited trade that existed was channeled through Macao. European visitors wrote scornfully of China's disdain for military advances. A Jesuit wrote that "the military . . . is considered mean among them." The Chinese were also disparaged for adhering to tradition. One Western missionary in the 17th century described how, in his opinion, the Chinese could not be persuaded "to make use of new instruments and leave their old ones without an especial order from the Emperor to that effect. They are more fond of the most defective piece of antiquity than of the most perfect of the modern, differing much in that from us who are in love with nothing but what is new."

So China managed to avoid trying to keep up with European developments while also avoiding subservience to European merchants. Chinese manufacturing gains led to a strong export position, which is why Europeans sent a great deal of American silver to China to pay for the goods they wanted. Indeed, at the end of the 18th century, a famous British mission, appealing to the government to open the country to greater trade, was rebuffed. The imperial court, after insisting on extreme deference from the British envoy, haughtily informed him that the Chinese had no need for outside goods. European eagerness for Chinese goods—attested to by the habit adopted in the 17th century of calling fine porcelain "china"—was simply not matched by Chinese enthusiasm, but a trickle of trade continued. Westerners compensated in part by developing their own porcelain industry by the 18th century, which contributed to the early Industrial Revolution, particularly in Britain. Still, there were hopes for commercial entry to China that remained unfulfilled.

Japan, although initially attracted by Western expeditions in the 16th century, pulled back even more fully. So did Korea. The Japanese showed some openness to Christian missions, and they were fascinated by Western advances in gunnery and shipping. Artists captured the interest in exotic foreigners. Guns had particular relevance to Japan's ongoing feudal wars, for there was no disdain here for military life. Yet Japanese leaders soon worried about undue Western influence and the impact this could have on internal divisions among warring lords, as well as the threat guns posed to samurai military dominance. They encouraged a local gunmaking industry that matched existing European muskets and small cannon fairly readily, but having achieved this, they cut off most contact with any world trade. Most Japanese were forbidden to travel or trade abroad, the small Christian minority was suppressed, and from the 17th until the 19th centuries Japan entered a period of almost complete isolation except for some Chinese contact and trading concessions to the small Dutch enclave near Nagasaki.

Other societies participated variously in world trade. The rulers of India's new Mughal empire in the 16th century were interested in Western traders and even encouraged the establishment of small port enclaves. India also sold goods—not only spices but also manufactured cottons textiles and other items—in return for New World silver. Most attention, however, was riveted on internal development and land-based expansion and commerce; world trade was a sideline. The same held true for the Ottoman and Safavid empires in the Middle East through the 17th century, despite the presence of small European enclaves in key cities. Russia lay partially outside the world economic orbit until the 18th century. A largely agricultural society, Russia conducted much of its trade with nomadic peoples in central Asia, which further insulated it from west European demands.

mestizos [mehs-TEE-zohs] People of mixed European and Indian ancestry in Mesoamerica and South America; particularly prevalent in areas colonized by Spain; often part of forced labor system.

Read the **Document** on **MyHistoryLab**: Multatuli, Max Havelaar: Or the Coffee Auctions of the Dutch Trading Company

The Expansionist Trend

The world economy was not stationary; it tended to gain ground over time, as the centerpiece of the process of proto-globalization. The process also linked to the formation of new kinds of empire. South America, the West Indies, a part of North America, and some regions in west Africa were first staked out as colonial dependencies beginning in the 16th century, and the list later expanded. Portions of southeast Asia that produced for world markets, under the dominance of the great Western trading companies, were brought into the orbit by the 17th century.

By the early 18th century, Western traders were advancing in India as the Mughal empire began to fall apart. The British and French East India Companies staked out increasing roles in internal trade and administration. Early in the 18th century, Britain passed tariffs against the import of cotton cloth made in India as a means of protecting Britain's own cotton industry. The intent was to use India as a market for British-processed goods and a source of outright payments of gold, which the British were requiring by the late 18th century. Indian observers were aware of the shifting balance. An 18th-century account noted,

> But such is the little regard which they [the British] show to the people of this kingdom, and such their apathy and indifference for their welfare, that the people under their dominion groan everywhere, and are reduced to poverty and distress.

India maintained a complex regional economy still, with much internal manufacturing and trade; it was not forced into such complete dependency as Latin America, for example. However, what had initially been a position outside the world economy was changing, to India's disadvantage. Manufacturing began to decline.

Eastern Europe also was brought into a growing relationship with the world economy and the west European core. The growth of cities in the West created a growing market for imported grains by the 18th century. Much of this demand was met by east European growers, particularly in Prussia and Poland but also in Russia. Export grains, in turn, were produced mainly on large estates by serfs, who were subjected to prolonged periods of labor service. This relationship was similar to that which prevailed in Latin America, with one exception: Outside of Poland, east European governments were much stronger than their Latin American counterparts.

COLONIAL EXPANSION

Europe's new naval power supported the establishment of several overseas empires, particularly in the Americas. Trade patterns and the results of the Columbian exchange helped shape colonial relationships.

21.4   Did the new European colonies constitute major expansions of state power?

Opportunities to establish colonies were particularly inviting in the Americas, where European guns, horses, and iron weapons offered special advantages and where political disarray and the population losses provided openings in many cases (see Chapter 24).

The Americas: Loosely Controlled Colonies

Spain moved first. The Spanish colonized several West Indian islands soon after Columbus's first voyage, starting with Hispaniola and then moving into Cuba, Jamaica, and Puerto Rico. Only in 1509 did they begin settlement on the mainland, in search of gold. The first colony was established in what is now Panama, under an able but unscrupulous adventurer, **Vasco de Balboa**. Several expeditions fanned out in Central America, and then a separate expedition from Cuba launched the Spanish conquest of the Aztecs in Mexico. Another expedition headed toward the Inca realm in the Andes in 1531, where hard fighting was needed before ultimate victory. From this base several colonial expeditions spread to Colombia, other parts of the Andes, and portions of Argentina.

Expansion resulted from the efforts of a motley crew of adventurers, many of them violent and treacherous, like **Francisco Pizarro** (1478–1541), admittedly one of the more successful examples (Figure 21.5). Pizarro first came to the Americas in 1502 and settled on the island of Hispaniola. Later, he joined Balboa's colony in Panama, where he received a cattle ranch. Learning of wealth in Peru, he joined with an illiterate soldier and a priest, mounting two expeditions that failed. In 1528

Balboa, Vasco de (c. 1475–1519) First Spanish captain to begin settlement on the mainland of Mesoamerica in 1509; initial settlement eventually led to conquest of Aztec and Inca empires by other captains.

Pizarro, Francisco Led conquest of Inca Empire of Peru beginning in 1535; by 1540, most of Inca possessions fell to the Spanish.

he returned to Spain to gain the king's support and also his agreement that he would be governor of the new province. With these pledges and a force of about 180 men, he attacked the divided Inca empire. Capturing Emperor Atahuallpa, he accepted a large ransom and then strangled him. Several revolts followed during Pizarro's rule from Lima, a coastal city he founded. But the Spanish king ennobled Pizarro for his success. At a dinner in 1541, Pizarro was assassinated by a group of Inca rebels.

Early colonies in the Americas typically were developed by small bands of gold-hungry Europeans, often loosely controlled by colonial administrations back home. Colonial rulers often established only limited controls over native populations at first, content to exact tribute without imposing detailed administration and sometimes leaving existing leaders in place. Gradually, more formal administration spread as agricultural settlements were established and official colonial systems took shape under control of bureaucrats sent from Spain and Portugal. Active missionary efforts, designed to Christianize the native peoples, added another layer of detailed administration throughout the Spanish holdings in North and South America.

France, Britain, and Holland, although latecomers to the Americas, also staked out colonial settlements. French explorations along the St. Lawrence River in Canada led to small colonies around Quebec, from 1608 onward, and explorations in the Mississippi River basin. Dutch and English settlers moved into portions of the Atlantic coastal regions early in the 17th century. Also in the 17th century, all three countries seized and colonized several West Indian islands, which they soon involved in the growing slave trade.

FIGURE **21.5** Francisco Pizarro.

British and French North America: Backwater Colonies

Colonies of European settlers developed in North America, where patterns differed in many respects from those in Latin America and the Caribbean. English colonies along the Atlantic received religious refugees, such as the Calvinists who fled religious tensions in Britain to settle in New England. Government grants of land to major proprietors such as William Penn led to explicit efforts to recruit settlers. New York began as a Dutch settlement but was taken over easily by an English expedition in 1664.

In Canada, the first substantial European settlements were launched by the French government under Louis XIV. The initial plan involved setting up manorial estates under great lords whose rights were carefully restricted by the state. French peasants were urged to emigrate, although it proved difficult to develop an adequate labor force. However, birth rates were high, and by 1755 **New France** had about 55,000 settlers in a peasant society that proved extremely durable as it fanned out around the fortress of Quebec. Strong organization by the Catholic Church completed this partial replica of French provincial society. Britain attacked the French strongholds (Figure 21.6) as part of a worldwide colonial struggle between the two powers. In the conflict, known as the **Seven Years War**, France lost its colony under the terms of the **Treaty of Paris**, which in 1763 settled the war. France eagerly regained its West Indian sugar islands, along with trading posts in Africa, and Britain took control of Canada and the Mississippi basin. Relations between British officials and the French Canadian community remained strained as British settlements developed in eastern Canada and in Ontario. The flight of many American loyalists after the 1776 revolution added to the English-speaking contingent in Canada.

Colonial holdings along the Atlantic and in Canada were generally of modest interest to Western colonial powers in the 17th and even the 18th centuries. The Dutch were more attached to their Asian colonies. British and French leaders valued their West Indian holdings much more than their North American colonies. The value of North American products, such as timber and furs, was not nearly as great as profits from the Caribbean or Latin America, so much less attention was given to economic regulation. As a result, some merchant and manufacturing activities emerged among the new Americans.

New France French colonies in North America; extended from St. Lawrence River along Great Lakes and down Mississippi River valley system.

Seven Years War Fought both in continental Europe and also in overseas colonies between 1756 and 1763; resulted in Prussian seizures of land from Austria, English seizures of colonies in India and North America.

Treaty of Paris Arranged in 1763 following Seven Years War; granted New France to England in exchange for return of French sugar islands in Caribbean.

DOCUMENT

Western Conquerors: Tactics and Motives

IN THE FIRST PASSAGE QUOTED HERE, Columbus writes to the Spanish monarchy on his way home from his 1492 expedition. In the second passage, the brother of Francisco Pizarro, the Spanish conqueror of Peru, describes in 1533 how the Inca ruler, Atahuallpa, was defeated.

COLUMBUS'S 1492 EXPEDITION

Sir, believing that you will take pleasure in hearing of the great success which our Lord has granted me in my voyage, I write you this letter, whereby you will learn how in thirty-three days' time I reached the Indies with the fleet which the most illustrious King and Queen, our Sovereigns, gave to me, where I found very many islands thickly peopled, of all which I took possession without resistance for their Highnesses by proclamation made and with the royal standard unfurled. To the first island that I found I gave the name of *San Salvador*, in remembrance of His High Majesty, who hath marvelously brought all these things to pass; the Indians call it *Guanaham*. . . .

Espanola is a wonder. Its mountains and plains, and meadows, and fields, are so beautiful and rich for planting and sowing, and rearing cattle of all kinds, and for building towns and villages. The harbours on the coast, and the number and size and wholesomeness of the rivers, most of them bearing gold, surpass anything that would be believed by one who had not seen them. There is a great difference between the trees, fruits, and plants of this island and those of *Juana*. In this island there are many spices and extensive mines of gold and other metals. The inhabitants of this and of all the other islands I have found or gained intelligence of, both men and women, go as naked as they were born, with the exception that some of the women cover one part only with a single leaf of grass or with a piece of cotton, made for that purpose. They have neither iron, nor steel, nor arms, nor are they competent to use them, not that they are not well-formed and of handsome stature, but because they are timid to a surprising degree. . . .

Although I have taken possession of all these islands in the name of their Highnesses, and they are all more abundant in wealth than I am able to express . . . yet there was one large town in *Espanola* of which especially I took possession, situated in a locality well adapted for the working of the gold mines, and for all kinds of commerce, either with the main land on this side, or with that beyond which is the land of the great Khan, with which there is great profit. . . .

I have also established the greatest friendship with the king of that country, so much so that he took pride in calling me his brother, and treating me as such. Even should these people change their intentions towards us and become hostile, they do not know what arms are, but, as I have said, go naked, and are the most timid people in the world; so that the men I have left could, alone, destroy the whole country, and this island has no danger for them, if they only know how to conduct themselves. . . . Finally, and speaking only of what has taken place in this voyage, which has been so hasty, their Highnesses may see that I shall give them all the gold they require, if they will give me but a very little assistance; spices also, and cotton, as much as their Highnesses shall command to be shipped; and mastic, hitherto found only in Greece . . . slaves, as many of these idolators as their Highnesses shall command to be shipped. . . .

But our Redeemer hath granted this victory our illustrious King and Queen and their kingdoms, which have acquired great fame by an event of such high importance, in which all Christendom ought to rejoice, and which it ought to celebrate with great festivals and the offering of solemn thanks to the Holy Trinity with many solemn prayers, both for the great exaltation which may accrue to them in turning so many nations to our holy faith, and also for the temporal benefits which will bring great refreshment and gain, not only to Spain, but to all Christians.

WHY AND HOW ATAHUALLPA WAS DEFEATED

The messengers came back to ask the Governor to send a Christian to Atahuallpa, that he intended to come at once, and that he would come unarmed. The Governor sent a Christian, and presently Atahuallpa moved, leaving the armed men behind him. He took with him about five or six thousand Indians without arms, except that under their shirts they had small darts and slings with stones.

He came in a litter, and before went three or four hundred Indians in liveries, cleaning straws from the road and singing. Then came Atahuallpa in the midst of his chiefs and principal men, the greatest among them being also borne on men's shoulders. . . . A Dominican Friar, who was with the Governor, came forward to tell him, on the part of the Governor, that he waited for him in his lodgings, and that he was sent to speak with him. The Friar then told Atahuallpa that he was a Priest, and that he was sent there to teach the things of the Faith, if they should desire to be Christians. He showed Atahuallpa a book . . . and told him that book contained the things of God. Atahuallpa asked for the book, and threw it on the ground, saying: "I will not leave this place until you have restored all that you have taken in my land. I know well who you are, and what you have come for." . . . The Friar went to the Governor and reported what was being done, and that no time was to be lost. The Governor sent to me; and I had arranged with the Captain of the artillery that, when a sign was given, he should discharge his pieces, and that, on hearing the reports, all the troops should come forth at once. This was done, and as the Indians were unarmed, they were defeated without danger to any Christian. Those who carried the litter, and the chiefs who surrounded Atahuallpa, were all killed, falling around him. The Governor came out and seized Atahuallpa, and in protecting him, he received a knife cut from a Christian in the hand. The troops continued the pursuit as far as the place where the armed Indians were stationed, who made

(continued on next page)

(continued from previous page)

no resistance whatever, because it was night. All were brought into town, where the Governor was quartered.

Next morning the Governor ordered us to go to the camp of Atahuallpa, where we found forty thousand pesos worth of gold and two or three pounds of silver. . . . The Governor said that he had not come to make war on the Indians, but that our Lord the Emperor, who was Lord of the whole world, had ordered him to come that he might see the land, and let Atahuallpa know the things of our Faith. . . . The Governor also told him that that land, and all other lands, belonged to the Emperor, and that he must acknowledge him as his Lord. He replied that he was content, and, observing that the Christians had collected some gold, Atahuallpa said to the Governor that they need not take such care of it, as if there was so little; for that he could give them ten thousand plates, and that he could fill the room in which he was up to a white line, which was the height of a man and a half from the floor.

QUESTIONS

- What were the main bases for initial European judgments about the characteristics of Native Americans?
- How might the native peoples have judged the Europeans?
- What motives does Columbus appeal to in trying to interest Spanish rulers in the new land?
- These documents raise obvious problems of interpretation. They interpret interactions with another, very foreign culture from the European standpoint only. They also attribute motives to the adventurers that may or may not have been predominant. Figuring out how to gain useful, valid information from documents of this sort, which are essential in interpreting key developments in world history, is a major challenge. What parts of the accounts seem most reliable, and what criteria can be used to sort out degrees of accuracy?

FIGURE **21.6** British naval power allowed the light infantry to scale the French fort from the St. Lawrence River and capture Quebec in 1759. The battle was a turning point in Canadian history: the beginning of the end of French rule.

However, the American colonies that would become the United States had a population of a mere 3 million, far smaller than the powerful colonies in Latin America. Southern colonies that produced tobacco and sugar, and then cotton, became important. Patterns there were similar to those of Latin America, with large estates based on imported slave labor, a wealthy planter class bent on importing luxury products from western Europe, and weak formal governments. Still, in world historical terms, the Atlantic colonies in North America were of limited value amid the larger colonial holdings staked out in the Early Modern centuries.

Yet European settlers did arrive. Driven by religious dissent, ambition, and other motives, Europeans, many from the British Isles, colonized the Atlantic coastal region, where native populations were quickly reduced by disease and war. The society that developed in the British colonies was far closer to west European forms than was that of Latin America. The colonies operated their own assemblies, which provided the people with political experience. Calvinist and Quaker church assemblies gave governing power to groups of elders or wider congregations. Many colonists thus had reason to share with some west Europeans a sense of the importance of representative institutions and self-government.

Colonists were also avid consumers of political theories written in Europe, such as the parliamentary ideas of John Locke. There was also wide reading and discussion of Enlightenment materials. Institutions such as the 18th-century American Philosophical Society deliberately imitated European scientific institutes, and hundreds of North Americans contributed scientific findings to the British Royal Society. The colonies remained modest in certain cultural attainments. Art was rather primitive, although many stylistic cues came from Europe. There was no question that in formal culture, North American leaders saw themselves as part of a larger Western world.

By the late 18th century, some American merchants were trading with China, their ships picking up medicinal herbs along the Pacific coast and exchanging them for Chinese artifacts and tea. Great Britain tried to impose firmer limits on this modestly thriving local economy after the Seven Years War. It hoped to win greater tax revenues and to guarantee markets for British goods and traders, but the effort came too late and helped encourage rebellion in key colonies. Unusual among the colonies, North America developed a merchant class and some stake in manufacturing in a pattern similar to that taking shape in western Europe itself.

The spread of Western values in the Atlantic colonies and in British and French settlements in Canada was facilitated by the modest impact of Native Americans in these settled areas (Figure 21.7). The native population of this part of North America had always been less dense than in Central America or the Andes region. Because few Native American groups in these regions practiced settled agriculture, instead combining hunting with slash-and-burn corn growing, European colonists found it easy to displace them from large stretches of territory. The ravages of European-imported disease reduced the indigenous population greatly. Many forest peoples were pushed westward. Some abandoned agriculture, turning to a new horse-based hunting economy on the plains (the horse was brought to Mexico by the Spaniards). Many territorial wars further distracted the Native American groups. The net result of these factors was that although European colonists interacted with Native Americans, learned from them, and feared and mistreated them, the colonists did not combine with them to forge new cultural groups like those emerging in much of Latin America.

By 1700, the importation of African slaves proved to be a more important addition to the North American experience, particularly in the southern colonies. The practice of slaveholding and interactions with

FIGURE **21.7** Watercolor by John White (c. 1590) of the Native American settlement of Secoton, Virginia. White was the governor of the pioneer colony of Roanoke, in what is now North Carolina. When he returned from a desperate voyage back to England to obtain supplies, he found the settlement abandoned. Historians have never been able to determine what happened to the men, women, and children of the "Lost Colony."

African culture distinguished North American life from its European counterpart. By the 18th century, 23 percent of the population of the English colonies was of African origin.

North America and Western Civilization

On balance, most white settlers intended to transplant key Western habits into their new setting. For example, family patterns were similar. American colonists were able to marry slightly earlier than ordinary western Europeans because of the greater abundance of land, and they had larger families. Still, they reproduced most features of the European-style family, including the primary emphasis on the nuclear unit. The new Americans did have unusual concern for children, if only because they depended so heavily on their work in a labor-scarce environment. European visitors commented on the child-centeredness of American families and the freedom of children to speak up. These variations, although significant, played on trends also becoming visible in Europe, such as the new emphasis on family affection.

Even when key colonies rebelled against European control, as they did in 1776, they moved in the name of Western political ideas and economic goals against the dependency the British tried to impose. They established a government that responded to the new Western political theories, implementing some key ideas for the first time.

Africa and Asia: Coastal Trading Stations

In Africa, Europeans for the most part contented themselves with small coastal fortresses, negotiating with African kings and merchants but not trying to claim large territories of their own. They sold Asian products, like Indian cotton, and European guns and decorative items in return for slaves. Generally, Europeans were deterred by climate, disease, and non-navigable rivers from trying to reach into the interior. Mostly, they dealt with West African governments and traders. There were two important exceptions. From initial coastal settlements, Portugal sent expeditions into Angola in search of slaves. These expeditions had a more direct and more disruptive impact in this part of southwestern Africa than elsewhere along the Atlantic coast. More important still was the **Cape Colony** planted by the Dutch on the Cape of Good Hope in 1652. The intent was to form another coastal station to supply Dutch ships bound for Asia. But some Dutch farmers were sent, and these **Boers** (the Dutch word for farmers) began to fan out on large farms in a region still lightly populated by Africans. They clashed with local hunting groups, enslaving some of them. Only after 1770 did the expanding Boer settlements directly conflict with Bantu farmers, opening a long battle for control of southern Africa that raged until the late 20th century in the nation of South Africa.

European colonies in Asia were also exceptional. Spain set up an administration for the Philippines and sent active Catholic missionaries. The Dutch East India company administered portions of the main islands of present-day Indonesia and also (for a time) Taiwan, off the China coast.

Colonization in Asia entered a new phase as the British and French began to struggle for control of India, beginning in the late 17th century when the Mughal empire weakened. Even before the Mughals faltered after the death in 1707 of their last great emperor, Aurangzeb, French and British forts dotted the east and west coasts, along with Portuguese Goa. As Mughal inefficiency increased, with a resultant surge of regional states ruled by Indians, portions of the subcontinent became an arena for the growing international rivalry between Britain and France.

The British East India Company had two advantages in this competition. Through negotiation with local princes, it had gained a station at **Calcutta**, which gave it some access to the great wealth of the Ganges valley. Furthermore, the company had enormous influence over the British government and, through Britain's superior navy, excellent communication on the ocean routes. Its French rivals, in contrast, had less political clout at home, where the government often was distracted by European land wars. The French also were more interested in missionary work than the British, for Protestants became deeply committed to colonial missions only in the 19th century. Before then, the British were content to leave Hindu customs alone and devote themselves to commercial profits.

French–British rivalry raged bitterly through the mid-18th century. Both sides recruited Indian princes and troops as allies. Outright warfare erupted in 1744 and then again during the Seven Years War. In 1756, an Indian ruler in Bengal attacked and captured the British base

Cape Colony Dutch colony established at Cape of Good Hope in 1652 initially to provide a coastal station for the Dutch seaborne empire; by 1770 settlements had expanded sufficiently to come into conflict with Bantus.

Boers Dutch settlers in Cape Colony, in southern Africa.

Calcutta Headquarters of British East India Company in Bengal in Indian subcontinent; located on Ganges; captured in 1756 during early part of Seven Years War; later became administrative center for all of Bengal.

FIGURE **21.8** This Indian portrait of two women in European dress illustrates the English influence in 18th-century India.

(V & A Images/Victoria and Albert Museum.)

at Calcutta. In the aftermath of the battle, English prisoners were placed in their own jail, where humidity and overcrowding led to perhaps as many as 120 deaths before Indian officials became aware of their plight and released them. The English used this incident, which they dubbed the "black hole of Calcutta," to rally their forces. The East India Company's army recaptured Calcutta and then seized additional Indian and French territory, aided by abundant bribes to many regional princes. French power in India was destroyed, and the East India Company took over administration of the Bengal region, which stretched inland from Calcutta. Soon after this, the British also gained the island of Ceylon (Sri Lanka) from the Dutch.

The full history of British India did not begin until late in the 18th century, when the British government took a more active hand in Indian administration, supplementing the unofficial government of the East India Company (Figure 21.8). Indeed, British control of the subcontinent was incomplete. The Mughal empire remained, although it was increasingly weak and it controlled scant territory, as did other regional kingdoms, including the Sikh state. Britain gained some new territories by force but was also content to form alliances with local princes without disturbing their internal administration.

In most colonies, European administration long remained fairly loose. Few settlers arrived, except in south Africa and the Americas. Outside the Americas, cultural impositions were slight. Missionary activity won many converts in the Philippines but not elsewhere in Asia or in Africa at this point. The main impact of colonies supplemented the more general development of the world economy: Colonial administrations pressed for economic advantage for the home country by opening markets and prompting commercial production of cheap foods and raw materials. Here, of course, the consequences to colonial peoples were very real.

Impact on Western Europe

Western Europe was hugely affected by its own colonial success, not only economically but also diplomatically. Colonial rivalries and wars added to the existing hostilities between key nation-states. England and Holland early turned against Spanish success, with great effect. The Dutch and the English competed, engaging in many skirmishes in the 17th century. Then attention turned to the growing competition between the British and the French. This contest had extensive geographic scope: the Seven Years War (1756–1763), fought in Europe, India, and North America, has been called the first world war.

There were also less obvious but equally dramatic effects on European society, including daily life. For example, from the mid-17th century onward, the use of colonially produced sugar spread widely. Previously, sugar had been a costly, upper-class item. Now for the first time (salt had been the one previous exception), a basic product available to ordinary people was being traded over long distances. The spread of sugar had cultural as well as social and economic significance in giving ordinary Europeans the ability to obtain pleasurable sensations in quick doses—an interesting foreshadowing of later features of Western consumer behavior. It also promoted a growing role for dentists by the 18th century.

More broadly, the profits Europeans brought in from world trade, including the African slave trade, added wealth and capital. Many Europeans turned to manufacturing operations, as owners and workers, partly because of opportunities for export in world trade. These developments enhanced Europe's commercial character, while reducing dependence on agriculture alone. They provided additional tax revenues for growing governments and their military ambitions.

The Impact of a New World Order

The development of the world economy and European colonialism had immense impact. The range of unfree labor systems to supply goods for world trade became more widespread than ever before. Slavery and serfdom deeply affected Latin America and eastern Europe, while the slave trade disrupted west Africa, and millions of individual lives as well.

Yet the world economy brought benefits as well as hardships, quite apart from the profits to Europe. New foods and wider trade patterns helped some societies deal with scarcity. Individual merchants and landowners gained new wealth virtually everywhere. China prospered from the imports of silver, although rapid population growth limited gains overall. The mixture of profits and compulsion brought more and more people and regions into the world economy network.

Global Connections and Critical Themes

THE WORLD ECONOMY—AND THE WORLD

Buoyed by its growing role in the world, western Europe unquestionably saw its economy and military power increase more rapidly than those of any other society during the Early Modern period. As the next chapter shows, Europe changed internally as well, often in dramatic ways. Because of these facts, it is tempting to see the Early Modern centuries as a European drama in which other regions either played supporting roles or watched in awe.

Yet the relationships to the world economy were in fact quite complex. They ranged from conscious isolation to controlled participation to undeniable dependency. Many societies retained vibrant political systems and internal economies. Some, although attracted to certain western features, wanted to stand apart from the values and institutions that world economic success seemed to involve.

Even societies that had changes thrust upon them, like Latin America, were hardly passive. Pressed by missionaries, Latin Americans did not simply adopt European-style Christianity, but rather blended in traditional beliefs and practices and many distinctive artistic forms. The world was growing closer, but it was not necessarily becoming simpler.

Further Readings

Excellent discussions of Western exploration and expansion are found in Kenneth Pomeranz and Steven Topik, *The World that Trade Created: Society, Culture, and the World Economy, 1400 to the Present* (2006); Carlo Cipolla, *Guns, Sails, and Empires: Technological Innovation and the Early Phases of European Expansion 1400–1700* (1997); J. H. Parry, *The Age of Reconnaissance* (1982); Richard S. Dunn, *Sugar and Slaves: The Rise of the Planter Class in the English West Indies, 1624–1713* (1972); and D. Boorstin, *The Discoverers* (1991). Other works include Alan K. Smith, *Creating a World Economy: Merchant Capital, Colonialism, and World Trade 1460–1825* (1991); and James Tracy, ed., *The Rise of Merchant Empires* (1986) and *The Political Economy of Merchant Empires* (1991). Somewhat more specific facets are treated in B. Bailyn and P. L. Denault, *Soundings in Atlantic History: Latent Structures and Intellectual Currents* (2009); Warren R. Hofstra, ed., *Cultures in Conflict: The Seven Years' War in North America* (2007); Daniel P. Barr, ed., *The Boundaries Between Us: Natives and Newcomers along the Frontiers of the Old Northwest Territory* (2006); Robert Ross, *Status and Respectability in the Cape Colony, 1750–1870: A Tragedy of Manners* (1999); Joseph E. Inikori, *Africans and the Industrial Revolution in England: A Study in International Trade and Economic Development* (2002); J. H. Parry, *The Discovery of South America* (1979); and S. Subrahmanyam, *The Portuguese Empire in Asia, 1500–1700* (1993). A vital treatment of the international results of new trading patterns of foods and disease is Alfred Crosby, *The Columbian Exchange: Biological and Cultural Consequences of 1492* (1972); see also Elinor G. Melville, *A Plague of Sheep: Environmental Consequences of the Conquest of Mexico* (1994). For a stimulating re-emphasis on Asia, see Andre Gunder Frank, *ReOrient: Global Economy in the Asian Age* (1998). See also Stephen Mosley, *Environment in World History* (2010).

On slavery and its trade, see Pamela Scully and Diana Paton, eds., *Gender and Slave Emancipation in the Atlantic World* (2005); H. S. Klein, *The Atlantic Slave Trade* (2010); Eric Williams, *Capitalism and Slavery* (1964); Orlando Patterson, *Slavery and Social Death: A Comparative Study* (1982); and D. B. Davis, *Slavery and Human Progress* (1984); the last two are important comparative and analytical statements in a major field of recent historical study. See also Philip D. Curtin, *Atlantic Slave Trade* (1972), and his edited volume, *Africa Remembered: Narratives by West Africans from the Era of the Slave Trade* (1967). A good recent survey of developments in Africa and in the period is Paul Bohannan and Philip Curtin, *Africa and Africans* (1988).

New world trading patterns, including Asia's role in them, are discussed in K. N. Chaundhuri, *Trade and Civilization in the Indian Ocean* (1985); Stephan Frederic Dale, *Indian Merchants and*

Eurasia Trade: 1600–1750 (1994); Scott Levi, *The Indian Diaspora in Central Asia and Its Trade 1550–1900* (2002); and S. Volmer, *Planting a New World: Letters and Languages of Transatlantic Botanical Exchange* (2008). A controversial theoretical statement about new trade relationships and their impact on politics and social structure is found in Immanuel Wallerstein, *The Modern World System: Capitalist Agriculture and the Origins of the European World Economy in the Sixteenth Century* (1974), and *The Modern World System: Mercantilism and the Consolidation of the European World*

Economy 1600–1750 (1980); see also his *Politics of the World Economy: The States, the Movements, and the Civilizations* (1984).

For discussions on where colonial North America fits in this period of world history, see Colin G. Calloway, *The Scratch of a Pen: 1763 and the Transformation of North America* (2006); Jack Greene and J. R. Pole, eds., *Colonial British America: Essays on the New History of the Early Modern Era* (1984); William J. Eccles, *France in America*, rev. ed. (1990); and Gary Nash, *Red, White, and Black: The Peoples of Early America*, rev. ed. (1982).

On MyHistoryLab

 Study and Review on MyHistoryLab

Critical Questions

1. Compare the Asian and the west European roles in the world economy that developed in the Early Modern period.

2. Did the Early Modern period see distinctive changes in human-environment interaction, or were only minor shifts involved?

3. What was the role of technological change in causing major developments during the Early Modern period?

4. Were the European settlements in North America an extension of Western civilization during the Early Modern period, or should they be seen as launching a new civilization pattern?

The Transformation of the West, 1450–1750

((• Listen to **Chapter 22**
on **MyHistoryLab**

Throughout the early modern period, Europe's growing involvement in world trade had important impacts on internal developments—on the economy, obviously, but also on government policy and even personal taste. A case in point involved the implications of brightly colored cotton cloth.

Cotton manufacturing had long been a specialty in India. Cheaper than silks, cotton fabrics could sport vivid dyes and designs. Indian cotton products had sold extensively in world trade during the postclassical period, reaching East Asia, the Middle East and, more tentatively, Europe. With Europe's new connections to India after 1498, availability of cottons, and consumer passion, both increased rapidly.

FIGURE **22.1** This tapestry with a Tree of Life design from India dates from the early 18th century. This particular design is on cotton, but it shows the colors and artistry that made Indian fabrics such a popular global commodity in the postclassical and Early Modern periods.

👁 Watch the Video Series on MyHistoryLab

Learn about some key topics related to this chapter with the *MyHistoryLab Video Series:*
Key Topics in World History

The contrast with conventional linen and woolen fabrics, with characteristically dull colors, was marked. One European traveler to India wrote ecstatically of "cloths of the whiteness of snow, and very delicate and fine" with other fabrics "bespangled and painted with various figures." Europeans were particularly taken with floral designs, and Indian manufacturers began to target part of their production specifically for the European market. Here was one of several examples where rising levels of global trade spurred new consumer tastes, allowing new levels of personal expression through clothing. By the 17th century another observer noted that "in some things the artists of India out-do all the ingenuity of Europe" as in cotton textiles, which Europeans could not match "in their brightness and life of colour."

Portuguese traders were the first to bring cottons directly to Europe, with peddlers taking them to more northern markets. By the 17th century Danish merchants and others were traveling direct to India to seek decorative textiles for homes as well as clothing.

Royal officials in several countries worried about the impact of Indian imports on domestic production and domestic profits. There was also some chiding by moral conservatives about this kind of showy display. By the later 17th century many governments passed rules against wearing brightly colored clothing, while even more laws tried to protect European industry by banning Indian textile imports.

By this point also, however, European manufacturers themselves were beginning to wonder if they could take advantage of consumer tastes directly. In southern France, several Armenian workmen brought in new techniques in partnership with local businessmen around 1650, and Armenians also helped set up production in Amsterdam. By 1750 a factory in Switzerland, although using manual operations, employed over 1300 workers. Only by this point were European methods adequate to match the best Indian colors and designs.

By the later 18th century, dramatic new printing processes, including use of a rotary press, moved European cottons directly into the industrial revolution. By this time as well, European consumers, now seeing access to colorful cottons as a routine need, became ever more demanding of dramatic new styles each year, indulging a taste for novelty that was built into modern consumerism. What began as a deferential contact with Asia turned into an engine for European change. ■

This chapter deals with a series of big changes in western Europe between 1450 and 1750. The specific new movements were diverse, but over the three centuries' span they added up to a novel cultural framework for intellectuals but also many ordinary people, some key political innovations, and a more commercially based social structure. In considering particular developments, it is vital to keep the larger ultimate directions of change in mind: What were the main ways western Europe in 1750 differed from western Europe in 1450? It's also important to remember that the developments occurred in a context of growing interaction with other parts of the world—even in areas as prosaic as new preferences for clothing.

During the Early Modern period major changes occurred in Europe's economy and culture, along with significant shifts in politics. Some innovations—like the idea of a nation-state or the scientific revolution—would later have global impacts. At the same time, it is important not to overdo European

1300 C.E.	1450 C.E.	1500 C.E.	1550 C.E.	1650 C.E.	1750 C.E.
1300–1450 Italian Renaissance	**1450–1519** Life of Leonardo da Vinci **1450–1600** Northern Renaissance **1455** First European printing press, Mainz, Germany **1475–1514** Life of Michelangelo **1490**s France and Spain invade Italian city-states; beginning of Italian decline	**1500–1600** Commercial revolution **1515–1547** Reign of Francis I, France **1517** Luther's 95 theses; beginning of Protestant Reformation **1534** Beginning of Church of England **1541–1564** Calvin in Geneva **1543** Copernican revolution; Copernicus's work on astronomy	**1550–1649** Religious wars in France, Germany, and Britain **1555–1603** Reign of Elizabeth I, England **1564–1642** Life of Galileo **1588** English defeat the Spanish Armada **17th century** Scientific Revolution **1609** Independence of Netherlands **1618–1648** Thirty Years War **1642–1649** English Civil War **1642–1727** Life of Isaac Newton **1643–1715** Reign of Louis XIV, France; absolute monarchy **1647–1648** Culmination of popular rebellions in western Europe	**1670–1692** Decline of witchcraft trials **1682–1699** Habsburgs drive Turks from Hungary **1688–1690** Glorious Revolution in Britain; parliamentary monarchy; some religious toleration; political writing of John Locke **18th century** Enlightenment **1712–1786** Life of Frederick the Great of Prussia, enlightened despot **1730–1850** European population boom **1733** James Kay invents flying shuttle loom **1736** Beginnings of Methodism	**1756–1763** Seven Years War: France, Britain, Prussia, and Austria **1776** Adam Smith's *Wealth of Nations* **1780–1790** Reign of Joseph II, first Habsburg emperor **1792** Mary Wollstonecraft's *Vindication of the Rights of Women*

dynamism. There were no fundamental changes, for example, in agriculture, at least until the final decades of the period, and agriculture remained basic. Furthermore, some changes saw Europe mainly catching up to achievements that many other societies had already established; not everything was really new or different, from a global perspective.

THE FIRST BIG CHANGES: CULTURE AND COMMERCE, 1450–1650

22.1   What was the relationship between the Renaissance and the Reformation as forces for cultural change?

> The Renaissance emphasized new styles and beliefs. Religious changes springing from the Protestant Reformation had an even wider impact.

The Italian writer Francesco Petrarch (1304–1374) once climbed Ventoux, a mountain in southern France. He wrote of his ascent, proud of his own skill and using the climb as a symbol of what he could achieve. There was a new spirit of individual pride expressed in this work, intended to be published, compared to the more humble and religious sentiments of the Middle Ages when individual artisans did not even put their names on the magnificent cathedrals they built. But Petrarch did not abandon religion, and in later life he talked about how he had given up poetry in favor of reading Christian texts, finding "hidden sweetness which I had once esteemed but lightly."

The Italian Renaissance

The move away from earlier European patterns began with the Renaissance, which first developed in Italy during the 14th and 15th centuries. Largely an artistic movement, the Renaissance challenged medieval intellectual values and styles. It also sketched a new, brasher spirit that may have encouraged a new Western interest in exploring strange waters or urging that old truths be re-examined.

Machiavelli, Niccolo [mak EE uh vel EE] (1469–1527) Author of *The Prince* (16th century); emphasized realistic discussions of how to seize and maintain power; one of most influential authors of Italian Renaissance.

 Read the **Document** on **MyHistoryLab:** The Prince (1519) Machiavelli

humanism Focus on humankind as center of intellectual and artistic endeavor; method of study that emphasized the superiority of classical forms over medieval styles, in particular the study of ancient languages.

 View the **Closer Look** on **MyHistoryLab:** Humanism and Renaissance Art

Northern Renaissance Cultural and intellectual movement of northern Europe; began later than Italian Renaissance (c. 1450); centered in France, Low Countries, England, and Germany; featured greater emphasis on religion than Italian Renaissance.

Francis I King of France in the 16th century; regarded as Renaissance monarch; patron of arts; imposed new controls on Catholic church; ally of Ottoman sultan against Holy Roman emperor.

Italy was already well launched in the development of Renaissance culture by the 15th century, based on its unusually extensive urban, commercial economy and its competitive city-state politics. Writers such as Petrarch and Boccaccio had promoted classical literary canons against medieval logic and theology, writing in Italian as well as the traditional Latin and emphasizing secular subjects such as love and pride. Painting turned to new realism and classical and human-centered themes. Religion declined as a central focus. The Italian Renaissance blossomed further in the 15th and early 16th centuries. This was a great age of Western art, as Leonardo da Vinci advanced the realistic portrayal of the human body and Michelangelo applied classical styles in painting and sculpture. In political theory, **Niccolo Machiavelli** emphasized realistic discussions of how to seize and maintain power. Like the artists, Machiavelli bolstered his realism with Greek and Roman examples.

Overall, Italian Renaissance culture stressed themes of **humanism**: a focus on humankind as the center of intellectual and artistic endeavor, as Francesco Petrarch's interests suggested. Religion was not attacked, but its principles were no longer predominant. Historians have debated the reasons for this change. Italy's more urban, commercial environment was one factor, but so was the new imitation of classical Greek and Roman literature and art.

These Renaissance themes had some bearing on politics and commerce. Renaissance merchants improved their banking techniques and became more openly profit-seeking than their medieval counterparts had been. City-state leaders experimented with new political forms and functions. They justified their rule not on the basis of heredity or divine guidance but more on the basis of what they could do to advance general well-being and their city's glory. Thus, they sponsored cultural activities, as states began to use art to gain greater popular support. They also tried to improve the administration of the economy. Resistance leaders developed more professional armies, for wars among the city-states were common, and gave new attention to military tactics and training. They also rethought the practice of diplomacy, introducing the regular exchange of ambassadors for the first time in the West. Clearly, the Renaissance encouraged innovation, although it also produced some dependence on classical models.

The Renaissance Moves Northward

Italy began to decline as a Renaissance center by about 1500. French and Spanish monarchs invaded the peninsula, reducing political independence. At the same time, new Atlantic trade routes reduced the importance of Mediterranean ports, a huge blow to the Italian economy.

As Renaissance creativity faded in its Italian birthplace, it passed northward. The **Northern Renaissance**—focused in France, the Low Countries, Germany, and England—began after 1450. Renaissance styles also affected Hungary and Poland in east central Europe. Classical styles in art and architecture became the rage. Knowledge of Greek and Latin literature gained ground, although many northern humanists wrote in their own languages (English, French, and so on). Northern humanists were more religious than their Italian counterparts, trying to blend secular interests with continued Christian devotion. Renaissance writers such as Shakespeare in England and Rabelais in France mixed classical themes with an earthiness—a joy in bodily functions and human passions—that maintained elements of medieval popular culture. Renaissance literature established a new set of classics for literary traditions in the major Western languages, such as the writings of Shakespeare in England and Cervantes in Spain.

The Northern Renaissance produced some political change, providing another move toward greater state powers. As their revenues and operations expanded, Renaissance kings increased their pomp and ceremony. Kings such as **Francis I** in France became patrons of the arts, importing Italian sculptors and architects to create their classical-style palaces. By the late 16th century, many monarchs were sponsoring trading companies and colonial enterprises. Interest in military conquest was greater than in the Middle Ages. Francis I was even willing to ally with the Ottoman sultan, the key Muslim leader. His goal was to distract his main enemy, the Habsburg ruler of Austria and Spain. In fact, it was an alliance in name only, but it illustrated how power politics was beginning to abandon the feudal or religious justifications that had previously clothed it in the West.

Yet the impact of the Renaissance should not be overstated, particularly outside Italy. Renaissance kings were still confined by the political powers of feudal landlords. Ordinary people were little touched by Renaissance values; the life of most peasants and artisans went on much as before. Economic life also changed little, particularly outside the Italian commercial centers. Even in the upper classes, women sometimes encountered new limits as Renaissance leaders touted men's public bravado over women's domestic roles.

Changes in Technology and Family

More fundamental changes were brewing in Western society by 1500, beneath the glittering surface of the Renaissance. Spurred by trading contacts with Asia, workers in the West improved the quality of pulleys and pumps in mines and learned how to forge stronger iron products. Printing was introduced in the 15th century when the German **Johannes Gutenberg** and other inventors introduced movable type, building on Chinese printing technology. Soon books were distributed in greater quantities in the West, which helped expand the audience for Renaissance writers and disseminated religious ideas. Literacy began to gain ground and became a fertile source of new kinds of thinking.

Family structure was also changing. A **European-style family** pattern came into being by the 15th century in the western part of the continent. This pattern involved a late marriage age and a primary emphasis on nuclear families of parents and children rather than the extended families characteristic of most agricultural civilizations. The goal was to limit family birth rates. By the 16th century, ordinary people usually did not marry until their late 20s—a marked contrast to most agricultural societies. These changes emphasized the importance of husband–wife relations. They also closely linked the family to individual property holdings, for most people could not marry until they had access to property.

The Protestant and Catholic Reformations

In the 16th century, religious upheaval and a new commercial surge began to define the directions of change more fully. In 1517, a German monk named **Martin Luther** issued a document containing 95 theses, or propositions. He was publicly protesting claims made by a papal representative in selling indulgences, or grants of salvation, for money, but in fact his protest went deeper. Luther's reading of the Bible convinced him that only faith could gain salvation. Church sacraments were not the path, for God could not be manipulated. Luther's protest, which was rebuffed by the papacy, soon led him to challenge many Catholic beliefs, including the authority of the pope. Luther would soon argue that monasticism was wrong, that priests should marry (as he did), and that the Bible should be translated from Latin so ordinary people could have direct access to its teachings. Luther did not want to break Christian unity, but the church he wanted should be on his terms (or, as he would have argued, the terms of the true faith).

Luther picked up wide support for his views during the mid-16th century and beyond. Many Germans, in a somewhat nationalist reaction, resented the authority and taxes of the Roman pope. German princes saw an opportunity to gain more power. Their nominal leader, the Holy Roman emperor, remained Catholic. Thus, princes who turned Protestant could increase their independence and seize church lands. The Lutheran version of **Protestantism** (as the general wave of religious dissent was called) urged state control of the church as an alternative to papal authority, and this had obvious political appeal.

There were reasons for ordinary people to shift their allegiance as well. Some German peasants saw Luther's attack on authority as a sanction for their own social rebellion against landlords, although Luther specifically renounced this reading. Some townspeople were drawn to Luther's approval of work in the world. Because faith alone gained salvation, Lutheranism could sanction moneymaking and other earthly pursuits more wholeheartedly than did traditional Catholicism. Unlike Catholicism, Lutherans did not see special vocations as particularly holy; monasteries were abolished, along with some of the Christian bias against moneymaking.

Once Christian unity was breached, other Protestant groups sprang forward (see Map 22.1). In England, Henry VIII began to set up an **Anglican church**, initially to challenge papal attempts to enforce his first marriage, which had failed to produce a male heir. (Henry ultimately had six wives in sequence, executing two of them, a particularly graphic example of the treatment of women in power politics.) Henry was also attracted to some of the new doctrines, and his most durable successor, his daughter Elizabeth I, was Protestant outright.

Still more important were the churches inspired by **Jean Calvin**, a French theologian who established his base in the Swiss city of Geneva. Calvinism insisted on God's *predestination*, or prior determination, of those who would be saved. Calvinist ministers became moral guardians and preachers of God's word. Calvinists sought the participation of all believers in local church administration, which promoted the idea of a wider access to government. They also promoted broader popular education so that more people could read the Bible. Calvinism was accepted not only in part of Switzerland but also in portions of Germany, in France (where it produced strong

Gutenberg, Johannes Introduced movable type to western Europe in 15th century; credited with greatly expanded availability of printed books and pamphlets.

 View the Closer Look on **MyHistoryLab:** A Renaissance Printing Press

European-style family Originated in 15th century among peasants and artisans of western Europe, featuring late marriage age, emphasis on the nuclear family, and a large minority who never married.

Luther, Martin (1483–1546) German monk; initiated Protestant Reformation in 1517 by nailing 95 theses to door of Wittenberg church; emphasized primacy of faith over works stressed in Catholic church; accepted state control of church.

 Read the Document on MyHistoryLab: Martin Luther's "Ninety-Five Theses," 1517

Protestantism General wave of religious dissent against Catholic church; generally held to have begun with Martin Luther's attack on Catholic beliefs in 1517; included many varieties of religious belief.

Anglican church Form of Protestantism set up in England after 1534; established by Henry VIII with himself as head, at least in part to obtain a divorce from his first wife; became increasingly Protestant following Henry's death.

Calvin, Jean French Protestant (16th century) who stressed doctrine of predestination; established center of his group at Swiss canton of Geneva; encouraged ideas of wider access to government, wider public education; Calvinism spread from Switzerland to northern Europe and North America.

Read the Document on MyHistoryLab: Calvin on Predestination (16th c.)

MAP **22.1 Western Europe During the Renaissance and Reformation** Different Protestant denominations made inroads in much of northwestern Europe with the Reformation, but Catholicism maintained its hold on significant portions of the continent.

Catholic Reformation Restatement of traditional Catholic beliefs in response to Protestant Reformation (16th century); established councils that revived Catholic doctrine and refuted Protestant beliefs.

Jesuits A new religious order founded during the Catholic Reformation; active in politics, education, and missionary work; sponsored missions to South America, North American, and Asia.

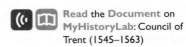

Read the Document on MyHistoryLab: Council of Trent (1545–1563)

Edict of Nantes Grant of tolerance to Protestants in France in 1598; granted only after lengthy civil war between Catholic and Protestant factions.

minority groups), in the Netherlands, in Hungary, and in England and Scotland. By the early 17th century, Puritan exiles brought it to North America.

The Catholic church did not sit still under Protestant attack. It could not restore religious unity, but it defended southern Europe, Austria, Poland, much of Hungary, and key parts of Germany for the Catholic faith. Under a **Catholic Reformation**, a major church council revived Catholic doctrine and refuted key Protestant tenets such as the idea that priests had no special sacramental power and could marry. They also attacked popular superstitions and remnants of magical belief, which meant that Catholics and Protestants alike were trying to find new ways to shape the outlook of ordinary folk. A new religious order, the **Jesuits**, became active in politics, education, and missionary work, regaining some parts of Europe for the church. Jesuit fervor also sponsored Catholic missionary activity in Asia and the Americas.

The End of Christian Unity in the West

The Protestant and Catholic Reformations had several results in Europe during the late 16th and early 17th centuries. Most obvious was an important series of bloody religious wars. France was a scene of bitter battles between Calvinist and Catholic forces. These disputes ended only with the granting of tolerance to Protestants through the **Edict of Nantes** in 1598, although in the next century French kings progressively cut back on Protestant rights. In Germany, the **Thirty Years War** broke out in 1618, pitting German Protestants and allies such as Lutheran Sweden against the Holy Roman emperor, backed by Spain. The war was so devastating that it reduced German power and prosperity for a full century, cutting population by as much as 60 percent in some regions. It was ended only by the 1648 **Treaty of Westphalia**, which agreed to the territorial tolerance concept: Some princely states and cities chose one religion, some another. This treaty also finally settled a rebellion of the Protestant Netherlands against Spain, giving the former its full independence.

Religious fighting punctuated British history, first before the reign of Elizabeth in the 16th century, then in the **English Civil War** in the 1640s. Calvinists, Anglicans, and some remaining Catholics locked in combat. There was also growing tension between the claims of parliament and some strong assertions of authority by a new line of English kings. The civil war ended in 1660 (well after King Charles I had been beheaded; Figure 22.2), but full resolution came only in 1688–1689, when limited religious toleration was granted to most Protestants, although not to Catholics.

Religious issues thus dominated European politics for almost a century. The religious wars led to a grudging and limited acceptance of the idea of religious pluralism. Christian unity could not be restored, although in most individual countries the idea of full religious liberty was still in the future. The religious wars persuaded some people that religion itself was suspect; if there was no dominant single truth, why all the cruelty and carnage? Finally, the wars affected the political balance of Europe, as Map 22.2 shows. After a period of weakness during its internal strife, France was on the upswing. The Netherlands and Britain were galvanized toward a growing international role. Spain, briefly ascendant, fell back. Internally, some kings and princes benefited from the decline of papal authority by taking a stronger role in religious affairs. This was true in many Catholic and Protestant domains. In some cases, however, Protestant dissent encouraged popular political movements and enhanced parliamentary power.

The impact of religious change went well beyond politics. Popular beliefs changed most in Protestant areas, but Catholic reform produced new impulses as well. Western people gradually became less likely to see an intimate connection between God and nature. Protestants resisted the idea of miracles or other interventions in nature's course. Religious change also promoted greater concentration on family life. Religious writers encouraged love between husband and wife. As one English Protestant put it, "When love is absent between husband and wife, it is like a bone out of joint: there is no ease, no order." This promotion of the family had ambiguous implications for women. Protestantism, abolishing religious convents, made marriage more necessary for women than before;

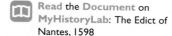

Read the Document on MyHistoryLab: The Edict of Nantes, 1598

Thirty Years War War within the Holy Roman Empire between German Protestants and their allies (Sweden, Denmark, France) and the emperor and his ally, Spain; ended in 1648 after great destruction with Treaty of Westphalia.

Treaty of Westphalia Ended Thirty Years War in 1648; granted right to individual rulers within the Holy Roman empire to choose their own religion—either Protestant or Catholic.

English Civil War Conflict from 1640 to 1660; featured religious disputes mixed with constitutional issues concerning the powers of the monarchy; ended with restoration of the monarchy in 1660 following execution of previous king.

FIGURE **22.2** Civil war over religious issues and the relative power of king and parliament resulted in the beheading of Charles I in London in 1649. As this painting suggests, the regicide was one of the most controversial events in English history.

MAP **22.2 Europe Under Absolute Monarchy, 1715** The rise of absolute monarchies led to consolidation of national borders as states asserted full control of areas within their boundaries. For example, a recent study shows that villages that straddled the French–Spanish border were undifferentiated before 1600, but by 1700 they showed marked national differences because of different state policies and the greater impact of belonging to one state or another.

there were fewer alternatives for women who could not marry. Fathers were also responsible for the religious training of the children. On the other hand, women's emotional role in the family improved with the new emphasis on affection.

Religious change accompanied and promoted growing literacy along with the spread of the printing press. In the town of Durham, England, around 1570, only 20 percent of all people were literate, but by 1630 the figure had climbed to 47 percent. Growing literacy opened people to additional new ideas and ways of thinking.

Overall, the European Reformation was a fascinating case where long-run consequences did not coincide entirely with the intentions of early leaders, or with initial, short-term change. This was a very different development from the Renaissance, but ultimately, by the 17th century, the two movements could combine to an extent in their effects on politics or culture.

THE COMMERCIAL REVOLUTION

Trade and manufacturing expanded rapidly. A more commercial economy also spurred protest.

22.2   How did Europe's commercial revolution affect social structure?

Along with religious upheaval during the 16th century, the economic structure of the West was fundamentally redefined. The level of European trade rose sharply, and many Europeans had new goods available to them. Involvement with markets and merchants increased. Here was the clearest impact of the new world economy in western Europe.

The Impact of the World Economy

A basic spur to greater commercialization was the price inflation that occurred throughout western Europe during the 16th century. The massive import of gold and silver from Spain's new colonies in Latin America forced prices up. The availability of more money, based on silver supply, generated this price rise. New wealth heightened demand for products to sell, both in the colonies and in Europe, but western production could not keep pace, hence the price inflation. Inflation encouraged merchants to take new risks, for borrowing was cheap when money was losing value. A sum borrowed one year would be worth less, in real terms, five years later, so it made sense to take loans for new investments.

Inflation and the new colonial opportunities led to the formation of the great trading companies, often with government backing, in Spain, England, the Netherlands, and France. Governments granted regional monopolies to these giant concerns; thus, the Dutch East India Company long dominated trade with the islands of Indonesia. European merchants brought new profits back to Europe and developed new managerial skills and banking arrangements.

Colonial markets stimulated manufacturing. Most peasants continued to produce mainly for their own needs, but agricultural specialty areas developed in the production of wines, cheeses, wool, and the like. Some of these industries favored commercial farming and the use of paid laborers on the land. Shoemaking, pottery, metalworking, and other manufacturing specializations arose in both rural villages and the cities. Technical improvements followed in many branches of manufacture, particularly in metals and mining.

Prosperity increased for many ordinary people as well as for the great merchants. One historian has estimated that by about 1600 the average Western peasant or artisan owned five times as many "things" as his or her counterpart in southeastern Europe. A 16th-century Englishman noted that whereas in the past a peasant and his family slept on the floor and had only a pan or two as kitchenware, by the final decades of the century a farmer might have "a fair garnish of pewter in his cupboard, three or four feather beds, so many coverlets and carpets of tapestry, a silver salt, a bowl for wine . . . and a dozen spoons." It was about this time that French peasants began to enjoy wine fairly regularly rather than simply at special occasions—the result of higher productivity and better trade and transport facilities.

Social Protest

There were victims of change as well. Growing commercialization created the beginnings of a new **proletariat** in the West—people without access to wealth-producing property. Population growth and rising food prices hit hard at the poor, and many people had to sell their small plots of land. Some proletarians became manufacturing workers, depending on orders from merchant capitalists to keep their tools busy in their cottages. Others became paid laborers on agricultural estates, where landlords were eager for a more manipulable workforce to take advantage of business opportunities in the cities. Others pressed into the cities, and a growing problem of beggars and wandering poor began to affect Western society (Map 22.3). By blaming the poor for moral failings, a new, tough attitude toward poverty took shape that has lasted to some extent to the present day.

Not surprisingly, the shifts in popular economic and cultural traditions provoked important outcries. A huge wave of popular protest in western Europe developed at the end of the 16th century and extended until about 1650. Peasants and townspeople alike rose for greater protection from poverty and loss of property. The uprisings did not deflect the basic currents of change, but they revealed the massive insecurity of many workers.

The popular rebellions of the 17th century revealed social tension and new ideas of equality. Peasant songs voiced such sentiments as this: "The whole country must be overturned, for we peasants are now to be the lords, it is we who will sit in the shade." Uprisings in 1648 produced demands for a popular political voice; an English group called the Levelers gained 100,000 signatures on a petition for political rights. Elsewhere, common people praised the kings while attacking their "bad advisors" and high taxes. One English agitator said that "we should cut off all the gentlemen's heads. . . . We

proletariat Class of working people without access to producing property; typically manufacturing workers, paid laborers in agricultural economy, or urban poor; in Europe, product of economic changes of 16th and 17th centuries.

People per square mile:
- Over 60
- 30 to 60
- 10 to 30
- Under 10

MAP **22.3 European Population Density, c. 1600** Europe experienced new levels of population concentration in some urban areas by 1600, although by Asian standards, city size remained fairly modest.

shall have a merrier world shortly." In France, Protestant and Catholic peasants rose together against landlords and taxes: "They seek only the ruin of the poor people for our ruin is their wealth."

An unprecedented outburst against suspected witches arose in the same decades in various parts of western Europe and also in New England. Although attacks on witches had developed before, the new scale reflected intense social and cultural upheaval. Between 60,000 and 100,000 suspected witches were accused and killed. The **witchcraft persecution** reflected new resentments against the poor, who were often accused of witchcraft by communities unwilling to accept responsibility for their poverty. The hysteria also revealed new tensions about family life and the role of women, who were the most common targets of persecution. A few of the accused witches actually believed they had magical powers, but far more were accused by fearful or self-serving neighbors. The whole witchcraft experience revealed a society faced with forces of unusual complexity.

witchcraft persecution Reflected resentment against the poor, uncertainties about religious truth; resulted in death of over 100,000 Europeans between 1590 and 1650; particularly common in Protestant areas.

A Balance Sheet

Changes in Europe between 1450 and 1650 were untidy. Renaissance secular interests clashed with Reformation spiritual emphases. The confusion of change helped explain sharp reactions, like the witchcraft trials. Still, there were some basic directions to change. Europe was becoming more commercial; even some of the implications of the Reformation pushed toward higher valuation of commercial success. The role of families was shifting. Religion remained strong, but its expressions and its political roles became more contested. All of this finally set the stage for further change.

THE SCIENTIFIC REVOLUTION: THE NEXT PHASE OF CHANGE

22.3   What were the most innovative features of Western science?

The revolution in science, culminating in the 17th century, set the seal on the cultural reorientation of the West. Although the **Scientific Revolution** most obviously affected formal intellectual life, it also promoted changes in popular outlook. At the same time, after the political upheavals of the Reformation, a more decisive set of new government forms arose in the West, centering on the emergence of the nation-state. The functions of the state expanded. The Western nation-state was not a single form, because key variants such as absolute monarchies and parliamentary regimes emerged, but there were some common patterns beneath the surface.

Did Copernicus Copy?

This is a chapter about big changes in western Europe during the early modern period. Big changes are always complex. One key development was the rise of science in intellectual life. A key first step here was the discovery by the Polish monk **Nicolaus Copernicus**, in the 16th century, that the planets moved around the sun rather than the earth, as the Greeks had thought. This discovery set other scientific advances in motion, and more generally showed that new thinking could improve on tradition. Copernicus is usually taken as a quiet hero of western science and rationalism.

Copernicus based his findings on mathematics, understanding that the Greek view of earth as central raised key problems in calculating planetary motion. Historians have recently uncovered similar geometrical findings by two Arabs, al-Urdi and al-Tusi, from the 13th and 14th centuries. Did Copernicus copy, as Westerners had previously done from the Arabs, while keeping quiet because learning from Muslims was now unpopular? Or did he discover independently? It's also worth noting that scientists in other traditions, such as Chinese, Indian, and Mayan, had already realized the central position of the sun.

What is certain is that based on discoveries like that of Copernicus, science began to take on more importance in Western intellectual life than had ever been the case in the intellectual history of other societies, including classical Greece. Change may be complicated but it does occur.

Science: The New Authority

During the 16th century, scientific research quietly built on the traditions of the later Middle Ages. After Copernicus, **Johannes Kepler** (1571–1630; Figure 22.3) was another important early figure in the study of planetary motion. Unusual for a major researcher, Kepler was from a poor family; his father abandoned the family outright, and his mother was once tried for witchcraft. But Kepler made his way to university on scholarship, aiming for the Lutheran ministry, but he was drawn to astronomy and mathematics. Using the work of Copernicus and his own observations, he resolved basic issues of planetary motion. He also worked on optics and, with the mixed interests so common in real intellectual life, also practiced astrology, casting horoscopes for wealthy patrons. Also around 1600, anatomical work by the Belgian Vesalius gained greater precision. These key discoveries not only advanced knowledge of the human body but also implied a new power for scientific research in its ability to test and often overrule accepted ideas.

A revolution in the nature and status of science occurred during the 17th century. The European state took on new forms and functions. This wave of change intensified after 1650.

Scientific Revolution Culminated in 17th century; period of empirical advances associated with the development of wider theoretical generalizations; resulted in change in traditional beliefs of Middle Ages.

Nicolaus Copernicus Polish monk and astronomer (16th century); disproved Hellenistic belief that the earth was at the center of the universe.

Read the **Document** on MyHistoryLab: Galileo Galilei, "Letter to Madame Christine of Lorraine, Grand Duchesse of Tuscany"

FIGURE **22.3** Johannes Kepler, one of the leading figures in the Scientific Revolution.

Kepler, Johannes (December 27, 1571–November 15, 1630) Was an astronomer and mathematician who was a prominent figure in the Scientific Revolution.

Galileo Galilei Published Copernicus's findings (17th century); added own discoveries concerning laws of gravity and planetary motion; condemned by the Catholic church for his work.

Harvey, William English physician (17th century) who demonstrated circular movement of blood in animals, function of heart as pump.

Bacon, Francis (January 22, 1561–April 9, 1626) English philosopher, statesman, author, and scientist; an influential member of the Scientific Revolution; best known for work on the scientific method.

Descartes, René [dAY kärt] Established importance of skeptical review of all received wisdom (17th century); argued that human reason could then develop laws that would explain the fundamental workings of nature.

Newton, Isaac (1643–1727) English scientist; author of *Principia*; drew together astronomical and physical observations and wider theories into a neat framework of natural laws; established principles of motion; defined forces of gravity.

Deism Concept of God current during the Scientific Revolution; role of divinity was to set natural laws in motion, not to regulate once process was begun.

Locke, John (1632–1704) English philosopher who argued that people could learn everything through senses and reason and that power of government came from the people, not divine right of kings; offered possibility of revolution to overthrow tyrants.

Read the Document on MyHistoryLab: John Locke, Essay Concerning Human Understanding

A series of empirical advances and wider theoretical generalizations extended the possibilities of science from the 1600s onward. New instruments such as the microscope and improved telescopes allowed gains in biology and astronomy. The Italian **Galileo Galilei** publicized Copernicus's discoveries while adding his own basic findings about the laws of gravity and planetary motion. Condemned by the Catholic Church for his innovations, Galileo proved the inadequacy of traditional ideas about the universe. He also showed the new pride in scientific achievement, writing modestly how he, "by marvelous discoveries and clear demonstrations, had enlarged a thousand times" the knowledge produced by "the wise men of bygone ages." Chemical research advanced understanding of the behavior of gasses. English physician **William Harvey** demonstrated the circular movement of the blood in animals, with the heart as the "central pumping station."

These advances in knowledge were accompanied by important statements about science and its impact. **Francis Bacon** urged the value of careful empirical research and predicted that scientific knowledge could advance steadily, producing improvements in technology as well. **René Descartes** established the importance of a skeptical review of all received wisdom, arguing that human reason could develop laws that would explain the fundamental workings of nature.

The capstone to the 17th-century Scientific Revolution came in 1687, when **Isaac Newton** published his *Principia Mathematica*. This work drew the various astronomical and physical observations and wider theories together in a neat framework of natural laws. Newton set forth the basic principles of all motion (for example, that a body in motion maintains uniform momentum unless affected by outside forces such as friction). Newton defined the forces of gravity in great mathematical detail and showed that the whole universe responded to these forces, which among other things explained the planetary orbits described by Kepler. Finally, Newton stated the basic scientific method in terms of a mixture of rational hypothesis and generalization and careful empirical observation and experiment. Here was a vision of a natural universe that could be captured in simple laws (although increasingly complex mathematics accompanied the findings). Here was a vision of a method of knowing that might do away with blind reliance on tradition or religious faith.

The Scientific Revolution was quickly popularized among educated westerners. Here was a key step in the cultural transformation of western Europe in the early modern period. New scientific institutes were set up, often with government aid, to advance research and disseminate the findings. Lectures and easy-to-read manuals publicized the latest advances and communicated the excitement that researchers shared in almost all parts of Europe. Beliefs in witchcraft began to decline and magistrates grew increasingly reluctant to entertain witchcraft accusations in court after about 1670. There were growing signs of a new belief that people could control and calculate their environment. Insurance companies sprang up to help guard against risk. Doctors increased their attacks on popular healers, promoting a more scientific diagnosis of illness. Newsletters, an innovation by the late 17th century, began to advertise "lost and found" items, for there was no point leaving this kind of problem to customary magicians, called "cunning men," who had poked around with presumably enchanted sticks.

By the 1680s writers affected by the new science, although not themselves scientists, began to attack traditional religious ideas such as miracles, for in the universe of the Scientific Revolution there was no room for disruption of nature's laws. Some intellectuals held out a new conception of God, called **Deism**, arguing that although there might be a divinity, its role was simply to set natural laws in motion. In England, **John Locke** argued that people could learn everything they needed to know through their senses and reason; faith was irrelevant. Christian beliefs in human sinfulness crumbled in the view of these intellectuals, for they saw human nature as basically good. Finally, scientific advances created wider assumptions about the possibility of human progress. If knowledge could advance through concerted human effort, why not progress in other domains? Even literary authorities joined this parade, and the idea that past styles set timeless standards of perfection came under growing criticism.

Science had never before been central to intellectual life. Science had played important roles in other civilizations, as in China, classical Greece, Central America, and Islam. Europe's science built in fact on continuing contacts with work in the Middle East. But while the West was not alone in developing crucial scientific ideas, it now became the leading center for scientific advance. Its key thinkers stood alone for some time in seeing science as the key to gaining and defining knowledge.

VISUALIZING THE PAST

Versailles

THIS PICTURE SHOWS LOUIS XIV'S GRAND 17th-century palace at Versailles. It displays the sheer opulence of this absolute monarchy, in what was Europe's richest and most populous and influential nation. It also shows the renewed hold of a classical style, seen to be most prestigious for public buildings. What else does it suggest?

Architecture is sometimes thought to be the most socially and historically revealing of all the arts because it depends most heavily on public support; it is harder for architects, particularly dealing with public buildings, to be as idiosyncratic as painters or poets.

🔍 **View the Closer Look on MyHistoryLab:** Versailles

The palace at Versailles.

QUESTIONS

- What kinds of intentions on the part of Louis and his advisors does this building represent?
- How can Versailles be interpreted as a statement of absolute monarchy?
- What would the palace represent to an ordinary French person? To an aristocrat?

POLITICAL CHANGE

| 22.4 | To what extent did European states begin to catch up with characteristics of effective states in various Asian societies? |

> As feudalism declined in western Europe, new political forms gained ground. Both absolute and parliamentary monarchies emerged.

Political change from 1600 to 1750 was complicated, even as religious strife gradually calmed. A tradition of strong monarchy developed in France and elsewhere, greatly adding to the functions of the central government. But in Britain and Holland a different emphasis emerged, providing a strong parliamentary check on royal power. Both traditions proved significant in shaping Europe's political future. More effective central governments and better-trained bureaucrats helped Europe catch up to political forms that had been developed earlier in countries like China. At the same time, growing suggestions of what would come to be called the nation-state provided a new element in politics that would later spread to other parts of the world.

Absolute Monarchies

New political currents took shape along with the rise of science, and at times the two trends connected. The feudal monarchy—the balance between king and nobles—that had defined Western politics since the late postclassical period finally came undone in the 17th century. In most countries, after the passions of religious wars finally cooled, monarchs gained new powers, curtailing the tradition of noble pressure or revolt. At the same time, more ambitious military organization, in states that defined war as a central purpose, required more careful administration and improved tax collection.

The model for this new pattern was France, now the West's largest and most powerful nation. French kings steadily built up their power in the 17th century. They stopped convening the medieval parliament and passed laws as they saw fit, although some provincial councils remained strong. They blew up the castles of dissident nobles, another sign that gunpowder was undercutting the military basis of feudalism. They appointed a growing bureaucracy drawn from the merchants and lawyers. They sent

THINKING HISTORICALLY

Elites and Masses

WHAT CAUSED THE END OF WITCHCRAFT hysteria in the West by the later 17th century? Did wise rulers calm a frenzied populace or did ordinary people themselves change their minds? One explanation focuses on new efforts by elites, such as local magistrates, to discipline mass impulses. Authorities stopped believing in demonic disruptions of natural processes, and so forced an end to persecutions. But many ordinary people were also thinking in new ways. Without converting fully to a scientific outlook, they became open to new ideas about how to handle health problems, reducing their belief in magical remedies; they needed witches less. Potential "witches" may have become more cautious. Older women, threatened by growing community suspicion, learned to maintain a lower profile and to emphasize benign, grandmotherly qualities rather than seeking a more independent role. Without question, there was a decline both in witchcraft beliefs, once a key element in the Western mentality, and in the hysteria specifically characteristic of the 16th and 17th centuries. This decline reflected new ways of thinking about strangeness and disruption. It involved complex interactions between various segments of Western society: magistrates and villagers, scientists and priests, husbands and widows.

The transformation of Western society after 1450 raises fascinating questions about the role of elites—particularly powerful groups and creative individuals—versus the ordinary people in causing change. The growing importance of social history has called attention to ordinary people, as we have seen, but it has not answered all the questions about their actual role. This role varies by place and time, of course. Some social historians tend to see ordinary people as victims of change, pushed around by the power groups. Others tend to stress the positive historical role of ordinary people in partly shaping the context of their own lives and affecting the larger course of history.

It is easy to read the early modern transformation of western Europe as an operation created by elites, with the masses as passively watching or futilely protesting. Not only the Renaissance and Reformation but also the commercial revolution required decisive action by key leadership groups. Leading merchants spurred economic change, and they ultimately began to farm out manufacturing jobs. The resultant rise of dependent wage labor, which tore a growing minority of western Europeans away from property and so from economic control of their lives, illustrates the power disparities in Western society. Ordinary people knuckled under or protested, but they were reacting, not initiating.

The rise of science rivets our attention on the activities of extraordinarily creative individuals, such as Newton, and elite institutions, such as the scientific academies. Some historians have suggested that the rise of science opened a new gap between the ways educated upper classes and masses thought.

> *Some historians have suggested that the rise of science opened a new gap between the ways educated upper classes and masses thought.*

Yet the ordinary people of western Europe were not passive, nor did they simply protest change in the name of tradition. Widespread shifts came from repeated decisions by peasants and artisans, not just from those at the top. The steady technological improvements in manufacturing thus flowed upward from practicing artisans, not downward from formal scientists. The European-style family that had taken shape by the 16th century was an innovation by ordinary people long ignored by the elite. It encouraged new parent–child relations and new tensions between young adults and the old that might spur other innovations, including a willingness to settle distant colonies in search of property. The fact that young people often had to wait to marry until their property-owning fathers died could induce many to seek new lands or new economic methods. In other words, ordinary people changed their habits too, and these changes had wide impact.

QUESTIONS

- Did elites gain new power over the masses in early modern Western society?
- Are ordinary people more conservative by nature, more suspicious of change, than groups at the top?
- Can you describe at least two other historical cases in which it is important to determine whether change was imposed on ordinary people from above or whether ordinary people themselves produced important innovations?

direct representatives to the outlying provinces. They professionalized the army, giving more formal training to officers, providing uniforms and support, and creating military hospitals and pensions.

So great was the power of the monarch, in fact, that the French system became known as **absolute monarchy**. Its most glorious royal proponent, King **Louis XIV**, summed up its principles succinctly: "I am the state." Louis became a major patron of the arts, giving government a cultural role beyond any previous levels in the West. His academies not only encouraged science but also worked to standardize the French language. A sumptuous palace at Versailles was used to keep nobles busy with social functions so that they could not interfere with affairs of state.

Using the new bureaucratic structure, Louis and his ministers developed additional functions for the state. They reduced internal tariffs, which acted as barriers to trade, and created new, state-run manufacturing. The reigning economic theory, mercantilism, held that governments should promote the internal economy to improve tax revenues and to limit imports from other nations, lest money be lost to enemy states. Therefore, absolute monarchs such as Louis XIV set tariffs on imported goods, tried to encourage their merchant fleets, and sought colonies to provide raw materials and a guaranteed market for manufactured goods produced at home.

The basic structure of absolute monarchy developed in other states besides France (Map 22.2). Spain tried to imitate French principles in the 18th century, which resulted in efforts to tighten control over its Latin American colonies. However, the most important spread of absolute monarchy occurred in the central European states that were gaining in importance. A series of kings in Prussia, in eastern Germany, built a strong army and bureaucracy. They promoted economic activity and began to develop a state-sponsored school system. Habsburg kings in Austria–Hungary, although still officially rulers of the Holy Roman empire, concentrated increasingly on developing a stronger monarchy in the lands under their direct control. The power of these Habsburg rulers increased after they pushed back the last Turkish invasion threat late in the 17th century and then added the kingdom of Hungary to their domains.

Most absolute monarchs saw a strong military as a key political goal, and many hoped for territorial expansion. Louis XIV used his strong state as the basis for a series of wars from the 1680s onward. The wars yielded some new territory for France but finally attracted an opposing alliance system that blocked further advance. Prussian kings, although long cautious in exposing their proud military to the risk of major war, turned in the 18th century to a series of conflicts that won new territory.

Parliamentary Monarchies

Britain and the Netherlands, both growing commercial and colonial powers, stood apart from the trend toward absolute monarchy in the 17th century. They emphasized the role of the central state, but they also built parliamentary regimes in which the kings shared power with representatives selected by the nobility and upper urban classes. The English civil wars produced a final political settlement in 1688 and 1689 (the so-called **Glorious Revolution**) in which parliament won basic sovereignty over the king. The English parliament no longer depended on the king to convene, because regular sessions were scheduled. Its rights to approve taxation allowed it to monitor or initiate most major policies.

Furthermore, a growing body of political theory arose in the 17th century that built on these parliamentary ideas. John Locke and others argued that power came from the people, not from a divine right to royal rule. Monarchs should therefore be restrained by institutions that protected the public interest, including certain general rights to freedom and property. A right of revolution could legitimately oppose unjust rule.

Overall, western Europe developed important diversity in political forms, between absolute monarchy and a new kind of **parliamentary monarchy**. It maintained a characteristic tension between government growth and the idea that there should be some limits to state authority. This tension was expressed in new forms, but it recalled some principles that had originated in the Middle Ages.

The Nation-State

The absolute monarchies and the parliamentary monarchies shared important characteristics as nation-states. Unlike the great empires of many other civilizations, they ruled peoples who shared a common culture and language, some important minorities apart. They could appeal to a certain loyalty that linked cultural and political bonds. This was as true of England, where the idea of special rights of Englishmen helped feed the parliamentary movement, as it was of France. Not surprisingly, ordinary people in many nation-states, even though not directly represented in government, increasingly believed that government should act for their interests. Thus, Louis XIV faced recurrent popular riots based on the assumption that when bad harvests drove up food prices, the government was obligated to help people out.

In sum, nation-states developed a growing list of functions, particularly under the banner of mercantilism, whose principles were shared by monarchists and parliamentary leaders alike. They also promoted new political values and loyalties that were very different from the political traditions of other civilizations. They kept the West politically divided and often at war.

absolute monarchy Concept of government developed during rise of nation-states in western Europe during the 17th century; featured monarchs who passed laws without parliaments, appointed professionalized armies and bureaucracies, established state churches, imposed state economic policies.

Louis XIV (1638–1715) French monarch of the late 17th century who personified absolute monarchy.

 Read the **Document** on **MyHistoryLab**: Jean Domat, On Social Order and Absolutist Monarchy

Glorious Revolution English overthrow of James II in 1688; resulted in affirmation of parliament as having basic sovereignty over the king.

parliamentary monarchy Originated in England and Holland, 17th century, with monarchs partially checked by significant legislative powers in parliaments.

THE WEST BY 1750

> Key changes gained further ground in the 18th century. Most importantly, the Enlightenment expanded the range of intellectual innovation.

During the first half of the 18th century, several basic changes continued in western Europe. The impact of absolutism and the parliamentary monarchies persisted, although outright political innovation slowed. Commercial changes, however, began to have even wider results, with an important expansion of manufacturing; new agricultural developments added an important element. Europe's cultural transformation, at both elite and popular levels, continued as well, with growing implications for political and social life. The Enlightenment, building on the earlier scientific revolution, had particularly important results on Europe and, ultimately, other parts of the world.

Political Patterns

During much of the 18th century, English politics settled into a parliamentary routine in which key political groups competed for influence without major policy differences. Absolute monarchy in France changed little institutionally, but it became less effective. It could not force changes in the tax structure that would give it more solid financial footing because aristocrats refused to surrender their traditional exemptions.

Frederick the Great Prussian king of the 18th century; attempted to introduce Enlightenment reforms into Germany; built on military and bureaucratic foundations of his predecessors; introduced freedom of religion; increased state control of economy.

Political developments were far livelier in central Europe. In Prussia, **Frederick the Great**, building on the military and bureaucratic organization of his predecessors, introduced greater freedom of religion while expanding the economic functions of the state. His government actively encouraged better agricultural methods; for example, it promoted use of the American potato as a staple crop. It also enacted laws promoting greater commercial coordination and greater equity; harsh traditional punishments were cut back. Rulers of this sort claimed to be enlightened despots, wielding great authority but for the good of society at large.

Enlightened or not, the policies of the major Western nation-states produced recurrent warfare. France and Britain squared off in the 1740s and again in the Seven Years War (1756–1763); their conflicts focused on battles for colonial empire. Austria and Prussia also fought, with Prussia gaining new land. Wars in the 18th century were not devastating, but they demonstrated the continued linkage between statecraft and war that was characteristic of the West.

Enlightenment Thought and Popular Culture

Enlightenment Intellectual movement centered in France during the 18th century; featured scientific advance, application of scientific methods to study of human society; belief that rational laws could describe social behavior.

In culture, the aftermath of the Scientific Revolution spilled over into a new movement known as the **Enlightenment**, centered particularly in France but with adherents throughout the Western world. Enlightenment thinkers continued to support scientific advance. Although there were no Newton-like breakthroughs, chemists gained new understanding of major elements, and biologists developed a vital new classification system for the natural species.

The Enlightenment also pioneered in applying scientific methods to the study of human society, sketching the modern social sciences. The basic idea was that rational laws could describe social as well as physical behavior and that knowledge could be used to improve policy. Thus, criminologists wrote that brutal punishments failed to deter crime, whereas a decent society would be able to rehabilitate criminals through education. Political theorists wrote about the importance of carefully planned constitutions and controls over privilege, although they disagreed about what political form was best. A new school of economists developed. In his classic book *Wealth of Nations*, Scottish philosopher **Adam Smith** set forth a number of principles of economic behavior. He argued that people act according to their self-interest but, through competition, promote general economic advance. Government should avoid regulation in favor of the operation of individual initiative and market forces. This was an important statement of economic policy and an illustration of the growing belief that general models of human behavior could be derived from rational thought.

Smith, Adam Established liberal economics (*Wealth of Nations*, 1776); argued that government should avoid regulation of economy in favor of the operation of market forces.

Diderot, Denis [duh-NEE DEE-duh-roh] (October 5, 1713–July 31, 1784) A French Enlightenment figure best known for his work on the first encyclopedia.

Single individuals could sum up part of the Enlightenment's impressive range. **Denis Diderot** (1713–1784) was a multifaceted leader of the French Enlightenment, best known for his editorial work on the *Encyclopédie* that compiled scientific and social scientific knowledge. Trained initially by the Jesuits, Diderot also wrote widely on philosophy, mathematics, and the psychology of deaf-mutes and also tried his hand at literature. An active friend of other philosophers, Diderot also traveled to foreign

DOCUMENT

Controversies About Women

CHANGES IN FAMILY STRUCTURE AND SOME shifts in the economic roles of women, as well as ambivalent Protestant ideas about women that emphasized the family context but urged affection and respect between wives and husbands, touched off new gender tensions in Western society by the 17th century. Some of these tensions showed in witchcraft trials, so disproportionately directed against women. Other tensions showed in open debate about women's relationships to men; women not content with a docile wifeliness vied with new claims of virtue and prowess by some women. Although the debate was centered in the upper class of Protestant nations such as England, it may have had wider ramifications. Some of these ramifications, although quieter during the 18th century, burst forth again in arguments about inequality and family confinement in the 19th century, when a more durable feminist movement took shape in the West. In the selections here, the antiwoman position is set forth in a 1615 pamphlet by Joseph Swetham; the favorable view implicitly urging new rights is in a 1640 pamphlet pseudonymously authored by "Mary Tattle-Well and Ioane Hit-Him-Home, spinsters."

SWETHAM'S "ARRAIGNMENT OF WOMEN"

Men, I say, may live without women, but women cannot live without men: for Venus, whose beauty was excellent fair, yet when she needed man's help, She took Vulcan, a clubfooted Smith. . . .

For women have a thousand ways to entice thee and ten thousand ways to deceive thee and all such fools as are suitors unto them: some they keep in hand with promises, and some they feed with flattery, and some they delay with dalliances, and some they please with kisses. They lay out the folds of their hair to entangle men into their love; betwixt their breasts in the vale of destruction; and in their beds there is hell, sorrow and repentance. Eagles eat not men till they are dead, but women devour them alive. . . .

It is said of men that they have that one fault, but of women it is said that they have two faults: that is to say, they can neither say well nor do well. There is a saying that goeth thus: that things far fetched and dear bought are of us most dearly beloved. The like may be said of women; although many of them are not far fetched, yet they are dear bought, yea and so dear that many a man curseth his hard pennyworths and bans his own heart. For the pleasure of the fairest woman in the world lasteth but a honeymoon; that is, while a man hath glutted his affections and reaped the first fruit, his pleasure being past, sorrow and repentance remaineth still with him.*

*Joseph Swetnam, *The Araignment of Lewde, Idle, Froward, and Unconstant Women* (London, 1615).

TATTLE-WELL AND HIT-HIM-HOME'S "WOMEN'S SHARP REVENGE"

But it hath been the policy of all parents, even from the beginning, to curb us of that benefit by striving to keep us under and to make us men's mere Vassals even unto all posterity.

How else comes it to pass that when a Father hath a numerous issue of Sons and Daughters, the sons forsooth they must be first put to the Grammar school, and after perchance sent to the University, and trained up in the Liberal Arts and Sciences, and there (if they prove not Blockheads) they may in time be book-learned? . . .

When we, whom they style by the name of weaker Vessels, though of a more delicate, fine, soft, and more pliant flesh therefore of a temper most capable of the best Impression, have not that generous and liberal Education, lest we should be made able to vindicate our own injuries, we are set only to the Needle, to prick our fingers, or else to the Wheel to spin a fair thread for our own undoing, or perchance to some more dirty and debased drudgery. If we be taught to read, they then confine us within the compass of our Mother Tongue, and that limit we are not suffered to pass; or if (which sometimes happeneth) we be brought up to Music, to singing, and to dancing, it is not for any benefit that thereby we can engross unto ourselves, but for their own particular ends, the better to please and content their licentious appetites when we come to our maturity and ripeness. And thus if we be weak by Nature, they strive to make us more weak by our Nurture; and if in degree of place low, they strive by their policy to keep us more under.

Now to show we are no such despised matter as you would seem to make us, come to our first Creation, when man was made of the mere dust of the earth. The woman had her being from the best part of his body, the Rib next to his heart, which difference even in our complexions may be easily decided. Man is of a dull, earthy, and melancholy aspect, having shallows in his face and a very forest upon his Chin, when our soft and smooth Cheeks are a true representation of a delectable garden of intermixed Roses and Lilies. . . . Man might consider that women were not created to be their slaves or vassals; for as they had not their Original out of his head (thereby to command him), so it was not out of his foot to be trod upon, but in a medium out of his side to be his fellow feeler, his equal, and companion. . . .

Thus have I truly and impartially proved that for Chastity, Charity, Constancy, Magnanimity, Valor, Wisdom, Piety, or any Grace or Virtue whatsoever, women have always been more than equal with men, and that for Luxury, Surquidant obscenity, profanity, Ebriety, Impiety, and all that may be called bad we do come far short of them.

QUESTIONS

- What conditions prompted a more vigorous public debate about gender in the 17th century?
- How did the pro-woman argument compare with more modern views about women?
- Did the new arguments about women's conditions suggest that these conditions were improving?

courts as advisor and visiting intellectual. He visited Catherine the Great of Russia in 1773–1774, for example, to thank her for generous patronage.

More generally still, the Enlightenment produced a set of basic principles about human affairs: Human beings are good, at least improvable, and they can be educated to be better; reason is the key to truth, and religions that rely on blind faith or refuse to tolerate diversity are wrong. Enlightenment thinkers attacked the Catholic Church with particular vigor, because it seemed to support older superstitions while wielding political power. Progress was possible, even inevitable, if people could be set free. Society's goals should center on improving material and social life.

Although it was not typical of the Enlightenment's main thrust, a few thinkers applied these general principles to other areas. A handful of socialists argued that economic equality and the abolition of private property must become important goals. A few feminist thinkers, such as **Mary Wollstonecraft** (Figure 22.4) in England, argued—against the general male-centered views of most Enlightenment thinkers—that new political rights and freedoms should extend to women. Several journals written by women for women made their first appearance during this extraordinary cultural period. Madame de Beaumere took over the direction of the French *Journal des Dames* from a man, and in Germany, Marianne Ehrmann used her journal to suggest that men might be partly to blame for women's lowly position.

Wollstonecraft, Mary (1759–1797) Enlightenment feminist thinker in England; argued that new political rights should extend to women.

The popularization of new ideas encouraged further changes in the habits and beliefs of many ordinary people. Reading clubs and coffeehouses allowed many urban artisans and businessmen to discuss the latest reform ideas. Leading writers and compilations of scientific and philosophical findings, such as the *Encyclopaedia Britannica*, won a wide audience and, for a few people, a substantial fortune from the sale of books.

Other changes in popular outlook paralleled the new intellectual currents, although they had deeper sources than philosophy alone. Attitudes toward children began to shift in many social groups. Older methods of physical discipline were criticized in favor of more restrained behavior that would respect the goodness and innocence of children. Swaddling—wrapping infants in cloth so they could not move or harm themselves—began to decline as parents became interested in freer movement and greater interaction for young children. Among wealthy families, educational toys and books for children reflected the idea that childhood should be a stage for learning and growth.

mass consumerism The spread of deep interest in acquiring material goods and services below elite levels, along with a growing economic capacity to afford some of these goods. While hints of mass consumerism can be found in several premodern societies, it developed most clearly beginning in Western Europe from the 18th century onward.

Family life generally was changed by a growing sense that old hierarchies should be rethought and revised toward greater equality in the treatment of women and children in the home. Love between family members gained new respect, and an emotional bond in marriage became more widely sought. Change affected older children as well: Parents grew more reluctant to force a match on a son or daughter if the emotional vibrations were not right. Here was a link not only with Enlightenment ideas of proper family relations but with novels such as Richardson's *Pamela* that poured out a sentimental view of life.

FIGURE **22.4** Portrait of feminist Mary Wollstonecraft.

Cultural changes during the 18th century were complex. They included continued religious vitality, as new groups like Methodists helped stimulate piety. Three points, however, stand out. First, mainly through the Enlightenment, many popular attitudes, as well as purely intellectual interests, were changing. Beliefs in magic, for example, began to decline. Second, in establishing a culture favorable to material progress, the Enlightenment helped set up a climate for further change in the West. And third, some Enlightenment ideas, like that notion that all people shared a fundamental rationality and human worth, had implications that spilled beyond Europe. Already in 1750, for example, new agitation began to develop against the institution of slavery, in the name of basic rights.

Ongoing Change in Commerce and Manufacturing

Ongoing economic change paralleled changes in popular culture and intellectual life. Commerce continued to spread. Ordinary Westerners began to buy processed products, such as refined sugar and coffee or tea obtained from Indonesia and the West Indies, for daily use. This was a sign of the growing importance of Europe's new colonies for ordinary life and of the beginnings of **mass consumerism** in Western society. The growing popularity of cotton textiles spread more widely, giving even relatively poor people the chance to express a sense of style. Theft of clothing increased in the 18th century, a clear indication of new consumer priorities. Another sign of change was the growing use of paid professional entertainment as part of popular leisure, even in rural festivals. Circuses, first introduced in France in the 1670s, began to redefine leisure to include spectatorship and a taste for the bizarre.

Agriculture began to change. Until the late 17th century, western Europe had continued to rely largely on the methods and techniques characteristic of the Middle Ages—a severe economic constraint in an agricultural society. The three-field system still meant that a full third of all farmland was left unplanted each year to restore fertility. First in the Netherlands and then elsewhere, new procedures for draining swamps added available land. Reformers touted nitrogen-fixing crops to reduce the need to leave land idle. Stockbreeding improved, and new techniques such as seed-drills and the use of scythes instead of sickles for harvesting increased productivity. Some changes spread particularly fast on large estates, but other changes affected ordinary peasants as well. Particularly vital in this category was the spread of the potato from the late 17th century onward.

A New World crop, the potato had long been shunned because it was not mentioned in the Bible and was held to be the cause of plagues. Enlightened government leaders, and the peasants' desire to win greater economic security and better nutrition, led to widespread use of this crop. In sum, the West improved its food supply and agricultural efficiency, leaving more labor available for other pursuits.

These changes, along with the steady growth of colonial trade and internal commerce, spurred increased manufacturing. Capitalism—the investment of funds in hopes of larger profits—also spread from big trading ventures to the production of goods. The 18th century witnessed a rapid spread of household production of textiles and metal products, mostly by rural workers who alternated manufacturing with some agriculture. Here was a key use of labor that was no longer needed for food. Hundreds of thousands of people were drawn into this domestic system, in which capitalist merchants distributed supplies and orders and workers ran the production process for pay. Although manufacturing tools were still operated by hand, the spread of domestic manufacturing spurred important technological innovations designed to improve efficiency. In 1733, John Kay in England introduced the flying shuttle, which permitted automatic crossing of threads on looms; with this, an individual weaver could do the work of two. Improvements in spinning and the mechanized printing of cotton cloth soon followed as the Western economy began to move toward a full-fledged Industrial Revolution (see Chapter 28).

Human changes accompanied and sometimes preceded technology. Around 1700, most manufacturers who made wool cloth in northern England were artisans, doing part of the work themselves. By 1720, a number of loom owners were becoming outright manufacturers with new ideas and behaviors. How were manufacturers different? They spent their time organizing production and sales rather than doing their own work. They moved work out of their homes. They stopped drinking beer with their workers. And they saw their workers as market commodities, to be treated as the conditions of trade demanded. In 1736, one such manufacturer coolly wrote that because of slumping sales, "I have turned off [dismissed] a great many of my makers, and keep turning more off weekly."

Finally, agricultural changes, commercialism, and manufacturing combined, particularly after about 1730, to produce a rapidly growing population in the West. With better food supplies, more people survived, particularly with the aid of the potato. Furthermore, new manufacturing jobs helped landless people support themselves, promoting earlier marriage and sexual relationships. Population growth, in turn, promoted further economic change, heightening competition and producing a more manipulable labor force. The West's great population revolution, which continued into the 19th century, both caused and reflected the civilization's dynamism, although it also produced great strain and confusion.

Innovation and Instability

By the 18th century, the various strands of change were increasingly intertwined in Western civilization. Stronger governments promoted agricultural improvements, which helped prod population growth. Changes in popular beliefs were fed by new economic structures; both encouraged a reevaluation of the family and the roles of children. New beliefs also raised new political challenges. Enlightenment ideas about liberty and fundamental human equality could be directed against existing regimes. New family practices might have political implications as well. Children, raised with less adult restraint and encouraged to value their individual worth through parental love and careful education, might see traditional political limitations in new ways.

There was no perfect fit, no inevitable match, in the three strands of change that had been transforming the West for two centuries or more: the commercial, the cultural, and the political. However, by 1750 all were in place. The combination had already produced an unusual version of an agricultural civilization, and it promised more upheaval in the future.

proto-globalization Proto-globalization is a term sometimes used to describe the increase of global contacts from the 16th century onward, particularly in trade, while also distinguishing the patterns from the more intense exchanges characteristic of outright globalization.

Global Connections and Critical Themes

EUROPE AND THE WORLD

In 1450, Europeans were convinced that their Christianity made them superior to other people. But they also understood that many societies were impressive in terms of cities and wealth and the strength of their governments. As Europe changed and prospered, participating strongly in the process of **proto-globalization**, its outlook toward the world changed as well. We saw in the previous chapter how Europeans began to use technology as a measure of society, arguing that other societies that were less interested in technological change were inferior. By the 18th century, criticisms of the superstitions of other people

began to surface among Europeans proud of their science and rationalism.

The wider world could still provide a sense of wonder, but increasingly this was focused on natural phenomena and the strange animals being imported to European zoos. The Enlightenment generated the idea of a "noble savage"—a person uncorrupted by advanced civilization and urban ways. But this was largely a fiction designed to comment on Europe itself, not a source of real admiration for other peoples. Increasingly, European power and the rapid changes within Western civilization led to a sense that many other societies were backward, perhaps not even civilized. The idea had powerful impact not only on European attitudes but also on the ways other societies perceived themselves and reacted.

Further Readings

For an overview of developments in Western society during this period, with extensive bibliographies, see Sheldon Watts, *A Social History of Western Europe, 1450–1720* (1984); Michael Anderson, *Approaches to the West European Family* (1980); Peter N. Stearns, *Life and Society in the West: The Modern Centuries* (1988); and J. L. Roark, M. P. Johnson, P. C. Cohen, *The American Promise* (2008). Charles Tilly, *Big Structures, Large Processes, Huge Comparisons* (1985), offers an analytical framework based on major change; see also Tilly's edited volume, *The Formation of National States in Western Europe* (1975).

On more specific developments and periods, see John Man, *Gutenberg, How One Man Remade the World with Words* (2002); J. R. Hale, *The Civilization of Europe in the Renaissance* (1994); J. H. Plumb, *The Italian Renaissance* (1986); F. H. New, *The Renaissance and Reformation: A Short History* (1977); O. Chadwick, *The Reformation* (1983); Richard A. Muller, *After Calvin: Studies in the Development of a Theological Tradition* (2003); and Steven Ozment, *Protestants: The Birth of a Revolution* (1992), are fine introductions to early changes. See also John W. O'Malley, *Trent and All That: Renaming Catholicism in the Early Modern Era* (2000); H. Baron, *The Crisis of the Early Italian Renaissance* (1996), examines the place of civic life in Italian humanism. A. Vickery, *The Gentleman's Daughter: Women's Lives in Georgian England* (1998) surveys the growth or retreat of opportunities for women over time.

Later changes are sketched in Thomas Munck, *Seventeenth Century Europe: 1598–1700* (1990); C. L. Johnson, *Cultural Hierarchy*

in 16th-century Europe (2011); and Jeremy Black, *Eighteenth Century Europe: 1700–1789* (1990). On England in the civil war period, see Christopher Hill, *A Nation of Change and Novelty* (1990). See also Julian Swann, *Provincial Power and Absolute Monarchy: The Estates General of Burgundy, 1661–1790* (2006). On key aspects of Enlightenment, see Darrin McMahon, *Happiness: A History* (2006); and Peter N. Stearns, *Human Rights in World History* (2012).

Key aspects of social change in this period can be approached through Gary S. De Krey, *Restoration and Revolution in Britain: A Political History of the Era of Charles II and the Glorious Revolution* (2007); Peter Burke, *Popular Culture in Early Modern Europe* (1978); Robin Biggs, *Communities of Belief: Cultural and Social Tensions in Early Modern France* (1989); Keith Thomas, *Religion and the Decline of Magic* (1971); Lawrence Stone, *The Family, Sex and Marriage in England 1500–1800* (1977); and James Sharpe, *Instruments of Darkness: Witchcraft in Early Modern England* (1997). On popular protest, see Charles Tilly, *The Contentious French* (1986); and H. A. F. Kamen, *The Iron Century: Social Change in Europe 1550–1660* (1971).

On science, Matthew L. Jones, *The Good Life in the Scientific Revolution: Descartes, Pascal, Leibniz, and the Cultivation of Virtue* (2006); John Marshall, *John Locke, Toleration and Early Enlightenment Culture: Religious Intolerance and Arguments for Religious Toleration in Early Modern and Early Enlightenment Europe* (2006); and Michael S. Reidy, Gary Kroll, and Erik M. Conway, *Exploration and Science: Social Impact and Interaction* (2007). See also N. J. G. Pounds, *A historical geography of Europe, 1500–1840* (2009).

On MyHistoryLab

 Study and Review on MyHistoryLab

Critical Thinking Questions

1. How did the Scientific Revolution compare with developments in science in other societies, during but also before the Early Modern period?

2. Amid many changes, what were two key continuities in European society during the Early Modern period?

3. What factors caused the Enlightenment in Europe?

4. Compare the institutions and assumptions of absolute versus parliamentary monarchy. Were there any similarities?

Glossary

Pronunciation guidance is supplied in square brackets, [ ], after difficult words. The symbols used for pronunciation are found in the table below. Syllables for primary stress are *italicized*.

a	act, bat, marry	h	here	ô	order, ball	zh	vision, pleasure
AY	age, rate	hw	which, when	oi	oil, joint	uh	*a*lone, syst*e*m,
är	ar, dare	i	if, big	oo	book, tour		eas*i*ly, gall*o*p, circ*u*s
ä	ah, part, calm	I	bite, ice	ou	plow, out	A	as in French *a*mi
ch	chief, beach	j	just, tragic	sh	she, fashion	KH	as in German
e	edge, set	k	keep, cop	th	thin, ether		a*ch*, i*ch*
EE	equal, seat, bee	ng	sing	u	sum, up	N	as in French bo*n*
EER	here, ear	o	ox, hot	U	sue, blew, through	OE	as in French d*eu*x
g	give, trigger	O	hope, over	ûr	turn, urge, cur	R	as in French *r*ouge
						Y	as in German f*ü*hlen

Abbasid [uh bas id, ab uh sid] Dynasty that succeeded the Umayyads as caliphs within Islam; came to power in 750 C.E.

Abelard, Peter (1079–1142) Author of *Yes and No*; university scholar who applied logic to problems of theology; demonstrated logical contradictions within established doctrine.

absolute monarchy Concept of government developed during rise of nation-states in western Europe during the 17th century; featured monarchs who passed laws without parliaments, appointed professionalized armies and bureaucracies, established state churches, imposed state economic policies.

Abu Bakr [ah-BOO BA-kuhr] The first caliph or leader of the Muslim faithful elected after Muhammad's death in 632. Renown for his knowledge of the nomadic tribes who then dominated the Islamic community.

acupuncture An ancient Chinese system of medicine that is centered on the insertion of special needles to relieve stress-related pain or ailments.

agrarian revolution Occurred between 8500 and 3500 B.C.E.; transition from hunting and gathering to sedentary agriculture.

Akhenaton {ah-ken-AH-tehn] (1379–1335 B.C.E.) Egyptian pharaoh of the New Kingdom; attempted to establish a one-god religion, replacing the traditional Egyptian pantheon of gods.

Alexander the Great Successor of Philip II; successfully conquered Persian Empire prior to his death in 323 B.C.E.; attempted to combine Greek and Persian cultures.

Alexandria, Egypt One of the cities founded by and named for Alexander the Great; site of ancient Mediterranean's greatest library; center of literary studies.

al-Ghazali [al Gaz-AHL-ee] (1058–1111) Brilliant Islamic theologian; struggled to fuse Greek and Qur'anic traditions; not entirely accepted by ulama.

Ali (c. 599–661) Cousin and son-in-law of Muhammad; one of orthodox caliphs; focus for Shi'a.

ali'i [ah-LEE-ee] High chiefs of Hawaiian society who claimed descent from the gods and rested their claims on their ability to recite in great detail their lineages.

Allah The Arab term for the high god in pre-Islamic Arabia that was adopted by the followers of Muhammad and the Islamic faith.

al-Mahdi [al-mä dEE] (r. 775–785) Third of the Abbasid caliphs; attempted but failed to reconcile moderates among Shi'a to Abbasid dynasty; failed to resolve problem of succession.

Almohadis [AHL-moh-HAH-dees] A reformist movement among the Islamic Berbers of northern Africa; later than the Almoravids; penetrated into sub-Saharan Africa.

Almoravids [al muh räv udz] A puritanical reformist movement among the Islamic Berber tribes of northern Africa; controlled gold trade across Sahara; conquered Ghana in 1076; moved southward against African kingdoms of the savanna and westward into Spain.

alpacas Along with llamas, domesticated animals of the Americas; basis for only form of nomadic pastoralism in the New World until European importation of larger animals in 15th century C.E.

Amaterasu [ä mä te Rä sU] Sun goddess of the Shinto religion.

Anasazi "The ancient ones" culture located in southwestern United States; flourished from 200 to 1200 C.E.; featured large multistory adobe and stone buildings built in protected canyons or cliffs.

Anglican church Form of Protestantism set up in England after 1534; established by Henry VIII with himself as head, at least in part to obtain a divorce from his first wife; became increasingly Protestant following Henry's death.

animism [AH-nuh-mih-zum] A religious outlook that sees gods in many aspects of nature and propitiates them to help control and explain nature; typical of Mesopotamian religions.

Antigonids One of the regional dynasties that followed the death of Alexander the Great; founded in Macedonia and Greece.

Aquinas, Thomas [Thomas ah-KWY-nuhs] (1225–1274) Creator of one of the great syntheses of medieval learning; taught at University of Paris; author of several *Summas;* believed that through reason it was possible to know much about natural order, moral law, and nature of God.

archaic cultures Hunting-and-gathering groups dispersed over the American continents by 9000 B.C.E.

Aristophanes [ar uh stof uh nEEz] (c. 448–380 B.C.E.) Greek writer of the comedies; author of *The Frogs.*

Aristotle (384–322 B.C.E.) Greek philosopher; teacher of Alexander the Great; espoused knowledge based on observation of phenomena in material world.

Arthashastra [är thä shäs trä] Political treatise written during reign of Chandragupta Maurya; advocated use of spies and assassins, bribery, and scientific forms of warfare.

Aryans [EH-ree-uhnz] Indo-European nomadic pastoralists who replaced Harappan civilization; militarized society.

ascetics Persons who had renounced the pleasures of the material world.

Ashikaga Shogunate [ah-she-kah-gah shoh-guh-nayt] Replaced the Kamakura regime in Japan; ruled from 1336 to 1573; destroyed rival Yoshino center of imperial authority.

Ashikaga Takuaji [ah-she-kah-gah tahk-oo-ah-jee] Member of the Minamoto family; overthrew the Kamakura regime and established the Ashikaga Shogunate from 1336–1573; drove emperor from Kyoto to Yoshino.

Ashoka [uh sO kuh] (r. 273–232 B.C.E.) Grandson of Chandragupta Maurya; completed conquests of Indian subcontinent; converted to Buddhism and sponsored spread of new religion throughout his empire.

Augustine (Saint)   Influential church father and theologian (354–430 C.E.); born in Africa and ultimately bishop of Hippo in Africa; champion of Christian doctrine against various heresies and very important in the long-term development of Christian thought on such issues as predestination.

Augustus Caesar   (63 B.C.E.–14 C.E.) Name given to Octavian following his defeat of Mark Antony and Cleopatra; first emperor of Rome.

Austronesian   Family of 30 related languages found in the Philippines, Indonesia, and southeast Asia; people of this linguistic group migrated throughout the Pacific.

Axum   Kingdom located in Ethiopian highlands; replaced Meroë in first century C.E.; received strong influence from Arabian peninsula; eventually converted to Christianity.

ayan   [ä yän] The wealthy landed elite that emerged in the early decades of Abbasid rule.

ayllus   [EYEL-lehs] Households in Andean societies that recognized some form of kinship; traced descent from some common, sometimes mythical ancestor.

ayllus   [eye-LUHS] Households in Andean societies that recognized some form of kinship; traced descent from some common, sometimes mythical ancestor.

Aztecs   The Mexica; one of the nomadic tribes that used political anarchy after fall of Toltecs to penetrate into the sedentary agricultural zone of Mesoamerican plateau; established empire after 1325 around shores of Lake Texcoco.

Babylonian Empire   Unified all of Mespotamia c. 1800 B.C.E.; collapsed due to foreign invasion c. 1600 B.C.E.

Bacon, Francis   (January 22, 1561–April 9, 1626) English philosopher, statesman, author, and scientist; an influential member of the Scientific Revolution; best known for work on the scientific method.

Baghdad   Capital of Abbasid dynasty located in Iraq near ancient Persian capital of Ctesiphon.

Baibars   [bI bars] (1223–1277) Commander of Mamluk forces at Ain Jalut in 1260; originally enslaved by Mongols and sold to Egyptians.

bakufu   Military government established by the Minamoto following the Gempei Wars; centered at Kamakura; retained emperor, but real power resided in military government and samurai.

Balboa, Vasco de   (c. 1475–1519) First Spanish captain to begin settlement on the mainland of Meso-america in 1509; initial settlement eventually led to conquest of Aztec and Inca empires by other captains.

ball games   Ritual elements of many American cultures; played on formal courts; religious significance required that losing teams pay a penalty of forfeiture of goods or their lives.

band   A level of social organization normally consist-ing of 20 to 30 people; nomadic hunters and gatherers; labor divided on a gender basis.

Bantu   Originated in eastern Nigeria in west Africa; migrated into central and southern Africa using rivers—particularly the Congo Basin; village dwellers who depended on agriculture and fishing.

Battle of Kulikova   Russian army victory over the forces of the Golden Horde; helped break Mongol hold over Russia.

Battle of Siffin   Fought in 657 between forces of Ali and Umayyads; settled by negotiation that led to frag-mentation of Ali's party.

Battle of the River Zab   Victory of Abbasids over Umayyads; resulted in conquest of Syria and capture of Umayyad capital.

Batu   [BAH-too] Ruler of Golden Horde; one of Chinggis Khan's grandsons; responsible for invasion of Russia beginning in 1236.

Bedouin   [BEHD-oo-ihn] Nomadic pastoralists of the Arabian peninsula; culture based on camel and goat nomadism; early converts to Islam.

Belisarius   (c. 505–565) One of Justinian's most important military commanders during period of reconquest of western Europe; commanded in north Africa and Italy.

Benedict of Nursia   Founder of monasticism in what had been the western half of the Roman Empire; established Benedictine Rule in the 6th century; paralleled development of Basil's rules in Byzantine Empire.

Benin   Powerful city-state (in present-day Nigeria) which came into contact with the Portuguese in 1485 but remained relatively free of European influence; important commercial and political entity until the 19th century.

Berke   [ber kuh] (r. 1257–1266) A ruler of the Golden Horde; converted to Islam; his threat to Hulegu combined with the growing power of Mamluks in Egypt forestalled further Mongol conquests in the Middle East.

Bernard of Clairvaux   [klehr-VOH] (1090–1153) Emphasized role of faith in preference to logic; stressed importance of mystical union with God; successfully challenged Abelard and had him driven from the universities.

bhaktic cults   [BAHK-teek] Hindu groups dedicated to gods and goddesses; stressed the importance of strong emotional bonds between devotees and the god or goddess who was the object of their veneration; most widely worshipped gods were Shiva and Vishnu.

bishops   Headed Christian churches and regional centers and supervised the activities of other churches within the jurisdictional area.

Black Death   Plague that struck Europe in 14th century; significantly reduced Europe's population; affected social structure.

bodhisattvas   [boh-dih-SAHT-vuh] Buddhist holy men and women; built up spiritual merits during their lifetimes; prayers even after death could aid people to achieve reflected holiness.

Boers   Dutch settlers in Cape Colony, in southern Africa.

boyars   Russian aristocrats; possessed less political power than did their counterparts in western Europe.

British East India Company   Joint stock company that obtained government monopoly over trade in India; acted as virtually independent government in regions it claimed.

Bulgaria   Slavic kingdom established in northern portions of Balkan peninsula; constant source of pressure on Byzantine empire; defeated by Emperor Basil II in 1014.

bushi   Regional warrior leaders in Japan; ruled small kingdoms from fortresses; administered the law, supervised public works projects, and collected revenues; built up private armies.

Buyids   [BOO-yihds] Regional splinter dynasty of the mid-10th century; invaded and captured Baghdad; ruled Abbasid Empire under title of sultan; retained Abbasids as figureheads.

Byzantine empire   Eastern half of Roman Empire following collapse of western half of old empire; retained Mediterranean culture, particularly Greek; later lost Palestine, Syria, and Egypt to Islam; capital at Constantinople.

Caesar, Julius   Roman general responsible for conquest of Gaul; brought army back to Rome and overthrew republic; assassinated in 44 B.C.E. by conservative senators.

Calcutta   Headquarters of British East India Company in Bengal in Indian subcontinent; located on Ganges; captured in 1756 during early part of Seven Years War; later became administrative center for all of Bengal.

caliph   The political and religious successor to Muhammad.

calpulli   [kal-PUHL-lee] Clans in Aztec society, later expanded to include residential groups that distributed land and provided labor and warriors.

Calvin, Jean   French Protestant (16th century) who stressed doctrine of predestination; established center of his group at Swiss canton of Geneva; encouraged ideas of wider access to government, wider public education; Calvinism spread from Switzerland to northern Europe and North America.

Cape Colony   Dutch colony established at Cape of Good Hope in 1652 initially to provide a coastal station for the Dutch seaborne empire; by 1770 settlements had expanded sufficiently to come into conflict with Bantus.

Cape of Good Hope   Southern tip of Africa; first circumnavigated in 1488 by Portuguese in search of direct route to India.

capitalism   Economic system based on profit-seeking, private ownership, and investment.

Carolingians   Royal house of Franks after 8th century until their replacement in 10th century.

Carthage   Originally a Phoenician colony in northern Africa; became a major port and commercial power in the western Mediterranean; fought the Punic Wars with Rome for dominance of the western Mediterranean.

Castile and Aragon   Regional kingdoms of the Iberian Peninsula; pressed reconquest of peninsula from Muslims and ultimately united under the Spanish monarchy.

Çatal Hüyük   Early urban culture based on sedentary agriculture; located in modern southern Turkey; was larger in population than Jericho, had greater degree of social stratification.

Catholic Reformation   Restatement of traditional Catholic beliefs in response to Protestant Reformation (16th century); established councils that revived Catholic doctrine and refuted Protestant beliefs.

Celts   Inhabited most of Britain and Ireland; organized in small regional kingdoms; featured mixed agricultural and hunting economies; replaced in most places by Germans.

Chabi   [CHAH-bee] Influential wife of Kubilai Khan; promoted interests of Buddhists in China; indicative of refusal of Mongol women to adopt restrictive social conventions of Chinese; died c. 1281.

Chams   Indianized rivals of the Vietnamese; driven into the highlands by the successful Vietnamese drive to the south.

Chan Buddhism   Known as Zen in Japan; stressed meditation and appreciation of natural and artistic beauty; popular with members of elite Chinese society.

Chandragupta Maurya   [chun druh gUp tuh mour EE uh] (r. 322–298 B.C.E.) Founder of Maurya dynasty; established first empire in Indian subcontinent; first centralized government since Harappan civilization.

Chang'an   [chahng-an] Capital of Tang dynasty; population of 2 million, larger than any other city in the world at that time.

Charlemagne   [SHAR-luh-mayn] Charles the Great; Carolingian monarch who established substantial empire in France and Germany c. 800.

Charles Martel   (686–741) Carolingian monarch of Franks; responsible for defeating Muslims in battle of Tours in 732; ended Muslim threat to western Europe.

Chavín culture   Appeared in highlands of Andes between 1800 and 1200 B.C.E.; typified by ceremonial centers with large stone buildings; greatest ceremonial center was Chavín de Huantar; characterized by artistic motifs.

Chichén Itzá   [chee-CHEHN-eet-she] Originally a Mayan city; conquered by Toltecs c. 1000 and ruled by Toltec dynasties; architecture featured pyramid of Feathered Serpent (Quetzalcoatl).

Chimu state   [chee-MOO] Regional Andean chiefdom that flourished from 800 to 1465 C.E.; fell to Incas.

chinampas   Beds of aquatic weeds, mud, and earth placed in frames made of cane and rooted in lakes to create "floating islands" system of irrigated agriculture utilized by Aztecs.

Chinggis Khan   [JEHNG-gihs KAHN] Born in 1170s in decades following death of Kabul Khan; elected khagan of all Mongol tribes in 1206; responsible for conquest of northern kingdoms of China, territories as far west as the Abbasid regions; died in 1227, prior to conquest of most of Islamic world.

Choson   [choh-suhn] Earliest Korean kingdom; conquered by Han armies in 109 B.C.E.

Cicero   (106–43 B.C.E.) Conservative Roman senator; Stoic philosopher; one of great orators of his day; killed in reaction to assassination of Julius Caesar.

city-state   A form of political organization typical of Mesopotamian civilizations; consisted of agricultural hinterlands ruled by an urban-based king.

civilization   Societies distinguished by reliance on sedentary agriculture, ability to produce food surpluses, and existence of non-farming elites, as well as merchant and manufacturing groups.

clientage   The social relationship whereby wealthy Roman landholders offered protection and financial aid to lesser citizens in return for political support and labor.

Clovis   Early Frankish king; converted Franks to Christianity c. 496; allowed establishment of Frankish kingdom.

Columbus, Christopher   Genoese captain in service of king and queen of Castile and Aragon; successfully sailed to New World and returned in 1492; initiated European discoveries in Americas.

concubine   A secondary wife, whose status is inferior to that of a ruler or wealthy man's primary wife.

Confucius   Also known as Kung Fuzi; major Chinese philosopher born in 6th century B.C.E.; author of Analects; philosophy based on need for restoration of order through advice of superior men to be found among the shi.

Constantine   Roman emperor from 312 to 337 C.E.; established second capital at Constantinople; attempted to use religious force of Christianity to unify empire spiritually.

consuls   Two chief executives or magistrates of the Roman republic; elected by an annual assembly dominated by aristocracy.

Copts   Christian sect of Egypt; tended to support Islamic invasions of this area in preference to Byzantine rule.

core nations   Nations, usually European, that enjoyed profit from world economy; controlled international banking and commercial services such as shipping; exported manufactured goods for raw materials.

Corinthian   Along with Doric and Ionian, distinct style of Greek and Hellenistic architecture; the most ornate of the three styles.

Council of Nicaea   Christian council that met in 325 C.E. to determine orthodoxy with respect to the Trinity; insisted on divinity of all persons of the Trinity.

Crusades   Series of military adventures initially launched by western Christians to free Holy Land from Muslims; temporarily succeeded in capturing Jerusalem and establishing Christian kingdoms; later used for other purposes such as commercial wars and extermination of heresy.

cuneiform   [kyoo-NAY-uh-form] A form of writing developed by the Sumerians using a wedge-shaped stylus and clay tablets.

curacas   [koo-RAH-kahs] Ayllu chiefs with privileges of dress and access to resources; community leaders among Andean societies.

Cyril   (827–869) Along with Methodius, missionary sent by Byzantine government to eastern Europe and the Balkans; converted southern Russia and Balkans to Orthodox Christianity; responsible for creation of written script for Slavic known as Cyrillic.

Cyrus the Great   Established massive Persian empire by 550 B.C.E.; successor state to Mesopotamian empires.

da Gama, Vasco   Portuguese captain who sailed for India in 1497; established early Portuguese dominance in Indian Ocean.

Dadu   Present-day Beijing; so-called when Kubilai Khan ruled China.

daimyos   [daim-yo] Warlord rulers of 300 small states following civil war and disruption of Ashikaga Shogunate; holdings consolidated into unified and bounded mini-states.

Damascus   Syrian city that was capital of Umayyad caliphate.

Dao   [dow] In Chinese, *the way*. A religious system that stresses contemplation, self-centering, and reverence for the natural world.

Dasas   Aryan name for indigenous people of Indus valley region; regarded as socially inferior to Indo-Aryans.

Deism   Concept of God current during the Scientific Revolution; role of divinity was to set natural laws in motion, not to regulate once process was begun.

Delian league   Alliance formed by Athens after the Persian Wars; cities contributed to unified treasury on island of Delos to support alliance fleet; later taken over by Athens and became Athenian empire.

Demak   Most powerful of the trading states on north coast of Java; converted to Islam and served as point of dissemination to other ports.

demographic transition   Shift to low birth rate, low infant death rate, stable population; first emerged in western Europe and United States in late 19th century.

demography   The study of population.

Descartes, René   [dAY kärt] Established importance of skeptical review of all received wisdom (17th century); argued that human reason could then develop laws that would explain the fundamental workings of nature.

Devi   Mother goddess within Hinduism; widely spread following collapse of Guptas; encouraged new emotionalism in religious ritual.

dharma   [där muh] The caste position and career determined by a person's birth; Hindu culture required that one accept one's social position and perform occupation to the best of one's ability in order to have a better situation in the next life.

dhimmi   [DIH-mee] Literally "people of the book" applied as inclusive term to Jews and Christians in Islamic territories; later extended to Zoroastrians and even Hindus.

dhows   Arab sailing vessels with triangular or lateen sails; strongly influenced European ship design.

Diderot, Denis   [duh-NEE DEE-duh-roh] (October 5, 1713–July 31, 1784) A French Enlightenment figure best known for his work on the first encyclopedia.

diffusion   The spread of ideas, technology, plants, or other productions of human fabrication across cultures and regions.

Diocletian   Roman emperor from 284 to 305 C.E.; restored later empire by improved administration and tax collection.

Doric   Along with Ionian and Corinthian, distinct style of Greek and Hellenistic architecture; the least ornate of the three styles.

Dutch East India Company   Joint stock company that obtained government monopoly over trade in Asia; acted as virtually independent government in regions it claimed.

Edict of Nantes   Grant of tolerance to Protestants in France in 1598; granted only after lengthy civil war between Catholic and Protestant factions.

Empress Wu   Tang ruler 690–705 C.E. in China; supported Buddhist establishment; tried to elevate Buddhism to state religion; had multistory statues of Buddha created.

English Civil War   Conflict from 1640 to 1660; featured religious disputes mixed with constitutional issues concerning the powers of the monarchy; ended with restoration of the monarchy in 1660 following execution of previous king.

Enlightenment   Intellectual movement centered in France during the 18th century; featured scientific advance, application of scientific methods to study of human society; belief that rational laws could describe social behavior.

Epic of Gilgamesh   The first literary epic in Western civilization; written down c. 2000 B.C.E.; included story of Great Flood.

Ethiopia   A Christian kingdom that developed in the highlands of eastern Africa under the dynasty of King Lalibela; retained Christianity in the face of Muslim expansion elsewhere in Africa.

Etruscans   Culture that ruled Rome prior to republic; ruled through powerful kings and well-organized armies; expelled by Romans c. 510 B.C.E.

eunuchs   Castrated males used within the households of Chinese emperors, usually to guard the emperors' concubines; became political counterbalance to powerful marital relatives during Later Han.

European-style family   Originated in 15th century among peasants and artisans of western Europe, featuring late marriage age, emphasis on the nuclear family, and a large minority who never married.

extended families   Consisted of several generations, including the family patriarch's sons and grandsons with their wives and children; typical of Shang China elites.

feudalism The social organization created by exchanging grants of land or fiefs for formal oaths of allegiance and promises of loyal service; typical of Zhou dynasty and European and Japanese "Middle Ages" greater lords provided protection and aid to lesser lords in return for military service.

five pillars The obligatory religious duties of all Muslims; confession of faith, prayer, fasting during Ramadan, zakat, and hajj.

flying money Chinese credit instrument that provided credit vouchers to merchants to be redeemed at the end of the voyage; reduced danger of robbery; early form of currency.

footbinding Practice in Chinese society of mutilating women's feet in order to make them smaller; produced pain and restricted women's movement; made it easier to confine women to the household.

Francis I King of France in the 16th century; regarded as Renaissance monarch; patron of arts; imposed new controls on Catholic church; ally of Ottoman sultan against Holy Roman emperor.

Frederick the Great Prussian king of the 18th century; attempted to introduce Enlightenment reforms into Germany; built on military and bureaucratic foundations of his predecessors; introduced freedom of religion; increased state control of economy.

Fujiwara Japanese aristocratic family in mid-9th century; exercised exceptional influence over imperial affairs; aided in decline of imperial power.

Galileo Galilei Published Copernicus's findings (17th century); added own discoveries concerning laws of gravity and planetary motion; condemned by the Catholic church for his work.

Gempei Wars [gehm-pay] Waged for five years from 1180, on Honshu between Taira and Minamoto families; resulted in destruction of Taira.

Ghana First great sub-Saharan state; created by Soninke people; by 9th century C.E. a major source of gold in the Mediterranean world.

Glorious Revolution English overthrow of James II in 1688; resulted in affirmation of parliament as having basic sovereignty over the king.

Golden Horde One of the four subdivisions of the Mongol empire after Chinggis Khan's death, originally ruled by his grandson Batu; territory covered much of what is today south central Russia.

Gothic An architectural style that developed during the Middle Ages in western Europe; featured pointed arches and flying buttresses as external supports on main walls.

Gracchus, Gaius (154–121 B.C.E.) Tribune who, along with Tiberius Gracchus, attempted to introduce land and citizenship reform within the Roman republic; killed on the command of the Senate.

Gracchus, Tiberius (163–132 B.C.E.) Along with Gaius Gracchus, tribune who attempted to introduce land and citizenship reform within the Roman republic; assassinated by conservatives.

Grand Canal Built in 7th century during reign of Yangdi during Sui dynasty; designed to link the original centers of Chinese civilization on the north China plain with the Yangtze river basin to the south; nearly 1200 miles long.

Great Zimbabwe Bantu confederation of Shona-speaking peoples located between Zambezi and Limpopo rivers; developed after 9th century; featured royal courts built of stone; created centralized state by 15th century; king took title of Mwene Mutapa.

Greek fire Byzantine weapon consisting of mixture of chemicals that ignited when exposed to water; utilized to drive back the Arab fleets that attacked Constantinople.

Gregory VII Pope during the 11th century who attempted to free church from interference of feudal lords; quarreled with Holy Roman Emperor Henry IV over practice of lay investiture.

griots [grEE O, grEE O, grEE ot] Professional oral historians who served as keepers of traditions and advisors to kings within the Mali Empire.

guilds Sworn associations of people in the same business or craft in a single city; stressed security and mutual control; limited membership, regulated apprenticeship, guaranteed good workmanship; often established franchise within cities.

Guptas   Dynasty that succeeded the Kushans, one of the Buddhist dynasties that emerged after the fall of the Mauryas in the 3rd century C.E.; built empire that extended to all but the southern regions of Indian subcontinent; less centralized than Mauryan Empire.

gurus   Originally referred to as brahmans who served as teachers for the princes of the imperial court of the Guptas.

Gutenberg, Johannes   Introduced movable type to western Europe in 15th century; credited with greatly expanded availability of printed books and pamphlets.

hadiths   [huh-DEETHs] Traditions of the prophet Muhammad.

Hagia Sophia   [hä juh sä FEE uh] New church constructed in Constantinople during reign of Justinian.

hajj   A Muslim's pilgrimage to the holy city of Mecca, to worship Allah at the Ka'ba.

Hammurabi   (r. 1792–1750 B.C.E.) The most important ruler of the Babylonian empire; responsible for codification of law.

Hannibal   Great Carthaginian general during Second Punic War; successfully invaded Italy but failed to conquer Rome; finally defeated at Battle of Zama.

Hanseatic League   An organization of cities in northern Germany and southern Scandinavia for the purpose of establishing a commercial alliance.

hapu   Primary social unit of Maori society in New Zealand; divisions of tribes consisting of extended families; land allotted to extended families in common.

Harsha   Ruler who followed Guptas in India; briefly constructed a loose empire in northern India between 616 and 657 C.E.

Harun al-Rashid   One of the great Islamic rulers of the Abbasid era.

Harvey, William   English physician (17th century) who demonstrated circular movement of blood in animals, function of heart as pump.

Hausa   Peoples of northern Nigeria; formed states following the demise of Songhay Empire that combined Muslim and pagan traditions.

Heian   [hay-yan] Capital city of Japan under the Yamato emperors, later called Kyoto; built in order to escape influence of Buddhist monks; patterned after ancient imperial centers of China; never fully populated.

Hellenism   Culture derived from the Greek civilization that flourished between 300 and 100 B.C.E.

helots   Conquered indigenous population of Spartan city-state; provided agricultural labor for Spartan landowners; only semifree; largest population of Spartan city-state.

Henry the Navigator   Portuguese prince responsible for direction of series of expeditions along the African coast in the 15th century; marked beginning of western European expansion.

Himalayas   Mountain region marking the northern border of the Indian subcontinent; site of the Aryan settlements that formed small kingdoms or warrior republics.

Hinduism   The name given to the mixture of forms of religious expression that became the predominant religion of India from last centuries B.C.E. Hinduism developed from the blending of sublime philosophical thinking, popular polythesistic cults, and mysticism.

Hittites   [HIT-eyet] An Indo-European people who entered Mesopotamia c. 1750 B.C.E.; destroyed the Babylonian empire; swept away c. 1200 B.C.E.

Hojo   Warrior family closely allied with Minamoto; dominated Kamakura regime and manipulated Minamoto rulers who claimed to rule in name of Japanese emperor at Kyoto.

Holy Roman emperors   Emperors in northern Italy and Germany following split of Charlemagne's empire; claimed title of emperor c. 10th century; failed to develop centralized monarchy in Germany.

Homo sapiens   The humanoid species that emerged as most successful at the end of the Paleolithic period.

Honshu   Largest of the Japanese islands; most heavily populated.

Hopewell culture   A North American mound-building culture; lasted from c. 200 to 500 C.E.

Horace   Poet who adapted Greek poetic meters to the Latin language; author of lyrical poetry laudatory of the empire; patronized by Augustus.

horizon   Archeological term for a period when a broad central authority seems to have integrated a widely dispersed region.

huacas   [WAH-kahs] Sacred spirits and powers that resided or appeared in caves, mountains, rocks, rivers, and other natural phenomena; typical of Andean societies.

Huari   [WAH-ree] Along with Tihuanaco, large center for regional chiefdoms between 300 and 900 C.E.; located in southern Peru; featured large ceremonial center supported by extensive irrigated agriculture; established widely diffused religious and artistic symbols spread all over Andean zone.

Huitzilopochtli   [WEE-tsuh-loh-POHKT-lee] Aztec tribal patron god; central figure of cult of human sacrifice and warfare; identified with old sun god.

Hulegu   [hoo-LAY-goo] (1217–1265) Ruler of the Ilkhan khanate; grandson of Chinggis Khan; responsible for capture and destruction of Baghdad in 1257.

humanism   Focus on humankind as center of intellectual and artistic endeavor; method of study that emphasized the superiority of classical forms over medieval styles, in particular the study of ancient languages.

Hundred Years' War   Conflict between England and France from 1337 to 1453; fought over lands England possessed in France and feudal rights versus the emerging claims of national states.

Ibn Battuta   (b. 1304) Arab traveler who described African societies and cultures in his travel records.

Ibn Khaldun   [i buhn kal dUn, KHUn] (1332–1406) A Muslim historian; developed concept that dynasties of nomadic conquerors had a cycle of three generations—strong, weak, dissolute.

icon   An icon is an artistic representation, usually of a religious figure.

ideographs   Pictographic characters grouped together to create new concepts; typical of Chinese writing.

Iliad   Greek epic poem attributed to Homer but possibly the work of many authors; defined gods and human nature that shaped Greek mythos.

Ifriqiya   [IHF-rih-kee-uh] The Arabic term for eastern north Africa.

Inca   Group of clans centered at Cuzco that were able to create empire incorporating various Andean cultures; term also used for leader of empire.

Inca socialism   A view created by Spanish authors to describe Inca society as a type of utopia; image of the Inca empire as a carefully organized system in which every community collectively contributed to the whole.

Indians   Misnomer created by Columbus referring to indigenous peoples of New World; implies social and ethnic commonality among Native Americans that did not exist; still used to apply to Native Americans.

Indra   Chief deity of the Aryans; depicted as a colossal, hard-drinking warrior.

investiture   Practice of state appointment of bishops; Pope Gregory VII attempted to ban the practice of lay investiture, leading to war with Holy Roman Emperor Henry IV.

Ionic   Along with Doric and Corinthian, distinct style of Greek and Hellenistic architecture; more ornate than Doric but less than Corinthian.

Islam   Major world religion having its origins in 610 C.E. in the Arabian peninsula; meaning literally submission; based on prophecy of Muhammad.

jatis   The multitude of occupational subgroups into which the Indian caste hierarchy is divided.

Jericho   Early walled urban culture site based on sedentary agriculture; located in modern Israeli-occupied West Bank near Jordan River.

Jesuits   A new religious order founded during the Catholic Reformation; active in politics, education, and missionary work; sponsored missions to South America, North American, and Asia.

Jesus of Nazareth   Prophet and teacher among the Jews; believed by Christians to be the Messiah; executed c. 30 C.E.

jihads [jih-HAHDs] Struggles; often used for wars in defense of the faith, but also a term to indicate personal quests for religious understanding.

Jin Kingdom north of the Song Empire; established by Jurchens in 1115 after overthrowing Liao dynasty; ended 1234.

jinshi [chin shEE] Title granted to students who passed the most difficult Chinese examination on all of Chinese literature; became immediate dignitaries and eligible for high office.

jizya [JIHZ-yuh] Head tax paid by all nonbelievers in Islamic territories.

Jomon culture [JOH-muhn] Created by early migrants to Japan after 3000 B.C.E.; hunting-and-gathering people, produced a distinctive pottery form.

junks Chinese ships equipped with watertight bulkheads, sternpost rudders, compasses, and bamboo fenders; dominant force in Asian seas east of the Malayan peninsula.

Jurchens [YUHR-chehns] Founders of the Jin kingdom that succeeded the Liao in northern China; annexed most of the Yellow River basin and forced Song to flee to south.

juula [JOO-luh] Malinke merchants; formed small partnerships to carry out trade throughout Mali Empire; eventually spread throughout much of west Africa.

Ka'ba Most revered religious shrine in pre-Islamic Arabia; located in Mecca; focus of obligatory annual truce among bedouin tribes; later incorporated as important shrine in Islam.

Kabir (1440–1518) Muslim mystic; played down the importance of ritual differences between Hinduism and Islam.

Kamasutra Written by Vatsayana during Gupta era; offered instructions on all aspects of life for higher-caste males, including grooming, hygiene, etiquette, selection of wives, and lovemaking.

Kamehameha I [kä mAY hä mAY hä, kuh mAY uh mAY uh] (1758–1819) Fought series of wars backed by British weapons and advisors resulting in unified Hawaiian kingdom by 1810; as king he promoted economic change by encouraging Western merchants to establish export trade in Hawaiian goods.

kapu [kah-POO] Complex set of social regulations in Hawaii that forbade certain activities and regulated social discourse.

Karakorum Capital of the Mongol empire under Chinggis Khan, 1162 to 1227.

Karbala Site of defeat and death of Husayn, son of Ali; marked beginning of Shi'a resistance to Umayyad caliphate.

karma The sum of merits accumulated by a soul at any given point in time; determined the caste to which the soul would be assigned in the next life.

Kautilya (350–275 B.C.E.) Political advisor to Chandragupta Maurya; one of the authors of Arthashastra; believed in the scientific application of warfare.

Kepler, Johannes (December 27, 1571–November 15, 1630) Was an astronomer and mathematician who was a prominent figure in the Scientific Revolution.

Khadijah [kah-DEE-juh] (555–619) First wife of the prophet Muhammad, who had worked for her as a trader.

khagan [KAH-gahn] Title of the supreme ruler of the Mongol tribes.

khanates [KAHN-ayts] Four regional Mongol kingdoms that arose following the death of Chinggis Khan.

Khitans [kiht-ahn] Nomadic peoples of Manchuria; militarily superior to Song dynasty in China but influenced by Chinese culture; forced humiliating treaties on Song China in 11th century.

Khmers [kuh-MEHRs] Indianized rivals of the Vietnamese; moved into Mekong River delta region at time of Vietnamese drive to the south.

Kiev Trade city in southern Russia established by Scandinavian traders in 9th century; became focal point for kingdom of Russia that flourished to 12th century.

Kievan Rus' The predecessor to modern Russia; a medieval state that existed from the end of the 9th to the middle of the 13th century; its territory spanned parts of modern Belarus, Ukraine, and Russia.

kiva Circular pit in Anasazi and other communities used for religious meetings by the men in the society.

Koguryo [koh-goor-yoo] Tribal people of northern Korea; established an independent kingdom in the northern half of the peninsula in 37 B.C.E.; began a process of Sinification.

Kongo Kingdom, based on agriculture, formed on lower Congo River by late 15th century; capital at Mbanza Kongo; ruled by hereditary monarchy.

Kubilai Khan [KOO-bluh KAHN] (1215–1294) Grandson of Chinggis Khan; commander of Mongol forces responsible for conquest of China; became khagan in 1260; established Sinicized Mongol Yuan dynasty in China in 1271.

Kumbi Saleh [KUHM-bee sah-LEH] Capital of empire of Ghana; divided into two adjoining cities— one for the king, court, and indigenous people, one for the merchants, scholars, and religious leaders; flourished 750–1240.

kuriltai [KURL-tuh] Meeting of all Mongol chieftains at which the supreme ruler of all tribes was selected.

Kush [kuhsh] An African state that developed along the upper reaches of the Nile c. 1000 B.C.E.; conquered Egypt and ruled it for several centuries.

Laozi [low-dzuh] Also known as Lao Tsu; major Chinese philosopher in 4th century B.C.E.; recommended retreat from society into nature; individual should seek to become attuned with Dao.

lateen Triangular sails attached to the masts of dhows by long booms, or yard arms, which extended diagonally high across the fore and aft of the ship.

Legalists Proponents of a political philosophy in 4th century B.C.E. that China's rulers should have absolute power.

Lepanto Naval battle between the Spanish and the Ottoman empire resulting in a Spanish victory in 1571.

Li Bo (701–762) Most famous poet of the Tang era; blended images of the mundane world with philosophical musings. The name is alternately spelled Li Po and Li Bai.

Li Yuan [lee wahn] (566–635) Also known as Duke of Tang; minister for Yangdi; took over empire following assassination of Yangdi; first emperor of Tang dynasty; took imperial title of Gaozu.

Liao [lyow] dynasty Founded in 907 by nomadic Khitan peoples from Manchuria; maintained independence from Song dynasty in China.

Liu Bang [lyoh-bahng] (247–195 B.C.E.) Founder of the Han dynasty in 202 B.C.E.

llamas Along with alpacas, domesticated animals of the Americas; basis for only form of nomadic pastoralism in the New World until European importation of larger animals in 15th century C.E.

Locke, John (1632–1704) English philosopher who argued that people could learn everything through senses and reason and that power of government came from the people, not divine right of kings; offered possibility of revolution to overthrow tyrants.

loess [LOH-ehs] Fine-grained soil deposited in Ordos region in China by winds from central Asia; created fertile lands for sedentary agricultural communities.

long count Mayan system of dating from a fixed date in the past, 3114 B.C.E.; marked the beginning of a great cycle of 5200 years; allowed precision dating of events in Mayan history.

Louis XIV (1638–1715) French monarch of the late 17th century who personified absolute monarchy.

lunar cycle One of the principal means of establishing a calendar; based on cycles of moon; differed from solar cycles and failed to provide accurate guide to round of the seasons; required constant revision or intercalation.

Luoyang Capital of China in the Classical Era.

Luther, Martin (1483–1546) German monk; initiated Protestant Reformation in 1517 by nailing 95 theses to door of Wittenberg church; emphasized primacy of faith over works stressed in Catholic church; accepted state control of church.

Macedon Kingdom located in northern Greece; originally loosely organized under kings, became centralized under Philip II; served as basis for unification of Greece and later Macedonian Empire.

Machiavelli, Niccolo [mak EE uh vel EE] (1469–1527) Author of *The Prince* (16th century); emphasized realistic discussions of how to seize and maintain power; one of most influential authors of Italian Renaissance.

Magellan, Ferdinand (1480–1521) Spanish captain who in 1519 initiated first circumnavigation of the globe; died during the voyage; allowed Spain to claim Philippines.

Maghrib [MAH-gribb] The Arabic word for western north Africa.

Magna Carta Great Charter issued by King John of England in 1215; confirmed feudal rights against monarchical claims; represented principle of mutual limits and obligations between rulers and feudal aristocracy.

Mahabharata [muh hä bär uh tuh] Indian epic of war, princely honor, love, and social duty; written down in the last centuries B.C.E.; previously handed down in oral form.

Mahayana Chinese version of Buddhism; placed considerable emphasis on Buddha as god or savior.

Mahmud of Ghazni [ma-MOOD of GAHZ-nee] (971–1030) Third ruler of Turkish slave dynasty in Afghanistan; led invasions of northern India; credited with sacking one of wealthiest of Hindu temples in northern India; gave Muslims reputation for intolerance and aggression.

maize One of the staple crops of sedentary agriculturists in the Americas; domesticated by 4000 B.C.E. in central Mexico.

Malacca Portuguese factory or fortified trade town located on the tip of the Malayan peninsula; traditionally a center for trade among the southeastern Asian islands.

Mali Empire centered between the Senegal and Niger rivers; creation of Malinke peoples; broke away from control of Ghana in 13th century.

Mamluks Muslim slave warriors; established a dynasty in Egypt; defeated the Mongols at Ain Jalut in 1260 and halted Mongol advance.

mana Power of Hawaiian ali'i; emanated from their lineages and enabled them to extract labor or tribute from their subjects.

mandalas Cosmic diagrams; part of the Hindu belief system.

Mandate of Heaven The divine source for political legitimacy of Chinese rulers; established by Zhou to justify overthrow of Shang.

manioc One of staple crops of sedentary agriculturists in the Americas; principal crop of peoples of the lowlands of South America and the islands of the Caribbean.

manorialism System that described economic and political relations between landlords and their peasant laborers during the Middle Ages; involved a hierarchy of reciprocal obligations that exchanged labor or rents for access to land.

Maori Residents of New Zealand; migrated to New Zealand from Society Islands as early as 8th century C.E.

Marius (157–86 B.C.E.) Successful Roman general who introduced the concept of using paid volunteers in his army rather than citizen conscripts; created military force with personal loyalties to commander.

mass consumerism The spread of deep interest in acquiring material goods and services below elite levels, along with a growing economic capacity to afford some of these goods. While hints of mass consumerism can be found in several premodern societies, it developed most clearly beginning in Western Europe from the 18th century onward.

matrilineal Family descent and inheritance traced through the female line.

matrilocal A culture in which young men upon marriage go to live with the brides' families.

Mauryan Dynasty established in Indian subcontinent in 4th century B.C.E. following invasion by Alexander the Great.

mawali Non-Arab converts to Islam.

Maya Classic culture emerging in southern Mexico and Central America contemporary with Teotihuacan;

extended over broad region; featured monumental architecture, written language, calendrical and mathematical systems, highly developed religion.

Mecca City located in mountainous region along Red Sea in Arabian peninsula; founded by Umayyad clan of Quraysh; site of Ka'ba; original home of Muhammad; location of chief religious pilgrimage point in Islam.

Medina Also known as Yathrib; town located northeast of Mecca; grew date palms whose fruit was sold to bedouins; became refuge for Muhammad following flight from Mecca (hijra).

Mencius [men-shee-us] Also known as Meng Ke; follower of Confucius; stressed consent of the common people.

mercantilism Economic theory that stressed governments' promotion of limitation of imports from other nations and internal economies in order to improve tax revenues; popular during 17th and 18th centuries in Europe.

Meroë [MEHR-oh-ee] An ancient city of the east bank of the Nile river in modern Sudan; served as the southern capital of the Kushite Kingdom from 800 B.C.E. to 350 C.E.

Mesoamerica Mexico and Central America; along with Peru, site of development of sedentary agriculture in Western hemisphere.

mestizos [mehs-TEE-zohs] People of mixed European and Indian ancestry in Mesoamerica and South America; particularly prevalent in areas colonized by Spain; often part of forced labor system.

Methodius (826–885) Along with Cyril, missionary sent by Byzantine government to eastern Europe and the Balkans; converted southern Russia and Balkans to Orthodox Christianity; responsible for creation of written script for Slavic known as Cyrillic.

Middle Ages The period in western European history from the decline and fall of the Roman Empire until the 15th century.

Minamoto Defeated the rival Taira family in Gempei Wars and established military government (bakufu) in 12th-century Japan.

Ming dynasty Succeeded Mongol Yuan dynasty in China in 1368; lasted until 1644; initially mounted huge trade expeditions to southern Asia and elsewhere, but later concentrated efforts on internal development within China.

Ministry of Rites Administered examinations to students from Chinese government schools or those recommended by distinguished scholars.

Minoan [mih-NO-un] A civilization that developed on the island of Crete c. 1600 B.C.E.; capital at the palace complex of Knossos.

Mira Bai [MIHR-uh Bay] (1498–1547) Celebrated Hindu writer of religious poetry; reflected openness of bhaktic cults to women.

miscegenation Practice of interracial marriage or sexual contact; found in virtually all colonial cultures.

Mississippian culture Last of the mound-building cultures of North America; flourished between 800 and 1300 C.E.; featured large towns and ceremonial centers; lacked stone architecture of Central America.

mita Labor extracted for lands assigned to the state and the religion; all communities were expected to contribute; an essential aspect of Inca imperial control.

moa Large, wingless birds native to New Zealand; hunted to extinction by early settlers; extinction established need to develop new sources of protein.

Mochica state [MOH-chay] Flourished in Andes north of Chavín culture in the Moche valley between 200 and 700 C.E.; featured great clay-brick temples; created military chiefdom supported by extensive irrigated agriculture.

moldboard Heavy plow introduced in northern Europe during the Middle Ages; permitted deeper cultivation of heavier soils; a technological innovation of the medieval agricultural system.

Mongols Central Asian nomadic peoples; smashed Turko-Persian kingdoms; captured Baghdad in 1258 and killed last Abbasid caliph.

monotheism The exclusive worship of a single god; introduced by the Jews into Western civilization.

monsoons   Seasonal winds crossing the Indian subcontinent and southeast Asia; during summer bring rains.

montaña   Located on eastern slopes of Andes mountains; location of cultivation and gathering of tropical fruits and coca leaf.

Monte Alban   Chief center of Zapotec culture in southern Mexico during preclassic period; contemporary with Olmec culture; based on irrigated agriculture and calendrical and writing systems.

Mu'awiya   [moo-UH-wee-uh] (602–680) Leader of Umayyad clan; first Umayyad caliph following civil war with Ali.

Muhammad ibn Qasim   [moh-HAM-ihd ihbn HAH-sihm] (661–750) Arab general; conquered Sind in India; declared the region and the Indus valley to be part of Umayyad Empire.

Muhammad of Ghur   (1173–1206) Military commander of Persian extraction who ruled small mountain kingdom in Afghanistan; began process of conquest to establish Muslim political control of northern India; brought much of Indus valley, Sind, and northwestern India under his control.

Muhammad the Great   Extended the boundaries of the Songhay Empire; Islamic ruler of the mid-16th century.

Muhammad   Prophet of Islam; born c. 570 to Banu Hashim clan of Quraysh tribe in Mecca; raised by father's family; received revelations from Allah in 610 C.E. and thereafter; died in 632.

mummification   The act of preserving the bodies of the dead; practiced in Egypt to preserve the body for enjoyment of the afterlife.

Nahuatl   [NAH-wahtl] Language spoken by the Toltecs and Aztecs.

Nara   Along with Heian, capital of the Yamato emperors; patterned after ancient imperial centers of China; never fully populated.

Narmer   First pharaoh of Egyptian Old Kingdom; ruled c. 3100 B.C.E.

Natufian complex   Preagricultural culture; located in present-day Israel, Jordan, Lebanon; practiced the collection of naturally present barley and wheat to supplement game; typified by large settlement sites.

neo-Confucians   Revived ancient Confucian teachings in Song era China; great impact on the dynasties that followed; their emphasis on tradition and hostility to foreign systems made Chinese rulers and bureaucrats less receptive to outside ideas and influences.

Nestorians   A Christian sect found in Asia; tended to support Islamic invasions of this area in preference to Byzantine rule; cut off from Europe by Muslim invasions.

New France   French colonies in North America; extended from St. Lawrence River along Great Lakes and down Mississippi River valley system.

Newton, Isaac   (1643–1727) English scientist; author of Principia; drew together astronomical and physical observations and wider theories into a neat framework of natural laws; established principles of motion; defined forces of gravity.

Nezhualcoyotl   [nehz-uh-WAHL-koh-YOH-tihl] Leading Aztec king of the 15th century.

Nguyen   [nhuwin] Rival Vietnamese dynasty that arose in southern Vietnam to challenge traditional dynasty of Trinh in north at Hanoi.

Nicolaus Copernicus   Polish monk and astronomer (16th century); disproved Hellenistic belief that the earth was at the center of the universe.

nirvana   The Buddhist state of enlightenment, a state of tranquility.

Nok   Culture featuring highly developed art style flourishing between 500 B.C.E. and 200 C.E.; located in forests of central Nigeria.

nomads   Cattle- and sheep-herding societies normally found on the fringes of civilized societies; commonly referred to as "barbarian" by civilized societies.

Northern Renaissance   Cultural and intellectual movement of northern Europe; began later than Italian Renaissance (c. 1450); centered in France, Low Countries, England, and Germany; featured greater emphasis on religion than Italian Renaissance.

Northern Wall   Chinese defensive fortification intended to keep out the nomadic invaders from the north; initiated during Qin dynasty and reign of Shi Huangdi.

nuclear families   Consisted of husband and wife, their children, and perhaps a grandmother or orphaned cousin; typical of Chinese peasantry.

Odyssey   Greek epic poem attributed to Homer but possibly the work of many authors; defined gods and human nature that shaped Greek mythos.

Ogedei   [OHGD-dih] (1186–1241) Third son of Chinggis Khan; succeeded Chinggis Khan as khagan of the Mongols following his father's death.

Olmec culture   Cultural tradition that arose at San Lorenzo and La Venta in Mexico c. 1200 B.C.E.; featured irrigated agriculture, urbanism, elaborate religion, beginnings of calendrical and writing systems.

Olympic Games   One of the pan-Hellenic rituals observed by all Greek city-states; involved athletic competitions and ritual celebrations.

oracle at Delphi   Person representing the god Apollo; allegedly received cryptic messages from the god that had predictive value if the seeker could correctly interpret the communication.

oracles   Shamans or priests in Chinese society who foretold the future through interpretations of animal bones cracked by heat; inscriptions on bones led to Chinese writing.

Ordos [OHR-dohs] bulge   Located on the Huanghe (Yellow River); region of fertile soil; site of Yangshao and Longshan cultures.

Pachacuti   [PACH-uh-KOO-tee] Ruler of Inca society from 1438 to 1471; launched a series of military campaigns that gave Incas control of the region from Cuzco to the shores of Lake Titicaca.

Paekche   [pah-EHK-chee] Independent Korean kingdom in southwestern part of peninsula; defeated by rival Silla kingdom and its Chinese Tang allies in 7th century.

pahi   Double canoes used for long-distance voyaging; carried a platform between canoes for passengers or cargo.

parliamentary monarchy   Originated in England and Holland, 17th century, with monarchs partially checked by significant legislative powers in parliaments.

parliaments   Bodies representing privileged groups; institutionalized feudal principle that rulers should consult with their vassals; found in England, Spain, Germany, and France.

pastoral nomads   An intermediate form of ecological adaptation dependent on domesticated animal herds that feed on the natural environment; typically more populous than shifting cultivation groups.

pastoralism   A nomadic agricultural lifestyle dependent on domesticated animal herds that feed on the natural environment; typically more populous than shifting cultivation groups.

patriarchal   Societies in which women defer to men; societies run by men and based on the assumption that men naturally directed political, economic, and cultural life.

patrilineal   Family descent and inheritance traced through the male line.

Paul   (3–67) One of the first Christian missionaries; moved away from insistence that adherents of the new religion follow Jewish law; use of Greek as language of the church.

Peloponnesian Wars   Wars from 431 to 404 B.C.E. between Athens and Sparta for dominance in southern Greece; resulted in Spartan victory but failure to achieve political unification of Greece.

Pericles   Athenian political leader during 5th century B.C.E.; guided development of Athenian Empire; died during early stages of Peloponnesian War.

Petrarch, Francesco   [PEE-trahrk] (1304–1374) One of the major literary figures of the Western Renaissance; an Italian author and humanist.

pharaoh   Title of kings of ancient Egypt.

Philip II   Ruled Macedon from 359 to 336 B.C.E.; founder of centralized kingdom; later conquered rest of Greece, which was subjected to Macedonian authority.

Phoenicians   [fih-NISH-unz] Seafaring civilization located on the shores of the eastern Mediterranean; established colonies throughout the Mediterranean.

Pizarro, Francisco   Led conquest of Inca Empire of Peru beginning in 1535; by 1540, most of Inca possessions fell to the Spanish.

Plato   Greek philosopher; taught knowledge based on consideration of ideal forms outside the material world; proposed ideal form of government based on abstract principles in which philosophers ruled.

plebeians   Ordinary citizens; originally those Roman families that could not trace their relationship to one of the major Roman clans.

pochteca   [pahk-TEHK-uh] Special merchant class in Aztec society; specialized in long-distance trade in luxury items.

polyandry   Marriage practice in which one woman had several husbands; recounted in Aryan epics.

polygamy   Marriage practice in which one husband had several wives; practiced in Aryan society.

Polynesia   Islands contained in a rough triangle whose points lie in Hawaii, New Zealand, and Easter Island.

pope   Bishop of Rome; head of the Christian Church in western Europe.

Prester John   In legends popular from 12th to 17th century, a mythical Christian monarch whose kingdom was cut off from Europe by Muslim conquests; Chinggis Khan was originally believed to be this mythical ruler.

proletariat   Class of working people without access to producing property; typically manufacturing workers, paid laborers in agricultural economy, or urban poor; in Europe, product of economic changes of 16th and 17th centuries.

Protestantism   General wave of religious dissent against Catholic church; generally held to have begun with Martin Luther's attack on Catholic beliefs in 1517; included many varieties of religious belief.

proto-globalization   Proto-globalization is a term sometimes used to describe the increase of global contacts from the 16th century onward, particularly in trade, while also distinguishing the patterns from the more intense exchanges characteristic of outright globalization.

Ptolemies   One of the regional dynasties that followed the death of Alexander the Great; founded in Egypt; flourished 305 to 30 B.C.E.

puna   High valleys and steppes lying between the two major chains of the Andes mountains; site of South American agricultural origins, also only location of pastoralism in Americas.

Punic Wars   Fought between Rome and Carthage to establish dominance in the western Mediterranean; won by Rome after three separate conflicts.

pure land Buddhism   Emphasized salvationist aspects of Chinese Buddhism; popular among masses of Chinese society.

Pygmies   One of few pure hunting societies left in Africa following Bantu migration.

pyramids   Monumental architecture typical of Old Kingdom Egypt; used as burial sites for pharaohs.

Quetzalcoatl   [keht-zahl-KOH-ah-tuhl] Toltec deity; Feathered Serpent; adopted by Aztecs as a major god.

quipu   [KEE-poo] System of knotted strings utilized by the Incas in place of a writing system; could contain numerical and other types of information for censuses and financial records.

Qur'an   [kuh-RAHN] Recitations of revelations received by Muhammad; holy book of Islam.

Quraysh [koo-RAYSH] Tribe of bedouins that controlled Mecca in 7th century C.E.

Qutb-ud-din Aibak [KUHTH-uhd-dihn ay-BAHK] Lieutenant of Muhammad of Ghur; established kingdom in India with capital at Delphi; proclaimed himself Sultan of India (r. 1206–1210).

Rajput [RAHJ-poot] Regional princes in western India; emphasized military control of their regions.

Rama Major figure in the popular Indian epic *Ramayana.*

Ramadan Islamic month of religious observance requiring fasting from dawn to sunset.

Ramayana One of the great epic tales from classical India; traces adventures of King Rama and his wife, Sita; written 4th to 2nd centuries B.C.E.

reincarnation The successive attachment of the soul to some animate form according to merits earned in previous lives.

Renaissance [REHN-uh-sahns] Cultural and political movement in western Europe; began in Italy c. 1400; rested on urban vitality and expanding commerce; featured a literature and art with distinctly more secular priorities than those of the Middle Ages.

Ridda Wars Wars that followed Muhammad's death in 632; resulted in defeat of rival prophets and some of larger clans; restored unity of Islam.

Roman republic The balanced constitution of Rome from c. 510 to 47 B.C.E.; featured an aristocratic Senate, a panel of magistrates, and several popular assemblies.

Romance of the West Chamber Chinese drama written during the Yuan period; indicative of the continued literary vitality of China during Mongol rule.

Rurik Legendary Scandinavian, regarded as founder of the first kingdom of Russia based in Kiev in 855 C.E.

Russian Orthodoxy Russian form of Christianity imported from Byzantine empire and combined with local religion; king characteristically controlled major appointments.

Sahara Desert running across northern Africa; separates the Mediterranean coast from southern Africa.

sahel The extensive grassland belt at the southern edge of the Sahara; a point of exchange between the forests to the south and northern Africa.

saints Holy men and women, often martyrs, who were revered in Christianity as models of Christian lifestyles; built up treasury of merit that could be tapped by more ordinary Christians.

Saladin Muslim leader in the last decades of the 12th century; reconquered most of the crusader outposts for Islam.

samurai Mounted troops of Japanese warrior leaders (bushi); loyal to local lords, not the emperor.

Sanskrit The sacred and classical Indian language.

Sargon I Ruler of city-state of Akkad; established the first empire in Mesopotamian civilization c. 2400 B.C.E.

Sasanian empires The dynasty that ruled Persia (contemporary Iran) in the centuries before the rise of Muhammad and the early decades of Islamic expansion.

savages Derogatory term wrongly applied to societies engaged in either hunting and gathering for subsistence or in migratory cultivation; not as stratified and specialized as sedentary and nomadic societies.

scholar-gentry Chinese class created by the marital linkage of the local land-holding aristocracy with the office-holding shi; superseded shi as governors of China.

scholasticism Dominant medieval philosophical approach; so called because of its base in the schools or universities; based on use of logic to resolve theological problems.

Scientific Revolution Culminated in 17th century; period of empirical advances associated with the development of wider theoretical generalizations; resulted in change in traditional beliefs of Middle Ages.

secret societies Chinese peasant organizations; provided financial support in hard times and physical protection in case of disputes with local aristocracy.

Seleucids [si lU sids, -cids] One of the regional dynasties that followed the death of Alexander the Great; founded in Mesopotamia.

Seljuk Turks [SEHL-jook Turks] Nomadic invaders from central Asia via Persia; staunch Sunnis; ruled in name of Abbasid caliphs from mid-11th century.

Senate Assembly of Roman aristocrats; advised on policy within the republic; one of the early elements of the Roman constitution.

seppuku Ritual suicide or disembowelment in Japan; commonly known in West as hara-kiri; demonstrated courage and a means to restore family honor.

serfs Peasant agricultural laborers within the manorial system of the Middle Ages.

Seven Years War Fought both in continental Europe and also in overseas colonies between 1756 and 1763; resulted in Prussian seizures of land from Austria, English seizures of colonies in India and North America.

Shah-Nama Written by Firdawsi in late 10th and early 11th centuries; relates history of Persia from creation to the Islamic conquests.

Shang First Chinese dynasty for which archeological evidence exists; capital located in Ordos bulge of the Huanghe; flourished 1600 to 1046 B.C.E.

Sharia [shä rEE ä] Islamic law; defined among other things the patrilineal nature of Islamic inheritance.

shaykhs [shAYks] Leaders of tribes and clans within bedouin society; usually men with large herds, several wives, and many children.

shi [shuh] Probably originally priests; transformed into corps of professional bureaucrats because of knowledge of writing during Zhou dynasty in China.

Shi'a Also known as Shi'ites; political and theological division within Islam; followers of Ali.

Shi Huangdi [shiuh-hwahng-dee] Founder of the brief Qin dynasty in 221 B.C.E.

shifting cultivation An intermediate form of ecological adaptation in which temporary forms of cultivation are carried out with little impact on the natural ecology; typical of rainforest cultivators.

Shinto Religion of early Japanese culture; devotees worshiped numerous gods and spirits associated with the natural world; offers of food and prayers made to gods and nature spirits.

Shiva Hindu god of destruction and reproduction; worshiped as the personification of cosmic forces of change.

shoguns Military leaders of the bakufu (military governments in Japan).

Shrivijaya [SHREE-vih-JAY-uh] Trading empire centered on Malacca Straits between Malaya and Sumatra; controlled trade of empire; Buddhist government resistant to Muslim missionaries; fall opened up southeastern Asia to Muslim conversion.

Signet Ring of Rakshasa One of the great Sanskrit dramas produced in the Gupta period; dramatized authority of brahmans.

Silla Independent Korean kingdom in southeastern part of peninsula; defeated Koguryo along with their Chinese Tang allies; submitted as a vassal of the Tang emperor and agreed to tribute payment; ruled united Korea by 668.

Sinification Extensive adoption of Chinese culture in other regions; typical of Korea, Japan, and Vietnam.

Skanda Gupta Last of the able rulers of the Gupta dynasty; following his late 5th-century reign, the empire dissolved under the pressure of nomadic invasions.

slash-and-burn agriculture A system of cultivation typical of shifting cultivators; forest floors cleared by fire are then planted.

Slavs An Indo-European group in Russia and the Balkans that ultimately dominated much of eastern Europe from the Balkans northward.

Smith, Adam Established liberal economics (*Wealth of Nations*, 1776); argued that government should avoid regulation of economy in favor of the operation of market forces.

Socrates   Athenian philosopher of later 5th century B.C.E.; tutor of Plato; urged rational reflection of moral decisions; condemned to death for corrupting minds of Athenian young.

solar cycle   Calendrical system based on solar year; typical of all civilizations; variations of solar calendars in Western civilization are Julian and Gregorian calendars; Mayas also constructed solar calendar.

Solon   Athenian reformer of the 6th century; established laws that eased burden of debt on farmers, forbade enslavement for debt.

Songhay   [sohng-HEYE] Successor state to Mali; dominated middle reaches of Niger valley; formed as independent kingdom under a Berber dynasty; capital at Gao; reached imperial status under Sunni Ali (r. 1464–1492).

Sophocles   (496–406 B.C.E.) Greek writer of tragedies; author of *Oedipus Rex*.

Southern Song   Rump state of Song dynasty from 1127 to 1279; carved out of the much larger domains ruled by the Tang and northern Song; culturally one of the most glorious reigns in Chinese history.

split inheritance   Inca practice of descent; all titles and political power went to successor, but wealth and land remained in hands of male descendants for support of cult of dead Inca's mummy.

stateless societies   African societies organized around kinship or other forms of obligation and lacking the concentration of political power and authority associated with states.

stelae   Large memorial pillars erected to commemorate triumphs and events in the lives of rulers or other ceremonial occasions.

Stoics   Hellenistic group of philosophers; emphasized inner moral independence cultivated by strict discipline of the body and personal bravery.

stupas   Stone shrines built to house pieces of bone or hair and personal possessions said to be relics of the Buddha; preserved Buddhist architectural forms.

Sudanic states   Kingdoms that developed during the height of Ghana's power in the region; based at Takrur on the Senegal River to the west and Gao on the Niger River to the east; included Mali and Songhay.

Sui   [sway] Dynasty that succeeded the Han in China; emerged from strong rulers in northern China; united all of northern China and reconquered southern China.

Sumerians   People who migrated into Mesopotamia c. 4000 B.C.E.; created first civilization within region; organized area into city-states.

Sundiata   The "Lion Prince" a member of the Keita clan; created a unified state that became the Mali Empire; died about 1260.

Sunnis   Political and theological division within Islam; supported the Umayyads.

Taika reforms   [tai kä] Attempt to remake Japanese monarch into an absolute Chinese-style emperor; included attempts to create professional bureaucracy and peasant conscript army.

Taira   [teye-ruh] Powerful Japanese family in 11th and 12th centuries; competed with Minamoto family; defeated after Gempei Wars.

Tale of Genji, The   Written by Lady Murasaki; first novel in any language; relates life history of prominent and amorous son of the Japanese emperor; evidence for mannered style of Japanese society.

tambos   Way stations used by Incas as inns and storehouses; supply centers for Inca armies on the move; relay points for system of runners used to carry messages.

Tang   Dynasty that succeeded the Sui in 618 C.E.; more stable than previous dynasty.

Tangut   Rulers of Xi Xia kingdom of northwest China; one of regional kingdoms during period of southern Song; conquered by Mongols in 1226.

Tatars   Mongols; captured Russian cities and largely destroyed Kievan state in 1236; left Russian Orthodoxy and aristocracy intact.

Temple of the Sun   Inca religious center located at Cuzco; center of state religion; held mummies of past Incas.

Tenochtitlan [teh-nahk-teet-LAHN] Founded c. 1325 on marshy island in Lake Texcoco; became center of Aztec power; joined with Tlacopan and Texcoco in 1434 to form a triple alliance that controlled most of central plateau of Mesoamerica.

Teotihuacan [tay-oh-tee-wah-KAHN] Site of classic culture in central Mexico; urban center with important religious functions; supported by intensive agriculture in surrounding regions; population of as much as 200,000.

Thirty Years War War within the Holy Roman Empire between German Protestants and their allies (Sweden, Denmark, France) and the emperor and his ally, Spain; ended in 1648 after great destruction with Treaty of Westphalia.

three estates The three social groups considered most powerful in Western countries: church, nobles, and urban leaders.

three-field system System of agricultural cultivation by 9th century in western Europe; included one-third in spring grains, one-third fallow.

Tian [tyahn] Heaven; an abstract conception in early Chinese religion; possibly the combined spirits of all male ancestors; first appeared during Zhou dynasty.

Tihuanaco [TEE-uh-wah-NAH-koh] Along with Huari, large center for regional chiefdoms between 300 and 900 C.E.; located in southern Peru; featured large ceremonial center supported by extensive irrigated agriculture; established widely diffused religious and artistic symbols spread all over Andean zone.

Timbuktu Port city of Mali; located just off the flood plain on the great bend in the Niger River; population of 50,000; contained a library and university.

Timur-i Lang Also known as Tamerlane; leader of Turkic nomads; beginning in 1360s from base at Samarkand, launched series of attacks in Persia, the Fertile Crescent, India, and southern Russia; empire disintegrated after his death in 1405.

Tlaloc [tlah-LOHK] Major god of Aztecs; associated with fertility and the agricultural cycle; god of rain.

Toltec culture Succeeded Teotihuacan culture in central Mexico; strongly militaristic ethic including human sacrifice; influenced large territory after 1000 C.E.; declined after 1200 C.E.

Toltecs [TOHL-tehks] Nomadic peoples from beyond the northern frontier of the sedentary agricultural area in Mesoamerica; established capital of Tula following migration into central Mesoamerican plateau.

Topiltzin [toh-PEYEL-tzihn] Religious leader and reformer of the Toltecs in 10th century; dedicated to god Quetzalcoatl; after losing struggle for power, went into exile in the Yucatan peninsula.

Trajan Roman emperor from 101 to 106 C.E.; instituted more aggressive imperial foreign policy resulting in expansion of empire to its greatest limits.

transhumant A form of pastoralism common to the Mediterranean basin and the Sahara; involves moving from one region to another according to the season.

transmigration Belief in a number of Indian religious traditions that the souls of living creatures persisted in supernatural realms and returned to inhabit other humans or animals after death.

Treaty of Paris Arranged in 1763 following Seven Years War; granted New France to England in exchange for return of French sugar islands in Caribbean.

Treaty of Westphalia Ended Thirty Years War in 1648; granted right to individual rulers within the Holy Roman empire to choose their own religion—either Protestant or Catholic.

tribunes Plebeian representatives in the Roman republic; elected in the Councilium Plebis Tributum on an annual basis.

Trinh Dynasty that ruled in north Vietnam at Hanoi, 1533 to 1772; rivals of Nguyen family in south.

Trung sisters Leaders of one of the frequent peasant rebellions in Vietnam against Chinese rule; revolt broke out in 39 C.E.; demonstrates importance of Vietnamese women in indigenous society.

tsetse fly [tsee-tsee] Flourished in wet lowlands; carried sleeping sickness that severely limited pastoralism in western and central Africa.

tumens Basic fighting units of the Mongol forces; consisted of 10,000 cavalrymen; each unit was further divided into units of 1000, 100, and 10.

Twantinsuyu [twahn-tihn-SOO-yoo] Word for Inca empire; region from present-day Colombia to Chile and eastward to northern Argentina.

ulama Orthodox religious scholars within Islam; pressed for a more conservative and restrictive theology; increasingly opposed to non-Islamic ideas and scientific thinking.

Umayyad [oo-MY-yad] Clan of Quraysh that dominated politics and commercial economy of Mecca; clan established a dynasty under this title as rulers of Islam, 661 to 750.

umma Community of the faithful within Islam; transcended old tribal boundaries to create degree of political unity.

untouchables Lowest social caste in Hindu culture; performed tasks that were considered polluting—street sweeping, removal of human waste, and tanning.

Upanishads [oo-PAHN-uh-shadz] Later books of the Vedas; contained sophisticated and sublime philosophical ideas; utilized by brahmans to restore religious authority.

Urban II Called for First Crusade in 1095; appealed to Christians to mount military assault to free the Holy Land from the Muslims.

Uthman Third caliph and member of Umayyad clan; murdered by mutinous warriors returning from Egypt; death set off civil war in Islam between followers of Ali and the Umayyad clan.

varnas Clusters of caste groups in Aryan society; four social castes—Brahmins (priests), warriors, merchants, and peasants; beneath four Aryan castes was a group of socially untouchable Dasas.

vassals Members of the military elite who received land or a benefice from a feudal lord in return for military service and loyalty.

Vedas Aryan hymns originally transmitted orally but written down in sacred books from the 6th century B.C.E.

Vergil (70–19 B.C.E.) One of greatest of Roman poets during "Golden Age" of Latin literature; patronized by Augustus; author of *Aeneid*.

Vikings Seagoing Scandinavian raiders from Sweden, Denmark, and Norway who disrupted coastal areas of western Europe from the 8th to the 11th centuries.

Vishnu The brahminical, later Hindu, god of sacrifice; widely worshiped.

Vivaldis Two Genoese brothers who attempted to find a western route to the "Indies" disappeared in 1291; precursors of thrust into southern Atlantic.

Vladimir I Ruler of Russian kingdom of Kiev from 980 to 1015; converted kingdom to Christianity.

Völkerwanderungen [fôlk er van der Un gen] Movement of Germanic peoples southward into the Roman Empire; resulted from population growth, pressure of Asian groups on eastern flanks of Germanic regions.

Wang Anshi Confucian scholar and chief minister of a Song emperor in 1070s; introduced sweeping reforms based on Legalists; advocated greater state intervention in society.

Wang Mang Member of one of the powerful families related to the Han emperors through marriage; temporarily overthrew the Han between 9 and 23 C.E.

wazir [wuh-ZEER] Chief administrative official under the Abbasid caliphate; initially recruited from Persian provinces of empire.

White Lotus Society Secret religious society dedicated to overthrow of Yuan dynasty in China; typical of peasant resistance to Mongol rule.

William the Conqueror Invaded England from Normandy in 1066; extended tight feudal system to England; established administrative system based on sheriffs; established centralized monarchy.

witchcraft persecution Reflected resentment against the poor, uncertainties about religious truth; resulted in death of over 100,000 Europeans between 1590 and 1650; particularly common in Protestant areas.

Wollstonecraft, Mary (1759–1797) Enlightenment feminist thinker in England; argued that new political rights should extend to women.

world economy Established by Europeans by the 16th century; based on control of seas, including the Atlantic and Pacific; created international exchange of foods, diseases, and manufactured products.

Wu First of the Zhou to be recognized as king, 1122 B.C.E.

Wuzong Chinese emperor of Tang dynasty who openly persecuted Buddhism by destroying monasteries in 840s; reduced influence of Chinese Buddhism in favor of Confucian ideology.

Xi Xia [shee-shyah] Kingdom of Tangut people, north of Song kingdom, in mid-11th century; collected tribute that drained Song resources and burdened Chinese peasantry.

Xi'an Along with Luoyang, capital of the Zhou dynasty.

Xia China's first, possibly mythical, kingdom; no archeological sites have been connected to it; ruled by Yu.

Xiongnu [shung-noo] A polyglot nomadic group that built an empire in central Asia in the last centuries B.C.E.

Xuanzong [shwant-song] Leading Chinese emperor of the Tang dynasty who reigned from 713 to 755, although he encouraged overexpansion.

Xunzi [shwuhn-dzee] Author of *The Art of War*, a classic book that revolutionized thinking about military organization and the conduct of war.

Yamato Japanese clan that gained increasing dominance in the 4th and 5th centuries C.E.; created imperial cult around Amaterasu and Shinto; brought most of the lowland plains of the southern islands under control.

yanas A class of people within Inca society removed from their ayllus to serve permanently as servants, artisans, or workers for the Inca or the Inca nobility.

Yang Guifei [yäng gwä fä] (719–756) Royal concubine during reign of Xuanzong; introduction of her relatives into royal administration led to revolt.

Yangdi Second member of Sui dynasty; murdered his father to gain throne; restored Confucian examination system; responsible for construction of Chinese canal system; assassinated in 618.

Yaroslav (978–1054) Last of great Kievan monarchs; issued legal codification based on formal codes developed in Byzantium.

Yayoi epoch [yay-YOH-ee] Last centuries B.C.E. in Japan; featured introduction of wet-rice cultivation, ironworking; produced wheel-turned pottery and sophisticated bronzeware.

Yellow Turbans Chinese Daoists who launched a revolt in 184 C.E. in China promising a golden age to be brought about by divine magic.

Yi Korean dynasty that succeeded Koryo dynasty following period of Mongol invasions; established in 1392; ruled Korea to 1910; restored aristocratic dominance and Chinese influence.

Yoruba City-states developed in northern Nigeria c. 1200 C.E.; Ife featured artistic style possibly related to earlier Nok culture; agricultural societies supported by peasantry and dominated by ruling family and aristocracy.

Yu A possibly mythical Chinese ruler c. 2070 B.C.E.; revered for the construction of an effective system of flood control along the Huanghe valley; founder of the Xia kingdom.

zakat Tax for charity; obligatory for all Muslims.

Zen Buddhism Known as Chan Buddhism in China; stressed meditation and the appreciation of natural and artistic beauty.

Zenj [zehnj] Arabic term for the east African coast.

Zhao Kuangyin [jaoo kwän yin] (r. 960–976) Founder of Song dynasty; originally a general following fall of Tang; took title of Taizu; failed to overcome northern Liao dynasty that remained independent.

Zheng He [jehng huh] Chinese Muslim admiral who commanded series of Indian Ocean, Persian Gulf, and Red Sea trade expeditions under third Ming emperor, Yunglo, between 1405 and 1433.

Zhu Xi [ju shEE] (1130–1200) Most prominent of neo-Confucian scholars during the Song dynasty in China; stressed importance of applying philosophical principles to everyday l
ife and action.

Zhu Yuanzhang The given name of the Hongwu emperor, the founder of the Ming dynasty.

ziggurats [ZIG-uh-rat] Massive towers usually associated with Mesopotamian temple complexes.

Zoroastrianism [zôr O as trEE uh niz uhm, zOr-] Animist religion that saw material existence as battle between forces of good and evil; stressed the importance of moral choice; righteous lived on after death in "House of Song" chief religion of Persian Empire.

Credits

Numismatics, Iconography. Epigraphy and History: Studies in Honor of George C. Miles, Ed. Dickran Kouymijian, (Beirut: American University of Beirut, 1974), 443–455. Reprinted by Permission of The American University of Beirut Press. Second column, *The Chronicle of Jean de Venette*, Richard A. Newhall, ed., Copyright © 1953, Columbia University Press. Reprinted with permission of the publisher.

PHOTO CREDITS

PART I

P. 1 Bridgeman Art Library, London/SuperStock; p. 2 Gianni Dagli Orti/Fine Arts/Corbis.

Chapter 1 Figure 1.1 Reeda Peel; **1.2** Newman and Associates/Phototake; **1.3** Scala/Art Resource, NY; **Document** Art Resource, NY; **1.4** Michael Jenner/Robert Harding; **Visualizing the Past Image 1** Riedmiller/Caro/Alamy; **Image 2** Superstock/Superstock; **Images 3 & 4** Erich Lessing/Art Resource, NY; **1.5** Marion Bull/Alamy.

Chapter 2 Figure 2.1 Erich Lessing/Art Resource, NY; **2.2** University of Pennsylvania Museum of Archaeology and Anthropology, Philadelphia/Courtesy of the Penn Museum; **2.4** Scala/Art Resource, NY; **2.5** Ian Stewart/Shutterstock; **2.6** Erich Lessing/Art Resource, NY; **2.7** Erich Lessing/Art Resource, NY.

Chapter 3 Figure 3.1 Travel India/Alamy; **3.2** Art Resource, NY; **3.3** Corbis; **3.4** Borromeo/Art Resource, NY; **3.5** Art Resource; **3.6** TAO Images Limited/Alamy; **3.7** Asian Art & Archaeology, Inc./Corbis; **3.8** Asian Art & Archaeology, Inc./Corbis.

PART I REVISITING

P. 66 DeAgostini/SuperStock.

PART II

P. 68 Robert Harding World Imagery; p. 72 Dorling Kindersley.

Chapter 4 Figure 4.1 Art Archive, The/SuperStock; **4.2** The Granger Collection; **4.3** Nancy McKenna/Photo Researchers, Inc.; **4.4** Graham Mulrooney/Alamy; **4.5** The Granger Collection, NYC; **4.6** Barney Burstein/Burstein Collection/Corbis.

Chapter 5 Figure 5.1 RMN-Grand Palais/Art Resource, NY; **5.2** Bridgeman-Giraudon/Art Resource, NY; **5.3** Bridgeman Art Library, London/SuperStock; **5.4** The British Museum; **5.5** Erich Lessing/ Art Resource, NY; **Visualizing the Past** National Museum of Iran, Tehran, Iran / The Bridgeman Art Library; **5.6 (top left)** Mimmo Jodice/Fine Art/Corbis; **(top right)** Alexander A.Trofimov/Shutterstock.com; **(bottom)** Image Source/Corbis; **5.7** Borromeo/Art Resource, NY.

Chapter 6 Figure 6.1 David Gurr/Eye Ubiquitous/Corbis.; **6.2** Smart-foto/Shutterstock; **6.3** PhotosIndia.com RM 20/Alamy; **6.4** Indian, (3rd century BC)/The Bridgeman Art Library Ltd./Alamy; **6.5** Christophe Boisvieux/Terra/Corbis; **6.6** Alamy Limited.

Chapter 7 Figure 7.1 Zev Radovan/www.BibleLandPictures.com/Alamy; **7.2** Araldo de Luca/Fine Art/Corbis; **7.3** Scala/Art Resource, NY; **Visualizing the Past** Gail Mooney-Kelly/Alamy; **7.4** Erich Lessing/Art Resource, NY.

Chapter 8 Figure 8.1 JTB Media Creation, Inc/Alamy; **8.2** Gianni Dagli Orti/The Art Archive at Art Resource, NY; **8.3** Ira Block/National Geographic Image Collection/Alamy; **8.4** Werner Forman/Art Resource, NY; **8.5** Steve Vidler/Alamy; **8.6** Vincent Palermo/Alamy; **8.7** Nathan Benn/Alamy; **8.8** Copyright April 2, 1990, *U. S. News & World Report*.

Chapter 9 Figure 9.1 Bridgeman-Giraudon/Art Resource, NY; **9.2** Jenny Matthews/Alamy; **9.3** RMN-Grand Palais/Art Resource, NY; **9.4** Bartlomiej K. Kwieciszewski/Shutterstock; **9.5** Sakamoto Photo Research Laboratory/Fine Art/Corbis; **9.6** Herb Kawainui Kane.

Chapter 10 Figure 10.1 (left) Mimmo Jodice/Fine Art/Corbis; (right) Borromeo/Art Resource, NY; **10.2** Courtesy of the Penn Museum, Image #C 395 S8-G2844; **10.3** Ancient Art & Architecture Collection Ltd.; **10.4** Chris Hellier/Fine Art/Corbis; **10.5** Amit Pashricha/Dorling Kindersley, Ltd.; **10.6** Bridgeman-Giraudon/Art Resource, NY.

PART II REVISITING

P. 231 Dorling Kindersley; p. 233 Andy Sotiriou/Photodisc/Getty Images.

PART III

P. 235 Age Fotostock/SuperStock; p. 236 British Library Board / Robana / Art Resource, NY.

Chapter 11 Figure 11.1 Ian Dagnall/Alamy; **11.2** Frederick Barry/Fine Art/Corbis; **11.3** Ursula Gahwiler/Robert Harding Picture Library Ltd/Alamy; **11.4** Werner Forman/Art Resource, NY; **11.5** The British Library Board; **11.6** Mohsin Raza/Corbis; **11.7** Bridgeman Art Library; **Visualizing the Past Image 1** Philip de Bay/Historical Picture Archive/Corbis; **Image 2** Terence Waeland/Alamy.; **Image 3** Pearson; **Image 4** Images & Stories/Alamy; **Image 5** Erich Lessing/Art Resource, NY.

Chapter 12 Figure 12.1 Heritage Images/Corbis; **12.2** Harvard Art Museums/Arthur M. Sackler Museum, Gift of John Goelet, formerly in the collection of Louis J. Cartier, 1958.76; **12.3** Digital Image © Museum Associates / LACMA. Licensed by Art Resource, NY; **12.4** The Granger Collection, NYC; **12.5** Ric Ergenbright/Corbis; **12.6** Pahari School (18th century) / British Library, London, UK / © British Library Board. All Rights Reserved / The Bridgeman Art Library.

Chapter 13 Figure 13.1 The Granger Collection New York; **13.2** George Steinmetz/Terra/Corbis; **Visualizing the Past Image 1** Bombaert Patrick/Alamy; **Image 2** Igor Alyukov/Shutterstock; **13.3** Brooklyn Museum L54.5 Collection of Robin B. Martin; **13.4** Werner Forman/Art Resource, NY; **13.5** Nick Greaves/Images of Africa Photobank/Alamy.

Chapter 14 Figure 14.1 Erich Lessing / Art Resource, NY; **14.2** B.O'Kane/Alamy; **Visualizing the Past** Erich Lessing/Art Resource, NY; **14.3** EvrenKalinbacak/Shutterstock; **14.4** Album/Art Resource, NY; **14.5** Gianni Dagli Orti / The Art Archive at Art Resource, NY.

Chapter 15 Figure 15.1 British Library/akg-images; **15.2** Snark / Art Resource, NY; **Visualizing the Past** RMN-Grand Palais/Art Resource, NY; **15.3** Bridgeman-Giraudon/Art Resource, NY; **15.4** The Art Archive at Art Resource, NY; **15.5** Elio Ciol/Fine Art/Corbis; **15.6** Ian Dagnall/Alamy; **15.7** akg-images/British Library/Newscom; **15.8** DeAgostini/SuperStock; **15.9** Snark/Art Resource, NY.

Chapter 16 Figure 16.1 Sucesores de Luis Covarrubias Duclaud, Sean Sprague/Mexicolore / The Bridgeman Art Library International; **16.2** SEF/Art Resource, NY; **16.3** Scala / Art Resource, NY; **16.4**

jejim/Shutterstock; **16.5** DeAgostini/SuperStock; **Visualizing the Past Image 1** Kevin Schafer/Corbis; **Image 2** Charles Lenars/Corbis; **16.6** Werner Forman/Art Resource, NY; **16.7** Chuck Pefley/Alamy.

Chapter 17 Figure 17.1 Eastphoto/Beijing Eastphoto stockimages Co.,Ltd/Alamy; **17.2** Image copyright © The Metropolitan Museum of Art. Image source: Art Resource, NY.; **17.3** Image copyright Â© The Metropolitan Museum of Art. Image source: Art Resource, NY; **17.4** The Granger Collection, NYC; **17.5** Art Archive, The/SuperStock; **17.6** Museum feur Asiatische Kunst, Staatliche Museen, Berlin, Germany/Juergen Lipe/Art Resource, NY; **Visualizing the Past** Library of Congress Prints and Photographs Division [LC-USZ62-49138] **17.7** Museum of Fine Arts, Boston.

Chapter 18 Figure 18.1 Art Archive, The/SuperStock; **18.2** DeA Picture Library/The Granger Collection; **18.3** Louis V. Ledoux and Asian Art/Department Funds/The Bridgeman Art Library; **18.4** Jon Arnold Images Ltd / Alamy; **18.5** The Nelson Atkins Museum of Art; **18.6** Free Agents Limited/Corbis;

18.7 Mr. and Mrs. Charles M. Endicott Fund/The Bridgeman Art Library; **18.8** David South/Alamy; **Visualizing the Past Image 1** The Granger Collection NYC; **Image 2** DeAgostini/SuperStock; **Image 3** akg-images/British Library/Newscom; **Image 4** Image copyright © The Metropolitan Museum of Art. Image source: Art Resource, NY.

Chapter 19 19.1 Scala/White Images / Art Resource, NY; **19.2** The Granger Collection, NYC; **19.3** The Granger Collection, NYC; **19.4** bpk, Berlin / Art Resource, NY; **19.5** The Granger Collection, NYC; **19.6** The Granger Collection, NYC; **19.7** De Agostini/Getty Images.

Chapter 20 Figure 20.1 The Granger Collection, NYC; **20.2** Scala/Art Resource, NY; **20.3** MasterLu/Fotolia; **20.4** The Granger Collection, NYC; **20.5** The Granger Collection, NYC.

PART III REVISITING

P. 454 Pascal Rateau/Shutterstock; **p. 455** Private Collection/akg-images; **p. 456** Image Asset Management Ltd. / Alamy.

P. 457 "Departure for the Cape," King Manuel I of Portugal blessing Vasco da Gama and his expedition, c.1935, Anonymous / University of Witwatersrand, Johannesburg, South Africa/The Bridgeman Art Library; **p. 458** Model of the slave ship 'Brookes' used by William Wilberforce (1759–1833) in the House of Commons to demonstrate conditions on the middle passage, 18th century (wood) (see also 112029, 136291 and 135589) / © Wilberforce House, Hull City Museums and Art Galleries, UK/ The Bridgeman Art Library.

Chapter 21 Figure 21.1 The Granger Collection, NYC; **21.2** The Granger Collection, NYC; **21.3** Art Resource, NY; **21.4** The Granger Collection, NYC; **21.5** The Granger Collection, NYC; **21.6** The Granger Collection, NYC; **21.7** National Gallery, London/Art Resource, NY; **21.8** V & A Images.

Chapter 22 Figure 22.1 V&A Images, London/Art Resource, NY; **22.2** The Granger Collection, NYC; **22.3** GL Archive/Alamy; **Visualizing the Past** RMN-Grand Palais/Art Resource, NY; **22.4** bpk, Berlin/National Portrait Gallery, London, Great Britain/Jochen Remmer/Art Resource, NY.

Index

Ayan, 265
Ayllus, 179, 180, 181, 362
Aztecs, 171, 354–361
    agriculture of, 357
    behavior for people in different roles, 360–361
    calendar, 357, 357f
    conquest and, ideology of, 355–357
    early civilization and, 21
    economy of, 357–358
    Incas compared to, 367–368
    men's roles in, 360–361
    population of, 359, 361
    power of, rise to, 354–355
    religion of, 355–357, 356f
    social classes, 358–359, 359f
    social contract of, 355
    social transition of, 358–360
    technological constraints of, 359, 361
    tributes in, 361
    women's rights and roles in, 359, 360–361

B

Babylonian Empire, 30, 31–33
Bacon, Francis, 496
Bactria, 106
Baghdad
    as Abbasid capital, 260
    elite in, 264
Baibars, 428, 429
Bakufu, 401
Balboa, Vasco de, 476
Ball games, 170
Bands of hunters and gatherers, 11
Banking, in western Europe, 344–345, 345f
Bantu migrations, 188–189, 189m, 191
Barbarians, 21–22, 98
Baths
    at Mohenjo Daro, 48
    Roman, 72f
Battle of Kulikova, 426
Battle of Siffin, 255
Battle of the River Zab, 259
Batu, 424
Bedouin culture, 245–246, 258–259. *See also* Arabia
Belisarius, 314, 315
Benedict of Nursia, 226
Benin, 304, 306
Beowulf, 342
Berke, 429
Bernard of Clairvaux, 340
Bet Giorgis, 295f
Bhagavad Gita, 125
Bhaktic cults, 285, 285f, 286

Bian Liang, 373f
Bindusara, 129
Bishops, 155
Black Death, 347, 348f, 442, 444
Bodhisattvas, 223
Boers, 481
Book of Lord Shang, The (Shang Yang), 81
Book of Odes, 58, 59
Book of Poetry, 88
Boyars, 324
Brahmans, 119–122
    Buddhism and, 126–128
    caste system and, 122–126
    in Gangetic plain, 120–121
    Mauryas, 128–131
    power, sources of, 121–122
    recovery of, 131, 133–135
British
    colonial expansion and, impact of, 477, 479f, 480–481
    West Indian slaveholding, 474
British East India Company, 469, 481
Bronze, 19, 22
Bronze Age, 15
Brookes (slave ship), 458
Brutus, 143, 143f
Bubonic plague, 442, 444
Buddha, 126–127, 224f
Buddhism
    bodhisattvas, 223
    challenge of, 127
    Christianity compared to, 223–225
    in classical India, 126–130, 130m
    distribution of, in world today, 227m
    emergence of, 127
    institutions, rituals, and symbols, 212–213
    in late classical period, 223–225
    Mahayana, 223
    Mauryas, 129–130
    rise of, 53
    spread of, 212–213, 215f, 216
Building materials, in Neolithic Age, 17
Bulgaria, 316
Bulgaroktonos, 316
Burial rituals and patterns
    in Çatal Hüyük, 20
    in Natufian complex, 12
    pyramids, 35, 35f
    in Russian settlements, 12
    Shang, 56
Bushi, 400
Buyids, 273
Byzantine empire, 222
    Arab pressure and empire's defense, 314–315, 316
    art in, 314, 314f, 317, 318f

    churches in, 221f
    decline of, 318–320
    under Justinian, 313–314, 314m
    politics in, 316–317
    power of, 311–312
    society in, 316–317
    women and power in, 315

C

Caesar, 316
Cahokia, 166, 167f, 175, 176
Calcutta, 481–482
Calendar systems
    Aztec, 357, 357f
    in historical perspective, 173–174
    lunar cycle, 171, 173
    Mayan, 169, 170
    Olmec, 168
    solar cycle, 171, 173
Caliphs
    in Abbasid era, 271–273, 278
    Muhammad and, 252
    in Sudan, 300
Calpulli, 358
Calvin, Jean, 489–490
Camel nomads, 16
Camels, domestication of, 15
Canterbury Tales (Chaucer), 342
Cape Colony, 481
Cape of Good Hope, 467
Capital cities
    Baghdad, 260
    Cahn-Chan, 363
    designs and patterns of, 91, 91m
    Hangzhou, 373–374
    Heian (Kyoto), 397–399
    Zhou, 54m, 57, 58, 62
Capitalism, 344–346
Carolingians, 331
Carthage, 143, 144
Caste system, 122–126
    family and changing status of women, 124–125
    inequality and, in historical perspective, 123
    inequality and, intensifying, 135–137
    social divisions, enforcing, 124
Castile, 447
Çatal Hüyük, 14, 18, 19, 20, 20f, 22
Catherwood, Frederick, 161
Catholic Reformation, 490
Cattle, domestication of, 15
Cattle-herding peoples, 16, 21
Causation, in historical perspective, 470
Cave paintings
    animal hunts and, 11, 13
    religion and, 10

overview of, 69
political units of the world, 70*m*
timeline, 72–73
trading routes in, 132–133, 132*m*
trends and societies, 73
triggers for change, 69, 71
Clientage, 143
Climatic variations in Africa, 186, 187*m*
Cloth, 274
"Cloud Messenger" (Kalidasa), 134, 136
Clovis, 330
Coeur, Jacques, 345
Columbian Exchange, 471–473
of animal husbandry, 472
of crops, 471–472
of disease, 471, 472*f*
environmental impact of, 472–473
Columbus, Christopher, 467
expedition of, 478
Commerce
commercialism, in western Europe, 443–445
commercial revolution, 492–495
balance sheet, 494–495
social protest, 493, 494
world economy and, impact of, 493
during 18th century, 502–503
in Western transformation, 487–492
Compass, 437–438
Complimentary husbands, 388
Concubines, 90, 93
Confessions of Augustine, 156
Confucius, 54, 67, 74–76, 74*f*
Analects, 75, 77
heirs of, 78
Laozi compared to, 79
portrait of, 78*f*
shi and, 77–78, 86
in Song era, 384
Constantine, 220
Consuls, 143
Copernicus, Nicolaus, 495
Copts, 254
Córdoba, 242*f*, 243
Core nations, 474
Corinthian, 110, 111*f*
Cotton, 485, 485*f*
Council of Nicaea, 226
Crops, Columbian Exchange of, 471–472
Cross-cultural exchange, Mongols and, 423–424
Crusades, 273
Culture
in age of innovation (4000 to 3000 B.C.E)., 22
in Andean civilization, regional, 178–179
archaic, 164–165

Aryan, 50–51
Babylonian, 30, 31
bedouin, 245–246, 258–259
in Çatal Hüyük, 20
Chavín, 178–179
Chinese, in historical perspective, 61–62
in Egypt, 33, 34, 35, 37
compared to Mesopotamia, 37
Harappan, 48–49
Hellenistic period, before and after Alexander the Great, 112
historical perspective of, 21–22
Hopewell, 175
in Inca empire, 367, 367*f*
Indian, in historical perspective, 61–62
indigenous, in Japan, 203–204
in Jericho, 19–20
Jewish, 40
Jomon, 203
in Kievan Rus', 323, 324
Longshan, 53
in Mediterranean, 39–41
Middle East, in 1450, 439–440
Mississippian, 175
of Mongols, Chinese influence of, 430
in Natufian complex, 12, 13
Neolithic revolution and, 15–17
Nok, 188
Olmec, 167–168, 168*f*, 169
in patriarchal societies, 36–37
Phoenician, 41
Renaissance, 445–446
Roman Empire, 146–148
Shang, 54, 56
spread of, 10–11, 12*m*
Sumerian, 27–28
on Swahili coast of East Africa, 302–303
Toltec, 353–354
in Western transformation, 487–492
Catholic Reformation, 490, 490*m*
Christian unity and, end of, 490–492
Italian Renaissance, 487–488
Northern Renaissance, 488
Protestantism, 489–490, 490*m*
technology and family, 489
writing and, 29, 31
Yangshao, 53
Cuneiform, 27, 27*f*, 31, 35, 66*f*
Cunningham, Alexander, 44–45
Curacas (leaders), 181, 364
Cyril, 321
Cyrus the Great, 98, 99

D

Dadu, 430
Da Gama, Vasco, 447, 448*f*
Daimyos, 403

Damascus, 256
Damask, 274
Dao, 78–79
Daoism, distribution in world today, 227*m*
Darius, 99, 99*f*, 103, 107, 113
Darwin, Charles, 21
Dasas, 51
Decimination, 141
Decline and fall of civilizations
in historical perspective, 222
Ibn Khaldun on, 274
Deforestation, 154
Deism, 496
Deities. *See* Gods/goddesses
Delian League, 102
Demak, 287
Democracy, origin of word, 102
Demographic transition, 305, 306
Demography, 304–306
Descartes, René, 496
Description of the World (Polo), 432*f*
Desert peoples, 175–177
Destruction of the Philosophers, The (Al-Ghazali), 439
Devi, 217
Dharma, 124
Dhimmi, 256
Dhows, 261, 268–269, 268*f*
Diderot, Denis, 500, 502
Diffusion, 65–66
Diocletian, 220
Diplomacy, in classical Greece
in Athens, rise of, 102
united effort and, tensions of, 103–104
Discourse between Muslim Sages, A, 276*f*
Disease, Columbian Exchange of, 471, 472*f*
Divine Comedy (Dante), 445*f*
Divorce, in Tang and Song eras, 388
Dogs, domestication of, 15
Doric, 110, 111*f*
Dowager Wang, 93
Drama, Greek, 109
Dry farming, 200
Du, Nguyen, 414
Dutch East India Company, 469
Dynamism, in western Europe, 442

E

Early modern period
big changes, 460–461
big concepts, 458
biological exchange, 461
continuity, 462
impact on daily life, work, 462
major political units of the world, c. 1450, 459*m*

North America
    colonial expansion and, impact of, 477, 480
    early civilization in
        in historical perspective, 21
        spread of culture in, 11
North American Indians, 175–177
    Anasazi, 176–177, 176f
    desert peoples, 175–177
    Hopewell culture, 175
    Mississippian culture, 175
    mound builders, 175
Northern European expeditions, 468–469,
        469f, 471m
Northern Renaissance, 488
Northern wall, 81, 82f
Notre-Dame, 342f
Nubia, 294
Nuclear families, Shang, 55

O

Oba, 307f
Oceania
    pastoralism in, 15–16
    spread of human populations in, 12m
Odyssey (Vergil), 146
Oedipus complex, 110
Ogedei, 424
Old Kingdom period, 26
Old Stone Age. See Paleolithic Age
Olmecs, 167–168, 168f, 169
Olympic Games, 96, 103
One-god religion of Akhenaton, 34
Oracle at Delphi, 103
Oracles, 56
Ordos bulge, 53, 54
Orejones, 367
Origin, myths of, 191–192
Orthodox Christianity, 311, 312, 316, 317,
        324, 325
Oyo, 304

P

Pachacuti, 362
Pacific voyagers, 207, 207f
Paekche, 406, 406m
Pahi, 207, 207f
Paintings
    cave, Paleolithic, 10, 11, 13
    wall
        in Çatal Hüyük, 20
        Egyptian, 39f, 40f
Palenque, 161, 169, 170, 171
Paleolithic Age, 9–14. See also Hunters and
        gatherers
    agrarian revolution, 11, 12
    animistic religions, 10
    art, 10

children's roles, 11
culture, 9–11
Natufian complex, 12, 13
Russian settlements, 12
society and life, 11
spread of, 10–11
timeline, 9
tools, 9, 10–11, 11f
women's roles, 11
Pamela (Richardson), 502
Pan, 283
Parliamentary monarchy, 499
Parliaments, 335
Pastoralism, 15–16, 17, 53
Pastoral nomads
    in early civilization, 8, 10, 15, 19
    human adaptation and, 195–196, 200–201
    migrations of, 195–196
Patriarchal societies, 36–37
Patrilineal descent and inheritance, 51
Paul, 151, 155, 156
Peasants
    Book of Odes and, 58, 59
    earthen dikes built by, 53
    Han, 89–90
    in nuclear families, in Shang, 55
    Shang, 55–56
    in western Europe, 331, 331f
    Zhou, 57, 58, 59, 60, 61
Peking Man, 53
Peloponnesian Wars, 103m, 104, 108
Pericles, 102
Periplus of the Erythraean Sea, The, 302
Persian empire, 97m, 98–100
    political innovations in, 99–100
    political rituals in, 107
    royal audience hall of Darius and
        Xerxes, 99f
Peru, 364m, 365, 367, 368
Petrarch, Francesco, 445
Pharaohs (kings), in Egypt, 33
Pheidippides, 96, 96f
Philip II, 105
Philosophers/philosophy
    in classical Greece, 107–110
    Confucius, 77–78, 79
    Dao, 78–79
    Harappan, 53
    in Hellenistic period, 107–110
    Indian, 51, 52
    Laozi, 78–79
    Legalists, 78, 81, 82, 86
    Mencius, 78, 79
    Shang, 61
    Shang Yang, 78, 79, 81
    Zhou, 61, 62, 77–79
Phoenicians, 41

Phúc, Ly Van, 394–395
Pi (π), 134
Pictographs (ideographs), 45, 49m, 56
Pigs, domestication of, 15
Pipiltin, 358
Pizarro, Francisco, 476–477, 477f
Plants, domestication of, 14–15
Plato, 108, 129
Plebeians, 142
Plow, introduction of, 15, 17, 19, 22
Pochteca, 357
Poetry
    Aeneid (Vergil), 148
    Arabian, 248
    "Cloud Messenger" (Kalidasa), 134, 136
    Iliad and Odyssey, 100
    neglected poets in Arabia, 248
    in praise of a war horse, Aryan, 52
Political organization
    in age of innovation (4000 to 3000
        B.C.E)., 22
    in Americas, in 1450, 449
    in Byzantine empire, 316–317
    in China
        compared with classical Greece, 102
        in historical perspective, 61–62
    in classical Greece, 100–104
    in classical period, 70m
    in Egypt, 33, 34
        compared to Mesopotamia, 37, 38
    during 18th century, 500
    feudalism, 57, 58
    in Japan, 204
    Jewish, 40
    Kushite, 39
    Legalists, 78, 81, 82, 86
    Mandate of Heaven and, 57–58, 61
    Minoan, 41
    in Neolithic revolution, 17
    patriarchalism and, 36
    in Persian empire, 99–100, 107
    in Song era, 383
    in Sudanic states, 300
    Sumerian, 27, 28
    in western Europe, 330, 334
    in Western transformation, 497–499
        absolute monarchies, 497, 498–499
        nation-state, 499
        parliamentary monarchies, 499
    Zhou, 57–58, 61
Polyandry, 51, 52
Polygamy, 51, 52
Polynesia, 205–209, 206m
    ancient Hawaii, 207–208
    in 1450
        conquest in, 449
        Maorian achievements in, 449–450

great migration, 206–207
New Zealand and Maori culture, 208–209
Pacific voyagers, 207, 207f
Pope, 225
Populations
    in Africa, in historical perspective, 304–306
    in Americas, in historical perspective, 304–306
    of Aztecs, 359, 361
    demographic transition and, 305, 306
    demography and, 304–306
    spread of *Homo sapiens sapiens*, 10–11, 12m
    trends, 443
    in Western transformation, 494m
Portugal, maritime power in, 466–467, 468m
Postclassical period
    in Americas, 351–372
    big changes, 238
    big concepts, 236
    in China, 373–393
    contacts and their limits, 453–454
    continuity and limitations, 240
    critical themes, 454–455
    critical thinking questions, 456
    eastern Europe in, 310–326
    impact on daily life, women and, 240–240
    Islam in, rise and spread of
        Africa, 290–309
        in Arabia, 237m, 242–267, 254m
        in middle and late Abbasid eras, 270–278, 271m
        in south Asia, 278–286
        in southeast Asia, 286–288, 287m
    main routes of Afro-Eurasian trade, c. 1250, 237m
    overview of, 236
    religion in, spread of, 237m
    timeline, 238–239
    transregional network, 239–240
    trends and societies in early modern period, 241
    triggers for change, 238
    in western Europe, 327–350, 336m
Potosi silver mine, 464f
Pottery, 17, 18
    ceramics, in Korea, 407f
    Harappan, 49
    in Meroë, 39
    pre-Harappan, 47
    Sumerian, 27
    terra-cotta, 303, 304f
Predestination, 489

Prefarming peoples, 11, 12
Prester John, 427
Priests, 10
    Aryan, 51
    Chinese, as oracles, 56
    Harappan, 48–49
    shi as, 58
    Vedic, 50–51, 52
Prince, The (Machiavelli), 488
Principia Mathematica (Newton), 496
Proletariat, 493
Protestantism, 489–490, 490m
Proto-Bantu language, 188
Proto-globalization, 460, 503, 504
Ptolemies, 106
Puna, 177
Punic Wars, 143, 144
Pure land Buddhism, 379
Pygmies, 189
Pyramids, 34, 35, 35f

Q

Qin, 75m, 80–83
    collapse of, 82–83
    Legalists, 78, 81, 82, 86
    Shi Huangdi, 76, 81–83, 83f, 86
Quetzalcoatl, 353
Quipu, 367
Qur'an, 249
Quraysh, 247
Qutb-ud-din Aibak, 282

R

Rain forests, spread of agriculture in, 16, 17
Rajas, 281
Rajput, 217
Rama, 124
Ramadan, 252
Ramayana, 119, 124–125
Reincarnation, 124
Religion, 51f. *See also* Buddhism; Christianity; Hinduism; Judaism
    animistic, 10
    Aryan, 50, 51–52
    of Aztecs, 355–357, 356f
    cave paintings and, 10
    Chinese, 61, 62
    in classical Greece, 107–110
    in classical India, 126–128 (*See also* Buddhism)
    in Egypt, 35
    Harappan, 49
    in Hellenistic period, 107–110
    in Inca empire, 362, 363–364
    in late classical period, 212–213, 216, 223–228

map of major religions of the world, 227, 227m, 228
    in Mesoamerican civilization, 170
    monotheistic, 40–41
    one-god religion of Akhenaton, 34
    reform in western Europe, 338
    in Roman Empire, 151
    Sumerian, 26–27, 28, 36
    in Tang era, 379, 380–381
    Tian, 62
    Vedas, 50–51, 52
    in wake of decline and fall, 228
    in western Europe, 341–342
        in art and literature, 341–342
        popular, 341
Renaissance
    Italian, 445
        culture of, 445–446
        secular directions in, 445–446
    Northern, 488
Republic, 129
Richard, King, 337f
Ridda Wars, 252
Rituals, political, in Persia, 107
Romance of the Rose, The (Villon), 342
Romance of the West Chamber, 432
Roman civilization, early, 21
Roman Empire, 140–159
    art, 146, 148, 148f
    Augustus and successors of, 149, 150m
    Christianity, 154–157
    crisis of, 145, 147
    culture, 146–148
    decline and fall of, 218–223
        Attila the Hun, 221
        causes of decline, 219–220
        Germanic kingdoms after invasions, 220m
        patterns of decline, 221
        problem of, in historical perspective, 222
        process of decline, 219–220
        results of, 221–222, 223
        signs of decline, 218
    decline of, 157
    economic structure, 152, 154
    environmental consequences, 154
    expansion of, 143–145, 144m
    government and expansion, 149–150
    in historical perspective, 153
    law, 150, 151
    literature, 148
    Mediterranean heritage and, 157
    Roman republic, 142–145
    Rome, 146
    rule of, 148–151
    slavery in, 152

Roman Empire (*cont.*)
  social structure, 151–152, 153
  timeline, 142
Roman republic, 142–145
Rome, 146
Royal houses, Zhou, 58
Rubaiyat (Khayyam), 275, 276
Rurik, 322–323
Russia, 323
  Mongols in, 425–427
  in postclassical period
    Christianity and, 323
    in Kiev, 323, 324–325
    in Kievan Rus', 323, 324
  world economy in, 475
Russian Orthodoxy, 323

S

Sacrifice, religious
  animal, 50, 52
  Aryan, 52
  Shang, 56
  Zhou, 62
Sahara, 186
Sahel, 186
Saints, 223–224
St. Sophia, 315*f*, 317*f*
Saladin, 273, 336, 337*f*, 338
Samurai, 400
San Salvador, 478
Sanskrit, 50, 194
Sargon I, 30, 30*f*
Sarmatians, 199
Sasanian empires, 249
Sati, 283
Savages, 21–22
Schism, 317–318
Scholar-gentry. *See also* Han
  defined, 87
  emergence of, 87–88
  gender roles, 88–89
  Mongols and, Chinese influence of, 431–432
  in Tang and Song eras, 390, 392
Scholasticism, 341
Schools
  Chinese, in classical period, 79
  Han, 86–87
Science
  in Abbasid era, 276
  in classical Greece, 107–110
  in Egypt compared to Mesopotamia, 37–38
  Han, 92–93
  in Hellenistic period, 107–110
  in Song era, 388, 389–390
  Sumerian, 28

in Tang era, 388, 389–390
  war as, Xunzi and, 85
Scientific Revolution, 495, 495–497
  Bacon and, 496
  Copernicus and, 495
  Deism and, 496
  Galileo and, 496
  Harvey and, 496
  Kepler and, 495, 495*f*
  Locke and, 496
  Newton and, 496
Scythians, 199
Secoton, Virginia, 480*f*
Secret societies, 90, 93
Sedentary agriculture, 14–19. *See also* Neolithic Age
  Aryan, 53
  domestication of plants and animals, 14–15
  in loess zone, 53
  pastoralism and, 15–16, 17
  wet-rice, 200
Seleucids, 106
Seljuk Turks, 273
Senate, 142
Seppuku, 400
Serfs, 329
  Aryan, 51
  Zhou, 58
Servants
  Shang, 55, 56
  Zhou, 58
Seven Years War, 477
Sexual relations
  miscegenation, 51
  in patriarchal societies, 36
Shah-Nama, 275–276
Shakuntala, 136
Shamanistic beliefs, 424
Shamans, 10, 56
Shang, early civilization in, 54–56, 54*m*, 57
  culture in, 56
  decline of, 57
  society in, 55–56
  warrior kings of, 54–55
Shang Yang, 78, 79, 81
Sharia, 300
Shaykhs, 247
Sheep, domestication of, 15
Sheep-herding peoples, 16, 21
Shelter. *See also* Houses
  in Neolithic Age, 15, 17, 17*f*, 19, 20, 20*f*
  in Paleolithic Age, 10–11, 13
Shi
  Confucius and, 77–78, 86
  defined, 58

in Han, dominance and revenge of, 86–87
  writing and, 58
Shi'a, 255
Shifting cultivation, 15, 200
Shi gentleman, 77–78
Shi Huangdi, 76, 81–83, 83*f*, 86
Shinto, 203, 204*f*
Shintoism, distribution in world today, 227*m*
Shiva, 121*f*, 131
Shoguns, 401
Shrivijaya, 286
Signet Ring of Rakshasa, 134
Silk, 54, 56
Silk Road, 196
Silla, 406, 406*m*
Silver, in new world economy, 464–465
  Potosi silver mine, 464*f*
Sinification, 406–409
  in Korea
    of elites, 407–409
    tribute system and, 406–408
  in Vietnam, 409–410
Sinified, 383
Skanda Gupta, 137
Slash-and-burn agriculture, 169–170, 200
Slaves
  Aryan, 51
  British West Indian slaveholding, 474
  in Egypt compared to Mesopotamia, 37
  Harappan, 49
  in Roman Empire, 152
  Shang, 56
  Zhou, 58, 58*f*
Slavic peoples, 199–200, 199*m*, 321, 322*m*
Smith, Adam, 500
Social class and organization. *See also* Elites; Peasants; Slaves
  administrative, 49
  in Americas, origins of, 162–167
  aristocrats, 47, 55
  Aryan, 51
  Aztec, 358–359, 359*f*
  caste system, 122–126
  Chinese writing and, 57
  in classical India, 122–126
  in Egypt, 33–34
  Hammurabi's law code and, 30, 32
  Han, 88–89
  Harappan, 48–49
  indigenous, in Japan, 203–204
  in Indus Valley cities, 47
  inequality, in historical perspective, 123
  in Japan, 204–205
  merchant, 48, 51
  in Mesoamerican civilization, 170–171

in Middle East
in classical period, 112–113
in Middle East in
1450, 439–440
of Mongols, Chinese influence on,
431–432
in Neolithic revolution, 17–19
in Paleolithic Age, 11
priestly, 48–49, 51
Shang, 55–56
in Song era, 387–388
in Sudanic states, 300
Sumerian, 27
in Tang era, 387–388
values, in Song era, 391
varnas, 51
warrior, 51, 53, 55
in western Europe, 343–344
Social history, defining, 114–115
Social protest, in commercial revolution,
493, 494
Socrates, 108
Solar cycle, 171, 173
Solon, 101
Song era, 382–392, 383*m*
agrarian production in, 386–387, 387*f*
artistic creativity and accomplishment
in, 388, 389–392
Confucian thought in, 384
decline of, 384–385
divorce in, 388
engineering in, 388, 390
expansion in, commercial, 386
family in, 387–388
founding of, 382–283
Golden Age of, 385–392
Hangzhou as capital of, 373–374
invention in, 388, 389–390
male dominance in, Neo-Confucian,
388, 389
marriage in, 388
politics in, 383
scholar-gentry elite in, 390, 392
science and technology in, 388,
389–390
social values in, 391
society in, 387–388
Southern Song era and, 385
state and religion in, 379, 380–381
Wang reforms in, 384–385
Songhay, 299–300
Song of Roland, The, 342
Sophocles, 110
South America, spread of culture in, 11
South Asia, Islam in, 278–286
accommodation patterns and, 283,
284–285

challenge of, 283, 285
conversion patterns and, 282–283,
284–285
Hindu revival and, 283, 285
Indian influences on, 281
Muslim invasions
Muslim presence in India and, 286
political divisions and, 280–281
second wave of, 281–282
political divisions and, 280
Southeast Asia, Islam in, 286–288, 287*m*
conversion and, 287
Sufi mystics and, 288
trade contacts and, 287
Southern Song era, 385
Spain, maritime power in, 467, 468*m*
Sparta
vs. Athens, 104
helots, 113
Sphinx, 35*f*
Spiritual power, in western Europe, 330
Split inheritance, 363
Stateless societies, 292
States
in Americas, 165, 166
Hellenistic, 105–106, 107
in Tang era, 379, 380–381
Stelae, 170
Stephens, John Lloyd, 161
Stilicho, 219*f*
Stoics, 108
Stonehenge, 198*f*
Stone relief, 140*f*, 217*f*
Stupas, 129*f*, 130
Sudanic states, 296–300
city dwellers and villagers, 297, 298
epic of Sundiata and, 298
"Lion Prince" and, 297
Mali Empire, 296–297
political and social life in, 300
Songhay, 299–300
Sufi mystics, 288
Sui dynasty, 215, 374–376
Sultans, 273
of Delhi, 282
Sumer, 26–29
art and, 28, 30
city-states and, 27
civilization and, 29
culture and, 27–28
gender roles and, 27
literature and, 28, 29
map of, 26*m*
political and social organization and, 27
pottery and, 27
religion and, 26–27, 28, 36
trade and, 26, 27, 28, 29

war activities and, 27, 28
writing and, 18, 27–28, 29, 66*f*
Summas (highest works), 340, 341
Sundiata, 297, 298
Sunnis, 255
Swahili coast of East Africa,
301–303, 302*m*
cultures on, 302–303
trading routes, 30*m*2, 302
Swetham, Joseph, 501
Syncretism, 69

T

Taffeta, 274
Taika reforms, 396
Taira, 400–401
Taizong, 217*f*
Tale of Genji, The (Murasaki), 398–399,
399*f*, 414
Tale of Kieu, The (Du), 414
Tambos, 364
Tang era, 215, 376–382, 385–392
agrarian production in, 386–387, 387*f*
anti-Buddhist backlash in, 381
artistic creativity in, 388, 389–392
decline of, 381–382
divorce in, 388
emergence of, 376–377
engineering in, 388, 390
expansion in, commercial, 386
family in, 387–388
Golden Age of, 385–392
invention in, 388, 389–390
Korea and, alliances and conquest of, 406
male dominance in, Neo-Confucian,
388, 389
marriage in, 388
meritocracy and examination system in,
377–378, 378*f*
rebuilding, 377
restoration of, 376–377
scholar-gentry elite in, 390, 392
science and technology in, 388, 389–390
society in, 387–388
state and religion in, 379, 380–381
Tangut tribes, 384
Tatars, 325
Technology
in Egypt, 34
compared to Mesopotamia, 37
in historical perspective, 21
in Kush, 39
in maritime power, 466
in Paleolithic Age, 9, 13
in Song era, 388, 389–390
in Tang era, 388, 389–390
in Western transformation, 489